INTERNATIONAL LAW ASPECTS OF THE EU'S SECURITY AND DEFENCE POLICY, WITH A PARTICULAR FOCUS ON THE LAW OF ARMED CONFLICT AND HUMAN RIGHTS

INTERNATIONAL LAW ASPECTS OF THE EU'S SECURITY AND DEFENCE POLICY, WITH A PARTICULAR FOCUS ON THE LAW OF ARMED CONFLICT AND HUMAN RIGHTS

Frederik NAERT

intersentia
Antwerp – Oxford – Portland

Distribution for the UK:
Hart Publishing Ltd.
16C Worcester Place
Oxford OX1 2JW
UK
Tel.: +44 1865 51 75 30
Fax: +44 1865 51 07 10

Distribution for Switzerland and Germany:
Schulthess Verlag
Zwingliplatz 2
CH-8022 Zürich
Switzerland
Tel.: +41 1 251 93 36
Fax: +41 1 261 63 94

Distribution for the USA and Canada:
International Specialized Book Services
920 NE 58th Ave Suite 300
Portland, OR 97213
USA
Tel.: +1 800 944 6190 (toll free)
Tel.: +1 503 287 3093
Fax: +1 503 280 8832
Email: info@isbs.com

Distribution for other countries:
Intersentia Publishers
Groenstraat 31
BE-2640 Mortsel
Belgium
Tel.: +32 3 680 15 50
Fax: +32 3 658 71 21

International Law Aspects of the EU's Security and Defence Policy, with a Particular Focus on the Law of Armed Conflict and Human Rights
Frederik Naert

Antwerp – Oxford – Portland
www.intersentia.com

ISBN 978-90-5095-771-7
D/2010/7849/1
NUR 828

TABLE OF CONTENTS

PART II
TO WHAT EXTENT ARE INTERNATIONAL ORGANIZATIONS BOUND BY INTERNATIONAL LAW?

TABLE OF ABBREVIATIONS AND ABBREVIATED CITATIONS

1. INTERNATIONAL AGREEMENTS AND INSTRUMENTS

1907 HC V	Convention (V) respecting the Rights and Duties of Neutral Powers and Persons in Case of War on Land (The Hague, 18 October 1907);
1907 HC XIII	Convention (XIII) concerning the Rights and Duties of Neutral Powers in Naval War (The Hague, 18 October 1907);
1969 VCLT	Vienna Convention on the Law of Treaties (Vienna, 23 May 1969, 1155 *U.N.T.S.* 331);
1975 VCRSIO	Vienna Convention on the Representation of States in their Relations with International Organizations of a Universal Character (Vienna, 14 March 1975, not yet entered into force);
1978 VCSST	Vienna Convention on Succession of States in Respect of Treaties (Vienna, 23 August 1978, 1946 *U.N.T.S.* 3 and 17 *I.L.M.* 1978, pp. 1488–1517);
1986 VCLT	Vienna Convention on the Law of Treaties between States and International Organizations or between International Organizations (Vienna, 21 March 1986, not yet entered into force);
ACHR	American Convention on Human Rights (San José, 22 November 1969, *OAS Treaties Series* No. 36);
Amended Brussels Treaty	Treaty of Economic, Social and Cultural Collaboration and Collective Self-Defence (Brussels, 17 March 1948), as amended by the Protocol Modifying and Completing the Brussels Treaty (Paris, 23 October 1954);
1977 Additional Protocols	Additional Protocols to the (1949) Geneva Conventions (API & APII, see *infra*);
API	Protocol additional to the Geneva Conventions of 12 august 1949, and Relating to the Protection

	of Victims of International Armed Conflicts (Protocol I) (8 June 1977, 1125 *U.N.T.S.* 3);
APII	Protocol Additional to the Geneva Conventions of 12 August 1949, and Relating to the Protection of Victims of Non-international Armed Conflicts (Protocol II) (8 June 1977, 1125 *U.N.T.S.* 609);
ECHR	(European) Convention for the Protection of Human Rights and Fundamental Freedoms (Rome, 4 November 1950, 5 *E.T.S*, as later amended);
EC Treaty	Treaty Establishing the European (Economic) Community (Rome, 25 March 1957, 298 *U.N.T.S.* 11, later repeatedly amended);
EDC Treaty	Treaty Setting Up the European Defence Community (Paris, 27 May 1952, not entered into force);
EU Constitution	Treaty establishing a Constitution for Europe (Rome, 29 October 2004, *O.J. C* 310, 16 December 2004, not entered into force);
EU SOFA	Agreement between the Member States of the European Union concerning the status of military and civilian staff seconded to the institutions of the European Union, of the headquarters and forces which may be made available to the European Union in the context of the preparation and execution of the tasks referred to in Article 17(2) of the Treaty on European Union, including exercises, and of the military and civilian staff of the Member States put at the disposal of the European Union to act in this context (Brussels, 16 November 2003, *O.J. C* 321, 31 December 2003, p. 6, not yet entered into force);
EU Treaty	Treaty on European Union (Maastricht, 7 February 1992, *O.J. C* 191, 29 July 1992, later repeatedly amended);
GATT 1947	General Agreement on Tariffs and Trade (Geneva, 30 October 1947, 55 *U.N.T.S.* 187);
Geneva Conventions	Geneva Conventions of 12 August 1949 (GCI, GCII, GCIII & GCIV, see *infra*);

GCI	Geneva Convention for the Amelioration of the Condition of the Wounded and Sick in Armed Forces in the Field (Geneva, 12 August 1949, 75 *U.N.T.S.* 31);
GCII	Geneva Convention for the Amelioration of the Condition of the Wounded, Sick and Shipwrecked Members of Armed Forces at Sea (Geneva, 12 August 1949, 75 *U.N.T.S.* 85);
GCIII	Geneva Convention Relative to the Treatment of Prisoners of War (Geneva, 12 August 1949, 75 *U.N.T.S.* 135);
GCIV	Geneva Convention Relative to the Protection of Civilian Persons in Time of War (Geneva, 12 August 1949, 75 *U.N.T.S.* 287);
Hague Regulations	Regulations concerning the Laws and Customs of War on Land. Annexed to Convention (IV) respecting the Laws and Customs of War on Land (The Hague, 18 October 1907);
ICC Statute	Statute of the International Criminal Court (Rome, 17 July 1998, 2187 *U.N.T.S.* 3 and 37 *I.L.M.* 1998, pp. 998–1069);
ICCPR	International Covenant on Civil and Political Rights (New York, 16 December 1966, 999 *U.N.T.S.* 171);
ICJ Statute	Statute of the International Court of Justice (Annexed to the UN Charter (*infra*));
Lisbon Treaty	Treaty of Lisbon amending the Treaty on European Union and the Treaty establishing the European Community (Lisbon, 13 December 2007, *O.J. C* 306, 17 December 2007; consolidated versions of the EU Treaty and the Treaty on the Functioning of the European Union as they would be amended by the Lisbon Treaty are published in *O.J. C* 115, 9 May 2008);
Maastricht Treaty	Treaty on European Union (original version, Maastricht, 7 February 1992, *O.J. C* 191, 29 July 1992, p. 1);
Ottawa Convention	Agreement on the Status of the North Atlantic Treaty Organization, National Representatives and International Staff (Ottawa, 20 September 1951);

Paris Protocol	Protocol on the Status of International Military Headquarters set up pursuant to the North Atlantic Treaty (Paris, 28 August 1952);
Treaty of Amsterdam	Treaty of Amsterdam (Amsterdam, 2 October 1997, *O.J. C* 340, 10 November 1997, amending EC and EU Treaties);
Treaty of Nice	Treaty of Nice Amending the Treaty on European Union, the Treaties Establishing the European Communities and Certain Related Acts (Nice, 26 February 2001, *O.J. C* 80, 10 March 2001);
UN Charter	Charter of the United Nations (San Francisco, 26 June 1945);

2. INTERNATIONAL JURISPRUDENCE

Bankovic	ECtHR, *Vlastimir and Borka Bankovic´ and Others v. Belgium, the Czech Republic, Denmark, France, Germany, Greece, Hungary, Iceland, Italy, Luxembourg, the Netherlands, Norway, Poland, Portugal, Spain, Turkey and the United Kingdom*, 12 December 2001 (admissibility decision);
Behrami & Saramati	ECtHR, Grand Chamber, *Behrami and Behrami v. France* (No. 71412/01) and *Saramati v. France, Germany and Norway* (No. 78166/01), 31 May 2007 (admissibility decision);
Bosphorus	ECtHR, *Bosphorus Hava Yolları Turizm ve Ticaret Anonim Şirketi v. Ireland*, judgment of 30 June 2005;
Issa	ECtHR, *Halima Musa Issa and Others v. Turkey*, judgment of 16 November 2004;
Kadi	ECJ (CFI), Case T-315/01, *Kadi v. Council and Commission*, judgment of 21 September 2005;
Kadi appeals judgment	Joined Cases C-402/05 P and C-415/05 P, *Yassin Abdullah Kadi and Al Barakaat International Foundation v. Council of the European Union and Commission of the European Communities*, judgment of 3 September 2008;
Matthews	ECtHR, *Matthews v. UK*, judgment of 18 February 1999;

Nicaragua Case	ICJ, *Case concerning the Military and Paramilitary Activities in and against Nicaragua*, judgment of 27 June 1986;
Nuclear Weapons Opinion	ICJ, *Legality of the Threat or Use of Nuclear Weapons*, advisory opinion of 8 July 1996;
Reparations Opinion	ICJ, *Reparation for Injuries Suffered in the Service of the United Nations*, Advisory opinion of 11 April 1949;
Yusuf	ECJ (CFI), Case T-306/01, *Yusuf and Al Barakaat International Foundation v. Council and Commission*, judgment of 21 September 2005;

3. BOOKS & PUBLICATIONS

AMERASINGHE	C.F. Amerasinghe, *Principles of the Institutional Law of International organisations*, Cambridge, Cambridge University Press, 2005 (2nd ed.);
AUST	A. Aust, *Modern Treaty Law and Practice*, Cambridge, Cambridge University Press, 2000;
BOSSUYT & WOUTERS	M. Bossuyt & J. Wouters, *Grondlijnen van international recht*, Antwerp/Oxford, Intersentia, 2005;
BROWNLIE	I. Brownlie, *Principles of Public International Law*, Oxford, Clarendon Press, 1998 (5th ed.);
COT & PELLET	J.-P. Cot, A. Pellet (eds.), M. Forteau (ass. ed.), *La Charte des Nations Unies: commentaire article par article*, Paris, Economica, 2005 (3rd ed.);
DAVID	E. David, *Principes de droit des conflits armés*, Brussels, Bruylant, 2002 (3rd ed.);
DE WET	E. de Wet, *The Chapter VII Powers of the United Nations Security Council*, Oxford, Hart, 2004;
DUPUY (ED.)	R.-J. Dupuy (ed.), *Manuel sur les organisations internationales/A Handbook on International Organizations*, Dordrecht, Nijhoff, 1998 (2nd ed.);
HÄUSSLER	U. Häußler, *Ensuring and Enforcing Human Security: The Practice of International Peace Missions*, Nijmegen, Wolf Legal Publishers, 2007;
ICRC COMMENTARY (GC)	J. Pictet (ed.), *The Geneva Conventions of 12 August 1949: Commentary*, Geneva, ICRC, 1958, 4 Vols. (available online at www.icrc.org/ihl);

ICRC Commentary (AP)	C. Pilloud *et al.* (eds.), *Commentary on the Additional Protocols of 8 June 1977 to the Geneva Conventions of 12 August 1949*, Geneva/Dordrecht, ICRC/Nijhoff, 1987 (available online at www.icrc.org/ihl);
Klabbers	J. Klabbers, *An Introduction to International Institutional Law*, Cambridge, Cambridge University Press, 2002;
Klein	P. Klein, *La Responsabilité des organisations internationales dans les ordres juridiques internes et en droit des gens*, Brussels, Bruylant, 1998;
Kolb, Porretto & Vité	R. Kolb, G. Porretto & S. Vité, *L'application du droit international humanitaire et des droits de l'homme aux organisations internationales. Forces de paix et administrations civiles transitoires*, Brussels, Bruylant, 2005;
Lawson	R. Lawson, *Het EVRM en de Europese Gemeenschappen: bouwstenen voor een aansprakelijkheidsregime voor het optreden van internationale organisaties*, Deventer, Kluwer, 1999 (with a summary in English);
Malanczuk	P. Malanczuk, *Akehurst's Modern Introduction to International Law*, London/New York, Routledge, 1997 (7th ed.);
Sands & Klein	P. Sands & P. Klein, *Bowett's Law of International Institutions*, London, Sweet & Maxwell, 2001 (5th ed.);
Schermers & Blokker	H.G. Schermers & N.M. Blokker, *International Institutional Law*, Boston *et al.*, Martinus Nijhoff, 2003 (4th ed.);
Shaw	M. Shaw, *International Law*, Cambridge, Cambridge University Press, 2003 (5th ed.);
Simma	B. Simma (ed.), *The Charter of the United Nations. A Commentary*, Oxford, Oxford University Press, 2002 (2nd ed.);
Trybus & White	M. Trybus & N. White (eds.), *European Security Law*, Oxford, Oxford University Press, 2007;
UK Manual	UK Ministry of Defence, *The Manual of the Law of Armed Conflict*, Oxford, Oxford University Press, 2004;

VANHAMME	J. Vanhamme, *Volkenrechtelijke beginselen in het Europees recht*, Groningen, Europa Law Publishing, 2001;
WESSEL	R.A. Wessel, *The European Union's Foreign and Security Policy. Legal Institutional Perspective*, Kluwer Law International, The Hague, 1999;
WHITE	N. White, *The Law of International Organisations*, Manchester, Manchester University Press, 1996;
ZWANENBURG	M. Zwanenburg, *Accountability under International Humanitarian Law for United Nations and North Atlantic Treaty Organization Peace Support Operations*, Leiden, E.M. Meijers Institute, 2004;

4. JOURNALS AND OTHER ABBREVIATIONS

ACLU	American Civil Liberties Union
African Y.I.L	African Yearbook of International Law
AI	Amnesty International
A.I.D.I.	Annuaire de l'Institut de droit international
A.J.I.L.	American Journal of International Law
AMM	Aceh Monitoring Mission
Appl.	Application
Art(s).	Article(s)
ASEAN	Association of Southeast Asian Nations
ASIL	American Society of International Law
ass. ed.	assistant editor
AU	African Union
A.U.I.L.R.	American University International Law Review
Australian Y.I.L.	Australian Yearbook of International Law
Austrian J. Pub. I.L.	Austrian Journal of Public and International Law
AVR	Archiv des Völkerrechts
BGBl.	Bundesgesetzblatt
BiH	Bosnia and Herzegovina
Boston C. I.C.L.R.	Boston College International and Comparative Law Review
Boston U.I.L.J.	Boston University International Law Journal
Bull. EC	Bulletin of the European Communities
Bull. EU	Bulletin of the European Union

BverfG	Bundesverfassungsgericht (German Constitutional Court)
BVerfGE	Entscheidungen des Bundesverfassungsgerichts
B.Y.I.L.	British Yearbook of International Law
California Western I.L.J	California Western International Law Journal
C.D.E.	Cahiers de droit européen
CESDP	Common European Security and Defence Policy (of the EU)
CESCR	(UN) Committee on Economic Social and Cultural Rights
C.E.T.S.	Council of Europe Treaties Series (succeeds *E.T.S.* as of 2004)
CFI	Court of First Instance (of the EC/EU)
CFSP	Common Foreign and Security Policy (of the EU)
Ch(s).	Chapter(s)
Chinese J.I.L.	Chinese Journal of International Law
C.M.L. Rev.	Common Market Law Review
Cmnd.	UK Command Papers
Colum. J. Transn. L.	Columbia Journal of Transnational Law
Colum. L Rev.	Columbia Law Review
COMESA	Common Market for Eastern and Southern Africa
COREPER	Committee of Permanent Representatives (EU)
Cornell I.L.J.	Cornell International Law Journal
CSCE	Conference for Security and Cooperation in Europe
CSDP	Common Security and Defence Policy (EU)
C.Y.I.L.	Canadian Yearbook of International Law
Denver J.I. L. & Policy	Denver Journal of International Law and Policy
Dept.	Department
Doc.	Document
DRC	Democratic Republic of the Congo
D-SACEUR	Deputy Supreme Allied Commander Europe
Duke J.C.I.L.	Duke Journal of Comparative & International Law
EC	European Community / Communities
E.C.H.R.	Reports of Judgments and Decisions (of the European Court of Human Rights)*

* Since 1 Nov. 1998 the *Reports of Judgments and Decisions* are no longer cited as *Rep.* (followed by the Volume) but as *ECHR* (followed by the Volume).

ECJ	European Court of Justice (EC/EU)
EComHR	European Commission of Human Rights (Council of Europe)
ECR	European Court Reports (EC/EU)
ECtHR	European Court of Human Rights (Council of Europe)
ed(s).	edition or editor(s)
E.F.A.R.	European Foreign Affairs Review
E.J.I.L.	European Journal of International Law
Emory I.L.R.	Emory International Law Review
Eur. L. Rev.	European Law Review
EPC	European Political Cooperation
E.H.R.L.R.	European Human Rights Law Review
E.H.R.R.	European Human Rights Reports
ESDP	European Security and Defence Policy (of the EU)
et al.	and others
E.T.S.	European Treaties Series (Council of Europe; as of 2004 renamed *C.E.T.S.*)
EU	European Union
EUBG	EU Battle Group
EU ISS	EU Institute for Security Studies
EUMC	EU Military Committee
EUMS	EU Military Staff
EUPM	EU Police Mission (in Bosnia and Herzegovina)
Eur. Gr. R.Z.	Europäische Grundrechte-Zeitschrift
EUSR	EU Special Representative
EWCA Civ.	England and Wales Court of Appeal (Civil Division)
EWHC Admin.	England and Wales High Court (Administrative Court)
EWHC (QB)	England and Wales High Court (Queen's Bench Division)
Florida J.I.L.	Florida Journal of International Law
Fordham I.L.J.	Fordham International Law Journal
F.Y.I.L.	Finnish Yearbook of International Law
FYROM	Former Yugoslav Republic of Macedonia
GAERC	(EU) General Affairs and External Relations Council
GAM	Free Aceh Movement (Gerakan Aceh Merdeka)

GATT	General Agreement on Tariffs and Trade (used as an overall term including all agreements related to GATT 1947 (see *supra*) before the establishment of the WTO)
Georgia J.I.C.L.	Georgia Journal of International and Comparative Law
George Washington I.L.R.	George Washington International Law Review
G.Y.I.L.	German Yearbook of International Law
Harvard I.L.J.	Harvard International Law Journal
Harvard L. Rev.	Harvard Law Review
HCNM	(OSCE) High Commissioner on National Minorities
Houston J.I.L.	Houston Journal of International Law
HPCR	Program on Humanitarian Policy and Conflict Research (Harvard University)
HRC	Human Rights Committee
H.R.L.J.	Human Rights Law Journal
H.R.L.R.	Human Rights Law Review
H.R.Q.	Human Rights Quarterly
HRW	Human Rights Watch
IACtHR	Inter-American Court of Human Rights
IAComHR	Inter-American Commission on Human Rights
IAEA	International Atomic Energy Agency
IBRD	International Bank for Reconstruction and Development (World Bank)
ICAO	International Civil Aviation Organization
ICC	International Criminal Court
ICJ	International Court of Justice
I.C.J. Reports	Reports of Judgments, Advisory Opinions and Orders of the International Court of Justice*
I.C.L.Q.	International & Comparative Law Quarterly
ICRC	International Committee of the Red Cross
ICSID	International Centre for the Settlement of Investment Disputes
ICTR	International Criminal Tribunal for Rwanda
ICTY	International Criminal Tribunal for the Former Yugoslavia
IGC	Intergovernmental Conference (in the EU)

* Where a volume of the *I.C.J. Reports* has both a continuing pagination and one starting at the beginning of each specific advisory opinion, decision or judgement, both page numbers are cited.

IHL	International Humanitarian Law
ILC	International Law Commission
I.L.M.	International Legal Material
ILO	International Labour Organization
I.L.R.	International Law Reports
IMO	International Maritime Organization
IMP	Initial Monitoring Presence (in the AMM)
Indian J.I.L.	Indian Journal of International Law
I.O.L.R.	International Organizations Law Review
I.R.R.C.	International Review of the Red Cross
ISAF	International Security Assistance Force (in Afghanistan)
Israel Y.H.R.	Israel Yearbook on Human Rights
Italian Y.I.L.	Italian Yearbook of International Law
J.C.M.S.	Journal of Common Market Studies
J.I.C.J.	Journal of International Criminal Justice
J.T.	Journal des tribunaux
J.T.T.	Journal des Tribunaux du Travail
KFOR	Kosovo Force
LCHR	Lawyers Committee for Human Rights
Leiden J.I.L.	Leiden Journal of International Law
LGDJ	Librairie Générale de Droit et de Jurisprudence
LOAC	Law of Armed Conflicts
Loyola L.A.I.C.L.R.	Loyola of Los Angeles International & Comparative Law Review
Melbourne J.I.L.	Melbourne Journal of International Law
MOU	Memorandum of Understanding
M.P.Y.U.N.L.	Max Planck Yearbook of United Nations Law
Michigan J.I.L.	Michigan Journal of International Law
Mil. L. Rev.	Military Law Review
NAC	North Atlantic Council (NATO)
NATO	North Atlantic Treaty Organization
N.J.B.	Nederlands Juristenblad
N.I.L.R.	Netherlands International Law Review
N.J.C.M.-Bulletin	Bulletin van het Nederlands Juristen Comité voor de Mensenrechten
N.J.W.	Neue Juristische Wochenschrift
No. / Nos	Number / Numbers
Nordic J.I.L.	Nordic Journal of International Law
N.Q.H.R.	Netherlands Quarterly of Human Rights
NRF	NATO Response Force

NVIR	Nederlandse Vereniging voor Internationaal Recht
N.Y.I.L.	Netherlands Yearbook of International Law
N.Y.U. J.I.L. Politics	New York University Journal of International Law & Politics
N. Z. Wehrrecht	Neue Zeitschrift für Wehrrecht
OAS	Organization of American States
OAU	Organization of African Unity
OECD	Organization for Economic Cooperation and Development
O.J.	Official Journal (of the EC/EU)
OSCE	Organization for Security and Cooperation in Europe
p(p).	page(s)
Polish Y.I.L	Polish Yearbook of International Law
POW(s)	prisoner(s) of war
PSC	Political and Security Committee
Publ. Court	Publications of the (European or Inter-American) Court (of Human Rights)
R.A.E. / L.E.A.	Revue des Affaires Européennes / Law & European Affairs
R.B.D.I./B.T.I.R.	Revue Belge de Droit International / Belgisch Tijdschrift voor Internationaal Recht (= Belgian Review of International Law)
R.D.U.E.	Revue du droit de l'Union Européenne
Rec. Cours	Recueil des Cours de l'Académie de droit international de La Haye
R.E.D.P./E.R.P.L.	Revue européenne de droit public/ European Review of Public Law
Res.	Resolution
R.D.M.D.G.	Revue de droit militaire et de droit de la guerre = The Military Law and the Law of War Review = Tijdschrift voor militair recht en oorlogsrecht = Zeitschrift für Wehrrecht und Kriegsvölkerrecht = Rivista di diritto militare e di diritto della guerra = Revista de derecho militar y derecho de la guerra (previously R.D.P.M.D.G.)
R.D.P.M.D.G.	Revue de droit pénal militaire et de droit de la guerre (later R.D.M.D.G.)
R.G.D.I.P.	Revue Générale de Droit International Public
R.I.C.R.	Revue internationale de la Croix-Rouge

R.M.C.	Revue du Marché Commun (later R.M.C.U.E.)
R.M.C.U.E.	Revue du Marché Commun et de l'Union Européenne (previously R.M.C.)
R.T.D.E.	Revue Trimestrielle de Droit Européen
R.T.D.H.	Revue trimestrielle des droits de l'homme
ROE	Rules of Engagement
SAARC	South Asian Association for Regional Cooperation
SACEUR	Supreme Allied Commander Europe
S.A.Y.I.L.	South African Yearbook of International Law
S.E.W.	Sociaal-economische wetgeving
SHAPE	Supreme Headquarters of Allied Powers Europe (NATO)
SOFA	Status of Forces Agreement
SOMA	Status of Mission Agreement
SOP	Standard Operating Procedure
Stanford J.I.L.	Stanford Journal of International Law
S.Z.I.E.R.	Schweizerische Zeitschrift für internationales und europäisches Recht = Revue suisse de droit international et de droit européen
Texas I.L.J.	Texas International Law Journal
UDHR	Universal Declaration of Human Rights (1948)
U.K.T.S.	United Kingdom Treaties Series
UN	United Nations
UNGA	United Nations General Assembly
UNHCHR	UN High Commissioner for Human Rights
UNIDO	United Nations Industrial Development Organization
UNMIK	United Nations Interim Administration Mission in Kosovo
UNSC	United Nations Security Council
U.N.T.S.	United Nations Treaties Series
US	United States (of America)
U.S.C.	United States Code
Vanderbilt J.T.L.	Vanderbilt Journal of Transnational Law
Virginia J.I.L.	Virginia Journal of International Law
V.N.	Vereinte Nationen
WEU	Western European Union
WEU ISS	WEU Institute for Security Studies
WHO	World Health Organization
Wisconsin I.L.J.	Wisconsin International Law Journal

WTO	World Trade Organization
Yale J.I.L.	Yale Journal of International Law
Y.E.L.	Yearbook of European Law
Y.I.H.L.	Yearbook of International Humanitarian Law
Y.I.L.C.	Yearbook of the International Law Commission
Z.a.ö.R.V.	Zeitschrift für ausländisches öffentliches Recht und Völkerrecht
Z. Eur. S.	Zeitschrift für Europarechtliche Studien
§(§)	paragraph(s)

INTRODUCTION

This book is an updated and slightly amended version of the thesis with the same title with which I obtained the degree of Doctor in Laws at the Faculty of Law of the Catholic University of Leuven in November 2008. I am grateful to the K.U.Leuven for the opportunity which it has given me to write and defend that thesis. I am also grateful to my successive superiors at the Legal Services of the Belgian Ministry of Defence/Defence Staff and the Council of the European Union for their support in my efforts to complete it and wish to express my thanks to my present and former colleagues, friends and family for all their support.

This short introduction explains how the European Security and Defence Policy (ESDP) raises international law questions (A) and addresses the methodology used and the research questions addressed in this book (B).

A. HOW THE DEVELOPMENT OF THE EUROPEAN SECURITY AND DEFENCE POLICY RAISES INTERNATIONAL LAW QUESTIONS

The European Union (EU), building on the European Political Cooperation developed since 1970, has been developing a Common Foreign and Security Policy (CFSP) since the EU was established by the Treaty on European Union (EU Treaty), which was signed in Maastricht on 7 February 1992 and which entered into force on 1 November 1993. Initially, the security and defence component of the CFSP was limited and the EU had to rely on the Western European Union (WEU), which in turn was to a significant extent dependent on the North Atlantic Treaty Organization (NATO). However, the amendments introduced by the Treaty of Amsterdam enabled a substantial development of this security and defence component. This potential was seized by the Cologne and Helsinki European Councils in June and December 1999, which initiated the development of a (Common) European Security and Defence Policy (ESDP).[1]

1 Initially, the term CESDP was used (the 1999 Cologne European Council used the term "Common European Policy on Security and Defence") but later on the term ESDP prevailed. However, under the Lisbon Treaty (Treaty amending the Treaty on European Union and the Treaty establishing the European Community, Lisbon, 13 December 2007, *O.J. C* 306, 17 December 2007; see also Doc. CIG 14/07 of 3 December 2007 and Doc. CIG 15/07 of

Subsequently, much of the institutional machinery was set in place, first on a provisional basis and later permanently, with some structures being anchored in the EU Treaty by the Treaty of Nice, and the EU took over most crisis management tasks and assets of the WEU. Subsequently, the ESDP was declared operational to an increasing extent in December 2001 and May 2003 and in 2003 the EU launched its first civilian and military ESDP operations, which have been increasing in number, variety and size since then (as of 31 August 2009, the EU has launched some 22 operations). Moreover, the December 2003 Brussels European Council adopted a *European Security Strategy*. These developments and the status of the ESDP are described in more detail in chapters 1 to 3 below.

As the ESDP is manifesting itself through an increasing number of ESDP operations, questions arise as to the legal basis for such operations under international law, the scope of the ESDP under the EU Treaty and the law governing the conduct of these ESDP operations. The *European Security Strategy* also raises the issue of when the EU should act and may act in the security field. While these questions are similar to questions raised regarding other security organizations, including the UN (see especially the debate over the applicability of international humanitarian law to UN forces) and NATO (for instance the debate over the legality of the Kosovo air campaign in 1999 (operation "Allied Force")), the peculiar legal nature of the EU[2] and its specificity justify a separate examination of the ESDP in this respect. This is especially the case with regard to human rights, where there is a large body of jurisprudence on human rights obligations of the European Communities (EC) and, albeit to a lesser extent, the EU. Moreover, while there is a significant body of legal literature on the ESDP,[3]

3 December 2007), this policy is renamed "Common Security and Defence Policy" (see the new Title V, Chapter 2, Section 2 of the EU Treaty as amended by the Lisbon Treaty; consolidated version in *O.J.* C 115, 9 May 2008).

2 By this I mean that the EU's constitutive instrument is rather elaborate and detailed in comparison with many other international organizations, and certainly compared to NATO, and that the powers of the EU and its organs and the EU's decision-making procedures are similarly defined in more detail, even in CFSP and ESDP. Obviously, in the latter two areas the enforcement of these rules is less judicial in nature than it is for the European Community and decision-making occurs mainly by unanimity, justifying their qualification as more intergovernmental than supranational. Nevertheless, even so CFSP and ESDP missions and instruments are better defined than their UN and NATO counterparts.

3 See, e.g. the references in Chapter 2, note 161 as well as A. Bashlinskaya, *Der rechtliche Gehalt der Gemeinsamen Sicherheits- und Verteidigungspolitik der Europäischen Union (GESVP) und ihre Vereinbarkeit mit dem deutschen Grundgesetz*, Bremen, May 2005, Zentrum für Europäische Rechtspolitik an der Universität Bremen, Diskussionspapier 2/2005 (available online at www.zerp.uni-bremen.de/english/pdf/dp2_2005.pdf); A. Deighton, 'The European Security and Defence Policy', 40 *J.C.M.S.* 2002, pp. 719–741; S. Grassi, 'L'introduzione delle operazioni di peace-keeping nel Trattato di Amsterdam: profili giuridici ed implicazioni politiche', 73(2) *La comunità internazionale* 1998, pp. 295–326; I. Österdahl, 'The EU and Its Member States, Other States, and International Organizations: The Common European

often covering both a European law perspective[4] and an international law perspective, only a few more recent publications discuss to some extent the considerable practice already developed so far in ESDP operations[5] and even those rarely analyze specific legal issues related thereto such as applicable law[6] or

Security and Defence Policy after Nice' 70 *Nordic J.I.L.* 2001, pp. 341–372; F. Pagani, 'A New Gear in the CFSP Machinery: Integration of the Petersberg Tasks in the Treaty on European Union', 9 *E.J.I.L.* 1998, pp. 737–749; L.N. Pnevmaticou, *Aspectes juridiques de la politique européenne de sécurité et de défense*, Paris, WEU ISS, 2001 (Occasional Paper 31) and M. Trybus, 'With or without the EU Constitutional Treaty: towards a Common Security and Defence Policy?', 31 *Eur. L. Rev.* 2006, pp. 145–166.

4 Most commentaries on the EU Treaty and handbooks on EU law include a section on the ESDP but this is usually rather short. Even books on EU external relations generally address the ESDP only briefly compared to other external relations aspects. For instance, P. Eeckhout, *External Relations of the European Union. Legal and Constitutional Foundations*, Oxford, Oxford University Press, 2004, devotes a mere 26 pages out of 484 pages to the CFSP and only marginally addresses the ESDP. P. Koutrakos, *EU International Relations Law*, Oxford, Hart, 2006, does somewhat better with 25 pages out of 506 specifically on the ESDP, although this is still rather limited.

5 E.g. J. Litten, *Beitrag der Westeuropäischen Union (WEU) zur Europäischen Sicherheits- und Verteidigungspolitik (ESVP): eine rechtspolitische Untersuchung*, Aachen, Shaker, 2005, does well compared to the other publications but still only devotes 13 pages of some 300 pages to the five ESDP operations that had been launched at the time. The main exceptions I am aware of are S. Lang, *Bestimmungsfaktoren und Handlungsfähigkeit der Europäischen Sicherheits- und Verteidigungspolitik*, Frankfurt, Peter Lang, 2007, pp. 189–262; my own chapter on ESDP operations ('ESDP in Practice: Increasingly Varied and Ambitious EU Security and Defence Operations') in Trybus & White, pp. 61–101; the Chapter by N. Tsagourias ('EU Peacekeeping Operations: Legal and Theoretical Issues') in that same publication (pp. 102–133); M. Merlingen & R. Ostrauskaite (eds.), *European Security and Defence Policy: An Implementation Perspective*, Abingdon, Routledge, 2008 and some chapters in S. Blockmans (ed.), *The European Union and International Crisis Management: Legal and Policy Aspects*, The Hague, TMC Asser Press, 2008. There are a number of Articles and chapters on specific operations or even providing an overview of several operations (see the references in Chapter 3), but very few of these are written from a legal perspective and go beyond one specific operation.

6 For an exception predating the first operations, see S. Bartelt, *Der rechtliche Rahmen für die neue operative Kapazität der Europäischen Union*, Münster, Lit Verlag, 2003, pp. 161–209. More recent exceptions include N. Ronzitti, 'L'applicabilità del diritto internazionale umanitario', in N. Ronzitti (ed.), *Le forze di pace dell'Unione Europea*, Roma, Rubbettino, 2005, pp. 165–194; the brief sections in N. Tsagourias, *supra* note 5, pp. 115–118 and in G.-J. Van Hegelsom, 'Relevance of IHL in the Conduct of Petersberg Tasks', in College of Europe & ICRC (eds.), *Proceedings of the Bruges Colloquium. The Impact of International Humanitarian Law on Current Security Policy Trends. 26th - 27th October 2001 / Actes du colloque de Bruges. L'impact du droit international humanitaire sur l'évolution des politiques de sécurité. 26-27 octobre 2001*, Bruges, College of Europe (*collegium* No. 25, available online at www.coleurop.be/template.asp?pagename=pub_collegium), 2002, pp. 109–120, as well as M. Zwanenburg, 'Toward a More Mature ESDP: Responsibility for Violations of International Humanitarian Law by EU Crisis Management Operations', in S. Blockmans (ed.), *The European Union and International Crisis Management: Legal and Policy Aspects*, The Hague, TMC Asser Press, 2008, pp. 395–416 and V. Falco, 'Old Continent, New Wars: The European Union and International Humanitarian Law', conference paper available online at www.ies.be/files/repo/conference2008/EUinIA_I_2_Falco.pdf. For publications on human rights, see *infra* note 2278. On the status of EU-led forces, see also the references *infra* notes 346–347. For a discussion of the role of international humanitarian law in the EU's CFSP more generally see T. Ferraro, 'Le droit international humanitaire dans la politique étrangère et de

do so only very briefly. This book does not intend to cover all international law issues relating to the ESDP but will address mainly the applicable international law in ESDP operations because this has been largely neglected in the literature so far. Moreover, the large degree of transparency in ESDP operations, which is visible in the publication in the *Official Journal* of many documents and agreements concerning such operations, offers a significant insight into legal aspects of ESDP crisis management operations that is not always so public in the case of operations conducted by other international organizations.[7] The precise scope of the questions analyzed in this book is set out in the next section.

B. METHODOLOGY AND RESEARCH QUESTIONS

As outlined above, the legal issues that arise in respect of the ESDP include the legal basis for ESDP operations under international law, the scope of the ESDP under the EU Treaty and the law applicable to the conduct of ESDP operations.

As this book deals with international law aspects of the ESDP, the EU law aspects are not its main focus. Admittedly, EU law, despite is specific nature, is a part of international law.[8] However, in (the title of) this book by international law I

---

sécurité commune de l'Union européenne', 84 No. 846 *R.I.C.R./I.R.R.C.* 2002, pp. 435–461 and for the EU's promotion of respect for this body of law *by other States or actors*, see the European Union Guidelines on promoting compliance with international humanitarian law (IHL), *O.J. C* 327, 23 December 2005, p. 4. It should also be noted that the Council has adopted a series of joint actions and decisions supporting and promoting the (universal) ratification and implementation of various weapons and disarmament treaties as well as UNSC Res. 1540 (28 April 2004); see, e.g. Council Joint Action of 23 July 2007 in support of the convention on prohibitions or restrictions on the use of certain conventional weapons which may be deemed to be excessively injurious or to have indiscriminate effects, in the framework of the European Security Strategy (2007/528/CFSP), *O.J. L* 194, 26 July 2008, p. 11 and Council Joint Action of 14 May 2008 in support of the implementation of United Nations Security Council Resolution 1540 (2004) and in the framework of the implementation of the EU strategy against the proliferation of weapons of mass destruction (2008/368/CFSP), *O.J. L* 127, 15 May 2008, p. 78. The wider interaction between the EU and the LOAC was the subject of a colloquium on 'Le droit international humanitaire et l'Union européenne' on 18–19 June 2009 in Nice, the proceedings of which will be published by Pedone.

7 On this transparency, see, e.g. the Decision of the Representatives of the Governments of the Member States of 29 October 2008 on the treatment of documents of EU civilian crisis management missions and military operations (2008/836), *O.J. L* 299, 8 November 2008, p. 34.

8 There is some discussion as to the position of EU law in relation to international law. More generally, while it now seems fairly generally accepted that international organizations (may) have a proper legal order, there is less agreement on the nature of that legal order and in particular the degree of its autonomy from general international law. This will be elaborated upon somewhat in Chapter 7.C below. It may be noted that the ILC is dealing with the topic 'Fragmentation of International Law: Difficulties Arising from the Diversification and Expansion of International Law', which covers this issue to some extent; see http://untreaty.

mean general public international law.[9] Nevertheless, where relevant for the international law issues, EU law aspects will be examined. This is for instance the case for the legal personality of the EU and its related treaty-making power, the scope of the ESDP missions under the EU Treaty and, in part, the status of international law in the EU, including the UN Charter and human rights. In contrast, legal issues primarily limited to EU law, such as defence procurement in light of Article 296 EC Treaty, the European Defence Agency (EDA), flexible or differentiated integration and delimitation of competences between the different Pillars of the EU and between EU organs will not be addressed or will be addressed only marginally.[10]

In respect of those EU law issues that are addressed, the focus is on the EU Treaty as in force on 31 August 2009. However, relevant changes that were envisaged under the abandoned EU Constitutional Treaty[11] and those set out in the Lisbon Treaty[12] are also analyzed. Since the Lisbon Treaty largely left intact the EU

---

un.org/ilc/guide/1_9.htm. See on this topic also A. Gattini, 'Un regard procédural sur la fragmentation du droit international', 110 *R.G.D.I.P.* 2006, pp. 303–336 and M. Prost & P. Kingsley Clark, 'Unity, Diversity and the Fragmentation of International Law: How Much Does the Multiplication of International Organizations Really Matter?', 5 *Chinese J.I.L.* 2006, pp. 341–370. Compare with regard to international organizations, N.M. Blokker & H.G. Schermers (eds.), *Proliferation of International Organizations: Legal Issues*, The Hague, Kluwer Law International, 2001.

9 In this book, the expression 'general international law' will be used *sensu stricto* as covering customary international law and general principles of law recognized in international law (I exclude multilateral codification conventions as such, which are sometimes included in this notion (e.g. VANHAMME, pp. 6 *juncto* 17), because most of their content will already be covered by customary international law) and *sensu lato* as covering international law, including treaties and decisions of international organizations, with the exception of the legal order of a given international organization from which it will then be distinguished (e.g. EC/EU law). It should be clear from the context in which sense these expressions are used.

10 See briefly Chapter 2 below.

11 For a general analysis, see, e.g. G. Amato, H. Bribosia & B. de Witte (eds.), *Genèse et destine de la Constitution européenne / Genesis and Destiny of the European Constitution*, Brussels, Bruylant, 2007; K. Lenaerts, 'La constitution pour l'Europe et l'Union comme entité politique et ordre juridique, 41 *C.D.E.* 2005, pp. 13–125; J.-C. Piris, *The Constitution for Europe: A Legal Analysis*, Cambridge, Cambridge University Press, 2006; J.-C. Piris, *Le traité constitutionnel pour l'Europe: une analyse juridique*, Brussels, Bruylant, 2006 and L. Burgorgue-Larsen, A. Levade & F. Picod (eds.), *Traité établissant une Constitution pour l'Europe*, Brussels, Bruylant (*Tome 1: Parties I et IV, Architecture constitutionnelle*, 2007; *Tome 2: Partie II: La Charte des droits fondamentaux de l'Union. Commentaire article par article*, 2005).

12 See generally R. Barents, *Het Verdrag van Lissabon*, Deventer, Kluwer, 2008; K.H. Fischer, *Der Vertrag von Lissabon*, Baden-Baden, Nomos, 2008; S. Griller & J. Ziller (eds.), *The Lisbon Treaty: EU Constitutionalism Without a Constitutional Treaty?*, Vienna, Springer, 2008; V. Hellmann, *Der Vertrag von Lissabon: vom Verfassungsvertrag zur Änderung der bestehenden Verträge: Einführung mit Synopse und Übersichten*, Berlin, Springer, 2009; I. Pernice (ed.), *Der Vertrag von Lissabon: Reform der EU ohne Verfassung? Kolloquium zum 10. Geburtstag des WHI*, Baden-Baden, Nomos, 2008; F.-X. Priollaud & D. Siritzky, *Le Traité de Lisbonne: commentaire, article par article, des nouveaux traités européens (TUE et TFUE)*, Paris, Documentation Française, 2008; R. Streinz *et al.*, *Der Vertrag von Lissabon zur Reform der*

Constitution's provisions on the ESDP as well as those on the legal status of the EU and on human rights, what has been written on the EU Constitution in this respect mostly remains very relevant. Just before this book was going in print, the Czech Republic deposited its instrument of ratification of the Lisbon Treaty on 13 November 2009, as the last Member State to do so. Therefore the Lisbon Treaty will enter into force on 1 December 2009.

In order to demonstrate how the above-mentioned international law issues arise and to provide the required background, I will first set out in Part I a short summary of the ESDP's genesis (Chapter 1), the key features of its present status, including an overview of possible future developments (Chapter 2), an overview of ESDP operations launched so far and the legal aspects thereof (Chapter 3), as well as the international law issues which the ESDP raises (Chapter 4). With respect to the latter, the focus will be on the scope of the ESDP and ESDP missions and the international legal basis for the latter,[13] as well as on neutrality. The international law applicable to ESDP operations will be analyzed extensively

---

EU: Einführung mit Synopse, Munich, Beck, 2008 (2nd ed.); X., *"Vertrag von Lissabon": der EU-Reformvertrag aus europäischer, verfassungsrechtlicher und wirtschaftspolitischer Sicht: 28. Februar 2008: Referate und Diskussionsbeiträge, Österreichischer Juristentag*, Vienna, Manz, 2008; X., 'Der Reformvertrag von Lissabon', *Europarecht* 2009, Beiheft 1/2009 and the series of contributions on different aspects of the Lisbon Treaty in 56 and 57 *S.E.W.* 2008 and 2009. On external relations, see, e.g. A. Ott & R.A. Wessel, 'Het Verdrag van Lissabon en de externe betrekkingen van de Europese Unie', 56 *S.E.W.* 2008, pp. 478–482 and A. Juncos & R. Whitman, 'The Lisbon Treaty and the Foreign, Security and Defence Policy: Reforms, Implementation and the Consequences of (non-)Ratification', 14 *E.F.A.R.* 2009, pp. 25–46. For a brief general survey, see P. Craig, 'The Treaty of Lisbon: Process, Architecture and Substance', 33 *Eur. L. Rev.* 2008, pp. 137–166; M. Dougan, 'The Treaty of Lisbon 2007: Winning Minds, Not Hearts', 45 *C.M.L. Rev.* 2008, pp. 617–703; J.P. Jacqué, 'Le traité de Lisbonne: une vue cavalière', 44 *R.T.D.E.* 2008, pp. 439–483; J.-V. Louis, 'Le traité de Lisbonne', 15 *Journal des tribunaux droit européen* 2007, pp. 289–298; G. Maganza, 'The Lisbon Treaty: A Brief Outline', 31 *Fordham I.L.J.* 2008, pp. 1603–1613; F.C. Mayer, 'Die Rückkehr der Europäische Verfasung?: ein Leitfaden zum Vertrag von Lissabon', 67 *Z.a.ö.R.V.* 2007, pp. 1141–1217; C. Reh, 'The Lisbon Treaty: Deconstitutionalizing the European Union', 47 *J.C.M.S.* 2009, pp. 625–650 and J.P. Terhechte, 'Der Vertrag von Lissabon: Grundlegende Verfassungsurkunde der europäischen Rechtsgemeinschaft oder technischer Änderungsvertrag?', 43 *Europarecht* 2008, pp. 143–189 (www.europarecht-online.info/eurecht/hefte/Aufsatz_EUR_08_02.pdf). See also the report by the UK House of Lords' European Union Select Committee on the Lisbon Treaty (*The Treaty of Lisbon: An Impact Assessment*, 10th Report, Session 2007–08, HL Paper 62, available online at www.parliament.uk/parliamentary_committees/lords_eu_select_committee.cfm) and the German Constitutional Court's judgement BVerfG, 2 BvE 2/08, 30 June 2009 (English translation at www.bundesverfassungsgericht.de/entscheidungen/es20090630_2bve000208en.html).

13 Initially, it was my intention to treat this legal basis more extensively in a distinct part. However, as the EU's position in this respect is less peculiar and as this issue has been analyzed quite extensively already in doctrine, I have opted for a short discussion only and have rather focused on the LOAC and human rights in ESDP operations, on which little research has been done so far.

in Part III, where the focus is on the law of armed conflict (LOAC[14]) and human rights.

However, before taking on these aspects in Part III, there is a preliminary question that must be tackled, namely what are the obligations incumbent upon international organizations under international law generally? It is submitted that this question has not received much attention yet even though it has profound implications for other aspects of the law of international organizations, such as their responsibility. The analysis of this problem in Part II will start with the legal status and personality of international organizations generally, as this would logically seem to be a prerequisite for an organization to be subject to obligations under international law (Chapter 5). This includes, by way of comparison, also an analysis of the legal status of NATO and the Organization for Security and Cooperation (OSCE). It is followed by a specific examination of the legal status of the EU (Chapter 6). Subsequently, I look at how international organizations may be bound by international law, both in general and for the EU specifically, *inter alia* covering the internal legal order of these organizations and their constitutional instruments, agreements entered into by international organizations, customary international law, general principles of law, with particular attention for the European Court of Justice's jurisprudence on human rights, treaties concluded by Member States, and decisions of international organizations, and also Member State responsibility in relation to conduct in the framework of international organizations (Chapter 7).

Part III on international law applicable to the conduct of ESDP operations will, after a short introduction to the complex legal framework in ESDP operations, focus on the law of armed conflict (Chapter 8) and human rights (Chapter 9). Concerning the LOAC, the main issues that will be addressed are its specific scope of application, the nature of armed conflicts in which EU-led forces might become engaged, the law of occupation, the impact of UN Security Council intervention and the degree of EU command and control and the impact thereof on the LOAC obligations of the EU itself and of the Member States, building on the conclusions of Chapter 7. Concerning human rights, specific attention will be paid to the controversial issue of their extraterritorial scope of application, derogations in times of war and emergencies, including the impact of UN Security Council intervention, the relationship between human rights and the LOAC, as well as the human rights obligations of the EU itself and of the Member States in light of command and control arrangements, again building on the conclusions of Chapter 7.

---

14 I use this term as interchangeable with 'international humanitarian law' or 'the law of war', even though distinctions are sometimes made between these terms.

Throughout this book the relevant texts, especially treaties and decisions of international organizations, are the starting point of the analysis but I equally take into account customary international law and general principles of law, as well as actual practice and doctrine.

My work as a legal advisor in the Directorate General Legal Support and Mediation of the Belgian Ministry of Defence/Defence Staff from September 2004 until October 2007 has been extremely valuable in gaining crucial insights into how peace operations are actually conducted and how legal issues pertaining thereto are dealt with in practice. In addition, my current position at the Legal Service of the Council of the European Union since November 2007 has permitted me to gain further insights into the practice of ESDP operations, even though the thesis on which this book is based had essentially been written by then.[15] While some aspects of this matter are not in the public domain and cannot be discussed in this book due to their classified nature, there are many aspects that are not classified but that are nevertheless simply not widely known outside the military (legal) community.[16] I have endeavoured to include these practical aspects as much as possible and to reconcile them with the theoretical legal framework. While the overall result is still fairly theoretical, I hope it nevertheless offers a theoretical framework that provides a workable basis for being applied in practice.

As a final point, I have chosen to include a table of cases but not a table of international instruments because the latter would be rather long, especially given the large number of EU decisions pertaining to ESDP operations, and yet would provide little added value. Neither have I included an index as I trust that the detailed table of contents will suffice to guide readers looking for a specific issue. The research was concluded on 31 August 2009.

The two main research questions which I analyze are:

1. To what extent and how are international organizations in general and the EU in particular bound by international law?
2. What international law is applicable to the conduct of ESDP operations, in particular what rules, if any, of the law of armed conflict and of international human rights law?

---

15 The views expressed in this book are solely my own and do not bind the Council or its Legal Service.

16 For a very useful publication discussing many of these issues from a more practical perspective, see U. Häußler, *Ensuring and Enforcing Human Security: The Practice of International Peace Missions*, Nijmegen, Wolf Legal Publishers, 2007.

Each of these main questions will raise many more specific questions that will be addressed throughout this book. In my conclusions of especially Chapters 6 to 9 and the general conclusions, I will answer these two key questions and the various more specific related questions.

PART I
THE ESDP AND ITS INTERNATIONAL LAW ASPECTS

INTRODUCTION

In order to set the scene for the international law questions that are the focus of this book, I will first set out in this part a brief historical overview of the development of the ESDP up to 2003, i.e. the year of the entry into force of the EU Treaty as it is in force on 31 August 2009 (subject to subsequent accessions) and the year in which the ESDP really became operational and launched its first operations (Chapter 1). This is followed by a brief survey of the main features of the ESDP as it stands (Chapter 2) and a detailed discussion of the ESDP operations launched so far, focusing on their legal aspects (Chapter 3). In Chapter 4, the key international legal issues arising from these developments are identified and those which are not dealt with more extensively in Parts II and III are analyzed to some extent, including the scope of the ESDP – both under the pre- and post-Lisbon EU Treaty – and the international legal bases for ESDP operations.

CHAPTER 1
BRIEF HISTORICAL EVOLUTION

The purpose of this brief overview of the genesis and development of the ESDP is merely to explain how the current status of the ESDP, and especially its relationship to NATO and WEU, came about, and to provide an overview of the European security architecture of which the ESDP is a part. It is therefore limited to what is deemed necessary for this purpose and is by no means comprehensive.

I have divided these developments into the following six periods: the failure of the European Defence Community and the establishment of the WEU in the aftermath of the post World War II period (A); the period in which the WEU was overshadowed by other international organizations (B); the era of the European Political Cooperation and the reactivation of the WEU (C), the setting up of the EU with a CFSP and the WEU as its defence component, that was also the European Security and Defence Identity in NATO (D); the Treaty of Amsterdam, the Cologne and Helsinki European Councils and the foundation of the ESDP (E) and the Treaty of Nice, the European Security Strategy and the first ESDP operations (F). That brings us up to 2003, the year of the entry into force of the Treaty of Nice's amendments of the EU Treaty – i.e. the pre-Lisbon version of the EU Treaty – and the year in which the ESDP really became operational and launched its first operations.

A. THE FAILURE OF THE EUROPEAN DEFENCE COMMUNITY AND THE ESTABLISHMENT OF THE WEU IN THE AFTERMATH OF POST WORLD WAR II

After World War II, various initiatives were launched towards European integration and several security arrangements were set up in and for Europe, the latter mostly in response to the Soviet threat. One of the first of these initiatives was the Treaty on Economic, Social and Cultural Collaboration and Collective Self-Defence signed in Brussels on 17 March 1948 between Belgium, France, Luxembourg, the Netherlands and the UK (hereinafter '1948 Brussels

Treaty').[17] Although it was concluded only between five States, it is interesting because of the broad nature of its *envisaged* scope of action, i.e. economic, social and cultural collaboration as well as collective defence. However, this treaty and the cooperation pursuant thereto were quickly overshadowed by other arrangements.

In the defence field, collaboration within the framework of the 1948 Brussels Treaty started off well, with the adoption of a plan for a common defence, involving an integrated military structure and the setting up of a Western Union Defence Organization in September 1948.[18] Nevertheless, in the security field, the primary security organization for Europe quickly became the North Atlantic Treaty Organization (NATO), established by the North Atlantic Treaty signed in Washington DC on 4 April 1949.[19] This evolution, coupled with the desire to integrate the Federal Republic of Germany in the new security structures, led to two further developments. On the one hand, the parties to the 1948 Brussels Treaty, all of which were also parties to the North Atlantic Treaty, decided to transfer their military structures to NATO in order to avoid duplication. On the other hand, France put forward proposals for a European Defence Community (EDC) and a proposal was also developed to set up a European Political Community. The former came close to success with the signature of the Treaty Setting Up the European Defence Community on 27 May 1952 in Paris (EDC Treaty),[20] only to be aborted when the French parliament rejected it on 30 August 1954.[21] The latter never became more than

---

17 19 *U.N.T.S.* 51, entered into force on 25 August 1948. See A. Dumoulin & E. Remacle, *L'Union de l'Europe occidentale. Phénix de la défense européenne*, Brussels, Bruylant, 1998, pp. 3–12.

18 See WEU, 'Origins of WEU', www.weu.int/History.htm#1 and A. Dumoulin & E. Remacle, *supra* note 17, pp. 14–16.

19 34 *U.N.T.S.* 243, entered into force on 24 August 1949 (available online at www.nato.int/docu/basictxt/treaty.htm). On NATO, see generally its website at www.nato.int; NATO, *NATO Handbook*, NATO Public Diplomacy Division, Brussels, 2006 edition, available online at www.nato.int/docu/handbook/2006/hb-en-2006.pdf; the *NATO Review* (available online at www.nato.int/docu/review.htm) and J.-C. Zarka, *L'OTAN*, Paris, PUF, 1997. On NATO and its early years, see, e.g. A.L. Goodhart, 'The North Atlantic Treaty', 79 *Rec. Cours* 1951-II, pp. 186–236. See also *infra*, Section D of this Chapter on NATO's evolution.

20 Traité instituant la Communauté européenne de défense, *inter alia* published in the Belgian Parliamentary document *Gedrukte Stukken* Kamer, 1952–1953, No. 163. For references to the various versions of the text of the treaty, see E. Fursdon, *The European Defence Community: A History*, London and Basingstoke, MacMillan Press, 1980, p. 188, note 1. The French text is available online at http://mjp.univ-perp.fr/europe/1952ced.htm.

21 It had obtained parliamentary assent in Belgium, Germany, Luxembourg and the Netherlands and was pending in the Italian Parliament: see A. Dumoulin & E. Remacle, *supra* note 17, p. 27, especially notes 80–81. See also K. Lenaerts & P. Van Nuffel, *Constitutional Law of the European Union*, London, Sweet & Maxwell, 2005 (2nd ed.) pp. 27–28. For an elaborate overview of the birth and death of the EDC, see E. Fursdon, *supra* note 20. On its conception, see also P. Reuter, 'L'origine du projet de communauté européenne de défense: souvenirs et réflexions', in R.-J. Dupuy (ed.), *Humanité et droit international: mélanges Rene-Jean Dupuy*, Paris, Pedone, 1991, pp. 241–248 and J. Legaret & E. Martin-Dumesnil, *La communauté*

a draft project.[22] The failure of these ambitious projects (the EDC had a very strong supranational nature and was based on numerous and very detailed provisions[23]) required another solution for the European security arrangements. Agreement on that solution was reached later in 1954 in the 'Paris Agreements'[24] which *inter alia* provided for the accession of Germany to NATO[25] and the modification of the 1948 Brussels Treaty by the Protocol signed in Paris on 23 October 1954[26] that established the Western European Union[27] but stated

---

européenne de défense: étude analytique du traité du 27 mai 1952, Paris, Vrin, 1953, pp. 41–51, who also provide an analysis from a French point of view (in 1953) at pp. 99–168. See also M. Trybus, *European Union Law and Defence Integration*, Oxford, Hart, 2005, pp. 22–43. For a very critical French view at the time, see J. Moch, *Alerte! Le problème crucial de la communauté européenne de defense*, Paris, Laffont, 1954.

22 Projet de traité portant statut de la Communauté Européenne, adopted by an *ad hoc* Assembly on 10 March 1953 in Strasbourg (available online at http://mjp.univ-perp.fr/europe/1953cpe.htm). For a discussion, see H.W. Briggs, 'The Proposed European Political Community', 48 *A.J.I.L.* 1954, pp. 110–122; R.T. Griffiths, *Europe's First Constitution: The European Political Community, 1952–1954*, London, Federal Trust for Education and Research, 2000; R. Griffiths, 'Europe's First Constitution: The European Political Community, 1952–1954', in S. Martin (ed.), *The Construction of Europe: Essays in Honour of Emile Noël*, Dordrecht, Kluwer Academic Publishers, 1994, pp. 19–39; B. Karp, 'The Draft Constitution for a European Political Community', 8 *International Organization* 1954, pp. 181–202; A.H. Robertsen, 'The European Political Community', 29 *B.Y.I.L.* 1952, pp. 383–401 and H. Ridder, 'Zur Problematik der Europäischen Politischen Gemeinschaft / Le problème de la Communauté politique européenne', *Internationales Jahrbuch der Politik* 1954, pp. 52–74.

23 The Treaty contained no less than 132 Articles, 12 Protocols and a number of other related instruments. For an extensive discussion of the EDC Treaty, see, e.g. E. Fursdon, *supra* note 20, pp. 150–188; J. Legaret & E. Martin-Dumesnil, *supra* note 21, pp. 53–96 and 181–271 and H. Leynen, *De Europese Defensie Gemeenschap*, Antwerpen, De Vlijt, 1953. For an analysis and appraisal, see A. De Smet, *La Communauté Européenne de Défense, expérience et leçons*, Heule, UGA, 1966. See also M. Trybus, 'The Vision of the European Defence Community and a Common Defence for the European Union', in Trybus & White, pp. 13–42.

24 See A. Bloed & R.A. Wessel (eds.), *The Changing Functions of the Western European Union (WEU): Introduction and Basic Documents*, Dordrecht, Nijhoff, 1994, pp. xiv-xvii. Some of the agreements not cited below are available at www.nato.int/docu/basics.htm; www.weu.int/Treaty.htm#2 or www.nato.int/archives/1st5years/index.htm.

25 See the Final Communiqué of the Meeting of the North Atlantic Council attended by Foreign and Defence Ministers of 22 October 1954 (available at www.nato.int/docu/basictxt/b541022e.htm) and the Protocol to the North Atlantic Treaty on the Accession of the Federal Republic of Germany, Paris, 23 October 1954, 243 *U.N.T.S.* 308 (1956) (also available online at www.nato.int/docu/basictxt/b541023v.htm).

26 Protocol(s) Modifying and Completing the Brussels Treaty, 211 *U.N.T.S.* 343 (1955), entered into force on 6 May 1955. The consolidated version of the Brussels Treaty is available online at www.weu.int/Treaty.htm#1.

27 On WEU and its development, see generally E. Birk, *Der Funktionswandel der Westeuropäischen Union (WEU) im europäischen Integrationsprozess*, Würzburg, Ergon, 1999; A. Bloed & R.A. Wessel (eds.), *supra* note 24; G. Brandstetter, *Die Westeuropäischen Union – Einfürung und Dokumente*, Baden-Baden, Nomos, 1999; A. Deighton & E. Remacle (eds.), 'The Western European Union, 1948–1998. From the Brussels treaty to the Treaty of Amsterdam', 51(1–2) *Studia Diplomatica* 1998 (special issue); A. Dumoulin & E. Remacle, *supra* note 17; A. Dumoulin, with a contribution by F. Gevers, *Union de l'Europe occidentale: La Déstructuration (1998-2006)*, Brussels/Paris, Bruylant/LGDJ, 2005; A. Imbert, *L'Union de l'Europe occidentale*, Paris, L.G.D.J., 1968; G. Lenzi (ed.), *WEU at Fifty*, Paris, WEU Institute for Security Studies, 1998; J. Litten, *Beitrag der Westeuropäischen Union (WEU) zur*

that the WEU would "*rely on the appropriate Military Authorities of NATO for information and advice on military matters*" (hereinafter the consolidated treaty is referred to as 'Amended Brussels Treaty').[28]

B. WEU IS SOON OVERSHADOWED BY OTHER ORGANIZATIONS

Thus in the military field, the WEU came second to NATO. In many of the other areas of (potential) activity of the WEU, other organizations took over.[29] For instance, a more prominent role was played by the Council of Europe, which was established in 1949 and has the aim "*to achieve a greater unity between its members for the purpose of safeguarding and realising the ideals and principles which are their common heritage and facilitating their economic and social progress*" through "*discussion of questions of common concern and by agreements and common action in economic, social, cultural, scientific, legal and administrative matters and in the maintenance and further realisation of human rights and fundamental freedoms*" but excluding national defence.[30] The Council of Europe quickly acquired significant expertise in the field of human rights, democracy and the rule of law, with as its main achievement the European Convention on Human Rights (ECHR) and its supervisory organs.[31] The importance of the ECHR for the ESDP will be discussed extensively in Chapter 9.

Europäischen Sicherheits- und Verteidigungspolitik (ESVP): eine rechtspolitische Untersuchung, Aachen, Shaker, 2005; G.W. Rees, *The Western European Union at the Crossroads: Between Trans-Atlantic Solidarity and European Integration*, Boulder, Westview, 1998; M.A. Robles Carrillo, *La Unión de la Europa occidental et la cooperación europea en materia de seguridad et defensa*, McGraw-Hill, Madrid, 1997; M. Saalfeld, *Entwicklung und Perspectiven der Westeuropäischen Union: völkerrechtliche und sicherheitspolitische Überlegungen zu einer künftigen Revision des WEU-Vertrags*, University of Tübingen (dissertation), 1992; P. Van Ackere, *L'Union de l'Europe occidentale, Que sais-je?*, Paris, PUF, 1995; M. Warnken, *Der Handlungsrahmen der Europäischen Union im Bereich der Sicherheits- und Verteidigingspolitik*, Baden-Baden, Nomos, 2002, pp. 83–140 and J. Varwick, *Sicherheit und Integration in Europa: zur Renaissance der Westeuropäischen Union*, Opladen, Leske und Budrich, 1998. See also various publications of the WEU Institute for Security Studies, which has now been transferred to the EU, available online at www.iss.europa.eu.

28 For a short summary of this era, see also WEU, 'Origins of WEU', www.weu.int/History.htm#1; A. Dumoulin & E. Remacle, *supra* note 17, pp. 14–44 and Lord Ismay, *NATO the First Five Years 1949–1954*, Part I, Chapter 1, 'Origins of the North Atlantic Treaty', available online at www.nato.int/archives/1st5years/index.htm. On the WEU-NATO relationship thus created, see A. Dumoulin & F. Gevers, *supra* note 27, pp. 13–16.

29 A. Bloed & R.A. Wessel (eds.), *supra* note 24, p. vx, write that "*the defence aspect of WEU is the only side which has not been abandoned*". See also A. Dumoulin & F. Gevers, *supra* note 27, pp. 7–13 and A. Dumoulin & E. Remacle, *supra* note 17, pp. 12–14.

30 Statute of the Council of Europe, London, 5 May 1949, 87 *U.N.T.S.* 103 and *E.T.S.* No. 1, entered into force on 3 August 1949 (subsequently amended).

31 (European) Convention for the Protection of Human Rights and Fundamental Freedoms, 4 November 1950, 213 *U.N.T.S.* 222 and *(C.)E.T.S.* No. 5, as amended and supplemented by several Protocols.

Specifically in the economic sphere, the Organization for European Economic Cooperation, established on 16 April 1948 on the basis of the Marshall Plan,[32] which would later become the Organization for Economic Cooperation and Development (OECD),[33] was of greater importance than the collaboration under the 1948 Brussels Treaty. The establishment of the European Coal and Steel Community in 1951[34] and subsequently also the European (Economic) Community[35] and the European Atomic Energy Community,[36] shifted the economic cooperation to these organizations, which would later broaden their scope of action far beyond economic matters.

Thus for a considerable era[37] and especially since the early 1970s, the WEU became a dormant organization (it played some role as a meeting place between the UK and the EC Member States before the UK's accession to the EC on 1 January 1973[38]) and NATO was the key institutional actor in the field of Western European security. Its counterpart in Central and Eastern Europe was

32 See the Convention for European Economic Cooperation, Paris, 16 April 1948, 888 *U.N.T.S.* 142 (1973), which was put into operation on a provisional basis from 16 April 1948 and which entered into force on 28 July 1948.

33 Established by the Convention on the Organization for Economic Cooperation and Development, Paris, 14 December 1960, 888 *U.N.T.S.* 181 (1973), which entered into force on 30 September 1961.

34 See the Treaty Establishing the European Coal and Steel Community, 18 April 1951, 261 *U.N.T.S.* 140 (1957), which entered into force on 23 July 1952. This Treaty expired on 23 July 2002, in conformity with its Article 97, which stated that this treaty was concluded for a period of 50 years from its entry into force. It may be noted that the ECSC Treaty did have objectives concerning security: its preamble *inter alia* states that "*world peace can be safeguarded only by creative efforts commensurate with the dangers that threaten it*" and that "*the contribution which an organized and vital Europe can make to civilization is indispensable to the maintenance of peaceful relations*". See also S. Sur, 'Aspects juridiques d'une politique européenne de sécurité et de défense', in C. Tomuschat & J.A. Frowein (eds.), *Rechtsprobleme einer europäischen Sicherheits- und Verteidigungspolitik*, Heidelberg, Müller, 1997, p. 133 ("*la construction européenne a toujours eu et conserve un objectif fondamental de sécurité*").

35 See the Treaty Establishing the European Economic Community, Rome, 25 March 1957, 294 *U.N.T.S.* 18 (1958), which entered into force on 1 January 1958. This treaty was renamed the Treaty Establishing the European Community by the EU Treaty (see Title I, Article A and Title II, Article G of the Maastricht version). Unless indicated otherwise, all subsequent references to the EC Treaty will be to the EC Treaty as subsequently modified and in force at the time of writing (see *O.J. C 325*, 24 December 2002, p. 33, as amended by subsequent accession treaties).

36 See the Treaty Establishing the European Atomic Energy Community, Rome, 25 March 1957, which entered into force on 1 January 1958 (subsequently amended).

37 A. Bloed & R.A. Wessel (eds.), *supra* note 24, p. xviii, speak of a period of 30 years during which "*the WEU was not given a chance to really develop itself into a fully-fledged security organizations*". See also A. Dumoulin & E. Remacle, *supra* note 17, pp. 55–85.

38 See WEU, 'WEU History. WEU from 1955 to 1984: The Saar, Arms Control, the UK and the EC Six', www.weu.int/History.htm#2 and A. Dumoulin & E. Remacle, *supra* note 17, pp. 77–85.

the Warsaw Treaty Organization.[39] In the 1970s, West and East met in the framework of the Conference on Security and Cooperation in Europe (CSCE), which first resulted in the 1975 Helsinki Final Act[40] and would gradually develop into a permanent forum and eventually, in 1994,[41] into the Organization on Security and Cooperation in Europe (OSCE),[42] which is a regional arrangement under Chapter VIII of the UN Charter.[43]

---

39 Established by the Treaty of Friendship, Cooperation and Mutual Assistance between the People's Republic of Albania, the People's Republic of Bulgaria, the Hungarian People's Republic, the German Democratic Republic, the Polish People's Republic, the Rumanian People's Republic, the Union of Soviet Socialist Republics, and the Czechoslovak Republic, signed in Warsaw on 14 May 1955 and which entered into force on 6 June 1955 ('Warsaw Pact'). No English text has been published in the *U.N.T.S.*; see the note at http://avalon.law.yale.edu/20th_century/warsaw.asp, where an English translation is available. For a comparative analysis of both alliances, see 'The Parallel History Project on NATO and the Warsaw Pact', at www.php.isn.ethz.ch.

40 1 August 1975.

41 CSCE, 'Towards a Genuine Partnership in a New Era', Budapest, 6 December 1994, §3 Summit Declaration. On the legal nature of the OSCE, see *infra*, Chapter 5.C.

42 The OSCE's website is at www.osce.org. On the CSCE/OSCE generally and its evolution, see G. Barberini, *Sicurezza e cooperazione da Vancouver a Vladivostok: introduzione allo studio dell'Organizzazione per la Sicurezze e la Cooperazione in Europe (OSCE)*, Giappichelli, 2004 (2nd ed.); A. Bloed (ed.), *From Helsinki to Vienna: Basic Documents of the Helsinki Process*, Dordrecht, Martinus Nijhoff, 1990; A. Bloed (ed.), *The Conference on Security and Cooperation in Europe: Analysis and Basic Documents, 1972–1993*, Dordrecht, Kluwer, 1993; A. Bloed (ed.), *The Challenges of Change: The Helsinki Summit of the CSCE and Its Aftermath*, Dordrecht, Martinus Nijhoff, 1994; A. Bloed (ed.), *The Conference on Security and Cooperation in Europe: Basic Documents, 1993–1995*, The Hague, Martinus Nijhoff, 1997; J. Bortloff, *Die Organisation für Sicherheit und Zusammenarbeit in Europa: eine völkerrechtliche Bestandsaufnahme*, Berlin, Duncker & Humblot, 1996; M. Bothe, N. Ronzitti & A. Rosas (eds.), *The OSCE in the Maintenance of Peace and Security: Conflict Prevention, Crisis Management and Peaceful Settlement of Disputes*, The Hague, Kluwer, 1997; E. Decaux, *Sécurité et coopération en Europe. Les textes officiels du processus de Helsinki (1973–1992)*, Paris, La documentation française, 1992; D.J. Galbreath, *The Organization for Security and Co-operation in Europe*, Abingdon, Routledge, 2007; V.-Y. Ghébali, *La diplomatie de la détente: la CSCE, d'Helsinki à Vienne (1973–1989)*, Brussels, Bruylant, 1989; V.-Y. Ghébali, *L'OSCE dans l'Europe post-communiste, 1990–1996. Vers une identité paneuropéenne de sécurité*, Brussels, Bruylant, 1996; J. Leatherman, *From Cold War to Democratic Peace: Third Parties, Peaceful Change, and the OSCE*, Syracuse, Syracuse University Press, 2003; M.R. Lucas (ed.), *The CSCE in the 90's: Constructing European Security and Cooperation*, Baden-Baden, Nomos, 1993; D.S. Lutz (ed.), *Perspektiven und Defizite der OSZE*, Baden-Baden, Nomos, 2000 and S. Trifunovska, *Organization for Security and Co-operation in Europe (OSCE)*, in J. Wouters (ed.) *International Encyclopaedia of Laws. Intergovernmental Organizations*, The Hague, Kluwer Law International, 2006. See also the journal *Helsinki Monitor*, the newsletter *OSCE Magazine* (available online at www.osce.org/publications/show_publication.php?grp=194, previously the *OSCE Newsletter*), the *OSCE-Jahrbuch/OSCE Yearbook* (published by the Institut für Friedensforschung und Sicherheitspolitik an der Universität Hamburg since 1995 in German and since 1996 in English and later also in Russian) and OSCE, *OSCE Handbook*, Vienna, OSCE Secretariat, 1999 (3rd ed.) (2007 version available online at www.osce.org/item/22000.html).

43 See, e.g. CSCE, 'Towards a Genuine Partnership in a New Era', *supra* note 41, Decision on Strengthening the CSCE, §26. For a discussion, see, e.g. H. Körbs, 'Ist die Organisation über

C. EUROPEAN POLITICAL COOPERATION AND THE REACTIVATION OF THE WEU

Also in the 1970s, the Member States of the European Communities started to develop intergovernmental consultation and cooperation mechanisms amongst themselves on matters relating to foreign policy and cooperation on law and order. Formally, these activities initially took place outside the institutional context of the European Communities.[44] The first of these mechanisms, and the one relevant for the development of the ESDP, was the European Political Cooperation (EPC), instituted in 1970.[45] The EPC dealt with certain foreign policy issues[46] and was given a treaty basis by the Single European Act in 1986.[47] The second such mechanism was the biannual meeting of the Home Affairs Ministers (or their equivalents) of the Member States on matters of law and order,

---

Sicherheit und Zusammenarbeit in Europa (OSZE) eine "regionale Abmachung oder Einrichtung" im Sinne des Kapitels VIII der UN-Charta?', 33 *A.V.R.* 1995, pp. 459–538. For the UN's reaction, see W. Hummer & M. Schweitzer, 'Article 52', in SIMMA, pp. 834–835 (who appear to see a mainly implicit UN recognition of this status). On this status and its relevance, see *infra*, Chapter 4.A.6.

44 Though obviously some links existed, especially after the adoption of the European Single Act, see, e.g. C. Reich, 'Le role de la Commission des Communautés européennes dans la Cooperation politique européenne', No. 331 *R.M.C.* 1989, pp. 560–563 and S. Nuttall, 'Interaction between European Political Cooperation and the European Community', 7 *Y.E.L.* 1987, pp. 211–249 and 8 *Y.E.L.* 1988, pp. 171–173.

45 The European Political Cooperation was adopted by a decision of the Foreign Affairs ministers of the Member States on 27 October 1970, see *Bull. EC* 11-1970, pp. 9–14.

46 On the EPC generally, see, e.g. E. Denza, *The Intergovernmental Pillars of the European Union*, Oxford, Oxford University Press, 2002, pp. 33–61; P. De Schoutheete de Tervarent, *La cooperation politique européenne*, Brussels, Editions Labor, 1986; J.K. De Vree *et al.* (eds.), *Towards a European Foreign Policy*, Dordrecht, Martinus Nijhoff, 1987; M. Holland (ed.), *The Future of European Political Cooperation*, Basingstoke, Macmillan, 1991; S. Nuttal, *European Political Co-operation*, Oxford, Clarendon Press, 1992; A. Pijpers, E. Regelsberger & W. Wessels (eds.), *European Political Cooperation in the 1980s: A Common Foreign Policy for Western Europe?*, Dordrecht, Nijhoff, 1988 and R. Rummel, *EPZ – Erfolgsformel für die gemeinsame Europäische Aussenpolitik?: Entwicklungsmöglichkeiten der Europäischen Politischen Zusammenarbeit auf der Basis der Einheitlichen Europäischen Akte*, Ebenhausen, Stiftung Wissenschaft und Politik, 1987. On the legal nature of the EPC, see also R. Gosalbo Bono, 'Some Reflections on the CFSP Legal Order', 43 *C.M.L. Rev.* 2006, pp. 338–339 and 342.

47 European Single Act, Luxembourg and The Hague, 17 and 28 February 1986, *O.J. L* 169, 29 June 1987, p. 1, which entered into force on 1 July 1987 (see especially the treaty provisions on European cooperation in the sphere of foreign policy in Article 30). On the impact of the Single European Act on the EPC, see D. Murphy, 'European Political Cooperation after the Single European Act; The Future of Foreign Affairs in the European Communities', 12 *Boston C. I.C.L.R.* 1989, pp. 335–355 and W. Wessels, 'EPC after the Single European Act: Towards a European Foreign Policy via Treaty Obligation?', in M. Holland (ed.), *supra* previous note, pp. 143–160.

set up by a European Council decision of December 1975, known as the TREVI-group.[48]

Shortly before the adoption of the Single European Act, an effort was made to 'reactivate' the WEU in the Rome Declaration of 27 October 1984.[49] While this reactivation was rather modest, it did produce some results.[50] For instance, on 27 October 1987, the WEU Ministerial Council adopted the Platform on European Security Interests, which *inter alia* recalled the commitment "*to build a European Union in accordance with the Single European Act ...*" and stated that the Member States were "*convinced that the construction of an integrated Europe will remain incomplete as long as it does not include security and defence*" and expressed the resolve "*to strengthen the European pillar of the Alliance*".[51] Furthermore, in 1990 Portugal and Spain acceded to the WEU. But most importantly, the WEU also became operational to some extent: it conducted mine-clearing naval operations in the Persian Gulf in 1987–1988, helped enforce the UN embargo following the Iraqi invasion of Kuwait in 1990 and helped enforce UN sanctions in the Yugoslav conflicts in the Adriatic Sea and on the Danube.[52]

48 See the Summary of the Conclusions of the European Council of Rome, 1–2 December 1975, *Bull. EC* 11–1975, p. 1104. TREVI stands for '*Terrorisme, Radicalisme, Extrémisme et Violence Internationale*'.

49 See WEU, 'WEU History. Reactivation of WEU', www.weu.int/History.htm#3. The Rome Declaration is available online at www.weu.int/documents/841024en.pdf.

50 For a general discussion of this reactivation, see A. Bloed & R.A. Wessel (eds.), *supra* note 24, pp. xviii-xix; A. Cahen, 'La Défense européene: Perspectives nouvelles ouvertes par la réactivation de l'Union de l'Europe Occidentale', 33 *Annuaire Europeen* 1986, pp. 15–38; A. Cahen, 'L'Union de l'Europe occidentale (UEO) et la mise en oeuvre de la future défense commune de l'Union européenne', No. 394 *R.M.C.U.E.* 1996, pp. 23–25; A. Dumoulin & E. Remacle, *supra* note 17, pp. 87–174; I. Gaias, 'Security in Europe: Reactivation of the WEU and the Process of European Integration', 20(3–4) *The International Spectator* 1985, pp. 27–33 and P. Tsakaloyannis, *La relance de l'union de l'Europe occidentale: implications pour la CE et ses institutions / The Reactivation of the Western European Union: The Effects on the EC and Its Institutions*, Maastricht, European Institute of Public Administration, 1985.

51 See the preamble and part III.a.2. The text is available online at www.weu.int/documents/871027en.pdf.

52 See generally A. Bloed & R. Wessel (eds.), *supra* note 24, pp. xvii-xxix; A. Dumoulin & E. Remacle, *supra* note 17, pp. 140–145, 231–234 and 239–242; J. Litten, *supra* note 27, pp. 96–98 and WEU, 'WEU History. Operational Role', www.weu.int/History.htm#4. The key WEU documents in this respect are mentioned and reproduced in A. Bloed & R. Wessel (eds.), *supra* note 24 and many of them are also available online at www.weu.int/Key%20texts.htm.

D. THE ESTABLISHMENT OF THE EU WITH A CFSP AND THE WEU AS ITS DEFENCE COMPONENT THAT IS ALSO THE EUROPEAN SECURITY AND DEFENCE IDENTITY IN NATO

However, it was especially following the end of the Cold War and the establishment of the European Union that a European security and defence policy started to develop. The Maastricht Treaty on European Union of 7 February 1992, which entered into force on 1 November 1993 (hereinafter 'Maastricht Treaty'[53]) established the EU, which is founded on the European Communities (as its so-called first pillar) supplemented by two other fields of policy and cooperation, namely the Common Foreign and Security Policy (hereinafter 'CFSP', also referred to as the second pillar of the EU)[54] and provisions on justice and home affairs (also referred to as the third pillar of the EU).[55] In essence, the Maastricht Treaty brought the EPC and TREVI into the institutional framework of the EU and broadened and deepened cooperation in these fields. The EPC was thereby replaced by the CFSP.

Before I continue with the development of the CFSP and eventually also the ESDP, let me return to the wider European and world scene. After the end of the Cold War the security situation, especially in Europe, evolved from a confrontation between two blocs that did not involve the direct use of force to a more diverse spectre of security challenges and conflicts, some of which became extremely violent, for instance in the former Yugoslavia. The new geopolitical situation made it possible for the former enemies to work together, which for

---

53 *O.J. C* 224, 31 August 1992, p. 1.

54 *Id.*, Article B and title V (Articles J-J.11), now Article 2 and Title V (Articles 11–28) EU Treaty. See generally E. Denza, *supra* note 46, pp. 33–61; M. Holland (ed.), *Common Foreign and Security Policy: The Record and Reforms*, London, Pinter, 1997; E. Regelsberger, P. De Schoutheete de Tervarent and W. Wessels (eds.), *Foreign Policy of the European Union: from EPC to CFSP and Beyond*, Boulder, Lynne Riennner, 1997; S.A. Pappas & S. Vanhoonacker (eds.), *The European Union's Common Foreign and Security Policy: The Challenges of the Future*, Maastricht, EIPA, 1996; G. Dattilo, *Politica estera e sicurezza comune nell'Unione europea*, Torino, Giappichelli, 1996; W. Carlsnaes & S. Smith (eds.), *European Foreign Policy: The EC and Changing Perspectives in Europe*, London, Sage, 1994; T. Jürgens, *Die gemeinsame Europäische Aussen- und Sicherheitspolitik*, Köln, Carl Heymanns, 1994 and T. Stein, *Die Gemeinsame Aussen- und Sicherheitspolitik der Union unter Berücksichtigung der Sanktionsproblematik*, Graz, Karl-Franzens-Universität, Forschungsinstitut für Europarecht, 1993.

55 Maastricht Treaty, Article B and title VI (Articles K-K.9), now Article 2 and Title VI (Articles 29–42) EU Treaty. Articles 1(11) and 2(15) of the Treaty of Amsterdam have incorporated some aspects initially covered under the third pillar in the first pillar (see title IV EC Treaty) and renamed the third pillar 'Police and Judicial Cooperation in Criminal Matters' (see Title VI EU Treaty), although the latter is often still referred to as 'JHA'.

instance permitted an increased UN Security Council involvement in conflict situations,[56] ranging from robust peace operations that go beyond traditional peacekeeping to authorizations to States and international organizations to conduct peace enforcement operations.[57] Also, most international organizations

---

56 The changed situation allowed the Security Council to start playing the central role which it had always been meant to play, especially under Chapter VII of the UN Charter, even if not always entirely in the way envisaged and sometimes even beyond what had been envisaged. See generally M. Berdal & S. Economides, *United Nations Interventionism, 1991-2004*, Cambridge, Cambridge University Press, 2007; O. Corten & P. Klein, 'Action humanitaire et chapitre VII – La redefinition du mandat et des moyens d'action des Forces des Nations Unies', 39 *A.F.D.I.* 1993, pp. 105–130; de Wet, pp. 149–177; P.-M. Dupuy, 'Le maintien de la paix' in Dupuy (ed.), pp. 561–604; P.-M. Dupuy, 'Securité collective et organisation de la paix', 97 *R.G.D.I.P.* 1993, pp. 617–627; R.-J. Dupuy (ed), *Le développement du rôle du Conseil de Sécurité: colloque, La Haye, 21–23 juillet 1992 = The Development of the Role of the Security Council: Workshop, The Hague, 21–23 July 1992: Peace-keeping and Peace-building*, Dordrecht, Martinus Nijhoff, 1993; W. Durch (ed.), *The Evolution of UN Peacekeeping: Case Studies and Comparative Analysis*, New York, St. Martin's Press, 1993; Y. Kerbrat, *La référence au Chapitre VII de la Charte des Nations Unies dans les résolutions à caractère humanitaire du Conseil de sécurité*, Paris, LGDJ, 1995; E. Lagrange, *Les opérations de maintien de la paix et le chapitre VII des Nations Unies*, Paris, Montchrestien, 1999 (especially pp. 7–46); D.M. Malone (ed.), *The UN Security Council: From the Cold War to the 21st Century*, Boulder, Rienner, 2004; D.M. Malone, 'The Security Council in the Post-Cold War Era: A Study in the Creative Interpretation of the U.N. Charter', 35 *N.Y.U. J.I.L. Politics* 2003, pp. 487–517; I. Österdahl, *Threat to the Peace: An Interpretation by the Security Council of Article 39 of the Charter*, Uppsala, Iustus Förlag, 1998; D. Sarooshi, *The United Nations and the Development of Collective Security: The Delegation by the UN Security Council of its Chapter VII Powers*, Oxford, Oxford University Press, 2000; A. Schäfer, *Der Begriff der "Bedrohung des Friedens" in Artikel 39 der Charta der Vereinten Nationen: die Praxis des Sicherheitsrates*, Frankfurt am Main, Lang, 2006; J.-M. Sorel (ed.), *Le Chapitre VII de la Charte des Nations Unies. Colloque de la Société Française pour le Droit international (02–06–1994; Rennes)*, Paris, Pedone, 1995 and M. Zambelli, *La constatation des situations de l'article 39 de la Charte des Nations Unies par le Conseil de sécurité: le champ d'application des pouvoirs prévus au chapitre VII de la Charte des Nations Unies*, Geneva, Helbing & Lichtenhahn, 2002. See also *infra* note 58. In addition, post '11 September' Security Council measures, which include quasi legislative resolutions such as UNSC Resolutions 1373 (28 September 2001) and 1540 (28 April 2004), have given rise to renewed debate and ample publications on the powers of the Security Council.

57 Traditionally, UN peacekeeping operations were based on consent of the parties involved, impartiality and a very limited use of force. Also the tasks of such operations were limited to creating a buffer zone and observing compliance with peace or ceasefire agreements. However, this has evolved significantly since the 1990s. I will discuss this in more detail below in Chapter 4.A.1 when addressing the scope of ESDP tasks.

adopted a broad concept of security, including the UN,[58] CSCE/OSCE,[59] NATO,[60] WEU[61] and EU.[62]

Although this changed environment offered new possibilities,[63] using these possibilities has not been an easy exercise as illustrated by the UN's (and other

58 See generally An Agenda for Peace, *infra* note 63, especially §§5, 12, 13 and 15. See also the practice of the Security Council, in particular relating to the expansion of the notion "threat to international peace and security", which has been held to (actually or potentially) cover, *inter alia*, terrorism (see, e.g. Resolutions 1269 (19 October 1999) and 1373 (28 September 2001); for a more comprehensive overview, see D. Leurdijk & G. Steeghs, *Decision-making by the Security Council: Terrorist Acts which Threaten International Peace and Security, 1989 – 2004*, Clingendeal Research Essay, January 2005, available online at www.clingendael.nl/publications/2005/20050100_cli_ess_leurdijk.pdf), internal conflicts or unrest (e.g. in Somalia: Resolutions 733 (23 January 1992) and 751 (24 April 1992) and following), the overturn of a democratically elected regime (Haiti, see Resolutions 841 (16 June 1993), 875 (16 October 1993), 917 (6 May 1994) and 940 (31 July 1994)) and the repression of civilians and/or minorities (see especially Resolutions 688 (5 April 1991, §1) and 1296 (19 April 2000, §5)). See also Resolutions 1308 (17 July 2000, concerning AIDS), 1325 (31 October 2000, on women and peace and security) and 1366 (30 August 2001, on conflict prevention). See furthermore the *Declaration and Programme of Action on a Culture of Peace*, 13 September 1999, UN Doc. A/RES/53/243 (6 October 1999). See also B. Ramcharan, *The Security Council and the Protection of Human Rights*, The Hague, Nijhoff, 2002 and some of the publications cited *supra* note 56.

59 See especially the Helsinki Final Act (*supra* note 40), *passim*; the Charter of Paris for a New Europe (Paris, 19–21 November 1990), §21 and the Charter for European Security (Istanbul, 18–19 November 1999), §§4, 5 and 9.

60 See especially The Alliance's Strategic Concept (*infra* note 68), §25.

61 See *European Security: A Common Concept of the 27 WEU Countries* (WEU, Extraordinary Council of Ministers, Madrid, 14 November 1995, available online at www.weu.int/documents/951114en.pdf), §1.

62 Such a broad security concept clearly underlies the *European Security Strategy* adopted at the December 2003 Brussels European Council (*A Secure Europe in a Better World*, available at www.consilium.europa.eu/showPage.aspx?id=266&lang=EN). Moreover, the EU's adherence to a broad security concept is also illustrated through the reference in Article 11(1) EU Treaty to the CSCE's Charter of Paris for a New Europe (which endorses a comprehensive security concept, see *supra*, note 59) and the EU's development of civilian crisis management instruments and its focus on conflict prevention. H. Neuhold, 'The European Union: A Major Actor in the Field of Security Policy', in W. Benedek, H. Isak & R. Kicker (eds.), *Development and Developing International and European Law: Essays in Honour of Konrad Ginther on the Occasion of his 65th Birthday*, Frankfurt am main, Lang, 1999, pp. 451–471 clearly sees an added value of the EU in the framework of a broader security concept.

63 In *An Agenda for Peace. Preventive Diplomacy, Peacemaking and Peacekeeping, Report of the Secretary-General pursuant to the statement adopted by the Summit Meeting of the Security Council on 31 January 1992*, UN Doc. A/47/277 – S/24111, 17 June 1992, the spirit of that time was captured in the following words: "*In these past months a conviction has grown [...] that an opportunity has been regained to achieve the great objectives of the Charter*" (§3). *See also Supplement to An Agenda for Peace* (UN Doc. A/50/60-S/1995/1, 3 January 1995), §5 ("*we still live in a new age that holds great promise for both peace and development*").

actors') failures in Bosnia and Herzegovina[64] and Rwanda[65] and has led to thorough studies and reform proposals and measures.[66] Be that as it may, in this environment NATO also changed and started to undertake, in addition to its collective defence role, operations other than self-defence, that are usually labelled 'non-article V', crisis response or peace support operations (starting with operations in Bosnia and Herzegovina, Kosovo and FYROM[67]).[68] It also started

64 See, e.g. *Report of the Secretary-General pursuant to General Assembly Resolution 53/35 (1998) ('Report on the fall of Srebrenica')*, UN Doc. A/54/549, 15 November 1999.

65 *Report of the Independent Inquiry into the Actions of the United Nations During the 1994 Genocide in Rwanda*, 15 December 1999, UN Doc. S/1999/1257, 16 December 1999.

66 See especially the *Report of the Panel on United Nations Peace Operations*, UN Doc. A/55/305-S/2000/809, 17 August 2000 and follow-up measures (available online at www.un.org/peace/reports/peace_operations); *A More Secure World: Our Shared Responsibility. Report of the High-level Panel on Threats, Challenges and Change*, UN Doc. A/59/565, 2 December 2004 (available online at www.un.org/secureworld) and *Report of the Secretary-General on "In larger freedom: towards development, security and human rights for all"*, UN Doc. A/59/2005, 21 March 2005 (available online at www.un.org/largerfreedom).

67 For a summary overview, see www.nato.int/issues/balkans/index.html.

68 This evolution in NATO's role was *inter alia* reflected in its revised Strategic Concepts of 1991 (*The Alliance's New Strategic Concept*, Rome, 7–8 November 1991) and 1999 (*The Alliance's Strategic Concept*, Washington DC, 24 April 1999). For NATO's evolution from the end of the Cold War to 11 September 2001, see, e.g. G. Bono, *NATO's 'Peace Enforcement' Tasks and "Policy Communities": 1990–1999*, Aldershot, Ashgate, 2003; M.J. Brenner (ed.), *NATO and Collective Security*, Basingstoke, Macmillan, 1998; A. Buzzi, *L'intervention armée de l'OTAN en République Fédérale de Yougoslavie*, Paris, Pedone, 2001; F. Carr & K. Ifantis, *NATO in the New European Order*, Basingstoke/New York, Macmillan/St. Martin's Press, 1996; R. de Wijk, B. Boxhoorn & N. Hoekstra (eds.), *NATO after Kosovo*, The Hague, Clingendael Institute, 2000; T. Gazzini, 'NATO Coercive Military Activities in the Yugoslav Crisis (1992–1999)', 12 *E.J.I.L.* 2001, pp. 391–435; X. Guérin, 'L'Organisation des Nations Unies, l'Organisation du Traité de l'Atlantique Nord et le maintien de la paix', 40 *A.F.D.I.* 1994, pp. 171–174; S. Kay, *NATO and the Future of European Security*, Lanham, Rowman & Littlefield, 1998; A. Krohn, 'NATO- und WEU-peacekeeping', in H.-G. Ehrhart & D. Haglund (eds.), *The 'New Peacekeeping' and European Security: German and Canadian Interests and Issues*, Baden-Baden, Nomos, 1995, pp. 91–105; R. Latter, *NATO in the New Europe*, London, HSMO, May 1995 (Wilton Park Paper 99); F.-J. Meiers, *NATO's Peacekeeping Dilemma*, Bonn, Europa-Union-Verlag, 1996; S.V. Papocosma *et al.* (eds.), *NATO after Fifty Years*, Wilmington, Scholarly Resources, 2001; P. Pascallon, *L'Alliance Atlantique et l'OTAN, 1949–1999: un demi-siècle de succès*, Brussels, Bruylant, 1999; T. Sandler, *The Political Economy of NATO: Past, Present, and into the 21st Century*, Cambridge, Cambridge University Press, 1999; H. Timmermann & A. Pradetto (eds.), *Die NATO auf dem Weg ins 21. Jahrhundert*, Münster, LIT Verlag, 2002; S. Trifunovska (ed.), *The Transatlantic Alliance on the Eve of the New Millennium*, The Hague, Kluwer Law International, 1996; S. Trifunovska, *North Atlantic Treaty Organization*, in J. Wouters (ed.) *International Encyclopaedia of Laws. Intergovernmental Organizations*, The Hague, Kluwer Law International, 2002; A. Van Staden, *Van collectieve verdediging naar collectieve veiligheid?: de aanpassing en uitbreiding van de NAVO*, The Hague, Adviesraad Vrede en Veiligheid, 1996; J. Woodliffe, 'The Evolution of a New NATO for a New Europe', 47 *I.C.L.Q.* 1998, pp. 174–192 and D.S. Yost, *NATO Transformed: The Alliance's New Roles in International Security*, Washington DC, United States Institute of Peace Press, 1998. For a legal analysis of these new NATO missions, see, e.g. B. Delcourt & F. Dubuisson, 'Contribution au débat juridique sue les missions 'non-article 5' de l'OTAN', 35 *R.B.D.I. / B.T.I.R.* 2002, pp. 439–467 and the discussion between I. Dekker & E. Myjer on the one hand

developing cooperation mechanisms with third countries and admitting new members.[69]

WEU reacted both to this new environment and to the establishment of the EU.[70] A first key text is this respect, the nature and content of which illustrates the close relationship that would exist henceforth between the EU and WEU, was the Declaration by Belgium, Germany, Spain, France, Italy, Luxembourg, the Netherlands, Portugal and the United Kingdom of Great Britain and Northern Ireland, which are members of the Western European Union and also members of the European Union on the role of the Western European Union and its relations with the Atlantic Alliance, adopted at the EC Summit in Maastricht on 10 December 1991, i.e. when the text of the EU Treaty had been agreed but the Treaty had not yet been signed. However, since the declaration was also annexed to the EU Treaty and is based on that treaty, I will first set out the provisions on security and defence in the EU Treaty and then turn to this declaration and the WEU.[71]

Pursuant to Article B of the Maastricht Treaty the EU's objectives included "*to assert its identity on the international scene, in particular through the implementation of a common foreign and security policy including the eventual framing of a common defence policy, which might in time lead to a common*

---

and N. Blokker & S. Muller on the other hand in 9 *Leiden J.I.L.* 1996, pp. 411–424. For an interesting discussion of notions like "collective security" in a European context, see S. Jaberg, *Systeme kollektiver Sicherheit in und für Europa in Theorie, Praxis und Entwurf: ein systemwissenschaftlicher Versuch*, Baden-Baden, Nomos, 1998. In addition, following '11 September', NATO's role changed further, see, e.g. A. Forster & W. Wallace, 'What is NATO for?", 43 *Survival* 2001, pp. 107–122; P.H. Gordon, 'NATO after 11 September', 43 *Survival* 2001, pp. 89–106 and T. Lansford, *All for One: Terrorism, NATO and the United States*, Ashgate, 2002.

69 These cooperation mechanisms include(d) the North Atlantic Cooperation Council, later succeeded by the Euro-Atlantic Partnership Council, the Partnership for Peace, specific Partnerships with Russia and Ukraine, the Mediterranean Dialogue, the South East Europe Initiative and, most recently, the Istanbul Cooperation Initiative (involving the broader Middle East region). See, e.g. NATO, 'NATO's Partner Countries', www.nato.int/issues/partners/index.html (with further references); Part VII of the *NATO Handbook* (*supra* note 19); A. Dumoulin & E. Remacle, *supra* note 17, pp. 332–339; S. Trifunovska, *supra* previous note (*International Encyclopaedia of Laws*), Chapter V, pp. 103–143 and A. Wenger, C. Breitenmoser & P. Lehmann, *Die Nato-Partnerschaft für den Frieden im Wandel: Entwicklung und Zukunft eines kooperativen Sicherheidtsinstrumentes*, Zürich, FSK, 1998. On NATO enlargement, see, e.g. R.D. Asmus, *Opening NATO's Door: How the Alliance Remade Itself for a New Era*, New York, Columbia University Press, 2002 and M.A. Smith & E. Timmin (eds.), *Building a Bigger Europe: EU and NATO Enlargement in Comparative Perspective*, Aldershot, Ashgate, 2000.

70 See generally A. Dumoulin & E. Remacle, *supra* note 17, pp. 177–354.

71 See also A. Collet, 'Le Traite de Maastricht et la défense', 29 *R.T.D.E.* 1993, pp. 225–233 and J. Litten, *supra* note 27, pp. 140–174.

defence".[72] According to Article J.1(1), the CFSP was to cover all areas of foreign and security policy. Article J.1(2) further defined the objectives of the CFSP as follows:

- to safeguard the common values, fundamental interests and independence of the Union;
- to strengthen the security of the Union and its Member States in all ways;
- to preserve peace and strengthen international security, in accordance with the principles of the United Nations Charter as well as the principles of the Helsinki Final Act and the objectives of the Paris Charter;
- to promote international cooperation;
- to develop and consolidate democracy and the rule of law, and respect for human rights and fundamental freedoms.

Article J.4 then spelled out in greater detail what the CFSP was to encompass in the area of security and defence.[73] It read, in relevant part, as follows:

> 1. The common foreign and security policy shall include all questions related to the security of the Union, including the eventual framing of a common defence policy, which might in time lead to a common defence.
> 2. The union requests the Western European Union (WEU), which is an integral part of the development of the Union, to elaborate and implement decisions and actions of the Union which have defence implications. The Council shall, in agreement with the institutions of the WEU, adopt the necessary practical arrangements.
> 3. Issues having defence implications dealt with under this Article shall not be subject to the procedures set out in Article J.3.
> 4. The policy of the Union in accordance with this Article shall not prejudice the specific character of the security and defence policy of certain Member States and shall respect the obligations of certain Member States under the North Atlantic Treaty and be compatible with the common security and defence policy established within that framework.
> 5. The provisions of this Article shall not prevent the development of closer cooperation between two or more Member States on a bilateral level, in the framework of the WEU and the Atlantic Alliance, provided such cooperation does not run counter to or impede that provided for in this Title.

---

72 Second hyphen.

73 See generally A. Collet, *supra* note 71, pp. 225–233; A. van Staden, 'After Maastricht: Explaining the Movement towards a Common European Defence Policy', in W. Carlsnaes & S. Smith (eds.), *supra* note 54, pp. 138–155 and C. Zanghì, 'La difesa europea: dall'UEO a Maastricht', 33(2) *Rivista di diritto europeo* 1993, pp. 211–222. For a more extensive analysis, see H. Schöllhorn, *Der sicherheitspolitische Handlungsrahmen der Europäischen Union: eine Darstellung der rechtlichen und tatsächlichen Möglichkeiten für operative Maßnahmen der Krisenbewältigung*, Baden-Baden, Nomos, 1996.

6. With a view to furthering the objective of this Treaty, and having in view the date of 1998 in the context of Article XII of the Brussels Treaty [[74]], the provisions of this Article may be revised as provided for in Article N(2) on the basis of a report to be presented in 1996 by the Council to the European Council, which shall include an evaluation of the progress made and the experience gained until then.

Therefore, the CFSP included all foreign policy and security issues, but when it came to decisions and actions of the EU having defence implications, it would ask the WEU, which was an integral part of the development of the EU, to elaborate and implement these decisions.[75] The framing of a common defence policy was only an "eventual" aim and that of a "common defence" only a possible future one. The safeguarding of the "*specific character of the security and defence policy of certain Member States*" is generally understood to concern especially the neutral EU Member States[76] but also France, which had a peculiar position in NATO.[77]

However, it is worth noting that the EC already conducted one crisis management operation before the conclusion and entry into force of the Maastricht Treaty: the European Community Monitoring Mission in the former Yugoslavia (ECMM, which would later evolve into the EU Monitoring Mission).[78]

---

74 This Article provides that after 50 years each party may withdraw from the Treaty.

75 Hence the appropriate title ('the EU with the WEU as security system') used by J.A. Frowein, 'Die Europaische Union mit WEU als Sicherheitssystem', in O. Due, M. Lutter & J. Schwarze (eds.), *Festschrift fur Ulrich Everling*, Baden-Baden, Nomos, 1995, Vol. 1, pp. 315–326.

76 On the issue of the compatibility of neutrality with EU membership, see *infra*, Chapter 4.A.5.ii.

77 See A. Collet, *supra* note 71, pp. 230–231. France is a NATO Member State but until recently did not fully participate in NATO's military structures (it withdrew in 1966, later partly rejoined in 1995–1996 and fully re-integrated only in 2009, see *infra* note 219). For its position prior to 2009, see A. Dumoulin & E. Remacle, *supra* note 17, pp. 363–366 and M. Vaïsse *et al.* (eds.), *La France et l'OTAN 1949–1996: actes du colloque tenu á l'Ecole militaire, 8, 9 et 10 février 1996, à Paris*, Brussels, Complexe, 1996. See also E. Stein & D. Carreau, 'Law and Peaceful Change in a Subsystem: "Withdrawal" of France for the North Atlantic Treaty Organisation', 62 *A.J.I.L.* 1968, pp. 577–640.

78 The ECMM was established by a Memorandum of Understanding signed on 13 July 1991 (however, on who the parties to this agreement were – the EC and/or its Member States, see *infra*, Chapter 6.B, note 1510) and was renamed EUMM by Council Joint Action of 22 December 2000 on the European Union Monitoring Mission (2000/811/CFSP), *O.J. L* 328, 23 December 2000, p. 53, last amended and extended by Council Joint Action of 21 November 2005 extending and amending the mandate of the European Union Monitoring Mission (EUMM) (2005/807/CFSP), *O.J. L* 303, 22 November 2005, p. 61; Council Joint Action of 30 November 2006 extending and amending the mandate of the European Union Monitoring Mission (EUMM) (2006/867/CFSP), *O.J. L* 335, 1 December 2006, p. 48 (*corrigendum O.J. L* 349, 12 December 2006, p. 59) and Council Joint Action of 22 January 2007 amending Joint Action 2002/921/CFSP extending the mandate of the European Union Monitoring Mission (EUMM) (2007/40/CFSP), *O.J. L* 17, 24 January 2007, p. 22. This mission was terminated on 31 December 2007: see EU Doc. S/375/07 of 27 December 2007. On the ECMM, see J. Wouters

The role of the WEU in this context was set out in more detail in the above-mentioned Maastricht declaration, which was also annexed to the Maastricht Treaty and which *inter alia* stated that:

> 1. WEU Member States agree on the need to develop a genuine European security and defence identity and a greater European responsibility on defence matters. This identity will be pursued through a gradual process involving successive phases. WEU will form an integral part of the process of the development of the European Union and will enhance its contribution to solidarity within the Atlantic Alliance. WEU Member States agree to strengthen the role of WEU, in the longer term perspective of a common defence policy within the European Union which might in time lead to a common defence, compatible with that of the Atlantic Alliance.
> 2. WEU will be developed as the defence component of the European Union and as a means to strengthen the European pillar of the Atlantic Alliance. To this end, it will formulate common European defence policy and carry forward its concrete implementation through the further development of its own operational role.
> [...]
> 3. The objective is to build up WEU in stages as the defence component of the European Union. To this end, WEU is prepared, at the request of the European Union, to elaborate and implement decisions and actions of the Union which have defence implications.
> To this end, WEU will take the following measures to develop a close working relationship with the Union [...]. The WEU Council shall, in agreement with the competent bodies of the European Union, adopt the necessary practical arrangements.
> 4. The objective is to develop WEU as a means to strengthen the European pillar of the Atlantic Alliance. Accordingly WEU is prepared to develop further the close working links between WEU and the Alliance and to strengthen the role, responsibilities and contributions of WEU Member States in the Alliance. This will be undertaken on the basis of the necessary transparency and complementarity between the emerging European security and defence identity and the Alliance. WEU will act in conformity with the positions adopted in the Atlantic Alliance.
> [...]
> 5. WEU's operational role will be strengthened by examining and defining appropriate missions, structures and means, covering in particular:
>
> - [...]
> - military units answerable to WEU.
>
> Other proposals will be examined further, including:

& F. Naert, 'How Effective is the European Security Architecture? Lessons from Bosnia and Kosovo', 50 *I.C.L.Q.* 2001, pp. 547–550, 558 and 560 and D. Lopandic, 'Les memorandums d'entente: des instruments juridiques spécifiques de la politique étrangere et de sécurite de l'Union Europeenne: le cas de l'ex-Yougoslavie', No. 392 *R.M.C.U.E.* 1995, pp. 557–562. The EUMM's website was www.eumm.org.

- enhanced co-operation in the field of armaments with the aim of creating a European armaments agency;
- development of the WEU Institute into a European Security and Defence Academy.

Arrangements aimed at giving WEU a stronger operational role will be fully compatible with the military dispositions necessary to ensure the collective defence of all Allies.

This text sets out the essence of the role the WEU would (attempt to) play in the European security architecture from then on until its functions were almost fully integrated into the EU later on (see *infra*): namely being the EU's defence component and NATO's European component.[79] The WEU would subsequently gradually increase its operational capacities and expand its military structures,[80] including by setting up a Satellite Centre,[81] and Member States would designate certain forces and headquarters as 'Forces Answerable to the WEU' for WEU operations (such forces would sometimes also be available to NATO).[82] The Eurocorps is an example of such a Headquarters.[83] The creation of a European

79 For a brief discussion, see A. Bloed & R.A. Wessel (eds.), *supra* note 24, pp. xxiv-xxvii and xxix-xxx and A. Dumoulin & E. Remacle, *supra* note 17, pp. 194–199. See also R.A. Wessel, 'Gemeenschappelijk defensiebeleid via een achterdeur. Een fusie van de Westeuropese Unie en de Europese Unie?', 24 *Transaktie* 1995, pp. 340–355.

80 See A. Cahen, *supra* note 50 (*R.M.C.U.E.*), pp. 31–33 and A. Dumoulin & E. Remacle, *supra* note 17, pp. 261–328.

81 See also A. Collet, *supra* note 73, p. 229; A. Dumoulin & E. Remacle, *supra* note 17, pp. 304–315 and J. Litten, *supra* note 27, pp. 79–96.

82 See A. Dumoulin & E. Remacle, *supra* note 17, pp. 263–277; J. Litten, *supra* note 27, pp. 80–89 and H. Schöllhorn, *supra* note 73, pp. 49–54.

83 Eurocorps was initially a French-German creation (see A. Collet, *supra* note 73, pp. 228–229) but these States were later joined by Belgium, Luxemburg and Spain. The Eurocorps Member States decided on 19 May 1993 to put it at the WEU's disposal. It is also at NATO's disposal and has served in a couple of NATO operations. See Traité entre le Royaume de Belgique, la République fédérale d'Allemagne, le Royaume d'Espagne, la République française et le Grand-Duché de Luxembourg relatif au Corps européen et au statut de son Quartier Général, Brussels, 22 November 2004, published in *Memorial. Journal Officiel du Grand-Duché de Luxembourg*, A, No. 63, 12 April 2006, pp. 1274–1284 (available online at www.legilux.public.lu/leg/a/archives/2006/0063/a063.pdf). See also generally A. Dumoulin & E. Remacle, *supra* note 17, pp. 266–272; E. Martin, (ed.), *Eurokorps und Europäische Einigung*, Bonn, Kunst & Kommunikation/ Edition Zeitgeschichte, 1996; T. Stein, 'Rechtsfragen des Eurokorps und der deutsch-französischen Brigade', in C. Tomuschat & J. Frowein (eds.), *supra* note 34, pp. 53–67 (available online at http://archiv.jura.uni-saarland.de/projekte/Bibliothek/text.php?id=334); M. Voelckel, 'La construction juridique du Corps européen: quelques remarques', 41 *A.F.D.I.* 1995, pp. 137–149; P. Wassenberg, *Das Eurokorps: sicherheitsrechtliches Umfeld und völkerrechtliche Bedeutung eines multinationalen Großverbands* , Baden-Baden, Nomos, 1999 and www.eurocorps.org. See also for Belgium, Loi du 19 juin 2008 portant assentiment au Traité relatif au Corps européen et au statut de son Quartier général entre la République française, la République fédérale d'Allemagne, le Royaume de Belgique, le Royaume d'Espagne et le grand-duché de Luxembourg, et à l'Acte final, faits à Bruxelles le 22 novembre 2004, *Moniteur belge*, 20 February 2009, p. 15822.

Armaments Agency would take considerable time and a European Defence Agency was only established in 2004 (see below). However, in between, various armaments cooperation mechanisms were set up in (the Independent European Programme Group (IEPG) established in 1976 between the European NATO Member States evolved into the Western European Armaments Group (WEAG) and Western European Armaments Organization (Research Cell) in the WEU[84]) or outside (OCCAR[85]) the framework of the WEU.[86]

The WEU also envisaged the new kind of operations that might be required in the new security environment outlined above and to that effect adopted the famous 'Petersberg tasks' in its 19 June 1992 Bonn Ministerial 'Petersberg Declaration', which provided that:

> Apart from contributing to the common defence in accordance with Article 5 of the Washington Treaty and Article V of the modified Brussels Treaty respectively, military units of WEU Member States, acting under the authority of WEU, could be employed for:
>
> - humanitarian and rescue tasks;
> - peacekeeping tasks;
> - tasks of combat forces in crisis management, including peacemaking.[87]

But most importantly, over the next years, the WEU intensified its relations with the EU and NATO. NATO in turn had accepted the idea of a European Security and Defence Identity (ESDI).[88] In particular, the 6–7 June 1991 North Atlantic Council final communiqué reads (in §§1 and 3):

> A transformed Atlantic Alliance constitutes an essential element in the new architecture of an undivided Europe ... An important basis for this transformation is the agreement of all Allies to enhance the role and responsibility of the European members. We welcome efforts further to strengthen the security dimension in the process of European integration and recognise the significance of the progress made by the countries of the European Community towards the goal of political union, including the development of a common foreign and security policy. These two

---

84 See generally www.weu.int/weag/ and www.weao.weu.int.

85 Organisation Conjointe de Coopération en matière d'Armement / Organization for Joint Armament Co-operation, see generally www.occar-ea.org.

86 See A. Dumoulin & E. Remacle, *supra* note 17, pp. 321–328.

87 See the part entitled 'On Strengthening WEU's Operational Role' (available online at www.weu.int/documents/920619peten.pdf), §4. See also L. Vierucci, 'The WEU and Peacekeeping', 51(1–2) *Studia Diplomatica* 1998, pp. 101–106.

88 For an extensive discussion of this identity from a mostly political perspective, see A. Dumoulin, *L''identité européenne de sécurité et de défense. Des coopérations militaries croisées au Livre blanc européen*, Brussels, Presses Interuniversitaires Européennes, 1999, especially pp. 31–40 and 99–128. See also A. Dumoulin & F. Gevers, *supra* note 27, pp. 18–26.

> positive processes are mutually reinforcing. The development of a European security identity and defence role, reflected in the strengthening of the European pillar within the Alliance, will reinforce the integrity and effectiveness of the Atlantic Alliance.
>
> Recognising that it is for the European Allies concerned to decide what arrangements are needed for the expression of a common European foreign and security policy and defence role, we further agree that, [...], we will develop practical arrangements to ensure the necessary transparency and complementarity between the European security and defence identity as it emerges in the Twelve and the WEU, and the Alliance. There will be a need, in particular, to [...] ensure that the Allies that are not currently participating in the development of a European identity in foreign and security policy and defence should be adequately involved in decisions that may affect their security.

Hence, the WEU became the security and defence component of the EU and the (Western) European pillar of NATO[89] and in reality the ESDI initially concentrated on the WEU.[90] To implement this role, the WEU established far-reaching cooperation mechanisms with NATO and the EU and developed special categories of membership for the non-WEU NATO and non-WEU EU members (associated members and observers respectively).[91]

The arrangements with NATO were adopted at the 11 January 1994 North Atlantic Council Meeting, which decided to endorse the concept of Combined Joint Task Forces (CFTF – combined means composed of elements from different countries and joint means including elements from different services/components (land, naval or air)[92]) and that (§3):

> We therefore stand ready to make collective assets of the Alliance available, on the basis of consultations in the North Atlantic Council, for WEU operations undertaken by the European Allies in pursuit of their Common Foreign and Security Policy. We support the development of separable but not separate capabilities which could

89 See generally K. Georgantzis, *Die WEU als sicherheitspolitische Säule der EU und als europäischer Pfeiler der NATO*, Universität der Bundeswehr München, München, 1998; G. Lenzi, 'The WEU between NATO and EU', 51(1–2) *Studia Diplomatica* 1998, pp.167–174; U. Schürr, *Der Aufbau einer europäischen Sicherheits- und Verteidigungsidentität: im Beziehungsgeflecht von EU, WEU, OSZE und NATO*, Frankfurt, Lang, 2003 and G.W. Rees, *supra* note 27.

90 See A. Collet, *supra* note 73, p. 227.

91 In addition, some third States that were neither members of NATO nor of the EU but could later become members obtained the status of associated partners. The basic features of the status of these forms of participation is laid down in the Ministerial declarations of Petersberg (19 June 1992), Kirchberg (9 May 1994) and Erfurt (18 November 1997), all available online at www.weu.int/Key%20texts.htm.

92 See, e.g. A. Dumoulin & E. Remacle, *supra* note 17, pp. 277–294 and J. Litten, *supra* note 27, pp. 98–94.

> respond to European requirements and contribute to Alliance security. Better European coordination and planning will also strengthen the European pillar and the Alliance itself. Integrated and multinational European structures, as they are further developed in the context of an emerging European Security and Defence Identity, will also increasingly have a similarly important role to play in enhancing the Allies' ability to work together in the common defence and other tasks.

The arrangements on NATO-WEU cooperation were further developed and agreed, especially at the 3 June and 10 December 1996 North Atlantic Council Meetings. The final communiqué of the latter had the following to say on this in its §17:

> We note in particular the steps taken towards implementing the concept of separable but not separate capabilities:
>
> - the decisions of the Council in Permanent Session on political guidance concerning the elaboration of European command arrangements within NATO able to prepare and conduct WEU-led operations;
> - the decisions of the Council in Permanent Session regarding the arrangements for identifying NATO capabilities and assets which might be made available to the WEU for a WEU-led operation;
> - the progress to date on arrangements for the release, monitoring and return or recall of Alliance assets and capabilities;
> - the decision of the Council in Permanent Session with respect to modalities of cooperation with the WEU;
> - the progress on work regarding planning and conducting exercising for WEU-led operations, following receipt of illustrative profiles for WEU missions.

The whole of these arrangements became known as the 'Berlin+ arrangements'. However, it would take another couple of years before they were really finalized: at NATO's April 1999 Washington summit it was said that "*the key elements of the Berlin decisions are being put in place*" but also that "*the decisions taken in Berlin in 1996, [...], should be further developed*".[93] The arrangements would first

---

93 On WEU-NATO cooperation, see, e.g. F. Burwell, 'WEU-NATO Cooperation', 51(1–2) *Studia Diplomatica* 1998, pp.125–130; A. Cahen, *The Western European Union and NATO: Building a European Defence Identity within the Context of Atlantic Solidarity*, London, Brassey's, 1989; A. Dumoulin, *supra* note 88, pp. 115–120; A. Dumoulin & E. Remacle, *supra* note 17, pp. 284–294 and 361–370; R. Hunter, 'ESDI and the Future of Transatlantic Relations', 51(1–2) *Studia Diplomatica* 1998, pp. 175–181; A. Kintis, 'NATO-WEU: An Enduring Relationship?', 3 *E.F.A.R.* 1998, pp. 537–562; A. Kintis, *NATO and the WEU: Interblocking or Interlocking Institutions. NATO research fellowship report (1996–1998), s.l.*, 1998 (available online at www.nato.int/acad/fellow/96-98/f96-98.htm); M.A. Robles Carrillo, 'L'identité européenne de sécurité et défense et les relations UEO-OTAN', 51(1–2) *Studia Diplomatica* 1998, pp. 107–124; W. Van Eekelen, 'WEU Missions and Cooperation with NATO – Comments', 51(1–2) *Studia Diplomatica* 1998, pp. 151–152; M. Warnken, *supra* note 27, pp. 121–135; R. Wegener, 'WEU: The European Pillar of the Atlantic Alliance', in S. Baierallen (ed.), *The Future of Euro-*

be tested in a joint exercise in 2000.[94] They have never been used in practice and by 2000, as we will see below, the EU was already busy incorporating the WEU *acquis* and taking charge itself.

The WEU also developed closer relations with the EU, but these were initially less elaborate[95] and rather of a political nature.[96] They are primarily reflected in the observer status of non-WEU EU members[97] (see *supra*) and more far-reaching permanent arrangements were adopted only in 1999 following the Amsterdam Treaty and developments thereunder (see *infra*). Nevertheless, there was already some cooperation regarding specific operations. In fact, under the Maastricht Treaty and already before the EU itself was given the authority to conduct crisis management operations (see *infra*), it administered the Bosnian city of Mostar[98] and it requested the WEU to conduct a police operation in

---

Atlantic Relations, Baden-Baden, Nomos, 2000, pp. 53–58 and J. Wouters & F. Naert, 'Europese defensie in de NAVO en de Europese Unie: eenheid en complementariteit', 31(2) *Vrede en Veiligheid* 2002, pp. 208–210.

94 NATO, 'First Ever Joint WEU/NATO Crisis Management Exercise, CMX/CRISEX 2000', fact sheet previously available online at www.nato.int/docu/pr/2000/p00-005e.htm.

95 See A. Cahen, *supra* note 50 (*R.M.C.U.E)*, pp. 27–28 and A. Dumoulin, *supra* note 88, p. 100. On EU-WEU relations up to 1996–1997, see also H. Van Der Woude, 'De samenwerking tussen de Europese Unie en de Westeuropese Unie', 90 *Militair Rechtelijk Tijdschrift* 1997, 33–37 and R.A. Wessel, 'De EU en de WEU op weg naar een Europese defensie-identiteit', 89 *Militair Rechtelijk Tijdschrift* 1996, pp. 353–358.

96 See A. Dumoulin & F. Gevers, *supra* note 27, pp. 26–33, especially p. 28, contrasting this with more functional and military NATO-WEU relations. See also A. Dumoulin & E. Remacle, *supra* note 17, pp. 213–217.

97 In a Declaration made together with that on the role of the WEU and its relations with NATO and the EU and also attached to the Maastricht Treaty, EU Member States that were not yet members of the WEU were invited to join, either as full members or as observers.

98 The initial basis was a Memorandum of Understanding approved by the Council at its meeting on 13 and 14 June 1994 and signed in Geneva on 5 July 1994 (*Tractatenblad* 1994, No. 183; the German text is included in C. Busse, *Die völkerrechtliche Einordnung der Europäischen Union*, Cologne, Carl Heymann, 1999, pp. 346–353). Subsequent decisions were Council Decision of 28 November 1994 appointing an Ombudsman for Mostar for the duration of the European Union administration of Mostar (94/776/EC), *O.J. L* 312, 6 December 1994, p. 34; Council Decision of 12 December 1994 concerning the joint action, adopted by the Council on the basis of Article J.3 of the Treaty on European Union, on continued support for European Union administration of the town of Mostar (94/790/CFSP), *O.J. L* 326, 17 December 1994, p. 2; Council Regulation of 6 February 1995 supplementing Decision 94/790/CFSP concerning the joint action, adopted by the Council on the basis of Article J.3 of the Treaty on European Union, on continued support for European Union administration of the town of Mostar (95/23/CFSP), *O.J. L* 33, 13 February 1995, p. 1; Council Decision of 4 December 1995 concerning the joint action, adopted by the Council on the basis of Article J.3 of the Treaty on European Union, on continued support for European Union administration of the town of Mostar (95/517/CFSP), *O.J. L* 298, 11 December 1995, p. 4; Council Decision of 19 December 1995 supplementing Decision 95/517/CFSP concerning the joint action, adopted by the Council on the basis of Article J.3 of the Treaty on European Union, on continued support for European Union administration of the town of Mostar (95/552/CFSP), *O.J. L* 313, 27 December 1995, p. 1 and Council Decision of 20 December 1996 on the phasing out of European Union

support of this administration, to which the WEU positively responded and effectively conducted a police operation.[99] A following request to the WEU in 1996 "*to examine as a matter of urgency how it can, for its part, contribute to the optimum use of the operational resources available*" in the framework of an EU Joint Action on the Great Lakes Region[100] appears to not have resulted in any WEU operation.[101] This was followed by two WEU operations at the request of the EU and both starting in 1998, i.e. between the adoption and entry into force of the Treaty of Amsterdam. These were a 'security surveillance mission' in Kosovo[102] and a de-mining mission in Croatia.[103] Finally, the WEU also sent a Multinational Advisory Police Element to Albania as part of EU and other efforts undertaken in that country and this mission was expanded in 1999 at the request of the EU.[104]

---

operations in Mostar (96/744/CFSP), *O.J. L* 340, 30 December 1996, p. 1. See C. Busse, *supra* this note, pp. 222–233; W. Hummer, 'Mostar: ein Beispiel internationaler Stadtverwaltung durch die Europäische Union', in W. Benedek, H. Isak & R. Kicker (eds.), *supra* note 62, pp. 377–419; J. Monar, 'Editorial Comment. Mostar: Three Lessons for the European Union', 2 *E.F.A.R.* 1997, pp. 1–5; F. Pagani, 'L'administration de Mostar par l'Union européenne', 42 *A.F.D.I.* 1996, pp. 234–254; J. Wouters & F. Naert, *supra* note 78, p. 555 and Court of Auditors, Special Report No 2/96, *O.J. C* 287, 30 September 1996, p. 1.

99 See WEU, 'WEU History. Operational Role', www.weu.int/History.htm#4A; A. Dumoulin & E. Remacle, *supra* note 17, pp. 247–249; W. Hummer, *supra* previous note, pp. 391–393; A. Preuss, *Friedensaufbau durch internationale Polizeieinsätze in ethnonationalen Konflikten Bosnien-Herzegowinas am Beispiel der WEU-Polizei in Mostar*, Münster, Lit, 2004 and J. Wouters & F. Naert, *supra* note 78, p. 555.

100 Council Decision of 22 November 1996 adopted on the basis of Article J.4 (2) of the Treaty on European Union on the elaboration and implementation of a Joint Action by the Union in the Great Lakes Region (96/670/CFSP), *O.J. L* 312, 2 December 1996, p. 3.

101 On this and the WEU's role in Africa at that time, see A. Dumoulin & E. Remacle, *supra* note 17, pp. 250–255.

102 See WEU, 'WEU History. Crisis Management Operations (1997–2001)', www.weu.int/History.htm#5 and Council Decision of 13 November 1998 adopted on the basis of Article J.4(2) of the Treaty on European Union, on the monitoring of the situation in Kosovo (98/646/CFSP), *O.J. L* 308, 18 November 1998, p. 1.

103 See WEU, 'WEU History. Crisis Management Operations (1997–2001)', www.weu.int/History.htm#5 and Council Decision of 9 November 1998 adopted on the basis of Article J.3 of the Treaty on European Union concerning a specific action of the Union in the field of assistance for mine clearance (98/627/CFSP), *O.J. L* 300, 11 November 1998, p. 1; Council Decision of 9 November 1998 adopted on the basis of Article J.4(2) of the Treaty on European Union on the implementation of a Council Decision concerning a specific action of the Union in the field of assistance for mine clearance (98/628/CFSP), *O.J. L* 300, 11 November 1998, p. 2; Council Decision of 20 March 2000 supplementing Decision 98/627/CFSP concerning a specific action of the Union in the field of assistance for mine clearance, *O.J. L* 73, 22 March 2000, p. 2 and Council Decision of 24 April 2001 supplementing Decision 98/627/CFSP concerning a specific action of the European Union in the field of assistance for mine clearance (2001/328/CFSP), *O.J. L* 116, 26 April 2001, p. 1.

104 See WEU, 'WEU History. Crisis Management Operations (1997–2001)', www.weu.int/History.htm#5 and Council Decision of 22 September 1998 adopted on the basis of Article J.4(2) of the Treaty on European Union on the study of the feasibility of international police operations to assist the Albanian authorities (98/547/CFSP), *O.J. L* 263, 26 September 1998, p. 1 and

E. THE TREATY OF AMSTERDAM, THE COLOGNE AND HELSINKI EUROPEAN COUNCILS AND THE FOUNDATION OF THE ESDP

This brings us to the changes introduced by the Treaty of Amsterdam,[105] already mentioned several times above, which enabled the EU to subsequently develop its ESDP. First, the Treaty of Amsterdam brought a number of improvements to the CFSP,[106] including notably the introduction of common strategies (in addition to the already existing joint actions and common positions, which were in turn better defined[107]),[108] the creation of a High Representative for the CFSP who would also be the Secretary-General of the Council (SG/HR)[109] and the

Council Decision of 9 March 1999 adopted on the basis of Article J.4(2) of the Treaty on European Union on the implementation of the joint action concerning a contribution by the European Union to the re-establishment of a viable police force in Albania (1999/190/CFSP), *O.J. L* 63, 12 March 1999, p. 3. See also A. Dumoulin & E. Remacle, *supra* note 17, p. 257.

105 Treaty of Amsterdam, 2 October 1997, *O.J C* 340, 10 November 1997, p. 1, entered into force on 1 May 1999.

106 See generally F. Dehousse, 'After Amsterdam: A Report on the Common Foreign and Security Policy of the European Union', 9 *E.J.I.L.* 1998, pp. 525–539; E. Denza, *supra* note 46, pp. 123–191; P. Des Nerviens, 'Les relations extérieures', 33 *R.T.D.E.* 1997, pp. 801–812; J. de Zwaan, 'Community Dimensions of the Second Pillar', in T. Heukels, N. Blokker & M. Brus (eds.), *The European Union after Amsterdam: A Legal Analysis*, The Hague, Kluwer Law International, 1998, pp. 179–193, especially pp. 180–186; R. Gosalbo Bono, *supra* note 46, pp. 347–351; S. Griller *et al.*, *The Treaty of Amsterdam. Facts, Analysis, Prospects*, Vienna, Springer, 2000, pp. 375–417; J. Monar, 'The European Union's Foreign Affairs System after the Treaty of Amsterdam: A 'Strengthened Capacity for External Action'?', 2 *E.F.A.R.* 1997, pp. 413–436; F. Naert 'De tenuitvoerlegging van het Gemeenschappelijk Buitenlands en Veiligheidsbeleid van de Europese Unie in het licht van de IGC 1996', 34 *Jura Falconis* 1997–1998, pp. 11–60 (available online at www.law.kuleuven.ac.be/jura/art/34n1/naert.htm) and 37 *R.D.M.D.G.* 1998, pp. 63–144 and H. Neuhold, 'The Provisions of the Amsterdam Treaty on the CFSP: Cosmetic Operation or Genuine Progress?', in G. Hafner *et al.* (eds.), *Liber Amicorum Professor Seidl-Hohenverldern – in Honour of His 80th Birthday*, The Hague, Kluwer Law International, 1998, pp 493–510. For more extensive discussion of the CFSP in this period, see S. Duke, *Between Vision and Reality: CFSP's Progress on the Path to Maturity*, Maastricht, EIPA, 2000; S. Nuttall, *European Foreign Policy*, New York, Oxford University Press, 2000; B. Soetendorp, *Foreign Policy in the European Union: Theory, History and Practice*, London, Longman, 1999; A. Cafruny & P. Peters (eds.), *The Union and the World: The Political Economy of a Common Foreign and Security Policy*, The Hague, Kluwer, 1998; K.A. Eliassen (ed.), *Foreign and Security Policy in the European Union*, London, Sage, 1998; S. Keukeleire, *Het buitenlands beleid van de Europese Unie*, Deventer, Kluwer, 1998; S. Semrau, *Die gemeinsame Außen- und Sicherheitspolitik der Europäischen Union*, Frankfurt am Main, Lang, 1998 and J. Zielonka (ed.), *Paradoxes of European Foreign Policy*, The Hague, Kluwer Law International, 1998.

107 Compare original Articles J.1(2), J.2(2) and J.3 with revised Articles 12 (ex J.2), 14 (ex J.4) and 15 (ex J.5) EU Teaty.

108 See revised Article 12 (ex J.2) EU Treaty.

109 See especially revised Articles 18(3) (ex J.8(3)) and 26 (ex J.16) EU Treaty.

formal recognition of the possibility to appoint special representatives,[110] the decision to set up a policy planning and early warning unit in the General Secretariat of the Council under the responsibility of the SG/HR,[111] the possibility of constructive abstention in CFSP decision-making[112] and the limited extension of qualified majority voting for implementing decisions,[113] the conclusion of treaties in the CFSP[114] and an expansion of the CFSP costs charged to the EC budget.[115]

There were also significant changes in the field of security and defence,[116] which were found in revised Article 17 (ex J.7, formerly J.4).[117] The key changes were the following. First, the European Council was empowered to decide to set up a common defence that might result from the progressive – thus no longer eventual – framing of a common defence policy, albeit that the European Council "*shall in that case recommend to the Member States the adoption of such a decision in accordance with their respective constitutional requirements*".[118] Second, the common defence policy was to take place in accordance with paragraph 2 of Article 17, which stated that "*Questions referred to in this Article shall include humanitarian and rescue tasks, peacekeeping tasks and tasks of combat forces in crisis management, including peacemaking*". This meant that the 'Petersberg tasks' adopted by the WEU (see above) were now also within the competences of

110 Article 18(5) (ex J.8(5)) EU Treaty. This practice already existed at the time; see, e.g. the references to 1996 decisions in E. Decaux, 'Le processus de decision de la PESC: vers une politique étrangère européenne?', in E. Cannizzaro (ed.), *The European Union as an Actor in International Relations*, The Hague, Kluwer Law International, 2002, p. 44 note 48.

111 Declaration on the establishment of a policy planning and early warning unit.

112 See revised Article 23(1) (ex J.13(1)) EU Treaty. It may be noted that the Declaration on voting in the field of the Common Foreign and Security Policy already stated that Member States would try to avoid posing a veto where a qualified majority existed in favour of a measure.

113 Compare original Article J.3(2) with revised Article 13(2) (ex J.3(2)) EU Treaty.

114 Revised Article 24 (ex J.14) EU Treaty. The EU's treaty-making power will be discussed extensively below in Chapter 6.B.

115 Compare original Article J.11(2) with revised Article 28(3) (ex J.18(3)) EU Treaty.

116 See, e.g. R. Doherty, *Ireland, Neutrality and European Security Integration*, Aldershot, Ashgate, 2002, pp. 142–169; A. Dumoulin & F. Gevers, *supra* note 27, pp. 34–38; P. d'Argent, 'Le traité d'Amsterdam et les aspects militaires de la PESC', in Y. Lejeune (ed.), *Le traité d'Amsterdam. Espoirs et déceptions*, Brussels, Bruylant, 1998, pp. 383–404; S. Griller *et al.*, *supra* note 106, pp. 417–431 and J. Litten, *supra* note 27, pp. 175–199. For a view on the EU in the wider European security architecture, see, e.g. K. Möttölä, 'Collective and Co-operative Security Arrangements in Europe', in M. Koskenniemi (ed.), *International Law Aspects of the European Union*, The Hague, Kluwer, 1998, pp. 87–97; M. Weller, 'The European Union within the "European Security Architecture"', in *id.*, pp. 57–85 and J. Wouters & F. Naert, *supra* note 78, pp. 540–576.

117 The Treaty of Amsterdam first amended and partially renumbered the CFSP Title in J-numbers and then again renumbered the entire EU Treaty in normal continuous numbers, hence the ex/former combination.

118 Revised Article 17(1) (ex J.7(1)). See also revised Article 2 (ex B).

the EU.[119] The scope of these tasks will be discussed below but it may already be noted here that the language does not appear to be exhaustive ("shall include"). I will therefore hereinafter use the term 'ESDP tasks' rather than 'Petersberg tasks'. It is also interesting to note two minor additions in the objectives of the CFSP that would appear to be at least potentially related to defence, namely safeguarding the integrity of the Union[120] and a specific inclusion of international law principles on external borders in relation to the objective to preserve peace and strengthen international security.[121] The progressive framing of a common defence policy was also to be supported "*as Member States consider appropriate*" by co-operation between them in the field of armaments. The relationship with the WEU was defined in Article 17(1), second subparagraph, and in Article 17(3) as follows:

> The Western European Union (WEU) is an integral part of the development of the Union providing the Union with access to an operational capability notably in the context of paragraph 2. It supports the Union in framing the defence aspects of the common foreign and security policy as set out in this Article. The Union shall accordingly foster closer institutional relations with the WEU with a view to the possibility of the integration of the WEU into the Union, should the European Council so decide. It shall in that case recommend to the Member States the adoption of such a decision in accordance with their respective constitutional requirements.
>
> ...
>
> The Union will avail itself of the WEU to elaborate and implement decisions and actions of the Union which have defence implications.
>
> The competence of the European Council to establish guidelines in [CFSP] shall also obtain in respect of the WEU for those matters for which the Union avails itself of the WEU.
>
> When the Union avails itself of the WEU to elaborate and implement decisions of the Union on the tasks referred to in paragraph 2 all Member States of the Union shall be entitled to participate fully in the tasks in question. The Council, in agreement with the institutions of the WEU, shall adopt the necessary practical arrangements to allow all Member States contributing to the tasks in question to participate fully and on an equal footing in planning and decision-taking in the WEU.

---

119 See on this S. Grassi, 'L'introduzione delle operazioni di peace-keeping nel Trattato di Amsterdam: profili giuridici ed implicazioni politiche', 53(2) *La comunità internazionale* 1998, pp. 295–326 and F. Pagani, 'A New Gear in the CFSP Machinery: Integration of the Petersberg Tasks in the Treaty on European Union', 9 *E.J.I.L.* 1998, pp. 737–749.

120 Revised Article 11 (ex J.1), 1st hyphen.

121 *Id.*, 3rd hyphen.

> Decisions having defence implications dealt with under this paragraph shall be taken without prejudice to the policies and obligations referred to in paragraph 1, third subparagraph.[122]

Therefore at this stage it was still envisaged that the EU would have recourse to the WEU for the capabilities required to conduct operations, with a right for non-WEU EU Member States to fully participate, and closer relations between the two organizations were therefore to be developed, with arrangements to that effect to be concluded within a year of the entry into force of the Treaty of Amsterdam.[123] This was elaborated in a declaration discussed below.[124] However, the – much debated[125] – integration of the WEU into the EU was explicitly mentioned as a possibility to be decided upon by the European Council. Furthermore, as before, specific security policies and NATO obligations were to be respected[126] and closer cooperation not contrary to the CFSP was permitted.[127] In addition, the 'Protocol on the Position of Denmark' consecrated one very specific position in respect of the ESDP: pursuant to its Article 6:

> With regard to measures adopted by the Council in the field of Articles J.3(1) and J.7 of the Treaty on European Union, Denmark does not participate in the elaboration and the implementation of decisions and actions of the Union which have defence implications, but will not prevent the development of closer co-operation between Member States in this area. Therefore Denmark shall not participate in their adoption. Denmark shall not be obliged to contribute to the financing of operational expenditure arising from such measures.[128]

---

122 This subparagraph read: "*The policy of the Union in accordance with this Article shall not prejudice the specific character of the security and defence policy of certain Member States and shall respect the obligations of certain Member States, which see their common defence realised in the North Atlantic Treaty Organisation (NATO), under the North Atlantic Treaty and be compatible with the common security and defence policy established within that framework*".

123 See Protocol on Article J.7.

124 Another attached declaration 'on enhanced co-operation between the European Union and the Western European Union' simply stated that with a view to enhanced co-operation the Council was invited to seek the early adoption of appropriate arrangements for the security clearance of the personnel of the General Secretariat of the Council.

125 See, e.g. S. Duke, 'The Second Death (or the Second Coming?) of the WEU', 34 *J.C.M.S.* 1996, pp. 167–190; R.A. Wessel, *supra* note 79, pp. 340–255 and R.A. Wessel, 'Merging WEU into EU: A Necessary Step Towards an Ever Closer Union?', in W.P. Heere (ed.), *Contemporary International Law Issues: Conflicts and Convergence. Proceedings of the Third Joint Conference Held in The Hague, The Netherlands, July 13–15, 1995*, The Hague, TMC Asser Institute, 1996, pp. 347–352.

126 See *supra* previous note.

127 Revised Article 17(4) (ex J.7(4)). Compare original Article J.4(5).

128 This position had in essence already been agreed to by the European Council in 1992, but not in the EU Treaty itself (or a Protocol thereto), see *O.J. C* 348, 31 December 1992, p. 1, section C ("*The Heads of State and Government note that ... nothing in the Treaty on European Union commits Denmark to become a member of the WEU. Accordingly, Denmark does not participate*

The 'Declaration relating to Western European Union' noted the 'Declaration of Western European Union on the role of Western European union and its relations with the European Union and with the Atlantic Alliance', adopted by the Council of Ministers of the WEU on 22 July 1997, which updated the 1991 Maastricht declaration on the same topic (see above), and read, in relevant part:

INTRODUCTION

1. ... WEU is an integral part of the development of the European Union (EU) providing the Union with access to an operational capability, notably in the context of the Petersberg tasks and is an essential element of the development of the ESDI within the Atlantic Alliance in accordance with the Paris Declaration and with the decisions taken by NATO ministers in Berlin.

...

A. WEU's RELATIONS WITH THE EUROPEAN UNION: ACCOMPANYING THE IMPLEMENTATION OF THE TREATY OF AMSTERDAM

4. In the "Declaration..." of 10 December 1991, WEU Member States set as their objective "to build up WEU in stages as the defence component of the European Union". They today reaffirm this aim as developed by the Treaty of Amsterdam.

5. When the Union avails itself of WEU, WEU will elaborate and implement decisions and actions of the EU which have defence implications. In elaborating and implementing decisions and actions of the EU for which the Union avails itself of WEU, WEU will act consistently with guidelines established by the European Council. WEU supports the Union in framing the defence aspects of the European Union Common Foreign and Security Policy as set out in Article J.7 of the Treaty on European Union.

6. WEU confirms that when the European Union avails itself of WEU to elaborate and implement decisions of the Union on the tasks referred to in Article J.7(2) of the Treaty on European Union, all Member States of the Union shall be entitled to participate fully in the tasks in question in accordance with Article J.7(3) of the Treaty on European Union. WEU will develop the role of the Observers in WEU in line with provisions contained in Article J.7(3) and will adopt the necessary practical arrangements to allow all Member States of the EU contributing to the tasks undertaken by WEU at the request of the EU to participate fully and on an equal footing in planning and decision-taking in the WEU.

---

in the elaboration and the implementation of decisions and actions of the Union which have defence implications, but will not prevent the development of closer cooperation between Member States in this area"). For a discussion, see D. Howarth, 'The Compromise on Denmark and the Treaty on European Union: A Legal and Political Analysis', 31 *C.M.L. Rev.* 1994, pp. 765–805.

7. Consistent with the Protocol on Article J.7 of the Treaty on European Union, WEU shall draw up, together with the European Union, arrangements for enhanced co-operation between them. In this regard, a range of measures, on some of which work is already in hand in WEU, can be taken forward now, such as:

- arrangements for improving the co-ordination of the consultation and decision making processes of the respective Organisations, in particular in crisis situations;
- holding of joint meetings of the relevant bodies of the two Organisations;
- harmonisation as much as possible of the sequence of the Presidencies of WEU and the EU, as well as the administrative rules and practices of the two Organisations;
- close co-ordination of the work of the staff of the Secretariat-General of the WEU and the General Secretariat of the Council of the EU, including through the exchange and secondment of personnel;
- arrangements to allow the relevant bodies of the EU, including its Policy Planning and Early Warning Unit, to draw on the resources of WEU's Planning Cell, Situation Centre and Satellite Centre;
- co-operation in the field of armaments, as appropriate, within the framework of the Western European Armaments Group (WEAG), as the European forum for armaments co-operation, the EU and WEU in the context of rationalisation of the European armaments market and the establishment of a European Armaments Agency;
- practical arrangements for ensuring co-operation with the European Commission reflecting its role in the CFSP as defined in the revised Treaty on European Union;
- improved security arrangements with the European Union.

It also set out WEU-NATO relations (see above), including (Part B, especially §12) mechanisms for consultation between the WEU and NATO in the context of a crisis; the WEU's active involvement in the NATO defence planning process; operational links between the WEU and NATO for the planning, preparation and conduct of operations using NATO assets and capabilities under the political control and strategic direction of the WEU, including military planning, conducted by NATO in co-ordination with the WEU, and exercises; a framework agreement on the transfer, monitoring and return of NATO assets and capabilities and liaison between the WEU and NATO in the context of European command arrangements. Finally, it also detailed the WEU's operational role and that it was to further enhance its capabilities (Part C).

The arrangements for enhanced cooperation between the EU and WEU and the practical arrangements for the participation of all Member States in tasks for which the Union avails itself of the WEU were adopted on 10 May 1999,[129] just ten days after the entry into force of the Treaty of Amsterdam. Less than one month later, the European Council would decide to integrate the WEU's crisis management functions into the EU.

The latter evolution, taking place around the period of the 1998–1999 Kosovo crisis, was made possible by a change in the UK position on European defence,[130] which manifested itself in the Anglo-French summit Declaration of Saint-Malo of 4 December 1998 and at the EU level in the conclusions of the Cologne European Council of 3 and 4 June 1999.[131]

At this Cologne summit, the European Council issued a declaration on the further development of a common European Security and Defence Policy and endorsed the Presidency report on this policy as a basis for further work. It also invited the Council "*to deal thoroughly with all discussions on aspects of security, with a view to enhancing and better coordinating the Union's and Member States' non-military crisis response tools. Deliberations might include the possibility of a stand-by capacity to pool national civil resources and expertise complementing other initiatives within the common foreign and security policy*".[132] The key provisions of this Declaration are the following:

> 1. We, the members of the European Council, are resolved that the European Union shall play its full role on the international stage. To that end, we intend to give the European Union the necessary means and capabilities to assume its responsibilities regarding a common European policy on security and defence. ...

---

129 Council Decision of 10 May 1999 concerning the arrangements for enhanced cooperation between the European Union and the Western European Union, *O.J. L* 153, 19 June 1999, p. 1, and annexed Arrangements for enhanced cooperation between the European Union and the Western European Union under the protocol on Article 17 of the Treaty on European Union, *id*, p. 2 and Council decision of 10 May 1999 concerning the practical arrangements for the participation of all Member States in tasks pursuant to Article 17(2) Treaty on European Union for which the Union avails itself of the WEU (1999/321/CFSP), *O.J. L* 123, 13 May 1999, p. 14. On EU-WEU relations post Amsterdam, see also S. Griller *et al.*, *supra* note 106, pp. 422–426.

130 See, e.g. S. Biscop, 'The UK's Change of Course: A New Chance for the ESDI', 4 *E.F.A.R.* 1999, pp. 253–268; A. Missiroli, *CFSP, Defence and Flexibility*, Paris, WEU ISS, Chaillot Paper No. 38, February 2000, pp. 24–25 (available online at www.iss.europa.eu/index.php?id=143&L=0#c893) and P. Teunissen, 'Het smalle pad naar Europese defensiesamenwerking', 53 *Internationale Spectator* 1999, pp. 92–97.

131 See generally J.-L. Sauron & G. Asseraf, 'Le conseil européen de Cologne des 3 et 4 juin 1999', No. 430 *R.M.C.U.E.* 1999, pp. 441–443 and P. Teunissen, 'Europese defensiepolitiek: plannen en realiteiten', 53 *Internationale Spectator* 1999, pp. 493–499.

132 Presidency conclusions, §§55–56 and Annex III.

In pursuit of our Common Foreign and Security Policy objectives and the progressive framing of a common defence policy, we are convinced that the Council should have the ability to take decisions on the full range of conflict prevention and crisis management tasks defined in the Treaty on European Union, the "Petersberg tasks". To this end, the Union must have the capacity for autonomous action, backed up by credible military forces, the means to decide to use them, and a readiness to do so, in order to respond to international crises without prejudice to actions by NATO. The EU will thereby increase its ability to contribute to international peace and security in accordance with the principles of the UN Charter.

2. We are convinced that to fully assume its tasks in the field of conflict prevention and crisis management the European Union must have at its disposal the appropriate capabilities and instruments. We therefore commit ourselves to further develop more effective European military capabilities ...

We also recognise the need to undertake sustained efforts to strengthen the industrial and technological defence base...

3. We welcome the results of the NATO Washington summit as regards NATO support for the process launched by the EU and its confirmation that a more effective role for the European Union in conflict prevention and crisis management will contribute to the vitality of a renewed Alliance. In implementing this process launched by the EU, we shall ensure the development of effective mutual consultation, cooperation and transparency between the European Union and NATO.

We want to develop an effective EU-led crisis management in which NATO members, as well as neutral and non-allied members, of the EU can participate fully and on an equal footing in the EU operations.

We will put in place arrangements that allow non-EU European allies and partners to take part to the fullest possible extent in this endeavour.

4. We therefore approve and adopt the report prepared by the German Presidency, which reflects the consensus among the Member States.

5. We are now determined to launch a new step in the construction of the European Union. To this end we task the General Affairs Council to prepare the conditions and the measures necessary to achieve these objectives, including the definition of the modalities for the inclusion of those functions of the WEU which will be necessary for the EU to fulfil its new responsibilities in the area of the Petersberg tasks. In this regard, our aim is to take the necessary decisions by the end of the year 2000. In that event, the WEU as an organisation would have completed its purpose. The different status of Member States with regard to collective defence guarantees will not be affected. The Alliance remains the foundation of the collective defence of its Member States.

Some of these points were elaborated in the Presidency Report, which *inter alia* stated that:

> 2. Guiding principles
>
> The aim is to strengthen the CFSP by the development of a common European policy on security and defence. This requires a capacity for autonomous action backed up by credible military capabilities and appropriate decision making bodies. Decisions to act would be taken within the framework of the CFSP according to appropriate procedures in order to reflect the specific nature of decisions in this field. …
>
> The focus of our efforts therefore would be to assure that the European Union has at its disposal the necessary capabilities (including military capabilities) and appropriate structures for effective EU decision making in crisis management within the scope of the Petersberg tasks. This is the area where a European capacity to act is required most urgently. The development of an EU military crisis management capacity is to be seen as an activity within the framework of the CFSP (Title V of the TEU) and as a part of the progressive framing of a common defence policy in accordance with Article 17 of the TEU.
>
> The Atlantic Alliance remains the foundation of the collective defence of its Members. The commitments under Article 5 of the Washington Treaty and Article V of the Brussels Treaty will in any event be preserved for the Member States party to these Treaties. The policy of the Union shall not prejudice the specific character of the security and defence policy of certain Member States.
>
> 3. Decision Making
>
> As regards EU decision making in the field of security and defence policy, necessary arrangements must be made in order to ensure political control and strategic direction of EU-led Petersberg operations so that the EU can decide and conduct such operations effectively.
>
> Furthermore, the EU will need a capacity for analysis of situations, sources of intelligence, and a capability for relevant strategic planning.
>
> This may require in particular:
>
> - regular (or ad hoc) meetings of the General Affairs Council, as appropriate including Defence Ministers;
> - a permanent body in Brussels (Political and Security Committee) consisting of representatives with pol/mil expertise;
> - an EU Military Committee consisting of Military Representatives making recommendations to the Political and Security Committee;
> - a EU Military Staff including a Situation Centre;
> - other resources such as a Satellite Centre, Institute for Security Studies.
>
> Further institutional questions may need to be addressed.

Decisions relating to crisis management tasks, in particular decisions having military or defence implications will be taken in accordance with Article 23 of the Treaty on European Union. Member States will retain in all circumstances the right to decide if and when their national forces are deployed.

4. Implementation

As regards military capabilities, Member States need to develop further forces (including headquarters) that are suited also to crisis management operations, without any unnecessary duplication. The main characteristics include: deployability, sustainability, interoperability, flexibility and mobility.

For the effective implementation of EU-led operations the European Union will have to determine, according to the requirements of the case, whether it will conduct:

- EU-led operations using NATO assets and capabilities or
- EU-led operations without recourse to NATO assets and capabilities.

For EU-led operations without recourse to NATO assets and capabilities, the EU could use national or multinational European means pre-identified by Member States. This will require either the use of national command structures providing multinational representation in headquarters or drawing on existing command structures within multinational forces. Further arrangements to enhance the capacity of European multinational and national forces to respond to crises situations will be needed.

For EU-led operations having recourse to NATO assets and capabilities, including European command arrangements, the main focus should be on the following aspects:

- Implementation of the arrangements based on the Berlin decisions of 1996 and the Washington NATO summit decisions of April 1999.
- The further arrangements set out by NATO at its summit meeting in Washington should address in particular:
- assured EU access to NATO planning capabilities able to contribute to military planning for EU-led operations;
- the presumption of availability to the EU of pre-identified NATO capabilities and common assets for use in EU-led operations.

5. Modalities of participation and cooperation

The successful creation of a European policy on security and defence will require in particular:

- the possibility of all EU Member States, including non-allied members, to participate fully and on an equal footing in EU operations;
- satisfactory arrangements for European NATO members who are not EU Member States to ensure their fullest possible involvement in EU-led operations, building on existing consultation arrangements within WEU;
- arrangements to ensure that all participants in an EU-led operation will have equal rights in respect of the conduct of that operation, without prejudice to the

principle of the EU's decision-making autonomy, notably the right of the Council to discuss and decide matters of principle and policy;
- the need to ensure the development of effective mutual consultation, cooperation and transparency between NATO and the EU;
- the consideration of ways to ensure the possibility for WEU Associate Partners to be involved.

The EU therefore decided to develop a (C)ESDP that should enable it to carry out the Petersberg tasks, either with or without recourse to NATO assets, and, to that effect, to set up the proper decision-making and expert bodies, to develop the required capabilities, to strengthen the industrial and technological defence base and to agree upon the appropriate cooperation arrangements with identified partners, including the non-EU European NATO members. This includes taking over the WEU's crisis management functions,[133] without fully integrating it, even though it would hardly have any functions left (as collective defence is implemented within NATO and armaments cooperation was also envisaged to take place within the EU).[134] However, the WEU *acquis* undoubtedly facilitated the speed of the development of the ESDP once it was launched.

At the Helsinki European Council of 10–11 December 1999, this was further elaborated.[135] In particular, it was decided that by March 2000, as an *interim* measure, and on the basis of the EU Treaty as in force, a standing interim Political and Security Committee and an interim body of military representatives of Member States' Chiefs of Defence would be set up within the Council and that the Council Secretariat would be strengthened by military experts seconded from Member States in order to assist in the work on the CESDP and to form the nucleus of the future Military Staff. Furthermore, the European Council decided that "*cooperating voluntarily in EU-led operations, Member States must be able, by 2003, to deploy within 60 days and sustain for at least 1 year military forces of up to 50,000–60,000 persons capable of the full range of Petersberg tasks*", with, "*as appropriate, air and naval elements*". To achieve this, a "headline goal" was to be defined as well as a process to ensure the necessary follow up and review. In order to deal with the envisaged participation of certain third States in EU-led operations, committees of contributors were to be set up. Finally, a non-military crisis management mechanism was to be established "*to coordinate and make*

133 See R.A. Wessel, 'The EU as a Black Widow: Devouring the WEU to Give Birth to a European Security and Defence Policy", in V. Kronenberger (ed.), *The European Union and the International Legal Order: Discord or Harmony?*, The Hague, Asser Press, 2001, pp. 405–434 and S. Biscop, *De integratie van de WEU in de Europese Unie: Europa op weg naar een Europese Defensie Organisatie*, Leuven, Acco, 2000.

134 On the demise of the WEU, see A. Dumoulin & F. Gevers, *supra* note 27, especially pp. 39–73 and R.A. Wessel, 'Afscheid van de West-Europese Unie', 28 *Transaktie* 1999, pp. 559–568.

135 Presidency Conclusions, §§25–29 and the reports in annex IV.

more effective the various civilian means and resources, in parallel with the military ones, at the disposal of the Union and the Member States". A first civilian 'headline goal' was defined at the Santa Maria da Feira European Council of 19–20 June 2000: Member States, cooperating voluntarily, undertook that by 2003 they would be able "*to provide up to 5000 police officers for international missions across the range of conflict prevention and crisis management operations*" and "*to be able to identify and deploy up to 1 000 police officers within 30 days*".[136]

In the course of 2000 and 2001, the institutional framework for the ESDP was gradually put in place. This framework includes especially the Political and Security Committee (PSC),[137] EU Military Committee (EUMC)[138] and EU Military Staff (EUMS),[139] all initially established on an interim basis and

136 Presidency Conclusions, §§6–12 and the reports in annex I. On the civilian aspects of the ESDP, see generally A. Nowak (ed.), *Civilian Crisis Management: The EU Way*, Chaillot Paper No. 90, Paris, EU ISS, June 2006 (available online at www.iss.europa.eu/index.php?id=143&L=0#c893); R. Rummel, 'Der zivile Gehalt der Europäischen Sicherheits- und Verteidigungspolitik', in L. Schröter (ed.), *Europa und Militär: europäische Friedenspolitik oder Militarisierung der EU?*, Schkeuditz, Schkeuditzer Buchverlag, 2005, pp. 83–105 and R. Rummel, 'Soft-Power EU: Interventionspolitik mit zivilen Mitteln', in H.-G. Ehrhart & B. Schmitt (eds.), *Die Sicherheitspolitik der EU im Werden: Bedrohungen, Aktivitäten, Fähigkeiten*, Baden-Baden, Nomos, 2004, pp. 259–279.

137 Council Decision of 14 February 2000 setting up the Interim Political and Security Committee (2000/143/CFSP), *O.J. L* 49, 22 February 2000, p. 1; later replaced by Council decision of 22 January 2001 setting up the Political and Security Committee (2001/78/CFSP), *O.J. L* 27, 30 January 2001, p. 1.

138 Council Decision of 14 February 2000 setting up the Interim Military Body (2000/144/CFSP), *O.J. L* 49, 22 February 2000, p. 2; later replaced by Council decision of 22 January 2001 setting up the Military Committee of the European Union (2001/79/CFSP), *O.J. L* 27, 30 January 2001, p. 4. See also Council decision of 9 April 2001 appointing the Chairman of the Military Committee of the European Union (2001/309/CFSP), *O.J. L* 109, 19 April 2001, p. 1; Council Decision of 19 May 2003 appointing the Chairman of the Military Committee of the European Union (2003/401/EC), *O.J. L* 139, 6 June 2003, p. 34; Council Decision of 27 June 2006 appointing the Chairman of the Military Committee of the European Union (2006/451/EC), *O.J. L* 179, 1 July 2006, p. 55 and Council Decision of 8 December 2008 appointing the Chairman of the Military Committee of the European Union (2009/22/EC), *O.J. L* 9, 14 January 2009, p. 51.

139 Council Decision of 14 February 2000 on the secondment of national experts in the military field to the General Secretariat of the Council during an interim period (2000/145/CFSP), *O.J. L* 49, 22 February 2000, p. 3; later replaced by Council decision of 22 January 2001 on the establishment of the Military Staff of the European Union (2001/80/CFSP), *O.J. L* 27, 30 January 2001, p. 7. The latter decision applied as of 11 June 2001; see Decision of the Secretary-General of the Council/High Representative for the Common Foreign and Security Policy of 8 June 2001 on the application of the Council Decision on the establishment of the Military Staff of the European Union (2001/442/CFSP), *O.J. L* 155, 12 June 2001, p. 18. See also Council decision of 28 February 2000 on the rules applicable to national experts in the military field on secondment to the General Secretariat of the Council during an interim period (2000/178/CFSP), *O.J. L* 57, 2 March 2000, p. 1; later replaced by Council decision of 25 June 2001 on the rules applicable to national military staff on secondment to the General Secretariat of the Council in order to form the European Union Military Staff (2001/496/

subsequently as permanent bodies. It also comprises an EU Satellite Centre[140] and EU Institute for Security Studies,[141] both taken over from the WEU,[142] and a Committee for Civilian Aspects of Crisis Management (CIVCOM).[143] The EC also set up a rapid reaction financing facility.[144] In parallel, the required military and civilian capacities were gradually made available by the Member States, including through capabilities commitment conferences on 20 November 2000[145] and 19 November 2001 and the EU Capability Action Plan (ECAP), agreed by the Council on 19–20 November 2001.[146] This made it possible for the

CFSP), *O.J. L* 181, 4 July 2001, p. 1, as amended by Council Decision of 20 December 2001 amending the Council Decisions of 25 June 2001, 22 December 2000, 25 June 1997 and 22 March 1999 with regard to the daily allowance received by national military staff and national experts on detachment to the General Secretariat of the Council (2002/34/EC:), *O.J. L* 15, 17 January 2002, p. 29 and Council Decision of 19 May 2003 amending Decision 2001/496/CFSP, Decision 2001/41/EC, the Council Decision of 25 June 1997 and the Council Decision of 22 March 1999 as regards the subsistence allowances of national military staff and experts on secondment to the General Secretariat of the Council (2003/400/EC), *O.J. L* 139 , 6 June 2003, p. 33. See *infra* Chapter 2.B, note 192 on further amendments to these EUMS decisions.

140 Council Joint Action of 20 July 2001 on the establishment of a European Union Satellite Centre (2001/555/CFSP), *O.J. L* 200, 25 July 2001, p. 5 as amended by Council Joint Action 2006/998/CFSP of 21 December 2006 amending Joint Action 2001/555/CFSP on the establishment of a European Union Satellite Centre, *O.J. L* 405, 30 December 2006, p. 60 (*corrigendum O.J. L* 29, 3 February 2007, p. 23 and *O.J. L* 240, 1 June 2007, p. 58). See also the Staff Regulations of the European Union Satellite Centre, *O.J. L* 39, 9 February 2002, p. 44, replaced by those in *O.J. L* 235, 12 September 2005, p. 28.

141 Council Joint Action of 20 July 2001 on the establishment of a European Union Institute for Security Studies (2001/554/CFSP), *O.J. L* 200, 25 July 2001, p. 1, as amended by Council Joint Action 2006/1002/CFSP of 21 December 2006 amending Joint Action 2001/554/CFSP on the establishment of a European Union Institute for Security Studies, *O.J. L* 409, 30 December 2006, p. 181 (*corrigendum O.J. L* 36, 8 February 2007, p. 66). See also the Staff Regulations of the European Union Institute for Security Studies, *O.J. L* 39, 9 February 2002, p. 18, replaced by those in *O.J. L* 235, 12 September 2005, p. 1.

142 See A. Dumoulin & F. Gevers, *supra* note 27, pp. 63–69.

143 Council Decision of 22 May 2000 setting up a Committee for Civilian Aspects of Crisis Management (2000/354/CFSP), *O.J. L* 127, 27 May 2000, p. 1.

144 Council Regulation (EC) No 381/2001 of 26 February 2001 creating a rapid-reaction mechanism, *O.J. L* 57, 27 February 2001, p. 5 (later repealed by Regulation (EC) No 1717/2006 of the European Parliament and of the Council of 15 November 2006 establishing an Instrument for Stability, *O.J. L* 327, 24 November 2006, p. 1). On the latter, see F. Hoffmeister, 'Das Verhältnis zwischen Entwicklungszusammenarbeit und Gemeinsamer Außen- und Sicherheitspolitik am Beispiel des EG-Stabilitätsinstruments', *Europarecht* 2008, pp. 55–75 and T. Hadden (ed.), *A Responsibility to Assist. Human Rights Policy and Practice in European Union Crisis Management Operations. A COST Report*, Oxford, Hart, 2009, pp. 16–21.

145 The declaration made at this conference is available online at www.consilium.europa.eu/uedocs/cmsUpload/Military%20Capabilities%20Commitment%20Declaration.pdf.

146 Council conclusions, *inter alia* available online at www.consilium.europa.eu/uedocs/cmsUpload/European%20Capability%20Action%20Plan%20-%20Excerpt%20Press%20Release%20November%202001.pdf. See also J. Lindley-French, 'Plugging the Expanded Petersberg Tasks Gap?: Europe's Capabilities and the European Capabilities Action Plan (ECAP)', in H.-G. Ehrhart & B. Schmitt (eds.), *supra* note 136, pp. 201–213.

ESDP to be declared operational to a limited extent at the Laeken European Council of 14–15 December 2001:

> Through the continuing development of the ESDP, the strengthening of its capabilities, both civil and military, and the creation of the appropriate structures …, the Union is now capable of conducting some crisis-management operations. … Development of the means and capabilities at its disposal will enable the Union progressively to take on more demanding operations.[147]

F. THE TREATY OF NICE, A EUROPEAN SECURITY STRATEGY AND THE FIRST ESDP OPERATIONS

The Treaty of Nice, adopted on 26 February 2001 and which entered into force on 1 February 2003,[148] essentially consolidated and affirmed the decisions already adopted and implemented in the field of security and defence.[149] In this context, it may be noted that the 'Declaration on the European security and defence policy' annexed to the Treaty of Nice states that a decision to declare the ESDP operational would be taken by the European Council as soon as possible in 2001 "*on the basis of the existing provisions of the Treaty on European Union*" and that "*Consequently, the entry into force of the Treaty of Nice does not constitute*

---

147 Presidency Conclusions, §6 and Annex II (Declaration on the operational capability of the Common European Security and Defence Policy). Compare J.P. Kelche, 'Vers une force européenne de réaction rapide', 57(2) *Défense Nationale* 2001, pp. 5–22.

148 Treaty of Nice Amending the Treaty on European Union, the Treaties Establishing the European Communities and Certain Related Acts, 26 February 2001, *O.J. C* 80, 10 March 2001, p. 1. A consolidated version of the EU Treaty including the amendments made by the Treaty of Nice is published in *O.J. C* 325, 24 December 2002, p. 5. On the CFSP from 2001 onwards, see, e.g. H. Smith, *European Union Foreign Policy. What It Is and What It Does*, London, Pluto Press, 2002; K. Smith, *European Union in a Changing World*, Cambridge, Polity Press, 2003; M.E. Smith, *Europe's Foreign and Security Policy. The Institutionalization of Cooperation*, Cambridge, Cambridge University Press, 2003 and B. White, *Understanding European Foreign Policy*, Basingstoke, Palgrave, 2001.

149 On the ESDP after Nice, see generally E. Blanc & M. Fennebresque, 'La défense européenne après le conseil européen de Nice', 57(2) *Défense Nationale* 2001, pp. 23–34; A. Cammilleri, 'Le traité de Nice et la politique européenne de défense', 10 *Revue des Affaires européennes* 2000, pp. 389–397; M. Cogen, 'De militaire integratie van de Europese Unie na Nice', 55(6) *Internationale Spectator* 2001, pp. 304–309 and 26(2) *VVN-Berichten* 2002, pp. 30–41; S. Duke, 'CESDP: Nice's Overtrumped Success?', 6 *E.F.A.R.* 2001, pp. 155–175; J. Litten, *supra* note 27, pp. 200–274; I. Österdahl, 'The EU and Its Member States, Other States, and International Organizations – The Common European Security and Defence Policy after Nice', 70 *Nordic J.I.L.* 2001, pp. 341–372; D. Thym, *Die Gemeinsame Sicherheits- und Verteidigungspolitik vor und nach Nizza*, WHI-Paper 3/01, April 2001 (available online at www.whi-berlin.de/documents/whi-paper0301.pdf) and M. Trybus, *supra* note 21, pp. 100–118. On the CFSP in/after this Treaty, see also R. Gosalbo Bono, *supra* note 46, pp. 351–353.

a precondition".[150] The main changes concerning the ESDP are the deletion of the references to the WEU[151] and the succession of the Political Committee by the newly established Political and Security Committee, the mandate of which explicitly includes to "*exercise, under the responsibility of the Council, political control and strategic direction of crisis management operations*" and which may be authorized by the Council "*for the purpose and for the duration of a crisis management operation, as determined by the Council, to take the relevant decisions concerning the political control and strategic direction of the operation*".[152] There are also some changes in the EU's treaty-making power in the CFSP, but these will be discussed below.[153] Furthermore, the Treaty of Nice also introduced the possibility of enhanced cooperation (i.e. some Member States integrating further within the framework of the EU) in the CFSP for the implementation of a joint action or a common position, though not regarding matters having military or defence implications.[154]

Furthermore, EU-NATO arrangements were negotiated and finally agreed upon in 2002–2003. It proved especially difficult to find, on the one hand, the "*satisfactory arrangements for European NATO members who are not EU Member States to ensure their fullest possible involvement in EU-led operations, building on existing consultation arrangements within WEU*" and to "*ensure that all participants in an EU-led operation will have equal rights in respect of the conduct of that operation, without prejudice to the principle of the EU's decision-making autonomy, notably the right of the Council to discuss and decide matters of principle and policy*" and, on the other hand, "*assured EU access to NATO planning capabilities able to contribute to military planning for EU-led operations and the presumption of availability to the EU of pre-identified NATO capabilities and common assets for use in EU-led operations*", set out in the 1999 Cologne Declaration and Presidency report (see above). In particular, finding a solution

150 See for a discussion, L.N. Pnevmaticou, *Aspectes juridiques de la politique européenne de sécurité et de défense*, Paris, WEU ISS, 2001 (Occasional Paper 31). See also below, Chapter 4.A.4.

151 Article 17 EU Treaty, with the exception of closer cooperation in the WEU, which is still mentioned as a possibility.

152 Article 25 EU Treaty.

153 See Article 24 EU Treaty and *infra* Chapter 6.B.

154 Article 27(a)-(b) EU Treaty. On attempts to already introduce enhanced cooperation in the Treaty of Amsterdam, see A. Missiroli, *supra* note 130 (Chaillot Paper No. 38), pp. 5–15. For a discussion of differentiated integration in ESDP, see, e.g. J. Howorth, 'The European Draft Constitutional Treaty and the Future of the European Defence Initiative', 9 *E.F.A.R.* 2004, pp. 483–508; K. Lenaerts, 'Cooperation in the Second and Third Pillars of the European Union', text presented at a colloquium on 'Models of Cooperation within an Enlarged European Union' in Brussels on 28 January 2003, on file with the author, and R. Wessel, 'Differentiation in EU Foreign, Security and Defence Policy: Between Coherence and Flexibility', in TRYBUS & WHITE, pp. 223–248.

that satisfied Turkey was not easy.[155] The arrangements on NATO-EU cooperation will be analyzed briefly below (Chapter 2.C).

The year 2003 not only saw the entry into force of the Treaty of Nice, but was also a key year for the ESDP.[156] First, the ESDP was declared more fully operational by the Council on 19–20 May 2003: "*the EU now has operational capability across the full range of Petersberg tasks, limited and constrained by recognised shortfalls. These limitations and/or constraints are on deployment time and high risk may arise at the upper end of the spectrum of scale and intensity, in particular when conducting concurrent operations*".[157] Second, in 2003 the EU launched its first civilian and military ESDP operations, which have been increasing in number, variety and size since then (by 31 August 2009, some 22 operations had been launched).[158] Third, the operational developments were matched by a strategic aspect when the 12–13 December 2003 Brussels European Council adopted the *European Security Strategy* entitled *A Secure Europe in a Better World*,[159] which

155 On the position of Turkey in relation to the ESDP, see, e.g. M. Aykan, 'Turkey and European Security and Defence Identity/Policy (ESDI/P): A Turkish View', 13 *J.C.M.S.* 2005, pp. 335–359; M. Cebeci, *A Delicate Process of Participation: The Question of Participation of WEU Associate Members in Decision-making for EU-led Petersberg Operations, with Special Reference to Turkey*, Paris, WEU ISS, Occasional Paper No. 10, November 1999; A. Dumoulin, R. Mathieu & G. Sarlet, *La Politique Européenne de Sécurité et de Défense. De l'opératoire à l'identitaire*, Brussels, Bruylant, 2003, pp. 708–723; P. Fitschen & S.A. Serdar, 'Die ESVP und die Türkei – Auf der Suche nach einer strategischen Partnerschaft', in H.-G. Ehrhart & B. Schmitt (eds.), *supra* note 136, pp. 118–129; A. Missiroli, 'EU-NATO Cooperation in Crisis Management: No Turkish Delight for ESDP', 33 *Security Dialogue* 2002, pp. 9–26; M. Müftüler-Bac, 'Turkey's Role in the EU's Security and Foreign Policies', 31 *Security Dialogue* 2000, pp. 489–502 and Ö. Orhun, 'European Security and Defence Identity: Common European Security and Defence Policy: A Turkish perspective', 5(3) *Perceptions* 2000, pp. 115–124.

156 Javier Solana, the SG/HR appropriately labelled it 'Politique européenne de sécurité et de défense: de l'opérationnalité aux opérations' (No. 466 *R.M.C.U.E.* 2003, pp. 148–150).

157 Conclusions *inter alia* available at www.consilium.europa.eu/uedocs/cmsUpload/Declaration%20on%20EU%20Military%20Capabilities%20-%20May%202003.pdf.

158 For an overview, see Chapter 3 below and www.consilium.europa.eu/cms3_fo/showPage.asp?id=268&lang=en&mode=g.

159 *A Secure Europe in a Better World. European Security Strategy*, *supra* note 62. See generally www.consilium.europa.eu/showPage.aspx?id=266&lang=EN; A. Bailes, *The European Security Strategy: An Evolutionary History*, Stockholm International Peace Research Institute, Policy Paper No. 10, February 2005 (available online at http://books.sipri.org/files/PP/SIPRIPP10.pdf); S. Biscop, *The ABC of European Union Strategy: Ambition, Benchmark, Culture*, Egmont Paper 16, Brussels, October 2007 (available online at www.egmontinstitute.be/paperegm/ep16.pdf); S. Biscop & J.J. Andersson (eds.), *The EU and the European Security Strategy – Forging a Global Europe*, London, Routledge, 2007; S. Biscop, *The European Security Strategy – A Global Agenda for Positive Power*, Aldershot, Ashgate Publishing, 2005; S. Biscop, 'The European Security Strategy. Implementing a Distinctive Approach to Security', No. 82 *Sécurité & Stratégie*, March 2004 (available online at www.irri-kiib.be/papers/Artikel%20V&S%20ESS.pdf); S. Biscop, 'In Search of a Strategic Concept for the ESDP', 7 *E.F.A.R.* 2002, pp. 473–490; S. Duke, 'The European Security Strategy in a Comparative Framework: Does it

was supplemented later by an implementation report of which the analysis was shared by the 11–12 December 2008 European Council.[160]

This concludes the short historical overview and brings us to the ESDP as it is currently regulated under the EU Treaty. In Chapters 2 to 4, I will analyze in more detail this current state of the ESDP, including the ESDP's future under the Lisbon Treaty, as well as the ESDP operations and I will identify the main international law aspects which these developments raise.

Make for Secure Alliances in a Better World?', 9 *E.F.A.R.* 2004, pp. 459–481; G. Quille, 'The European Security Strategy: A Framework for EU Security Interests?', 11 *International Peacekeeping* 2004, pp. 422–438 and A. Toje, 'The 2003 European Union Security Strategy: A Critical Appraisal', 10 *E.F.A.R.* 2005, pp. 117–133. See also G. Bono, 'The EU's Military Doctrine: An Assessment', 11 *International Peacekeeping* 2004, pp. 439–456 (noting *inter alia* that the EU developed a military doctrine before it had a security strategy) and J. Solana, 'The Common Foreign and Security Policy and the European Security and Defence Policy: Current Status and Perspectives', in K. von Wogau (ed.), *The Path to European Defence*, Antwerp, Maklu, 2004, pp. 36–43.

160 Report on the Implementation of the European Security Strategy – Providing Security in a Changing World, EU Council Doc. 17104/08 of 10 December 2008 / S407/08, available online at www.consilium.europa.eu/showPage.aspx?id=266&lang=EN and §30 of the 11–12 December European Council conclusions. See also the Council declaration of 8 December 2008 on international security (EU Council Doc. 16751/08 of 3 December 2008), endorsed by the 11–12 December 2008 European Council (EU Council Doc. 17271/1/08 REV 1, §30 and Annex 6).

CHAPTER 2
THE STATE OF THE ESDP

In this Chapter, I will briefly summarize the present status of the ESDP under the EU Treaty as last substantially amended by the Treaty of Nice, focusing on those issues that have legal significance, especially under international law. It is therefore not a systematic and comprehensive description of the state of the ESDP.[161]

---

161 For more comprehensive overviews, see, e.g. S. Blockmans (ed.), *The European Union and International Crisis Management: Legal and Policy Aspects*, The Hague, TMC Asser Press, 2008; G. Bono & S. Ulriksen (eds.), 'The EU, Crisis Management and Peace Support Operations', 11 No. 3 *International Peacekeeping* 2004 (special issue); M. Britz & A. Eriksson, 'The European Security and Defence Policy: A Fourth System of European Foreign Policy?', in B. Irondelle & F. Petiteville (eds.), *A la recherche de la politique étrangère européenne*, Paris, L'Harmattan, 2005, pp. 35–62; P. Buffotot (ed.), *La défense en Europe: avancées et limites*, Paris, La Documentation Française, 2005; S. Duke, *The EU and Crisis Management. Development and Prospects*, EIPA, Maastricht, 2002; A. Dumoulin, R. Mathieu & G. Sarlet, *La Politique Européenne de Sécurité et de Défense. De l'opératoire à l'identitaire*, Brussels, Bruylant, 2003; H.-G. Ehrhart & B. Schmitt (eds.), *Die Sicherheitspolitik der EU im Werden: Bedrohungen, Aktivitäten, Fähigkeiten*, Baden-Baden, Nomos, 2004; N. Gnesotto (ed.), *EU Security and Defence Policy. The First Five Years (1999–2004) / La politique de sécurité et de défense de l'UE Les cinq premières années (1999–2004)*, Paris, EU Institute for Security Studies, 2004 (available online at www.iss.europa.eu); J. Howorth, *Security and Defence Policy in the European Union*, Basingstoke, Palgrave, 2007; S. Lang, *Bestimmungsfaktoren und Handlungsfähigkeit der Europäischen Sicherheits- und Verteidigungspolitik*, Frankfurt, Peter Lang, 2007; M. Merlingen & R. Ostrauskaite (eds.), *European Security and Defence Policy: An Implementation Perspective*, Abingdon, Routledge, 2008; A. Missiroli & A. Pansa, *La difesa europea*, Il melangolo, Genova, 2007 and K. von Wogau (ed.), *The Path to European Defence*, Antwerp, Maklu, 2004. For overviews from a legal perspective, see S. Bartelt, *Der rechtliche Rahmen für die neue operative Kapazität der Europäischen Union*, Münster, Lit Verlag, 2003; S. Dietrich, *Europäische Sicherheits- und Verteidigungspolitik (ESVP). Die Entwicklung der rechtlichen und institutionellen Strukturen der sicherheits- und verteidigungspolitischen Zusammenarbeit im Europäischen Integrationsprozess von den Brüsseler Verträgen bis zum Vertrag über eine Verfassung für Europa*, Nomos, Baden-Baden, 2006; S. Dietrich, 'Die rechtlichen Grundlagen der Verteidigungspolitik der Europäischen Union', 66 *Z.a.o.R.V.* 2006, pp. 663–695 (English summary at pp. 696–697); K. Gerteiser, *Die Sicherheits- und Verteidigungspolitik der Europäischen Union. Rechtliche Analyse der gegenwärtigen Struktur und der Optionen zur weiteren Entwicklung*, Frankfurt am Main, Peter Lang, 2002; C. Gramsch, *Europa auf dem Weg zu einer gemeinsamen Sicherheits- und Verteidigungspolitik: eine juristische Analyse der Europäischen Sicherheits- und Verteidigungspolitik (ESVP) im Lichte der Beschlüsse von Köln bis Laeken* (dissertation), Bonn, 2003; E. Kirchner, 'The Challenge of European Union Security Governance', 44 *J.C.M.S.* 2006, pp. 947–968; P. Koutrakos, 'Which Policy for which Europe?: The Emerging Security and Defence Policy of the European Union', in T. Tridimas & P. Nebbia (eds.), *European Union Law for the Twenty-*

The issues that are covered are the basic principles (A); institutions (B); cooperation with NATO (C); cooperation with other actors, including third States, the UN, the OSCE and the AU (D); capabilities (E); the European Defence Agency and defence industry and procurement (F); financing (G) and the status of forces (H).

I have included future developments where I think this is useful. In this respect, the Treaty establishing a Constitution for Europe signed in Rome on 29 October 2004[162] (hereinafter 'EU Constitution') is mentioned at various instances despite the fact that it has now been adandoned, because a discussion of its provisions on ESDP remains almost entirely relevant as the Lisbon Treaty, which will enter into force on 1 December 2009, which is also discussed where relevant, includes virtually all the elements of the EU Constitution's security and defence provisions.[163] Moreover, as will become clear further on, some of the steps taken

---

first Century: Rethinking the New Legal Order, Oxford, Hart, 2004, Vol. 1, pp. 273–289; P. Koutrakos, 'Constitutional Idiosyncrasies and Political Realities: The Emerging Security and Defense Policy of the European Union', 10 *Columbia Journal of European Law* 2003–2004, pp. 69–96; J. Litten, *Beitrag der Westeuropäischen Union (WEU) zur Europäischen Sicherheits- und Verteidigungspolitik (ESVP): eine rechtspolitische Untersuchung*, Aachen, Shaker, 2005; N. Ronzitti (ed.), *Le forze di pace dell'Unione Europea*, Roma, Rubbettino, 2005 (available online at www.difesa.it/backoffice/upload/allegati/2006/%7BEA8BC1A6-47B4-4A78-B563-BB9E5C9741F6%7D.pdf with an executive summary in English); H. Schöllhorn, *Der sicherheitspolitische Handlungsrahmen der Europäischen Union: eine Darstellung der rechtlichen und tatsächlichen Möglichkeiten für operative Maßnahmen der Krisenbewältigung*, Baden-Baden, Nomos, 1996; H. Sjursen, 'Security and Defence', in W. Carlsnaes, H. Sjursen & B. White (eds.), *Contemporary European Foreign Policy*, London, Sage, 2004, pp. 59–74; C. Tomuschat & J.A. Frowein (eds.), *Rechtsprobleme einer europäischen Sicherheits- und Verteidigungspolitik* (36 Berichte der Deutschen Gesellschaft für Völkerrecht), Heidelberg, Müller, 1997; Trybus & White; M. Trybus, *European Union Law and Defence Integration*, Oxford, Hart, 2005; S. Graf von Kielmansegg, *Die verteidigungspolitik der Europäischen Union*, Stuttgart, Boorberg, 2005; S. Graf von Kielmansegg, 'The Meaning of Petersberg: Some Considerations on the Legal Scope of ESDP Operations', 44 *C.M.L. Rev.* 2007, pp. 629–648; S. Graf von Kielmansegg, 'Die verteidigungspolitischen Kompetenzen der Europäischen Union', 41 *EuR.* 2006, pp. 182–200 and M. Warnken, *Der Handlungsrahmen der Europäischen Union im Bereich der Sicherheits- und Verteidigingspolitik*, Baden-Baden, Nomos, 2002, especially pp. 141-212. For compilations of key documents, see (W)EU ISS, Chaillot papers Nos. 47, 51, 57, 67, 75, 87, 98 and 112, available at www.iss.europa.eu. The Presidency Reports on ESDP to the successive European Councils offer an excellent overview of the evolution and state of affairs; they are available at www.consilium.europa.eu/showPage.aspx?id=700&lang=en. The most recent ones at the time of writing can be found in EU Council Documents 10415/08 of 16 June 2008, 16686/08 of 9 December 2008 and 10748/09 of 15 June 2009. See also the *ESDP Newsletters*, available online at www.consilium.europa.eu/showPage.aspx?id=1090&lang=en and more generally the Council's ESDP website at www.consilium.europa.eu/showPage.aspx?id=261&lang=EN.

162 *O.J. C* 310, 16 December 2004, p. 1.

163 For a discussion of some of the Lisbon Treaty's provisions on security and defence, see, e.g. B. Angelet & I. Vrailas, *European Defence in the Wake of the Lisbon Treaty*, Egmont Paper 21, May 2008 (www.egmontinstitute.be/paperegm/ep.21.pdf) and S. Biscop & F. Algieri (eds.),

in the EU Constitution can also be, and have been to some extent, taken under the present EU Treaty.[164]

A. BASIC PRINCIPLES

As the previous Chapter has shown, the EU now has a European Security and Defence Policy. The key features of the ESDP are the following:

First, this policy is part of the comprehensive CFSP and includes the progressive framing of a common defence policy under Articles 2 and 17 EU Treaty (from here on, all references to the EU Treaty are to this Treaty as amended by the Treaty of Nice, unless indicated otherwise), which includes humanitarian and rescue tasks, peacekeeping tasks and tasks of combat forces in crisis management, including peacemaking, and which might lead to a common defence if the European Council so decides. What exactly is covered by this will be addressed below in some detail (Chapter 4.A). However, it may be noted here that the ESDP being part of the CFSP entails an outward focus: the ESDP only covers crisis management outside the EU (and possibly in the future a common defence

The Lisbon Treaty and ESDP: Transformation and Integration, Egmont Paper 24, June 2008 (www.egmontinstitute.be/paperegm/ep24.pdf). For a discussion of the security and defence related provisions of the EU Constitution, see L. Benoit, 'La politique de sécurité et de défense commune dans le traité instituant une Constitution pour l'Europe', No. 486 *R.M.C.U.E.* 2005, pp. 155–162; G. Bono, 'La PESC et la PESDC dans la Constitution européenne: evalution sur la base du projet de la Convention', 5 *Annuaire français de relations internationales* 2004, pp. 556–563; H. Bribosia, 'Les coopérations renforcées et les nouvelles formes de flexibilité en matière de défense dans la Constitution européenne', *R.D.U.E.* 2004(4), pp. 647–709; S. Dietrich, *supra* note 161 (66 *Z.a.o.R.V.* 2006), pp. 692–694; F. Goudappel, 'Prospects of the European Common Defence Policy', 16 *R.E.D.P.* 2004, pp. 245–260; J. Howorth, 'The European Draft Constitutional Treaty and the Future of the European Defence Initiative', 9 *E.F.A.R.* 2004, pp. 483–508; M. Koopmann, 'Notwendige Fortschritte, verpasste Chancen: die ESVP im Verfassungsentwurf des Europäischen Konvents', in H.-G. Ehrhart & B. Schmitt (eds.), *supra* note 161, pp. 78–90; F. Naert, 'European Security and Defence Policy in the EU Constitutional Treaty', 10 *J.C.S.L.* 2005, p. 187–207; R. Schmidt-Radefeldt, 'Die Weiterentwicklung der Europäischen Sicherheits- und Verteidigungspolitik im EU-Verfassungsvertrag: Auf dem zu einer Europäischen Armee?', *Unterrichtsblättern für die Bundeswehrverwaltung* 2005(6), pp. 201–208 (available online at www.deutsches-wehrrecht.de/Aufsaetze/UBWV_2005_201.pdf); T. Stein, 'Sicherheits- und Verteidigungspolitik nach der geplannten EU-Verfassung: nur virtuell?', in R. Hofmann & A. Zimmermann (eds.), *Eine Verfassung für Europa: Die Rechtsordnung der Europäischen Union unter dem Verfassungsvertrag*, Berlin, Duncker & Humblot, 2005, pp. 179–195; M. Trybus, 'On the Common Security and Defence Policy of the EU Constitutional Treaty', in TRYBUS & WHITE, pp. 43–58; M. Trybus, 'With or without the EU Constitutional Treaty: towards a Common Security and Defence Policy?', 31 *Eur. L. Rev.* 2006, pp. 145–166 and M. Trybus, *supra* note 161, pp. 293–399.

164 See also M. Trybus, *supra* previous note, pp. 145–166.

against outside aggression, see *infra*).[165] Also, as already noted in Chapter 1, the ESDP includes both civilian and military crisis management.

Second, the EU may conduct ESDP operations conducted either autonomously or with recourse to NATO assets.[166] Furthermore, the obligations and role of NATO are not affected;[167] there will be no *unnecessary* duplication[168] and the EU will only act when NATO as a whole is not engaged.[169] However, the latter element has been narrowed down to some extent, see *infra*, Section C of this

---

165 This does not appear to be explicitly stated but is clear nonetheless. Similarly, K. Gerteiser, *supra* note 161, p. 143 ("*mit ihrer eindeutigen Ausrichtung auf Konflikte außerhalb der Union*"); I. Österdahl, 'The EU and Its Member States, Other States, and International Organizations – The Common European Security and Defence Policy after Nice', 70 *Nordic J.I.L.* 2001, p. 369 and M. Weller, 'The European Union within the "European Security Architecture"', in M. Koskenniemi (ed.), *International Law Aspects of the European Union*, The Hague, Kluwer Law International, 1998, pp. 62–63. Article 27(1) (renumbered 42(1)) EU Treaty as amended by the Lisbon Treaty (and Article I-41(1) EU Constitution) explicitly provides that "*The Union may use [civil and military assets] on missions outside the Union ...*". But see H. Neuhold, 'The Provisions of the Amsterdam Treaty on the CFSP: Cosmetic Operation or Genuine Progress?', in G. Hafner *et al.* (eds.), *Liber Amicorum Professor Seidl-Hohenverldern – in Honour of His 80th Birthday*, The Hague, Kluwer Law International, 1998, p. 500, who seems to see room for *intra*-EU operations, and A. Abas, *infra* note 438, pp. 144–145, who writes that the choice to deploy where NATO cannot go could mean an internal competence (this should be rejected as the deference to NATO is not related to a geographical competence, see *infra* next paragraph). Compare, with respect to the WEU, J. Litten, *supra* note 161, pp. 68 and 73–74, who does not seem to exclude an internal focus on the basis of the Amended Brussels Treaty, but acknowledges that this is not mentioned in the Petersberg Declaration and would in any event be excluded without the consent of the Member State concerned given that WEU decisions must be taken unanimously.

166 According to §1 of the Cologne Declaration of the European Council and Presidency report on strengthening the European common policy on security and defence (3–4 June 1999, Presidency conclusions, Annex III), the EU "*must have the capacity for* autonomous *action*" (emphasis added). According to §4 of the Presidency report annexed thereto, the European Union "*will have to determine, according to the requirements of the case, whether it will conduct: EU-led operations using NATO assets and capabilities or EU-led operations without recourse to NATO assets and capabilities*". The autonomy is stressed by L. Balmond, 'L'Union européenne, une organisation de défense?', in R. Ben Achour & S. Laghmani (eds.), *Le droit international à la croisée des chemins: force du droit et droit de la force: VIe Rencontre internationale de la Faculté des Sciences juridiques, politiques et sociales de Tunis, 14, 15 et 16 avril 2004*, Paris, Pedone, 2004, pp. 291–314. See also *supra*, Chapter 1, Sections D-E.

167 See Article 17(1), 2nd subparagraph EU Treaty. This is maintained under the Lisbon Treaty: see Article 27(2), 2nd subparagraph (renumbered 42(2), 2nd subparagraph) EU Treaty as amended (see also Article I-41(2), 2nd subparagraph EU Constitution). See also *supra*, Chapter 1.E.

168 See §3 *in fine* of the 1999 Cologne Presidency Report: "*As regards military capabilities, Member States need to develop further forces (including headquarters) that are suited also to crisis management operations,* without any unnecessary duplication" and Helsinki European Council Presidency Conclusions, 10–11 December 1999, §27: "*This process* will avoid unnecessary duplication *and does not imply the creation of a European army*" (emphasis added).

169 Helsinki European Council Presidency Conclusions, 10–11 December 1999, §27: "*The European Council underlines its determination to develop an autonomous capacity to take*

Chapter. Moreover, non-EU European NATO members should be able to participate in ESDP operations, though without affecting the EU's decision-making autonomy.[170] To ensure that all of this works, close cooperation with NATO is a key element. This will be explored below (Section C of this Chapter).

Third, the ESDP shall respect the principles of the United Nations Charter and the primary role of the UN Security Council. This not only results from Article 11 EU Treaty,[171] but was also specifically confirmed with regard to the ESDP[172] and is reinforced under the Lisbon Treaty.[173] This is relevant to the international

decisions and, where NATO as a whole is not engaged, *to launch and conduct EU-led military operations in response to international crises*" (emphasis added).

170 According to §1 of the Cologne European Council Declaration on strengthening the European common policy on security and defence (*supra* note 166) the EU wants to develop an effective EU-led crisis management "*in which NATO members, as well as neutral and non-allied members, of the EU can participate fully and on an equal footing in the EU operations*" and the EU "*will put in place arrangements that allow non-EU European allies and partners to take part to the fullest possible extent in this endeavour*". The annexed Presidency Report adds in §5 that a successful ESDP will require "*satisfactory arrangements for European NATO members who are not EU Member States to ensure their fullest possible involvement in EU-led operations, building on existing consultation arrangements within WEU*" and "*arrangements to ensure that all participants in an EU-led operation will have equal rights in respect of the conduct of that operation, without prejudice to the principle of the EU's decision-making autonomy, notably the right of the Council to discuss and decide matters of principle and policy*".

171 Article 11(1), 1st and 3rd hyphen EU Treaty state that the objective "*to safeguard the common values, fundamental interests, independence and integrity of the Union*" shall be pursued "*in conformity with the principles of the United Nations Charter*" and the objective "*to preserve peace and strengthen international security*" shall likewise be pursued "*in accordance with the principles of the United Nations Charter, as well as the principles of the Helsinki Final Act and the objectives of the Paris Charter, including those on external borders*".

172 See §2 of the 1999 Cologne Presidency Report: "*The European Union is committed to preserve peace and strengthen international security in accordance with the principles of the UN Charter as well as the principles of the Helsinki Final Act and the objectives of the Charter of Paris, as provided for in Article 11 of the [EU Treaty]*" and §26 of the Helsinki European Council Presidency Conclusions, 10–11 December 1999: "*The Union will contribute to international peace and security in accordance with the principles of the United Nations Charter. The Union recognises the primary responsibility of the United Nations Security Council for the maintenance of international peace and security*".

173 See also Article 3(5) (renumbered 3(5)) EU Treaty as amended under the Lisbon Treaty ("*In its relations with the wider world, the Union shall uphold and promote its values and interests. It shall contribute to peace, security, ..., solidarity and mutual respect among peoples, ... and the protection of human rights, in particular the rights of the child, as well as to the strict observance and the development of international law, including respect for the principles of the United Nations Charter*") and especially the Declaration (No. 13) concerning the common foreign and security policy annexed to the Lisbon Treaty in which it is stated that "*[The Conference] stresses that the EU and its Member States will remain bound by the provisions of the Charter of the United Nations and, in particular, by the primary responsibility of the Security Council and of its Members for the maintenance of international peace and security*".

legal basis for ESDP operations and will be addressed below (Chapter 4.A.6; see also Chapter 7.G.4).

Fourth, as a matter of EU law, the ESDP is part of the CFSP.[174] It is therefore subject to the CFSP rules, except where stipulated otherwise.[175] This means, for instance, that constructive abstention is possible in the ESDP.[176] One of the ESDP exceptions is the exclusion of qualified majority voting for "*decisions having military or defence implications*".[177] Another specific ESDP rule is that the sending of armed forces requires a decision by each Member State for its forces (even when it has consented to an ESDP operation).[178] The relevance of the latter rule will become clear in Chapter 3 and Chapter 4.A.2 on operations and the scope of the ESDP below. Another ESDP exception is that enhanced cooperation in the CFSP for the implementation of a joint action or a common position "*shall not relate to matters having military or defence implications*".[179] Finally, it may be recalled that Denmark does not participate in the elaboration and the implementation of decisions and actions of the Union which have defence implications,[180] a position which remains the same under the Lisbon Treaty.[181]

In the remainder of this section, I will mainly address those issues that are of legal significance or necessary for a proper understanding of the ESDP but that will not be discussed more extensively below.

---

174 The provisions on the ESDP are in the EU Treaty Title on the CFSP. In the EU Treaty as amended by the Lisbon Treaty, the CSDP will be a sub-policy of the CFSP (see Title V, Chapter 2, Section 2).

175 See the 1999 Cologne Presidency Report, §2 ("*The aim is to strengthen the CFSP by the development of a common European policy on security and defence. ... Decisions to act would be taken within the framework of the CFSP according to appropriate procedures in order to reflect the specific nature of decisions in this field*").

176 See *supra*, Chapter 1.E and Article 23(1) EU Treaty.

177 Article 23(2) EU Treaty.

178 See §3 *in fine* of the 1999 Cologne Presidency Report: "*Decisions relating to crisis management tasks, in particular decisions having military or defence implications will be taken in accordance with Article 23 of the Treaty on European Union.* Member States will retain in all circumstances the right to decide if and when their national forces are deployed" (emphasis added) and the title on 'decision-making' in the Helsinki Presidency Report on ESDP: "*The commitment of national assets by Member States to such operations will be based on their sovereign decision*".

179 Article 27(a)-(b) EU Treaty, see *supra*, Chapter 1.F.

180 Article 6 Protocol on the Position of Denmark attached to the EU Treaty since the Treaty of Amsterdam, see *supra*, Chapter 1.E.

181 See Article 5 Protocol on the Position of Denmark as amended by the Lisbon Treaty. See also Article 5 of the Protocol on the Position of Denmark attached to the EU Constitution. However, the Danish government is reportedly considering holding a referendum on ending this opt-out; see J. Hetland, 'Nordics Take a Global Perspective', *European Voice*, 10 July 2008, p. 24.

B. INSTITUTIONS[182]

In order to adequately develop the ESDP and conduct operations pursuant to this policy, the Council may meet composed of Defence Ministers, albeit formally not entirely autonomously.[183] Furthermore, as described above, a Political and Security Committee (PSC), EU Military Committee (EUMC), EU Military Staff (EUMS)[184] and Committee for Civilian Aspects of Crisis Management (CIVCOM)[185] are now functioning.

However, so far the EU has no standing military military command structure and headquarters[186] and it should be stressed that the EUMC and EUMS may provide advice and strategic planning but their mandate does not include

182 See generally E. Decaux, 'Le processus de decision de la PESC: vers une politique étrangère européenne?', in E. Cannizzaro (ed.), *The European Union as an Actor in International Relations*, The Hague, Kluwer Law International, 2002, pp. 25–33; S. Dietrich, *supra* note 161 (66 *Z.a.o.R.V.* 2006), pp. 684–686; S. Duke, 'Peculiarities in the Institutionalisation of CFSP and ESDP', in S. Blockmans (ed.), *The European Union and International Crisis Management: Legal and Policy Aspects*, The Hague, TMC Asser Press, 2008, pp. 75–105; A. Dumoulin, R. Mathieu & G. Sarlet, *supra* note 161, pp. 285–347 (and their discussion of institutional rivalries at pp. 551–595); J. Litten, *supra* note 161, pp. 214–223; R. Matarazzo, 'Le strutture istituzionale della Pesd', in N. Ronzitti (ed.), *supra* note 161, pp. 21–48 and M. Trybus, *supra* note 161, pp. 108–112. See also H. Dijkstra, 'The Council Secretariat's Role in the Common Foreign and Security Policy', 13 *E.F.A.R.* 2008, pp. 149–166.

183 The Defence ministers have met informally since 1998 (for the first time on 3–4 November 1998). Subsequently they also met within the General Affairs/External Relations Council together with the Foreign Affairs Ministers. This was agreed by the 11 October 1999 Council ("*Work will continue in the Council bodies and on 15 November at the General Affairs Council with the participation of Defence Ministers*") and first implemented at the 15 November 1999 Council (the Conclusions read "*The General Affairs Council, with the participation of Defence Ministers, discussed the follow-up to the Cologne conclusions on strengthening the ESDP .*"). Moreover, on 18–19 February 2002 the Council decided that they could also meet formally by themselves, albeit within the framework of the General Affairs/External Relations Council (EU Council Doc. 6247/02 (Presse 30), p. 26: "*Regarding the participation of Ministers of Defence at the General Affairs Council in May, the Council noted the Presidency's intention to enable Defence Ministers to discuss certain agenda items, limited to issues covering military capabilities. Discussion on these issues will be chaired by the Minister of Defence of the Presidency*"), which they did for the first time on 13 May 2002 (see the list of participants in EU Council Doc. 8649/02 (Presse 124) and pp. 13–15). See A. Dumoulin, R. Mathieu & G. Sarlet, *supra* note 161, pp. 71, 277–248 and 299–306 and J. Litten, *supra* note 161, pp. 214 and 227.

184 On the EUMS, see www.consilium.europa.eu/showPage.aspx?id=1039&lang=en (including all issues of the EUMS Bulletin, entitled 'Impetus').

185 See *supra*, Chapter 1, notes 137–138 and 143 for the relevant decisions and *infra* note 192 for further amendments to the EUMS decisions.

186 See also *infra* on the EU Operations Centre. It may be noted that even where there is common funding of the acquisition of some materiel for military operations, the financing mechanism regards such common costs as costs shared by the Member States jointly rather than by the EU (see the Athena decision, *infra* note 342, Article 2(3)).

operational planning[187] and they do not command or conduct an operation – they are not included in the chain of command. For military operations, the latter goes from the PSC (which exercises political control and strategic direction) over the Operation Commander (and his headquarters), who has the highest level of *military command*, to the Force Commander (and his headquarters) and to subordinate commanders and forces.[188] Therefore the arrangements for commanding an operation and in particular its headquarters are each time determined on an *ad hoc* basis (similar to the generation of the necessary forces[189]) and headquarters have to be made available by NATO or by Member States individually or jointly. Nevertheless, as the ESDP has evolved, there has been a greater acceptance for the nucleus of a proper headquarters within the EU in defined circumstances.[190] To this effect, a civilian military (planning) cell has been set up in the EUMS and the mandate of the EUMS[191] has been amended: the EUMS now also has the responsibility through the Civil/Military Cell "*of generating the capacity to plan and run an autonomous EU military operation, and maintains the capacity within EUMS rapidly to set up an operations centre for a specific operation, in particular where a joint civil/military response is required and where no national HQ is identified, once a decision on such an operation has been taken by the Council, upon the advice of the EUMC*".[192] The EU Operations

187 G.-J. Van Hegelsom, 'Relevance of IHL in the Conduct of Petersberg Tasks', in College of Europe & ICRC (eds.), *Proceedings of the Bruges Colloquium. The Impact of International Humanitarian Law on Current Security Policy Trends. 26th – 27th October 2001 / Actes du colloque de Bruges. L'impact du droit international humanitaire sur l'évolution des politiques de sécurité. 26–27 octobre 2001*, Bruges, College of Europe (*collegium* No. 25, available online at www.coleurop.be/template.asp?pagename=pub_collegium), 2002, p. 113. However, the role of the EUMS in the early stages of planning for a military ESDP operation has recently been enhanced, see, e.g. the EU Concept for Military Planning at the Political and Strategic Level, Council Doc. 10687/08 of 16 June 2008.

188 On the command and control (C2) arrangements in military ESDP operations, see Council Doc. 11096/03 EXT 1 (26 July 2006; this is a partially declassified version). See also P. Petrov, 'The ESDP in motion: Opportunities and constraints for the application of an integrated Civil-Military Operational Scenario', 60(3) *Studia Diplomatica* 2007, pp. 157–181.

189 See on this the EU Concept for Force Generation, Council Doc. 10690 of 16 June 2008.

190 This development is closely linked to the degree of autonomy that the ESDP should have and the demand to avoid unnecessary duplication and has been the subject of much debate. See also the section on EU-NATO relations below (Section C of this Chapter) and M. Reichard, *infra* note 204, pp. 81–88.

191 Council fact sheet on EU Battle Groups and the EU Civilian and Military Cell (February 2005), available online at www.consilium.europa.eu/uedocs/cmsUpload/Battlegroups.pdf. See also the December 2003 European Council approved document on NATO-EU Consultation, Planning and Operations, available online at www.consilium.europa.eu/uedocs/cmsUpload/78414%20-%20EU-NATO%20Consultation,%20Planning%20and%20Operations.pdf and *ESDP Newsletter* No. 2, June 2006, pp. 7–9 (www.consilium.europa.eu/showPage.aspx?id=1090&lang=en) as well as P. Petrov, *supra* note 188, pp. 172–182.

192 See Council Decision of 10 May 2005 amending Decision 2001/80/CFSP on the establishment of the Military Staff of the European Union (2005/395/CFSP), *O.J. L* 132, 26 May 2005, p. 17. For the previous mandate, see the decisions cited *supra*, Chapter 1, note 139. This decision

Centre, which reached operational capability on 1 January 2007, has been successfully activated for the first time during the EU's military exercise 2007 (MILEX 07) in June 2007.[193]

In addition, in 2007, new guidelines were adopted for the Command and Control Structure for EU Civilian Operations in Crisis Management,[194] including the establishment of the Civilian Planning and Conduct Capability.[195] They *inter alia* provide that:

---

was subsequently replaced by Council Decision of 7 April 2008 amending Decision 2001/80/CFSP on the establishment of the Military Staff of the European Union (2008/298/CFSP), *O.J. L* 102, 12 April 2008, p. 25 (to take into account an enhanced planning role and changes in the General Secretariat of the Council; see also Council Doc. 10687/08 of 16 June 2008, *supra* note 187). On the Civ-Mil Cell and the EU Operations Centre, see also EU Council Doc. 13990/04 EXT 1 of 28 January 2005. Furthermore, the rules applicable to seconded (military) staff have been altered by Council Decision of 16 June 2003 concerning the rules applicable to national experts and military staff on secondment to the General Secretariat of the Council and repealing the Decisions of 25 June 1997 and 22 March 1999, Decision 2001/41/EC and Decision 2001/496/CFSP (2003/479/EC), *O.J. L* 160, 28 June 2003, p. 72, subsequently amended by Council Decision of 8 March 2004 amending Decision 2003/479/EC concerning the rules applicable to national experts and military staff on secondment to the General Secretariat of the Council (2004/240/EC), *O.J. L* 74, 12 March 2004, p. 17; by Council Decision of 30 May 2005 adjusting the allowances provided for in Decision 2003/479/EC concerning the rules applicable to national experts and military staff on secondment to the General Secretariat of the Council (2005/442/EC), *O.J. L* 153, 16 June 2005, p. 32; by Council Decision of 27 June 2006 adjusting the allowances provided for in Decision 2003/479/EC concerning the rules applicable to national experts and military staff on secondment to the General Secretariat of the Council (2006/471/CFSP), *O.J. L* 187, 8 July 2006, p. 32 and by Council Decision of 18 June 2007 adjusting the allowances provided for in Decision 2003/479/EC concerning the rules applicable to national experts and military staff on secondment to the General Secretariat of the Council (2007/456/EC), *O.J. L*. 173, 3 July 2007, p. 27. This decision was in turn replaced by Council Decision of 5 December 2007 concerning the rules applicable to national experts and military staff on secondment to the General Secretariat of the Council and repealing Decision 2003/479/EC (2007/829/EC), *O.J. L* 327, 13 December 2007, p. 10 as amended by Council Decision of 16 June 2008 adjusting the allowances provided for in Decision 2003/479/EC and Decision 2007/829/EC concerning the rules applicable to national experts and military staff on secondment to the General Secretariat of the Council (2008/451/EC), *O.J. L* 158, 18 June 2008, p. 56 and by Council Decision of 27 April 2009 adjusting the allowances provided for in Decision 2003/479/EC and Decision 2007/829/EC concerning the rules applicable to national experts and military staff on secondment to the General Secretariat of the Council (2009/399/EC), *O.J. L* 127, 26 May 2009, p. 8. Specific rules apply to staff seconded to the EDA, see *infra*, Section F of this Chapter, note 323.

193 External Relations Council of 19–20 November 2007, conclusions on ESDP, §32.

194 On civilian crisis management by the EU, see generally A. Nowak (ed.), *Civilian Crisis Management: The EU Way*, Chaillot Paper No. 90, Paris, EU ISS, June 2006 (available online at www.iss.europa.eu/index.php?id=143&L=0) and R. Rummel, 'Soft-Power EU: Interventionspolitik mit zivilen Mitteln', in H.-G. Ehrhart & B. Schmitt (eds.), *Die Sicherheitspolitik der EU im Werden: Bedrohungen, Aktivitäten, Fähigkeiten*, Baden-Baden, Nomos, 2004, pp. 259–279.

195 See, e.g. External Relations Council of 19–20 November 2007, conclusions on ESDP, §36; Council Doc. 9919/07 EXT 1 of 6 July 2007 and Council Doc. 11277/07 of 28 June 2007. See

> a Civilian Operation Commander will exercise command and control at strategic level for the planning and conduct of all civilian crisis management operations, under the political control and strategic direction of the [PSC] and the overall authority of the [SG/HR]; these Guidelines further provide that the Director of the Civilian Planning and Conduct Capability (CPCC) established within the Council Secretariat will, for each civilian crisis management operation, be the Civilian Operation Commander.[196]

Furthermore, the 11–12 December 2008 European Council "*would encourage the efforts of the Secretary-General/High Representative to establish a new, single civilian-military strategic planning structure for ESDP operations and missions*".[197]

The PSC plays a key role in the ESDP and especially in the conduct of ESDP operations. Pursuant to Article 25 EU treaty, it "*shall exercise, under the responsibility of the Council, political control and strategic direction of crisis management operations*" and "*the Council may authorise the Committee, for the purpose and for the duration of a crisis management operation, as determined by the Council, to take the relevant decisions concerning the political control and strategic direction of the operation ...*". The practice of ESDP operations so far has confirmed this key role. In particular, the PSC is usually granted the authority to amend the operation plan, the chain of command, sometimes including the appointment of the Head of Mission or the Operation and Force Commander, and the rules of engagement, to accept third States' contributions and to set up a committee of contributors, while the powers of decision concerning the objectives and termination of the operation remain vested in the Council.[198] The role of the PSC essentially remains the same under the Lisbon Treaty.[199]

---

also *ESDP Newsletter* No. 6, July 2008, pp. 24–25 (www.consilium.europa.eu/showPage.aspx?id=1090&lang=en).

196 See, e.g. Council Joint Action of 13 November 2007 amending Joint Action 2007/369/CFSP on the establishment of the European Union Police Mission in Afghanistan (EUPOL AFGHANISTAN) (2007/733/CFSP), *O.J. L* 295, 14 November 2007, p. 31 (2nd consideration of the preamble). Decisions implementing these changes in specific operations which have already been adopted are included in Chapter 3 below. See also EU Council Doc. 10116/07 (5 June 2007) on the 'Watchkeeping Capability (WKC) for ESDP Operations within the General Secretariat of the Council' (partially public).

197 See §30 of the Presidency Conclusions and §6 of the Declaration by the European Council on the Enhancement of the European Security and Defence Policy in Annex II thereto (EU Council Doc. 17271/1/08 REV 1).

198 See *infra* Chapter 3 and F. Naert, 'ESDP in Practice: Increasingly Varied and Ambitious EU Security and Defence Operations', in Trybus & White, pp. 61–101.

199 See Article 23 (renumbered 38) EU Treaty as amended by the Lisbon Treaty. See also Article III-307(2) EU Constitution.

Furthermore, mention should be made of the EU Satellite Centre, the EU Institute for Security Studies[200] and the European Defence Agency[201] as well as the European Security and Defence College.[202] The role of the European Commission and of the European Parliament is rather limited (as is the case under the CFSP more generally).[203]

---

200 See for both *supra*, Chapter 1.E, notes 140–141 and accompanying text. On their status, see also *infra*, Chapter 6.D. On the EU Satellite Centre, see also *ESDP Newsletter* No. 8, Summer 2009, pp. 22–23 (www.consilium.europa.eu/showPage.aspx?id=1090&lang=en) and www.eusc.org/.

201 See *infra*, Section F of this Chapter.

202 Council Joint Action of 18 July 2005 establishing a European Security and Defence College (ESDC) (2005/575/CFSP), *O.J. L* 194, 26 July 2005, p. 15; replaced by Council Joint Action of 23 June 2008 establishing a European Security and Defence College (ESDC) and repealing Joint Action 2005/575/CFSP (2008/550/CFSP), *O.J. L* 176, 4 July 2008, p. 20. See also *ESDP Newsletter* No. 2, June 2006, pp. 10–12 (www.consilium.europa.eu/showPage.aspx?id=1090&lang=en). Furthermore, "*As regards the future format of the ESDC, work is ongoing on the elaboration of a new Council Decision evolving the European Security and Defence College in line with the ESDC Steering Committee recommendations approved by Council in December 2008*", see EU Council Doc. 10748/09 of 15 June 2009, §99.

203 On the role of the European Parliament and of the European Commission in the CFSP, see Article 21 EU Treaty on the one hand (it must be consulted on the main aspects and basic choices, its views are to be duly taken into consideration, it is to be kept informed, may ask questions and make recommendations and shall hold an annual debate; see also its budgetary powers) and Articles 18(4), 22 and 27 EU Treaty on the other hand (it shall be "*fully associated with the work carried out in the common foreign and security policy field*" and specifically in the representation of the Union and in the implementation of CFSP decisions and has a (non-exclusive) right of initiative). Compare renumbered Article 24 (pointing out the specificity of the CFSP) as well as Articles 36 (European Parliament) and Articles 22(2), 27(3), 30(1), 42(4) and 45(2) (Commission) of the EU Treaty as they are amended by the Lisbon Treaty as well as Declaration (14) concerning the common foreign and security policy (which reads in part "*The Conference also notes that the provisions covering the Common Foreign and Security Policy do not give new powers to the Commission to initiate decisions nor do they increase the role of the European Parliament*"). On parliamentary oversight over the ESDP, see, e.g. G. Bono, 'The European Union as an International Security Actor: Challenges for Democratic Accountability', in H. Born & H. Hänggi (eds.), *The "Double Democratic Deficit": Parliamentary Accountability and the Use of Force Under International Auspices*, Aldershot, Ashgate, 2004, pp. 163–181; C. Gourlay, 'Parliamentary Accountability and ESDP: The National and the European Level', in *id.*, pp. 183–200 and K. Raube, 'European Parliamentary Oversight of Crisis Management', in S. Blockmans (ed.), *The European Union and International Crisis Management: Legal and Policy Aspects*, The Hague, TMC Asser Press, 2008, pp. 181–198 and *infra*, note 1136. See also D. Nickel & G. Quille, *In the Shadow of the Constitution: Common Foreign and Security Policy/European Security and Defence Policy Adapting to a Changing External Environment*, Jean Monnet Working Paper 02/2007 (available online at www.jeanmonnetprogram.org/papers/07/070201.pdf). Obviously, when actions in the field of the ESDP are accompanied or followed by measures under the first pillar, close coordination is required with the European Commission.

C. COOPERATION WITH NATO[204]

The key principles defining the EU-NATO relationship have already been set out above. First, NATO remains responsible for the implementation of collective defence, even under the Lisbon Treaty. However, as will be noted below (Chapter 4.A.5.iv), this might cause some difficulty if the EU does decide to have a common defence and it would have to be put in practice in defence of a Member State that is not a NATO member.

Second, the ESDP is complementary to NATO and the EU should only conduct ESDP operations where NATO as a whole is not engaged.[205] In this respect, one cannot avoid the impression that there is, or was, some competition, e.g. in the case of the parallel EU and NATO support for AMIS II.[206] Similarly, EUJUST LEX and NATO's training mission in Iraq[207] also raise the question of duplication, although the kind of training provided and the target audiences in this case seem to correspond to the expertise of each of the organizations involved. It is submitted that complementarity does not hinder concurrent operations as long as they are sufficiently distinct in nature and reflect the strengths of the two organizations. Thus the EUPM being deployed while NATO was still leading S-FOR is not problematic, nor are the concurrent EULEX

---

204 For an extensive overview, including from a legal perspective, see M. Reichard, *The EU-NATO Relationship: A Legal and Political Perspective*, Aldershot, Ashgate, 2006 and M. Reichard, 'The EU-NATO "Berlin Plus" Agreement: The Silent Eye of the Storm', in S. Blockmans (ed.), *The European Union and International Crisis Management: Legal and Policy Aspects*, The Hague, TMC Asser Press, 2008, pp. 233–253. See furthermore generally the websites www.consilium.europa.eu/showPage.aspx?id=282&lang=en and www.nato.int/issues/nato-eu/index.html; F. Burwell *et al.*, *Transatlantic Transformation: Building a NATO-EU Security Architecture*, Atlantic Council of the US, Policy Paper, March 2006 (available online at www.acus.org/docs/0603-Transatlantic_Transformation.pdf#search=%22malta%2C%20cyprus%2C%20nato%2C%20security%20agreement%2C%20esdp%20%20%22); M. Comelli, 'Gli interventi dell'Unione europea e la cooperazione con la Nato', in N. Ronzitti (ed.), *supra* note 161, pp. 137–164; A. Dumoulin, R. Mathieu & G. Sarlet, *supra* note 161, pp. 356–365; J.-Y. Haine, 'ESDP and NATO' in N. Gnesotto (ed.), *supra* note 161, pp. 131–143; H. Krieger, 'Common European Defence: Competition or Compatibility with NATO?', in Trybus & White, pp. 174–197; J. Litten, *supra* note 161, pp. 237–243; F. Terpan, 'EU-NATO Relations: Consistency as a Strategic Consideration and a Legal Requirement', in Trybus & White, pp. 270–294 and the fact sheet 'NATO-EU relations' at www.wsibrussels.org/eu_nato_relations.htm.

205 On differences of interpretation of this principle, see D. Keohane, 'Unblocking EU-NATO Co-operation', *Centre for European Reform Bulletin* Issue 48, June/July 2006, www.cer.org.uk/articles/48_keohane.html (mentioning that the US perceived this as a right of first refusal for NATO) and M. Reichard, *supra* previous note, pp. 147–170, especially pp. 162–170. See also H. Krieger, *supra* previous note, pp. 193–194.

206 NATO was providing air lift and training to AU forces, see www.nato.int/issues/darfur/index.html.

207 NATO's Training Mission in Iraq is providing training in the security sector; see www.nato.int/issues/iraq-assistance/index.html.

Kosovo and KFOR missions. In contrast, the continued presence in Bosnia and Herzegovina (BiH) of a small NATO mission concurrently with Althea seems less logical, although it may be based on political considerations such as a continued US involvement and BiH's relations with NATO. Most recently, there has been some overlap between EU and NATO anti-piracy operations off the coast of Somalia, although there have been efforts to de-conflict and coordinate and the area is big enough for both operations to operate without unnecessary overlap.

Third, while the arrangements for the EU to conduct operations with access to NATO assets proved a tough challenge and could only be agreed upon in March 2003, they have since been applied in Concordia and are being applied in Althea and seem to function well.[208] The package on these relations was finalized on 17 March 2003[209] and *inter alia* consists of the 16 December 2002 NATO-EU 'Berlin Plus' agreement governing EU access to NATO planning, NATO European command options and EU use of NATO assets and capabilities,[210] the 16 December 2002 EU-NATO Declaration on ESDP setting out the principles governing their mutual relations[211] and the EU-NATO Security Agreement of 14 March 2003[212].[213] However, Cyprus, an EU but not NATO member, still does not have a security agreement with NATO and is not involved in NATO's Partnership for Peace programme and therefore cannot participate in EU operations with recourse to NATO assets, such as ALTHEA (this was also the case for Malta until it rejoined NATO's Partnership for Peace programme in 2008).[214]

208 Although it may be noted that both cases concerned operations taken over from NATO rather than operations in which NATO was not involved at all.

209 See www.nato.int/issues/nato-eu/chronology.html.

210 The agreement itself is not in the public domain. Its content is summarized in the background note entitled 'EU-NATO: The Framework for Permanent Relations and Berlin Plus' and available online at www.consilium.europa.eu/uedocs/cmsUpload/03-11-11%20Berlin%20Plus%20press%20note%20BL.pdf. For a discussion from a legal perspective, see M. Reichard, 'Some Legal Issues Concerning the EU-NATO Berlin Plus Agreement', 73 *Nordic J.I.L.* 2004, pp. 37–67 and M. Reichard, *supra* note 204, pp. 273–310.

211 42 *I.L.M.* 2003, p. 242. See also www.nato.int/docu/pr/2002/p02-142e.htm.

212 Agreement between the European Union and the North Atlantic Treaty Organisation on the Security of Information, *O.J. L* 80, 27 March 2003, p. 35/36, entered into force 14 March 2003. The agreement supersedes the Interim Security Arrangement concluded between the General Secretariat of the Council of the EU and NATO through an Exchange of Letters dated 26 July 2000.

213 See also the background note entitled 'EU-NATO: The Framework for Permanent Relations and Berlin Plus', *supra* note 210.

214 The Berlin Plus arrangements (*supra* this section) are limited to Partnership for Peace members; see NATO Parliamentary Assembly, report 176 PCNP 05 E on NATO-EU Security Co-operation (2005, available online at www.nato-pa.int/default.Asp?SHORTCUT=675), §3. See also F. Burwell *et al.*, *supra* note 204, p. 25. In the case of Cyprus, Turkey has so far

More generally, Cyprus' accession to the EU has created an obstacle to better EU-NATO relations as long as Turkish-Cypriot relations do not improve. In particular, it has prevented the release of some NATO documents to the EU or at least to all EU Member States. In return, Cyprus has rejected NATO-EU discussions without the presence of Cyprus (and Malta) except concerning Berlin Plus issues.[215] Insiders have stated that strategic cooperation is therefore seriously hampered, whereas cooperation in the field has so far worked quite well.[216] However, they have expressed concern that the consequences of the strategic obstacles are increasingly being felt at the operational level too. For instance, NATO-EU arrangements for cooperation between both organizations' Kosovo and Afghanistan missions[217] are not yet concluded at headquarters level because of these political controversies.[218] France's re-integration into NATO's military structures in 2009[219] may have a positive impact upon EU-NATO relations, but this remains to be seen.[220]

Fourth, and closely related to this, agreement was reached on the participation of the European non-EU NATO members in the ESDP (Bulgaria and Romania, who have become EU Member States in the meantime, and Iceland (which applied for EU membership in July 2009), Norway and Turkey[221]). All of these countries have participated quite actively in ESDP operations and have concluded

opposed the conclusion of a security agreement. Malta reactivated its participation in the Partnership for Peace (which it had joined in 1995 but suspended in 1996) in 2008, see §32 of NATO's 3 April 2008 Bucharest Summit Declaration and www.nato.int/docu/update/2008/04-april/e0403e.html. On security of information in NATO and the EU, see generally M. Reichard, *supra* note 204, pp. 311–351.

215 For a short analysis, see D. Keohane, *supra* note 205 (also blaming French resistance to a global security role for NATO and hence to EU-NATO discussions on global security issues).

216 See, e.g. the assessment made by the Dutch Minister of Foreign Affairs in the annotated agenda of the 26–27 April 2007 NATO Ministerial meeting in Oslo sent to the Dutch Parliament on 23 April 2007 (available online at www.minbuza.nl/nl/Actueel/Kamerstukken/2007/04/Kamerbrief_betreffende_informele_NAVO_bijeenkomst_van_ministers_van_Buitenlandse_Zaken_Oslo_26_en_27_april_2007).

217 See below, Chapter 3, Sections T and Q. The EUPOL Afghanistan Joint Action (*infra* note 734) envisages arrangements with the NATO-led ISAF on various forms of support; see its Article 5(2).

218 See also J. Dempsey, 'Letter from Germany: Bickering between NATO and EU Hampers Training of Afghan Police', *International Herald Tribune*, 23 August 2007, noting that arrangements with regard to Afghanistan have not been concluded at EU-NATO level, and A. Toje, *The EU, NATO and European Defence – A Slow Train Coming*, Paris, EU ISS, Occasional Paper No. 74, December 2008, p. 19.

219 France's decision to fully participate in NATO's military structures, was welcomed by the 3–4 April 2009 NATO Summit. See www.nato.int/cps/en/natolive/news_52837.htm?mode=pressrelease and www.diplomatie.gouv.fr/fr/actions-france_830/defense-securite_9035/france-otan_9044/sommet-otan-strasbourg-kehl-03-04.04.09_70821.html. See also *supra* note 77.

220 Compare A. Toje, *supra* note 218.

221 See generally *supra* Chapter 1, note 155 and the accompanying text.

a permanent agreement on their participation in such operations.[222] The same is true for Canada,[223] for which separate arrangements have been adopted[224] and which has also concluded a generic participation agreement.[225]

Fifth, unnecessary duplication of capabilities was to be avoided. This has given rise to considerable debate, including within the EU, and is closely related to the degree of autonomy of the ESDP. A compromise was adopted in late 2003 to have a small civil/military planning cell at the EU Military Staff and an EU planning cell at SHAPE.[226] While the EU initially had to rely either on NATO or on Member States for Operation Headquarters, it is now also envisaged that the civil/military planning cell in the EUMS might serve as the core of an Operation Headquarters to be activated and reinforced on an *ad hoc* basis.[227] Also, the efforts to enhance Member States' capabilities in both organizations should be complementary,[228] including through the EU-NATO Capability Group.[229]

Finally, there are arrangements on permanent consultations and cooperation, including regular joint meetings of the North Atlantic Council and the PSC and of the North Atlantic Council and the EU Council.[230] However, as indicated above, it appears that in respect of these political high level contacts significant

222 See *infra* Section D of this Chapter and Chapter 3.

223 See generally A. Dumoulin, R. Mathieu & G. Sarlet, *supra* note 161, pp. 683–690 and J. Fraterman, *Canada-EU Cooperation in Military Crisis-Management: Principles, Modalities and Practice*, European Foreign Policy Unit Working Paper 2006/1, *s.d.*, available online at www2.lse.ac.uk/internationalRelations/centresandunits/EFPU/EFPUpdfs/EFPUworkingpaper 2006-1.pdf.

224 See EU Council Doc. 8721/02 of 6 May 2002.

225 Agreement between the European Union and Canada establishing a framework for the participation of Canada in the European Union crisis management operations, 24 November 2005, *O.J. L* 315, 1 December 2005, p. 20/21, entered into force 1 December 2005.

226 Presidency Conclusions, 12–13 December 2003, §90. The document agreed upon is available online at www.consilium.europa.eu/uedocs/cmsUpload/78414%20-%20EU-NATO%20 Consultation,%20Planning%20and%20Operations.pdf. See also EU Council Doc. 13990/04 EXT 1 of 28 January 2005. Compare the Presidency Conclusions, 17–18 June 2003, §65 and the annexed document 'European Defence: NATO/EU Consultation, Planning and Operations'. See also J.-Y. Haine, *supra* note 204, pp. 140–141.

227 See the documents cited *supra* previous note, second sentence. See also *supra*, Section B of this Chapter, on the EUMS's role in this context.

228 See the 16 December 2002 EU-NATO Declaration on ESDP (*supra* note 211). On ESDP capabilities, see *infra*, next section. On NATO's capabilities, see www.nato.int/issues/capabilities/index.html.

229 See, e.g. EU Council Doc. 6805/03 (26 February 2003), pp. 4 (especially note 2), 13 and 15–17.

230 This was first laid down in an exchange of letters between the NATO Secretary-General and the EU Council Presidency in January 2001; see the reference thereto in §42 of the final communiqué of the North Atlantic Council of 29 May 2001. The arrangements provide that "*Not less than three meetings between the North Atlantic Council and the EU Political and Security Committee and not less than one Ministerial meeting will be held during each EU Presidency. Either organisation may request additional meetings as necessary. Both*

obstacles to better cooperation still exist. The December 2008 European Council stated that:

> The European Council ... reaffirms the goal of strengthening the strategic partnership between the EU and NATO in order to address current needs, in a spirit of mutual enhancement and respect for their decision-making autonomy. To this end, it backs the setting up of an informal EU-NATO high-level group to improve cooperation between the two organisations on the ground in a pragmatic manner. It recalls the need to exploit fully the approved framework that enables European allies which are not members of the EU to be associated with the ESDP, in compliance with EU procedures.[231]

It remains to be seen whether this latest attempt to overcome these obstacles will succeed.

D. COOPERATION WITH OTHER ACTORS

It is clear that in its historical development, the ESDP was closely related to the WEU and the WEU was, from the Maastricht Treaty until approximately late 2000, an integral part of the ESDP. Indeed, in all probability the quick progress that has been made in the ESDP since it was launched in 1999 would not have been possible if the WEU *acquis* had not been available. However, the WEU currently does not play any significant role anymore although the collective defence clause in its constitutive treaty remains relevant as a legal commitment in force (but one that will be implemented within NATO). As I will show below (Section F of this Chapter), its armaments cooperation activities have also been taken over by the EU. I will therefore not address EU-WEU cooperation.

However, three other aspects of external cooperation merit some discussion. First, there is extensive cooperation with third States in ESDP operations. This will be elaborated below in Chapter 3, but I will summarize its main features here. Second, the relationship with the UN will be outlined briefly. Third, some attention will be paid to the relationship with other international organizations, in particular the OSCE and the AU but also very briefly ASEAN.

---

organisations are committed to stepping up contacts and meetings in the emergency phase of a crisis" (*id.*). The text of the letters in reproduced in M. Reichard, *supra* note 204, pp. 399–402.

231 Declaration European Council on the Enhancement of the European Security and Defence Policy in Annex II to the 11–12 December 2008 European Council Presidency Conclusions, §7 (EU Council Doc. 17271/1/08 REV 1).

1. THIRD STATE PARTICIPATION[232]

The larger and more traditional types of EU operations so far have been reinforced by third States' participation, while a number of the smaller and newer ones have not. Many of these participations came from candidate member States (including Turkey), most of which have now acceded to the EU. However, the non-EU NATO Member States Iceland, Canada and Norway have also been active participants, as has Switzerland. Finally, an increasing number of countries have participated in one or just a few of the operations, including Ukraine,[233] Russia,[234] Albania, Croatia (which is now a candidate Member State), Brazil, South Africa, Argentina, Chile, FYROM, Morocco, New Zealand, Malaysia, Brunei, Singapore, the Philippines, Thailand, Angola, Honduras, Guatemala, El Salvador and the Dominican Republic. It is also worth noting the first US participation (in EULEX Kosovo).

This openness to third States provides an added value and may be enhanced by the full participation in the day-to-day running of the operation, including for small contributors,[235] and the tendency in the more recent participation agreements to not demand a contribution in the common costs. Obviously, the latter somewhat increases the share in the common costs for the participating EU Member States. However, if this helps to attract contributions from third States, which in any event pay the non-common costs for their forces/personnel, it is probably more advantageous in the end. The inclusion of mutual waivers of claims or best efforts to obtain such waivers reflects the position between Member States under the EU Claims Agreement concluded between the Member States on 28 April 2004.[236]

The participation agreements that are concluded with third States to regulate their participation in EU-led operations do not seem to differ very much, except

232 See generally A. Dumoulin, R. Mathieu & G. Sarlet, *supra* note 161, pp. 697–701.

233 For an analysis of Ukraine's participation in and views on the ESDP, see A. Dumoulin, R. Mathieu & G. Sarlet, *supra* note 161, pp. 377–379.

234 For an analysis of Russia's participation in and views on the ESDP, see A. Dumoulin, R. Mathieu & G. Sarlet, *supra* note 161, pp. 365–377; M. Webber, 'Third-Party Inclusion in European Security and Defence Policy: A Case Study of Russia', 6 *E.F.A.R.* 2001, pp. 407–426 and A. Zagorski, 'Russo-European Security Co-operation: Is the Glass Half Full or Half Empty', in H.-G. Ehrhart & B. Schmitt (eds.), *supra* note 161, pp. 176–185. On 11 May 2007, in the margin of the EU Member States' Chiefs of Defence Staff meeting, the Member States' Chiefs of Defence Staff held an exchange of views with the Chief of the General Staff of the Russian Armed Forces; see EU press release of 10 May 2007, www.consilium.europa.eu/uedocs/cms_Data/docs/pressdata/en/sg/94058.pdf.

235 I.e. by not reserving this participation for those who provide "significant" contributions or by judging that all contributions are significant, see Chapter 3 below.

236 *Infra* note 348, especially Articles 3–4 (not yet entered into force).

where they reflect specificities proper to an operation. In fact, in addition to mission specific model participation agreements,[237] there now exist general (draft) model participation agreements for military and civilian ESDP missions.[238] Moreover, an increasing number of third States have now concluded framework agreements on participation in ESDP operations, thereby avoiding the need to conclude a specific agreement for every operation (these countries were/are the former acceding States Bulgaria[239] and Romania,[240] the candidate Member State and NATO member Turkey,[241] the NATO members Iceland,[242] Norway[243] and Canada[244] and Ukraine[245]).

2. THE UN AND THE ESDP

As far as EU-UN relations in the field of security and defence are concerned, three elements may be distinguished. One is the attitude of the EU towards the UN Charter rules on the use of force and the authority of the UN Security Council (see *infra*, Chapter 4.A.6). A second aspect is the EU's actions within the UN and especially the Security Council.[246] This aspect will not be explored in

237 See *infra* notes 471 (ARTEMIS) and 575 (ALTHEA).

238 The most recent versions listed in the Council's register appear to be respectively EU Documents 12047/04 (3 September 2004) and 12050/04 (3 September 2004).

239 Agreement between the European Union and the Republic of Bulgaria establishing a framework for the participation of the Republic of Bulgaria in the EU crisis management operations, *O.J. L* 46, 17 February 2005, p. 49/50, which was provisionally applied as from 24 January 2005 and entered into force on 1 August 2006.

240 Agreement between the European Union and Romania establishing a framework for the participation of Romania in the European Union crisis-management operations, *O.J. L* 67, 14 March 2005, p. 1/14, which entered into force on 1 December 2004.

241 Agreement between the European Union and the Republic of Turkey establishing a framework for the participation of the Republic of Turkey in the European Union crisis management operations, Brussels, 29 June 2006, *O.J. L* 189, 12 July 2006, p. 16/17, which entered into force on 1 August 2007.

242 Agreement between the European Union and the Republic of Iceland establishing a framework for the participation of the Republic of Iceland in the European Union crisis-management, 21 February 2005, *O.J. L* 67, 14 March 2005, p.1/2, which entered into force on 1 April 2005 (and was provisionally applied as of the date of signature).

243 Agreement between the European Union and the Kingdom of Norway establishing a framework for the participation of the Kingdom of Norway in the European Union crisis-management operations, 3 December 2004, *O.J. L* 67, 14 March 2005, p. 1/8, which entered into force on 1 January 2005.

244 *Supra* note 225.

245 Agreement between the European Union and Ukraine establishing a framework for the participation of Ukraine in the European Union crisis management operations, 13 June 2005, *O.J. L* 182, 13 July 2005, p. 28/29, which entered into force on 1 May 2008.

246 See, e.g. several chapters in K. Laatikainen & K. Smith (eds.), *The European Union at the United Nations. Intersecting Multilateralisms*, Basingstoke, Palgrave Macmillan, 2006 and in J. Wouters, F. Hoffmeister & T. Ruys (eds.), *The United Nations and the European Union: An*

this book, except incidentally when it touches upon one of the other two aspects. The third element, which will be analyzed briefly in this section, is the cooperation between the EU and the UN[247] in relation to the ESDP.[248]

Ever Stronger Partnership, The Hague, T.M.C. Asser Press, 2006; as well as M.B. Rasch, *The European Union at the United Nations. The Functioning and Coherence of EU External Representation in a State-Centric Environment*, UN University, 2008; A. Hamonic, *L'Union européenne à l'ONU: perspectives ouvertes par le Traité constitutionnel*, Rennes, Éd. Apogée, 2007; A. Degrand-Guillaud, 'Actors and Mechanisms of EU Coordination at the UN', 14 *E.F.A.R.* 2009, pp. 405–430; B. Fassbender, 'The Better Peoples of the United Nations? Europe's Practice and the United Nations', 15 *E.J.I.L* 2004, pp. 873–876 and 880–882; K. Lenaerts & E. de Smijter, 'The United Nations and the European Union: Living Apart Together', in K. Wellens (ed.), *International Law: Theory and Practice: Essays in Honour of Eric Suy*, The Hague, Nijhoff, 1998, pp. 442–447 and H. Portocarero, 'De EU in de Veiligheidsraad', 26(2) *VVN-Berichten* 2002, pp. 7–13. For the EC/EU in the UN General Assembly; see K.-D. Stadler, *Die Europäische Gemeinschaft in den Vereinten Nationen: die Rolle der EG im Entscheidungsprozess der UN-Hauptorgane am Beispiel der Generalversammlung*, Baden-Baden, Nomos, 1993 and J. Wouters, "The European Union as an Actor within the United Nations General Assembly", in V. Kronenberger (ed.), *The EU and the International Legal Order: Discord or Harmony?*, The Hague, T.M.C. Asser Press, 2001, pp. 375–404. Pursuant to Article 302 EC Treaty, "*It shall be for the Commission to ensure the maintenance of all appropriate relations with the organs of the United Nations and of its specialised agencies*". Since 1974, the EC has been an observer in the UN General Assembly (see UNGA Res. 3208 (XXIX) of 11 October 1974).

247 On EU-UN relations generally, see, e.g. the websites http://ec.europa.eu/external_relations/organisations/un/index_en.htm; www.europa-eu-un.org and www.consilium.europa.eu/showPage.aspx?id=403&lang=EN. See also EU, *The Enlarging European Union and the United Nations: Making Multilateralism Matter*, January 2004 (available online at www.medea.be/files/EU_and_UN_1_2004.pdf and www.europa-eu-un.org/articles/en/article_1001_en.htm); European Commission, *The European Union and the United Nations: The Choice of Multilateralism*, COM(2003)526, 10 September 2003; the Council conclusions of 8 December 2003 on EU-UN relations; European Commission, *Relations between the European Community and International Organisations*, Luxembourg, Office for Official Publications of the EC, 1989, pp. 23–188; Part II in D. Dormoy (ed.), *L'Union européenne et les organisations internationales*, Brussels, Bruylant, 1997, pp. 275–458; K. Laatikainen & K. Smith (eds.), *supra* previous note; K. Lenaerts & E. de Smijter, *supra* previous note, pp. 439–458; A. Schnabel, '"The Choice of Multilateralism": zum Verhältnis EU/UN nach dem Irak-Krieg', in H.-G. Ehrhart & B. Schmitt (eds.), *supra* note 161, pp. 186–198 and J. Wouters, F. Hoffmeister & T. Ruys (eds.), *supra* previous note.

248 This section is to some extent based on J. Wouters & F. Naert, 'Linking Global and Regional Organizations: The Case of the United Nations and the European Union', April 2004, available online at www.law.kuleuven.be/iir/nl/onderzoek/opinies/FNJWeuun.pdf. See generally J. Coelmont, 'De verhouding EU-VN, de militaire aspecten', 26(2) *VVN-Berichten* 2002, pp. 14–17; U. Villani, 'La politica europea in materia di sicurezza e di difesa e i suoi rapporti con le Nazioni Unite', 59 *La Comunità internazionale* 2004, pp. 63–90; J. Wouters & T. Ruys, 'UN-EU Cooperation in Crisis Management: Partnership or Rhetoric?', in S. Blockmans (ed.), *The European Union and International Crisis Management: Legal and Policy Aspects*, The Hague, TMC Asser Press, 2008, pp. 215–232 and J. Wouters, 'De verhouding tussen de Europese Unie en de Verenigde Naties op het gebied van vrede en veiligheid', 26(2) *VVN-Berichten* 2002, pp. 18–29. Specifically on EU-UN cooperation in conflict prevention, see J. Wouters, 'The United Nations, the EU and Conflict Prevention: Interconnecting the Global and Regional Levels', in V. Kronenberger & J. Wouters (eds.), *The European Union and Conflict Prevention. Legal and Policy Aspects*, T.M.C. Asser Press, 2004, pp. 369–392.

In the area of the ESDP, EU-UN cooperation has grown in practice, particularly in BiH[249] and Kosovo[250] (and hence to some extent already before the launching of the ESDP), as well as on a more systematic basis following political initiatives.

More systematic EU-UN relations in the field of peace and security were set in motion by a speech by the then French EU Council Presidency at the UN General Assembly in 2000, *inter alia* inviting Kofi Annan to meet with EU institutions,[251] which he did that very month. The call for exploring cooperation in crisis management was taken up by the December 2000 Nice European Council.[252] Subsequently, concrete arrangements were agreed in this field and approved by the EU General Affairs Council on 11 June 2001[253] and by the Göteborg European Council later that month.[254] They stated that the EU-UN partnership "*is further strengthened by the mutually reinforcing approaches to conflict prevention and by ensuring that the European Union's evolving military and civilian capacities provide real added value for UN crisis management activities*", gave priority to the Western Balkans, the Middle East and Africa, stressed the importance of a comprehensive approach and envisaged the "*conclusion of framework agreements between the European Community and relevant UN organisations*". The conclusions spell out three specific themes and areas of cooperation:

1. *Conflict prevention*, in particular ensuring mutually reinforcing approaches; exchange of information and analyses concerning on-going and potential crises; co-operation on fact-finding; co-ordination of diplomatic activity and messages, including consultations between Special Representatives; field co-ordination and training; increased co-operation in electoral assistance and election monitoring.
2. *Civilian and military aspects of crisis management*, in particular ensuring that EU's evolving military and civilian capacities provide real added value for the UN, i.a. by enhancing compatibility of training standards for civilian crisis management personnel, and exchange of information on questions related to the planning and implementation of crisis management; co-ordination in the field.

---

249 On the EU's and the UN's role there, see J. Wouters & F. Naert, 'How Effective is the European Security Architecture? Lessons from Bosnia and Kosovo', 50 *I.C.L.Q.* 2001, pp. 540–576.

250 *Id.* See also the reference to the EU in §17 of UNSC Res. 1244 (10 June 1999).

251 Speech of 12 September 2000, available online at www.un.int/france/eu/speeches/debat/0912F.htm.

252 Presidency Conclusions, Annex VI, part VIII, inviting the Swedish Presidency to report on "*the identification of possible areas as well as modalities of cooperation between the European Union and the United Nations in crisis management*".

253 *Bull. EU*, 6–2001, §I.31.53. For details, see EU Council Doc. 9528/2/01 REV 2, 7 June 2001. See also Council Secretariat, Relations between the European Union and the United Nations in crisis management and conflict prevention, Doc. 12969/01, 7 November 2001.

254 Conclusions, §53 and the annexed Council conclusions on EU-UN co-operation in conflict prevention and crisis management.

> 3. *Particular regional issues*, Western Balkans, Middle East and Africa, in particular the Great Lakes, Horn of Africa and West Africa, will be for the time being the priority areas of reinforced co-operation between the EU and the UN.

On a practical level, measures were adopted to ensure a more continuous and coherent cooperation. They include meetings of the EU Ministers with the UN Secretary-General, contacts between the SG/HR and the external relations Commissioner on the one hand and the UN Secretary-General and Deputy Secretary-General on the other hand, meetings of the EU's PSC with the UN Deputy Secretary-General and Under Secretaries-General and at other levels as appropriate (including with the UN Department of Peacekeeping Operations) and contacts between the EU Council Secretariat and the Commission's services on the one hand, and the UN Secretariat on the other hand.

In the meantime, the EU had taken over the UN's police mission in the BiH and had conducted operation Artemis in support of the UN's operation in the Democratic Republic of Congo (DRC; see *infra*, Chapter 3.B and D). The next step was the adoption of the EU-UN Joint Declaration on cooperation in crisis management of 24 September 2003.[255] After an introductory part, this Declaration states:

> 3. Further practical steps should be taken to build on the momentum of the positive co-operation between the United Nations and the European Union. To this end, the United Nations and the European Union agree to establish a joint consultative mechanism at the working level to examine ways and means to enhance mutual co-ordination and compatibility in the following areas:
>
> - *Planning*: including reciprocal assistance in assessment missions and greater contact and co-operation between mission planning units, specifically with regard to logistical resource allocation and inventory as well as interoperability of equipment.
> - *Training*: the establishment of joint training standards, procedures and planning for military and civilian personnel; the synchronisation of pre-deployment training for civilian police, military liaison officers and military observers; and the institutionalisation of training seminars, conferences and exercises.
> - *Communication*: greater co-operation between situation centers; exchange of liaison officers whenever required (military, civilian police, situation center, political/headquarters officials); establishment of desk-to-desk dialogue through the respective liaison offices in New York and Brussels.

[255] Text at www.europa-eu-un.org/articles/en/article_2768_en.htm and at www.consilium.europa.eu/showPage.aspx?id=1289&lang=en. Originally, a treaty had been envisaged rather than a mere declaration; see EU Council Documents 12338/03, 8 September 2003 and 12466/03, 11 September 2003.

- *Best Practices*: regularised and systematic exchange of lessons learned and best practices information, including sharing of information on mission hand-over and procurement.

To further this cooperation, a joint consultative mechanism (also known as "Steering Committee") was established at working level.[256] On 17–18 June 2004, the European Council endorsed the elaboration of modalities under which the EU could provide military capabilities in support of the UN (while work on a complementary document on civilian aspects of EU-UN co-operation was in progress[257]).[258] These modalities under which the EU could provide military capabilities in support of the UN are either the provision of national military capabilities in the framework of a UN operation, in which case the EU could not do much more than set up a 'clearing house process' that would be activated upon request or an EU operation in answer to a request from the UN but always under the political control and strategic direction of the EU. For the latter option, two modalities are put forward: either the EU could conduct operations under a UN mandate as a standalone operation or it could take responsibility for a specific component within the structure of a UN mission. Special consideration is given to operations calling for a rapid response, where the EU would bring a particular added value. Such operations could in turn comprise two broad categories: the "bridging model" (giving the UN time to launch or reorganize its mission; this could include subsequent 'rehatting' of personnel of the EU operation) and the "standby model" (i.e. an "over the horizon reserve" or extraction force). In addition, general cooperation measures that are envisaged include better knowledge of each other's procedures, concepts and structures, intelligence sharing and cooperation between the EU Satellite Centre and the UN, including possibly the conclusion of an MOU on this.

On the operational side, in the spring of 2006 the EU again launched an operation to support the UN mission in the DRC, namely EUFOR DR Congo (see *infra*, Chapter 3.P). In addition, there are/were support arrangements between EUPOL Kinshasa and the UN mission in the DRC and between EUSEC DRC and the UN mission in the DRC.[259] Moreover, in August 2006 the EU

---

256 See the document 'EU-UN co-operation ...', *infra* note 258, §2.

257 See EU Council Doc. 11022/1/03, 4 July 2003.

258 Presidency Conclusions, §62. The modalities are apparently contained in the Document 'EU-UN co-operation in Military Crisis Management Operations. Elements of Implementation of the EU-UN Joint Declaration' (available online at www.consilium.europa.eu/uedocs/cms Upload/EU-UN%20co-operation%20in%20Military%20Crisis%20Management%20Operations.pdf). Compare the wide range of options identified in EU Council Doc. 12969/01, 7 November 2001.

259 EU Council Doc. 10418/06 of 12 June 2006, §85. See also EU Council Doc. 7390/06 of 14 March 2006 (classified).

coordinated to some extent the contributions of the EU Member States to the reinforced UN peacekeeping operation in Lebanon following the end of the hostilities between Israel and Hezbollah.[260]

Furthermore, on 7 November 2005, the Council adopted Conclusions on the UN World Summit, which *inter alia* state that "*As endorsed by the Summit, the EU supports a stronger relationship between the UN and regional and subregional organisations, pursuant to Chapter VIII of the UN Charter. It is ready, for its part, to expand consultation and cooperation with the UN, through a possible formalised agreement*".[261] It seems to have been considered to conclude a Technical arrangement between the General Secretariat of the Council and the UN Department of Peacekeeping Operations (DPKO) Situation Centres.[262] The scope and meaning of Chapter VIII of the UN Charter and the status of the EU thereunder will be addressed briefly below in Chapter 4.A.6. It may suffice to note here that the UN has gradually been enhancing its cooperation with regional and subregional organizations since the 1990s. This is, for instance, reflected in the adoption of a UN Security Council Resolution 1631 of 17 October 2005 on this topic, which calls for closer cooperation and more consultation and specifies this in a number of ways.

On 7 June 2007, a new Joint Statement on UN-EU cooperation in Crisis Management was signed[263] and work on its implementation has been taken forward.[264] Subsequently, there was again close EU-UN cooperation in operations, especially in Chad and the CAR (see below, Chapter 3.S) but also in Kosovo (see below, Chapter 3.T).

It is therefore submitted that, despite some initial hesitations, especially from the UN side where fears existed that the ESDP might develop to the detriment of

260 See, e.g. the Conclusions of the extraordinary Council meeting of 25 August 2006, following consultations with the UN Secretary-General.

261 Available online at www.consilium.europa.eu/uedocs/cmsUpload/COUNCIL_CONCLUSIONS_ON_UN_WORLD_SUMMIT-NOV05.pdf.

262 See EU Council Doc. 12094/06 of 28 July 2006. As this document is not public, it cannot be ascertained whether the agreement has actually been concluded.

263 Available online at www.consilium.europa.eu/showPage.aspx?id=1289&lang=en. See also EU Council Doc. 10310/07 of 5 June 2007 and *ESDP Newsletter* No. 3, January 2007, pp. 15–17 (www.consilium.europa.eu/showPage.aspx?id=1090&lang=en).

264 See, e.g. EU Council documents 5293/1/08 (28 July 2008; p. 7 *inter alia* lists "*Exploring the possibility of having a framework arrangement on mutual logistical support or a model arrangement on logistical support*" and to "*consider: • the conditions under which the EU might transfer materiel to the UN following the termination of an EU mission or operation, and vice-versa*") and 17317/08 (15 December 2008, partially available to the public).

contributions to UN peace operations,[265] the EU-UN relationship is a good one and is improving.

3. ESDP AND OTHER INTERNATIONAL ORGANIZATIONS

i. The OSCE[266]

As the only European Security organization with full membership of all European States and the status of a regional arrangement under Chapter VIII of the UN Charter (see *supra*, Chapter 1.B *in fine* and *infra*, Chapter 4.A.6), the OSCE is clearly a candidate for close cooperation with the EU in the area of the EDSP and CFSP more generally. In fact, one of the CFSP's objectives under the EU Treaty, namely to preserve peace and strengthen international security, is to be pursued in accordance with the CSCE/OSCE "*principles of the Helsinki Final Act and the objectives of the Paris Charter, including those on external borders*".[267]

Cooperation with the OSCE was mentioned in the Presidency Report to the Helsinki European Council.[268] This was elaborated somewhat in respect of

---

265 See T. Tardy, *Limits and Opportunities of UN-EU Relations in Peace Operations: Implications for DPKO*, September 2003 (available online at http://pbpu.unlb.org/pbps/Library/Artemis.pdf), pp. 3–4 and EU Council Doc. 12969/01, 7 November 2001, §6.

266 See generally http://ec.europa.eu/external_relations/organisations/osce/index_en.htm; A. Bailes, J.-Y. Haine & Z. Lachowski, 'Reflections on the OSCE-EU Relationship', 13 *OSCE Yearbook* 2007, pp. 65–77; H. Borchert & D. Maurer, 'Kooperation, Rivalität oder Bedeutungslosigkeit? Fünf Szenarien zur Zukunft der Beziehungen zwischen OSZE und EU', 9 *OSZE-Jahrbuch* 2003, pp. 441–458 = 'Co-operation, Rivalry or Insignificance? Five Scenarios for the Future of Relations between the OSCE and the EU', *OSCE Yearbook* 2003, pp. 403–420; F. Cameron, 'The European Community and the CSCE', in M.R. Lucas (ed.), *The CSCE in the 90's: Constructing European Security and Cooperation*, Baden-Baden, Nomos, 1993, pp. 265–277; V. de Graaf & A. Verstichel, 'OSCE Crisis Management and OSCE-EU Relations', in S. Blockmans (ed.), *The European Union and International Crisis Management: Legal and Policy Aspects*, The Hague, TMC Asser Press, 2008, pp. 255–276 and G. Nesi, 'The Relations between the European Union and the OSCE in Crisis Management', in E. Cannizzaro (ed.), *The European Union as an Actor in International Relations*, The Hague, Kluwer Law International, 2002, pp. 271–277. For cooperation in the area of conflict prevention, see E. Bakker, 'A Culture of Conflict Prevention: OSCE Experiences and Cooperation with the EU', in V. Kronenberger & J. Wouters (eds.), *supra* note 248, pp. 393–413. On the OSCE's role in the broader European security architecture, see, e.g. I. Peters, 'OSZE, NATO und EU im "Geflecht europäischer Sicherheitsinstitutionen": Hierarchisierung, Flexibilisierung, Marginalisierung', 9 *OSZE-Jahrbuch* 2003, pp. 419–440 = 'The OSCE, NATO and the EU within the "Network of Interlocking European Security Institutions": Hierarchization, Flexibilization, Marginalization', *OSCE Yearbook* 2003, pp. 381–402.

267 Article 11(1), 3rd hyphen.

268 Presidency Conclusions, Annex IV *in fine*.

civilian missions, where one of the aims was to enhance and facilitate "*the EU's contributions to, and activities within, other organisations, such as the UN and the OSCE whenever one of them is the lead organisation in a particular crisis, as well as EU autonomous actions*" and to that end, Member States and the EU were, *inter alia*, to "*develop a rapid reaction capability by defining a framework and modalities, as well as by pre-identifying personnel, material and financial resources that could be used in response to a request of a lead agency like the UN or the OSCE, or, where appropriate, in autonomous EU actions*".[269] In fact, the EC/EU had already cooperated with the CSCE/OSCE in the Yugoslav conflicts, including by putting ECMM (see *supra*, Chapter 1.D) monitors at the disposal of CSCE/OSCE missions, by collaborating on monitoring the implementation of sanctions and more generally in the post-conflict international civilian presence in BiH and Kosovo, including through the Stability Pact for South Eastern Europe.[270]

Some more specific proposals were endorsed by the 2000 Santa Maria da Feira[271] and Nice[272] and the 2001 Göteberg European Councils.[273] However, structural

---

269 Id., Annex 2 to Annex IV.

270 See J. Wouters & F. Naert, *supra* note 249, pp. 547–550, 553–557 and 561–568.

271 Annex I, Presidency Report on Strengthening the Common European Security and Defence Policy, §8 ("*the importance has been underlined of ensuring an extensive relationship in crisis management by the Union between the military and civilian fields, as well as cooperation between the EU rapidly-evolving crisis management capacity and the UN, OSCE and the Council of Europe*"); Appendix 3.B.2 ("*(ii) the EU could aim at promoting guidelines for the selection and training of international judges and penal experts in liaison with the United Nations and regional organisations (particularly the Council of Europe and the OSCE)*") and Appendix 4, A.3 ("*Member States and the EU can play a catalysing role in raising standards for international police operations, including within and through the United Nations and the OSCE*" – however, in what immediately follows only close cooperation with the UN is envisaged) and B ("*[to develop] the EU's contributions to international organisations, in particular the UN and OSCE, as well as its capabilities for EU autonomous actions ... the EU will coordinate closely with the United Nations Department of Peace Keeping Operations (UN/ DPKO), the OSCE, notably the REACT Task Force, and with the Council of Europe and Member States contact points, in order to ensure that EU efforts and those of these organisations are compatible and mutually reinforcing, to avoid duplication as well as to facilitate the exchange of information relating to new police missions*").

272 Annex II to Annex VI, III ("*A seminar entitled "Strengthening the rule of law in the context of crisis management – What are the specific targets of the European Union?" was held on 25 October 2000 [with] Initial exchanges between the EU and representatives of ... the OSCE ... International personnel should be selected according to common standards. The European Union's work should here take full account of the body of experience built up by the United Nations, the OSCE and the Council of Europe*") and Annex V to Annex VI, (listing as an EUMS function to establish "*appropriate relations with identified correspondents within the UN and OSCE, subject to an agreement from these organisations*").

273 See especially the EU Programme for the Prevention of Violent Conflicts, §§14 ("*The EU must build and sustain mutually reinforcing and effective partnerships for prevention with the UN, the OSCE and other[s] .... Increased co-operation is needed at all levels, from early warning and analysis to action and evaluation. Field co-ordination is of particular importance. EU action*

cooperation seems to have grown only slowly and modestly[274] and only in November 2003 did the Council adopt more detailed conclusions on EU-OSCE Cooperation. The Guiding Principles state:

> 3. ... the Council affirms its determination to continue enhancing its relationship with the OSCE with a view to further develop the existing co-operation between the EU and the OSCE. Co-operation should take into account the different nature of the EU and the OSCE.
> 4. Co-ordination between the EU and the OSCE should also be based on the principle of avoiding duplication and identifying comparative advantages and added value, leading to effective complementarity. Moreover, co-ordination should develop as a process in the light of changing needs within the EU Common Foreign and Security Policy, including European Security and Defence Policy as well as within the OSCE.

Moreover, specific areas of co-operation are listed:

> 5. EU-OSCE co-operation should encompass the politico-military, economic and environmental and human dimensions, which characterise both the EU and the OSCE, as well as the specific tasks of conflict prevention, crisis management and post-conflict rehabilitation. In particular:
>
> (i) Enhanced co-operation should include: exchange of information and analyses, co-operation on fact finding missions, co-ordination of diplomatic activity and statements, including consultations between special representatives, training and in-field co-ordination.
> (ii) Mutually reinforcing initiatives could include inter alia:
>
> - possible contribution by the EU to the OSCE's operational efforts in crisis management
> - joint and/or co-ordinated programmes on post-conflict rehabilitation
> - EU crisis management operations following a request from the OSCE

The conclusions then elaborate on the modalities for EU-OSCE co-operation, which include regular contacts and meetings between the relevant EU and OSCE

should be guided by principles of value added and comparative advantage") and 15 ("*In order to increase co-operation and build effective partnerships [t]he EU will intensify its exchange of information and practical co-operation with the UN system, the OSCE, ..., making full use of recent work on intensified EU-UN and EU-OSCE co-operation in the field of conflict prevention and crisis management; ... joint training programmes for EU, UN and OSCE field and headquarters personnel should be developed ...*").

274 In a speech to the OSCE Permanent Council on 25 September 2005 (available online at www.consilium.europa.eu/uedocs/cmsUpload/72254.pdf), the SR/HR listed what had been achieved as "*exchanging information and expertise in developing our crisis management tools; cooperating on the ground and between headquarters to increase our efficiency and developing compatible methods and standards to allow for this co-operation to develop*".

bodies at Political level (including the EU and OSCE Troika, Secretary-General, Presidency, Chairman-in-Office and PSC and coordination among the EU Member States' representations to the OSCE and the EC delegation in Vienna (a Council Secretariat's liaison officer could be posted to Vienna) and coordination between them and the EU institutions and bodies in Brussels), field level (EU Special Representatives,[275] heads of EU crisis management operations, Member State embassies, EC delegations, OSCE field presences and special representatives) and staff-to-staff level (at all levels between the EU Council General Secretariat, the European Commission services and the OSCE Secretariat and other OSCE institutions). The Council requested the Presidency, assisted by the SG/HR and in full association with the Commission, to implement these general guidelines in coordination with the OSCE and requested the PSC to monitor the implementation of these guidelines, to identify further potential cooperation areas and priorities for EU-OSCE cooperation, to closely monitor emerging or potential crises within the OSCE's areas of activity and to examine possible EU contributions to relevant OSCE mechanisms already in place.[276] In 2004, the Council assessed the EU's role in relation to the OSCE, but this contained relatively few aspects concerning the ESDP.[277]

In practice, it would appear that the EU and the OSCE have significant overlapping civilian capabilities[278] and that the EU has conducted proper operations rather than contributing to an OSCE operation, although there is cooperation when both operate in the same area. The former may be justified in order to maintain a capability for EU action when the OSCE is unwilling to act. The latter may be linked to the crisis which the OSCE has been going through.[279] As an example of cooperation, one may cite the efforts of both organizations in FYROM in relation to the 13 August 2001 Ohrid Framework Agreement: the EU has contributed to the implementation of this agreement through its ESDP

275 On EU Special Representatives, see generally G. Grevi, *Pioneering Foreign Policy: The EU Special Representatives*, Chaillot Paper No. 106, Paris, EU ISS, October 2007 (available online at www.iss.europa.eu/index.php?id=143&L=0).

276 See EU Council Documents 14527/1/03 REV 1, 10 November 2003 and 14512/03 of 10 November 2003. See also the advice of the Committee for Civilian Aspect of Crisis Management in EU Council Doc. 14168/03 of 30 October 2003.

277 See also the Draft assessment report of the EU's role vis-à-vis the OSCE, EU Council Doc. 15387/1/04 REV 1 of 10 December 2004.

278 At its 1999 Istanbul Summit, the OSCE decided to "*Create Rapid Expert Assistance and Co-operation Teams (REACT), thereby enabling the OSCE to respond quickly to demands for assistance and for large civilian field operations*" (Charter for European Security, 8–19 November 1999).

279 See on that crisis, e.g. P. Dunay, *The OSCE in Crisis*, Chaillot Paper No. 88, Paris, EU ISS, April 2006 (available online at www.iss.europa.eu/index.php?id=143&L=0). See also M. Odello, 'Thirty Years after Helsinki: Proposals for OSCE's Reform', 10 *J.C.S.L.* 2005, pp. 435–449.

operations in FYROM (see *infra*, Chapter 3.C, E and N).[280] Another example, albeit a more modest one, was the EU's support of reinforcing the capacity of the Georgian authorities to support and protect the OSCE Observer Mission on the border of the Republic of Georgia with the Chechen Republic of the Russian Federation.[281] Finally, the EU has submitted to the OSCE a proposal for a Joint Declaration on Enhanced EU-OSCE Co-operation, laying the ground for further and stronger co-operation.[282]

ii. The African Union

The EU has long had close relations with many African countries.[283] This is for instance reflected in the relationship with the ACP group.[284] Moreover, one of the first explicit conflict prevention initiatives of the EU concerned Africa.[285] This initiative started at the Essen European Council of December 1994, which advocated "*an intensive political dialogue between the European Union and the Organization for African Unity (OAU) in particular regarding conflict prevention in Africa*".[286] This eventually *inter alia* led to the adoption and implementation of a common position concerning conflict prevention and resolution in Africa in 1997.[287] It may be noted that this occurred in parallel with initiatives taken

280 For the OSCE's mission in FYROM, see www.osce.org/skopje/13165.html.

281 See Council Joint Action of 20 July 2000 regarding a contribution of the European Union towards reinforcing the capacity of the Georgian authorities to support and protect the OSCE Observer Mission on the border of the Republic of Georgia with the Chechen Republic of the Russian Federation (2000/456/CFSP), *O.J. L* 183, 22 July 2000, p. 3; Council Joint Action of 26 July 2001 regarding a contribution of the European Union towards reinforcing the capacity of the Georgian authorities to support and protect the OSCE Observer Mission on the border of the Republic of Georgia with the Chechen Republic of the Russian Federation (2001/568/CFSP), *O.J. L* 202, 27 July 2001, p. 2 and Council Joint Action of 21 May 2002 regarding a contribution of the European Union towards reinforcing the capacity of the Georgian authorities to support and protect the OSCE observer mission on the border of Georgia with the Ingush and Chechen Republics of the Russian Federation (2002/373/CFSP), *O.J. L* 134 , 22 May 2002, p. 1.

282 EU Council Doc. 10418/06 of 12 June 2006, §88.

283 See generally www.consilium.europa.eu/showPage.aspx?id=400&lang=en.

284 See generally www.ue-acp.org and http://ec.europa.eu/development/geographical/cotonouintro_en.cfm?CFID=29173983&CFTOKEN=11575942&jsessionid=0806918082181492a447.

285 This section is based on J. Wouters & F. Naert, 'The EU and Conflict Prevention: A Brief Historic Overview', in V. Kronenberger & J. Wouters (eds.), *supra* note 248, pp. 45–48 (also available as K.U. Leuven, Institute for International Law, Working paper No. 52 at www.law.kuleuven.be/iir/nl/onderzoek/wp/WP52e.pdf).

286 Presidency Conclusions, 9–10 December 1994, title 'External relations', §8.

287 Council Common position of 2 June 1997 defined by the Council on the basis of Article J.2 of the Treaty on European Union, concerning conflict prevention and resolution in Africa (97/356/CFSP), *O.J. L* 153, 11 June 1997, p. 1, implemented by the Council decision of 20 October 1997 concerning the implementation of Common Position 97/356/CFSP defined by the Council on the basis of Article J.2 of the Treaty on European Union, concerning

within the UN.[288] In addition, in 2001 African leaders launched the New Partnership for Africa's Development (NEPAD),[289] which, *inter alia*, includes 'Strengthening mechanisms for conflict prevention, management and resolution at the subregional and continental levels, and to ensure that these mechanisms are used to restore and maintain peace'.[290]

The EU's efforts in the field of peace and security include the 'Peace Facility for Africa', financed through the European Development Fund, which is to support African-led peace support operations and to enhance the institutional capacities of the African Union (AU; the AU succeeded the OAU) and sub-regional organizations in relation to peacekeeping and conflict prevention.[291] This Facility was *inter alia* used to help finance the AU's operation in Darfur, Sudan (AMIS), to which the EU also contributed through its AMIS Supporting Mission (see *infra*, Chapter 3.K, including on its extension to also include support for the AU mission in Somalia).

The primary focus of the ESDP concerning Africa is to reinforce African capabilities and to act at the request and in cooperation with the UN or African regional organizations.[292] Indeed, the EU's military operations ARTEMIS and

---

conflict prevention and resolution in Africa (97/690/CFSP), *O.J. L* 293, 27 October 1997, p. 3 and later replaced by updated common positions in 2001 and 2004.

288 A main starting point was the Report of the Secretary-General on the Causes of Conflicts and the Promotion of Durable Peace and Sustainable Development in Africa (UN Doc. A/52/871-S/1998/318, 16 April 1998). See furthermore several Security Council Resolutions and Presidential statements, e.g. UNSC Res. 1170 (28 May 1998) and 1318 (7 September 2000), the UN General Assembly's annual resolutions on Causes of conflict and the promotion of durable peace and sustainable development in Africa (starting with UNGA Res. 53/92 of 16 December 1998) and the Millennium Declaration (UNGA Res. 55/2 of 18 September 2000, Part VII). Furthermore, the Security Council established, in 2002, an Ad Hoc Working Group on Conflict Prevention and Resolution in Africa; see UN press release SC/7632, 14 January 2003 (and, for the terms of reference of this working group, UN Doc. S/2002/207, 1 March 2002).

289 See generally www.nepad.org.

290 The New Partnership for Africa's Development (NEPAD), October 2001, available at www.nepad.org, §49. See also §§71–78.

291 See European Commission, Securing peace and Stability for Africa. The EU-funded African Peace Facility, July 2004, available online at http://ec.europa.eu/comm/development/body/publications/docs/flyer_peace_en.pdf. For a brief discussion, see R. Keane, 'The EU's African Peace Facility Uncovered: Better Late than Never?' No. 24 *European Security Review* 2004 (previously available online at www.isis-europe.org/ftp/Download/ESR%2024%20-%20APF.PDF). See also more generally N. Pirozzi, *EU Support to African Security Architecture: Funding and Training Components*, Paris, EU ISS, Occasional Paper No. 76, February 2009.

292 See Council conclusions on Peace and Security in Africa of 22 November 2004, EU Council Doc. 15132/4 of 23 November 2004; Action Plan for ESDP support to Peace and Security in Africa, EU Council Documents 10538/4/04 of 16 November 2004 and Guidelines for implementing ESDP support to Peace and Security in Africa, EU Council Doc. 15542/1/04 REV 1 of 9 December 2004. On EU-UN-AU cooperation, see M. Mubiala, 'Cooperation

EUFOR DR Congo both supported the UN mission in the Democratic Republic of Congo (DRC) (see *infra*, Chapter 3.D and P) and its Chad/Central African Republic operation is part of a "multidimensional presence" that also comprises a UN component.[293] It is only when this is not an adequate solution that the EU will itself conduct a standalone ESDP operation. However, even the EU's stand alone operations in Africa usually support UN efforts. See, e.g. the police and security sector reform missions in the DRC (EUPOL Kinshasa and its DRC-wide follow-up operation EUPOL RD Congo and EUSEC DRC, see *infra*, Chapter 3.H, I and R).

It may also be noted that a further step in the EU-AU partnership was made at the EU-AU Summit on 8–9 December 2007, at which a "strategic partnership" was adopted.[294]

iii. ASEAN

A further step involved close cooperation with the Association of South East Asian Nations (ASEAN), bringing a new dimension to EC/EU-ASEAN relations.[295]

---

between the United Nations, the European Union and the African Union for Peace and Security in Africa', 60(3) *Studia Diplomatica* 2007, pp. 111–121. These efforts include the EURO RECAMP – AMANI AFRICA training and exercise cycle, see www.eurorecamp.org.

293 See UNSC Res. 1778 (25 September 2007), §§1–9. On this operation, see very briefly *infra* note 171 and accompanying text.

294 See the Joint Africa-EU Strategy and the Lisbon Declaration, Documents 16343/07 (Presse 290) and 16344/07 (Presse 291), both of 9 December 2007; www.eu2007.pt/UE/vEN/Reunioes_Eventos/ChefesEstado/EUAfrica.htm and *ESDP Newsletter* No. 5, December 2007, pp. 6–21 (www.consilium.europa.eu/showPage.aspx?id=1090&lang=en). See also generally A. Abass, 'EU Crisis Management in Africa: Progress, Problems and Prospects', in S. Blockmans (ed.), *The European Union and International Crisis Management: Legal and Policy Aspects*, The Hague, TMC Asser Press, 2008, pp. 327–343. See also http://africa-eu-partnership.org. Moreover, in early December 2007, the Council and the Commission, in two distinct but closely related decisions, appointed Koen Vervaeke as EUSR to the AU and as Head of the Commission delegation to the AU, thus effectively creating the EU's first integrated mission (see EU Doc. S355/07 of 6 December 2007 and Council Joint Action of 6 December 2007 appointing a European Union Special Representative to the African Union (2007/805/CFSP), *O.J. L* 323, 8 December 2007, p. 45 as amended by Council Joint Action of 29 May 2008 amending Joint action 2007/805/CFSP appointing a European Union Special Representative to the African Union (2008/403/CFSP), *O.J. L* 140, 30 May 2008, p. 35 and by Council Joint Action of 1 December 2008 extending the mandate of the European Union Special Representative to the African Union (2008/898/CFSP), *O.J. L* 322, 2 December 2008, p. 50; see also www.consilium.europa.eu/showPage.aspx?id=1397&lang=EN).

295 See D. Thym, 'Interregional Cooperation in Crisis Management: EU Support for the AU, ASEAN and Other Regional Organisations', in S. Blockmans (ed.), *The European Union and International Crisis Management: Legal and Policy Aspects*, The Hague, TMC Asser Press, 2008, pp. 277–290. On EU-ASEAN relations more generally, see http://ec.europa.eu/comm/external_relations/asean/intro/index.htm.

E. CAPABILITIES

Capabilities (both civilian and military) and objectives in this field are also evolving continuously. I will not address this extensively,[296] as it has, as such, little to do with (international) law.[297]

Based on the military objectives defined at the 1999 Helsinki European Council (see above, Chapter 1.E), the 'Helsinki Headline Goal' was set.[298] Also, a Capability Development Mechanism was established.[299] Subsequently, the Headline Goal 2010[300] and a Capability Development Plan[301] were adopted. Consistency with capability development in NATO is *inter alia* ensured through the EU-NATO Capability Group.[302]

---

296 A good overview with some reference documents is available online at www.consilium.europa.eu/showPage.aspx?id=437&lang=en. For recent discussions, see, e.g. J.-Y. Haine, 'Assessing the Union's Military Capabilities: ESDP and the European Crisis of Liberal Internationalism', in S. Blockmans (ed.), *The European Union and International Crisis Management: Legal and Policy Aspects*, The Hague, TMC Asser Press, 2008, pp. 107–134 and J. Schuyer, 'The Civilian Headline Goal 2008: Developing Civilian Crisis Management Capabilities for the EU', in *id.*, pp. 135–142. See also the Dutch Advisory Council on International Affairs, *Military Cooperation in Europe. Possibilities and Limitations*, Advice No. 31 of April 2003 (available online at www.aiv-advies.nl/ContentSuite/upload/aiv/doc/nr31eng(1).pdf); S. Biscop, 'Able and Willing? Assessing the EU's Capacity for Military Action', 9 *E.F.A.R.* 2004, pp. 509–527; M. Clarcke *et al.*, *The ERRF and the NRF. The European Rapid Reaction Force and the NATO Response Force: Compatibilities and Choices*, Military Centre for Strategic Studies & Centre for Defence Studies, Rome/London, Rubbettino, 2004 (available online at www.difesa.it/backoffice/upload/allegati/2006/{18301FFC-4C79-42E4-945C-726795767A7B}.pdf); A. Dumoulin, R. Mathieu & G. Sarlet, *supra* note 161, pp. 258–285 (with an overview of various European multinational forces at pp. 105–121); B. Schmitt, 'European Capabilities: How Many Divisions?' in N. Gnesotto (ed.), *supra* note 161, pp. 89–110; R. Ferretti, 'Capacità operative e impiego delle Forze di pace', in N. Ronzitti (ed.), *supra* note 161, pp. 81–112; H.-B. Weisserth, 'The European Headline Goal: Current and Future Crisis Managament Capacilities' in K. von Wogau (ed.), *supra* note 161, pp. 115–130 and the proceedings of the Brussels symposiums of the Centre for Defence Studies 'Able and Willing' (16 March 2004) and 'E Pluribus Unum? Military Integration in the European Union' (28 February 2005), both available online at www.mil.be/rdc/subject/index.asp?LAN=en&ID=433&page=3. For a perspective on the financial implications, see A. Missiroli & B. Schmitt, 'More Euros for European Security and Defence Policy: What Convergence, What Criteria?', in K. von Wogau (ed.), *supra* note 161, pp. 284–294.

297 Although the civilian capabilities include experts on the rule of law and civilian administration.

298 See www.consilium.europa.eu/uedocs/cmsUpload/Helsinki%20Headline%20Goal.pdf.

299 See EU Council documents 6805/03 (26 February 2003) and COR 1 and 6867/03 (28 February 2003).

300 See www.consilium.europa.eu/uedocs/cmsUpload/2010%20Headline%20Goal.pdf.

301 See www.consilium.europa.eu/uedocs/cmsUpload/080708-PR_Capability_plan.pdf.

302 See, e.g. EU Council Doc. 6805/03 (26 February 2003), pp. 4 (especially note 2), 13 and 15–17.

Furthermore, it is worth pointing out that the EU has developed a 'Battle Group' concept that has been integrated in its Headline Goal 2010. An EU Battle Group (EUBG) is designed for a range of possible missions and is described as "*the minimum militarily effective, credible, rapidly deployable, coherent force package capable of stand-alone operations, or for the initial phase of larger operations (30 days initially, extendable to 120, if re-supplied appropriately), based on a combined arms, battalion sized force and reinforced with Combat Support and Combat Service Support elements (meaning some 1500 troops), of a multinational nature and able to be formed by a Framework Nation or a multinational coalition and associated with a (Force)Headquarters and pre-identified operational and strategic enablers, such as strategic lift and logistics*".[303] At least two EUBGs should be on standby at all times (for a six-month period) and it should be possible to deploy two EUBG size operations simultaneously.[304] It was to be ensured that from January 2007 onwards the EU has the Full Operational Capability to undertake two Battlegroup sized rapid response operations, including the ability to launch two such operations nearly simultaneously.[305] The ambition of the EU is to be able to take the decision to launch an operation within five days of the approval of the Crisis Management Concept by the Council and that the forces start implementing their mission on the ground no later than ten days after the EU decision to launch the operation.[306]

---

303 See EU Battlegroup Concept (declassified sections), Council Doc. 13618/06 EXT 1 of 27 April 2007 and the Council fact sheet on EU Battle Groups (EU BG 01, November 2005), available online at www.consilium.europa.eu/uedocs/cmsUpload/BattlegroupsNov05factsheet.pdf. See generally G. Lindstrom, *Enter the EU Battle Groups*, Chaillot Paper No. 97, Paris, EU ISS, February 2007 (available online at www.iss.europa.eu/index.php?id=143&L=0).

304 Fact sheet on EU Battle Groups, *supra* previous note. See also *ESDP Newsletter* No. 2, June 2006, pp. 24–25 and *ESDP Newsletter* No. 3, January 2007, pp. I-IV (after p. 14) (both www.consilium.europa.eu/showPage.aspx?id=1090&lang=en).

305 EU Council Doc. 10418/06 of 12 June 2006, §41.

306 Headline Goal 2010, approved by General Affairs and External Relations Council on 17 May 2004 and endorsed by the European Council of 17 and 18 June 2004, §4 (available online at www.consilium.europa.eu/uedocs/cmsUpload/2010%20Headline%20Goal.pdf). See also the Council fact sheet on EU Battle Groups and the EU Civilian and Military Cell, *supra* note 191; 'The EU battlegroups: approaching full operational capability', *ESDP Newsletter* No. 2, June 2006, pp. 24–25 (available online at www.consilium.europa.eu/uedocs/cmsUpload/ESDP_Newsletter_ISSUE2.pdf) and the Dutch Letter to Parliament dated 4 November 2005 (*Kamerbrief over de Nederlandse toewijzing aan EU Battlegroup Duitsland-Nederland-Finland*, previously available online at www.mindef.nl/actueel/parlement/kamerbrieven/2005/4/20051104_battlegroup.aspx (last consulted in November 2007)). See also EU Military Rapid Response Concept (EU Council Doc. 5654/1/09 REV 1, 27 April 2009) and EU Air and Martime Rapid Response Concepts (respectively EU Council documents 16838/07, 21 December 2007 and 15294/07, 15 November 2007; both partially available in the Council's register). For an example of an agreement on a specific EUBG, see the Estonian-Finnish-Norwegian-Swedish Memorandum of Understanding dated 17 May 2005, previously available online at www.dep.no/filarkiv/247184/MOU_nordisk-estisk_innsatsstyrke_230505.doc.

One issue that has legal implications in this context, however, is the putting on standby of pre-composed EUBGs for six months. This might create some tension between on the one hand the choice that Member States have on whether or not to participate in a given operation (and if so, to what extent), a fundamental principle of the ESDP (see *supra*) which may facilitate decision-making, and on the other hand the idea that if the EU decides upon a rapid reaction operation (EUBGs are only intended to be used for such operations[307]), one of the EUBGs on standby will be deployed (at least initially). This may make it difficult for a Member State which has an EUBG on standby to agree to an operation without participating in it. This could force it to (i) block the operation, (ii) participate reluctantly or (iii) agree to the operation but not participate and thereby disable the EUBG in which it participates.[308] As long as only one EUBG at the time is concerned, this may be solved by using the other one, but this may not always be a solution.

The EUBG concept is also included in the permanent structured cooperation under the Lisbon Treaty.[309] The Lisbon Treaty in fact contains obligations in respect of capabilities as Member States "*undertake progressively to improve their military capabilities*"[310] and, with the exception of Denmark,[311] have to make civilian and military capabilities, which may include multinational forces, available to the Union for the implementation of the CSDP (under the Lisbon Treaty, the ESDP is renamed the Common Security and Defence Policy or

307 This has led to some questions as force generation for onging or new but non-rapid reaction operations has sometimes proven difficult while standby EUBGs are ready but are not deployed because they are reserved for rapid reaction operations. There is a similar debate with regard to NATO's NATO response Force (NRF).

308 The problem is discussed in a Dutch Letter to Parliament dated 26 April 2005 which stresses the retention of national decision-making authority but acknowledges that participation in an EUBG does create some expectations (*Kamerbrief over besluitvorming snelle reactiemachten*, available online at www.nieuwsbank.nl/inp/2005/04/26/F087.htm and previously at www.mindef.nl/actueel/parlement/kamerbrieven/2005/2/20050426_reactiemachten.aspx (last consulted in November 2007)) and was already identified by the Dutch Advisory Council on International Affairs in its Advice No. 34 of March 2004 on *The Netherlands and Crisis Management. Three Issues of Current Interest*, available online at www.aiv-advies.nl/ContentSuite/upload/aiv/doc/nr34eng(1).pdf, pp. 29–30 (in respect of the NATO Response Force, but the issue is the same as for the EUBGs).

309 See Protocol (No. 4) on permanent structured cooperation established by Article 27 of the Treaty on European Union, as added by the Lisbon Treaty (see renumbered Articles 42(6) and 46 EU Treaty). See also the Protocol on permanent structured cooperation established by Article I-41(6) and Article III-312 of the EU Constitution (*O.J.* C 310, 16 December 2004, p. 364), Article 1(b).

310 Article 27(3) (renumbered 42(3)) EU Treaty as amended by the Lisbon Treaty. See also Article I-41(3) EU Constitution.

311 See Article 5 of the Protocol on the position of Denmark as amended by the Lisbon Treaty (and the EU Constitution): "*Denmark shall not be obliged [...] to make military capabilities available to the Union*".

CSDP).[312] Under the Lisbon Treaty, those Member States whose military capabilities fulfil higher criteria and which have made more binding commitments to one another in this area with a view to the most demanding missions shall establish a permanent structured cooperation within the Union framework.[313]

Also, it may be noted that six EU Member States which have 'gendarmerie' or similar police forces with a military status (the Spanish Guardia Civil, the French Gendarmerie nationale, the Italian l'Arma dei Carabinieri, the Dutch Maréchaussée, the Portuguese Guardia Nacional Republicana and the Romanian Gendarmerie), have established a 'Force de gendarmerie européenne', based on a declaration of intent dated 17 September 2004,[314] followed by a treaty signed on 18 October 2007,[315] and of which the headquarters were inaugurated on 23 January 2006.[316] They could be especially deployed for ESDP police operations wherein EU police forces have to temporarily replace the local police (as opposed to monitoring, advising and training them).[317]

On the civilian side, on 22 November 2004 Member States' voluntary commitments of staff were 5,761 in the area of police, 631 for rule of law, 562 for civilian administration, 4,988 for civil protection and 505 for monitoring, exceeding the targets set.[318] Subsequently, the EU set itself a Civilian Headline Goal 2008 (including a follow-up process)[319] and started to develop 'civilian response teams' (CRTs), which are civilian crisis management rapid reaction

312 Title V, Chapter 2, Section 2 EU Treaty as amended by the Lisbon Treaty. See also Article I-41(3) EU Constitution.

313 Articles 27(6) and 31 (renumbered 42(6) and 46) EU Treaty as they are amended by the Lisbon Treaty and Protocol (No. 4) on permanent structured cooperation established by Article 27 of the Treaty on European Union. Article 1 of the said Protocol specifies the commitments that participants must undertake. See also Articles I-41(6)) and III-312 EU Constitution and the Protocol on permanent structured cooperation established by Article I-41(6) and Article III-312 of the Constitution and S. Biscop, 'Permanent Structured Cooperation and the Future of the ESDP: Transformation and Integration', 13 *E.F.A.R.* 2008, pp. 431–448.

314 Available online at www.eurogendfor.org/referencetexts/EGF%20declaration%20of%20 intent.pdf.

315 Treaty between the Kingdom of Spain, the French Republic, the Italian Republic, the Kingdom of The Netherlands and the Portuguese Republic, establishing the European Gendarmerie Force (EUROGENDFOR), Velsen, 18 October 2007, available online at www.eurogendfor.org/referencetexts/EGF%20Treaty%20english%20version.pdf. Romania joined later.

316 See www.eurogendfor.eu/.

317 Declaration of intent, *supra* note 314, 'scope' and 'missions'.

318 Civilian Capabilities Commitment Conference: Ministerial Declaration, §§3–4, available onlineatwww.consilium.europa.eu/uedocs/cmsUpload/COMMITMENT%20CONFERENCE %20MINISTERIAL%20DECLARATION%2022.11.04.pdf.

319 See, e.g. EU Council Documents 15863/04 of 7 December 2004; 15428/05 of 5 December 2005 and 15325/05 of 7 December 2005.

capabilities of flexible size and composition, consisting of Member State experts with, in principle, Council Secretariat participation, and drawn from an EU-wide pre-selected pool of experts,[320] to be able to quickly launch civilian ESDP missions. The current objective is the Civilian Headline Goal 2010.[321]

Finally, the 11–12 December 2008 European Council adopted a Declaration on the enhancement of the European Security and Defence Policy (16840/08), which *inter alia* states:

> 3. … the European Council … subscribes to the declaration on capabilities adopted by the Council, which sets numerical and precise targets to enable the EU, in the coming years, to conduct simultaneously, outside its territory, a series of civilian missions and military operations of varying scope, corresponding to the most likely scenarios.[1]
> 4. This renewed goal requires a commitment to develop robust, flexible and interoperable capabilities. This will entail, on a voluntary basis, innovative forms of specialisation, pooling and sharing of major equipment projects, with priority being given to planning, crisis management, space and maritime security. In this respect the declaration on capabilities highlights several concrete projects in key sectors. The European Council voices its determination to support this effort in the long term and calls on the Member States to convert these commitments into national requirements in terms of equipment.
> …
> 1. Europe should actually be capable, in the years ahead, in the framework of the level of ambition established, inter alia of deploying 60 000 men in 60 days for a major operation, within the range of operations envisaged within the headline goal for 2010 and within the civilian headline goal for 2010, of planning and conducting simultaneously:
>
> - two major stabilisation and reconstruction operations, with a suitable civilian component, supported by a maximum of 10 000 men for at least two years;
> - two rapid response operations of limited duration using inter alia the EU's battle groups;
> - an emergency operation for the evacuation of European nationals (in less than ten days), bearing in mind the primary role of each Member State as regards its nationals and making use of the consular lead State concept;
> - a maritime or air surveillance/interdiction mission;
> - a civilian-military humanitarian assistance operation lasting up to 90 days;
> - around a dozen ESDP civilian missions (inter alia police, rule of law, civil administration, civil protection, security sector reform and observation missions) of varying formats, inter alia in a rapid reaction situation, including a major mission (possibly up to 3 000 experts), which could last several years.

320 See EU Council Documents 10462/05 of 23 June 2005 and 10670/05 of 28 June 2005.
321 External Relations Council, 19–20 November 2007, conclusions on ESDP, §35.

For its operations and missions, the European Union uses, in an appropriate manner and in accordance with its procedures, the resources and capabilities of Member States, of the European Union and, if appropriate for its military operations, of NATO.[322]

F. THE EUROPEAN DEFENCE AGENCY, DEFENCE INDUSTRY AND PROCUREMENT

In a development related to capabilities, a European Defence Agency was set up in 2004.[323] Its mission is to "*support the Council and the Member States in their effort to improve the EU's defence capabilities in the field of crisis management and to sustain the ESDP as it stands now and develops in the future*".[324] To this effect, it shall work in the fields of defence capabilities development, armaments co-operation, the European defence technological and industrial base and defence equipment market.[325] The actual development of the ESDP outpaced the

322 Annex II to the Presidency Conclusions (EU Council Doc. 17271/1/08 REV 1). See also §30 of these conclusions as well as the Council declaration of 8 December 2008 on the enhancement of the capabilities of the European Security and Defence Policy (16840/08) listed in Annex 6 to these conclusions.

323 Council Joint Action of 12 July 2004 on the establishment of the European Defence Agency (2004/551/CFSP), *O.J. L* 245, 17 July 2004, p. 17 as amended by Council Joint Action of 7 April 2008 amending Joint Action 2004/551/CFSP on the establishment of the European Defence Agency (2008/299/CFSP), *O.J. L* 102, 12 April 2008, p. 34 (minor amendment to create the post of a second deputy chief executive). See also Council Decision of 24 September 2004 concerning the Rules applicable to national experts and military staff on secondment to the European Defence Agency (2004/677/EC), *O.J. L* 310, 7 October 2004, p. 64 as amended by Council Decision of 29 January 2007 amending Decision 2004/677/EC with regard to a minimal period of secondment of national experts and military staff seconded to the European Defence Agency (2007/216/EC), *O.J. L* 95, 5 April 2007, p. 24; Council Decision of 24 September 2004 concerning the Staff Regulations of the European Defence Agency (2004/676/EC), *O.J. L* 310, 7 October 2004, p. 9 as amended by Council Decision of 29 January 2007 amending Decision 2004/676/EC concerning the Staff Regulations of the European Defence Agency (2007/215/EC), *O.J. L* 95, 5 April 2007, p. 21; and Council Decision of 13 September 2004 laying down the financial provisions applicable to the general budget of the European Defence Agency (2004/658/CFSP), *O.J. L* 300, 25 September 2004, p. 52 as amended by Council decision of 21 November 2005 amending Decision 2004/658/CFSP on the financial provisions applicable to the general budget of the European Defence Agency (2005/821/CFSP), *O.J. L* 305, 24 November 2005, p. 43 and replaced by Council Decision of 18 September 2007 on the financial rules of the European Defence Agency and on the procurement rules and rules on financial contributions from the operational budget of the European Defence Agency (2007/643/CFSP), *O.J. L* 269, 12 October 2007, p. 1. The EDA's website is at www.eda.europa.eu. See also A. Georgopoulos, *infra* note 328, pp. 215–219; J. Howorth, 'The European Draft Constitutional Treaty and the Future of the European Defence Initiative', 9 *E.F.A.R.* 2004, pp. 496–499; A. Roth, 'L'Agence européenne de défense: virage vers l'avenir ou de Vénus à Mars?', 6 *Annuaire français de relations internationales* 2005, pp. 615–631 and B. Schmitt, *supra* note 296, pp. 100–101.

324 Article 2(1) Council Joint Action 2004/551/CFSP, *supra* previous note.

325 *Id.*, Article 5.

ESDP provisions in the EU Constitution, in which the EDA would still have to be set up but would otherwise perform more or less the same functions.[326] This has been accommodated in the Lisbon Treaty.[327] Moreover, the EDA is also gradually taking over some of the existing European armaments cooperation forums, especially the WEAG and WEAO that operated in the framework of the WEU (see *supra*, Chapter 1.D).[328]

In respect of the European defence technological and industrial base things are also moving. A key provision in this respect is Article 296 EC Treaty, according to which:

> 1. The provisions of this Treaty shall not preclude the application of the following rules: (a) no Member State shall be obliged to supply information the disclosure of which it considers contrary to the essential interests of its security; (b) any Member State may take such measures as it considers necessary for the protection of the essential interests of its security which are connected with the production of or trade in arms, munitions and war material; such measures shall not adversely affect the conditions of competition in the common market regarding products which are not intended for specifically military purposes.
> 2. The Council may, acting unanimously on a proposal from the Commission, make changes to the list, which it drew up on 15 April 1958, of the products to which the provisions of paragraph 1(b) apply.

Article 296 EC Treaty was included in Article III-436 EU Constitution without substantive changes and is left untouched by the Lisbon Treaty (renumbered Article 346 Treaty on the Functioning of the European Union). On the basis of Article 296 EC Treaty, Member States have largely exempted defence

---

326 See Articles I-43(3) and III-311 EU Constitution.

327 See Articles 17(3) and 28 D (renumbered 42(3) and 45) EU Treaty as amended by the Lisbon Treaty.

328 Pursuant to the 8th consideration of the preamble of the EDA Joint Action (*supra* note 323), "*The Agency should develop close working relations with existing arrangements, groupings and organisations such as Letter of Intent (LoI), Organisation de coopération conjointe en matière d'armement (OCCAR) and Western European Armaments Group (WEAG)/Western European Armaments Organisation (WEAO), with a view to assimilation or incorporation of relevant principles and practices as appropriate*". In light thereof, The Ministers of Defence of the 19 WEAG Nations held their last meeting in Brussels on 22 November 2004 and recognized that European armaments co-operation in the future would take place within the EU and therefore decided to close WEAG (see www.weu.int/weag/whatsnew.htm). According to the WEAO website, "*After 11 years serving the Defence R&T community in Europe, the Research Cell will cease its activities on 30 June 2006*" (see www.weao.weu.int). See also A. Dumoulin, with a contribution by F. Gevers, *Union de l'Europe occidentale: La Déstructuration (1998–2006)*, Brussels/Paris, Bruylant/LGDJ, 2005, pp. 119–156. OCCAR (see A. Georgopoulos, 'The European Armaments Policy: A *conditio sine qua non* for the European Security and Defence Policy?', in Trybus & White, pp. 209–121) will most likely continue to exist.

industry and procurement from the normal rules under European law.[329] However, initiatives have been taken to limit the scope of this

---

329 Sometimes even where the conditions of Article 296 are not met, see, e.g. ECJ, Case C-414/97, *Commission v. Spain*, judgment of 16 September 1999, §§17–24; Case C-337/05, *Commission v. Italy*, 8 April 2008, especially §§42–54 and Case C-157/06, *Commission v. Italy*, 2 October 2008. See also Cases C-186/01, *Dory*, 11 March 2003, §29–42 (especially 30–31) and T-26/01, *Fiocchi Munizioni SpA v Commission*, 30 September 2003, §§56–64 and M. Trybus, 'Case C-337/05, *Commission v. Italy (Agusta and Agusta Bell Helicopters)*, judgment of the Court (Grand Chamber) of 8 April 2008, not yet reported; and Case C-157/06, *Commission v. Italy*, judgment of the Court (Second Chamber) of 2 October 2008, not yet reported', 46 *C.M.L. Rev.* 2009, pp. 973–990. On defence procurement and industry in the EU, see generally H. Bühl, 'Operational Requirements and Industrial Competitiveness', in K. von Wogau (ed.), *supra* note 161, pp. 278–283; P. Busquin, 'Security Research in the European Union: Current Status and Strategic Prospects', in K. von Wogau (ed.), *supra* note 161, pp. 54–60; D. Coulmy, 'Europe de l'armement et Europe de la défense', 6(1) *Revue des affaires européennes* 1996, pp. 19–24; H. Davies, 'Defence Research and Technology', in K. von Wogau (ed.), *supra* note 161, pp. 265–277; A. Dumoulin, R. Mathieu & G. Sarlet, *supra* note 161, pp. 635–660; D. Eisenhut, 'The Special Security Exemption of Article 296 EC: Time for a New Notion of "Essential Security Interests"?', 33 *Eur. L. Rev.* 2008, pp. 577–585; A. Georgopoulos, 'Defence Procurement and EU Law', 30 *Eur. L. Rev.* 2005, pp. 559–572; A. Georgopoulos, *supra* previous note, pp. 198–222; P. Gilsdorf, 'Les reserves de securite du traite CEE, a la lumiere du traite sur l'Union europeenne', No. 374 *R.M.C.U.E.* 1994, pp. 17–25; T.R. Guay, *At Arm's Length: The European Union and Europe's Defence Industry*, Basingstoke, Macmillan, 1998; B. Heuninckx, 'Defence Procurement: The Most Effective Way to Grant Illegal State Aid and Get Away with It ... or Is It?', 46 *C.M.L. Rev.* 2009, pp. 191–211; D. Keohane (ed.), *Towards a European Defence Market*, Paris, EU ISS, Chaillot Paper No. 113, November 2008; X. Lebacq, 'Cooperation technologique et industries de défense', No. 396 *R.M.C.U.E.* 1996, pp. 244–250; O. Lhoest, 'La production et le commerce des armes, et l'article 223 du traité instituant la Communauté européenne', 26 *R.B.D.I./B.T.I.R.* 1993, pp. 176–207; E. Liikanen, 'Industrial Aspects of a European Defenece Policy', in K. von Wogau (ed.), *supra* note 161, pp. 44–53; R.M. Lutje Schipholt, 'De ontwikkeling van een Europees militair-industrieel beleid', 111(4) *Marineblad* (April) 2001, pp. 112–122; G. Merritt, 'Cross-Border Cooperation in Europe', in K. von Wogau (ed.), *supra* note 161, pp. 229–238; M. Nones, 'A Test Bed for Enhanced Cooperation: The European Defence Industry', 35(3) *International Spectator* 2000, pp. 25–35; B. Schmitt, 'Rüstungszusammenarbeit in Europa: Zeit für Reformen', in H.-G. Ehrhart & B. Schmitt (eds.), *supra* note 161, pp. 214–229; S. Trombetta, 'La protection des intérêts nationaux de la défense quand la défense devient européenne: les évolutions de l'article 296 TCE', No. 490 *R.M.C.U.E.* 2005, pp. 441–450; M. Trybus, 'The Limits of European Community Competence for Defence', 9 *E.F.A.R.* 2004, pp. 189–217; M. Trybus, 'Procurement for the Armed Forces: Balancing Security and the Internal Market', 27 *Eur. L. Rev.* 2002, pp. 692–713; M. Trybus, 'The EC Treaty as an Instrument of European Defence Integration: Judicial Scrutiny of Defence and Security Exceptions', 39 *C.M.L. Rev.* 2002, pp. 1347–1372; M. Trybus, 'On the Application of the E.C. Treaty to Armaments', 25 *Eur. L. Rev.* 2000, pp. 663–668; M. Trybus, *European Defence Procurement Law: International and National Procurement Systems as Models for a Liberalised Defence Procurement Market in Europe*, The Hague, Kluwer Law International, 1999; M. Trybus, 'Developing a Model for the Regulation of European Defence Procurement', 11 *R.E.D.P./E.R.P.L.* 1999, pp. 115–145; M. Trybus, 'European Defence Procurement: towards a Comprehensive Approach', 4 *European Public Law* 1998, pp. 111–133 and M. Trybus, *supra* note 161, pp. 123–261. See also (W)EU ISS, Chaillot papers Nos. 21, 27, 40 and 63, and, for a collection of key documents, No. 59, all available at www.iss.europa.eu/index.php?id=143. For arms exports, see the code of conduct and the Common Position replacing it (*infra* note 1283) and Article 11 Regulation (EEC) No 2603/69 of the Council of 20 December 1969 establishing common rules for exports, *O.J. L* 324, 27 December 1969, p. 25 (as subsequently amended).

exceptional regime. Two complementary initiatives are worth mentioning in particular.

First on 1 July 2006, a regime was introduced to increase transparency and competition in the European Defence Equipment Market segment covered by Article 296 EC Treaty. It is a voluntary,[330] inter-governmental regime managed by the EDA that operates on the basis of the Code of Conduct on Defence Procurement, approved by the Defence Ministers in November 2005[331] and a Code of Best Practice in the Supply Chain, approved in May 2006[332].[333]

Second, the European Commission, following earlier initiatives such as the *Communication on European Defence Industrial and Market Issues – Towards an EU Defence Equipment Policy*,[334] launched a *Green Paper on Defence Procurement* on 23 September 2004[335] and reported on the results of the consultations thereon on 6 December 2005.[336] In the latter report, it announced that it would adopt in 2006 an "Interpretative Communication on the application of Article 296 of the Treaty in the field of defence procurement" and might propose a directive on defence procurement not covered by Article 296 EC Treaty.[337] In December 2007, the Commission published a further communication on the matter and proposals for a Directive on intra-EU transfers of Defence Products and a Directive on Defence Procurement.[338] This has led to the adoption of Directive 2009/81/EC of the European Parliament and of the Council of 13 July 2009 on the coordination of procedures for the award of certain works contracts, supply contracts and service contracts by contracting authorities or entities in the fields of defence and security, and amending Directives 2004/17/EC and 2004/18/EC[339] and Directive 2009/43/EC of the European Parliament and of the Council of 6 May 2009 simplifying terms and conditions of transfers of defence-related products within the Community.[340]

---

330 Apart from Denmark, which does not take part in the military side of the ESDP, only Spain and Hungary have opted out for the time being.

331 See www.eda.europa.eu/genericitem.aspx?area=Organisation&id=154.

332 See www.eda.europa.eu/genericitem.aspx?area=Organisation&id=159.

333 EDA press release, 'Birth of European Defence Equipment Market with Launch of Code of Conduct', 30 June 2006, www.eda.europa.eu/newsitem.aspx?id=43. See also A. Georgopoulos, *supra* note 328, pp. 217–219.

334 COM (2003) 113 final, 11 March 2003, available online at eur-lex.europa.eu/LexUriServ/LexUriServ.do?uri=COM:2003:0113:FIN:en:PDF.

335 COM(2004)608 final.

336 COM(2005)626.

337 *Id.*, p. 9. See also A. Georgopoulos, *supra* note 328, pp. 214–215.

338 See http://ec.europa.eu/enterprise/sectors/defence/documents/index_en.htm.

339 *O.J. L* 216, 20 August 2009, p. 76.

340 *O.J. L* 146, 10 June 2009, p. 1.

G. FINANCING

Another issue for which arrangements had to be adopted is the financing of ESDP operations. This too will only briefly be addressed here. Where costs are not charged to the EC budget under Article 28 EU Treaty, as is the case for expenditure arising from operations having military or defence implications (not all ESDP operations have "military or defence implications"; see below),[341] they are charged to the Member States. In this respect, an agreement was reached that some costs were common (in part always and in part when this is agreed for a specific operation) and would be administered by a separate mechanism called Athena (and involving third States that participate in an EU-led operation)[342] and that other costs would 'lie where they fall' and therefore be financed by the Member State(s) concerned.[343] The

---

341 And for other ESDP operations if the Council unanimously decides not to charge the costs thereof to the EC budget. This means civilian ESDP operations are normally charged to the EC budget. For an overview of the financing of ESDP operations, see EU Council Secretariat, 'Financing of ESDP Operations', fact sheet, June 2007, www.consilium.europa.eu/uedocs/cmsUpload/ATHENA_june_2007.pdf.

342 See Council Decision of 23 February 2004 establishing a mechanism to administer the financing of the common costs of European Union operations having military or defence implications (2004/197/CFSP), *O.J. L* 63, 28 February 2004, pp. 68–82, subsequently amended by Council Decision of 22 December 2004 amending Decision 2004/197/CFSP establishing a mechanism to administer the financing of the common costs of the European Union operations having military or defence implications (ATHENA) (2004/925/EC), *O.J. L* 395, 31 December 2004, p. 68; by Council Decision of 24 January 2005 amending Decision 2004/197/CFSP establishing a mechanism to administer the financing of the common costs of the European Union operations having military or defence implications (Athena) (2005/68/CFSP), *O.J. L* 27, 29 January 2005, p. 59 and by Council Decision of 12 February 2007 amending Decision 2004/197/CFSP establishing a mechanism to administer the financing of the common costs of European Union operations having military or defence implications Athena (2007/91/CFSP), *O.J. L* 41, 13 February 2007, p. 11 (consolidated version in *O.J. L* 152, 13 June 2007, p. 14); replaced by Council Decision 2008/975/CFSP of 18 December 2008 establishing a mechanism to administer the financing of the common costs of European Union operations having military or defence implications (Athena), *O.J. L* 345, 23 December 2008, p. 96. For an interesting explanatory note, see EU Council Doc. 13668/03 of 16 October 2003. See also the Decision of the Representatives of the Governments of the Member States, meeting within the Council of 28 April 2004 concerning privileges and immunities granted to ATHENA (2004/582/EC), *O.J. L* 261, 6 August 2004, p. 125 and various Athena documents at www.consilium.europa.eu/showPage.aspx?id=746&lang=en. In operations before the establishment of this mechanism, an *ad hoc* arrangement was set up.

343 The principle decision in this respect was adopted on 17 June 2002 and laid down in EU Council Doc. 10155/02 of 18 June 2002. See generally A. Missiroli, 'Financing ESDP: The Operational Dimension', in H.-G. Ehrhart & B. Schmitt (eds.), *supra* note 161, pp. 245–258; A. Missiroli, *€uros for ESDP: Financing EU Operations*, Paris, EU ISS, Occasional Paper No. 45, June 2003; A. Missiroli, 'Ploughshares into Swords? Euros for European Defence', 8 *E.F.A.R.* 2003, pp. 14–16 and D. Scannell, 'Financing ESDP Military Operations', 9 *E.F.A.R.* 2004, pp. 529–549. On CFSP financing more generally, see also J. Monar, 'The Finances of the Union's Intergovernmental Pillars: Tortuous Experiments with the Community Budget', 35 *J.C.M.S.* 1997, pp. 57–78.

Lisbon Treaty changes little, except for a rapid financing mechanism in the CFSP/ESDP.[344]

Aside from this, it may be noted that the EC has re-inforced its rapid reaction financing mechanisms through the 'Instrument for Stability'.[345]

H. STATUS OF FORCES

Foreign officials in a host State often enjoy certain privileges and immunities, as do officials of international organizations. The same goes for armed forces, which are usually accorded certain privileges and immunities under 'status of forces agreements' (SOFAs).[346] It is therefore no surprise that the EU Member States have concluded an Agreement between the Member States of the European Union concerning the status of military and civilian staff seconded to the institutions of the European Union, of the headquarters and forces which may be made available to the European Union in the context of the preparation and execution of the tasks referred to in Article 17(2) of the Treaty on European Union, including exercises, and of the military and civilian staff of the Member States put at the disposal of the European Union to act in this context (EU SOFA).[347] This agreement has still not yet entered into force. It is supplemented by the Agreement between the Member States of the European Union concerning

344 See Article 28(3) (renumbered 41(3)) EU Treaty as amended by the Lisbon Treaty. Compare Article III-313(3) EU Constitution.

345 Regulation (EC) No 1717/2006 of the European Parliament and of the Council of 15 November 2006 establishing an Instrument for Stability, *O.J. L* 327, 24 November 2006, p. 1 (this regulation *inter alia* repeals Council Regulation (EC) No 381/2001 of 26 February 2001 creating a rapid-reaction mechanism, *O.J. L* 57, 27 February 2001, p. 5).

346 With regard to the EU, see A. Sari, 'Status of Forces and Status of Mission Agreements under the ESDP: The EU's Evolving Practice', 19 *E.J.I.L.* 2008, pp. 67–100. See more generally D. Fleck (ed.), *The Handbook of the Law of Visiting Forces*, Oxford, Oxford University Press, 2001 (focusing mostly on the peacetime status between allies). With regard to NATO, the standard (albeit dated) work is S. Lazareff, *Le statut des forces de l'O.T.A.N.*, Paris, Association des Etudes Internationales, 1965. Compare P. Weckel, 'Le statut des capacités militaires européennes', in C. Tomuschat & J.A. Frowein (eds.), *Rechtsprobleme einer europäischen Sicherheits- und Verteidigungspolitik*, Heidelberg, Müller, 1997, pp. 39–52. See also the introduction to Part III.

347 Brussels, 16 November 2003, *O.J. C* 321, 31 December 2003, p. 6. The EU SOFA is based on the NATO SOFA (Agreement between the Parties to the North Atlantic Treaty regarding the Status of their Forces, London, 19 June 1951, 199 *U.N.T.S.* 67 (1954), which entered into force on 23 August 1953, available online at www.nato.int/docu/basictxt/b510619a.htm). For a discussion of the EU SOFA, see A. Sari, 'The European Union Status of Forces Agreement (EU SOFA)' 13 *J.C.S.L.* 2008, pp. 353–391; J. Voetelink, 'The EU SOFA: The European Union Status of Forces Agreement', 44 (3–4) *The Military Law and the Law of War Review* 2005, pp. 17–30; J. Voetelink, 'De EU SOFA: Status of Forces Agreement van de Europese Unie', 98 *Militair Rechtelijk Tijdschrift* 2005, pp. 89–100 and, very extensively, A. Sari, 'The EU Status of Forces

claims introduced by each Member State against any other Member State for damage to any property owned, used or operated by it or injury or death suffered by any military or civilian staff of its services, in the context of an EU crisis management operation.[348] However, the ratification process of these two agreements is taking a long time.

In addition, the status of forces/missions in third States, especially the States in which operations take place, also has to be determined. This is usually done through the conclusion of status of forces/mission agreements (SOFAs/SOMAs) or other arrangements to this effect (see the sections on applicable law for each of the operations discussed in Chapter 3 below as well as Chapter 4.B).

Agreement: Continuity and Change in the law of Visiting Forces', 46 *R.D.M.D.G.* 2007, pp. 9–254.

348 Brussels, 28 April 2004, *O.J. C* 116,30 April 2004, p. 1 (also not yet entered into force).

CHAPTER 3
ESDP OPERATIONS[349]

In this chapter, I will give an overview of the ESDP operations conducted up to 31 August 2009, with particular attention to the legal issues involved. The section is quite long but I believe this is justified because the actual operations best illustrate both where the ESDP stands and what it means and also what legal issues arise and how they have been handled. Moreover, this is one of the aspects of the ESDP on which there have been few publications, certainly from a legal perspective. The structure of this chapter is straightforward: after a short introduction and overview of the legal framework for ESDP operations (A), the operations will be reviewed more or less in chronological order (B-W). In principle, in addition to a general description,[350] the focus is on the mandate, legal status and applicable law and the participation of third States,[351] if applicable, and an attempt is made to point to both particular and recurrent features. However, especially in the more recent operations some standard features are no longer repeated, including the role of the PSC and the chain of command in the civilian operations following its reform as explained above (Chapter 2.B). While the budget for each operation will be specified to give an idea of the operation's costs, financing issues will otherwise only be dealt with marginally.[352] The conclusions from this chapter are drawn in Chapter 4.

A. OVERVIEW

As of 31 August 2009, the EU has launched some 22 ESDP operations (sometimes the term operations is reserved for military operations and missions for civilian

349 This chapter is partially based on F. Naert, *supra* note 198.

350 While this will usually include the number of forces/personnel and the contributing States, I have not always been able to collect this information and no breakdown is provided for each contributing State. Moreover, the number of personnel involved may change over time. For this information the reader is referred to the publications listed in note 5 and in the general note accompanying the title of each operation. It may be noted that the Conference of Committees for European and Community Affairs of the European Parliaments (COSAC) has welcomed the Council's decision to publish information on which Member States participate in which ESDP operations, see *O.J. C* 322, 17 December 2005, p. 1, §1.

351 The data on this point is to some extent indicative only, as third country participation may evolve throughout an operation, notably if an operation lasts several years.

352 See on this *supra* Chapter 2.G.

missions but I will use both interchangeably):[353] the military operations CONCORDIA in the Former Yugoslav Republic of Macedonia (FYROM), ARTEMIS and EUFOR DR Congo in the Democratic Republic of the Congo (DRC), ALTHEA in Bosnia and Herzegovina (BiH), EUFOR Tchad/RCA in Chad and in the Central African Republic (CAR) and EUNAVFOR Somalia / Atalanta in the waters off the coast of Somalia, which was preceded by the military coordination action EU NAVCO; the police operations EUPM in BiH, PROXIMA in FYROM, succeeded by the EU Police Advisory Team EUPAT there, EUPOL KINSHASA in the DRC, followed by the police security sector reform mission EUPOL RD Congo, EUPOL COPPS for the Palestinian Territories and EUPOL Afghanistan; the rule of law missions EUJUST THEMIS in Georgia and EULEX KOSOVO in Kosovo and the integrated rule of law mission EUJUST LEX*for* Iraq; the security sector reform missions EUSEC DRC in the DRC and EU SSR GUINEA-BISSAU in Guinea Bissau; the mixed civilian-military EU *Support* to AMIS II (African Union (AU) Mission in the Darfur region of Sudan); the EU monitoring mission AMM in Aceh (Indonesia) and EUMM Georgia in Georgia and the EU Border Assistance Mission at Rafah Crossing Point in the Palestinian Territories (EU BAM Rafah). Furthermore, this list excludes European Community (EC)/EU missions launched before 1999 which would probably qualify as crisis management operations today, in particular the EU's administration of the city of Mostar and the EC/EU Monitoring Mission (ECMM/EUMM) in the former Yugoslavia.[354] It also excludes the EU Border Assistance Mission to Moldova and Ukraine, which is not an ESDP operation.[355]

353 The number depends to some extent on how one counts, including whether successor operations are counted as distinct ones and whether or not supporting and coordinating actions are included. See on ESDP operations generally http://ue.eu.int/cms3_fo/showPage.asp?id=268&lang=en&mode=g; COSAC Secretariat, *Fourth Bi-Annual Report*, October 2005, available online at www.cosac.eu/en/documents/biannual/; M. Bacot-Décriaud, 'La PESD: montée en puissance et perfectibilité', in P. Buffotot (ed.), *supra* note 161, pp. 192–198; G. Grevi, D. Lynch & A. Missiroli, *ESDP Operations*, EU ISS, previously available online at www.iss-eu.org/esdp/09-dvl-am.pdf (last consulted in November 2007); G. Lindstrom, 'On the Ground: ESDP Operations', in N. Gnesotto (ed.), *supra* note 161, pp. 111–130; J. Litten, *supra* note 161, pp. 247–259 and UK FCO, 'ESDP Operations', previously available online at www.fco.gov.uk/servlet/Front?pagename=OpenMarket/Xcelerate/ShowPage&c=Page&cid=1077042145284 (last consulted in November 2007). See also EU Council Doc. 10418/06 of 12 June 2006 and the Annex to the Dutch Letter to Parliament on ESDP dated 10 July 2006 (*Kamerbrief over het Europese Veiligheids- en Defensiebeleid*, available online at www.minbuza.nl/nl/Actueel/Kamerstukken/2006/07/Kamerbrief_inzake_het_Europese_Veiligheids_en_Defensiebeleid). See also the overview in *ESDP Newsletter* No. 8, Summer 2009, p. 28 (www.consilium.europa.eu/showPage.aspx?id=1090&lang=en).

354 See *supra*, Chapter 1.D, notes 78 and 98 and accompanying text. The EUMM was only terminated on 31 December 2007, see EU Doc. S/375/07 of 27 December 2007.

355 See on this mission generally www.eubam.org; www.consilium.europa.eu/showPage.aspx?id=986&lang=EN and X. Kurowska & B. Tallis, 'EU Border Assistance Mission: Beyond Border Monitoring?', 14 *E.F.A.R.* 2009, pp. 47–64. It would seem that this mission is distinct

However, let me first provide a short introduction to the legal framework of ESDP operations. First, the international mandate will usually be based on a United Nations (UN) Security Council mandate, peace agreement and/or host State consent. Second, the EU will normally conclude a Status of Mission/Forces Agreement (SOMA/SOFA) with the host State which will regulate the status and activities of an operation in the host State.[356] Pending the conclusion or entry into force of such agreements (which may not occur in time, especially if the operation is launched on short notice), host States may grant certain privileges and immunities through unilateral declarations. Alternative arrangements on the status may also be put in place, including the extension of a SOFA for a non-EU operation to an EU operation by the UN Security Council. There may also be transit agreements with third States.[357] Third, there will be an EU Council Joint Action establishing the operation and in some cases a separate Council Decision launching the operation. Fourth, there may be various decisions of the PSC, which exercises political control and strategic direction of EU crisis management operations (see *supra*), e.g. a decision setting up a Committee of Contributors, accepting a third State contribution or appointing the Head of Mission or Operation or Force Commander. Fifth, there are often agreements between the EU and third States participating in an operation and/or partner organizations.[358] Sixth, there will be an Operation Plan and rules of

---

from, but cooperates closely with, the Border Support Team within the team of the EUSR for Moldova (see currently EU Council Joint Action of 16 February 2009 extending the mandate of the European Union Special Representative in the Republic of Moldova (2009/132/CFSP), *O.J. L* 46, 17 February 2009, p. 50, especially Article 2(1)g and 3(1)e) and that it is headed by the Senior Political Advisor to the EUSR. See, e.g. the 27 October 2005 Commission note at www.eubam.org/files/0-99/79/information%20note%20to%20Council.pdf. However, the mission is mentioned in an ESDP report; see EU Council Doc. 10418/06 of 12 June 2006, §11.

356 It should be noted that while a SOFA/SOMA includes, at least implicitly, the host State's consent, such consent is usually already given before the conclusion of the SOFA/SOMA, which primarily aims at regulating the precise modalities of the operation's presence and status (compare ICJ, *Case concerning armed activities on the territory of the Congo (DRC v. Uganda)*, judgment of 19 December 2005, §47). Thus even when there is a Chapter VII mandate and consent is not necessary, a SOFA/SOMA may be concluded, though obviously this will not be possible in the case of a pure peace enforcement action against the will of the host State (this seems to be misunderstood by A. Abas, *infra* note 438, pp. 140–141). See on such agreements generally T. Burkhardt, 'Die Entwicklung der Rechtsverhältnisse auslandischer Streitkräfte in den Aufnahmestaaten, insbesodere außerhalb der NATO', in H. Fischer (ed.), *Krisensicherung und humanitärer Schutz: Festschrift für Dieter Fleck*, Berlin, Berliner Wissenschafts-Verlag, 2004, pp. 53–54.

357 However, there appear to have been few such agreements in ESDP operations. To my knowledge, there has been one in the form of a Technical Arrangement for EUFOR DR Congo and in the framework of EUFOR TCHAD/RCA, a transit agreement under Article 24 EU Treaty was concluded with Cameroon (see Chapter 3.S.2 below).

358 These often take the form of Technical Arrangements. The status of such Technical Arrangements is interesting: at first sight, their conclusion outside Article 24 EU Treaty suggests that they are not treaties but if their conclusion is authorized by an agreement concluded under Article 24 EU Treaty (e.g. a SOFA), this does not necessarily seem to be the case.

engagement,[359] at least for military operations, but these are not in the public domain, as well as a number of decisions and documents implementing this, including standard operating procedures (SOPs; taking into account generic ESDP documents[360]). Seventh, there may be additional agreements (usually memoranda of understanding) between Participating States, which are often not in the public domain either, as well as technical arrangements implementing any of the above agreements.[361] Eighth, other rules of EU law may also be relevant, e.g. on financing or human rights. Finally, staff and especially military forces will remain bound by a significant part of the domestic law of their sending State; host State domestic law will also be relevant and *respect* for this law will usually be required by the SOFA/SOMA and general international law may include further rules that are relevant, including the law of armed conflict and human rights law (see extensively Part III below).

B. EUPM (BiH)[362]

The EU/EC has been involved in BiH for quite some time.[363] Especially after the end of the NATO military operation over Kosovo in 1999, the EU adopted a

359 The Operation Plan contains the specifics of the operation and is often lengthy, in part due to many annexes, which normally *inter alia* address legal issues and the use of force, at least for military operations. The rules of engagement may be described in short as instructions concerning the use of force. For an example of a 'sanitized' (main body of an) Operation Plan, see EU Doc. 7855/03 of 28 March 2003 (on Concordia).

360 For examples of relevant generic documents, see EU Concept for Logistic Support for EU-led Military Operations (Council Doc. 10963/08 of 19 June 2008); EU Concept for Reception, Staging, Onward Movement & Integration (RSOM&I) for EU-led Military Operations (Council Doc. 10971/08 of 19 June 2008) and EU Concept for Strategic Movement and Transportation for EU-led Military Operations (Council Doc. 10967/08 of 19 June 2008).

361 For an example, see the Estonian-Finnish-Norwegian-Swedish Memorandum of Understanding on an EUBG dated 17 May 2005 and previously available online at www.dep.no/filarkiv/247184/MOU_nordisk-estisk_innsatsstyrke_230505.doc. J. Dempsey, 'Letter from Germany: Bickering between NATO and EU Hampers Training of Afghan Police', *International Herald Tribune*, 23 August 2007, notes that absent EU-NATO agreements on cooperation between their respective Afghanistan missions (see *supra* Chapter 2.C, notes 216–218 and accompanying text), efforts are being made by the EU (mission) to conclude separate agreements with individual Proviancial Reconstruction Teams (which are part of the NATO mission).

362 See generally A. Hansen, 'Security and Defence: The EU Police Mission in Bosnia-Herzegovina', in W. Carlsnaes, H. Sjursen & B. White (eds.), *Contemporary European Foreign Policy*, London, Sage, 2004, pp. 173–185; C. Kouyoudjian, 'La mission de police de l'Union européenne en Bosnie-Herzégovine (MPUE)', in J. Tercinet (ed.), *Les relations transatlantiques et l'environnement international*, Brussels, Bruylant, 2005, pp. 215–241; A. Nowak, *L'Union en action: la mission de police en Bosnie*, EU ISS, Occasional Paper No. 42, January 2003; K.M. Osland, 'The EU Police Mission in Bosnia and Herzegovina', 11 *International Peacekeeping* 2004, pp. 544–560 and the websites www.eupm.org and www.consilium.europa.eu/showPage.aspx?id=585&lang=en.

363 See J. Wouters & F. Naert, *supra* note 249, pp. 553 and 555. The EU's involvement included the ECMM (discussed above), humanitarian aid, political and diplomatic involvement,

broad and ambitious regional approach to South-Eastern Europe, including the Stability Pact for South-Eastern Europe and the Stabilisation and Association Process, with the aim of eventually integrating the countries of this area in the EU.[364] There is also an EU Special Representative for BiH,[365] who is at the same time High Representative for BiH.[366]

Subsequently, on 1 January 2003 the EU launched its first ESDP operation, the EU Police Mission in Bosnia and Herzegovina (EUPM), which succeeded the UN's International Police Task Force (IPTF).[367] In December 2004, the EU also took over the military stabilization force from NATO through operation ALTHEA (discussed below in Section G of this chapter). The EUPM was planned well in advance: the EUPM Joint Action was adopted already on 11 March 2002 and established a planning team.[368] The Head of Mission would lead the planning team and was appointed on that day too.[369] This timely preparation also made possible the timely conclusion and entry into force of a SOMA.[370]

(monitoring of) sanctions, substantial financial support and leading the reconstruction efforts (together with the World Bank). For a recent appraisal, see S. Recchia, *Beyond International Trusteeship: EU Peacebuilding in Bosnia and Herzegovina*, Paris, EU ISS, Occasional Paper No. 66, February 2007 (available online at www.iss.europa.eu/index.php?id=154&L=0).

364 See J. Wouters & F. Naert, *supra* note 249, pp. 566–568 and http://ec.europa.eu/enlargement/enlargement_process/accession_process/how_does_a_country_join_the_eu/sap/index_en.htm. The Stabilisation and Association Agreement with BiH was signed on 16 June 2008, together with an interim trade agreement; see Council Presidency press release of that day (available online at www.eu2008.si/en/News_and_Documents/Press_Releases/June/0616GAERC_BIH.html) and *O.J. L* 169, 30 June 2008, pp. 10 and 13 and *O.J. L* 233, 30 August 2008, pp. 1, 5 and 6.

365 See generally www.consilium.europa.eu/showPage.aspx?id=1617&lang=EN. For his current mandate, see Council Joint Action of 11 March 2009 appointing the European Union Special Representative in Bosnia and Herzegovina (2009/181/CFSP), *O.J. L 67*, 12 March 2009, p. 88.

366 See UNSC Res. 1869 of 25 March 2009. The High Representative has important powers under the Dayton Agreement (*infra* note 1399) and the conclusions of the Peace Implementation Council (PIC). See generally www.ohr.int. For the most recent (29–30 June 2009) PIC communiqué, see www.ohr.int/pic/default.asp?content_id=43665. The High Representative has made use of the "Bonn powers" as recently as 20 June 2009, see www.ohr.int/decisions/statemattersdec/default.asp?content_id=43633. See also Article 5 Joint Action 2009/181/CFSP (*supra* previous note).

367 The IPTF was a part of the UN Mission in Bosnia and Herzegovina, see generally www.un.org/Depts/dpko/missions/unmibh/.

368 Council Joint Action of 11 March 2002 on the European Union Police Mission (2002/210/CFSP), *O.J. L* 70, 13 March 2002, p. 1.

369 Council Decision of 11 March 2002 concerning the appointment of the Head of Mission/Police Commissioner of the European Union Police Mission (EUPM) (2002/212/CFSP), *O.J. L* 70, 13 March 2002, p. 8.

370 Agreement between the European Union and Bosnia and Herzegovina (BiH) on the activities of the European Union Police Mission (EUPM) in BiH, *O.J. L* 293, 29 October 2002, p. 1/2, concluded in accordance with Article 11(1) EUPM Joint Action (*supra* note 368).

The EUPM is part of the broader EU rule of law follow up in BiH.[371] This was *inter alia* reflected in the chain of command, where the EU Special Representative (EUSR) for Bosnia and Herzegovina acted as an intermediary between the High Representative for the Common Foreign and Security Policy and Secretary-General of the Council of the EU (SG/HR) on the one hand and the Head of Mission on the other hand.[372]

The objective of the mission originally was "*to establish sustainable policing arrangements under BiH ownership in accordance with best European and international practice, and thereby raising current BiH police standards*" through monitoring, mentoring and inspecting and the mission does not include executive powers or the deployment of an armed component.[373]

The mission was foreseen to run from 2003 till 2005,[374] but was extended (with a revised mandate) for another two years late 2005[375] and subsequently again until the end of 2009.[376] For its initial duration, it had an estimated total budget of 129.7 million euros, including 75.7 million euros from the Community budget.[377] The amount funded by the Community budget was reduced by approximately

371 Article 7 EUPM Joint Action, *supra* note 368.

372 *Id.*, Articles 6–7. See also Council Joint Action of 7 February 2007 amending and extending the mandate of the European Union Special Representative in Bosnia and Herzegovina (2007/87/CFSP), *O.J. L* 35, 8 February 2007, p. 35. This has been affected by the changes in the chain of command (see *infra* note 386 and accompanying text).

373 EUPM Joint Action, *supra* note 368, annexed mission statement and Article 1 EUPM SOMA, *supra* note 370. Its revised mission statement for 2006–2007 amended the objective to read "*through mentoring, monitoring and inspecting, to establish in BiH a sustainable, professional and multiethnic police service operating in accordance with best European and international standards*" (Article 1(1) Joint Action 2005/824/CFSP, *infra* note 375).

374 Article 1(3) EUPM SOMA, *supra* note 370.

375 Council Joint Action of 24 November 2005 on the European Union Police Mission (EUPM) in Bosnia and Herzegovina (BiH) (2005/824/CFSP), *O.J. L* 307, 25 November 2005, p. 55, Articles 1 and 15. For the budget in the following years, see also Council Decision of 28 November 2006 implementing Joint Action 2005/824/CFSP on the European Union Police Mission (EUPM) in Bosnia and Herzegovina (BiH) (2006/865/CFSP), *O.J. L* 335, 1 December 2006, p. 46; Council Decision of 4 December 2007 implementing Joint Action 2007/749/CFSP on the European Union Police Mission (EUPM) in Bosnia and Herzegovina (BiH) (2007/791/CFSP), *O.J. L* 317, 5 December 2007, p. 83 and Council Decision of 27 November 2008 implementing Joint Action 2007/749/CFSP on the European Union Police Mission (EUPM) in Bosnia and Herzegovina (BiH) (2008/890/CFSP), *O.J. L* 318, 28 November 2008, p. 14.

376 External Relations Council of 19–20 November 2007, conclusions on ESDP, §18 and Council Joint Action of 19 November 2007 on the European Union Police Mission (EUPM) in Bosnia and Herzegovina (BiH) (2007/749/CFSP), *O.J. L* 303, 21 November 2007, p. 40.

377 Article 9 EUPM Joint Action, *supra* note 368; Council Joint Action of 27 February 2003 amending Joint Action 2002/210/CFSP on the European Union Police Mission (2003/141/CFSP), *O.J. L* 53, 28 February 2003, p. 63 and Council Decision of 10 December 2002 concerning the implementation of Joint Action 2002/210/CFSP on the European Union Police Mission (2002/968/CFSP), *O.J.* L 335, 12 December 2002, p. 1.

2.5 million euros for 2004 and 2005,[378] presumably reflecting the amount paid by third States participating in the mission (as explained below).[379]

The mission was initially led by Commissioner Sven Frederiksen,[380] who was succeeded by Assistant Commissioner Kevin Carty,[381] Mr. Vincenzo Coppola[382] and Mr. Stefan Feller,[383] and it numbers about 500 police officers from 33 countries (detailed below) with headquarters in Sarajevo and 24 monitoring units co-located within police units throughout BiH.[384] The PSC exercises political control and strategic direction of the operation.[385] The command structure was amended in November 2007 to reflect the new policy on command in civilian operations.[386] Moreover, coordination with other EU missions and activities has been improved.[387]

378 Council Decision of 8 December 2003 concerning the implementation of Joint Action 2002/210/CFSP on the European Union Police Mission (2003/856/CFSP), *O.J. L* 323, 10 December 2003, p. 13 and Council Decision of 6 December 2004 concerning the implementation of Joint Action 2002/210/CFSP on the European Union Police Mission (2004/837/CFSP), *O.J. L* 360, 7 December 2004, p. 32.

379 Information previously available at http://europa.eu.int/comm/external_relations/cfsp/fin/actions/eupm03.htm.

380 Council Decision 2002/212/CFSP, *supra* note 369.

381 Council Decision of 23 February 2004 concerning the appointment of the Head of Mission/Police Commissioner of the European Union Police Mission (EUPM) (2004/188/CFSP), *O.J. L* 58, 26 February 2004, p. 27, extended by Council Decision of 31 January 2005 extending the mandate of the Head of Mission/Police Commissioner of the European Union Police Mission (EUPM) in Bosnia-Herzegovina (2005/81/CFSP), *O.J. L* 29, 2 February 2005, p. 48.

382 PSC Decision of 25 November 2005 concerning the appointment of the Head of Mission/Police Commissioner of the European Union Police Mission (EUPM) in Bosnia and Herzegovina (BiH) (EUPM/1/2005–2005/922/CFSP), *O.J. L* 335, 21 December 2005, p. 58 (*corrigendum O.J. L* 188, 11 July 2006, p. 14: EUPM/1/2005 should read EUPM/2/2005), extended by PSC Decision of 5 December 2006 extending the mandate of the Head of Mission/Police Commissioner of the European Union Police Mission (EUPM) in Bosnia and Herzegovina (BiH) (EUPM/1/2006–2006/979/CFSP), *O.J. L* 365, 21 December 2006, p. 87 and by PSC Decision of 30 November 2007 extending the mandate of the Head of Mission/Police Commissioner of the European Union Police Mission (EUPM) in Bosnia and Herzegovina (BiH) (EUPM/1/2007), *O.J. L* 329, 14 December 2007, p. 63 (corrig. *O.J. L* 330, 15 December 2007, p. 60).

383 PSC Decision of 24 October 2008 concerning the appointment of the Head of Mission/Police Commissioner of the European Union Police Mission (EUPM) in Bosnia and Herzegovina (EUPM/1/2008 – 2008/835/CFSP), *O.J. L* 298, 7 November 2008, p. 30.

384 Article 3 EUPM Joint Action, *supra* note 368 and Article 1(2) EUPM SOMA, *supra* note 370.

385 Article 7 EUPM Joint Action, *supra* note 368.

386 Joint Action 2007/749/CFSP, *supra* note 376.

387 See *infra* note 553.

1. MANDATE

The Council of the EU expressed its readiness to take over the UN's IPTF on 18 February 2002, an offer that was accepted by the Peace Implementation Council Steering Board (which supervises the implementation of the General Framework Agreement for Peace in Bosnia and Herzegovina (Dayton Peace Agreement)[388]) ten days later and welcomed by the UN Security Council on 5 March 2002 in Resolution 1396.[389] On 4 March 2002, the Bosnian authorities invited the EU to undertake this mission. The EUPM is therefore based on the consent of the authorities of Bosnia and Herzegovina. This is reflected in the wording of UN Security Council Resolution 1396, which *welcomes* rather than *authorizes* the EUPM.[390]

2. LEGAL STATUS AND APPLICABLE LAW

The EUPM SOMA was concluded well in time[391] and entered into force before the start of the mission. The key provision on the status of the mission is Article 4, which grants the EUPM the status equivalent to that of a diplomatic mission, makes all its offices and means of transport inviolable and gives EUPM personnel all privileges and immunities equivalent to those of personnel of embassies (differentiating between EUPM personnel, administrative and technical staff and locally hired auxiliary personnel), adding that the EU Member States and other Sending Parties shall have priority of jurisdiction. It may be noted that it is common for States and international organizations to seek privileges and immunities for the personnel participating in operations/missions (and even exercises) abroad. Some reflections on this point are included in Chapter 4 below. Remarkably (SOFAs/SOMAs usually stipulate respect for local law), there is no provision at all on applicable law (applicable law refers to the law applicable to the personnel of an operation and usually is a complex mix of international law, the law of the State(s) sending the personnel and local (meaning host State) law).[392] Equally remarkable, the SOMA contains no claims provisions. However, the Joint Action does stipulate that a State or Community institution having seconded a staff member is responsible for answering any claims linked to the secondment from or concerning the staff member and is also responsible for bringing any action against the secondee.[393]

---

388 Paris, 14 December 1995, 35 *I.L.M.* 1996, p. 75.

389 EUPM Joint Action, *supra* note 368, preamble.

390 For a more thorough analysis of this distinction, see *infra*, Chapter 4.A.6.

391 *Supra* note 370.

392 See Section A above and the discussion below in this chapter on the SOFAs/SOMAs for other missions, Chapter 4.B and the introduction to Part III.

393 EUPM Joint Action, *supra* note 368, Article 11(2).

In line with the nature of the mission (as discussed above, it does not have executive functions), Article 5(1) EUPM SOMA states that "*Members of the EUPM shall not carry arms*". It is for BiH to take "*all necessary measures for the protection, safety and security of the EUPM and its members*" (Article 6(1) EUPM SOMA). Furthermore, according to Article 6(2) EUPM SOMA "*Members of the EUPM shall not undertake any action or activity incompatible with the impartial nature of their duties*".

3. PARTICIPATION OF THIRD STATES

All 15 'old'[394] EU Member States (including Denmark) participate in the EUPM, as well as the 12 'new' Member States, the candidate Member State Turkey, the NATO Member States Iceland, Norway and Canada and also Russia, Switzerland and Ukraine.[395] The participation of Denmark is not evident given its special status (see *supra*[396]) but it indicates that decisions or matters having "defence implications" do not cover the entire ESDP and notably do not cover the civilian side of the ESDP.[397]

The participation of third States that are members of the OSCE was permitted by Article 8 EUPM Joint Action, which also provided for the conclusion of detailed agreements to be concluded with those States. Such agreements were indeed concluded.[398] On the basis of a selective survey, they share the following elements: the participating State associates itself with the Joint Action establishing the EUPM and commits itself to seconding a specified number of personnel to this mission. It bears the costs thereof and it pays a share in the common costs. Its personnel are covered by the EUPM SOMA. EU decision-making autonomy is safeguarded but all Participating States have the same rights and obligations in terms of day-to-day management of the operation as participating EU Member States,[399] and the EU will consult with Participating States when ending the mission. The agreements also contain a clause on

394 I.e. the EU Member States before the 2004 accession wave.

395 Fact sheet previously available at www.eupm.org/FactSheet.asp?lang=eng.

396 Chapter 1.E.

397 This will be discussed in more detail below in Chapter 4.A.

398 Most of the agreements have been published in *O.J. L* 239, 25 December 2003, pp. 1–44. For the agreement with Poland, see *O.J. L* 64, 7 March 2003, p. 37/38 and for that with Russia, see *O.J. L* 197, 5 August 2003, p. 37/38. I have not been able to find an agreement with Canada. For more details on the agreements, see the *O.J.* and the Council's agreements database (www.consilium.europa.eu/showPage.aspx?id=252&lang=en).

399 It was apparently decided that all contributions are significant in the sense of Article 8 EUPM Joint Action, *supra* note 368.

classified information[400] and on claims linked to the secondment of personnel to the EUPM. Also, a committee of contributors was set up.[401]

C. CONCORDIA (FYROM)[402]

CONCORDIA was the EU's second ESDP operation and its first military one. The EU had already played a role in FYROM at the time of the crisis in Kosovo[403] and following its regional approach to South-Eastern Europe (mentioned above in Section B of this chapter) and when tensions increased in early 2001, the EU and NATO undertook coordinated efforts to avoid an escalation,[404] resulting in the 13 August 2001 Ohrid Framework Agreement.[405]

The EU was involved in the implementation and supervision of this agreement, but the military presence was initially led by NATO, which conducted operations Essential Harvest, Amber Fox and Allied Harmony in FYROM.[406] However, on 31 March 2003 the EU took over NATO's peacekeeping mission.[407] The Operation plan and rules of engagement were adopted on 18 March 2003.[408] CONCORDIA was initially to last six months[409] but was extended until 15 December 2003.[410] It

400 The sharing of classified information with non-Member States requires regulation and can be problematic (compare the position of Cyprus and until recently Malta in EU-led operations with recourse to NATO assets, discussed below in note 544).

401 PSC Decision on the setting up of the Committee of Contributors for the European Union Police Mission (EUOM) in Bosnia and Herzegovina (EUPM/1/2005), EU Council Doc. 6914/05, 3 March 2005.

402 See generally G. Lindstrom, *supra* note 353, pp. 116–118; C. Mace, 'Operation Concordia: Developing a "European" Approach to Crisis Management?', 11 *International Peacekeeping* 2004, pp. 474–490; P. Maral, 'Vers une union opérationnelle?: Concordia', 60(5) *Défense nationale* 2004, pp. 15–41 and www.consilium.europa.eu/showPage.aspx?id=594&lang=en.

403 J. Wouters & F. Naert, *supra* note 249, pp. 559–560.

404 J. Wouters & F. Naert, 'Europese defensie in de NAVO en de Europese Unie: eenheid en complementariteit', 31 *Vrede en Veiligheid* 2002, pp. 215 and 223 (note 71).

405 Text at http://faq.macedonia.org/politics/framework_agreement.pdf.

406 See www.nato.int/fyrom/home.htm and W. Hermsdörfer, 'Die NATO-geführte Operation Harvest in der Republik Mazedonien', 46 *N.Z. Wehrrecht* 2004, pp. 23–30.

407 Article 1 Council Decision of 18 March 2003 relating to the launch of the EU military operation in the Former Yugoslav Republic of Macedonia (2003/202/CFSP), *O.J. L* 76, 22 March 2003, p. 43. See also Council Joint Action of 27 January 2003 on the European Union military operation in the Former Yugoslav Republic of Macedonia (2003/92/CFSP), *O.J. L* 34, 11 February 2003, p. 26.

408 18 March 2003 Council conclusions. For the 'sanitized' Operation Plan, see EU Doc. 7855/03 of 28 March 2003.

409 Article 3 Council Decision 2003/202/CFSP, *supra* note 407.

410 Council Decision of 29 July 2003 on the extension of the European Union military operation in the Former Yugoslav Republic of Macedonia (2003/563/CFSP), *O.J. L* 190, 30 July 2003, p. 20.

was then followed by EUPOL PROXIMA and EUPAT (discussed below in Sections E and N of this chapter).

The aim of the operation was to contribute to stability and security in FYROM and to further the implementation of the Ohrid Agreement.[411]

CONCORDIA was an operation with recourse to NATO assets and only became possible once EU-NATO arrangements had been agreed upon – a difficult process only successfully concluded in March 2003 (see *supra* Chapter 2.C). A specific EU-NATO exchange of letters was concluded for CONCORDIA on 17 March 2003.[412] The EU operational headquarters were located at (NATO's) Supreme Headquarters of Allied Powers in Europe (SHAPE) and the Operation Commander was the Deputy Supreme Allied Commander for Europe (D-SACEUR).[413] The responsibilities at Force Headquarters level were first exercised by France as 'framework nation' and as of 1 October 2003 by EUROFOR (the French – Spanish – Italian – Portuguese European Force established to conduct peace support operations).[414]

The PSC, under the responsibility of the Council, exercised the political control and strategic direction of the operation and was authorized to take "*the relevant decisions*", including the powers to amend the operation plan, the chain of command and the rules of engagement, whereas the powers of decision with respect to the objectives and termination of the operation remained vested in the Council.[415]

Some 400 military personnel from 27 countries were engaged in this operation,[416] i.e. all the "old" EU Member States except Denmark, which does not participate in the elaboration and the implementation of decisions and actions of the Union which have defence implications,[417] and except Ireland, which, under Irish law,

---

411 Joint Action 2003/92/CFSP, *supra* note 407, 1st consideration preamble.

412 Council Decision 2003/202/CFSP, *supra* note 407, 4th consideration preamble. This agreement was extended with CONCORDIA's extension; see Council Decision 2003/563/CFSP, *supra* note 410, 6th consideration preamble.

413 EU Doc. 6158/03, 7 February 2003 and Article 2 Joint Action 2003/92/CFSP, *supra* note 407.

414 EU Doc. 11881/03, 29 July 2003; Article 2 Council Decision 2003/563/CFSP, *supra* note 410 and information previously available at www.eurofor.it/Mission_CONCORDIA_03%20 INDEX.htm (last consulted in November 2007).

415 Article 4(1) Joint Action 2003/92/CFSP, *supra* note 407.

416 Information previously available at www.consilium.europa.eu/showPage.aspx?id=594 &lang=en.

417 See *supra* Chapter 1.E. This is recalled in the 8th consideration of the preamble of Council Decision 2003/202/CFSP, *supra* note 407.

can only take part in missions with a UN mandate,[418] and 14 third States (detailed below).

The budget for the common costs amounted to 6.2 million euros[419] and was managed through a specific financial mechanism. The other costs were funded by the Participating States on a "*costs lie where they fall*" basis.[420]

1. MANDATE

CONCORDIA was undertaken following a request by the FYROM President.[421] In addition, UN Security Council Resolution 1371 of 26 September 2001 welcomed the presence of international observers (§4) and strongly supported "*the establishment of a multinational security presence in [FYROM] at the request of its Government to contribute towards the security of the observers*" (§5). So here too the main legal basis was the consent of the government and the UN Security Council merely endorsed the operation rather than authorized it. The significance of the latter point will be addressed below (in Chapter 4.A.6).

2. LEGAL STATUS AND APPLICABLE LAW

Article 12 of Joint Action 2003/92/CFSP[422] provided for a SOFA. On this basis, the CONCORDIA SOFA was concluded on 21 March 2003[423] and entered into force on 31 March 2003,[424] i.e. the day the operation started. This agreement

---

418 E.g. Parliamentary debates, 24 November 2004 (http://debates.oireachtas.ie/DDebate.aspx?F=JUS20041124.xml&Ex=All&Page=2). Even a positive UN attitude and host State consent did not suffice. This is a specific restraint under Irish law which is distinct from restraints under international law that will be discussed *infra*, Chapter 4.A.6. See also R. Murphy, 'Ireland Withdraws from Participation in EU Peacekeeping Mission to Macedonia', 9 *International Peacekeeping (Yearbook)* 2003, pp. 123–138 (noting that Ireland had initially committed itself to participating and discussing the need for a UN mandate).

419 Information previously available at www.consilium.europa.eu/showPage.aspx?id=594&lang=en. Initially, only 4.7 million euros had been allocated: see Article 9(3) Joint Action 2003/92/CFSP, *supra* note 407.

420 Article 9 and 11th consideration preamble Joint Action 2003/92/CFSP, *supra* note 407.

421 18 March 2003 Council conclusions. The CONCORDIA extension was also based on such a request: see EU Doc. 11881/03, 29 July 2003.

422 *Supra* note 407.

423 *O.J. L* 285, 1 November 2003, p. 47 and Annex to Council Decision of 21 March 2003 concerning the conclusion of the Agreement between the European Union and the Former Yugoslav Republic of Macedonia on the status of the European Union-led Forces (EUF) in the Former Yugoslav Republic of Macedonia (2003/222/CFSP), *O.J. L* 82, 29 March 2003, p. 45 (agreement at p. 46) (this SOFA appears to have been published twice, the first time with the Council decision and an exchange of letters).

424 See the Council's agreements database, *supra* note 398.

also covered personnel and assets of a third State participating in CONCORDIA.[425]

Pursuant to Article 2 of this SOFA, the European Union-led forces (EUF) were to respect FYROM laws and regulations and Article 9 added an obligation to respect international conventions and FYROM laws regarding the protection of the environment and cultural heritage, albeit "*subject to the requirements of the operation*". Furthermore, Article 2 obliged mission staff to refrain from any activity incompatible with the impartial and international nature of the operation. Pursuant to Article 5, EUF premises, accommodation, archives and documents were inviolable, its premises and accommodations and assets thereon and their means of transport were immune from search, execution, etc. and EUF correspondence was granted a status equivalent to that of diplomatic correspondence. Article 6 granted EUF personnel treatment, including immunities and privileges, equivalent to that of diplomatic agents. Article 7(2) permitted EUF personnel to carry arms and ammunitions "*on condition that they [were] authorised to do so by their orders*". In respect of claims for death, injury, damage or loss, Article 13 distinguished between two categories of claims. Claims arising out of activities in connection with civil disturbances, protection of the EUF or which were incidental to operational necessities were not to be the subject of any reimbursement by States participating in the operation or by the EU financing mechanism. All other claims were to be dealt with by a Joint Claims Commission composed of representatives of the EUF and FYROM authorities. Settlement of the latter claims was to occur after previous consent of the State concerned or the mechanism. In contrast with the EUPM, there was no provision on (*intra*-EU responsibilities with respect to) claims in the Joint Action.

Finally, Article 16 provided that a number of separate implementing agreements were to be concluded, *inter alia* on the status of local staff and contractors, on procedures for addressing and settling claims and on the exchange of information.

3. PARTICIPATION OF THIRD STATES

The CONCORDIA Joint Action provided for the participation of third States, in particular non-EU European NATO members, candidate EU Member States and other "*potential partners*".[426]

425 Article 1(3)(c) and (g) CONCORDIA SOFA.
426 Joint Action 2003/92/CFSP, *supra* note 407, Article 8.

This participation was without prejudice to EU decision-making autonomy and third States making "*significant military contributions*" were to have the same rights and obligations in the day-to-day management of the operation as participating EU Member States.[427] The PSC was authorized to take the relevant decisions on acceptance of the proposed contributions, upon the recommendation of the Operation Commander and the EU Military Committee (EUMC).[428]

On 18 March 2003, the Council welcomed the participation of 14 third States.[429] These States were the (then) acceding/candidate Member States Bulgaria, the Czech Republic, Estonia, Hungary, Latvia, Lithuania, Poland, Romania, Slovakia, Slovenia and Turkey and the NATO Member States Iceland and Norway. Canada initially intended to participate but later withdrew.[430]

Detailed arrangements regarding third State participation were to be the subject of an agreement under Article 24 EU Treaty, and the SG/HR, "*assisting the Presidency*", was authorized to negotiate such arrangements on the Presidency's behalf.[431] It seems that agreements were concluded with 12 third States.[432]

On the basis of a selective survey, these agreements share the following elements: the participating State associates itself with the Joint Action establishing the

---

427 *Id.*, Articles 8(1) and (4).

428 *Id.*, Article 8(2).

429 Council conclusions of 18 March 2003. See also PSC Decision of 10 March 2003 on the acceptance of third States contributions to the European Union military operation in the Former Yugoslav Republic of Macedonia (FYROM/2/2003–2003/497/CFSP), *O.J. L* 170, 9 July 2003, p. 15 as amended by PSC Decision of 11 March 2003 amending the Political and Security Committee Decision FYROM/2/2003 of 10 March 2003 on the acceptance of third States contributions to the European Union military operation in the Former Yugoslav Republic of Macedonia (FYROM/3/2003–2003/498/CFSP), *id.*, p. 17.

430 Canada was initially listed (see www.consilium.europa.eu/uedocs/cmsUpload/Fourteen%20 non-EU%20countries.pdf) but no longer afterwards (see information previously available at www.eurofor.it/Mission_CONCORDIA_03%20INDEX.htm; last consulted in November 2007). Its withdrawal is reflected in PSC Decision of 17 June 2003 amending the Decision FYROM/2/2003 on the acceptance of third States contributions to the European Union military operation in the Former Yugoslav Republic of Macedonia (FYROM/4/2003–2003/499/CFSP), *O.J. L* 170, 9 July 2003, p. 19 (the 3rd consideration of the preamble states that "*by letter of 29 April 2003 the Canadian Representative to the EU has informed the EU that it is unable to participate in Operation Concordia on the current terms*"). According to G. Lindstrom, *supra* note 353, p. 125, Canada withdrew over financing arrangements. Also, the author has not found an EU-Canada participation agreement for CONCORDIA.

431 Joint Action 2003/92/CFSP, *supra* note 407, Article 8(3).

432 Czech Republic (*O.J. L* 229, 13 September 2003, p. 38/39), Estonia (*O.J. L* 216, 28 August 2003, p. 60/61), Latvia (*O.J. L* 313, 28 November 2003, p. 78/79), Lithuania (*O.J. L* 234, 20 September 2003, p. 18/19), Poland (*O.J. L* 285, 1 November 2003, p. 43/44), Romania (*O.J. L* 120, 24 April 2004, p. 61/62), Slovak Republic (*O.J. L* 12, 17 January 2004, p. 53/54) and Turkey (*O.J. L* 234, 20 September 2003, p. 22/23). The agreements with Hungary (18 June 2003), Iceland (3 July 2003), Norway (17 June 2003) and Slovenia (31 July 2003) do not seem to have been published in the *O.J.* The author has not found any agreement with Bulgaria or Canada.

operation and commits itself to seconding personnel to this mission (in most cases to be determined at a Force Generation Conference[433]). It bears the costs thereof, except common costs, and pays a specified share in the common costs. Participating State personnel are covered by the CONCORDIA SOFA and the participating third State exercises jurisdiction over its personnel. All forces and personnel remain under the full command of their national authorities, who transfer operational control to the EU operation commander.[434] EU decision-making autonomy is safeguarded, but all Participating States have the same rights and obligations in day-to-day management of the operation as participating EU Member States.[435] The agreements also contain a clause on classified information and on claims for damage to the local population caused by personnel seconded by a third State to the operation.

Furthermore, a Committee of Contributors for this operation was set up by the PSC,[436] which had been authorized to do so by the Council.[437]

D. ARTEMIS (DRC)[438]

ARTEMIS was an operation in an area where the EU was already involved: the EU had taken initiatives at the continental level,[439] at the (sub)regional level of

433 Such conferences are held to generate the forces and assets required to fulfil the mission. On force generation for military ESDP operations, see EU Concept for Force Generation, EU Council doc. 10690/08 of 16 June 2008.

434 For more details on kinds of command and control and their relevance, see *supra*, Section B of this Chapter, notes 188 and accompanying text and *infra*, Chapter 8.F-G, especially notes 2200–2217 and the accompanying text.

435 It again was apparently decided that all contributions were significant in the sense of Article 8(4) Joint Action 2003/92/CFSP, *supra* note 407.

436 PSC Decision of 18 February 2003 on the setting up of the Committee of Contributors for the European Union Military Operation in the Former Yugoslav Republic of Macedonia (FYROM/1/2003), *O.J. C* 62, 15 March 2003, p. 1.

437 Joint Action 2003/92/CFSP, *supra* note 407, Article 8(5).

438 See generally www.consilium.europa.eu/showPage.aspx?id=605&lang=en; A. Abass, 'Extraterritorial Collective Security: The European Union and Operation ARTEMIS', in Trybus & White, pp. 134–156; C. Mace, 'Operation Artemis: Mission improbable?', *European Security Review* No 18, July 2003, available at www.isis-europe.org; B. Neveux, 'Vers une union opérationnelle?: Artémis', 60(5) *Défense nationale* 2004, pp. 11–24; S. Ulriksen, C. Gourlay & C. Mace, 'Operation Artemis: The Shape of Things to Come?', 11 *International Peacekeeping* 2004, pp. 508–525; UN Peacekeeping Best Practices Unit (PBPU), *Operation Artemis: The Lessons of the Interim Emergency Multinational Force*, October 2004, available at http://pbpu.unlb.org and A. Vahlas, 'Le prototype Artémis d'agencement multinational et la diversification de l'action militaire européenne', 6 *Annuaire français de relations internationales* 2005, pp. 262–275.

439 E.g. Council Common Position of 26 January 2004 concerning conflict prevention, management and resolution in Africa and repealing Common Position 2001/374/CFSP

the Great Lakes region[440] and specifically regarding the DRC,[441] which has long suffered from internal armed conflicts with foreign interventions. Obviously, operation ARTEMIS signified a greater EU involvement on the field. Moreover, the EU later also launched a Police operation in Kinshasa (and in 2007 in the wider DRC), a security sector reform mission in the DRC and a second military operation (discussed below in Sections H, I and P of this chapter).

In May 2003, intense fighting erupted in and around Bunia in the DRC's Ituri region, leading to many deaths and refugees. As the United Nations Organization Mission in the DRC (MONUC) was unable to deal with the situation, the UN Secretary-General called for "*the rapid deployment to Bunia of a highly trained and well-equipped multinational force, under the lead of a Member State, to provide security at the airport as well as to other vital installations in the town and to protect the civilian population*".[442] Subsequently, France indicated its readiness to deploy a force to Bunia and on 30 May 2003 in Resolution 1484, the Security Council authorized the deployment, until 1 September 2003, by which date MONUC was to be sufficiently reinforced, of an International Emergency Multinational Force (IEMF) in Bunia "*to contribute to the stabilization of the security conditions and the improvement of the humanitarian situation in Bunia, to ensure the protection of the airport, the internally displaced persons in the camps in Bunia and, if the situation requires it, to contribute to the safety of the civilian population, [UN] personnel and the humanitarian presence in the town*".

France successfully appealed to the EU Member States to make this an EU operation. The preparations took place very quickly[443] and the decision to undertake the operation was adopted on 5 June.[444] The operation plan and rules of engagement were adopted on 12 June and on that same day the operation was formally launched,[445] although French forces were already on the ground on 6 June.[446]

(2004/85/CFSP), *O.J. L* 21, 28 January 2004, p. 25. See also www.consilium.europa.eu/showPage.aspx?id=400&lang=en.

440 E.g. the EU Special Representative for this region; see www.consilium.europa.eu/showPage.aspx?id=1212&lang=EN. See also M. Martinelli, 'Helping Transition: The EU Police Mission on the Democratic Republic of the Congo (EUPOL Kinshasa) in the Framework of the EU Policies in the Great lakes', 11 *E.F.A.R.* 2006, pp. 381–386.

441 See generally M. Martinelli, *supra* previous note, pp. 386–393.

442 UN Doc. S/2003/574, 15 May 2003.

443 The Council asked the SG/HR for a feasibility study on 19 May 2003.

444 Council Joint Action of 5 June 2003 on the European Union military operation in the Democratic Republic of Congo (2003/423/CFSP), *O.J. L* 143, 11 June 2003, p. 50.

445 Council Decision of 12 June 2003 on the launching of the European Union military operation in the Democratic Republic of Congo (2003/432/CFSP), *O.J. L* 147, 14 June 2003, p. 42. By 13 June, 400 troops were in Bunia, see www.reliefweb.int/rw/rwb.nsf/AllDocsByUNID/af53b8f764b3e760c1256d470029cff1.

446 UNPBPU, *supra* note 438, p. 19.

ARTEMIS was an autonomous EU operation without recourse to NATO assets. This required the designation of a "Framework Nation" since the EU itself had no proper headquarters.[447] France was the "Framework Nation" and contributed the multinationalized Headquarters, the Operation and Force Commanders (Generals Bruno Neveu and Jean-Paul Thonier) and the majority of the forces.[448] The operational Headquarters, which became operational on 16 June 2003,[449] were located in Paris and the Force Headquarters in Entebbe, Uganda, with an outpost in Bunia. ARTEMIS' full strength was 1,800 troops and these were all deployed by early July.[450] The mission ended on 1 September 2003 with a handover to MONUC and the last ARTEMIS troops left Bunia on 7 September. The political control and strategic direction of the operation was exercised by the PSC under the responsibility of the Council and the PSC was authorized to take "*the relevant decisions*", including the powers to amend the operation plan, the chain of command and the rules of engagement, but excluding the powers of decision with respect to the objectives and termination of the operation, which remained vested in the Council.[451]

Six EU Member States participated both in the headquarters and with forces (Belgium, France, Germany, Greece, Sweden and the UK) and another six participated in the headquarters only (Austria, Ireland, Italy, Netherlands, Portugal and Spain).[452] Obviously, Denmark did not participate in this military operation (as explained above),[453] and neither did Luxemburg and Finland.[454] The then candidate Member States Cyprus and Hungary participated in the headquarters and Canada, South Africa and Brazil participated too (as explained below).

---

447 ARTEMIS Joint Action, *supra* note 444, 5th consideration preamble. See also *supra*, Chapter 2.B-C.

448 ARTEMIS Joint Action, *supra* note 444, Articles 2–5.

449 French Defence Ministry press release, 16 June 2003, previously available at www.defense.gouv.fr/sites/ema/enjeux_defense/operations_exterieures/documentation/republique_democratique_du_congo.

450 Council fact sheet on ARTEMIS, July 2003 and H.L. Stimson Center, 'Review of European Union Field Operations', March 2004, www.stimson.org/fopo/pdf/Factsheet_EUField Operations.pdf, p. 4. The total number of personnel involved may have run up to 2,200; see J. Howorth, 'The Capacities at Europe's Disposal', in Royal Defence College and (eds.), *Able and Willing ...*, Brussels, Belgian Ministry of Defence, 2004, previously available online at www.mil.be/rdc (last consulted in November 2007), p. 25.

451 ARTEMIS Joint Action, *supra* note 444, Article 7.

452 G. Lindstrom, *supra* note 353, p. 120.

453 ARTEMIS Joint Action, *supra* note 444, 13th consideration preamble.

454 The author is not aware of the reasons for this non-participation, nor of those that led some Member States to only participate in the headquarters. However, the speed with which the operation was set up in combination with the recourse to *ad hoc* internationalized French headquarters might have been among these reasons.

The Council set up an arrangement for the common costs, estimated at 7 million euros, and the remaining costs were born by the Participating States on a "*costs lie where they fall*" basis.[455] In contrast to earlier operations, third Participating States did not contribute to the common costs.[456]

1. MANDATE

Operation ARTEMIS was based on UN Security Council Resolution 1484 of 30 May 2003, adopted under Chapter VII[457] of the UN Charter and authorizing the Participating States to "*take all necessary measures to fulfil [the Force's] mandate*" (§4). However, in the preamble of this Resolution, the Security Council took note of the support of the DRC, Rwanda, Uganda and the Ituri parties for the deployment of the force.

Hence the operation contains both elements of peacekeeping with consent of the parties and Chapter VII peace enforcement. ARTEMIS was conducted in a dangerous environment, as was shown by the subsequent heavy MONUC fighting with various militias,[458] but was not confronted with major hostile actions against it.[459]

UN support for ARTEMIS was renewed in Security Council Resolutions 1493 (28 July 2003) and 1505 (26 August 2003). The latter Resolution authorized ARTEMIS to provide assistance to MONUC in and around Bunia if MONUC requested such assistance during the period of ARTEMIS' disengagement, until 15 September 2003 at the latest.

455 ARTEMIS Joint Action, *supra* note 444, Article 11.

456 C. Mace, *supra* note 438, p. 2.

457 This chapter allows the Security Council to determine the existence of any threat to the peace, breach of the peace, or act of aggression and to make recommendations or decide upon measures to be taken to maintain or restore international peace and security, including sanctions and the use of force.

458 MONUC later regularly conducted significant combat operations against certain rebel groups. For instance, on 1 March 2006, MONUC provided some details on an operation conducted by 500 UN forces and 2,500 DRC armed forces against rebel forces in which the UN had to engage attack helicopters and mortar fire (information previously available at www.monuc.org/news.aspx?newsID=10105; last consulted in November 2007). On this more robust UN approach, see also A. Zeebroek, 'Un premier pas vers une doctrine des opérations robustes?', 60(3) *Studia Diplomatica* 2007, pp. 5–16. MONUC also conducted a joint military operation with the Congolese Armed Forces against illegal armed groups in 2009; see UN press releases of 20 April and 8 June 2009.

459 However, on 14 June a patrol was attacked by rebel militias and returned fire ('Une patrouille d'Artemis prise à partie', 14 June 2003, previously available at the French ARTEMIS web page, *supra* note 449) and on 16 June EU forces under attack returned fire and killed two attackers (C. Mace, *supra* note 438, p. 3, note 3).

2. LEGAL STATUS AND APPLICABLE LAW

Article 13 of the ARTEMIS Joint Action[460] provided that "*If required, the status of the EU-led forces in the [DRC] shall be the subject of an agreement with the Government of the [DRC] ... on the basis of Article 24 [EU Treaty]*". However, a SOFA was only concluded with Uganda, or rather, the SOFA between France and Uganda was extended to the EU,[461] and none was concluded with the DRC.

3. PARTICIPATION OF THIRD STATES[462]

Article 10 of the ARTEMIS Joint Action[463] provided for the participation of third States, without prejudice to the EU's decision-making autonomy. It authorized the PSC to "*take appropriate action with regard to participation arrangements*", to take, upon the recommendation of the Operation Commander and the EUMC, the relevant decisions on the acceptance of proposed contributions and to set up a Committee of Contributors, in case the third States provided significant military contributions.

Pursuant to this authority, the PSC accepted contributions from Hungary, Canada, Brazil and South Africa on 1 July[464] and established a Committee of Contributors on 11 July.[465] On 31 July it accepted the Cypriot participation.[466] Cyprus and Hungary only participated in the headquarters, whereas Canada and South Africa sent troops and Brazil did both.[467] The participation of Canada, South Africa and Brazil lasted until 5 July.[468]

---

460 *Supra* note 444.

461 See EU Documents 12225/03 (4 September 2003) and 10773/03 (26 June 2003, partially in the public domain) and the text of and information on the French-Ugandan SOFA of 18 June 2003 (2227 *U.N.T.S.* 267 and *Journal Officiel de la République Française*, 29 August 2003) available online at www.doc.diplomatie.fr/BASIS/pacte/webext/bilat/DDD/20030063.pdf.

462 See also A. Abas, *supra* note 438, pp. 150–152.

463 *Supra* note 444.

464 PSC Decision of 1 July 2003 on the acceptance of third States' contributions to the European Union military operation in the Democratic Republic of Congo (DRC/1/2003–2003/500/CFSP), *O.J. L* 170, 9 July 2003, p. 19.

465 PSC Decision of 11 July 2003 on the setting up of the Committee of Contributors for the European Union military operation in the Democratic Republic of Congo (DRC 2/2003–2003/529/CFSP), *O.J. L* 184, 23 July 2003, p. 13.

466 PSC Decision of 31 July 2003 amending the Political and Security Committee Decision DRC/1/2003 on the acceptance of third States' contributions to the EU military operation in the Democratic Republic of Congo (DRC/3/2003–2003/605/CFSP), *O.J. L* 206, 15 August 2003, p. 32.

467 Council fact sheet on ARTEMIS, July 2003.

468 G. Lindstrom, *supra* note 353, p. 120.

The short time limits may explain why no participation agreements seem to have been concluded (the ARTEMIS Joint Action did not provide for agreements under Article 24 EU Treaty[469]), except with Cyprus,[470] even though the Council did adopt a model participation agreement specifically for this operation.[471] Alternatively, the agreements exist but are not in the public domain. Either way, only the agreement with Cyprus can be discussed. This agreement more or less follows the agreements on CONCORDIA (discussed above), with the exception of the lack of contribution to the common costs.[472]

E. PROXIMA (FYROM)[473]

The EU Police Mission PROXIMA in FYROM was launched on 15 December 2003 as the EU's military operation CONCORDIA there ended.[474] It was initially established for 12 months[475] but was later extended by one year.[476] After its termination on 14 December 2005, it was followed by the EU Police *Advisory* Team EUPAT (discussed below in Section N of this chapter).

PROXIMA had the competences to monitor, mentor and advise the local police, in order to support, *inter alia*, the consolidation of law and order, including the

---

469 This provision reads: "*1. When it is necessary to conclude an agreement with one or more States or international organisations in implementation of this title, the Council may authorise the Presidency, assisted by the Commission as appropriate, to open negotiations to that effect. Such agreements shall be concluded by the Council on a recommendation from the Presidency. 2. The Council shall act unanimously when the agreement covers an issue for which unanimity is required for the adoption of internal decisions. 3. When the agreement is envisaged in order to implement a joint action or common position, the Council shall act by a qualified majority in accordance with Article 23(2). […] 5. No agreement shall be binding on a Member State whose representative in the Council states that it has to comply with the requirements of its own constitutional procedure; the other members of the Council may agree that the agreement shall nevertheless apply provisionally. 6. Agreements concluded under the conditions set out by this Article shall be binding on the institutions of the Union*". See extensively *infra*, Chapter 6.B.

470 Agreement between the European Union and the Republic of Cyprus on the participation of the Republic of Cyprus in the European Union Forces (EUF) in the Democratic Republic of Congo, *O.J. L* 253, 7 October 2003, p. 22/23.

471 EU Doc. 11468/03, 16 July 2003.

472 The agreement is also less extensive, but this is logical as it only concerns participation in a headquarters.

473 See generally www.consilium.europa.eu/showPage.aspx?id=584&lang=en.

474 Council Joint Action of 29 September 2003 on the European Union Police Mission in the Former Yugoslav Republic of Macedonia (EUPOL "Proxima") (2003/681/CFSP), *O.J. L* 249, 1 October 2003, p. 66. On the EU's involvement in FYROM and CONCORDIA, see above, I.2.

475 *Id.*, Article 14 .

476 Council Joint Action of 22 November 2004 on the extension of the European Union Police Mission in the Former Yugoslav Republic of Macedonia (EUPOL PROXIMA) (2004/789/CFSP), *O.J. L* 348, 24 November 2004, p. 40.

fight against organized crime, the implementation of the comprehensive reform of the Ministry of the Interior, including the police, the creation of a border police, the local police in building confidence within the population and enhanced police cooperation with neighbouring States.[477] Although executive functions were excluded (i.e. the mission police would not itself maintain law and order), PROXIMA was authorized to have an armed protection unit, unlike the EUPM.[478]

The strength of the mission was up to around 200 police officers and civilians,[479] coming from the 15 'old' Member States, nine 'new' Member States and Turkey, Norway, Switzerland and Ukraine (see also below) and 140 local staff.[480] The operation was initially led by Commissioner Bart D'Hooge,[481] who was succeeded by Mr. Jürgen Paul Scholz.[482] PROXIMA had, in principle, a headquarters in Skopje, one central co-location unit at the Ministry of Interior level and other units co-located within FYROM at appropriate levels.[483] The PSC exercised, under the responsibility of the Council, the political control and strategic direction of the mission, and was authorized to take the relevant decisions.[484] The PSC could therefore amend the operation plan, the chain of command and the rules of engagement, but the powers of decision with respect to the objectives and termination of the operation remained vested in the Council.[485] The Joint Action extending the mission added that the EUSR for FYROM "*shall provide local political guidance to the Police Head of Mission [and] shall ensure coordination with other EU actors as well as relations with host party authorities and media*".[486] The EUSR also acted as the communication channel between the SG/HR and the Head of Mission.[487]

---

477 Joint Actions 2003/681/CFSP and 2004/789/CFSP, *supra* notes 474 and 476, Article 3.

478 Articles 9(3) and 8(3)-(7) PROXIMA SOMA, *infra* note 494.

479 See the fact sheet at www.consilium.europa.eu/uedocs/cmsUpload/ProximaBrochure.pdf. This number was not maintained throughout the operation.

480 See www.eupol-proxima.org (last visited 25 September 2005, no longer active). Ireland was not represented anymore in the later stages of the operation.

481 Council Decision of 29 September 2003 concerning the appointment of the Head of Mission/Police Commissioner of the European Union Police Mission (EUPOL) in the Former Yugoslav Republic of Macedonia (2003/682/CFSP), *O.J. L* 249, 1 October 2003, p. 70.

482 PSC Decision of 30 November 2004 concerning the appointment of the Head of Mission of the EU Police Mission in the former Yugoslav Republic of Macedonia, EUPOL Proxima (PROXIMA/2/2004–2004/846/EC), *O.J. L* 367, 14 December 2004, p. 29.

483 Joint Actions 2003/681/CFSP and 2004/789/CFSP, *supra* notes 474 and 476, Article 4.

484 *Id.*, Article 8.

485 Joint Action 2003/681/CFSP, *supra* note 474, Article 8. Under Joint Action 2004/789/CFSP, *supra* note 476, the power to appoint the Head of Mission was added (and was exercised by the PSC, see *supra* note 482) but rules of engagement were dropped. However, since the listing does not appear to have been exhaustive and the latter power was not explicitly reserved for the Council, this may not have made a difference.

486 Joint Action 2004/789/CFSP, *supra* note 476, Article 8(2).

487 Joint Actions 2003/681/CFSP and 2004/789/CFSP, *supra* notes 474 and 476, both Article 7.

The mission costs initially foreseen were up to 15.006 million euros out of the Community budget,[488] while costs related to the police officers seconded by Participating States were to be borne by them, except *per diems*.[489] In January 2004, up to 6.555 million euros for *per diems* of EUR 100 per person for 2004 out of the Community budget were added[490] and the Joint Action extending the mission fixed the financial reference amount covering the expenditure related to the extended mission at 15.95 million euros.[491]

1. MANDATE

PROXIMA, like CONCORDIA, was undertaken following a request by FYROM[492] and was, at least partly, covered under the EU's role welcomed in UN Security Council Resolution 1371 of 26 September 2001 (as noted above in I.2). Consequently, the main legal basis for the operation was the consent of the FYROM government.

2. LEGAL STATUS AND APPLICABLE LAW

Article 13 of the PROXIMA Joint Action provided for the conclusion of a SOMA in accordance with Article 24 EU Treaty, and the SG/HR was authorized to negotiate such arrangements on the Presidency's behalf.[493] The SOMA was concluded only four days before the start of the mission.[494]

Pursuant to Article 2 of this SOMA, the mission forces, headquarters and assets (EUPOL PROXIMA) were to respect the laws and regulations of FYROM, including those regarding the protection of the environment and cultural

488 Joint Action 2003/681/CFSP, *supra* note 474, Article 10.

489 Joint Actions 2003/681/CFSP and 2004/789/CFSP, *supra* notes 474 and 476, both Article 6(2).

490 Council Joint Action of 26 January 2004 amending Joint Action 2003/681/CFSP on the European Union Police Mission in the Former Yugoslav Republic of Macedonia (EUPOL Proxima) (2004/87/CFSP), *O.J. L* 21, 28 January 2004, p. 31.

491 Joint Action 2004/789/CFSP, *supra* note 476, Article 10.

492 Joint Action 2003/681/CFSP, *supra* note 474, 6th consideration preamble. The extension of the operation was also based on such a request, see Joint Action 2004/789/CFSP, *supra* note 476, 8th consideration preamble.

493 *Supra* note 474, Article 13(1).

494 Agreement between the European Union and the Former Yugoslav Republic of Macedonia on the status and activities of the European Union Police Mission in the Former Yugoslav Republic of Macedonia (EUPOL Proxima), *O.J. L* 16, 23 January 2004, p. 65/66. Pursuant to its Article 18(1), this agreement shall enter into force upon written notification of the Parties that the internal requirements have been complied with. However, the EU Council's agreements database (*supra* note 398) does not mention a FYROM notification.

heritage, and mission staff were to refrain from any activity incompatible with the impartial and international nature of their duties or inconsistent with the SOMA.

The privileges and immunities of EUPOL PROXIMA and EUPOL PROXIMA personnel were governed by respectively Articles 5 and 6. EUPOL PROXIMA was granted the status equivalent to that of a diplomatic mission, with the corresponding inviolability and immunity from the criminal, civil, and administrative jurisdiction of FYROM, in accordance with the Vienna Convention on Diplomatic Relations.[495] EUPOL PROXIMA personnel were granted all privileges and immunities of diplomatic agents and the mission's administrative and technical staff enjoyed a status equivalent of that of administrative and technical staff from sending States employed in diplomatic missions. However, for the first time in an EU SOMA/SOFA, it was stipulated that the SG/HR "*shall, with the explicit consent of the competent authority of the Sending State, waive the immunity enjoyed by EUPOL Proxima personnel where such immunity would impede the course of justice and it can be waived without prejudice to the interests of the EU*". Local personnel employed by EUPOL PROXIMA who were nationals of or permanently resident in the Host Party enjoyed the status enjoyed by locally employed staff in diplomatic missions in FYROM (Article 7).

While FYROM was responsible for the security of EUPOL PROXIMA personnel, EUPOL PROXIMA did have the right to establish, within the Mission, an armed protection element of around 30 police officers to ensure the protection and possible rescue of EUPOL PROXIMA and local personnel, as well as EUMM or OSCE personnel and this element had the right to use all means necessary, including weapons (see also Article 9(3)), to perform its tasks in accordance with rules determined by the EU, though it did not have an executive policing role (Article 8).

In respect of claims for death, injury, damage or loss, Article 14 distinguished between two categories of claims. Participating States or the EU were not obliged to reimburse claims arising out of activities in connection with civil disturbances, protection of the EU mission (personnel) or which were incidental to operational necessities. Any other claim of a civil law character, to which the Mission or any member thereof was a party and over which the courts of the Host Party did not have jurisdiction because of the SOMA, was to be submitted to the Head of Mission and was to be dealt with by separate arrangements establishing procedures for settling claims, after previous consent of the State concerned.

---

495 Vienna, 18 April 1961, 500 *U.N.T.S.* 95.

As in the EUPM, a State or Community institution having seconded a staff member was responsible for answering any claims linked to the secondment, from or concerning the staff member and was also responsible for bringing any action against the secondee.[496]

3. PARTICIPATION OF THIRD STATES

Article 9 of the PROXIMA Joint Action[497] provided for the participation of third States, distinguishing between the acceding States which were invited and other States which could be invited, without prejudice to EU decision-making autonomy. It authorized the PSC to take, upon the recommendation of the Head of Mission and the Committee for Civilian Aspects of Crisis Management, the relevant decisions on acceptance of proposed contributions and to take "*appropriate action with regard to participation arrangements*". Furthermore, third Participating States were to bear the cost of sending the police officers and/or civilian staff seconded by them and were to contribute to the running costs of PROXIMA "*as appropriate*". Moreover, third Participating States had the same rights and obligations in day-to-day management of the operation as participating EU Member States. Article 9(4) did not require a "significant" contribution, as was demanded in the previous operations but ignored or liberally interpreted in practice (as noted above), thus reflecting existing practice. A committee of contributors was set up.[498]

Detailed arrangements regarding third State participation were to be the subject of an agreement under Article 24 EU Treaty. On 10 February 2004, the PSC accepted the participation of Turkey, Norway, Switzerland and Ukraine,[499] and agreements with these countries were concluded.[500] These agreements are very similar to the ones for the EUPM, although the number of staff to be seconded was not specified and for the common costs only a voluntary contribution was requested. All personnel remained under the full command of their national

---

496 Joint Actions 2003/681/CFSP and 2004/789/CFSP, *supra* notes 474 and 476, both Article 13(2).

497 *Supra* note 474 and Joint Action 2004/789/CFSP, *supra* note 476, Article 9.

498 PSC Decision on the setting-up of the Committee of Contributors for the European Union Police Mission (EUPOL PROXIMA) in the former Yugoslav Republic of Macedonia (FYROM) (PROXIMA/3/2005), EU Council Doc. 6915/05, 3 March 2005.

499 PSC Decision of 10 February 2004 on the acceptance of non-acceding third States' contributions to the European Union Police Mission in the former Yugoslav Republic of Macedonia (EUPOL "Proxima") (PROXIMA/1/2004–2004/190/CFSP), *O.J. L* 60, 27 February 2004, p. 54.

500 All published in *O.J. L* 354, 30 November 2004 (respectively at pp. 89/90, 85/86, 77/78 and 81/82). According to the EU Council's agreements database (*supra* note 398) the agreement with Turkey only entered into force on 1 April 2008 and that with Ukraine did not enter into force but was provisionally applied from 8 July 2004.

authorities, who transferred operational control to the Head of Mission. The clause on claims included a mutual waiver for most claims between Participating States, which was not the case in participation agreements for earlier operations.

In addition, nine acceding Member States participated (all but Malta).[501] There seem to have been no agreements with the acceding States, so presumably this was not deemed necessary in light of their imminent accession.

F. EUJUST THEMIS (GEORGIA)[502]

After two military and two police operations, the EU launched its first rule of law mission, EUJUST THEMIS in Georgia, in June 2004.[503] The mission could to some extent be seen as a conflict prevention effort: according to the preamble of the THEMIS Joint Action "*The security situation in Georgia is stable but may deteriorate with potentially serious repercussions on regional and international security and the strengthening of democracy and the rule of law. A commitment of EU political effort and resources will help to embed stability in the region*".[504] In any event, this operation clearly intensified the EU's role in this country.[505]

On 16 July, the Council approved the Operational Plan for EUJUST THEMIS and launched the mission, which lasted 12 months and was successfully concluded on 14 July 2005.[506] Ms. Sylvie Pantz was the Head of Mission of THEMIS,[507] which had a Head Office in Tbilisi and experts co-located at several key positions with the Georgian authorities.[508] Mission experts were seconded

501 See www.eupol-proxima.org (last visited 25 September 2005; no longer active).

502 See generally www.consilium.europa.eu/showPage.aspx?id=701&lang=EN and *ESDP Newsletter* No. 1, December 2005, pp. 24–25 (www.consilium.europa.eu/showPage.aspx?id=1090&lang=en).

503 Council Joint Action of 28 June 2004 on the European Union Rule of Law Mission in Georgia, EUJUST THEMIS (2004/523/CFSP), *O.J. L* 228, 29 June 2004, p. 21.

504 *Id.*, 3rd consideration preamble.

505 On EU relations with Georgia, see http://ec.europa.eu/world/where/georgia/index_en.htm and the EU fact sheet of 26 October 2004 at www.consilium.europa.eu/uedocs/cmsUpload/Factsheet%20THEMIS%20041026.pdf, pp. 4–5.

506 EU fact sheet, *supra* previous note, and EU Doc. THE/03 (update 3), 22 July 2005, available online at www.consilium.europa.eu/uedocs/cmsUpload/050722_Themis_UPDATE_3_final_briefing.pdf. The mission was followed by an enhanced mandate of the EUSR for the South Caucasus; see Council conclusions of 18 July 2005, EU Doc. 10813/05 (Presse 177); the SOMA for this follow on action (Agreement between the European Union and the Government of Georgia on the status in Georgia of the European Union Special Representative (EUSR) for the South Caucasus and his/her support team, Brussels, 12 May 2006, *O.J. L* 135, 23 May 2006, p. 14/15), entered into force on 11 August 2006.

507 PSC Decision of 30 June 2004 concerning the appointment of the Head of Mission of the EU Rule of Law Mission in Georgia, in the context of ESDP, EUJUST THEMIS (THEMIS/1/2004–2004/540/CFSP), *O.J. L* 239, 9 July 2004, p. 35.

508 THEMIS Joint Action, *supra* note 503, Article 3.

by EU Member States or institutions and international and local staff were recruited on a contractual basis as required[509] and would number about ten, plus some local staff.[510] As in other missions, the PSC exercised, under the responsibility of the Council, the political control and strategic direction of the mission and was authorized to take the relevant decisions, including the powers to appoint a Head of Mission and to amend the operation plan and the chain of command but excluding the powers of decision with respect to the objectives and termination of the operation.[511] In this mission too, an EUSR functioned at the level between the SG/HR and the Head of Mission.[512] There was no participation of third States due to the limited size of the mission.[513]

The mission of THEMIS was, in coordination with and complementary to EC and other donors' programmes, to assist in "*the development of a horizontal governmental strategy guiding the reform process for all relevant stakeholders within the criminal justice sector*". It was also to "*help develop an overall policy and improve top-level planning and performance capabilities in the areas identified as requiring urgent assistance*".[514]

The financial reference amount intended to cover the expenditure related to the mission was initially set at 2.05 million euros.[515] It was later raised to 2,307,873 euros.[516] Member States – apparently in contrast to institutions – bore the costs related to the mission experts seconded by it, except *per diem* allowances.[517] Themis was followed by a reinforced EUSR support team and a Border Support Team[518] and, in 2008, by EUMM Georgia (see below, Section V of this chapter).

1. MANDATE

THEMIS was undertaken at the request of the Georgian authorities,[519] which forms the legal basis for this mission.

509 *Id.*, Article 6(2)-(3).
510 Information previously available at http://ue.eu.int/cms3_fo/showPage.asp?id=701&lang=en &mode=g.
511 THEMIS Joint Action, *supra* note 503, Article 9.
512 *Id.*, Article 8.
513 *Id.*, 6th consideration preamble.
514 *Id.*, Article 2.
515 *Id.*, Article 10.
516 Council Joint Action of 13 September 2004 amending Joint Action 2004/523/CFSP on the European Union Rule of Law Mission in Georgia, EUJUST THEMIS (2004/638/CFSP), *O.J. L* 291, 14 September 2004, p. 17.
517 THEMIS Joint Action, *supra* note 503, Article 6(2).
518 See EU Council Doc. 10418/06 of 12 June 2006, §10. See also *infra* note 881.
519 THEMIS Joint Action, *supra* note 503, 4th consideration preamble.

2. LEGAL STATUS AND APPLICABLE LAW

Pursuant to Article 7 of the THEMIS Joint Action,[520] a SOMA was concluded on 3 December 2004, i.e. more than four months after the start of the mission.[521] It is not clear whether this SOMA ever entered into force.[522]

Article 2 of the SOMA demanded that the mission and mission personnel respect the laws and regulations of Georgia and obliged mission staff to refrain from any activity incompatible with the impartial and international nature of their duties or inconsistent with the SOMA. Moreover, under the THEMIS Joint Action, "*both during and after the mission, the mission experts shall exercise the greatest discretion with regard to all facts and information relating to the mission*".[523]

The privileges and immunities of THEMIS and THEMIS personnel were governed by respectively Articles 5 and 6 THEMIS SOMA and seem identical to those of EUPOL PROXIMA.[524] EUPOL PROXIMA personnel were granted all privileges and immunities of diplomatic agents and the clause on waiver of immunity[525] was, *mutatis mutandis*, identical to that in the PROXIMA SOMA.[526] Apparently, there was some discussion over the extent of staff immunities, since delegations noted in the Council that the provisions of the draft Agreement were without prejudice to provisions that might be agreed for future missions and that, in particular "*the extent of the privileges and immunities foreseen for staff of the Mission [did] not constitute a precedent*".[527] Since the only difference with PROXIMA was the broader immunity of administrative and technical staff,[528] this was presumably what was referred to.

In respect of claims for death, injury, damage or loss, Article 13 distinguishes between two categories of claims similarly to the PROXIMA SOMA. It may be added that a State or Community institution having seconded a staff member was responsible for answering any claims linked to the secondment, from or

---

520 *Supra* note 503.

521 Agreement between the European Union and Georgia on the status and activities of the European Union Rule of Law Mission in Georgia, EUJUST THEMIS, *O.J. L* 389, 30 December 2004, p. 41/42.

522 The Council's agreements database (*supra* note 398) does not give a date of entry into force nor does it mention a provisional application.

523 THEMIS Joint Action, *supra* note 503, Article 4(3).

524 See the PROXIMA SOMA, *supra* note 494, discussed above in I.4.

525 Article 6(2) THEMIS SOMA.

526 Compare with Article 6(3) PROXIMA SOMA (*supra* note 494).

527 EU Doc. 10651/04, 18 June 2004, §3.

528 Compare Article 6 THEMIS SOMA with Article 6 PROXIMA SOMA (*supra* note 494).

concerning the staff member and was responsible for bringing any action against the secondee.[529]

Finally, on 10 July, the Government of Georgia adopted a decree on co-operation between EUJUST THEMIS and all the major stakeholders in Georgia.[530]

G. ALTHEA (BiH)[531]

By taking over, on 2 December 2004, the military presence in BiH from, the NATO-led Stabilisation Force (SFOR)[532] through operation ALTHEA, the EU was undertaking its biggest and most challenging mission at the time and was further enhancing its role in BiH, where it was already very active, including with the EUPM (see above, Section B of this chapter).

ALTHEA had been prepared for quite some time and the Council adopted a Joint Action on this operation already in July 2004, appointing the Operation Commander, D-SACEUR,[533] and the EU Force Commander (initially General A. David Leakey) and designating the EU Operational Headquarters as being located at SHAPE.[534] The Head of the EU Command Element at Naples, General

---

529 THEMIS Joint Action, *supra* note 503, Article 7(2).

530 EU fact sheet on THEMIS, *supra* note 505, p. 2.

531 See generally www.consilium.europa.eu/showPage.aspx?id=745&lang=en; http://euforbih.org/eufor; the three-monthly reports on Althea to the UN Security Council, most recently UN Doc. S/2009/525 of 8 October 2009; K. Prieur, 'Europäische Sicherheits- und Verteidigungspolitik in der Praxis: der Einsatz "ALTHEA" in Bosnien und Herzegowina', in D. Weingärtner (ed.), *Einsatz der Bundeswehr im Ausland: Rechtsgrundlagen und Rechtspraxis*, Baden-Baden, Nomos, 2007, pp. 29–34 and *ESDP Newsletter* No. 1, December 2005, pp. 20–23 and *ESDP Newsletter* No. 4, Summer 2007, pp. 16–18 (both www.consilium.europa.eu/showPage.aspx?id=1090&lang=en).

532 On SFOR, see www.nato.int/issues/sfor/index.html.

533 Consequently, following appointment of a new D-SACEUR, the Operation Commander was also replaced; see PSC Decision of 24 September 2004 on the appointment of an EU Operation Commander for the European Union military operation in Bosnia and Herzegovina (BiH/2/2004–2004/733/CFSP), *O.J. L* 324, 27 October 2004, p. 22 and PSC Decision of 25 September 2007 on the appointment of an EU Operation Commander for the European Union military operation in Bosnia and Herzegovina (BiH/10/2007–2007/724/CFSP), *O.J. L* 293, 10 November 2007, p. 8.

534 Council Joint Action of 12 July 2004 on the European Union military operation in Bosnia and Herzegovina (2004/570/CFSP), *O.J.* L 252, 28 July 2004, p. 10, especially Articles 2–4. General Leakey was succeeded as Force Commander by General Gian Marco Chiarini (PSC Decision of 14 June 2005 on the appointment of an EU Force Commander for the European Union Military Operation in Bosnia and Herzegovina (BiH/6/2005 – 2005/483/CFSP), *O.J. L* 173, 6 July 2005, p. 14); Rear Admiral Hans-Jochen Witthauer (PSC Decision of 27 June 2006 on the appointment of an EU Force Commander for the European Union Military Operation in Bosnia and Herzegovina (BiH/9/2006–2006/497/CFSP), *O.J. L.* 196, 18 July 2006, p. 25); Major

Ciro Cocozza, was appointed in October 2004[535] and the operation plan was adopted that same month.[536] The decision on the launching of ALTHEA was made on 27 November 2004 and the operation commenced on 2 December 2004.[537] No date was fixed for the end of this operation.[538] ALTHEA is a mission with recourse to NATO assets and is governed by the EU-NATO arrangements mentioned above (Chapter 2.C) but the entire chain of command of the EU Force remains under the political control and strategic direction of the EU, after consultation with NATO, and NATO is only informed by the PSC and by the Chairman of the EUMC (CEUMC).[539] Initially, 7,000 troops were deployed[540] from more than 30 countries.[541] The Force headquarters are established in Sarajevo.[542] Twenty-two Member States participate(d) in ALTHEA (all but Denmark,[543] Cyprus and Malta[544]), as did 11 third States (see details below).[545] The force includes an Integrated Police Unit (IPU) style capability with executive

General Ignacio Martin Villalain (PSC Decision of 25 September 2007 on the appointment of an EU Force Commander for the European Union military operation in Bosnia and Herzegovina (BiH/11/2007–2007/711/CFSP), *O.J. L* 288, 6 November 2007, p. 60) and Major General Stefano Castagnotto (PSC Decision of 21 November 2008 on the appointment of an EU Force Commander for the European Union military operation in Bosnia and Herzegovina (BiH/14/2008–2008/895/CFSP), *O.J. L* 319, 29 November 2008, p. 80). At least pending the entry into force of the EU SOFA, the status of the Operational Headquarters required an *ad hoc* status agreement, which took the form of an Exchange of Letters between Belgium and the Althea Commander concerning the privileges and immunities of the Althea OHQ at SHAPE and of its staff, dated 10 and 14 July 2006.

535 PSC Decision of 19 October 2004 on the appointment of the Head of the EU Command Element at Naples for the European Union military operation in Bosnia and Herzegovina (BiH/4/2004 – 2004/821/CFSP), *O.J. L* 357, 2 December 2004, p. 38. He was succeeded by Lieutenant General Eduardo Zamarripa; see PSC Decision of 25 September 2007 on the appointment of the Head of the EU Command Element at Naples for the European Union military operation in Bosnia and Herzegovina (BiH/12/2007–2007/725/CFSP), *O.J. L* 293, 10 November 2007, p. 9.

536 Council Conclusions of 11 October 2004.

537 Council Decision of 25 November 2004 on the launching of the European Union military operation in Bosnia and Herzegovina (2004/803/CFSP), *O.J. L* 353, 27 November 2004, p. 21.

538 The operation shall end on a date to be decided by the Council, see ALTHEA Joint Action, *supra* note 534, Article 17(2). See also Council Decision 2004/803/CFSP, *supra* previous note, Article 3.

539 ALTHEA Joint Action, *supra* note 534, Articles 1(3) and 13(1).

540 See the Council fact sheet of 29 November 2004 at www.consilium.europa.eu/uedocs/cmsUpload/041129%20Althea%20update%203.pdf.

541 EU Doc. S0337/04, 2 December 2004.

542 See the Council fact sheet on ALTHEA, *supra* note 540.

543 ALTHEA Joint Action, *supra* note 534, 19th consideration preamble.

544 Cyprus, and until recently Malta, did not have a security agreement with NATO and could not participate in EU operations with recourse to NATO assets, such as ALTHEA. See also *supra* note 214.

545 Information previously accessible at www.euforbih.org/organisation/organisation.htm. On 31 July 2009, five third States participated; see www.euforbih.org/eufor/index.php?option=com_content&task=view&id=144&Itemid=58.

powers.[546] By the end of 2007, the number of troops had been reduced to some 2,450 (from 31 countries)[547] and by May 2009 to 2,200 (from 27 countries).[548]

ALTHEA's mission is twofold: first, to provide deterrence and continued compliance with Annexes 1A and 2 of the Dayton Agreement and second, to contribute to a safe and secure environment in BiH.[549]

As in previous operations, the PSC, under the responsibility of the Council, exercises the political control and strategic direction of the EU military operation and is authorized to take the relevant decisions, which include amending the Operation Plan, the chain of command and the rules of engagement and decisions on the appointment of the EU Operation and Force Commander, while the powers of decision with respect to the objectives and termination of the EU military operation remain vested in the Council.[550] The EUMC monitors the proper execution of the operation conducted under the responsibility of the EU Operation Commander, with the Chairman of the EUMC acting as point of contact for the Operation Commander.[551] There is a six-monthly review.[552]

A number of measures have been adopted to ensure coherence of ALTHEA with other EU actions in BiH, including the EUPM, with a key role for the EUSR.[553]

As to financing, the common costs are administered by Athena, i.e. the financing mechanism set up to administer common costs of ESDP operations,[554] and the initial financial reference amount for the common costs was set at 71.7 million euros.[555]

---

546 See the Council fact sheet on ALTHEA, *supra* note 540. An Integrated Police Unit is a multinational force composed mainly of police forces, but includes military components (see www.euforbih.org/forum/special/html/t241a.htm, no longer active). On the IPU, see www.euforbih.org/eufor/index.php?option=com_content&task=view&id=16&Itemid=32.

547 See www.euforbih.org/eufor/index.php?option=com_content&task=view&id=145&Itemid=62 as consulted in December 2007.

548 Factsheet Althea/15, May 2009, www.consilium.europa.eu/uedocs/cmsUpload/090514-Factsheet_EUFOR_Althea-version15_EN.pdf.

549 ALTHEA Joint Action, *supra* note 534, art 1(1).

550 *Id.*, Article 6.

551 *Id.*, Article 8.

552 *Id.*, Article 16.

553 *Id.*, Article 7. See also Council Joint Action of 8 November 2007 amending Joint Action 2004/570/CFSP on the European Union military operation in Bosnia and Herzegovina (2007/720/CFSP), *O.J. L* 291, 9 November 2007, p. 29 and Council Joint Action of 19 November 2007 amending Joint Action 2007/87/CFSP amending and extending the mandate of the European Union Special Representative in Bosnia and Herzegovina (2007/748/CFSP),*O.J. L* 303, 21 November 2007, p. 38.

554 See the Council Decisions cited *supra* note 342.

555 ALTHEA Joint Action, *supra* note 534, Article 12.

A possible evolution of the operation to a non-executive capacity-building and training operation is under consideration and the ongoing planning for this is kept under regular review so that a decision on the future of the operation can be made once the necessary conditions have been met, having taken into account political developments, including the future role of the EU Special Representative.[556]

1. MANDATE

The EU's intention to take over from SFOR was welcomed in UN Security Council Resolution 1551 of 9 July 2004 (§10). However, the legal situation is somewhat complicated since SFOR, although mandated by the UN Security Council, also worked on the basis of the Dayton Agreements, which specifically envisaged a NATO-led force.[557] This was solved by the Security Council, which, in its Resolution 1575 of 22 November 2004 authorized "*the Member States acting through or in cooperation with the EU to establish for an initial planned period of 12 months a multinational stabilization force (EUFOR) as a legal successor to SFOR under unified command and control, which will fulfil its missions in relation to the implementation of Annex 1-A and Annex 2 of the Peace Agreement in cooperation with the NATO HQ presence in accordance with the arrangements agreed between NATO and the EU as communicated to the Security Council in their letters of 19 November 2004, which recognize that the EUFOR will have the main peace stabilization role under the military aspects of the Peace Agreement*" (§10). However, the Security Council did acknowledge the support of the Bosnian authorities for this solution and their confirmation that both the EU force and the remaining NATO presence are the legal successors to SFOR (§7).[558] Consequently, the combination of the Dayton Agreement and Resolution 1575 constitutes the legal basis for ALTHEA.

Resolution 1575 also authorized the new NATO presence (§11). Furthermore, it stated that references in the Dayton Agreement and relevant Resolutions to IFOR (Implementation Force, SFOR's predecessor) and/or SFOR, NATO and the North Atlantic Council (NAC, NATO's main political decision-making body) shall henceforth be read as applying, as appropriate, to the NATO presence, EUFOR,

---

556 Conclusions of the External Relations Council of 18–19 May 2009 (EU Council Doc. 10009/09 (Presse 137), p. 16). On the role of the EUSR/High Representative, see *supra* notes 365–366 and the accompanying text.

557 See *supra* note 388, Annex 1-A, Article 1. While Article 1(a) seems sufficiently general to cover an EU force ("*Member States or regional organizations and arrangements*"), the remainder of Article 1 frequently refers to NATO.

558 This will also be discussed below in Chapter 6.F.

the EU and the PSC and Council of the EU (§12, see also below) and accorded both missions the necessary powers under the Dayton Agreements and the relevant Security Council Resolutions (§§14–16). It also expressed the intention to consider the terms of further authorization as necessary in the light of developments in the implementation of the Dayton agreement and the situation in BiH (§13). Indeed, this UN mandate was subsequently extended for one-year periods by UN Security Council Resolutions 1639 of 21 November 2005, 1722 of 21 November 2006, 1785 of 21 November 2007 and 1845 of 20 November 2008.

2. LEGAL STATUS AND APPLICABLE LAW

Regarding the SOFA, a similar problem arose as with the mandate because the SFOR SOFA was included in the Dayton Agreement and only applies to a NATO-led force.[559] Here to, the two Security Council Resolutions already cited provide a solution. Firstly, pursuant to §20 of Resolution 1551 the status of forces agreements currently contained in the Dayton Agreement applies provisionally in respect to the (then) proposed EU mission and its forces, including from the point of their build-up in BiH, in anticipation of the concurrence of the parties to those agreements to that effect. Secondly, according to §12 of Resolution 1575, all references to (the) NATO (operation) in the Dayton Agreement, "*in particular in Annex 1-A and its appendices*" – which include the SFOR SOFA – shall henceforth be read as applying, as appropriate, to (the) NATO (presence) and to the EU (mission). The SFOR SOFA is thereby made applicable to ALTHEA.

It may suffice to mention the key elements of the SOFA, replacing 'NATO' by 'EU'. The SOFA makes applicable, *mutatis mutandis*, the provisions of the Convention on the Privileges and Immunities of the United Nations[560] to the EU and those concerning experts on mission to EU personnel involved in the Operation, except as otherwise provided for in the SOFA (§2). As experts on mission, EU personnel are immune from personal arrest or detention (§8) and EU military personnel are subject to the exclusive jurisdiction of their national elements in respect of any offences committed by them in BiH (§7). All mission personnel must respect the laws of BiH "*insofar as it is compatible with the entrusted tasks/mandate*" and shall refrain from activities not compatible with the nature of the Operation (§3). EU personnel may possess and carry arms if authorized to do so by their orders (§4). Local personnel hired also enjoy some privileges and immunities (§16). The SOFA also applies to the civilian and military personnel, property and assets of national elements/units of EU States,

---

559 See ***supra*** note 388, Appendix B to Annex 1A, especially §1.
560 13 February 1946, 1 *U.N.T.S.* 15.

acting in connection with the Operation or the relief for the civilian population (§19) and BiH shall accord non-EU States and their personnel participating in the Operation the same privileges and immunities as those accorded under this agreement to EU States and personnel (§21). Claims for damage or injury to government personnel or property, or to private personnel or property of BiH shall be submitted through Bosnian governmental authorities to the designated NATO Representatives (§15). Finally, supplemental arrangements may be concluded (§20).

3. PARTICIPATION OF THIRD STATES

The non-EU European NATO members and Canada are allowed to participate if they so wish and candidate Member States, potential partners and other third States may also be invited to participate in the operation, obviously without prejudice to the decision-making autonomy of the EU.[561] Third States making "*significant military contributions*" have the same rights and obligations in day-to-day management of the operation as participating EU Member States.[562] The PSC is authorized to take the relevant decisions on acceptance of proposed contributions, upon the recommendation of the Operation Commander and the EUMC, and to set up a committee of contributors.[563] As in previous missions, detailed arrangements regarding third State participation are to be the subject of an agreement under Article 24 EU Treaty, but where the EU and a third State have concluded an agreement establishing a framework for the participation of this State in the EU operations, such an agreement shall apply.[564] This presumably applied to Bulgaria and Romania (who have become EU Member States in the meantime) and to Norway and Turkey.[565]

On 21 September 2004, the PSC accepted contributions from Argentina, Bulgaria, Canada, Chile, Morocco, New Zealand, Norway, Romania, Switzerland and Turkey[566] and on 3 November 2004 also from Albania.[567] A committee of

561 ALTHEA Joint Action, *supra* note 534, Article 11(1).

562 *Id.*, Article 11(4).

563 *Id.*, Article 11(2) and (5).

564 *Id.*, Article 11(3).

565 See *supra*, Chapter 2.D.1, especially notes 239, 240, 243 and 241.

566 PSC Decision of 21 September 2004 on the acceptance of third States' contributions to the European Union military operation in Bosnia and Herzegovina (BiH/1/2004 – 2004/732/CFSP), *O.J. L* 324, 27 October 2004, p. 20.

567 PSC Decision of 3 November 2004 amending Decision BiH/1/2004 on the acceptance of third States' contributions to the European Union military operation in Bosnia and Herzegovina and Decision BiH/3/2004 on the setting-up of the Committee of Contributors for the

contributors was set up on 29 September 2004.[568] So far, agreements have been concluded with Switzerland,[569] Morocco,[570] Albania,[571] New Zealand,[572] Chile[573] and Argentina,[574] apparently on the basis of a mission specific model participation agreement.[575] FYROM was later added as a participant and also concluded an agreement.[576] At first sight, these agreements do not substantially differ from participation agreements in previous missions but they require no contribution to the common costs from the participating State and provide for the transfer of operational and tactical command and/or control to the EU Operation Commander,[577] who is entitled to delegate his authority. Furthermore, in July

European Union military operation in Bosnia and Herzegovina (BiH/5/2004 – 2004/822/CFSP), *O.J. L* 357, 2 December 2004, p. 39.

568 PSC Decision of 29 September 2004 on the setting-up of the Committee of Contributors for the European Union military operation in Bosnia and Herzegovina (BiH/3/2004 – 2002/739/CFSP), *O.J. L* 325, 28 October 2004, p. 64.

569 Agreement between the European Union and the Swiss Confederation on the participation of the Swiss Confederation in the European Union military crisis management operation in Bosnia and Herzegovina (operation ALTHEA), *O.J. L* 20, 22 January 2005, p. 41/42, which entered into force on 1 February 2005 and was provisionally applied from 22 December 2004.

570 Agreement between the European Union and the Kingdom of Morocco on the participation of the Kingdom of Morocco in the European Union military crisis management operation in Bosnia and Herzegovina (Operation Althea), *O.J. L* 34, 8 February 2005, p. 46/47, which has not yet entered into force but was provisionally applied from 1 February 2005.

571 Agreement between the European Union and the Republic of Albania on the participation of the Republic of Albania in the European Union military crisis management operation in Bosnia and Herzegovina (Operation Althea), *O.J. L* 65, 11 March 2005, p. 34/35, which entered into force on 1 August 2005, and was provisionally applied from 7 March 2005.

572 Agreement between the European Union and New Zealand on the participation of New Zealand in the European Union military crisis management operation in Bosnia and Herzegovina (Operation Althea), *O.J. L* 127, 20 May 2005, p. 27/28, which has not yet entered into force, but was provisionally applied from 4 May 2005.

573 Agreement between the European Union and the Republic of Chile on the participation of the Republic of Chile in the European Union military crisis management operation in Bosnia and Herzegovina (Operation ALTHEA), 25 July 2005, *O.J. L* 202, 3 August 2005, p. 39/40, which entered into force on 1 February 2009.

574 Agreement between the European Union and the Argentine Republic on the participation of the Argentine Republic in the European Union military crisis management operation in Bosnia and Herzegovina (Operation Althea), *O.J. L* 156, 18 June 2005, p. 21/22, which entered into force on 9 June 2005.

575 EU Doc. 12382/04, 14 September 2004, listed but not published in the Council's register.

576 PSC Decision of 15 March 2006 amending Decision BiH/1/2004 on the acceptance of third States' contributions to the European Union military operation in Bosnia and Herzegovina and Decision BiH/3/2004 on the setting-up of the Committee of Contributors for the European Union military operation in Bosnia and Herzegovina (BiH/8/2006–2006/267/CFSP), *O.J. L* 96, 5 April 2006, p. 14 and Agreement between the European Union and the former Yugoslav Republic of Macedonia on the participation of the former Yugoslav Republic of Macedonia in the European Union military crisis management operation in Bosnia and Herzegovina (Operation ALTHEA), *O.J. L* 188, 11 July 2006, p. 9/10 as corrected and replaced by the agreement in *O.J. L* 203, 26 July 2006, p. 11 (which has not yet entered into force).

577 For more details on kinds of command and control and their relevancy, see *supra*, Section B of this chapter, notes 188 and the accompanying text and *infra*, Chapter 8.F-G, especially notes 2200–2217 and the accompanying text.

2008, contributions by Honduras, Guatemala, El Salvador and the Dominican Republic were accepted.[578] No participation agreements appear to have been concluded with these States so far nor does it seem to be stipulated that they are exempt from common costs.

H. EUPOL KINSHASA (DRC)[579]

The EU Police Mission to Kinshasa (DRC) had its antecedents in the DRC peace and transition agreement of 17 December 2002 and especially the Memorandum on Security and the Army of 29 June 2003, which provided for the establishment of an Integrated Police Unit (IPU).[580] Following a DRC government request for EU assistance in October 2003, the PSC agreed in December 2003 that the EU should support the establishment of the IPU.[581] EUPOL KINSHASA was the third EU initiative in support of the IPU, following an initiative under the European Development Fund and an earlier Council Joint Action assisting the establishment of the IPU by contributions with funds and/or in kind to provide the government of the DRC with the law enforcement equipment, arms and ammunition necessary for the establishment of the IPU.[582]

The mission was prepared by a Planning Team[583] and was launched on 30 April 2005.[584] It was only intended to be active until the end of 2005[585] but was

---

578 PSC Decision of 29 July 2008 amending Decision BiH/1/2004 on the acceptance of third States' contributions to the European Union military operation in Bosnia and Herzegovina and Decision BiH/3/2004 on the setting-up of the Committee of Contributors for the European Union military operation in Bosnia and Herzegovina (BiH/13/2008 – 2008/712/CFSP), *O.J. L* 237, 4 September 2009, p. 90, with an up-to-date list of third States participating at the time in its Annex.

579 See generally www.consilium.europa.eu/showPage.aspx?id=788&lang=en; M. Martinelli, *supra* note 440, pp. 379–399, especially pp. 390–392 and M. Martinelli, 'Les opérations Eupol et Eusec au Congo: L'UE entre engagement et apprentissage', in B. Delcourt, M. Martinelli & E. Klimis, *L'Union européenne et la gestion de crises*, Brussels, Editions de l'Université de Bruxelles, 2008, pp. 85–101.

580 On the role of the IPU, see H. Boshoff, *Summary Overview of the Security Sector Reform Process in the DRC. ISS Situation Report*, 6 January 2005, www.iss.co.za/af/current/2005/050110DRC.pdf, pp. 11–13.

581 See the preamble of Council Joint Action of 9 December 2004 on the European Union Police Mission in Kinshasa (DRC) regarding the Integrated Police Unit (EUPOL Kinshasa) (2004/847/CFSP), *O.J. L* 367, 14 December 2004, p. 30. The EU's involvement in the DRC is discussed above in section D of this chapter.

582 Council Joint Action of 17 May 2004 on European Union support to the establishment of the Integrated Police Unit in the Democratic Republic of the Congo (DRC) (2004/494/CFSP), *O.J. L* 182, 19 May 2004, p. 41.

583 Joint Action 2004/847/CFSP, *supra* note 581, Article 1.

584 See EU Doc. S173/05 of that date, available online at www.consilium.europa.eu/uedocs/cmsUpload/050430_Visite_Afrique.en.pdf.

585 See Article 14 Joint Action 2004/847/CFSP, *supra* note 581 (expired 31 December 2005).

extended by a further 12-month period,[586] counted about 30 staff[587] under the command of the Head of Mission (Police Commissioner Adilio Custodio)[588] and was to cost no more than 4.37 million euros.[589] The mission's objective was to "*monitor, mentor, and advise the setting up and the initial running of the IPU in order to ensure that the IPU acts following the training received in the Academy Centre and according to international best practices in this field*" and was focused on the IPU chain of command.[590] As usual, the PSC exercised political control and the strategic direction of the mission.[591] Furthermore, in April 2006, the operation was reinforced and received an additional mission and mandate, namely: "*For ... the temporary reinforcement ... during the electoral process, EUPOL "Kinshasa" shall establish, as an integral part of EUPOL "Kinshasa" and under the overall security framework for the elections, a police coordination support element in order to ensure an enhanced and coordinated response of the Congolese crowd control units in Kinshasa, in case of disturbances during the electoral period. The area of responsibility shall be limited to Kinshasa. The police coordination support element, as part of EUPOL "Kinshasa", shall not have executive powers*".[592] The mandate was again extended by six months in

586 See Council Joint Action of 21 November 2005 amending and extending Joint Action 2004/847/CFSP on the European Union Police Mission in Kinshasa (DRC) regarding the Integrated Police Unit (EUPOL Kinshasa) (2005/822/CFSP), *O.J. L* 305, 24 November 2005, p. 44, 3rd consideration preamble *juncto* Article 1(6).

587 EU Doc. 15855/04 (Presse 349), 9 December 2004 (www.consilium.europa.eu/ueDocs/cms_Data/docs/pressData/en/misc/83090.pdf). On 31 August 2005, only staff from six Members States had been contracted or seconded to the mission: Belgium, France, Italy, the Netherlands, Portugal and Sweden; see COSAC Secretariat, *supra* note 353, p. 15.

588 See PSC Decision of 9 December 2004 concerning the appointment of the Head of Mission of the EU Police Mission in Kinshasa (DRC), EUPOL 'Kinshasa' (EUPOL Kinshasa/1/2004-2004/931/CFSP), *O.J. L* 396, 31 December 2004, p. 61. This appointment was extended by PSC Decision of 22 November 2005 extending the mandate of the Head of Mission of the EU Police Mission in Kinshasa (DRC), EUPOL Kinshasa (EUPOL KINSHASA/2/2005-2005/921/CFSP), *O.J. L* 335, 21 December 2005, p. 57.

589 Joint Action 2004/847/CFSP, *supra* note 581, Article 10.

590 *Id.*, Article 3. This was slightly broadened by Article 1(2) Council Joint Action 2005/847/CFSP, *supra* note 581 to include "*further advice on other issues complementary to the effective conduct of policing in DRC, and shall enhance liaison with EUSEC RD CONGO in the field of security sector reform*".

591 Joint Action 2004/847/CFSP, *supra* note 581, Articles 7 and 8.

592 See Article 1(2) Council Joint Action of 21 April 2006 amending and extending Joint Action 2004/847/CFSP on the European Union Police Mission in Kinshasa (DRC) regarding the Integrated Police Unit (EUPOL Kinshasa) (2006/300/CFSP), *O.J. L* 111, 25 April 2006, p. 12. This reinforcement was subsequently extended until the end of 2006 by Council Joint Action of 30 November 2006 amending Joint Action 2004/847/CFSP on the European Union Police Mission in Kinshasa (DRC) regarding the Integrated Police Unit (EUPOL Kinshasa) (2006/868/CFSP), *O.J. L* 335, 1 December 2006, p. 50 and then for a further three months (see next note).

December 2006.[593] This mission was then succeeded by the security sector reform police mission EUPOL RD Congo (see below, Section R of this chapter).

1. MANDATE, LEGAL STATUS, APPLICABLE LAW AND PARTICIPATION OF THIRD STATES

As noted above, this EU operation was based on the consent of the DRC government.

Article 13 of the EUPOL KINSHASA Joint Action[594] provided for the conclusion of a SOMA. A SOMA was concluded but only on 1 September 2005. It *inter alia* granted the mission and its staff protection equivalent to that of diplomatic missions and staff, including the possibility of waiver, demands respect for local law, allows the carrying of sidearms for self-defence, and contained a claims provision.[595]

The participation of third States was provided for in Article 9 EUPOL KINSHASA Joint Action,[596] and the participation of African partner nations was welcomed.[597]

I. EUSEC DRC[598]

The EU's involvement in the DRC discussed above (sections D and H of this chapter) was further extended by the launching of yet another new type of mission, namely a security sector reform mission (EUSEC DRC), in response to a

593 Council Joint Action of 7 December 2006 amending and extending Joint Action 2004/847/CFSP on the European Union Police Mission in Kinshasa (DRC) regarding the Integrated Police Unit (EUPOL Kinshasa) Extension into 2007 (2006/913/CFSP), *O.J. L* 346, 9 December 2006, p. 67, also extending the reinforcement for three months.

594 *Supra* note 581.

595 Agreement between the European Union and the Democratic Republic of the Congo on the status and activities of the European Union police mission in the Democratic Republic of the Congo (EUPOL Kinshasa), *O.J. L* 256, 1 October 2005, p. 57/58, which entered into force 1 September 2005.

596 *Supra* note 581.

597 Council Conclusions of 17 July 2006 on the DRC (available online at www.consilium.europa.eu/uedocs/cms_Data/docs/pressdata/en/gena/90562.pdf), p. 2. EU Council Doc. 10418/06 of 12 June 2006, §19 notes that Angola, Cape Verde, Mali, Morocco, Senegal and South Africa were invited to participate. However, I have not found any agreements with third States on their participation or involvement in this operation.

598 See generally www.consilium.europa.eu/showPage.aspx?id=909&lang=en and M. Martinelli, *supra* note 579, 2008, pp. 85–101.

DRC government request in April 2005.[599] This operation was launched on 8 June 2005, was initially to cover a period of 12 months,[600] was initially led by General Pierre Joana, comprises eight experts seconded by the Member States and by the EU institutions and had an initial estimated cost of 1.6 million euros.[601] The mission initially aimed "*to provide advice and assistance for security sector reform in the [DRC] with the aim of contributing to a successful integration of the army in the DRC [...], while taking care to promote policies compatible with human rights and international humanitarian law, democratic standards and the principles of good governance, transparency and respect for the rule of law*".[602] As usual, the PSC exercises political control and strategic direction of the operation.[603] The mission is formally a civilian one but its activities concern security sector reform of the armed forces and its command and control arrangements do not follow the new standard arrangements for civilian missions. The eventual merger with EUPOL RD Congo which was considered,[604] has not (yet) taken place. Mid-2006, the mission was extended until 30 June 2007 with a somewhat amended structure and additional expenditure of 4.75 million euros.[605] The mandate was also somewhat altered in March and June 2007 with

---

599 Council Joint Action of 2 May 2005 on the European Union mission to provide advice and assistance for security sector reform in the Democratic Republic of the Congo (DRC) (2005/355/CFSP), *O.J. L* 112, 3 May 2005, p. 20, especially 8th consideration preamble, as corrected by Corrigendum to Council Joint Action 2005/355/CFSP of 2 May 2005 on the European Union mission to provide advice and assistance for security sector reform in the Democratic Republic of the Congo (DRC) (*OJ L* 112, 3.5.2005), *O.J. L* 169, 22 June 2006, p. 60 and later amended by Council Joint Action of 1 December 2005 amending Joint Action 2005/355/CFSP on the European Union mission to provide advice and assistance for security sector reform in the Democratic Republic of the Congo (DRC) with regard to setting up a technical assistance project on improving the chain of payments of the Ministry of Defence in the DRC (2005/868/CFSP), *O.J. L* 318, 6 December 2005, p. 29.

600 Council Joint Action 2005/355/CFSP, *supra* previous note, Article 15.

601 See EU Doc. RDC/00 (initial), 23 May 2005 (www.consilium.europa.eu/uedocs/cmsUpload/Background-23.5.05.en.pdf). The size of the mission dictates that only some Member States will participate in it. General Joana was succeeded by Mr. Michel Sido (PSC Decision of 12 February 2008 on the appointment of the Head of Mission for the European Union mission to provide advice and assistance for security sector reform in the Democratic Republic of the Congo (EUSEC RD Congo) (2008/171/CFSP – EUSEC/1/2008), *O.J. L* 56, 29 February 2008, p. 63) and subsequently by Mr. Jean-Paul Michel (PSC Decision of 24 June 2008 on the appointment of the Head of Mission for the European Union mission to provide advice and assistance for security sector reform in the Democratic Republic of the Congo (EUSEC RD Congo) (2008/490/CFSP – EUSEC/2/2008), *O.J. L* 168, 28 June 2008, p. 41).

602 EUSEC Joint Action (*supra* note 599), Article 1.

603 *Id.*, Articles 7 and 8.

604 See Council Joint Action of 12 June 2007 on the European Union mission to provide advice and assistance for security sector reform in the Democratic Republic of the Congo (EUSEC RD Congo) (2007/406/CFSP), *O.J. L* 151, 13 June 2007, p. 52, 8th consideration of the preamble.

605 Council Joint Action of 25 April 2006 amending and extending Joint Action 2005/355/CFSP on the European Union mission to provide advice and assistance for security sector reform in

further extensions until 30 June 2008, 30 June 2009 and 30 September 2009.[606] It was subsequently extended yet again until 30 September 2010 with a revised mandate.[607]

1. MANDATE, LEGAL STATUS, APPLICABLE LAW AND PARTICIPATION OF THIRD STATES

As noted above, the mission is based on the consent of the DRC government.

The SOMA for this mission should be the same one as that for EUPOL KINSHASA[608] and there was initially no participation of third States in EUSEC DRC.[609]

Interestingly, in one of the amending joint actions, a clause was inserted which stipulates that "*Under no circumstances may the European Union or the Secretary-General/High Representative for the [CFSP] be held liable by contributing Member States as a result of acts or omissions by the Head of Mission in the use of funds from those States [providing financial contributions for specific projects]*". This seems to be a rare instance, related to this specific context, where the potential responsibility of the *EU* is recognized.[610]

---

the Democratic Republic of the Congo (DRC) (2006/303/CFSP), *O.J. L* 112, 26 April 2006, p. 18 (*corrigendum* in *O.J. L* 169, 22 June 2006, p. 60).

606 See Council Joint Action of 27 March 2007 amending Joint Action 2005/355/CFSP on the European Union mission to provide advice and assistance for security sector reform in the Democratic Republic of the Congo (DRC) (2007/192/CFSP), *O.J. L* 87, 28 March 2007, p. 22; Council Joint Action 2007/406/CFSP of 12 June 2007 (*supra* note 604); Council Joint Action of 26 June 2008 amending and extending Council Joint Action 2007/406/CFSP on the European Union mission to provide advice and assistance for security sector reform in the Democratic Republic of the Congo (EUSEC RD Congo) (2008/491/CFSP), *O.J. L* 168, 28 June 2008, p. 42 (expanding the mandate to *inter alia* also include work on drawing up the arrangements for the organization of the future Rapid Reaction Force specified by the Government of the DRC as part of the overall plan for reforming the army) and Council Joint Action of 25 June 2009 amending and extending Joint Action 2007/406/CFSP on the European Union mission to provide advice and assistance for security sector reform in the Democratic Republic of the Congo (EUSEC RD Congo) (2009/509/CFSP), *O.J. L* 172, 2 July 2009, p. 36.

607 Council Joint Action 2009/709/CFSP of 15 September 2009 on the European Union mission to provide advice and assistance for security sector reform in the Democratic Republic of the Congo (EUSEC RD Congo) (2009/709/CFSP), *O.J. L* 246, 18 September 2009, p. 33.

608 EUSEC Joint Action (*supra* note 599), 11th consideration preamble: "*The status of the mission will be subject to consultation with the DRC government with a view to ensuring that the [SOMA] relating to EUPOL 'Kinshasa' is applicable to the mission and its staff*".

609 However, Article 1(3) of Council Joint Action 2005/868/CFSP (*supra* note 599) inserted an amendment allowing for the participation of third States in the chain of payments project set up by this Joint Action.

610 Council Joint Action 2007/192/CFSP, *supra* note 606, Article 1(1) (adding new paragraphs to Article 2 of the initial Joint Action).

J. EUJUST LEX (IRAQ)[611]

As part of the EU's support for post-Saddam Iraq,[612] the EU decided late 2004 to set up an expert team to consider an integrated rule of law mission for Iraq[613] and early 2005 indeed decided to establish such a mission.[614] The aim of EUJUST LEX is to address the urgent needs in the Iraqi criminal justice system through providing training for some 770 senior and high potential officials primarily from the police, judiciary and penitentiary[615] in senior management and in skills and procedures in criminal investigation, in full respect for the rule of law and human rights, in order to improve the capacity, coordination and collaboration of the different components of the Iraqi criminal justice system.[616]

EUJUST LEX comprises a planning phase which was to begin no later than 9 March 2005 and an operational phase which was to begin no later than 1 July 2005 and was to last one year.[617] A particular feature of this operation is that it takes place mostly outside Iraq: the training activities take place in the EU (with a Coordinating office in Brussels employing 16 staff) or in the region and there is only a liaison office in Baghdad (five staff), although depending on developments in Iraq, the Council was to examine the possibility of training within Iraq and, if necessary, was to amend the Joint Action accordingly.[618] It seems this might partially be done through contracting out these services.[619] Mr. Stephen White was appointed Head of Mission[620] and the financial reference amount from the

---

611 See generally www.consilium.europa.eu/showPage.aspx?id=823&lang=en and *ESDP Newsletter* No. 1, December 2005, pp. 26–27 and *ESDP Newsletter* No. 4, Summer 2007, pp. 21–23 (both www.consilium.europa.eu/showPage.aspx?id=1090&lang=en).

612 For the EU's role in Iraq, see generally 'EU support for Iraq', fact sheet, June 2005, www.consilium.europa.eu/uedocs/cmsUpload/Factsheet-Iraq-June2005.pdf. As EU Member States were divided on the legality and opportunity of the 2003 war against Iraq, the EU played hardly any role before and during this war. Even in the aftermath of that war, its role has remained limited.

613 Council Joint Action of 26 November 2004 on establishing an expert team with a view to a possible European Union integrated police, rule of law and civilian administration mission for Iraq (2004/909/CFSP), *O.J. L* 381, 28 December 2004, p. 84.

614 Council Joint Action of 7 March 2005 on the European Union Integrated Rule of Law Mission for Iraq, EUJUST LEX (2005/190/CFSP), *O.J. L* 62, 9 March 2005, p. 37.

615 See the fact sheet *supra* note 612.

616 EUJUST LEX Joint Action, *supra* note 614, Article 2.

617 *Id.*, Articles 1 and 14. The Council welcomed the first training sessions in its 18 July 2005 conclusions.

618 EUJUST LEX Joint Action, *supra* note 614, Articles 2 and 3.

619 The extending decision (*infra* note 623) in its Article 1(3) states that, given the security situation, "*services in Baghdad shall be provided through the contracts entered into by the United Kingdom with the companies providing and invoicing for these services*" (for up to 2.5 million euros).

620 PSC Decision of 8 March 2005 concerning the appointment of the Head of Mission of the EU Integrated Rule of Law Mission for Iraq, EUJUST LEX (EUJUST LEX/1/2005 – 2005/232/

EU budget was initially EUR 10 million, with Member States contributing training courses and trainers as well as some additional financial support.[621] The PSC exercises the political control and strategic direction of the mission.[622] On 12 June 2006, the Council decided to extend the mission by 18 months and adopted a Joint Action on its functioning in a first phase until 31 October 2006 and on 17 October 2006 a Joint Action covering the next phase until the end of 2007.[623] It was further extended until 30 April 2008, 30 June 2008 and 30 June 2009[624] and its command structure was amended in November 2007 to reflect the new guidelines in this respect.[625] It was subsequently further extended until 30 June 2010[626] and it was decided that "*During the period from 1 July 2009 until 30 June 2010, EUJUST LEX shall start a pilot phase of activities in Iraq, including providing strategic advice, follow-up mentoring and training activities, as and where security conditions and resources allow*".[627] In June 2009, the number of persons trained was 2,446.[628]

CFSP), *O.J. L* 72, 18 March 2005, p. 29, extended by PSC Decision of 13 June 2006 extending the mandate of the Head of Mission for the European Union Integrated Rule of Law Mission for Iraq, EUJUST LEX (EUJUST LEX/1/2006-2006/449/CFSP), *O.J. L* 176, 30 June 2006, p. 111 and by PSC Decision of 3 July 2009 appointing the Head of Mission for the European Union Integrated Rule of Law Mission for Iraq, EUJUST LEX (EUJUST LEX/1/2009-2009/596/CFSP), *O.J. L* 202, 4 August 2009, p. 82.

621 EUJUST LEX Joint Action, *supra* note 614, Article 11, and the fact sheet *supra* note 612.

622 EUJUST LEX Joint Action, *supra* note 614, Articles 8(2) and 9.

623 Council Joint Action of 12 June 2006 amending and extending Joint Action 2005/190/CFSP on the European Union Integrated Rule of Law Mission for Iraq, EUJUST LEX (2006/413/CFSP), *O.J. L* 163, 15 June 2006, p. 17 and Council Joint Action of 17 October 2006 amending and extending Joint Action 2005/190/CFSP on the European Union Integrated Rule of Law Mission for Iraq, EUJUST LEX (2006/708/CFSP), *O.J. L* 291, 21 October 2006, p. 43.

624 See External Relations Council of 19–20 November 2007, conclusions on ESDP, §22; Council Joint Action 2007/760/CFSP (*infra*, next note); Council Joint Action of 14 April 2008 amending and extending Joint Action 2005/190/CFSP on the European Union Integrated Rule of Law Mission for Iraq, EUJUST LEX (2008/304/CFSP), *O.J. L* 105, 15 April 2008, p. 10 and Council Joint Action of 23 June 2008 amending and extending Joint Action 2005/190/CFSP on the European Union Integrated Rule of Law Mission for Iraq, EUJUST LEX (2008/480/CFSP), *O.J. L* 163, 24 June 2008, p. 43.

625 Council Joint Action of 22 November 2007 amending and extending Joint Action 2005/190/CFSP on the European Union Integrated Rule of Law Mission for Iraq, EUJUST LEX (2007/760/CFSP), *O.J. L* 305, 23 November 2007, p. 58.

626 Council Joint Action of 11 June 2009 on the European Union Integrated Rule of Law Mission for Iraq, EUJUST LEX (2009/475/CFSP), *O.J. L* 156, 19 June 2009, p. 57.

627 *Id.*, Article 2(3).

628 FactsheetIraq/12,June2009,www.consilium.europa.eu/uedocs/cmsUpload/090611FACTSHEET_EUJUST_LEX-version12_EN.pdf.

1. MANDATE, LEGAL STATUS, APPLICABLE LAW AND PARTICIPATION OF THIRD STATES

The operation was undertaken with the consent of the Iraqi government.[629]

As to the SOMA, the situation is not very clear. Article 7(1) of the EUJUST LEX Joint Action states that "*[w]here required, the status of EUJUST LEX staff, including where appropriate the privileges, immunities and further guarantees necessary for the completion and smooth functioning of EUJUST LEX shall be agreed in accordance with ... Article 24 [EU Treaty]*".[630] However, to the author's knowledge, at the time of writing no such agreements have been concluded. Given that the training will take place in different countries, both EU Member States and third States, and as it may be necessary to also regulate the status of Iraqi trainees and not just the trainers, any SOMAs concluded are likely to contain peculiar features. Furthermore, the EUJUST LEX Joint Action devotes considerable attention to the security of the mission and its staff, e.g. "*Member States shall endeavour to provide EUJUST LEX, in particular the Liaison Office, secure accommodation, body armour and close protection within Iraq*".[631]

Participation of third States is not provided for, although training in the region will obviously require the cooperation of some third States.

K. EU SUPPORT AMIS II (SUDAN)[632]

The EU support for the peace process in Sudan[633] culminated in a mission in support of the AU mission to Sudan (AMIS II),[634] at the request of the

---

629 See EUJUST LEX Joint Action, *supra* note 614, 2nd and 5th considerations preamble and EU Doc. S211/05, 9 June 2005, www.consilium.europa.eu/ueDocs/cms_Data/docs/pressData/en/declarations/85157.pdf.

630 *Supra* note 614.

631 *Id.*, Article 10, especially Article 10(8).

632 See generally www.consilium.europa.eu/showPage.aspx?id=956&lang=en and *ESDP Newsletter* No. 1, December 2005, pp. 30–33 (www.consilium.europa.eu/showPage.aspx?id=1090&lang=en).

633 For other EU actions, see the preamble of Council Joint Action of 18 July 2005 on the European Union civilian-military supporting action to the African Union mission in the Darfur region of Sudan (2005/557/CFSP), *O.J. L* 188, 20 July 2005, p. 46. See also Council Joint Action of 18 July 2005 appointing a Special Representative of the European Union for Sudan (2005/556/CFSP), *O.J. L* 188, 20 July 2005, p. 43, replaced by Council Joint Action of 5 July 2006 renewing and revising the mandate of the Special Representative of the European Union for Sudan (2006/468/CFSP), *O.J. L* 184, 6 July 2006, p. 38 (see for further amendments *infra* note 640).

634 Council Joint Action 2005/557/CFSP, *supra* previous note, p. 46.

AU,[635] which had taken the lead in attempting to bring security to the population of the Darfur region in Sudan, where international crimes against the population have been committed in recent years.[636] One of the peculiar elements of this mission was its clearly mixed civil-military nature: it consisted of a civilian (police) and a military component, with different tasks and financing arrangements.[637] This has been the only (formally) mixed operation to date. The PSC exercised political control and strategic direction and was advised by both the Committee for Civilian Aspects of Crisis Management and the EUMC (assisted by the EU Military Staff (EUMS)), in the field of their respective competences.[638] It would seem that at least the mission staff incorporated in AMIS was part of the AU/AMIS chain of command and under some degree of AU/AMIS command and control.[639] The EUSR for Sudan, Mr. Pekka Haavisto, who was succeeded by Mr. Torben Brylle,[640] was assisted by a police advisor,[641] who was the Head of the police team, and by a military advisor,[642] who was to "*help to ensure coherence of the military component of the EU supporting*

---

635 *Id.*, 11th consideration preamble.

636 The Darfur situation has been referred to the International Criminal Court by the UN Security Council, see http://www2.icc-cpi.int/menus/icc/situations%20and%20cases/situations/situation%20icc%200205 and UNSC Res. 1593 of 31 March 2005.

637 Council Joint Action 2005/557/CFSP, *supra* note 633, respectively Sections II and III. See also Council Decision of 21 November 2005 implementing Joint Action 2005/557/CFSP on the European Union civilian-military supporting action to the African Union mission in the Darfur region of Sudan (2005/806/CFSP), *O.J. L* 303, 22 November 2005, p. 60.

638 AMIS Joint Action, *supra* note 633, Article 4.

639 See AMIS Joint Action, *supra* note 633, Articles 5(2) ("[*the EU Coordination Cell in Addis Ababa] ... shall manage the day-today coordination with all relevant EU actors and with the Administrative Control and Management Centre (ACMC) within the chain of command of the AU in Addis Ababa in order to ensure coherent and timely EU support to AMIS II*") and 11(1)(a) ('*EU officers operating in the AMIS II chain of command*').

640 Council Decision of 19 April 2007 appointing the European Union Special Representative for Sudan (2007/238/CFSP), *O.J. L* 103, 20 April 2007, p. 52 (later amended by Council Joint Action of 6 December 2007 amending Joint Action 2007/108/CFSP extending the mandate of the European Union Special Representative for Sudan (2007/809/CFSP), *O.J. L* 323, 8 December 2007, p. 57). See generally www.consilium.europa.eu/showPage.aspx?id=1227&lang=EN (with references to the subsequent extensions and amendments of his mandate).

641 Douglas Brand, appointed by PSC Decision of 29 July 2005 appointing a Head of the EU Police Team/Police Advisor to the European Union Special Representative for Sudan (DARFUR/2/2005 – 2005/654/CFSP), *O.J. L* 241, 17 September 2005, p. 58.

642 Philippe Mendez, appointed by PSC Decision of 29 July 2005 appointing a Military Adviser to the European Union Special Representative for Sudan (DARFUR/1/2005 – 2005/653/CFSP), *O.J. L* 241, 17 September 2005, p. 57; succeeded by Colonel Marc Boileau, appointed by PSC Decision of 25 July 2006 appointing a Military Advisor to the European Union Special Representative for Sudan (Darfur/3/2006–2006/634/CFSP), *O.J. L* 258, 21 September 2006, p. 13 and subsequently by Colonel François Amelineau, appointed by PSC Decision of 16 January 2007 appointing a Military Adviser to the European Union Special Representative for Sudan (DARFUR/5/2007 – 2007/34/CFSP), *O.J. L* 13, 19 January 2007, p. 9 and by Colonel Michel Billard, appointed by PSC Decision of 18 July 2007 appointing a Military Advisor to

action".[643] The duration of the mission had not been determined in advance[644] and was linked to the evolution of the situation in Sudan and the replacement of AMIS by a hybrid UN-AU peace operation as of 31 December 2007.[645] Indeed, as of that date the mission has been terminated.[646] The support was varied and

the European Union Special Representative for Sudan (DARFUR/6/2007–2007/537/CFSP), *O.J. L* 196, 28 July 2007, p. 48.

643 AMIS Joint Action, *supra* note 633, respectively Articles 7 and 10.

644 *Id.*, Article 16(2). It was extended until 31 October 2006 by Council Decision of 11 July 2006 concerning the implementation of Joint Action 2005/557/CFSP on the European Union civilian-military supporting action to the African Union mission in the Darfur region of Sudan (2006/486/CFSP), *O.J. L* 192, 13 July 2006, p. 30; until 31 December 2006 by Council Decision of 17 October 2006 implementing Joint Action 2005/557/CFSP on the European Union civilian-military supporting action to the African Union mission in the Darfur region of Sudan (2006/725/CFSP), *O.J. L* 296, 26 October 2006, p. 24 and until 31 October 2007 by Council Decision of 23 April 2007 implementing Joint Action 2005/557/CFSP on the European Union civilian-military supporting action to the African Union mission in the Darfur region of Sudan (2007/244/CFSP), *O.J. L* 106, 24 April 2007, p. 64. Indeed, it was subsequently decided that the civilian component of the mission would end upon the transfer of authority from AMIS to the new AU-UN force, which was to – and did – take place by 31 December 2007: see Council Decision of 22 October 2007 implementing Joint Action 2005/557/CFSP on the European Union civilian-military supporting action to the African Union missions in the Darfur region of Sudan and in Somalia (2007/690/CFSP), *O.J. L* 282, 26 October 2007, p. 62 (3rd and 4th considerations of the preamble).

645 In November 2007, the Sudanese government had consented to a hybrid UN-AU operation (though initially the intention seems to have been a transfer to a UN-only operation; see, e.g. UNSC Resolutions 1663 of 24 March 2006 and 1679 of 16 May 2006) but only after considerable international pressure and long discussions; Sudan had unconditionally accepted transition to the final phase of this hybrid operation in June 2007 (UN press release, 17 June 2007) and that operation was authorized by the UN Security Council in Resolution 1769 of 31 July 2007. The mission was slowly deployed in late October 2007 (UN press release of 31 October 2007) despite lacking key assets (see UN press releases of 8 October and 10 November 2007) and concern that it might not obtain an adequate strength and the Sudanese government is apparently given a say over which nations can participate (see UN pres release of 14 November 2007). In addition, an AMIS position was attacked by a significant rebel force in late September 2007, which resulted in some ten peacekeepers being killed (see UN press releases of 30 September and 2 October 2007 and UNSC Presidential Statement of 2 October 2007 (UN Doc/ S/PRST/2007/35)). See the contributions on developments in Sudan in the *Newsletters* 2006 No. 1 and following of the International Society for Military Law & the Law of War (available online at http://home.scarlet.be/~ismllw/publication/bulletin_info.htm). For the latest developments, see www.un.org/apps/news/infocusRel.asp?infocusID=88&Body=Sudan&Body1= and www.africa-union.org/DARFUR/homedar.htm. For an EU perspective; see, e.g. EU Council Doc. 11501/06 of 10 July 2006. For an earlier overview, see J.I. Levitt, 'The Peace and Security Council of the African Union and the United Nations Security Council: The Case of Darfur, Sudan', in N. Blokker & N. Schrijver (eds.), *The Security Council and the Use of Force: Theory and Reality: A Need for Change?*, Leiden, Nijhoff, 2005, pp. 236–249.

646 See EU Doc. S/374/07 of 27 December 2007 and Council Joint Action of 20 December 2007 repealing Joint Action 2005/557/CFSP on the European Union civilian-military supporting action to the African Union missions in the Darfur region of Sudan and in Somalia (2007/887/CFSP), *O.J. L* 346, 29 December 2007, p. 28.

included assistance in the field of training, planning and transport.[647] The mission reportedly counted 30 military personnel and up to 50 police officers (but this number was not always filled).[648]

In April 2007, the mandate of this mission was broadened to also include support for the AU mission in Somalia.[649]

1. MANDATE

As already mentioned, the mandate was based on an AU request for assistance to the AU mission, which in turn was based on a UN Security Council mandate adopted on the basis of a ceasefire/peace agreement and a Sudanese request.[650] Moreover, EU support to AMIS I was welcomed by the UN Security Council in its Resolution 1556 of 30 July 2004 (§3).

2. LEGAL STATUS AND APPLICABLE LAW

Pursuant to Article 12 of the AMIS II Joint Action,[651] the SG/HR was to secure legally binding assurances from the African States on the territory of which EU supporting action personnel was or would be deployed that their status was/would be governed by the Status of Mission Agreement (SOMA) on the Establishment and Management of the Ceasefire Commission in the Darfur area of Sudan (CFC),[652] and by the General Convention on the Privileges and Immunities of the Organization of African Unity.[653] These assurances appear to have been obtained, as the 15th consideration of the preamble of this Joint Action

647 AMIS Joint Action, *supra* note 633, respectively Articles 6 and 9 and EU Doc. AMIS II/01, July 2005, www.consilium.europa.eu/uedocs/cmsUpload/AMIS_II_July.pdf.

648 COSAC Secretariat, *supra* note 353, p. 11. See also the fact sheet attached to EU Doc. S/374/07 of 27 December 2007.

649 Council Joint Action of 23 April 2007 amending Joint Action 2005/557/CFSP on the European Union civilian-military supporting action to the African Union mission in the Darfur region of Sudan with regard to the inclusion of a military support element providing assistance to the setting up of the African Union Mission in Somalia (AMISOM) (2007/245/CFSP), *O.J. L* 106, 24 April 2007, p. 65. On AMISOM, see generally www.africa-union.org/root/AU/AUC/Departments/PSC/AMISOM/amisom.htm.

650 See Resolutions 1547 (11 June 2004), 1556 (30 July 2004), 1564 (18 September 2004, especially §3), 1574 (19 November 2004) and 1590 (24 March 2005). See also Resolution 1706 of 31 August 2006.

651 *Supra* note 633.

652 Concluded between the AU and the Government of Sudan on 4 June 2004 and available online at www.africa-union.org/DARFUR/Agreements/soma.pdf.

653 Accra, 25 October 1965, available online at www.africa-union.org/Official_documents/Treaties_%20Conventions_%20Protocols/offTreaties_Conventions_&_Protocols.htm. It would

stated that "*The exchange of letters between the SG/HR and the President of the [AU] Commission confirming the arrangements for the EU supporting action to AMIS II also confirms that all EU personnel already deployed or to be deployed in Sudan and other African States in the context of the EU supporting action are covered, as far as their status is concerned, by the agreement between the AU and Sudan on the status of the AU mission*". As with ALTHEA and ARTEMIS, this was a SOMA construction of a particular nature. Moreover, in addition to privileges and immunities, the AU SOMA contained some peculiar elements, such as respect for international humanitarian law (the significance thereof is discussed below).[654]

3. PARTICIPATION OF THIRD STATES

The AMIS II Joint Action did not mention the participation of third States but did refer to the need for coordination with the UN and NATO, in addition to the AU.[655]

L. EU AMM (INDONESIA)[656]

The EU, together with countries from the Association of Southeast Asian Nations (ASEAN) and Norway and Switzerland, deployed a monitoring mission in Aceh (Indonesia) to monitor the implementation of various aspects of the peace agreement set out in the Memorandum of Understanding between the Government of Indonesia and the Free Aceh Movement of 15 August 2005 (hereinafter in this section 'the MoU'[657]),[658] which appears to have brought an end to the lengthy conflict in this Indonesian province.

---

seem that this convention is applicable to the AU. This convention may be especially relevant for personnel located at the AU Headquarters in Ethiopia.

654 *Supra* note 652, Title IV, §§8–9.

655 *Supra* note 633, Article 3. On NATO's assistance to AMIS, see www.nato.int/issues/darfur/index.html.

656 See generally the websites www.aceh-mm.org and www.consilium.europa.eu/showPage.aspx?id=961&lang=en; P.-A. Braud & G. Grevi, *The EU Mission in Aceh: Implementing Peace*, Paris, EU ISS, Occasional Paper No. 61, December 2005 (available online at www.iss.europa.eu/index.php?id=154&L=0) and *ESDP Newsletter* No. 2, June 2006, pp. 18–23 and *ESDP Newsletter* No. 4, Summer 2007, pp. 19–20 (both www.consilium.europa.eu/showPage.aspx?id=1090&lang=en).

657 Text at www.consilium.europa.eu/uedocs/cmsUpload/MoU_Aceh.pdf.

658 Council Joint Action of 9 September 2005 on the European Union Monitoring Mission in Aceh (Indonesia) (Aceh Monitoring Mission–AMM) (2005/643/CFSP), *O.J. L* 234, 10 September 2005, p. 13.

The AMM, led by Pieter Feith,[659] became operational on 15 September 2005, i.e. the date on which the decommissioning of the Free Aceh Movement (GAM) armaments and the relocation of non-organic military and policy forces began,[660] although an initial monitoring presence (IMP) of 80 staff was already deployed on 15 August 2005.[661] The mission was estimated to cost 15 million euros, including 9 million euros out of the EU budget, and was to end in March 2006.[662] However, on 27 February, 7 June and 7 September 2006 it was extended by three months each time.[663]

In order to monitor the implementation of the commitments under the MoU, the AMM's tasks *inter alia* included monitoring the GAM demobilization and decommissioning, the re-location of non-organic military forces and non-organic police troops, the reintegration of active GAM members and the process of legislation change as well as monitoring the human rights situation and providing assistance in this field in the context of the other tasks, ruling on disputed amnesty cases and investigating and ruling on complaints and alleged violations of the MoU.[664]

The mission consisted of 226 international unarmed personnel (130 from EU Member States and from Norway and Switzerland and 96 from the participating ASEAN countries), spread over the Headquarters in Banda Aceh, 11 geographically distributed District Offices conducting monitoring tasks and 4 Decommissioning Teams.[665] The PSC exercised political control of and provided strategic direction to the mission.[666] The mission was formally a civilian one but arguably also included military aspects.

---

659 *Id.*, Article 5(1).

660 In the MoU (*supra* note 657), 'organic' police/military forces seems to refer to officially recognized and constituted police/military forces.

661 EU Doc. ACH/02, 15 September 2005, available online at www.consilium.europa.eu/uedocs/cmsUpload/AcehCouncil%20FactsheetREV2bis.pdf.

662 *Id.* and Articles 12(1) and 16 AMM Joint Action, *supra* note 658.

663 Council Joint Action of 27 February 2006 amending and extending Joint Action 2005/643/CFSP on the European Union Monitoring Mission in Aceh (Indonesia) (Aceh Monitoring Mission–AMM) (2006/202/CFSP), *O.J. L* 71, 10 March 2006, p. 57; Council Joint Action of 7 June 2006 amending and extending Joint Action 2005/643/CFSP on the European Union Monitoring Mission in Aceh (Indonesia) (Aceh Monitoring Mission–AMM) (2006/407/CFSP), *O.J. L* 158, 10 June 2006, p. 20 and Council Joint Action of 7 September 2006 amending and extending Joint Action 2005/643/CFSP on the European Union Monitoring Mission in Aceh (Indonesia) (Aceh Monitoring Mission–AMM) (2006/607/CFSP), *O.J. L* 246, 8 September 2006, p. 16.

664 AMM Joint Action, *supra* note 658, Article 2.

665 *Id.*, Article 4 and EU Doc. ACH/02, *supra* note 661.

666 AMM Joint Action, *supra* note 658, Articles 8 and 9.

1. MANDATE, LEGAL STATUS AND APPLICABLE LAW

The mission was based on the MoU[667] and therefore on the consent of the Indonesian government[668] and GAM. Both the MoU and the AMM Joint Action[669] provided for the conclusion of a SOMA, which was signed on 14 September and 3 October 2005 and provisionally applied from 15 September 2005.[670] It is not clear under what status the IMP operated. The SOMA had to be extended repeatedly as the mission itself was extended.[671] It differed from early SOMAs (see *supra*) in that it no longer referred to an application by analogy of diplomatic immunities but rather set out proper privileges and immunities, which entailed some differences notably with regard to the status of mission personnel. In particular, while it provided for immunity from host State criminal jurisdiction as before (and subject to any waiver), it included a more differentiated rule of limited functional immunity from the civil and administrative jurisdiction of the host State: if the Head of Mission and the authority having seconded the staff member certified that conduct was not performed in the exercise of official functions, local court proceedings could take place.[672]

2. PARTICIPATION OF THIRD STATES

Pursuant to Article 10 of the AMM Joint Action,[673] acceding States were to be invited and third States could be invited to participate in the AMM and all third States making contributions (whether significant or not) to the AMM would have the same rights and obligations in terms of the day-to-day management of the mission as participating EU Member States. Only Norway and Switzerland participated.[674] In addition, this operation was conducted under EU leadership

---

667 *Supra* note 657, title V.

668 See also AMM Joint Action, *supra* note 658, 3rd consideration preamble.

669 Respectively in §5(3) and Article 7.

670 Agreement in the form of an exchange of letters between the European Union and the Government of Indonesia on the tasks, status, privileges and immunities of the European Union Monitoring Mission in Aceh (Indonesia) (Aceh Monitoring Mission–AMM) and its personnel, *O.J. L* 288, 29 October 2005, p. 59/60. The Agreement entered into force on 3 October 2005.

671 See Exchange of Letters concerning the extension of the Agreement in the form of an Exchange of Letters between the European Union and the Government of Indonesia on the tasks, status, privileges and immunities of the European Union Monitoring Mission in Aceh (Indonesia) (Aceh Monitorino Mission—AMM) and its personnel, *O.J. L* 71, 10 March 2006, p. 53/55; O.J. L 176, 30 June 2006, p. 107/108 and O.J. L 273, 4 October 2006, p. 8/9.

672 AMM SOMA, *supra* note 670, section 6, especially (c) and (d).

673 AMM Joint Action, *supra* note 658.

674 EU Doc. ACH/02, *supra* note 661 and Agreement between the European Union and the Swiss Confederation on the participation of the Swiss Confederation in the European Union

but jointly with the ASEAN Member States Brunei, Malaysia, the Philippines, Singapore and Thailand. Agreements with the ASEAN Participating States were adopted in the form of exchanges of letters.[675] There was one deputy Head of Mission from an ASEAN country[676] and the PSC set up a Committee of Contributors in November 2005.[677]

M. COPPS (PALESTINIAN TERRITORIES)[678]

The EU is one of the members of the 'Quartet' (along with the US, the UN and Russia) and has been involved in the Middle East peace process for some time[679] and also has an EUSR for this peace process.[680]

COPPS stands for the EU Coordinating Office for Palestinian Police Support and was initially not a formal ESDP operation.[681] It was established as an ESDP operation in November 2005 with an operational phase beginning no later than on 1 January 2006 and it mission is "*to contribute to the establishment of sustainable and effective policing arrangements under Palestinian ownership in accordance with best international standards, in cooperation with the Community's institution building programmes as well as other international efforts in the wider context of Security Sector including Criminal Justice Reform*" by assisting the Palestinian Civil Police (PCP) in implementation of the Police Development Programme by advising and closely mentoring the PCP, and specifically senior

Monitoring Mission in Aceh (Indonesia) (Aceh Monitoring Mission–AMM), *O.J. L* 349, 31 December 2005, p. 30/31.

675 For the Council decision approving the conclusion of the agreements, see Council Doc. 12321/05 of 4 October 2005. The agreement with the Philippines is in *id.*, add 5, that with Malaysia in *id.*, add 3, and that with Thailand in *id.*, add 4. The agreements with Singapore and Brunei are listed but were classified (*id.*, add 2 and 1). The Council Decision of 11 October 2005 concerning the conclusion of an Agreement in the form of an Exchange of Letters between the European Union and Brunei, Singapore, Malaysia, Thailand and the Philippines on the participation of those States in the European Union Monitoring Mission in Aceh (Indonesia) (Aceh Monitoring Mission–AMM) (2005/495/CFSP) and the agreements were ultimately published in the *O.J. L* 183, 13 July 2007, pp. 51, 52, 58, 64, 70 and 76 (for Brunei with a corrig. in *O.J.* L. 208, 9 August 2007, p. 16).

676 EU Doc. ACH/02, *supra* note 661.

677 PSC Decision of 15 November 2005 on the establishment of the Committee of Contributors for the European Union Monitoring Mission in Aceh (Indonesia) (Aceh Monitoring Mission–AMM) (ACEH/1/2005 – 2005/860/EC), *O.J. L* 317, 3 December 2005, p. 16.

678 See www.consilium.europa.eu/showPage.aspx?id=974&lang=en.

679 See generally http://ec.europa.eu/external_relations/mepp/index_en.htm and especially http://ec.europa.eu/external_relations/mepp/political/political_en.htm.

680 See www.consilium.europa.eu/showPage.aspx?id=452&lang=en.

681 See EU Doc. S308/05, 26 September 2005, available online at www.consilium.europa.eu/uedocs/cms_Data/docs/pressdata/fr/discours/86356.pdf.

officials at District, Headquarters and Ministerial level, coordinating and facilitating EU and Member State assistance, and where requested, international assistance to the PCP and advising on police-related Criminal Justice elements.[682]

This operation had a planned duration of three years and the financial reference amount was EUR 2.5 million for 2005, EUR 3.6 million for 2006,[683] EUR 2.8 million for 2007 and early 2008, EUR 6 million for the remainder of 2008 and EUR 6.2 million for 2009.[684] COPPS was initially led by Mr. Jonathan McIvor[685] and should have had some 33 unarmed staff.[686] Its command structure was adapted in December 2007 to reflect the new EU policy on command and control in civilian ESDP missions.[687] The operation was subsequently extended for another two years, with strengthened action in the area of the rule of law.[688]

---

682 Articles 1 and 2 Council Joint Action of 14 November 2005 on the European Union Police Mission for the Palestinian Territories (2005/797/CFSP), *O.J. L* 300, 17 November 2005, p. 65.

683 *Id.*, Articles 3 and 14.

684 Council Decision of 6 December 2007 amending Decision 2006/807/CFSP on the European Union Police Mission for the Palestinian Territories (2007/808/CFSP), *O.J. L* 323, 8 December 2007, p. 56, Article 1; Council Decision of 18 February 2008 implementing Joint Action 2005/797/CFSP on the European Union Police Mission for the Palestinian Territories (2008/134/CFSP), *O.J. L* 43, 19 February 2008, p. 38; Council Decision of 23 June 2008 amending Decision 2008/134/CFSP on the European Union Police Mission for the Palestinian Territories (2008/482/CFSP), *O.J. L* 163, 24 June 2008, p. 52 and Council Joint Action 2008/958/CFSP, *infra* note 688, Article 2.

685 PSC Decision of 16 November 2005 concerning the appointment of the Head of Mission/ Police Commissioner of the European Union Police Mission for the Palestinian Territories (EUPOL COPPS) (EUPOL COPPS/1/2005–2005/836/CFSP), *O.J. L* 312, 29 November 2005, p. 57. He was succeeded by Mr. Colin Smith, see PSC Decision of 21 November 2006 concerning the appointment of the Head of Mission/Police Commissioner of the European Union Police Mission for the Palestinian Territories (EUPOL COPPS) (EUPOL COPPS/2/2006–2006/853/CFSP), *O.J. L* 331, 29 November 2006, p. 21 and PSC Decision EUPOL of 30 October 2007 concerning the extension of the mandate of the Head of Mission/ Police Commissioner of the European Union Police Mission for the Palestinian Territories (EUPOL COPPS) (COPPS/1/2007–2007/737/CFSP), *O.J. L* 298, 16 November 2007, p. 22. The latter was in turn succeeded by Mr. Paul Kernaghan, see PSC Decision of 16 December 2008 concerning the appointment of the Head of the European Union Police Mission for the Palestinian Territories (EUPOL COPPS/1/2008 – 2008/970/CFSP), *O.J. L* 344, 20 December 2008, p. 139.

686 EU Council factsheet, 'European Union Police Mission for the Palestinian Territories (EUPOL-COPPS)', EUPOL-COPPS/02, 9 February 2006, available online at www.consilium.europa.eu/uedocs/cmsUpload/051222-EUPOL-COPPS.pdf.

687 Council Joint Action 2007/806/CFSP of 6 December 2007 amending Joint Action 2005/797/ CFSP on the European Union Police Mission for the Palestinian Territories (2007/806/CFSP), *O.J. L* 323, 8 December 2007, p. 50.

688 Council Joint Action of 16 December 2008 amending Joint Action 2005/797/CFSP on the European Police Mission for the Palestinian Territories (2008/958/CFSP), *O.J. L* 338, 17 December 2008, p. 75, Article 1.

1. MANDATE, LEGAL STATUS AND APPLICABLE LAW AND PARTICIPATION OF THIRD STATES

The European Union Coordinating Office for Palestinian Police Support was formally established by an Exchange of Letters on 20 April 2005 between the Palestinian Prime Minister Ahmed Qurei and the EU Special Representative to the Middle-East Peace Process Marc Otte and was initially not an ESDP operation.[689] It was turned into an ESDP operation at the invitation of the Palestinian Authority.[690] It is therefore based on the consent of the Palestinian Authority. There appear to have been problems of accreditation by Israel that were only resolved in December 2007.[691]

The participation of third States is permitted[692] but there does not appear to be such participation, although a Committee of Contributors was set up in 2009.[693] The conclusion of a SOMA under Article 24 EU Treaty is foreseen "*where required*"[694] but the Council's agreements database does not list one.[695]

N. EUPAT (FYROM)[696]

EUPAT was a follow-on mission in FYROM after CONCORDIA and PROXIMA (see above, Sections C and E of this chapter), which aimed to further support the development of an efficient and professional police service based on European

689 See the 3rd consideration of the preamble of Council Joint Action 2005/797/CFSP, *supra* note 682, and EU Doc. S163/05, www.consilium.europa.eu/ueDocs/cms_Data/docs/pressData/en/declarations/84603.pdf.

690 See the 6th consideration of the preamble of Council Joint Action 2005/797/CFSP, *supra* note 682.

691 External Relations Council of 19–20 November 2007, conclusions on ESDP, §20. The resolution of this problem was welcomed in EU Doc. S/376/07 of 28 December 2007.

692 Council Joint Action 2005/797/CFSP, *supra* note 682, Articles 8(4) and 12.

693 PSC Decision of 27 May 2009 on the establishment of the Committee of Contributors for the European Union Police Mission for the Palestinian Territories (EUPOL COPPS) (EUPOL COPPS/1/2009 – 2009/412/CFSP), *O.J. L* 132, 29 May 2009, p. 18 (no list of participating third States is attached).

694 *Id.*, Article 9(1).

695 The database (*supra* note 398) can be searched by party and the parties listed include the Palestinian Authority. However, on the Israeli side, the agreement on the accreditation (*supra* note 691 and the accompanying text) should be mentioned (it is not (yet) listed in the database).

696 Established by Council Joint Action of 24 November on the establishment of an EU Police Advisory Team (EUPAT) in the Former Yugoslav Republic of Macedonia (fYROM) (2005/826/CFSP), *O.J. L* 307, 25 November 2005, p. 61. See generally www.consilium.europa.eu/showPage.aspx?id=994&lang=en and www.eu-pat.org (the latter website is no longer active).

standards of policing from 15 December 2005 until 14 June 2006,[697] after which EC support initiatives for FYROM were planned, and was estimated to cost 1.5 million euros.[698] It consisted of some 30 police advisors led by Mr. Jürgen Scholtz (who was also the last Proxima Head of Mission; see *supra*).[699]

1. MANDATE, LEGAL STATUS AND APPLICABLE LAW AND PARTICIPATION OF THIRD STATES

EUPAT took place with the consent of the FYROM government.[700] The EUPAT Joint Action provided for efforts to extend the Proxima SOMA[701] to EUPAT. No participation of third States was foreseen.

O. EU BAM RAFAH (PALESTINIAN TERRITORIES)[702]

After COPPS, the EU launched a second ESDP operation in the Palestinian Territories, namely the EU Border Assistance Mission at Rafah (EU BAM Rafah). The aim of EU BAM Rafah is "*to provide a Third Party presence at the Rafah Crossing Point between Egypt and the Palestinian Territories in order to contribute, in cooperation with the Community's institution-building efforts, to the opening of the Rafah Crossing Point and to build up confidence between the Government of Israel and the Palestinian Authority*", by actively monitoring, verifying and evaluating the Palestinian Authority's performance with regard to the implementation of the Framework, Security and Customs Agreements concluded between the Parties on the operation of the Rafah terminal, contributing, through mentoring, to building up the Palestinian capacity in all aspects of border management at Rafah and contributing to the liaison between the

---

697 It closed down on that date as foreseen; see EU Council Doc. 10418/06 of 12 June 2006, §8.

698 Council Joint Action 2005/826/CFSP, *supra* note 696, 8th consideration preamble and Articles 1–2, 8 and 12.

699 PSC Decision EUPAT/1/2005 of 7 December 2005 concerning the appointment of the Head of the EU Police Advisory Team Mission in the former Yugoslav Republic of Macedonia (fYROM), EUPAT, *O.J. L* 346, 29 December 2005, p. 46 and Council fact sheet 'EU police advisory team (EUPAT) in the former Yugoslav Republic of Macedonia', EUPAT/00, December 2005, available online at www.consilium.europa.eu/uedocs/cmsUpload/Factsheet_EUPAT_fYROM_051215.pdf.

700 Council Joint Action 2005/826/CFSP, *supra* note 696, 8th consideration preamble ("*During consultations with the EU, the Government of the former Yugoslav Republic of Macedonia (fYROM) have indicated they would welcome, under certain conditions, a EU Police Advisory Team bridging between the end of EUPOL Proxima and a planned project funded by CARDS aiming at providing technical assistance in the field*").

701 *Id.*, Article 11(1).

702 See generally www.consilium.europa.eu/showPage.aspx?id=979&lang=en.

Palestinian, Israeli and Egyptian authorities in all aspects regarding the management of the Rafah Crossing Point.[703] It was to start on 25 November 2005 and was planned to last one year, with a budget of EUR 1,696,659 for 2005 and EUR 5,903,341 for 2006.[704] Major General Pietro Pistolese was the Head of Mission,[705] leading up to 75 police officers (initially only 55).[706] The mission was later extended until 24 May 2007,[707] 24 May and 24 November 2008 and 24 November 2009.[708] However, it has been suspended in practice following the closure of the border crossing point in June 2007.[709] Its command structure was also adapted in December 2007 to reflect the new policy thereon.[710]

---

703 Article 2 Council Joint Action of 12 December 2005 on establishing a European Union Border Assistance Mission for the Rafah Crossing Point (EU BAM Rafah) (2005/889/CFSP), *O.J. L* 327, 14 December 2005, p. 28. This Joint Action was corrected by *Corrigendum* to Council Joint Action 2005/889/CFSP of 12 December 2005 on establishing a European Union Border Assistance Mission for the Rafah Crossing Point (EU BAM Rafah) (OJ L 327, 14.12.2005), *O.J. L* 5, 10 January 2006, p. 20 (stating that the date of the Joint Action should be read as 25 November 2005 instead of 12 December 2005).

704 Council Joint Action 2005/889/CFSP, *supra* previous note, Articles 1(2) and 3 and 13.

705 *Id.*, Article 5(1). He was succeeded by Mr. Alain Faugeras; see PSC Decision of 11 November 2008 concerning the appointment of the Head of Mission of the European Union Border Assistance Mission at the Rafah Crossing Point (EUBAM Rafah) (EUBAM Rafah/1/2008 – 2008/863/CFSP), *O.J. L* 306, 15 November 2008, p. 99.

706 Council factsheet, 'European Union Border Assistance Mission for the Rafah Crossing Point (EU BAM Rafah)', EU BAM Rafah/02, 7 February 2006, available online at www.consilium.europa.eu/uedocs/cmsUpload/060206%20EU%20_BAM_RAFAnew.pdf.

707 Council Joint Action 2006/773/CFSP of 13 November 2006 amending and extending Joint Action 2005/889/CFSP on establishing a European Union Border Assistance Mission for the Rafah Crossing Point (EU BAM Rafah), *O.J. L* 313, 14 November 2006, p. 15 (*corrigendum O.J. L* 17, 24 January 2007, p. 23).

708 Council Joint Action of 23 May 2007 amending and extending Joint Action 2005/889/CFSP on establishing a European Union Border Assistance Mission for the Rafah Crossing Point (EU BAM Rafah) (2007/359/CFSP), *O.J. L* 133, 25 May 2007, p. 51 (setting the financial reference amount for the period from 25 May 2007 until 24 May 2008 at EUR 7 million); Council Joint Action of 19 May 2008 amending Joint Action 2005/889/CFSP on establishing a European Union Border Assistance Mission for the Rafah Crossing Point (EUBAM Rafah) (2008/379/CFSP), *O.J. L* 130, 20 May 2008, p. 24 (extending this amount to also cover the period up to 24 November 2008) and Council Joint Action of 10 November 2008 amending Joint Action 2005/889/CFSP on establishing a European Union Border Assistance Mission for the Rafah Crossing Point (EUBAM Rafah) (2008/862/CFSP), *O.J. L* 306, 15 November 2008, p. 98 (setting the financial reference amount for 25 November 2008 until 24 November 2009 at EUR 2.5 million).

709 External Relations Council of 19–20 November 2007, conclusions on ESDP, §21.

710 Council Joint Action of 6 December 2007 amending Joint Action 2005/889/CFSP on establishing a European Union Border Assistance Mission for the Rafah Crossing Point (EU BAM Rafah) (2007/807/CFSP), *O.J. L* 323, 8 December 2007, p. 53.

1. MANDATE, LEGAL STATUS AND APPLICABLE LAW AND PARTICIPATION OF THIRD STATES

The mission is based on the invitation and consent of the Israeli government and Palestinian Authority and on an agreement between these two on the Rafah crossing point.[711] The participation of third States is permitted[712] but there does not appear to be such participation. The conclusion of a SOMA under Article 24 EU Treaty is foreseen "*where required*"[713] but the Council's agreements database does not list one.[714]

P. EUFOR DR CONGO[715]

After ARTEMIS, EUPOL Kinshasa and EUSEC DRC (see *supra*, Sections D, H and I), the EU launched its fourth mission the DRC, namely the military operation EUFOR DR Congo. It was an autonomous EU operation with the aim to support the UN mission (MONUC) in that country during the 2006 elections.[716] UN Security Council Resolution 1671 of 25 April 2006, adopted under Chapter VII of the UN Charter, in §8 authorized EUFOR R.D.Congo "*to take all necessary measures, within its means and capabilities, to carry out the following tasks*", in accordance with the agreement to be reached between the EU and the UN:

(a) to support MONUC to stabilize a situation, in case MONUC faces serious difficulties in fulfilling its mandate within its existing capabilities,
(b) to contribute to the protection of civilians under imminent threat of physical violence in the areas of its deployment, and without prejudice to the responsibility of the Government of the Democratic Republic of the Congo,
(c) to contribute to airport protection in Kinshasa,

---

711 Council Joint Action 2005/889/CFSP, *supra* note 703, 8th and 9th consideration of the preamble.

712 *Id.*, Articles 7(4) and 11.

713 *Id.*, Article 8(1).

714 The database (*supra* note 398) can be searched by party and the parties listed include the Palestinian Authority.

715 See generally www.consilium.europa.eu/showPage.aspx?id=1091&lang=en; A. Mattelaer, 'EUFOR RDC and the Development of the ESDP', 60(3) *Studia Diplomatica* 2007, pp. 73–89; R. Yakemtchouk, 'L'Union européenne face à la République démocratique du Congo – L'opération "EUFOR R.D. Congo"', No. 501 *R.M.C.U.E.* 2006, pp. 512–518 and *ESDP Newsletters* No. 2, June 2006, pp. 14–17 and No. 3, January 2007, pp. 10–11 (both www.consilium.europa.eu/showPage.aspx?id=1090&lang=en).

716 Article 1 Council Joint Action of 27 April 2006 on the European Union military operation in support of the United Nations Organisation Mission in the Democratic Republic of the Congo (MONUC) during the election process (2006/319/CFSP), *O.J. L* 116, 29 April 2006, p. 98.

(d) to ensure the security and freedom of movement of the personnel as well as the protection of the installations of Eufor R.D.Congo,
(e) to execute operations of limited character in order to extract individuals in danger,

EUFOR R.D.Congo was launched on 12 June 2006,[717] is was fully operational in July 2006 and ended four months after the date of the first round of elections in the DRC (which started on 30 July 2006).[718] Lieutenant General Karlheinz Viereck was the Operation Commander. Major General Christian Damay the Force Commander and the EU Operational Headquarters were located at the German Armed Forces Operations Command (Einsatzführungskommando der Bundeswehr) in Potsdam (reflecting the German lead).[719] The Operation Headquarters counted some 140 personnel from 19 States.[720] EUFOR RD Congo included the deployment of an advance element to Kinshasa of several hundred military personnel, and a battalion-size "on-call" force over the horizon outside the country (in Libreville, Gabon), but which was quickly deployable if necessary.[721] The financial reference amount for the common costs for the four-month period was 16.7 million euros.[722]

As usual, under the responsibility of the Council, the PSC exercised the political control and strategic direction of the operation and was authorized to take the relevant decisions in accordance with Article 25 EU Treaty, including to amend the planning documents, the Chain of Command and the Rules of Engagement

717 Council Decision of 12 June 2006 on the launching of the European Union military operation in support of the United Nations Organisation Mission in the Democratic Republic of the Congo (MONUC) during the election process (Operation EUFOR RD Congo) (2006/412/CFSP), *O.J. L* 163, 15 June 2006, p. 16. See also EU Council Documents 9652/06 of 2 June 2006 and 10366/06 (Presse 180) of 12 June 2006 (available online at www.consilium.europa.eu/ueDocs/cms_Data/docs/pressData/en/esdp/89995.pdf).

718 Council Joint Action 2006/319/CFSP, *supra* note 716, Article 15(2), subsequently repealed by 2007/147/CFSP of 27 February 2007 repealing Joint Action on the European Union military operation in support of the United Nations Organisation Mission in the Democratic Republic of the Congo (MONUC) during the election process (2006/319/CFSP), *O.J. L* 64, 2 March 2007, p. 44. See also Council conclusions on the DRC of 17 July 2006. The end on 30 November 2006 was reportedly insisted upon by Germany which had the lead of this operation and for which this time limit appears to have been a condition for accepting to take this lead role, even though the situation in Kinshasa might have warranted a short extension. This abrupt end also caused some problems as the forces still had to redeploy (this redeployment explains why the repealing Joint Action was only adopted in Feburary 2007).

719 Council Joint Action 2006/319/CFSP, *supra* note 716, Articles 2–4.

720 'Javier Solana visits the EU OHQ (Operation Headquarters) in Potsdam', Potsdam, 8 June 2006, available online at www.consilium.europa.eu/uedocs/cmsUpload/Potsdam_08.06.06.pdf.

721 Doc. 10366/06 (Presse 180), *supra* note 717 and 'EUFOR DR Congo: The Mission', available online at www.consilium.europa.eu/uedocs/cmsUpload/The_mission.pdf.

722 Council Joint Action 2006/319/CFSP, *supra* note 716, Article 13.

and to decide on the Commanders, while the powers of decision with respect to the objectives and termination of the operation remained vested in the Council.[723]

The SG/HR, assisted by the EUSR, acted as a primary point of contact with the UN, the DRC authorities and other relevant actors, while the Operation Commander liaised with the UN Department of Peacekeeping Operations and MONUC and the Force Commander maintained close contacts with MONUC, local authorities and other international actors, as appropriate, all in close coordination, including with EUPOL Kinshasa, EUSEC DRC and the (EU Council's) Presidency.[724]

1. MANDATE AND PARTICIPATION OF THIRD STATES

The operation was authorized by UN Security Council Resolution 1671 of 25 April 2006, which refers to the consent of the DRC government and a request of the UN. Third States were allowed to participate in the operation[725] but only Turkey and Switzerland participated.[726] Consequently, a Committee of Contributors was set up.[727]

---

723 *Id.*, Article 6.

724 *Id.*, Article 9. See also Article 8 on coherence of EU activities. On the cooperation with the UN in this operation, see C. Major, *EU-UN Cooperation in Military Crisis Management: The Experience of EUFOR RD Congo in 2006*, Paris, EU ISS, Occasional Paper No. 72, September 2008.

725 *Id.*, Article 10.

726 PSC Decision of 30 May 2006 on the acceptance of third States' contributions to the European Union military operation in support of the United Nations Organisation Mission in the Democratic Republic of the Congo (MONUC) during the election process (MONUC SPT/1/2006–2006/499/CFSP), *O.J. L* 197, 19 July 2006, p. 14 and Council Decision of 10 August 2006 concerning a contribution by the Swiss Confederation to the European Union military operation in support of the United Nations Organisation Mission in the Democratic Republic of the Congo (MONUC) during the election process (Operation EUFOR RD Congo) (2006/675/CFSP), *O.J. L* 276, 7 October 2006, p. 109 and Agreement in the form of an Exchange of Letters between the European Union and the Government of the Swiss Confederation on the participation of the Swiss Confederation in the European Union military operation in support of the United Nations Organisation Mission in the Democratic Republic of the Congo (MONUC) during the election process (Operation EUFOR RD Congo), *id.*, p. 110/111.

727 PSC Decision of 30 May 2006 on the setting up of the Committee of Contributors for the European Union military operation in support of the United Nations Organisation Mission in the Democratic Republic of the Congo (MONUC) during the election process (MONUC SPT/2/2006–2006/492/CFSP), *O.J. L* 194, 14 July 2006, p. 31.

2. LEGAL STATUS AND APPLICABLE LAW

The status of the EU-led forces was determined in accordance with the relevant provisions of UN Security Council Resolution 1671.[728] The latter stated in §12 that the Security Council "*Urges the Government of the [DRC] and the [EU] to conclude a status-of-forces agreement before the deployment of advance elements of Eufor R.D.Congo as referred to in paragraph 6 above, and decides that, until such an agreement is concluded, the terms of the status-of-forces agreement for MONUC dated 4 May 2000 shall apply mutatis mutandis between the [EU] and the Government of the [DRC] in respect of Eufor R.D.Congo, including possible third-country contributors*".[729] It may be recalled that for ARTEMIS no SOFA was concluded with the DRC (see *supra*, section D.2 of this chapter).

In addition, a SOFA with Gabon was concluded (as part of the force remained there; see *supra*).[730] This SOFA *inter alia* demanded that EUFOR and EUFOR personnel respect the laws and regulations of the Host State and refrain from any action or activity incompatible with the objectives of the operation (Article 2(1)), and set out the privileges and immunities of EUFOR (Article 5) and EUFOR personnel (Article 6). As to the latter, EUFOR personnel were not liable to any form of arrest or detention and enjoyed immunity from the criminal jurisdiction of the Host State, although this could be expressly waived by the Sending State or EU institution concerned. EUFOR personnel enjoyed immunity from the civil and administrative jurisdiction of the Host State in respect of words spoken or written and all acts performed by them in the exercise of their official functions. In civil cases, the latter were to be determined in a binding way by the EU Force Commander and the competent authority of the Sending State or EU institution and outside such acts a trial could take place and lead to measures of execution on private property of EUFOR personnel that was not certified by the EU Force Commander to be necessary for the fulfilment of their official function (this is similar to the AMM SOMA, see *supra*). There was also a claims clause (Article 15) which exempted claims for damage resulting from EUFOR protection, established the role of EUFOR and Host State as channels for processing claims as well as a claims commission and an arbitral tribunal as an appeals instance for cases above a certain amount.

---

728 *Id.*, Article 12.

729 Agreement between the United Nations and the Democratic Republic of the Congo on the status of the United Nations Mission in the Democratic Republic of the Congo. Kinshasa, 4 May 2000, 2106 *U.N.T.S.* (registration No. 36644, limited publication – not published in *U.N.T.S.*'s online version); French version on file with the author.

730 Agreement between the European Union and the Gabonese Republic on the status of the European Union-led forces in the Gabonese Republic, *O.J. L* 187, 8 July 2006, p. 42/43. See also Council Documents 10307/06 of 8 June 2006; 10542/06 of 16 June 2006 and especially 10256/06 of 8 June 2006.

Q. EUPOL AFGHANISTAN[731]

In the framework of the EU's broader support for and relations with Afghanistan,[732] also reflected in the appointment of an EU Special Representative for Afghanistan (and Pakistan),[733] the EU decided in May 2007 to set up an EU police mission in Afghanistan.[734]

---

731 See generally www.consilium.europa.eu/showPage.aspx?id=1268&lang=en and www.eupol-afg.eu. See also *ESDP Newsletter* No. 4, Summer 2007, pp. 10–11 and *ESDP Newsletter* No. 8, Summer 2009, pp. 7–11 (both www.consilium.europa.eu/showPage.aspx?id=1090&lang=en); E. Gross, *Security Sector Reform in Afghanistan: The EU's Contribution*, Paris, EU ISS, Occasional Paper No. 78, April 2009 and the Letter by the Dutch Minsters of Defence, Foreign Affairs and Development Cooperation to the Dutch Parliament on Afghanistan and the Dutch ISAF participation (*Kamerbrief inzake actuele stand van zaken over Afghanistan en de Nederlandse missie Uruzgan*, available online at www.minbuza.nl/nl/Actueel/Kamerstukken/2007/06/Kamerbrief_inzake_actuele_stand_van_zaken_over_Afghanistan_en_de_Nederlandse_missie_Uruzgan), 20 June 2007, section 'EU Politiemissie Afghanistan'.

732 See generally http://ec.europa.eu/external_relations/afghanistan/index_en.htm. It may suffice to mention the 16 November 2005 EU-Afghanistan Joint Declaration Committing to a new EU-Afghan Partnership (Doc. 14519/05 (Presse 299) of the same date); EC assistance to the Afghan justice sector (see http://europa.eu/rapid/pressReleasesAction.do?reference=IP/07/990&format=HTML&aged=0&language=EN&guiL)anguage=en and www.delafg.ec.europa.eu/en/downloadable_documents/Nov_2008/Press_Release/PR_30mar09.pdf) and the Council Conclusions for enhanced EU engagement in Afghanistan and Pakistan adopted by the 15 June 2009 General Affairs Council. For the wider international community involvement, see also the 2006 Afghanistan Compact (available online at www.ands.gov.af/admin/ands/ands_docs/upload/UploadFolder/The%20Afghnistan%20Compact%20-%20Final%20English.pdf) and the UN Assistance Mission in Afghanistan (UNAMA, see generally http://unama.unmissions.org).

733 Council Joint Action of 10 December 2001 concerning the appointment of the Special Representative of the European Union [for Afghanistan] (2001/875/CFSP), *O.J. L* 326, 11 December 2001, p. 1, as subsequently amended/extended/repealed/replaced, including recently by Council Joint Action of 24 July 2008 concerning the appointment of the European Union Special Representative for Afghanistan (2008/612/CFSP), *O.J. L* 197, 25 July 2008, p. 60; Council Joint Action of 16 February 2009 extending the mandate of the European Union Special Representative for Afghanistan (2009/135/CFSP), *O.J. L* 46, 17 February 2009, p. 61 and Council Joint Action of 15 June 2009 appointing the European Union Special Representative for Afghanistan and Pakistan and repealing Joint Action 2009/135/CFSP (2009/467/CFSP), *O.J. L* 151, 16 June 2009, p. 41. See generally www.consilium.europa.eu/showPage.aspx?id=1509&lang=EN.

734 Council Joint Action of 30 May 2007 on [the] establishment of the European Union Police Mission in Afghanistan (EUPOL AFGANISTAN) (2007/369/CFSP), *O.J. L* 139, 31 May 2007, p. 33 as amended by Council Joint Action of 13 November 2007 amending Joint Action 2007/369/CFSP on the establishment of the European Union Police Mission in Afghanistan (EUPOL AFGHANISTAN) (2007/733/CFSP), *O.J. L* 295, 14 November 2007, p. 31 (reflecting changes to the command structure and activating the Watch-Keeping Capability for this mission); by Council Joint Action of 17 March 2008 amending Joint Action 2007/369/CFSP on the establishment of the European Union Police Mission in Afghanistan (2008/229/CFSP), *O.J. L* 75, 18 March 2008, p. 80 and by Council Joint Action of 4 August 2008 amending Joint Action 2007/369/CFSP on [the] establishment of the European Union Police Mission in Afghanistan (EUPOL AFGHANISTAN) (2008/643/CFSP), *O.J. L* 207, 5 August 2008, p. 43.

The objective of the mission is to "*significantly contribute to the establishment under Afghan ownership of sustainable and effective civilian policing arrangements, which will ensure appropriate interaction with the wider criminal justice system*", in keeping with the policy advice and institution building work of other international actors and to "*support the reform process towards a trusted and efficient police service, which works in accordance with international standards, within the framework of the rule of law and respects human rights*". The focus is on the strategic level and it is a non-executive Mission which carries out its tasks through, amongst other means, monitoring, mentoring, advising and training.[735]

The mission's operational phase started mid-June 2007 and it was established for an initial period of three years.[736] The financial reference amount for the expenditure until 29 March 2008 was EUR 43.6 million but this amount later appeared to be sufficient to cover the period up to 30 September 2008 and even 30 November 2008.[737] The financial reference amount for the period from 1 December 2008 until 30 November 2009 is EUR 64 million.[738]

Brigadier General Friedrich Eichele, the first Head of Mission, was succeeded rather quickly by Brigadier-General Jürgen Scholz (as of 1 November 2007), who was succeeded in turn by Mr. Kai Vittrup (as of 16 October 2008).[739] The initial aim seems to have been some 160 expert staff but in March 2009, the authorized strength was said to be some 400 personnel and the actual strength 225 international and 123 local staff.[740] The mission's headquarters are in Kabul and

---

735 See Articles 3 and 4 of Joint Action 2007/369/CFSP (*supra* note 734).

736 See *id.*, Article 1(1) and EU Council Doc. 10939/07 (Presse 140), 15 June 2007, www.consilium.europa.eu/ueDocs/cms_Data/docs/pressData/en/esdp/94719.pdf.

737 Article 13(1) Joint Action 2007/369/CFSP (*supra* note 734) as amended by Article 1 Joint Action 2008/229/CFSP (*supra* note 734) and Article 1 Joint Action 2008/643/CFSP (*supra* note 734).

738 Article 1 Council Decision of 21 November 2008 implementing Joint Action 2007/369/CFSP on the establishment of the European Union Police Mission in Afghanistan (EUPOL AFGHANISTAN) (2008/884/CFSP), *O.J. L* 316, 26 November 2008, p. 21.

739 See Article 6(1) Joint Action 2007/369/CFSP (*supra* note 734); PSC Decision of 16 October 2007 concerning the appointment of the Head of Mission of EUPOL AFGHANISTAN (EUPOL AFG/1/2007–2007/685/CFSP), *O.J. L* 281, 25 October 2007, p. 37 and PSC Decision of 3 October 2008 concerning the appointment of the Head of Mission of the European Union Police Mission in Afghanistan (EUPOL AFGHANISTAN) (EUPOL AFGHANISTAN/1/2008 – 2008/821/CFSP), *O.J. L* 285, 29 October 2008, p. 20. It seems that the mission got off to a difficult start; see J. Dempsey, 'German General to Leave Afghan Mission amid Dispute', *The International Herald Tribune*, 11 September 2007.

740 See EU Council Doc. 10939/07 (Presse 140), 15 June 2007, www.consilium.europa.eu/ueDocs/cms_Data/docs/pressData/en/esdp/94719.pdf, p. 3 and Factsheet, Afghanistan/14, March 2009, www.consilium.europa.eu/uedocs/cmsUpload/090330-FACTSHEET_EUPOL_Afghanistan-version14_EN.pdf. The decision to double the authorized strength to some 400 staff was

mission staff are deployed at the central, regional and provincial level in light of the security assessment.[741] In March 2009, the mission was deployed in 16 Afghan provinces.[742]

It was provided for that technical arrangements would be sought with ISAF (the NATO-led military International Security Assistance Force[743]) and Regional Command/Provincial Reconstruction Team (PRT) Lead Nations for information exchange, medical, security and logistical support including accommodation by Regional Commands and PRTs.[744] Obstacles in EU-NATO cooperation[745] have prevented the conclusion of cooperation agreements at headquarters level between both organizations.[746] In April 2009, NATO decided to establish a NATO Training Mission for Afghanistan which will complement existing training and capacity development programmes, including EUPOL Afghanistan.[747]

1. MANDATE, LEGAL STATUS AND APPLICABLE LAW AND PARTICIPATION OF THIRD STATES

The mission is conducted at the invitation of the Afghan government[748] and was welcomed by UN Security Council Resolution 1746.[749]

The Joint Action envisages the conclusion of a SOMA but it does not seem that a SOMA has been concluded so far.[750]

referred to in the conclusions of the External Relations Council of 10 November 2008 (EU Council Doc. 15396/08 (Presse 319), p. 17).

741 Article 5(1)-(2) Joint Action 2007/369/CFSP (*supra* note 734).

742 Factsheet, Afghanistan/14, March 2009, *supra* note 740.

743 See generally www.nato.int/ISAF/.

744 Article 5(2) Joint Action 2007/369/CFSP (*supra* note 734).

745 See *supra*, Chapter 2, Section C.

746 See, e.g. the answer to parliamentary questions in the Netherlands (Beantwoording vragen van het lid Pechtold over het aftreden van het hoofd van de politietrainingsmissie in Afghanistan van de Europese Unie, 19 October 2007, www.minbuza.nl/nl/Actueel/Kamerstukken/2007/10/Beantwoording_vragen_van_het_lid_Pechtold_over_het_aftreden_van_het_hoofd_van_de_politietrainingsmissie_in_Afghanistan_van_de_Europese_Unie).

747 See www.nato.int/cps/en/natolive/news_52802.htm?selectedLocale=en.

748 See the 8th consideration of the preamble of Joint Action 2007/369/CFSP (*supra* note 734).

749 23 March 2007, §11. See also UNSC Res. 1806 of 20 March 2008, §17.

750 Article 8(1) Joint Action 2007/369/CFSP (*supra* note 734). At the time of writing, there is no reference to a SOMA in the Council's treaty database (www.consilium.europa.eu/showPage.aspx?id=252&lang=en) nor in the Council register nor on the mission's website.

The Joint Action provided for the participation of third States upon PSC decision.[751] *Ad hoc* participation agreements have been concluded with Croatia[752] and New Zealand[753] and a committee of contributors has been set up.[754] Canada and Norway also participate.[755]

R. EUPOL RD CONGO[756]

The security sector reform police mission EUPOL RD Congo[757] in the DRC succeeded the police mission EUPOL Kinshasa (see above, Section H of this chapter) as of 1 July 2007.

Its mission is to provide advice and assistance for security sector reform in the DRC, with the aim of contributing to Congolese efforts to reform and restructure the National Congolese Police and its interaction with the judicial system, while taking care to promote policies compatible with human rights and international humanitarian law, democratic standards and the principles of good governance, transparency and respect for the rule of law.[758] It complements EUSEC DRC, the

751 Joint Action 2007/369/CFSP (*supra* note 734), Article 12.

752 Agreement between the European Union and the Republic of Croatia on the participation of the Republic of Croatia in the European Union Police Mission in Afghanistan (EUPOL AFGHANISTAN), *O.J. L* 270, 13 October 2007, p. 27/28.

753 Agreement between the European Union and New Zealand on the participation of New Zealand in the European Union Police Mission in Afghanistan (EUPOL AFGHANISTAN), *O.J. L* 274, 18 October 2007, p. 17/18 (*corrigendum O.J. L* 290, 8 November 2007, p. 22).

754 PSC Decision of 30 November 2007 on the establishment of the Committee of Contributors for the European Union Police Mission in Afghanistan (EUPOL AFGHANISTAN) (2007/886/CFSP – EUPOL AFGH/2/2007), *O.J. L* 346, 29 December 2007, p. 26.

755 Factsheet, Afghanistan/14, *supra* note 740.

756 See generally www.consilium.europa.eu/showPage.aspx?id=1303&lang=en.

757 See Council Joint Action of 12 June 2007 on the European Union police mission undertaken in the framework of reform of the security sector (SSR) and its interface with the system of justice in the Democratic Republic of the Congo (EUPOL RD Congo) (2007/405/CFSP), *O.J. L* 151, 13 June 2007, p. 46 as amended by Council Joint Action of 20 December 2007 amending Joint Action 2007/405/CFSP on the European Union police mission undertaken in the framework of reform of the security sector (SSR) and its interface with the system of justice in the Democratic Republic of the Congo (EUPOL RD Congo) (2008/38/CFSP), *O.J. L* 9, 12 January 2008, p. 18 (adapting the command and control arrangements and activating the Watch-Keeping Capability for this mission) and by Council Joint Action of 23 June 2008 amending and extending Joint Action 2007/405/CFSP on the European Union police mission undertaken in the framework of reform of the security sector (SSR) and its interface with the system of justice in the Democratic Republic of the Congo (EUPOL RD Congo) (2008/485/CFSP), *O.J. L* 164, 25 June 2008, p. 44 (slightly expanding the tasks, restructuring the mission, extending it and determining the further financial reference amount).

758 See Article 1 Joint Action 2007/405/CFSP (*supra* previous note).

mandate of which concerns reform of the armed forces (see above, section I of this chapter).

The mission's headquarters are located in Kinshasa and movement or the presence of staff beyond Kinshasa was initially only provided for under specified conditions[759] but was subsequently expanded to include a permanent presence in Goma and Bukavu, in the eastern part of the DRC.[760] Superintendent Adílio Ruivo Custódio – who was already the Head of Mission of EUPOL Kinshasa – was appointed Head of Mission.[761] The initial financial reference amount was 5.5 million Euros.[762] No duration was determined but the initial Joint Action expired on 30 June 2008.[763] This was subsequently extended to 30 June 2009, with a financial reference amount of 6.92 Euros for the second year,[764] and to 30 June 2010 with a financial reference amount to be determined.[765] In March 2009 the mission counted 53 international staff.[766]

1. MANDATE, LEGAL STATUS AND APPLICABLE LAW AND PARTICIPATION OF THIRD STATES

The mission is conducted with the consent of the DRC government.[767]

Pursuant to Article 13(1) of the Joint Action, the status of mission staff was to be "*agreed in accordance with the procedure laid down in Article 24 of the Treaty on European Union*". However, a specific SOMA does not seem to have been concluded. Presumably, the EUPOL Kinshasa SOMA has been extended to EUPOL RD Congo.

---

759 Article 3 Joint Action 2007/405/CFSP (*supra* note 757).

760 Article 3 Joint Action 2007/405/CFSP (*supra* note 757) as amended by Joint Action 2008/485/CFSP (*supra* note 757).

761 Article 5(1) Joint Action 2007/405/CFSP (*supra* note 757).

762 *Id.*, Article 9(1).

763 *Supra* note 757, see its Article 16.

764 Respectively Articles 16 and 9(1) of Joint Action 2007/405/CFSP (*supra* note 757) as amended by Joint Action 2008/485/CFSP (*supra* note 757).

765 Respectively Articles 16 and 9(1) of Joint Action 2007/405/CFSP (*supra* note 757) as amended by Council Joint Action of 15 June 2009 amending and extending Joint Action 2007/405/CFSP on the European Union police mission undertaken in the framework of reform of the security sector (SSR) and its interface with the system of justice in the Democratic Republic of the Congo (EUPOL RD Congo) (2009/466/CFSP), *O.J. L* 151, 16 June 2009, p. 40. Pursuant to the latter provision, the financial reference amount for the second year also covers the period up to 31 October 2009.

766 Fact sheet EUPOL RDC/05, March 2009, www.consilium.europa.eu/uedocs/cmsUpload/090325%20Factsheet%20EUPOL%20RD%20Congo%20-%20version%205_EN.pdf.

767 Joint Action 2007/405/CFSP (*supra* note 757), 13th consideration of the preamble.

The participation of third States is provided for upon PSC approval.[768] It seems that Angola is the only third State participating.[769]

S. EUFOR TCHAD/RCA[770]

In the framework of its regional policy towards the crisis in Sudan[771] and in order to help provide security in Eastern Chad and in the North-Eastern of the Central African Republic (CAR) as part of a wider international presence also including a UN component, the EU decided in September 2007 to establish a military operation in Chad and the CAR (EUFOR Tchad/RCA).[772]

EUFOR Tchad/RCA was a bridging operation for an envisaged follow-on arrangement and was to be conducted in accordance with the mandate set out in UN Security Council Resolution 1778 (25 September 2007) and in accordance with the political and strategic objectives approved by the Council on 12 September 2007.[773] In Resolution 1778 (§6) the UN Security Council, acting under Chapter VII of the UN Charter:

> (a) *Authorizes* the European Union to deploy, for a period of one year from the date that its initial operating capability is declared by the European Union in consultation with the Secretary-General, an operation (hereinafter referred to as "the European Union operation") aimed at supporting the elements referred to in paragraphs 2 to 4, and *decides* that this operation shall be authorized to take all necessary measures, within its capabilities and its area of operation in eastern Chad and the north-eastern

768 Article 10 Joint Action 2007/405/CFSP (*supra* note 757).

769 Factsheet EUPOL RDC/05, *supra* note 766. Compare with EUPOL Kinshasa, *supra* note 597.

770 See generally www.consilium.europa.eu/showPage.aspx?id=1366&lang=EN. See also R. Yakemtchouk, 'La force européenne Eufor au Tchad et en République Centrafricaine', No. 519 *R.M.C.U.E.* 2007, pp. 365–369 and the contributions in *ESDP Newsletter* No. 5, December 2007, pp. 12–16; *ESDP Newsletter* No. 6, July 2008, pp. 7–16 and *ESDP Newsletter* No. 8, Summer 2009, pp. 17–21 (all www.consilium.europa.eu/showPage.aspx?id=1090&lang=en).

771 The EUSR for Sudan was to give political guidance to the operation; see the 10th consideration of the preamble and Article 8(2) Joint Action 2007/677/CFSP (*infra* note 772). See also the amendments to the mandate of this EUSR introduced by Council Joint Action of 6 December 2007 amending Joint Action 2007/108/CFSP extending the mandate of the European Union Special Representative for Sudan (2007/809/CFSP), *O.J. L* 323, 8 December 2007, p. 57 (the mandate of this EUSR was most recently extended by Council Joint Action 2009/134/CFSP of 16 February 2009, *O.J. L* 46, 17 February 2009, p. 57). On this EUSR, see generally www.consilium.europa.eu/showPage.aspx?id=1227&lang=EN.

772 Council Joint Action of 15 October 2007 on the European Union military operation in the Republic of Chad and in the Central African Republic (2007/677/CFSP), *O.J. L* 279, 23 October 2007, p. 21 (for the context, see the preamble of this Joint Action).

773 *Id.*, Article 1. These strategic objectives, adopted as part of the planning procedure, are not as such in the public domain.

> Central African Republic, to fulfil the following functions, in accordance with the arrangement to be concluded between the European Union and the United Nations, in liaison with the Governments of Chad and the Central African Republic:
> (i) To contribute to protecting civilians in danger, particularly refugees and displaced persons;
> (ii) To facilitate the delivery of humanitarian aid and the free movement of humanitarian personnel by helping to improve security in the area of operations;
> (iii) To contribute to protecting United Nations personnel, facilities, installations and equipment and to ensuring the security and freedom of movement of its staff and United Nations and associated personnel;
> (b) *Authorizes* the European Union operation, at the close of the period referred to in subparagraph a, to take all appropriate measures to achieve an orderly disengagement, by means including fulfilment of the functions indicated in subparagraph a, and within the limits of its residual capacity;

The operation was conducted in a challenging environment in which several armed conflicts were ongoing.[774] However, the operation was not to get involved in these conflicts and the EU stressed repeatedly that in observance of its mandate, EUFOR Tchad/RCA would act with full independence, impartiality and neutrality.[775] Although a number of incidents occurred, it seems that this approach was well understood and the operation did not get involved in the conflict.[776]

---

774 In particular, there was an internal armed conflict in Chad as well as in Sudan, and both countries accused each other of supporting rebels fighting the respective governments. For some information on this, see UN Documents S/2008/215 of 1 April 2008, §§7–14 and S/2008/444 of 8 July 2008, §§10–15. In fact, it would seem that on two occasions, EUFOR personnel/assets were attacked by Sudanese armed forces. See UN Doc. S/2008/215, 1 April 2008, §35 ("*A French special force reconnaissance team, under EUFOR command, mistakenly crossed into the Sudan on 3 March and came under fire from Sudanese Armed Forces about 3 km into Darfur, near the Chadian town of Tissi. One French soldier was killed and another wounded*") and UN Doc. S/2008/760, 4 December 2008, §14 ("*On 15 November, EUFOR reported that two Sudanese MI-24 helicopters had fired upon its road patrol, near Birak in eastern Chad. No casualties were sustained but two EUFOR vehicles were destroyed*"). These appear to have been isolated incidents that have not led to any escalation. On the former incident, see also the OHQ press releases of 3, 4, 5 and 10 March 2008 (available at www.consilium.europa.eu/showPage.aspx?id=1368&lang=en).

775 See, e.g. the Conclusions of the External Relations Council of 26–27 May 2008 on EUFOR Tchad/RCA (EU Council Doc. 9868/08 (Presse 141), p. 33: "*In observance of its mandate EUFOR Tchad/RCA will act in an impartial, neutral and independent manner*") and of 15–16 October 2007 (EU Council Doc. 13720/07 (Presse 227), p. 10, §3: "*The operation will be conducted with full independence, impartiality and neutrality*").

776 For a summary account of the two incidents, see the OHQ press releases of 14 June and 19 August 2008, both available at www.consilium.europa.eu/showPage.aspx?id=1368&lang=en. According to the former "*In the midst of an engagement between unidentified armed groups and the Chadian National Army, EUFOR Irish troops deployed to protect Djabal IDP's/ refugee camps ... were confronted and fired upon. They returned warning fire and no casualties were sustained by them*". According to the latter "*on 18 August 2008 ... an EUFOR patrol was fired on and returned fire. ... The EUFOR patrol had earlier encountered a car in which two of the seven civilian occupants had received wounds, having previously been ambushed. After*

The UN part of the multidimensional presence was, for a(n initial) period of one year, the United Nations Mission in the Central African Republic and Chad (MINURCAT).[777] In addition, there is a UN Peacebuilding Support Office in CAR (BONUCA) and CAR is on the agenda of the UN Peacebuilding Commission.[778]

The EUFOR Tchad/RCA Joint Action provided for close coordination, contacts and liaison with the UN and local authorities, as well as other relevant actors, and specifically provided for the SG/HR and the EU Commanders to enter into the necessary arrangements with the UN regarding the modalities for mutual assistance and cooperation.[779]

Lieutenant General Patrick Nash was appointed EU Operation Commander and Brigadier General Jean-Philippe Ganascia EU Force Commander and the EU Operational Headquarters were located at Mont Valérien (near Paris, France).[780] When fully deployed, the operation numbered 3,700 troops.[781] The financial reference amount for the common costs of the EU military operation, which were administered by ATHENA, was EUR 99.2 million.[782]

The operation was launched on 28 January 2008[783] and was to end no later than 12 months after having reached Initial Operating Capability,[784] which was reached on 15 March 2008.[785] Interestingly, the execution of the mandate during the recovery phase, within residual capabilities, was explicitly provided for and the Joint Action "*shall be repealed following the recovery of the EU force*".[786]

rendering first aid to the injured civilians, the EUFOR patrol went to observe the ambush site, witnessing two cars and 8 to 10 unidentified persons there. Approaching within 80 meters of them and identifying themselves as EUFOR, the patrol was fired upon and in response returned fire following which the ambushers withdrew". See also *supra* note 774.

777 Established by UNSC Res. 1778, §§2–5. See generally www.un.org/Depts/dpko/missions/minurcat.

778 See www.un.org/peace/peacebuilding/car.shtml and the latest report in UN Doc. S/2009/309 of 12 June 2009.

779 Joint Action 2007/677/CFSP (*supra* note 772), Article 9.

780 *Id.*, respectively Articles 2, 4 and 3.

781 EU Factsheet Tchad-RCA/9, March 2009, www.consilium.europa.eu/uedocs/cmsUpload/Final_FACTSHEET_EUFOR_TCHAD-RCA-version9_EN.pdf.

782 Joint Action 2007/677/CFSP (*supra* note 772), Article 13.

783 Council Decision of 28 January 2008 on the launching of the European Union military operation in the Republic of Chad and in the Central African Republic (Operation EUFOR Tchad/RCA) (2008/101/CFSP), *O.J. L* 34, 8 February 2008, p. 39 and conclusions of the GAERC of that day (Doc. 5624/08 (Presse 19), pp. 14 and 20).

784 Joint Action 2007/677/CFSP (*supra* note 772), Article 15.

785 UN Doc. S/2008/215, 1 April 2008, §§36–37 (adding that as of that date, EUFOR personnel present in Chad and the Central African Republic numbered over 1,500).

786 Joint Action 2007/677/CFSP (*supra* note 772), Article 15 ("*The EU force shall begin recovery at the end of the EU military operation. During the period of recovery, the EU force may continue to perform the tasks entrusted to it in accordance with UNSCR 1778 (2007), within the limits of*

After the end of the mission, the UN reinforced MINURCAT[787] and a transfer of authority took place at midnight of 14–15 March 2009, following close EU-UN coordination and the 're-hatting' of 1877 EUFOR personnel to MINURCAT.[788]

1. MANDATE, LEGAL STATUS AND APPLICABLE LAW AND PARTICIPATION OF THIRD STATES

As already mentioned above, UN Security Council Resolution 1778 (25 September 2007, §6) authorized the EU to conduct the operation.[789] The EUFOR Tchad/RCA Joint Action also noted that "*the authorities of Chad and the Central African Republic have welcomed a possible EU military presence in their respective countries*".[790]

The EU concluded SOFAs with the two host States.[791] They probably offer the best picture of what the EU regards as a standard SOFA for its military ESDP

its residual capabilities; in particular, the chain of command for the EU military operation shall continue to apply"). See also §6(b) UNSC Res. 1778, cited above, and UNSC Res. 1861 of 14 January 2009, §9. The OHQ was closed on 31 May 2009; see www.consilium.europa.eu/showPage.aspx?id=1373&lang=en.

787 See especially UNSC Res. 1861 of 14 January 2009 and UN Doc. S/2008/760, 4 December 2008, §§39–71.

788 See UN Doc. S/2009/199, 14 April 2009, especially §§24–26 (also mentioning strong cooperation between EUFOR and MINURCAT headquarters – in particular through a joint Core Planning Team, and noting that Italy will remain in theatre under EUFOR command to support MINURCAT until the deployment of a Norwegian level II hospital in mid-May) and §23 (referring to a MINURCAT-EUFOR Technical Arrangement for the handover of the operation, covering operational issues, force protection, information-sharing, as well as command, control and coordination during the transitional period, in order to ensure a seamless transfer from EUFOR to MINURCAT and UN reverse support for the EUFOR phased withdrawal). In an unfortunate incident, on 7 April 2009, a French EUFOR Tchad/RCA soldier killed two fellow French EUFOR soldiers, a Togolese MINURCAT peacekeeper and a local peasant in Abeché (eastern Chad). He was apprehended by Chadian gendarmes on 9 April and was subsequently transferred to EUFOR/French authorities. See UN press release of 8 April 2009; www.lefigaro.fr/international/2009/04/07/01003-20090407ARTFIG00578-tchad-un-militaire-francais-tue-trois-autres-soldats-.php; http://minurcat.unmissions.org/Portals/MINURCAT/PR-%2008-04-2009-%20Minurcat%20mourns%20the%20victims%20of%20recent%20events%20in%20Abeche.pdf and www.france-info.com/spip.php?article276789&theme=14&sous_theme=18.

789 See also Joint Action 2007/677/CFSP (*supra* note 772), 9th and 5th considerations of the preamble.

790 *Id.*, 8th consideration of the preamble.

791 Agreement between the European Union and the Republic of Chad on the status of the European Union-led forces in the Republic of Chad (N'Djamena, 6 March 2008, provisionally applicable as of the date of signature), *O.J. L* 83, 26 March 2008, p. 39/40 and Agreement between the European Union and the Central African Republic on the status of the European Union-led forces in the Central African Republic (Bangui, 16 April 2008, entered into force on this date), *O.J. L* 136, 24 May 2008, p. 45/46.

operations.[792] In addition, a transit agreement/SOFA was concluded with Cameroon.[793] To my knowledge, it is the first such agreement concluded under Article 24 EU Treaty. It contains some provisions adapted to the transit function: e.g. there is no exclusion of liability for claims related to operational necessities or caused by activities in connection with civil disturbances or protection of EUFOR (Article 15) and the provisions on security specifically mention the right of EUFOR to take the measures necessary to protect its facilities *and convoys*, albeit in close cooperation with the competent authorities of Cameroon and they do not grant the Force Commander the right to establish military police units (Article 13).

The Joint Action provided for third State participation upon PSC decision.[794] The PSC accepted contributions by Russia, Croatia and Albania and set up a committee of contributors.[795] *Ad hoc* participation agreements were concluded with Russia,[796] Croatia[797] and Albania.[798]

---

792 The Concordia SOFA was an early one and, as described above in this chapter, in most of its other military operations, existing non-EU SOFAs were extended to the EU operation: this was the case for Artemis with Uganda (with the DRC there was no SOFA), Althea and EUFOR RD Congo with the DRC (there was a SOFA with Gabon). Given the maritime context, the SOFAs for Atalanta contain some specific features (see below, Section W.2 of this chapter).

793 Agreement between the European Union and the Republic of Cameroon on the status of the European Union-led Forces in transit within the territory of the Republic of Cameroon (Yaoundé, 6 February 2008, entered into force on this date), *O.J. L* 57, 1 March 2008, p. 30/31.

794 Joint Action 2007/677/CFSP (*supra* note 772), Article 10.

795 PSC Decision of 13 February 2008 on the acceptance of third States' contributions to the European Union military operation in the Republic of Chad and in the Central African Republic (2008/172/CFSP – CHAD/1/2008), *O.J. L* 56, 29 February 2008, p. 64 and PSC Decision of 18 March 2008 on the setting-up of the Committee of Contributors for the European Union military operation in the Republic of Chad and in the Central African Republic (2008/313/CFSP – CHAD/2/2008), *O.J. L* 107, 17 April 2008, p. 60, both amended by PSC Decision 2008/412/CFSP – CHAD/3/2008 of 28 May 2008 (*O.J. L* 144, 4 June 2008, p. 82; *corrigendum O.J. L* 180, 9 July 2008, p. 22) and by PSC Decision 2008/731/CFSP – CHAD/4/2008 of 2 September 2008 (*O.J. L* 247, 16 September 2008, p. 54).

796 Agreement between the European Union and the Russian Federation on the participation of the Russian Federation in the European Union military operation in the Republic of Chad and in the Central African Republic (EUFOR Tchad/RCA), *O.J. L* 307, 18 November 2008, p. 15/16.

797 Agreement between the European Union and the Republic of Croatia on the participation of the Republic of Croatia in the European Union military operation in the Republic of Chad and in the Central African Republic (Operation EUFOR Tchad/RCA), *O.J. L* 268, 9 October 2008, p. 32/33.

798 Agreement between the European Union and the Republic of Albania on the participation of the Republic of Albania in the European Union military operation in the Republic of Chad and in the Central African Republic (Operation EUFOR Tchad/RCA), *O.J. L* 217, 13 August 2008, p. 18/19 (*corrigendum O.J. L* 219, 14 August 2008, p. 74).

T. EULEX KOSOVO[799]

The European Union Rule of Law Mission in Kosovo, EULEX KOSOVO, is by far the largest civilian ESDP operation established so far. It had been planned for quite some time (a planning team had been set up already in 2006[800]) but the protracted negotiations over the final status of Kosovo that ended unsuccessfully[801] delayed its launch for some time. Nevertheless, despite the still

799 See generally www.consilium.europa.eu/showPage.aspx?id=1458&lang=EN; www.eulex-kosovo.eu; the reports in Annex 1 to UN Documents UN Doc. S/2009/149 of 17 March 2009 and S/2009/300 of 10 June 2009; A. Braem & B. Bilquin, 'L'Union européenne au Kosovo et sa mission "État de droit": entre voie diplomatique étroite et voix politique s'affirmant', 53 *Revue de la Faculté de droit de l'Université de Liège* 2008, pp. 385–399; Y. de Kermabon, 'Opération civiles de l'UE: perspectives d'EULex Kosovo', 64(7) Défense nationale 2008, pp. 46–54 and *ESDP Newsletter* No. 3, January 2007, pp. 13–14; *ESDP Newsletter* No. 4, Summer 2007, pp. 12–13; *ESDP Newsletter* No. 6, July 2008, pp. 17–20 and *ESDP Newsletter* No. 7, Winter [2008], pp. 9–13 (all www.consilium.europa.eu/showPage.aspx?id=1090&lang=en). See also B. Delcourt, 'La gestion de crises: un nouvel élan pour l'Europe?: analyse de l'implication de l'UE au Kosovo', in P. Magnette & A. Weyembergh (eds.), *L'Union européenne: la fin de la crise?*, Brussels, Éditions de l'Université de Bruxelles, 2008, pp. 103–114 and R. Yakemtchouk, 'Une décennie de participation de l'UE au règlement de la question du Kosovo', No. 512 *R.M.C.U.E.* 2007, pp. 556–564.

800 Council Joint Action of 10 April 2006 on the establishment of an EU Planning Team (EUPT Kosovo) regarding a possible EU crisis management operation in the field of rule of law and possible other areas in Kosovo (2006/304/CFSP), *O.J. L* 112, 26 April 2006, p. 19 as extended and amended by Council Joint Action of 11 December 2006 (2006/918/CFSP), *O.J. L* 349, 12 December 2006, p. 57; by Council Joint Action of 14 May 2007 (2007/334/CFSP), *O.J. L* 125, 15 May 2007, p. 29; by Council Joint Action of 23 July 2007 (2007/520/CFSP), *O.J. L* 192, 24 July 2007, p 28; by Council Joint Action of 29 November 2007 (2007/778/CFSP), *O.J. L* 312, 30 November 2007, p. 68 (including changes reflecting the new civilian command structure) and by Council Joint Action of 17 March 2008 (2008/228/CFSP), *O.J. L* 75, 18 March 2008, p. 78 (addressing third State participation and providing for the possibility of contracting staff who are nationals of third States). See also PSC Decision of 2 May 2006 concerning the appointment of the Head of the EU Planning Team (EUPT Kosovo) regarding a possible EU crisis management operation in the field of rule of law and possible other areas in Kosovo (EUPT/1/2006–2006/353/CFSP), *O.J. L* 130, 18 May 2006, p. 42, extended by PSC Decision of 12 December 2006 (EUPT/2/2006–2006/980/CFSP), *O.J. L* 365, 21 December 2006, p. 88 and by PSC Decision of 15 May 2007 (EUPT/1/2007–2007/358/CFSP), *O.J. L* 133, 25 May 2007, p. 49 and replaced by PSC Decision of 18 December 2007 concerning the appointment of the Head of the European Union Planning Team (EUPT Kosovo) (2007/888/CFSP – EUPT/2/2007), *O.J. L* 346, 29 December 2007, p. 29, as amended by PSC Decision of 6 June 2008 (2008/545/CFSP – EUPT/1/2008), *O.J. L* 173, 3 July 2008, p. 30.

801 After the end of the 1999 war over Kosovo, UNSC Res. 1244 (10 June 1999) authorized the establishment of an international security presence and a civilian international interim administration, "*under which the people of Kosovo can enjoy substantial autonomy within the Federal Republic of Yugoslavia, and which will provide transitional administration while establishing and overseeing the development of provisional democratic self-governing institutions*", "*pending a final settlement*" (see *inter alia* §§10, 11(a), (c) and (f), 6th hyphen of Annex 1 and §§5 and 8 of Annex 2). The final status of Kosovo therefore remained to be settled. In March 2007, the UN Secretary General's Special Envoy for the future status process for Kosovo, Martti Ahtisaari, submitted a Comprehensive Proposal for the Kosovo Status Settlement (see UN Documents S/2007/168 and S/2007/168/Add.1, both 26 March 2007), but this proposal was not accepted by all parties and was not endorsed by the Security Council. The EU was part of a 'troika' with Russia and the US that led further negotiations on the

open issue of Kosovo's status,[802] the operation was established in February 2008,[803] reached its initial operational capability in early December 2008,[804] was launched throughout Kosovo on 9 December 2008[805] and achieved its full operational capability on 6 April 2009.[806]

---

future status of Kosovo (see, e.g. UN press release of 1 August 2007 and EU Council Doc. 12369/07 of 13 August 2007), but there was no agreed solution by the 10 December 2007 deadline. See also M. Weller, 'The Vienna Negotiations on the Final Status for Kosovo', 84 *International Affairs* 2008, pp. 659–682 and M. Weller, *Negotiating the Final Status of Kosovo*, Paris, EU ISS, Chaillot Paper No. 114, December 2008.

802 After the failure of negotiations, on 17 February 2008 Kosovo declared its independence, which was recognized by a number of States (UN Doc. S/2009/300 of 10 June 2009, §2, mentions 60 recognitions), including a number of EU Member States (the Conclusions of the 18 February 2008 External Relations Council on Kosovo state that "*The Council notes that member states will decide, in accordance with national practice and international law, on their relations with Kosovo. ... The Council reiterates the EU's adherence to the principles of the UN Charter and the Helsinki Final Act, inter alia the principles of sovereignty and territorial integrity and all UN Security Council resolutions. It underlines its conviction that in view of the conflict of the 1990s and the extended period of international administration under SCR 1244, Kosovo constitutes a sui generis case which does not call into question these principles and resolutions*"; early June 2008, 20 Member States had recognized Kosovo; see EU Council Doc. 10219/08, 2 June 2008). See also C. Warbrick, 'Kosovo: The Declaration of Independence', 57 *I.C.L.Q.* 2008, pp. 675–690. On 9 April 2008, the Kosovo Assembly adopted the 'Constitution of the Republic of Kosovo', which came into force on 15 June 2008 (see UN Doc. S/2008/458 of 15 July 2008, §4). The UN General Assembly has asked the International Court of Justice for an advisory opinion on the question "*Is the unilateral declaration of independence by the Provisional Institutions of Self-Government of Kosovo in accordance with international law?*"; see UNGA Res. 63/3 (8 October 2008) and www.icj-cij.org/docket/index.php?p1=3&p2=4&code=kos&case=141&k=21. See also generally M. Weller, *Contested Statehood: Kosovo's Struggle for Independence*, Oxford, Oxford University Press, 2009; O. Corten, 'Déclarations unilatérales d'indépendance et reconnaissances prématurées: du Kosovo, à L'Ossétie du sud et à l'Abkhazie', 112 *R.G.D.I.P.* 2008, pp. 721–759; P. Hilpold, 'Das Kosovo-Problem: ein Testfall für das Völkerrecht', 68 *Z.a.ö.R.V.* 2008, pp. 779–801; A. Orakhelashvili, 'Statehood, Recognition and the United Nations System: A Unilateral Declaration of Independence in Kosovo', 12 *M.P.Y.U.N.L.* 2008, pp. 1–44; J. Vidmar, 'International Legal Responses to Kosovo's Declaration of Independence', 42 *Vanderbilt J.T.L.* 2009, pp. 779–851 and the Agora on Kosovo in 8 *Chinese J.I.L.* 2009, pp. 1–61 (R. Müllerson, 'Precedents in the Mountains: On the Parallels and Uniqueness of the Cases of Kosovo, South Ossetia and Abkhazia', pp. 2–25; B.B. Jia, 'The Independence of Kosovo: A Unique Case of Secession?', pp. 27–46 and P. Hilpold, 'The Kosovo Case and International Law: Looking for Applicable Theories', pp. 47–61).

803 Council Joint Action of 4 February 2008 on the European Union Rule of Law Mission in Kosovo, EULEX KOSOVO (2008/124/CFSP), *O.J. L* 42, 16 February 2008, p. 92. See also EU Council Doc. 6613/08 (Presse 43) of 16 February 2008. A partially declassified version of the Concept of Operations is contained in EU Council Documents 5978/08 EXT 1 and 5204/08 EXT 1 and revisions, all 27 March 2008.

804 EU Council Doc. S/400/08, 5 December 2008, www.consilium.europa.eu/uedocs/cms_Data/docs/pressdata/en/declarations/104524.pdf.

805 UN Doc. S/2009/149 of 17 March 2009, Annex 1, §3. Pursuant to Article 5(1) of Joint Action 2008/124/CFSP (*supra* note 803); the decision to launch EULEX KOSOVO was to be taken by the Council upon approval of the OPLAN and the operational phase of EULEX KOSOVO was to start upon transfer of authority from UNMIK.

806 See www.consilium.europa.eu/showPage.aspx?id=1458&lang=EN and EU Council Doc.S/095/09, 6 April 2009, www.consilium.europa.eu/uedocs/cms_Data/docs/pressdata/en/esdp/107145.pdf.

EULEX Kosovo is part of a wider engagement of the EU in relation to Kosovo.[807] In particular, the EU has also appointed an EU Special Representative for Kosovo (Mr. Pieter Feith)[808] and this person also heads the 'International Civilian Office' there,[809] as had been planned for quite some time.[810] Furthermore, "*[t]he Stabilisation and Association Process is the strategic framework of the EU's policy towards the Western Balkan region, and its instruments apply to Kosovo, including a European partnership, political and technical dialogue under the SAP Tracking Mechanism, and related Community assistance programmes*".[811] Obviously, the EU's relations with Kosovo are closely linked to its relations with Serbia, at least as long as the issue of Kosovo's status is open and EU Member States do not all have the same position on Kosovo's status.[812]

---

807 See generally www.euinkosovo.eu/ and http://ec.europa.eu/enlargement/potential-candidate-countries/kosovo/eu_kosovo_relations_en.htm.

808 Council Joint Action of 4 February 2008 appointing a European Union Special Representative in Kosovo (2008/123/CFSP), *O.J. L* 42, 16 February 2008, p. 88, as extended by Council Joint Action of 16 February 2009 extending the mandate of the European Union Special Representative in Kosovo (2009/137/CFSP), *O.J. L* 46, 17 February 2009, p. 69 and amended by Council Joint Action of 7 August 2009 amending Joint Action 2009/137/CFSP extending the mandate of the European Union Special Representative in Kosovo (2009/605/CFSP), *O.J. L* 206, 8 August 2009, p. 20 (increasing the financial reference amount in order to cover expenditure related to the reinforced liaison presence in Belgrade). See generally http://consilium.europa.eu/cms3_fo/showPage.aspx?id=1445&lang=EN and www.eusrinkosovo.eu/en/. The EUSR is to give local political guidance to the EULEX Head of Mission: see Article 3(c) Joint Action 2008/124/CFSP (*supra* note 803) and Article 12(2) 2009 EUSR Joint Action (*supra* this note).

809 The 8th consideration of the preamble of the current 2009 EUSR Joint Action (*supra* previous note) states that "*The Council foresees that the powers and authorities of the EUSR and the powers and authorities of an International Civilian Representative shall be vested in the same person*". Nonetheless, Article 6(2) of the same Joint Action only provides for contracted personnel with the nationality of EU Member States and personnel seconded by EU institution or Member States.

810 See Council Joint Action of 15 September 2006 on the establishment of a EU-team to contribute to the preparations of the establishment of a possible international civilian mission in Kosovo, including a European Union Special Representative component (ICM/EUSR Preparation Team) (2006/623/CFSP), *O.J. L* 253, 16 September 2006, p. 29; extended (and amended) by Council Joint Action of 27 March 2007 (2007/203/CFSP), *O.J. L* 90, 30 March 2007, p. 94; by Council Joint Action of 16 July 2007 (2007/517/CFSP), *O.J. L* 190, 21 July 2007, p. 38 and by Council Joint Action of 19 November 2007 (2007/744/CFSP), *O.J. L* 301, 20 November 2007, p. 27.

811 See the 6th consideration of the preamble of the current 2009 EUSR Joint Action (*supra* note 808). The Instrument for Pre-accession Assistance (set up by Council Regulation (EC) No 1085/2006 of 17 July 2006 establishing an Instrument for Pre-Accession Assistance (IPA), *O.J. L* 210, 31 July 2006, p. 82; *corrigendum O.J. L* 18, 25 January 2007, p. 11), which came into force on 1 January 2007 and brought all pre-accession support into one single instrument, also covers the countries with potential candidate status, including "*Serbia including Kosovo[, a]s defined in UNSCR 1244*" (Annex II of this Regulation and the footnote thereto). See also www.delprn.ec.europa.eu/?cid=2,97.

812 The Stabilization and Association Agreement with Serbia provides in its Article 135 that it "*shall not apply in Kosovo which is at present under international administration pursuant to*

EULEX KOSOVO's mission is to "*assist the Kosovo institutions, judicial authorities and law enforcement agencies in their progress towards sustainability and accountability and in further developing and strengthening an independent multi-ethnic justice system and multi-ethnic police and customs service, ensuring that these institutions are free from political interference and adhering to internationally recognised standards and European best practices ... through monitoring, mentoring and advising, while retaining certain executive responsibilities*".[813] Its tasks which include executive responsibilities appear to be primarily to "*monitor, mentor and advise the competent Kosovo institutions on all areas related to the wider rule of law (including a customs service), whilst retaining certain executive responsibilities*" and to "*ensure the maintenance and promotion of the rule of law, public order and security including, as necessary, in consultation with the relevant international civilian authorities in Kosovo, through reversing or annulling operational decisions taken by the competent Kosovo authorities*".[814] The mission has taken over significant aspects of the mandate of the UN Mission in Kosovo (UNMIK) (see below, under mandate), which had already transferred large parts of its tasks to the local authorities.[815]

The Mission has its main Headquarters in Pristina, regional and local offices across Kosovo, a Brussels support element and liaison offices as required and consists of the Head of Mission and staff, a police component, a justice

United Nations Security Council Resolution 1244 of 10 June 1999" and that this "*is without prejudice to the current status of Kosovo or the determination of its final status under that Resolution*" (29 April 2008, text available online at http://ec.europa.eu/enlargement/pdf/serbia/key_document/saa_en.pdf). On the Stabilization and Association Process, see generally http://ec.europa.eu/enlargement/enlargement_process/accession_process/how_does_a_country_join_the_eu/sap/index_en.htm (where Kosovo is listed separately from Serbia as 'Kosovo under UNSCR 1244'). Council Decision 2008/213/EC of 18 February 2008 on the principles, priorities and conditions contained in the European Partnership with Serbia including Kosovo as defined by United Nations Security Council Resolution 1244 of 10 June 1999 and repealing Decision 2006/56/EC and its annexes (*O.J. L* 80, 19 March 2008, p. 46), set out principles, priorities and conditions in the European Partnership with "*Serbia including Kosovo under UNSCR 1244*". Council Joint Action 2009/445/CFSP of 9 June 2009 amending Joint Action 2008/124/CFSP on the European Union Rule of Law Mission in Kosovo(1), EULEX KOSOVO, *O.J. L* 148, 11 June 2009, p. 33, contains a footnote after Kosovo adding/specifying "*Under United Nations Security Council Resolution 1244 (1999)*". This seems to be the EU agreed wording that is now used. On Kosovo's status, see *supra* notes 801–802 and the accompanying text.

813 Joint Action 2008/124/CFSP (*supra* note 803), Article 2.

814 *Id.*, Article 3(a) and (b). EULEX already had to use these powers: e.g. it dispersed demonstrators (including with tear gas) on a number of occasions (UN Doc. S/2009/300 of 10 June 2009, §12).

815 On the role of both organizations, see also M. Karnitschnig, 'The UN and the EU in Kosovo – the Challenges of Joint Nation-Building', in J. Wouters, F. Hoffmeister & T. Ruys (eds.), *supra* note 246, pp. 323–351, especially p. 341–351.

component and a customs component.[816] On 31 May 2009, mission staffing was 2,569 staff (1,651 international staff and 918 local staff),[817] headed by Mr. Yves de Kermabon.[818]

The initial duration of the mission is some two years and the Joint Action expires 28 months from the date of approval of the OPLAN,[819] i.e. on 14 June 2010.[820] The financial reference amount for the 16 months starting from the approval of the OPLAN was EUR 205 million[821] and the financial reference amount for the entire period up to 14 June 2010 was later fixed at EUR 265 million.[822]

Cooperation was envisaged with the NATO-led Kosovo Force (KFOR) and cooperation in the field between EULEX Kosovo and KFOR appears to work fine.[823] However, as in Afghanistan, no overarching EU-NATO arrangement on the cooperation between their respective operations appears to have been concluded.

1. MANDATE

The EULEX Kosovo Joint Action[824] refers to UN Security Council Resolution 1244 (10 June 1999) and the UN Secretary-General's authority under this resolution, suggesting these are considered to be the legal basis for this mission.[825]

---

816 *Id.*, Article 6. For more details, see www.eulex-kosovo.eu/home/docs/EULEXOrgChart.pdf.

817 UN Doc. S/2009/300 of 10 June 2009, Annex I (p 12). The final staff target is about 3,000 (1,900 international and 1,100 local staff according to the EU Factsheet, EULEX/04, December 2008, www.consilium.europa.eu/uedocs/cms_Data/docs/pressdata/en/declarations/104524.pdf and www.eulex-kosovo.eu/?id=2 and 1.950 international and 1,200 local staff according to the EU Factsheet, EULEX/07, April 2009, www.consilium.europa.eu/uedocs/cmsUpload/090406-FACTSHEET_EULEX_Kosovo-version7_EN.pdf).

818 See PSC Decision of 7 February 2008 concerning the appointment of the Head of Mission of the European Union Rule of Law Mission in Kosovo, EULEX KOSOVO (2008/125/CFSP – EULEX/1/2008), *O.J. L* 42, 16 February 2008, p. 99.

819 Article 20 Joint Action 2008/124/CFSP (*supra* note 803).

820 Council Joint Action 2009/445/CFSP of 9 June 2009 amending Joint Action 2008/124/CFSP on the European Union Rule of Law Mission in Kosovo[(1)], EULEX KOSOVO ([(1)] Under United Nations Security Council Resolution 1244 (1999)), *O.J. L* 148, 11 June 2009, p. 33, 1st consideration of the preamble and Article 1(2).

821 Article 16(1) Joint Action 2008/124/CFSP (*supra* note 803).

822 Joint Action 2009/445/CFSP (*supra* note 820), Article 1(1).

823 See, e.g. reporting on a joint exercise at www.nato.int/kfor/docu/inside/2009/01/i090127a.htm.

824 *Supra* note 803.

825 The Netherlands has clearly expressed the view that Resolution 1244 constitutes the legal basis for EULEX Kosovo: see the 18 July 2008 letter by the ministers concerned to parliament on the preparations for the July 2008 GAERC (*Kamerbrief betreffende verslag schriftelijk overleg inzake de RAZEB d.d. 22 en 23 juli 2008*, www.minbuza.nl/nl/Actueel/

The first consideration of the preamble mentions Resolution 1244 and its authorization for the UN Secretary-General, "*with the assistance of relevant international organisations, to establish an international civil presence in Kosovo*" as well as the responsibility of the international civilian presence to "*in a final stage, oversee[...] the transfer of authority from Kosovo's provisional institutions to institutions established under a political settlement*" and the 7th consideration of the preamble states that "*The United Nations Secretary-General also noted the readiness of the EU to play an enhanced role in Kosovo, as reflected in the conclusions of the Brussels European Council on 14 December*".[826] Furthermore, pursuant to Article 5(1) of this Joint Action, "*The operational phase of EULEX KOSOVO shall start upon transfer of authority from the United Nations Mission in Kosovo, UNMIK*". In addition, the 2nd consideration of the preamble defines the Kosovo organs, institutions and authorities referred to in the Joint Action as the "*institutions created on the basis of Resolution 1244*" and the SG/HR has declared that the EULEX mission operates "*in the framework of the UNSC 1244*"[827] and under the overall authority of the UN.[828]

This transfer of authority initially proved somewhat difficult and the international legal basis for EULEX Kosovo was initially not undisputed.[829] E.g. in late 2007 Russia argued that any EU mission without some form of UN Security Council approval and Serbian consent would be illegal.[830] However, these initial discussions have been overcome and especially as of June 2008 a number of successive reports by the UN Secretary-General on UNMIK[831] and their

Kamerstukken/2008/07/Kamerbrief_betreffende_verslag_schriftelijk_overleg_inzake_de_RAZEB _d_d_22_en_23_juli_2008): "*EULEX Kosovo vindt haar rechtsbasis in VNVR-resolutie 1244 (1999)*".

826 See UN Doc. S/2007/768 of 3 January 2008, §35.

827 EU Council Doc. S223/08, 21 June 2008, www.consilium.europa.eu/uedocs/cms_Data/docs/pressdata/en/esdp/101372.pdf.

828 "*... pour la mission EULEX, il fixe son cadre d'opération sous l'autorité de la résolution 1244. En clair, EULEX opèrera* sous l'autorité globale des Nations unies *et je veillerai à fournir tous les rapports nécessaires à leur Secrétaire Général*": EU Council Doc. S257/08, 18 July 2008, www.consilium.europa.eu/uedocs/cms_Data/docs/pressdata/en/esdp/101884.pdf (emphasis added).

829 Compare E. de Wet, 'The Governance of Kosovo: Security Council Resolution 1244 and the Establishment and Functioning of EULEX', 103 *A.J.I.L.* 2009, pp. 83–96 and A. de Guttry, 'The EU Rule of Law Mission in Kosovo. Remarks on Its Legality', International Training Programme for Conflict Management, Vol. 7 No. 1 *Newsletter*, April 2009, www.sssup.it/UploadDocs/4217_ITPCM_Newsletter_April_2009.pdf, pp. 3–6.

830 See, e.g. O. Shchedrov, 'Russia Says New EU Role in Kosovo "Not Impossible"', Reuters, 21 December 2007, www.alertnet.org/thenews/newsdesk/L21190769.htm.

831 See especially UN Documents S/2008/354 of 12 June 2008, §§10–20; S/2008/458 of 15 July 2008, §§3 and 30–33 and UN Doc. S/2008/692, 24 November 2008, §§23–29 and 50–52 and the more recent reports cited below.

implementation, as well as an endorsement thereof by the Security Council,[832] have taken forward this process, which is accompanied by a reconfiguration of UNMIK.[833]

From these reports, it appears that both the UN and Serbia have accepted the reconfiguration of UNMIK and the enhanced role of EULEX Kosovo, under the overall authority of the United Nations, under a UN umbrella headed by the UN Secretary General's Special Representative, within the status neutral framework of the UN and in accordance with Resolution 1244 (1999).[834] To quote from the most recent report:

> In line with my reports … and the Security Council's presidential statement of 26 November 2008 … EULEX … has continued to operate under the overall authority of the United Nations and within the status-neutral framework of Security Council resolution 1244 (1999). … I welcome the assumption of full operational capability by EULEX. Its operational role in the rule of law sector, under the overall authority and within the status-neutral framework of the United Nations, is key to the maintenance of stability on the ground. … I am encouraged by the level of cooperation between

---

832 S/PRST/2008/44, 26 November 2008 ("*The Security Council welcomes … Report … S/2008/692 … and, taking into account the positions of Belgrade and Pristina …, welcomes their intentions to cooperate with the international community. The Security Council welcomes the cooperation between the UN and other international actors, within the framework of Security Council Resolution 1244 (1999), and also welcomes the continuing efforts of the European Union to advance the European perspective of the whole of the Western Balkans, thereby making a decisive contribution to regional stability and prosperity*").

833 See also generally E. Milano, 'Il trasferimento di funzioni da UMNIK a EULEX in Kosovo', 91 *Rivista di diritto internazionale* 2008, pp. 967–990 and X., 'Editorial Comments. And in the meantime … Kosovo …', 46 *C.M.L. Rev.* 2009, pp. 377–382.

834 See especially UN Doc. S/2008/692, 24 November 2008, §§23, 28 ("*all parties have accepted the reconfiguration of the structure and profile of the international presence … to one that corresponds to the evolving situation in Kosovo and enables the [EU] to assume an enhanced operational role throughout Kosovo, in particular in the areas of international policing, justice and customs*"), 29, 50 ("*my Special Representative and Head of UNMIK is facilitating the [EU] preparations to undertake an enhanced operational role in Kosovo in the rule of law area. EULEX will fully respect Security Council resolution 1244 (1999) and operate under the overall authority and within the status neutral framework of the United Nations. EULEX will submit reports to the [UN] on a regular basis*") and 52 ("*The Government of Serbia has accepted … the arrangements set out in the present report*") and UN Doc. S/2009/149 of 17 March 2009, §§5 ("*the Government of Serbia and a majority of Kosovo Serbs have accepted the deployment of … (EULEX) on condition that it would fully respect resolution 1244 (1999) and that it would operate under the overall authority of the [UN] and within its status-neutral framework*"), 12 ("*In line with the presidential statement of 26 November 2008 … EULEX assumed full operational responsibility in the area of rule of law on 9 December within the framework of resolution 1244 (1999) and under the overall authority of the United Nations*") and 37 ("*I have noted the commitment of EULEX to fully respect resolution 1244 (1999) and operate under the overall authority and within the status-neutral framework of the [UN]. … EULEX has begun to submit reports to the [UN] on its activities on a regular basis*").

UNMIK and EULEX on the ground, and expect that such cooperation will continue and be strengthened in all relevant areas.[835]

The Kosovo authorities have stated that they are "*in favour of a quick deployment of EULEX in Kosovo in accordance with the mandate foreseen in the Declaration of Independence, the Comprehensive Proposal for a Kosovo Status Settlement, the Constitution of the Republic of Kosovo, Kosovo legislation, the European Union Joint Action of 4 February 2008 and Kosovo's institutions' invitation to EULEX*".[836] Presumably, for those States having recognized Kosovo, this invitation (also) constitutes an adequate legal basis for the mission.[837]

The transfer process has included the conclusion of a number of arrangements, e.g. on the handover of assets and of justice-related investigative and case files between UNMIK and EULEX.[838] It also seems that pragmatic solutions have been developed to deal with difficulties arising from the status question. For instance, UNMIK continues to exercise certain responsibilities with regard to external relations in the justice area, including requests for international legal assistance from and to non-recognizing countries even after local authorities took over responsibility for international legal assistance requests to and from countries which have recognized Kosovo as of 19 March 2009 and UNMIK also continues to play a role in facilitating contacts with INTERPOL and with the ICTY.[839] At the time of writing, the reconfiguration and downsizing of UNMIK is close to finalization and it is envisaged that the Mission will be reduced from a personnel strength of 4,911 to 507 to perform the residual UNMIK tasks.[840]

Interestingly, the 3rd consideration of the preamble of the Joint Action adds that "*There is a need to prevent, on humanitarian grounds, possible outbreaks of violence, acts of persecution and intimidation in Kosovo, taking account, as appropriate, of the responsibility towards populations as referred to in Resolution 1674 by the United Nations Security Council on 28 April 2006*" (the latter Resolution deals with the protection of civilians in armed conflict and refers to the "the responsibility to protect" in its §4).[841]

---

835 UN Doc. S/2009/300 of 10 June 2009, §§6 and 41.

836 UN Doc. S/2008/692, 24 November 2008, §52 and especially Annex I, §1.

837 Compare C. Schaller, 'Die Sezession des Kosovo und der völkerrechtliche Status der internationalen Präsenz', 46 *A.V.R.* 2008, pp. 131–171.

838 See respectively UN Doc. S/2009/300 of 10 June 2009, §20 and UN Doc. S/2009/149 of 17 March 2009, §13 as well as UN Doc. S/2008/692, 24 November 2008, §§23–24.

839 UN Doc. S/2009/300 of 10 June 2009, §22.

840 *Id.*, §§18–19.

841 The responsibility to protect is also referred to in the 2008 ESS Implementation Report (*supra* note 160, 3rd last paragraph) but only in general terms and with a reference to the agreement reached at the UN World Summit in 2005. On the latter, see UNGA Res. 60/1 (16 September

2. LEGAL STATUS AND APPLICABLE LAW

Article 10(1) of the Joint Action[842] provides that "*The status of EULEX KOSOVO and its staff, including the privileges, immunities and further guarantees necessary for the completion and smooth functioning of EULEX KOSOVO, shall be agreed as appropriate*". The usual reference to an agreement under Article 24 EU Treaty is absent, undoubtedly because of the disputed status of Kosovo. The participation agreement with the US states that "*seconded personnel serving in Kosovo ... shall enjoy privileges and immunities accorded on the basis of relevant UN documents including UNSCR 1244, relevant provisions of the law applicable in Kosovo, and other pertinent documents and correspondence*".[843] The Kosovar authorities have granted EULEX Kosovo and its staff privileges and immunities.[844]

As regards the applicable law, it is worth noting that pursuant to Article 3(i) of the Joint Action,[845] the mission is to "*ensure that all its activities respect international standards concerning human rights and gender mainstreaming*". This is consistent with the rule enacted by UNMIK that "*In exercising their functions, all persons undertaking public duties or holding public office in Kosovo*

2005), §§138–140 ("*139. The international community, through the United Nations, also has the responsibility to use appropriate diplomatic, humanitarian and other peaceful means, ..., to help to protect populations from genocide, war crimes, ethnic cleansing and crimes against humanity. In this context, we are prepared to take collective action, in a timely and decisive manner, through the Security Council, in accordance with the Charter, including Chapter VII, on a case-by-case basis and in cooperation with relevant regional organizations as appropriate, should peaceful means be inadequate and national authorities are manifestly failing to protect their populations from genocide, war crimes, ethnic cleansing and crimes against humanity*"). See also generally A.J. Bellamy, *Responsibility to Protect: The Global Effort to End Mass Atrocities*, Cambridge, Polity, 2009; G. Evans, *The Responsibility to Protect: Ending Mass Atrocity Crimes Once and For All*, Washington DC, Brookings Institution Press, 2008; P. Niemelä, *The Politics of Responsibility to Protect: Problems and Prospects*, Helsinki, Erik Castrén Institute of International Law and Human Rights, 2008 and Société française pour le Droit international (ed.), *La responsabilité de protéger – Colloque de Nanterre. (41e Colloque de la Société française pour le Droit international, Paris X-Nanterre, 7–9 juin 2007)*, Paris, Pedone, 2008. See also the report of the International Commission on Intervention and State Sovereignty, entitled *The Responsibility to Protect*, available online at www.iciss.ca.

842 Joint Action 2008/124/CFSP (*supra* note 803).

843 *Infra* note 851, Article 2(1). The privileges and immunities of UNMIK are set out in UNMIK Regulation 2000/47, 18 August 2000, especially section 3, www.unmikonline.org/regulations/2000/re2000_47.htm. See also International Crisis Group, *Kosovo's Fragile Transition. Crisis Group Europe Report N°196*, 25 September 2008. Some EULEX invitations to tender also refer to an UNMIK executive decision on privileges, see, e.g. http://eulexkosovo.org/tenders/docs/fuel/Tender-Dossier.pdf (p. 18 note 1).

844 See especially the Law No. 03/L-033 on the Status, Immunities and Privileges of Diplomatic and Consular Missions and Personnel in Republic of Kosovo and of the International Military Presence and Its Personnel, 20 February 2008 (www.gazetazyrtare.com/e-gov/ahtisari/033-Eng.swf), which explicitly covers EULEX (see Article 3(2)b).

845 Joint Action 2008/124/CFSP (*supra* note 803).

shall observe internationally recognized human rights standards", as reflected in particular in a series of international human rights instruments.[846]

3. PARTICIPATION OF THIRD STATES

The Joint Action provides for third State participation upon PSC decision.[847] Norway, Turkey and Canada participate[848]and *ad hoc* participation agreements have been concluded with Switzerland,[849] Croatia[850] and the US (which is participating for the first time in an ESDP operation).[851] Also, a Committee of Contributors has been set up.[852]

U. EU SSR GUINEA-BISSAU[853]

In February 2008, the EU decided to conduct a civilian security sector reform mission in Guinea-Bissau (EU SSR GUINEA-BISSAU) to complement European

846 Section 1(3) of UNMIK Regulation 2000/59, 27 October 2000, amending UNMIK Regulations 1999/24 (12 December 1999) and 1999/1 (25 July 1999), all available online at www.unmikonline.org/regulations/index.htm.

847 Article 13 Joint Action 2008/124/CFSP (*supra* note 803). Furthermore, pursuant to Article 9(4) of this Joint Action, third States may also, as appropriate, second staff to EULEX KOSOVO and exceptionally, in duly justified cases, where no qualified applications from Member States are available, nationals from participating third States may be recruited on a contractual basis, as appropriate. See already the possibility of third State participation in the EUPT, *supra* note 800.

848 See www.eulex-kosovo.eu/?id=2.

849 Agreement between the European Union and the Swiss Confederation on the participation of the Swiss Confederation in the European Union Rule of Law Mission in Kosovo, EULEX KOSOVO, *O.J. L* 217, 13 March.2008, p. 23/24 (corrigendum *O.J. L* 219, 14 August 2008, p. 77).

850 Agreement between the European Union and the Republic of Croatia on the participation of the Republic of Croatia in the European Union Rule of Law Mission in Kosovo, EULEX KOSOVO, *O.J. L* 317, 27 November 2008, p. 19/20.

851 Agreement between the European Union and the United States of America on the participation of the United States of America in the European Union Rule of Law Mission in Kosovo, EULEX KOSOVO, *O.J. L* 282, 25 October 2008, p. 32/33. See also the joint press statement in EU Council Doc. 14619/08 (Presse 295), 22 October 2008, www.consilium.europa.eu/uedocs/cmsUpload/103487.pdf.

852 PSC Decision of 22 April 2008 on the establishment of the Committee of Contributors for the European Union Rule of Law Mission in Kosovo (EULEX KOSOVO) (EULEX/2/2008 – 2008/356/CFSP), *O.J. L* 118, 6 May 2008, p. 33.

853 See generally www.consilium.europa.eu/showPage.aspx?id=1413&lang=en and *ESDP Newsletter* No. 7, Winter [2008], pp. 22–25 (www.consilium.europa.eu/showPage.aspx?id=1090&lang=en). For the EU's relations with the country, see generally http://ec.europa.eu/development/geographical/regionscountries/countries/country_profile.cfm?cid=GW&type=short&lng=en.

Development Fund and EC activities.[854] Guinea-Bissau is also on the agenda of the UN Peacebuilding Commission.[855]

The mission is to "*provide local authorities with advice and assistance on [Security Sector Reform] in the Republic of Guinea-Bissau, in order to contribute to creating the conditions for implementation of the National SSR Strategy, in close cooperation with other EU, international and bilateral actors, and with a view to facilitating subsequent donor engagement*".[856]

The operation was launched on 16 June 2008[857] and was initially established for a duration of up to one year from the declaration of initial operational capability, with the Joint Action expiring on 31 May 2009.[858] It was subsequently extended for six months until 30 November 2009.[859] The financial reference amount is EUR 5.65 million.[860]

The mission counts some 32 staff,[861] headed by Mr. Juan Esteban Verástegui.[862] It consists of military and civilian advisers assigned to work with the Army, the Navy, the Air Force, the Judicial Police, the Public Order Police, the Prosecution Services and the Secretariat of the Steering Committee for the Security Sector Reform process.[863]

---

854 Council Joint Action of 12 February 2008 on the European Union mission in support of security sector reform in the Republic of Guinea-Bissau (EU SSR GUINEA-BISSAU) (2008/112/CFSP), *O.J. L* 40, 14 February 2008, p. 11. See the 8th consideration of the preamble.

855 See www.un.org/peace/peacebuilding/guinea-bissau.shtml and *Report of the Secretary-General on developments in Guinea-Bissau and on the activities of the United Nations Peacebuilding Support Office in that country*, UN Doc. S/2009/302 of 10 June 2009.

856 Joint Action 2008/112/CFSP (*supra* note 854), Article 2.

857 EU Council Doc. 10415/08 of 16 June 2008, §§39–42.

858 Joint Action 2008/112/CFSP (*supra* note 854), Articles 1(1) and 17.

859 Council Joint Action 2009/405/CFSP of 18 May 2009 amending Joint Action 2008/112/CFSP on the European Union mission in support of security sector reform in the Republic of Guinea-Bissau (EU SSR GUINEA-BISSAU), *O.J. L* 128, 27 May 2009, p. 60.

860 Joint Action 2008/112/CFSP (*supra* note 854), Article 9(1).

861 EU Factsheet Guinea-Bissau/04, March 2009, www.consilium.europa.eu/uedocs/cmsUpload/090325%20FACTSHEET%20EU%20SSR%20Guinea-Bissau%20-%20version%205_EN.pdf.

862 See PSC Decision of 5 March 2008 concerning the appointment of the Head of Mission of the European Union mission in support of security sector reform in the Republic of Guinea-Bissau (EU SSR GUINEA-BISSAU) (2008/226/CFSP – EU SSR GUINEA-BISSAU/1/2008), *O.J. L* 73, 15 March 2008, p. 34.

863 Joint Action 2008/112/CFSP (*supra* note 854), Article 3 and EU Factsheet Guinea-Bissau/04, *supra* note 861.

1. MANDATE, LEGAL STATUS AND APPLICABLE LAW AND PARTICIPATION OF THIRD STATES

The mission is conducted at the invitation of the Government of Guinea-Bissau[864] and a status of mission agreement has been concluded.[865] The PSC was authorized to accept third State contributions.[866]

V. EUMM GEORGIA[867]

In August 2008, an armed conflict erupted between Georgian security forces on the one hand and Russian armed forces and separatist forces in South Ossetia and Abkhazia on the other hand.[868] The latter two regions within Georgia had already been outside Georgian government control for a number of years following earlier fighting and a number of cease-fire agreements,[869] accompanied by international peacekeeping and monitoring missions.[870] The EU already supported the conflict settlement process in South Ossetia.[871] The EU, and

---

864 Joint Action 2008/112/CFSP (*supra* note 854), 10th consideration of the preamble.

865 Agreement between the European Union and the Republic of Guinea-Bissau on the Status of the European Union Mission in Support of Security Sector Reform in the Republic of Guinea-Bissau, *O.J. L* 219, 14 August 2008, p. 65/66.

866 Joint Action 2008/112/CFSP (*supra* note 854), Article 10. It would seem that the only third State which might effectively participate is the US: EU Factsheet Guinea-Bissau/04, *supra* note 861.

867 See generally www.consilium.europa.eu/showPage.aspx?id=1512&lang=EN; www.eumm.eu and *ESDP Newsletter* No. 7, Winter [2008], pp. 14–19 (www.consilium.europa.eu/showPage.aspx?id=1090&lang=en).

868 See, e.g. the account in UN Doc. S/2008/631 of 3 October 2008, §§5–15. See also J. Kranz, 'Der Kampf um den Frieden und sein besonderer Facilitator: Anmerkungen zur Georgienkrise', 46 *A.V.R.* 2009, pp. 481–501 and O. Luchterhandt, 'Völkerrechtliche Aspekte des Georgien-Krieges', 46 *A.V.R.* 2008, pp. 435–480.

869 Including the 1993 Sochi Agreement (see http://smr.gov.ge/uploads/file/annex/annex4.pdf); the 1994 Moscow Agreement (UN Doc. S/1994/583 of 17 May 1994, Annex) and the 2001 Yalta Declaration (UN Doc. S/2001/242 of 19 March 2001, Annex).

870 These include(d) the UN Observer Mission in Georgia (UNOMIG), the OSCE Mission to Georgia and Commonwealth of Independent States peacekeeping forces. UNOMIG was established in August 1993 to verify compliance with the ceasefire agreement between the Government of Georgia and the Abkhaz authorities in Georgia. UNOMIG's mandate was expanded following the signing by the parties of the 1994 Agreement on a Ceasefire and Separation of Forces. Due to a failure among Security Council members to agree on its extension, the mission came to an end on 15 June 2009. See www.un.org/Depts/dpko/missions/unomig and www.unomig.org. The OSCE mission in Georgia was established in 1992 and ended late 2008 when no agreement could be reached on its extension. It *inter alia* monitored the Joined Peacekeeping Forces. See www.osce.org/georgia.

871 See Council Joint Action of 29 October 2001 regarding a contribution from the European Union to the conflict settlement process in South Ossetia (2001/759/CFSP), *O.J. L* 286, 30 October 2001, p. 4 as extended by Joint Action 2003/473/CFSP of 25 June 2003 (*O.J. L* 157,

especially the then French Council Presidency, tried to mediate in the conflict and contributed to the conclusion of a six-point cease-fire plan and implementing agreement, respectively dated 12 August and 8 September 2008,[872] which ended the fighting.[873] As part of these efforts, the EU committed itself to deploying a monitoring mission.[874]

This led to the establishment of the EU Monitoring Mission in Georgia, EUMM Georgia, in September 2008.[875] In addition, the EU appointed a Special representative for the crisis in Georgia (Pierre Morel) with the mandate "*to help prepare for the international talks to be held under point 6 of the settlement plan of 12 August 2008*[876] *and to help establish the EU's position and represent it, at his level, in those talks and to facilitate the implementation of the two agreements in close coordination with the UN and the OSCE*".[877] It also established an independent international fact-finding mission on the conflict in Georgia, headed by Ms. Heidi Tagliavini (a Swiss national[878]) with the aim "*to investigate the origins and the course of the conflict in Georgia, including with regard to international law, humanitarian law and human rights, and the accusations made in that context*" in complete independence with a view to presenting its findings in a report to the parties to the conflict, the EU Council, the OSCE and the

26 June 2003, p. 72); by Joint Action 2005/561/CFSP of 18 July 2005 (*O.J. L* 174, 28 June 2006, p. 9); by Joint Action 2006/439/CFSP of 27 June 2006 (*O.J. L* 174, 28 June 2006, p. 9); by Joint Action 2007/484/CFSP of 10 July 2007 (*O.J. L* 181, 11 July 2007, p. 14) and by Joint Action 2008/450/CFSP of 16 June 2008 (*O.J. L* 157, 17 June 2008, p. 110).

872 The French text of the six-point plan is available online at www.diplomatie.gouv.fr/fr/IMG/pdf/Accord_6_points_signe_PR.pdf. The points are reproduced in English in the Conclusions of the 13 August 2008 extraordinary GAERC (EU Council Doc. 12453/08 (Presse 236)). The English text of the implementation agreement is available at www.mid.ru/brp_4.nsf/e78a48070f128a7b43256999005bcbb3/eb7add059a673d09c32574bf00258898?OpenDocument.

873 See UN Doc. S/2008/631 of 3 October 2008, §§11–16.

874 See point 2 of the implementation agreement. See also §§4–5 of the Conclusions of the Extraordinary European Council of 1 September 2008 and the Conclusions of the External Relations Council of 15–16 September 2008 on Georgia (EU Council Doc. 13030/08 (Presse 255)).

875 Council Joint Action 2008/736/CFSP of 15 September 2008 on the European Union Monitoring Mission in Georgia, EUMM Georgia, *O.J. L* 248, 17 September 2008, p. 26.

876 The 'Geneva talks', which are co-chaired by the EU (see, e.g. UN Doc. S/2009/69 of 3 February 2009, §64).

877 Council Joint Action 2008/760/CFSP of 25 September 2008 appointing the European Union Special Representative for the crisis in Georgia, *O.J. L* 259, 27 September 2008, p. 16, especially Article 3 as extended by Council Joint Action 2009/131/CFSP of 16 February 2009 extending the mandate of the European Union Special Representative for the crisis in Georgia, *O.J. L* 46, 17 February 2009, p. 47 and by Council Joint Action 2009/571/CFSP of 27 July 2009 extending the mandate of the European Union Special Representative for the crisis in Georgia, *O.J. L* 197, 29 July 2009, p. 109. See generally www.consilium.europa.eu/showPage.aspx?id=1523&lang=EN.

878 See http://eu2008.fr/PFUE/lang/en/accueil/PFUE-11_2008/PFUE-21.11.2008/PESC_HT_Georgie.html.

UN.[879] Furthermore, the EU already had an EU Special Representative for the South-Caucasus (currently Peter Semneby).[880] In the framework of this EUSR's mandate, there is also a Border Support Team.[881] Previously, the EU had conducted the rule of law mission EUJUST Themis in Georgia (see above, Section F of this chapter).

The EUMM was deployed in phases, with deployment beginning in September 2008 and the operational phase beginning on 1 October 2008.[882] This was a remarkably quick launch, namely within two weeks of the decision to establish the mission. Its initial duration was 12 months[883] but it was extended for a second year.[884]

The EUMM has as its mission to *"provide civilian monitoring of Parties' actions, including full compliance with the six-point Agreement and subsequent implementing measures throughout Georgia, working in close coordination with partners, particularly the [UN and OSCE] and consistent with other EU activity, in order to contribute to stabilisation, normalization and confidence building*

879 Council Decision 2008/901/CFSP of 2 December 2008 concerning an independent international fact-finding mission on the conflict in Georgia, *O.J. L* 323, 3 December 2008, p. 66, especially Article 1. See also Council Decision of 27 July 2009 amending and extending Decision 2008/901/CFSP concerning the independent international fact-finding mission on the conflict in Georgia (2009/570/CFSP), *O.J. L* 197, 29 July 2009, p. 108. See generally www.ceiig.ch (including the mission's report presented on 30 September 2009).

880 Joint Action of 7 July 2003 concerning the appointment of the European Union Special Representative for the South Caucasus (2003/496/CFSP), *O.J. L* 169, 8 July 2003, p. 74 as extended/amended by Joint Actions 2003/872/CFSP of 8 December 2003 (*O.J. L* 326, 13 December 2003, p. 44); 2004/532/CFSP of 28 June 2004 (*O.J. L* 234, 3 July 2004, p. 16); 2005/100/CFSP of 2 February 2005 (*O.J. L* 31, 4 February 2005, p. 74); 2005/330/CFSP of 26 April 2005 (*O.J. L* 106, 27 April 2005, p. 36); 2005/582/CFSP of 28 July 2005 (*O.J. L* 199, 29 July 2005, p. 92); 2006/121/CFSP of 20 February 2006 (*O.J. L* 49, 21 February 2006, p. 14); 2007/111/CFSP of 15 February 2007 (*O.J. L* 46, 16 February 2007, p. 75); 2008/132/CFSP of 18 February 2008 (*O.J. L* 43, 19 February 2008, p. 30); 2008/796/CFSP of 13 October 2008 (*O.J. L* 272, 14 October 2008, p. 19, *corrigendum O.J. L* 301, 12 November 2008, p. 40) and 2009/133/CFSP of 16 February 2009 (*O.J. L* 46, 17 February 2009, p. 53). See generally www.consilium.europa.eu/showPage.aspx?id=1037&lang=EN.

881 Established by Council Joint Action of 28 July 2005 amending and extending the mandate of the European Union Special Representative for the South Caucasus (2005/582/CFSP), *O.J. L.* 199, 29 July 2005, p. 92, Article 2. Its mandate was most recently extended together with the EUSR's mandate (see *supra* previous note). See generally www.consilium.europa.eu/showPage.aspx?id=1319&lang=EN.

882 Joint Action 2008/736/CFSP (*supra* note 875), Article 1(1) and the 1 October 2008 Head of Mission press statement, available at www.consilium.europa.eu/uedocs/cmsUpload/081001_HoM_Press_stakeout_1.pdf.

883 Joint Action 2008/736/CFSP (*supra* note 875), Article 18.

884 Council Joint Action 2009/572/CFSP of 27 July 2009 amending and extending Joint Action 2008/736/CFSP on the European Union Monitoring Mission in Georgia, EUMM Georgia, *O.J. L* 197, 29 July 2009, p. 110.

whilst also contributing to informing European policy in support of a durable political solution for Georgia" and as particular objectives " *to contribute to long-term stability throughout Georgia and the surrounding region*" and "*in the short term, the stabilisation of the situation with a reduced risk of a resumption of hostilities, in full compliance with the six-point Agreement and the subsequent implementing measures*".[885]

It counts 340 staff, including 236 monitors[886] and Mr. Hansjörg Haber was appointed Head of Mission.[887] The initial financial reference amount of EUR 31 million[888] was subsequently increased to EUR 35 million and then to EUR 37.1 million,[889] as well as by a further EUR 12.5 for its second year.[890]

On 10 October 2008, the EUMM confirmed that Russian armed forces had completed their planned withdrawal from the areas adjacent to Abkhazia and South Ossetia.[891] EUMM access to the two breakaway regions appears to be problematic.[892]

1. MANDATE, LEGAL STATUS AND APPLICABLE LAW AND PARTICIPATION OF THIRD STATES

The legal framework which governs the two breakaway Georgian regions is a very complex one, *inter alia* comprising a number of old agreements and UN Security Council Resolutions[893] whose continued relevance is questionable,[894]

885 Joint Action 2008/736/CFSP (*supra* note 875), Article 2.

886 See http://eumm.eu/en/about_eumm/facts_and_figures and http://eumm.eu/en/eumm_in_action.

887 PSC Decision EUMM/1/2008 of 16 September 2008 appointing the Head of the European Union Monitoring Mission in Georgia (EUMM Georgia), *O.J. L* 319, 29 November 2008, p. 79 and PSC Decision of 31 July 2009 concerning the extension of the mandate of the Head of Mission of the European Union Monitoring Mission in Georgia (EUMM Georgia) (EUMM Georgia/1/2009–2009/619/CFSP), *O.J. L* 214, 19 August 2009, p. 40.

888 Joint Action 2008/736/CFSP (*supra* note 875), Article 14(1).

889 Council Joint Action 2008/759/CFSP of 25 September 2008 amending Joint Action 2008/736/CFSP on the European Union Monitoring Mission in Georgia, EUMM Georgia, *O.J. L* 259, 27 September 2008, p. 15 and Council Joint Action 2009/294/CFSP of 23 March 2009 amending Joint Action 2008/736/CFSP on the European Union Monitoring Mission in Georgia, EUMM Georgia, *O.J. L* 79, 25 March 2009, p. 60.

890 Council Joint Action 2009/572/CFSP (*supra* note 884).

891 See EU Council Doc. S332/08 of that day.

892 See EUMM press release 06/08 of 5 November 2008, www.consilium.europa.eu/uedocs/cmsUpload/081105-HoM_on_ABK.pdf.

893 E.g. UNSC Res. 934 (30 June 1994); UNSC Res. 1808 (15 April 2008) and 1866 (13 February 2009).

894 See, e.g. UN Doc. S/2009/69 of 3 February 2009, §§61 and 63.

the August 2008 plan and agreement and the ongoing Geneva talks following them and declarations of independence that have only been recognized by Russia and Nicaragua.[895]

In any event, the 8 September 2008 implementation agreement[896] in its point 2 provides for "*the deployment of international mechanisms in [the zones adjoining South Ossetia and Abkhazia], including at least 200 observers from the European Union, no later than October 1, 2008*". This is also confirmed in its point 3 and its point 4 states that "*As guarantor of the principle of non-aggression, the European Union will actively prepare the deployment of an observer mission in addition to the existing observer mechanisms*". In addition, the EUMM is conducted upon the invitation of the Georgian government.[897]

A SOMA has been concluded with Georgia.[898] The Joint Action provides for third State participation upon PSC acceptance[899] but no third States seem to participate.

W. EU NAVCO & EUNAVFOR SOMALIA / ATALANTA[900]

As the number of acts of piracy and armed robbery off the coast of Somalia increased in 2007 and 2008, several individual States (France, Denmark, the Netherlands and Canada[901]) conducted naval operations to escort the World

895 On the latter, see, e.g. X. 'Nicaragua Recognizes Independence of South Ossetia and Abkhazia', www.nytimes.com/2008/09/04/world/americas/04iht-georgia.4.15904253.html.
896 *Supra* note 872.
897 See the preamble of the SOMA, *infra* next note.
898 Agreement between the European Union and Georgia on the status of the European Union Monitoring Mission in Georgia, *O.J. L* 310, 21 November 2008, p. 30/31.
899 Joint Action 2008/736/CFSP (*supra* note 875), Article 11.
900 See generally www.consilium.europa.eu/showPage.aspx?id=1518&lang=en; www.eunavfor.eu; www.mschoa.eu; T. Heinicke, 'Piratenjagd vor der Küste Somalias: Überlegungen zu den rechtlichen Rahmenbedingungen der EU NAVFOR Somalia/ATALANTA-Operation', 42 *Kritische Justiz* 2009, pp. 178–195; WEU Assembly, *The Role of the European Union in Combating Piracy*, Document A/2037, 4 June 2009 (available online at www.assembly-weu.org/en/documents/sessions_ordinaires/rpt/rpt.php?annee=2009) and *ESDP Newsletter* No. 7, Winter [2008], pp. 20–21 and *ESDP Newsletter* No. 8, Summer 2009, pp. 12–16 (both www.consilium.europa.eu/showPage.aspx?id=1090&lang=en).
901 See, e.g. Dutch Ministry of Foreign Affairs, 7 March and 1 July 2008 letters to the Dutch parliament ('Kamerbrief inzake inzet marine voor bescherming humanitaire hulp Somalië tegen piraterij', www.minbuza.nl/nl/Actueel/Kamerstukken/2008/03/Kamerbrief_inzake_inzet_marine_voor_bescherming_humanitaire_hulp_Somalië_tegen_piraterij and 'Kamerbrief inzake beëindiging inzet marine voor bescherming van humanitaire hulptransporten Somalië tegen piraterij', www.minbuza.nl/nl/Actueel/Kamerstukken/2008/07/

Food Programme's shipping to Somalia, as provided for by UN Security Council Resolutions 1772 (20 Augustus 2007, §18), 1801 (20 February 2008, §12) and 1814 (15 May 2008, §11). The UN Security Council subsequently called for and authorized further anti-piracy cooperation and activities in Resolutions 1816 (2 June 2008; including in the territorial waters of Somalia with the consent of its Transitional Federal Government), 1838 (7 October 2008), 1846 (2 December 2008; extending the substance of UNSCR 1816 for 12 months) and 1851 (16 December 2008; also covering the land territory of Somalia). Moreover, the latter Resolution encourages all States and regional organizations fighting piracy and armed robbery at sea off the coast of Somalia to establish an international cooperation mechanism to act as a common point of contact between and among them (§4). This has led to the setting up of a Contact Group on Piracy off the Coast of Somalia in January 2009 in which the EU participates and which has four Working Groups, including one on legal aspects of piracy and one on military and operational coordination and information sharing.[902] The International Maritime Organization and the United Nations Office on Drugs and Crime are also involved in efforts to combat piracy and in the Contact Group work.[903]

In this wider framework, the European Union first set up *EU NAVCO*, a military Coordination Action in support of UNSCR 1816, with the mandate to support UN Security Council Resolution 1816 by supporting the activities of Member States deploying military assets in theatre, with a view to facilitating the availability and operational action of those assets, in particular by setting up a coordination cell, which was to perform the tasks set out in an implementation plan.[904] The Cell essentially served as a channel of communication and coordination between MS with warships in the area and the maritime community and also facilitated the provision of support for WFP escorts.[905]

Kamerbrief_inzake_beëindiging_inzet_marine_voor_bescherming_van_humanitaire_hulp_transporten_Somalië_tegen_piraterij) and www.wfp.org/content/canada-saves-lives-extending-naval-escorts-somalia.

902 See, e.g. the statement following the 14 January 2009 meeting at www.africom.mil/getArticle.asp?art=2466&lang=0 and the statement following the 29 May 2009 meeting at http://allafrica.com/stories/200905300009.html. See also www.state.gov/r/pa/prs/ps/2009/05/123584.htm.

903 See, e.g. the statements *supra* previous note, as well as www.imo.org/TCD/mainframe.asp?topic_id=362; www.unodc.org/unodc/en/press/releases/2008-12.16.html and www.unodc.org/unodc/en/frontpage/ship-riders-tackling-somali-pirates-at-sea.html.

904 Council Joint Action 2008/749/CFSP of 19 September 2008 on the European Union military coordination action in support of UN Security Council resolution 1816 (2008) (EU NAVCO), *O.J. L* 252, 20 September 2008, p. 39, especially Articles 1 and 2.

905 See Factsheet Somalia/01, 19 September 2008, www.consilium.europa.eu/uedocs/cmsUpload/080919factsheetEUNAVCO_EN22092008.pdf and the presentation available at www.consilium.europa.eu/uedocs/cmsUpload/081015_EU_naval_coordination_cell.ppt.

Captain Andrés A. Breijo Claúr was appointed Head of the EU Coordination Cell, which was located in Brussels.[906] The coordination action was launched on 19 September 2008, on the same day on which an implementation plan was adopted (there does not seem to have been an OPLAN).[907] The PSC and EUMC played their usual roles.[908] The coordination cell was closed after the launch of Atalanta, which took over the tasks of the military coordination cell.[909] The costs for communications, transport/travel and administration were defined as common costs, to be administered by Athena and the financial reference amount for these common costs was EUR 60,000.[910] The management by Athena was decided even though "*expenditure arising from an EU military coordination action such as that envisaged by this Joint Action is not provided for under [the Athena Decision 2007/384/CFSP of 14 May 2007]*".[911]

At around the same time that EU NAVCO was set up, Standing NATO Maritime Group 2[912] conducted operation 'Allied Provider' to provide close protection to WFP chartered ships and to conduct deterrence patrols in the areas most susceptible to criminal acts against merchant shipping from 24 October to 12 December.[913]

On 10 November 2008, the EU decided to set up operation *EUNAVFOR Somalia / Atalanta*, in order to contribute to the protection of vessels of the WFP delivering food aid to displaced persons in Somalia and the protection of vulnerable vessels cruising off the Somali coast, and the deterrence, prevention and repression of acts of piracy and armed robbery off the Somali coast[914] and launched this operation on 8 December 2008[915] – around the time the NATO operation ended.[916]

---

906 *Id.*, Articles 3 and 4.

907 *Id.*, Article 5.

908 *Id.*, Articles 6 and 7.

909 Joint Action 2008/851/CFSP (*infra* note 914), Article 16(2) and 8th consideration of the preamble.

910 Joint Action 2008/749/CFSP (*supra* note 904), Article 12.

911 *Id.*, 6th consideration of the preamble.

912 See generally www.nato.int/shape/news/2008/10/docs/factsheet-The_Standing_NATO_Maritime_Group_2.pdf.

913 See www.nato.int/shape/news/2008/12/081212a.html and www.afsouth.nato.int/JFCN_Operations/allied_provider/index.htm.

914 Council Joint Action 2008/851/CFSP of 10 November 2008 on a European Union military operation to contribute to the deterrence, prevention and repression of acts of piracy and armed robbery off the Somali coast, *O.J. L* 301, 12 November 2008, p. 33 (*corrig. O.J. L* 253, 25 September 2009, p. 18).

915 Council Decision 2008/918/CFSP of 8 December 2008 on the launch of a European Union military operation to contribute to the deterrence, prevention and repression of acts of piracy and armed robbery off the Somali coast (Atalanta), *O.J. L* 330, 9 December 2008, p. 19.

916 There was a meeting between both force commanders to facilitate a smooth transition; see www.nato.int/docu/update/2008/12-december/e1215a.html.

Atalanta is conducted in support of UN Security Council Resolutions 1814, 1816 and 1838, in a manner consistent with action permitted with respect to piracy under Article 100 *et seq.* of UNCLOS[917] and by means, in particular, of commitments made with third States, in order to contribute to the protection of vessels of the WFP delivering food aid to displaced persons in Somalia and the protection of vulnerable vessels cruising off the Somali coast, and the deterrence, prevention and repression of acts of piracy and armed robbery off the Somali coast, in accordance with the mandate laid down in UNSC Resolution 1816 (2008) and the forces deployed to that end shall operate, up to 500 nautical miles off the Somali coast and neighbouring countries, in accordance with the crisis management concept approved by the Council on 5 August 2008 (the specific mandate is addressed below in subsection 2).[918] In this framework, the operation has *inter alia* protected ships supplying AMISOM.[919]

Rear Admiral Philip Jones was the Operation Commander.[920] He was succeeded by Rear Admiral Peter Hudson on 3 June 2009.[921] Commodore Antonios Papaioannou was appointed Force Commander.[922] He was succeeded by Commander Juan Garat Caramé as of 7 April 2009[923] and by Commodore Peter Bindt as of 13 August 2009.[924] The EU Operational Headquarters are located at Northwood (in the UK)[925] and the Force Headquarters are on board a ship.[926] The number of assets deployed – essentially ships, maritime patrol aircraft and

917 United Nations Convention on the Law of the Sea, Montego Bay, 10 December 1982, 1833 *U.N.T.S.* 3.
918 Joint Action 2008/851/CFSP (*supra* note 914), Article 1.
919 See, e.g. the EU (Council) Presidency Statement to the UNSC dated 13 May 2009, www.eu-un.europa.eu/articles/en/article_8727_en.htm.
920 Joint Action2008/851/CFSP (*supra* note 914), Article 3.
921 PSC Decision of 27 May 2009 on the appointment of an EU Operation Commander for the European Union military operation to contribute to the deterrence, prevention and repression of acts of piracy and armed robbery off the Somali coast (Atalanta) (2009/413/CFSP – ATALANTA/4/2009), *O.J. L* 132, 29 May 2009, p. 20.
922 PSC Decision of 18 November 2008 on the appointment of an EU Force Commander for the European Union military operation to contribute to the deterrence, prevention and repression of acts of piracy and armed robbery off the Somali coast (Atalanta) (2008/888/CFSP – ATALANTA/1/2008), *O.J. L* 317, 27 November 2008, p. 24.
923 PSC Decision of 17 March 2009 on the appointment of an EU Force Commander for the European Union military operation to contribute to the deterrence, prevention and repression of acts of piracy and armed robbery off the Somali coast (Atalanta) (2009/288/CFSP – ATALANTA/1/2009), *O.J. L* 76, 24 March 2009, p. 45.
924 PSC Decision of 22 July 2009 on the appointment of an EU Force Commander for the European Union military operation to contribute to the deterrence, prevention and repression of acts of piracy and armed robbery off the Somalia coast (Atalanta) (2009/559/CFSP – Atalanta/6/2009), *O.J. L* 192, 24 July 2009, p. 68.
925 Joint Action2008/851/CFSP (*supra* note 914), Article 4.
926 See EU Council Doc. 5178/09, 12 January 2009.

vessel protection detachments – has varied throughout the operation.[927] The common costs are administered by Athena and the financial reference amount for these common costs is EUR 8.3 million.[928]

Atalanta's mandate also includes liaising with organizations and entities, as well as States, working in the region to combat acts of piracy and armed robbery off the Somali coast, in particular the 'Combined Task Force 150' maritime force which operates within the framework of 'Operation Enduring Freedom'[929] and at the operational level, the EU Operation Commander shall act as the contact point with, in particular, ship-owners' organizations, as well as with the relevant departments of the UN General Secretariat and the WFP.[930] Indeed, Atalanta is not the only actor active in this area. In particular, NATO subsequently conducted further counter-piracy operations named 'Allied Protector' and 'Ocean Shield'.[931] Furthermore, several States (including Russia, India and China) have sent warships to the region to deter and combat piracy.[932] Efforts to coordinate these different operations include 'Shared Awareness and Deconfliction' (SHADE) meetings.[933] Also, "cooperative frameworks" have been adopted concerning the cooperation with some of these other actors.[934] The contacts with the ship-owners' associations and the maritime sector more generally build upon the work of EU NAVCO (see above) and include a dedicated website.[935]

Atalanta was to terminate 12 months after the initial operating capability was declared, subject to the prolongation of UN Security Council Resolutions

---

927 Late March 2009, eight frigates and two maritime patrol aircraft were participating in Atalanta (30 March 2009 press release, www.consilium.europa.eu/uedocs/cms_data/docs/pressdata/en/esdp/106976.pdf). Mid-July 2009 this was 14 ships and three maritime patrol aircraft ('current total strength', www.consilium.europa.eu/uedocs/cmsUpload/naviresjuin.pdf, visited on 12 July 2009).

928 Joint Action2008/851/CFSP (*supra* note 914), Article 14.

929 See generally www.cusnc.navy.mil/command/ctf150.html. In 2009, CTF-151 was formed to combat piracy, see http://en.wikipedia.org/wiki/Combined_Task_Force_151 and www.cusnc.navy.mil/command/ctf151.html.

930 Joint Action2008/851/CFSP (*supra* note 914), respectively Articles 2(f) and 9(2).

931 See, e.g. www.manw.nato.int/page_operation_allied_protector.aspx (SNMG1, March – June 2009); www.nato.int/cps/en/natolive/news_55594.htm; www.nato.int/cps/en/natolive/news_56035.htm (SNMG2 to continue the operation) and www.nato.int/cps/en/natolive/news_56991.htm (Ocean Shield). See also www.shipping.nato.int/CounterPir.

932 See also E. Kontorovich, 'International Legal Responses to Piracy off the Coast of Somalia', 13(2) *ASIL Insight*, 6 February 2009, www.asil.org/insights090206.cfm.

933 See the 29 May 2009 Contact Group statement at http://hongkong.usconsulate.gov/uscn_state_2009052901.html.

934 See, e.g. EU Council Documents 6218/09 EXT 1 and 5838/09 EXT 1, both 23 April 2009 and partially declassified, respectively concerning Japan, Malaysia, India, Yemen, Oman and Egypt; and Saudi Arabia, Russia and China.

935 Maritime Security Centre Horn of Africa, www.mschoa.eu.

1814 and 1816,[936] but in June 2009 the EU decided to extend it by another year.[937]

1. MANDATE

The Atalanta Joint Action repeatedly refers to UN Security Council Resolutions 1814 and 1816 as well as to UNCLOS, which are clearly regarded as the legal basis for the operation.[938] To repress acts of piracy, which, by definition take place on the high seas or in a place outside the jurisdiction of any State,[939] and by extension also to the exclusive economic zone,[940] UNCLOS alone provides a sufficient legal basis.[941]

However, operating in the territorial waters of coastal States against pirates seeking refuge there or armed robbers at sea normally requires the consent of the coastal State. It is here that the UN Security Council Resolutions come into play. In particular, in paragraph 7 of Resolution 1816 the Security Council decided that:

> ... for a period of six months from the date of this resolution, States cooperating with the TFG [Transitional Federal Government] in the fight against piracy and armed robbery at sea off the coast of Somalia, for which advance notification has been provided by the TFG to the Secretary-General, may:

---

936 Joint Action2008/851/CFSP (*supra* note 914), Article 16(3).

937 See the conclusions of the General Affairs Council of 15 June 2009 (EU Council Doc. 10938/09 (Presse 173), p. 15: "*The Council noted that the Operation ATALANTA had demonstrated its ability to act effectively against piracy, that piracy off the coast of Somalia was likely to remain a serious threat beyond Operation ATALANTA's current end date of 13 December 2009, and that early agreement on extending the operation would facilitate the necessary force generation. In this context, the Council agreed that Operation ATALANTA should be extended for one year from its current end date*').

938 *Supra* note 914, *inter alia* the 1st to 3rd and 12th considerations of the preamble and Article 16(3), which makes the duration of the operation "*subject to the prolongation of UNSC Resolutions 1814 (2008) and 1816 (2008)*".

939 See Article 101 UNCLOS.

940 UNCLOS, Articles 100–107 and 110 *juncto* Article 58(2).

941 See Articles 100–107 and 110 UNCLOS. On piracy generally, see, e.g. R. Collins & D. Hassan, 'Applications and Shortcomings of the Law of the Sea in Combating Piracy: A South East Asian Perspective', 40 *Journal of Maritime Law and Commerce* 2009, pp. 89–114; P. Lehr (ed.), *Violence at Sea: Piracy in the Age of Global Terrorism*, New York, Routledge, 2007 and A. Morita, 'Piracy Jure Gentium Revisited', 51 *Japanese Yearbook of International Law* 2008, pp. 76–97. Specifically with regard to Somalia, see T. Treves, 'Piracy, Law of the Sea, and Use of Force: Developments off the Coast of Somalia', 20 *E.J.I.L.* 2009, pp. 399–414 and X., 'United States Joins International Response to Somali Pirates', 103 *A.J.I.L.* 2009, pp. 146–148. See also G.-J. Knoops, 'The War on Piracy: rechtspolitieke dilemma's en oplossingen', *N.J.B.* 2009, pp. 1273–1276 and G. Strijards, 'Piraten en hun berechting', *N.J.B.* 2009, pp. 1143–1144.

> (a) Enter the territorial waters of Somalia for the purpose of repressing acts of piracy and armed robbery at sea, in a manner consistent with such action permitted on the high seas with respect to piracy under relevant international law; and
> (b) Use, within the territorial waters of Somalia, in a manner consistent with action permitted on the high seas with respect to piracy under relevant international law, all necessary means to repress acts of piracy and armed robbery;

By requiring TFG notification, which took place for Atalanta,[942] the Resolution essentially sets up a simplified form of consent.[943] The territorial waters of neighbouring States are not covered by this Resolution but obviously these States can give their consent to certain Atalanta operations in their territorial waters.

2. LEGAL STATUS AND APPLICABLE LAW

From the initial planning stages, it was clear that legal issues would play an important role in this operation.[944] This is reflected in the Joint Action,[945] which contains several provisions that are particularly relevant for the purpose of this book and that go into more detail than is usually the case in the Joint Action for an operation. For instance, in addition to the references to relevant UN Security Council Resolutions and UNCLOS already referred to above, Article 2 gives the following mandate:

> Under the conditions set by [applicable] international law[, in particular the United Nations Convention on the Law of the Sea,] and by UNSC Resolutions 1814 (2008), 1816 (2008) and 1838 (2008), Atalanta shall, as far as available capabilities allow:[946]
> (a) provide protection to vessels chartered by the WFP, including by means of the presence on board those vessels of armed units of Atalanta, in particular when cruising in Somali territorial waters;
> (b) provide protection, based on a case-by-case evaluation of needs, to merchant vessels cruising in the areas where it is deployed;
> (c) keep watch over areas off the Somali coast ...;
> (d) take the necessary measures, including the use of force, to deter, prevent and intervene in order to bring to an end acts of piracy and armed robbery which may be committed in the areas where it is present;
> (e) in view of prosecutions potentially being brought by the relevant States under the conditions in Article 12, arrest, detain and transfer persons who have committed, or

942 See Council Decision 2008/918/CFSP (*supra* note 915), 4th consideration of the preamble. See also Joint Action 2008/851/CFSP (*supra* note 914), Article 5.

943 On this Resolution, see generally D. Guilfoyle, 'Piracy Off Somalia: UN Security Council Resolution 1816 and IMO Regional Counter-Piracy Efforts', 57 *I.C.L.Q.* 2008, pp. 690–699.

944 See, e.g. EU Council Doc. 14491/1/08 (21 October 2008).

945 *Supra* note 914.

946 The text between square brackets reflects the *corrigendum* (*O.J. L* 253, 25 September 2009, p. 18).

> are suspected of having committed, acts of piracy or armed robbery in the areas where it is present and seize the vessels of the pirates or armed robbers or the vessels caught following an act of piracy or an armed robbery and which are in the hands of the pirates, as well as the goods on board; ....

Furthermore, Article 12 sets out the rules regarding transfer of persons arrested and detained with a view to their prosecution, in the following terms:

> 1. On the basis of Somalia's acceptance of the exercise of jurisdiction by Member States or by third States, on the one hand, and Article 105 of [UNCLOS], on the other hand, persons having committed, or suspected of having committed, acts of piracy or armed robbery in Somali territorial waters or on the high seas, who are arrested and detained, with a view to their prosecution, and property used to carry out such acts, shall be transferred:
> – to the competent authorities of the [Member State or of the third State participating in the operation, of which the vessel which took them captive flies the flag], or[947]
> – if this State cannot, or does not wish to, exercise its jurisdiction, to a Member States or any third State which wishes to exercise its jurisdiction over the aforementioned persons and property.
> 2. No persons referred to in paragraphs 1 and 2 may be transferred to a third State unless the conditions for the transfer have been agreed with that third State in a manner consistent with relevant international law, notably international law on human rights, in order to guarantee in particular that no one shall be subjected to the death penalty, to torture or to any cruel, inhuman or degrading treatment.

Article 10(6) adds that "*The conditions for the transfer to a State participating in the operation of persons arrested and detained, with a view to the exercise of jurisdiction of that State, shall be established when the participation agreements ... are concluded or implemented*". This has already been implemented with regard to Croatia.[948] Furthermore, Article 13 provides that "*The conditions governing the presence on board merchant ships, particularly those chartered by the WFP, of units belonging to Atalanta, including privileges, immunities and other guarantees relating to the proper conduct of the operation, shall be agreed with the flag States of those vessels*". To this effect, a model/template declaration for a flag State of merchant ships on which a Vessel Protection Detachment (VPD) is embarked has been developed.[949]

Pursuant to Article 12 of the Joint Action and on the basis of Article 24 EU Treaty, the EU concluded an agreement in the form of an exchange of letters with

947 *Id.*
948 See Article 3 of the participation agreement with Croatia (*infra* note 977) and the Annex to this agreement.
949 See EU Council Doc. 17468/08, 18 December 2008.

Kenya on the conditions and modalities for the transfer of suspected pirates.[950] Section 2 of the Agreement sets out the following general principles:

> (a) Kenya will accept, upon the request of EUNAVFOR, the transfer of persons detained by EUNAVFOR in connection with piracy and associated seized property by EUNAVFOR and will submit such persons and property to its competent authorities for the purpose of investigation and prosecution.
> (b) EUNAVFOR will ... transfer persons or property only to competent Kenyan law enforcement authorities.
> (c) The signatories confirm that they will treat persons transferred under this Exchange of Letters, both prior to and following transfer, humanely and in accordance with international human rights obligations, including the prohibition against torture and cruel, inhumane and degrading treatment or punishment, the prohibition of arbitrary detention and in accordance with the requirement to have a fair trial.

Section 7 clarifies that "*Nothing in this Exchange of Letters is intended to derogate, or may be construed as derogating, from any rights that a transferred person may have under applicable domestic or international law*". Section 3 contains elaborate provisions on the treatment, prosecution and trial of transferred persons, including detailed fair trial guarantees and also provides that "*(h) Kenya will not transfer any transferred person to any other State for the purposes of investigation or prosecution without prior written consent from EUNAVFOR*". Section 4 states that "*No transferred person will be liable to suffer the death sentence. Kenya will, in accordance with the applicable laws, take steps to ensure that any death sentence is commuted to a sentence of imprisonment*". There are also provisions on records and notifications (section 5), EUNAVFOR assistance to Kenya (section 6; in particular, "*(a) EUNAVFOR, within its means and capabilities, will provide all assistance to Kenya with a view to the investigation and prosecution of transferred persons*") and provides for implementing arrangements (section 9). The issue of

950 Exchange of Letters between the European Union and the Government of Kenya on the conditions and modalities for the transfer of persons suspected of having committed acts of piracy and detained by the European Union-led naval force (EUNAVFOR), and seized property in the possession of EUNAVFOR, from EUNAVFOR to Kenya and for their treatment after such transfer, *O.J. L* 79, 25 March 2009, p. 47/49. See also EU Council Doc. 6381/09 ADD 1, 24 February 2009 and ADD 2, 25 February 2009. See more generally F. Naert, 'Setting the Scene: Transfers and Humanitarian Concerns – An EU Perspective' and 'Ways Forward. How to Operationalise the Legal Obligations?', forthcoming in the proceedings of the 9th Bruges Colloquium on 'Transfers of Persons in Situations of Armed Conflict' organized in Bruges on 16–17 October 2008 by the ICRC and the College of Europe, 2009 (which will be available online at www.coleurop.be/template.asp?pagename=pub_collegium). For a critical view, see the comments on the agreement by the Meijers Committee (Standing committee of experts on international immigration, refugee and criminal law), www.commissie-meijers.nl/assets/commissiemeijers/Commentaren/2009/CM0904%20Comments%20on%20the%20agreement%20between%20the%20EU%20and%20Kenya%20on%20piracy.pdf.

detention and transfer of detainees is addressed more generally below (see Chapter 9.D.2.iv.b). On 23 October 2009, the Council adopted a decision approving the signing of a similar exchange of letters with the Seychelles (Council conclusions of this date).

Status of Forces Agreements have been concluded with Somalia[951] and Djibouti (which serves as a logistical base).[952] The agreements both contain some specific features. For instance, the definition of "national contingents" specifically includes "vessels, aircraft and elements, in particular protection detachments and embarked military forces on board merchant vessels" (Article 1(3)f of both SOFAs). The Djibouti SOFA provides that "*should a police authority of the Host State observe an offence in the act of being committed on a public thoroughfare, it shall be allowed, where the offender has violated the physical integrity of a Host State national, to detain him in order to ensure his protection pending the arrival of the competent EUNAVFOR authorities*" (Article 6(1)).[953] It also authorizes EUNAVFOR "*on the land territory of the Host State and its internal waters, to take the measures necessary to protect its facilities, vessels and aircraft*, as well as the vessels that it protects, *against any external attack or intrusion, in cooperation with the Host State's competent authorities*" and authorizes EUNAVFOR personnel transiting through the territory of Djibouti to escort persons arrested by EUNAVFOR "*to apply the necessary measures of restraint with respect to these persons*" (Article 13(2) and (5); emphasis added). Furthermore, this SOFA does not exempt EUNAVFOR from claims relating to operational necessity (Article 15). The Somalia SOFA grants EUNAVFOR personnel "*immunity from the criminal, civil and administrative jurisdiction of the Host State under all circumstances*" and rules out any measures of execution in respect of them (Article 6(3) and (6)).[954] It also authorizes EUNAVFOR "*on the land territory of the Host State and its internal waters, to take the measures necessary to protect its vessels, aircraft and assets* as well as the vessels that it protects, *against any*

---

951 Agreement between the European Union and the Somali Republic on the status of the European Union-led naval force in the Somali Republic in the framework of the EU military operation Atalanta, *O.J. L* 10, 15 January 2009, p. 27/29.

952 Agreement between the European Union and the Republic of Djibouti on the status of the European Union-led forces in the Republic of Djibouti in the framework of the EU military operation Atalanta, *O.J. L* 33, 3 February 2009, p. 41/43.

953 This is exceptional as the SOFAs usually provide that EUFOR personnel shall not be liable to any form of arrest or detention. However, this provision may correspond to an unwritten exception also known with regard to diplomatic inviolability/immunity (see ICJ, *Case Concerning United States Diplomatic and Consular Staff in Teheran*, 24 May 1980, *I.C.J. Reports* 1980, §86 and E. Denza, *Diplomatic Law. A Commentary on the Vienna Convention on Diplomatic Relations*, Oxford, Clarendon Press, 1998 (2nd ed.), pp. 218–220). It may be noted that in the Chad incident referred to above (note 788), the French EUFOR soldier sought for four killings was taken into custody and held by the Chadian authorities before being handed over to EUFOR after a joint manhunt.

954 This is wider than usual in that the immunity from civil jurisdiction also covers acts not performed in an official capacity.

external attack or intrusion" (Article 11; emphasis added). Its claims procedure is also not the usual one in that it only provides for diplomatic means and that "*In the event of legal action instituted in connection with a prejudice caused to third parties, the Republic of Somalia shall stand in lieu of EUNAVFOR in the proceedings. In all events, the Republic of Somalia shall pay any compensation due as redress for prejudice caused to third parties other than those [from which it is exempted under the SOFA]. If such compensation is attributable to EUNAVFOR, the amount of compensation shall be totally or partially refunded by EUNAVFOR*" (Article 13). On 23 October 2009, the Council adopted a decision approving the conclusion of a SOFA with the Seychelles (Council conclusions of this date).

Press releases provide information on a number of incidents in which pirate attacks have been foiled and in which pirates have been arrested. E.g. on 24 December 2008, a German frigate assisted an Egyptian bulk carrier in fighting off a pirate attack and a number of pirates were subsequently detained and later released after their arms and equipment had been confiscated.[955] In another incident, on 3 March 2008 a German warship, helped by an American CTF 151 destroyer, successfully fended off a pirate attack on a German owned ship and nine suspects were arrested and a large amount of fuel, weapons and ladders were discovered and confiscated.[956] On 29 March 2009, a German warship took into custody a number of pirates who had attempted to attack a German tanker operating under Atalanta command.[957] On 15 April 2009, a French vessel intercepted 11 suspected pirates spotted the day before when its helicopter had helped to thwart an attack against a container ship.[958] On 3 May 2009, the same frigate again intercepted 11 suspected pirates who had been spotted the day before by a Spanish maritime patrol aircraft.[959] On 22 May 2009, an Italian warship took into custody nine suspected pirates following unsuccessful attacks on two merchant vessels.[960] On 26 May 2009, another seven suspected pirates were taken into custody on board a Swedish warship following an attack on a Greek merchant vessel.[961] Most of the suspected pirates captured in the

955 25 December 2009 press release, www.consilium.europa.eu/uedocs/cmsUpload/081226_1st_pirate_engagement.pdf.

956 4 March 2009 press release, www.consilium.europa.eu/uedocs/cms_data/docs/pressdata/en/esdp/106500.pdf.

957 30 March 2009 press release, www.consilium.europa.eu/uedocs/cms_data/docs/pressdata/en/esdp/106976.pdf.

958 15 April 2009 press release, www.consilium.europa.eu/uedocs/cmsUpload/090415FregateNivoseEN.pdf.

959 3 May 2009 press release, www.consilium.europa.eu/uedocs/cmsUpload/090503-Interception_pirates-EN.pdf.

960 22 May 2009 press release, www.consilium.europa.eu/uedocs/cms_Data/docs/pressdata/en/esdp/107974.pdf.

961 26 May 2009 press release, www.consilium.europa.eu/uedocs/cms_data/docs/pressdata/en/esdp/108084.pdf.

framework of Atalanta have been transferred to Kenya pursuant to the transfer agreement.[962]

It appears that the arrangements put in place for Atalanta have worked fairly well so far, although detainees rather seem to be transferred to Kenya[963] and Member States do not seem to be eager to prosecute themselves.[964] However, some Member States have adapted their domestic legislation or are in the process of doing so with a view to such prosecutions.[965] Moreover, under the Instrument for Stability,[966] the European Community is providing support to enhance the Kenyan capacity to detain and try suspects.[967]

There are relatively few cases in which suspected pirates have been released by Atalanta forces (see, e.g., the case mentioned above). In contrast, in some of the other counter-piracy operations, warships have had to release captured pirates

---

962 See, e.g. the press releases dated 8 May 2009 (11 suspects held on board a French ship); 16 May 2009 (13 suspects held on board a Spanish ship), all available at www.consilium.europa.eu/showPage.aspx?id=1520&lang=en. On 16 May 2009, a total of 52 suspects had been transferred to Kenya (16 May 2009 press release). On one of these cases, see M. Gebauer & H. Stark, 'Somali Pirate Trial Tests Limits of EU Mission", *Spiegel Online*, 1 April 2009, www.spiegel.de/international/world/0,1518,616760,00.html.

963 See also J. Gettleman, 'The West Turns to Kenya as Piracy Criminal Court', *New York Times*, 24 April 2009.

964 There are some cases of prosecution but they do not concern Atalanta so far. E.g. in early January 2009, five pirates who attempted to attack a vessel flying the Netherlands flag and registered in the Antilles were captured by the Danish warship Absalon. They were subsequently arrested by Dutch authorities on board the Danish ship and brought to the Netherlands to stand trial for piracy. See the reply by the Dutch Minister of Justice to parliamentary questions dated 25 February 2009, www.justitie.nl/images/zeeslag%20tussen%20Denemarken%20en%20Nederland_13370_tcm34-170824.pdf; http://news.bbc.co.uk/2/hi/africa/7883493.stm; http://rawstory.com/news/afp/Dutch_extradite_five_Somali_pirates_02102009.html; www.nrc.nl/binnenland/article2121260.ece/Nederland_gaat_piraten_berechten and http://jurist.law.pitt.edu/paperchase/2009_05_18_indexarch.php#4888936211045454993. France is also prosecuting two groups of pirates; see, e.g. AFP, 'Trois pirates somaliens inculpés et écroués en France', 17 April 2009, www.24heures.ch/actu/monde/trois-pirates-somaliens-inculpes-ecroues-france-2009-04-17; X., 'Les trois pirates somaliens du "Tanit" placés en garde à vue en France', *Le Monde online*, 14 April 2009 and BBC, 'France Charges Somali 'Pirates", 18 April 2008, http://news.bbc.co.uk/2/hi/europe/7355598.stm (this concerns the cases also referred to *infra* note 970).

965 E.g. in Belgium the government agreed on a bill to be submitted to Parliament in July 2009; see http://presscenter.org/archive/20090710/c6eaed2bc305fa1245c346cdd6b37333/?lang=nl. In France, ironically, it seems that the piracy offences established by Loi n°1825-04-10 du 10 avril 1825 pour la sûreté de la navigation et du commerce maritime (title I) were abolished in late 2007 (see www.legifrance.gouv.fr/affichTexte.do;jsessionid=B6354BE3145A3E9ABCF69CAE77FC7F38.tpdjo09v_1?cidTexte=LEGITEXT000006074265&dateTexte=20071221).

966 Regulation (EC) No 1717/2006 of the European Parliament and of the Council of 15 November 2006 establishing an Instrument for Stability, *O.J. L* 327, 24 November 2006, p. 1.

967 See, e.g. the 3 June 2009 speech by European Commissioner Benita Ferrero-Waldner, available at www.europa-nu.nl/9353000/1/j9vvh6nf08temv0/vi5llcnnx7nx?ctx=vha2fzq7xwz8.

more often.[968] Also, a few pirates were killed in the course of such other operations,[969] which have also led to the liberation of a few vessels which had already been "pirated", including by French forces (the *Ponant* and the *Tanit*[970]) and by Yemeni forces.[971]

Atalanta ships also rescued some one hundred victims of human trafficking in March 2009[972] and a number of shipwrecked sailors.[973]

3. PARTICIPATION OF THIRD STATES

The Joint Action provides for the participation of third States upon PSC decision.[974] A Committee of Contributors has been established[975] and contributions from Norway and Croatia have been accepted.[976] A participation agreement has been concluded with Croatia.[977]

---

968 See, e.g. www.nato.int/cps/en/natolive/news_53310.htm; www.dw-world.de/dw/article/0,,4222757,00.html and http://news.sky.com/skynews/Home/World-News/Somali-Pirates-Crisis-Dutch-Commandos-Catch-Seven-Pirates-But-Are-Forced-To-Release-Them-Says-Nato/Article/200904315264346.

969 See, e.g. R.D. McFadden & S. Shane, 'In Rescue of Captain, Navy Kills 3 Pirates', *New York Times*, 13 April 2009 and www.lanouvellegazette.be/actualite/monde/2009-04-27/petrolier-yemenite-repris-pirates-somaliens-698635.shtml. See also X., 'United States Joins International Response to Somali Pirates', 103 *A.J.I.L.* 2009, pp. 146–148.

970 See www.meretmarine.com/article.cfm?id=107429; www.lefigaro.fr/international/ 2008/04/12/01003-20080412ARTFIG00187-l-armee-francaise-libere-les-otages-du-ponant.php and www.dorffer-patrick.over-blog.fr/article-30122446.html. In the latter case, one hostage died. See also *supra* note 964.

971 See www.lanouvellegazette.be/actualite/monde/2009-04-27/petrolier-yemenite-repris-pirates-somaliens-698635.shtml.

972 20 March 2009 press release, www.consilium.europa.eu/uedocs/cmsUpload/Floreal.pdf.

973 7 June 2009 press release, www.consilium.europa.eu/uedocs/cms_data/docs/pressdata/en/esdp/108361.pdf.

974 Joint Action 2008/851/CFSP (*supra* note 914), Article 10.

975 PSC Decision of 21 April 2009 on the setting up of the Committee of Contributors for the European Union military operation to contribute to the deterrence, prevention and repression of acts of piracy and armed robbery off the Somali coast (Atalanta) (2009/369/CFSP-ATLANTA/3/2009), *O.J. L* 112, 6 May 2009, p. 9 and Addendum to PSC Decision of 21 April 2009 on the setting up of the Committee of Contributors for the European Union military operation to contribute to the deterrence, prevention and repression of acts of piracy and armed robbery off the Somali coast (Atalanta) (2009/369/CFSP-ATLANTA/3/2009) (*O.J. L* 112, 6.5.2009), *O.J. L* 119, 14 May 2009, p. 40.

976 PSC Decision of 21 April 2009 on the acceptance of third States' contributions to the European Union military operation to contribute to the deterrence, prevention and repression of acts of piracy and armed robbery off the Somali coast (Atalanta), (2009/356/CFSP-ATLANTA/2/2009) *O.J. L* 109, 30 April 2009, p. 52.

977 Agreement between the European Union and the Republic of Croatia on the participation of the Republic of Croatia in the European Union military operation to contribute to the deterrence, prevention and repression of acts of piracy and armed robbery off the Somali coast (Operation Atalanta), *O.J. L* 202, 4 August 2009, p. 83/84.

CHAPTER 4
SOME CONCLUSIONS AND LEGAL ISSUES RAISED

In this chapter, some conclusions will be drawn from the two preceding chapters and their significance regarding the scope of the ESDP (A) and the legal status and applicable law (B) will be analyzed in more detail. As to the former, I will successively discuss the scope of the ESDP under the text of the present EU Treaty, its scope in practice (i.e. the ESDP operations), the scope of the CSDP under the Lisbon Treaty, the integration of the WEU, the issue of solidarity, neutrality and the development towards a common defence and the international legal basis for ESDP operations, to round off with some final conclusions on the scope of the ESDP. As to the latter, I will address both what the SOFA/SOMAs say and what the SOFA/SOMAs are silent on, in particular the law of armed conflict and human rights law.

As a general remark, it is submitted that the survey above clearly shows that the ESDP works in practice and is developing steadily. Moreover, in this process, the EU is gradually developing doctrines and model documents/agreements, some of which are relevant to legal issues. In this respect, it is commendable that many EU documents relating to ESDP operations are in the public domain. Nevertheless, some relevant documents are not[978] and some aspects of the practice therefore cannot be addressed in as much detail as they deserve.

A. THE SCOPE OF THE ESDP

1. THE SCOPE OF THE ESDP UNDER THE TEXT OF THE EU TREATY

I will take as a starting point the EU Treaty as amended by the Treaty of Amsterdam, as this was when the enabling clauses of the ESDP were inserted into the EU Treaty (see *supra*, Chapter 1.E). According to Article 17 EU Treaty, the European Council was empowered to decide to set up a *common defence* that

978 This includes the EU's doctrine on the use of force and rules of engagement. It normally also includes the rules of engagement and operation plan.

might result from the *progressive framing of a common defence policy*, albeit that in that case Member States' constitutional requirements would have to be fulfilled. Moreover, in the framework of the *common defence policy* "*Questions referred to ... include[d] humanitarian and rescue tasks, peacekeeping tasks and tasks of combat forces in crisis management, including peacemaking*". Furthermore, the WEU was an integral part of the development of the Union providing the Union with access to an operational capability, supported the Union in framing the defence aspects of the CFSP and the EU was to "*foster closer institutional relations with the WEU with a view to the possibility of the integration of the WEU into the Union, should the European Council so decide*", albeit that in that case too the Member States' constitutional requirements would have to be fulfilled.

i. A Common Defence Policy

A first question this raises is what exactly is covered by "*the progressive framing of a common defence policy*", which is being developed,[979] and by the "*humanitarian and rescue tasks, peacekeeping tasks and tasks of combat forces in crisis management, including peacemaking*" which are part of it.[980]

A first point in this respect is the meaning of the terms 'security' and 'defence'. Sometimes, defence is equated with territorial defence,[981] whereas security is in that view the broader concept including the use of military resources for non-territorial defence operations.[982] This is a view that has been adopted by the European Parliament at least at one stage[983] and that seems to be supported by

979 See also S. Graf von Kielmansegg, *supra* note 161 (41 *Europarecht* 2006), pp. 185–187.

980 Pursuant to Article 17(1) the progressive framing of a common defence policy is to take place in accordance with the second subparagraph, which reads "*Questions referred to in this Article shall include humanitarian and rescue tasks, peacekeeping tasks and tasks of combat forces in crisis management, including peacemaking*". For a good discussion, see S. Graf von Kielmansegg, *supra* note 161 (44 *C.M.L. Rev.* 2007), pp. 631–644.

981 See, e.g. H. Schöllhorn, *supra* note 161, pp. 33–34, who narrowly defines the common defence policy under the Maastricht Treaty as a common policy to react against direct military threats ("*eine gemeinsame Politik zur Reaktion auf unmittelbare militärische Bedrohungen*"). However, when it comes to decisions/matters with defence implications, this author broadens the term defence to include military aspects of security *id.*, pp. 35–36. Note, moreover, that the notion of territorial defence is itself being challenged, notably by the evolution in combating terrorism: see *infra* on the solidarity clause.

982 For an extensive discussion of the notion 'security' in a broader context, see, e.g. S. Jaberg, *Systeme kollektiver Sicherheit in und für Europa in Theorie, Praxis und Entwurf: ein systemwissenschaftlicher Versuch*, Baden-Baden, Nomos, 1998, pp. 95–140.

983 European Parliament Resolution on the Gradual Establishment of a Common Defence Policy for the European Union, 14 May 1998, *O.J. C* 167, 1 June 1998, p. 190, §7 ("*a clear distinction should be made between security and defence, with the concept of security covering Petersberg operations and the concept of defence including territorial defence and the protection of the vital interests of the Member States*"), also cited in K. Lenaerts & P. Van Nuffel, *Constitutional*

the clauses in the EU Treaty that create specific rules for matters or decisions having "military or defence" implications and thereby do not equate military and defence.[984] It also seems to be or have been the UK view.[985] However, this meaning would imply that a common defence policy refers to a policy concerning territorial defence.[986] Yet, this can hardly be the case as that policy, i.e. the ESDP that is being progressively framed, notably largely excludes, at least so far, defence in this sense (see *infra*). In addition, the distinction between defence and other aspects of military security becomes harder to make as the two categories overlap (e.g. in relation to terrorism) and both call to some extent on similar capabilities (i.e. expeditionary forces). This view would also imply that under the Maastricht Treaty non-territorial defence military operations would have fallen under 'security' and therefore under the CFSP generally,[987] which was clearly not the intention: in the Amsterdam version of the EU Treaty there is an explicit need to have recourse to the WEU both for Article 17(2) missions and for defence aspects. An alternative meaning would be to read 'defence' as including all military matters.[988] This would be more in line with practice under the WEU,[989] with

Law of the European Union, London, Sweet & Maxwell, 2005 (2nd ed.), p. 871. However, in that same resolution this distinction does not appear to be maintained very strictly, since its §4 reads "*under a* common defence policy *the European Union will be able to contribute to* peace and stability in the world, *primarily in the areas located on its land and sea borders,* under a mandate issued by the UN or the OSCE" (emphasis added) and the reference to a UN or OSCE mandate and world peace suggests this does include peace operations other than defence as defined in §7.

984 See Articles 23(2) *in fine* and 28(3) EU Treaty (Amsterdam version) and see *supra*.

985 See House of Commons, Select Committee on Defence, *Eighth Report*, 11 May 2000 (available online at www.parliament.the-stationery-office.co.uk/pa/cm199900/cmselect/cmdfence/264/26402.htm), §§39–42 (noting e.g. that "*The Secretary of State confirmed that the ends not the means ... is the distinction between defence and crisis management*").

986 Some support for this may be provided by two minor additions by the Treaty of Amsterdam to the objectives of the CFSP that would appear to be at least potentially related to defence, namely safeguarding the integrity of the Union (revised Article 11, 1st hyphen) and a specific inclusion of international law principles on external borders in relation to the objective to preserve peace and strengthen international security (*Id.*, 3rd hyphen) (see also *supra*, Chapter 1.E). On whether the first of these changes is relevant in this context, compare Wessel, p. 61, with S. Griller *et al.*, *infra* note 1062, p. 376.

987 The Maastricht Treaty only mentioned recourse to the WEU for decisions with defence implications. Compare the discussion and references in S. Graf von Kielmansegg, *supra* note 161 (41 *EuR*. 2006), p. 187.

988 In that sense S. Graf von Kielmansegg, *supra* note 161 (41 *Europarecht* 2006), pp. 188–189. See also H. Krieger, *supra* note 204, pp. 180–181.

989 See especially the preliminary conclusions on the formulation of a Common European Defence Policy, approved by the WEU Ministerial Council in Noordwijk on 14 November 1994; see §5 of the Noordwijk Declaration (available online at www.weu.int/documents/941114en.pdf) and these preliminary conclusions (available online in French at http://mjp.univ-perp.fr/defense/ueo94f.htm). The latter clearly regard a common defence policy as including both elements of a collective defence in the strict sense and crisis management in the broad sense.

what the ESDP stands for at present, with the Danish position,[990] and with the meaning of defence as used in most Member States' ministries of defence.[991] However, it ignores the difference between military and defence that is still expressed in the Treaty (see *supra*), except if one were to read defence (only) in these instances in the strict sense. The inclusion of military security better corresponds to practice and it is submitted that this is clearly covered by the common defence policy.[992] What is less clear, ironically, is whether this policy also includes defence in the strict sense. Some subscribe to the view that a 'common defence policy' and also the 'defence' in 'common security and defence policy' is a misnomer.[993] But the term 'defence *policy*' may not have been that ill chosen and may leave room for defence aspects to be discussed at the policy level and in terms of capabilities as long as this does not amount to a common defence decision or operation.[994] While practice so far may not support this, it should be kept in mind that the common defence policy will only be framed progressively.[995]

990 Denmark does not participate in the elaboration and the implementation of decisions and actions of the Union "*which have defence implications*" and this is seen as including all military operations even those not of a territorial defence nature (see *supra*, Chapter 3).

991 Compare S. Duke, 'CESDP: Nice's Overtrumped Success?', 6 *E.F.A.R.* 2001, pp. 157–159, noting this tendency but apparently himself viewing defence in the strict meaning.

992 Similarly, K. Gerteiser, *supra* note 161, pp. 95–97.

993 As was expressed by the House of Commons, Select Committee on Defence in its *Eighth Report*, *supra* note 985, §42: "*To that extent we consider it in some ways regrettable that 'defence' crops up in the title of the ESDI and the CESDP at all—what they are both about is the use of military means for crisis management, not for 'defence' in the traditionally understood sense of collective self-defence*". This also seems to be the view of S. Duke, see *supra* previous note. I have supported this view myself in the past; see J. Wouters & F. Naert, *supra* note 404, p. 211.

994 Compare M. Warnken, *supra* note 1, pp. 142–145, for whom the common defence policy includes the maintaining of armed forces and the conduct of peace operations but also and reactions to an immediate military threat, though presumably without an actual military operation in self-defence. In that sense also J. Frowein, 'Auf dem Weg zu einer gemeinsamen Sicherheits- und Verteidigungspolitik', in C. Tomuschat & J.A. Frowein (eds.), *Rechtsprobleme einer europäischen Sicherheits- und Verteidigungspolitik*, Heidelberg, Müller, 1997, p. 12 (considering that all military preparations are included in a common defence policy) and J. Litten, *supra* note 161, pp. 144–148, for whom it includes not just crisis management (including civilian aspects) but also all military preparations. Compare also A. Dumoulin, R. Mathieu & G. Sarlet, *supra* note 161, pp. 25–34, seeing the terminology as unclear; M. Trybus, *supra* note 161, pp. 64–66, viewing the matter as not very clear; and H. Krieger, *supra* note 204, pp. 181–182 (seeing a common defence as including aspects such as an automatic action commitment and/or integrated forces/structures and arguing that a voluntary territorial defence operation with non-integrated forces would be possible under a common defence *policy*). R. Gosalbo Bono, 'Some Reflections on the CFSP Legal Order', 43 *C.M.L. Rev.* 2006, pp. 343–344 note 12, distinguishes the two notions as follows: a common defence policy refers to "*the creation of structures providing for coordination of the defence policies of the Member States*" wheras a common defence points to "*the creation of an integrated command structure under whose orders a European army would operate*".

995 See also S. Graf von Kielmansegg, *supra* note 161 (41 *Europarecht* 2006), pp. 188–192, who regards the concept of 'defence' ("*der Verteidigungsbegriff*") in the EU Treaty as encompassing territorial defence but also the military side of CFSP more generally and then tries to define the difference between a common defence policy and a common defence.

In any event, as long as the ESDP comprises less than would seem to be permitted, the discussion is of little importance. It may, however, have an impact on the debate over a common defence, which, at present, is clearly excluded (see *infra*).

A second point in this respect is whether the listed "*humanitarian and rescue tasks, peacekeeping tasks and tasks of combat forces in crisis management, including peacemaking*" are exhaustive or not and what they mean. As the progressive framing of a common defence policy is the key provision and it is merely stated that this "*shall include*" the listed tasks, the latter tasks do not seem exhaustive.[996] None of the other language versions I can read seem to preclude a non-exhaustive reading either.[997] In any event, this question seems to have been clearly answered by the adoption of the European Security Strategy in December 2003, as this document states that "*we should think in terms of a wider spectrum of missions. This might include joint disarmament operations, support for third countries in combating terrorism and security sector reform*"[998] and by the reality of some ESDP operations putting this into practice (e.g. EUSEC DRC and the AMM, see *supra*, Chapter 3.I and L).

Moreover, the listed tasks themselves may be interpreted widely, in particular the words "*peacekeeping tasks and tasks of combat forces in crisis management, including peacemaking*".

---

996 See also P. Koutrakos, *EU International Relations Law*, Oxford, Hart, 2006, p. 455 and G.-J. Van Hegelsom, *supra* note 187, p. 113. S. Graf von Kielmansegg, *supra* note 161 (41 *Europarecht* 2006), pp. 185–192, also supports a broader reading of the common defence policy. *Contra*: K. Gerteiser, *supra* note 161, p. 137 and M. Trybus, *supra* note 161, p. 102.

997 In the languages I understand, it reads in: Dutch ("*De in dit artikel bedoelde aangelegenheden* omvatten ..."), French ("*Les questions visées au présent Article* incluent ..."), German ("*Die Fragen, ...,* schließen ... ein"), Italian ("*Le questioni cui si riferisce il presente articolo* includono ..."), Portuguese ("*As questões a que se refere o presente artigo* incluem ...") and Spanish ("*Las cuestiones a que se refiere el presente artículo* incluirán ...") (emphasis added). For an Italian author supporting the non exhaustive reading, see N. Ronzitti, 'L'applicabilità del diritto internazionale umanitario', in N. Ronzitti (ed.), *supra* note 161, p. 172.

998 *Supra*, Chapter 1.F, note 159, part III ('policy implications'). See also M. Roscini, 'L'articolo 17 del Trattato sull'Unione europea e i compiti delle Forze di pace', in N. Ronzitti (ed.), *supra* note 161, pp. 49–80 (see the English summary at p. 17 of this book). On security sector reform in the EU, see EU Concept for ESDP support to Security Sector Reform (EU Council Doc. 12566/4/05, 13 October 2005); European Commission, A Concept for European Community Support for Security Sector Reform (COM(2006) 253 final, 24 May 2006, http://eur-lex.europa.eu/LexUriServ/site/en/com/2006/com2006_0253en01.pdf) and the 12 June 2006 General Affairs Council Conclusions on a Policy Framework for Security Sector Reform (EU Council Doc. 9946/06 (Presse 161), pp. 16–17). See also D. Spence & P. Fluri, (eds.), *The European Union and Security Sector Reform*, London, John Harper Publishing, 2008. For the UN, see, e.g. *Report of the Secretary-General, Securing peace and development: The role of the United Nations in supporting security sector reform*, 23 January 2008, UN Doc. A/62/659 – S/2008/39 of 23 January 2008.

ii. A Terminological Intermezzo

At this stage, some remarks on terminology are in order. As every organization has its own constitutive instruments and develops its own terminology, there is not really a common terminology in the field of security.[999] It is neither my ambition to treat this comprehensively nor to develop fully a proper terminology for the purposes of this book. However, I will try to convey a rough idea of the key terms and how I will use them as this is necessary for the subject matter addressed.

The oldest relevant notion of those currently used is probably '*peacekeeping*', a practice developed by the UN (and not based on any explicit provision in the UN Charter but now well established[1000]). It was initially used for military operations that were conducted with the consent of the parties involved in an impartial manner, with a very limited authority to use force and a narrow mandate to monitor peace agreements and/or to establish a buffer zone.[1001] This classical notion was nicely codified in the framework of the CSCE.[1002] It was also reflected in the UN Secretary-General's 1992 *Agenda for Peace*, which defined peacekeeping as "*the deployment of a [UN] presence in the field, hitherto with the consent of all the parties concerned, normally involving [UN] military and/or police personnel and frequently civilians as well. Peace-keeping is a technique that expands the possibilities for both the prevention of conflict and the making of peace*".[1003]

---

999 See also ZWANENBURG, pp. 11–12.

1000 See, e.g. R. Ben Achour, 'Les opérations de maintien de la paix', in COT & PELLET, pp. 265–283; M. Bothe, 'Peacekeeping', in SIMMA, pp. 648–700 (with a select bibliography) and E. Suy, 'Peace-Keeping Operations', in DUPUY (ED), pp. 542–544. On the legality of UN peacekeeping operations, see, e.g. ICJ, *Certain Expenses of the United Nations*, Advisory Opinion of 20 July 1962, *I.C.J. Rep.* 1962, pp. 150–181.

1001 See, e.g. E. Suy, *supra* note 1000, pp. 548–554 and S. Vohra, 'Impartiality in United Nations Peace-Keeping', 9 *Leiden J.I.L.* 1996, pp. 63–85. See also N. Tsagourias, 'Consent, Neutrality/Impartiality and the Use of Force in Peacekeeping: Their Constitutional Dimension', 11 *J.C.S.L.* 2006, pp. 465–482.

1002 CSCE, The Challenges of Change, Helsinki Document 1992, Decision III on Early warning, conflict prevention and crisis management (including fact-finding and rapporteur missions and CSCE peacekeeping), 9–10 July 1992, §§17–56, especially §§22–24 ("*CSCE peacekeeping operations will not entail enforcement action; Peacekeeping operations require the consent of the parties directly concerned; Peacekeeping operations will be conducted impartially*") (available online at www.osce.org/documents/mcs/1992/07/4046_en.pdf). On OSCE peacekeeping, see generally N. Ronzitti, 'OSCE Peace-keeping', in M. Bothe, N. Ronzitti & A. Rosas (eds.), *The OSCE in the Maintenance of Peace and Security: Conflict Prevention, Crisis Management and Peaceful Settlement of Disputes*, The Hague, Kluwer, 1997, pp. 237–255.

1003 *An Agenda for Peace. Preventive Diplomacy, Peacemaking and Peacekeeping. Report of the Secretary-General pursuant to the statement adopted by the Summit Meeting of the Security Council on 31 January 1992*, UN Doc. A/47/277 – S/24111, 17 June 1992, §20.

However, as the security challenges evolved and the Security Council started to play its envisaged role,[1004] the mandate was broadened to include a great variety of new tasks, up to the interim administration[1005] of territories in Kosovo[1006]

1004 On the reactivation of the Security Council, see, e.g. *supra*, Chapter 1.D, notes 56–57 and the accompanying text.

1005 See generally E. De Brabandere, *The United Nations, International Administrations, the 'Light Footprint Approach', and beyond. A Comparative Legal Analysis of the International Reconstruction of Post-Conflict Kosovo, East-Timor, Afghanistan and Iraq*, Ghent, University of Ghent, 2007 (dissertation); R. Caplan, *A New Trusteeship?: The International Administration of War-Torn Territories*, Oxford, Oxford University Press, 2002; S. Chesterman, *You, the People: The United Nations, Transitional Administration, and State-building*, Oxford, Oxford University Press, 2004; H.K. Dickerson, 'Assumptions of Legitimacy: and the Foundations of International Territorial Administration', 34 *Denver J.I. L. & Policy* 2007, pp. 161–196; B. Knoll, *The Legal Status of Territories Subject to Administration by International Organisations*, Cambridge, Cambridge University Press, 2008; Kolb, Porretto & Vité; C. Stahn, 'Justice under the Transitional Administration: Contours and Critique of a Paradigm', 27 *Houston J.I.L.* 2005, pp. 311–344; C. Stahn, *The law and practice of international territorial administration. Versailles to Iraq and beyond*, Cambridge, Cambridge University Press, 2008; C. Stahn, 'Governance Beyond the State: Issues of Legitimacy in International Territorial Administration', 2 *I.O.L.R.* 2005, pp. 9–56; R. Wilde, *International Territorial Administration: How Trusteeship and the Civilizing Mission Never Went Away*, Oxford, Oxford University Press, 2008; R. Wilde, 'Representing International Territorial Administration: A Critique of Some Approaches', 15 *E.J.I.L.* 2004, pp. 71–96; R. Wilde & B. Delcourt, 'Le retour des "protectorats": l'irrésistible attrait de l'administation de territoires étrangers', in B. Delcourt, D. Duez & É. Remacle (eds.), *La guerre d'Irak: prélude d'un nouvel ordre international?*, Brussels, Lang, 2004, pp. 219–247; R. Wolfrum, 'International Administration in Post-conflict Situations by the United Nations and other International Actors', 9 *M.P.Y.U.N.L.* 2005, pp. 649–696 and A. Yokaris, 'Intervention et administration internationale du territoire', 59 *Revue hellénique de droit international* 2006, pp. 407–414.

1006 The UN Interim Administration Mission in Kosovo (UNMIK); see generally www.unmikonline.org and K. Ardault *et al.*, 'L'administration internationale de territoire à l'épreuve du Kosovo et du Timor oriental: la pratique à la recherche d'une théorie', 39 *R.B.D.I./B.T.I.R.* 2006, pp. 300–383; M. Bothe & T. Marauhn, 'UN Administration of Kosovo and East Timor: Concept, Legality and Limitations of Security Council-Mandated Trusteeship Administration', in C. Tomuschat (ed.), *Kosovo and the International Community: A Legal Assessment*, The Hague, Kluwer Law International, 2002, pp. 217–242; M. Brand, 'Institution-Building and Human Rights Protection in Kosovo in the Light of UNMIK Legislation', 70 *Nordic J.I.L.* 2001, pp. 461–488; M. Brand, 'Effective Human Rights Protection when the UN "Becomes the State": Lessons from UNMIK', in N. White & D. Klaasen (eds.), *The UN, Human Rights and Post-conflict Situations*, Manchester, Manchester University Press, 2005, pp. 347–375; E. Franckx, A. Pauwels & S. Smis, 'An International Trusteeship for Kosovo: Attempt to Find a Solution to the Conflict', 52(5–6) *Studia diplomatica* 1999, pp. 155–166; J. Friedrich, 'UNMIK in Kosovo: Struggling with Uncertainty', 9 *M.P.Y.U.N.L.* 2005, pp. 225–293; T. Garcia, 'La mission d'administration intérimaire des Nations Unies au Kosovo (MINUK)', 104 *R.G.D.I.P.* 2000, pp. 61–71; L. Henry, 'L'administration exercée par les Nations Unies sur un territoire: démocratisation et respect de la souveraineté ou le paradoxe de l'histoire juridique internationale: étude comparée de trois administrations temporaires des Nations Unies (APRONUC, MINUK et ATNUTO)', in R. Mehdi (ed.), *La contribution des Nations Unies à la démocratisation de l'état ...*, Paris, Pedone, 2002, pp. 161–188; T. Irmscher, 'The Legal Framework for Activities of the United Nations Interim Administration Mission in Kosovo: The Charter, Human Rights, and the Law of Occupation', 44 *G.Y.I.L.* 2002, pp 353–395; R.A. Kristensen, 'Administering Membership of International Society : The Role and Function of UNMIK', in T.B. Knudsen & C.B. Laustsen (eds.), *Kosovo between War and Peace: Nationalism, Peacebuilding and International Trusteeship*, London, Routledge, 2006, pp. 135–

and East-Timor[1007], [1008] and some peacekeeping operations were authorized to enforce, including by force, some of their tasks under Chapter VII of the UN Charter (under this chapter the Security Council may take or authorize action, including by air, sea, or land forces, as may be necessary to maintain or restore international peace and security when it determines that there is a threat to the peace, a breach of the peace, or an act of aggression). This blurred the line between peacekeeping and peace enforcement (on this term, see *infra*).[1009] However, peacekeepers were not always appropriately equipped and armed or

---

155; E. Lagrange, 'La Mission intérimaire des Nations Unies au Kosovo, nouvel, essai d'administration directe d'un territoire', 45 *A.F.D.I.* 1999, pp. 335–370; J. Nilsson, 'UNMIK and the Ombudsperson Institution in Kosovo: Human Rights Protection in a United Nations "Surrogate State"', 22 *N.Q.H.R.* 2004, pp. 389–411; D. Rossbacher, *Friedenssicherung – am Beispiel der Interimsverwaltung der Vereinten Nationen im Kosovo (UNMIK): die Zivilverwaltung als neue Form der Friedenssicherung*, Hamburg, Kovac, 2004; M. Ruffert, 'The Administration of Kosovo and East Timor by the International Community', 50 *I.C.L.Q.* 2001, pp. 613–631; C. Stahn, 'The United Nations Transitional Administrations in Kosovo and East Timor: A First Analysis', 5 *M.P.Y.U.N.L. Law* 2001, pp. 105–183; C. Stahn, 'International Territorial Administration in the Former Yugoslavia: Origins, Developments and Challenges Ahead', 61 *Z.a.ö.R.V.* 2001, pp. 107–176; L. von Carlowitz, 'UNMIK Lawmaking Between Effective Peace Support and Internal Self-Determination', 41 *A.V.R.* 2003, pp. 336–393 and J. Wouters & F. Naert, *supra* note 249, pp. 557–568.

1007 UN Transitional Administration in East-Timor (UNTAET); see generally www.un.org/peace/etimor/etimor.htm and K. Ardault *et al.*, *supra* note 1006, pp. 301–383; M. Bothe & T; Marauhn, *supra* note 1006, pp. 217–242; A. de Hoogh, 'Attribution or Delegation of (Legislative) Power by the Security Council?: The Case of the United Nations Transitional Adminstration in East Timor (UNTAET)', 7 *International Peacekeeping* 2002, pp. 1–41; W. Hayde, 'Ideals and Realities of the Rule of Law and Administration of Justice in Post Conflict East Timor', 8 *International Peacekeeping* 2004, pp. 65–97; L. Henry, *supra* note 1006, pp. 161–188; M.Kelly, T. McCormack, P. Muggleton & B. Oswald, 'Legal Aspects of Australia's Involvement in the International Force for East Timor', No. 841 *I.R.R.C./R.I.C.R.* 2001, pp. 101–139; S. Linton, 'Rising From The Ashes: The Creation Of A Viable Criminal Justice System In East Timor', 5 *Melbourne University Law Review* 2001, pp. 122–180 (available online at www.austlii.edu.au/au/journals/MULR/2001/5.html); M. Ruffert, *supra* note 1006, pp. 613–631 and C. Stahn, *supra* previous note (5 *M.P.Y.U.N.L. Law* 2001), pp. 105–183.

1008 On some of the legal challenges resulting from these broader tasks, see, e.g. M.J. Kelly, *Restoring and Maintaining Order in Complex Peace Operations. The Search for a Legal Framework*, The Hague, Kluwer, 1999.

1009 A good example is the UN peacekeeping operation in the former Yugoslavia, UNPROFOR. It was initially a more or less traditional peacekeeping operation, but was later turned into a Chapter VII operation, for the first time by UNSC Res. 807 (19 February 1993, see the 5th and the final consideration of its preamble). On the evolved nature of UNPROFOR and the problems connect with it, see the UN Secretary-General's report of 30 May 1995 (UN Doc. S/1995/444), §§56–79 and M. Weller, 'Peace-keeping and Peace-enforcement in the Republic of Bosnia and Herzegovina', 56 *Z.a.ö.R.V.* 1996, pp. 70–177, especially pp. 96–163. On the evolution of the use of force in UN peace operations, see especially T. Findlay, *The Use of Force in UN Peace Operations*, Oxford, Oxford University Press, 2002; S. Chesterman, *The Use of Force in UN Peace Operations*, External Study for the UN Department of Peacekeeping Operations Best Practices Unit, 2004 (available online at http://pbpu.unlb.org/pbps/Library/Chesterman%20External%20Paper%20(31-08-2004).pdf); S. Chesterman, *supra* previous note, pp. 99–125; K. Cox, 'Beyond Self-Defence: United Nations Peacekeeping Operations and the Use of Force', 27 *Denver J.I. L. & Policy* 1999, pp. 239–273 and R. Zacklin, 'The Use of Force in Peacekeeping Operations', in N. Blokker & N. Schrijver (eds.), *supra* note 645, pp. 91–106.

deployed with sufficient forces for this task, leading to unrealistic expectations with disastrous consequences (e.g. the non-defending of 'safe areas' such as Srebrenica[1010]) and even violence against peacekeepers in some cases (e.g. their kidnapping and use as human shields in BiH[1011]).

The 2000 *Brahimi Report* proposed some measures in this respect in order to create more robust and capable operations without abandoning the key principles of "*consent of the local parties, impartiality and use of force only in selfdefence*" (see however *infra*, Chapter 8.B on this notion), *inter alia* stating that "*Impartiality for such operations must therefore mean adherence to the principles of the Charter and to the objectives of a mandate ... [and] is not the same as neutrality or equal treatment of all parties in all cases for all time, which can amount to a policy of appeasement*".[1012] Indeed, in practice since then, UN peacekeeping operations have continued to have broad mandates with sometimes peace enforcement elements but have generally been somewhat better equipped when this was the case.[1013] Thus I will use peacekeeping as covering operations based on the consent of the parties or the host State but that may comprise peace enforcement elements.[1014] Where necessary, I will distinguish this from 'pure' or 'traditional'

1010 See, e.g. Report of the Secretary-General pursuant to General Assembly resolution 53/35 (1998) ('Report on the fall of Srebrenica'), UN Doc. A/54/549, 15 November 1999.

1011 See J. Wouters & F. Naert, *supra* note 249, pp. 548–549.

1012 See especially the Report of the Panel on United Nations Peace Operations, UN Doc. A/55/305-S/2000/809, 17 August 2000, §§48 and 50 (available online with follow-up measures at www.un.org/peace/reports/peace_operations/). For a discussion of this distinction between peacekeeping and peace enforcement in the UN, see A. Sitkowski, 'Reflections on the Peacekeeping Doctrine', 7 *International Peacekeeping (Yearbook)* 2001, pp. 181–196.

1013 The combat operations conducted by MONUC in the DRC (see *supra* note 458) are a good illustration.

1014 A 1998 UN Glossary (available online at www.un.org/Depts/dpko/glossary) distinguishes between a peacekeeping (defined as "*hybrid politico-military activity aimed at conflict control, which involves a United Nations presence in the field (usually involving military and civilian personnel), with the consent of the parties, to implement or monitor the implementation of arrangements relating to the control of conflicts (cease-fires, separation of forces etc.), and their resolution (partial or comprehensive settlements) and/or to protect the delivery of humanitarian relief*") and a peacekeeping *operation* (defined as "*a noncombat military operations undertaken by outside forces with the consent of all major belligerent parties and designed to monitor and facilitate the implementation of an existing truce agreement in support of diplomatic efforts to reach a political settlement; ... covers: peace-keeping forces, observer missions and mixed operations*") on the one hand and a 'peace-restoration and conflict-mitigation operation' (defined as "*a new and tentative concept applying to the multidimensional operations which, while originally mandated under chapter VI, are forced by realities in the field to turn into a chapter VII operations, as when humanitarian convoys need to be defended by force of arms, or exclusion zone enforced by air strikes*") on the other hand. However, the latter term does not appear to be in use. NATO uses a similar distinction between peacekeeping (defined as "*A peace support operation following an agreement or ceasefire that has established a permissive environment where the level of consent and compliance is high, and the threat of disruption is low. The use of force by a peace support force is normally limited to self-defence*") and 'peace enforcement' (defined as "*A peace support operation conducted to maintain a ceasefire or peace agreement where the level of consent and compliance is uncertain and the threat of disruption is* peacekeeping, meaning entirely consensual operations without any enforcement powers.

In contrast, 'pure' '*peace enforcement*' means imposing a UN mandated objective by force against the will of one or more parties involved. The *Brahimi Report* correctly recognized that "*the United Nations does not wage war. Where enforcement action is required, it has consistently been entrusted to coalitions of willing States, with the authorization of the Security Council, acting under Chapter VII of the Charter*"[1015] (authorization of regional action will be discussed below, see Section A.6 of this chapter). While it may have been the intention of the Charter that the UN would do so, reality has shown this is not the case and that it outsources this task. While the term is relatively clear, there may be some debate as to whether it includes action by some Member States to enforce Security Council demands in cases where the Security Council has not authorized their forceful imposition (e.g. the 1999 NATO air campaign against Yugoslavia over Kosovo). While many see this as illegal, it is sometimes qualified as unilateral enforcement of a collective will[1016] and in that sense could be qualified as 'unauthorized peace enforcement'.

In contrast, '*peace-making*' means, in the UN context, "*action to bring hostile parties to agreement, essentially through such peaceful means as those foreseen in Chapter VI of the Charter of the United Nations*".[1017] However, in the EU it has a different meaning, as will be shown below (see subsection iii of this section).

In addition, the term *peace building* is used. It was initially related to a post-conflict situation and was defined as "*action to identify and support structures which will tend to strengthen and solidify peace in order to avoid a relapse into conflict*".[1018] However, it may also take place preventively before a conflict erupts as a conflict prevention measure and therefore the second part of this definition

---

high. The peace support force must be capable of applying credible coercive force and must apply the provisions of the ceasefire or peace agreement impartially"), see NATO, *NATO Glossary of Term and Definitions*, AAP-6(2006), p. 2-P-2 (2009 edition available online at www.nato.int/docu/stanag/aap006/aap6.htm). However, as I will explain below, peace enforcement is usually defined more restrictively.

1015 Report of the Panel on United Nations Peace Operations, *supra* note 1012, §53. See also G. Oliver, 'The Other Side of Peacekeeping: Peace Enforcement and Who Should Do It', 8 *International Peacekeeping (Yearbook)* 2002, pp. 99–117 (discussing the origins of this term at pp. 101–103).

1016 See on this notion N. Krisch, 'Unilateral Enforcement of the Collective Will: Kosovo, Iraq, and the Security Council', 3 *M.P.Y.U.N.L.* 1999, pp. 59–103 and C. Stahn, 'Enforcement of the Collective Will after Iraq', 97 *A.J.I.L.* 2003, pp. 804–823.

1017 An Agenda for Peace, *supra* note 1003, §20.

1018 An Agenda for Peace, *supra* note 1003, §21.

may, in my view, be dropped.[1019] This brings us to '*conflict prevention*', which may seem self-explanatory but may nevertheless be defined in different ways, e.g. as "*measures that are aimed at or contribute to preventing the outbreak, escalation, spreading or recurrence of violent conflict*".[1020]

Moreover, the UN uses '*peace operations*' as an overall term for the various peace related operations. It is defined as "*peace support operations, include[ing] preventive deployments, peacekeeping and peace-enforcement operations, diplomatic activities such as preventive diplomacy, peacemaking and peace building, as well as humanitarian assistance, good offices, fact-finding, electoral assistance*".[1021] From this definition it results that the term '*peace support operations*' is also used as a synonym. The latter term is also used by NATO as an overarching term and is defined there as "*An operation that impartially makes use of diplomatic, civil and military means, normally in pursuit of United Nations Charter purposes and principles, to restore or maintain peace. Such operations may include conflict prevention, peacemaking, peace enforcement, peacekeeping, peacebuilding and/or humanitarian operations*".[1022]

iii. Peacekeeping Tasks and Tasks of Combat Forces in Crisis Management, Including Peacemaking

One of the key terms in the ESDP tasks, namely peacekeeping, has been dealt with above. However, already it is clear that depending on how one defines this term the missions at hand will either have to be limited to pure peacekeeping or may contain enforcement elements. However, it is submitted that deciding this point is not necessary, given that the ESDP tasks in any event also include "*tasks of combat forces in crisis management, including peacemaking*" and that the latter include at least peacekeeping with peace enforcement elements. This requires some explanation as it is often said that the EU only does 'soft' or low intensity peacekeeping.[1023]

1019 NATO defines peace building as "*A peace support operation employing complementary diplomatic, civil and – when necessary – military means, to address the underlying causes of conflict and the longer-term needs of the people. It requires a commitment to a long-term process and may run concurrently with other types of peace support operations*", see the NATO Glossary, *supra* note 1014.

1020 Compare V. Kronenberger & J. Wouters, 'Introduction', in V. Kronenberger & J. Wouters, *supra* note 248, pp. xxii-xxv. NATO defines 'conflict prevention' as "*A peace support operation employing complementary diplomatic, civil, and – when necessary – military means, to monitor and identify the causes of conflict, and take timely action to prevent the occurrence, escalation, or resumption of hostilities*", see NATO Glossary, *supra* note 1014.

1021 UN Glossary, *supra* note 1014.

1022 NATO Glossary, *supra* note 1014.

1023 Compare N. Tsagourias, 'EU Peacekeeping Operations: Legal and Theoretical Issues', in Trybus & White, pp. 106–107 and 131–133, who sees EU peacekeeping as an expression of

As noted above, within the UN, peacemaking refers to the peaceful settlement of disputes. However, the NATO definition indicates that it may mean more than this by including the use of military assets.[1024] In the EU Treaty, peacemaking is considered a task of combat forces in crisis management (also a rather general term[1025]), thus also implying the use of armed force. Since peacekeeping is already mentioned separately and peacemaking is apparently something for combat forces, it must *at least* mean peacekeeping with peace enforcement elements.[1026] Moreover, the words used in some other language versions of the EU Treaty suggest it also/rather refers to pure peace enforcement,[1027] although some have argued that peace enforcement was deliberately excluded.[1028]

Perhaps most importantly, it is viewed by at least a number of Member States as including pure peace enforcement.[1029] For instance, the UK Secretary of State in 2000 stated before the UK Parliament that in his view an operation like NATO's Kosovo air campaign (which clearly went beyond peacekeeping and constituted (unauthorized) peace enforcement) would fall within the ESDP tasks, though the

---

the EU civilian identity notwithstanding the fact that he seems to consider that the EU could be engaged in coercive peace operations (*id.*, pp. 129–130).

1024 NATO defines 'peacemaking' as "*A peace support operation, conducted after the initiation of a conflict to secure a ceasefire or peaceful settlement, that involves primarily diplomatic action supported, when necessary, by direct or indirect use of military assets*", see NATO Glossary, *supra* note 1014.

1025 In the EU it is used as an overall term for ESDP operations. See, e.g. §1 of the Cologne ESDP Declaration: "*In pursuit of our [CFSP] objectives and the progressive framing of a common defence policy, we are convinced that the Council should have the ability to take decisions on the full range of conflict prevention and crisis management tasks defined in the Treaty on European Union, the "Petersberg tasks"*". It is defined by NATO as "*The coordinated actions taken to defuse crises, prevent their escalation into an armed conflict and contain hostilities if they should result*", see NATO Glossary, *supra* note 1014.

1026 Similarly, H. Schöllhorn, *supra* note 161, pp. 44–45. In this sense also M. Roscini, *supra* note 998, p. 60, arguing that tasks of combat forces is hard to reconcile with peacemaking in the UN sense.

1027 Especially in the French ("*les missions de rétablissement de la paix*"; see also D. Vignes, 'Réflexions sur l'intégration européenne dans les domaines de leations extérieures et de la défense', in E. Ando *et al.* (eds.), *Liber Amicorum Judge Shigeru Oda*, The Hague, Kluwer Law International, 2002, pp. 1633–1634) and Dutch ("*het tot stand brengen van vrede*") versions. See also the German version ("*friedensschaffender Maßnahmen*").

1028 See, e.g. F. Pagani, 'A New Gear in the CFSP Machinery: Integration of the Petersberg Tasks in the Treaty on European Union', 9 *E.J.I.L.* 1998, pp. 741–742. But see W. Van Eekelen, *Debating European Security*, 1948–1998, The Hague, SDU, 1998, p. 127, stating that in his view in the WEU 'peace-making' was interpreted as 'peace enforcement' (also cited in M. Roscini, *supra* note 998, p. 60). See also G.-J. Van Hegelsom, *supra* note 187, p. 114, noting that in WEU documents the term 'peace-making' was usually accompanied by a note explaining that it meant peace enforcement.

1029 Though there does appear to be some disagreement, see M. Comelli, *supra* note 204, p. 159 and M. Roscini, *supra* note 998, p. 59 note 46.

UK Parliament Committee itself was less convinced of this.[1030] Belgium also adheres to this view.[1031] Moreover, the Member States appear to have agreed in 2000 that the most demanding Petersberg tasks are understood to mean missions in the course of which selective/targeted high intensity military operations are necessary in particular to re-establish the peace and that Kosovo would represent the upper limit to such operations.[1032] There are also indications that the EUBGs should be able to conduct peace enforcement operations.[1033] Commentators appear to be divided or uncertain on whether peace enforcement is included.[1034]

1030 House of Commons, Select Committee on Defence, *Eighth Report*, *supra* note 985, §41 (on the one hand "*the Secretary of State was prepared to say that Operation Allied Force (the campaign against Serbia in March to June of 1999) "could have been" a Petersberg task*" and "*the Secretary of State responded – there is not ... a rigid distinction between ... peace keeping and high intensity conflict. A Petersberg task can involve quite intensive conflict*" whereas on the other hand "*In our view, the Secretary of State's claim that the Operation Allied Force "could have been" a Petersberg task is already pushing at the limits of the definition of 'peace making' ... it needs to be driven home harder that this is not about waging war or defending territory*").

1031 For instance, in a presentation on 8 March 2001 for Belgian officers, the Belgian representative to the PSC at that time, ambassador Brouhns, expressed this view.

1032 Déclaration d'engagement de capacités – Glossaire thématique (Brussels, 21 November 2000, available online at http://ihedn.lorraine.free.fr/GroupTrav/D%E9fense%20europ%E9enne/Politique%20de%20d%E9fense%20europ%E9enne/001121%20-%20glossaire%20th%E9matique.pdf#search=%22%22le%20kosovo%20repr%C3%A9sente%20la%20borne%20haute%22%22 – previously available for free but now requiring user name and password): "*On entend par 'missions de Petersberg les plus exigeantes' les missions au cours desquelles des opérations militaires de haute intensité sont ponctuellement nécessaires en particulier pour rétablir la paix ; le Kosovo représente la borne haute de cette expression*", also cited in A. Dumoulin, R. Mathieu & G. Sarlet, *supra* note 161, p. 774 (I have been unable to find this document in the Council's register).

1033 For instance, the Dutch Letter to Parliament dated 4 November 2005 (*supra* note 306) mentions as possible missions 'initial entry'-operations, which are defined as the starting phase of an operation aimed at obtaining access to an area, if necessary by force ("*de beginfase van crisisbeheersingsoperaties die gericht zijn op het zonodig gewapenderhand verkrijgen van toegang tot een gebied*").

1034 *Pro*: A. Dumoulin, R. Mathieu & G. Sarlet, *supra* note 161, p. 241; R. Ferretti, *supra* note 296, pp. 90 and 92–93; R. Gosalbo Bono, *supra* note 994, p. 349 note 28 and pp. 391–392; S. Graf von Kielmansegg, *supra* note 161 (41 *Europarecht*, 2006), p. 200; I. Österdahl, *supra* note 165, pp. 365–366 and M. Roscini, *supra* note 998, pp. 59–66. *Contra*: S. Duke, *The EU and Crisis Management. Development and Prospects*, EIPA, Maastricht, 2002, p. 206 note 122 (noting that 'peace enforcement' is not *officially* a Petersberg task); K. Gerteiser, *supra* note 161, p. 137 and F. Pagani, *supra* note 1028, p. 741 (though seemingly doubtful on whether an exclusion will be tenable). Uncertain: S. Blockmans, 'A New Crisis Manager at the Horizon – The Case of the European Union', 13 *Leiden J.I.L.* 2000, p. 259. Compare A. Missiroli, *CFSP, Defence and Flexibility*, Paris, WEU ISS, Chaillot Paper No. 38, February 2000 (available online at www.iss.europa.eu/index.php?id=143&L=0), p. 17 (submitting this may be a case of 'constructive ambiguity' but apparently considering that at least peacekeeping with peace enforcement elements is covered) and M. Ortega, 'Beyond Petersberg: Missions for the EU Military Forces', in N. Gnesotto (ed.), *supra* note 161, pp. 73–74 (noting that different interpretations are possible and that hardly any attempts were made to clarify the scope of the tasks). On the scope of these tasks before the Treaty of Amsterdam, see, e.g. H. Schöllhorn, *supra* note 161, pp. 35–36, and within the WEU, see J. Litten, *supra* note 161, pp. 62–63 and 68

On balance, it is submitted that peace enforcement, even in its pure form, is included.

2. THE SCOPE OF THE ESDP IN PRACTICE: ESDP OPERATIONS

The ESDP tasks have already been applied in practice as at least comprising peacekeeping with peace enforcement elements. This is clearly illustrated by operations ARTEMIS and EUFOR DR Congo, since both, while conducted with the consent of the parties involved, acted under a Chapter VII mandate and had an enforcement mission,[1035] albeit a limited one, and were called in precisely because the UN peacekeeping force in place was (expected to be) unable to cope with the situation.

Second, the operations the EU has undertaken in the first six years after the launch of its first operation illustrate quite well the broad variety of possible ESDP tasks and the advantage which this choice of instruments offers. Operations such as EUJUST THEMIS (which, moreover, may be regarded as a conflict prevention mission), EUSEC DRC, EUJUST LEX, the AMM, the AMIS II Supporting Mission, EUPAT, EU BAM Rafah and EULEX Kosovo, reflect the flexibility of these instruments. In the military field, the maritime counter-piracy operation EUNAVFOR Somalia / Atalanta also breaks new ground. Moreover, in most cases both military and civilian operations have been or are being conducted in the same country, though the relationship in time varies: in BiH the EUPM is now accompanied by ALTHEA; in the DRC, ARTEMIS was, after a time gap, followed by EUPOL KINSHASA, EUSEC DRC, EUPOL DRC and EUFOR DR Congo, and in FYROM CONCORDIA was immediately succeeded by PROXIMA, which was in turn followed by EUPAT. In fact, the AMIS II Supporting mission was even a mixed mission from the start, albeit with two quite distinct elements and the AMM also can be regarded as having had both military and civilian features. This development of a more integrated approach, based on a broad security concept,[1036] is a positive development but brings with it new challenges, especially given the institutional differences between military

---

and M. Warnken, *supra* note 1, p. 114 (both taking the view that peace enforcement was included). J. Frowein, *supra* note 994, p. 14 notes that a 1993 document adopted by both the EU and the WEU explicitly included peace enforcement.

1035 See, concerning Artemis, A. Abas, *supra* note 438, pp. 141–143 and 146–148 (arguing that it was a peace enforcement mission) and M. Roscini, *supra* note 998, p. 66 (noting the above-mentioned difference between Security Council authorization and welcoming).

1036 See *supra*, Chapter 1.

and civilian missions.[1037] Moreover, the different status of EU BAM Rafah, which is an ESDP operation, and the EU Border Assistance Mission to Moldova and Ukraine, which is not,[1038] raises the question when, as a matter of EU law, an operation must be regarded as an ESDP operation.[1039] It would appear that the security situation in the operation zone and the potential harm to CFSP objectives are among the relevant elements in this respect.[1040]

Third, the geographical reach of the ESDP is clearly expanding: after starting with the Balkans, the EU now also conducts operations in Africa and Asia, including the Middle East. While it is sometimes questioned whether regional organizations should act outside their own region,[1041] it is submitted that there is no *a priori* obstacle to such actions as long as they are based on an appropriate international mandate (as discussed below[1042]). Furthermore, the AMIS Support Mission and AMM illustrate the EU's readiness to support other regional organizations and to cooperate with them.

Fourth, in parallel, as regards the military operations, there is the increasing size and difficulty of the missions: while CONCORDIA was very limited, ARTEMIS was already bigger and fairly challenging given its autonomous nature, the distance involved, the quick deployment and the dangerous environment, as was EUFOR DR Congo, and ALTHEA as also a significant challenge in light of the

1037 For a critical view, see C. Gourlay, 'European Union Procedures and Resources for Crisis Management', 11 *International Peacekeeping* 2004, pp. 404–421 (also adding the challenge of coherence between EC and EDSP activities).

1038 See *supra* note 355 and the accompanying text.

1039 The broader debate on the delimitation of first and second pillars is relevant in this respect (see on this *infra*, Chapter 6, note 1586 and especially ECJ, Case C-91/05, *Commission of the European Communities v. Council of the European Union*, 20 May 2008 as well as the Opinion of Advocate-General Mengozzi of 19 September 2007 in this case). For one perspective, see F. Hoffmeister, 'Inter-pillar Coherence in the European Union's Civilian Crisis Management', in S. Blockmans (ed.), *The European Union and International Crisis Management: Legal and Policy Aspects*, The Hague, TMC Asser Press, 2008, pp. 157–180.

1040 See, e.g. the 13th consideration of the preamble of the EU BAM Rafah Joint Action, *supra* note 703 ("*The mission will implement its mandate in the context of a situation which poses a threat to law and order, the security and safety of individuals, and to the stability of the area and which could harm the objectives of the Common Foreign and Security Policy as set out in Article 11 of the Treaty*").

1041 See the discussion in A. Abass, *supra* note 438, pp. 136 and 145 and K. Graham, 'UN-EU Cooperation on Security: In Search of "Effective Multilateralism" and a Balanced Division of Tasks', in J. Wouters, F. Hoffmeister & T. Ruys (eds.), *supra* note 246, pp. 292–294, who qualifies the EU and NATO as "other intergovernmental organisations" rather than regional or subregional organizations because they can act "out of area"; however, Graham does not seem to contest the legitimacy of them acting out of area. Compare the discussion in A. Dumoulin, R. Mathieu & G. Sarlet, *supra* note 161, pp. 452–457. Such a limitation is rejected by F. Pagani, *supra* note 1028, p. 741.

1042 See Section A.6 of this chapter.

size of the mission and the possibly considerable duration, although it relies on NATO assets. EUFOR Tchad/RCA was also quite demanding and with EUNAVFOR Somalia / Atalanta the EU ventured into maritime operations. Admittedly, it remains to be seen whether the EU could deal with a high-intensity conflict and/or a significantly larger military operation. However, this is essentially a military issue.[1043] From an institutional perspective, the main question would seem to be whether the EU has adequate headquarters and planning and command structures at its disposal for such an eventuality.

Fifth, practice shows that not all Member States participate in every mission and that even when this is the case, contributions may differ greatly. This does not seem to have caused any problems and reflects what Member States have always envisaged by retaining a sovereign right to decide upon engaging their forces (see *supra*, Chapter 2.A[1044]). It is also perfectly normal for Denmark given its special position (see *supra*) and seems logical for those Member States which have a security and defence policy with a "*specific character*",[1045] such as Ireland[1046] and other neutral States (see below, Section A.5.ii of this chapter, for an analysis of the impact of neutrality). It is also permitted for States that make use of the 'constructive abstention' mechanism (see *supra*). However, for *military operations* outside these cases, at first sight, it seems to sit uneasy with the letter of the EU Treaty given that it is not specifically authorized in the EU Treaty and that Article 27B EU Treaty only permits enhanced cooperation in the CFSP for the implementation of a Joint Action or Common Position and excludes such cooperation for matters having military or defence implications (see *supra*).[1047] Nevertheless, it seems to be what was intended and what does occur and it is apparently not regarded as a form of enhanced cooperation. Moreover, if there were a requirement for all non-exempted Member States to participate, this could easily be met by providing for a symbolic participation only (e.g. a

1043 See *supra* Chapter 2.E. However, it is submitted that the usual comparison with the US is not the most relevant one and that a comparison with potential hostile forces in potential ESDP operation zones would be more relevant.

1044 E.g. the Presidency report on ESDP to the 10–11 December 1999 Helsinki European Council states that "*The commitment of national assets by Member States to such operations will be based on their sovereign decision*" (Annex 1 to Annex IV of the Presidency conclusions of this European Council, under 'Decision-making').

1045 See Article 17(1), second subparagraph EU Treaty, as discussed *infra* notes 1116–1121 and the accompanying text.

1046 Ireland is both neutral and has a specific constitutional requirement for a UN mandate, see *supra* note 418 and the accompanying text and *infra* Section A.5.i-ii of this chapter.

1047 On differentiation and flexibility in ESDP generally, see R. Wessel, 'Differentiation in EU Foreign, Security, and Defence Policy: between Coherence and Flexibility', in TRYBUS & WHITE, pp. 225–248.

liaison officer in the operation headquarters). Be that as it may, under the Lisbon Treaty, entrusting a mission to a group of Member States is clearly possible.[1048]

3. THE SCOPE OF THE CSDP'S CRISIS MANAGEMENT COMPONENT UNDER THE LISBON TREATY

Under Article 27(1) (renumbered 42(1)) EU Treaty as it is amended by the Lisbon Treaty, "*[the CSDP] shall provide the Union with an operational capacity drawing on civil and military assets. The Union may use them on missions outside the Union for peace-keeping, conflict prevention and strengthening international security in accordance with the principles of the United Nations Charter*". These missions are further defined in Article 28(1) (renumbered 43) of this Treaty: they "*shall include joint disarmament operations, humanitarian and rescue tasks, military advice and assistance tasks, conflict prevention and peace-keeping tasks, tasks of combat forces in crisis management, including peace-making and post-conflict stabilisation*" and may all "*contribute to the fight against terrorism, including by supporting third countries in combating terrorism in their territories*".[1049] Furthermore, in the preamble of the Protocol on permanent structured cooperation (both under the EU Constitution and the Lisbon Treaty), it is recognized that the EU may be called upon by the UN to assist in implementation of missions undertaken under *Chapter VI or VII* of the UN Charter. It is therefore submitted that under the Lisbon Treaty, the CSDP also encompasses peace enforcement. The Lisbon Treaty's defence provisions in the strict sense are addressed below (see Section A.5.iv of this chapter).

4. THE INTEGRATION OF THE WEU

As mentioned above, the Treaty of Amsterdam made it possible for the European Council to decide *to integrate the WEU into the EU*, albeit that in that case the

---

1048 See Articles 27(5) and 29 (renumbered 42(5) and 44) EU Treaty as amended by the Lisbon Treaty. See also Articles I-41(5) and III-310 EU Constitution. See also R. Wessel, *supra* previous note, pp. 232–248.

1049 See also Articles I-41(1) and III-309(1) EU Constitution. Compare S. Graf von Kielmansegg, *supra* note 161 (44 *C.M.L. Rev.* 2007), pp. 644–648, arguing that the main change in this respect is an extension to situations that are less linked to an acute or latent crisis. On the ESDP and the fight against terrorism, see generally M. Sossai, 'The Anti-Terrorism Dimension of ESDP', in Trybus & White, pp. 157–173. See also S. Duke, 'CESDP and the EU Response to 11 September: Identifying the Weakest Link', 7 *E.F.A.R.* 2002, pp. 153–169 and J. Howorth, 'The European Union, Peace Operations and Terrorism' in T. Tardy (ed.), *Peace Operations after 11 September 2001*, London, Cass, 2004, pp. 80–97.

Member States' constitutional requirements would have to be fulfilled. However, the European Council did not decide upon a full integration, but rather upon "*the inclusion of those functions of the WEU which will be necessary for the EU to fulfil its new responsibilities in the area of the Petersberg tasks*", although it also held that "*In that event, the WEU as an organisation would have completed its purpose*".[1050] Indeed, as described above (Chapter 1.E-F), the EU did take over the WEU's crisis management capabilities but the WEU continued to exist, albeit in a minimal manner. Did this require going through the constitutional procedures of the Member States?

The question whether the development of the ESDP as envisaged required any Treaty changes was raised and examined. The December 1999 Helsinki European Council invited the next Presidency to draw up a report by mid-2000 containing "*an indication of whether or not Treaty amendment is judged necessary*".[1051] The excerpt from that report read:

> The existing provisions of the TEU define the questions relating to the security of the Union, including the progressive framing of a common defence policy as part of the Common Foreign and Security Policy governed by Title V of the Treaty. On this basis, the Council has decided to establish the interim Political and Security Committee and the Interim Military Body, and to reinforce the Council Secretariat with military experts seconded from Member States. Article 17 TEU expressly includes the Petersberg tasks in the CFSP. The Presidency took note of the opinion of the Council Legal Service the conclusion of which reads as follows:
>
> "The Council's Legal Service is of the opinion that the conclusions of the Cologne and Helsinki European Councils regarding European security and defence policy can be implemented without it being legally necessary to amend the Treaty on European Union. However, such amendments would be necessary if the intention is to transfer the Council's decision-making powers to a body made up of officials, or to amend the Treaty's provisions regarding the WEU. Furthermore, it is for Member States to determine whether amendments to the Treaty would be politically desirable or operationally appropriate."
>
> The Presidency suggests that the issue of Treaty revision should continue to be examined between the Feira and Nice European Councils.[1052]

1050 Cologne ESDP Declaration, §5.

1051 Presidency conclusions, §29.

1052 Strengthening the Common European Security and Defence Policy – Presidency Report to the Feira European Council, EU Council Doc. 9149/00 of 15 June 2000, Part II.E, pp. 9–10. See also L.N. Pnevmaticou, *Aspectes juridiques de la politique européenne de sécurité et de défense*, Paris, WEU ISS, 2001, pp. 12–13, citing the advice as No. 8332/08.05.2000 (Occasional Paper 31, available online at www.iss.europa.eu/index.php?id=154&L=0).

The advice of the Council legal service was followed and the ESDP was further developed, without the PSC having any decision-making authority.[1053] However, it is questionable whether the way the ESDP was being developed did not in fact amend the Treaty provisions on the WEU and therefore would have required a Treaty amendment or perhaps rather the national constitutional procedures.[1054]

In any event, any legal difficulties that may have existed, were overcome with the entry into force of the Treaty of Nice, which removed the references to the WEU and gave the PSC a Treaty basis (see *supra*, Chapter 1.F), including a decision-making power in respect of ESDP operations when authorized by the Council,[1055] a power it has consistently been given by the Council and has exercised frequently since then (see *supra*, Chapter 2.A and Chapter 3).

Moreover, although the EU Treaty provisions on the ESDP are not always very precise and there are a few instances where they seem to have been construed and applied in a rather extensive way, the development of the ESDP is based on Treaty provisions that have been amended time upon time according to the proper treaty amendment procedure. Likewise, the EU's decisions in the field of the ESDP are often quite legal and precise in nature (e.g. they always mention their legal basis), reflecting a strong legal nature of and culture within the EU.

This can be most clearly seen when comparing the legal framework of the ESDP with that which formerly existed in the WEU and that which still exists within NATO. Indeed, apart from the collective self-defence clause, the provisions in

---

1053 See the interim and permanent decisions on the PSC cited *supra*, Chapter 1, note 137.

1054 L.N. Pnevmaticou, *supra* note 1052, pp. 12–13, is rather of the view that the existing Treaty provisions did not suffice. See also the references in A. Dumoulin & F. Gevers, *supra* note 328, pp. 70–73 to reports insisting that the competences of the WEU be respected until the entry into force of the Treaty of Nice. Compare E. Decaux, *supra* note 182, pp. 20–21 and 28–30 and R.A. Wessel, 'De Europese Unie in de internationale rechtsorde', in NVIR (ed.), *De plaats van de Europese Unie in het veranderende bestel van de volkenrechtelijke organisatie. Preadvies* (123 Mededelingen van de NVIR), The Hague, TMC Asser Press, 2001, pp. 55–56 (rather doubtful). J. Litten, *supra* note 161, p. 228 is of the opinion that it was not an integration of the WEU in the sense of Article 17 EU Treaty.

1055 See Article 25 EU Treaty: "…*Within the scope of this title, this Committee shall exercise, under the responsibility of the Council, political control and strategic direction of crisis management operations. The Council may authorise the Committee, for the purpose and for the duration of a crisis management operation, as determined by the Council, to take the relevant decisions concerning the political control and strategic direction of the operation, without prejudice to Article 47*".

the constitutive treaties of the WEU[1056] and NATO[1057] on other forms of cooperation are rather vague and broad and the crisis management functions have been granted to these organizations by decisions of their decision-making bodies (the Council of Ministers and North Atlantic Council respectively) (see *supra*, Chapter 1.D).[1058] Nevertheless, this appears to have raised no major objections. In fact, the German Constitutional Court on 22 November 2001 ruled that the German government did not act *ultra vires* when it approved the new NATO missions.[1059]

1056 The only provisions in the Amended Brussels Treaty that seem capable of providing some legal basis for the WEU to conduct operations other than collective self-defence entitling are Article VIII, paragraph 1 ("*For the purposes of strengthening peace and security and of promoting unity and of encouraging the progressive integration of Europe and closer co-operation between Them and with other European organisations, the High Contracting Parties ... shall create a Council to consider matters concerning the execution of this Treaty and of its Protocols and their Annexes*") and 3 ("*At the request of any of the High Contracting Parties the Council shall be immediately convened in order to permit Them to consult with regard to any situation which may constitute a threat to peace, in whatever area this threat should arise, or a danger to economic stability*"). See also J. Litten, *supra* note 161, pp. 63–66; R.A. Wessel, 'The Legality of the New Functions of the Western European Union. The Attribution of Powers Reconsidered on the Occasion of the 50th Anniversary of the Brussels Treaty', 51(1–2) *Studia Diplomatica* 1998, pp. 21–22 and M. Warnken, *supra* note 1, pp. 98–109. Compare W. Heintschel von Heinegg, 'Rechtsprobleme einer deutsch-franzözischen Zusammenarbeit bei Friedenssicherungsaktionen der Vereinte Nationen', in C. Tomuschat & J.A. Frowein (eds.), *supra* note 994, pp. 105 and 113–114, who argues that the new tasks are covered by the Amended Brussels Treaty only if they are conducted in the framework of the UN, to which this treaty refers. J. Frowein, *supra* note 994, pp. 13–14 argues that the Amended Brussels Treaty was amended by the later EU-WEU arrangements.

1057 Provisions that might support non-Article V operations are the preamble ("*...resolved to unite their efforts for collective defence* and for the preservation of peace and security"; emphasis added) read together with Article 2 ("*The Parties will contribute toward the further development of peaceful and friendly international relations by strengthening their free institutions, ..., and by promoting conditions of stability and well-being*"), Article 3 ("*In order more effectively to achieve the objectives of this Treaty, the Parties, separately and jointly, ..., will maintain and develop their individual and collective capacity to resist armed attack*") and Article 4 ("*The Parties will consult together whenever, in the opinion of any of them, the territorial integrity, political independence or security of any of the Parties is threatened*").

1058 For a legal analysis of the expansion of WEU and NATO tasks, see generally B. Delcourt & F. Dubuisson, 'Contribution au débat juridique sue les missions 'non-Article 5' de l'OTAN', 35 *R.B.D.I./B.T.I.R.* 2002, pp. 439–467; F. Daigeler, *Parlamentarische Kontrollrechte beim Abschluss völkerrechtlicher Verträge: am Beispiel der Neubestimmung der Aufgaben der NATO und der Entwicklungen im Rahmen der OSZE*, Hamburg, Kovac, 2005; G. Geiger, 'Die völker- und verfassungsrechtlich wirksame Erweiterung des Aufgabensspektrums von NATO und WEU um Krisenmanagementaufgaben', 43 *Neue Zeitschrift für Wehrrecht* 2001, pp. 133–150; E. Myjer, *NAVO, WEU en Nederland: is "out-of-area" -optreden geoorloofd?, Europa Instituut*, Rijksuniversiteit Utrecht, 1991; See also de Wet, pp. 292–293 (arguing that the North Atlantic Treaty has been amended through practice); G. Nolte, 'Die "neuen Aufgaben" von NATO und WEU: Völker- und verfassungsrechtliche Fragen', 54 *Z.a.ö.R.V.* 1994, pp. 95–123 and R.A. Wessel, *supra* previous note, pp. 15–28.

1059 BVerfG, 2 BvE 6/99, available online in German at www.bundesverfassungsgericht.de/entscheidungen/es20011122_2bve000699.html and in English translation at www.

5. OF SOLIDARITY, NEUTRALITY AND THE WAY TOWARDS A COMMON DEFENCE

i. No Common Defence Yet

Even after the Treaty of Amsterdam, a common defence was still only a possibility that might result from a common defence policy. This remained the same after the Treaty of Nice. Moreover, the Seville European Council of June 2002 clearly affirmed that the step towards a common Defence had not yet been made.[1060] It is worth quoting part of the National Declaration by Ireland and the Declaration of the European Council in response:[1061]

> NATIONAL DECLARATION BY IRELAND
>
> 3. Ireland confirms that its participation in the [EU's CFSP] does not prejudice its traditional policy of military neutrality. The [EU Treaty] makes clear that the Union's security and defence policy shall not prejudice the specific character of the security and defence policy of certain Member States.
>
> 4. In line with its traditional policy of military neutrality, Ireland is not bound by any mutual defence commitment. Nor is Ireland party to any plans to develop a European army. Indeed, the Nice European Council recognised that the development of the Union's capacity to conduct humanitarian and crisis management tasks does not involve the establishment of a European army.
>
> 5. The Treaty on European Union specifies that any decision by the Union to move to a common defence would have to be taken by unanimous decision of the Member States and adopted in accordance with their respective constitutional requirements. The Government of Ireland have made a firm commitment to the people of Ireland, solemnized in this Declaration, that a referendum will be held in Ireland on the

---

bundesverfassungsgericht.de/entscheidungen/es20011122_2bve000699en.html (while the court held that "*The possibility of so-called crisis response operations, however, constitutes an important expansion of NATO's tasks, which has not been implied in the Treaty*" (§12), it nevertheless decided that "*it cannot be inferred that an objective amendment of the NATO Treaty has taken place. The definitions of content that have been made can still be understood as a further development and a concretisation of the open wording of the NATO Treaty*" (§16)). See on this H. Sauer, 'Die NATO und das Verfassungsrecht: neues Konzept – alte Fragen', 62 *Z.a.ö.R.V.* 2002, pp. 317–346 and M. Rau, 'NATO's New Strategic Concept and the German Federal Government's Authority in the Sphere of Foreign Affairs: The Decision of the German Federal Constitutional Court of 22 November 2001', 44 *G.Y.I.L.* 2002, pp. 544–575. See also W. Lang, 'Sind WEU und NATO noch Allianzen?', 13 *Österreichisches Jahrbuch für internationale Politik*, 1996, pp. 1–14.

1060 For a discussion of an incident in which the question might have been relevant but no significant EU action was taken, see J. Monar, 'The CFSP and the Leila/Perejil Island Incident: The Nemesis of Solidarity and Leadership', 7 *E.F.A.R.* 2002, pp. 251–255.

1061 21–22 June 2002, Annex III-IV to the Presidency Conclusions, EU Council Doc. 13463/02, 24 October 2002.

adoption of any such decision and on any future treaty which would involve Ireland departing from its traditional policy of military neutrality.

6. Ireland reiterates that the participation of contingents of the Irish Defence Forces in overseas operations, including those carried out under the [ESDP], requires (a) the authorisation of the operation by the Security Council or the General Assembly of the United Nations, (b) the agreement of the Irish Government and (c) the approval of Dáil Éireann, in accordance with Irish law.

7. The situation set out in this Declaration would be unaffected by the entry into force of the Treaty of Nice. ...

DECLARATION BY THE EUROPEAN COUNCIL

1. The European Council takes cognisance of the National Declaration by Ireland...

2. The European Council notes that the Treaty on European Union provides that any decision to move to a common defence shall be adopted in accordance with the respective constitutional requirements of the Member States.

3. The European Council recalls that under the terms of the Treaty on European Union the policy of the Union shall not prejudice the specific character of the security and defence policy of certain Member States. Ireland has drawn attention, in this regard, to its traditional policy of military neutrality.

4. The European Council acknowledges that the Treaty on European Union does not impose any binding mutual defence commitments. Nor does the development of the Union's capacity to conduct humanitarian and crisis management tasks involve the establishment of a European army.

5. The European Council confirms that the situation referred to in paragraphs 2, 3 and 4 would be unchanged by the entry into force of the Treaty of Nice.

6. The European Council recognises that, like all Member States of the Union, Ireland would retain the right, after the entry into force of the Treaty of Nice, to take its own sovereign decision, in accordance with its constitution and its laws, whether to commit military personnel to participate in any operation carried out under the European Security and Defence Policy. Ireland, in its National Declaration, has clearly set out its position in this regard.

Hence, for the time being Article V of the North Atlantic Treaty and of the Amended Brussels Treaty remain the relevant collective defence provisions, both being implemented only in NATO. However, this situation does raise the question of delimitation between the common defence policy, which is being realized (see *supra*), and the common defence, which is not (yet) an EU competence. I will return to this below when treating the defence provisions in the Lisbon Treaty and EU Constitution.

ii. A Confirmation of the Decline of Neutrality?

The above-mentioned declarations relating to Ireland raise the issue of the compatibility of neutrality[1062] with involvement in the ESDP. The question is not new and has repeatedly been debated, including in respect of EC and EU membership.[1063]

1062 Sometimes the term 'non-aligned' is used, but as pointed out by H. Neuhold, *supra* note 165, p. 499 note 17, this term already has a distinct meaning associated to a movement of mainly developing countries (see www.nam.gov.za/); see H. Neuhold, 'Permanent Neutrality and Non-alignment: Similarities and Differences', 35 *India Quarterly* 1979, pp. 285–308. The expression "non-allied" States mentioned in S. Griller *et al.*, *The Treaty of Amsterdam. Facts, Analysis, Prospects*, Vienna, Springer, 2000, p. 420 may be more appropriate. Nevertheless, I will only use the term "neutral".

1063 See, e.g. F. Cede, 'Osterreichs Neutralitat und Sicherheitspolitik nach dem Beitritt zur Europaischen Union', 36 *Zeitschrift fur Rechtsvergleichung, Internationales Privatrecht und Europarecht* 1995, pp. 142–148; R. Doherty, *Ireland, Neutrality and European Security Integration*, Aldershot, Ashgate, 2002 (noting that Ireland has adapted somewhat slower than the other European neutrals); G.P. Elliott, 'Neutrality, the Acquis Communautaire and the European Union's Search for a Common Foreign and Security Policy under Title V of the Maastricht Treaty: The Accession of Austria, Finland and Sweden', 25 *Georgia J.I.C.L.* 1996, pp. 601–639; K. Ginther, 'Neutralitatsrecht – Volkerrecht – Europarecht: zur Diskussion der Vereinbarkeit von dauernder Neutralitat und Mitgliedschaft in der EG', in W. Haller *et al.* (eds.), *Im Dienst an der Gemeinschaft: Festschrift fur Dietrich Schindler zum 65. Geburtstag*, Basel, Helbing & Lichtenhahn, 1989, pp. 373–388 (arguing at pp. 380–386 that the answer might depend upon whether Article 297 EC Treaty can be invoked for neutrality reasons); H.-J. Glaesner *et al.*, *Aussen- und Sicherheitspolitische Aspekte des Vertrages von Maastricht und seine Konsequenzen für neutrale Beitrittswerber*, Graz, Forschungsinstitut für Europarecht, Karl-Franzens-Universität, 1993; H.J. Glaesner, 'Gemeinschaftsrecht und dauernde Neutralitat', in J.F. Baur *et al.* (eds.), *Europarecht, Energierecht, Wirtschaftsrecht: Festschrift fur Bodo Borner zum 70. Geburtstag*, Cologne, Carl Heymann, 1992, pp. 89–97; S. Griller *et al.*, *supra* note 551, pp. 431–440; G. Hafner & P. Schulz, 'La neutralité de l'Autriche après son adhésion à l'Union Européenne', 40 *A.F.D.I.* 1994, pp. 287–325; S. Harden (ed.), *Neutral States and the European Community*, London, Brassey's, 1994; W. Hummer, 'Annaherung zwischen EG und EFTA-Staaten: aussen-, neutralitats- und wirtschaftliche Problemfelder', 4 *Veroffentlichungen der Kommission fur Europarecht* 1991, pp. 7–52; P. Luif, *Neutrale in die EG?: die westeuropäische Integration und die neutralen Staaten*, Vienna, Verlag Wilhelm Braumüller, 1988; P. Luif, 'The Western European Union and the Neutrals. The Security Policy of Europe's Non-Aligned Countries in the Context of the EU's Common Foreign and Security Policy', 51 *Studia Diplomatica* 1998, pp.77–98; G. Lysen, 'Some Views on Neutrality and Membership of the European Communities: The Case of Sweden', 29 *C.M.L. Rev.* 1992, pp. 229–255; D. O'Connor, 'Ireland's Neutrality under the Amsterdam Treaty', 18 *Irish Law Times* 2000, pp. 283–291; I. Österdahl, 'The Neutral Ally: The European Security and Defence Policy and the Swedish Constitution', 78 *Nordic J.I.L.* 2009, pp. 95–132; K. Schilcher, 'GASP und neutrale Staaten', 2 *Z. Eur. S.* 1999, pp. 609–651 (*inter alia* pointing to the relevance of Article 297 EC Treaty and noting that to the extent that sanctions would involve a breach of impartiality, this only poses a real problem for neutrality in the case of EU/EC sanctions not based on a UN obligation and taken in relation to an international armed conflict; see pp. 637–639); P. Schröter, T. Cottier & A. Kopse, *Neutralität und GASP: erste Erfahrungen Finnlands, Österreichs und Schwedens*, 11 Swiss papers on European integration, Zürich/Bern, Schulthess/Stämpfli, 1997; M. Schweitzer, 'GASP und dauernde Neutralitat Osterreichs', in O. Due *et al.* (eds.), *Festschrift fur Ulrich Everling*, Baden-Baden,

Nowadays, neutrality is often defined as that part of the law of war governing the relationship under international law between States engaged in an armed conflict and those that are not participating in that conflict.[1064] However, the law of neutrality has evolved considerably throughout time.[1065] What is now regarded as 'traditional neutrality' is the law codified in two 1907 Hague Conventions.[1066] It was a very strict regime associated with the freedom to wage war[1067] and based on the two notions of impartiality towards the parties to a conflict and abstention from engaging in hostilities.[1068] It *inter alia* required that a State wishing to be neutral in relation to a conflict not take part in that conflict[1069] and behave in a very strict even-handed manner towards all belligerents involved in the conflict[1070] and that neutral states prohibit the use of their territory by belligerents and safeguard their territory[1071] and intern all armed forces of a belligerent on their territory.[1072] Moreover, one was either a party to a conflict or

---

Nomos, 1995, pp. 1379–1391; S.P. Subedi, 'The Common Foreign and Security Policy of the European Union and Neutrality: towards Co-existence?', 42 *N.I.L.R.* 1995, pp. 399–412; S.P. Subedi, 'Neutrality in a Changing World: European Neutral States and the European Community', 42 *I.C.L.Q.* 1993, pp. 238–268 and M. Thaler, "Zur Frage der Vereinbarkeit von EWG-Mitgliedschaft und dauernder Neutralitat", 39 *Osterreichische Zeitschrift fur offentliches Recht*, 1988, pp. 303–311.

1064 See, e.g. UK MANUAL, §1.42, p. 19 and M. Bothe, 'The Law of Neutrality', in D. Fleck (ed.), *The Handbook of Humanitarian Law in Armed Conflicts*, Oxford, Oxford University Press, 1995, p. 485. This is also reflected in the ILA's 1998 Helsinki Principles on the Law of Martitime Neutrality (68 *ILA Report of the 1998 Conference*, pp. 496–497), §1.1: defining a neutral State as "*any State which is not party to an international armed conflict*" (see also the commentary to this paragraph, *id.*).

1065 See, e.g. E. Chadwick, *Traditional Neutrality Revisited. Law, theory and Case Studies*, The Hague, Kluwer Law International, 2002, especially pp. 182–215 and T. Komarnicki, 'The Place of Neutrality in the Modern System of International Law', 80 *Rec. Cours* 1952-I, pp. 398–510.

1066 Convention (V) respecting the Rights and Duties of Neutral Powers and Persons in Case of War on Land, The Hague, 18 October 1907 (1907 HC V) and Convention (XIII) concerning the Rights and Duties of Neutral Powers in Naval War, The Hague, 18 October 1907 (1907 HC XIII), both available online at www.icrc.org/ihl. On their customary status, see briefly K. Schilcher, *supra* note 1063, p. 613.

1067 See, e.g. T. Komarnicki, *supra* note 1065, pp. 401–418 and *Rapport sur la neutralité. Publié en annexe du "rapport sur la politique extérieure de la Suisse dans les années 90" du 29 novembre 1993* (available online at www.eda.admin.ch/etc/medialib/downloads/edazen/topics/intla/cintla.Par.0031.File.tmp/Rapport_sur_la_neutralite_fr.pdf). On the relevance of the concept of war in this context, see G.C. Petrochilos, 'The Relevance of the Concepts of War and Armed Conflict to the Law of Neutrality', 31 *Vanderbilt J.T.L.* 1998, pp. 575–615.

1068 See, e.g. M. Bothe, *supra* note 1064, p. 485; C. Chaumont, 'Nations Unies et neutralité', 89 *Rec. Cours* 1956-I, p. 9; T. Komarnicki, *supra* note 1065, p. 406 and M. Torrelli, 'La neutralite en question', 96 *R.G.D.I.P.* 1992, pp. 7–10. See also Convention on Maritime Neutrality, Havana, 20 February 1928 (available online at www.icrc.org/ihl), preamble ("*Considering that neutrality is the juridical situation of states which do not take part in the hostilities, and that it creates rights and imposes obligations of impartiality*").

1069 See, e.g. Article 16 1907 HC V.

1070 See, e.g. Article 9 1907 HC V.

1071 Articles 1–5 and 10 1907 HC V.

1072 Article 11 1907 HC V.

a neutral and there was no intermediate status.[1073] Furthermore, it may be noted that the rules of neutrality are particularly developed in respect of naval warfare.[1074]

In addition to this 'occasional' neutrality which relates to a given conflict, some States were permanent neutrals, either as a legal requirement under domestic and/or international law, or as a matter of long standing policy.[1075] Permanent neutrality included some additional obligations such as not being part of a military alliance and not having foreign military bases on one's territory,[1076]

1073 T. Komarnicki, *supra* note 1065, pp. 403–405..

1074 As is rightly noted by M. Torelli, *supra* note 1068, pp. 7–10. See 1907 HC XIII and the San Remo Manual (*infra* note 1090).

1075 M. Bothe, *supra* note 1064, §§1105, pp. 489–490. For the origins of Swiss and Austrian neutrality, see C. Chaumont, *supra* note 1068, pp. 24–26 and 27–29. For a discussion of the various permanent neutrals, see, e.g. Y. Beignbeder, 'La neutralité suisse en question: isolement ou solidarité internationale', 24 *R.B.D.I./B.T.I.R.* 1991, pp. 27–45; N. Blanc-Noël, *La politique suédoise de neutralité active: de la Seconde Guerre mondiale à l'entrée dans l'Union européenne*, Paris, Institut de Stratégie Comparée, EPHE IV, Sorbonne, 1997; R. Doherty, *supra* note 1063; D. Keohane, *Realigning Neutrality? Irish Defence Policy and the EU*, Paris, WEU ISS, Occasional Paper No. 24, March 2001; W. Lang, 'L'Autriche entre la neutralite et l'integration', 42 *Actualites du Droit: Revue de la Faculte de Droit de Liege* 1997, pp. 693–699; R. Lippold, 'Strukturfragen der Verfassung am Beispiel der immerwahrenden Neutralitat Osterreichs', 42 *Austrian J. Pub. I.L.* 1991, pp. 295–318; S. Martens, 'Autriche: la neutralité: vers la fin d'un mythe', in P. Buffotot (ed.), *supra* note 161, pp. 27–32; J. Ross, *Neutrality and International Sanctions: Sweden, Switzerland and Collective Security*, New York, Praeger, 1989; K. Schilcher, *supra* note 1063, pp. 626–633; D. Schindler, 'Neue Falle dauernder Neutralitat: Malta und Costa Rica', in B. Dutoit & E. Grisel (eds.), *Melanges Georges Perrin*, Lausanne, Payot, 1984, pp. 277–291; D. Schindler, 'Kollektive Sicherheit der Vereinten Nationen und dauernde Neutralität der Schweiz', 2 *S.Z.I.E.R.* 1992, pp. 435–479; B. Sundelius (ed.), *The Committed Neutral: Sweden's Foreign Policy*, Boulder, Westview Press, 1989; D. Thurer, 'Neutralitat der Schweiz – Illusionen oder (humanitäre) Chance?', in W. Benedek, H. Isak & R. Kicker (eds.), *Development and Developing International and European Law: Essays in Honour of Konrad Ginther on the Occasion of his 65th Birthday*, Frankfurt am main, Lang, 1999, pp. 741–755; D. Thurer, 'Humanitat und Neutralitat – zum politischen und volkerrechtlichen Spannungsverhaltnis zweier Grundprinzipien der schweizerischen Aussenpolitik', in Y. Hangartner & S. Trechsel (eds.), *Volkerrecht im Dienste des Menschen. Festschrift fur Hans Haug*, Bern, Verlag Paul Haupt, 1986, pp. 279–308 and M. von Grunigen, 'Finnische Neutralitat -- Kontinuitat im Wandel', in W. Haller *et al.* (eds.), *supra* note 1063, pp. 389–403. On Malta, see *infra*, note 1104.

1076 See S. Griller *et al.*, *supra* note 1062, p. 436; K. Ginther, *supra* note 1063, p. 379–380, and, with regard to Austria, C. Chaumont, *supra* note 1068, pp. 27. M. Bothe, *supra* note 1064, §1105, pp. 489–490 only mentions the first requirement. Compare M. Torelli, *supra* note 1068, pp. 31–37. On permanent neutrality, see generally S. Griller, 'Vom Wandel der immerwahrenden Neutralitat', in G. Schefbeck (ed.), *75 Jahre Bundesverfassung: Festschrift aus Anlass des 75. Jahrstages der Beschlussfassung uber das Bundes-Verfassungsgesetz*, Vienna, Verlag Osterreich, 1995, pp. 727–753; B. Havel, 'An International Law Institution in Crisis: Rethinking Permanent Neutrality', 61 *Ohio State Law Journal* 2000, pp. 167–266; M. Rotter, *Die dauernde Neutralität*, Berlin, Duncker & Humblot, 1981 and L. Wildhaber, 'Muss die dauernde Neutralitat bewaffnet sein?', in W. Haller *et al.* (eds.), *supra* note 1063, pp. 429–441.

although it has been argued that there is no customary regime but rather a variety of specific regimes.[1077]

However, the UN Charter with its rules on the *ius ad bellum* (i.e. the rules on the (il)legality of having recourse to the use of force) and its collective security system (with the Security Council as key actor), fundamentally challenged the traditional laws of neutrality.[1078] Nevertheless, several permanent neutral States clearly did not regard their permanent neutral status as incompatible with UN membership,[1079] as did the other UN Member States by admitting known permanent neutral States to membership.[1080] Furthermore, some rules regarding neutrality, essentially those of a humanitarian nature,[1081] were included in post UN Charter international humanitarian law treaties, including the 1949 Geneva Conventions[1082] and the 1977 First Additional Protocol.[1083]

1077 K. Schilcher, *supra* note 1063, pp. 614–615 (but see p. 17).

1078 For a thorough treatment of this problem concluding that there is substantial incompatibility between both, see A.R. Schaub, *Neutralität und kollektive Sicherheit: Gegenüberstellung zweier unvereinbarer Verhaltenskonzepte in bewaffneten Konflikten und Thesen zu einem zeit- und völkerrechtsgemässen modus vivendi*, Basel / Frankfurt am Main, Helbing & Lichtenhahn, 1995. In the same sense also H. Kelsen, *The Law of the United Nations*, New York, Praeger, 1951, pp. 94 and 108 (holding the view that membership of the UN was incompatible with permanent neutrality). But see C. Chaumont, *supra* note 1068, pp. 1–59, rejecting the incompatibility of neutrality and UN membership (by reducing the scope of neutrality). Compare also T. Komarnicki, *supra* note 1065, pp. 464–502 (seeing little but still some room for neutrality). On neutrality and UN membership and collective security, see also generally E. Diez, 'UNO-Beitritt und Neutralitatserklarung', in B. Dutoit & E. Grisel (eds.), *Melanges Georges Perrin*, Lausanne, Payot, 1984, pp. 77–90; A. Greber, *Die dauernde Neutralität und das kollektive Sicherheitssystem der Vereinten Nationen*, Zurich, Juris Druck, 1967; J. Ross, *supra* note 1075; H. Schmid, *Dauernd neutrale Staaten im Sicherheitsrat der Vereinten Nationen*, Winterthur, Schellenberg, 1984; H. Turk, 'Neutralitat und Mitgliedschaft bei den Vereinten Nationen', in K. Ginther *et al.* (eds.), *Volkerrecht zwischen normativem Anspruch und politischer Realitat: Festschrift fur Karl Zemanek zum 65. Geburtstag*, Berlin, Duncker & Humblot, 1994, 439–463 and K. Zemanek, 'The Changing International System: A New Look at Collective Security and Permanent Neutrality', 42 *Austrian J. Pub. I.L.* 1991, pp. 277–294.

1079 Switzerland was long a non-UN member (until 2002) but this seems at most only partially to have been based on its neutral status, at least in more recent times, since it did participate, e.g. in UN mandated sanctions even before its UN membership. See, e.g. the 1993 Swiss Report (*supra* note 1067).

1080 But see K. Zemanek, *supra* note 1078 (*Austrian J. Pub. I.L.*), pp. 280–281 questioning the awareness by UN Member States of the (scope of) Austrian neutrality. See also R. Doherty, *supra* note 1063, pp. 46–47, noting that Ireland was initially not admitted to the UN, though it appears this only refers to admission as a founding member as the subsequent admission was held hostage to a broader admission issue opposing the two cold war blocs.

1081 E. Chadwick, *supra* note 1065, p. 201.

1082 See, e.g. Articles 4, 27, 32, 37 and 43 GC I; 5, 15, 17, 21, 25, 32 and 40 GC II; 111 GC III and 4 and 132–135 GC IV.

1083 See, e.g. Article 31 AP I.

The continued existence of occasional neutrality is said to have revived with the failure of the UN collective security system[1084] and may indeed easily be understood given that it is not always clear which State is the aggressor in an international armed conflict, especially where the Security Council makes no determination in this respect. The continued existence of *permanent* neutrality is, however, much more difficult to justify. In any event, as a result of these developments, while neutrality still exists, it has repeatedly been said that the law of neutrality is to some extent in a state of chaos.[1085] While the impact of the UN Charter and the *ius ad bellum* does not yet appear to have been fully clarified, it would appear that there is a growing consensus that the UN Charter and the *ius ad bellum* have primacy and will prevail in the case of conflicts with those rules of neutrality that still apply.[1086] This is a logical consequence of the primacy of the UN Charter[1087] and its *lex specialis* and *lex posterior* nature vis-à-vis traditional neutrality law.[1088] For instance, the UK MANUAL notes that "*the*

1084 See, e.g. K. Ipsen *et al.*, *Völkerrecht*, München, CH Beck, 2004 (5th ed.), pp. 1273–1275 and 1281. K. Schilcher, *supra* note 1063, pp. 624–625 also points to a converse relation between collective security and neutrality.

1085 See, e.g. K. Zemanek, 'The Chaotic Status of the Laws of Neutrality', in W. Haller *et al.* (eds.), *supra* note 1063, pp. 443–454 (seeing problems with regard to the substitution of war by armed conflict, economic warfare and new weapons in particular in relation to safeguarding the inviolability of airspace). See already C. Chaumont, *supra* note 1068, pp. 10–13. The 1993 Swiss Report (*supra* note 1067, p. 7 online version) states that "*le droit de la neutralité n'a jamais été actualisé depuis sa codification en 1907. Il a de ce fait perdu de sa pertinence et de son efficacité, il comporte de nombreuses lacunes et n'est plus adapté au monde actuel*".

1086 M. Bothe, *supra* note 1064, §§1103–1104, pp. 487–489 and K. Ipsen *et al*, *supra* note 1084, p. 1274. This seems also to have been recognized, albeit rather cautiously, in the ILA's 1998 Helsinki Principles on the Law of Martitime Neutrality (*supra* note 1064), §1.2 and commentary thereto (p. 499). For the evolution of the Austrian position, see K. Zemanek, *supra* note 1078, pp. 277–294, concluding in 1991 that if the collective security system effectively started functioning, the priority of the Charter over the rules of neutrality long resisted by Austria and Austrian scholars merited serious consideration. It would appear that the neutrals have since then increasingly accepted this. For instance, the 1993 Swiss report (*supra* note 1067, especially pp. 15–20), which also refers to the Austrian position, states that participation in UN mandated sanctions, even military ones (although it is not clear to what extent), is not contrary to neutrality, arguing that such UN mandated measures do not amount to participating in a war in the sense of neutrality. The report also views participation in some regionally mandated sanctions as not incompatible with neutrality (*id.*, pp. 20–21; see also *Pratique suisse de la neutralité – aspects actuels. Rapport du groupe de travail interdépartemental du 30 août 2000,* available online at www.eda.admin.ch/etc/medialib/downloads/edazen/topics/intla/cintla.Par.0032.File.tmp/Bericht_zur_Neutralitaetspraxis_Kosovo_2000_fr.pdf).

1087 See Article 103 UN Charter, discussed below in Section A.6 of this chapter and in Chapters 8.E and 9.C.5. In the same sense, T. Komarnicki, *supra* note 1065, p. 473.

1088 The *lex posterior* nature is obvious. In addition, in respect of initiating armed force, the *ius ad bellum* is also to be considered as *lex specialis* and prevails on that basis too. On these relationship rules, see more extensively *infra*, Chapter 9.D.2 (albeit with regard to the relationship between the LOAC and human rights). Finally, to the extent that the rules of the *ius ad bellum* are part of *ius cogens* (see *infra*, Section A.6 of this chapter), they also prevail in *traditional law of neutrality has been affected by and, to a large extent, superseded by the UN Charter*".[1089] Also, the 1994 San Remo Manual on International Law Applicable to Armed Conflicts at Sea provides that:

> SECTION III: ARMED CONFLICTS IN WHICH THE SECURITY COUNCIL HAS TAKEN ACTION
>
> 7. Notwithstanding any rule in this document or elsewhere on the law of neutrality, where the Security Council, acting in accordance with its powers under Chapter VII of the Charter of the United Nations, has identified one or more of the parties to an armed conflict as responsible for resorting to force in violation of international law, neutral States:
> (a) are bound not to lend assistance other than humanitarian assistance to that State; and
> (b) may lend assistance to any State which has been the victim of a breach of the peace or an act of aggression by that State.
>
> 8. Where, in the course of an international armed conflict, the Security Council has taken preventive or enforcement action involving the application of economic measures under Chapter VII of the Charter, Member States of the United Nations may not rely upon the law of neutrality to justify conduct which would be incompatible with their obligations under the Charter or under decisions of the Security Council.
>
> 9. Subject to paragraph 7, where the Security Council has taken a decision to use force, or to authorize the use of force by a particular State or States, the rules set out in this document and any other rules of international humanitarian law applicable to armed conflicts at sea shall apply to all parties to any such conflict which may ensue.[1090]

A key point is also whether there is an intermediary status between neutrality and being a party to a conflict.[1091] While this was not the case under traditional neutrality (see *supra*), it results from the UN Charter rules that a State which

---

that capacity; see Article 64 1969 VCLT. For an analysis of neutrality from the perspective of the use of force rules as *ius cogens* and *erga omnes*, see K. Doehring, 'Neutralitat und Gewaltverbot', 31 *A.V.R.* 1993, pp. 193–205.

1089 §1.42.2, p. 20.

1090 This manual was adopted on 12 June 1994 by experts and aims to provide a contemporary restatement of international law applicable to armed conflicts at sea, though it includes a few provisions which might be considered progressive developments (see its introduction). It has been published together with a commentary in L. Doswald-Beck (ed.), *San Remo Manual on International Law Applicable to Armed Conflicts at Sea*, Cambridge, Cambridge University Press, 1995. The Manual itself is also published in No. 309 *I.R.R.C./R.I.C.R.* 1995, pp. 583–594 and is also available online at www.icrc.org/ihl.

1091 See already the discussion in C. Chaumont, *supra* note 1068, pp. 10–13, and, for an extensive discussion, including from a historical perspective, T. Komarnicki, *supra* note 1065, pp. 419–502.

assists one party to a conflict but not to the extent that it uses force itself or becomes (co-)responsible for the use of force by the State it is supporting[1092] and is thereby no longer fully neutral, may not be attacked under the *ius ad bellum*[1093] and is therefore neither neutral in the traditional sense, nor a party to such conflict.[1094]

Indeed, recognition of this intermediate status may be found in AP I, which in some instances uses the term "*neutral or other Sate not party to the conflict* ....".[1095] The ICRC COMMENTARY states in this respect that "*In fact, other forms of non-participation in a conflict have been added to neutrality as defined by treaty [...] and customary law*" and that "*while assigning them equal significance, the Conference considered it appropriate to make a separate mention of non-participation in the conflict in general, and of neutrality in the true sense of the word -- whether this is neutrality in a particular conflict, or permanent neutrality*". It added: "*The fact that the Protocol thus gave restrictive meaning to the term "neutral" by using this new wording, does not affect the meaning of the term in the Conventions, where it should be interpreted as covering non-participation in conflicts in general, as well as neutrality in the proper sense of the word*".[1096] In fact, GC III already mentions "*neutral or non-belligerent powers*".[1097] However, this begs the question what exactly would be the distinction between 'strict neutrality' and the intermediate status of non-belligerency and what the latter would entail. It was in order to avoid uncertainty in this respect that the San Remo Manual did not recognize such a distinction.[1098]

1092 The degree of support that will give rise to such reponsibility is somewhat uncertain. While the ICJ posed a high threshold in the *Nicarague Case*, the ICTY appears to have lowered it in the *Tadic case* (Appeals Chamber, *Prosecutor v. Dusko Tadic*, IT-94-1, 15 July 1999, §§97–145) and post '11 September' developments also suggest a lowered threshold, at least in the case of terrorism. See for a more extensive discussion with further references, F. Naert, 'The Impact of the Fight against International Terrorism on the *Ius ad Bellum* after '11 September'', 43(3–4) *R.D.M.D.G.* 2004, pp. 60–61 and 80 (also available as Institute for International Law Working Paper No 68 at www.law.kuleuven.be/iir/nl/onderzoek/wp/WP68e.pdf).

1093 In this sense the UK MANUAL, §1.43, p. 20, stating that a Party to a conflict attacked by forces from another Party to the conflict operating from neutral territory may be entitled to attack these forces on neutral territory under the ordinary rules of the *ius ad bellum*.

1094 See also K. Ipsen *et al*, *supra* note 1084, p. 1280, recognizing intermediate positions between being party to a conflict and neutral. A Dutch manual also notes a development towards non belligerency; see The Koninklijke Landmacht (Netherlands Army), *Humanitair oorlogsrecht. Handleiding*, *s.l.*, *s.n.*, 2005, pp. 139–152, §§0901–0944.

1095 E.g. Articles 2(c), 9(2)a and 31. See UK MANUAL, §1.42.3, p. 20.

1096 ICRC COMMENTARY TO THE AP, commentary to Article 2(c), p. 61. Compare E. Kussbach, 'Le Protocole additionnel I et les Etats neutres', 62 No. 725 *R.I.C.R.* 1980, pp. 231–251, especially pp. 232–235.

1097 Article 4.B.2 and 122. See UK MANUAL, §1.42.3, p. 20. However, the ICRC commentaries do not discuss the relevance thereof.

1098 See its commentary in L. Doswald-Beck (ed.), *supra* note 1090, p. 68. The ILA's 1998 Helsinki Principles on the Law of Martitime Neutrality (*supra* note 1064), §1.1 and commentary

Two views are therefore possible: either some form of strict neutrality still exists next to a status of non-belligerency but may only be possible in very few cases or neutrality has been reduced so much that it simply equals not being a party to a conflict.[1099] In fact, the latter corresponds to the present definition of neutrality given above and is in line with the meaning of 'neutral' in the GC and AP I defended in the ICRC Commentary (see *supra*) and therefore seems to be the better view. In any event, to the extent that strict neutrality still exists, the primacy of the *ius ad bellum* rules dictates that violations thereof short of becoming a party to the conflict can only be subject to international responsibility and counter-measures short of the use of force.[1100]

---

thereto also do not recognize such a distinction (pp. 496–497) and state that it contains "*principles which apply to all States not parties to a conflict even if a State considers itself authorised to depart from the rules of abstention and impartiality*".

1099 K. Ipsen *et al.*, *supra* note 1084, p. 1280 appears to support the former view. C. Chaumont, *supra* note 1068, pp. 12–22 already suggested that ultimately, the latter was the core principle of neutrality. The UK MANUAL, at §1.43, p. 20, while perhaps not intending to be exhaustive, cites only one fundamental obligation for a neutral State under neutrality law: to refrain from allowing its territory to be used by belligerent States for military operations (obviously in addition to not engaging in such operations against one of the parties itself). The Dutch manual cited *supra* note 1094, pp. 139–152, §§0901–0944 identifies as the core content the inviolability of the territory and the prohibition of direct military support. However, M. Bothe, *supra* note 1064, §§1108–1114, pp. 494–499 still lists more extensive obligations. W. Heintschel von Heinegg, 'Wider die Mär vom Tode des Neutralitätsrecht', in H. Fischer (ed.), *supra* note 356, pp. 221–241, submits that the scope of the law of neutrality has survived more or less intact but that its automatic applicability has disappeared. In another publication (W. Heintschel von Heinegg, '"Benevolent" Third States in International Armed Conflicts: The Myth of the Irrelevance of the Law of Neutrality', in M. Schmitt & J. Pejic (eds.), *International Law and Armed Conflict: Exploring the Faultlines. Essays in Hounor of Yoram Dinstein*, Nijhoff, Leiden, 2007, pp. 543–568), this author seems to distinguish exceptional cases of full neutrality from more common cases in which only the "*essentialia neutralitatis*" are applied and stresses the functional and differentiated nature of neutrality, which he sees as resulting from the aim of the neutrality rules, i.e. (in his view) protection of the interests of belligerents and preventing an escalation of the armed conflict (pp. 565–567). The 1993 Swiss report (*supra* note 1067) also seems to list more than just non-participation, but does acknowledge that the content of neutrality may evolve except for the key pinciple of non-participation ("*Le seul principe immuable qui soit inhérent à la neutralité est celui de la non-participation d'un Etat aux conflits armés opposant d'autres Etats*", p. 6 *in fine* online version). K. Schilcher, *supra* note 1063, pp. 618–625 identifies a tendency towards a reduction to non participation in combat actions.

1100 Such counter-measures might in turn be illegal under other rules of international law if carried out by an aggressor that has in a sense provoked the breach of neutrality. Compare the discussion in M. Bothe, *supra* note 1064, §1107, pp. 492–494. The solution might be different if one regards neutrality law as containing an element of *ius ad bellum* providing a specific additional exception to the prohibition of the use of force (this argument was mentioned by W. Heintschel von Heinegg in a lecture in Sanremo in October 2006, though he did not make it clear whether he supported this argument himself). However, there is little evidence that this argument reflects States' views.

The situation is somewhat different for permanent neutrality. There the key additional duty appears to be not to enter into military assistance or collective defence engagements that would make it impossible to remain neutral if a conflict breaks out.[1101]

If these principles adequately reflect the present law of neutrality, EU membership as such does not seem problematic for a neutral State, especially in light of the freedom neutral States now have to maintain their neutral status, for instance by not participating in peace enforcement operations.[1102] This clearly is also the present[1103] view of the EU Member States that are neutral.[1104] However, if the EU

1101 M. Bothe, *supra* note 1064, §1105, pp. 489–494; R. Doherty, *supra* note 1063, pp. 24–25 and 127–136 (arguing that neutrality has been reduced to the core of non-participation in military alliances and that "*any connection between neutrality and impartiality has been lost since the end of the Cold War*") and S. Griller *et al.*, *supra* note 1062, p. 436. K. Ginther, *supra* note 1063, p. 379, identifies the obligation not to enter into alliances, not to have foreign military bases on its territory, to maintain a certain defence and to conduct a peace policy. Along the same lines, M. Warnken, *supra* note 1, p. 184 lists non-participation in armed conflicts, the obligation not to enter into alliances and not to have foreign military bases on its territory as the key elements. G. Hafner & P. Schulz, *supra* note 1063, p. 310, cite the Austrian government as having identified the latter three elements as the core of permanent neutrality. M. von Grunigen, *supra* note 1075, p. 400 describes the obligations of a permanent neutral as doing nothing in times of peace that would prevent neutrality in times of war and making the preparations necessary to be able to uphold its neutrality in times of war. L. Wildhaber, *supra* note 1076, pp. 434–441 argues that there is European regional customary law that permanent neutrality must be armed and discusses the scope of this perceived obligation. On neutrality and alliances, see A. Vanheusden, 'Neutraliteit en militaire allianties', in Studiecentrum voor Militair Recht en Oorlogsrecht (ed.), *Neutraliteit en militaire allianties. Studiedag van 4 december 2003/ Neutralité et alliances militaires. Journée d'étude du 4 décembre 2003*, Brussels, 2004, pp. 25–31.

1102 See also M. Warnken, *supra* note 1, pp. 185–186. Compare K. Schilcher, *supra* note 1063, pp. 636–651, who seems to see a legal compatibility but questions whether this is politically tenable. *Contra*: S. Griller *et al.*, *supra* note 1062, pp. 434–440. For an analysis of neutrality and peacekeeping generally, see S. Dragon, 'Permanent Neutrality and Peacekeeping', 5 *International Peacekeeping* 1999, pp. 37–41.

1103 This was not always so; see for instance S. Griller *et al.*, *supra* note 1062, p. 433 and K. Schilcher, *supra* note 1063, p. 629 (with an overview of the position of the neutral acceding/ Member States at pp. 626–633). For a discussion of the neutrals in the ESDP, see also A. Dumoulin, R. Mathieu & G. Sarlet, *supra* note 161, pp. 54–63 and 603–608.

1104 For instance, Malta apparently did not see any problem in its accession; see Declaration (35) by the Republic of Malta on neutrality, annexed to the Final Act to the Treaty of Accession to the European Union (Athens, 16 April 2003, *O.J. L* 236, 23 September 2003, p. 982): "*Malta affirms its commitment to the common foreign and security policy of the European Union as set out in the Treaty on European Union. Malta confirms that its participation in the European Union's common foreign and security policy does not prejudice its neutrality. The Treaty on European Union specifies that any decision by the Union to move to a common defence would have to be taken by unanimous decision of the European Council adopted by the Member States in accordance with their respective constitutional requirements*" (see on Maltese neutrality D. Schindler, *supra* note 1075 (1984), pp. 277–291 and the webpage previously available at www.forummalta.gov.mt/fme/364/DesktopDefault.aspx?PageID=364#FAQ3068-108; last consulted in *November 2007*). Similarly, in the Joint Declaration (1) on Common Foreign and would move towards a collective defence (see on this *infra*), this would be different as entering into a collective defence commitment still is regarded as incompatible with a permanent neutral status.[1105] If the EU would move towards such a commitment, the neutrals would have to obtain an opt-out or would have to consider giving up their neutrality.[1106] That being said, it seems politically most unlikely that if an EU Member State were the victim of a serious attack, the neutral Member States would indeed remain neutral even today.[1107]

iii. Solidarity against Terrorism

While a common defence remains out of bounds for the time being, the European Council of 25 March 2004, in response to the Madrid train bombings of 11 March 2004, welcomed "*the political commitment of the member States and of the acceding States, taken as of now, to act jointly against terrorist acts, in the spirit of the Solidarity Clause contained in Article 42 of the draft Constitution for Europe*" reflected in an attached Declaration on solidarity against terrorism reading as follows:

> We, the Heads of State or Government of the Member States ..., and of the States acceding ... on 1 May, have declared our firm intention as follows:
>
> In the spirit of the solidarity clause laid down in Article 42 of the draft Treaty establishing a Constitution for Europe, the Member States and the acceding States shall accordingly act jointly in a spirit of solidarity if one of them is the victim of a terrorist attack. They shall mobilise all the instruments at their disposal, including military resources to:

Security Policy attached to the Final Act concerning the conditions of accession of the Kingdom of Norway, the Republic of Austria, the Republic of Finland and the Kingdom of Sweden and the adjustments to the Treaties on which the European Union is founded (*O.J. C* 241, 29 August 1994, p. 381), states that "*the new Member States will, from the time of their accession, be ready and able to participate fully and actively in the Common Foreign and Security Policy as defined in the Treaty on European Union*" and that "*With regard to Member States' obligations deriving from the [EU Treaty] concerning the implementation of the Union's [CFSP] it is understood that on the day of accession the legal framework of the acceding countries will be compatible with the 'acquis'*". For an analysis regarding Ireland, see R. Doherty, *supra* note 1063, especially pp. 192–224. See also the view expressed in the 1993 Swiss report, *supra* note 1067, pp. 21–26.

1105 See, e.g. the 1993 Swiss report, *supra* note 1067, p. 25 ("*Tant que l'UE ne se sera pas dotée d'un système de sécurité assurant la défense militaire de ses membres, la neutralité permanente et armée de manière crédible de notre pays conserverait sa justification*") and R. Doherty, *supra* note 1063, pp. 192–192 and 224. In this sense also O. Karas, 'Neutrality: A Non-Concept for the 21st Century?', in K. von Wogau (ed.), *supra* note 161, pp. 185–194.

1106 Whether and under what conditions the latter is possible, would depend upon the basis of this neutrality. For a brief analysis, see, e.g. K. Schilcher, *supra* note 1063, p. 615; M. Warnken, *supra* note 1, p. 183 and L. Wildhaber, *supra* note 1076, pp. 430–432.

1107 Similarly R. Doherty, *supra* note 1063, pp. 223–224 (mentioning a 1996 opinion poll in which 57% of the Irish would be in favour of supporting a Member State if it were attacked).

> - prevent the terrorist threat in the territory of one of them;
> - protect democratic institutions and the civilian population from any terrorist attack;
> - assist a Member State or an acceding State in its territory at the request of its political authorities in the event of a terrorist attack.
>
> It shall be for each Member State or acceding State to the Union to choose the most appropriate means to comply with this solidarity commitment towards the affected State.[1108]

As stated, this declaration closely mirrors the 'solidarity clause' contained in the Lisbon Treaty.[1109] While the clause leaves open the choice of means to provide assistance, it contains a political commitment and mentions the possibility of the use of military resources, including to protect from attack. It may therefore raise issues of a common defence since terrorist attacks may in some cases also be regarded as armed attacks giving rise to self-defence.[1110]

iv. The Lisbon Treaty: Towards a Common Defence?[1111]

The EU's objectives in the field of the CFSP under the Lisbon Treaty correspond more or less with the EU's present external relations objectives, although matters are spelled out in more detail and occasionally in stronger terms in the Lisbon Treaty.[1112] However, when it comes to the meaning and scope of the CSDP, and

1108 Available online at www.consilium.europa.eu/ueDocs/cms_Data/docs/pressData/en/ec/79637.pdf. For a discussion, see M. Sossai, *supra* note 1049, pp. 159–160 and 168–172.

1109 See Article 188R (renumbered 222) Treaty on the Functioning of the European Union as inserted by the Lisbon Treaty and the Declaration (No. 37) on Article 188R of the Treaty on the Functioning of the European Union and Declaration (No. 48) concerning the Protocol on the position of Denmark. See also Articles I-43 and III-329 EU Constitution, the Declaration on Articles I-43 and III-329 and the Declaration concerning the Protocol on the position of Denmark.

1110 See on this F. Naert & J. Wouters, 'Shockwaves through International Law after 11 September: Finding the Right Responses to the Challenges of International Terrorism', in C. Fijnaut, J. Wouters & F. Naert (eds.), *Legal Instruments in the Fight against International Terrorism. A Transatlantic Dialogue*, Martinus Nijhoff, Leiden/Boston, 2004, pp. 427–470 (available online at www.law.kuleuven.ac.be/iir/eng/research/publications/NaertWoutersIL.pdf); F. Naert, *supra* note 1092, pp. 55–110 and M. Sossai, *supra* note 1049, pp. 169–170.

1111 See also A. Dumoulin, 'Traité de Lisbonne: de l'assistance mutuelle à la défense mutuelle: oscillations et interprétations', No. 519 *R.M.C.U.E.* 2007, pp. 351–355; H. Krieger, *supra* note 204, pp. 183–187 and M. Reichard, *supra* note 204, pp. 201–224. For a pre-EU Constitution analysis of the implications of a collective defence clause in the EU Treaty or an optional protocol thereto, see K. Gerteiser, *supra* note 161, pp. 213–251 and 153–211.

1112 Compare Articles 2 and especially 11 pre-Lisbon EU Treaty with Articles 3(5) and 10(a) (renumbered 3(5) and 21) EU Treaty as amended by the Lisbon Treaty (and Articles I-3(4) and III-292 EU Constitution). The relevance of the provisions on international law and the UN Charter will be addressed below in Chapter 7.

especially its defence component (on its security component, see *supra*, Section A.3 of this chapter), there are significant changes.

First, Articles 11(1) and 27(2) (renumbered 24(1) and 42(2)) are crucial, but unfortunately slightly divergent. Both of these provisions state that the CSDP includes "*the progressive framing of a common Union defence policy*" (see also Articles I-16(1) and I-41(2) EU Constitution). However, according to Article 27(2) (renumbered 42(2)) this "will *lead to a common defence*", whereas Article 11(1) (renumbered 24(1)), like the present Article 17(1) EU Treaty, only provides that it "might *lead to a common defence*" (emphasis added). This discrepancy is also present in other language versions.[1113] It is submitted that Article 11(1) (renumbered 24(1)) probably best reflects what was intended because it is most in line with the position of the neutral Member States as set out below.[1114] Of course, in practical terms, there is hardly any difference between both provisions since Article 27(2) (renumbered 42(2)) does not specify a timetable and it requires a unanimous decision of the European Council which must then recommend to the Member States the adoption of such a decision "*in accordance with their respective constitutional requirements*".

Second, another and more important innovation is the mutual assistance clause in Article 27(7) (renumbered 42(7)) EU Treaty as it is amended under the Lisbon Treaty (see also Article I-41(7) EU Constitution). This clause reads as follows:

> If a Member State is the victim of armed aggression[1115] on its territory, the other Member States shall have towards it an obligation of aid and assistance by all the means in their power, in accordance with Article 51 of the United Nations Charter. This shall not prejudice the specific character of the security and defence policy of certain Member States.
>
> Commitments and cooperation in this area shall be consistent with commitments under the North Atlantic Treaty Organisation, which, for those States which are

---

1113 E.g. in the French (respectively "*conduira*" and "*peut conduire*"), Dutch (respectively "*zal leiden*" and "*kan leiden*") and German (respectively "*führt*" and "*führen kann*") versions.

1114 Compare J. Howorth, 'The European Draft Constitutional Treaty and the Future of the European Defence Initiative', 9 *E.F.A.R.* 2004, pp. 493–494, who describes the formulation in Article I-41(2) as "*considerably stronger than the wishy-washy wording in Article 17 of the [EU Treaty]*" but who does not discuss the discrepancy with Article I-16.

1115 On the term 'armed aggression' in relation to 'armed attack' (the latter is used in Article 51 UN Charter), see M. Reichard, *supra* note 204, pp. 209–210. In addition, the formulation armed aggression *on its territory* raises the question whether this is an intentional limitation or a case of bad drafting (if interpreted strictly, it would, e.g. exclude an armed attack against a State's warships on the high seas; however, it is questionable whether such a restrictive scope was intended).

members of it, remains the foundation of their collective defence and the forum for its implementation.

However, while Article 27(7) (renumbered 42(7)) certainly is a step ahead in the construction of the CSDP, it is phrased rather ambiguously. First of all, the stipulation that this obligation of aid and assistance "*shall not prejudice the specific character of the security and defence policy of certain Member States*" raises questions as to the precise scope of this obligation. This is so because the said mutual assistance obligation, if not qualified, is incompatible with the neutrality of the neutral Member States as conceived so far.[1116] There appear to be two possible interpretations of the 'safeguard' clause. The first one is that the obligation of assistance is not binding on the neutral Member States. To achieve this result, one can either regard the safeguard clause as a derogation or exception from the mutual assistance obligation for those Member States,[1117] or interpret "*all the means* in their power" (emphasis added) as taking into account restrictions resulting from neutrality.[1118] Either way, the effect is an exemption of the neutral Member States and this is probably what was envisaged.[1119] Indeed, the neutral Member States were opposed to an earlier proposal to include a mutual assistance obligation during the 2003–2004 IGC on the grounds that "*provisions containing formal binding security guarantees would be inconsistent with our security policy or with our constitutional requirements*".[1120] The alternative is that both clauses are incompatible and that the safeguard clause is a

1116 See especially the position of Ireland set out *supra* note 418 and accompanying text and the document cited *supra* note 1061 and accompanying text. Indeed, as K. Schilcher, *supra* note 1063, p. 651 notes (not aimed at the EU Constitution but nevertheless entirely to the point), a State cannot in good faith underwrite a collective defence commitment and in spite of this claim to abstain from participation in a conflict if it is activated. Compare M. Trybus, *supra* note 161, p. 336, who seems to consider that the safeguard clause saves neutrality without any real problem. H. Krieger, *supra* note 204, pp. 185–186, regards this clause as an automatic action commitment.

1117 That seems to be the view of I. Österdahl, 'The Neutral Ally: The European Security and Defence Policy and the Swedish Constitution', 78 *Nordic J.I.L.* 2009, p. 99.

1118 In this sense J. Howorth, *supra* note 1114, pp. 495–496, who, in respect of Article I-41(2) generally, discerns a "*recognition that, in the event of attack against a Member State, the others will do what they feel they can (or wish to) do to help out*". However, in view of the textual obligation to provide aid and assistance "*by all the means in their power*" such a general freedom of response does not seem correct; see also M. Reichard, *supra* note 204, p. 210, arguing that military means are included when available to the States concerned (albeit not in the specific context of the safeguard clause).

1119 Similarly M. Reichard, *supra* note 204, pp. 211–214, arguing that the wording leads to a result which is manifestly absurd but that on the basis of the travaux preparatoires the clause does exempt the neutral Member States (including Malta, see *supra* note 1104) but noting that in addition, the open wording may also exempt Member States who specifically see their mutual defence realized in NATO, although Reichard (rightly) maintains that such flexibility is contradictory to the essence of a mutual defence clause.

1120 See Doc. CIG 62/03 DELEG 30, 5 December 2003.

symbolic statement that does not affect the obligation of aid and assistance.[1121] However, this is most unlikely given the position of the neutral Member States.

The meaning of this provision was clarified at the 18–19 June 2009 European Council, in a Decision of the Heads of State or Government of the 27 Member States of the European Union, meeting within the European Council, on the concerns of the Irish people on the Treaty of Lisbon, which is compatible with the Treaty of Lisbon, will not necessitate any reratification of that Treaty, will take effect on the same date as the Treaty of Lisbon and will, at the time of the conclusion of the next accession Treaty, be included in a Protocol to be attached, in accordance with their respective constitutional requirements, to the Treaty on European Union and the Treaty on the Functioning of the European Union that will clarify but not change either the content or the application of the Treaty of Lisbon.[1122] This decision *inter alia* states that:

> The Union's common security and defence policy... does not prejudice the security and defence policy of each Member State, including Ireland, or the obligations of any Member State. The Treaty of Lisbon does not affect or prejudice Ireland's traditional policy of military neutrality. It will be for Member States – including Ireland, acting in a spirit of solidarity and without prejudice to its traditional policy of military neutrality – to determine the nature of aid or assistance to be provided to a Member State which is the object of a terrorist attack or the victim of armed aggression on its territory.
>
> Any decision to move to a common defence will require a unanimous decision of the European Council. It would be a matter for the Member States, including Ireland, to decide, in accordance with the provisions of the Treaty of Lisbon and with their respective constitutional requirements, whether or not to adopt a common defence.[1123]

1121 O. Karas, *supra* note 1105, pp. 191–192, apparently regards a similar safeguard clause in the present EU Treaty and in an earlier Draft of the EU Constitution as not pertaining to neutrality because subsequently only obligations relating to NATO are specifically mentioned. However, this view does not seem to be correct.

1122 Presidency Conclusions of the European Council of 18–19 June 2009, EU Council Doc. 11225/2/09 REV 2, 10 July 2009, §§3–5 and Annex I, Section C.

1123 It also adds that "*Nothing in this Section affects or prejudices the position or policy of any other Member State on security and defence. It is also a matter for each Member State to decide, in accordance with the provisions of the Treaty of Lisbon and any domestic legal requirements, whether to participate in permanent structured cooperation or the European Defence Agency. The Treaty of Lisbon does not provide for the creation of a European army or for conscription to any military formation. It does not affect the right of Ireland or any other Member State to determine the nature and volume of its defence and security expenditure and the nature of its defence capabilities. It will be a matter for Ireland or any other Member State, to decide, in accordance with any domestic legal requirements, whether or not to participate in any military operation*".

This is supplemented by a National Declaration by Ireland, which *inter alia* states that:

> Ireland confirms that its participation in the European Union's common foreign and security policy does not prejudice its traditional policy of military neutrality. The Treaty on European Union makes clear that the Union's security and defence policy shall not prejudice the specific character of the security and defence policy of certain Member States.
>
> In line with its traditional policy of military neutrality, Ireland is not bound by any mutual defence commitment. The Treaty on European Union specifies that any decision by the Union to move to a common defence would have to be taken by unanimous decision of the Member States and adopted in accordance with their respective constitutional requirements. The Constitution of Ireland requires that a referendum be held on the adoption of any such decision applicable to Ireland and this requirement will not be affected should Ireland ratify the Treaty of Lisbon....
>
> The situation set out in this Declaration would be unaffected by the entry into force of the Treaty of Lisbon. In the event of Ireland's ratification of the Treaty of Lisbon, this Declaration will be associated with Ireland's instrument of ratification.[1124]

Thus the Lisbon Treaty clearly preserves the neutrality of neutral Member States but also suggests that all Member States have a choice as to how they assist an attacked Member State. The latter is somewhat surprising given that there is an obligation of assistance "*by all the means in their power*".[1125]

1124 Presidency Conclusions of the European Council of 18–19 June 2009, EU Council Doc. 11225/2/09 REV 2, 10 July 2009, Annex 3. The declaration also states that "*Ireland ... reiterates that the participation of contingents of the Irish Defence Forces in overseas operations, including those carried out under the European common security and defence policy requires (a) the authorisation of the operation by the Security Council or the General Assembly of the United Nations, (b) the agreement of the Irish Government, and (c) the approval of Dáil Éireann, in accordance with Irish law. Ireland notes that nothing obliges it to participate in permanent structured cooperation as provided for in the Treaty on European Union. Any decision enabling Ireland to participate will require the approval of Dáil Éireann in accordance with Irish law. Ireland notes also that nothing obliges it to participate in the European Defence Agency, or in specific projects or programmes initiated under its auspices. Any decision to participate in such projects or programmes will be subject to national decision-making and the approval of Dáil Éireann in accordance with Irish law. Ireland declares that it will participate only in those projects and programmes that contribute to enhancing the capabilities required for participation in UN-mandated missions for peace-keeping, conflict prevention and strengthening international security, in accordance with the principles of the United Nations Charter*". See also D. de Bréadún, 'Bill Sets Conditions for Army Role in EU Defence Body', *Irish Times online*, 17 June 2009, www.irishtimes.com/newspaper/frontpage/2009/0617/1224248984008.html and 'Government Approves Draft Bill that Restricts State's role in EU Defence', *Irish Times online*, 1 July 2009, www.irishtimes.com/newspaper/ireland/2009/0701/1224249837738.html.

1125 The German Constitutional Court's judgment on the Lisbon Treaty (BVerfG, 2 BvE 2/08, 30 June 2009, English translation at www.bundesverfassungsgericht.de/entscheidungen/

Second, the provision that NATO "*for those States which are members of it, remains the foundation of their collective defence and the forum for its implementation*" also raises questions, in particular in relation to the scope of the "common defence" envisaged in Article 27(2) (renumbered 42(2)). At present, a common defence is usually understood to mean a collective defence commitment.[1126] Safeguarding NATO as the forum for implementing the collective defence of its Member States appears to aim at avoiding duplication.[1127] As a majority of EU Member States are also Member States of NATO,[1128] this would imply that the EU will not use its military organs and structures for collective defence.[1129] This view appears to be supported by the fact that the PSC is only empowered to exercise political control and strategic direction over "*the crisis management operations referred to in Article 28 [renumbered 43]*",[1130] which apparently excludes collective defence operations since Article 28 (renumbered

es20090630_2bve000208en.html), §386, also goes in this direction ("*From the wording and the location of Article 42 TEU Lisbon it becomes clear at any rate that the Member States' obligation of assistance does not go beyond the obligation of assistance pursuant to Article 5 of the North Atlantic Treaty ... This obligation does not forcibly encompass the use of military means but grants the States Party to this Treaty a scope of assessment as regards the content of the assistance to be rendered (...). In addition, the obligation of mutual assistance explicitly shall not prejudice 'the specific character of the security and defence policy of certain Member States' ... This provides the Member States with the possibility, which is secured by primary law, of invoking fundamental content-related reservations as regards the obligation of assistance*"). However, the comparison with Article 5 North Atlantic Treaty is not persuasive given the different wording. Compare I. Österdahl, *supra* note 1117, pp. 100 and 110.

1126 See, e.g. J. Litten, *supra* note 161, pp. 144 and 148 (though leaving open whether this is limited to the legal obligation or also includes the military implementation) and M. Trybus, *supra* note 161, p. 103.

1127 See Foreign and Commonwealth Office, *White Paper on the Treaty establishing a Constitution for Europe*, September 2004, Cm 6309 (available online at www.fco.gov.uk/Files/kfile/White%20Paper_Treaty%20establishing%20a%20Constitution%20for%20Europe.pdf), p. 34, §79: "*the Government secured the deletion of any reference in the draft Treaty to an EU mutual defence commitment which would have been divisive and a duplication of NATO. The text now makes it clear that for those States which are members of NATO, NATO "remains the foundation of their collective defence" and the instrument for implementing that commitment (Article I-40.7)*". Compare A. Baggett, 'The Development of the European Union Common Defense and its Implications for the United States and NATO", 31 *Georgia J.I.C.L.* 2003, pp. 355–384 and H. Ojanen, 'The EU and Nato: Two Competing Models for a Common Defense Policy', 44 *J.C.M.S.* 2006, pp. 57–76.

1128 Only the five neutral EU Member States and Cyprus are not members of NATO.

1129 Similarly, H. Krieger, *supra* note 204, p. 186. An implementation of a collective self-defence obligation only seems sensible if all, or at least most (see France's position in NATO until recently) of the States bound by this obligation participate in it. But compare M. Trybus, *supra* note 161, pp. 335–336, who sees the relationship with NATO rather as an obligation to first invoke the collective defence clause in NATO but leaves open it being invoked in the EU if it is rejected in NATO. However, such a hypothesis seems unlikely and would imply a difference of opinion between all EU (NATO) members on the one hand and one or more other NATO members on the other hand over whether there is a situation giving rise to self-defence.

1130 See Article 25 (renumbered 38) EU Treaty as amended by the Lisbon Treaty and compare Article III-307(2) EU Constitution.

43) only refers to Article 27(1) (renumbered 42(1)) and the restriction of Article 27(1) (renumbered 42(1)) to missions *outside the Union* – whereas Article 27(7) (renumbered 42(7)) is activated by an aggression *on the territory of a Member State* (although the reaction need not be subject to such a restriction) – suggests that both provisions cover different situations. In fact, no arrangements at all are provided for the implementation of the mutual assistance clause in Article 27(7) (renumbered 42(7)) – in contrast with the solidarity clause and with missions for peace-keeping, conflict prevention and strengthening international security (see *supra*). Assuming the neutral Member States are exempted from the mutual assistance clause (see *supra*), this leaves Cyprus in a peculiar position: if it is attacked, an *ad hoc* implementation of the mutual assistance clause would appear to be the only solution available, unless the involvement of States that are members of both the EU and NATO leads to NATO involvement.[1131] Likewise, any assistance by Cyprus to EU Member States which are also members of NATO and which are attacked would have to be arranged on an *ad hoc* basis.

However, one may wonder what the envisaged "common defence" means if not the implementation of collective self-defence.[1132] The sole Article of the Protocol to Article I-41(2) EU Constitution was of some relevance in this respect. It read: "*The Union shall draw up, together with the Western European Union, arrangements for enhanced cooperation between them*".[1133] Since the WEU's only remaining substantive competences concern its mutual assistance clause,[1134] the envisaged EU-WEU cooperation could only concern the mutual assistance clause. However, if, as I have argued above, the EU's competence does not include the implementation of this clause, as is also the case for the WEU,[1135] it is hard to see the value of EU-WEU cooperation in this field. One might rather expect that

1131 M. Reichard, *supra* note 204, pp. 222–223, argues that since the assistance by EU Member States would include NATO Members States and thus implicate NATO and effectively entail a back door extension of the NATO collective defence clause to Cyprus. However, this will not necessarily always be the case since the NATO collective defence clause only covers an armed attack in Europe or North America and, especially in the case of armed attacks by non-State actors (see on this *supra* note 1110 and the accompanying text), allies defending Cyprus outside Europe (in a situation similar to operation Enduring Freedom in Afghanistan) would not necessarily themselves be attacked in Europe.

1132 See also H. Krieger, *supra* note 204, pp. 186–187.

1133 Protocol on Article I-41(2) of the Constitution.

1134 See *supra*, Chapter 1.E and F and WEU, Council of Ministers, Marseille Declaration, 13 November 2000, available at www.weu.int/documents/001113en.pdf (its armaments functions which initially also remained are now being taken over by the EDA too; see *supra*, Chapter 2,.F). See generally A. Dumoulin & F. Gevers, *supra* note 328, pp. 48–62 and 70–163, especially pp. 76–86 on the future of the mutual assistance clause.

1135 See Article IV modified WEU Treaty (*supra* note 16): "*Recognising the undesirability of duplicating the military staffs of NATO, the Council and its Agency will rely on the appropriate Military Authorities of NATO for information and advice on military matters*".

the mutual defence clause in WEU – and even the WEU as a whole – be abolished once the EU Constitution or Lisbon Treaty with a similar clause enters into force.[1136] Yet under the Lisbon Treaty a Protocol on Article 42 EU Treaty copies that text.[1137] Moreover, given that the EU mutual defence clause will be implemented in NATO for most EU Member States, it is quite remarkable that there is no provision on EU-NATO cooperation in this field instead. In light of

1136 Similarly, M. Trybus, *supra* note 161, p. 337, arguing that this clause would constitute a transfer of the WEU collective security element, and p. 399, pleading for dissolving the WEU once all its elements have been integrated into the EU. It is submitted that this would be the case if the EU undertakes a collective defence commitment because the WEU's other residual functions have already been transferred. Compare M. Reichard, *supra* note 204, pp. 216–220, arguing that the EU Constitution would terminate the mutual defence clause in the WEU under the law of treaties and arguably even the entire WEU. The added value that is sometimes perceived to exist in WEU's Parliamentary Assembly (e.g. M. Trybus, *supra* note 161, pp. 106–108; compare A. Dumoulin, R. Mathieu & G. Sarlet, *supra* note 161, pp. 201–206 and 562–581) does not appear to really exist since its powers (see, e.g. E. Lotter, 'WEU Assembly: Parliamentary Control of European Security Policy?', 51(1–2) *Studia Diplomatica* 1998, pp. 31–40) are essentially the same as and arguably even more limited than those of the European Parliament (which, e.g. also has budgetary powers, even if these are limited in the ESDP), namely to be informed, to debate, to question and to make recommendations (compare Article IX Amended Brussels Treaty with Article 21 EU Treaty) and its composition of members of national parliaments is hardly sufficient by itself (the national parliaments can be involved at the national level and via the Conference of Committees for European and Community Affairs of the European Parliaments, which has already discussed the ESDP; see, e.g. *supra* notes 350 and 353). This does not mean that the democratic control and parliamentary oversight in the ESDP cannot be improved, only that the WEU Parliamentary forum is not in a privileged position in this respect. On parliamentary oversight generally, see R. Schmidt-Radefeldt, 'EU-Militäreinsätze unter demokratischer Kontolle?: Überlegungen zur parlamentarischen Dimension der Europäischen Sicherheits- und Verteidigungsarchitektur', in H. Fischer (ed.), *supra* note 356, pp. 489–504. A. Dumoulin & F. Gevers, *supra* note 328, pp. 83–84 note that disbanding the WEU was considered, but ultimately not decided. It may be recalled that the Cologne ESDP Declaration stated that "*WEU as an organisation would have completed its purpose*" upon the EU taking over the WEU's crisis management functions even before the EU has a collective defence clause (§5). This is all the more so since WEU full membership (only full members are bound by the mutual defence clause) has not expanded in parallel with the expansion of EU and NATO membership: according to a statement on the WEU website "*Following a decision taken on 14 June 2001, the Secretary-General stated during the 1352nd meeting of the Council of Western European Union on 28 June 2001 that, with regard to the period from 1 January 2002, the Member States deemed it unnecessary, in present and foreseeable circumstances, to make any formal change to the statuses of non-full members*" (www.weu.int/Delegations.htm). One might have expected States that have acceded to both the EU and NATO to become full members of the WEU. See also A. Dumoulin & F. Gevers, *supra* note 328, pp. 110–119. For a recent discussion of the WEU, see A. Dumoulin, 'L'UEO crépusculaire', 62(2) *Défense nationale* 2006, pp. 25–33 and A. Dumoulin, 'L'Union de l'Europe occidentale: anniversaire du Phénix ou chant du cygne?', No. 486 *R.M.C.U.E.* 2005, pp. 163–171.

1137 One can only wonder what added value such enhanced cooperation with a dormant organisation could possibly provide. In addition, the Protocol refers to Article 42(2) and not the mutual defence clause in Article 42(7). Perhaps it simply survived because the IGC mandate did not include dropping it. Only practice will tell whether it will ever be implemented and be of any use.

the interpretation advanced above that (a) a mutual assistance clause exists but exempts the neutral Member States and (b) a common defence will not include the implementation of collective self-defence,[1138] the most sensible meaning of the future common defence appears to be a mutual defence clause in which *all* Member States, including the present neutrals, will participate but which will not cover the implementation of this clause.

6. THE INTERNATIONAL LEGAL BASIS FOR ESDP OPERATIONS

In addition to the question of the scope of the ESDP under EU law, which has been the subject of this section so far, the question arises whether this scope is compatible with international law. In other words, what is the international law basis for the EU's ESDP and especially its ESDP operations? A first aspect of this, namely the neutral status of some EU Member States, has already been addressed but is more concerned with the status of the Member States concerned than with the EU as such.

Except for some initial discussions with regard to EULEX Kosovo, the problem has not arisen so far and all ESDP missions launched up till now have (had) a clear basis in international law.[1139] Invariably, this was the invitation or consent of the host State government and other parties involved, sometimes in the form of a peace agreement and often reinforced by Security Council support or endorsement and, in some cases, by Security Council authorization.[1140]

1138 But see H. Krieger, *supra* note 204, pp. 186–187, who seems to consider that it would mean the creation of a 'european army', apparently including the implementation of a common defence.

1139 On the discussion over EULEX Kosovo, see *supra*, Chapter 3.T.1.

1140 On Security Council authorization for the use of force, see generally N. Blokker, 'Is the Authorization Authorized?: Powers and Practice of the UN Security Council to Authorize the Use of Force by "Coalitions of the Able and Willing"', 11 *E.J.I.L.* 2000, pp. 541–568; O. Corten & F. Dubuisson, 'L'hypothèse d'une règle émergente fondant une intervention militaire sur une "autorisation implicite" du Conseil de Sécurité', 104 *R.G.D.I.P.* 2000, pp. 873–910; DE WET, pp. 256–310; R. Durward, 'Security Council Authorization for Regional Peace Operations: A Critical Analysis', 13 *International Peacekeeping* 2006, pp. 350–365; H. Freudenschuß, 'Between Unilateralism and Collective Security: Authorizations of the Use of Force by the UN Security Council', 5 *E.J.I.L.* 1994, pp. 492–531; C. Gray, *International Law and the Use of Force*, Oxford, Oxford University Press, 2004 (2nd ed.), pp. 252–281 and 322–325; E. Kalkku, 'The United Nations Authorisation to Peace Enforcement with the Use of Armed Forces in the Light of the Practice of the UN Security Council', 9 *F.Y.I.L.* 2000, pp. 349–405; M.E. O'Connell, 'The United Nations Security Council and the Authorization of Force: Renewing the Council through Law Reform', in N. Blokker & N. Schrijver (eds.), *supra* note 645, pp. 47–63; I. Österdahl, 'Preach What You Practice: The Security Council and the Legalisation ex Post Facto of the Unilateral Use of Force', 74 *Nordic J.I.L.* 2005, pp. 231–260;

However, NATO's air campaign in the 1999 Kosovo crisis illustrates that the question may arise.[1141] This is particularly the case for peacekeeping operations with enforcement elements and pure peace enforcement operations.

I will now briefly analyze the limits of the EU's competence in this respect under international law. This question is distinct from requirements that might exist in the domestic law of some Member States, e.g. in the above-mentioned case of Ireland.[1142]

Much can be written about the legal bases under international law for intervention, especially armed intervention. However, this would far exceed the scope of this work.[1143] What I will briefly discuss here is the status of the rules concerning the use of force in international law, as this status is essential for the applicability of these rules to international organizations, including the EU (see extensively *infra*, Chapter 7).

D. Sarooshi, *The United Nations and the Development of Collective Security: The Delegation by the UN Security Council of its Chapter VII Powers*, Oxford, Oxford University Press, 2000 (addressing delegation to regional organizations at pp. 247–284); L.-A. Sicilianos, 'L'autorisation par le Conseil de sécurité de recourir à la force: une tentative d'évalation', 106 *R.G.D.I.P.* 2002, pp. 5–50; G. Troost, *Die Autorisierung von UN-Mitgliedstaaten zur Durchführung militärischer Zwangsmaßnahmen des Sicherheitsrates in Recht und Praxis der Vereinten Nationen*, Aachen, Shaker, 1997 and U. Villani, 'The Security Council's Authorization of Enforcement Action by Regional Organizations', 6 *M.P.Y.U.N.L.*2002, pp. 535–557.

1141 See *supra* Chapter 3.T.1 (showing that it may even arise in respect of a civilian operation) and also N. Tsagourias, *supra* note 1023, pp. 129–130, who considers that a coercive EU operation without Security Council mandate cannot be ruled out and argues that it may even be legal. With regard to NATO's intervention in the Kosovo crisis, see, e.g. (the literature is vast) P.E. Auerswald & D.P. Auerswald, *The Kosovo Conflict: A Diplomatic History Through Documents*, The Hague, Kluwer Law International, 2000; H. Krieger (ed.), *The Kosovo Conflict and International Law. An Analytical Documentation 1974-1999*, Cambridge, Cambridge University Press, 2001; D.S. Lutz, *Der Kosovo- Krieg. Rechtliche und rechtsethische Aspekte*, Baden-Baden, Nomos, 2000; R. Merkel, *Der Kosovo- Krieg und das Völkerrecht*, Frankfurt-am-Main, Suhrkamp, 2000 and C. Tomuschat (ed.), *Kosovo and the International Community: A Legal Assessment*, The Hague, Kluwer Law International, 2002.

1142 See *supra*, note 418 and the accompanying text on its position in respect of Operation Concordia and its Neutrality. For an analysis of the legality of the ESDP under German law, see A. Bashlinskaya, *Der rechtliche Gehalt der Gemeinsamen Sicherheits- und Verteidigungspolitik der Europäischen Union (GESVP) und ihre Vereinbarkeit mit dem deutschen Grundgesetz*, Bremen, May 2005, Zentrum für Europäische Rechtspolitik an der Universität Bremen, Diskussionspapier 2/2005 (available online at www.zerp.uni-bremen.de/english/pdf/dp2_2005.pdf).

1143 In fact, it was originally my intention to explore this more fully in a separate Part of my thesis. However, due to mainly time constraints and the considerable body of literature that already exists on this point, I have limiting myself to this very modest section.

First, in light of the conclusions drawn in Chapter 7 below, these rules are binding on the EU to the extent that they constitute customary international law, regardless of whether they are also considered to be *ius cogens*. There is no doubt that the rules on the *ius ad bellum* can perfectly be applied to and by international organizations.[1144] The main question which arises is the scope of the *ius ad bellum* under customary international law[1145] and especially to what extent these customary rules correspond to those in the UN Charter. It may suffice to say here that although there appears to be a large convergence between the UN Charter and customary international law concerning the *ius ad bellum*, there may not be a complete parallelism.[1146] This is problematic in the light of the primacy of the UN Charter over other international law, at least if one accepts that Article 103 of the Charter extends this primacy also over customary international law.[1147] Despite numerous studies on the *ius ad bellum*, this aspect

---

1144 See, e.g. M. Gestri, 'ECOWAS Operations in Liberia and Sierra Leone: Amnesty for Past Unlawful Acts or Progress toward Future Rules?', in M. Bothe, M.E. O'Connell & N. Ronzitti (eds.), *Redefining Sovereignty: The Use of Force after the Cold War*, Ardsley, Transnational, 2005, p. 229 and P. Menon, *The Law of Treaties between States and International Organizations*, Lewiston, Mellen Press, 1992, p. 111. This also seems to be the view of U. Villani, *infra* note 1153, pp. 358–359.

1145 See generally E. Cannizzaro & P. Palchetti (eds.), *Customary International Law on the Use of Force. A Methodological Approach*, Martinus Nijhoff, 2005. See also H. McCoubrey & N. White, *International Law and Armed Conflict*, Dartmouth, Aldershot, 1992, pp. 26–35 and N. Schrijver, 'Article 2, Paragraphe 4', in Cot & Pellet, pp. 449–466 . For an analysis of the methodologies used in the debate over the scope of customary international law on the use of force, see O. Corten, 'The Controversies over the Customary Prohibition on the Use of Force: A Methodological Debate', 16 *E.J.I.L.* 2005, pp. 803–822.

1146 The ICJ ruled in the *Case concerning the Military and Paramilitary Activities in and against Nicaragua*, 27 June 1986, *I.C.J. Reports* 1986, §§174–175, that there was substantial overlap between the two regimes concerning the use of force but that they were not identical. Compare the ILC's view as discussed in P. Palchetti, 'Customary Rules on the Use of Force in the Work of Codification of the International Law Commission', in E. Cannizzaro & P. Palchetti (eds.), *supra* previous note, pp. 233–241. See also F. Naert, *supra* note 1092, pp. 68–69. Compare also Y. Dinstein, *War, Aggression and Self-Defence*, Cambridge, Cambridge University Press, 2001 (3rd ed.), pp. 90–91 and S. Murase, 'The Relationship between the UN Charter and General International Law Regarding Non-Use of Force: The Case of NATO's Air Campaign in the Kosovo Crisis of 1999', in E. Ando *et al.* (eds.), *Liber Amicorum Judge Shigeru Oda*, The Hague, Kluwer Law International, 2002, Vol. 2, pp. 1543–1554 (the latter author argues that customary international law on the use of force differs from the Charter rules and that it may come into play when in specified circumstances the Charter law becomes inoperative). The ECtHR recently considered that "*The responsibility of the UNSC ... has evolved as a counterpart to the prohibition, now customary international law, on the unilateral use of force*" (decision of 31 May 2007 in joined cases *Behrami and Behrami v. France* (No. 71412/01) and *Saramati v. France, Germany and Norway* (No. 78166/01), §148).

1147 This question is addressed in some detail below in Chapter 8.E, where I argue that Article 103 does cover customary international law. The problem of Charter change through customary law in the light of Article 103 (and 108) of the Charter is rightly identified by Simma, Brunner & Kaul in respect of Article 27 UN Charter (B. Simma, S. Brunner & H.-P; Kaul, 'Article 27', in Simma, pp. 495–498). It is also examined by J.-M. Thouvenin, 'Article 103', in Cot & Pellet, p. 2141, who considers that custom can change the Charter and in that case has not been analyzed as thoroughly as one might expect,[1148] except to some extent in respect of self-defence, where the reference in Article 51 of the Charter to an inherent right of self-defence is usually considered to refer to self-defence under customary international law.[1149]

Second, it must be verified whether the EU is bound by the rules on the *ius ad bellum* in the UN Charter in any other way. As is explained below in Chapter 7.G.4, the EU is bound through the EU Treaty to respect the principles of the UN Charter, which include the prohibition of the threat or use of force. This is clear as a matter of EU law, i.e. between the EU and its Member States. The same can be said of the Lisbon Treaty.[1150] Yet the relevant provisions in the EU Treaty do not appear to have an external effect. The closest we have at present to unilateral acts *by the EU* binding itself externally are European Council conclusions on the

---

Article 103 would not be relevant. This supposes, however, that the relevant customary rule has also changed the Charter, which is precisely the question here. On the possibility and limits of Charter change through custom, see, e.g. B. Conforti, *The Law and Practice of the United Nations*, The Hague, Kluwer Law International, 2000 (2nd ed.), pp. 10–11 and 66–68; G. Cahin, 'Le droit de la Charte et la coutume internationale', in Cot & Pellet, pp. 85–86 and 103–109; J. Kammerhofer, 'Uncertainties of the Law on Self-Defence in the United Nations Charter', 35 *N.Y.I.L.* 2004, pp. 146–149 and W. Karl, B. Mützelburg & G. Witschel, 'Article 108', in Simma, pp. 1346–1347. Compare O. Corten, 'La participation du Conseil de sécurité à l'élaboration, à la cristallisation ou à la consolidation de règles coutumières', 37 *R.B.D.I./B.T.I.R.* 2004, pp. 554–555 on institutional custom. Moreover, N. Ronzitti, 'The Current Status of Legal Principles prohibiting the Use of Force and Legal Justifications of the Use of Force', in M. Bothe, M.E. O'Connell & N. Ronzitti (eds.), *supra* note 1144, pp. 93–94, rightly points out that changes in the *ius as bellum* are also more difficult to the extent that it is considered to be *ius cogens* (on the latter, see briefly *infra* notes 1171–1172).

1148 For a brief discussion of the problem, see F. Naert, *supra* note 1092, pp. 68–69. Even in a work specifically devoted to customary international law on the use of force such as E. Cannizzaro & P. Palchetti (eds.), *supra* note 1145, the relationship with the Charter is addressed only to a limited extent (in some ten pages) and Article 103 does not seem to be mentioned in this context at all. Obviously, the problem may be circumvented if changes are at the same time regarded as re-interpretations of or amendments to the Charter (in this sense G.P. Buzzini, 'Les comportements passifs des états et leur incidence sur la règlementation de l'emploi de la force en droit international général', in *id.*, p. 102), but this implies a parallelism between both regimes and has limits too, in particular as to amendment. On Charter change through interpretation, see also T. Franck, *Recourse to Force*, Cambridge, Cambridge University Press, 2002, pp. 5–9. The most comprehensive analysis I have found is that by S. Ford, 'Legal Processes of Change: Article 2(4) and the Vienna Convention on the Law of Treaties', 4 *Journal of Armed Conflict* 1999, pp. 75–116, who, while citing Article 103 (at p. 97) only in relation to the difficulty of changing the Charter via treaties (and apparently deeming it inapplicable to custom), discusses the legal process through which the Charter rules on the use of force could change and seems to see interpretation through subsequent practice as the most likely venue.

1149 See, e.g. the ICJ in the *Nicaragua case*, *supra* note 1146, §176.

1150 Of which Article 3(5) (renumbered 3(5)) provides that "*In its relations with the wider world, the Union shall … contribute to … the strict observance and the development of international law, including respect for the principles of the United Nations Charter*". See also Article 1(3) EU Constitution.

ESDP proclaiming that the ESDP will be conducted in accordance with the principles of the UN Charter and recognizing the primary responsibility of the UN Security Council for the maintenance of international peace and security,[1151] but it is doubtful that this is sufficiently precise and was intended to (legally) bind the EU. However, under the Lisbon Treaty there is a Declaration (No. 13) concerning the common foreign and security policy in which it is stated that "*[The Conference] stresses that the [EU] and its Member States will remain bound by the provisions of the Charter of the United Nations and, in particular, by the primary responsibility of the Security Council and of its Members for the maintenance of international peace and security*".[1152] This is remarkable because of the binding of the *EU* (albeit by the Member States) to the *provisions* of the Charter. While perhaps not intended to be a unilateral act, its more precise language and public nature in the context of the Lisbon Treaty arguably means it amounts to just that, although it is the Member States who bind the EU.

Third, the question arises whether the EU is a regional agency or arrangement in the sense of Chapter VIII of the UN Charter and whether this matters.[1153] The

1151 See, e.g. §2 of the 1999 Cologne Presidency Report and §26 of the Helsinki European Council Presidency Conclusions, 10–11 December 1999.

1152 *O.J. C* 306, 17 December 2007, p. 255.

1153 On the role of regional organizations in the maintenance of peace and security, see generally, e.g. A. Abass, *Regional Organisations and the Development of Collective Security: beyond Chapter VIII of the UN Charter*, Oxford, Hart, 2004; Z. Deen-Racsmány, 'A Redistribution of Authority between the UN and Regional Organizations in the Field of the Maintenance of Peace and Security', 13 *Leiden J.I.L.* 2000, pp. 297–331; J. Delbrück, 'The Role of Regional Organizations in Maintaining Peace and Security', in M. Bothe, M.E. O'Connell & N. Ronzitti (eds.), *supra* note 656, pp. 145–160; E. de Wet, 'The Relationship between the Security Council and Regional Organizations during Enforcement Action under Chapter VII of the United Nations Charter', 71 *Nordic J.I.L.* 2002, pp. 1–37; A. Gioia, 'The United Nations and Regional Organizations in the Maintenance of Peace and Security', in M. Bothe, N. Ronzitti & A. Rosas (eds.), *supra* note 1002, pp. 191–236; C. Gray, *supra* note 1140, pp. 282–327; A. Holstein, *Das Verhältnis des Sicherheitsrates der Vereinten Nationen zu NATO und OSZE*, Stuttgart, Boorberg, 1996; M. Kamto, 'Le rôle des "accords et organismes régionaux" en matière de maintien de la paix et de la sécurité internationales à la lumière de la charte des nations unies et de la pratique internationale', 111 *R.G.D.I.P.* 2007, pp. 771–802; H. Körbs, *Die Friedenssicherung durch die Vereinten Nationen und Regionalorganisationen nach Kapitel VIII der Satzung der Vereinten Nationen*, Bochum, Brockmeyer, 1997; H. McCoubrey & J. Morris, *Regional Peacekeeping in the Post-Cold War*, Kluwer Law International, 2000; I. Österdahl, 'The Continued Relevance of Collective Security under the UN: The Security Council, Regional Organizations and the General Assembly', 10 *F.Y.I.L.* 2002, pp. 103–140; F. Olonisakin, *Reinventing Peacekeeping in Africa. Conceptual and Legal Issues in ECOMOG Operations*, The Hague, Kluwer Law International, 2000; S.R. Pemmaraju, 'International Organizations and Use of Force', in N. Ando *et al.* (eds.), *supra* note 1146, pp. 1575–1608; U. Villani, *supra* note 1140, pp. 535–557; U. Villani, 'Les rapports entre l'ONU et les organisations régionales dans le domaine du maintien de la paix', 290 *Rec. Cours* 2001, pp. 225–436, especially pp. 324–425; C. Walter, 'Security Council Control over Regional Action', 1 *M.P.Y.U.N.L.* 1997, pp. 129–193; R. Wolfrum, 'Der Beitrag regionaler Abmachungen zur

Charter itself does not define what is meant by such agencies or arrangements and the matter is not clear.[1154] Subsequent practice by both the UN and regional organizations *sensu lato* (i.e. not limited to the purpose of Chapter VIII UN Charter) indicates that while the UN has increasingly developed cooperation with a significant number of regional and international organizations,[1155] there are only a small number of cases in which this has clearly been acknowledged by both[1156] as falling under Chapter VIII of the UN Charter, namely the OAU/AU, the OAS, the OSCE and the Arab League.[1157] It would appear that the EU,

---

Friedenssicherung: Möglichkeiten und Grenzen', 53 *Z.a.ö.R.V.* 2001, pp. 576–602 and X., 'Symposium: The United Nations, Regional Organizations, and Military Operations', 7 *Duke J.C.I.L.* 1996, pp. 1–270. For some early dicussion, see J. Yepes, 'Les accords régionaux et le droit international', 71 *Rec. Cours* 1947-II, pp. 233–344 and H. Saba, 'Les accords régionaux dans la Charte de l'O.N.U.', 80 *Rec. Cours* 1952-I, pp. 637–721.

1154 See also K. Graham, *supra* note 1041, pp. 292–296. For a more extensive discussion, see, e.g. W. Hummer & M. Schweitzer, 'Article 52', in Simma, pp. 816–838; E. Kodjo, 'Article 52', in Cot & Pellet, pp. 1371–1385 and U. Villani, *supra* previous note, pp. 271–297. Compare R. Kolb, 'Article 53', in Cot & Pellet, pp. 1406–1410, arguing that Articles 52 and 53 may cover different concepts of regional organizations and that for Article 53 there now essentially only remains a functional criterion, namely a peace and security function in conformity with the purposes and principles of the Charter.

1155 For instance, every few years since 1994 the UN Secretary General has held High Level meetings with Regional and other International Organizations (e.g. the seventh such meeting in September 2006); the Security Council has convened meetings too (see K. Graham, *supra* note 1041, p. 291) and its Counter-Terrorism Committee closely cooperates with such organizations (see www.un.org/sc/ctc/cooperation.html) and the Security Council has adopted a number of documents on the role of these organizations (see, e.g. UN Security Council Resolutions 1631 of 17 October 2005 and 1809 of 16 April 2008; S/PRST/2004/27 of 20 July 2004; S/PRST/2007/7 of 28 March 2007 and S/PRST/2006/39 of 20 September 2006). See K. Graham, *supra* note 1041, p. 291.

1156 A. Geslin, 'Le pouvoir d'habilitation du Conseil de sécurité: la délégation des pouvoirs du Conseil aux organisations internationales', 37 *R.B.D.I./B.T.I.R.* 2004, pp. 485–491 discerns a reluctance to acknowledge the applicability of Chapter VIII by both the Security Council and regional organizations.

1157 W. Hummer & M. Schweitzer, *supra* note 1154, pp. 828–831 and 832–835. This suggests that regional arrangement or agency in the sense of Chapter VIII UN Charter has a distinct meaning from the ordinary meaning accorded to these notions. Alternatively, any organization with some regional focus and a security function would qualify. Compare E. Kodjo, *supra* note 1154, pp. 1371–1385, describing the evolution toward relaxation of the requirements (while citing the ICJ's restrictive view in its judgment of 26 November 1984 in the *Case concerning Military and Paramilitary Activities in and against Nicaragua (Nicaragua v. U.S.)* (jurisdiction and admissibility), §107: "*The Court does not consider that the Contadora process ... can properly be regarded as a "regional arrangement" for the purposes of Chapter VIII*") and wondering whether the notion of regional arrangements/agencies still has a distinct meaning under Chapter VIII UN Charter. However, this is doubtful and would seem to negate the distinct (indirect) recourse to international organizations foreseen in Article 48 UN Charter. On the Chapter VII status of the OSCE, see, e.g. T. Lohmann, 'The OSCE and Chapter VIII of the UN Charter: Some Consequences for the Architecture of European Security', in W.P. Heere (ed.), *Contemporary International Law Issues: Conflicts and Convergence. Proceedings of the Third Joint Conference Held in The Hague, The Netherlands, July 13–15, 1995*, The Hague, TMC Asser Institute, 1996, pp. 340–346. On OSCE – UN relations more generally, see, e.g. G.L. Burci, 'Division of Labour between the UN and the similarly to NATO,[1158] has not declared itself a regional agency or arrangement in the sense of Chapter VIII UN Charter[1159] and that it has not been so designated by the UN either, though some commentators have qualified it as such.[1160]

While it is interesting to look into whether the EU meets the conditions to be a Chapter VIII agency or arrangement,[1161] absent EU and UN recognition of such a status, this has little practical value. Moreover, one may question whether this status has any substantial implications.[1162] In particular, while it is sometimes

---

OSCE in Connection with Peace-keeping', in M. Bothe, N. Ronzitti & A. Rosas (eds.), *supra* note 1002, pp. 289–313.

1158 See also K. Graham, *supra* note 1041, p. 294; D. Sarooshi, *supra* note 1140, p. 251 and M. Zwanenburg, 'NATO, Its Member States, and the Security Council', in N. Blokker & N. Schrijver (eds.), *supra* note 645, pp. 193–195 and 200–201 (noting the apparent NATO view that it is not such an agency/arrangement as well as some indications that the UN disagreed/disagrees) and 201–203 (discussing NATO's ambiguity as to the need for a Security Council mandate). Compare DE WET, pp. 293–294 (arguing that Article 53 only concerns authorizations to regional organizations to act against one of their Member States – an argument rejected by H. Helsen, *infra* this note, p. 165); W. Hummer & M. Schweitzer, *supra* note 1154, p. 819; C Gray, 'Regional Arrangements and the United Nations Collective Security System', in H. Fox (ed.), *The Changing Constitution of the United Nations*, London, British Institute of International & Comparative Law, 1997, p. 115 and A. Holstein, *supra* note 1153, pp. 111–116. For an early discussion, see A.L. Goodhart, 'The North Atlantic Treaty of 1949', 79 *Rec. Cours* 1951-II, pp. 204–209 and 232–235 (arguing that the treaty is not a regional arrangement under Chapter VIII because it has no inward focus) and H. Kelsen, 'Is the North Atlantic Treaty a Regional Arrangement', 45 *A.J.I.L* 1952, pp. 162–166 (concluding that NATO was a Chapter VIII regional organization).

1159 See also K. Graham, *supra* note 1041, p. 294. But see S. Bartelt, *supra* note 161, p. 143. The matter has been the subject of some discussion within the EU but this discussion does not seem to have been conducted in public.

1160 E.g. S. Bartelt, *supra* note 161, pp. 139–143 (noting the Security Council's apparent qualification of the EC as a Chapter VIII agency in the preamble of several Resolutions on the former Yugoslavia in the early 1990s, e.g. UNSC Resolutions 727 of 8 January 1992 and 752 of 15 May 1992); S. Dietrich, *supra* note 161 (66 *Z.a.o.R.V.* 2006), p. 691; K. Gerteiser, *supra* note 161, pp. 142–145 and J. Litten, *supra* note 161, pp. 245–246 (and pp. 69–75 with regard to the WEU). Compare N. Tsagourias, *supra* note 1023, p. 126, 'functionally' qualifying the EU as a Chapter VIII agency when it exercises relevant functions.

1161 The EC/EU certainly conforms to the purposes and principles of the UN Charter and has well developed internal dispute settlement mechanisms. However, the latter are limited and do not primarily concern political and security disputes that might arise between Member States (the whole idea being to prevent such disputes from arising in the first place). Also, the internal sanctions mechanism in case of a security threat is essentially limited to Article 7 EU Treaty and the CFSP and ESDP have an external focus. Moreover, one might wonder whether it is possible to have a regional agency or arrangement with a membership that is a subgroup of the membership of another such agency or arrangement (*in casu* the OSCE). Thus it is debatable whether the EU meets the conditions usually read into Chapter VIII. Compare N. White, 'The EU as a Regional Security Actor within the Intenational Legal Order', in TRYBUS & WHITE, pp. 329–349, especially pp. 332–335.

1162 In this sense also C Gray, *supra* note 1158, p. 113 and C. Gray, *supra* note 1140, p. 325. Compare A. Gioia, *supra* note 1153, pp. 200–202 ("*In the final analysis, the real question is ... whether a regional union ... functions as [a regional arrangement or agency or an alliance] in a given situation*") and N. Tsagourias, *supra* note 1023, p. 126.

argued that a Chapter VIII status implies some kind of subordination to the UN,[1163] the actual provisions of the Charter only attach to it a reporting duty (Article 54, which does not necessarily imply subordination[1164]) and require a Security Council authorization for enforcement action (Article 53). However, the latter is generally held to be a requirement irrespective of the Chapter VIII status (but see *infra*).[1165] Therefore the Chapter VIII status seems merely to formalize a willingness to integrate in the UN system without any significant rights or obligations other than a reporting duty. Moreover, it should be noted that even organizations that have a Chapter VIII status have not always strictly respected the Charter rules concerning enforcement action. This can notably be seen for the OAS in the Cuban missile crisis.[1166] Commentators have also suggested that the OAU and AU Charters were drawn up so as to leave some room for freedom to these organizations vis-à-vis the UN that might exceed what the Charter envisaged.[1167]

1163 W. Hummer & M. Schweitzer, *supra* note 1154, p. 828 seem to take this view by retaining as part of their definition the primary task the maintenance of peace and security "*under the control and within the framework of the UN*". A. Geslin, *supra* note 1156, pp. 492–496 argues in favour of a re-interpretation towards cooperation rather than hierarchy.

1164 Similarly J. Yepes, *supra* note 1153, pp. 280–281. W. Hummer & M. Schweitzer, *supra* note 1154, pp. 893–894 identify Security Council control as the aim of this obligation. However, nowhere in the Charter can one find of what this control could consist and how it could in any way differ from the authority which the Security Council has in any event irrespective of Chapter VIII.

1165 See also R. Kolb, *supra* note 1154, p. 1409 and D. Sarooshi, *supra* note 1140, pp. 248–249, who argues that a Chapter VIII status does not add any rights nor any obligations compared to Member States' actions.

1166 See on this, e.g. A. Gioia, *supra* note 1153, pp. 217–218; E. Kwam Kouassi, *Les rapports entre l'Organisation des Nations Unies et l'Organisation de l'Unité Africaine*, Brussels, Bruylant, 1978, pp. 59–61; H. McCoubrey & N. White, *supra* note 1145, pp. 59–60 and 90; P. Pirrone, 'The Use of Force in the Framework of the O.A.S.', in A. Cassese (ed.), *The Current Legal Regulation of the Use of Force*, Dordrecht, Nijhoff, 1986, pp. 225–228 (and 236 on the OAS' ambiguous attitude towards the need for a Security Council mandate more generally; the OAS' somewhat independent stance is also noted by E. Kodjo, *supra* note 1154, pp. 1400–1401) and L.C. Wilson, 'The Settlement of Conflicts within the Framework of Relations between Regional Organizations and the United Nations: The Case of Cuba, 1962–1964', 22 *N.I.L.R.* 1975, pp. 282–318.

1167 See for the OAU, E. Kwam Kouassi, *supra* previous note, pp. 72–82. For a good discussion regarding the AU, see A. Abass & M. Baderin, 'Towards Effective Collective Security and Human Rights Protection in Africa: An Assessment of the Constitutive Act of the New African Union', 49 *N.I.L.R.* 2002, pp. 13–24 and J.I. Levitt, *supra* note 645, pp. 228–236, submitting that the provisions in the AU Constitutive Act (Lomé, 11 July 2000 (available online at www.africa-union.org/root/au/AboutAU/Constitutive_Act_en.htm), which entered into force on 25 May 2001 with the formal succession of the OAU by the AU taking place on 9 July 2002; Articles 4(h) and (j)) and especially in the Protocol Relating to the Establishment of the Peace and Security Council of the African Union (Durban, 10 July 2002, which entered into force on 26 December 2003, available online at www.africa-union.org/root/au/Documents/Treaties/Text/Protocol_peace%20and%20security.pdf), are ambiguous (e.g. the AU's "*primary responsibility for promoting peace, security and stability in* Africa" in

There is, however, one possible argument according to which a Chapter VIII status could have an important impact. It relates to the issue of consent to intervention by force given in advance in a treaty. While consent is normally a circumstance precluding wrongfulness and considered a distinct legal basis for military intervention (see, e.g. the cases discussed above where the Security Council welcomed or endorsed rather than authorized an ESDP operation), the question arises whether consent can be given *in advance* between States, as is in fact the case for the UN Charter itself.

The question is more general and not limited to Chapter VIII UN Charter but its relevance for that Chapter will be explained below. There has been rather little discussion of this possibility[1168] and some have rejected it on the basis that consent cannot justify a violation of *ius cogens*.[1169] A related issue of consent was recently addressed in the International Court of Justice's judgment on the DRC

Article 16(1) compared to the recognition of the UN Security Council's "*primary responsibility for the maintenance of* international *peace and security*" in Article 17(1) (emphasis added) and the provision in Article 17(2) that "*Where necessary, recourse will be made to the [UN]* to provide the necessary financial, logistical and military support *for the [AU's peace and security activities] in Africa, in keeping with the provisions of Chapter VIII of the UN Charter* ..." (emphasis added); thus omitting any legal requirement for authorization despite the reference to Chapter VIII) but on the whole were intended to preserve freedom of action of the AU even for peace enforcement without a UN Security Council mandate. See also B. Kioko, 'The Right of Intervention under the African Union's Constitutive Act: From Non-interference to Non-intervention', 85 No. 852 *I.R.R.C.* 2003, pp. 807–825, especially pp. 820–824. Compare H. Strydom, 'Peace and Security under the African Union', 28 *S.A.Y.I.L.* 2003, pp. 70–76, especially p. 71, arguing that the AU must respect Article 53 UN Charter. For an appraisal of OAU/AU-UN Security Council relations, see also N.-M. Mulikita, 'Cooperation versus Dissonance: The UN Security Council and the Evolving African Union', 9 *African Y.I.L.* 2001, pp. 75–99. For UN-OAU relations; see B. Andemicael, *The OAU and the UN*, New York, Africana Publishing, 1976, especially pp. 30 and 156–163.

1168 With the exception of N. Ronzitti, 'Use of Force, Jus Cogens and State Consent', in A. Cassese (ed.), *supra* note 1166, pp. 147–166. The question is also analyzed in some detail by A. Abass, *supra* note 1153, pp. 183–208 and A. Abass & M. Baderin, *supra* note 1167, pp. 16–20. J. Frowein, 'Zwangsmaßnahmen von Regionalorganisationen', in U. Beyerlin et al. (eds.), *Recht zwischen Umbruch und Bewahrung – Festschift für Rudolf Bernhardt*, Berlin, Springer, 1995, pp. 67–69 seems inclined to accept conventional intervention rights, without, however, discussing enforcement actions against a government. R. Wolfrum, *supra* note 1153, p. 597, rejects such a right, as does R. Bernhardt, 'Article 103', in SIMMA, p. 1297. A. Tanca, *infra* note 1191, pp. 13–50 and especially pp. 44–46 seems doubtful on treaty-based consent. D. Wippman, 'Military Intervention, Regional Organizations, and Host-State Consent', 7 *Duke J.C.I.L.* 1996, pp. 237–238 sees the matter as uncertain (with further references).

1169 E.g. F. Rajower, *Das Recht des bewaffneten nicht-internationalen Konflikts seit 1949*, Zürich, Schulthess, 1990, p. 117. On the exclusion of consent as a justification for violations of *ius cogens*, see ILC, Draft Articles on Responsibility of States for Internationally Wrongful Acts, adopted on 31 May and 3 August 2001, *Report of the International Law Commission. Fifty-third session*, UN Doc. A/56/10, pp. 173–177 and 206–209, Articles 20 *juncto* 26 (especially commentary 4).

case but it does not seem conclusive as to the point at issue.[1170] However, while there is considerable support for the view that some rules of the *ius ad bellum* have attained the status of *ius cogens*,[1171] it is not clear at all whether the rules that have achieved this status include the exclusion of consent.[1172] It is submitted that the latter is clearly not the case and that the *ius ad bellum* clearly recognizes consent as a justification for the use of force in at least some cases.[1173]

The question is whether this is also the case for *prior treaty-based* consent. The system of the Charter itself indicates that prior consent can hardly be contrary to *ius cogens* as such, unless the Charter rule prohibiting prior consent *except for*

1170 *Case concerning armed activities on the territory of the Congo (DRC v. Uganda)*, judgment of 19 December 2005, §§42–54. In particular, the Court held that the consent given to the presence of Ugandan forces in the DRC was initially given informally and that its later confirmation in an agreement did not mean that the initial consent could not be informally withdrawn (i.e. there was no need to terminate the later agreement). The case does not seem conclusive for the question at stake here, since in the case of a treaty-based intervention right, the conventional consent would exist first.

1171 I will not elaborate on this. See, e.g. H. McCoubrey & N. White, *supra* note 1145, pp. 27–28; N. Schrijver, 'Challenges to the Prohibition to Use Force: Does the Straitjacket of Article 2(4) UN Charter Begin to Gall too Much?', in N. Blokker & N. Schrijver (eds.), *supra* note 645, pp. 39–43; N. Schrijver, *supra* note 1145, pp. 459–462 and N. Ronzitti, *supra* note 1168, pp. 149–163 (submitting at p. 150 that those rules that are part of *ius cogens* are more limited than Article 2(4) UN Charter).

1172 A. Abass, *supra* note 1153, pp. 191–201, considers especially the ICJ's and the ILC's views and concludes that only the prohibition of aggression belongs to *ius cogens* and goes on (at pp. 201–208) that therefore consent may well justify other *prima facie* violations of the wider prohibition on the use of force, including treaty-based intervention rights.

1173 See also A. Tanca, *infra* note 1191, pp. 13–22 and D. Wippman, *supra* note 1168, pp. 209–239, especially p. 209 ("*That consent may validate an otherwise wrongful military intervention into the territory of the consenting state is a generally accepted principle*"). Thus the ILC has correctly noted that "*One State cannot dispense another from the obligation to comply with a peremptory norm, ... But in applying some peremptory norms the consent of a particular State may be relevant. For example, a State may validly consent to a foreign military presence on its territory for a lawful purpose*" (*Report of the International Law Commission. Fifty-third session*, UN Doc. A/56/10, pp. 208–209). The issue of consent in relation to *ius cogens* and the use of force is explored in some detail by N. Ronzitti, *supra* note 1168, pp. 149–163, who persuasively argues that a number of rules of the *ius ad bellum* permit consent as a legal basis. One of the clear cases, in addition to consensual peacekeeping (see *infra*), is the evacuation of nationals abroad, which cannot (always) be brought under self-defence. While such evacuations without consent are controversial, their legality with consent does not appear to be disputed and those arguing in favour of its legality absent consent sometimes consider it as a distinct legal basis rather than self-defence; for a brief overview, see, e.g. F. Naert, 'Juridische aspecten van Non-Combatant Evacuation Operations (NEOs)', in Royal Defence College (ed.), *NEO – Represailles – Command responsibility. Studiedag voor Raadgevers in, het Recht van de Gewapende Conflicten – 29/04/2005. Teksten*, Brussels, Royal Defence College, 2005, pp. 3–11 (separate pagination). For a more comprehensive discussion, see N. Ronzitti, *Rescuing Nationals Abroad through Military Coercion and Intervention on Grounds of Humanity*, Nijhoff, Dordrecht, 1985.

the UN is *ius cogens*.[1174] It is submitted that this is not the case: practice suggests there are cases of prior treaty consent which, while controversial, do not seem to have met the uniform and qualified rejection that would indicate a violation of *ius cogens*. This practice consists of a few largely historical examples, including the still relevant Treaty of Guarantee concerning Cyprus.[1175] Moreover, Article 4(h) of the Constitutive Act of the African Union stipulates that the AU has "*The right ... to intervene in a Member State pursuant to a decision of the Assembly in respect of grave circumstances, namely war crimes, genocide and crimes against humanity*".[1176] Two interpretations of this provision are possible: either this right is dependent upon a Security Council mandate or it is not. In the former interpretation, the provision merely lays down the internal AU decision making procedure without affecting the external legal basis and there is no incompatibility with the UN Charter.[1177] In the latter interpretation, however, there does seem to be a conflict. Despite its apparent Chapter VIII status,[1178] there are indications that the AU follows the latter interpretation.[1179] This case is

---

1174 The latter position seems to be the view of N. White, *supra* note 1161, pp. 343–344 and 348–349. Compare A. Orakhelashvili, 'The Impact of Peremptory Norms on the Interpretation and Application of United Nations Security Council Resolutions', 16 *E.J.I.L.* 2005, p. 63, who considers that the prohibition of the use of force is peremptory but "*linked to, and qualified by the powers of the Security Council*".

1175 Treaty of Guarantee, Nicosia, 16 August 1960 (available online at www.mfa.gov.cy/mfa/mfa2006.nsf/All/484B73E4F0736CFDC22571BF00394F11/$file/Treaty%20of%20Guarantee.pdf). Pursuant to Article IV, second paragraph of this treaty, "*In so far as common or concerted action may not prove possible, each the three guaranteeing Powers reserves the right to take action with the sole aim of re-establishing the state of affairs created by the present Treaty*". Its compatibility with the Charter is questioned by R. Bernhardt, 'Article 103', in Simma, p. 1297 and C. Walter, *supra* note 1153, p. 149 (who sees treaty-based intervention as questionable given the reactions to the Cyprus intervention) but N. Ronzitti, *supra* note 1168, pp. 157–160 supports its validity and points to various instances of UN recognition of the Treaty. Also, its conclusion in 1960, i.e. well after the entry into force of the UN Charter, implies that the parties to this treaty considered it to be valid.

1176 Lomé, 11 July 2000, entered into force on 26 May 2001 (and formally replaced the OAU Charter on 9 July 2002). N.-M. Mulikita, *supra* note 1167, p. 81 argues that this is cancelled out by Article 4(g), which affirms "*non-interference by any Member State in the internal affairs of another*" but this can hardly be correct given the clear text of Article 4(h).

1177 For this reason R. Kolb, *supra* note 1154, pp. 1421–1422 sees this interpretation as the better one.

1178 As a successor to the OAU and confirmed by the references to this Chapter in its Constituent Act cited above. See also A. Abass & M. Baderin, *supra* note 1167, pp. 20–21.

1179 See also A. Abass, *supra* note 1153, pp. 187 and 165–167; A. Abass & M. Baderin, *supra* note 1167, pp. 20–24 and especially p. 23 ("*the Union has empowered itself to undertake enforcement action* without *the authorisation of the Security Council*"; emphasis in the original) and J.I. Levitt, *supra* note 645, pp. 228–236 (see also *supra* note 1167), who argues that African state practice and resulting treaty law as well as retroactive authorizations by the UN Security Council have created African customary international and treaty law, in particular on (humanitarian) intervention, that the latter prevails over Article 103 UN Charter (as to customary law on the basis of the argument that it is not covered by Article 103 UN Charter – a view I argue against *infra*, Chapter 8.E). See in that sense also M. Gestri, *supra* note 1144, particularly interesting because it arguably illustrates that a right to intervention based on prior consent in a treaty even without a Security Council mandate need not be regarded as so dangerous or hostile to international law and need not necessarily be condemned, which would most likely be different if it violated *ius cogens*. Although this AU stance (assuming it is indeed the AU's view or that of a number of AU Member States) would weaken the central role of the UN Security Council,[1180] it can be argued to be a step towards bringing peace and security to Africa,[1181] which would hardly be contrary to the *principles and purposes* of the UN.[1182] It is also clearly a case where the treaty was concluded by all States concerned in a free manner and without any coercion. Another fairly recent example of a treaty-based right of intervention seems to exist within ECOWAS.[1183]

The matter is relevant for Chapter VIII of the UN Charter because of the Charter's requirement of Security Council authorization for regional enforcement action in Article 53(1). If prior treaty-based consent is generally not a violation of

---

pp. 211–250, especially pp. 247–250. Compare J. Delbrück, *supra* note 1153, pp. 157–159, arguing that there is insufficient practice to have changed Article 53. A. Geslin, *supra* note 1156, pp. 491–496, argues in favour of a re-interpretation/novation rather than a change by customary law.

1180 R. Kolb, *supra* note 1154, pp. 1404–1405, 1412–1413 and 1436–1437 points out that the essence of Article 53 UN Charter is striking a balance between the UN and regional level that is constantly adjusted with a tendency towards less UN control but very much stresses the primacy of the Security Council and opposes decentralization of peace enforcement. Compare U. Villani, *supra* note 1153, pp. 390–391, arguing that the Security Council could not issue a general authorization to a regional organization – a view shared by R. Kolb, *supra* note 1154, p. 1431. Note the hostility toward regionalism during the Charter negotiations cited by A. Geslin, *supra* note 1156, p. 492, who rightly argues that the changed circumstances no longer justify such hostility.

1181 But see C. Heyns, E. Baimu & M. Killander, 'The African Union', 46 *G.Y.I.L* 2003, pp. 276–277, who consider that the right to intervention poses both a danger and opportunity and submit that it remains to be seen whether it will be used to protect human rights or retain in power unpopular regimes.

1182 One could argue that the purposes and principles of the UN are worded broad enough to accomodate some regional collective action. Compare N. Ronzitti, *supra* note 1168, pp. 154–163, who accords much importance to the conformity of the aims of an action with the principles and purposes of the UN and international law.

1183 See especially the Protocol relating to the Mechanism for Conflict Prevention, Management, Resolution, Peacekeeping and Security (Lomé, 10 December 1999, available online at www.sec.ecowas.int/sitecedeao/english/ap101299.htm) and its Articles 3 (listing as objectives to "*maintain and consolidate peace, security and stability within the Community*" and to "*constitute and deploy a civilian and military force to maintain or restore peace within the sub-region, whenever the need arises*") *juncto* 9 (voting of the Mediation and Security Council by a two-thirds majority) and 10 (power of the Mediation and Security Council to "*authorise all forms of intervention and decide particularly on the deployment of political and military missions*"); see the discussion in A. Abass, *supra* note 1153, pp. 162–164 and M. Gestri, *supra* note 1144, pp. 211–250, especially pp. 247–250.

the UN Charter and of the customary international law rules on the use of force, this would mean that this Charter obligation is a specific and additional restriction *only* intended for regional arrangements or agencies in the sense of Chapter VIII. It might be objected that the Charter does not as such bind an international organization (see *supra* and Chapter 7.G for the EU).[1184] However, this may be countered by regarding the acceptance of Chapter VIII status as an acceptance of the provisions of this Chapter of the Charter, which would thereby become binding. This would mean that a Chapter VIII status would impose restrictions upon an organization that it would not otherwise have. It is doubtful whether this was really envisaged[1185] – and is desirable[1186] – but it does seem to have some support in the developments and arguments set out above, as well as in the opposition of some organizations to a Chapter VIII status. Alternatively, one might argue that intervention based on treaty-based consent, like intervention based on *ad hoc* consent,[1187] is not peace enforcement and therefore does not require Security Council authorization under Article 53 UN Charter. Yet this seems artificial and cannot be correct as it would mean that under the Charter there could be no UN mandated enforcement action at all (since such actions are based on prior treaty-based consent as well), even though it could provide a more flexible way of changing Article 53 through a re-interpretation rather than by superseding custom which arguably requires more practice and greater consensus.[1188] In any event, such a right of intervention is unlikely to be granted to the EU, including by reason of the outward scope of the ESDP, and is therefore hardly relevant. Nevertheless, the Chapter VIII status could also be relevant more generally in respect of any military operation other than in self-defence that would qualify as an enforcement action and that is or might one

1184 Similarly for the OAU, E. Kwam Kouassi, *supra* note 1166, p. 57.

1185 U. Villani, *supra* note 1153, pp. 359–360 argues that it was not intended to impose more restrictions on States when they act collectively (albeit not in relation to this specific point).

1186 C. Walter, *supra* note 1153, pp. 162–171 submits that humanitarian intervention by a regional organization may be preferable to global inaction on the one hand and unilateral action more prone to abuse on the other hand. But see the restrictive view in *A More Secure World: Our Shared Responsibility. Report of the High-level Panel on Threats, Challenges and Change*, UN Doc. A/59/565 (17 November 2004), §272(a): "*Authorization from the Security Council should in all cases be sought for regional peace operations, recognizing that in some urgent situations that authorization may be sought after such operations have commenced*". Compare A. Geslin, *supra* note 1156, p. 496. However, as M. Zwanenburg, *infra* note 1190, especially p. 508, points out, this seems overly restrictive, at least as regards *ad hoc* consensual operations, and has not been included in the 2005 World Summit Outcome document (UNGA Res. 60/1, 24 October 2005, especially §§77–80, 93 and 170).

1187 See *supra*, Chapter 3.

1188 In addition to the problem of custom changing the Charter in the light of Article 103 of the Charter discussed above (*supra* note 1147–1149 and the accompanying text). On change through interpretation, see also S. Ford, *supra* note 1148, pp. 100–116.

day be legal under the *ius ad bellum* without a UN Security Council mandate.[1189]

Fourthly, given the frequent reliance on host State consent in ESDP operations,[1190] mention must be made of the issue of intervention in civil war.[1191] In particular, while intervention directed against a government is clearly illegal,[1192] there is some debate over intervention on the invitation and in support of a government. While one might expect such intervention to be lawful (why should a government not be entitled to ask for assistance?[1193]), the contrary has often been argued,

---

1189 E.g. humanitarian intervention, still controversial at present; see, e.g. International Commission on Intervention and State Sovereignty, *The Responsibility to Protect*, Ottawa, International Development Research Centre, 2001 (available online at www.iciss.ca/pdf/Commission-Report.pdf). Compare R. Kolb, *supra* note 1154, pp. 1414–1426, especially p. 1426, stating that there is no need for Security Council authorization when the use of force is otherwise lawful.

1190 See on such consent A. Geslin, *supra* note 1156, p. 489; E. Lagrange, *Les opérations de maintien de la paix et le chapitre VII des Nations Unies*, Paris, Montchrestien, 1999, pp. 13–33 (qualifying host State consent as legally necessary except where a Chapter VII mandate is given by the UN security Council); N. Tsagourias, *supra* note 1023, pp. 126–127 (seeing consent as sufficient even for a coercive but consensual mandate) and U. Villani, *supra* note 1153, pp. 395–397 and 407–416 (arguing that consent suffices only for non-coercive mandates). In its Advisory opinion of 20 July 1962 on *Certain Expenses of the United Nations (Article 17, paragraph 2, of the Charter)*, *I.C.J. Rep.* 1962, pp. 164–166, 170–171 and 177, the ICJ clearly distinguished consensual peacekeeping from peace enforcement undertaken against a State; see also G. Nolte, *supra* note 1058, p. 105. For a recent appraisal in the context of regional organizations, see M. Zwanenburg, 'Regional Organisations and the Maintenance of International Peace and Security: Three Recent Regional African Peace Operations', 11 *J.C.S.L.* 2006, pp. 483–508, arguing that there is no need for Security Council authorization when there is consent by the parties to the conflict or by the government, possibly even when the latter is no longer in effective control.

1191 See generally M. Bennouna, *Le consentement à l'ingérence militaire dans les conflits internes*, Paris, LGDJ, 1974; L. Doswald-Beck, 'The Legal Validity of Military Intervention by Invitation of the Government', 56 *B.Y.I.L.* 1985, pp. 189–252 (concluding at pp. 251–252 that new customary norms had developed and had set aside the older rule permitting support of a government and there was at least serious doubt whether support of a government to suppress a rebellion was legal, particularly if the rebellion was widespread, but that the provision of advice and arms short of direct action was acceptable); T.J. Farer, 'The Regulation of Foreign Intervention in Civil Armed Conflict', 142 *Rec. Cours* 1974-II, pp. 291–406; C. Gray, *supra* note 1140, pp. 59–94; H. McCoubrey & N. White, *supra* note 1145, pp. 71–86; G. Nolte, *Eingreifen auf Einladung. Zur völkerrechtlichen Zulässigkeit des Einsatzes fremder Truppen im internen Konflikt auf Einladung der Regierung*, Berlin, Springer, 1999; F. Rajower, *supra* note 1169, pp. 107–128 and A. Tanca, *Foreign Armed Intervention in Internal Conflict*, Dordrecht, Martinus Nijhoff, 1993.

1192 E.g. ICJ, *Nicaragua* case, *supra* note 1146, §§206–209 and UNGA Res. 2625(XXV), 24 October 1970, Annex (Friendly Relations Declaration): "*no State shall organize, assist, foment, finance, incite or tolerate subversive, terrorist* or armed activities directed towards the violent overthrow of the regime of another State" (emphasis added).

1193 In fact, C. Walter, *supra* note 1153, p. 144 points out that the classical view was that a government could indeed invite intervention, *inter alia* citing ICJ, *Nicaragua* case, *supra* note 1146, §246 ("*it is difficult to see what would remain of the principle of non-intervention in* especially once an internal conflict reaches the level of a civil war.[1194] For instance, a Resolution of the Institute of International Law in 1975 prohibited any outside assistance to parties in a civil war (except when supported by the UN).[1195] The key question seems to be one of legitimacy:[1196] the underlying argument of opponents against supporting governments in civil wars essentially appears to be that in a civil war no side has the necessary legitimacy to invite and receive outside support. However, it may be questioned whether this is correct, both as a matter of principle and of practice. As to the former, there may clearly be cases of civil war where one side is quite generally internationally recognized as the international representative of the State concerned.[1197] While some argue it is not for outside powers to intervene in favour of one side in such an internal matter,[1198] this is hardly convincing: if taken to its full consequences, it would mean that a State in civil war cannot have any international representation at all.[1199] This is clearly not supported by State practice, where one might agree that there is a rebuttable presumption in favour of the vested government.[1200] Also,

---

international law if intervention, which is already allowable at the request of the government of a State, *were also to be allowed at the request of the opposition*"; emphasis added).

1194 See also UNGA Res. 2625(XXV), *supra* note 1192: "*no State shall ... interfere in civil strife in another State*" and a 1984 UK document cited in C. Gray, *supra* note 1140, pp. 68–69. C. Byron, 'Armed Conflicts: International or Non-International', 6 *J.C.S.L.* 2001, pp. 82–83 regards pro government intervention as illegal, citing the risk of fake consent. C. Walter, *supra* note 1153, p. 143 submits that such intervention has become less problematic since the end of the Cold War.

1195 Resolution on The Principle of Non-Intervention in Civil Wars, adopted at the Wiesbaden session, Article 2.

1196 F. Rajower, *supra* note 1169, pp. 113–120 and A. Tanca, *supra* note 1191, pp. 138–140.

1197 See, e.g. several instances in the conflict(s) in the DRC in which the UN Security Council seems to have distinguished between States intervening at the invitation of the government and States intervening against this government, as described in C. Gray, *supra* note 1140, pp. 60–63. In the *Case concerning armed activities on the territory of the Congo (DRC v. Uganda)*, judgment of 19 December 2005, the ICJ appears to have accepted that the DRC government was entitled to invite the presence of foreign forces; see §§42–54. M. Zwanenburg, *supra* note 1190, pp. 505–506 adds that this was so despite indications that the DRC government was not in control of parts of its territory.

1198 This seems to be the view taken in the Friendly relations Declaration, *supra* note 1192, where the prohibition is found under the broader duty not to intervene in matters within the domestic jurisdiction of any State.

1199 Similarly, S. Wollenberg, *Die Regierung von Konfliktgebieten durch die Vereinten Nationen*, Baden-Baden, Nomos, 2007, p. 177 (regarding refusal of the right to ask for intervention as curtailing the legal freedom of action of the State).

1200 See F. Rajower, *supra* note 1169, pp. 113–120. Compare N. Ronzitti, *supra* note 1168, pp. 154–157, arguing that support for a government in a civil war is unlawful if the government does not have the "*legitimate right to express the will of the State according to international law*", which, however, simply shifts the question. R. Kolb, *supra* note 1154, pp. 1425–1426 and C. Walter, *supra* note 1153, pp. 146–148 submit that the legitimate government is the one exercising effective control. M. Gestri, *supra* note 1144, p. 244, also considers that effectiveness is still the prevailing test despite challenges from a democracy perspective. On pro-democratic intervention, including on a prior treaty basis, see, e.g. J. Wouters & C. Ryngaert, *Democracy* practice seems to indicate that intervention in favour of a government is regularly relied upon by States, especially but not only where there is no full civil war.[1201] It may also be noted that the Constitutive Act of the AU includes "*the right of Member States to request intervention from the Union in order to restore peace and security*".[1202] That being said, in some cases it may indeed be difficult to determine who may legitimately claim to represent a State at the international level. However, this is a problem in applying the law rather than one of (determining the) applicable law. Moreover, when this is possible, consent from all the parties and not just the host State can be sought.[1203] In conclusion, the EU can arguably rely on host government consent as long as there is an established government that is internationally recognized, even in cases of civil war. Obviously, support of a government is not permitted where this would be contrary to the right to self-determination.[1204]

7. CONCLUSIONS ON THE SCOPE OF THE ESDP

I conclude that the ESDP as it stands under the EU Treaty as last substantially amended by the Treaty of Nice is operational, as manifested through its rapidly increasing number and variety of operations, and constitutes part of the progressive framing of a common defence policy within the CFSP. However, it would probably better be described as a common security policy with a civilian and military component as it presently excludes a common defence, thereby

---

and International Law, Leuven Interdisciplinary Research Group on International Agreements and Development, Working Paper No. 5, June 2004 (available online at http://ghumweb2.ghum.kuleuven.ac.be/ggs/publications/workingpapers/archive/WP05.pdf), pp. 24–33. M. Zwanenburg, *supra* note 1190, pp. 505–507 submits that the requirement of effectiveness is being eroded; see also *supra* note 1197. On democracy and legitimacy of governments and international law, see also generally S. Marks, *The Riddle of All Constitutions: International Law, Democracy, and a Critique of Ideology*, Oxford, Oxford University Press, 2000; G.H. Fox & B.R. Roth (eds.), *Democratic Governance and International Law*, Cambridge, Cambridge University Press, 2000 and B. Roth, *Governmental Illegitimacy in International Law*, Oxford, Clarendon Press, 1999.

1201 See the examples discussed by C. Gray, *supra* note 1140, pp. 71–75. See also M. Zwanenburg, *supra* note 1190, pp. 483–508, especially pp. 505–507. One might also add US support for the Colombian government. Efforts to combat terrorism have arguably reinforced the acceptability of support of a government fighting rebel forces when the latter are perceived as terrorists.

1202 Article 4(j).

1203 Though as E. Lagrange, *supra* note 1190, pp. 28–32 points out, it may be politically difficult for an international organization to seek consent from rebel movements, at least where no peace agreement has been agreed (where such an agreement exists, it may include the consent of all parties to an international mission; see, e.g. the AMM, *supra*, Chapter 3.L).

1204 See also S. Wollenberg, *supra* note 1199, pp. 177–179, who rightly stresses, however, that this right will not necessarily be applicable in every civil war.

remaining compatible with the neutral status of some of the EU Member States. The ESDP does include at least peacekeeping with peace enforcement elements and in my view also pure peace enforcement, as well as a broad range of other, mostly consensual tasks.

The ESDP has an institutional setup revolving around the Council and PSC, supported by the SG/HR, EUMC, EUMS, CIVCOM and CPCC. Member States put at the disposal military and civilian capabilities on a voluntary basis and retain the decision over whether or not to deploy them and participation in operations may be limited to only a number of Member States. Operations may rely on NATO assets or may be autonomous, in which case Headquarters have to be provided by one or more Member States or constituted by the EU Operations Centre. The ESDP is based on complementarity with NATO and allows for a significant participation of third States and cooperation with other international organizations.

Under the Lisbon Treaty, the key innovations are the solidarity clause – providing for a common reaction to terrorist attacks – and a mutual defence clause, albeit one that exempts the neutral Member States and that does not yet constitute a common defence, as well as the possibility for some Member States to accept more far-reaching commitments via permanent structured cooperation. There are also various less fundamental changes, e.g. the possibility of entrusting the execution of an operation to a group of Member States, the commitment to improve capabilities and the role of the EDA and the possibility of enhanced cooperation on military and defence matters.

B. LEGAL STATUS AND APPLICABLE LAW

1. WHAT THE SOFA/SOMAs DO SAY

In the SOFAs and SOMAs, there has been some evolution but there are also a number of common elements. First, in the first (EUPM) SOMA, it was striking that there was no reference to an obligation to respect local law, a clause which is common in SOFAs.[1205] However, this obligation was introduced in later SOMA/SOFAs, and in two instances specific mention was additionally made of respect for local laws regarding environmental protection and the protection of cultural heritage, albeit in the case of CONCORDIA "*subject to the requirements of the operation*".

1205 See, e.g. §6 UN Model SOFA, UN Doc. A/45/594, 9 October 1990, and §3 SFOR SOFA, *supra* note 559 (where this is, however, qualified somewhat).

Second, the frequent granting of privileges and immunities equivalent to that of a diplomatic mission and diplomatic personnel is also unusual,[1206] though perhaps less so for the smaller civilian missions like THEMIS. It is particularly unusual for a military operation like CONCORDIA, where it is normally rather stipulated that the forces shall be under the exclusive criminal jurisdiction of their sending State.[1207] Indeed, it does not seem to have been followed any more in later SOFAs. The inclusion of a clause providing for a waiver of immunity in most of the later SOMAs is a welcome development. However, it would be very exceptional for such a waiver to be granted. To the author's knowledge, this has not yet happened and States are very reluctant to grant a waiver. Obviously, to the extent that they take the necessary remedial or judicial actions themselves, this need not be a problem.[1208] Moreover, in many cases the reluctance to hand over personnel to local jurisdictions is understandable given that such jurisdictions do not always exist and rarely function in accordance with international human rights standards in conflict zones in which operations usually take place. Taking into consideration the fact that staff of international organizations generally enjoy wide immunities in a host State and that personnel of an operation will usually be called upon to take more intrusive actions than such staff, such immunities do not seem excessive. Nevertheless, there may be cases in which a waiver is appropriate. The more differentiated immunity from local civilian and administrative courts in the more recent SOMAs is also an interesting development but it remains to be seen how it will be applied.[1209]

Third, for claims, the SOMA/SOFAs usually distinguish between two categories of claims: claims arising out of activities in connection with the operation are not subject to any reimbursement by Participating States or the EU, whereas all other claims, if they are not within the jurisdiction of the local courts, are dealt with by specific mechanisms. The issue of claims is complex and deserves further

1206 It is more common to reserve the diplomatic status for the top officials of a mission and accord other mission members somewhat less extensive immunities; see, e.g. §§24–28 UN Model SOFA, *supra* note 1205, and §§2 and 8 SFOR SOFA, *supra* note 559.

1207 E.g. §§27 and 47(b) UN Model SOFA, *supra* note 1205 and §7 SFOR SOFA, *supra* note 559.

1208 Admittedly, the immunities of international organizations are being increasingly challenged from a human rights perspective. However, the jurisprudence suggests that there is no problem where an adequate alternative remedy is available (see especially ECtHR, *Beer and Regan v. Germany* and *Waite en Kennedy v. Germany*, both 18 February 1999, and *McElhinney v. Ireland*, *Fogarty v. United Kingdom* and *Al-Adsani v. United Kingdom*, all three 21 November 2001). Court proceedings in the sending State of personnel concerned could be such a remedy, although in civil suits for damages this avenue may be very difficult to pursue for host State residents. Obviously, this supposes that the human rights obligation applies in the first case, an issue that will be explored below in Chapter 9.

1209 See also *infra* note 2222.

discussion, but is addressed here only very briefly.[1210] In any event, the treaty texts do not reflect the full reality on the ground and in at least one NATO-led operation, compensation is sometimes awarded even where a SOFA does not require it.[1211] Hence one has to look beyond the texts and take into account practice in this field. However, the author has not been able to verify whether such a practice has also occurred in EU-led operations. Finally, while in light of human rights considerations,[1212] a complete exclusion of some categories of claims may be problematic, a mission specific SOFA/SOMA is normally only applicable in the host State and may not preclude claims in the States participating in an operation, although this course of action may be very difficult to pursue for host State residents.

Fourth, the mechanisms used to make applicable SOFA/SOMAs of related missions and of other international organizations or countries constitute an interesting and practical approach to the status issue.

Fifth, it should be noted that there exist model SOFAs and SOMAs for civilian[1213] and military[1214] ESDP operations, but only the former is (or was) in the public domain.

2. WHAT THE SOFA/SOMAs DO NOT SAY: THE LAW OF ARMED CONFLICT AND HUMAN RIGHTS LAW

It is remarkable that respect for the law of armed conflict or human rights law is never mentioned in SOFA/SOMAs or participating State agreements, except in the case of the AMIS Supporting Mission via the AU SOMA and for EUFOR DR

1210 See more generally B. Amrallah, 'The International Responsibility of the United Nations for Activities Carried out by UN Peace-Keeping Forces', 32 *Revue égyptienne de droit international* 1976, pp. 57–82; K. Schmalenbach, *Die Haftung Internationaler Organisationen im Rahmen von Militäreinsätzen und Territorialverwaltungen*, Peter Lang, 2004 and K. Schmalenbach, 'Third Party Liability of International Organizations: A Study on Claim Settlement in the Course of Military Operations and International Administrations', 10 *International Peacekeeping* 2006, pp. 33–51.

1211 See, e.g. L. Kjelgaard, 'HQ ISAF Claims Office', Issue 19 *NATO Legal Gazette*, 7 April 2009, pp. 12–14.

1212 See *supra* note 1208.

1213 See EU Council Doc. 17141/08 of 15 December 2008.

1214 See EU Council Documents 12616/07 of 6 September 2007 *juncto* 11894/07 of 20 July 2007 and COR 1 (5 September 2007).

Congo via the MONUC SOFA[1215]. [1216] However, the provisions on respect for human rights in the EULEX Kosovo and Atalanta Joint Actions[1217] are a positive development.

While the applicability of the law of armed conflict to UN operations has long been debated and is still not quite settled,[1218] the UN has moved towards the acceptance of the applicability of at least some principles and rules of the law of armed conflict to its operations[1219] and this has been reflected in SOFAs, albeit only fairly recently, and in agreements with Participating States.[1220] However, within the UN too the texts have so far been silent on the applicability of human rights to UN operations even though they are usually more relevant.

Obviously, the general lack of any references in the EU legal instruments surveyed above, with only a few exceptions, does not necessarily mean that the law of armed conflict or human rights law is not mentioned anywhere or is not deemed to be applicable. Indeed, the EU has a doctrine on the use of force in military ESDP operations which *inter alia* addresses this very issue. Unfortunately, it is a classified document. Likewise, this issue is usually dealt with in the Operation Plan and reflected in the Rules of Engagement, but these documents too are normally classified.

1215 See for the latter Article 6(a) of this SOFA, *supra* note 729 ("*L'Organisation des Nations Unies s'assure que la MONUC s'acquitte de sa mission dans la République démocratique du Congo dans le plein repect des principes et règles des conventions internationales relatives à la conduite du personnel militaire. Ces conventions internationales comprennent les quatre Conventions de Genève du 12 août 1949 et leurs Protocoles additionnels du 8 juin 1977 et la Convention internationale de l'UNESCO pour la protection des biens culturels en cas de conflit armé*").

1216 See the similar comment by N. Ronzitti, *supra* note 997, pp. 181–182.

1217 See above, Chapter 3, respectively Sections T.2 and W.2.

1218 For two recent elaborate studies with further references, see Zwanenburg, also published in an amended version as M . Zwanenburg, *Accountability of Peace Support Operations*, Leiden, Martinus Nijhoff, 2005 and Kolb, Porretto & Vité, especially pp. 117–232.

1219 See especially the UN Secretary-General Bulletin on Observance by United Nations Forces of International Humanitarian Law, UN Doc. ST/SGB/1999/13, 6 August 1999, available online at www.icrc.org/Web/Eng/siteeng0.nsf/iwpList367/711A2C1A3BD7FA2EC1256B66005DD94 A.

1220 See Part X, section 28 of the Model Agreement between the United Nations and Member States Contributing Personnel and Equipment to the United Nations Peace-keeping Operation, UN Doc. A/46/185, 23 May 1991, Annex ("*[The … operation] shall observe and respect the principles and spirit of the general international conventions applicable to the conduct of military personnel. The international conventions referred to above include the four Geneva Conventions of 12 August 1949 and their Additional Protocols of 8 June 1977 and the UNESCO Convention of 14 May 1954 on the Protection of Cultural Property in the event of armed conflict. [The Participating State] shall therefore ensure that the members of its national contingent … be fully acquainted with the principles and spirit of these Conventions*"). There is no corresponding provision in the Model Status-of-Forces Agreement between the United Nations and Host Countries (UN Doc. A/45/594, 9 October 1990, Annex) but it became common practice to include such a clause from 1992 onwards: see Zwanbenburg, p. 175.

Fortunately, the EU Treaty itself says something on this point: its Article 6(2) states that "*The Union shall respect fundamental rights, as guaranteed by the European Convention for the Protection of Human Rights and Fundamental Freedoms signed in Rome on 4 November 1950 and as they result from the constitutional traditions common to the Member States, as general principles of Community law*". This provides an excellent starting point for examining in Part III whether the EU is bound by any human rights obligations in the context of ESDP operations. That this question is not a theoretical one is easily illustrated by some of the recent law suits and court decisions dealing with military operations, including the 1999 NATO air campaign over Kosovo,[1221] British forces deployed in Iraq[1222] and France, Germany and Norway in respect of conduct of peacekeepers in Kosovo.[1223]

Does Article 6 EU Treaty also have some relevance for the applicability of the law of armed conflict? And are human rights the appropriate standard for ESDP operations, or should it be international humanitarian law, or both? The answer will require an analysis of the relationship between both bodies of law and their respective scope of applicability. Therefore, the applicability of these two bodies of law and their mutual relationship will be explored extensively in Part III below.

1221 See especially ECtHR, *Vlastimir and Borka Bankovic´ and Others v. Belgium, the Czech Republic, Denmark, France, Germany, Greece, Hungary, Iceland, Italy, Luxembourg, the Netherlands, Norway, Poland, Portugal, Spain, Turkey and the United Kingdom*, 12 December 2001 (decision on admissibility).

1222 See, e.g. *R (Al-Skeini and others) v Secretary of State for Defence* ([2004] EWHC 2911 (Admin)), 14 December 2004 (available online at www.bailii.org/ew/cases/EWHC/Admin/2004/2911.html), upheld on appeal on 21 December 2005 in [2005] EWCA Civ 1609 (available online at www.bailii.org/ew/cases/EWCA/Civ/2005/1609.html) and upheld by the House of Lords on 13 June 2007 ([2007] UKHL 26, available online at www.publications.parliament.uk/pa/ld200607/ldjudgmt/jd070613/skeini-1.pdf).

1223 On 31 May 2007, the Grand Chamber of the ECtHR declared inadmissible the applications brought in the cases *Behrami and Behrami v. France* (No. 71412/01) and *Saramati v. France, Germany and Norway* (No. 78166/01), both concerning conduct of personnel of the international presence in Kosovo (the former concerning the death and wounding of children due to unexploded ordinance and the latter concerning security detention).

PART II
TO WHAT EXTENT ARE INTERNATIONAL ORGANIZATIONS BOUND BY INTERNATIONAL LAW?

INTRODUCTION

As noted at the outset, before analyzing the key issue in Part III, I will address the preliminary question of what obligations are incumbent upon international organizations under international law generally. This requires consideration because, although it is clear that international organizations may be subjects of international law, they are nevertheless subjects different from States, which have been the traditional subjects of international law. This leads to the question whether one may simply apply the rules applicable to States to international organizations, either as such or *mutatis mutandis*, or whether international organizations are subject to proper rules only, or a combination of the two.

This analysis will start with the international legal status of international organizations in Chapter 5 and of the EU in particular in Chapter 6, as international legal subjectivity or personality would logically seem to be a prerequisite for an organization to be subject to obligations under international law.[1224] In Chapter 7, I will then look at how international organizations may be bound by international obligations, both in general and specifically for the EU. This will include consideration of a range of sources, including *inter alia* constitutional instruments and agreements entered into by international organizations, customary international law and general principles of law as a potential source of obligations, with particular attention to the ECJ's jurisprudence on human rights.

As a preliminary remark, in the absence of a generally accepted definition of international organizations,[1225] I will define international organizations as

---

1224 P. Bekker, *Legal Position of Intergovernmental Organisations-A Functional Necessity Analysis of Their Legal Status and Immunities*, Dordrecht, Nijhoff, 1994, p. 52 rightly points out that "*the legal status of an international organization is a starting-point whenever we are concerned with rights and duties of an organization*". For a critical view on the focus on legal personality/subjectivity, see A. Clapham, *Human Rights Obligations of Non-State Actors*, Oxford, Oxford University Press, 2006, pp. 59–82, arguing that capacity is more important. However, the author himself seems to associate capacity to personality (at pp. 82–83) and his criticism may be countered by distinguishing between subjectivity, personality, capacity and competence (see *infra*, Chapter 5.A.1).

1225 Schermers & Blokker, §32, p. 26 and I. Seidl-Hohenveldern, 'Internationale Organisationen aufgrund von Soft Law', in U. Beyerlin *et al.* (eds.), *Recht zwischen Umbruch und Bewahrung. Festschift für Rudolf Bernhardt*, Berlin, Springer, 1995, p. 229. Treaties offer little help in this respect: Article 2(1)i of both the 1969 and 1986 VCLT simply state that "'*international organization' means an intergovernmental organization*". The same definition is used in "*forms of international cooperation founded on an international instrument creating a new entity, usually a legal person, having at least one organ with a will of its own and not established under the domestic law of a State*".[1226] As in the definition provisionally adopted by the ILC for the purposes of the responsibility of international organizations,[1227] I have chosen "international instrument" rather than treaty because that expression covers, in addition to treaties, both decisions of international organizations setting up another international organization[1228] and non-legally binding agreements establishing an international organization (such as the OSCE; see *infra*).[1229] The latter reason is

---

Article 1(1)1 of the 1975 VCRSIO (not yet entered into force) and in Article 2(1)n of the 1978 VCSST (which entered into force on 6 November 1996). In respect of the 1986 VCLT, this was identical to the provision in the ILC's 1982 draft Articles on the subject, the commentary to which makes it clear that some States suggested additional elements but that it was nevertheless deemed sufficient for the purposes of this instrument (*Y.I.L.C.* 1982-II, Part 2, pp. 20–21). For an extensive discussion, see M. Virally, 'Definition and Classification of International Organizations: A Legal Approach', in G. Abi-Saab (ed.), *The Concept of International Organization*, Paris, UNESCO, 1981, pp. 50–66. But see C. Brölmann, *The Institutional Veil in Publmic International Law. International Organizations and the Law of Treaties*, Amsterdam, University of Amsterdam, Faculty of Law (dissertation), 2005, p. 15, arguing that common elements may be discerned in the various definitions.

1226 Inspired by Schermers & Blokker, §§33–45, pp. 26–37, especially §33 p. 26 ("*forms of cooperation founded on an international agreement usually creating a new legal person having at least one organ with a will of its own, established under international law*") but with some modifications, though to some extent in line with these authors' intentions. Compare Amerasignhe, pp. 9–11 ("*normally created by a treaty*" and identifying legal personality and treaty-making power as "*sometimes mentioned in connection with*" international organizations but regarding these elements rather as consequences of being an organization). Sands & Klein, pp. 16–17 are more exigent and demand establishment by treaty and the possession of legal personality. For the definition used by the ILC, see *infra*, note 1233.

1227 Provisional Article 2 of the draft Articles on this matter reads: "*For the purposes of the present draft Articles, the term "international organization" refers to an organization established by a treaty* or other instrument *governed by international law and possessing its own international legal personality …*" (*Report of the International Law Commission on the Work of its fifty-fifth Session*, UN Doc. A/58/10, 2003, §53, p. 33; emphasis added). Commentary 4 thereto (*id.*, pp. 39–40) explains that this is meant to cover organizations established on a non-treaty basis, e.g. by a decision of another international organization or a non-legally binding act. Nevertheless, there is some ambiguity in this definition in that there remains the element "*governed by international law*" and it is remarked in respect of the OSCE that "*although an implicit agreement may be held to exist, member States insisted that there was no treaty concluded to that effect*" (on the OSCE, see *infra*, Chapter 5.C).

1228 Though in this case too the basis will, indirectly, be a treaty.

1229 See also I. Seidl-Hohenveldern, *supra* note 1225, pp. 232–233 and F. Seyersted, *Objective International Personality of Intergovernmental Organizations: Do Their Capacities Really Depend Upon the Conventions Establishing Them?*, Copenhagen, *s.n.*, 1963, pp. 48–55. Compare Klabbers, pp. 7–13, especially pp. 10–12, identifying the treaty basis as a characteristic but stressing that this criterion essentially refers to the creation by an intentional act. F. Morgenstern, *Legal Problems of International Organizations*, Cambridge, Grotius, 1986, pp. 19–22 also mentions inroads into the need for establishement by treaty.

also the reason why I chose "*not established under domestic law*"[1230] rather than "*established under international law*": while both serve primarily to distinguish an international organization from an entity that fully functions under the domestic law of a State[1231] the wording used here does not preclude establishment at the international level but not under legally binding arrangements.[1232] It is submitted that the elements retained here suffice to ensure the public and international nature of the organization and are adequate for the purposes of this book. Although I will conclude in Chapter 5 that being a subject of international law is needed to have obligations under international law, I do not see this as an absolute requirement for being an international organization.[1233]

1230 Similary F. Seyersted, *supra* note 1229, p. 47 ("*not ... subject to the authority of any one State*").

1231 See, e.g. Schermers & Blokker, §45, pp. 36–37.

1232 Compare the ambiguity in the ILC's definition noted *supra* note 1227. For a critical analysis of such 'organizations', see J. Klabbers, 'Institutional Ambivalence by Design: Soft Organizations in International Law', 70 *Nordic J.I.L.* 2001, pp. 403–421.

1233 The ILC's inclusion of this element in its provisional Article 2 of the draft Articles on the responsibility of international organizations ("*For the purposes of the present draft Articles, the term "international organization" refers to an organization ... possessing its own international legal personality ...*" (*Report of the International Law Commission on the Work of its fifty-fifth Session*, UN Doc. A/58/10, 2003, §53, p. 33)) is linked to the specific subject matter of these draft Articles: international responsibility of the organization can only arise when the organization has proper obligations under international law. See, e.g. comment 3 to this draft Article (*id.*, p. 39): "*No additional element would be required [compared to the definition as an 'intergovenmental organization'] in the case of international responsibility apart from possessing an obligation under international law*". This point is more clearly made in the *First Report of the Special Rapporteur* on this topic (UN Doc. A/CN.4/532, 27 March 2003, §15, pp. 8–9): "*When considering a definition of international organizations that is functional to the purposes of draft Articles on responsibility of international organizations, one has to start from the premise that responsibility under international law may arise only for a subject of international law. Norms of international law cannot impose on an entity "primary" obligations or "secondary" obligations in case of a breach of one of the "primary" obligations unless that entity has legal personality under international law*". Compare the ILA's 2004 *Final Report on the Accountablity of International Organisations* (available online at www.ila-hq.org): p. 4 (introduction): "*intergovernmental organisations in the traditional sense [are] created under international law by an international agreement amongst States, possessing a constitution and organs separate from its Member States. The Committee's work is intended also to cover organisations where not only States are members, but not to cover anomalous cases in which intergovernmental organisations do not possess a legal personality of their own in international law*". Compare F. Seyersted, *supra* note 1229, especially pp. 45–56, who regards legal personality as a consequence, albeit a necessary one, of being an international organization, and C. Brölmann, *supra* note 1225, pp. 22–23 and 95–97, who regards legal personality as an external attribute that may be granted to an international organization by the international legal order and sees a difficulty in conceptualizing an intergovernmental organization without legal personality. *Contra* P. Dailler & A. Pellet, *Droit international public*, Paris, L.G.D.J., 2002 (7th ed.), pp. 578 and 593 who regard legal personality as an element of the definition of an international organization.

CHAPTER 5
THE INTERNATIONAL LEGAL STATUS OF INTERNATIONAL ORGANIZATIONS

In this chapter, I will analyze the legal status of international organizations, which will be applied to the EU in the next chapter as a prelude to looking into the international obligations of international organizations and the EU in Chapter 7.

After an introductory and terminological section (A), I examine international organizations as subjects of international law (B). Subsequently, the legal status of the OSCE (which has or at least had some features in common with the EU) is analyzed and I argue that it is not merely political in nature (C). This is followed by a brief section on the uncontroversial consideration that international organizations may possess international legal personality, even by implication, (D) and by a closer look at the contents of the international legal personality of international organizations, including its elements and consequences and treaty-making capacity as one decisive element (and dealing briefly with NATO and the Eurocorps) (E). Attention is then paid to the question whether international legal personality is objective (F) and the main findings are summarized in the preliminary conclusions (G).

A. TERMINOLOGY: LEGAL PERSONALITY, SUBJECTIVITY, LEGAL CAPACITIES AND COMPETENCE

As mentioned above in the introduction to this chapter, the international legal subjectivity or personality of international organizations is discussed here because it would logically seem to be a prerequisite for an organization to be bound by proper obligations under international law, at least if one defines either of these two notions, at least in part, as the capacity to have international rights and duties. But since the law is not always logical, this first needs to be verified. Moreover, the nature of the legal status will already reveal some issues of applicable law.

The problem is that just as there is no generally accepted definition of an international organization, there also appear to exist various terms related to international legal status that do not always have identical meanings.[1234] The main terms used in English are 'subject of international law', 'international legal/ juridical person(ality)', 'international person(ality)' and '(international) legal capacity'. Obviously, the matter becomes more complex if one looks at other languages. In this respect, one must mention the German term 'völkerrechtliche Handlungsfähigkeit' as a term covering an additional notion.

Lacking any treaty definitions, I will start with the ICJ's *Reparations Opinion*, usually considered the leading precedent on the legal status of international organizations. In this opinion, the ICJ was *inter alia* asked whether the UN had the "*capacity to bring an international claim*" against a government that was deemed responsible for damages which the UN had suffered. The Court first considered the characteristics of the UN so as to determine whether these included a right to present an international claim. It looked at whether the UN was given with regard to its members "*rights which it is entitled to ask them to respect*", or, "*in other words*", whether the UN possessed "*international personality*". It acknowledged that the latter term was a doctrinal expression which had given rise to controversy and stated that it meant being an entity capable of availing itself of obligations incumbent upon its members. It then noted that "*the subjects of law in any legal system are not necessarily identical in their nature or in the extent of their rights*". Holding that the UN exercised and enjoyed "*functions and rights which can only be explained on the basis of the possession of a large measure of international personality and the capacity to operate upon an international plane*", the Court concluded that the UN was an international person and that this meant "*that it is a subject of international law and capable of possessing international rights and duties, and that it has the capacity to maintain its rights by bringing international claims*". The ICJ then considered whether the sum of the UN's international rights included the right to bring an international claim, finding that it did.[1235]

The opinion provides some help as to the terms used. First, several of its considerations suggest that capacity is usually used in relation to a specific right

[1234] For a brief discussion, see H.-H. Nöll, *Die Völkerrechtssubjektivität der Europäischen Gemeinschaften und deren Bindung an das allgemeine Völkerrecht*, Baden-Baden, Nomos, 1986, pp. 32–33. For an elaborate analysis of international legal personality from a broader perspective, see, e.g. J.E. Nijman, *The Concept of International Legal Personality: An Inquiry into the History and Theory of International Law*, The Hague, T.M.C. Asser Press, 2004.

[1235] *I.C.J. Reports* 1949, pp. 177/7–180/10.

and in such cases is a narrow notion,[1236] as opposed to a subject of international law or international person, which would have a broader meaning.[1237] Second, by saying that international personality means being a subject of international law and listing additional elements, the notion of international personality would appear to be broader than that of a subject of international law. Alternatively, the further elements listed – i.e. being capable of possessing international rights and duties and having the capacity to maintain its rights by bringing international claims – are already comprised in the notion of a subject of international law.[1238] While the latter is indeed likely for being capable of possessing international rights and duties (see *infra*), this is less clear for having the capacity to maintain its rights by bringing international claims. Indeed, it is not entirely clear whether the Court sees that element as a condition for or a consequence of international personality: on the one hand, it seems to include it as part of the definition of this term, while on the other hand, it still inquires whether the international personality includes the possibility to bring a claim.[1239] Moreover, one may put the question what it means to be capable of bringing an international claim, especially given the absence of a general compulsory dispute settlement mechanism in international law.[1240]

1236 However, in one instance ("*by giving the [UN] legal capacity and privileges and immunities in the territory of each of its Members*", *id.*, p. 179/9), the term capacity is apparently used in a broader sense.

1237 Similarly, though not related to this opinion, Sands & Klein, pp. 472–474 ("*specific* capacities *have sometimes been inferred from the recognition of personality*" and "*[the] difference between the attribution of personality, on the one hand, and of specific capacities, on the other,...*") (emphasis in original).

1238 This might be concluded from the phrase in which the Court equated "*rights which it is entitled to ask them to respect*" with the UN possessing "*international personality*" (*id.*, p. 178/8). It would mean that the 'and' is to be read as a further clarification rather than an additional element.

1239 Admittedly, it is possible to read the Court's inquiry on this point as only concerning the "kind *of international claim*" in question (*id.*, p. 179/9 *in fine*, emphasis added). However, the Court's argumentation and conclusion do not seem to be limited to a particular kind of claim (*id.*, p. 180/10: "*the functions of the UN] ... could not be effectively discharged if they involved the concurrent action ... of [58] Foreign Offices, and the Court concludes that the Members have endowed the [UN] with the capacity to bring international claims when necessitated by the discharge of its functions*"). Compare Sands & Klein, pp. 472–473, apparently viewing the Court as having inferred the right to bring an international claim from the personality. M. Rama-Montaldo, 'International Legal Personality and Implied Powers of International Organizations', 44 *B.Y.I.L.* 1970, pp. 124–131 also convincingly makes the latter argument, adding that only the Court's inquiry into the kind of claim related to the UN's specific functions. It would therefore appear that the Court saw the right to bring a claim as a consequence of international legal personality, and the right to bring this specific kind of claim as specifically linked to the UN's functions.

1240 Malanczuk, p. 93, rightly notes that the ICJ only treated the claims aspect in the abstract since the UN could not enforce its claim before the ICJ (nor, one might add, elsewhere).

Thus all in all, this opinion does not shed that much light on the notions of international personality and a subject of international law and leaves open two possibilities to define these two concepts, and even three if they are not identical:[1241] one that is limited to the capacity to possess rights and duties under international law[1242] and one also requiring the capacity to bring a claim to enforce such rights.[1243] It is therefore not surprising that both definitions can be found in the literature.[1244]

For the purpose of this book, namely determining the key rights and duties of an international organization under international law, and more specifically those of the EU in the area of the ESDP, the discussion is of little relevance as the focus

---

1241 Some scholars use the terms interchangeably, e.g. Bossuyt & Wouters, p. 177; Malanczuk, p. 91; Schermers & Blokker, p. 985 note 3; I. Seidl-Hohenveldern & G. Loibl, *Das Recht der Internationalen Organisationen einschlieblich der Supranationalen Gemeinschaften,* Cologne, Carl Heymanns, 1992 (6th ed.), pp. 35, 102 and 107 and Shaw, pp. 175–177 (who immediately jumps to legal personality in a chapter entitled 'the subjects of international law', thus apparently equating the two notions). In contrast, the American Law Institute's *Restatement of the Foreign Relations Law of the United States* (St. Paul, American Law Institute Publishers, 1990 (3rd ed.; student ed.), introductory note to Part II ('Persons in International Law'), p. 70), makes a distinction and regards subject as possibly having more limited implications. A. Leenen, *Gemeenschapsrecht en volkenrecht*, Deventer/'s-Gravenhage, Kluwer/TMC Asser Institute, 1984, pp. 10–12 also makes a distinction. C. Brölmann, *supra* note 1225, p. 88 notes that although commonly used interchangeably, more extensive definitions appear to use different meanings. D. Feldman, 'International Personality', 191 *Rec. Cours* 1985-II, pp. 351–352 records different views on whether the two notions differ or not. P. Pescatore, 'Les relations extérieures des communautés européennes: contribution à la doctrine de la personnalité des organisations internationales', 103 *Rec. Cours* 1961-II, pp. 29–32 also distinguishes between the two notions. I will distinguish both notions; see *infra* further down this section.

1242 E.g. Malanczuk, p. 91 ("*a capacity to enter into legal relations and to have legal rights and duties*"; though see *infra* on this first element) and Sands & Klein, p. 473 ("*international legal personality simply means that the entity is a subject of international law and that it is capable of possessing international rights and duties*"). See also Klabbers, p. 42 ("*subjects of international law ... in accordance with the standard definition of 'subject', ... are deemed capable of independently bearing rights and obligations under international law*"). However, this author subsequently speaks of conflation between subjects and international personality, stating that the latter is conferred by a legal system and the former is an academic label (in the sense of a subject of legal study). While 'subject' may sometimes be used in that sense (notably by those who refer to acting on an international plane generally rather than in international legal relations; see, e.g. the definition by Greig cited in A. Leenen, *supra* note 1241, p. 12: "*an international person is an entity having the power of independent action on the international plane*" – see *infra* note 1250), this appears to be less the case in recent writings on legal personality.

1243 E.g. Brownlie, p. 57 ("*A subject of law is an entity capable of possessing international rights and duties and having the capacity to maintain its rights by bringing international claims*"), though noting that the definition is somewhat circular as the *indicia* referred to depend upon the existence of a legal person, and Bossuyt & Wouters, p. 177 ("*de bekwaamheid hebben drager van internationaalrechtelijke rechten en plichten te zijn en onder het international recht een vordering kunnen instellen tot vrijwaring van [zijn] rechten*").

1244 See, e.g. Shaw, p. 176, himself submitting that there is no fixed definition.

will be on substantive rights and duties and not on their enforcement. Nevertheless, I will define a *subject of international law* as an entity possessing rights and/or duties directly under international law.[1245] I will use a different definition for *international legal personality*, namely the ability to possess rights and duties directly under international law *and to exercise proper powers on the international plane and/or enter into international legal relations*,[1246] the key

1245 Similarly J. Barberis, 'Nouvelles questions concernant la personnalité juridique internationale', 179 *Rec. Cours* 1983-I, pp. 161–170; G. Gaja, *First Report on the Responsibility of International Organisations*, UN Doc. A/CN.4/532, 27 March 2003, §15, p. 8 ("*an entity has to be regarded as a subject of international law even if only a single obligation is imposed on it under international law*"); H. Krück, *Völkerrechtliche Verträge im Recht de Europäischen Gemeinschaften*, Berlin, Springer, 1977, p. 8, in respect of *Völkerrechtsfähigkeit* (equated below to general international legal capacity, see *infra* note 1251) and M. Rama-Montaldo, *supra* note 1239, pp. 137–138. See also the *Restatement of the Foreign Relations Law of the United States* (*supra* note 1241), introductory note to Part II ('Persons in International Law'), p. 70. Compare P. Pescatore, *supra* note 1241, pp. 29–32, who regards subjects as referring only to being the addressee of a specific rule. Compare also C. Dominicé, 'La personnalité juridique dans le système des droits de gens', in J. Makarczyk (ed.), *Theory of International Law at the Threshold of the 21st Century: Essays in Honour of Krzysztof Skubiszewski*, The Hague, Kluwer Law International, 1996, p. 154, who distinguishes between being the addressee of rules of international law and being a subject of international law, arguing that the latter only comes about following the rules set out by international law. For a recent extensive discussion on subjects of international law, see Société Française pour le Droit International (ed.), *Colloque du Mans. Le sujet en droit international*, Paris, Pdeone, 2005.

1246 This is inspired by H. Kelsen, *The Law of the United Nations*, New York, Praeger, 1951, p. 329 ("*Juridical personality means the capacity of being a subject of legal duties and rights, of performing legal transactions and of suing and being sued at law*"); MALANCZUK, p. 91 ("*a capacity to enter into legal relations and to have legal rights and duties*"); M. Rama-Montaldo, *supra* note 1239, pp. 131–139, especially p. 137 ("*the capacity to enjoy international rights and duties and be considered a distinct entity able to create and extinguish legal relationships within [the international] legal order*"); I. Seidl-Hohenveldern & G. Loibl, *supra* note 1241, pp. 2–7 (noting as an element the (revocable) renunciation by the founding entities of the exercise of certain sovereign rights and their replacement by the exercise of similar rights by the organizations: "*Die Partner ... verzichten – ... nicht unwiderruflich – auf die Ausübung souveräner Rechte, über die sie ... verfügen können, wobei an deren Stelle gleichartige Rechte des von Ihnen geschaffenen Gebildes treten*") and C. Trüe, 'Rechtspersönlichkeit der Europäischen Union nach dem Vertragsänderungen von Amsterdam: Wer handlt in GASP und PJZ', 3 *Z. Eur. S.* 2000, p. 159 (identifying "*Kompetenzen zu rechtlich verbindlichem Handeln nach innen und/oder nach außen*" as sufficient). See also A. Leenen, *supra* note 1241, pp. 10–12 ("*het vermogen, om zelfstandig in het internationale rechtsverkeer zekere functies of bevoegdheden uit te oefenen*") and J. de Zwaan, 'The Legal Personality of the European Communities and the European Union', 30 *N.Y.I.L.* 1999, p. 77. Exercising *powers* must be distinguished from exercising *rights* in that the contents of the latter are fixed. C. Brölmann, *supra* note 1225, p. 92 correctly points out that an examination of international organizations within the positive law paradigm has to give a central place to legal personality because it is usually coupled with the ability to perform juristic acts. Compare P. Pescatore, *supra* note 1241, pp. 29–32, who requires more than just being the addressee of rights and obligations and adds competences, functions or powers but sees this as broader than participating in norm creation, and F. Seyersted, *supra* note 1229, pp. 28–29, 46–47 and 58–61, who lists the performance of sovereign and/or international acts as a criterion for being an international organization (entailing international legal personality) but considers that it results from distinction and additional element being that an entity with international legal personality may, within its powers, to some extent create new international obligations and rights (though not necessarily new *law*).[1247] This is closely related to decision-making (as an internal manifestation thereof) and treaty-making capacity (as an external manifestation thereof) and especially the latter will be discussed more extensively below.[1248] I exclude the specific requirement of the capacity to make an international claim as a constitutive element because, as noted above, I do not find it very clear or helpful in light of the freedom of choice of how to bring such claims and the absence of a general compulsory dispute settlement mechanism.[1249] I will not use the term *international person* as it seems to be used either as a synonym for international legal person or in a less legal sense.[1250] I will avoid as much as possible the term *international legal capacity* in general, which probably corresponds to 'international legal personality' rather than 'subject of international law'[1251] and will rather reserve *legal capacity*

having distinct organs that act on behalf of the organization and is therefore superfluous. For P.R. Menon, 'The Legal Personality of International Organizations', 4 *Sri Lanka Journal of International Law* 1992, p. 93, the capacity to enter into legal relations with other legal persons is an essential condition *for* being a *subject* of international law. Compare generally D. Feldman, *supra* note 1241, pp. 351–362.

1247 See also R. Gosalbo Bono, 'Some Reflections on the CFSP Legal Order', 43 *C.M.L. Rev.* 2006, p. 354, who seems to define international legal personality as "*the capacity ... to create rights and obligations on the international scene*".

1248 While individuals, companies and NGOs are, or may be, subjects of international law with rights and duties and, when specifically provided for, even a right to bring an international claim (especially before international human rights bodies, albeit normally only after exhausting 'local remedies') or the capacity to be held internationally responsible (in particular for individuals before international tribunals and companies in competition cases before EC bodies – albeit, as noted by O. Elias, 'General International Law in the European Court of Justice: from Hypothesis to Reality?', 31 *N.Y.I.L.* 2000, p. 31, that even there they are granted a less privileged postition than the EU institutions and the Member States), the international legal order has not given them the power to create new international rights and obligations, e.g. by concluding binding agreements under international law. Therefore they are not international legal persons in the sense defined here.

1249 However, I will argue below (Section E.2 of this chapter) that this capacity is inherent in any international organization having international legal personality. The difference is that I regard it as a *consequence* rather than a *constitutive element.*

1250 See, e.g. the remark by Klabbers discussed *supra* note 1242 and the definition by Greig, cited in A. Leenen, *supra* note 1241, p. 12: "*an international person is an entity having the power of independent action on the international plane*". Regardless of whether it was meant to be understood in a less legal way, it is submitted that acting on the international plane is to be broadly phrased and may cover behaviour on the international scene that has nothing to do with international law (e.g. a coalition of prominent people and/or NGOs may champion a given cause at the international level but purely on the political field, for instance by campaigning for a ban on cluster bombs).

1251 Some authors seem to use the terms interchangeably; see, e.g. Schermers & Blokker, §1569, p. 991, first two phrases. For an example of an apparently interchangeable use in treaties, compare Article X of the Paris Protocol (*infra* note 1413, in English 'juridical personality' but in French 'la capacité juridique') with Article IV of the Ottawa Convention (*infra* note 1415, for use in relation to specific rights such as treaty-making capacity,[1252] which, in turn, should be distinguished from *material competences* that relate to subject matter competence.[1253] In German doctrine, there is also a term used for the ability of an entity to itself *exercise* its own international rights, namely *völkerrechtliche Handlungsfähigkeit*.[1254] As there does not appear to be an easy English equivalent (except perhaps capacity to act or exercise rights) and the concept may be relevant to international organizations,[1255] I will use a description of the term when necessary.

---

in English 'juridical personality' and in French 'la personnalité juridique') despite the fact that no differences in meaning can be discerned (*infra*, Section E.3.ii of this chapter; compare P. Weckel, 'Le statut des capacités militaires européennes', in C. Tomuschat & J.A. Frowein (eds.), *Rechtsprobleme einer europäischen Sicherheits- und Verteidigungspolitik*, Heidelberg, Müller, 1997, pp. 47–48). Compare also the use of both terms in respect of EC agencies as discussed in G. Schusterschitz, 'European Agencies as Subjects of International Law', 1 *I.O.L.R.* 2004, pp. 168 and 171. Compare at the domestic level the Irish Diplomatic Relations and Immunities Act 1967 (available online at www.irishstatutebook.ie/1967/en/act/pub/0008/index.html), section 41 (*"An organisation to which this Part applies shall have the legal capacity of a body corporate"*). The German term 'Völkerrechtsfähigkeit' would seem to best correspond to 'international legal capacity' in a general sense: see H.-H. Nöll, *supra* note 1234, p. 33 and H. Krück, *supra* note 1245, p. 7 (*"Völkerrechtsfähigkeit bedeuted ganz allgemein die Fähigkeit, Träger völkerrechtlicher Rechte und Zuordnungsobjekt völkerrechtlicher Pflichten zu sein, bzw. die Fähigkeit, rechtlich an den internationalen Beziehungen teilzunehmen"*).

1252 For a discussion of the difference between capacities and personality, see also Wessel, pp. 245–251.

1253 See, e.g. P. Bekker, *supra* note 1224, pp. 63–93, especially pp. 63 and 75; C. Brölmann, *supra* note 1225, pp. 117–121 (making a further distinction between subject matter competence and division of competences between organs or organs and Member States); Wessel, pp. 245–251 (qualifying capacity as a general competence that exists only in relation to specific attributed competences) and R.A. Wessel, 'De Europese Unie in de internationale rechtsorde', in NVIR (ed.), *De plaats van de Europese Unie in het veranderende bestel van de volkenrechtelijke organisatie. Preadvies* (123 Mededelingen van de NVIR), The Hague, TMC Asser Press, 2001, pp. 15–17. F. Seyersted, *supra* note 1229, pp. 30–31 does not use these terms but nevertheless implicitly seems to make the same distinction by writing that restrictions in constitutent instruments *"usually do not preclude the performance of specific types of legal acts, but the performance of any acts for the purposes other than those authorised"*). For the relevance of this distinction, see, e.g. *infra* notes 1349 and 1386 and the accompanying text.

1254 H. Krück, *supra* note 1245, p. 8. See also K. Ipsen *et al.*, *Völkerrecht*, München, CH Beck, 2004 (5th ed.), p. 58.

1255 For instance, where the conclusion of an agreement on a certain subject matter is (in whole or in part) within the power of the EC as a matter of EC law but the agreement is only open to States and the EC therefore cannot become a party to it for external reasons, it can authorize its Member States to become parties in its interest. See, e.g. ECJ, *Opinion 2/91*, 19 March 1993, §5 of the Court's reasoning (*"although, under the ILO Constitution, the Community cannot itself conclude Convention No 170, its external competence may, if necessary, be exercised through the medium of the Member States acting jointly in the Community's interest"*) and Council Decision of 2 March 2004 authorising the Member States to sign, ratify or accede to, in the interest of the European Community, the Protocol of 2003 to the International Convention on the Establishment of an International Fund for Compensation for Oil Pollution Damage, 1992, and authorising Austria and Luxembourg, in the interest of the European Community, to accede to the underlying instruments (2004/246/EC), *O.J. L* 78,

For the purpose of this book, the key notion is therefore international organizations as subjects of international law. However, the international legal personality of international organizations is also relevant inasmuch as it relates to their capacity to enter into international agreements and thereby accept international obligations. Moreover, as the ESDP involves a number of other actors, both third States and international organizations, and is focused on operating outside the Union, the international legal personality is certainly relevant. In the remainder of this section, I will address international organizations as subjects of international law (2), deal with the OSCE as an alleged political entity (3), confirm that international organizations may possess international legal personality, including by implicit grant (4), analyze the contents of this concept, including treaty-making capacity (5) as well as the question of its objective or relative reach (6) and draw some preliminary conclusions (7).

B. INTERNATIONAL ORGANIZATIONS AS SUBJECTS OF INTERNATIONAL LAW

Having defined a subject of international law, I will now analyze when international organizations are such subjects. It suffices that an organization has been directly granted some rights or duties under international law, even if it is only in relation to its Member States or its own staff. This will easily be met: almost all organizations have at least some rights and duties under their constitutive instrument and related instruments, which usually are treaties, e.g. privileges and immunities,[1256] the right to receive financial contributions, the duty to convene meetings of organs at set times or occasions and the duty to respect certain rules in relation to the hiring and treatment of staff.

International organizations that may not have any rights and duties under international law can mostly be divided into two categories: those established on the basis of non-legal international commitments[1257] and those who only act on behalf of the Member States and do not possess any proper rights and duties. The latter is possible but exceptional, though it has been alleged of the EU and is perhaps to some extent the case for the Eurocorps. It will be examined below in

16 March 2004, p. 22. See generally I. MacLeod, I.D. Henry & S. Huett, *The External Relations of the European Communities*, Oxford, Clarendon Press, 1996, pp. 236–237.

1256 Though it is feasible that these operate only at the domestic level, as is generally the case for the OSCE (see *infra*, Section C of this chapter), they are usually granted in a treaty and are then rights under international law. See the *Reparations opinion*, p. 179/9.

1257 That this is possible results from my definition of international organizations, *supra*, introduction to Part II.

Chapter 6 (and for the Eurocorps in Section E.3.iii of this Chapter). The issue of non-legal commitments has arisen especially in respect of the OSCE, which I will therefore examine in some detail in the next section.

C. THE OSCE: NOT MERELY POLITICAL IN NATURE?

On the one hand, the CSCE gradually developed from a conference with a follow-up mechanism to an increasingly institutionalized organization,[1258] a change reflected in it being renamed OSCE, and has performed a number of acts, including the conclusion of international agreements,[1259] that suggest is has international legal personality. On the other hand, it is not based on legally binding agreements (even if some seem to contest this)[1260] and the question of its

---

1258 See generally C. Bertrand, 'La nature juridique de l'organisation pour la sécurité et la coopération en Europe (OSCE)', 102 *R.G.D.I.P.* 1998, pp. 365–406; J. Bortloff, *Die Organisation für Sicherheit und Zusammenarbeit in Europa: eine völkerrechtliche Bestandsaufnahme*, Berlin, Duncker & Humblot, 1996; E. Decaux, 'La CSCE au lendemain du Conseil de Rome: un bilan de la transition institutionnelle', 5 *E.J.I.L.* 1994, pp. 267–284; I.F. Dekker & R.A. Wessel, 'Van CVSE naar OVSE. De sluipende institutionalisering en onvermijdelijke juridisering van een internationale conferentie', 31 *Vrede en Veiligheid* 2002, pp. 425–438; M. Sapiro, 'Current Developments. Changing the CSCE into the OSCE: Legal Aspects of a Political Transformation', 89 *A.J.I.L.* 1995, pp. 631–637; T. Schweisfurth, 'Die juristische Mutation der KSZE: eine internationale Organisation in statu nascendi', in U. Beyerlin (ed.), *Recht zwischen Umbruch und Bewahrung*, Berlin, Springer, 1995, pp. 213–228; S. Trifunovska, *Organization for Security and Co-operation in Europe (OSCE)*, in J. Wouters (ed.) *International Encyclopaedia of Laws. Intergovernmental Organizations*, The Hague, Kluwer Law International, 2006, pp. 23–31 and M. Wenig, 'Der völkerrechtliche Status der OSZE: gegenwärtiger Stand und Perspektiven', 3 *OSZE-Jahrbuch* 1997, pp. 393–411.

1259 Apart from various Memorandums of Understanding, of which the legal nature is generally more debatable, these include some agreements that at the very least strongly look like legally binding treaties; see notably an agreement with Denmark on the status of the OSCE Parliamentary Assembly and an agreement with the FRY on the status of the Kosovo Verification Mission (*infra*, notes 1270 and 1290 and the accompanying text).

1260 CSCE and OSCE documents, with the exception of a few treaties, are deemed to be only political in nature and not legally binding. For instance, the 1975 Helsinki Final act explicitly stated that "*The ... text of this Final Act ... is not eligible for registration under Article 102 of the Charter of the United Nations*" (see the final sections of the Final Act) a formula that has been repeated consistently, for instance in the final section of the 1990 Charter of Paris for a new Europe and of the 1994 Budapest Summit Declaration (the summit which transformed the CSCE into the OSCE, see §3 of this Declaration). Likewise, the 3 December 1994 Code of Conduct on Politico-Military Aspects of Security contains a provision (section X, §39) stating "*The provisions adopted in this Code of Conduct are politically binding. Accordingly, this Code is not eligible for registration under Article 102 of the [UN] Charter*" (available online at www1.osce.org/documents/fsc/1994/12/4270_en.pdf). This nature seems to be contested by I. Dekker & R. Wessel, *supra* note 1258, pp. 430–431. However, it is submitted that one must accept that States occasionally chose to adopt decisions which they regard as politically binding but not legally binding. I will come back on this point *infra*, Section C.3 of this chapter. For a more legal status has always been the subject of debate and suggests that its Participating States have not intended to accord it international legal personality.[1261]

1. LEGAL CAPACITIES, PRIVILEGES AND IMMUNITIES

In a document annexed to the 1990 Charter of Paris, it was stated that "*The host countries undertake to enable the institutions to function fully and enter into contractual and financial obligations and to accord them appropriate diplomatic status*" and that "*Staff will be accredited by the seconding State to the host country where they will enjoy full diplomatic status*".[1262] Thus there was a political commitment that host States should grant adequate legal capacities in domestic law and that staff would have diplomatic status through accreditation to the host State (rather than to the OSCE proper). The issue of legal status was subsequently debated and led to a Decision at the 1993 Rome Ministerial Meeting stating that:

> The Ministers have taken note with appreciation of the report of the ad hoc Group of Legal and Other Experts. The Ministers adopted a decision on legal capacity and privileges and immunities that recommends implementation of the following three basic elements (CSCE/4-C/Dec.2):
>
> - The CSCE participating States will, subject to their constitutional, legislative and related requirements, confer legal capacity on CSCE institutions in accordance with the provisions adopted by the Ministers;
> - The CSCE participating States will, subject to their constitutional, legislative and related requirements, confer privileges and immunities on CSCE institutions, permanent missions of the participating States, representatives of participating States, CSCE officials and members of CSCE missions in accordance with the provisions adopted by the Ministers; ….[1263]

---

extensive discussion, see J. Bortloff, *supra* note 1258, pp. 322–369; U. Fastenrath, 'The Legal Significance of CSCE/OSCE Documents', 1/2 *OSCE Yearbook*, 1995/96, pp. 411–427 = 'Rechtliche Bedeutung der KSZE/OSZE-Dokumente', 2 *OSZE-Jahrbuch* 1996, pp. 447–464 and S. Trifunovska, *supra* note 1258, pp. 71–72. Specifically on the 1975 Helsinki Final Act, see T. Schweisfurth, 'Zur Frage der Rechtsnatur, Verbindlichkeit und völkerrechtlichen Relevanz der KSZE-Schlußakte. Ein Diskussionsbeitrag zum Phänomen der außerrechtlichen (non-legal) zwischenstaatlichen Abmachung', 36 *Z.a.ö.R.V.* 1976, pp. 681–726. For a critical view, see J. Klabbers, *supra* note 1232, pp. 409–412.

1261 See generally S. Trifunovska, *supra* note 1258, pp. 61–63.

1262 Supplementary document to give effect to certain provisions contained in the Charter of Paris for a New Europe, section H. Procedures and modalities concerning CSCE Institutions, §§11 and 9.

1263 30 November and 1 December 1993, Decision VII (CSCE Structures and operations), §11 (available online at www.osce.org/documents/mcs/1993/11/4165_en.pdf).

The decision referred to *inter alia* states that:

> 5. The Ministers agreed on the usefulness of *legal capacity* being granted to the CSCE institutions *in the territories of all the CSCE participating States*, in particular the capacity to contract, to acquire and dispose of movable and immovable property, and to institute and participate in legal proceedings.
> 6. The Ministers further agreed that it was appropriate that certain *privileges and immunities* be granted to the CSCE institutions and their officers and staffs, as well as to the Secretary General of the CSCE and the High Commissioner on National Minorities and their staffs, members of CSCE missions and the representatives of the participating States to the extent necessary to the exercise of their duties.
> 7. In most participating States, however, the competence to make rules concerning the legal status of the CSCE institutions and privileges and immunities rests with the legislature.
> 8. In view of these considerations and in order to assist in harmonizing the rules to be applied, the Ministers adopted the provisions set out in Annex 1. They *recommend* that participating States implement these provisions, subject to their constitutional and related requirements.
>
> Annex 11. PROVISIONS CONCERNING THE LEGAL CAPACITY OF THE CSCE INSTITUTIONS AND PRIVILEGES AND IMMUNITIES
>
> LEGAL CAPACITY OF THE CSCE INSTITUTIONS
>
> 1. The CSCE participating States will, subject to their constitutional, legislative and related requirements, confer such legal capacity as is necessary for the exercise of their functions, and in particular the capacity to contract, to acquire and dispose of movable and immovable property, and to institute and participate in legal proceedings, on the following CSCE institutions:
>
> - The CSCE Secretariat,
> - The Office for Democratic Institutions and Human Rights (ODIHR),
> - Any other CSCE institution determined by the CSCE Council.
>
> PRIVILEGES AND IMMUNITIES
>
> General
> 2. The CSCE participating States will, subject to their constitutional, legislative and related requirements, confer the privileges and immunities as set out in paragraphs 4–16 below.
> 3. Privileges and immunities will be accorded to the CSCE institutions in the interests of those institutions. Immunity may be waived by the Secretary General of the CSCE in consultation with the Chairman-in-Office.
> Privileges and immunities will be accorded to individuals not for the personal benefit of the individuals concerned, but in order to safeguard the independent exercise of their functions. Immunity will be waived in any case where the immunity would

impede the course of justice and can be waived without prejudice to the purpose for which the immunity is accorded. Decision to waive immunity will be taken:

- with respect to officers and staff of the CSCE institutions and to members of CSCE missions, by the Secretary General of the CSCE in consultation with the Chairman-in-Office;
- with respect to the Secretary General and the High Commissioner on National Minorities, by the Chairman-in-Office.
- The Government concerned may waive immunity with respect to its representatives.[1264]

The document then sets out in some detail the scope of the privileges and immunities to be accorded. Thus once again there only was a political decision, even framed merely as a recommendation, to grant 'legal capacity' in the domestic law of Participating States as well as privileges and immunities. Thus, instead of the normal mechanism whereby privileges and immunities and legal status are imposed under international law and then merely implemented in the domestic legal orders, here the legal obligation is found exclusively in the domestic legal order. Pursuant to this decision, several Participating States adopted national legislation according to the status set out.[1265] In at least some cases, the 'legal capacities' were regarded as being equivalent to legal personality in domestic law.[1266] An exception to this mechanism is the OSCE Court of

1264 CSCE/4-C/Dec.2, reproduced in CSCE, *From Rome to Budapest. 1993–1994, CSCE Decision Reference Manual*, CSCE, *s.l.*, *s.d.*, pp. 37–42; available online as Annex A to attachment 1 to the Annex to Doc. PC.DEC/383 of 26 November 2000 at www.osce.org/documents/pc/2000/11/2163_en.pdf (emphasis added).

1265 For an overview in 2000, see OSCE Legal Capacity and on Privileges and Immunities, section I.1, attachment 1 to the Annex to PC.DEC/383 of 26 November 2000 (available online at www.osce.org/documents/pc/2000/11/2163_en.pdf). For the Netherlands, see the Wet van 31 oktober 2002, houdende bepalingen inzake rechtspersoonlijkheid, privileges en immuniteiten van de Hoge Commissaris inzake Nationale Minderheden (*Wet HCNM*), 31 October 2002, *Staatsblad van het Koninkrijk der Nederlanden* 2002, No. 580 (available online at www.st-ab.nl/wetten/0528_Wet_HCNM.htm), entered into force on 1 January 2003 (see Besluit van 18 november 2002, houdende vaststelling van het tijdstip van inwerkingtreding van de Wet HCNM, *Staatsblad van het Koninkrijk der Nederlanden*, 5 December 2002, No. 581, available online at https://zoek.officielebekendmakingen.nl/stb-2002-581.pdf). The explanatory note to the Dutch Bill also included an overview of the status in other OSCE host States in 2003; see Wet HCNM, Memorie van Toelichting, *Tweede Kamer, vergaderjaar 1999–2000, 27 194, nr. 3*, section 1.6 (available online at https://zoek.officielebekendmakingen.nl/kst-27194-3.pdf). However, as noted in Chapter 7.B.1, in some cases the immunities granted vary from those set out in the decision.

1266 Namely in the Netherlands (see the Wet HCNM, *supra* previous note, Article 2(1)) and in Austria (see I. Seidl-Hohenveldern, *supra* note 1225, p. 239 and Bundesgesetz über die Rechtsstellung von Einrichtungen der KSZE in Österreich, *Bundesgesetzblatt* No. 511/1993, available online at www.ris.bka.gv.at/Dokumente/BgblPdf/1993_511_0/1993_511_0.pdf and at www.ena.lu/bundesgesetz_rechtsstellung_einrichtungen_ksze_osterreich_30_juli_1993-030006812.html, §1(1), amended in 1995 to take into account the name change but without

Conciliation and Arbitration, which was established by one of the few legally binding conventions between (some) OSCE Participating States. Its Article 6 directly provides that "*The conciliators, the arbitrators, the Registrar and the agents and counsel of the parties to a dispute shall enjoy, while performing their functions in the territory of the States parties to this Convention, the privileges and immunities accorded to persons connected with the International Court of Justice*".[1267]

2. FROM CSCE TO OSCE

The change from CSCE to OSCE apparently did not change the (non-)legal regime, as it was declared in Budapest that "*The change in name from CSCE to OSCE alters neither the character commitments nor the status of the CSCE and its institutions*", albeit also that "*The CSCE will review implementation of the Rome Decision on Legal Capacity Immunities and explore if necessary the possibility of further arrangements. Participating States will, furthermore, examine possible ways of incorporating into national legislation and, where appropriate, of concluding treaties*".[1268] However, it is submitted that the OSCE is at least since then (regarded as) an international organization, albeit one regarded by most States as lacking (international) legal personality (but see *infra*, subsection 4).[1269]

---

substantive amendments). On the distinction between legal capacity and legal personality, see *supra*, Section A of this chapter.

1267 Convention on Conciliation and Arbitration within the CSCE, Stockholm, 15 December 1992, which entered into force on 5 December 19994 (see generally www.osce.org/cca).

1268 CSCE Summit, 5–6 December 1994, Budapest Decision I. Strengthening the CSCE (available online at www.osce.org/documents/mcs/1994/12/4048_en.pdf), §29. C. Bertrand, *supra* note 1258, p. 378 interprets the latter phrase as a possible avenue to enable the OSCE to sign agreements, but it may also refer to the possibility of the Participating States signing an agreement.

1269 See, e.g. M. Sapiro, *supra* note 1258, pp. 631–637 (writing especially from a US perspective) and the view of the Dutch government expressed in a further explanation following the advice of the *Raad Van State* on the Bill concerning the HCNM (Wet HCNM, Advies Raad van State en Nader Rapport, *Tweede Kamer, vergaderjaar 1999–2000, 27 194, A*, §3.a, available online at https://zoek.officielebekendmakingen.nl/kst-27194-A.pdf). But see *Common Purpose, Towards a More Effective OSCE, Final Report and Recommendations of the Panel of Eminent Persons On Strengthening the Effectiveness of the OSCE*, 25 June 2005 (available online at www.osce.org/documents/cio/2005/06/15432_en.pdf), sections 3.1, §§28 ("*The OSCE's development from a conference to a full-fledged international organisation must now be completed, finally making "participating States" into "member States"*") and 30(a) ("*Participating States should devise a concise Statute or Charter of the OSCE containing its basic goals, principles and commitments, as well as the structure of its main decision-making bodies. This would help the OSCE to become a full-scale regional organisation*"), which suggest that it is not yet a fully-fledged international organization. Compare also the ILC's commentary to its provisional draft Article 2 on the responsibility of international organizations (*Report of the International Law Commission on the Work of its fifty-fifth*

However, it must be noted that Denmark does appear to consider that the OCSE has international legal personality and has concluded an international agreement with the OSCE Parliamentary Assembly on the legal status of the latter.[1270]

Although the issue of the legal status has been under discussion since the transition to OSCE, hardly any progress has been achieved. The most extensive analysis that seems to have been undertaken is an inconclusive 2000 report endorsed by the Permanent Council, which essentially notes that during the work of the group "*there was a growing awareness among delegations that something ought to be done, but opinions differed as to the direction to be chosen. A first informal discussion of possible options ... showed an overwhelming majority in favour of a convention on the legal personality and the privileges and immunities of the OSCE. The core issue is that the OSCE does not enjoy the legal status of an*

Session, UN Doc. A/58/10, 2003, pp. 39–40): "*In other cases, although an implicit agreement may be held to exist, member States insisted that there was no treaty concluded to that effect, as for example in respect of the [OSCE]*". For a more extensive analysis, see C. Bertrand, *supra* note 1258, pp. 365–406 (who concludes that the OSCE clearly is an international organization with legal personality (*id*, p. 381: "*Au total donc, l'effectivité institutionnelle de l'OSCE ne fait aucun doute: ... status et personnalité juridique interne et internationale*") but struggles with the (perceived) requirement in (French) doctrine that such an organization be established by treaty) and J. Bortloff, *supra* note 1258, pp. 370–402 (concluding that the OCSE is an international organization but without international legal personality). Compare E. Decaux, *supra* note 1258, pp. 267–284 (especially at p. 269, writing before Budapest that "*La CSCE reste une 'non institution' mais une consolidation progressive de sa personnalité juridique est évidente, sur le plan extérieur, comme sur le plan interne*") and I.F. Dekker & R.A. Wessel, *supra* note 1258, pp. 425–438 (questioning whether the OSCE does not possess international legal personality despite Participating States' efforts to deny this). Somewhat surprisingly, SANDS & KLEIN, p. 201, consider that the OSCE is "*obviously able to undertake international legal commitments in its own name on the international plane*" (though without supporting this by evidence and in fact only listing one source questioning this). KLABBERS, pp. 11–12 and 338 seems undecided. A.S. Muller, *International Organizations and Their Host States: Aspects of Their Legal Relationship*, The Hague, Kluwer Law International, 1995, pp. 79–80 writes that for the OSCE "*some form of international legal personality has grown over the years*". Compare SCHERMERS & BLOKKER, §30 p. 23 and §1569, pp. 991–992. G. Hafner, *infra* note 1290, pp. 35–57, argues that the OCSE is not an international organization and does not possess international legal personality, as did T. Schweisfurth, *supra* note 1258, pp. 223–227 concerning the CSCE just before its change to OSCE. In contrast, I. Seidl-Hohenveldern, *supra* note 1225, pp. 229–239 argued that even the CSCE just before its transformation into the OCSE already was an international organization with international legal personality. M. Odello, 'The Organization for Security and Co-operation in Europe and European Security Law', in TRYBUS & WHITE, p. 308 does not take a position on this.

1270 Wet HCNM, Memorie van Toelichting, *supra* note 1265, section 1.6. Ironically, the Dutch government qualified this as the use of a fiction that the OSCE possesses international legal personality and stated that it would itself adopt the strict and formal legal criterion (*id.*, and Wet HCNM, Nota naar aanleiding van het verslag, *Tweede Kamer, vergaderjaar 1999–2000, 27 194, nr.* 6, pp. 1–3).

international organization".[1271] The latter proved a stumbling block also for the conclusion of bilateral agreements: "*In addition ... a majority of delegations pointed out the necessity that the OSCE be recognized as having the possibility of entering into bilateral arrangements with individual participating States in the context of the establishment of an OSCE Institution or Mission on their territories, particularly in order to be granted additional privileges and immunities. As this issue depends to some extent on the issue of the legal personality/capacity of the OSCE, it is also still open*".[1272] In 2003 the Chairmanship regretted "*that no progress has been made regarding the OSCE's legal capacity*" and "*while most of the drafting of a convention on privileges and immunities had been completed in previous years, the issue of the OSCE's legal capacity itself remain[ed] deadlocked on grounds of political principle*".[1273]

The issue was revived due to its inclusion in the 2005 *Final Report and Recommendations of the Panel of Eminent Persons on Strengthening the Effectiveness of the OSCE*, which stated that "*The OSCE's standing as an international organisation is handicapped by its lack of a legal personality. The lack of a clear status also affects OSCE personnel when stationed in crisis areas without the protection that diplomatic recognition would give them*" and recommended that "*Participating States agree on a convention recognising the OSCE's legal capacity and granting privileges and immunities to the OSCE and its officials. Such a convention would not diminish in any way the politically binding character of OSCE commitments*".[1274] In response, in December 2005, the Ministerial Council tasked the Permanent Council to continue to work on the basis of this report and report to the 2006 Ministerial Council on, *inter alia*, "*Examining the possibility of providing the OSCE with legal status and granting privileges and immunities, taking into consideration advice of legal experts*".[1275] However, it remains to be seen whether this will change anything.

1271 PC.DEC/383 of 26 November 2000 and annexes, §3 (available online at www.osce.org/documents/pc/2000/11/2163_en.pdf).

1272 *Id.*, §8. See also §4.

1273 Ministerial Meeting, Maastricht, 1 December 2003, Chairmanship's Report on Reform Issues, section 7 (Organizational reform and conclusion), final paragraph (available online at www1.osce.org/documents/mcs/2003/12/4175_en.pdf).

1274 *Supra* note 1269, section 3.1, §§29–30.

1275 Decision No. 17/05 Strengthening the Effectiveness of the OSCE, MC.DEC/17/05 of 6 December 2005, §1 (available online at www1.osce.org/documents/mcs/2005/12/18653_en.pdf).

3. NON-LEGAL OBLIGATIONS AND AGREEMENTS?

The discussion of the legal status of the OCSE raises a few points that are interesting from a more general perspective and also in relation to the EU's legal status. The first one is the proclaimed political nature of OSCE documents and commitments.[1276] This nature has been questioned by some, including in relation to the OSCE.[1277] Some critics rely *inter alia* on the ICJ's judgment in the case of the *Maritime Delimitation and Territorial Questions between Qatar and Bahrain (Qatar v. Bahrain)*.[1278] While it is true that the Court in this case held that "*The Court does not find it necessary to consider what might have been the intentions of the Foreign Minister of Bahrain or, for that matter, those of the Foreign Minister of Qatar*" (§27), it would appear from other instances in the judgment that this was not an absolute statement but rather one related to the specific facts of the case and especially the actual terms of the agreement. See, e.g. the Court's statements that "*In order to ascertain whether an agreement of that kind has been concluded, "the Court must have regard above all to its actual terms and to the particular circumstances in which it was drawn up*" [Aegean Sea Continental Shelf, Judgment, I.C.J. Reports 1978, *p. 39, para. 96*]" (§23) and that "*Nor is there anything in the material before the Court which would justify deducing ... that [Qatar] did not intend to conclude, and did not consider that it had concluded, an [international agreement]; nor could any such intention, even if shown to exist, prevail over the actual terms of the instrument in question*" (§29). Moreover, in this case, the commitment that was found to exist, namely to refer a dispute to the ICJ, can indeed hardly be regarded as not being of a legal nature.[1279] But most importantly, it is quite common in practice that States accept commitments that are political and not legal in nature[1280] and there is no objection to this in principle.[1281] For instance, it was recognized by the Institut de Droit

1276 See *supra* note 1260 and accompanying text. Compare, with regard to NATO, A. Bouter, 'Volkenrechtelijke binding van Nederland aan de inhoud van NAVO-besluiten', 34 *Internationale Spectator* 1980, pp. 292–296.

1277 See I. Dekker & R. Wessel, *supra* note 1258, pp. 430–431. The authors *inter alia* refer to J. Klabbers, *The Concept of Treaty in International Law*, The Hague, Kluwer Law International, 1996 and J. Klabbers, 'Qatar v. Bahrain: The Concept of "Treaty" in International Law', 33 *A.V.R.* 1995, pp. 361–376.

1278 1 July 1994, especially §§21–30. See also the two publications by J. Klabbers cited *supra* previous note.

1279 See also the arguments put forward by Aust, pp. 41–44, against Klabber's position.

1280 See also D. Verwey, *The European Community, the European Union and the Law of Treaties*, The Hague, TMC Asser Press, 2004, pp. 93–94 (noting that "*the purpose of [frequently used informal non treaty-instruments] is very clear, namely, the creation of a non-binding instrument, usually expressing a political position without the assumption of any legal obligations*").

1281 For a discussion, see also R. Müllerson, 'NATO Enlargement and Russia', 47 *I.C.L.Q.* 1998, pp. 197–201. See also A. Aust, 'The Theory and Practice of Informal International Instruments',

International, which stated in 1983 that "*Subject to [paragraphs 5 and 6], texts containing commitments which States that accepted them intended to be binding solely at the political level and which have all their effects at that level (hereafter referred to as "purely political commitments") do not constitute international texts of legal import in the mutual relations between their authors*".[1282] Indeed, also in the EPC but even within the framework of the EC and EU, it has been argued that a number of agreements and declarations have been political rather than legal in nature.[1283]

---

35 *I.C.L.Q.* 1986, pp. 804–806. J. Klabbers, 'The Undesirabilty of Soft Law', 67 *Nordic J.I.L.* 1998, pp. 381–391 makes an interesting criticism on the notion of 'soft law', arguing that there should be either law or non-law but not something in between. But see the defence of soft law by I. Seidl-Hohenveldern, *supra* note 1225, pp. 232–233 and P. Kooijmans, 'Some Thoughts on the Relation between Extra-legal Agreements and the Law-creating Process', in J. Makarczyk (ed.), *supra* note 22, pp. 425–437 (seeing a role for the borderland between legal and non-legal texts). However, whatever opinion one holds in this respect, it is different from objecting to non-law (W. Wengler, 'Die Wirkungen nichtrechtlicher Verträge zwischen Staaten', 22 *A.V.R.* 1984, p. 312 also distinguishes non-binding agreement from soft law).

1282 See the Resolution of the Institut de Droit International on International Texts of Legal Import in the Mutual Relations of their Authors and Texts Devoid of Such Import, adopted at its 1983 Cambridge session (available online at www.idi-iil.org/idiE/resolutionsE/1983_camb_02_en.PDF), §4. Paragraphs 5–6 essentially deal with countermeasures that remain within international law (i.e. presumably that do not rely on previous illegal conduct as a justification), peaceful settlement, good faith, estoppel and waiver of certain pleas in defence of requests for enforcement (e.g. domestic jurisdiction).

1283 See, e.g. R. Gosalbo Bono, *supra* note 1247, pp. 338 and 342 (on the EPC), pp. 360–361 (on European Council conclusions) and pp. 362–363 (on the Berlin Plus agreement, see also *supra* Chapter 2.C, note 210 and *infra* Section E.3.ii of this chapter, note 1423). See also on the discussion on the "Luxembourg compromise", e.g. A. Leenen, *supra* note 1241, pp. 240–241 and W. Meng, *Das Recht der Internationalen Organisationen – eine Entwicklungsstufe des Völkerrechts*, Baden-Baden, Nomos, 1979, pp. 106–108. An example in the framework of the EU is the European Union Code of Conduct on Arms Exports, adopted by the Council on 8 June 1998 (available online at www.consilium.europa.eu/uedocs/cmsUpload/08675r2en8.pdf) and the related Common Military List of the European Union (equipment covered by the European Union Code of Conduct on Arms Exports; latest version adopted by the Council on 10 March 2008, *O.J. C* 98, 18 April 2008, p. 1), which have the status of a political commitment (see the Council Declaration of 13 June 2000 in *O.J. C* 191, 8 July 2000, p. 1). This code of conduct was replaced by Council Common Position 2008/944/CFSP defining common rules governing the control of exports of military technology and equipment, *O.J. L* 335, 13 December 2008, p. 99 (see A.-S. Millet-Devalle, 'A propos de la position commune de l'Union européenne relative aux règles communes régissant le contrôle des exportations de technologie et d'équipements militaires du 8 décembre 2008', 113 *R.G.D.I.P.* 2009, pp. 95–112). This common position is regarded as a legally binding instrument (see, e.g. the 11 February 2009 letter by the Dutch Minister of Foreign Affairs to the Dutch parliament, *Kamerbrief over de aanvaarding van de EU-Gedragscode tot het EU-Gemeenschappelijk Standpunt m.b.t. het Wapenexportbeleid*, www.minbuza.nl/nl/Actueel/Kamerstukken/2009/02/Kamerbrief_over_de_aanvaarding_van_de_EU_Gedragscode_tot_het_EU_Gemeenschappelijk_Standpunt_m_b_t_het_Wapenexportbeleid). See also *infra*, Chapter 6.A on the discussion over the legal nature of certain EU acts and *infra*, Chapter 7.F.2.i, notes 1783–1785 and the accompanying text on the nature of the EU Charter of Fundamental Rights.

The practice on non-legal commitments is also reflected in the (widespread but not widely known) practice of concluding arrangements that are not regarded as legally binding,[1284] as is often the case with Memorandums of Understanding,[1285] although the name of the agreement is not

1284 For some examples of State views, see Commonwealth of Australia, *Review of the Treaty-Making Process*, August 1999 (available online at www.austlii.edu.au/au/other/dfat/reports/infokit.html#Heading692), §7.15 ("*instruments of less than treaty status [...] are often titled 'memoranda of understanding', 'arrangements' or 'declarations'. They [...] are not intended to be legally binding*") and the UK Foreign & Commonwealth Office Treaty Section, *Treaties and MOUs. Guidance on Practice and Procedures*, 2nd ed. (April 2000, revised May 2004, available online at www.fco.gov.uk/resources/en/pdf/pdf8/fco_pdf_treatymous), pp. 1–2 ("*An MOU records international "commitments", but in a form and with wording which expresses an intention that it is not to be legally binding ... The term "MOU" is short for Memorandum of Understanding, which is the most common name for non-legally binding instruments. (NB: Confusingly some treaties also have that name.)*" and "*It is becoming generally accepted international practice to show clearly by the form of the document and its terminology the intention either to create legally binding obligations, or not, i.e. either a treaty or an MOU*"). Long excerpts of a 27 April 1981 US State Department Regulation on the matter (codified in Part 181 of Chapter 22 of the Code of Federal Regulations (available online in enclosure 3 of the Department of Defense Directive 5530.3 of 11 June 1987 as amended, previously available online at www.dtic.mil/whs/directives/corres/html2/d55303x.htm); current version available onlineathttp://ecfr.gpoaccess.gov/cgi/t/text/text-idx?c=ecfr&tpl=/ecfrbrowse/Title22/22cfr181_main_02.tpl) are included in A. Aust, *supra* note 1281, pp. 797–800, who also briefly comments on Dutch and Israeli practice (*id.*, pp. 796–797). See also the 'Treaty Affairs' section of the US department of State's Office of the Legal Advisor website at www.state.gov/s/l/treaty/c175/ ("*Thus, statements of intent or documents of a political nature not intended to be legally binding are not covered by the Circular 175 procedure*"); www.state.gov/s/l/treaty/ ("*[The Office] ... reviews hundreds of non-binding instruments annually, to ensure that they do not contain binding language that would create legal obligations for the United States*") and www.state.gov/s/l/treaty/faqs/ ("*Why does the Office of Treaty Affairs have to review documents between governments that are not legally binding under international law? Governments frequently wish to record in writing the terms of an understanding or arrangement between them without, by so doing, creating obligations that would be binding under international law. The language, titles, and techniques used for this purpose vary considerably. While not binding under international law, a nonbinding instrument may carry significant moral or political weight. Such instruments are often used in our international relations to establish political commitments. When negotiating a nonbinding instrument, it must be confirmed that both/all sides understand that the instrument does not give rise to binding obligations under international law. ... In U.S. practice, certain terminology is used in the drafting of nonbinding documents to indicate that they are not binding international agreements. Generally, the provisions of a document should be cast as expressions of intent rather than as obligations*"). E. Barconcini, *infra* note 1285, p. 394 writes that "*La technique des 'non-binding administrative agreements' ... est bien connue et pratiquée par tous les Etats mebres [de l'Union européenne] et sa caractéristique est présisément l'absence d'intention ... d'assumer des liens juridiques internationaux*" and cites EU Doc. PESC/SEC/899 of 9 August 1996 as evidence.

1285 On such non-binding international agreements, see, e.g. Aust, pp. 17–18, 19–21 and especially 26–46, with further references; A. Aust, *supra* note 1281, pp. 878–812; P.-M. Eisemann, 'Le *gentlemen's agreement* comme source de droit international' 106 *J.D.I.* 1979, pp. 326–348 (concluding at p. 347 that such agreements create rights and obligations but do not give rise to direct international responsibility if breached); H. Hillgenberg, 'Soft Law im Völkerrecht', 1 *Z. Eur. S.* 1998, pp. 81–102 (accepting non-binding agreements outside international law); J. Klabbers, 'Informal Agreements in International Law: Towards a Theoretical Framework', 5 *F.Y.I.L.* 1994, pp. 267–387; F. Münch, 'Comments on the 1968 Draft Convention on the Law of decisive.[1286] An example of an MOU that was clearly not intended to be legally binding was the Estonian – Finnish – Norwegian – Swedish MOU on their EU Battle Group, which explicitly stated that "*This MOU does not constitute a treaty in accordance with the Vienna Convention on the Law of Treaties of 23 May 1969*".[1287] Such provisions are, among others, quite frequently included in the numerous agreements that are concluded between participants to multinational military operations, although they are mostly not made public and are little known outside the military (legal) community and foreign affairs ministries.

This brings us to the matter of MOUs and agreements concluded by the OSCE. As just argued, practice clearly supports that such agreements may be legally non-binding. Moreover, the conclusion of MOUs seems to be a common practice in the relations between international organizations.[1288] They also appear to be a

---

Treaties; Non-binding Agreements', 29 *Z.a.ö.R.V.* 1969, pp. 1–11 (accepting that agreements may be non binding but holding that the intent is only decisive if clearly expressed by all the parties); O. Schachter, 'Editorial Comment. The Twilight Existence of Nonbinding International Agreements', 71 *A.J.I.L.* 1977, pp. 296–304; J. Van Den Brandhof, 'Administratieve overeenkomsten in het internationaal publiekrecht', 61 *N.J.B.* 1986, pp. 1277–1282; W. Wengler, *supra* note 1281, pp. 306–327 (seeming to accept non-binding agreements and perceiving their increased popularity at the time at p. 313), and, in relation to the EC/EU, A.-P. Allo, 'Les accords administratifs entre l'Union européenne et les organisations internationales', in D. Dormoy (ed.), *L'Union européenne et les organisations internationales*, Brussels, Bruylant, 1997, pp. 56–67; E. Barconcini, 'La Cour de justice et le *treaty making power* de la Commission européenne depuis l'Accord de coopération dans l'application des régimes antitrust jusqu'à l'Accord sur les orientations en matière de coopération normative et de transparence', *R.D.U.E.* 2006, pp. 369–430 and D. Lopandic, 'Les memorandums d'entente: des instruments juridiques spécifiques de la politique étrangere et de sécurite de l'Union Europeenne: le cas de l'ex-Yougoslavie', No. 392 *R.M.C.U.E.* 1995, pp. 557–562.

1286 See Article 2(1)a 1969 VCLT: "... *whatever its particular designations*".

1287 *Supra* Chapter 2, notes 306 and 361.

1288 For examples involving the OSCE, see a 26 May 1993 exchange of letters between the UN Secretary-General and the CSCE Chairman-in-Office, Annexed to UN Doc. A/48/185, 1 June 1993 (and cited in E. Decaux, *supra* note 1258, p. 270 and S. Trifunovska, *supra* note 1258, p. 104; on CSCE/OSCE – UN relations in this period, see, e.g. F.D. Gaer, 'The United Nations and the CSCE: Cooperation, Competition, or Confusion?', in M.R. Lucas (ed.), *The CSCE in the 90's: Constructing European Security and Cooperation*, Baden-Baden, Nomos, 1993, pp. 161–206); the MOU between the OSCE and the UNECE Secretariats of 6 December 2004 (available online at www.unece.org/ead/osce/osceunece/MoU.pdf); a 1997 MOU with the UN Human Rights Office in Abkhazia (cited in OSCE Doc. SEC.INF/33/05, 26 August 2005, previously available online at www.osce.org/documents/sg/2004/05/3242_en.pdf, p. 13); a June 2006 MOU between the OSCE and UNDP (mentioned in a statement on behalf of the OSCE at the UN Conference to Review Progress Made in the Implementation of the Programme of Action to Prevent, Combat and Eradicate the Illicit Trade in Small Arms and Light Weapons in All Its Aspects (New York, 26 June – 7 July 2006), available online at www.un.org/events/smallarms2006/pdf/arms060629osce-eng.pdf) and an October 1998 UNHCR-OSCE MOU (mentioned in UN Doc. A/AC.96/SR.540, 12 October 1999, p. 4, which also contains references to other MOUs between the UNHCR and other international common instrument between the OSCE and States hosting missions or offices.[1289] However, absent specific stipulations, it may be difficult to establish whether or not a given MOU or agreement is legally binding and not all parties may have the same view on this. A good example in the case of the OSCE is the Agreement on the OSCE Kosovo Verification Mission concluded on 16 October 1998 between the OSCE and the Federal Republic of Yugoslavia (FRY).[1290] While the OSCE's proclaimed lack of legal personality suggests this agreement cannot be a treaty, its terms indicate that it is one. In particular, it *inter alia* provides that the FRY government "*hereby guarantees the safety and security of the Verification mission and all its Members*" (I.6) and "*will accept the OSCE Verification Mission as a diplomatic entity in terms of the Vienna Convention on Diplomatic Relations*" (I.8), in addition to various detailed provisions on the mission's mandate and composition. There is no clause excluding the agreement's legal nature. One may also refer to the agreement with Denmark on the status of the OSCE Parliamentary Assembly which even more clearly would appear to be a treaty.[1291]

Moreover, there are indications that various MOUs may well qualify as treaties too. For instance, the Council of Europe's Venice Commission issued an opinion holding that a Memorandum of Understanding between the OSCE and the Federation of Bosnia and Herzegovina dated 9 October 2001 was binding upon the Bosnian authorities and therefore presumably constitutes a treaty.[1292] Also,

---

organizations). See also C. Brölmann, *supra* note 1225, pp. 161–164. For the EC/EU, see, e.g. A.-P. Allo, *supra* note 1285, pp. 56–67.

1289 For instance, various MOUs with Host States of Offices and Missions are mentioned in OSCE Doc. SEC.INF/33/05, *supra* note 1288. See also S. Trifunovska, *supra* note 1258, p. 63 and the OSCE-Bosnian, OSCE-Azerbaijan and OSCE-Armenian MOUs mentioned *infra* notes 1292 and 1293. For a general overview of MOUs concluded by the OSCE, see OSCE Doc. SEC. GAL/92/03/Rev. 1, Table I, circulated in July 2003 according to G. Schusterschitz, *supra* note 1251, p. 183 note 104.

1290 UN Doc. S/1998/978, 20 October 1998, Annex, Enclosure and 38 *I.L.M.* 1999, pp. 24–27. The preamble identifies the OSCE as a party (alongside the FRY government). For an extensive discussion, see G. Hafner, 'Did the FR Yugoslavia Make the OSCE an International Organization?', in W. Benedek, H. Isak & R. Kicker (eds.), *Development and Developing International and European Law: Essays in Honour of Konrad Ginther on the Occasion of his 65th Birthday*, Frankfurt am Main, Lang, 1999, pp. 35–57, who concludes that this is not a legally binding treaty.

1291 See *supra* note 1270.

1292 Opinion on the Rank and Status of the Ombudsman of the Federation of Bosnia and Herzegovina, CDL-AD (2002) 8, Opinion no. 193/2002_bih, 17 May 2002 (available online at www.venice.coe.int/docs/2002/CDL-AD(2002)008-e.asp?PrintVersion=True), §26–27 ("... *the [MOU] ... was duly signed, and thus concluded, by competent representatives for the OSCE Mission to Bosnia and Herzegovina on the one hand and by the Government of the Federation of Bosnia and Herzegovina on behalf of the Federation of Bosnia and Herzegovina, on the other. Accordingly, the Federation of Bosnia and Herzegovina in bound by this Agreement*"). See also the Comments by Mr Hans-Heinrich VOGEL, CDL (2002) 35, 1 March 2002 (available online at www.venice.coe.int/docs/2002/CDL(2002)035-e.asp), §3 ("... *the [MOU] ... was duly signed,* there are instances of MOUs relating to a mission being approved by host State parliaments, notably of Participating States, which may indicate that they are considered by the host State as being legally binding (although this would depend upon these States' domestic law).[1293] It may also be noted that generally, where an agreement with a host State determines the status of the OSCE's presence in that State, e.g. by according privileges and immunities, a legally binding agreement (as is normally pursued by the EU[1294]), would seem appropriate because such rights should be enforceable in the domestic courts.[1295] In this respect there is, or has been, some discussion over similar 'administrative agreements' concluded by the European Commission on the status of its delegations in third States.[1296] While the OSCE may be in a position to demand

---

and thus concluded, by competent representatives for the OSCE Mission to Bosnia and Herzegovina on the one hand and for the Federation of Bosnia and Herzegovina on the other, and the signing of the agreement had been preceded by extensive negotiations and deliberations of its material contents. In view of this, I cannot at present find any reason why the agreement on minimum salaries, as documented in the Memorandum of Understanding, should be seen as not to provide a sufficient legal basis of what has been agreed upon, which – among other things – expressly is to equate salaries of the Ombudsmen with those of the ordinary court judges mentioned in Article 4 of the Memorandum").

1293 See, e.g. 'Azerbaijan and Organization for Security and Cooperation in Europe (OSCE)', available online at www.azembvienna.at/en/osce.htm ("*The [OSCE] Office [in Baku] initiated its official activities on July 18, 2000 following the ratification by the Parliament of Azerbaijan of the Memorandum of Understanding between the OSCE and the Republic of Azerbaijan*"); the MOU is dated 19 June 2000; see 'OSCE Chairperson-in-Office welcomes signing of Memorandum of Understanding with the Republic of Azerbaijan', press release, 20 June 2000 (available online at www.eurasianet.org/resource/azerbaijan/hypermail/200006/0028.html) and www.osce.org/yerevan/13204.html ("*The [OSCE] Office [in Yerevan] started operations on 9 February 2000 following the ratification by the Armenian National Assembly of the Memorandum of Understanding between the OSCE and the Armenian Ministry of Foreign Affairs*"). This point is also made by G. Schusterschitz, *supra* note 1251, p. 184 note 105.

1294 See *supra* Chapter 3.

1295 Similarly, in respect of privileges and immunities of international organizations generally, Sands & Klein, p. 489.

1296 See A.-P. Allo, *supra* note 1285, pp. 56–67; I. MacLeod, I.D. Henry & S. Huett, *supra* note 1255, pp. 166–167 and D. Verwey, *supra* note 1280, pp. 97–99 and 217. The problem is not limited to such status agreements but also relates to cooperation agreements with other international organizations (see, e.g. J. Rideau, 'La participation de l'Union européenne aux organisations internationales. Rapport général', in J.-C. Gautron & L. Grard (eds.), *Droit international et droit communautaire, perspectives actuelles. Société Française pour le Droit Interntional. Colloque de Bordeaux*, Paris, Pedone, 2000, pp. 314 and 318–320). Moreover, it is somewhat different because the EC may and does conclude treaties (see Article 300 EC treaty) but the agreements at stake are concluded by the Commission without recourse to the normal treaty-making procedure but relying in part on its powers to maintain relations with other international organizations under Articles 302–304 EC Treaty and in part on its power to conclude agreements for *laissez-passer* to be recognized as valid travel documents within the territory of third countries (Article 7(1) Protocol on the Privileges and Immunities of the European Communities, *infra* note 1380). A first question is thus whether these powers include the power to conclude the agreements concerned. Article 300(2) grants the Council the treaty-making power but "*subject to the powers vested in the Commission in this field*", raising the question what the Commission powers are. Other than those for the *laissez-passer* respect for such arrangements even if they are not of a legal nature, the OSCE's commitment to the rule of law and independence of the judiciary should lead it to put in place legal arrangements that are in conformity with the rule of law.

4. THE OSCE DOES HAVE LEGAL PERSONALITY

The treaty practice sheds a different light on the question of the OSCE's international legal personality. While Participating States may be able to enter into political commitments only, especially when they explicitly so qualify these commitments, various agreements do not seem to include such explicit clauses excluding their legal nature[1297] and, in light of their content and the

they seem rather limuted, see the ECJ judgment *infra* this note. In addition, there is the question whether such agreements bind the EC (which would be normal given that it is the EC which has international legal personality; see the ECJ judgment *infra* this note) or only the Commission. The question whether organs of an international organization may themselves be party to agreements is not settled; see C. Brölmann, *supra* note 1225, pp. 171–173; KLEIN, pp. 323–325; F. Morgenstern, *supra* note 1229, pp. 23–26 and SCHERMERS & BLOKKER, §1571, pp. 993–994. Compare G. Schusterschitz *supra* note 1251, pp. 163–188 in respect of EC agencies and F. Naert, *De bevoegdheid van de NAVO inzake het sluiten van internationale overeenkomsten*, Brussels, Belgian Ministry of Defence/Federal Public Service Personnel and Organization, 2005, pp. 10–11, concerning NATO, where the question appears to be settled for certain international Headquarters but not for some NATO agencies. Also, the question may arise whether the agreement is legally binding. The ECJ ruled on an agreement concluded by the Commission with the US concerning competition (Case 327/91, *French Republic v Commission of the European Communities*, Judgment of 9 August 1994) that the agreement (was intended to) produce(d) legal effects (§§15 and 23) and was a treaty under international law binding the EC as a legal person (§§24–25) despite the fact that the Commission did not have the competence to conclude such an agreement (§§26–43). In response, the Commission has largely resorted to non-binding agreements; see E. Barconcini, *supra* note 1285, pp. 369–430, especially pp. 392–394, citing various examples. The ECJ ruled that at least one of these agreements (concerning Guidelines on regulatory cooperation and transparency concluded with the US) was indeed not legally binding; see Case C-233/02, *French Republic v. Commission of the European Communities*, judgment of 23 March 2004, §§42–45 ("*... the intention of the parties must in principle be the decisive criterion for the purpose of determining whether or not the Guidelines are binding ... In the present case, that intention is clearly expressed ... in the text of the Guidelines itself ... In those circumstances, and without its being necessary to consider the specific importance which the use of the terms 'should' or 'will' rather than 'shall' could assume in an international agreement concluded by the Community, it need only be stated that on the basis of that information, the parties had no intention of entering into legally binding commitments ... the history of the negotiations confirms [this] ... It follows that the Guidelines do not constitute a binding agreement and therefore do not fall within the scope of Article 300 EC*") , also discussed in E. Barconcini, *supra* note 1285, pp. 404–425.

1297 To my knowledge, the agreements that are in the public domain do not include such stipulations. Moreover, if they existed, they would probably have been taken into consideration in the Venice Commission's opinion cited *supra* note 1292, *quod non*.

understanding of their legal nature by the other party to the agreement,[1298] would seem to be legally binding treaties.[1299]

This implies that the OSCE is a subject of international law and has international legal personality, at least if one accepts, as I will argue below, that treaty-making power requires international legal personality (see *infra* Section E.3 of this chapter on the latter point). However, the expressed view of the Participating States to the contrary should lead to a narrow reading of the legal *capacities* resulting from this personality for the OSCE. Interestingly, the case of the OSCE thus shows a certain parallelism with that of the EU (see *infra*, Chapter 6).

D. INTERNATIONAL ORGANIZATIONS MAY POSSESS INTERNATIONAL LEGAL PERSONALITY – EVEN BY IMPLICATION

In this section, I will illustrate that it is no longer contested that international organizations may possess international legal personality (1) and that this personality may be granted implicitly (2).

However, there is one more terminological issue that should be clarified first: I will use the term '(international) agreement' as a generic term including both legally binding and non-legally binding (international) agreements and the term 'treaty' for international agreements binding under international law.[1300]

1298 See also 'Minister Oskanian and Yerevan OSCE Head Sign Memorandum of Understanding', press release dated 9 June 2006 (available online at www.armeniaforeignministry.com/pr_06/060609_osce_agreement.html), noting the conclusion of "*an additional protocol to the Memorandum of Understanding between the OSCE and Armenia which creates the* legal basis *for establishing presences to implement OSCE programs in regions of Armenia*" (emphasis added).

1299 Therefore the assertion by S. Trifunovska, *supra* note 1258, p. 63, §79 *in fine* that "*Due to the absence of legal personality of the OSCE this Memorandum and other OSCE agreements concluded by OSCE cannot be considered to be treaties under international law and have no legally binding power*" does not seem entirely correct, despite its logic. See also F. Münch, *supra* note 1285, pp. 1–11, holding that the intent is only decisive if clearly expressed by all the parties, and J. Klabbers, 'Informal Instruments before the European Court of Justice', 31 *C.M.L. Rev.* 1994, pp. 1019–1023, arguing that the ECJ applies a presumption that agreements (in the broad sense, including various informal instruments) are legally binding.

1300 Compare Schermers & Blokker, §1744, pp. 1111–1112 and C. Brölmann, *supra* note 1225, pp. 80–81 and 257–261.

1. INTERNATIONAL ORGANIZATIONS MAY POSSESS INTERNATIONAL LEGAL PERSONALITY

First, although it was once debated,[1301] it is presently beyond any doubt that international organizations may possess international legal personality. This possibility was confirmed by the ICJ already in its 1949 *Reparations* advisory opinion[1302] and is generally accepted by scholars.[1303] Moreover and above all, its acceptance by States is evidenced by the increase of explicit grants of international legal personality to international organizations in their constituent instruments, a practice that was rather exceptional before the 1990s (for some of the early exceptions, see the ECSC[1304] and, interestingly, the EDC[1305] and the proposed draft European Political Community[1306]).[1307] More recent examples include

1301 See, e.g. C. Brölmann, *supra* note 1225, pp. 72–81.

1302 *Reparations Opinion*, pp. 7/177–9/179.

1303 Amerasinghe, implicitly at pp. 69 ("*what is useful or even necessary is that states have the option of creating an organisation which has personality...* ") and 79 (identifying two approaches that both accept the possibility of international organizations having international legal personality); Klabbers, pp. 42–43 ("*International organizations are generally counted among the subject of international law ... Thus, ... they are deemed capable of independently bearing rights and obligations under international law ...* ") and pp. 52–57 (implicitly by identifying two approaches that both accept the possibility of international organizations having international legal personality); Sands & Klein, pp. 469–470 (noting a "*more general acceptance*" of this possibility); Schermers & Blokker, §§1562–1590, pp. 987–1011, especially §1569, p. 991 (even submitting that "*It is generally recognised that organizations have [international legal personality], unless there is clear evidence to the contrary*") and White, pp. 27–56, especially p. 52 (submitting that "*Conceptually, the international legal personality of international organisations is equivalent to that of States*").

1304 See Article 6 Treaty Establishing the European Coal and Steel Community, 18 April 1951, 261 *U.N.T.S.* 140 (1957), which entered into force on 23 July 1952 and expired on 23 July 2002 (in conformity with its Article 97): "*The Community shall have legal personality. In international relations, the Community shall enjoy the legal capacity it requires to perform its functions and attain its objectives*".

1305 Article 7 EDC Treaty reads: "*La Communauté a la personnalité juridique. Dans les relations internationales, la Communauté jouit de la capacité juridique nécessaire pour exercer ses fonctions et atteindre ses buts ...*".

1306 Projet de traité portant statut de la Communauté Européenne, adopted by an *ad hoc* Assembly on 10 March 1953 in Strasbourg (available online at http://mjp.univ-perp.fr/europe/1953cpe.htm), Article 4 (cited in H.W. Briggs, 'The Proposed European Political Community', 48 *A.J.I.L.* 1954, p. 113 as reading as follows in English: "*The Community shall have juridical personality. In international relationships the Community shall enjoy the juridical personality necessary to the exercise of its functions and the attainment of its ends*"). Moreover, Article 5 is quoted by A.H. Robertsen, 'The European Political Community', 29 *B.Y.I.L.* 1952, p. 388 as providing that "*The Community, together with the E.C.S.C. and the E.D.C., shall constitute a single legal entity*". On the context of the proposed European Political Community, see *supra*, Chapter 1.A.

1307 See, with further examples, Sands & Klein, pp. 470–471 and Schermers & Blokker, §1564, p. 988. But see Klabbers, p. 53 and Amerasinghe, pp. 78 and 84.

the African Development Bank,[1308] Andean Community,[1309] Mercosur,[1310] IFAD,[1311] ISA,[1312] COMESA,[1313] ICSID[1314] and ICC.[1315] There are also examples of explicit recognition of such personality in other instruments, for instance in the case of the Bank for International Settlements[1316]. [1317] While such an explicit grant of international legal personality is still not that common, it shows that most States accept that international organizations may have international legal

---

1308 See Article 50 of the Agreement Establishing the African Development Bank, Khartoum, 4 August 1963, which entered into force on 10 September 1964, as subsequently amended (available online at www.afdb.org/fileadmin/uploads/afdb/Documents/Legal-Documents/30718627-EN-AGREEMENT-ESTABLISHING-THE-AFRICAN-DEVELOPMENT-BANK-6TH-EDITION.PDF): "*To enable it to fulfil its purpose and the functions with which it is entrusted, the Bank shall possess full international personality. To those ends, it may enter into agreements with members, non-member States and other international organizations*".

1309 Article 48 Andean Community Constitution (available online at www.comunidadandina.org/ingles/normativa/ande_trie1.htm): "*The Andean Community is a subregional organization with an international legal capacity or status*".

1310 Article 34 Protocolo Adicional al Tratado de Asuncion sobre la Estructura Institucional del Mercosur, Ouro Preto, 17 December 1994 (available online at www.mininterior.gov.ar/migraciones/inter_pdf/mercosur/protocolodeouropreto.pdf): "*El Mercosur tendrá personalidad jurídica de Derecho Internacional*".

1311 Article 10 section 1 Agreement Establishing the International Fund for Agricultural Development (13 June 1976, available online at www.ifad.org/pub/basic/agree/e/!01agree.pdf): "*The Fund shall possess international legal personality*".

1312 Article 176 UN Convention on the Law of the Sea (Montego Bay, 10 December 1982, 1833 *U.N.T.S.* 3): "*The Authority shall have international legal personality and such legal capacity as may be necessary for the exercise of its functions and the fulfilment of its purposes*". Although this Article is part of the controversial Part XI of this Convention, it is not affected by the Agreement relating to the implementation of Part XI of the United Nations Convention on the Law of the Sea (10 December 1982, New York, 28 July 1994, Annex to UNGA Res. 48/263).

1313 Article 186(1) COMESA Treaty (available online at http://about.comesa.int/lang-en/publications/comesa-treaty): "*The Common Market shall enjoy international legal personality*".

1314 Article 18 Convention on the Settlement of Investment Disputes between States and Nationals of Other States (Washington DC, 18 March 1965, which entered into force on 14 October 1966, available online at http://icsid.worldbank.org/ICSID/FrontServlet): "*The Centre shall have full international legal personality*".

1315 Article 4(1) ICC Statute: "*The Court shall have international legal personality*".

1316 See Article 1 of the Agreement between the Swiss Federal Council and the Bank for International Settlements to determine the Bank's legal status in Switzerland, 10 February 1987: "*The Swiss Federal Council acknowledges the international legal personality and the legal capacity within Switzerland of the Bank for International Settlements [...]*" (available online at www.bis.org/about/headquart-en.pdf).

1317 See also the reference to the recognition by Switzerland, the host State, of the "*international personality and legal capacity*" of the League of Nations in a bilateral treaty: 7 *Official Journal of the League of Nations* 1926, Ann. 911a, 1422, cited in Sands & Klein, p. 471 and in D.A. Ijalaye, *The Extension of Corporate Personality in International Law*, Dobbs Ferry/Leiden, Oceana/Sijthoff, 1978, p. 13. The latter author also mentions a recommendation of the Governing Board of the Pan-American Union that the governments should recognize that this Union was "*an institution having international juridical personality*" (*id.*, p. 16).

personality.[1318] This is also recognized in the preamble of the 1986 VCLT.[1319] Moreover, there are also a number of constitutive acts that grant legal personality without explicitly specifying whether this includes international legal personality, but where it is fairly clear from other provisions and subsequent practice that this is indeed the case, e.g. the E(E)C (although Article 281 EC Treaty only provides that "*The Community shall have legal personality*" without specifying whether this is at the domestic and/or international level, it is generally accepted that it includes international legal personality),[1320] WEU,[1321]

1318 The examples listed bring together most countries. E.g. in July 2009, the ICSID Constitution was ratified by 144 parties (http://icsid.worldbank.org/ICSID/FrontServlet?requestType=ICSIDDocRH&actionVal=ContractingStates&ReqFrom=Main), the UN Convention on the Law of the Sea was ratified by 159 States (*U.N.T.S.*) and IFAD had 165 Member States (www.ifad.org/governance/ifad/ms.htm). While other considerations may have led some parties/Member States to accept the legal personality provision in a constitutive act despite objections to it, there are no such objections to my knowledge.

1319 See the 10th consideration: "Having in mind *the specific features of treaties to which international organizations are parties as subjects of international law distinct from States*". Admittedly, this refers to a subject of international law rather than an international legal person, but as noted above (Section A of this chapter), the two terms are often used interchangeably.

1320 Indeed, various provisions of the EC Treaty support this view, including those on the EC's treaty-making power (see, e.g. Articles 133, 300 and 310 EC Treaty, initially 113, 228 and 238 EEC Treaty) as well as those on cooperation with the UN, Council of Europe, OECD and other international organizations (Articles 302–304 EC Treaty, initially 229–231 EEC Treaty). For an affirmation by the ECJ, see, e.g. Case C-22/70, *Commission of the European Communities v Council of the European Communities, European Agreement on Road Transport (AETR)*, Judgment of 31 March 1971, §§13–14 ("*Article 210 provides that "The Community shall have legal personality". This provision, ... means that in its external relations the Community enjoys the capacity to establish contractual links with third countries over the whole field of objectives defined in Part one of the Treaty* ..."). But see J. Klabbers, 'Presumptive Personality: The European Union in International Law', in M. Koskenniemi (ed.), *International Law Aspect of the European Union*, The Hague, Martinus Nijhoff, 1998, pp. 248–249. It is often held that Article 281 even exclusively refers to international legal personality, due to its contrast with Article 282 EC Treaty, which is restricted to the domestic legal personality/capacity; see, e.g., H. Krück, *supra* note 1245, p. 20 note 102; N. Neuwahl, 'Legal Personality of the European Union – International and Institutional Aspects', in V. Kronenberger (ed.), *The European Union and the International Legal Order: Discord or Harmony?*, The Hague, T.M.C. Asser Press, 2001, p. 10; H.-H. Nöll, *supra* note 1234, p. 125 note 2; A.S. Muller, *supra* note 1269, p. 69 note 2; C. Tomuschat, 'Artikel 281 EG', in H. von der Groeben & J. Schwarze (eds.), *Kommentar zum Vertrag über die Europäische Union und zur Gründung der Europäischen Gemeinschaft*, Baden-Baden, Nomos, 2003 (6th ed.), p. 1241 and J. Ukrow, 'Article 281', in C. Calliess & M. Ruffert (eds.), *Kommentar des Vertrages üder die Europäische Union und des Vertrages zur Gründung der Europäischen Gemeinschaft*, Zurich, Schulthess/Luchterhand, 1999, p. 2045. Compare P. Pescatore, *supra* note 1241, pp. 39–40, arguing that Article 281 EC Treaty accords a comprehensive legal personality in the different legal orders, domestic and international.

1321 Agreement on the Status of the Western European Union, National Representatives and International Staff (Paris, 11 May 1955, 1258 *U.N.T.S.* 312 (1981), which entered into force on 19 July 1956), Articles 3 *juncto* 27 ("*The Organisation shall possess juridical personality; it shall have the capacity to conclude contracts, to acquire and dispose of movable and immovable*

CARICOM,[1322] SADC[1323] and the Joint Vienna Institute.[1324] Likewise, there are acts of recognition of legal personality that implicitly but quite clearly concern international legal personality.[1325] Also, in the discussions on the international legal personality of the EU since the Treaty of Maastricht, it was, to my knowledge, never disputed at all that the EU *could* be endowed with international legal personality.

---

property and to institute legal proceedings" and "*The Council acting on behalf of the Organisation may conclude with any Member State or States supplementary agreements adjusting the provisions of the present Agreement, so far as that State or those States are concerned*" (see also Article 10(3)). For an example of such an agreement, see the WEU-NATO security agreement of 6 May 1996 (mentioned in the Final Communiqué of the WEU Council of Ministers, Birmingham, 7 May 1996, available online at www.weu.int/documents/960507en.pdf#search=%22security%2C%20weu%2C%20nato%2C%20agreement%22, §18). See also J. Litten, *Beitrag der Westeuropäischen Union (WEU) zur Europäischen Sicherheits- und Verteidigungspolitik (ESVP): eine rechtspolitische Untersuchung*, Aachen, Shaker, 2005, p. 55 and M. Warnken, *infra* note 1472, p. 95.

1322 See Article 228(1) *juncto* (3) Revised Treaty of Chaguaramas Establishing the Caribbean Community, Including the CARICOM Single Market and Economy (initially Article 20(1) *juncto* (3) Treaty establishing the Caribbean Community, Chaguaramas, 4 July 1973, which entered into force on 1 August 1973, available online at www.sice.oas.org/trade/ccme/ccmetoc.asp): "*The Community shall have full juridical personality*" and "*The Community may also conclude agreements with States and International Organisations*" (available online at untreaty.un.org/unts/158780_159109/1/4/132.pdf; it is not clear whether the revised agreement has been concluded but the provision on the legal status is almost identical in both versions).

1323 See Articles 3 and 24(1) Treaty of the Southern African Development Community (Windhoek, 17 August 1992, as amended, available online at www.sadc.int/index/browse/page/58): "*SADC [...] shall have legal personality*" and "*SADC [...] may enter into agreements with other states, regional and international organisations, whose objectives are compatible with the objectives of SADC and the provisions of this Treaty*".

1324 Its initial constitutive instrument is annexed to UN Doc. E/1994/115 and Article 1(1) thereof establishes this institute as an "*international organization with full juridical personality*" and under Articles 4 and 8 it may conclude a headquarters agreement and agreements on its privileges and immunities. See also A.S. Muller, *supra* note 1269, pp. 5–6 and 80–81.

1325 See the Agreement Recognising the International Legal Personality of the International Rice Research Institute, Manila, 19 May 1995, *Australian Treaties Series* 2001 No. 6 (available online at www.austlii.edu.au/au/other/dfat/treaties/2001/6.html). Despite the title of this treaty, the relevant provision itself (Article I) does not explicitly grant *international* legal personality and only states that "*The Institute shall have a juridical personality*" (§1). However, its §2 makes it clear that what is envisaged is indeed international legal personality, by stipulating that "*In order to fulfill its purpose, the Institute may cooperate and/or conclude agreements or arrangements with governments and/or organizations*". See also the following consideration in the preamble: "*Whereas, it is to the benefit of the rice producing and consuming peoples of the world that the Institute be provided with the status and characteristics appropriate to its international mandate, its international sources of financing, its international operations and the international character of its Board of Trustees and staff, so that it may more effectively pursue its international activities*".

2. INTERNATIONAL LEGAL PERSONALITY MAY BE GRANTED TO INTERNATIONAL ORGANIZATIONS IMPLICITLY

It is also well established that international legal personality need not be granted explicitly,[1326] as was held by the ICJ in its *Reparations opinion*.[1327] This concerns not so much the already mentioned case of an explicit granting of legal personality of which it is not clear whether this includes international legal personality, but rather the lack of a provision on legal personality or the explicit granting of legal personality that by its wording is limited to legal personality under domestic law.[1328] Indeed, whereas an explicit grant is still not that frequent (see previous subsection), an implicit grant is, or at least was, more common. The UN is an example of an explicit grant of legal personality that by its wording is limited to domestic legal personality.[1329] An example of the absence of a provision on legal personality for organizations that have such personality is the EU (at least since the Treaty of Amsterdam, see *infra*). It should be noted that in some cases the provision(s) on legal personality are not included in the constitutive instrument of an organization, but rather in

---

1326 AMERASINGHE, pp. 77–87 (not explicitly saying so – though nearly at p. 78: "*international personality of organizations has evolved, as necessary, rather than emanated from explicit statements in constitutions*" – but it clearly underlies the text); KLABBERS, pp. 49–57 (identifying in practice a presumptive personality that would operate as soon as an organization acts in a way that requires such personality); SANDS & KLEIN, pp. 471–472; SCHERMERS & BLOKKER, §§1565–1569, pp. 988–992 (even submitting that "*It is generally recognised that organizations have [international legal personality], unless there is clear evidence to the contrary*") and WHITE, pp. 27 ("*there appears to be no need for an express provision in the constituent treaty of an organisation for it to be deemed to possess personality*") and 52 (conceptually equating the international legal personality of international organizations to that of States).

1327 ICJ, *Reparations opinion*, pp. 7–89/177–179.

1328 This assumes that domestic legal personality is largely irrelevant to international legal personality. See in this sense, AMERASINGHE, pp. 78–79. However, see SHAW, p. 241 and A.S. Muller, *supra* note 1269, p. 70, who argues that international legal personality always entails domestic legal personality in the host State. E. Lauterpacht, 'The Development of the Law of International Organization by the Decisions of International Tribunals', 152 *Rec. Cours* 1976-IV, p. 412 regards the matter as open.

1329 See Article 104 UN Charter: "*The Organization shall enjoy in the territory of each of its Members such legal capacity as may be necessary for the exercise of its functions and the fulfilment of its purposes*". See also I. Seidl-Hohenveldern & K. Rudolp, 'Article 104' in SIMMA, pp. 103–104, rightly stating that this limitation was confirmed by the ICJ's reasoning in the *Reparations opinion* as it found that the international legal personality was implied on the basis of other elements. Compare AMERASINGHE, pp. 78–79.

a separate agreement on its privileges and immunities. This is, for instance, the case for NATO[1330] and the AU.[1331]

E. THE CONTENTS OF THE INTERNATIONAL LEGAL PERSONALITY OF INTERNATIONAL ORGANIZATIONS

The purpose of this section is to examine when international organizations have not just rights and duties under international law but also the capacity to enter into international legal relations or to exercise powers on the international level and hence to create international rights and duties. This is why I will pay particular attention to the treaty-making capacity of international organizations, as it is the one of the most obvious ways to enter into international legal relations, in addition to having regulatory or decision-making powers. I will look at what are said to be the *indicia* of the international legal personality of international organizations and also address the question whether the international legal personality of international organizations comprises some inherent legal capacities. While the latter is partly related to the consequences rather than the elements, to the extent that capacities are inherent they may be relevant to the determination of international legal personality. The legal position of NATO and the Eurocorps will be analyzed in the section on treaty-making capacity.

1330 See the Agreement on the Status of the North Atlantic Treaty Organization, National Representatives and International Staff, Ottawa, 20 September 1951, 200 ***U.N.T.S.*** 3 (1954) (available online at www.nato.int/docu/basictxt/b510920a.htm), Article IV ("*The Organization shall possess juridical personality; it shall have the capacity to conclude contracts, to acquire and dispose of movable and immovable property and to institute legal proceedings*"). See *infra* on whether this includes international legal personality.

1331 See Article 1 of the General Convention on the Privileges and Immunities of the [Organization of African Unity], Accra, 25 October 1965, which would seem to be applicable to the AU (see K. Magliveras & G. Naldi, *The Organization of African Unity / African Union*, in J. Wouters (ed.), *International Encyclopaedia of Laws. Intergovernmental Organisations*, The Hague, Kluwer Law International, 2004, §92, pp. 53). The text of the provision cited suggests only legal personality under domestic law is concerned (Article 1: "*The Organization of African Unity shall possess juridical personality and shall have the capacity: (a) To enter into contacts including the rights to acquire and dispose of movable and immovable property; (b) To institute legal proceedings*"). The AU Constitution itself only hints at some legal personality since its Article 33(1) reads "*the [OAU] Charter shall remain operative for a transitional period ... for the purpose of enabling the OAU/AEC to undertake the necessary measures regarding the devolution of its assets and liabilities to the Union and all matters relating thereto*". The OAU Constitution did not mention legal personality.

1. TWO THEORIES

If an international organization is implicitly granted international legal personality, there must be certain elements on the basis of which this may be inferred. While this appears to be the prevailing view,[1332] there is less agreement on what these indicators are. Doctrine mainly identifies two current schools of thought:[1333] on the one hand, one seeing 'objective' international legal personality, meaning derived from international law when (limited) conditions are met irrespective of the will of the founding entities (the 'objective theory'),[1334] and on the other hand one for whom the international legal status is given by and derived from the founding entities ('will theory' or 'subjective theory').[1335] Both are said to rely to some extent on the ICJ's *Reparations opinion*,[1336] though the latter is primarily regarded as supporting the subjective theory,[1337] which also appears to have stronger support.[1338]

As Klabbers notes in a short but to-the-point discussion of both theories, the subjective theory is most in line with the view that international law is based

1332 Klabbers, p. 44, identifies three indicators. Shaw, p. 241, mentions three significant factors or *indicia*.

1333 See, e.g. Amerasinghe, p. 79; Klabbers, pp. 52–56 and Schermers & Blokker, §1564, pp. 988–989. Also, sometimes two further theories are added which relate to the consequences of international legal personality, but this will be addressed below (Section E.2 of this chapter). Compare M. Hartwig, *Die Haftung der Mitgliedstaaten für Internationale Organisationen*, Berlin, Springer, 1993, pp. 36–38 and 336, who advocates a hybrid construction combining elements of both.

1334 The main proponent of the former theory is Seyersted: see, e.g. F. Seyersted, *supra* note 1229 and F. Seyersted, 'International Personality of Intergovernmental Organizations. Do Their Capacities Really Depend upon Their Constitutions.', 4 *Indian J.I.L.* 1964, pp. 1–97. White appears to be a present adherent to this theory; see White, pp. 27–53 (concluding at pp. 52–53 that "*Conceptually, the international legal personality of international organisations is equivalent to that of States. In other words, organisations have, in theory, the same rights and duties as States. However, constitutional and practical limitations – the 'functional limitation' – on the capacity of international organisations signifies that it is only possible to identify a common core of rights* ...").

1335 E.g. P. Pescatore, *supra* note 1241, pp. 36–39; Sands & Klein, p. 475 ("*Whether it flows directly from the constituent instrument or other multilateral agreements, or whether it arises by implication ... the international legal personality of international organisations is based upon the will of the founders*") and I. Seidl-Hohenveldern & G. Loibl, *supra* note 1241, pp. 38–39. Amerasinghe, pp. 81–83, also seems to take this view but seems to try to make somewhat objective the intention of the founders.

1336 Klabbers, p. 52.

1337 See Amerasinghe, pp. 79–81 and Schermers & Blokker, §§1564–1565, pp. 989–990. But see H.-H. Nöll, *supra* note 1234, p. 38 (however, acknowledging in note 3 that others read the opinion differently).

1338 Klabbers, p. 53 and Schermers & Blokker, §1565, p. 989.

primarily, in one way or another, on State consent.[1339] Nevertheless, he sees a problem in the position of other States, which, due to the lack of objective personality in the sense of personality opposable to third States, are often believed to need to recognize an organization before it may be opposed to them and could therefore make it ineffective by not recognizing it.[1340] However, this does not seem to be an insurmountable obstacle as one can distinguish between an organization having international legal personality vis-à-vis its Member States on the one hand, and the opposability thereof against third States on the other hand.[1341] Even assuming that the founders' will alone may not be able to create an objective legal personality in the sense of one opposable to third States (this will be considered below, Section F of this chapter), that is not contrary to the subjective theory as such but illustrates the limits of the will of States. Klabbers also identifies key problems with the objective theory, namely on the one hand the question of a distinct will of the organization (which, one might add, is not limited to this theory) but most fundamentally that this theory claims it may override a clear will of the founders and thereby runs counter to States' freedom to set up an organization that does not possess international legal personality.[1342] Klabbers argues that practice has adopted a pragmatic solution which he captures in the term 'presumptive personality', meaning "*as soon as an organization performs acts which can only be explained on the basis of international legal personality, such an organization will be presumed to be in possession of international legal personality*".[1343] However, while this view may well be correct,[1344] it is not clear how it is different from the subjective theory since if an organization acts in such a way, this must be based on it having been granted the power to do so and hence, ultimately, upon the will of the Member

1339 Klabbers, p. 53.

1340 Klabbers, p. 54.

1341 In this sense M. Bettati, 'Création, personnalité juridique et structure des organisations internationales', in Dupuy (ed), pp. 50–51; R.J. Dupuy, 'Le Droit des relations entre les organisations internationales', 100 *Rec. Cours* 1960-II, pp. 555–557; H. Krück, *supra* note 1245, pp. 11–12 and especially the authors cited there (Zemanec and Mosler) and Schermers & Blokker, §1568, pp. 990–991 (submitting that international organizations are no different in this respect from non-universally recognized States).

1342 Klabbers, p. 55.

1343 Klabbers, pp. 55–57 and *supra* note 1320, pp. 231–253. This appears to be quite close to M. Rama-Montaldo, *supra* note 1239, who concludes at p. 155 that "*[international] personality is dependent upon international law in the sense that it is customary to assume that States creating an organization with the characteristics defined above endow it with a full legal capacity. But since it is for them to create the organization, they might also limit some rights arising from personality if particular provisions of the constitution so specify*" (see also *id.*, p. 147).

1344 According to M. Bettati, *supra* note 1341, pp. 51–52, this presumptive theory is even the majority view among scholars and best corresponds to practice.

States. Moreover, since it is only a presumption, it is implied that the presumption may be rebutted,[1345] thus reintroducing the 'will'.

An interesting recent defence of the objective theory is that by Brölmann, who argues that although doctrine and State views remain divided, the objective theory is the more logical one since the determination of who is a subject of a legal order must be made by that legal order and cannot depend upon the will of its creators.[1346] While she rightly situates the determining rule in general international law, this arguably only shifts the question to what general international law has to say on this: does it accord legal personality exclusively on the basis of objective criteria or does it accord a role to the will of Member States?

Klabbers' view of presumptive personality may be the most accurate one by accepting that in most cases, if an international organization meets certain criteria, it will have international legal personality, while acknowledging that States still have the freedom to deny such status if they so wish. However, it is submitted that, as the examples of the OSCE (*supra*, Section C of this chapter) and EU (*infra*, Chapter 6) show, there is a limit to this State power in the sense that if Member States enable an organization to perform certain acts that necessarily imply international legal personality, they cannot deny such personality.[1347] Nevertheless, in this case the expressed denial should be taken into account when considering the capacities of an international organization. I will proceed on this basis.

1345 This is the view of M. Bettati, *supra* note 1341, pp. 51–52. Similarly A.S. Muller, *supra* note 1269, p. 78, who seems to consider than there is a presumption if these elements are met but that this may be rebutted, albeit only explicitly. See also M. Rama-Montaldo, *supra* note 1239, p. 155.

1346 C. Brölmann, *supra* note 1225, *inter alia* at pp. 86–87, 92 and 105–114. Similarly J. Barberis, *supra* note 1245, p. 176.

1347 Similarly, C. Busse, *Die völkerrechtliche Einordnung der Europäischen Union*, Cologne, Carl Heymann, 1999, pp. 155–156, accepting legal personality despite Member State opposition where competences/capacities that imply such personality are granted and where the exercise thereof is not opposed by the Member States. It is submitted that C. Brölmann, *supra* note 1225, pp. 109–110 is therefore only partially correct in asserting that organizations proclaiming their non-personality seem to incur a legal identity against their will and giving the EU and OSCE as an example: as illustrated above and below (Sections C of this chapter and Chapter 6), the case of the OSCE is not yet settled (as she admits) and in the EU it was ultimately the acceptance in practice by the Member States which arguably played a determining role in more or less ending the debate.

2. ELEMENTS AND CONSEQUENCES OF INTERNATIONAL LEGAL PERSONALITY

Under both the objective and the subjective theories, the problem remains what elements lead to international legal personality. However, this question is made particularly difficult in the subjective theory because it regards the international legal personality of international organizations, in contrast to that of States, as variable, both in terms of material competences, where the principles of speciality and conferred (explicit or implicit) powers entail limitations[1348] and in terms of specific capacities[1349]. [1350]

1348 The principle of speciality means that unlike States, which can act in any substantive area (e.g. environmental matters, military issues, economic policy, etc.), international organizations can only act in those areas within the scope of their competences as conferred upon them explicitly of implicitly and is related to the principle of attributed or conferred powers. It was clearly endorsed by the ICJ in its advisory opinion on the *Legality of the Use by a State of Nuclear Weapons in Armed Conflict* of 8 July 1996 (preliminary objections – not to be confused with the ICJ's other *Nuclear Weapons opinion*), in which it ruled that the WHO was not competent to ask for an advisory opinion on the legality of the use of nuclear weapons (§§18–31) and stated that "*International organizations are governed by the "principle of speciality", that is to say, they are invested by the States which create them with powers, the limits of which are a function of the common interests whose promotion those States entrust to them*" and that "*the necessities of international life may point to the need for organizations, in order to achieve their objectives, to possess subsidiary powers which are not expressly provided for in the basic instruments which govern their activities. It is generally accepted that international organizations can exercise such powers, known as "implied" powers*" (both §25). See also *Reparations Opinion*, pp. 182/12–183/13. See generally SCHERMERS & BLOKKER, §§206–236, pp. 154–183. Compare R.J. Dupuy, *supra* note 1341, pp. 533–542, who argues that the speciality rule is tempered by the 'effet utile' rule (similar to implied powers), resulting in a functional competence. Compare R. Wessel, 'Lowering the corporate veil. Het recht der internationale organisaties vanuit de institutionele rechtstheorie', in M.A. Heldeweg, R.J.P. Schobben & W.G. Werner (eds.), *De Regel Meester. Opstellen voor Dick W.P. Ruiter*, Enschede, Twente University Press, 2001, p. 18, who distinguishes the attribution principle from the speciality principle, arguing that the latter suggests a more objective approach to the determination of competences.

1349 The ICJ's *Reparations opinion* concerned legal personality in general and the specific capacity to bring an international claim. Moreover, not all authors distinguish between material competences on the one hand and capacities or powers on the other hand (for this distinction, see *supra* note 1253 and accompanying text); see note 2 in SCHERMERS & BLOKKER, §206, p. 154 and the brief discussion in KLABBERS, pp. 279–280. See, e.g. *infra* note 1386 and the accompanying text on how this distinction may be useful.

1350 In the *Reparations opinion*, the ICJ noted that "*The subject of law in any legal system are not necessarily identical in their nature or in the extent of their rights*" (p. 178/8) and although this was mainly to distinguish the UN from States (*id.*, p. 179/9), it also said that "*Whereas a State possesses the totality of international rights and duties recognized by international law, the rights and duties of an entity such as the [UN] must depend upon its purposes and functions as specified or implied in its constituent documents and developed in practice*" (*id.*, p. 180/10). See also MALANCZUK, pp. 92–93 ("*[international] legal personality must be treated as a relative concept ... it is futile to ask whether an international organization has legal personality in the abstract*"); SANDS & KLEIN, p. 473 ("*legal personality has no pre-determined content in international law*") and SCHERMERS & BLOKKER, §1570, pp. 992–993.

Moreover, the discussion becomes more complex through it being linked to the *consequences* of legal personality. While most proponents of the objective theory regard most or even all legal capacities as inherent to international organizations with international legal personality,[1351] although this is almost invariably tempered somewhat by the acceptance that these capacities may be limited by the constituent documents of an organization,[1352] most proponents of the subjective theory do not consider that any capacities are inherent in such organizations.[1353] However, it may be questioned whether there are not some capacities which may be regarded as inherent in the international legal personality of an international organization.[1354] In this respect, a persuasive

1351 E.g. F. Seyersted, *supra* note 1229, pp. 15–45 and White, pp. 28–29 ("*It would seem therefore that the weight of theory not only supports an 'objective approach', but also a 'material approach' to personality, which, in contrast to the formal approach, identifies 'a certain category of rights and duties which' 'arise from the very personality of the organization, and thus to be enjoyed by every organization constituting an international person irrespective, in principle, of the particular provisions of the constitution'*"). But see *infra*, next note. Sometimes this view was labelled a distinct 'material' theory that relates to the consequences of legal personality (see, e.g. M. Rama-Montaldo, *supra* note 1239, pp. 116–122), but it is usually adhered to by those who support the objective theory, see H.-H. Nöll, *supra* note 1234, pp. 53–57.

1352 See especially F. Seyersted, *supra* note 1229, p. 28 note 51 and pp. 29–31 and 44 (moreover, it may be noted that for an organization to bind its Member States and their nationals/residents, Seyersted requires a specific legal basis, see *id.*, pp. 29–31, 37–40 and 95–96). See also White, pp. 52–53 ("*constitutional and practical limitations – the 'functional limitation' – on the capacity of international organisations signifies that it is only possible to identify a common core of rights such as treaty-making capacity and privileges and immunities*"). For an analysis of constitutional limitations focused on European international organizations, see H. Hahn, 'Constitutional Limitations in the Law of the European Organisations', 108 *Rec. Cours* 1963-I, pp. 189–306.

1353 E.g. E. Lauterpacht, *supra* note 1328, pp. 403–413; P. Pescatore, *supra* note 1241, pp. 44–46; Sands & Klein, p. 473 and Schermers & Blokker, §1570, p. 992 and note 29 (but see their views on a treaty-making capacity and international responsibility, *infra* notes 1363 and 1371). See also L. Grard, *infra* note 1465, p. 370. Compare Klabbers, p. 57: "*After all is said and done, personality in international law, like 'subjectivity', is but a descriptive notion: useful to describe a state of affairs, but normatively empty, as neither rights nor obligations flow automatically from a grant of personality[, e]xcept, arguably, a very abstract sort of rights, such as the right to conclude treaties …*". C.F. Amerasinghe, 'Legal Rights and Capacity', in Dupuy (ed.), pp. 349–365, especially pp. 361–362 ("*… [capacities] of international organizations derive in the last analysis … from the constituent instruments*") also seems to rather reject the notion of inherent capacities (but see *infra* notes 1361 and 1365). Sometimes this view was regarded as a distinct 'formal' theory that relates to the consequences of legal personality (see, e.g. M. Rama-Montaldo, *supra* note 1239, pp. 112–116), but it is usually adhered to by those who support the subjective theory; see H.-H. Nöll, *supra* note 1234, pp. 43–44.

1354 For instance, A. Cassese, *International Law*, Oxford, Oxford University Press, 2001, pp. 73–75, lists four rights as being among those that "*we may safely regard as belonging to international bodies*" and C. Dominicé, *supra* note 1245, pp. 158–163, lists three inherent capacities (treaty-making power, having diplomatic relations and participating in general mechanisms of State responsibility). The position of I. Seidl-Hohenveldern & G. Loibl, *supra* note 1241, pp. 41–42 and 82–83 is less clear: on the one hand they state without qualification that international organizations possess certain rights and duties such as privileges and immunities and an argument is made by Rama-Montaldo that there are, in addition to functions and powers specific to each organization, also on the one hand rights inherent to international legal personality, irrespective of whether it is that of States or international organizations, and, on the other hand, rights that arise from their character as international organizations and which to a limited extent are common to such organizations.[1355] Another analysis worth mentioning is that of Bekker, who argues in favour of inherent capacities based on functional necessity, but which appear to be variable,[1356] which is therefore not very helpful when looking for general elements. I will now briefly discuss some of the rights that may be inherent before continuing.

The capacity to bring an international claim to uphold its rights is arguably an inherent capacity.[1357] There is no reason why the ICJ's analysis in the *Reparations*

---

active and passive right of mission yet they name these as other rights after a discussion of the treaty-making capacity which they do not regard as inherent. Also somewhat unclear is A.S. Muller, *supra* note 1269, pp. 82–83 who seems to recognize some inherent capacities but only in a very general sense (e.g. "*capacities are both evidence and consequence of the legal personality ... albeit in a more general sense. A specific competence, such as the power to conclude treaties, cannot be deduced simply from the possession of legal personality*"). J. Boulois, 'Le droit des Communautés européennes dans ses rapports avec le droit international général', 235 *Rec. Cours* 1992-IV, pp. 55–64 seems to regard a capacity for representation, treaty-making power and the capacity to bring an international claim as inherent ("*leur personnalité juridique comporte les attributes qui y sont traditionnellement attachées ...*").

1355 M. Rama-Montaldo, *supra* note 1239, pp. 111–155, especially pp. 131–155. See also J. Barberis, *supra* note 1245, pp. 160–178, trying to define subjects of international law, which he seems to equate to international legal persons and noting the variety of such subjects, some of which are unique and some of which can be brought together in categories of subjects. Compare D. Feldman, *supra* note 1241, pp. 351–361 (trying to define international legal personality generally) and the reference to Anzilotti in C. Brölmann, *supra* note 1225, p. 79 who is cited as having presented legal capacity as resulting from international legal subjectivity rather than from sovereignty. F. Seyersted (*supra* note 1229) also recognizes that there is a core of international legal personality, which he sees as sovereign organs (p. 48: "*the only criterion which is common to [States and international organisations] is the fact that they have organs which are sovereign (or self-governing) or not subject to the jurisdiction of any one other organized community. Indeed, these criteria are common to all subjects of international law and ... appea[r] to be the crucial and only condition for international personality*"). However, when it comes to capacities, he largely (e.g. pp. 88–93) and arguably too strongly (e.g. the application of state immunity rules at p. 56, see *infra*, Chapter 7.B.1) equates international organizations to States, accepting essentially only factual differences or limits imposed in the constituent document. In the same vein, I. Pernice, *infra* note 1376, pp. 229–250 argues that the 1986 VCLT is a development which better assimilates international organizations to States and pleads for further steps in this direction, thereby seeming to ignore in part the proper nature of international organizations.

1356 P. Bekker, *supra* note 1224, pp. 57–83. However, it is not entirely clear whether he applies the functional necessity test only to the material competences or also to the capacities but the latter seems to be the case and would appear to be the most logical approach in view of his functional necessity perspective.

1357 See also J. Boulois, *supra* note 1354, pp. 55 and 61–64; A. Cassese, *supra* note 1354, p. 74 and D.A. Ijalaye, *supra* note 1317, p. 41. R. Wessel, *supra* note 1253, p. 17 seems inclined to accept *opinion* in respect of the UN cannot or should not be applied to other international organizations that have international rights and duties. While it must be conceded[1358] that this opinion is not very clear on whether the right to bring an international claim is inherent in international legal personality[1359] or is linked to an analysis based on requirements proper to the UN, it is submitted that, given the non-specific nature of this capacity in general[1360] as opposed to more specific capacities related to this capacity, such as the *ius standi* before a specific judicial organ, the same reasoning may be applied to all international organizations possessing international legal personality.[1361] Indeed, it may even be said to be inherent in the notion of international legal personality more generally.[1362]

The same is arguably also the case for the capacity to have its international responsibility engaged.[1363] This seems to be the view of the ILC in its work on

---

this too. P.R. Menon, *supra* note 1246, p. 93 sees it as one of three essential *conditions f*or being a subject of international law.

1358 As Amerasinghe, pp. 94–95 points out.

1359 A point apparently reflected in some definitions of international legal personality, see *supra*, Section A of this chapter, although it seems more correct to regard this right as a consequence rather than a constitutive requirement.

1360 Already noted *supra* note 1249 and accompanying text. See also C. Dominicé, *supra* note 1245, pp. 162–163, who regards participating in *general* mechanisms of State responsibility (apparently both active and passive) as inherent.

1361 See also *supra* note 14. Compare Amerasinghe, pp. 98–99, and his discussion of a possible 'skeleton' right that would require further definition. Moreover, Amerasinghe, p. 395 remarks that "*capacity [to bring a claim under international law for damage suffered by an organisation itself] is easy to concede because it is really a necessary attribute of the corporate character of the [UN] and its possession of international legal personality*". But see Brownlie, pp. 684–685, not viewing this right as inherent. Compare ECJ, Case C-131/03, *R.J. Reynolds Tobacco Holdings, Inc. et al. v. Commission of the European Communities*, Judgment of 12 September 2006, §§86 and 94.

1362 M. Rama-Montaldo, *supra* note 1239, pp. 127–129 and 139–140. See also H. Kelsen, *supra* note 1246, p. 329: "*Juridical personality* means *the capacity … of suing … at law*" (emphasis added). Compare C. Eustathiades, 'Les sujets du droit international et la responsabilité internationale: nouvelles tendances', 84 *Rec. Cours* 1953-III, pp. 412–428 and 607–608, especially pp. 412–414, who defines a subject of international law as having a right under international law and being entitled to claim it on the international level and/or being the addressee of an obligation under international law and capable of breaching it and being held internationally responsible. I regard the right to bring an international claim as inherent to international legal personality but not to being a subject of international law because in respect of the latter even though rights exist under international law, they are not necessarily accompanied by the right to bring an *international* claim. See on the latter also A. Clapham, *supra* note 1224, pp. 74–75 and Elias, *supra* note 1248, pp. 30–31.

1363 See also C. Dominicé, *supra* note 1245, pp. 162–163, who regards participating in *general* mechanisms of State responsibility as inherent. P.R. Menon, *supra* note 1246, p. 93 sees it as one of three essential *conditions f*or being a subject of international law. On claims against international organizations, see generally M.H. Arsanjani, 'Claims against International Organizations: Quis Custodiet Ipsos Custodes', 7 *Yale Studies in World Public Order* 1980–1981, pp. 131–176; Klein; A. Reinisch, *International Organizations before National Courts*, this topic[1364] and has rightly been considered *"as simple as logical"* in view of the notion of a separate legal personality.[1365] One may also cite the UN Secretariat's view that it is *"an attribute of [the UN's] international legal personality and its capacity to bear international rights and duties"*.[1366] This right too may be said to be inherent in the notion of international legal personality generally.[1367]

Furthermore, it is submitted that the capacity to enter into international relations with States and other international organizations is also inherent.[1368] In

---

Cambridge, Cambridge University Press, 2000 and K. Wellens, *Remedies against International Organisations*, Cambridge, Cambridge University Press, 2002. On the responsibility of international organizations generally, see, e.g. C. Eagleton, "International Organizations and the Law of Responsibility", 76 *Rec. Cours* 1950-I, pp. 319–425; M. Hirsch, *infra* note 1367; W. Meng, 'Internationale Organisationen im völkerrechtlichen Deliktsrecht', 45 *Z.a.ö.R.V.* 1985, pp. 324–357; M. Perez Gonzalez, 'Les organisations internationales et le droit de la responsabilité', 92 *R.G.D.I.P.* 1988, pp. 63–102 and H.G. Schermers, 'Liability of International Organizations', 1 *Leiden J.I.L.* 1988, pp. 3–14.

1364 Pursuant to the provisional version of the ILC's Draft Articles on the responsibility of international organizations, *"Every internationally wrongful act of an international organization entails the international responsibility of the international organization"* and *"There is an internationally wrongful act of an international organization when conduct consisting of an action or omission: (a) Is attributed to the international organization under international law; and (b) Constitutes a breach of an international obligation of that international organization"*, without any further requirements (Article 3, see *Report of the International Law Commission on the Work of its fifty-fifth Session*, UN Doc. A/58/10, 2003, §53 p. 33). Although the precise scope and consequences obviously will have to be described in detail, it is the principle that matters for the present purposes.

1365 Schermers & Blokker, §§1582–1584, pp. 1004–1007. See also Amerasinghe, pp. 386, 399 and 406; M. Hartwig, *supra* note 1333, pp. 45 and 336; D.A. Ijalaye, *supra* note 1317, p. 41; I. Scobbie, 'International Organizations and International Relations', in Dupuy (ed.), pp. 885–887 (submitting that the core principles concerning State responsibility also apply to international organizations but that some modalities are unclear) and R. Wessel, *supra* note 1253, pp. 17 and 50–51 (perceiving, however, limited means of enforcement – though this is hardly proper to international organizations only). Compare Brownlie, pp. 686–687 apparently supporting this principle but showing some reservations on applying it.

1366 UN Doc. A/51/389, 20 September 1996, p. 4, also cited in Schermers & Blokker, §§1582–1584, pp. 1004–1007.

1367 See also H. Kelsen, *supra* note 1246, p. 329: *"Juridical personality* means *the capacity ... of ... being sued at law"* (emphasis added) and C. Tomuschat, *supra* note 1320, p. 1246 (*"Völkerrechtsfähigkeit ist ohne Haftung nicht denkbar"*). Compare also Eustathiades' view mentioned *supra* note 1362 and M. Hirsch, *The Responsibility of International Organizations Towards Third Parties: Some Basic Principles*, Dordrecht, Nijhoff, 1995, pp. 8–10 (noting divergent views on whether the basis for the international responsibility of international organizations is inherent but deeming that this responsibility may now be safely regarded as customary). J. Barberis, *supra* note 1245, p. 165 notes that Wengler even argued that to be a potential target of the sanction resulting from international responsibility means to be a subject of international law.

1368 M. Rama-Montaldo, *supra* note 1239, p. 139. See *a fortiori* Schermers & Blokker, §1770, p. 1131, who argue that there is an inherent right to conclude treaties on this matter (see *infra* note 1371). The capacity to enter into such relations must also be an inherent capacity *a fortiori* for those who regard the treaty-making capacity more generally as inherent. Compare J. Boulois, *supra* note 1354, pp. 55–58, deeming some form of international respresentation as particular, some form of such relations is necessary to exercise the right to make an international claim and to be held internationally responsible, both of which I regard as inherent (see above).[1369] However, as with the capacity to bring an international claim, this may be a case of a 'skeleton' right that will be further defined on a case-by-case basis and need not necessarily comprise the right to send or receive formal delegations.[1370]

Although it is sometimes alleged that the treaty-making capacity is inherent,[1371] this is more often denied.[1372] The relevant provisions in the 1986 VCLT, which

inherent. On diplomatic relations, including of international organizations, see also generally L. Dembinski, *The Modern Law of Diplomacy: External Missions of States and International Organizations*, Dordrecht, Nijhoff, 1988.

1369 Compare the dissenting opinion by Judge Hackworth to the *Reparations opinion, I.C.J. Reports* 1949, pp. 199/26–197/27.

1370 See the discussion of this notion by Amerasinghe, mentioned *supra* note 1361. Compare M. Bettati, *supra* note 1341, p. 53, who seems to regard the latter right as inherent ("*la reconnaissance de chaque organisation entraîne l'exercice d'un droit de légation actif et passif*"), as does M. Rama-Montaldo, *supra* note 1239, p. 140.

1371 E.g. A. Cassese, *supra* note 1354, p. 73; M. Rama-Montaldo, *supra* note 1239, pp. 139–140 and C. Tomuschat, *supra* note 1320, p. 1244. This view was also taken by some within the ILC during the drafting of the Draft Articles on the law of treaties between States and international organizations or between international organizations that would later become the 1986 VCLT; see comment 1 to draft Article 6 (*Y.I.L.C.* 1982-II, Part 2, p. 24). The view of SCHERMERS & BLOKKER, §§1748–1755, pp. 1114–1121 is not entirely clear (on the one hand, "*There can be no doubt that international organizations generally have the capacity to enter into agreements*" and "*the right to conclude agreements relating to its headquarters and to the privileges and immunities of its staff can probably be seen as inherent to any public international organization*" (see also *id.*, §1770, p. 1131: "*All international organisations enjoy the competence to conclude agreements on their status [and] also have an inherent right to enter into agreements with other international organizations on their mutual relations ...*") but on the other hand "*[Article 6 1986 VCLT] implies that there can be organizations without the power to conclude agreements*"). On the latter point, see however, *infra* note 1376. As to agreements relating to headquarters and to privileges and immunities, treated more extensively by A.S. Muller, *supra* note 1269, pp. 25–67 and 268, there may be an exception, at least vis-à-vis Member States, where Member States themselves conclude an agreement on this status or expressly reserve this power for themselves, as would seem to be the case for the Eurocorps (see *infra*, Section E.3.iii of this chapter). Compare KLABBERS, p. 57 ("*neither rights nor obligations flow automatically from a grant of personality [e]xcept, arguably, a very abstract sort of rights, such as the right to conclude treaties ...*") and pp. 279–280 (noting, with further references, that the leading theory is that the capacity is derived from general international law and the competence from the rules of the organization, but stating that practice has largely ignored this distinction which he finds somewhat artificial). Compare generally H. Chiu, *The Capacity of International Organizations to Conclude Treaties, and the Special Legal Aspects of the Treaties so Concluded*, The Hague, Nijhoff, 1966; H.J. Geiser, *Les effets des accords conclus par des organisations internationales: étude en droit des traités des organisations internationales à la lumière de la Convention de Vienne de 1969*, Bern, Lang, 1977; J.W. Schneider, *Treaty-making Power of International Organizations*, Geneva, Droz, 1959 and Y. Souliotis, 'La capacité des organisations internationales de conclure des accords d'après leurs actes constitutifs et la pratique', 25 *Revue hellénique de droit international* 1972, pp. 194–223.

1372 E.g. BROWNLIE, pp. 681–682; D.A. Ijalaye, *supra* note 1317, pp. 18–19; SANDS & KLEIN, p. 480 and I. Seidl-Hohenveldern & G. Loibl, *supra* note 1241, pp. 82–83.

has not yet entered into force[1373] but the substantive provisions of which are very similar to those in the 1969 VCLT[1374] and may mostly be applied as customary international law,[1375] are not very helpful and have given rise to different

---

1373 Pursuant to its Article 85 it requires 35 State Parties and as of 24 July 2009 there were only 29 (see *U.N.T.S.*), although it has been ratified by a number of important international organizations, mainly within the 'UN family' (12 as of this same date, including the UN, the IAEA, ICAO, IMO, ILO, UPU, WHO and WIPO) and has been signed by four others (the FAO, ITU, UNESCO and WMO).

1374 Aust, pp. 7–8 and Schermers & Blokker, §1743, p. 1111. This can easily be verified by comparing the structure and provisions of the two conventions. C. Brölmann, *supra* note 1225, *inter alia* at pp. 167–169, 216 and 224 argues that this is necessarily so because of the nature of treaty law in a single international legal order. For a detailed comparison, see G.E. do Nascimento e Silva, 'The 1969 and the 1986 Conventions on the Law of Treaties: A Comparison', in Y. Dinstein (ed.), *International Law at a Time of Perplexity: Essays in Honour of Shabtai Rosenne*, Dordrecht, Nijhoff, 1989, pp. 461–487.

1375 Aust, pp. 10–11, notes that the ICJ has accepted that various provisions of the 1969 VCLT reflect customary international law; see, e.g. *Fisheries Jurisdiction Case (United Kingdom v Iceland)*, judgment of 2 February 1973 (*I.C.J. Reports* 1973, pp. 18–19, §36) and *Case concerning the Gabcíkovo-Nagymaros Project (Hungary/Slovakia)*, Judgment of 25 September 1997, §46. Therefore most substantive rules of the 1969, and also of the 1986 VCLT since they are largely identical, may be applied as customary international law to treaties concluded by international organizations. See, e.g. Aust, pp. 7–8; C. Brölmann, *supra* note 1225, pp. 248–249 and I. Scobbie, *supra* note 1365, pp. 868–870. See also the arbitral award of 29 June 1990, *European Molecular Biology Laboratory v. Germany* (105 *I.L.R.* 1997, pp. 25, 30 and 53, accepting Articles 7, 31 and 46 of the two conventions as customary international law) and ECJ, Case C-162/96, *Racke / Hauptzollamt Mainz*, 16 June 1998, especially §§24, 53 and 59 (accepting as customary law the *pacta sunt servanda* rule and *rebus sic stantibus* exception but not some procedural requirements as to a period between notification and effect) and Case 327/91, *French Republic v Commission of the European Communities*, Judgment of 9 August 1994 (applying Article 2(1)(a)(i) 1986 VCLT). For a brief discussion of the ECJ's application of provisions of the two conventions as customary law to agreements concluded by the EC with further references, see D. Verwey, *supra* note 1280, p. 88 (also noting that the Commission's legal service's official position is to adhere to the 1969 VCLT) and C. Kaddous, *Le droit des relations extérieures dans la jurisprudence de la Cour de justice des Communautés européennes*, Brussels/Basel, Bruylant/Helbing & Lichtenhahn, 1998, pp. 440–442. For a more extensive analysis concerning the EC, see F. Hoffmeister, 'Die Bindung der Europäischen Gemeinschaft and das Völkergewohnheitsrecht der Verträge', 10 *Europäisches Wirtschafts- und Steuerrecht* 1998, pp. 365–371; P.J. Kuijper, 'The Court and the Tribunal of the EC and the Vienna Convention on the Law of Treaties 1969', 25 *Legal Issues of European Integration* 1998, pp. 1–23 and Vanhamme, pp. 19–26. For the EC's attitude towards the 1986 VCLT, see, e.g. P. Manin, 'The European Communities and the Vienna Convention on the Law of Treaties between States and International Organizations or between International Organizations', 24 *C.M.L. Rev.* 1987, pp. 457–481. In 1973 the Institut de Droit International stated in Article I of its resolution of 14 September 1973 on The Application of the Rules of the General International Law of Treaties to International Agreements Concluded by International Organizations (available online at www.idi-iil.org/idiE/resolutionsE/1973_rome_01_en.pdf) that: "*The provisions of the Vienna Convention on the Law of Treaties, of 23 May 1969, are in principle applicable to international agreements concluded by International Organizations either with other International Organizations or with one or several States*".

interpretations.[1376] In fact, treaty-making capacity may rather be a case where one may find, to apply Klabber's expression in a more limited manner, a presumptive capacity that can be rebutted by express or clearly implied exclusion.[1377]

The position in respect of privileges and immunities is unclear, with some States and scholars accepting that there are customary international law immunities, at least in relation to Member and host States,[1378] and others denying

1376 Article 6 of this Convention reads: "*The capacity of an international organization to conclude treaties is governed by the rules of that organization*", implying, according to SCHERMERS & BLOKKER, §1748, p. 1115 and I. Seidl-Hohenveldern & G. Loibl, *supra* note 1241, pp. 82–83 that not all organizations have this capacity. However, the commentary to the corresponding provision in the Draft Articles on the law of treaties between States and international organizations or between international organizations (Article 6) notes that the wording did not intend to settle the question whether this capacity was inherent or not, see *Report of the International Law Commission on the work of its thirty-fourth session* (*supra* note 1371), p. 24. The discussion on this point has been analyzed extensively by C. Brölmann, *supra* note 1225, pp. 169–173 and especially pp. 227–230 and 261–264. See also F. Seyersted, 'Treaty-making Capacity of Intergovernmental Organizations: Article 6 of the International Law Commission's Draft Articles on the Law of Treaties between States and International Organizations or between International Organizations', 34 *Österreichische Zeitschrift für öffentliches Recht und Völkerrecht* 1983, pp. 261–267 and I. Pernice, 'Völkerrechtliche Verträge internationaler Organisationen', 48 *Z.a.ö.R.V.* 1988, pp. 229–250, especially pp. 235–236 (stressing the limited external effect of any limitation on the basis of Article 27 and 46 of the convention). Also, KLABBERS, p. 279, with further references, notes that the consideration in the preamble of this Convention that "*international organizations possess the capacity to conclude treaties, which is necessary for the exercise of their functions and the fulfilment of their purposes*" may be read as confirming a general international law basis of the treaty-making capacity. This is treated somewhat more elaborately by I. Scobbie, *supra* note 1365, pp. 870–875, who also points to the clause in the preamble "*Recognizing that the practice of international organizations in concluding treaties with States or between themselves should be in accordance with their constituent instruments*" and specifically the use of the term 'should'. G. Hafner, 'The Amsterdam Treaty and the Treaty-Making Power of the European Union', in G. Hafner *et al.* (eds.), *Liber Amicorum Professor Seidl-Hohenverldern – in Honour of His 80th Birthday*, The Hague, Kluwer Law International, 1998, p. 260 concludes that the first cited preambular clause refers to the fundamental capacity, whereas the one cited second as well as Article 6 deal with the scope of this right.

1377 Similarly, C.F. Amerasinghe, *supra* note 1353, pp. 363–364, seeing a strong presumption. Compare P. Pescatore, *supra* note 1241, pp. 57–62, who acknowledges a practice apparently exceeding constitutional provisions but downplays the nature of this practice and argues that a treaty-making power with third States binding Member States should not be presumed, thereby seeming to leave open the possibility of a presumption in other cases (moreover, this distinction relates to competence and legal effect rather than to legal capacity).

1378 A State adhering to this view is the Netherlands; see, e.g. the references in SANDS & KLEIN, pp. 489–490. See also a German case cited in A.S. Muller, *supra* note 1269, p. 49 note 79. For scholars, see, e.g. *Restatement of the Foreign Relations Law of the United States* (*supra* note 1241), introductory note p. 492 and §467(1) and comment (a) thereto at pp. 493–494; BROWNLIE, pp. 682–683 (though noting a lack of agreement on the specific content of such immunities); A. Cassese, *supra* note 1354, pp. 73–74; I. Scobbie, *supra* note 1365, pp. 833–867 (arguing that the functional privileges and immunities have a customary law status and giving as specific examples inviolability of archives and premises and some jurisdictional this[1379] or, and perhaps this is the majority opinion, viewing the matter as uncertain.[1380] Although the references to 'customary' privileges and immunities

immunity); I. Seidl-Hohenveldern, 'Functional Immunity of International Organizations and Human Rights', in W. Benedek, H. Isak & R. Kicker (eds.), *supra* note 1290, p. 138 and R. Wessel, *supra* note 1348, p. 21. KLABBERS, pp. 164–165 seems inclined to accept a rule of customary international law, but submits it would be so abstract that it would not be helpful, except if one were to retain absolute immunity of jurisdiction for international organizations, which he questions (see *infra*, Chapter 7.B.1, on the latter point). See also the references to 'customary' privileges and immunities *infra* note 1380 and in §1(2) of Austria's Bundesgesetz vom 14. Dezember 1977 über die Einräumung von Privilegien und Immunitäten an internationale Organisationen, *Bundesgesetzblatt* No. 677/1977 (available online at www.ris.bka.gv.at/Dokumente/BgblPdf/1977_677_0/1977_677_0.pdf: "*Den ... internationalen Organisationen ... können auch jene Privilegien und Immunitäten eingeräumt werden (Abs. 1), die entweder ... oder nach den allgemein anerkannten Regeln des Völkerrechts zur Erfüllung ihrer Aufgaben vorgesehen sind*"). For a comprehensive analysis from the perspective of host States, see A.S. Muller, *supra* note 1269, especially at pp. 47–51 (concluding that there are customary privileges and immunities at least for host States that may be especially important in the initial stages of an international organization if no specific agreement has yet been concluded or entered into force).

1379 For instance, SANDS & KLEIN, pp. 489–490, deny that there is such a rule under customary international law, although they indicate that there may be specific implied obligations to grant privileges and immunities where States accept the presence of an international organization on their territory. For a court decision denying immunity, see the judgment of the Belgian *Cour de cassation* of 12 March 2001 concerning the Arab League (reported in 120 *J.T.* 2001, p. 610 and 8 *Algemeen Juridisch Tijdschrift* 2001–2002, pp. 493–497, and available online at www.juridat.be/juris/jucn.htm), in which the Court ruled that the Arab League did not enjoy privileges and immunities under general principles of law (while the Court did not discuss the issue from a customary international law perspective, it is doubtful whether it did distinguish between these two sources of law). See also the arbitral award of 29 June 1990, *European Molecular Biology Laboratory v. Germany*, 105 *I.L.R.* 1997, pp. 55–56 (no customary international law immunity for Directors of international organizations due to the great variety of immunities).

1380 AMERASINGHE, pp. 344–348, seems doubtful but inclined to accept that there may be a rule of customary international law, especially vis-à-vis Member States and based on good faith and functionalism. The latter argument is also made by R. Higgins, *infra* note 1396, p. 91. I. Seidl-Hohenveldern & G. Loibl, *supra* note 1241, p. 262 also seem inclined to accept a customary rule but only in relation to Member States, referring to Article 17(2) Vienna Convention on Consular Relations (24 April 1963, 596 *U.N.T.S.* p. 261 (1967)), which entitles a consular officer who is also accredited to an international organization "*to enjoy any privileges and immunities accorded ... by customary international law*" (see also the declaration made by Vietnam to the 1975 VCRSIO stressing that "*the absolute inviolability privilege accorded the offices and residences of the representations of member States at International Organizations has been established as a principle in the practice of international law and therefore must be strictly observed by all States*") and to Article 12(c) Protocol on the Privileges and Immunities of the European Communities (Brussels, 8 April 1965, *O.J. L* 152, 13 July 1967, p. 13, as subsequently amended, available online at http://eur-lex.europa.eu/LexUriServ/LexUriServ.do?uri=CELEX:12006E/PRO/36:EN:NOT), which provides that officials and other servants of the Communities shall "*in respect of currency or exchange regulations, be accorded the same facilities as are customarily accorded to officials of international organizations*" (see also *id.*, Articles 11 and 17, respectively according "*the customary privileges, immunities and facilities*" to representatives of Member States and "*the customary diplomatic immunities and privileges*" to missions of third countries accredited to the EC). On the meaning of these expressions in this Protocol, see C. Schmidt, 'Le protocole sur les privilèges et immunités des Communautés in some treaties support the existence of at least certain immunities under customary international law,[1381] I will leave this issue open here as it is of less importance for this book, though I will return to it below (Chapter 7.B.1) from a different perspective. It may be noted that following Rama-Montaldo's distinction, this would be a capacity linked to the specific nature of international organizations rather than to legal personality more generally.[1382]

Although 'inherent' capacities are normally associated with the objective theory,[1383] it is submitted that they are not *per se* incompatible with the subjective theory as it concerns specific capacities that exist if the will to grant international legal personality is found to be present. Amerasinghe's perceived problem that, unlike implied powers, inherent capacities may result in unlimited powers[1384] may be countered by distinguishing between capacity and (material) competence: finding than an organization has a treaty-making capacity does not mean that capacity is unlimited, rather, it will be limited by the principle of speciality/attribution[1385] *ratione materiae* to those matters that fall within the organization's material competences.[1386]

However, in line with the position adopted above, the question must be raised if Member States may withhold capacities that would normally be inherent. This

---

Européennes. Commentaire de l'article 218 du Traité de Rome et de l'article 28, premier alinéa, du Traité de fusion', 27 *C.D.E.* 1991, pp. 80, 84–85 and 93. Also uncertain: Malanczuk, p. 127 and Shaw, p. 692. Similarly, E. David, 'Le droit à un juge ne se réalise pas seulement dans la prononcé d'un jugement mais implique aussi son exécution', annotation of a judgment of the Belgian *Cour de cassation* of 12 March 2001, 120 *J.T.* 2001, p. 611 note 4 mentions divergent state practice. P. Bekker, *supra* note 1224, pp. 144–151 is certain for the UN but more hesitant for other organizations, where he sees room only vis-à-vis Member States, though he seems to accept a minimum customary immunity based on functional necessity.

1381 See *supra* previous note.

1382 M. Rama-Montaldo, *supra* note 1239, p. 152. Indeed, despite the fact there is still some confusion in this regard, the immunities of international organizations are a distinct category of immunities proper to these entities and not simply an application by analogy or extension of state or diplomatic immunity; see, e.g. P. Bekker, *supra* note 1224, pp. 3–8 and 152–180. I will come back to this in Chapter 7.B.1 below.

1383 See *supra* note 1351. See also C. Brölmann, *supra* note 1225, pp. 117–121, who considers that capacities may have their basis in general international law, whereas competences would be defined by the specific law of the organization (she then further distinguishes between material competences and other elements of competence such as the division of powers between organs or between organs and Member States).

1384 Amerasinghe, p. 99. See also Klabbers, p. 280, note 9.

1385 See *supra* note 1348. Klabbers, p. 280, note 9, submits that an inherent treaty-making power negates the distinction between capacity and competence. However, it is difficult to see why this is so: it is perfectly possible to accept that an organization has an inherent capacity to conclude treaties but can only use this within its material competences.

1386 This distinction (see *supra* notes 1253 and 1349 and the accompanying text) is also made by Sand & Klein, p. 481 and Schermers & Blokker, §1748, p. 1115, in respect of treaty-making capacity.

does not seem impossible, except to some extent vis-à-vis third States. In particular, Member States cannot prevent a third State from bringing a claim against an international organization with international legal personality, except if it relates to a breach of a treaty with that State in which it has been agreed that such claims are excluded, for instance providing that the claim must be brought against the Member States instead.[1387] Likewise, Member States cannot force a third State to accept that they bring a claim in respect of an obligation owed to an international organization with international legal personality, unless this has been agreed or perhaps where they are authorized to act on behalf of the organization, although the latter may raise questions as to opposability versus third Parties if they have not agreed to this.[1388]

3. TREATY-MAKING CAPACITY AS ONE DECISIVE ELEMENT

This still doesn't clarify when an international organization has international legal personality. Admittedly, the presence of those capacities identified above as inherent or presumptive in international organizations with international legal personality does offer some help. However, those capacities that *necessarily* imply international legal personality, apart from the treaty-making capacity to some extent, are rarely expressly regulated, especially the capacities to bring an international claim and to be held internationally responsible.[1389] Provisions may more often be found on the international relations of an international organization, but these do not only exist in organizations with international legal personality,[1390] and can therefore mostly not be decisive as to the existence of international legal personality, except where they would include a formal right of mission. Most scholars only provide some indicators and rarely demand much more than a distinct international legal rights and duties and powers on the international plane.[1391] The ILC has recently

---

1387 See, e.g. W. Meng, *supra* note 1363, p. 327 (who sees this, however, as a limitation to recognition by the third party, which he deems necessary for responsibility of an organization towards that party).

1388 For a brief discussion, see *id.*, pp. 337–338 and 344–347.

1389 See F. Seyersted, *supra* note 1229, p. 26 and D.A. Ijalaye, *supra* note 1317, p. 41, noting that "*hardly any constitution of an inter-governmental organization ... authorizes [it] to [present international claims]*".

1390 E.g. the OSCE and even CSCE before it could perfectly maintain international relations without having international legal personality, including through non-legal memoranda of understanding (see *supra*, Section C.3 of this chapter).

1391 Amerasinghe, pp. 80–84, essentially retains, in addition to elements required for an international organization (including a proper organ), "*the existence of a distinction between the organization and its members in respect of legal rights, duties and liabilities, etc. (...) on the international plane ...*". Brownlie, pp. 679–680 adopts a similar approach, essentially adding stressed,[1392] with reference to a couple of ICJ *dicta* suggesting that international organizations simply are subjects of international law,[1393] that there do not appear to be very stringent requirements.[1394] Some commentators are more specific and require a distinct will which they essentially define as the possibility to adopt binding decisions (vis-à-vis the Member States, or, more generally one might argue, within its own legal order[1395]).[1396] The latter indeed

---

"*the existence of legal powers exercisable on the international plane*". KLABBERS, pp. 44–45, lists as indicators the right to enter into international agreements, to send and receive legations and to bring and receive international claims and apparently regards them as alternative rather than cumulative in nature; he even turns around the proposition that international legal personality is required to participate in international legal relations, holding instead that "*once an entity does participate, it may be usefully described as having a degree of international legal personality*" (*id.*, p. 58). SHAW, p. 241 states that: "*significant factors ... will include the capacity to enter into relations with states and other organisations and conclude treaties with them, and the status it has been given under domestic law*".

1392 Provisional Article 2 of the ILC's Draft Articles on the responsibility of international organizations includes a proper international legal personality in the definition of international organization (*Report of the International Law Commission on the Work of its fifty-fifth Session*, UN Doc. A/58/10, 2003, §53, p. 33). Comment 8 thereto (*id.*, p. 41–42) in part reads as follows: "... *While the International Court of Justice has not identified particular prerequisites, its dicta on the legal personality of international organizations do not appear to set stringent requirements for this purpose. In its advisory opinion on the Interpretation of the Agreement of 25 March 1951 between the WHO and Egypt the Court stated: 'International organizations are subjects of international law and, as such, are bound by any obligations incumbent upon them under general rules of international law, under their constitutions or under international agreements to which they are parties.' In its advisory opinion on the Legality of the Use by a State of Nuclear Weapons in Armed Conflict, the Court noted: 'The Court need hardly point out that international organizations are subjects of international law which do not, unlike States, possess a general competence.' While it may be held that, when making both these statements, the Court had an international organization of the type of the World Health Organization (WHO) in mind, the wording is quite general and appears to take a liberal view of the acquisition by international organizations of legal personality under international law*" (notes omitted).

1393 See the ICJ's advisory opinions on the *Interpretation of the Agreement of 25 March 1951 between the WHO and Egypt* (20 December 1980, *I.C.J. Reports* 1980, §37, pp. 89/20–90/21) and on the *Legality of the Use by a State of Nuclear Weapons in Armed Conflict* (8 July 1996, preliminary objections – not to be confused with the ICJ's other *Nuclear Weapons opinion*), §§19 ("*the constituent instruments of international organizations are ... treaties of a particular type; their object is to create new subjects of law endowed with a certain autonomy, to which the parties entrust the task of realizing common goals*") and 25 both also cited *supra* previous note.

1394 In its comment 2 on Article 57 of the 2001 Draft Articles on State Responsibility (*Report of the International Law Commission on the Work of its fifty-third Session*, UN Doc. A/56/10, 2001, p. 361), the ILC even simply and shortly noted that "*[an international organization, meaning an intergovernmental organization] possesses separate legal personality under international law*".

1395 On the specificity of this legal order, see *infra*, Chapter 7.C.2.

1396 E.g. R. Higgins, *Problems and Process. International Law and How We Use It*, Oxford, Clarendon Press, 1994, p. 46 (in addition to elements that seems to relate primarily to domestic legal personality, i.e. capacity to contract, own property and sue and be sued). Similarly, WESSEL, pp. 252–256, stressing the decision of an organ as opposed to agreement between Member States (see also R. Wessel, *supra* note 1253, pp. 19–22), but apparently not seems to be a *sufficient* element, but not a *necessary* one, since treaty-making power is also regarded as conclusive evidence. I will discuss the decision-making power below (Chapter 6.A) in respect of the EU and will focus here on the treaty-making capacity.

The latter capacity may well be the key indicator of the international legal personality of international organizations (it is no longer contested that international organizations can have this capacity[1397]). Although it may only be deemed a presumptive capacity of international organizations with international legal personality (see *supra*), conversely its possession by an international organization necessarily means that that organization possesses international legal personality.[1398] Admittedly, as Klabbers notes, in some cases "*entities of doubtful legal personality engage in acts such as treaty-making*".[1399] However, in

---

requiring a legally binding decision. However, it is submitted that a legally binding decision is indeed required to be able to speak of international *legal* personality (as opposed to international *personality*, see *supra*, Section A of this chapter). For instance, the OSCE may exceptionally make a decision with unanimity minus the State(s) concerned (see I. Dekker & R. Wessel, *supra* note 1258, p. 428) but where such a decision is only political in nature (see *supra*, Section C.3 of this chapter) it cannot be a basis for concluding that the OCSE has legal personality. Compare C. Brölmann, *supra* note 1225, pp. 25–26 and 97, noting that the notion of autonomy that is central to international organizations is often linked to legal personality but that these are not identical. But see F. Seyersted, *supra* note 1229, *inter alia* pp. 28–31, who argues that it is not necessary that the decisions be binding for the Member States.

1397 This is *inter alia* recognized in the 1986 VCLT, in the ICJ's advisory opinion *on the Interpretation of the Agreement of 25 March 1951 between the WHO and Egypt* (*supra* note 1393), §37, pp. 89/20–90/21 and in the constituent documents of international organizations that explicitly include some treaty-making capacity (e.g. the references *supra* notes 1320–1323) as well as in the practice of most international organizations. See also KLABBERS, p. 278 and SCHERMERS & BLOKKER, §§1748–1755, pp. 1114–1121.

1398 See, e.g. the ILC's observation that "*all entities having treaty-making capacity necessarily had international personality*" (*Y.I.L.C.* 1959, Vol. II, p. 96, comment 8(a) to draft Article 2 on the law of treaties, also cited in SANDS & KLEIN, p. 473). See also D.A. Ijalaye, *supra* note 1317, p. 16 ("*The most salient evidence of legal personality under public international law is the right to conclude treaties*"); SCHERMERS & BLOKKER, §1745, pp. 1112–1113 ("*It is generally assumed that only subjects of international law have treaty-making capacity*", though admitting some arguable exceptions; see *infra* next note) and I. Seidl-Hohenveldern & G. Loibl, *supra* note 1241, p. 41 ("*Den Nachweis der eigenen Völkerrechtssubjektivität ... erbringt erst der Abschluß solcher völkerrechtlicher Verträge ... bei denen die Organisation selbst ... als Vertragspartner auftritt*"). Similarly KLABBERS, p. 44, listing as one indicator the right to enter into international agreements and regarding the possession of one of these indicators as sufficient for being a subject of international law (but see his doubts *infra* next note). Compare J. Carroz & Y. Probst, *Personnalité juridique internationale et capacité de conclure des traités de l'ONU et des institutions spécialisées*, Paris, Foulon, 1953, pp. 83–88.

1399 KLABBERS, p. 57, note 56, referring as an example to the Dayton peace agreements on Bosnia and Herzegovina (General Framework Agreement for Peace in Bosnia and Herzegovina with Annexes, Paris, 14 December 1995, 35 *I.L.M.* 1996, p. 75, available online at www.ohr.int/dpa/default.asp?content_id=380), *inter alia* discussed in P. Gaeta, 'The Dayton Agreements and International Law', 7 *E.J.I.L.* 1996, pp. 147–163 and J.-M. Sorel, 'L'accord de paix sur la Bosnie-such cases, which mostly deal with state-like entities rather than international organizations (with the exception perhaps of the ICRC[1400]), the entities in question may be regarded as having international legal personality, but with only very specific and limited legal capacities and competences.[1401]

Given the extensive practice of the conclusion of international agreements by international organizations (it may be hard to find an organization which has not concluded at least one international agreement),[1402] the main fundamental difficulties that can arise in relation to legal personality are the questions whether such agreements are legally binding under international law (the point of discussion in respect of the OSCE, see *supra*, Section C of this chapter, and one which may be raised regarding NATO, see *infra*, Section E.3.ii of this chapter), and whether they are concluded on behalf of the organization or on behalf of its Member States (long the key point regarding the EU, see *infra*, Chapter 6.A-B and a point which may be raised regarding the Eurocorps, see *infra*, Section E.3.iii of this chapter).[1403] The former is among others important in order to avoid a circular argument that would deduce international legal personality from the power or practice to conclude international agreements to then qualify the agreement as a treaty because it is concluded by an entity with international legal personality.[1404]

i. Will Contradicted by Capacities and Treaties or Non-Binding Agreements

At first sight, the subjective theory does not solve what is the situation when Member States on the one hand explicitly deny an organization international

---

Herzégovine du 14 décembre 1995: un traité sous bénéfice d'inventaire', 41 *A.F.D.I.* 1995, pp. 65–99.

1400 The ICRC has concluded agreements with various States in which it has offices or operates in the field; see J. P. Lavoyer, 'The International Committee of the Red Cross: Legal Status and Headquarters Agreements', in D. Fleck (ed.), *The Handbook of the Law of Visiting Forces*, Oxford, Oxford University Press, 2001, pp. 475–484.

1401 See P. Gaeta, *supra* note 1399, pp. 158 ("*The Dayton negotiations bear out ... that entities which exercise de facto control over a specific territory may be regarded as subjects of international law, even if they enjoy a limited international personality*"). In the same sense Schermers & Blokker, §1745, p. 1113 ("*Perhaps such entities [not recognized as subjects of international law] should be accepted as de facto subjects of international law for the particular matter in respect of which agreements are concluded with them*").

1402 See, e.g. the already impressive overview of agreements between international organizations in C.W. Jenks, 'Co-ordination: A New Problem of International Organization', 77 *Rec. Cours* 1950-II, pp. 205–252.

1403 See also I. Seidl-Hohenveldern & G. Loibl, *supra* note 1241, p. 41 ("*Den Nachweis der eigenen Völkerrechtssubjektivität ... erbringt erst der Abschluß solcher völkerrechtlicher Verträge ... bei denen die Organisation selbst ... als Vertragspartner auftritt*").

1404 See I. Seidl-Hohenveldern & G. Loibl, *supra* note 1241, p. 40. Compare Sands & Klein, pp. 472–473, who also warn of a circular reasoning but a somewhat different one.

legal personality (while they did not do so using these actual words in an agreed OSCE document, they all but did so and repeatedly confirmed the political and non-legal nature of the OSCE and its constituent documents) but on the other hand allow that organization to act in a manner that requires international legal personality, in particular by concluding international agreements which, due to the circumstances, cannot be qualified as anything else but treaties by those who conclude agreements with it (mostly third States but occasionally also Participating States[1405]).

In this respect, one cannot avoid the impression, having regard to the OSCE (and even more so the EU, see *infra*, Chapter 6), that a number of States either do not understand the concept of international legal personality of international organizations in the same way as it appears to be seen by the ICJ and most commentators,[1406] i.e. as being of a limited nature, or, and this is more likely, perhaps to some extent combined with the first element, do understand this but for political reasons do not wish to endow certain organizations with such personality even where they know that by giving it certain legal capacities (especially treaty-making capacity) and functions they are in fact implicitly granting it such personality and actively cooperating or at least acquiescing in the exercise thereof.[1407]

1405 E.g. all States hosting OSCE missions are OSCE Participating States.

1406 For instance, regarding the UN, during the negotiations on the UN Charter, one of the reasons for not explicitly granting international legal personality was to avoid any implication that the UN would in a sense be a super State; see the statement by the Chairman of the US delegation cited in AMERASINGHE, p. 78. See also J. de Zwaan, *supra* note 1246, p. 86, citing J. Cloos *et al*, *Le Traité de Maastricht, genèse, analyse, commentaries*, Brussels, Bruylant, 1993, p. 115, who write "*L'Union ... est un concept politique bien plus que juridique, et elle ne dispose dès lors pas de la personnalité juridique. On n'est pas arrivé au stade où les Etats membres seraient prêts à transférer leurs compétences en matière de politique étrangère à une entité juridique distincte. Ils sont d'accord pour agir collectivement ... mais non pas pour disparaître en tant qu'acteurs juridiquement distincts*". This is clearly a misconception as conferring international legal personality on the EU would not entail the disappearance of the Member States any less than that is the case following conferral of such personality upon the UN, the EC and various other international organizations (all the more so if the competences are not exclusive).

1407 E.g. G. Hafner, *supra* note 1376, p. 266 quotes a report in the framework of the EU that states "*Others consider that the creation of international legal personality for the Union could risk confusion with the legal prerogatives of Member States*". A.S. Muller, *supra* note 1269, pp. 85 note 46 aptly used the expression "*fiction of 'non personality' of the EU*" (an expression also used by A. Tizzano, *infra* note 1543, p. 144) and, rightly, believed that it would be defeated by practice. L. Grard, 'La condition internationale de l'Union européenne après Nice', 10 *R.A.E. / L.E.A.* 2000, p. 377 in respect of the EU speaks of mainly symbolic opposition and of a "*personnification de l'Union masquée*". R. Wessel, 'The International Legal Status of the European Union', 2 *E.F.A.R.* 1997, p. 129 believes that some Member States were not aware of the implications of the CFSP, though it seems more likely that they were but did not explicitly want to acknowledge it, at least since the Treaty of Amsterdam.

It is submitted that where capacities are exercised that necessarily require international legal personality, in particular treaty-making capacity, such personality is present. However, where a clear reluctance nevertheless exists to admit international legal personality in such cases, this will be an element supporting a limitation of this personality to capacities that are effectively exercised or that are undoubtedly inherent and that remain within the material competences of the organization.

ii. International Legal Personality and Treaty-Making Power of NATO

Just like the OSCE, NATO's status is worth discussing in some detail, both because it is a partner of the EU in the ESDP and agreements between both organizations exist and because it seems to be a good example of implied international legal personality, or at least a very extensive treaty practice based on implied powers.

The international legal personality of NATO has been discussed rather little until recently.[1408] The North Atlantic Treaty is silent on this matter, but various agreements concluded between the Member States (and in some cases third States[1409]), as well as some agreements between NATO or NATO organs and

1408 See generally U. Erberich, *Auslandseinsätze der Bundeswehr und Europäische Menschenrechtskonvention*, Cologne, Carl Heymanns, 2004, pp. 113–122; Zwanenburg, pp. 67–68 and A. Pellet, 'L'imputabilité d'éventuels actes illicites: responsabilité d'OTAN ou des états membres', in C. Tomuschat (ed.), *Kosovo and the International Community. A Legal Assessment*, The Hague, Kluwer Law International, 2002, p. 198 (all three arguing that NATO has international legal personality) and S. Lüder, *Völkerrechtliche Verantwortlichkeit bei Teilnahme an 'Peace-keeping'-Missionen der Vereinten Nationen,* Berlin, Berliner Wissenschaftsverlag, 2004, pp. 165–167 (submitting that NATO has partial international legal personality). T. Stein, 'The Attribution of Possible Internationally Wrongful Acts: Responsibility of NATO or of its Member States?', in C. Tomuschat (ed.), *supra* this note, pp. 181–192, also seems to accept this; see especially p. 183, as does A. Holstein, *Das Verhältnis des Sicherheitsrates der Vereinten Nationen zu NATO und OSZE*, Stuttgart, Boorberg, 1996, pp. 159–161. Brownlie, p. 680, note 9, notes some early conflicting Italian decisions on the status of NATO. R.J. Dupuy, *supra* note 1341, p. 534 considered (in 1960) that NATO did not have international legal personality. M. Reichard, *The EU-NATO Relationship: A Legal and Political Perspective*, Aldershot, Ashgate, 2006, pp. 134–135 writes that "*NATO's quality as a subject of international law is today undisputed*".

1409 Especially the non-Member States participating in the Partnership for Peace cooperation programme (see generally www.nato.int/issues/pfp/index.html); see, e.g. the PfP SOFA, *infra* note 1416.

Member[1410] and third[1411] States deal with the legal status of NATO and its headquarters and forces.[1412] The key agreements are the Ottawa Convention (for NATO, its international staff and Member State representatives),[1413] the NATO SOFA (for NATO forces)[1414] and Paris Protocol (for NATO headquarters)[1415] and their extensions to non-Member States participating in the Partnership for Peace,[1416] and the agreement on the status of representatives of third States.[1417]

However, most of these agreements are largely limited to legal status under domestic law and jurisdictional rules, with just a few exceptions concerning treaty-making. For instance, the Ottawa Agreement's basic provision, Article IV, states that "*The Organization shall possess juridical personality; it shall have the capacity to conclude contracts, to acquire and dispose of movable and immovable*

1410 Especially Member States hosting NATO institutions or headquarters. See, e.g. the agreements between Belgium and SHAPE (Overeenkomst tussen het Koninkrijk België en het Algemeen Hoofdkwartier van de Geallieerde Strijdkrachten in Europa inzake bijzondere voorwaarden voor de vestiging en het functioneren van dit Hoofdkwartier op het grondgebied van het Koninkrijk België, Brussels, 12 May 1967) and between the Netherlands and SHAPE (Agreement on the special conditions applicable to the establishment and operations of International Military Headquarters within the European territory of the Kingdom of the Netherlands (with related letters), Paris, 25 May 1964, 544 *U.N.T.S.* 245 (1965), applied provisionally as of 25 May 1964 and which entered into force on 13 April 1965). See also the NATO-Dutch agreement cited in ZWANENBURG, p. 67 note 68.

1411 Notably SOFAs with States in which NATO conducts operations or through which its forces transit; see *infra*.

1412 For a partial overview, see www.nato.int/docu/basics.htm, Part II.B-C. For a discussion of some of these agreements, see M. Johnson, 'NATO Military Headquarters', in D. Fleck (ed.), *The Handbook of the Law of Visiting Forces*, Oxford, Oxford University Press, 2001, pp. 257–320 (with an interesting discussion of why different arrangements were developed at pp. 258–262).

1413 Agreement on the Status of the North Atlantic Treaty Organisation, National Representatives and International Staff, Ottawa, 20 September 1951, 200 *U.N.T.S.* 3 (1954), which entered into force on 18 May 1954.

1414 Agreement between the Parties to the North Atlantic Treaty regarding the Status of their Forces, London, 19 June 1951, 199 *U.N.T.S.* 67 (1954), which entered into force on 23 August 1953. For a detailed analysis, see S. Lazareff, *Le statut des forces de l'O.T.A.N.*, Paris, Association des Etudes Internationales, 1965 and various chapters and sections in D. Fleck (ed.), *supra* note 1400. See also P. Weckel, *supra* note 1251, pp. 41–46.

1415 Protocol on the Status of International Military Headquarters set up pursuant to the North Atlantic Treaty, Paris, 28 August 1952, 200 *U.N.T.S.* 340 (1954), which entered into force on 10 April 1954.

1416 See Agreement among the States Parties to the North Atlantic Treaty and the other States participating in the Partnership for Peace regarding the Status of their Forces, Brussels, 19 June 1995 and Further Additional Protocol to the Agreement among the States Parties to the North Atlantic Treaty and the other States participating in the Partnership for Peace regarding the Status of their Forces, Brussels, 19 December 1997, both available online at www.nato.int/docu/basics.htm.

1417 Agreement on the Status of Missions and Representatives of Third States to the North Atlantic Treaty Organisation, Brussels, 14 September 1994, 2158 *U.N.T.S.* 113, which entered into force on 28 March 1997.

property and to institute legal proceedings" and its only provision hinting at *international* legal personality, is Article XXV, which reads "*The Council acting on behalf of the Organization may conclude with any Member State or States supplementary agreements modifying the provisions of the present Agreement, so far as that State or those States are concerned*". Similarly, Article X of the Paris Protocol provides that "*Each Supreme Headquarters shall possess juridical personality; it shall have the capacity to conclude contracts and to acquire and dispose of property. The receiving State may, however, make the exercise of such capacity subject to special arrangements between it and the Supreme Headquarters or any subordinate Allied Headquarters acting on behalf of the Supreme Headquarters*" and its Article XVI(2) adds that "*The present Protocol may be supplemented by bilateral agreement between the receiving State and a Supreme Headquarters, and the authorities of a receiving State ...*".[1418] One may read the first phrases in Articles IV Ottawa Agreement and X Paris Protocol as partly or solely referring to international legal personality in contrast with the phrases that follow them, or read the latter as elaborating the former and thus referring to domestic legal personality only.[1419]

In any event, the treaty-making power suggests that both NATO as such and the Headquarters covered by the Paris Protocol possess international legal personality.[1420] This is explicitly accepted by the NATO Member States in respect of the Headquarters.[1421] There are various elements that confirm this also for NATO as such. They include the frequent conclusion of international agreements.[1422] Admittedly, many may not be legally binding,[1423] as would, e.g.

1418 For instances of such agreements between a headquarters and a host State, see *supra* note 1410.

1419 One could draw the comparison with Articles 281 and 282 EC Treaty, see *supra* note 1320, but the provisions here are much less distinct from one another than is the case in the EC Treaty (they are not even in separate paragraphs). S. Lüder, *supra* note 1408, p. 167 also infers (partial) international legal personality from these agreements.

1420 M. Johnson, *supra* note 1412, pp. 257–258 points out that the separate legal personality of the two headquarters concerned includes that of their respective subordinate headquarters.

1421 See *Allied Joint Publication 4.5 (A), Host Nation Support Doctrine & Procedures* (AJP 4.5(A)), May 2005, available online at www.nato.int/docu/stanag/ajp45/ajp45.htm, §0126, B ("*The Paris Protocol and the companion Further Additional (Headquarters) Protocol to the PfP SOFA, among other things, establish the Bi-SCs and subordinate Headquarters as legal entities in International Law and the domestic law of ratifying nations*") and §0127.B ("*The [Paris] Protocol ... establishes the Strategic Commands' legal rights and obligations and grants SHAPE its own juridical (legal) personality to enter into binding agreements with other nations, organisations or individuals*"). But see P. Weckel, *supra* note 1251, pp. 45–49, seeing headquaters rather as common organs.

1422 See also Zwanenburg, p. 67 and M. Johnson, *supra* note 1412, pp. 305 and 317 (citing bilateral agreements between the headquarters and host nations).

1423 For instance, in the case of the Founding Act on Mutual Relations, Cooperation and Security between the Russian Federation and the North Atlantic Treaty Organisation, Paris, 27 May generally seem to be NATO's view on Host Nation Support Arrangements.[1424] However, several are quite clearly legally binding. The latter include the EU-NATO Security Agreement.[1425] They would also seem to include the Agreement between the Republic of Bosnia and Herzegovina and the North Atlantic Treaty Organisation (NATO) concerning the Status of NATO and its Personnel,[1426] the Kosovo Verification Mission Agreement between the North Atlantic Treaty Organization and the Federal Republic of Yugoslavia[1427] and perhaps the Military Technical Agreement between the International Security Force ("KFOR") and the Governments of the Federal Republic of Yugoslavia and the Republic of Serbia.[1428] Moreover, some transit agreements have had to be

---

1997 (36 *I.L.M.* 1997, pp. 1006–1015, also available online at www.nato.int/docu/basictxt/fndact-a.htm), it was reported that there was a deliberate choice not to conclude a legally binding agreement; see AUST, p. 42; R. Müllerson, 'NATO Enlargement and Russia', 47 *I.C.L.Q.* 1998, pp. 197–198 (noting that the first consideration of the preamble mentions "*an enduring political commitment undertaken at the highest political level*") and SCHERMERS & BLOKKER, §1783, p. 1140. The same goes for the Charter on a Distinctive Partnership between the North Atlantic Treaty Organisation and Ukraine (Madrid, 9 July 1997, available online at www.nato.int/docu/basictxt/ukrchrt.htm; see its preamble language "*building on a political commitment at the highest level*" noted in R. Müllerson, *supra* this note, p. 198) and for the 2002 NATO-EU Berlin Plus agreement (see *supra*, Chapter 2.C, note 210; for an elaborate analysis, see M. Reichard, 'Some Legal Issues Concerning the EU-NATO Berlin Plus Agreement', 73 *Nordic J.I.L.* 2004, pp. 37–67). M. Warnken, *infra* note 1472, pp. 124–130 qualifies earlier NATO-WEU arrangements as a treaty, although this seems questionable.

1424 On these arrangements, see, e.g. AJP 4.5(A), *supra* note 1421. In §0305.1 this document states that "*NATO considers these MOU to be politically binding whereas some HN(s) consider them legally binding*" (in the previous edition, it was stated in §1–15 that "*HNSAs are not, in themselves, legally binding*" and that "*to be relied on they must conform to the domestic law and practices of a HN and SN(s) and rules applicable to NATO activities. There also may be international legal considerations for certain nations*"). See in this context also the US reservation that "*USA does not agree with the wording incorporated in several chapters and annexes regarding the legal character of prospective MOUs and Technical Arrangements, which implies an obligation without express acceptance of the USA. USA will not be obligated by any MOU or subsequent Technical Arrangement, agreed to by NATO unless the USA expressly has accepted the obligation in writing after review of the MOU or subsequent Technical Arrangement*".

1425 See *supra*, Chapter 2.C, note 212.

1426 Appendix B to Annex 1A to the General Framework Agreement for Peace in Bosnia and Herzegovina, *supra* note 1399.

1427 15 October 1998, Annex to UN Doc. S/1998/991, 23 October 1998. Compare with the similar OSCE agreement discussed above, note 1290 and the accompanying text: there is a similar safety and security guarantee but also a clause on determining liability, albeit through bilateral channels.

1428 9 June 1999, 38 *I.L.M.* 1999, pp. 1217–1221 (also available online at www.nato.int/kosovo/docu/a990609a.htm). Article V of this agreement provides that: "*The international security force ("KFOR") commander is the final authority regarding interpretation of this Agreement and the security aspects of the peace settlement it supports. His determinations are binding on all Parties and persons*". For another example, see 'NATO and Iraq to Sign a Legal Agreement', NATO press release, 24 July 2009, www.nato.int/cps/en/SID-6ECF86D2-0AA1D9AC/natolive/news_56617.htm.

approved by Parliaments in the transit State,[1429] indicating a legally binding nature (although again, as with the OSCE, this would depend on the domestic law of the State concerned). Moreover, the comment made above in the previous section on the OSCE concerning the desirability of legally binding agreements with a host State on the status of an international presence in that State are equally valid for NATO.[1430] Finally, it should be noted in this respect that although the Ottawa Convention and Paris Protocol only explicitly grant a specific treaty-making power, this need not be read as an exhaustive provision and practice clearly shows it is not exhaustive.[1431]

In addition, and as argued by Zwanenburg,[1432] there are other indications of NATO's legal personality, such as an ICTY decision *inter alia* addressed to "*SFOR and its responsible authority, the North Atlantic Council*"[1433] and the submissions of some NATO Member States in the *Bankovic case* before the ECtHR,[1434] to

1429 For an example of a transit agreement, see the agreement signed on 2 March 205 between NATO and Georgia (NATO press release (2005)026 of 2 March 2005, available online at www.nato.int/docu/pr/2005/p05-026e.htm). This agreement was included in the 'Agreements and Treaties ratified by Parliament of Georgia. 2005 Year', available online at www.parliament.ge/files/544_7353_359339_2005-agr.doc (the list of ratified agreements that year includes one other agreement with NATO and one more with a NATO Agency). This is not a unique case.

1430 An example in which a SOFA is clearly regarded by NATO as legally binding is the SOFA with FYROM on KFOR, since Austria, as a non-Member State participating in the operation was asked to, and did, "*subscribe to the obligations, rights, privileges and immunities of KFOR and its members when present in the territory of [FYROM] as defined in the agreement*": see Zustimmungserklärung der Österreichischen Bundesregierung zum Abkommen zwischen der NATO und FYROM über den Status des KFOR-Personals in FYROM vom 18. Mai 2001, *Bundesgesetzblatt* No. 90/2003, available online at www.ris.bka.gv.at/Dokumente/BgblPdf/2003_90_3/2003_90_3.pdf.

1431 On NATO's treaty practice, see also M. Reichard, *supra* note 1408, pp. 141–143. In this respect there is a parallel with the EC, which also has an implied treaty-making power exceeding to some extent the specifically listed cases. See, e.g. ECJ, e.g. Case C-22/70, *Commission of the European Communities v Council of the European Communities, European Agreement on Road Transport (AETR)*, Judgment of 31 March 1971, §§13–14; P. Eeckhout, *External Relations of the European Union. Legal and Constitutional Foundations*, Oxford, Oxford University Press, 2004, pp. 58–137 and P. Koutrakos, *EU International Relations Law*, Oxford, Hart, 2006, pp. 77–134 (both with further references).

1432 Zwanenburg, pp. 67–68.

1433 ICTY, *Prosecutor v. Blagoje Simic, Milan Simic, Mirosllav Tadic, Stevan Todorovic and Simo Zaric*, Decision on Motion for judicial Assistance to be provided by SFOR and others, 18 October 2000, IT-95-9, §§38–58 and especially §§46–48 (the quote is from §1 of the disposition). This decision was also endorsed in ICTY, *Prosecutor v. Dragan Nikolic*, Decision on Defence Motion Challenging the Exercise of Jurisdiction by the Tribunal, 9 October 2002, IT-94-2-PT, §49.

1434 ECtHR, Grand Chamber, Decision as to the admissibility of Application No. 52207/99 by *Vlastimir and Borka Bankovic, Živana Stojanovic, Mirjana Stoimenovski, Dragana Joksimovic and Dragan Sukovic against Belgium, the Czech Republic, Denmark, France, Germany, Greece, Hungary, Iceland, Italy, Luxembourg, the Netherlands, Norway, Poland, Portugal, Spain, Turkey and the United Kingdom*, 12 December 2001, §§31–32. France argued that the actions which may be added similar submissions before the ICJ.[1435] Furthermore, Security Council Resolution 1575 of 22 November 2004 also recognized NATO's legal personality by regarding the EU's operation Althea as a "*legal successor to SFOR*"[1436] (since SFOR is to be regarded as a subsidiary organ of NATO[1437]). It may therefore be concluded on the basis of the above that NATO and some NATO Headquarters possess international legal personality.

---

concerned were attributable to NATO itself (§32) and several States submitted that the Court would determine the rights and obligations of NATO if it would adjudicate the merits of the case (§31).

1435 Schermers & Blokker, §1590A, p. 1010, note 106, point out that Canada made a similar argument before the ICJ in the *Legality of Use of Force case (Serbia and Montenegro v. Canada)*; see the public sittings of 10 and 12 May 1999 on Yugoslavia's request for provisional measures, documents CR 99/16, p. 15, §34 (implicitly) and especially CR 99/27, p. 10, both available online at www.icj-cij.org. See also A. Geslin, 'Réflexions sur la repartition de la responsabilité entre l'organisation internationale et ses Etats membres', 109 *R.G.D.I.P.* 2005, pp. 556–558, citing the submission by the Netherlands in its written pleadings of 5 July 2000 (available online at www.icj-cij.org), §§7.1.5 ("*the actions complained of by the FRY are or have been collective actions. The "imputability thesis" of the FRY wrongly ignores the collective nature of NATO decision-making and the organic nature of NATO decisions, involving both Operation Allied Force and KFOR. NATO and KFOR acts are not simply directly imputable to one or some of the States involved in their preparation and adoption*") and 7.2 (more extensively developing this argument).

1436 §10. See also UNSC Res. 1088 (12 December 1996), §18, which "*Authorizes the Member States acting through or in cooperation with [NATO] to establish ... a multinational stabilization force (SFOR) as the legal successor to IFOR*". See *infra* next note on the legal relationship between NATO and SFOR.

1437 See Zwanenburg, pp. 42–45 for a more extensive discussion. *Contra*, N. Figà-Talamanca, 'The Role of NATO in the Peace Agreement for Bosnia and Herzegovina', 7 *E.J.I.L.* 1996, pp. 164–175; W. Heintschel von Heinegg, 'Rechtsprobleme einer deutsch-franzözischen Zusammenarbeit bei Friedenssicherungsaktionen der Vereinte Nationen', in C. Tomuschat & J.A. Frowein (eds.), *supra* note 1251, pp. 101–103 and S.R. Lüder, 'Die völkerrechtliche Verantwortlichkeit der Nordatlantikvertrags-Organisation bei der militärischen Absicherung der Friedensvereinbarung von Dayton', 43 *N. Z. Wehrrecht* 2001, pp. 107–117, especially pp. 113–116 (available online at www.deutsches-wehrrecht.de/Aufsaetze/NZWehrr_2001_107.pdf). The ICTY apparently sees SFOR as an organ of NATO by qualifying the NAC as its responsible authority (see the *Simic et al.* decision cited *supra* note 1433, e.g §48: "*an international organization or its competent organ such as SFOR*"). While this seems correct given the role of NATO in the operation, the separate legal personality of NATO headquarters might also mean that SFOR is rather an organ of the Headquarters by which it is commanded. The latter view seems to underlie a letter by the SHAPE legal advisor cited in this decision (at §45) stating that "*It is understood that relevant nations and international military headquarters, not the UN, remain legally responsible for the acts or omissions of IFOR personnel*". Compare J.A. Burger, 'Headquarters IFOR/SFOR', in D. Fleck (ed.), *supra* note 1412, pp. 328–339, especially p. 329, seeing SFOR as a part of NATO's legal personality while admitting that it is not a NATO body set up in accordance with NATO's normal internal rules. On the question of the status of organs in relation to legal personality, see *supra* note 1296.

iii. The Eurocorps

Another example that is relevant in the context of the ESDP is the Eurocorps.[1438] Its 2004 Constitution,[1439] *inter alia* provides that:

> Article 5. 1. Le Quartier général a la capacité juridique. Il a la capacité de contracter, d'acquérir et d'aliéner.
> ...
> Article 6. 1. La capacité juridique du Quartier général est exercée par le Général commandant le Corps européen ou par toute personne désignée expressément par lui pour agir en son nom.
> 2. Le Général commandant le Corps européen peut recevoir mandat du Comité commun pour négocier des accords relatifs à l'organisation et à la conduite d'exercices ou d'opérations sur le territoire d'un Etat tiers.
> ...
> Article 20. ... 3. S'agissant des dommages pouvant être causés à des tiers par le Corps européen ou causés au Corps européen par des tiers en dehors du territoire d'une des Parties contractantes, le Comité commun est chargé par les Parties contractantes d'élaborer des procédures communes.
> ...
> Article 42. 1. Le Comité commun peut accepter la désignation de personnels d'Etats tiers auprès du Quartier général.
> 2. Le statut de ces personnels est fixé par accord entre l'Etat qui les désigne et l'Etat de séjour.
> 3. Les modalités de participation de personnels d'Etats tiers aux activités du Corps européen sont arrêtées par les Parties contractantes.

Here the situation is less clear. While on the domestic level legal capacity presumably may be equated to legal personality more generally, it would appear that the Parties have not intended to grant the Eurocorps international legal personality. Although Article 6(2) states that the Eurocorps Commander may receive a mandate from the Common Committee to negotiate some international agreements, it does not clarify whether such agreements would be concluded on behalf of the Eurocorps or on behalf of its Member States. The provisions of

---

1438 See generally *supra* Chapter 1.D, note 83.

1439 Traité entre le Royaume de Belgique, la République fédérale d'Allemagne, le Royaume d'Espagne, la République française et le Grand-Duché de Luxembourg relatif au Corps européen et au statut de son Quartier Général, Brussels, 22 November 2004, which entered into force on 26 February 2009, published in *Memorial. Journal Officiel du Grand-Duché de Luxembourg, A*, No. 63, 12 April 2006, pp. 1274–1284 (available online at www.legilux.public.lu/leg/a/archives/2006/0063/a063.pdf).

Articles 20(3) and 42(2–3) cited above suggest the overall aim is that international agreements are concluded on behalf of the Member States.[1440]

F. OBJECTIVE INTERNATIONAL LEGAL PERSONALITY?

A final point which does not appear to be quite settled in doctrine, is whether the international legal personality of an international organization is objective, in the sense that it may be invoked vis-à-vis non-Member States, or whether these States have to recognize the international legal personality in some way before it may be opposed to them.

Many commentators supporting the subjective theory submit that a treaty, including one setting up an international organization, cannot impose obligations upon third States without their acceptance,[1441] and that therefore the international legal personality of an international organization cannot be invoked against third States that have not recognized it.[1442] In this context, it is sometimes held that obtaining reparation from an international organization

1440 The French explanatory report explicitly confirms this, see projet de loi autorisant la ratification du traité relatif au Corps européen et au statut de son Quartier général entre la République française, la République fédérale d'Allemagne, le Royaume de Belgique, le Royaume d'Espagne et le Grand-Duché de Luxembourg, exposé des motifs (Sénat, Session 2005–2006, No. 478, available online at www.senat.fr/leg/pjl05-478.html): "*La capacité juridique du Quartier général du Corps européen ne lui permet pas de conclure des engagements internationaux. Le général commandant le Corps européen peut toutefois recevoir mandat du Comité commun pour négocier des accords relatifs à l'organisation et à la conduite d'exercices ou d'opérations sur le territoire d'un État tiers*". See also J. Rios Rodriguez, 'France: Projet de loi autorisant la ratification du traité relatif au corps européen et au statut de son quartier général', *Sentinelle* No. 78, 17 September 2006, www.sfdi.org/actualites/a2006/Sentinelle%2078.htm#eurocorps. The Luxembourg *Exposé des motifs* (Chambre des Députés, session 2004–2005, Doc. 5463, previously available online at www.chd.lu/servlet/DisplayServlet?id=39819&path=/export/exped/sexpdata/Mag/016/471/041750.pdf) is silent on his point. Compare, with regard to the Eurocorps before the conclusion of this treaty, P. Weckel, *supra* note 1251, pp. 41 and 45–49 (not seeing the Eurocorps as an international organization and taking the view that it did not possess international legal personality).

1441 See Article 35 1969 VCLT ("*An obligation arises for a third State from a provision of a treaty if the parties to the treaty intend the provision to be the means of establishing the obligation and the third State expressly accepts that obligation in writing*") and Article 35 1986 VCLT ("*An obligation arises for a third State or a third organization from a provision of a treaty if the parties to the treaty intend the provision to be the means of establishing the obligation and the third State or the third organization expressly accepts that obligation in writing. Acceptance by the third organization of such an obligation shall be governed by the rules of that organization*").

1442 E.g. K. Ipsen *et al.*, *supra* note 1254, pp. 85–86; Malanczuk, p. 92; Sands & Klein, p. 476 (and the authors cited there in note 34) and I. Seidl-Hohenveldern & G. Loibl, *supra* note 1241, pp. 42–43 and 78–83.

will be more difficult than from States.[1443] However, it is doubtful that this is necessarily so given, among other considerations, that there exists no compulsory dispute settlement vis-à-vis States.[1444] Moreover, the objection may be countered in that either the obligation will have been contracted with the organization, in which case the third party has recognized it, or the obligation existed before and in principle still exists on the part of the State that originally undertook it (as in that case one must distinguish between opposability of the existence of the organization and of all the rules pertaining thereto).[1445] In any event, it is accepted that such recognition may be, and in fact almost invariably is,[1446] implicit, e.g. by concluding a treaty with an organization.[1447] Occasionally, it is argued that recognition is necessary but that refusal of recognition would amount to interference in the domestic affairs of the Member States who may decide to exercise their rights as they see fit.[1448]

However, these same authors mostly accept the ICJ's opinion that in the case of the UN the Member States were in a position to establish an organization with objective personality in the sense of being opposable to third States,[1449] although they differ over whether, or to what extent, this also applies to other international

---

1443 E.g. K. Ipsen *et al.*, *supra* note 1254, pp. 85–86 and I. Seidl-Hohenveldern & G. Loibl, *supra* note 1241, pp. 79–81.

1444 While it is true that State immunity is nowadays limited to sovereign acts of a State and the immunity of jurisdiction of international organizations is often more comprehensive (see *infra*, Chapter 7.B.1), a number of international organizations have some specific dispute settlements in place. E.g. K. Lenaerts & E. De Smijter, 'The European Community's Treaty-Making Competence', 16 *Y.E.L.* 1996, pp. 54–57 note that agreements concluded by the EC almost always include dispute settlement mechanisms, including, ultimately, arbitration or submission to the ECJ. See more generally A.N. Papadopoulos, 'Procedures for the Settlement of Disputes concerning International Organisations Arising out of Treaties to Which They are Parties', 24 *Revue hellénique de droit international* 1971, pp. 235–266. Also, disputes between States and international organizations will most likely concern sovereign rights. C. Tomuschat, *supra* note 1320, p. 1254 submits that the EC is an extraordinarily positive carrier of responsibility.

1445 See F. Seyersted, *supra* note 1229, pp. 62–75 and 96–97. One may note that the ECJ, when it ruled that the EC had replaced or succeeded the Member States in the GATT, stressed and seemed to consider it necessary that the other parties had accepted this (see *infra*, Chapter 7.G.2).

1446 As pointed out by KLABBERS, p. 54, note 46, explicit recognitions in this field are very rare.

1447 E.g. SANDS & KLEIN, p. 476. M. Bothe, 'Die Stellung der Europäischen Gemeinschaften im Völkerrecht', 37 *Z.a.ö.R.V.* 1977, p. 130 notes, rightly in my view, that recognition is, in principle, not limited to certain capacities or competences (although he does seem to accept a reconsidering in the case of a fundamental change of competences, which is doubtful).

1448 P. Pescatore, *supra* note 1241, pp. 41–43. See also the view of R. Bernhardt, *infra* note 1450.

1449 *Reparations opinion*, pp. 184/14–185/15: *"fifty States, representing the vast majority of the members of the international community had the power, in conformity with international law, to bring into being an entity possessing objective international personality, and not merely personality recognized by them alone"*.

organizations: some authors say only the UN,[1450] some accept this only for universal organizations,[1451] whereas still others broaden it to include also 'closed' and regional organizations.[1452] For those who support the objective theory, there logically is no need for recognition as the international legal personality results from general international law.[1453]

Even though the issue rarely poses a problem in practice any more,[1454] it is relevant for the purposes of this book, as it primarily deals with the relations

1450 E.g. I. Seidl-Hohenveldern & G. Loibl, *supra* note 1241, p. 78. This also appears to be the view of SANDS & KLEIN, p. 476 (see also the authors cited in note 33 there). For a very peculiar view, see R. Bernhardt, 'Die Europäische Gemeinschaft als neuer Rechtsträger im Geflecht der traditionellen zwischenstaatlichen Rechtsbeziehungen', 18 *Europarecht* 1983, pp. 203–204, arguing that the ICJ's considerations cannot be transposed on other organizations, certainly not on regional ones but that the EC is special because it has been granted sovereign powers formerly exercised by the Member States and that to not make this opposable would be to accept interference in internal decisions.

1451 E.g. SCHERMERS & BLOKKER, §1568, pp. 990–991. See also P. Dailler & A. Pellet, *supra* note 1233, pp. 596–597, who consider that the representativeness was crucial for the ICJ and therefore extend the objective personality to all universal international organizations; however, they personally believe that the objective personality as a fact can be extended to most international organizations.

1452 E.g. AMERASINGHE, pp. 89–91; R. Higgins, *supra* note 1396, pp. 47–48 and R.A. Wessel, *supra* note 1407, p. 112 ("*recognition ... is never a prerequisite for the enjoyment of international legal personality*"). BROWNLIE, p. 692, does not take a position, arguing that the ICJ's opinion did not provide guidance for other cases, but does state that, "*Whilst third states are not in principle bound by the basic treaty of an international organization, the possession of legal personality by an organization may give rise to certain obligations on the part of non-member states under general international law. Thus, an organization may possess a capacity to bring claims against both members and non-members*". SHAW, p. 241, writes that "*In principle, it is now well established that international organisations may indeed possess objective international legal personality*". Compare *Restatement of the Foreign Relations Law of the United States* (*supra* note 1241), §223 and comment (e) thereto, pp. 140–141 (accepting objective international legal personality of international organizations with substantial membership and apparently including regional organizations with substantial membership in a region vis-à-vis States in that region). Categorically *contra* in respect of regional organizations: H. Hahn, *supra* note 1352, p. 294 and P. Pescatore, *supra* note 1241, p. 71.

1453 See, e.g. F. Seyersted, *supra* note 1229, pp. 45–98; F. Seyersted, 'Is the International Personality of Intergovernmental Organizations Valid vis-à-vis Non-Members?', 4 *Indian J.I.L.* 1964, pp. 233–265, reprinted in J. Klabbers (ed.), *International Organizations*, Aldershot, Ashgate, 2005, pp. 207–239 and R. Gosalbo Bono, *supra* note 1247, p. 355. See also KLABBERS, pp. 54–55, noting that the objective theory meets some of the objections to the subjective one, one of which, according to Klabbers, is precisely the issue of recognition. Compare M. Hartwig, *supra* note 1333, pp. 38–45 and 336.

1454 AMERASINGHE, p. 87, writes that "*No recent instances are known of a non member state refusing to acknowledge the personality of an organisation on the ground that it was not a member state and had not given the organization specific recognition*". The one example that is often cited (e.g. SANDS & KLEIN, p. 476 note 36) is the non-recognition by the Soviet Union and its allies of the EC, which was, however, formally abandoned in 1988 (see the Joint Declaration on the establishment of official relations between the European Economic Community and the Council for Mutual Economic Assistance, *O.J. L* 157, 24 June 1988, p. 35, between an international organization and third States or other international organizations, which are the focus of the ESDP. I submit that probably the better view in this matter is to accept an objective international legal personality. The objection that this imposes obligations on third States is not convincing.

Firstly, holding that the personality may be invoked against third States does not imply that they are bound by all the rules laid down in the constituent instruments of the organization. Rather, it means that they must accept the organization's existence as a separate legal person[1455] and respect those rights which it consequently has under general international law when they deal with it. In the words of Seyersted: "*objective international personality merely means that the State or Organization is subject to the rights and duties of international law and that it must be treated as a subject of international law by any other subject of international law which has relations to it*".[1456] Second, it is submitted that having to deal with an international organization rather than its members is not necessarily disadvantageous.[1457] Third, a parallel may de drawn with States, in respect of which recognition is nowadays mostly regarded as declaratory rather than constitutive.[1458] Fourth, it is hard to see how, as a matter of law, the objective effect vis-à-vis third States would be dependent upon the number of States establishing an organization.[1459] However, I would accept that the entities

especially §1: "*The European Economic Community and the Council for Mutual Economic Assistance establish official relations with each other by adopting this Declaration*"). Moreover, J. Verhoeven, *La reconnaissance internationale dans la pratique contemporaine*, Paris, Pedone, 1975, pp. 193–194, has questioned the legal relevance of this non-recognition.

1455 In this sense also R. Higgins, *supra* note 1396, pp. 47–48 and C. Tomuschat, *supra* note 1320, p. 1252.

1456 F. Seyersted, *supra* note 1229, pp. 97–98.

1457 See *supra* note 1443. Moreover, these members may in turn include international organizations, in which case the argument is even less convincing.

1458 See also Amerasinghe, pp. 90–91 and, more extensively, J. Verhoeven, *supra* note 1454, pp. 182–219, especially pp. 217–219.

1459 Similarly, Amerasinghe, pp. 89–90 and R.J. Dupuy, *supra* note 1341, pp. 555–557. While most authors requiring recognition mostly invoke the *res inter alios acta* rule, this rule is not subject to an exception in the case where the vast majority of States decide something. Compare P. Pescatore, *supra* note 1241, p. 70, who regards the ICJ's argumentation as political rather than legal. There appear to be only two other ways to justify the ICJ's view in the *Reparations opinion*. The first is to rely on a specific rule of customary international law accepting the international legal personality of the UN, and possibly other universal organizations, but the ICJ gave no indications that such an argument was the basis of its decision. Moreover, given the lack of recent objections (*supra* note 1454) one might in that case equally argue that there is a customary law rule in favour of objective international legal personality more generally. The second is to base its view on the nature of the UN Charter, with its primacy over other international agreements (Article 103) and its intended limited effect vis-à-vis non-Member States (Article 2(6)). However, there is no indication either that the Court based itself on this element, except in the individual opinion by Judge Alvarez (*I.C.J. Reports* 1949, p. 191/21, referring to Article 2(6) and "*the highest international institution*"), and textually Article 103 applies only to UN Member States and Article 2(6) is establishing an international organization for fraudulent or illegal purposes are *themselves* internationally responsible for the reparation of any violations of international law resulting from such *establishment*.[1460]

G. PRELIMINARY CONCLUSIONS

Starting from a definition of a subject of international law as an entity directly possessing rights and/or duties under international law, it is clear that most international organizations will be such subjects. If there is doubt, it will either result from a non-legal nature or because it is questioned whether the organization is not in fact only acting on behalf of the Member States. The former is usually alleged of the OSCE, and may be accepted in principle, but cannot be maintained in the face of this organization's treaty practice. The latter issue is probably the case for the Eurocorps and is examined below in respect of the EU.

In contrast, I have defined international legal personality as the ability to directly possess rights and duties under international law and to exercise proper powers on the international plane and/or enter into international legal relations, which I distinguish from specific legal capacities (e.g. treaty-making capacity) and material competences relating to the subject matter (e.g. defence). It is no longer contested that international organizations may possess international legal personality and that this need not be granted explicitly.

However, when it comes to defining what the elements and consequences of international legal personality are, there are different views, including especially those placing the will of the founders central, leading to a variable content with few or no inherent consequences and limited opposability, and those objectively

---

limited to aspects necessary for the maintenance of international peace and security (see on the latter the dissenting opinion by Judge Krylov to the Reparations opinion, *I.C.J. Reports* 1949, p. 218/48). There is therefore no convincing legal argument for limiting the ICJ's conclusion to the UN or universal organizations. Obviously, one could argue that the ICJ was wrong, but its ruling – which was unanimous on this point – does not appear to be contested.

1460 I do not see this as a case of responsibility of Member States for acts of international organizations, a complex and controversial issue currently being studied by the ILC, but rather as a distinct issue because the act of establishing an organization for illegal or fraudulent purposes *ab initio* is one attributable to the entities setting up such an organization. Compare Amerasinghe, p. 90, who seems willing, though hesitantly, to admit an exception in such cases to the objective personality. On whether acts of representatives of Member States in an international organization are/remain acts of that State, see E. Lagrange, *La représentation institutionnelle dans l'ordre international: une contribution à la théorie de la personnalité morale des organisations internationales*, The Hague, Kluwer Law International, 2002, pp. 135–167 and 310–357; I. Pernice, *supra* note 1376, p. 240 note 44 and W. Meng, *supra* note 1363, p. 343. I will briefly address this issue below in Chapter 7.H.

basing personality on given criteria and general international law, resulting in (wide) inherent capacities and general opposability, but also some alternative views.

I have argued that the presumptive personality put forward by Klabbers may be the most accurate one subject to the possibility of rebuttal except where Member States enable an organization to perform certain acts that necessarily imply international legal personality. Nevertheless, in that case the expressed denial should be taken into account when considering the legal capacities of an international organization.

When it comes to the consequences of international legal personality of international organizations, I submit that a number of legal capacities are inherent, arguably even in the very notion of international legal personality more generally (following Rama-Montaldo), in particular the right to bring an international claim, international responsibility and the right to conduct international relations. The treaty-making capacity is probably better described as presumptive and the better view is that privileges and immunities (distinct from those of States and diplomats) are customary and proper to international legal personality of international organizations, although this is not quite settled, especially in relation to non-Member States. Inherent capacities may be limited by the Member States but only to some extent vis-à-vis third parties. These elements will be particularly important for the analysis of what rules of international law are binding on international organizations undertaken below in Chapter 7.

Returning to the *indicia* of international legal personality of international organizations, two capacities stand out and are each sufficient: the power to take legally binding decisions and treaty-making capacity. The former is examined below in relation to the EU and the latter is widely spread but entails one problem to avoid a circular argument, namely that agreements concluded are binding under international law. This is studied in relation to NATO, which has an extensive agreements practice including at least some legally binding treaties and has international legal personality. The treaty-making power also raises the issue of whether agreements are concluded on behalf of the organization, which does not seem to be the case in respect of the Eurocorps and is examined below regarding the EU.

As a final point, I argue that the international legal personality of international organizations is objective in the sense that the *existence* of an organization with such personality is opposable to all and the rights and obligations resulting from it must be respected by other international legal persons, especially if they enter into relations with it. In contrast, rights and obligations resulting from the specific constituent instrument are not so opposable without some form of recognition or acceptance.

CHAPTER 6
THE INTERNATIONAL LEGAL STATUS OF THE EU[1461]

As noted above, the ECSC had explicitly been granted international legal personality[1462] and the legal personality granted to the E(E)C has always been understood to include international legal personality.[1463] In contrast, the EU, even after the entry into force of the Treaty of Nice, has not explicitly been given legal personality, nor has it explicitly been denied such personality.[1464] The question whether the EU nevertheless possesses international legal personality by an implicit grant, and also the related question whether it is a subject of international law, has long been debated and given rise to an impressive body of literature.[1465] While the issue now appears to have been

1461 I am grateful to Tim Corthaut for his valuable comments on an earlier draft of this chapter.

1462 See *supra* note 1304 and Article 6 ECSC Treaty ("*The Community shall have legal personality. In international relations, the Community shall enjoy the legal capacity it requires to perform its functions and attain its objectives*").

1463 See *supra* note 1320: while Article 281 EC Treaty only provides that "*The Community shall have legal personality*", the contrast with Article 282 EC Treaty, which concerns domestic legal personality and elements such as the EC's explicit treaty-making capacity have led to a general agreement that the EC possesses international legal personality.

1464 With one possible exception at the beginning: I. MacLeod, I.D. Henry & S. Huett, *supra* note 1255, p. 25 note 152 report that when deciding to change its name (see *infra* note 1473), the Council declared that this did not change its legal status and that the EU had no legal personality (citing *Agence Europe* of 9 November 1993). A.S. Muller, *supra* note 1269, pp. 78–79 sees an explicit denial but does not cite any primary source for this.

1465 See, e.g. J. de Zwaan, *supra* note 1246, pp. 75–113 (listing further references at pp. 85–87 and arguing that European lawyers rather view the EU as lacking international legal personality whereas international lawyers generally hold the opposite view; see also p. 110); O. Dörr, 'Zur Rechtsnatur der Europäischen Union', 30 *Europarecht* 1995, pp. 334–348; O. Dörr, 'Noch einmal: die Europäische Union und die Europäischen Gemeinschaften', 48 *N.J.W.* 1995, pp. 3162–3165; L. Grard, 'L'Union européenne, sujet de droit international', 110 *R.G.D.I.P.* 2006, pp. 337–372; G. Hafner, *supra* note 1376, pp. 257–284; J. Klabbers, *supra* note 1320, pp. 231–253; N. Neuwahl, *supra* note 1320, pp. 3–22; N. Neuwahl, 'A Partner With a Troubled Personality: EU Treaty Making in Matters of CFSP and JHA after Amsterdam', 3 *E.F.A.R.* 1998, pp. 177–195; M. Pachinger, *Die Völkerrechtspersönlichkeit der Europäischen Union*, Frankfurt am Main, Lang, 2003; M. Pechstein, 'Rechtssubjektivität für die Europäische Union?', 31 *Europarecht* 1996, pp. 137–144; G. Ress, 'Ist die Europäische Union eine juristische Person?', 30 *Europarecht* 1995, Beiheft 2, pp. 27–40; C. Trüe, *supra* note 1246, pp. 127–176; H. Wagner, 'Die Rechtsnatur der EU. Anmerkungen zu einer in Deutschland stattfindenden Debatte', 9 *Z. Eur. S.* 2006, pp. 287–300; WESSEL, pp. 242–318; R.A. Wessel, *supra* note 1407, pp. 109–129 and R.A. Wessel, 'Revisiting the International Legal Status of the EU', 5 *E.F.A.R.*

settled,[1466] especially since the entry into force of the Treaty of Nice early 2003 and the practice of the EU since roughly 2001,[1467] there is still denial in some quarters and for the purposes of this book it is worth briefly discussing the evolution of the EU's legal status since the Maastricht Treaty on European Union. It may also be noted that the debate is settled by the Lisbon Treaty.[1468] I will discuss elements relating to being a subject of international law and having international legal personality together and distinguish between them at the end of this chapter.

2000, pp. 507–537. Those who have taken a position more briefly (at one time or another) include, in favour of international legal personality: Brownlie, p. 680 ("*undoubtedly*"); I. Govaere, J. Capiau & A. Vermeersch, 'In-Between Seats: The Participation of the European Union in International Organizations',' 9 *E.F.A.R.* 2004, pp. 158 and 160–161; S. Griller *et al.*, *The Treaty of Amsterdam. Facts, Analysis, Prospects*, Vienna, Springer, 2000, pp. 54–55 and White, p. 50 ("*no doubt*"), and against: D. Curtin, 'The Constitutional Structure of the Union: A Europe of Bits and Pieces', 30 *C.M.L. Rev.* 1993, p. 27; E. Denza, 'Two Legal Orders: Divergent or Convergent', 48 *I.C.L.Q.* 1999, p. 282, K. Ipsen *et al.*, *supra* note 1254, pp. 91–92; I. MacLeod, I.D. Henry & S. Huett, *supra* note 1255, p. 3 and 25 and Sands & Klein, p. 174. The view of some has changed with the developments over time, especially the EU's treaty practice; compare, e.g. K. Lenaerts & E. De Smijter, *supra* note 1444, pp. 5–6 with K. Lenaerts & P. Van Nuffel, *Constitutional Law of the European Union*, London, Sweet & Maxwell, 2005 (2nd ed.), pp. 816–817 and H.G. Schermers & N. Blokker, *International Institutional Law*, Boston, Martinus Nijhoff, 1995 (3rd ed.), §1562, p. 977 with Schermers & Blokker, §1569, p. 992. Some see the matter as still unsettled; see, e.g. H.-J. Cremer, 'Anmerkungen zur GASP – Eine rechtspolitische Perspektive', 31 *Eur. Gr. R.Z.* 2004, p. 588 note 3.

1466 See, e.g. P. Eeckhout, *supra* note 1431, p. 155 ("*as time goes by, the debate seems ever more irrelevant, in light of Article 24 [EU Treaty], the effective use made of that provision, and the draft Constitution*"); R. Gosalbo Bono, *supra* note 1247, pp. 353–357; D. Verwey, *supra* note 1280, pp. 6 and 59–61 and W. Wormuth, *Die Bedeutung des Europarechts für die Entwicklung des Völkerrechts*, Frankfurt am Main, Peter Lang, 2004, pp. 102–110. See also J.-C. Piris, *The Constitution for Europe: A Legal Analysis*, Cambridge, Cambridge University Press, 2006, pp. 60–61, especially note 9.

1467 See especially the many treaties concluded in the framework of the ESDP and ESDP operations, notably SOFA/SOMAs and agreements with third States on their participation in ESDP operations discussed *supra*, Chapter 3.

1468 See Articles 1(3) (renumbered 1, third paragraph) ("... *The Union shall replace and succeed the European Community*") and 32 (renumbered 47) ("*The Union shall have legal personality*") EU Treaty as they are amended/inserted by the Lisbon Treaty. Article IV-438(1) EU Constitution provided that "*The European Union established by this Treaty shall be the successor to the European Union established by the Treaty on European Union and to the European Community*" and I-7 EU Constitution read "*The Union shall have legal personality*". While this is no explicit grant of international legal personality, it was never questioned that Article I-7 included international legal personality (see, e.g. the Final report of Working Group III on Legal Personality, EU Doc. CONV 305/02, 1 October 2002, available at http://european-convention.eu.int, *inter alia* at §10 ("*With a single legal personality the subject of international law will be the Union*") and §§19–46). Moreover, this also results from the EU succeeding the EC, of which it is generally accepted that it has international legal personality (see *supra*, notes 1320 and 1463). See on the relevant provisions in the (draft) EU Constitution, P. Eeckhout, *supra* note 1431, pp. 162–163; B. Fassbender, 'Die Völkerrechtssubjektivität der Europäischen Union nach dem Entwurf des Verfassungsvertrages', 42 *A.V.R.* 2004, pp. 26–43 and L. Grard, *supra* note 1465, pp. 357–370.

As a preliminary issue, it is submitted that the EU was, from its establishment, an international organization[1469] as I have defined it above (i.e. without necessarily possessing international legal personality[1470]): it clearly is a form of international cooperation, founded on an international instrument (undeniably a treaty[1471]), endowed with several organs (especially the European

---

1469 Similarly, W. Devroe & J. Wouters, *De Europese Unie. Het verdrag van Maastricht en zijn uitvoering: analyse en perspectieven*, Peeters, Leuven, 1996, pp. 65–66 and G. Hafner, *supra* note 1376, pp. 262–265, both with further references, including of opposing views. See also B. de Witte, 'The Pillar Structure and the Nature of the European Union: Greek Temple or Drench Gothic Cathedral' in T. Heukels, N. Blokker & M. Brus (eds.), *The European Union after Amsterdam: A Legal Analysis*, The Hague, Kluwer Law International, 1998, pp. 57–66 (also distinguishing with the issue of legal personality at pp. 61–62); S. Griller *et al.*, *supra* note 1465 pp. 52–53; D. Verwey, *supra* note 1280, pp. 63–65 (writing at p. 65 that "*Although questions remain as to what kind of international organisation the European Union is, its status as an international organisation is beyond dispute*") and W. Wormuth, *supra* note 1466, pp. 98–122. R. Gosalbo Bono, *supra* note 1247, pp. 346 and 353 is of the view that the EU was not initially a fully-fledged international organization but became one under the Amsterdam and Nice Treaties. Compare the German Constitutional Court's 'Maastricht judgment', in which it qualified the EU as a European 'Staatenverbund' (BVerfG, 12 October 1993, *BVerfGE* 89, 155, *inter alia* part III.C, available online at www.servat.unibe.ch/law/dfr/bv089155.html), which cannot easily be traslated (see, e.g. B. de Witte, *supra* note 1467, p. 659, situating it somewhere between a confederation and a federation). In the same vein, A. Pliakos, 'La nature juridique de l'Union européenne', 29 *R.T.D.E.* 1993, pp. 187–224, especially pp. 208–215 (seeing federal objectives but not the corresponding powers and means) and S. Breitenmoser, 'Die Europäische Union zwischen Völkerrecht und Staatsrecht', 55 *Z.a.ö.R.V.* 1995, pp. 951–992 (distinguishing the EU from a State and an international organization). On statehood elements in the EU, see S. Griller *et al.*, *supra* note 1465 pp. 65–88 and T. Tiilikainen, 'To Be or Not to Be?: An Analysis of the Legal and Political Elements of Statehood in the EU's External Identity', 6 *E.F.A.R.* 2001, pp. 223–241.

1470 See also O. Dörr, *supra* note 1465 (30 *Europarecht* 1995), pp. 335–337, concluding that the EU certainly is an international organization if this does not require international legal personality. Compare J.-C. Gautron, 'L'Union européenne et le concept d'organisation internationale', in D. Dormoy (ed.), *supra* note 1285, pp. 15–35, denying that the EU is an international organization esentially because it has no legal personality whereas this is deemed to be an element of the definition of an international organization (and noting that while the EU may look weak compared to the EC, this is not so compared to other international organizations). G. Ress, *supra* note 1465, p. 32 also requires legal personality.

1471 See, e.g. the German Constitutional Court, in its Maastricht judgment (*supra* note 1469), part III.C.II.d.2.1: "*Der Vertrag über die Europäische Union trifft eine völkerrechtliche Vereinbarung*" and Wessel, pp. 150–151. That the EU Treaty, like the constituent instruments of other international organizations, could at the same time, have served as the constitution of the EU, does not detract from this (see Article 5 1969 VCLT: "*The present Convention applies to any treaty which is the constituent instrument of an international organization … without prejudice to any relevant rules of the organization*", and, with regard to the EC Treaty, ECJ, Opinion 1/91, 14 December 1991, *Draft agreement between the Community, on the one hand, and the countries of the European Free Trade Association, on the other, relating to the creation of the European Economic Area*, §21: "*le traité CEE, bien que conclu sous la forme d'un accord international, n'en constitue pas moins la charte constitutionnelle d'une communauté de droit*"; see also J. Boulois, *supra* note 1354, pp. 23–24 and 27–39, using the notion of a material constitution that formally remains a treaty), though it is often argued that such texts are interpreted somewhat differently from other treaties: see, e.g. the discussion in

Council which mainly plays a role in the non-EC elements of the EU,[1472] but also the other organs)[1473] at least some of which have a will of their

---

AMERASINGHE, pp. 24–65; C. Brölmann, *supra* note 1225, pp. 141–155; E. Lauterpacht, *supra* note 1328, pp. 414–465 and SCHERMERS & BLOKKER, §§1346–1350, pp. 840–846. This was endorsed by the ICJ in its advisory opinion on the *Legality of the Use by a State of Nuclear Weapons in Armed Conflict* of 8 July 1996 (preliminary objections – not to be confused with the ICJ's other *Nuclear Weapons opinion*), §19: "*From a formal standpoint, the constituent instruments of international organizations are multilateral treaties, to which the well-established rules of treaty interpretation apply ... But the constituent instruments of international organizations are also treaties of a particular type; their object is to create new subjects of law endowed with a certain autonomy, to which the parties entrust the task of realizing common goals. Such treaties can raise specific problems of interpretation owing, inter alia, to their character which is conventional and at the same time institutional; the very nature of the organization created, the objectives which have been assigned to it by its founders, the imperatives associated with the effective performance of its functions, as well as its own practice, are all elements which may deserve special attention when the time comes to interpret these constituent treaties*". For a discussion regarding amendments to the EU constituent instruments and the law of treaties, see B. de Witte, 'Treaty Revision in the European Union: Constitutional Change through International Law', 35 *N.Y.I.L.* 2004, pp. 51–84. I will return to this specific nature and that of the legal order based on it below in Chapter 7.C.2.

1472 See especially Articles D, J.3(1) and J.8(1) Maastricht Treaty, now Articles 4 and 13 EU Treaty. This is admitted by J. de Zwaan, *supra* note 1246, pp. 89–90, who regards the other institutions as being borrowed from the EC, a view which is not very persuasive, though also adopted by others; see, e.g. D. Curtin, *supra* note 1465, pp. 26–30 and U. Everling, 'Reflections on the Structure of the European Union', 29 *C.M.L. Rev.* 1992, p. 1061. The better view is that the organs are simply shared, see notably C. Trüe, *supra* note 1246, pp. 144–149, who uses the expression "*Doppelorganschaft*". Moreover, M. Warnken, *Der Handlungsrahmen der Europäischen Union im Bereich der Sicherheits- und Verteidigingspolitik*, Baden-Baden, Nomos, 2002, pp. 64–66, who also supports the "dual organ" theory, submits that even the borrowing thesis would require legal personality by the borrowing EU as the actions of the organs in their capacity of being borrowed would be attributable to the EU and not the EC.

1473 The EU and EC are "*served by a single institutional framework*" (Article C Maastricht Treaty, now Article 3 EU treaty) and the European Parliament, the Council, the Commission and the ECJ have a role to play in the EU, albeit one different from that which they play in the EC (see Article E Maastricht Treaty: they "*exercise their powers under the conditions and for the purposes provided for, on the one hand, by the provisions of the Treaties establishing the European Communities and of the subsequent Treaties and Acts modifying and supplementing them and, on the other hand, by the other provisions of [the EU Treaty]*"; now Article 5 EU Treaty with a slightly amended but essentially the same text). The role of the ECJ was initially limited to cases where Member States had adopted a convention which included a clause accepting the ECJ's jurisdiction (Article K.2(3)c Maastricht Treaty) but is now much larger (see Article 35 EU Treaty). On the role of the ECJ in the CFSP, see M.-G. Garbagnati Ketvel, 'The Jurisdiction of the European Court of Justice in Respect of the Common Foreign and Security Policy', 55 *I.C.L.Q.* 2006, pp. 77–120. The situation is similar to the existence of distinct European Communities with common institutions (since the Convention on Certain Common Institutions, Rome, 25 March 1957, 294 *U.N.T.S.* 413 (1958) and the Treaty establishing a Single Council and a Single Commission of the European Communities, Brussels, 8 April 1965). Moreover, the Council formally renamed itself 'Council of the EU' (Council Decision of 8 November 1993 concerning the name to be given to the Council following the entry into force of the Treaty on European Union (93/591/EC), *O.J. L* 281, own,[1474] and it is not governed by the domestic law of a State but instead by international law.[1475] Although this was sometimes contested,[1476] it is submitted that most of the opposition stems from the complexity involving the relationship with the EC. If one were to think away the EC and simply imagine the EU with all the organs in their capacity of organs of the Union,[1477] it would be hard to see how it could not be an international organization.

I will now examine the legal status of the EU on the basis of the following elements: the rights and duties of the EU itself under international law and its power to adopt binding decisions (A), the EU's treaty-making capacity (B), the question of its privileges and immunities (C), the legal status of the EU agencies and the implications thereof for the EU's legal personality (D), the relationship between the EU and the EC and between the EU and the agencies (E) and the status of ESDP operations (F). On the basis of these findings, I conclude that the EU is a subject of international law with international legal personality (G).

16 November 1993, p. 18) and the Political Committee established by Article J.8(5) only functions in the EU (it was later succeeded by the PSC, see *supra*, Chapter 1.E-F). On the Council, see generally F. Hayes-Renshaw & H. Wallace, *The Council of Ministers*, Basingstoke, Palgrave/Macmillan, 2006 (2nd ed.) and M. Westlake & D. Galloway, *The Council of the European Union*, London, Harper, 2004 (3rd ed.). See also various *EU* agencies discussed *infra*, Section D of this chapter. *Contra*: D. Vignes, 'L'absence de personnalité juridique de l'Union européenne: Amsterdam persiste et signe', in G. Hafner *et al.* (eds.), *supra* note 1376, p. 759. Also critical, A. Pliakos, *supra* note 1469, p. 206. B. de Witte, *supra* note 1467, pp. 59–62, especially p. 61 points out that several authors who argue that the EU has no proper institutions reason backwards: because they feel the EU is not an international organization, it cannot have its own institutions. For a more extensive discussion, see Wessel, pp. 74–100 and various contributions in G. Ress, J. Schwarze & T. Stein (eds.) *Die Organe der Europäischen Union im Spannungsfeld zwischen Gemeinschaft und Zusammenarbeit*, 30 *Europarecht* 1995, Beiheft 2.

1474 For instance, under Article J.8(3) Maastricht Treaty the Commission, consisting of independent persons who may not take instructions for the Member States (see Article 213(2) (ex 157(2)) EC Treaty) was allowed to refer to the Council any question or proposal relating to the CFSP and already pursuant to Article J.3(2) Maastricht Treaty the Council could in specified circumstances adopt decisions by a qualified majority, which it now can in more cases under Article 23 EU Treaty. The Commission also had a right of initiative under Article K.3(2) Maastricht Treaty. When the ECJ is competent in the framework of the EU, it obviously also has a will of its own.

1475 While it has been argued that a number of instruments adopted within the EU under the EU Treaty were not legally binding (see *infra*, Section A of this chapter), it is clear that the EU Treaty as such, being a treaty, is legally binding, including its provisions on the EU.

1476 See the references to opposing views in the publications cited *supra* note 1469.

1477 In which case the 'borrowing thesis' (*supra* note 1472) would clearly be inapplicable.

A. RIGHTS AND OBLIGATIONS UNDER INTERNATIONAL LAW AND THE POWER TO ADOPT BINDING DECISIONS

Pursuant to Article A of the Maastricht Treaty, the *EU*'s task "*shall be to organize, in a manner demonstrating consistency and solidarity, relations between the Member States and between their peoples*". Pursuant to Article B of this treaty the *Union's* objectives include "*to assert its identity on the international scene*". In the same vein, under Article J.1, the *Union* and its Member States shall define and implement a CFSP which *inter alia* has as objectives "*to safeguard the common values, fundamental interests and independence of the* Union" and "*to strengthen the security* of the Union and its Member States *in all ways*" (emphasis added).[1478] Thus the EU had an identity and a task and was distinguished from its Member States. Yet this is not conclusive for legal purposes, as the separate identity might also be of a political nature rather than a legal one.[1479] This is why identifying rights and obligations of the EU is crucial.

In fact, there were also provisions which seemed to impose obligations upon the EU as distinct from the Member States. For instance, under Article F Maastricht Treaty, the "*Union shall respect the national identities of its Member States*" as well as "*fundamental rights, as guaranteed by the [ECHR] and as they result from the constitutional traditions common to the Member States, as general principles of Community law*". In particular the latter obligation of the Union[1480] can hardly be qualified as anything else than an obligation under international law.[1481] Conversely, Article J.1(4) provided that "*the member States shall support the Union's external and security policy actively and unreservedly in a spirit of loyalty and mutual solidarity*".[1482] In addition, Article 23 of the German constitution, inserted to permit the ratification of the EU Treaty, provides that Germany may transfer sovereign rights to the *Union*, though the provision has, at least initially,

---

1478 For a more extensive analysis, see Wessel, pp. 48–70. For a rather critical view, see M. Koskenniemi, 'International Law Aspects of the Common Foreign and Security Policy', in M. Koskenniemi (ed.), *supra* note 1320, pp. 27–44.

1479 A possibility pointed out by O. Dörr, *supra* note 1465 (30 *Europarecht* 1995), pp. 339–340. C. Trüe, *supra* note 1246, pp. 130–136 argues that the ordinary meaning suggests that the EU is a separate entity, including in legal terms.

1480 While these are to be respected as principles of *Community* law, the obligation rests upon the *Union*. This will be addressed more extensively in Chapter 7.F.2.i below.

1481 In this case EU law as a subset of international law. That it is an obligation vis-à-vis the Member States matters little.

1482 C. Trüe, *supra* note 1246, pp. 152–153, points out that this obligation, as well as other specific ones along the same lines, exists towards the Union and thereby corresponds to a right of the Union.

been interpreted differently.[1483] Moreover, pursuant to Article O of the Treaty of Maastricht (now Article 49 EU Treaty), new Member States could join the Union and, although the modalities would be agreed between the applicant and the Member States, it would first require the assent of the European Parliament, which is clearly an organ with a distinct will, acting in this case as an EU organ.[1484]

There were equally other provisions in the Maastricht Treaty that could indicate that the EU had rights under international law, in particular the right to adopt legally binding decisions. For instance, under Article J.2(2) the Council could define a common position and Member States were to ensure that their national policies conformed to the common positions, and under Article J.3(4) joint actions committed the Member States in the positions they adopted and in the conduct of their activity. However, there was initially disagreement among Member States and commentators over whether these instruments were legally binding.[1485]

1483 The provision reads: "*Zur Verwirklichung eines vereinten Europas wirkt die Bundesrepublik Deutschland bei der Entwicklung der Europäischen Union mit, die demokratischen, rechtsstaatlichen, sozialen und föderativen Grundsätzen und dem Grundsatz der Subsidiarität verpflichtet ist und einen diesem Grundgesetz im wesentlichen vergleichbaren Grundrechtsschutz gewährleistet. Der Bund kann hierzu ... Hoheitsrechte übertragen*". The German Constitutional Court, in its Maastricht judgment (*supra* note 1469), part III.C, read this as including a transfer of sovereign rights to the *Union and* the Communities. However, and in apparent contradiction, the Court ruled in this same judgment (*id.*, part III.C.II.b.1–2) that the Union was not a proper subject of law and did not itself possess any competences ("*der Unions-Vertrag [läßt] an keiner Stelle den übereinstimmenden Willen der Vertragsparteien erkennbar werden ..., mit der Union ein selbständiges Rechtssubjekt zu gründen, das Träger eigener Kompetenzen sein soll. Die Union besitzt nach Auffassung der Bundesregierung weder im Verhältnis zu den Europäischen Gemeinschaften noch zu den Mitgliedstaaten eine gesonderte Rechtspersönlichkeit. Diese Auffassung hat auch Generaldirektor Dewost in der mündlichen Verhandlung bestätigt*" and "*Die Union stattet "sich" in gleicher Weise mit Mitteln aus, wie sie "sich" in Article B Ziele setzt: Der Unions-Vertrag versteht hier die Union nicht als eigenständiges Rechtssubjekt, sondern als Bezeichnung für die gemeinsam handelnden Mitgliedstaaten; diese geben der Union Ziele und Mittel vertraglich vor*").

1484 Similarly, C. Trüe, *supra* note 1246, pp. 161–163.

1485 See N. Blokker, 'Decisions of International Organizations: The Case of the European Union', 30 *N.Y.I.L.* 1999, pp. 28–29 and 31–32 and Wessel, pp. 150–185 (*inter alia* mentioning a Council Legal Service opinion that Joint Actions were legally binding, at pp. 151–152, and noting that the Dutch government, which initially regarded Joint Actions as politically binding only, accepted that they were, or at least could be, legally binding already in 1995). M. Koskenniemi, *supra* note 1478, p. 30 notes that the Finnish govenrment stated that practice would provide an answer. Compare also P.-C. Müller-Graf, 'The Legal Bases of the Third Pillar and its Position in the Framework of the Union Treaty', 31 *C.M.L. Rev.* 1994, pp. 493–510 (noting that the Third Pillar is governed by international law (p. 495) and arguing that is doubtful whether joint actions were binding in the Third Pillar in contrast to the CFSP but that a legally binding effect under international law could not be excluded and might depend upon practice and the type of act (pp. 509–510; *a contario* implying that CFSP joint actions are legally binding)) and D. O'Keeffe, 'Recasting the Third Pillar', 32 *C.M.L. Rev.* 1995, pp.

The latter argument reveals an interesting parallel with the OSCE (see *supra*, Chapter 5.C), but with the fundamental difference that in the case of the EU, the constituent instrument clearly is a legally binding treaty.[1486] This does not necessarily mean that instruments adopted by EU organs are legally binding. Indeed, most organizations may only adopt non-binding instruments (except to some extent concerning their own functioning). However, there is no explicit denial of the legal nature of the EU instruments in the EU Treaty[1487] and the use of terms such as "*shall ensure*" conformity (Article J.2(2)) and "*shall commit the Member States*" (Article J.3(4)) suggest that common positions and especially joint actions[1488] were and are binding.[1489]

893–920 (arguing that Third Pillar joint actions are legally binding at p. 914). I. MacLeod, I.D. Henry & S. Huett, *supra* note 1255, pp. 417–418 and 423–424 seem to accept that joint actions and common positions under the CFSP may impose rights and obligations under international law (and rightly stress that the absence of jurisdiction of the ECJ is not relevant in this respect), as does F. Fink-Hooijer, 'The Common Foreign and Security Policy of the European Union', 5 *E.J.I.L.* 1994, pp. 178, 181 and 183, at least in respect of joint actions (noting their compulsory and binding character). G. Burghardt, G. Tebbe & S. Marquardt, 'Artikel 14 EU' and 'Artikel 15 EU', in H. von der Groeben & J. Schwarze (eds.), *supra* note 1320, Vol. I, pp. 211 and 216 regard joint actions as legally binding. For K. Schilcher, 'GASP und neutrale Staaten', 2 *Z. Eur. S.* 1999, pp. 643–644, joint actions are legally binding but common positions not.

1486 See *supra* note 1471.

1487 Unlike, e.g. Article 249 EC Treaty which states which instruments listed there are binding and which are not.

1488 For an extensive analysis of joint actions, see L. Münch, 'Die gemeinsame Aktion im Rahmen der GASP: Inhalt, Rechtsnatur und Reformbedürftigkeit', 31 *Europarecht* 1996, pp. 415–426, especially pp. 418–421 (concluding that a joint action is binding under international law but rather, so it seems, as an agreement between the member States than as an act of the Union) and L. Münch, *Die gemeinsame Aktion als Mittel der Gemeinsamen Außen- und Sicherheitspolitik*, Berlin, Duncker & Humblot, 1997. Compare A. Dashwood, 'The Law and Practice of CFSP Joint Actions', in M. Cremona & B. De Witte (eds.), *EU Foreign Relations Law: Constitutional Fundamentals*, Oxford, Hart, 2008, pp. 53–77.

1489 See also S. Griller *et al.*, *supra* note 1465, p. 54 and Wessel, pp. 154–155 and 172. R. Gosalbo Bono, *supra* note 1247, p. 364 regards CFSP instruments as being legally binding. According to Aust, p. 27, 'shall' is an indication of legally binding nature. The German Constitutional Court, in its Maastricht judgment (*supra* note 1469), part III.B.2.c, seemed to accept that common positions and joint actions could be binding under international law, though they would not enjoy the direct effect and primacy accorded to EC law ("*Ungeachtet einer völkerrechtlichen Bindung der Mitgliedstaaten durch [gemeinsame Aktionen und gemeinsame Maßnahmen in den Titeln V und VI des Unions-Vertrags] diese Ratsbeschlüsse (vgl. Article J.3 Nr. 4; ohne ausdrückliche Regelung Article K.3 Abs. 2 Buchst. b EUV), ..., kann durch sie kein in den Mitgliedstaaten unmittelbar anwendbares und Vorrang beanspruchendes Recht gesetzt werden ... Verpflichten gemeinsame Aktionen und Maßnahmen nach den Titeln V und VI des Unions-Vertrags die Mitgliedstaaten völkerrechtlich verbindlich zu grundrechtserheblichen Eingriffen, so können alle diese Eingriffe, wenn sie in Deutschland vorgenommen werden, von der deutschen Gerichtsbarkeit voll überprüft werden*"). Compare J. Klabbers, *supra* note 1299, pp. 997–1023, arguing that the ECJ applies a presumption that agreements (in the broad sense, including various informal instruments) are legally binding.

In any event, the changes introduced by the Treaty of Amsterdam clarified the situation in the Third Pillar by explicitly stating that the new category of framework decisions, as well as other decisions (than common positions), were binding (thereby implying that (Third Pillar) common positions were not).[1490] The binding nature of common positions and joint actions in the Second Pillar was not clarified (but see *infra*, further down this Section).[1491] However, for the purpose of the question at stake here, the acceptance of the binding nature of some EU instruments suffices. It means that the EU has the right to adopt a legally binding decision.[1492] It also means that the EU as such clearly has a number of competences.[1493]

Moreover, at least some of the decisions adopted grant the Council, and hence the Union, a number of specific rights,[1494] such as the right (and duty) to adopt staff regulations,[1495] or to receive the products of the EU Satellite Centre.[1496] The preamble of a 1994 EC Regulation recognizes that the EU has commitments by stating "*Whereas an effective system of export control ... is also necessary to ensure*

1490 Article 34(2)(b)-(c) EU Treaty. See also B. de Witte, *supra* note 1467, p. 56. On framework decisions, see, e.g. C. Schönberger, 'Der Rahmenbeschluss: Unionssekundärrecht zwischen Völkerrecht und Gemeinschaftsrecht', 67 *Z.a.ö.R.V.* 2007, pp. 1107–1139.

1491 Compare B. de Witte, *supra* note 1467, p. 52 ("*The fact remains that, whether or not the ECJ exercises judicial control, binding law is produced within each of the pillars*") and C. Trüe, *supra* note 1246, pp. 154–157 (arguing that common positions and joint actions in the CFSP are binding). Compare also N. Lavranos, *Legal Interaction between Decisions of International Organizations and European Law*, Groningen, Europa Law Publishing, 2004, pp. 192–210, especially pp. 193, 197–198, 201–202 and 210 (distinguishing general obligations towards joint actions and common positions and specific obligations in respect of specific ones and accepting that the latter may be legally binding and seeing common strategies as legally binding but noting other views).

1492 Similarly W. Wormuth. *supra* note 1466, p. 103.

1493 Similarly, A.S. Muller, *supra* note 1269, p. 85 note 46. *Contra*, J. de Zwaan, *supra* note 1246, pp. 88–91 and 97–99.

1494 Compare N. Neuwahl, *supra* note 1465, pp. 185–186, who argues that obligations may be imposed upon organs of the Union even without the latter having legal personality. This is correct only inasmuch as legal personality is deemed to include more than just rights and duties, in contrast to merely being a subject of international law (as I have defined it, see *supra*, Chapter 5.A). But see M. Koskenniemi, *supra* note 1478, pp. 33–35, who found only one joint action in the period 1994–1996 that imposed an independent obligation, namely Council Decision of 12 May 1995 concerning the joint action adopted by the Council on the basis of Article J.3 of the Treaty on European Union on anti-personnel mines (95/170/CFSP), *O.J. L* 115, 22 May 1995, p. 1 (which, in its Article 2, provides that "*A common moratorium on exports of anti-personnel mines shall hereby be implemented by Member States .... This moratorium shall comprise a total ban on exports of non-detectable anti-personnel mines and non-self-destructing anti-personnel mines to all destinations, as well as a ban on exports of all other types of anti-personnel mines ...*").

1495 E.g. Article 8 EU ISS Joint Action (*infra* note 1567) and Article 9(3) EU Satellite Centre Joint Action (*infra* note 1566).

1496 Article 5 EU Satellite Centre Joint Action (*infra* note 1566).

that the international commitments of the Member States and the European Union, ..., are complied with".[1497] There is even at least one common position which looks rather similar to a framework decision.[1498] The contrast with documents of which the political nature is much clearer[1499] also supports the binding legal nature of at least some of these EU legal instruments.

In addition, the distinction with conventions concluded between the Member States[1500] and decisions by the Member States meeting in the Council[1501] clearly implies that Council decisions must be regarded as acts of the Union and not as agreements between the Member States.[1502] This is further supported by the

1497 Council Regulation (EC) No 3381/94 of 19 December 1994 setting up a Community regime for the control of exports of dual-use goods, *O.J. L* 367, 31 December 1994, p. 1, also cited by O. Dörr, *supra* note 1465 (30 *Europarecht* 1995), p. 334 and R. Wessel, *supra* note 1407, p. 127. However, commitments might also cover political commitments so this is not entirely conclusive.

1498 Council Common Position of 23 June 2003 on the control of arms brokering (2003/468/CFSP), *O.J. L* 156, 25 June 2003, p. 79. According to the second consideration of its preamble, "*Member States ... have reached agreement on a set of provisions for controlling these activities* through national legislation, *as set out below*" (emphasis added) and its Article 1(2) stipulates that "*... Member States will ensure that their existing or future national legislation on arms brokering is in conformity with the provisions set out below*". While the terms "will" and "should" are used and are normally regarded as less strong than "shall", the similarity of this common position to a framework decision is unmistakable. The Netherlands considers that common positions can be legally binding; see 11 February 2009 letter by the Dutch Minister of Foreign Affairs to the Dutch parliament, *Kamerbrief over de aanvaarding van de EU-Gedragscode tot het EU-Gemeenschappelijk Standpunt m.b.t. het Wapenexportbeleid*, www.minbuza.nl/nl/Actueel/Kamerstukken/2009/02/Kamerbrief_over_de_aanvaarding_van_de_EU_Gedragscode_tot_het_EU_Gemeenschappelijk_Standpunt_m_b_t_het_Wapenexportbeleid.

1499 E.g. the 1998 European Union *Code of Conduct* on Arms Exports, *supra* note 1283 (now replaced by a common position), and the resolutions and recommendations in the Third Pillar mentioned by D. O'Keeffe, *supra* note 1485, pp. 894 and 915–916.

1500 See Article K.3(2) Treaty of Maastricht, now Article 34(2) EU Treaty.

1501 See, e.g. *infra*, Section D of this chapter, on the use of such decisions for granting privileges and immunities to EU agencies. See on such decisions, e.g. W. Meng, *supra* note 1283, pp. 94–95, situating them on the borderline between international agreements and decisions of an organization.

1502 In this sense, with regard to the EC, the ECJ's ruling on EC measures adopted pursuant to ex Article 235 EC Treaty in Case 38/69, *Commission of the European Communities v Italian Republic*, Judgment of 18 February 1970, §§10–11 ("*The ... decision was taken by virtue of Article 235, ... The power to take the measures envisaged by this Article is conferred, not on the member States acting together, but on the Council in its capacity as a Community institution. ... In these circumstances, a measure which is in the nature of a community decision on the basis of its objective and of the institutional framework within which it has been drawn up cannot be described as an 'international agreement'*"). See also, with regard to the EU, Advocate-General Mengozzi's opinion in of 19 September 2007 in Case C-91/05 (*Commission v. Council*), §114 ("*as the Commission submits and as admitted by the Council ..., the Member States do not exercise their competence collectively when an action is adopted by an act of the Council by virtue of Title V of the EU Treaty, still less when that act, like the contested decision, can be adopted by a qualified majority*"). See more generally R.J. Dupuy, *supra* note 1341, p. 544 and Wessel, p. 255. Compare C. Brölmann, *supra* note 1225, pp. 136–140 and F.

possibilities of majority voting, even though they are limited, and arguably by the possibility of enhanced cooperation.[1503] It is also reflected by the fact that in the case of qualified constructive abstention, introduced by the Treaty of Amsterdam in Article 23(1) EU Treaty, the Member State which is not obliged to apply a decision, shall accept that the decision commits *the Union* (and not the other Member States).[1504]

In addition, the Treaty of Amsterdam also inserted Article 7 EU Treaty (which was later amended somewhat by the Treaty of Nice), which allowed the Council, after obtaining the assent of the European Parliament, to determine the existence of a serious and persistent breach by a Member State of the principles of liberty, democracy, respect for human rights and fundamental freedoms, and the rule of law, and to suspend in that case certain of the rights deriving from the application of the EU Treaty to the Member State in question, including the voting rights of the representative of the government of that Member State in the Council. The Council was to act by unanimity (for the determination of a breach) or qualified majority (for imposing sanctions) without taking into account the vote of the representative of the government of the Member State in question.[1505] The latter element, and the required assent of the European Parliament, clearly implies that this is a power exercise by the Union, not the Member States acting in the framework of the Council.[1506]

Therefore, under the Treaty of Amsterdam and the practice pursuant thereto, the Union has been granted increasingly more rights under international law and at the latest from then on it is hardly possible to deny that it had become a subject

Seyersted, *supra* note 1229, pp. 40–44 (noting that it is possible that an organ acts on behalf of the Member States, but that this should not be presumed). But see M. Koskenniemi, *supra* note 1478, pp. 31–32 (suggesting that they may be agreements); J. Klabbers, *supra* note 1299, pp. 997–1023 (suggesting that the case discussed above in this note does not preclude qualification as a binding agreement) and L. Münch, *supra* note 1488 (*Europarecht* 1996), pp. 418–421 (seeing the Council as an executive organ of the Member States rather than an independent organ).

1503 A point made by L. Grard, *supra* note 1407, p. 377. See especially Articles 23(2), 24(3)-(4), 27(a)-(e), 34(2)(c) and (3) and 40–40(b) EU Treaty.

1504 See also G. de Kerchove & S. Marquandt, 'Les accord internationaux conclus par l'Union européenne', 50 *A.F.D.I.* 2004, p. 805 and C. Trüe, *supra* note 1246, pp. 271–274.

1505 See also Article 309 (ex Article 236) EC Treaty. On this mechanism, see, e.g. M. Hofstötter, 'Suspension of Rights by International Organisations: The European Union, the European Communities and Other International Organisations', in V. Kronenberger (ed.), *supra* note 1320, pp. 23–52.

1506 In this sense also C. Trüe, *supra* note 1246, p. 160.

of international law. That the rights primarily exist toward Member States matters little.[1507]

B. TREATY-MAKING CAPACITY

Under the Treaty of Maastricht, the EU was not explicitly granted treaty-making capacity. It also did not exercise any such capacity[1508] and it did not seem to have been implicitly granted treaty-making capacity either.[1509] When the conclusion of an agreement in the framework of the CFSP was deemed necessary, it was concluded by the Member States.[1510] However, the Treaty of Amsterdam introduced a significant novelty in this respect by inserting Article 24 (ex J.14) in the EU treaty. This provision read:

> When it is necessary to conclude an agreement with one or more States or international organisations in implementation of this Title, the Council, acting unanimously, may authorise the Presidency, assisted by the Commission as appropriate, to open negotiations to that effect. Such agreements shall be concluded by the Council acting unanimously on a recommendation from the Presidency. No agreement shall be binding on a member State whose representative in the Council

1507 Indeed, because of the relative nature of treaties, including those setting up international organizations, rights and duties deriving from them will mostly concern Member States. External rights and obligations only arise to a limited extent from the objective existence of an international organization with international legal personality, its exercise of sovereign powers if it exceptionally has such powers or from agreements concluded by such an organization. But see O. Dörr, *supra* note 1465 (30 *Europarecht* 1995), pp. 337–344, who seems to regard the internal aspect as insufficient.

1508 But see C. Trüe, *supra* note 1246, pp. 166–168; M. Trybus, *European Union Law and Defence Integration*, Oxford, Hart, 2005, p. 82; M. Warnken, *supra* note 1472, pp. 75–76 and 147–164 and R.A. Wessel, *supra* note 1465 (5 *E.F.A.R.* 2000), pp. 531–533 arguing that the parallel adoption of EU and WEU decisions on mutual relations (*inter alia* in 1993) constituted a treaty. On parallel decisions as an agreement, see R.J. Dupuy, *supra* note 1341, pp. 523–525. However, even assuming such parallel decisions constituted a legally binding agreement, it would have to be proven that the EU rather than the Member States was a party to it; see *infra*.

1509 Although I have argued above that treaty-making capacity is probably presumptive for organizations that possess international legal personality, the latter was precisely debated in respect of the EU. Moreover, it could be argued by comparison to the EC that *a contrario* the EU had no treaty-making power (this reasoning seems more acceptable for specific capacities than for international legal personality generally, especially in an organization regulated in such a detailed manner as the EC/EU).

1510 E.g. in the context of the conflict in the former Yugoslavia, see D. Lopandic, *supra* note 1285, pp. 557–562, especially pp. 559–560 and, specifically with regard to the MOU on the administration of Mostar (see on this MOU and administration *supra* Chapter 1.D *in fine*, notes 78 and 98–99 and the accompanying text), C. Busse, *supra* note 1347, pp. 222–233 and W. Hummer, 'Mostar: ein Beispiel internationaler Stadtverwaltung durch die Europäische Union', in W. Benedek, H. Isak & R. Kicker (eds.), *supra* note 1290, pp. 386–388. A model MOU (formerly available online at http://europa.eu.int) identified as one of the "*Participating Parties*" "*The European Union Member States*" and not the EU itself.

> states that it has to comply with the requirements of its own constitutional procedure; the other members of the Council may agree that the agreement shall apply provisionally to them. The provisions of this Article shall also apply to matters falling under Title VI.[1511]

However, the scope of this Article gave rise to extensive debate, focusing especially on whether the agreements concluded under this provision by the Council were concluded on behalf of the Union or of the Member States (I will focus on Article 24, but most of what is said in this respect also applies to Article 38[1512]).[1513] A comparison with Article 300 EC Treaty concerning treaties concluded by the EC offers some support for the latter view. In particular, there was initially no provision in Article 24 EU Treaty stating that agreements concluded were binding on the institutions of the Union and only the binding of Member States is mentioned. On the other hand, as with other instruments in EU law, the comparison with the EC Treaty can hardly be decisive. Moreover, at least *prima facie*, the Council must de deemed, as an organ of the Union, to be acting on behalf of the Union rather than the Member States,[1514] as the EU Treaty distinguishes between the two (see *supra*, Section A of this chapter). Moreover, the agreement is to be negotiated by the Presidency, which represents the Union, not the Member States.[1515] However, this presupposes that the Union

1511 See also Article 38 (ex K.10). There appears to have been some confusion over whether the reference in Article 38 to Article 24 concerns only the procedure or whether a substantive link to the CFSP is required. The former seems to be the better view and seems to have been adopted in practice; see D. Verwey, *supra* note 1280, pp. 75–77. Compare J. de Zwaan, *supra* note 1246, pp. 103–104.

1512 But see *supra* previous note and *infra* note 1552, on the invoking of constitutional requirements. For a more extensive overview specifically related to Article 38, see S. Marquardt, 'La capacité de l'Union européenne de conclure des accords internationaux dans le domaine de la cooperation policière et judiciaire en matière pénale', in G. de Kerchove & A. Weyembergh (eds.), *Sécurité et justice: enjeu de la politique extérieure de l'Union européenne*, Brussels, Editions de l'ULB, 2003, pp. 179–194 and P. de Koster, 'Bref état des lieux sur les accords de coopération conclus sur la base de l'article 38 du traité UE', in G. de Kerchove & A. Weyembergh (eds.), *supra* this note, pp. 195–199.

1513 See, e.g. in addition to the post Amsterdam literature on the Union's legal personality cited *supra* note 1465, S. Marquardt, 'The Conclusion of International Agreements under Article 24 of the Treaty on European Union', in V. Kronenberger (ed.), *supra* note 1320, pp. 333–349; S. Marquardt, *supra* note 1512, pp. 179–194; S. Marquardt, 'Artikel 24 EU', in H. von der Groeben & J. Schwarze (eds.), *supra* note 1320, pp. 245–251 and D. Verwey, *supra* note 1280, pp. 59–83.

1514 Similarly, P. Des Nerviens, 'Les relations extérieures', 33 *R.T.D.E.* 1997, pp. 805–806; B. de Witte, *supra* note 1467, p. 63; S. Marquardt, *supra* note 1512, p. 186 and Wessel, pp. 261–262. See more generally R.J. Dupuy, *supra* note 1341, pp. 543–545 and F. Seyersted, *supra* note 1229, pp. 40–44 (noting that it is possible that an organ acts on behalf of the Member States, but that this should not be presumed).

1515 See Article 18 EU Treaty; P. Eeckhout, *supra* note 1431, p. 159 and S. Marquardt, *supra* note 1512, p. 186.

is a separate legal person, a point which is precisely contested,[1516] though hard to maintain since the Treaty of Amsterdam (see previous section).

The provision that "*No agreement shall be binding on a Member State whose representative in the Council states that it has to comply with the requirements of its own constitutional procedure; the other members of the Council may agree that the agreement shall apply provisionally to them*" rendered Article 24 especially ambiguous.[1517]

On the one hand, it has been argued that this does not affect the agreement being applicable to the Union, or even *a contrario* that this implies that the Union is bound, in addition to the Member States where no constitutional obstacle is raised. This might be supported by viewing the binding nature for the Member States as a rule of EU law only which does not make them parties to the treaty under international law vis-à-vis the other contracting party/parties.[1518] It could also be supported by the fact that, if the Member States are the parties, one might expect the requirements of constitutional procedures to be the rule rather than

1516 A point made by D. Vignes, *supra* note 1472, p. 758 ("*identité n'est pas personnalité et est plus une notion politique que juridique*"). Similarly, the German Constitutional Court, in its Maastricht judgment (*supra* note 1469, part III.C.II.b.2) stated that, at least in some instances, the Union in the Treaty of Maastricht had to be read as the Member States acting jointly ("*Der Unions-Vertrag versteht hier die Union nicht als eigenständiges Rechtssubjekt, sondern als Bezeichnung für die gemeinsam handelnden Mitgliedstaaten*").

1517 It has *inter alia* been described as a provision that "*could hardly be more enigmatic*" (P. Eeckhout, *supra* note 1431, p. 158) and as "*rais[ing] more problems than it solves*" (G. Hafner, *supra* note 1376, p. 276). Nevertheless, it helps at least a little by implying that the agreements are clearly meant to be, or at least may be, legally binding (though Wessel, pp. 260–261 note 71 points out that the Dutch government initially held the opposite view). The entire Article 24 has also been described as an "*opaque provision*" with an "*inelegance and the inevitable appearance of trying to square the circle*": M. Cremona, 'The European Union as an International Actor: The Issues of Flexibility and Linkage', 3 *E.F.A.R.* 1998, p. 70 (although this author did contend that the provision would nevertheless be useful). See also generally R.A. Wessel & G. Fernandez Arribas, 'EU Agreements with Third Countries: Constitutional Reservations by Member States', in S. Blockmans (ed.), *The European Union and International Crisis Management: Legal and Policy Aspects*, The Hague, TMC Asser Press, 2008, pp. 291–308.

1518 See G. de Kerchove & S. Marquandt, *supra* note 1504, p. 818 and W. Wormuth, *supra* note 1466, pp. 103–106. This is generally the view with regard to the Member States being bound by treaties concluded by the EC under Article 300 EC Treaty; see, e.g. W. Wormuth, *supra* note 1466, pp. 117–121; P. Eeckhout, *supra* note 1431, p. 276; I. MacLeod, I.D. Henry & S. Huett, *supra* note 1255, pp. 125–128; I. Pernice, *supra* note 1376, p. 238; D. Verwey, *supra* note 1280, pp. 149–151 and Wessel, p. 262. Compare also F. Seyersted, *supra* note 1229, pp. 40–44, who also makes the comparison with the OECD (at pp. 42–43), in respect of which he writes that Member States by agreeing that the OECD concludes an agreement for which their cooperation is required undertake to provide such cooperation (citing Article 5(c) OECD Constitution *juncto* Article 19(a) Rules of Procedure and the interpretation thereof (at that time)).

the exception,[1519] although this may be countered by the argument that, similarly to joint actions and other decisions, the Member States will normally be committed by virtue of granting the Council treaty-making power in the EU Treaty (regardless of whether the EU or the Member States are bound) and that only exceptionally an agreement may still require the submission to constitutional procedures.[1520] It has also been argued that the unanimity requirement supports action on behalf of the Union as otherwise some Member States might authorize the Council to conclude an agreement on their behalf,[1521] though this is not convincing as it was probably only the intention to allow the Council to act on behalf of *all* the Member States.[1522] Arguments based on the limitation to the scope of the CFSP (and Third Pillar)[1523] are not persuasive either since these would equally apply to the Member States when acting within the Union in these fields.[1524] An argument that is more convincing is the one that if the Member States were intended to be bound, the agreements would rather have to be concluded by the 'Member States acting in the Council' rather than the Council.[1525]

On the other hand, the second sentence of the quote seems to make the definitive applicability to the Member States dependent upon the applicability to all members of the Council if one of them raises a constitutional requirement, implying that if a Member State declares that it has to comply with constitutional

1519 P. Eeckhout, *supra* note 1431, p. 158. Compare WESSEL, pp. 261–262, who argues that this provision only makes sense if the Members States themselves are not a party. However, this is not convincing: it may make sense in that normally the Member States will all be bound by agreeing to conclude an agreement, but that the situation is different where a Member State has to follow constitutional procedures. Compare J. de Zwaan, *supra* note 1246, pp. 104–105.

1520 G. Hafner, *supra* note 1376, pp. 273–275 also discusses a further ambiguity, namely whether the constitutional 'reservation' concerns the binding nature of the agreement for a Member State or only its effects within the legal order of a Member State, concluding convincingly in favour of the former.

1521 G. Hafner, *supra* note 1376, p. 271 and WESSEL, p. 262.

1522 A point, ironically, also noted by WESSEL, p. 262 (but on the basis of which Wessel concludes that the Council must be acting on behalf of the Union). The will to act only on behalf of all the Member States would moreover be consistent with the interpretation of the remainder of the text proposed below. This objection may therefore also be opposed to the argument that the "*agency-theory would not be consistent with … a double system of unanimous decision and partial exclusion of the legal effect*" (G. Hafner, *supra* note 1376, p. 271). However, N. Neuwahl, *supra* note 1465, pp. 186–187 and 192 argues that while the intention is to bind all the Member States, it may still be possible for the Council to decide unanimously to allow only some Member States to be bound; moreover, failing agreement, some Member States could also become parties themselves outside the framework of the Union.

1523 G. Hafner, *supra* note 1376, p. 271.

1524 Thus N. Neuwahl, *supra* note 1465, pp. 187–188 has no trouble discussing these limits even though she argues that only the Member States are parties to the agreements.

1525 S. Marquardt, *supra* note 1512, p. 186. See also the similar argument relating to other CFSP acts *supra* note 1501 and the accompanying text.

requirements and cannot obtain such compliance, the agreement will not enter into force *for any of* the members of the Council[1526] (it seems unlikely that this hypothesis of a Member State not obtaining approval under the constitutional procedures has not been considered[1527]). This would suggest that agreements are concluded on behalf of the Member States because it is unlikely to have been the intention to bind the EU when none of the members of the Council are bound, as the EU would in that case likely face serious difficulties in being able to respect the agreement, at least where the cooperation of the Member States is required. This has been countered by arguing that the provisional application cannot be the provisional application as understood in the law of treaties and pertaining to the applicability of the agreement in the relations with the other party to the agreement,[1528] because it would make the provision incomprehensible due to uncertainty over the temporal limit,[1529] but rather as a rule of EU law having

1526 This depends on how one reads the alternative for the permitted provisional application. The most logical reading is that there then is no application at all (in this sense also N. Neuwahl, *supra* note 1465, p. 191), which would presumably preclude definitive application if the reason for provisional application continues to exist (in this sense S. Griller *et al.*, *supra* note 1465 p. 256, arguing that in this case the agreement must be renounced). See also G. de Kerchove & S. Marquandt, *supra* note 1504, p. 813 and S. Marquardt, *supra* note 1512, pp. 187–188, who submit that if the constitutional procedure ends negatively, the Member State concerned will have to vote against a Council decision concluding the agreement or abstain. However, it is questionable whether abstention is possible in relation to Article 24, see *infra* this note. The provisional application would be terminated upon notification of the intention not to become a party to the agreement; see the second paragraph of the provisions cited *infra* note 1528. G. Hafner, *supra* note 1376, p. 277 admits that this interpretation solves at least part of the (perceived) problem with the provisional application. The second possible alternative is that absent provisional application, the agreement applies in full. However, this seems unlikely to have been the intention in light of the wording (if this was the intended meaning, the language more likely would have been something along the lines of "*the agreement shall apply to the other members of the Council, except if they agree that the agreement shall only apply provisionally to them*"), although it would be comparable to a constructive abstention. It may be noted that there are divergent views on whether the general rule on constructive abstention in the CFSP applies or whether Article 24 contains a *lex specialis* excluding the general rule, with the latter view seeming to be the better one; compare, e.g N. Neuwahl, *supra* note 1465, pp. 191 and C. Trüe, *supra* note 1246, pp. 164–165, with G. Hafner, *supra* note 1376, pp. 277–280 and Wessel, p. 261. The case of the EU-US extradition and mutual legal assistance agreements (*infra* note 1546), supports the view that the intention is for all the Member States to be bound before binding the Union: in this case 12 Member States invoked the clause (see EU Council Documents 10409/03 of 13 June 2003 and 9163/04 of 7 May 2004) and the agreement was only *signed* subject to subsequent *conclusion* (see the Decision in the *O.J. L* 181, 19 July 2003, p. 25) which will require that all Member States can apply the agreements (see respectively Articles 3(2) *juncto* 22 and 3(2)-(3) *juncto* 18 and EU Council Doc. 9163/04 of 7 May 2004).

1527 G. Hafner's, *supra* note 1376, p. 275 writes that "*theoretically [a parliament's] consent cannot be anticipated*" but also acknowledges that a Member State ultimately could remain not bound by the agreement. J. de Zwaan, *supra* note 1246, pp. 104–105, seems to regard the non-application by a Member State as only temporary.

1528 See Article 25 1969 VCLT and 1986 VCLT.

1529 Wessel, p. 263.

only internal effect.[1530] However, it is not clear how there is necessarily such uncertainty as to the temporal element in this regard if one requires that the invoking is to be made before the expression of consent to be bound by the agreement by the Council,[1531] since then the other members of the Council may decide to apply the agreement provisionally, presumably from the moment of conclusion.[1532] The expression of consent to be bound by the treaty would then follow later, if the constitutional obstacle is lifted.[1533] Moreover, making the binding of the Member States a matter of EU law doesn't solve the problem in the case where they are not bound yet: the EU as such would be bound.[1534] A more valid concern regarding the provisional application is that it may not unilaterally be decided by one party,[1535] although this is not insurmountable as the provisional application is only an option and may, if need be, be agreed with the other contracting parties. Another counter argument could be that the second phrase cited concerns provisional application to the *members of the Council* rather than the *Member States*. The provisional application may then mean that

---

1530 Wessel, pp. 263–264. Compare G. Hafner, *supra* note 1376, p. 283.

1531 G. Hafner, *supra* note 1376, p. 275, considers that such a declaration may also be made after the conclusion of an agreement, but advises the EU to verify it before the conclusion of the agreement. While a post-conclusion declaration is not precluded by the text, it is submitted that good faith and a consistent interpretation would support the proposed approach as even being obligatory under Article 24. In fact, Hafner (*id.*) invokes these considerations in order to argue that a Member State making a declaration is obliged to submit an agreement to the constitutional procedures. In the case of the EU-US extradition and mutual legal assistance agreements (*infra* note 1546) the declarations were made together with the approval of the decision to sign the agreements (see EU Council Documents 10409/03 of 13 June 2003 and 9163/04 of 7 May 2004).

1532 D. Verwey, *supra* note 1280, p. 71, note 61 submits that the right to decide upon provisional application only comes into effect after the agreement has been concluded internally but before the EU expresses its consent to be bound.

1533 As is the case for States, consent to be bound by an international organization may be expressed in many ways; see Articles 11–16 1969 VCLT and 1986 VCLT. Hence the problem apparently perceived by G. Hafner, *supra* note 1376, p. 277 is easily overcome. See also D. Verwey, *supra* note 1280, p. 71, note 61, who clearly implies that the internal conclusion of the agreement and the expression of the EU's consent to be bound (which he both regards as aspects of 'conclusion', see *id.*, p. 74, note 73) may differ in time, as does S. Griller *et al.*, *supra* note 1465 p. 388. For an example, see the EU-US extradition and mutual legal assistance agreements (*infra* note 1546) which were first signed subject to later conclusion (see the Decision in the *O.J. L* 181, 19 July 2003, p. 25 and EU Council Doc. 9163/04 of 7 May 2004). It may be noted that the possibility of separated signature and conclusion as an expression of consent to be bound was already EC practice and has also been codified in Article 300(2) (ex 228) EC Treaty by the Treaty of Amsterdam (see A. Dashwood, 'EC External Relations Provisions Post-Amsterdam', in A. Dashwood & C. Hillion (eds.), *The General Law of EC External Relations*, London, Sweet & Maxwell, 2000, p. 282).

1534 The problem is identified by G. Hafner, *supra* note 1376, pp. 281–283 but with the conclusion merely that the EU must assure it can apply the agreement before concluding it. Similarly, C. Trüe, *supra* note 1246, p. 164, pointing out, however, that the general loyalty obligation remains applicable and may limit the problem to some extent.

1535 G. Hafner, *supra* note 1376, pp. 282–283, pointing to Articles 25 1969 VCLT and 1986 VCLT.

the Council, somehow minus one member, will be bound provisionally until the constitutional procedure has been followed by the Member State concerned. However, this does not lead to a result when this constitutional procedure does not lead to approval of the agreement, and more importantly, when one so 'divides' the Council, the expression 'members of the Council' must be read as Member States for if the Council acts on behalf of the EU, it cannot be divided.[1536] The most persuasive counter argument to the Member State provision implying a binding of the Member States only is that recourse to a two-stage conclusion procedure in the case of a Member State invoking the clause – as defended above – precludes the EU from being bound if its Member States are not. If one combines this with the view that the binding of the Member States is only a rule of EU law, the clause does not pose an obstacle to the EU being the party bound by the agreement on the international plane.

As a last point in this respect, Declaration (No. 4) on Articles J.14 and K.10 of the Treaty on European Union attached to the Treaty of Amsterdam provided that "*The provisions of Articles J.14 and K.10 of the Treaty on European Union and any agreements resulting from them shall not imply any transfer of competence from the Member States to the European Union*". Depending on the meaning of competence, this can either be restricted to material competences,[1537] or also to legal capacity. In the latter case it would *prima facie* support the view that agreements concluded under Article 24 EU Treaty bind only the Member States. However, the latter view may be countered by the argument that when an organization is granted a treaty-making power, in particular a non-exclusive one (as is the case in the CFSP[1538]), this is an autonomous power and not one transferred from the Member States, thus leading to the same interpretation in this case, i.e. only material competences are covered by this declaration.[1539]

All said, the Amsterdam version of Article 24 EU Treaty reflected a compromise and was undoubtedly unclear and open to two interpretations. However, the ordinary meaning suggests that the Council acts as an EU organ on behalf of the EU (as argued in Section A of this chapter above, because since the Treaty of Amsterdam it can no longer be claimed that the Council normally acts on behalf of the Member States) and the provision may be interpreted in a manner consistent with this view (notably by only binding the Member States under EU

1536 Even where it votes by majority or in the case of qualified constructive abstention, it is the Council and the EU as a whole which are bound (though in the latter case an individual Member State will not be bound).

1537 See WESSEL, p. 262.

1538 G. de Kerchove & S. Marquandt, *supra* note 1504, p. 821 and S. Marquardt, *supra* note 1512, p. 190.

1539 G. Hafner, *supra* note 1376, pp. 271–272.

law and requiring a two-step conclusion procedure if a constitutional procedure must be followed by a Member State). Therefore it is submitted that this is the better view.[1540]

In any event, practice has clarified the matter:[1541] to my knowledge, all agreements concluded under Article 24 EU Treaty[1542] name the EU as a party

1540 Compare, e.g. on the one hand, P. Des Nerviens, *supra* note 1514, pp. 805–806; R. Genson, 'Les accords d'extradition et d'entraide judiciare signés le 25 juin 2003 à Washington entre l'Union européenne et les États-Unies d'Amérique', No. 470 *R.M.C.U.E.* 2003, p. 428; S. Griller *et al.*, *supra* note 1465 pp. 55–59 and 390–391; G. Hafner, *supra* note 1376, p. 272; S. Marquardt, *supra* note 1512, pp. 185–187; M. Pachinger, *supra* note 1465, pp. 90–108; C. Trüe, *supra* note 1246, pp. 163–165; D. Verwey, *supra* note 1280, pp. 60–61 and 72–75 and W. Wormuth. *supra* note 1466, pp. 104–106, concluding that the agreements are concluded on behalf of the Union, with, on the other hand, M. Cremona, *supra* note 1517, pp. 68 and 70–71; E. Denza, *supra* note 1465, p. 282; E. Denza, *The Intergovernmental Pillars of the European Union*, Oxford, Oxford University Press, 2002, pp. 173–174; J. de Zwaan, *supra* note 1246, pp. 101–103; L. Grard, *supra* note 1407, pp. 375–377; J. Monar, 'The European Union's Foreign Affairs System after the Treaty of Amsterdam: A 'Strengthened Capacity for External Action'?', 2 *E.F.A.R.* 1997, p. 427; N. Neuwahl, *supra* note 1465, pp. 184–186; H.-J. Cremer, 'Article 24' in C. Calliess & M. Ruffert (eds.), *supra* note 1320, pp. 174–175 and D. Vignes, *supra* note 1472, p. 760, concluding that they are concluded on behalf of the Member States.

1541 Similarly, D. Thym, 'Die Völkerrechtlichen Verträge der Europäischen Union', 66 *Z.a.ö.R.V.* 2006, pp. 863–915 (English summary at pp. 913–915), who lists over 60 agreements and also discusses the value of practice in the EU (at pp. 868–870). Thus D. Vignes, *supra* note 1472, p. 770 was right in stating that only to the extent that the Member States would deem it necessary to project the Union on the international scene, would they interpret the texts in a way so as to recognize the Union's legal personality if necessary, as was A.S. Muller, *supra* note 1269, p. 85 note 46 by deeming it not unlikely that the "*fiction of 'non personality' of the EU*" would be defeated by practice. Compare A. Sari, 'The Conclusion of International Agreements by the European Union in the Context of the ESDP', 56 *I.C.L.Q.* 2007, pp. 53–86, who concludes at pp. 85–86 that the EU has become a subject of international law but that the discussion has shifted to the area of responsibility.

1542 There is one case where this is perhaps not so, but it concerns two agreements based on Article 6 of the Protocol Integrating the Schengen *acquis* into the Framework of the European Union (annexed to the Treaty of Amsterdam, *O.J. C* 340, 10 November 1997, p. 93) rather than Article 24 (or 38) EU Treaty: The Agreement concluded by the Council of the European Union and the Republic of Iceland and the Kingdom of Norway concerning the latter's association with the implementation, application and development of the Schengen acquis (Brussels, 18 May 1999, entered into force on 26 June 2000, *O.J. L* 119, 7 May 1999, p. 35/36) and Agreement concluded by the Council of the European Union and the Republic of Iceland and the Kingdom of Norway on the establishment of rights and obligations between Ireland and the United Kingdom of Great Britain and Northern Ireland, on the one hand, and the Republic of Iceland and the Kingdom of Norway, on the other, in areas of the Schengen acquis which apply to these States (Brussels, 30 June 1999, which entered into force on 26 June 2000 (see *O.J. L* 149, 23 June 2000, p. 36), *O.J. L* 15, 20 January 2000, p. 1/2). This case is more complex as it involved 13 of the then 15 Member States acting in closer cooperation (A.G. Toth, 'The Legal Effects of the Protocols Relating to the United Kingdom, Ireland and Denmark', in T. Heukels, N. Blokker & M. Brus (eds.), *supra* note 1467, pp. 246–247 argues that under the Schengen Protocol it is the Member States concerned that act and not the EC or EU; for the opposing view, see D. Thym, *supra* note 1541, pp. 894–896) and covers both EC and Third Pillar Issues (as Schengen is spread over these two pillars, see, e.g. the cross-pillar and not the Member States, often distinguishing between the EU and its Member States in their provisions.[1543] The first agreement so concluded seems to have been the 25 April 2001 EUMM SOMA with the Federal Republic of Yugoslavia.[1544] It is interesting to note that Article 24 EU Treaty was thus first applied only after the signature of the Treaty of Nice on 23 February 2001, but before the latter's entry into force on 1 February 2003.[1545] The first agreements in

---

agreement with Switzerland, *infra* note 1556). Both agreements list the Council as a party rather than the Union and under Article 8(3) of the first agreement "*The acceptance by Iceland and Norway of the content of acts and measures referred to in paragraph 2 shall create rights and obligations between Iceland and Norway, and between Iceland and Norway on the one hand, and the European Community and those of its Member States bound by those acts and measures, on the other hand*". For a discussion, see J. de Zwaan, *supra* note 1246, pp. 101–102; G. de Kerchove & S. Marquandt, *supra* note 1504, pp. 819–820 and D. Verwey, *supra* note 1280, pp. 74–75.

1543 See also P. Eeckhout, *supra* note 1431, pp. 159–160, citing as an example of the distinction between the EU and the Member States the difference between staff appointed by the EU and staff seconded from the Member States; I. Govaere, J. Capiau & A. Vermeersch, *supra* note 1465, pp. 160–161; K. Lenaerts & P. Van Nuffel, *supra* note 1465, pp. 810–811 and D. Thym, *supra* note 1541, pp. 868–870. But see S. Marquardt, *supra* note 1512, p. 185 noting that in 2003 at least some Member States, as well as Commission services, still maintained that the agreements were concluded by the Member States. The Commission's position may perhaps result from an unwarranted fear that the recognition of the legal personality of the Union would affect that of the Communities: A. Tizzano, 'The Foreign Relations Law of the EU Between Supranationality and Intergovernmental Model', in E. Cannizzaro (ed.), *The European Union as an Actor in International Relations*, The Hague, Kluwer Law International, 2002, p. 143 identifies this concern as one of the key considerations underlying opposition to a Union legal personality, though without saying that this would apply to the Commission, and G. de Kerchove & S. Marquandt, *supra* note 1504, p. 807 attribute the Commission's opposition to a fear for its external relations competences. In any event, such resistance cannot be maintained in the face of clear practice to the contrary. For instance, the recent Agreement between the International Criminal Court and the European Union on Cooperation and Assistance (10 April 2006, *O.J. L* 115, 28 April 2006, p. 49/50) provides in its Article 2(1) that "*'EU' shall mean the Council of the [EU], the Secretary General/High Representative and the General Secretariat of the Council, and the Commission of the [EC]. 'EU' shall not mean the Member States in their own right*"; see also R. Wessel, 'The European *Union* as a Party to International Agreements: Shared Competences, Mixed Responsibilities?', in A. Dashwood and M. Maresceau (eds.), *The Law and Practice of EU External Relations – Salient Features of a Chaging Landscape*, Cambridge, Cambridge University Press, 2008, pp. 152–187, also published in the conference reader of the 37th Asser Colloquium on European Law on 'The European Union and International Crisis Management: Legal and Policy Aspects' (The Hague, 11–12 October 2007), p. 14. For an overview of EU pratice, see G. de Kerchove & S. Marquandt, *supra* note 1504, pp. 814–820 and D. Thym, *supra* note 1541, pp. 863–913, especially pp. 875–899, all rightly noting the frequent use in the ESDP (see *supra*, Chapter 3).

1544 Agreement between the European Union and the Federal Republic of Yugoslavia on the Activities of the European Union Monitoring Mission (EUMM) in the Federal Republic of Yugoslavia, *O.J. L* 125, 5 May 2001, p. 1/2. See also X., 'Editorial Comments. The European Union – A New International Actor', 38 *C.M.L. Rev.* 2001, p. 825.

1545 Other early examples include the 31 August 2001 Agreement between the European Union and the Former Yugoslav Republic of Macedonia on the Activities of the European Union Monitoring Mission (EUMM) in the Former Yugoslav Republic of Macedonia, *O.J. L* 241, 11 September 2001, p. 1/2; a 17 June 2002 Agreement in the Form of an Exchange of Letters the Third Pillar were only concluded after the entry into force of the Treaty of Nice.[1546]

Indeed, the Treaty of Nice made some changes to Article 24 EU Treaty that lend further support to the view that agreements under that provision are concluded by the EU rather than the Member States.[1547] These include the possibility of voting by qualified majority in the implementation of joint actions or common positions under Article 23(2) EU Treaty (new paragraph 3) and in Third Pillar issues that permit qualified majority decisions under Article 34(2) EU Treaty (new paragraph 4) but most importantly, a new paragraph 6 stating that "*Agreements concluded under the conditions set out by this Article shall be binding on the institutions of the Union*". The constitutional procedure and provisional application clause is left intact, with the exception of a minor but nevertheless suggestive amendment, namely that the decision on provisional application is no

---

between the European Union and the Republic of Lebanon concerning Cooperation in the Fight against Terrorism (EU Council Doc. 7494/02, 17 April 2002, as corrected by Doc. 10574/02, 9 July 2002); the 4 October 2002 Agreement between the European Union and the Bosnia and Herzegovina (BiH) on the Activities of the European Union Police Mission (EUPM) in BiH (*O.J. L* 293, 29 October 2002, p. 1/2) and a significant number of participation agreements with third States concerning the EUPM (see *supra*, Chapter 3.B.3, note 398).

1546 To my knowledge (see also P. Eeckhout, *supra* note 1431, p. 161), these are the Agreement on Extradition between the [EU] and the [USA], Washington, DC, 25 June 2003, *O.J. L* 181, 19 July 2003, p. 25/27, and Agreement on Mutual Legal Assistance between the [EU] and the [USA], Washington, DC, 25 June 2003, *O.J. L* 181, 19 July 2003, p. 25/34. Both clearly name the EU as a party and distinguish between the Member States and the Union, as do subsequent Third Pillar agreements. For a discussion of these two agreements, see, e.g. R. Genson, *supra* note 1540, pp. 427–432; V. Mitsilegas, 'The New EU-USA Cooperation on Extradition, Mutual Legal Assistance and the Exchange of Police Data', 8 *E.F.A.R.* 2003, pp. 523–533; G. Stessens, 'The EU-US Agreements on Extradition and on Mutual Legal Assistance: How to Bridge Different Approaches', in G. de Kerchove & A. Weyembergh (eds.), *supra* note 1512, pp. 263–273; J. Wouters & F. Naert, 'Of Arrest Warrants, Terrorist Offences and Extradition Deals. An Appraisal of the EU's Main Criminal Law Measures against Terrorism after '11 September'', 41 *C.M.L. Rev.* 2004, pp. 930–934 and J. Wouters & F. Naert, 'Police and Judicial Cooperation in the European Union and the Fight Against International Terrorism', in C. Fijnaut, J. Wouters & F. Naert (eds.), *Legal Instruments in the Fight against International Terrorism. A Transatlantic Dialogue*, Martinus Nijhoff, Leiden/Boston, 2004, pp. 142–146.

1547 See also P. Eeckhout, *supra* note 1431, p. 160 and X., *supra* note 1544, pp. 826–827 (writing, after considering practice and the Treaty of Nice, that "*intentions ... though they may once have seemed obscure, have now been made manifest*"). For post-Nice commentaries, see also G. de Kerchove & S. Marquandt, *supra* note 1504, pp. 803–825; T. Georgopoulos, 'What Kind of Treaty-making Power for the EU?: Constitutional Problems related to the Conclusion of the EU-US Agreements on Extradition and Mutual Legal Assistance', 30 *Eur. L. Rev.* 2005, pp. 190–208 (focusing on human rights and legitimacy concerns and taking the surprising view that the EU has treaty-making capacity but no international legal personality); L. Grard, *supra* note 1407, pp. 375–377; S. Marquardt, 'The Conclusion of International Agreements under Article 24 of the Treaty on European Union', in V. Kronenberger (ed.), *supra* note 1320, pp. 333–349 (discussing the impact of the Treaty of Nice amendments at pp. 348–349) and M. Pachinger, *supra* note 1465, pp. 105–108.

longer worded as concerning provisional application between the other members of the Council but simply provisional application, which suggests that it means provisional application by the EU.[1548] Nevertheless, the amendments are not entirely conclusive.[1549] The majority voting possibility implies that it is the Union that is bound, in addition, normally, to the Member States.[1550] The provision binding the institutions of the Union, and thus the Union,[1551] confirms this explicitly, and must, in light of the foregoing, probably be considered as referring to being bound internationally rather than as a matter of EU law only. Moreover, even if it were to refer to EU law only, it still clearly indicates that the Union as distinct from the Member States is bound under EU law. However, the retention of the constitutional procedure and provisional application clause means, as explained above, that there is a risk of the Union being bound when the Member States are not, which may give rise to difficulties, though this can easily be avoided if the EU obtains assurances that this clause will not be invoked before concluding an agreement or only signs an agreement subject to a later conclusion if it is invoked, as seems to happen. That being said, this provision has not been invoked very often, albeit relatively frequently in respect of the few agreements concluded under Article 38,[1552] which has given rise to the question whether

1548 S. Marquardt, *supra* note 1512, p. 188 an X., *supra* note 1544, p. 827.

1549 In this sense L. Grard, *supra* note 1407, pp. 375–377, arguing that the changes conserve the Amsterdam choice but that other elements introduced by the Treaty of Nice nevertheless may be analyzed as contributing to the formation of a customary international legal personality.

1550 S. Marquardt, *supra* note 1512, p. 186 and X., *supra* note 1544, p. 826. *Contra*: L. Grard, *supra* note 1407, pp. 375–376, at least in respect of the CFSP as the majority vote there is limited to an agreement necessary for the implementation of a common position or joint action. Indeed, it cannot be precluded that it still was the intention to bind the Member States, even, in this specific case, against their will. However, this is most doubtful, especially given the broader possibility for majority votes in Article 38, a point admitted by Grard.

1551 E.g. M. Pachinger, *supra* note 1465, p. 106. *Contra*: L. Grard, *supra* note 1407, p. 376, apparently not regarding the institutions as representing the Union and not considering the Union as being bound. However, this is an unlikely interpretation for which there seem to be no convincing arguments. In contrast, one might ask whether, given the single institutional framework, this also implies that the EC is bound (for an affirmative answer in respect of EU legal acts generally, see C. Trüe, *supra* note 1246, p. 157). On the one hand, the separation between the pillars and the primacy of the EC Pillar imply that agreements under the Second or Third Pillar should not affect the First Pillar. On the other hand, one may question whether this should go so far that it precludes the binding effect on the EC of measures adopted within the Second or Third Pillar (though the impact on the EC would in that case presumably be limited), in particular having regard to the requirement of consistency and coherence (on the latter, see *infra* notes 1586 and 1592).

1552 Similarly, L. Grard, *supra* note 1407, p. 377. D. Verwey, *supra* note 1280, pp. 6 and 60–61, writes that at the time no Member State had yet invoked this clause (though it is unclear whether this pertains to Article 24 only or also includes Article 38). However, in respect of the EU-US extradition and mutual legal assistance agreements (*supra* note 1546), 12 Member States have invoked this clause; see R. Genson, *supra* note 1540, p. 428 and EU Council Documents 10409/03 of 13 June 2003 and 9163/04 of 7 May 2004. See G. de Kerchove & S.

such agreements should not be mixed agreements including the Member States as parties in addition to the EU and the third party.[1553]

The clause disappears under the Lisbon Treaty, which, with its EC and EU merger, will have a unified set of treaty-making rules subject only to some specific exceptions.[1554] This may also take care of the difficulties that could arise in the case of a cross-pillar agreement involving the EC and the EU (and, possibly, also the Member States) and thus being based on Article 300 EC Treaty and 24 or 38 EU Treaty. Although it has been noted that such new 'mixed agreements' (a term use to refer to agreements to which both the Member States and the EC are a party because the subject matter is not exclusively within the competences of the EC) are possible,[1555] only two such agreements appear to have been concluded so far.[1556]

Marquandt, *supra* note 1504, pp. 822–823 for the relatively frequent use in respect of Third Pillar agreements.

1553 T. Georgopoulos, *supra* note 1547, pp. 207–208.

1554 See Article 22 (renumbered 37) EU Treaty ("*The Union may conclude agreements with one or more States or international organisations in areas covered by this Chapter*") and Articles 3(2) (renumbered 3(2)) (defining when the EU's treaty power is exclusive); 188 L (renumbered 216) ("*1. The Union may conclude an agreement with one or more third countries or international organisations where the Treaties so provide or where the conclusion of an agreement is necessary in order to achieve, within the framework of the Union's policies, one of the objectives referred to in the Treaties, or is provided for in a legally binding Union act or is likely to affect common rules or alter their scope. 2. Agreements concluded by the Union are binding upon the institutions of the Union and on its Member States*") and 188N (renumbered 218) (replacing Article 300 EC treaty and setting out the procedure) and 188O (renumbered 219) (relating to the ECB) Treaty on the Functioning of the European Union as they are amended/inserted by the Lisbon Treaty. Compare Articles III-323; III-325 and I-13(2) EU Constitution. For a brief discussion of these provisions in the draft EU Constitution, see R. Barents, 'Een grondwet voor Europa (VII): de externe betrekkingen', 11 *Nederlands tijdschrift voor Europees recht* 2005, pp. 89–90; L. Grard, *supra* note 1465, pp. 365–367 and D. Verwey, *supra* note 1280, pp. 78–82.

1555 E.g. M.-G. Garbagnati Ketvel, *supra* note 1473, pp. 92–94; L. Grard, *supra* note 1407, pp. 377–378; D. Thym, *supra* note 1541, pp. 908–912; D. Verwey, *supra* note 1280, p. 83 and X., *supra* note 1544, pp. 827–828 (even pleading for the conclusion of all external agreements by the EU under international law, with the question who is specifically bound to be regulated by EU law as an internal matter, but acknowledging that this would be going too fast). For an interesting discussion of the cross-pillar effect of common strategies, see C. Hillion, 'Common Strategies and the Interface between EC External Relations and the CFSP: Lessons of the Partnership between the EU and Russia', in A. Dashwood & C. Hillion (eds.), *supra* note 1533, pp. 287–301. For a brief discussion focused on human rights in the external relations, see E. Cannizzaro, 'The Scope of the EU Foreign Power. Is the EC Competent to Conclude Agreements with Third States Including Human Rights Clauses', in E. Cannizzaro (ed.), *supra* note 1543, pp. 305–307, who, however, does not seem to consider a mixed EU-EC agreement (based on Articles 11(1) and 24 EU Treaty on the EU side as well as relevant provisions from the EC Treaty) but rather an EC agreement based on EU provisions, which obviously posed problems and should be rejected.

1556 Namely the Agreement between the European Union, the European Community and the Swiss Confederation on the latter's association with the implementation, application and

One may therefore conclude that the Treaty of Amsterdam was very ambiguous on treaty-making capacity, but that the extensive practice under this provision since 2001, as well as its amendment by the Treaty of Nice, now undoubtedly confirm that agreements under Article 24 EU Treaty are concluded on behalf of the EU, which therefore has treaty-making power, and must be a subject of international law and have international legal personality.

C. PRIVILEGES AND IMMUNITIES

Interestingly, the Maastricht Treaty did not include any provisions on privileges and immunities, which remained therefore limited to those granted under the 1965 Protocol on the Privileges and Immunities of the European Communities.[1557] This means that the EU itself did not have any treaty-based privileges and immunities. It would also imply that representatives of Member States taking part in EU activities, such as the members of the Political Committee, were, strictly speaking, not covered by these immunities (though they may be covered by customary law immunities of State representatives), since these immunities only apply to "*Representatives of Member States taking part in*

development of the Schengen acquis (Luxembourg, 26 October 2004; see EU Council Doc. 13054/04 for the text; *O.J. L* 368, 15 December 2004, p. 26 for the EU signature decision and *O.J. L* 370, 17 December 2004, p. 78, for the EC signature decision, both providing for provisional application; *O.J. L* 53, 27 February 2008, p. 50 (corrig. *O.J. L* 110, 22 April 2008, p. 16) for the EU conclusion decision and *O.J. L* 53, 27 February 2008, p. 1 for the EC conclusion decision) and the Protocol between the European Union, the European Community, the Swiss Confederation and the Principality of Liechtenstein on the accession of the Principality of Liechtenstein to the Agreement between the European Union, the European Community and the Swiss Confederation on the Swiss Confederation's association with the implementation, application and development of the Schengen acquis (EC and EU signature decisions, in *O.J. L* 83, 26 March 2008, respectively p. 3 and p. 5 (corrig. *O.J. L* 110, 22 April 2008, p. 16)). See also G. de Kerchove & S. Marquandt, *supra* note 1504, p. 820; M.-G. Garbagnati Ketvel, *supra* note 1473, pp. 93–94 and S. Marquardt, *supra* note 1512, p. 189. A second case which comes close is the Agreement between the EU and Lebanon concerning Cooperation in the Fight against Terrorism (*supra* note 1546) because of its close connection to the Euro-Mediterranean Agreement establishing an Association between the EC and its Member States, of the one part, and Lebanon, of the other, yet it does not quite constitute such a mixed agreement because it is formally separated from the latter (compare D. Thym, *supra* note 1541, pp. 898–899, seeing this as an exceptional case that has not been followed since). It may be noted that even treaties covered by the EC Treaty may be subject to split signature decisions in a number of cases where they pertain to different parts of the EC Treaty that are subject to different regimes; see, e.g. the split decisions concerning the Protocols Against the Smuggling of Migrants by Land, Sea and Air, and to Prevent, Suppress and Punish Trafficking in Persons, Especially Women And Children, both supplementing the UN Convention Against Transnational Organised Crime, in *O.J. L* 262, 22 September 2006, pp. 24 and 34 and 44 and 51 respectively.

1557 *Supra* note 1380. This point is also raised by N. Neuwahl, *supra* note 1320, p. 13.

the work of the institutions of the Communities, *their advisers and technical experts shall*".[1558] Similarly, all EU staff would legally have to be regarded as EC staff to enjoy privileges and immunities under the Protocol,[1559] and presumably also more generally when they are recruited given the EU's lack of domestic legal personality.[1560]

The Treaty of Amsterdam did not make any changes in this regard concerning the *Union* and neither did the Treaty of Nice. While this seems possible because of the single institutional framework, it is rather strange considering that entire parts of the Council's staff are exclusively devoted to non-EC activities, most notably the military organs. It shows perhaps best of all how the existence of the EC is arguably the main element that has allowed for the EU's true status to have been denied for so long (which should not be read as a criticism of the continued existence of the EC). This situation is remedied under the Lisbon Treaty.[1561]

D. EU AGENCIES

Since the entry into force of the Treaty of Amsterdam, the EU has set up various entities in both the CFSP/ESDP and the Third Pillar by EU instruments (not by agreements concluded between the Member States, as was the case for Europol[1562]), possessing legal personality (mostly under domestic law, but in the

---

1558 Article 11, emphasis added.

1559 *Id.*, Article 12.

1560 In a sense D. Curtin, *supra* note 1465, p. 26 was therefore right that the EU is borrowing EC civil servants. However, see A.S. Muller, *supra* note 1269, p. 70, who argues that international legal personality always entails domestic legal personality in the host State. Since the EU's organs are distributed over most of its Member States, this would imply, if correct, that the EU would enjoy domestic legal personality in most Member States if it has international legal personality. In practice, the problem can largely be avoided because of the common institutions and the separate legal personality (and privileges and immunities) of various agencies (see *infra*, next Section).

1561 See Article 291 (renumbered 343) Treaty on the Functioning of the European Union and the Protocol on the Privileges and Immunities of the Union, as they are amended by the Lisbon Treaty. Compare Article III-434 EU Constitution ("*The Union shall enjoy in the territories of the Member States such privileges and immunities as are necessary for the performance of its tasks, under the conditions laid down in the Protocol on the privileges and immunities of the European Union*") and the Protocol (No. 7) on the privileges and immunities of the European Union.

1562 Convention on the establishment of a European Police Office, 1995 *O.J. C* 316, 27 November 1995, p. 1/2, which entered into force on 1 October 1998, as amended, Article 26. It may be noted that the Europol Convention will be replaced by a Council Decision; see Council Decision of 6 April 2009 establishing the European Police Office (Europol), *O.J. L* 121, 15 May 2009, p. 37.

case of Europol and Eurojust clearly also on the international plane[1563]). This is for instance the case for Eurojust,[1564] the EDA,[1565] the EU Satellite Centre,[1566] the EU ISS[1567] and the Athena financing mechanism for military operations.[1568] The European Police College (CEPOL) initially did not have legal personality[1569] but this was later changed.[1570]

Most of these agencies have separate arrangements for privileges and immunities, on the basis of different legal instruments: in most cases agreements between

1563 Since both organizations conclude international agreements, apparently in their own name, that appear to be legally binding, see Article 26 and 37 Europol Convention, *supra* note 1562 (and implementing Council decisions; for a discussion of some of the agreements concluded pursuant to Article 26; see J. Wouters & F. Naert, *supra* note 1546, pp. 140–142; for a list with the texts, see www.europol.europa.eu/index.asp?page=agreements; see also Article 42 Europol Convention) and Article 27(3) Eurojust Decision (*infra* note 1564), which, however, requires Council approval of such agreements (for an application, see the Eurojust agreements with Iceland and Romania signed on 2 December 2005 and mentioned in a Eurojust press release of that day, www.eurojust.europa.eu/press_releases/2005/02-12-2005.htm). See also the Europol-Eurojust cooperation agreement of 9 June 2004, available online at www.europol.europa.eu/legal/agreements/Agreements/17374.pdf. See also D. Thym, *supra* note 1541, pp. 892–893. For a brief discussion of the role of EU Third Pillar agencies in the Union's external relations, see, e.g. H.G. Nilsson, 'Organs and Bodies of the Third Pillar as Instruments of External Relations of the Union?', in G. de Kerchove & A. Weyembergh (eds.), *supra* note 1512, pp. 201–209. For a discussion of Europol in this respect, see C. Rijken, 'Legal and Technical Aspects of Co-operation between Europol, Third States, and Interpol', in V. Kronenberger (ed.), *supra* note 1320, pp. 577–603, especially pp. 582–583 and 586–603, *inter alia* mentioning a draft model agreement on cooperation with third States. See also more generally A. Ott, 'EU Regulatory Agencies in EU External Relations: Trapped in a Legal Minefield between European and International Law', 13 *E.F.A.R.* 2008, pp. 515–540.

1564 Council Decision of 28 February 2002 setting up Eurojust with a view to reinforcing the fight against serious crime (2002/187/JHA), *O.J. L* 63, 6 March 2002, p. 1, Article 1.

1565 Council Joint Action of 12 July 2004 on the establishment of the European Defence Agency, (2004/551/CFSP) *O.J. L* 245, 17 July 2004, pp. 17–28, Article 6. On the EDA, see *supra*, Chapter 2.F. On the basis of Articles 6 and 25 of this Joint Action, it can be argued that the EDA has international legal personality, see D. Thym, *supra* note 1541, p. 894.

1566 Council Joint Action of 20 July 2001 on the establishment of a European Union Satellite Centre (2001/555/CFSP), *O.J. L* 200, 25 July 2001, p. 5, Article 6. See also *supra*, Chapter 1.E, note 140 and the accompanying text.

1567 Council Joint Action of 20 July 2001 on the establishment of a European Union Institute for Security Studies (2001/554/CFSP), *O.J. L* 200, 25 July 2001, p. 1, Article 4. See also *supra*, Chapter 1.E, note 141 and the accompanying text.

1568 Council Decision of 23 February 2004 establishing a mechanism to administer the financing of the common costs of European Union operations having military or defence implications (2004/197/CFSP), *O.J. L* 63, 28 February 2004, pp. 68–82, as subsequently amended, Article 3 (which uses the term legal capacity).

1569 Council Decision of 22 December 2000 establishing a European Police College (CEPOL) (2000/820/JHA), *O.J. L* 336, 30 December 2000, p. 1.

1570 See Council Decision of 20 September 2005 establishing the European Police College (CEPOL) and repealing Decision 2000/820/JHA (2005/681/JHA), *O.J. L* 256, 1 October 2005, p. 63, Article 2.

(participating) Member States[1571] or decisions of the Member States meeting within the Council (which arguably amounts to the same),[1572] in one case an agreement between the body and the host State,[1573] and in still another the applicability of the Protocol on the Privileges and Immunities of the European Communities by a Council Decision.[1574] The latter has given rise to concern for

---

1571 See Article 41 Europol Convention, *supra* note 1562, and Protocol drawn up, on the basis of Article K.3 of the Treaty on European Union and Article 41 (3) of the Europol Convention, on the privileges and immunities of Europol, the members of its organs, the deputy directors and employees of Europol, *O.J. C* 221, 19 July 1997, p. 1/2, as amended (on the initial legal status and immunities of Europol, see A.S. Muller, *supra* note 1269, pp. 85–86). This was also envisaged in Article 26 EDA Joint Action (*supra* note 1565), Article 16 EU Satellite Centre Joint Action (*supra* note 1566) and Article 15 EU ISS Joint Action (*supra* note 1567), but in these cases a decision of the Member States was adopted instead, although this may in fact amount to an agreement (see *infra* next note). For the impact of the replacement of the Europol Convention by a Council Decision (see *supra* note 1562), see Article 51 of the latter decision.

1572 See Decision of the Representatives of the Governments of the Member States, meeting within the Council of 28 April 2004 concerning privileges and immunities granted to ATHENA (2004/582/EC), *O.J. L* 261, 6 August 2004, p. 125 (in its Article 6, this decision provides for entry into force on 1 November 2004 provided that all Member States have given notification that their internal procedures have been complied with, highlighting the similarity to a treaty); Decision of the representatives of the Governments of the Member States, meeting within the Council, on the privileges and immunities granted to the European Defence Agency and to its staff members (10 November 2004; it does not seem to have been published in the *O.J.* but is listed in the Council's agreements database; the most recent version available in the Council's register is EU Council Doc. 11502/1/04 REV 1, 9 September 2004; see also the supplementary Protocol *infra* next note) and Decision of the Representatives of the Governments of the Member States on the privileges and immunities granted to the European Union Institute for Security Studies and the European Union Satellite Centre, and to their bodies and staff members (15 October 2001; it does not seem to have been published in the *O.J.* but is listed in the Council's agreements database; the most recent version available in the Council's register is EU Council Doc. 11639/01, 19 September 2001; the French and Dutch texts are published together with the Belgian Act of Parliamentary assent (Wet van 13 juli 2004 houdende instemming met het Besluit van de vertegenwoordigers van de Regeringen der lid-Staten van de Europese Unie, in het kader van de Raad bijeen, betreffende de voorrechten en immuniteiten die aan het Instituut voor veiligheidsstudies en het Satellietcentrum van de Europese Unie, alsmede aan hun organen en de leden van hun personeel worden verleend, gedaan te Brussel op 15 oktober 2001) in the *Official Gazette* (*Belgisch Staatsblad*) of 13 October 2004; this (late) Parliamentary assent also indicates that the decision is a treaty).

1573 Namely Eurojust, see the Exchange of letters with the Netherlands dated 22 November/6 December 2005 published in the *Tractatenblad* 2005 No. 315 and Agreement of 15 March 2006, published in the *Tractatenblad* 2006 No. 68 (replacing the Exchange of letters dated 13/20 December 2002, published in the *Tractatenblad* 2003 No. 7). There is also an additional protocol between the EDA and Belgium concluded on 22 June 2005 in Brussels and supplementing the agreement between the Member States (*supra* note 1572); to my knowledge, this protocol has not yet been published.

1574 Article 3 CEPOL Decision, *supra* note 1570. This is also the solution adopted in the EC for the European Agency for the Management of Operational Cooperation at the External Borders; see Article 18 Council Regulation (EC) No 2007/2004 of 26 October 2004 establishing a European Agency for the Management of Operational Cooperation at the External Borders of some Member States[1575] and, incidentally, raises the question why instead of artificially and indirectly extending the privileges and immunities of the EC to the EU through the shared institutions (see preceding Section), the Council and the Member States have not simply decided to openly extend these immunities to the EU.

It is hard to see how the EU can have the power to establish entities with legal personality and accord them privileges and immunities if it does not itself have such personality,[1576] except perhaps where a body is specifically mentioned in the EU Treaty before its establishment.[1577] Moreover, such decisions clearly are legally binding and create rights and obligations under international law. They clearly illustrate that joint actions in the area of the CFSP are also (or at the very least can be) legally binding. This must also be true for the various Council decisions regulating the status of the staff of such agencies.[1578]

the Member States of the European Union, *O.J. L* 349, 25 November 2004, p. 1. On whether subsidiary bodies of an organization may participate in its privileges and immunities more generally, see F. Morgenstern, *supra* note 1229, pp. 24–26.

1575 See EU Council Doc. 11567/04, 7 September 2004, §3: "*It was noted by delegations ... that, for the purpose of implementing Article 3 of the Decision, the Agency would be assimilated to an international organisation by the Member States concerned. During the proceedings, some delegations furthermore recalled that the Commission had committed itself to initiate, within a reasonable deadline, a general reflection on the issue of the application of the 'Protocol on the Privileges and Immunities of the European Communities' on decentralised bodies, such as agencies. In this context, France and Sweden made the statement to the minutes of the meeting of the Representatives of the Governments of the Member States of the European Union, meeting within the Council, as set out in Annex to this note. ... Annex: La France et la Suède acceptent de lever leurs réserves sur le projet de décision relative aux privilèges et immunités accordés à l'Agence européenne de défense et à son personnel, en raison de la priorité politique accordée au lancement effectif de cette agence. Elles soulignent la nécessité d'un débat général sur le bien fondé de l'extension systématique du protocole sur les privilèges et immunités des Communautés européennes aux organes déconcentrés de l'UE, tels que les agences, et à leurs agents. Elles notent avec satisfaction que la Commission s'est engagée, lors de l'examen de la proposition de règlement sur l'Agence européenne des frontières le 18 mars 2004, à organiser un tel débat dans un délai raisonnable. Elles attachent une grande importance à la mise en oeuvre rapide de cet engagement*".

1576 L. Grard, *supra* note 1407, p. 377 mentions this development as a factor supporting the international legal personality of the EU. In the EC, the ECJ has confirmed that the EC may participate in agreements setting up international organizations or organs as long as certain limits are observed to safeguard EC law (see, e.g. Opinion 1/76, *Draft Agreement establishing a European laying-up fund for inland waterway vessels*, 26 April 1977; Cases 3–4/76 and 6/76 (*Cornelis Kramer and others*, 14 July 1976) and I. Govaere, J. Capiau & A. Vermeersch, *supra* note 1465, p. 157) and various agencies have also been established by EC instruments (see G. Schusterschitz *supra* note 1251, pp. 163–188).

1577 As was the case for Europol (see Article K.1(9) Maastricht Treaty) but not for other bodies. Eurojust was only given a treaty basis in Articles 29 and 31 EU Treaty by the Treaty of Nice, which entered into force after Europol's establishment.

1578 In the area of the ESDP, these decisions are listed *supra*, Chapter 1.E-F and Chapter 2.B.

E. HOW DOES THE EU RELATE TO THE EC AND THE AGENCIES?

Pursuant to Article A of the Maastricht Treaty "*By this Treaty, the High Contracting Parties establish among themselves a European Union ...*", which "*shall be founded on the European Communities, supplemented by the policies and forms of cooperation established by this Treaty*". This foundation of the EU on the EC supplemented by the other policies and forms of cooperation, including the CFSP, poses a challenge for considering the legal personality of the EU in relation to that of the EC.

In particular, this structure suggests that the EU *includes* the EC. Moreover, the two organizations "*are served by a single institutional framework*"[1579] and under Article O of the Maastricht Treaty, new Member States had to accede to the EU and this would entail their accession to the European Communities. However, it is quite clear that the European Communities continue to exist as separate international legal persons.[1580] Therefore, if the EU is the overall entity, it includes separate entities at least some of which possess their own international legal personality. Although this may appear strange, it is possible[1581] and would in fact reflect the situation within the EC,[1582] within the EU *sense stricto* (i.e.

1579 Article C Maastricht Treaty.

1580 Article 281 EC Treaty is left intact. However, a few authors have argued that despite this continued formal separate legal personality, the Communities have been absorbed by the Union as a single international organization with a single legal order; see notably A. von Bogdandy, 'The Legal Case for Unity: The European Union as Single Organization with a Single Legal System', 36 *C.M.L. Rev.* 1999, pp. 887–910 and A. von Bogdandy & M. Nettesheim, 'Die Europäische Union: Ein einheitlicher Verband mit eigener Rechtsordnung', 31 *Europarecht* 1996, pp. 3–26. A particularly interesting point in their thesis is the fact that before the ECJ cases are always brought against individual institutions rather than the organization in the framework of which they act (see *C.M.L. Rev.* 1999, pp. 906–907). For all their arguments, their analysis is, however, hard to square with the separate legal personalities. That being said, the resulting consequences on the internal level would seem to be much the same as in the thesis of a layered EU defended below.

1581 There is some uncertainty in doctrine over the extent to which entities of an international organization may possess proper international legal personality but it rather concerns organs which have no proper legal personality, see *supra* note 1296.

1582 For a discussion concerning the situation of agencies of the EC vis-à-vis the EC, see G. Schusterschitz *supra* note 1251, pp. 163–188 (concluding that at least some EC agencies have separate international legal personality). See also A.S. Muller, *supra* note 1269, pp 85–86; U. Everling, *supra* note 1472, p. 1064 (mentioning ECJ, Case 85/86, *Commission of the European Communities v Board of Governors of the European Investment Bank*, Judgement of 3 March 1988) and J. de Zwaan, *supra* note 1246, pp. 84–85, mentioning *inter alia* the European Central Bank (Article 107(2) EC Treaty provides that "*The ECB shall have legal personality*"; however, treaties concerning ECB matters are to be concluded by the Council on behalf of the EC; see Article 111 EC Treaty; see also J.-V. Louis, 'Les relations interntionales de l'Union économique et monétaire', in J.-C. Gautron & L. Grard (eds.), *supra* note 1296, pp. 399–400) without the EC)[1583] and within the 'UN family'.[1584] The main objection to this is that in this case the EC would be a part of the EU despite the EC's 'legally superior' status,[1585] but this, by itself, can hardly be conclusive, and is, moreover, somewhat mitigated by the requirement of consistency.[1586]

Alternatively, the EU as a legal person is to be regarded *sense stricto* as only consisting of the non-EC elements of the EU.[1587] That the two organizations

---

and the European Investment Bank (see Article 266 EC Treaty: "*The European Investment Bank shall have legal personality*") as well as over ten EC agencies, though not necessarily all with international legal personality.

1583 See the discussion of EU agencies *supra*, preceding section.

1584 Where the UN itself possesses international legal personality but also its specialized organizations; see, e.g. explicitly IFAD (*supra* note 1311) and ICSID (*supra* note 1314).

1585 See especially the provisions on respect for the *acquis communautaire* in Articles C and M Maastricht Treaty: now Articles 3 and 47 EU Treaty.

1586 As stipulated in Article 3 (ex Article C) EU Treaty. See, e.g. R. Wessel, 'The Inside Looking Out: Consistency and Delimitation in EU External Relations', 37 *C.M.L. Rev.* 2000, pp. 1135–1171, arguing persuasively against a full separation between the pillars and stressing that the overall consistency of the EU legal order should also be pursued, even though this creates a tension between consistency and delimitation. See also C. Herrmann, 'Much ado about Pluto?: The "Unity of the Legal Order of the European Union" revisited', in M. Cremona & B. De Witte (eds.), *EU Foreign Relations Law: Constitutional Fundamentals*, Oxford, Hart, 2008, pp. 19–51 and the focus on coherence by Pechstein, *infra* note 1592. For an interesting application of the principle of consistency and the interaction between EC and EU objectives and competences, see Cases T-306/01 (*Yusuf and Al Barakaat International Foundation v. Council and Commission*, especially §§231–259 and 277–282) and T-315/01 (*Kadi v. Council and Commission*, especially §§181–208 and 226–231), judgments of the ECJ's Court of First Instance of 21 September 2005 and the *Kadi* appeals judgment, all discussed more extensively *infra*, in Chapter 7.G.4.iii (linking Articles 60, 301 and 308 EC Treaty to the EU Treaty's foreign relations objectives). On cross-pillar consistency generally, see also E. Denza, *supra* note 1540, pp. 289–309. On consistency of the ESDP with EC/EU external relations generally, see P. Koutrakos, 'Security and Defence Policy within the Context of EU External Relations: Issues of Coherence, Consistency, and Effectiveness', in Trybus & White, pp. 249–269 and P. Koutrakos, 'Inter-Pillar Approaches to the European Security and Defence Policy: The Economic Aspects of Security', in V. Kronenberger (ed.), *supra* note 1320, pp. 435–453. The ECJ has clarified to some extent the issue of delimitation between the Second and First Pillar in Case C-91/05, *Commission of the European Communities v. Council of the European Union*, 20 May 2008 (the case concerns measures to combat the proliferation of small arms and light weapons; Advocate-General Mengozzi's opinion in the case was delivered on 19 September 2007). See, e.g. C. Hillion & R. Wessel, 'Competence Distribution in EU External Relations after *ECOWAS*: Clarification or Continued Fuzziness?', 46 *C.M.L. Rev.* 2009, pp. 551–586; R. van Ooik, 'Cross-Pillar Litigation before the ECJ: Demarcation of Community and Union Competences', 4 *European Constitutional Law Review* 2008, pp. 399–419; B. Van Vooren, 'EU-EC External Competences after the Small Arms Judgment', 14 *E.F.A.R.* 2009, pp. 7–24 and R.A. Wessel, 'Veiligheidsbeleid of toch ontwikkelingssamenwerking? De afbakening van de externe bevoegdheden tussen de EU, de EG en de lidstaten', 14 *Nederlands Tijdschrift voor Europees Recht* 2008, pp. 292–299. On the question under the EU Constitution, see T. Corthaut, 'An Effective Remedy for All?: Paradoxes and Controversies in Respect of Judicial Protection in the Field of the CFSP under the European Constitution', 12 *Tilburg Foreign Law Review* 2004, pp. 117–120.

1587 See the references in D. Curtin & I. Dekker, 'The EU as a "Layered" International Organization: Institutional Unity in Disguise', in P. Craig & G. de Búrca (eds.), *The Evolution* share a single institutional framework poses no obstacle to this: the European Communities also had separate international legal personalities despite common institutions[1588] and the institutions were to *"exercise their powers under the conditions and for the purposes provided for, on the one hand, by the provisions of the Treaties establishing the European Communities and of the subsequent Treaties and Acts modifying and supplementing them and, on the other hand, by the other provisions of [the EU Treaty]"*.[1589] A third possibility could be to regard the EU as a sub-entity of the EC, but this is not a plausible construction in the light of the additional features which the EU includes.[1590]

It is submitted that the better view is that the EU is the overall or parent organization but one which does include the European Communities (with a separate legal personality) as well as various agencies (at least some with their separate legal personality too)[1591] and may therefore be qualified, in a view that

---

of EU Law, Oxford, Oxford University Press, 1999, pp. 83–84 note 1 and in W. Schroeder, *European Union and European Communities*, in J.J.H. Weiler & A. von Bogdandy (eds.), *Jean Monnet Working Papers*, 2003 (available online at www.jeanmonnetprogram.org/papers/03/030901-08.pdf), p. 8 note 21. It is not very clear whether L. Grard, *supra* note 1465, pp. 355–357 adheres to this view or sees the EU as an overarching legal person. Compare F. Hoffmeister & P.J. Kuyper, 'The Status of the European Union at the United Nations: Institutional Ambiguities and Political Realities,' in J. Wouters, F. Hoffmeister & T. Ruys (eds.), *The United Nations and the European Union: An Ever Stronger Partnership*, The Hague, T.M.C. Asser Press, 2006, pp. 12–13, who consider that the EU as an entity with legal personality and treaty-making power is the "2nd pillar Union". However, that is unlikely as it seems to imply that there is also a separate Third Pillar Union and there seems to be little evidence of several European Unions with legal personality. Nevertheless, for an extensive argument in favour of the latter view, see C. Busse, *supra* note 1347, pp. 162–309, submitting that the Second and Third Pillars have distinct international legal personalities and that the overarching EU is a form of international cooperation without legal personality.

1588 On international organizations sharing common institutions, see also R.J. Dupuy, *supra* note 1341, pp. 484–488, who also mentions the ILO Administrative Tribunal, which also has competences in relation to some 50 other international organizations (see www.ilo.org/public/english/tribunal).

1589 Article E Maastricht Treaty.

1590 See also O. Dörr, *supra* note 1465 (30 *Europarecht* 1995), p. 344.

1591 In this sense also D. Curtin & I. Dekker, *supra* note 1587, pp. 83–136, especially pp. 101–103 (who qualify opposing views by European legal circles as "*fairly stubborn resistance*" at p. 83); W. Devroe & J. Wouters, *supra* note 1469, pp. 65–66 (though less certain at pp. 69–71); B. de Witte, *supra* note 1467, pp. 58–59 and 64–65; R.A. Wessel, *supra* note 1465 (5 *E.F.A.R.* 2000), p. 536; R.A. Wessel, 'The Constitutional Relationship between the European Union and the European Community: Consequences for the Relationship with the Member States', in J.J.H. Weiler & A. von Bogdandy (eds.), *Jean Monnet Working Papers*, 2003 (available online at www.jeanmonnetprogram.org/papers/03/030901-09.html), especially pp. 3–9 and W. Wormuth, *supra* note 1466, pp. 110–112 (who also makes the comparison with the UN). Compare U. Everling, *supra* note 1472, pp. 1061–1064 (writing that the EU, despite lacking international legal personality, has to be viewed as a unity with the Communities, *"also juridically, even though as separate legal persons they each possess formal autonomy"*); C. Hillgruber, 'Das Verhältnis der Europäischen Gemeinschaften under der Europäischen Union seems to gain increasing acceptance, as a "layered international organization" or "gestufte internationale organisation".[1592] It may also be noted that in everyday language[1593] and even among many lawyers,[1594] this is how the Union is usually

---

zu ihren Mitgliedstaaten – staats- und völkerrechtlich betrachtet', 34 *A.V.R.* 1996, pp. 347–375 (seeing no merger of the EC and EU and apparently according the latter legal personality); A. Tizzano, *supra* note 1543, pp. 135–147 (seeing the EU as the overall organization but arguing that it in fact has absorbed the EC even though it formally continues to exist separately) and W. Schroeder, *supra* note 1587.

1592 See D. Curtin & I. Dekker, *supra* note 1587, pp. 83–136; O. Dörr, *supra* note 1465 (30 *Europarecht* 1995), pp. 344–348; M. Pachinger, *supra* note 1465, pp. 41–53; C. Trüe, *supra* note 1246, pp. 175–176; M. Warnken, *supra* note 1472, pp. 79–82; R. Wessel, *supra* note 1586, pp. 1135–1171 (also stressing the need for consistency, see *supra* note 1586); R. Wessel, *supra* note 1253, pp. 7–11 and W. Wormuth, *supra* note 1466, pp. 110–112. Compare M. Pechstein, *supra* note 1465, pp. 137–144 (arguing that the EU has no international legal personality, but seeing it instead as a substantive legal order including the EC and the Member States) and M. Pechstein, 'Das Kohärenzgebot als entscheidende Integrationsdimension der Europäischen Union', 30 *Europarecht* 1995, pp. 247–258 (stressing the importance of coherence in this legal order). In fact, there seem to be a few indications in practice that support this view; see, e.g. EU Council Doc. 15782/1/06 REV 1 of 6 December 2006, p. 3, note 2 and the accompanying text ("*the Commission, the Presidency and the SG/HR will sit behind a single nameplate reading "European Union"* and "*In this context, the term "European Union" is used in the sense of Article 1 of the TEU, as meaning that* "The Union shall be founded on the European Communities, supplemented by the policies and forms of cooperation established in this Treaty"").

1593 For instance, the EU's website (http://europa.eu) is entitled 'gateway to the European Union' and does not have a separate subsite of the EC. To cite just one other example, the US mission is named US Mission to the European Union and on its website it is said that "*The United States has maintained diplomatic relations with the European Union and its forerunners since 1953*" and only mentions the European Communities in the past tense; see http://useu.usmission.gov/About_The_Mission/default.asp. More generally, missions of third States or other international organizations are said to be missions to the EU (see, e.g. L. Grard, *supra* note 1407, p. 377 and X., *supra* note 1544, p. 827), although it appears that they are formally still accredited to the European Communities (see R. Wessel, *supra* note 1253, p. 67). Moreover, in early December 2007, the Council and the Commission, in two distinct but closely related decisions, appointed Koen Vervaeke as EUSR to the AU and as Head of the Commission delegation to the AU, thus effectively creating the EU's first integrated mission (see EU Doc. S355/07 of 6 December 2007 and Council Joint Action of 6 December 2007 appointing a European Union Special Representative to the African Union (2007/805/CFSP), *O.J. L* 323, 8 December 2007, p. 45). See also F. Hoffmeister, 'Outsider or Frontrunner?: Recent Developments Under International and European Law on the Status of the European Union in International Organizations and Treaty Bodies', 44 *C.M.L. Rev.* 2007, pp. 41–68, who mentions at p. 53 a December 2006 COREPER decision that an EC/EU delegation to a specific meeting of the UN Peacebuilding Commission would sit behind the nameplate "European Union" within the meaning of Article 1(3) EU Treaty. On the latter, see also A. Hamonic, 'La représentation de l'Union européenne au sein de la commission de consolidation de la paix des Nations Unies: entre anticipation et continuité', 44 *C.D.E.* 2008, pp. 591–627 and M. Spernbauer, 'Musical Chairs Revisited: Status and Terms of Participation of the European Union in the UN Peacebuilding Commission', 5 *I.O.L.R.* 2009, pp. 299–322.

1594 Something I have, for instance, personally experienced in editorial work. Also, when Professor de Witte suggested in the Netherlands Society for International Law that lawyers should try to consistently distinguish between the EC and EU (though he admitted finding this difficult himself – understandably so), this gave rise to some debate illustrating different views (see perceived. The expression 'French gothic cathedral' used by de Witte is therefore a more apt metaphor[1595] than the more current Greek temple one. In this light one can also see the whole of the EU's constituent instruments as a 'multilevel constitution'.[1596]

F. THE STATUS OF ESDP OPERATIONS

A final aspect which must be discussed, particularly in a study focusing on the ESDP, is the legal status of ESDP operations. As described above,[1597] SOMA/SOFAs normally set out the rights and obligations of the operation, its personnel and its assets, including that of third States participating in such operations. The relevant provisions imply that at least to some extent the rights are granted to the operation, either as a separate legal entity or as an organ of the EU,[1598] and not to the Participating States for/via their participating forces or personnel.[1599]

The following elements support this view. First of all, the rights and obligations are almost always granted to the operation and its facilities and personnel and where this is otherwise, the sending States are specifically mentioned.[1600] Second,

NVIR (ed.), *De plaats van de Europese Unie in het veranderende bestel van de volkenrechtelijke organisaties* (124 Mededelingen van de NVIR), The Hague, TMC Asser Press, 2002, pp. 24–25 and 43). I have tried to take this suggestion to heart in this book but may not have been fully successful either.

1595 B. de Witte, *supra* note 1467, pp. 64–65.

1596 In this sense I. Pernice, 'Multilevel Constitutionalism and the Treaty of Amsterdam: European Constitution-Making Revisited?', 36 *C.M.L. Rev.* 1999, pp. 703–750, who also includes the member States' constitutions.

1597 Chapter 3.

1598 See the discussion *supra* Chapter 5.E.3.ii on the status of SFOR in relation to NATO and especially the view by J.A. Burger, *supra* note 1437, p. 329, that NATO-led operations share in the legal personality of NATO even though they are not subsidiary bodies established in accordance with the normal rules. Compare the ICTY's view in relation to the ECMM (which, however, had a peculiar status because while it was named an EC mission it may have been to some extent a Member State mission; see also *supra* Chapter 1, note 78 and *infra* note 1510) in the *Kordic and Cerkez* case, in which the ICTY first requested and then ordered the production of documents from the EC Member States at the time and the EU Council Presidency and the Commission; see *Prosecutor v. Dario Kordic and Mario Cerkez*, Case No. IT-95-14/2-T, Order for the Production of Documents by the European Community Monitoring Mission and its Member States, 4 August 2000. Compare also N. Tsagourias, 'EU Peacekeeping Operations: Legal and Theoretical Issues', in TRYBUS & WHITE, pp. 121–122, who, while undecided as to whether the EU exercises effective control, seems inclined to qualify ESDP operations as EU organs.

1599 Even though in some cases rights are granted to Participating States, e.g. concerning waivers of immunity.

1600 E.g. Article 1(2) Model Police SOMA (EU Doc. 14612/4/02 REV 4, 29 April 2003) defines and distinguishes 'EU Mission', 'EU Mission Personnel' and 'Sending Parties', defining the latter as "*EU Member States and Non EU States that have seconded EU Mission personnel*".

in the case of civilian operations, the personnel are normally hired or appointed by the EU and/or seconded by the Member States and thus clearly act on behalf of the EU and not of any single State.[1601] The situation in respect of military operations is somewhat less clear, because in such operations, in addition to appointed, hired and seconded personnel, that clearly act on behalf of the EU,[1602] there will normally also be national contingents, of which it is less clear whether they always engage the Union or sometimes (also) the Sending State (see *infra*, Chapter 8.G.1). However, at least for the former categories of personnel the EU will be the responsible entity. It seems that in their internal relations, when responsibility is settled in Joint Actions concerning ESDP operations, there are usually only references to the Institutions and the Member States. Nevertheless, with regard to EUSEC DRC, a clause was included which stipulates that "*Under no circumstances may the European Union or the Secretary-General/High Representative for the [CFSP] be held liable by contributing Member States as a result of acts or omissions by the Head of Mission in the use of funds from those States [providing financial contributions for specific projects]*". This implies a recognition of the potential responsibility of the *EU* since otherwise there would be no need to exclude its liability.[1603] Third, it appears from the claims settlement provisions that towards third parties the EU is the entity that may be held responsible.[1604] Fourth, the UN Security Council has qualified the EU operation

1601 E.g. pursuant to Article 1(2) Model Police SOMA (*supra* note 1600) it is the SG/HR who may waive the immunity of mission personnel, albeit with the consent of the sending State. Moreover, it appears that the new guidelines for command and control in civilian operations provide for a transfer of operational control to the EU chain of command; see, e.g. Council Joint Action of 13 November 2007 amending Joint Action 2007/369/CFSP on the establishment of the European Union Police Mission in Afghanistan (EUPOL AFGHANISTAN) (2007/733/CFSP), *O.J. L* 295, 14 November 2007, p. 31 (inserting Article 5a, paragraph 4 of which provides for this transfer of operational control).

1602 This is inherent in secondments. E.g. Article 5(1)a of Council Decision of 16 June 2003 concerning the rules applicable to national experts and military staff on secondment to the General Secretariat of the Council and repealing the Decisions of 25 June 1997 and 22 March 1999, Decision 2001/41/EC and Decision 2001/496/CFSP (2003/479/EC), *O.J. L* 160, 28 June 2003, p. 72, stipulates that a seconded national expert "*shall carry out his duties and shall behave solely with the interests of the Council in mind*". It may be noted that the ILC in the comments on Article 5 of the provisional version of the ILC's Draft Articles on the Responsibility of International Organizations is of the view that in the case of secondment the conduct of a seconded person is to be considered as that of an agent or organ of the organization without a need to have recourse to the separate rule on organs put at the disposal of an organization (*Report of the International Law Commission. Fifty-sixth session*, UN Doc. A/59/10, p. 110).

1603 Council Joint Action of 27 March 2007 amending Joint Action 2005/355/CFSP on the European Union mission to provide advice and assistance for security sector reform in the Democratic Republic of the Congo (DRC) (2007/192/CFSP), *O.J. L* 87, 28 March 2007, p. 22 (adding new paragraphs to Article 2 of the initial Joint Action).

1604 E.g. in the claims procedure under Article 15 of the EUFOR DR Congo SOFA with Gabon (Agreement between the European Union and the Gabonese Republic on the status of the

Althea in BiH as the "*legal successor to SFOR*", thereby also seeming to recognize its legal personality.[1605]

For the purpose of the issue at stake here, the above illustrates that an EU operation, as an organ of the EU and/or a separate entity established by the EU and in effective control over staff put at its disposal, has distinct rights and duties, which implies that the EU has legal personality.

European Union-led forces in the Gabonese Republic, *O.J. L* 187, 8 July 2006, p. 42/43.) there is nowhere any mention of (a representative of) the sending State but only of mission or EU (representatives) for the operation side (though this could be dealt with in implementing arrangements). References to the responsibility of a third participating State for claims concerning its personnel in participation agreements or to such responsibility of sending States or institutions in Joint Actions setting up operations (see the discussion of third State participation and of applicable law *supra* Chapter 2.B; it may be added that the latter kind of clauses only seem to be included in respect of civilian missions although there does not appear to be any obvious reason for this), appear to deal with the internal distribution of responsibility only, though this is not always very clear (N. Tsagourias, *supra* note 1598, p. 125, appears to see this also as pertaining to external responsibility but seems to overlook that there are claims procedures not dissimilar to those of the UN). For a similar view with regard to the UN, see see also UN Doc. A/CN.4/545, 25 June 2004, pp. 17–18 ("*While the agreements between the United Nations and contributing States divide the responsibility in the relationship between them, they are not opposable to third States. Vis-à-vis third States and individuals, therefore, where the international responsibility of the Organization is engaged, liability in compensation is, in the first place, entailed for the United Nations, which may then revert to the contributing State concerned and seek recovery on the basis of the agreement between them*"). Only in Article 3(4) of the generic participation agreement with Canada (*supra*, Chapter 2, note 225), is this responsibility qualified as being "*Without prejudice to the agreement on the status of mission/forces*". The financing rules and practice suggest that payment for claims resulting from an action of a national contingent are ultimately paid by the Member State concerned and that claims with regard to headquarters are paid "*through Athena [but] by the contributing States*" (see Article 43 Council Decision of 18 December 2008 establishing a mechanism to administer the financing of the common costs of European Union operations having military or defence implications (2008/975/CFSP), *O.J. L* 345, 23 December 2008, p. 96), but this is arguably an internal matter that does not determine the responsible entity. The clause "*through Athena [but] by the contributing States*" may reflect continuing reluctance to recognize the distinct legal status of the EU as such or its lack of a distinct budget and proper assets. But note the exceptional recognition of the EU's *potential* own liability in Council Joint Action 2007/192/CFSP of 27 March 2007 amending Joint Action 2005/355/CFSP on the European Union mission to provide advice and assistance for security sector reform in the Democratic Republic of the Congo (DRC), *O.J. L* 87, 28 March 2007, p. 22, Article 1(1) *in fine* ("*Under no circumstances may the European Union or the [SG/HR] be held liable by contributing Member States as a result of acts or omissions by the Head of Mission in the use of funds from those States*").

1605 See Resolution 1575 of 22 November 2004, authorizing "*the Member States acting through or in cooperation with the EU to establish for an initial planned period of 12 months a multinational stabilization force (EUFOR) as a legal successor to SFOR under unified command and control, ...*" (§10, see also §7 and *supra*, Chapter 3.G). While the resolution refers to the Member States acting through or in cooperation with the EU, it is EUFOR which is identified as the "*legal successor*".

G. CONCLUSION: A SUBJECT OF INTERNATIONAL LAW WITH INTERNATIONAL LEGAL PERSONALITY

From its establishment, the EU has been an international organization. However, the Member States initially seem to have viewed it not as a *legally* distinct entity, but rather as a forum for coordinating their actions in the fields covered by the CFSP and the Third Pillar. In this view, the EU might have been described as perhaps an *international* person, but not a *legal* person.[1606] This position could only be taken because the Union could rely on organs of the EC, which in that capacity enjoyed the legal status required to perform their functions, including privileges and immunities and the power to contract. However, this view was hard to square with some provisions that did seem to recognize the Union as a distinct legal entity, including the obligation to respect fundamental rights and the apparently binding nature of at least some EU instruments, notably joint actions in the CFSP. Nevertheless, the legal nature of such instruments was unclear and contested, at least initially, and the practice reveals rather few and mostly limited rights being created before the Treaty of Amsterdam. As international legal subjectivity and personality are not a question of the *number* of rights or legal capacities, the latter is not decisive but the intended limits show that even if one were to consider the EU as a subject of international law at that stage, its rights and duties would have been very limited, and if it was an international legal person, many of the legal capacities arguably inherent to this quality or presumed present therein seem to have been intended to be withheld.

The amendments introduced by the Treaty of Amsterdam should have settled the issue, as the EU clearly was given the right to adopt at least some legally binding decisions (notably the framework decisions in the Third Pillar). In addition, in Articles 24 and 38 EU Treaty it was also granted treaty-making capacity. However, the provision introducing this capacity was very ambiguous and gave rise to different interpretations, including one that the treaties were concluded on behalf of the Member States. Also, the situation whereby the EU and its staff only enjoyed privileges and immunities via their concurrent EC quality endured. These elements show that the Member States persisted in what some have called with reason "*the fiction of non personality*". Yet in the face of a power to adopt binding decisions that are clearly distinguished from treaties, such resistance entailed a legal contradiction and could not be upheld. However, it could and arguably did limit the legal capacities which the Union enjoyed.

1606 In the sense defined *supra* Chapter 5.A.

It seems that Member States finally caught up with the reality they created once the Treaty of Nice was signed, with the treaty-making capacity now textually and in practice being granted and exercised by the Union in its own name and the increasing adoption of EU instruments that clearly entail rights and obligations, including the setting up of EU agencies with separate legal personality and according them privileges and immunities, and the establishment of ESDP operations with distinct rights and duties. Therefore the EU now undoubtedly is a subject of international law and possesses international legal personality, despite the lingering reluctance of some Member States illustrated by the lack of an explicit grant of legal personality and of privileges and immunities for the EU in its own name in the Treaty of Nice. This final resistance appeared to have been overcome somewhere in 2003–2004, as manifested by the explicit provision on the EU's legal personality in the EU Constitution and subsequently in the Lisbon Treaty. Nevertheless, this resistance did not seem to have been fully withdrawn before the entry into force of the Lisbon Treaty.

Pursuant to the conclusions reached in Chapter 5.G on the international legal personality of international organizations generally, this means that the EU's legal personality is opposable to all States[1607] and international organizations and that the EU possesses a right to bring international claims (e.g. in ESDP operations), may be held internationally responsible[1608] (e.g. for breaching its treaty obligations) and may maintain international relations. Its treaty-making capacity is now beyond doubt. In respect of its privileges and immunities it arguably would be entitled to customary privileges and immunities if the present solution via the EC organs were to pose a problem.

Since the European Communities continue to exist as separate legal persons, it is necessary to define the Union in relation to the Communities. It is submitted that, despite the Communities' "stronger" legal nature, the Union is the overall 'layered' organization, sheltering within it a variety of other entities, including

1607 Moreover, in the context of ESDP operations P.J. Kuijper rightly remarked (at the 37th Asser Colloquium on European Law on 'The European Union and International Crisis Management: Legal and Policy Aspects', The Hague, 11–12 October 2007) that the States most concerned will usually in any event have recognized the legal personality of the EU through the conclusion of SOFA/SOMAs or participation agreements (see Chapter 2.D.1 and Chapter 3 on such agreements).

1608 As the European Commission stated to the ILC, "*it is clear that all international actors, be they States or organizations, need to recognize their international responsibility in the event of any wrongful acts*" (UN Doc. A/CN.4/545, 25 June 2004, p. 5). On the international responsibility of the EC, see, e.g. A. Conze, *Die völkerrechtliche Haftung der Europäischen Gemeinschaft*, Baden-Baden, Nomos, 1987. A. Sari, *supra* note 1541, pp. 53–86, concludes at pp. 85–86 that this is now the point on which the discussion with regard to the EU is focusing.

EU agencies and the Communities, which in turn comprise various agencies. The picture that emerges is, for all its differences, somewhat similar to that of the UN family at the world level.

CHAPTER 7
HOW ARE INTERNATIONAL ORGANIZATIONS BOUND BY INTERNATIONAL LAW?[1609]

The analysis in Part I has shown that international law issues may arise in respect of the ESDP. Furthermore, the conclusions in Chapter 6 that the EU is a subject of international law and possesses international legal personality mean that it is possible to examine such issues in respect of rights and obligations of the EU itself and not just of its Member States. However, before examining the rights and obligations arising under international law in respect of the ESDP, and in particular the law of armed conflict and human rights, one preliminary issue has to be dealt with, namely the extent to which international organizations are bound by international law.

In order to illustrate the nature of this problem, I will first discuss the fairly casual way in which doctrine and jurisprudence have usually dealt with the issue (A) and contrast this with the difficulties that have arisen when this theory meets practice, more specifically with regard to the immunities of international organizations and the applicability of the law of armed conflict to UN forces (B). I will then set out how I will approach the general question, which will include a short discussion of the importance of the internal legal order of international organizations (C) and will subsequently address obligations entered into by the organization itself (international agreements concluded by it and unilateral acts; D); obligations imposed upon an organization by its Member States (including through the constitutive instruments of international organizations; E) and obligations under general international law, especially customary international law, general principles of law and *ius cogens* (F). After that I will study the binding of international organizations to international agreements concluded by their Member States (discussing in particular the GATT, ECHR and UN Charter; G) and offer some reflections on the responsibility of Member States for their actions in the framework of international organizations (H). This chapter

1609 I am grateful to the members of the working group on the law of international organizations of the Netherlands Society for International Law (NVIR) for their valuable comments on an earlier draft of this chapter.

concludes with some general conclusions (I) and an application of the main findings to the EU (J).

A. A GENERAL BUT QUALIFIED ACCEPTANCE IN DOCTRINE AND JURISPRUDENCE

It is often taken for granted that (general) international law *does* apply to international organizations in the literature although usually it is acknowledged that limits may result from the nature and activities of international organizations and this view is sometimes limited to the external relations of international organizations.[1610] The same view appears to have been expressed in jurisprudence of the International Court of Justice and the European Court of Justice. For instance, the former has held that "*International organizations are subjects of international law and, as such, are bound by any obligations incumbent upon them under general international law, under their constitutions or under international agreements to which they are parties*"[1611] and the latter that "*the European Community must respect international law in the exercise of its powers*".[1612] In contrast, a few authors have adopted the view that international

1610 See, e.g. R. Higgins, *Problems and Process. International Law and How We Use It*, Oxford, Clarendon Press, 1994, p. 12; A. Leenen, *supra* note 1241, pp. 58–62; C. Tomuschat, 'Artikel 281 EG', in H. von der Groeben & J. Schwarze (eds.), *Kommentar zum Vertrag über die Europäische Union und zur Gründung der Europäischen Gemeinschaft*, Baden-Baden, Nomos, 2003 (6th ed.), pp. 1256–1257; D. Verwey, *supra* note 1280, p. 96 ("*the fact that rules of public international law are binding on the [European] Community*"). SCHERMERS & BLOKKER, §§1572–1581, pp. 994–1004, briefly identify the issue and develop the argument why organizations may be bound without their consent. The discussion in SANDS & KLEIN, pp. 456–461 is rather limited. The ILA in its 2004 *Final Report on the Accountability of International Organisations* (available online at www.ila-hq.org) is somewhat ambiguous on whether its view is that international organizations are bound or (also) that their Member States remain bound and responsible even when acting in the framework of an international organization: the latter is explicitly stated several times (see more extensively *infra*, section H of this chapter) but the former remains largely implicit, except in respect of *ius cogens* (at pp. 18–19). Despite this ambiguity it seems that the ILA view is that international organizations are also bound themselves. While this ILA report is not confined to legal considerations (see pp. 5–6), some of the rules included and comments concerned do belong to the legal domain.

1611 ICJ, Advisory opinion on the *Interpretation of the Agreement of 25 March 1951 between the WHO and Egypt*, 20 December 1980, *I.C.J. Reports* 1980, §37, pp. 89/20–90/21. Admittedly, as pointed out to me during a discussion of the working group on the law of international organizations of the Netherlands Society of International Law, the ICJ does not say "*are bound by general international law*" but rather by "*any obligations* incumbent upon them under *general international law*" (emphasis added), a point often overlooked. However, the ICJ's summing up of this basis next to the constituent instruments and international agreements suggests the Court meant at least part of general international law.

1612 Case C-286/90, *Anklagemyndigheden v Peter Michael Poulsen and Diva Navigation Corp.*, Judgment of 24 November 1992, §9. See also Case C-308/06, *International Association of* organizations are only bound by those rules to which they have consented[1613] or regard the matter as uncertain.[1614]

The question has rarely been examined thoroughly,[1615] except to some extent from particular perspectives, e.g. in the context of the EC/EU, albeit mostly with a focus on the binding nature of international law in *intra*-EC/EU relations and/or the question to what extent the EC/EU is bound by treaties concluded by its Member States,[1616] and in respect of specific issues such as the applicability of

---

Independent Tanker Owners (Intertanko) and Others, 3 June 2008, §51 ("*as is clear from settled case-law, the powers of the Community must be exercised in observance of international law, including provisions of international agreements in so far as they codify customary rules of general international law*") and Joined Cases C-402/05 P and C-415/05 P, *Yassin Abdullah Kadi and Al Barakaat International Foundation v. Council of the European Union and Commission of the European Communities*, 3 September 2008, §291.

1613 E.g. R.A. Wessel, 'Revisiting the International Legal Status of the EU', 5 *E.F.A.R.* 2000, p. 511 ("*international organizations as independent legal persons are not by definition bound to the same international legal obligations as their Member States. Apart from ius cogens, [they] too can only be bound on the basis of their own free will*"). However, Wessel later seems to have adopted a different position (or expressed his views differently), accepting that international organizations are bound by general international law in their external relations: see R.A. Wessel, *supra* note 1253, especially p. 39.

1614 See, e.g. A. Weber, *Schutznormen und Wirtschaftsintegration; zur völkerrechtlichen, europarechtlichen und innerstaatlichen Problematik von Schutzklauseln und ordre public-Vorbehalten*, Baden-Baden, Nomos, 1982, p. 435 ("*Die Frage, ob und im welchem Umfang Regeln des Völkergewohnheitsrechts und allgemeine Rechtsgrundsätze auf internationale Organisationen anwendbar sind, ist noch nicht geklärt*"), also cited in Vanhamme, p. 94.

1615 The main exceptions appear to be A. Bleckmann, 'Zur Verbindlichkeit des allgemeinen Völkerrechts für internationale Organisationen', 37 *Z.a.ö.R.V.* 1977, pp. 107–121; E. David, 'Le droit international applicable aux organisations internationales', in M. Dony (ed.), A. De Walsche (ass. ed.), *Mélanges en hommage à Michel Waelbroeck*, Brussels, Bruylant, 1999, pp. 3–22; Klein, pp. 311–375; F. Morgenstern, *supra* note 1229, pp. 3–36 and H.G. Schermers, 'The Legal Bases of International Organization Action', in Dupuy (ed), pp. 401–411. Amerasinghe, pp. 386–387, merely states that generally international law will govern the relations between international organizations and States or other international organizations. The question does not appear to be treated at all in Klabbers and White. It is addressed briefly in the ILA's 2004 *Final Report on the Accountability of International Organisations* (*supra* note 1610), pp. 18–19. In the context of the international responsibility of the UN, C. Dominicé, 'Le responsabilité internationale des Nations Unies', in Cot & Pellet, pp. 143–146, lists various sources binding international organizations and adds that the problem is often determining the applicable law. A. Reinisch, 'Securing the Accountability of International Organizations', in J. Klabbers (ed.), *International Organizations*, Aldershot, Ashgate, 2005, p. 539 also notes the general acceptance despite problematic aspects.

1616 For an overview and analysis concerning the EU, see R.A. Wessel, *supra* note 1253, pp. 1–77, especially pp. 37–52. See further, e.g. A. Bleckmann, 'Die Position des Völkerrechts im inneren Rechtsraum der Europäischen Gemeinschaften. Monismus oder Dualismus der Rechtsordnungen?', *Jahrbuch für Internationales Recht* 1975, pp. 300–319; M. Bothe, 'Die Stellung der Europäischen Gemeinschaften im Völkerrecht', 37 *Z.a.ö.R.V.* 1977, pp. 122–137; J. Boulois, 'Le droit des Communautés européennes dans ses rapports avec le droit international général', 235 *Rec. Cours* 1992-IV, pp. 13–79; P. Eeckhout, *supra* note 1431, pp. 167–344; O. Elias, *supra* note 1248, pp. 3–34; W. Ganshof van der Meersch, 'L'ordre juridique international humanitarian law to UN forces[1617] (and to a lesser extent NATO forces[1618]) or that of human rights to certain international organizations.[1619] Moreover, the discussion in Chapter 3 has revealed that differences of opinion exist regarding the international legal capacities of international organizations. It would therefore not be surprising if similar difficulties arise concerning the extent to which international law, which was traditionally made by and for States, is binding on international organizations.

---

des Communautés européennes et le droit international', 148 *Rec. Cours* 1975-V, pp. 1–433; J.-C. Gautron & L. Grard (eds.), *supra* note 1296; O. Jacot-Guillarmod, *Droit communautaire et droit international public – Etude des sources internationales de l'ordre juridique des Communautés européennes*, Genève, Georg, 1979; H. Krück, *supra* note 1245; P.J. Kuijper, 'From Dyestuffs to Kosovo Wine: From Avoidance to Acceptance by the Community Courts of Customary International Law as a Limit to Community Action', in I. Dekker & H. Post (eds.), *On the Foundations and Sources of International Law*, The Hague, TMC Asser Press, 2003, pp. 149–172 and the 'Comments' thereto by D. Curtin, *id.*, pp. 173–176; A. Leenen, *supra* note 1241; K. Meessen, 'The Application of Rules of Public International Law Within Community Law', 13 *C.M.L.Rev.* 1976, pp. 485–501; H.-H. Nöll, *supra* note 1234; A. Ott, 'Thirty Years of Case-Law by the European Court of Justice on International Law: A Pragmatic Approach towards Its Integration', in V. Kronenberger (ed.), *The EU and the International Legal Order: Discord or Harmony?*, The Hague, Asser Press, 2001, pp. 95–140; A. Peters, 'The Position of International Law Within the European Community Legal Order', 40 *G.Y.I.L.* 1997, pp. 9–77; H.G. Schermers, "Community Law and International Law", 12 *C.M.L.Rev.* 1975, pp. 77–90; J. Schwarze, 'Das allgemeine Völkerrecht in den innergemeinschaftlichen Rechtsbeziehungen', 18 *Europarecht* 1983, pp. 1–39; C. Timmermans, 'The EU and Public International Law', 4 *E.F.A.R.* 1999, pp. 181–194; R. Uerpmann, *International Law as an Element of European Constitutional Law: International Supplementary Constitutions*, Jean Monnet Working Paper 9/03 (available online at www.jeanmonnetprogram.org/papers/03/030901-02.pdf); D. Van Eeckhoutte & J. Wouters, 'Enforcement of Customary International Law through European Community Law' in J.M. Prinssen & A. Schrauwen (eds.), *Direct effect. Rethinking a Classic of EC Legal Doctrine*, Groningen, European Law Publishing, 2002, pp. 183–234; Vanhamme (noting at p. 4 note 7 that the ECJ has often motivated its pronouncements on this matter rather summarily); H.F. van Panhuys, 'Conflicts between the Law of the European Communities and Other Rules of International Law', 3 *C.M.L.Rev.* 1965–1966, pp. 420–449; R. Voss, 'Die Bindung der Europäischen Gemeinschaft and vorgemeinschaftliche Verträge ihrer Mitgliedstaaten', 35 *S.Z.I.E.R.* 1996, pp. 161–189 and J. Wouters, A. Nollkaemper & E. De Wet (eds.), *The Europeanisation of International Law: The Status of International Law in the EU and its Member States*, The Hague, T.M.C. Asser Press, 2008. Moreover, there is a significant body of more specific literature on the ECHR and human rights and the EC/EU, UN sanctions in the EC/EU legal order and the applicability of GATT/WTO rules within the EC, which will be discussed below when relevant.

1617 See Chapter 8 and especially the references in Chapter 8.A, notes 1998 and 2021.

1618 See the references in Chapter 8.A, note 1999.

1619 E.g. A. Clapham, *supra* note 1224, pp. 109–159; R. Dañino, 'The Legal Aspects of the World Bank's Work on Human Rights', 41 *The International Lawyer* 2007, pp. 21–25 and S. Skogly, *The Human Rights Obligations of the World Bank and the International Monetary Fund*, London, Cavendish, 2001. See also the interesting reflections in L. Gradoni, 'International Criminal Courts and Tribunals: Bound by Human Rights Norms … or Tied Down?', 19 *Leiden J.I.L.* 2006, pp. 847–873. For the EC/EU, see the comment *supra* note 1616 *in fine*. For a broader accountability perspective on human rights violations by international organizations, see the contributions in 1 *Human Rights & International Legal Discourse* 2007, pp. 209–423.

B. DIFFICULTIES IN PRACTICE

The two examples that will now be discussed suffice to illustrate that the question is not that simple and does give rise to problems.

1. IMMUNITIES OF INTERNATIONAL ORGANIZATIONS

First, although it is generally accepted that international organizations may enjoy privileges and immunities,[1620] there is uncertainty as to whether this is inherently so and/or whether it is based on customary law or requires a specific treaty basis.[1621] To the extent that the privileges and immunities are inherent or part of customary law, they are different from the rules of State or diplomatic immunities. Indeed, although in a few early cases international organizations have been granted the same immunities as States[1622] and State or diplomatic

---

1620 A further distinction has to be made between the privileges and immunities of the organizations themselves, those of their officials and those of representatives of (Member and third) States to international organizations. However, for the purposes of this book I will only address the immunities of international organizations themselves. On the privileges and immunities of international organizations generally, see, e.g. K. Ahluwalia, *The Legal Status, Privileges and Immunities of the Specialized Agencies of the United Nations and Certain Other International Orqanisations,* The Hague, Nijhoff, 1964; S. De Bellis, *L'immunità delle organizzazioni internazionali dalla giurisdizione,* Bari, Cacucci, 1992; C. Dominicé, 'L'immunité de jurisdiction et d'execution des organizations internationales', 187 *Rec. Cours* 1984-IV, pp. 145–238; J. Duffar, *Contribution à l'étude des privilèges et immunités des organisations internationales*, Paris, LGDJ, 1982; E. Gaillard & I. Pingel-Lenuzza, 'International Organisations and Immunity from Jurisdiction: to Restrict or to Bypass', 51 *I.C.L.Q.* 2002, pp. 1–15; J.-F. Lalive, 'L'immunité de juridiction et d'exécution des États et des organisations internationales', 84 *Rec. Cours* 1953-III, pp. 205–395; C. Sato, *Immunität internationaler Organisationen*, Frankfurt am Main, Peter Lang, 2004; M. Singer, 'Jurisdictional Immunity of International Organizations: Human Rights and Functional Necessity Concerns', 36 *Virginia J.I.L.* 1995, pp. 53–165 and the references below in this subsection.

1621 See *supra*, Chapter 5.E.2, notes 1378–1382 and the accompanying text.

1622 See, e.g. Article 95(1) Benelux Statute (Traité instituant l'Union économique Benelux, The Hague, 3 February 1958, entered into force on 1 November 1960): "*The Union shall enjoy in the territory of each High Contracting Party the same immunities as are accorded to foreign States*" (translation available at www.benelux.be/en/rgm/rgm_vdg_deel4.asp) and 22 U.S.C. §288a (available online at www.law.cornell.edu/uscode/uscode22/usc_sec_22_00000288---a000-.html): "*International organizations, their property and their assets, wherever located and by whomsoever held, shall enjoy the same immunity from suit and every form of Judicial process as is enjoyed by foreign governments, except to the extent that such organizations may expressly waive their immunity for the purpose of any proceedings or by the terms of any contract*". For a more recent example, see the Decision at the 1993 Rome Ministerial Meeting on the legal capacity and privileges and immunities of the CSCE, Doc. CSCE/4-C/Dec.2 (reproduced in CSCE, *From Rome to Budapest. 1993–1994, CSCE Decision Reference Manual,* CSCE, *s.l.*, *s.d.*, pp. 37–42 and available online as Annex A to attachment 1 to the Annex to PC.DEC/383 of 26 November 2000 at www.osce.org/documents/pc/2000/11/2163_en.pdf), immunities are still occasionally applied by analogy to international organizations in the literature[1623] or jurisprudence,[1624] in the vast majority of cases the immunity of international organizations is different from these other international immunities.[1625]

For instance, while the immunity from jurisdiction of States is now relative and only pertains to sovereign activities (*acta iure imperii*) to the exclusion of commercial activities,[1626] the immunity from jurisdiction of most international organizations is absolute, subject only to waiver.[1627] E.g. section 2 of the

---

Annex, §4: "*The CSCE institutions, their property and assets, wherever located and by whomsoever held, will enjoy the same immunity from legal process as is enjoyed by foreign States*". However, it appears that in practice at least some States which have implemented this decision have granted the immunity normally granted to international organizations rather than state immunity; see, e.g. §3(1) of the 1993 Austrian Act (*supra* Chapter 5 note 1266, applying the same immunities the UN has in Vienna), the Dutch HCNM Act (*supra* Chapter 5 note 1265, especially Articles 2(2) and 7) and Attachment 1 to the Annex to PC.DEC/383 (*supra* this note), §§20–21 (referring to Poland and the Czech Republic as having granted the OSCE the same immunities as accorded to the UN).

1623 See, e.g. M. Bothe, *supra* note 1616, p. 131; M. Hirsch, *The Responsibility of International Organizations towards Third Parties: Some Basic Principles*, Dordrecht, Nijhoff, 1995, p. ix and H.G. Schermers & H. Van Houtte, *Internationaal en Europees Recht. Compendium voor de Rechtspraktijk*, Antwerpen, Kluwer, 1985, p. 139. Compare F. Schröer, 'De l'application de l'immunité juridictionnelle des Etats étrangers aux organizations internationales', 75 *R.G.D.I.P.* 1971, pp. 712–741, especially pp. 724 and 738, who seems to argue in favour of an application of State immunity to international organizations under customary international law (at least in part based on his perception of international organizations as extensions of States) despite acknowledging that treaty based immunities of international organizations are usually different.

1624 For an example of such a Belgian case, see the judgment of the Brussels labour appeals court (*Arbeidshof*) of 27 November 1996 (*J.T.T.* 1997, p. 435). In the UK one of the judges in one of the International Tin Council cases reportedly also exclusively referred to sovereign or diplomatic immunity; see AMERASINGHE, p. 347.

1625 The point is made clearly by P. Bekker, *supra* note 1224, pp. 3–8 and 152–180, who puts forward "functional necessity" as the basis and standard for these immunities. See also AMERASINGHE, pp. 316–317; I. Scobbie, 'International Organizations and International Relations', in DUPUY (ED.), pp. 834–851, especially pp. 834 and 840 and I. Seidl-Hohenveldern, 'Functional Immunity of International Organizations and Human Rights', in W. Benedek, H. Isak & R. Kicker (eds.), *Development and Developing International and European Law: Essays in Honour of Konrad Ginther on the Occasion of His 65th Birthday*, Frankfurt am Main, Lang, 1999, pp. 139–141. Compare KLABBERS, pp. 146–168, who questions the utility of "functional necessity". See also F. Morgenstern, *supra* note 1229, pp. 5–10, for a discussion of objections by international organizations to cases where States applied rules of State or diplomatic immunity that fell short of the proper immunities of international organizations.

1626 This is *inter alia* reflected in the European Convention on State Immunity (Basel, 16 May 1972, *E.T.S.* No. 74, entered into force 11 June 1976) and the recent UN Convention on Jurisdictional Immunities of States and Their Properties (New York, 2 December 2004, Annex to UNGA Res. 59/38 of 2 December 2004), especially Part III.

1627 For some additional examples to the UN conventions cited *infra* next notes, see, e.g. Article 3 General Agreement on Privileges and Immunities of the Council of Europe (Paris, 2 September 1949, *E.T.S.* No. 2, which entered into force on 10 September 1952) and Article 2

Convention on the Privileges and Immunities of the United Nations provides that "*The United Nations, its property and assets wherever located and by whomsoever held, shall enjoy immunity from every form of legal process except insofar as in any particular case it has expressly waived its immunity shall extend to any particular case it has expressly waived its immunity*"[1628] and section 4 of the Convention on the Privileges and Immunities of the Specialized Agencies stipulates the same for the specialized agencies, their property and assets.[1629] Although it is sometimes argued that the State immunity restrictions should also be applied to international organizations,[1630] there are very few international

---

of the Agreement on Privileges and Immunities of the Organization of American States (Washington DC, 15 May 1949, 1438 *U.N.T.S.* 83 (1986) and *OAS Treaty Series* No. 22, available online at www.oas.org/juridico/english/sigs/c-13.html, which entered into force on 4 June 1951). For a more recent example, see Article VIII(2)-(4) Agreement Establishing the World Trade Organization (Marrakesh, 15 April 1994, available online at www.wto.org/english/docs_e/legal_e/04-wto.pdf), which provides for such privileges and immunities as are necessary for the exercise of the WTO's functions and adds that these shall be similar to the privileges and immunities stipulated in the Convention on the Privileges and Immunities of the (UN) Specialized Agencies. For an example in domestic law, see the Australian International Organisations (Privileges and Immunities) Act 1963, First Schedule, §1 (available online at www.austlii.edu.au/au/legis/cth/consol_act/ioaia1963558/): "*Immunity of the organisation, and of the property and assets of, or in the custody of, or administered by, the organisation, from suit and from other legal process*". See also R. Oparil, 'Immunity of International Organizations in United States Courts: Absolute or Restrictive ?', 24 *Vanderbilt J.T.L.* 1991, pp. 689–710 and SANDS & KLEIN, pp. 490–494. But see KLABBERS, p. 165.

1628 New York, 13 February 1946, 1 *U.N.T.S.* 15 (1946–1947), which entered into force on 17 September 1946.

1629 New York, 21 November 1947, 33 *U.N.T.S.* 261 (1949), which entered into force on 2 December 1948.

1630 This seems to be the view advocated by R. Sadurska & C. Chinkin, 'The Collapse of the International Tin Council: A Case of State Responsibility?', 30 *Virginia J.I.L.* 1990, pp. 852–855. For an argument in favour of restrictions, including on the basis of human rights considerations, see M. Singer, 'Jurisdictional Immunity of International Organizations: Human Rights and Functional Necessity Concerns', 36 *Virginia J.I.L.* 1995, pp. 53–165. Also in favour of restriction, see K. Cully, 'Jurisdictional Immunities of Intergovernmental Organizations', 91 *Yale Law Journal* 1982, pp. 1166–1195. Compare I. Scobbie, *supra* note 1625, pp. 834–851, especially pp. 835 and 846–851, who stresses the autonomous nature of the immunities of international organizations but seems willing to nevertheless accept an analogy with State immunity in some respects. The position in the US is problematic: 22 U.S.C. §288a grants international organizations the same immunities as foreign governments (see *supra* note 1622) but this immunity has evolved towards a limited immunity (endorsed in the US by the Foreign Sovereign Immunities Act 1976, 28 U.S.C. §§1602–1611, available online at www.law.cornell.edu/uscode/html/uscode28/usc_sec_28_00001611----000-.html, which only contains a specific provision (§§1611(a)) safeguarding international organizations' immunity from execution, not jurisdiction) whereas international agreements usually still provide for absolute immunity or an immunity subject to specifically defined exceptions. This raises the question as to the relations between these instruments under US law. See American Law Institute, *Restatement of the Foreign Relations Law of the United States*, St. Paul, American Law Institute Publishers, 1990 (3rd ed.; student ed.), §467 and the comments thereon at pp. 493–504. See also I. Seidl-Hohenveldern, *supra* note 1625, pp. 139–140, who notes that (at least some) US courts have ruled that the intention of the Act at the time was to grant the then agreements in that sense[1631] and, as Bekker has argued persuasively, to the extent that restrictions are justified, the test should be a different one.[1632] In addition, immunities need not necessarily be incompatible with human rights concerns. For instance, they can be consistent with the right of access to a court as part of the right to fair trial when alternative dispute settlement mechanisms are provided for.[1633]

---

absolute immunity to international organizations irrespective of later changes in State immunity and have therefore continued to apply absolute immunity. Compare also the analysis by R. Oparil, *supra* note 1627, pp. 696–710 also arguing in favour of this conclusion and K. Cully, *supra* this note, pp. 1166–1195. The Italian *Corte Suprema di Cassazione* in 1992 overruled earlier decisions and endorsed absolute immunity; see *FAO v. Colagrossi*, Judgment of 19 May 1992, No. 5942, 101 *I.L.R.* 1995, pp. 385–394 (393), also cited in AMERASINGHE, p. 322.

1631 Where treaty-based exceptions exist, they are specifically defined; see, e.g. AMERASINGHE, pp. 320–321 and SANDS & KLEIN, pp. 490–494, noting exceptions for a number of international financial institutions. These include *inter alia* Article VII(3) Articles of Agreement of the International Bank for Reconstruction and Development (Washington DC, 27 December 1945, available online at http://web.worldbank.org/WBSITE/EXTERNAL/EXTABOUTUS/ORGANIZATION/BODEXT/0,,contentMDK:50004943~menuPK:64020045~pagePK:64020054~piPK:64020408~theSitePK:278036,00.html); Article VI(3) Articles of Agreement of the International Finance Corporation (Washington DC, 11 April 1955, available online at *id.*); Article VIII(3) Articles of Agreement of the International Development Association (Washington DC, 26 January 1960, available online at *id.*); Article 44 Convention Establishing the Multilateral Investment Guarantee Agency (Seoul, 11 October 1985, available online at *id.*) and Article 46 Agreement Establishing the European Bank for Reconstruction and Development (Paris, 29 May 1990, available online at www.ebrd.com/pubs/insti/basics.pdf) and a specific regime in the EC with a key role for the ECJ (based on Articles 235, 238 and 240 EC Treaty). An exception would also seem to be those cases in which organizations enjoy the same immunity as States (e.g. the Benelux, *supra* note 1622), although it might be argued that a broader customary rule of immunity of international organizations has now developed which might prevail over the developments towards restrictive *State* immunity (such a rule would certainly be a *lex posterior* and in line with the original scope of the immunity, but the question would be whether it is also *lex specialis*: the specific regime of the Benelux would normally be regarded as the more specific, yet in this case because of its reference to State immunity one might question this). Compare the state of affairs in the US discussed above.

1632 P. Bekker, *supra* note 1224, pp. 152–180. AMERASINGHE, pp. 321–322 also rejects the application of the State immunity criteria.

1633 See ECtHR, *Beer & Regan v. Germany* and *Waite & Kennedy v. Germany*, both 18 February 1999. For a discussion from a human rights perspective, see generally A. Reinisch & U. Weber, 'In the Shadow of Waite and Kennedy: The Jurisdictional Immunity of International Organizations, the Individual's Right of Access to the Courts and Administrative Tribunals as Alternative Means of Dispute Settlement', 1 *I.O.L.R.* 2004, pp. 59–110; H.G. Schermers, 'Diplomatic Immunity in Modern International Law', in E. Denters & N. Schrijver (eds.), *Reflections on International Law from the Low Countries*, The Hague, Martinus Nijhoff, 1998, pp. 156–164; I. Seidl-Hohenveldern, *supra* note 1625, pp. 137–149, especially pp. 145–149 and H. Tigroudja, 'L'immunité de juridiction des organisations internationales et le droit d'accès à un tribunal', 11 *R.T.D.H.* 2000, pp. 83–106. With regard to peace operations, see J. Werzer, 'The UN Human Rights Obligations and Immunity: An Oxymoron Casting a Shadow on the Transitional Administrations in Kosovo and East Timor', 77 *Nordic J.I.L.* 2008, pp. 105–140. Similar issues arise regarding other international immunities and their relationship to human rights and international criminal law; see, e.g. ECtHR, *McElhinney v. Ireland*; *Fogarty v. UK*

That being said, privileges and immunities seem to be considered legal capacities rather than substantive law and differences between States and international organizations may therefore simply result from the different nature of States and international organizations even though they both (may) possess international legal personality. Nevertheless, this suggests that a distinction may have to be made between capacities and substantive law.

2. UN FORCES AND THE LAW OF ARMED CONFLICT

The second example concerns the applicability of the law of armed conflict to UN forces.[1634] The UN has long resisted being bound by the law of armed conflict, citing perceived practical and legal problems which would hinder it from fully applying this body of law.[1635] Nevertheless, it has gradually entered into commitments to respect the spirit and principles of the law of armed conflict, sometimes specifically mentioning some key treaties in this field.[1636] This has culminated, so far, in the notorious UN Secretary-General Bulletin on Observance by United Nations forces of international humanitarian law.[1637]

---

and *Al-Adsani v. UK*, all 21 November 2001 and the references in Bossuyt & Wouters, p. 432 (including J. Bröhmer, *State Immunity and the Violation of Human Rights*, The Hague, Kluwer Law International, 1997; L.M. Caplan, 'State Immunity, Human Rights, and Jus Cogens: A Critique of the Normative Hierarchy Theory', 97 *A.J.I.L.* 2003, pp. 741–781; M. Karagiannakis, 'State Immunity and Fundamental Human Rights', 11 *Leiden J.I.L.* 1998, pp. 9–43; M. Kloth, 'Immunities and the Right of Access to Court under the European Convention on Human Rights', 27 *Eur. L. Rev.* 2002, pp. 33–46; D. Lloyd Jones, 'Article 6 ECHR and Immunities Arising in Public International Law', 52 *I.C.L.Q.* 2003, pp. 463–472; D. Robinson, 'The Impact of the Human Rights Accountability Movement on the International Law of Immunities', 40 *C.Y.I.L.* 2003, pp. 151–193; I. Seidl-Hohenveldern, 'International Immunity Law and Human Rights', in H.-W. Arndt (ed.), *Völkerrecht und deutsches Recht. Festschrift für Walter Rudolf zum 70. Geburtstag*, Munich, Beck, 2001, pp. 95–104; F. Vicuna, 'Diplomatic and Consular Immunities and Human Rights', 40 *I.C.L.Q.* 1991, pp. 34–48 and E. Voyiakis, 'Access to Court v State Immunity', 52 *I.C.L.Q.* 2003, pp. 297–332).

1634 This section is based on the literature cited in Chapter 8.A, notes 1998 and 2021.

1635 See especially the legal opinion in the 1972 *UN Juridical Yearbook*, pp. 153–154, also cited in A. Reinisch, 'Developing Human Rights and Humanitarian Law Accountability of the Security Council for the Imposition of Economic Sanctions', 95 *A.J.I.L* 2001, p. 854.

1636 This is reflected in Part X, section 28 of the Model Agreement between the United Nations and Member States Contributing Personnel and Equipment to the United Nations Peace-keeping Operation, UN Doc. A/46/185, 23 May 1991, Annex ("*[The operation] shall observe and respect the principles and spirit of the general international conventions applicable to the conduct of military personnel. The international conventions referred to above include the four Geneva Conventions of 12 August 1949 and their Additional Protocols of 8 June 1977 and the UNESCO Convention of 14 May 1954 on the Protection of Cultural Property in the event of armed conflict. [The Participating State] shall therefore ensure that the members of its national contingent ... be fully acquainted with the principles and spirit of these Conventions*").

1637 UN Doc. ST/SGB/1999/13, 6 August 1999 (available online at www.icrc.org/Web/Eng/siteeng0.nsf/iwpList367/711A2C1A3BD7FA2EC1256B66005DD94A).

However, the Bulletin does not require respect for the entire body of the law of armed conflict[1638] and may be criticized on various points. In contrast, the *de iure* applicability of the law of armed conflict to some UN operations was recognized in Article 2(2) of the 1994 Convention on the Safety of United Nations and Associated Personnel, which stipulates that "*This Convention shall not apply to a United Nations operation authorized by the Security Council as an enforcement action under Chapter VII of the Charter of the United Nations in which any of the personnel are engaged as combatants against organized armed forces and to which the law of international armed conflict applies*".[1639] Moreover, the ICC Statute also recognizes that there may be situations in which UN forces are bound by the law of armed conflict.[1640] Furthermore, many commentators have argued that the UN is bound by at least the customary law of armed conflict.

Some of the more specific points of controversy will be addressed in more detail below in Chapter 8. For the present purpose, it may suffice that apparently the UN did not accept that it was bound by the entire set of rules of the customary law of armed conflict and to the extent that it did accept being bound by the law of armed conflict, has limited itself to referring to the spirit and principles and, more recently, the fundamental principles and rules, which it has identified only to a minor extent rather than identifying in detail which provisions it claims not being able to apply.[1641]

1638 Pursuant to its section 1(1) "*The fundamental principles and rules of international humanitarian law set out in the present bulletin are applicable to United Nations forces when in situations of armed conflict they are actively engaged therein as combatants, to the extent and for the duration of their engagement. They are accordingly applicable in enforcement actions, or in peacekeeping operations when the use of force is permitted in self-defence*". While section 2 provides that "*The present provisions do not constitute an exhaustive list of principles and rules of international humanitarian law binding upon military personnel, and do not prejudice the application thereof, nor do they replace the national laws by which military personnel remain bound throughout the operation*" and thereby does not preclude a broader applicability of international humanitarian law, the Bulletin's limitation to *fundamental principles and rules* is rather meagre.

1639 New York, 9 December 1994, 2051 *U.N.T.S.* 363, annexed to UNGA Res. 49/59, which entered into force on 15 January 1999.

1640 Articles 8(2)(b)iii and (e)iii prohibit "*Intentionally directing attacks against personnel, installations, material, units or vehicles involved in a humanitarian assistance or peacekeeping mission in accordance with the Charter of the United Nations*" but only "*as long as they are entitled to the protection given to civilians or civilian objects under the international law of armed conflict*", implying that they are not always protected as civilians and that when they are not, they are rather combatants and as such bound to respect the law of armed conflict.

1641 The Bulletin contains five sections on substantive law, compared to a few hundred Articles in the 1949 Geneva Conventions alone. The ICRC study on customary international humanitarian law (J.-M. Henckaerts & L. Doswald-Beck (eds.), *Customary International Humanitarian Law. Volume I: Rules*, Cambridge, Cambridge University Press, 2005) lists no less than 161 rules. On this study, see generally www.icrc.org/eng/customary-law; E.

C. APPROACH OF THE QUESTION AND THE INTERNAL LEGAL ORDER OF INTERNATIONAL ORGANIZATIONS

1. APPROACH

These two examples show that problems have indeed arisen. While they should not be exaggerated and in other cases the law has proved less problematic,[1642] the matter clearly deserves more attention that it has received so far and is a preliminary question to any determination of the law applicable to international organizations in a given field of international law. I will therefore now examine whether general rules can be established as to which sources of international law are binding upon international organizations and to what extent and how[1643] they may generally bind themselves or may be bound.[1644]

The most systematic and comprehensive treatment so far appears to be that by Klein, who successively discusses treaties concluded by an organization itself, obligations resulting from treaties concluded by its Member States, acts of other international organizations, customary international law, general principles of law, unilateral acts, international judicial decisions and succession of international organizations.[1645] However, I will adopt a different approach and analyze the sources and mechanisms under four headings: (D) obligations entered into by the organization itself (treaties and unilateral acts); (E) obligations

---

Wilmshurst & S. Breau (eds.), *Perspectives on the ICRC Study on Customary International Humanitarian Law*, Cambridge, Cambridge University Press, 2007 and P. Tavernier & J.-M. Henckaerts (eds.), *Droit international humanitaire coutumier: enjeux et défis contemporains*, Brussels, Bruylant, 2008. For a critical response, see the initial US response to the study, in 89 No. 866 *I.R.R.C.* 2007, pp. 443–471. For an earlier assessment of customary international humanitarian law, see, e.g. E. Kwakwa, *The International Law of Armed Conflict: Personal and Material Fields of Application*, Dordrecht, Kluwer Academic Publishers, 1992, pp. 29–42 and T. Meron, *Human Rights and Humanitarian Norms as Customary Law*, Oxford, Clarendon Press, 1989, pp. 3–78.

1642 For instance, the substantive rules of treaty law that do not concern the treaty-making capacity of international organizations appear to have largely become customary international law for both States and international organizations alike despite the non-entry into force of the 1986 VCLT; see *supra*, Chapter 5, notes 1373–1375 and the accompanying text.

1643 Compare R. Uerpmann, *supra* note 1616, p. 7, who lists accession, succession and incorporation by reference and by general principles of law as ways of binding international organizations.

1644 Compare F. Morgenstern, *supra* note 1229, pp. 3–4, who addresses "*to what extent are the rules of general international law suitable to international organizations; to what extent have rules of international law evolved which are responsive to specific problems posed by international organizations; and in what manner can international law be made applicable to international organizations?*".

1645 Klein, pp. 311–375.

imposed upon the organization by the Member States; (F) obligations under general international law (customary international law, general principles of law and *ius cogens*) and (G) Member State treaty obligations. This will be followed by some reflections on Member State responsibility for their actions in the framework of international organizations (H), general conclusions (I) and an application of these conclusions to the EU (J).

I will not specifically discuss the international constitutional law thesis that has gained some currency[1646] because either it is based on the particular status of certain norms under existing international law (especially the UN Charter, *ius cogens* and *erga omnes* obligations[1647]), each of which are discussed below in their own right in any event, or it introduces new categories which do not seem to have acquired a particular status and moreover may well entail further questions as to their scope in addition to those that already exist with regard to extant special categories.[1648] That is not to say that this approach has no merit but merely that I do not consider that it need be addressed as such in the context of the legal analysis of the subject matter discussed here.[1649]

Nor will I generally discuss decisions of international organizations and of international tribunals separately, because they are always based on other sources. The former result from the constituent instrument of the organization adopting the decision[1650] and will only be binding upon another international organization as such when the latter organization is a member of the former organization[1651] or when there is a specific acceptance by the latter organization (e.g. on the basis of its constituent instrument, a cooperation or relationship

---

1646 See, e.g. R.St.J. Macdonald & D. Johnston (eds.), *Towards World Constitutionalism: Issues in the Legal Ordering of the World Community*, Leiden, Brill, 2005; E.-U. Petersmann, 'Constitutionalism and International Organizations', 17 *Northwestern Journal of International Law and Business* 1997, pp. 398–469 and E. de Wet, *infra* notes 1684 and 1687. Compare E. Suy, 'The Constitutional Character of Constituent Treaties of International Organizations and the Hierarchy of Norms', in U. Beyerlin *et al.* (eds.), *Recht zwischen Umbruch und Bewahrung - Festschift für Rudolf Bernhardt*, Berlin, Springer, 1995, pp. 267–277.

1647 This essentially seems to be the approach adopted by E. de Wet, *infra* notes 1684 and 1687 (but see *infra* next note).

1648 See the consideration by E. de Wet, *infra* note 1687 of a possible *sui generis* character of (core rights in the) ECHR. On the uncertain nature of some existing notions, see *infra* note 1685 and the accompanying text.

1649 Similarly, I do not consider it important from a legal perspective (as opposed to an emotional, political or symbolic perspective) whether the proposed future EU Treaty is called just that or 'EU Constitution' or still something else. What matters in law is the substance and legal status of the instrument.

1650 See MALANZCUK, p. 53, who, on this basis, even questions whether they constitute a separate source of law.

1651 KLEIN, p. 350, points out that such binding effect is a matter of the internal law of the organization adopting the decision. For the EC, see generally B. Martenczuk, 'Decisions of agreement or by voluntary incorporation) that it is bound by certain decisions of the former organization.[1652] There is only one instance in which a rule of general international law might bind international organizations to decisions of another international organization irrespective of whether specific provisions so stipulate, namely the rule laid down in Article 30(6) 1986 VCLT, according to which the rules pertaining to successive treaties "*are without prejudice to the fact that, in the event of a conflict between obligations under the Charter of the United Nations and obligations under a treaty, the obligations under the Charter shall prevail*".[1653] However, not only is this only a priority rule imposing only an indirect binding effect at best, it is also textually not conclusive in that it only sets out a priority rule in the event of a conflict with obligations under the Charter but does not determine whether the latter obligations exist for international organizations.[1654] In fact, in the drafting of this provision there was a discussion within the ILC on whether Article 103 UN Charter applied to international organizations and the ILC was unable to agree and chose language which left the matter open.[1655] Nevertheless, the very open ILC language was amended during the later negotiations and in the final text and it would seem to have been the intention to bind international organizations to Article 103.[1656] Yet even so, since the 1986 VCLT has not yet entered into force and this specific rule does not appear to be widely adhered to in practice,[1657] it is probably not part of general international law binding international organizations.[1658]

Bodies Established by International Agreements and the Community Legal Order', in V. Kronenberger (ed.), *supra* note 1616, pp. 141–163.

1652 Compare KLEIN, pp. 349–359. For an acceptance of certain decisions of the EU by third States, see V. Kronenberger, 'Common Foreign and Security Policy: International Law Aspects of the Association of Third States with the Common Positions of the Council of the European Union', in V. Kronenberger (ed.), *supra* note 1616, pp. 351–373.

1653 See generally E. Sciso, 'On Article 103 of the Charter of the United Nations in the Light of the Vienna Convention on the Law of Treaties', 38 *Österreichische Zeitschrift für öffentliches Recht und Völkerrecht* 1987–1988, pp. 161–179.

1654 See I. Pernice, 'Völkerrechtliche Verträge internationaler Organisationen', 48 *Z.a.ö.R.V.* 1988, p. 240.

1655 See *Y.I.L.C.* 1982-II, Part 2, pp. 40–41. The ILC draft text read "*The preceding paragraphs are without prejudice to Article 103 of the Charter of the United Nations*".

1656 See E. Lagrange, *La représentation institutionnelle dans l'ordre international: une contribution à la théorie de la personnalité morale des organisations internationales*, The Hague, Kluwer Law International, 2002, pp. 514–517 and especially LAWSON, pp. 154–157 (arguing in favour of the interpretation binding international organizations to Article 103 but not to the entire UN Charter). M. Kotzur, *infra* note 1890, p. 24 rejects a binding of international organizations to the (entire) UN Charter via Article 103 of the Charter.

1657 See *infra*, Section F.G.5 of this chapter.

1658 In this sense, E. Sciso, *supra* note 1653, pp. 164–168 (*inter alia* citing the Swiss position at the time) and E. Lagrange, *supra* previous note, pp. 514–517. But see A. Toublanc, 'L'Article 103 et la valeur juridique de la Charte des Nations Unies', 108 *R.G.D.I.P.* 2004, p. 459, who seems inclined to regard Article 103 as customary international law (referring *inter alia* to UNGA Res. 2625(XXV), 24 October 1970, which is not persuasive since it merely restates that "*Where*

The binding nature of international judicial decisions, including arbitral awards, *as such*, also depends upon other sources. Thus, if the EC concludes a treaty with a third State providing for a binding dispute settlement mechanism with jurisdiction over the EC, the decisions of that mechanism will bind the EC (the question of the effect of such decisions in the EC legal order is more complex and will not be treated here).[1659] The value of jurisprudence as "*subsidiary means for the determination of rules of law*",[1660] e.g. customary international law, will be the same as with respect to States.[1661]

Neither will I treat succession separately because it will normally be governed by specific arrangements either agreed by the organizations and/or imposed by their Member States.[1662] This should not be taken to mean that this is not an important issue. Indeed, it arises in respect of the EU under the Lisbon Treaty[1663] and has also arisen recently with the AU's succession of the OAU.

---

obligations arising under international agreements are in conflict with the obligations of Members of the United Nations *under the Charter of the United Nations, the obligations under the Charter shall prevail*" (emphasis added)).

1659 E.g. the ECJ stated in Opinion 1/91, 14 December 1991, *Draft agreement between the Community, on the one hand, and the countries of the European Free Trade Association, on the other, relating to the creation of the European Economic Area*, §39, that "*lorsqu'un accord international prévoit un système juridictionnel propre qui comprend une Cour compétente pour régler les différends entre les parties contractantes à cet accord et, par conséquent, pour en interpréter les dispositions, les décisions de cette Cour lient les institutions de la Communauté*". See also Klein, pp. 369–370.

1660 Article 38(1)d ICJ Statute.

1661 Similarly, Klein, p. 370. With regard to the ECJ, see A. Rosas, 'With a Little Help from My Friends: International Case-Law as a Source of Reference for the EU Courts', *The Global Community Yearbook of International Law and Jurisprudence* 2005, pp. 203–230.

1662 J.F. Weiss, 'Succession of States in Respect of Treaties Concluded by the European Communities', 42 *S.E.W.* 1994, p. 668, submits that "*there are no general legal rules on ... succession between international organisations*". Compare A. Bleckmann, *supra* note 1615, pp. 107–108, submitting that succession of international organizations is subject to distinct rules from State succession to the extent that proper rules have been formed in this respect. See also more generally P.R. Myers, *Succession between International Organizations*, London, Kegan Paul International, 1993 and R. Ranjeva, *La succession d'organisations internationales en Afrique*, Paris, Pedone, 1978. Klein, p. 371, mentions that some scholars have applied by analogy the rules on succession in respect of treaties in the 1978 VCSST. However, given the uncertain status of these rules (the convention only entered into force in 1996 and counts a mere 20 parties; see more generally on the lack of agreed rules on succession J.F. Weiss, *supra* this note, pp. 669–670), this is not obvious. Also, one may wonder to which case of State succession the succession of an international organization should be assimilated (similarly, concerning State succession rules, Member State treaties and international organizations, W. Wormuth, *supra* note 1466, pp. 175–177).

1663 See Article 1(3) (renumbered 1, paragraph 3) EU Treaty as amended/inserted by the Lisbon ("... *The Union shall replace and succeed the European Community*"). Compare Article IV-438 EU Constitution.

2. THE INTERNAL LEGAL ORDER OF INTERNATIONAL ORGANIZATIONS

Before undertaking this analysis, a particular difficulty must be addressed, namely the legal order of international organizations. While it appears to be generally accepted that international organizations (may) have a proper legal order,[1664] there is less agreement on its precise scope, nature and implications.[1665] For instance, it is a matter of debate how this legal order relates to other legal orders, especially the (general) international legal order.[1666] In the case of the EC there has been a particularly strong tendency to stress the autonomy of the EC legal order,[1667] which appeared to be

---

1664 See, e.g. AMERASINGHE, pp. 271–274 (with further references); SANDS & KLEIN, pp. 441–453 and SCHERMERS & BLOKKER, §§1139–1144, pp. 719–722. See also generally G. Balladore-pallieri, 'Le droit interne des organisations internationales', 127 *Rec. Cours* 1969-II, pp. 1–36; P. Cahier, 'L'ordre juridique interne des organisations internationales', in DUPUY (ED.), pp. 377–400; P. Cahier, 'Le droit interne des organisations internationales', 67 *R.G.D.I.P.* 1963, pp. 563–602; W. Jenks, *The Proper Law of International Organisations*, London, Stevens, 1962 and J. Kolasa, 'La notion de droit interne des organisations internationales', 3 *Polish Y.I.L.* 1970, pp. 95–110.

1665 See, e.g. SCHERMERS & BLOKKER, §1142, pp. 720–721. For an extensive analysis, see W. Meng, *supra* note 1283. For a recent analysis concerning the EC/EU, see W. Wormuth, *supra* note 1466, pp. 57–96.

1666 See, e.g. SCHERMERS & BLOKKER, §1142, pp. 720–721. F. Morgenstern, *supra* note 1229, p. 32, submits that because the key element of an international organization's internal legal order is usually a treaty, the role of international law in these legal orders may call for a different hierarchy of norms from that between municipal law and international law. The ILA in its 2004 *Final Report on the Accountability of International Organisations* (*supra* note 1610) states that rules of general international law are part of the rules governing the relations between an international organization and its members because the internal legal order of an international organization is not free from international law as it is free from domestic law (pp. 19–20) but also states that a constituent instrument *can* (only) "*depart from otherwise applicable rules of international law as between the members of the IO*" (p. 18). F. Seyersted, 'Basic Distinctions', in J. Makarczyk (ed.), *supra* note 22, pp. 697–699 argues that the internal legal order is neither part of international law, nor of domestic law. On autonomous legal orders and self-contained regimes, see generally A. Lindroos & M. Mehling, 'Dispelling the Chimera of "Self-contained Regimes". International Law and the WTO', 16 *E.J.I.L.* 2005, pp. 857–877; M. Noortmann, *Enforcing International Law: from Self-Help to Self-Contained Regimes*, Aldershot, Ashgate, 2005; B. Simma, 'Self-contained Regimes', 16 *N.Y.I.L.* 1985, pp. 112–136; B. Simma & D. Pulkowski, 'Of Planets and the Universe: Self-contained Regimes in International Law', 17 *E.J.I.L.* 2006, pp. 483–529 and M. Sørensen, 'Autonomous Legal Orders: Some Considerations Relating to a Systems Analysis of International Organisations in the World Legal Order', 32 *I.C.L.Q.* 1983, pp. 559–576. With regard to the EC/EU, see also G. Conway, 'Breaches of EC Law and the International Responsibility of Member States, 13 *E.J.I.L.* 2002, pp. 679–695.

1667 The argument in favour of (almost complete) autonomy appeared to have been defended by the ECJ. In particular, after having ruled in *Van Gend en Loos / Administratie der Belastingen* (Case 26/62, judgment of 5 February 1963) that "*the Community constitutes a new legal order* of *international law*" (emphasis added), in *Costa / E.N.E.L.* (Case, 6/64, judgement of 15 July 1964) it seemed to endorse a legal order separated from international law by holding that "*By contrast with ordinary international treaties, the EEC Treaty has created its* own legal system ... *The law stemming from the Treaty,* an independent source of law, *could not, because of its special and original nature, be overridden by domestic legal provisions, however framed*" somewhat softened over time[1668] but was firmly reasserted in the ECJ's recent *Kadi* appeals judgment.[1669]

(emphasis added). See also J. Boulois, *supra* note 1616, pp. 40–41; J. Schwarze, *supra* note 1616, p. 12 and W. Wormuth, *supra* note 1466, p. 63 (who adds, however, that the ECJ never explicitly said that the EC legal order was outside the international legal order). Compare, e.g. M. Bothe, *supra* note 1616, p. 123, who discerned a tendency to exclude international law but argued that it could not be entirely excluded and wondered whether, where it still applied, this was as such or only by analogy; J. Boulois, *supra* note 1616, pp. 13–79 (who seems fairly open to international law in EC law as long as its rules are not contrary to EC legal principles, in part because he sees the EC legal order as not sufficiently complete to avoid recourse to other legal orders (at pp. 45–47)); K. Meessen, *supra* note 1616, p. 485 (writing that the EC legal order was soon "*emancipated from its origins*" and that "*inside Community Law rules of international law ... are only applicable insofar as they happen to coincide with principles of Community Law*") and J. Schwarze, *supra* note 1616, pp. 1–39, who saw no room for international law within the EC legal order. In an interesting analysis, J.-C. Gautron & L. Grard ('Rapport général: Le droit international dans la construction européenne', in J.-C. Gautron & L. Grard (eds.), *supra* note 1296, pp. 16–29) describe the treaty basis of the EC as the 'given' (*le donné*) and the autonomy of the EC legal order as 'constructed' (*le construit*).

1668 It was increasingly questioned, with good reason, whether the EC legal order was indeed quite as special as was often said and it has been argued that the ECJ's approach at the time may have been primarily based on policy considerations out of concern for safeguarding the legal force of EC law. See, e.g. B. de Witte, 'Retour à Costa', 20 *R.T.D.E.* 1984, pp. 425–454; R. Gosalbo Bono, *supra* note 1247, pp. 366–675; O. Elias, *supra* note 1248, p. 5 (with further references in note 5) and W. Wormuth, *supra* note 1466, pp. 57–96, especially pp. 91–95. Moreover, the ECJ had, more recently, arguably become more open to international law. See, e.g. O. Elias, *supra* note 1248, pp. 33–34 (arguing that the ECJ "*is becoming a court that applies general international law*" albeit sometimes 'internalized" as with customary international law) and P.J. Kuijper, *supra* note 1616, pp. 149–172 (showing, however, some hesitation as to the legitimacy of an unfiltered reception of customary international law in the EC legal order). Compare Vanhamme, pp. 333–336, who concludes that the ECJ gives more effect to international law when third States are concerned but less regarding Member States. Furthermore, the establishment of the EU with non/less 'supranational' forms of cooperation, such as the ESDP, also leaves more room for general international law. See G. Conway, *supra* note 1666, pp. 693–695; E. Denza, 'Two legal Orders: Divergent or Convergent', 48 *I.C.L.Q.* 1999, pp. 257–284 (who, after discussing similarities, differences and convergence, concludes that the EU consists of a mix of methods and regrets that EC law "*ever ceased to be regarded as a vanguard system of international law*"; see also E. Denza, *The Intergovernmental Pillars of the European Union*, Oxford, Oxford University Press, 2002, pp. 5–32); J.-C. Gautron & L. Grard, *supra* note 1667, pp. 13 and 43 (seeing more room for international law in the EU than in the EC) and Vanhamme, pp. 6–7 (submitting that cooperation in the second and third pillars must take place in accordance with general international law). D. Curtin, *supra* note 1616, pp. 173–176 welcomes the ECJ's openness to international law which she sees as a potential source of restraints on not only EC but also EU actions, including for EU agencies. R. Uerpmann, *supra* note 1616, pp. 43–46 argues that the EC seems to try and maintain a certain degree of autonomy from general international law and its Member State obligations. See also J. Allain, 'The European Court of Justice Is an International Court', 68 *Nordic J.I.L.* 1999, pp. 249–274 and H. Isak, 'Europa und die europäische Integration, Völkerrecht und Europarecht - eine untrennbare Einheit', in W. Benedek, H. Isak & R. Kicker (eds.), *supra* note 1625, pp. 421–440 and compare A. Rosas, 'The European Court of Justice and Public International Law', in J. Wouters, A. Nollkaemper & E. de Wet (eds.), *The Europeanisation of International Law: The Status of International Law in the EU and its Member States*, The Hague, T.M.C. Asser Press, 2008, pp. 71–85.

1669 See *infra* notes 1906–1910 and the accompanying text. See also *Intertanko*, *infra* note 1908 and the accompanying text.

Often, a distinction is made between internal and external relations of an international organization.[1670] E.g. in the case of the EC, a distinction is usually made between *intra*-EC relations and external relations of the EC, it being accepted that in the external relations the EC is subjected to general international law whereas general international law is only accorded a limited role (or even no role at all according to some) within the EC legal order.[1671] However, this distinction is not without problems. A key difficulty concerns its delimitation: while some authors limit the internal legal order to the functioning of the organization itself, others include also its relations vis-à-vis its members.[1672] The latter is usually the case in writings on the EC/EU[1673] but is more difficult in relation to (quasi) universal international organizations, especially the UN. The most appropriate distinction would seem to be to include relations between an organization and its members in the internal legal order but only to the extent that it concerns their capacity as a member of the organization.[1674] Moreover, in its external relations an international organization may also derogate from general international law *inter se* with one or more third parties, e.g. in a treaty (subject to the limits set out in the next paragraph).

Furthermore, and irrespective of which delimitation is used, this distinction is not entirely conclusive because even though States are generally free to agree to deviate from general international law by agreement among them,[1675] there are

1670 See also the ILA's view in its 2004 *Final Report on the Accountablity of International Organisations* (*supra* note 1610) that a constituent instrument *can* (only) "*depart from otherwise applicable rules of international law as between the members of the IO*" (p. 18).

1671 See (with variations but all accepting a large role for international law in the EC's external relations but a much more limited one, if any, within the EC legal order), e.g. M. Bothe, *supra* note 1616, pp. 123–127; J. Boulois, *supra* note 1616, pp. 22–25; O. Elias, *supra* note 1248, pp. 5–6; O. Jacot-Guillarmod, *supra* note 1616, especially pp. 248–254 (who also notes at p. 211 that all international law may potentially apply to the EC's external relations); A. Leenen, *supra* note 1241, pp. 56–59; K. Meessen, *supra* note 1616, pp. 485–487; J. Schwarze, *supra* note 1616, p. 4 and H.F. van Panhuys, *supra* note 1616, pp. 425–426.

1672 See Amerasinghe, pp. 272–274, and the references in note 4 there. Compare the ILA's views cited *supra* note 1666.

1673 See most of the references *supra* note 1671, where the distinction is made between *intra*-EC relations, including between Member States and the EC, and external relations with third parties.

1674 Compare H. Krück, *supra* note 1245, p. 23, who leaves open whether relations between an organization and its Member States outside the framework of membership are subject to the internal or external rules. In contrast, P. Pescatore, 'Les relations extérieures des communautés européennes: contribution à la doctrine de la personnalité des organisations internationales', 103 *Rec. Cours* 1961-II, pp. 22–23 and 32–36 seems to regard the relations between an organization and its members as always governed by the rules of the organization only. For a discussion with regard to agreements concluded between EC/EU Member States that are connected to EC/EU law but are/were not (fully) part of the latter, see J.-C. Gautron & L. Grard, *supra* note 1667, pp. 127–149, especially pp. 140–149.

1675 See, in respect of treaties, Article 41 1969 VCLT. See also E. Lagrange, 'Le Conseil de sécurité des Nations Unies peut-il violer le droit international?', 37 *R.B.D.I./B.T.I.R.* 2004, pp. 570–574.

exceptions to this freedom. First, they cannot derogate from peremptory norms of international law (*ius cogens*).[1676] Second, they can only derogate from treaties to which one or more third States are a party if such treaties explicitly permit such derogation or, absent such permission, when such derogation is not prohibited and neither affects "*the enjoyment by the other parties of their rights under the treaty or the performance of their obligations*" (a rule partially reflected in Article 307 (ex 234) EC Treaty[1677]) nor relates "*to a provision, derogation from which is incompatible with the effective execution of the object and purpose of the treaty as a whole*".[1678] The best known example of a prohibition is Article 103 of the UN Charter, although it works as a priority clause rather than a clause prohibiting amendment.[1679] It is submitted that derogation from provisions in human rights and international humanitarian law treaties will, in principle, be "*incompatible with the effective execution of the object and purpose of the treaty as a whole*" and is therefore not permissible.[1680] Third, rules of international law

---

1676 See Articles 53 and 64 1969 VCLT. E. Lagrange, *supra* previous note, pp. 572–574 sees this as less certain or absolute but mainly seems to envisage cases where *ius cogens* itself makes an exception for a given international organization, especially the UN.

1677 The first sentence of which reads: "*The rights and obligations arising from agreements concluded before 1 January 1958 or, for acceding States, before the date of their accession, between one or more Member States on the one hand, and one or more third countries on the other, shall not be affected by the provisions of this Treaty*". H.F. van Panhuys, *supra* note 1616, p. 427 aptly suggests that this provision "*recognizes*" a fundamental rule of international law.

1678 Article 41(1)b 1969 VCLT. See H.M. Haugen, 'The Nature of Social Human Rights Treaties and Standard-Setting WTO Treaties: A Question of Hierarchy', 76 *Nordic J.I.L.* 2007, pp. 453–464, discussing "multilateral obligations". See also the use of so-called "disconnection" clauses by the EC/EU (Member States) in which they attempt to safeguard the *inter se* application of EC law in treaties to which other States are also a party and the critical reflections on this by C. Economides & A. Kolliopoulos, 'La clause de déconnexion en faveur du droit communautaire: une pratique criticable', 110 *R.G.D.I.P.* 2006, pp. 273–302. For an EC law perspective on such clauses, see ECJ, Opinion 1/03 (*Competence of the Community to conclude the new Lugano Convention on jurisdiction and the recognition and enforcement of judgments in civil and commercial matters*), 7 February 2006, §§78–85 and 130 and ECJ, Case C-205/06, *Commission v. Austria*, 3 March 2009, §§41–42. See also more generally M. Licková, 'European Exceptionalism in International Law', 19 *E.J.I.L* 2008, pp. 463–490.

1679 On the nature of Article 103 UN Charter, see A. Toublanc, *supra* note 1658, pp. 439–460.

1680 Compare the discussion between Flinterman and Wessel in NVIR (ed.), *De plaats van de Europese Unie in het veranderende bestel van de volkenrechtelijke organisaties* (124 Mededelingen van de NVIR), The Hague, TMC Asser Press, 2002, pp. 27–29 and 37, in which Flinterman, citing Seiderman, argues in favour of deeming the ICCPR (among others) to be superior to 'normal' international law yet distinct from *ius cogens* and Wessels submits that this amounts to turning it into *ius cogens*. I would argue that going this far is not necessary if one accepts that *inter se* derogations are not possible for such treaties. F. Morgenstern, *supra* note 1229, pp. 26–28 notes that the ILO made a submission to the Vienna Conference on the Law of Treaties arguing that *inter se* derogations from ILO conventions were not permissible. Similarly, within the EC it does not appear to be excluded that Member States can invoke their prior treaty obligations towards third States even in relations between Member States where the respect of such obligations between Member States has an interest for those third States: see, e.g. P. Eeckhout, *supra* note 1431, p. 337 (with further references), mentioning from which derogation is permitted will also apply where no derogation has actually been made (neither explicitly nor implicitly).[1681] Fourth, it might be that some other rules of general international law may also not be derogated from between some States, even when they have not obtained the status of *ius cogens*, notably those rules with an *erga omnes* character[1682] but perhaps also rules that have been labelled "intransgressible"[1683]. [1684] However, the precise nature and

environmental agreements. The ECJ appears to have accepted this, e.g. in Case C-158/91 (*Criminal proceedings against Jean-Claude Levy*, Judgment of 2 August 1993, §§10–22) by ruling that if a prohibition on night work for women in ILO Convention 89 was still binding upon France, it prevailed over EC law (in a situation which was essentially internal to France). Compare also an opinion submitted by Switzerland in respect of the Rhine regime discussed in H.F. van Panhuys, *supra* note 1616, p. 431. Compare also the discussion by LAWSON, pp. 178–183, of "integral" treaties or obligations and Karl's view of international humanitarian law as more than mere inter-State law (W. Karl, 'Das Humanitäre Völkerrecht auf dem Weg vom Zwischenstaats- zum Weltrecht', in W. Benedek, H. Isak & R. Kicker (eds.), *supra* note 1625, pp. 577–593). See also E. Bates, 'Avoiding Legal Obligations Created by Human Rights Treaties', 57 *I.C.L.Q.* 2008, pp. 751–788.

1681 On this basis, VANHAMME, pp. 98–101, submits that international organizations are, in both their external and internal relations, bound by those rules of international law from which they cannot derogate and from which they have not derogated, referring to Articles 5 and 53 1969 VCLT. For an ECJ case in this sense, see Case 41/74, *Yvonne van Duyn v Home Office*, Judgment of 4 December 1974, §22: "*it is a principle of international law, which the EEC Treaty cannot be assumed to disregard in the relations between member States, that a State is precluded from refusing its own nationals the right of entry or residence*".

1682 The seminal case is ICJ, *Barcelona Traction, Light and Power Company Ltd. (Belgium v. Spain)*, 5 February 1970, §33–34 ("*an essential distinction should be drawn between the obligations of a State towards the international community as a whole, and those arising vis-à-vis another State in the field of diplomatic protection. By their very nature the former are the concern of all States. In view of the importance of the rights involved, all States can be held to have a legal interest in their protection; they are obligations erga omnes*"). See also ICJ, Advisory Opinion on the *Legal consequences of the construction of a wall in the occupied Palestinian territory*, 9 July 2004, §§88 and 155–159. See generally M. Ragazzi, *The Concept of International Obligations "Erga Omnes"*, Oxford, Clarendon Press, 1997 and C. Tams, *Enforcing Obligations Erga Omnes in International Law*, Cambridge, Cambridge University Press, 2005.

1683 See ICJ, *Legality of the Threat or Use of Nuclear Weapons*, Advisory Opinion, 8 July 1996, §79 ("*these fundamental rules are to be observed by all States whether or not they have ratified the conventions that contain them, because they constitute intransgressible principles of international customary law*"). For a discussion of this notion and its relation with related concepts, see R. Kolb, 'Jus cogens, intangibilité, intransgressibilité, dérogation "positive" et "negative"', 109 *R.G.D.I.P.* 2005, pp. 305–330, especially pp. 324–326. In its Advisory Opinion on the *Legal consequences of the construction of a wall in the occupied Palestinian territory*, 9 July 2004, §157, the ICJ seems to link this concept to *erga omnes* obligations.

1684 Compare E. de Wet, 'The Emergence of International and Regional Value Systems as a Manifestation of the Emerging International Constitutional Order', 19 *Leiden J.I.L.* 2006, pp. 611–632, who argues that international human rights constitute the core content of an international value system which accords a special but fragile hierarchical status to those human rights norms that qualify as *jus cogens* and/or *erga omnes* norms but admits that this is much more the case in Europe with the ECHR than in the international legal order more generally. Moreover, even with regard to the ECHR the author has to admit, quite rightly, that the ECtHR has not always been consistent in this respect (*id*, pp. 620–622) and that the ECtHR has a task to supervise respect for the ECHR and that, while it does this in the context consequences of these qualifications are not very clear.[1685] In particular, on the one hand an *erga omnes* character entailing obligations towards the international community as a whole suggests that they have a particular value and this could mean that no *inter se* derogation is possible.[1686] On the other hand, if the notion is distinct from that of *ius cogens*, as is usually argued,[1687] the difference might precisely pertain to the hierarchy with obligations of an *erga omnes* character that are not *ius cogens* only benefiting from an enhanced invokability and/or *ius standi*.[1688]

---

of general international law to the extent possible, a finding of a violation of the ECHR where it conflicts with another rule of international law does not necessarily reflect a hierarchy (*id.*, p. 618), in particular when a conflicting rule is one between a party and a non-party to the ECHR and where absent any relationship rule there is no choice but to violate one of the two rules (compare *id.*, p. 629).

1685 R. Kolb, *supra* note 1683, pp. 305–329, especially pp. 324–329.

1686 Compare E. de Wet, *supra* note 1684, pp. 631–632: "*it is not yet possible to argue that all erga omnes human rights norms would, by definition, enjoy normative superiority vis-a`-vis other obligations under public international law. This, on the other hand, does seem to be the case with the erga omnes partes obligations flowing from the ECHR. ... it cannot be denied that [the (core content) of the rights in the ECHR] have a special – perhaps sui generis – normative standing in international law. It is possible that, over time, the spill-over effect of the ECHR on the international value system would strengthen the latter to the point where all customary human rights obligations with erga omnes effect enjoy a similar superior standing – regardless of whether they strictly qualify as peremptory norms of international law. The true test for this development would lie in the extent to which courts and tribunals outside the system of human rights ... acknowledge the normatively superior standing of human rights obligations*".

1687 E. de Wet, 'The International Constitutional Order', 55 *I.C.L.Q.* 2006, p. 61, writes that *ius cogens* norms have *erga omnes* effect but that the reverse is not necessarily true. Malanczuk, pp. 57–60 treats the two concepts apart but writes that they are connected. Shaw, pp. 116–119, regards *erga omnes* as a matter of *locus standi* and *ius cogens* as a matter of hierarchy but notes that the two may be linked. Brownlie, pp. 514–517, treats both concepts under one heading but does not explicitly equate or distinguish them. Compare the ILC's views on the relationship between both concepts in its comments on Part II, Chapter 3 of its Draft Articles on Responsibility of States for Internationally Wrongful Acts, adopted on 31 May and 3 August 2001, *Report of the International Law Commission. Fifty-third session*, UN Doc. A/56/10, pp. 278–282 ("*Whether or not peremptory norms of general international law and obligations to the international community as a whole are aspects of a single basic idea, there is at the very least substantial overlap between them. ... But there is at least a difference in emphasis. While peremptory norms of general international law focus on the scope and priority to be given to a certain number of fundamental obligations, the focus of obligations to the international community as a whole is essentially on the legal interest of all States in compliance ... Consistently with the difference in their focus, it is appropriate to reflect the consequences of the two concepts in two distinct ways. First, serious breaches of obligations arising under peremptory norms of general international law can attract additional consequences, not only for the responsible State but for all other States. Secondly, all States are entitled to invoke responsibility for breaches of obligations to the international community as a whole*"). See generally C. Tomuschat & J.-M. Thouvenin (eds.), *The Fundamental Rules of the International Legal Order: Jus Cogens and Obligations Erga Omnes*, Leiden, Nijhoff, 2006.

1688 That seems to be Shaw's view on the matter (*supra* previous note). See also H.M. Haugen, *supra* note 1678, pp. 452–453. Another difference might be that in the case of a violation of *ius cogens*, the consequence is *invalidity* of the conduct, whereas in the case of a breach of an *erga*

I will come back to some aspects of the openness of the legal order to general international law in the following sections. At this stage, the difficulty that may be identified is whether the binding of an international organization other than through treaties which it concludes, in which case the external dimension is normally clear,[1689] is binding only in the internal legal order of the organization and/or in the (general) international legal order.[1690] An example may clarify the question and its importance: when the Member States bind the EU to certain human rights in Article 6 EU Treaty, is this a matter of EU law only or does it bind the EU in relation to third parties also and is a third country legally[1691] entitled to demand such respect from the EU?[1692] The same question arises when an international organization binds itself though a unilateral statement or act.

The question seems of little importance in substantive terms: what matters is that the organization is bound. However, it may have an impact on the effect of the norm in the organization's legal order and in the (general) international legal order. It is difficult to give a general answer. Rather, the answer will primarily depend upon who receives rights from the act, is intended to benefit from it, might legitimately rely upon it or is addressed by it. In some cases, the powers of the organization may offer some guidance, notably where an organization has primarily only an internal (like the OSCE) or external (like NATO) focus. However, where an organization exercises both internal and external powers, as is the case for the EC/EU, this may be more difficult.

A final point that may be raised here is whether an international organization that is not a member of another international organization may nevertheless be a subject of the internal legal order of the latter. I leave aside the situation of agencies that are part of a larger legal order, as discussed above in relation to the EU, because they are in a specific position,[1693] although even there the issue may not always be that clear.[1694] This question arose with regard to Eurocontrol in

omnes rule, there is a violation but not necessarily an invalidity (unless the rule is at the same time *ius cogens*) but perhaps rather a non-*opposability* vis-à-vis any third State.

1689 Although with regard to treaties with Member States the matter is not so clearly external.

1690 See on this also Klein, p. 369. Compare Schermers & Blokker, §1200, p. 754.

1691 As opposed to merely politically.

1692 R. Uerpmann, *supra* note 1616, p. 39 regards it as an internal obligation only. H.F. van Panhuys, *supra* note 1616, p. 447, questions whether the envisaged binding of European forces to law of war rules under customary international law and Member State treaties in Article 80 of the EDC Treaty, which he argues to some extent would have had the character of a "novation", would be binding on third States.

1693 *Supra*, Chapter 6.D-E.

1694 See notably the position of the UN specialized agencies in relation to decisions of UN organs; see *infra*, Section G.5 of this chapter.

the EC (Eurocontrol had at the time members that were not EC Member States). While the ECJ held that competition law did not apply to Eurocontrol because it was not an undertaking exercising a commercial activity,[1695] it was apparently of the opinion that Eurocontrol was a subject of the EC legal order.[1696] From the perspective of the legal order of the EC this poses no fundamental problem as the EC legal order can determine that another international organization is a subject of its legal order.[1697] However, from the perspective of the organization that is being subjected to this legal order, this is less obvious.[1698] Indeed, one may wonder whether the autonomy of an international organization that is sought to be guaranteed by privileges and immunities vis-à-vis States (leaving aside cases where the immunity does not apply[1699]) is not undermined if those States can assert jurisdiction over it via another international organization. The relationship between both constitutive instruments, given the different membership, does not offer a basis for according priority to either constitutive instrument.[1700] One does get the impression that the ECJ proceeded in this case on a basis which the EC does not accept when it comes to the EC's position in relation to the ECHR,[1701] the general international legal order or the legal order of other organizations, including the UN.

1695 Case C-364/92, *SAT Fluggesellschaft mbH v Eurocontrol*, Judgment of 19 January 1994, especially §§30–31.

1696 In §§11 and 14 it regarded this question as linked to the substance and on the substance the ECJ simply applied EC competition law. Because the ECJ found that this law did not apply as Eurocontrol was not an undertaking, it did not explicitly address the issue of whether EC law could be applied at all, which would logically have to be dealt with first. Nevertheless, it seems that the Court felt it did apply.

1697 In this sense Klein, p. 351.

1698 Indeed, Eurocontrol had argued that relations between itself and the EC (legal order) were governed by international law (*ECR* 1994, p. I-59, §8).

1699 For a discussion of this case from the perspective of immunities, see I. Scobbie, *supra* note 1625, pp. 848–851.

1700 Compare Vanhamme, pp. 144–148, who concludes from the rule that no obligations can be imposed upon third parties against their will that third States or international organizations cannot be subjected to EC law but nevertheless seems to accept the applicability of EC law to their economic activities.

1701 Compare the argument by C. Kaddous, *supra* note 1739, pp. 307–308 that the EC is bound by the ECHR because the Member States have committed themselves to respecting the human rights to anyone within their jurisdiction.

D. OBLIGATIONS ENTERED INTO BY THE ORGANIZATION

1. INTERNATIONAL AGREEMENTS CONCLUDED BY THE ORGANIZATION

I will be brief about this source. The capacity of international organizations to conclude international agreements has already been discussed above (Chapter 5.E.2–3) and I have argued there that this capacity may be presumed but that it must obviously be exercised in accordance with the organization's material competences (and applicable procedures). I have also mentioned already that despite the non-entry into force of the 1986 VCLT,[1702] most substantive rules of treaty law reflected in this convention and in the 1969 VCLT are deemed to apply as customary international law.[1703] The position of organs or agencies in relation to treaty making has also been touched upon above.[1704]

It should also be noted that, while there seems to be a reluctance to allow international organizations to participate in multilateral agreements and such participation has been limited, there is no obstacle to international organizations becoming a party to such treaties unless their terms preclude ratification or accession by international organizations.[1705] Indeed, a number of more recent treaties permit 'regional economic integration organizations',[1706]

1702 On this convention, see generally G.E. do Nascimento e Silva, 'The 1986 Vienna Convention and the Treaty-making Power of International Organizations', 29 *G.Y.I.L.* 1986, pp. 68–85; G.E. do Nascimento e Silva, 'The 1969 and the 1986 Conventions on the Law of Treaties: A Comparison', in Y. Dinstein (ed.), *International Law at a Time of Perplexity: Essays in Honour of Shabtai Rosenne*, Dordrecht, Nijhoff, 1989, pp. 461–487; G. Gaja, 'A "new" Vienna Convention on Treaties between States and International Organizations or between International Organizations: A Critical Commentary', 58 *B.Y.I.L.* 1987, pp. 253–269; P. Manin, 'La Convention de Vienne sur le droit des traités entre Etats et organisations internationales ou entre organisations internationales', 32 *A.F.D.I.* 1986, pp. 454–473 and F. Morgenstern, 'The Convention on the Law of Treaties between States and International Organizations or between International Organizations', in Y. Dinstein (ed.), *supra* this note, pp. 435–447. Compare R.-J. Dupuy, 'L'application des règles du droit international général des traités aux accords conclus par les organisations internationales', 55 *A.I.D.I.* 1973, pp. 214–415 and N. Sybesma-Knol, 'The New Law of Treaties: The Codification of the Law of Treaties Concluded between States and International Organizations or between Two or More International Organizations', 15 *Georgia J.I.C.L.* 1985, pp. 425–452.

1703 *Supra*, Chapter 5, note 1375 and the accompanying text.

1704 *Supra*, Chapter 5, note 1296 and the accompanying text.

1705 In this sense also KLEIN, pp. 318–322, seeing the problem as more political than anything else, and H. Krück, *supra* note 1245, pp. 98–101 and 180. For an early study, see M. Lachs, 'Les conventions multilatérales et les organisations internationales contemporaines', 2 *A.F.D.I.* 1956, pp. 334–342.

1706 See, e.g. United Nations Framework Convention on Climate Change (New York, 9 May 1992, 1771 *U.N.T.S.* 107, entered into force on 21 March 1994), Articles 20 and 22; United Nations and, less frequently, international organizations more generally,[1707] to become a party.

A further point that needs to be mentioned here is the binding nature of such agreements vis-à-vis the organization's Member States. This issue was controversial during the preparation and negotiations of the 1986 VCLT[1708] and a provision on the matter in the ILC draft convention[1709] was rejected and not included in this convention.[1710] As we have seen above, within the EC/EU the Member States are bound by agreements concluded by the EC/EU pursuant to Article 300(7) EC Treaty and Article 24 EU Treaty (with possibly some exceptions) but only under EC/EU law and not at the international level. In other words, they are not parties to the agreement, although the ECJ has not been somewhat ambiguous with regard to the scope of Article 300(7) EC Treaty.[1711]

Convention against Transnational Organized Crime (New York, 15 November 2000, Annex I to UNGA Res. 55/25 and 2225 *U.N.T.S.* 209), Article 36 and Convention on the Rights of Persons with Disabilities, New York, 13 December 2006 (Annex I to UNGA Res. 61/106; entered into force on 3 May 2008), Article 44. On the latter, see also *infra* note 2677.

1707 E.g. United Nations Convention on the Law of the Sea (Montego Bay, 10 December 1982, 1833 *U.N.T.S.* 3, entered into force on 16 November 1994), Article 305 and Annex IX.

1708 According to the ILC commentary to the 1982 draft convention, the relevant provision was "*unquestionably the one that has aroused most comment, controversy and difficulty, both in and outside the Commission*" (*Y.I.L.C.* 1982-II, Part 2, p. 43, first comment).

1709 Article 36*bis* ("*Obligations and rights arise for States members of an international organization from the provisions of a treaty to which that organization is a party when the parties to the treaty intend those provisions to be the means of establishing such obligations and according such rights and have defined their conditions and effects in the treaty or have otherwise agreed thereon, and if: (a) the States members of the organization, by virtue of the constituent instrument of that organization or otherwise, have unanimously agreed to be bound by the said provisions of the treaty; and (b) the assent of the States members of the organization to be bound by the relevant provisions of the treaty has been duly brought to the knowledge of the negotiating States and negotiating organizations*"), see *Y.I.L.C.* 1982-II, Part 2, pp. 43–47 (including comments). It may also be noted that in 1973 the Institut de Droit International left open this issue in Article V of its resolution of 14 September 1973 on the Application of the Rules of the General International Law of Treaties to International Agreements Concluded by International Organizations (available online at www.idi-iil.org/idiE/resolutionsE/1973_rome_01_en.pdf), which provided that "*An agreement concluded by an organ in accordance with II and III above is binding on the Organization as such. This applies without prejudice to any obligation that may arise from such agreement for Member States either under the relevant rules of the Organization or under any general rule of international law*". See generally C. Brölmann, 'The 1986 Vienna Convention on the Law of Treaties: The History of Draft Article 36bis', in J. Klabbers & R. Lefeber (eds.), *Essays on the Law of Treaties: A Collection of Essays in Honour of Bert Vierdag*, The Hague, Nijhoff, 1998, pp. 121–140.

1710 For a discussion, see, e.g. C. Brölmann, *The Institutional Veil in Public International Law. International Organizations and the Law of Treaties*, Amsterdam, University of Amsterdam, Faculty of Law (thesis), 2005, pp. 273–290 and P. Manin, 'The European Communities and the Vienna Convention on the Law of Treaties between States and International Organizations or between International Organizations', 24 *C.M.L. Rev.* 1987, pp. 468–471.

1711 See *supra*, Chapter 6.B especially note 1518 and the accompanying text for the view that this is an obligation under EU law only. However, as *inter alia* pointed out by W. Wormuth, *supra*

This solution is also most in line with the separate legal personality of international organizations with treaty-making capacity[1712] and the relative nature of treaties, even if Member States may in fact not entirely be strangers to such agreements. Indeed, the combination of Articles 2(1)h and 34–35 of the 1986 VCLT arguably confirms this view,[1713] despite the stipulation in its Article 74(3) that its provisions "*shall not prejudge any question that may arise in regard to the establishment of obligations and rights for States members of an international organization under a treaty to which that organization is a party*". Thus, whether Member States of an international organization are bound by an agreement concluded by an international organization is up to the rules of the organization and is an internal matter. At best, it may be argued that, absent a specific rule confirming such binding effect in a given organization, membership only implies a good faith duty not to hinder the organization to give effect to agreements it

note 1466, pp. 117–121, the ECJ has been ambiguous by holding in its judgment of 26 October 1982 in Case 104/81 (*Hauptzollamt Mainz v C.A. Kupferberg & Cie KG a.A.*), §13, that "*In ensuring respect for commitments arising from an agreement concluded by the Community institutions the member States fulfil an obligation* not only in relation to the non-member *but* also and above all in relation to the Community which has assumed responsibility for the due performance of the agreement" (emphasis added). This has given rise to some debate over the nature of this obligation of Member States. Essentially, it boils down to the question (discussed generally *supra* Section C.2 of this Chapter) whether this provision confers rights only upon the EC or also upon third Parties. The practice of mixed agreements implies that Article 300(7) does not make the Member States formal parties to agreements concluded by the EC only and would suggest that this provision only binds the Member States vis-à-vis the EC. Compare J. Boulois, *supra* note 1616, p. 63 (taking the view that if third parties are granted rights, this would be a provision of EC law granting a right to a third party and doubting whether this is the case); J.-C. Gautron & L. Grard, *supra* note 1667, pp. 59–62 and 200 (considering that a majority sees the Member States as internationally bound but themselves rather seeing it as a matter of EC law only) and K. Schmalenbach, 'Article 300', in C. Calliess & M. Ruffert (eds.), *Kommentar des Vertrages üder die Europäische Union und des Vertrages zur Gründung der Europäischen Gemeinschaft*, Zurich, Schulthess/Luchterhand, 1999, p. 2147 (regarding it as an obligation on the Member States under EC law only).

1712 Similarly, Sands & Klein, pp. 482–483 derive from the separate legal personality that the Member States are not directly bound.

1713 Article 2(1)(h) defines "third State" and "third organization" respectively as "*(i) a State, or (ii) an international organization, not a party to the treaty*"; Article 34 reads "*A treaty does not create either obligations or rights for a third State or a third organization without the consent of that State or that organization*" and Article 35 stipulates that "*An obligation arises for a third State or a third organization from a provision of a treaty if the parties to the treaty intend the provision to be the means of establishing the obligation and the third State or the third organization expressly accepts that obligation in writing ...*". This implies that Member States, if they are not formally a party to an agreement concluded by an international organization, are third parties in respect of that agreement and are, in principle, not bound by it. Compare Klabbers, pp. 289–291, who seems to rather accept that Member States are not bound but submits that whether Member States are third parties is precisely the question. In contrast, Schermers & Blokker, §1787, p. 1143 consider that the Member States are bound, but it is not clear whether they see this as a rule of internal or international law.

has lawfully entered into.[1714] Moreover, it should be recalled that many agreements concluded by an international organization will not require specific action by the Member States.

A further point that needs to be mentioned is that in a few cases, organizations have been granted possibilities to accept a treaty or consent thereto without being a party in the same sense as States.[1715] This is for instance the case under the 1975 VCRSIO.[1716]

2. UNILATERAL ACTS

States may, under certain conditions, internationally bind themselves by unilateral acts.[1717] I will not generally discuss these conditions here but only those that pose specific problems in their application to international organizations. However, I would caution against too easily deriving an intention to be legally bound.[1718]

1714 Schermers & Blokker, §1787, p. 1143 see this as one reason for considering that the Member States are bound. For the EU/EC, such an obligation may, in addition to the specific rule concerning treaties, be derived from the loyalty obligation laid down in Article 10 EC Treaty ("*Member States shall take all appropriate measures, whether general or particular, to ensure fulfilment of the obligations arising out of this Treaty or resulting from action taken by the institutions of the Community. They shall facilitate the achievement of the Community's tasks. They shall abstain from any measure which could jeopardise the attainment of the objectives of this Treaty*") and Article 11(2) EU Treaty ("*The Member States shall support the Union's external and security policy actively and unreservedly in a spirit of loyalty and mutual solidarity. The Member States shall work together to enhance and develop their mutual political solidarity. They shall refrain from any action which is contrary to the interests of the Union or likely to impair its effectiveness as a cohesive force in international relations. The Council shall ensure that these principles are complied with*"). Indeed, D. Verwey, *supra* note 1280, p. 46 regards Article 300(7) as a specific application of Article 10 EC Treaty. Compare M. Hirsch, *supra* note 1623, pp. 27–30.

1715 See on this, e.g. Klein, pp. 354 and 365–366 and F. Morgenstern, *supra* note 1229, pp. 35–36.

1716 Articles 86–89 of this convention reserve signature and ratification/accession for States and only take into account the number of State Parties for entry into force but pursuant to Article 90 "*After the entry into force of the present Convention, the competent organ of an international organization of a universal character may adopt a decision to implement the relevant provisions of the Convention*".

1717 This was recognized by the ICJ in *Nuclear Test (Australia v. France)*, judgment of 20 December 1974, especially §§42–46. See also Bossuyt & Wouters, pp. 127–131 and Shaw, pp. 114–115. This topic is currently under consideration by the ILC, see http://untreaty.un.org/ilc/guide/9_9.htm.

1718 For instance, A. Clapham, *supra* note 1224, p. 137 argues that the UN's willingness to accept obligations in the field of human rights, including in manuals and codes of conduct, suggests that it is bound by such human rights law, whereas such internal documents, in particular in the form of non-legally binding instruments, may very well merely reflect policy that need not be based on a belief that legal obligations exist. See also Klein, p. 369, arguing that internal documents will not normally create external obligations.

Obviously, international organizations may be empowered to adopt decisions, including decisions binding themselves. However, one may wonder whether international organizations have an inherent capacity to perform unilateral acts binding themselves. I would argue that if they possess international legal personality, they must be presumed to have this capacity similarly to the treaty-making capacity.[1719]

A second issue that poses a particular challenge in the context of international organizations is the addressee of a unilateral act: as noted above (Section C.2 of this chapter), one will have to analyze whether the organization is bound only in its internal legal order or externally.[1720] In some cases this may be clear, e.g. where the EC pledges to contribute certain amounts of money for humanitarian or reconstruction aid to a third party at an international conference (assuming it is the intention to *legally* commit the EC) or where the PSC or Council adopts a decision permitting or accepting the participation of a third State in an ESDP operation, this is clearly aimed (at least in part) externally. However, in other cases it may be more difficult. For instance, when a decision is made to finance certain initiatives in a third country, even if it is published in the *Official Journal*, this would not seem to give rights to this third party absent an additional element to that effect,[1721] although it might in some cases give rise to estoppel. Likewise, when the UN Secretary-General issues a Bulletin on Observance by United Nations forces of international humanitarian law,[1722] this is an internal instruction that would not seem to have external effect (although the UN's quasi universal membership complicates the matter somewhat as few entities remain really external).[1723]

1719 Klein, pp. 365–369, especially p. 365, also seems to take this view. Compare A. Reinisch, *supra* note 1615, pp. 540–541 and see more generally M. Virally, 'Unilateral Acts of International Organizations', in M. Bedjaoui (ed.), *International Law: Achievements and Prospects*, Paris/Dordrecht, UNESCO/Nijhoff, 1991, pp. 241–263 and 'Les actes unilatéraux des organisations internationales', in M. Bedjaoui (ed.), *Droit international: bilan et perspectives*, Paris, UNESCO/Pedone, 1991, pp. 253–276.

1720 This difference is also briefly mentioned by E. Lagrange, *supra* note 1656, p. 436. See also generally J.A. Frowein, 'The Internal and External Effects of Resolutions by International Organisations', 49 *Z.a.ö.R.V.* 1989, pp. 778–790. For an analysis of how the EC can bind itself (and its Member States) on the international plane specifically in relation to (the formation or scope of) customary international law, see V. Lowe, 'Can the European Community Bind the Member States on Questions of Customary International Law?', in M. Koskenniemi (ed.), *International Law Aspects of the European Union*, The Hague, Kluwer Law International, 1998, pp. 149–168, especially pp. 157–161.

1721 In particular, the EC/EU might later decide to amend such a decision. Accepting that it creates a right for a third party would make this more difficult. Binding external effect should therefore not be presumed. Compare R.A. Wessel, *supra* note 1253, pp. 49–50. On the repudiation of a prior position, see also V. Lowe, *supra* previous note, pp. 161–162.

1722 *Supra* note 1637.

1723 E.g. Zwanenburg, p. 184, does not see it as a unilateral act of the UN but merely as an internal administrative UN document. D. Shraga, 'UN Peacekeeping Operations:

On the practical side, a problem may arise as to whom (which organ) is entitled to perform such an act, but I will not explore this.

A final point in respect of unilateral acts is that an international organization may incorporate international agreements or decisions of international organizations, irrespective of whether they bind the organization or even whether they are legally binding at all, through a unilateral act. This mechanism is often overlooked but is surprisingly common, among others in the EC/EU.[1724] It would seem that in most cases this kind of commitment is limited to the internal legal order of the organization concerned. This is different where there are clear outside addressees: for instance when the UN's administration in Kosovo decreed that all persons exercising authority in Kosovo were bound by a series of human rights instruments,[1725] this was not merely internal (though in this case the external effect may have been limited to the Kosovo legal order).

E. OBLIGATIONS IMPOSED UPON THE ORGANIZATION BY THE MEMBER STATES

It is clear that the members of an international organization may impose upon it certain obligations in constituent instruments,[1726] including as interpreted or expanded by subsequent practice.[1727] For instance, Article 6 EU Treaty obliges the EU to respect fundamental rights (see more extensively *infra*, Sections F.2 and G.3 of this chapter and Chapter 9). Similarly, Article 11(1) EU Treaty requires

Applicability of International Humanitarian Law and Responsibility for Operations-Related Damage', 94 *A.J.I.L.*, 2000, p. 409 regards it as any other Secretary-General instruction. Compare the discussion of a UN Secretary General declaration to the ICRC in M. Hirsch, *supra* note 1623, p. 38.

1724 For a brief survey, see J.-C. Gautron & L. Grard, *supra* note 1667, pp. 124–127, *inter alia* providing examples with regard to treaties and decisions of ICAO and IMO and technical rules adopted by standardization agencies. For an example in the UN system, see Klein, pp. 354 and 364–366.

1725 See UNMIK Regulations 1999/1 (25 July 1999, section 2, referring only generally to "*internationally recognized human rights standards*") and 1999/24 (12 December 1999, section 1(3), listing eight instruments and a number of protocols), both available online at www.unmikonline.org/regulations/index.htm and also cited by A. Clapham, *supra* note 1224, pp. 128–131.

1726 On the importance of such restraints, see E. de Wet, *supra* note 1687, p. 53.

1727 That is, unless the rules of the organization preclude or limit the effect of subsequent practice, as is the case in the EC, where the ECJ has repeatedly refused to accept the legal force of mere practice *contra legem*; see, e.g. Case 68/86 (*United Kingdom of Great Britain and Northern Ireland v Council of the European Communities*, Judgment of 23 February 1988, §§23–24) and J.-C. Gautron & L. Grard, *supra* note 1667, p. 117. Compare more generally T. Sato, *Evolving Constitutions of International Organizations: A Critical Analysis of the Interpretative Framework of the Constituent Instruments of International Organizations*, The Hague, Kluwer Law International, 1996.

that the EU's CFSP be conducted in accordance with the principles of the UN Charter (see more extensively *infra*, Section G.4 of this chapter) and Article 63(1) EC Treaty stipulates that it shall adopt a number of measures concerning asylum "*in accordance with the Geneva Convention of 28 July 1951 and the Protocol of 31 January 1967 relating to the status of refugees and other relevant treaties*".[1728] A historical example of particular relevance to the subject matter of this book is the envisaged binding of European forces to law of armed conflict rules under customary international law and Member State treaties in Article 80 of the EDC Treaty.[1729] While such provisions pose no problem in principle, there are instances where it has been debated whether or to what extent certain provisions impose obligations on an organization.

The question whether the UN is bound by human rights and international humanitarian law under the UN Charter is an illustration of a case giving rise to discussion. Article 1(3) UN Charter lists as one of the purposes of the UN "*To achieve international cooperation in ... promoting and encouraging respect for human rights and for fundamental freedoms for all without distinction as to race, sex, language, or religion*", Article 55(c) provides that the UN shall *promote* "*universal respect for, and observance of, human rights and fundamental freedoms for all without distinction as to race, sex, language, or religion*" and Article 56 that "*All Members pledge themselves to take joint and separate action in cooperation with the Organization for the achievement of the purposes set forth in Article 55*". In addition, various human rights instruments have been adopted by UN organs, especially the UN General Assembly.[1730] Nevertheless, these provisions and instruments do not *explicitly* oblige *the UN itself* to *respect* these rights.[1731] However, on the basis of the *travaux préparatoires* it seems that the intention

1728 See on the latter also R. Uerpmann, *supra* note 1616, pp. 40–41.

1729 This provision reads as follows:
Article 80. 1. Dans l'exercice de la compétence qui lui est conféré par le présent traité, et sans préjudice des droits et obligations des États membres:
- la Communauté a, en ce qui concerne les Forces européennes de défense et leurs membres, les mêmes droits et obligations que les États en ce qui concerne leurs forces nationales et les membres de ces Forces, d'après le droit coutumier des gens;
- la Communauté est tenue au respect des règles de droit conventionnel de la guerre qui obligent un ou plusieurs États membres.

1730 E.g. the Universal Declaration on Human Rights (UNGA Res. 217(III), A, 10 December 1948), the ICCPR and the International Covenant on Economic, Social and Cultural Rights (New York, 16 December 1966, 993 *U.N.T.S.* 3).

1731 A. Reinisch, *supra* note 1635, p. 857 and Zwanenburg, p. 154. The situation may to some extent be compared to the lack of an explicit prohibition for *States* to *commit* genocide in the Convention on the Prevention and Punishment of the Crime of Genocide (Paris, 9 December 1948, 78 *U.N.T.S.* 277) in contrast with the explicit obligation to *prevent and punish* this crime. Yet is is clear that this obligation is implict in this convention; see *Application of the Convention on the Prevention and Punishment of the Crime of Genocide (Bosnia and Herzegovina v. Serbia and Montenegro)*, judgment of 26 February 2007, §§166–167.

was to bind the UN[1732] and this seems to be the prevailing view in the literature.[1733] Yet even if the UN is held to be bound by human rights, the question arises which human rights[1734] and whether this also includes international humanitarian law (as a distinct but related body of law).[1735] Moreover, on the basis of Article 1(1) of the Charter,[1736] it has been argued that the Security Council may disregard international law when acting under Chapter VII of the UN Charter because Article 1(1) only seems to require it to act "*in conformity with the principles of justice and international law*" when engaged in the peaceful settlement of disputes.[1737] It is not necessary to discuss this in

---

1732 Zwanenburg, p. 154.

1733 See, e.g. A. Reinisch, *supra* note 1635, p. 857; de Wet, p. 199; E. Riedel, 'Article 55(c)', in Simma, pp. 920 and 922–923 and E. Sciso, 'Fundamental Rights and Article 103 of the UN Charter Before the Court of First Instance of the European Communities', 15 *Italian Y.I.L.* 2006, pp. 148–149. Compare de Wet, pp. 198–204, who argues that by virtue of Articles 1(3) and 2(2) UN Charter, the UN has created an expectation that it will respect core human rights and that it is under a good faith obligation to meet this expectation.

1734 See, e.g. E. Riedel, *supra* previous note, pp. 922–923 and E. Sciso, *supra* previous note, pp. 148–149. T. Ahmed & I. de Jesús Butler, *infra* note 1773, p. 787, argue that this includes the Universal Declaration of Human Rights and the ICCPR. For a specific application, see ICJ, *United States Diplomatic and Consular Staff in Tehran (United States of America v. Iran)*, judgment of 24 May 1980, §91 ("*Wrongfully to deprive human beings of their freedom and to subject them to physical constraint in conditions of hardship is in itself manifestly incompatible with the principles of the Charter of the United Nations, as well as with the fundamental principles enunciated in the Universal Declaration of Human Rights*"). See also T. Meron, *Human Rights and Humanitarian Norms as Customary Law*, Oxford, Clarendon Press, 1989, pp. 81–85 on UN human rights instruments as authentic interpretations or elaborations of UN Charter provisions on human rights.

1735 See on the latter H.-P. Gasser, 'The International Committee of the Red Cross and the United Nations Involvement in the Implementation of International Humanitarian Law', in L. Condorelli, A.-M. La Rosa & S. Scherrer (eds.), *Les Nations Unies et le droit international humanitaire: actes du Colloque international à l'occasion du cinquantième anniversaire de l'ONU (Genève – 19,20 et 21 octobre 1995)*, Paris, Pedone, 1996, pp. 261–262 (who considers that human rights law includes (at least part of) the law of armed conflict); de Wet, pp. 204–215 (arguing that core principles of the law of armed conflict are included) and J. Gardam, 'Legal Restraints on Security Council Military Enforcement Action', 17 *Michigan J.I.L.* 1996, pp. 300–305 and 317–321 (who is in favour of including international humanitarian law). See also V. Gowlland-Debbas, 'Security Council Enforcement Action and Issues of State Responsibility', 43 *I.C.L.Q.* 1994, pp. 91–93, who seems to include international humanitarian law under the UN's human rights obligations. Zwanenburg, pp. 153–155, seems undecided. E. Riedel, *supra* note 1733, p. 932 mentions the 1977 Additional Protocols and the ICC Statute in the framework of his discussion of Article 55(c). Compare also *infra*, Chapter 8, Section G.2.iii and viii, in respect of the EU.

1736 Which reads: "*To maintain international peace and security, and to that end: to take effective collective measures for the prevention and removal of threats to the peace, and for the suppression of acts of aggression or other breaches of the peace, and to bring about by peaceful means, and in conformity with the principles of justice and international law, adjustment or settlement of international disputes or situations which might lead to a breach of the peace*".

1737 See, e.g. H. Kelsen, *The Law of the United Nations*, New York, Praeger, 1951, pp. 16–18 and, more extensively, Zwanenburg, pp. 144–155 (arguing that although Article 1(3) is not further detail at this stage (I will return to some of the issues raised here in Part III below) and it may suffice to note that this example illustrates that relevant provisions in constituent instruments may raise significant questions of interpretation.

Obligations may also be imposed on an international organization in related documents, e.g. on privileges and immunities. Thus section 20 of the Convention on the Privileges and Immunities of the United Nations[1738] provides that the UN Secretary-General "*shall have the right* and the duty *to waive the immunity of any official in any case where, in his opinion, the immunity would impede the course of justice and can be waived without prejudice to the interests*" of the UN (emphasis added).

F. OBLIGATIONS UNDER GENERAL INTERNATIONAL LAW

1. CUSTOMARY INTERNATIONAL LAW

In the general statements cited above (Section A of this chapter) and elsewhere,[1739] it is usually accepted that international organizations are, in their external relations, bound by customary international law. This is often qualified as only pertaining to those rules that are relevant to the activities of international organizations and to the latter being able, by their nature and powers, to apply

explicitly subject to a Chapter VII exception, such an exception is implicit on the basis of a rejection of a specific clause confirming the applicability of human rights to the Security Council during the *travaux préparatoires* and taking into account Article 1(1)). On human rights in these *travaux préparatoires*, see also K. Mansson, 'Reviving the "Spirit of San Francisco": The Lost Proposals on Human Rights, Justice and International Law to the UN Charter', 76 *Nordic J.I.L.* 2007, pp. 217–239.

1738 *Supra* note 1628.

1739 E.g. C. Dominicé, *supra* note 1615, p. 144; M. Hirsch, *supra* note 1623, pp. 31–37; C. Kaddous, *Le droit des relations extérieures dans la jurisprudence de la Cour de justice des Communautés européennes*, Brussels/Basel, Bruylant/Helbing & Lichtenhahn, 1998, pp. 437–442, especially p. 442; A. Reinisch, *supra* note 1615, p. 540; H. Schermers, *supra* note 1615, pp. 84–87 and Vanhamme, pp. 96–98 (with further references).

these rules.[1740] There are also indications that this is accepted by international organizations.[1741]

That international organizations may be bound by customary international law also seems to be confirmed by Article 38 of the 1986 VCLT, which stipulates that "*Nothing in Articles 34 to 37 precludes a rule set forth in a treaty from becoming binding upon a third State or a third organization as a customary rule of international law, recognized as such*". However, the ILC commentary on the identical draft Article indicates that the provision primarily intends to exclude that this binding be denied and not necessarily confirms that it exists in relation to international organizations.[1742]

1740 See, e.g. M. Bothe, *supra* note 1616, pp. 126–128. E. Cannizzaro, 'The Scope of the EU Foreign Power. Is the EC Competent to Conclude Agreements with Third States Including Human Rights Clauses', in E. Cannizzaro (ed.), *The European Union as an Actor in International Relations*, The Hague, Kluwer Law International, 2002, pp. 313–319 argues that international organizations (*in casu* specifically the EC) are addressees (only) of those rules of general international law that affect their sphere of competence. K. Meessen, *supra* note 1616, p. 487 submits that general international law is binding on the EC in its relations with third States "*to the extent that it pertains to subjects of international law which are not states*". F. Morgenstern, *supra* note 1229, pp. 3–19, especially pp. 3–5, looks at the extent to which international law is suitable for international organizations and states that "*large areas of international law are patently inapplicable to international organizations, which have no territory, confer no nationality and do not exercise jurisdiction in the same sense as States. Other rules ... either lack relevance ... or meet practical difficulties of implementation*" and retains only three subjects that are *prima facie* suitable, i.e. State immunity, diplomatic relations and the law of treaties. However, this seems overly restrictive, e.g. the perceived problems with key concepts of State responsibility arguably are less fundamental and I fail to see why an international organization administering a territory is acting that differently from a State (even if one were to regard it as exercising the functions of a government as this author submits). Compare also the broader spectre of law deemed applicable to the EC by M. Bothe, *supra* note 1616, pp. 128–137. H.-H. Nöll, *supra* note 1234, pp. 65–122 inquires into the *anwendbarkeit* of rules, i.e. can the norm materially/factually be applied to/by international organizations. Compare for a more extensive analysis G. Cahin, *La coutume internationale et les organisations internationales: l'incidence de la dimension institutionnelle sur le processus coutumier*, Paris, Pedone, 2001, pp. 512–527, concluding that it is not contested that customary international law applies to international organizations inasmuch as it is not set aside by their constituent instrument and is adapted to their needs; that international organizations as legal persons cannot escape the binding force of customary international law any less than States, irrespective of their consent, but that their functional nature and degree of autonomy in relation to international law (in the latter case apparently especially within their legal order) prevent a full application and may require an adaptation; seeing a binding of the rules concerning the 'techniques' of international relations (as adapted) and of those rules that apply in specific areas in which they exercise competences.

1741 E.g. the IMF's General Counsel in a legal brief dated 30 May 2001 reportedly seemed to concede that the IMF would be bound by rules of general international (human rights) law to the extent that the IMF's activities overlap with the content of these norms; see A. Clapham, *supra* note 1224, p. 147.

1742 *Y.I.L.C.* 1982-II, Part 2, pp. 47–48: "*The present draft Articles does not prejudge in one way or the other the possibility that the effects of the process of the formulation of customary law might extend to international organizations*".

Moreover, the basis for this apparently obvious binding nature is rarely mentioned or examined in detail and the scholars who have studied this matter more extensively come to different conclusions. For instance, David regards the (presumed) will of the Member States to be that the organization respect customary international law as the basis for it being bound by this source of law and rejects arguments based on analogies with State succession and the rule *nemo plus iuris dat quam ipse habet*,[1743] whereas Klein sees the latter rule as the basis for binding international organizations to customary international law.[1744] Morgenstern takes still another view and seems to see as the most convincing argument for organizations that are distinct legal entities "*a necessary implication of legal capacity and activity in the international legal order*".[1745] Schermers provides three (apparently alternative) grounds: either as a result of being a subject of international law, or because the Member States must be presumed to have bound the organization or because customary international law also constitutes general principles binding upon international organizations.[1746] Bleckmann offers a range of arguments in support of the binding nature of customary international law for international organizations, namely on the one hand analogy, based on equality before the law as a general principle inherent in any legal order, and on the other hand various dogmatic constructions all based on the continuity of the international legal order, which would be endangered and characterized by gaps if it did not adapt, the avoidance of an "escape in the

1743 E. David, *supra* note 1615, pp. 3–15. For a rare case where the Member States *expressed* a will to this effect, see Article 80 of the EDC Treaty ("*1. Dans l'exercice de la compétence qui lui est conféré par le présent traité, et sans préjudice des droits et obligations des États membres: – la Communauté a, en ce qui concerne les Forces européennes de défense et leurs membres, les mêmes droits et obligations que les États en ce qui concerne leurs forces nationales et les membres de ces Forces, d'après le droit coutumier des gens; ...*"). The (presumed) will to bind is sometimes also found elsewhere, including occasionally in the ECJ's jurisprudence; see, e.g. Case 41/74 (*supra* note 1681), §22: "*it is a principle of international law, which the EEC Treaty cannot be assumed to disregard in the relations between member States, that a State is precluded from refusing its own nationals the right of entry or residence*".

1744 Klein, pp. 359–362. This argument is also occasionally reflected elsewhere; see, e.g. the ILA's 2004 *Final Report on the Accountability of International Organisations* (*supra* note 1610), p. 25, stating that Member States cannot entrust international organizations with functions without "*the attendant duties and responsibilities*", quoting from the ICJ's *Reparations Opinion, I.C.J. Reports* 1949, p. 179/9. However, the full quote from this opinion is arguably somewhat less clear: it reads "*by entrusting certain functions to [the UN], with the attendant duties and responsibilities, [its Members] have clothed it with the competence required to enable those functions to be effectively discharged*" and does not make it clear whether the attendant duties and responsibilities are only those in fact entrusted or are deemed to be automatically entrusted. E. Lagrange, *supra* note 1675, pp. 570–571, rejects this theory as she considers that the establishment of international organizations (and presumably also the extension of their powers by subsequent amendment) are acts of creation and not of transfer.

1745 F. Morgenstern, *supra* note 1229, p. 32. This author also mentions the fact that Member States must not be able to collectively evade their obligations, but seems to accept this mainly where an organization is not a distinct legal entity.

1746 H. Schermers, *supra* note 1615, p. 402.

international organization" (*die Flucht in die internationale Organisation*)[1747] that would require a piercing of the organizational veil when it comes to the applicable law, the view of international organizations as situated between States and federal States which are both subject to international law, a functional succession (*Funktionsnachfolge*)[1748] and the presumed will of the Member States to bind organizations.[1749] However, he adds that there was no general rule yet supporting a general applicability of customary international law to international organizations and that these grounds only provide a potential that may either be confirmed (e.g. in treaty law) or contradicted (e.g. concerning immunities) by practice and that the rules should not be contrary to the nature of international organizations.[1750]

It is submitted that the better basis for holding that international organizations are bound by (relevant) customary international law (subject to any necessary modifications) is the argument that this simply derives from their international legal personality as I have defined it above, i.e. the ability to possess rights and duties directly under international law and to exercise proper powers on the international plane and/or enter into international legal relations.[1751] Thus this only applies to organizations that possess such personality. In contrast, organizations that are subjects of international law but lack international legal personality only have defined and limited rights and/or duties and the more general question does not arise in respect of them. Organizations that are not even subjects of international law can simply not be bound by international law and for them the question is thus legally irrelevant. Indeed, an international organization with international legal personality exists in the international legal order by virtue of this legal order, even if it refers to some extent to the will of the

1747 See also D. Lorenz, *Der territoriale Anwendungsbereich der Grund- und Menschenrechte - zugleich ein Beitrag zum Individualschutz in bewaffneten Konflikten*, Berlin, Berliner Wissenschafts-Verlag, 2005, pp. 266 and 281–282 (though rather in respect of treaty obligations).

1748 Vanhamme, p. 96 seems to take a similar view by attaching being subjected to international law to the exercise of sovereign powers. He adds that obligations follow rights on the basis of the nature of international law.

1749 A. Bleckmann, *supra* note 1615, pp. 113–120.

1750 *Id.*, pp. 113 and 120–121.

1751 *Supra*, Chapter 5.A. See also A. Reinisch, *supra* note 1615, p. 540; R.A. Wessel, *supra* note 1253, p. 39 and K. Osteneck, *infra* note 1850, pp. 130–131. This is also essentially similar to Morgenstern's view (*supra* note 1745 and the accompanying text), since she requires legal capacity and activity in the international legal order and also seems close to one of Schermers' arguments (*supra* note 1746 and the accompanying text) and to the view of C. Kaddous, *supra* note 1739, p. 442 ("*En tout état de cause, il ne fait pas de doute que la Communauté européenne, en tant que sujet de droit international, est soumise au respect du droit international général*") and of Hirsch (*supra* note 1623, p. 17: "*there is no doubt that intergovernmental organizations which exist under international law and are considered subjects of this law are bound to respect it*") . This argument is also mentioned by F. Schröer, *supra* note 1623, p. 713.

Member States on this existence,[1752] and must accept the rules of that legal order as applicable to it. In this respect, it does not differ from new States: although the latter's position was not undisputed in this respect, especially at the time of decolonization, there is hardly any evidence that a new State is free to reject general international law.[1753] There is also an important policy consideration in favour of binding international organizations to customary international law: if they are not so bound, they would be subject to very few rules in a number of areas of activity given that their constitutive instruments only very partially bind them to substantive rules governing their areas of activity (as opposed to provisions on competences and procedure) and that they often do not, and in many cases even cannot, become a party to international agreements in these areas.

However, it is also clear that the nature of international organizations means that the wholesale application of customary international law is not always feasible.[1754] Firstly, as has been argued above,[1755] there are differences in respect of the possession of certain legal capacities, which are automatically held to be possessed by States but not necessarily also all by international organizations. Secondly, even where a given legal capacity is possessed by an organization, it may be subject to some modification (e.g. immunities) or specific rules (e.g. some rules of treaty law and international responsibility). Thirdly, only those rules that concern the sphere of competence of a specific organization will be relevant. While arguably fewer rules than is often assumed may be regarded as *a priori* irrelevant for international organizations,[1756] many rules will be irrelevant for many specific organizations. Fourthly, even when rules are relevant and applicable, they may require some adaptation,[1757] including possibly (partial) non-application, as is the case with some rules concerning legal capacities. However, the impossibility or difficulty to apply a given rule as such should not too easily be permitted as an excuse for non-application.[1758] Rather, solutions will have to be sought to ensure respect, where necessary by resorting to implied powers and/or the internal rules of the organization, including obligations for

1752 See *supra*, Chapter 5.E.

1753 In this sense G. Cahin, *supra* note 1740, pp. 485–512, especially pp. 493–495, although leaving some room for specific and 'reasonable' objections. But see KLEIN, p. 363, who takes the view that State sovereignty stands in the way of a complete application of all customary international law to new States.

1754 Similarly, G. Cahin, *supra* note 1740, p. 513.

1755 See *supra*, Chapter 5.E.

1756 As the ILA notes in its 2004 *Final Report on the Accountability of International Organisations* (*supra* note 1610), p. 26: "*The expansion in the activities of IO-s widens the range of substantive primary rules of international law applicable to [international organisations]*".

1757 See also G. Cahin, *supra* note 1740, pp. 521–525, using the expression "*obligatoriété adaptée*".

1758 In this sense also A. Bleckmann, *supra* note 1615, pp. 120–121.

the Member States under this law to help ensure respect for a rule.[1759] For instance, a number of the UN's concerns that it lacks various powers to ensure respect for the obligations under international humanitarian law by UN forces[1760] are not convincing in light of the UN's extensive powers and its possibility to include relevant clauses in agreements with troop contribution States.[1761]

These considerations illustrate that it may not be that easy to determine which specific rules of customary international law apply to a particular international organization. The problem could be solved by international organizations becoming a party to multilateral law-making treaties, but as noted above (section D.1 of this chapter), this is not always permitted by such treaties and except for the EC to some extent there is very little practice in this direction. However, it is likely to increase as more and more 'regional integration organizations' are granted more extensive competences. Moreover, organizations seem very reluctant to accept that they are bound by treaties to which they are not formally a party (see especially *infra* section G of this chapter concerning treaties concluded by their Member States). It would appear that one must therefore hope that practice will clarify the applicable customary rules over time. Given the limited judicial oversight in this matter, jurisprudence is not likely to provide much guidance. The main alternatives seem to be binding an organization in its constituent instrument (see *supra*, Section E of this chapter) or via decisions of an organization that detail, at least to some extent, the applicable rules (e.g. the UN Secretary-General's Bulletin on UN forces and international humanitarian law[1762]).

Finally, it may be added that widespread practice, especially by international organizations, may give rise to new and specific rules of customary international law that concern the position and functioning of international organizations.[1763] This is, e.g. arguably the case for privileges and immunities.[1764]

2. GENERAL PRINCIPLES OF LAW

As with customary international law, it is generally assumed that general principles of law also apply to international organizations, at least in their

1759 See also KLEIN, pp. 319–321.
1760 See, e.g. the references in KLEIN, p. 319 note 67.
1761 Similarly, among others, KLEIN, pp. 319–320.
1762 *Supra* note 1637.
1763 See also A. Bleckmann, *supra* note 1615, p. 113 and KLEIN, p. 364.
1764 See *supra*, Section B.1 of this chapter and Chapter 5.E 2.

external relations.[1765] At first sight, since they both belong to general international law *sensu stricto*,[1766] there seems no reason not to accord them a different status from customary law as regards their effect for international organizations. However, it may be that their more fundamental or general nature[1767] in practice makes a derogation less likely than is the case for customary international law, including in the internal legal order. Apart from this consideration and the question of the legal effect (especially in terms of hierarchy), I submit that the binding nature of general principles of law for international organizations is the same as that of customary international law, and for the same reasons.[1768]

However, there is a peculiar phenomenon in the internal legal order of international organizations, especially within the EC/EU, that deserves some comment: namely general principles of law proper to the legal order of an international organization. I will first briefly sketch these principles within the EC/EU legal order and then consider to what extent the rules elaborated there are or could be applied in other international organizations.

i. General Principles in EC/EU Law

The ECJ has, in the course of its duty to ensure that in the interpretation and application of the EC/EU Treaties "*the law is observed*",[1769] developed an

[1765] See, e.g. A. Bleckmann, *supra* note 1615, p. 109; C. Dominicé, *supra* note 1615, p. 146; J.-C. Gautron & L. Grard, *supra* note 1667, pp. 117–118; M. Hirsch, *supra* note 1623, p. 37; Klein, pp. 364–365; H. Schermers, *supra* note 1615, pp. 401–402; Sands & Klein, pp. 458–460 and S. Skogly, *supra* note 1619, pp. 87–90. See also the ILA's 2004 *Final Report on the Accountability of International Organisations* (*supra* note 1610), p. 27 ("*[international organisations] may incur international legal responsibility if the exercise of their powers is not in compliance with general principles of law ...*").

[1766] The "*general principles of law recognized by civilized nations*" are included in Article 38(1) ICJ Statute next to treaties and customary international law as a primary source of international law. For a discussion, see A. Pellet, 'Article 38', in A. Zimmermann *et al.* (eds.), *The Statute of the International Court of Justice. A Commentary*, Oxford, Oxford University Press, 2006, pp. 764–773.

[1767] For a brief discussion of the notion 'principle' compared to 'rules', see A. Pellet, *supra* previous note, pp. 766–767; O. Wiklund & J. Bengoetxea, 'General Constitutional Principles of Community Law', in U. Bernitz & J. Nergelius (eds.), *infra* note 1769, pp. 121–124 and S. Skogly, *supra* note 1619, pp. 88–89.

[1768] It is sometimes argued that it is not always easy to distinguish general principles from customary international law; see, e.g. O. Elias, *supra* note 1248, p. 5 note 4; H. Schermers, *supra* note 1615, p. 402 and S. Skogly, *supra* note 1619, pp. 88–89.

[1769] See Article 220 (ex 164) EC Treaty, which is generally considered to be the basis for the ECJ's recognition of general principles of EC law. See, e.g. M. Herdegen, 'The Origins and Development of General Principles of Community Law', in U. Bernitz & J. Nergelius (eds.), *General Principles of European Community Law: Reports from a Conference in Malmö, 27–28 August 1999, Organised by the Swedish Network for European Legal Studies and the Faculty of Law, University of Lund*, The Hague, Kluwer Law International, 2000, pp. 15–17 and A. Toth, 'Human Rights as General Principles of Law, in the Past and in the Future', *id.*, extensive case law on general principles of EC law.[1770] I will use the term principles of EC law because it is most common, although the increased scope of the jurisdiction of the ECJ over *extra*-EC EU matters raises the question to what extent these principles are also general principles of EU law.[1771] The answer is likely to be a nuanced one: while some principles may easily be applied in the broader EU framework,[1772] including human rights,[1773] especially with a view to

---

p. 77. These authors *inter alia* cite ECJ, Joint Cases C-46/93 and C-48/93, *Brasserie du Pêcheur SA v Bundesrepublik Deutschland* and *The Queen v Secretary of State for Transport, ex parte: Factortame Ltd and others*, Judgement of 5 March 1996, §27 (which reads: "*Since the Treaty contains no provision expressly and specifically governing the consequences of breaches of Community law by Member States, it is for the Court, in pursuance of the task conferred on it by Article 164 of the Treaty of ensuring that in the interpretation and application of the Treaty the law is observed, to rule on such a question in accordance with generally accepted methods of interpretation, in particular by reference to the fundamental principles of the Community legal system and, where necessary, general principles common to the legal systems of the Member States*"). See also K. Lenaerts & P. Van Nuffel, *supra* note 1465, p. 711. In Opinion 2/94 of 28 March 1996 on *Accession by the Community to the European Convention for the Protection of Human Rights and Fundamental Freedoms*, the ECJ ruled that the EC did not have a general human rights competence permitting it to accede to the ECHR (for a discussion with further references, see C. Kaddous, *supra* note 1739, pp. 309–318). Toth (*supra* this note, pp. 78–81), is critical of this decision inasmuch as he sees a paradox with the ECJ deeming itself competent to ensure respect for human rights.

1770 See generally U. Bernitz & J. Nergelius (eds.), *supra* note 1769; K. Lenaerts & P. Van Nuffel, *supra* note 1465, pp. 711–739; R.-E. Papadopoulou, *Principes généraux du droit et droit communautaire: origines et concretisation*, Brussels/Athens, Bruylant/Sakkoulas, 1996; T. Tridimas, *The General Principles of EU Law*, Oxford, Oxford University Press, 2006 (2nd ed.) and J. Usher, *General Principles of EC Law*, London, Longman, 1998.

1771 This question does not appear to have attracted much attention yet. For some exceptions, see N. Lavranos, *infra* note 1860, pp. 211–230; K. Lenaerts & T. Corthaut, 'Of Birds and Hedges: The Role of Primacy in Invoking Norms of EU Law', 31 *Eur. L. Rev.* 2006, pp. 287–315, especially pp. 289–292 and S. Peers, 'Salvation Outside the Church: Judicial Protection in the Third Pillar After the Pupino and Segi Judgments', *C.M.L. Rev.* 2007, pp. 926–928 (pleading for the application of all general principles of EC law to the third pillar).

1772 E.g. proportionality, non-discrimination and fundamental rights. On these principles, see, e.g. G. de Búrca, 'Proportionality and Subsidiarity as General Principles of Law', in U. Bernitz & J. Nergelius (eds.), *supra* note 1769, pp. 95–112; H. Ragnemalm, 'Leading by Example or Leaning on Supremacy? Some Reflections on the Union, the Individual and the Protection of Fundamental Rights', *id.*, pp. 49–60; H. Schermers, 'Human Rights as General Principles of Law', *id.*, pp. 61–72; A. Toth, *supra* note 1769, pp. 73–92; R.-E. Papadopoulou, *supra* note 1770, pp. 243–265, 59–80 and 137–165 and J. Usher, *supra* note 1770, pp. 37–51 and 16–36.

1773 See, e.g. ECJ, Case C-105/03 (*Maria Pupino*, Judgment of 16 June 2005), §58 ("*in accordance with Article 6(2) EU, the* Union *must respect fundamental rights, ..., as general principles of law*" (emphasis added); this case concerned a Third Pillar framework decision) and Case C-354/04, *Gestoras Pro Amnistía and Others v Council of the European Union*, 27 February 2007, §§49–57, especially §51 ("*the institutions are subject to review of the conformity of their acts with the treaties and the general principles of law, just like the Member States when they implement* the law of the Union" (emphasis added); the case concerned a mixed Second-Third Pillar common position). See also the Opinion of Advocate General Maduro of 16 December 2004 in Case C-160/06 (*Kingdom of Spain v. Eurojust*), §§32–33 (the ECJ did not address this point in its judgment in this case). Similarly, with regard to the Third Pillar, S. Peers, *supra* note 1771, pp. 926–928 (who also extensively discusses the *Pupino* case at pp. 909–924). For C.

consistency and coherence,[1774] the wholesale extension of others to the EU may be less obvious.[1775]

These principles are derived from a variety of sources, especially the legal systems of the Member States, the EC legal order itself, general principles recognized by

---

Kaddous, *supra* note 1739, p. 306, Article 6 EU Treaty implies respect for human rights in all EU activities. Similarly, B. Beutler, 'Artikel 6 EU', in H. von der Groeben & J. Schwarze (eds.), *supra* note 1610, p. 95; T. Kingreen, 'Article 6', in C. Calliess & M. Ruffert (eds.), *supra* note 1711, p. 70; K. Lenaerts & P. Van Nuffel, *supra* note 1465, p. 723 and Wessel in 124 Mededelingen van de NVIR, *supra* note 1680, p. 40. Similarly, with regard to the EU Constitution, D. Scheuing, *infra* note 1803, p. 184, and with regard to the Charter of Fundamental Rights, D. Curtin & R. van Ooik, 'The Sting is Always in the Tail: The Personal Scope of Application of the EU Charter of Fundamental Rights', 8 *Maastricht Journal of European and Comparative Law* 2001, pp. 105–108 (also arguing that it covers all EU bodies) and H.D. Jarass, *infra* note 1802, p. 35 (arguing that it covers all EU bodies and agencies and the entire range of EU activities). Compare M. Fouwels, 'The European Union's Common Foreign and Security Policy and Human Rights', 15 *Netherlands Quarterly of Human Rights* 1997, pp. 293–296, arguing that although Article 6 requires respect for human rights as general principles of Community law, the inclusion of this obligation in the provisions common to all EU areas of activities suggests respect for human rights is also mandatory in non-EC EU competences, including the CFSP, at least as a source of inspiration. T. Ahmed & I. de Jesús Butler, 'The European Union and Human Rights: An International Law Perspective', 17 *E.J.I.L.* 2006, pp. 771–802 seem to use EC and EU interchangeably. R. Gosalbo Bono, *supra* note 1247, pp. 347–348, is of the view that the Amsterdam Treaty made the rule of law principle applicable also to CFSP law and qualifies the CFSP since then as "*founded on the rule of law but without judicial review by the Court of Justice*". See also the status of human rights in the ECJ's *Kadi* appeals judgment, *infra* notes 1906 and 1910 and accompanying text. On the applicability of fundamental rights as general principles within the ESDP, see more extensively *infra*, Chapter 9. On human rights and EU/EC external relations generally, see, e.g. W.S. Heinz, 'EU External Relations and Human Rights', in M. Brosig (ed.), *Human Rights in Europe: A Fragmented Regime?*, Frankfurt am Main, Lang, 2006, pp. 184–207; P. Leino, 'The Journey towards All that Is Good and Beautiful: Human Rights and "Common Values" as Guiding Principles of EU Foreign Relations Law', in M. Cremona & B. De Witte (eds.), *EU Foreign Relations Law: Constitutional Fundamentals*, Oxford, Hart, 2008, pp. 259–289; D. Napoli, 'The European Union's Foreign Policy and Human Rights', in N. Neuwahl & A. Rosas (eds.), *The European Union and Human Rights*, The Hague, Nijhoff, 1995, pp. 297–312 and E. Spaventa, 'Fundamental What?: The Difficult Relationship between Foreign Policy and Fundamental Rights', in M. Cremona & B. De Witte (eds.), *EU Foreign Relations Law: Constitutional Fundamentals*, Oxford, Hart, 2008, pp. 233–255.

1774 See on this *supra*, Chapter 6, notes 1586 and 1592 and the accompanying text.

1775 E.g. the institutional balance (see, e.g. B. de Witte, 'Institutional Principles: A Special Category of General Principles of EC Law', in U. Bernitz & J. Nergelius (eds.), *supra* note 1769, pp. 150–152; R.-E. Papadopoulou, *supra* note 1770, pp. 118–126 and J. Usher, *supra* note 1770, pp. 37–51 and 16–36) is quite different in the CFSP although it may lend itself to a variable content (it may be noted that this principle is contained in the ILA's 2004 *Final Report on the Accountability of International Organisations* (*supra* note 1610), pp. 12–13) and the primacy of EU law as opposed to EC law (B. de Witte, *supra* this note, pp. 147–148, questioning, however, whether this is a principle or rather a meta-norm) may not be quite that acceptable to Member States.

international law and derived from treaties concluded by the Member States (especially in the field of human rights[1776]).[1777]

It is through this mechanism that the ECJ has introduced human rights protection in the EC,[1778] which was initially not explicitly included in the E(E)C Treaty.[1779] This protection was only subsequently endorsed at the political level

---

1776 See especially Case C-4/73, *J. Nold, Kohlen- und Baustoffgroßhandlung v Commission of the European Communities*, Judgment of 14 May 1974, §13 ("*... fundamental rights form an integral part of the general principles of law ... In safeguarding these rights, the Court is bound to draw inspiration from constitutional traditions common to the member States ... Similarly, international treaties for the protection of human rights on which the member States have collaborated or of which they are signatories, can supply guidelines which should be followed within the framework of Community law*").

1777 See U. Bernitz, 'Preface', in U. Bernitz & J. Nergelius (eds.), *supra* note 1769, p. ix (listing the first three of these); T. Koopmans, 'General Principles of Law in European and National Systems of Law', *id.*, pp. 32–33 (listing the first two of these and human rights); J.-C. Gautron & L. Grard, *supra* note 1667, p. 25 (listing all of them) and A. Toth, *supra* note 1769, p. 78 note 14 (listing the first two of these, as well as public international law and Roman law). But see O. Elias, *supra* note 1248, p. 5 note 4, who seems to reject principles of international law as a source but does admit Member State treaties.

1778 After initial refusals to take into account human rights based on national constitutions (see, e.g. Case 1/58, *Friedrich Stork & Cie v High Authority of the European Coal and Steel Community*, Judgement of 4 February 1959, §3(A)), the ECJ first recognized human rights in Case 29/69 (*Erich Stauder v City of Ulm – Sozialamt*, Judgment of 12 November 1969, §7: "*Interpreted in this way the provision at issue contains nothing capable of prejudicing the fundamental human rights enshrined in the general principles of Community law and protected by the Court*") and since then the protection of fundamental rights has become established case law. Further early cases include Cases 11/70 (*Internationale Handelsgesellschaft mbH v Einfuhr- und Vorratsstelle für Getreide und Futtermittel*, Judgement of 17 December 1970, §§3–4, in which the ECJ distinguished invoking human rights as formulated by the constitution of a particular Member State from those shared by the Member States: "*the validity of a Community measure or its effect within a member State cannot be affected by allegations that it runs counter to ... fundamental rights formulated by the constitution of that State ... respect for fundamental rights forms an integral part of the general principles of law protected by the [ECJ]. The protection of such rights, whilst inspired by the constitutional traditions common to the member States, must be ensured within the framework of the structure and objectives of the Community*"); 4/73 (*supra* note 1776) and 44/79 (*Liselotte Hauer v Land Rheinland-Pfalz*, Judgement of 13 December 1979, §§13–15). See generally the references *supra* note 1772; K. Lenaerts & P. Van Nuffel, *supra* note 1465, pp. 719–739; P. Alston, with M. Bustelo & J. Heenan, *The EU and Human Rights*, Oxford, Oxford University Press, 1999 and N. Neuwahl & A. Rosas (eds.), *supra* note 1773 (the literature on this matter is vast but for the purposes of the issue at stake these references may suffice).

1779 Although it may be noted that the draft proposals for a European Political Community (see *supra*, Chapter 1.A, note 22) did contain a clause imposing respect for human rights, see A.H. Robertsen, 'The European Political Community', 29 *B.Y.I.L.* 1952, pp. 388 and 396 (the promotion of human rights was listed as the first aim in draft Article 1; draft Article 3 incorporated by reference the ECHR and draft Article 45 provided for judicial review of measures affecting human rights).

in 1977,[1780] mentioned in the preamble of the Single European Act[1781] and eventually included in what is now Article 6 EU Treaty. Moreover, while Article F Maastricht Treaty only provided that the EU was to respect human rights, the Treaty of Amsterdam added in Article 6 EU Treaty that the EU was also founded on respect for human rights and Article 7 EU Treaty introduced a sanctions mechanism for dealing with a serious and persistent breach of human rights or one of the other founding principles of the EU. It has been argued that this elevation of human rights to a founding principle has permitted the ECJ to accord it an enhanced status and to test whether EC law is in conformity with human rights rather than to test to what extent human rights can be incorporated within the EC system and only to test EC law against human rights as incorporated subject to this test.[1782] More recently, human rights in the EU were codified in the Charter of Fundamental Rights of the European Union,[1783] which was solemnly proclaimed by the European Parliament, the Council and the Commission in Nice on 7 December 2000, but of which the legal nature as such has, however, not yet determined.[1784] The Lisbon Treaty incorporates the Charter

---

1780 See the Joint Declaration by the European Parliament, the Council and the Commission of 5 April 1977, *O.J. C* 103, 27 April 1977, p. 1 ("*Whereas, as the Court of Justice has recognized, that law comprises, over and above the rules embodied in the treaties and secondary Community legislation, the general principles of law and in particular the fundamental rights, principles and rights on which the constitutional law of the Member States is based; Whereas, in particular, all the Member States are Contracting Parties to the [ECHR] ... 1. The European Parliament, the Council and the Commission stress the prime importance they attach to the protection of fundamental rights, as derived in particular from the constitutions of the Member States and the [ECHR]. 2. In the exercise of their powers and in pursuance of the aims of the European Communities they respect and will continue to respect these rights*"). For a discussion of the legal effect of this declaration in international law, see KLEIN, p. 368, who argues that it is a unilateral act creating international obligations, including towards third States. However, this seems questionable, including from the perspective of whom the addressees were intended to be (see *supra*, Section C.2 of this chapter).

1781 Luxembourg and The Hague, 17 and 28 February 1986, *O.J. L* 169, 29 June 1987, p. 1, 3rd consideration: "*Determined to work together to promote democracy on the basis of the fundamental rights recognized in the constitutions and laws of the Member States, in the [ECHR] and the European Social Charter, notably freedom, equality and social justice*".

1782 See F. Sudre, 'L'apport du droit international et européen à la protection communautaire des droits fondamentaux', in J.-C. Gautron & L. Grard (eds.), *supra* note 1296, pp. 188–193.

1783 *O.J. C* 364, 18 December 2000, p. 1.

1784 In §2 of the Presidency Conclusions of the 7–9 December Nice European Council, it is stated that "*the question of the Charter's force will be considered later*". In Case C-540/03 (*European Parliament v. the Council of the European Union*, Judgement of 27 June 2006), §38, the ECJ held that "*the Charter is not a legally binding instrument*", while stressing its importance, including as reaffirming rights already laid down elsewhere. On the latter basis, K. Lenaerts & P. Van Nuffel, *supra* note 1465, pp. 722 *juncto* 732–733 seem to consider that the rights laid down in the Charter are binding, referring *inter alia* to European Commission Communication COM 2000(644) of 11 October 2000 (which states in §10 that "*it is highly likely that the Court of Justice will seek inspiration in it, as it already does in other fundamental rights instruments. It can reasonably be expected that the Charter will become mandatory through the Court's interpretation of it as belonging to the general principles of Community* in the EU Treaty by way of reference, subject to some modifications, and makes it legally binding.[1785]

For our purposes, four aspects of the ECJ's jurisprudence on general principles of EC law are of particular importance.

First, as mentioned above, one category of principles is derived from the legal systems of the Member States. At first sight, there is a parallel with general principles of law in international law, which are also, at least mainly, derived from the domestic legal systems (but arguably in part include principles proper to international law).[1786] However, the key distinction is that within the EC the

---

law") and to Cases T-54/99 (*max.mobil Telekommunikation Service GmbH v. Commission of the European Communities*, Judgment of 30 January 2002, §§48 and 57) and T-177/01 (*Jégo-Quéré et Cie SA v. Commission of the European Communities*, Judgment of 3 May 2002, §§42 and 47, set aside by Case C-263/02, *Commission of the European Communities v. Jégo-Quéré et Cie SA*, Judgment of 1 April 2004; the appeals judgment does not mention the Charter) and various opinions of Advocates General. Compare F. Debusseré, 'Het Handvest van de grondrechten van de Europese Unie', 38 *Jura Falconis* 2001–2002 (available online at www.law.kuleuven.ac.be/jura/art/38n1/debussere.htm), section 5.

1785 See Article 6(1) EU Treaty as it would be amended *juncto* the amended Charter ("*The Union recognises the rights, freedoms and principles set out in the Charter of Fundamental Rights of 7 December 2000, as adapted at Strasbourg, on 12 December 2007, which shall have the same legal value as the Treaties. The provisions of the Charter shall not extend in any way the competences of the Union as defined in the Treaties. The rights, freedoms and principles in the Charter shall be interpreted in accordance with the general provisions in Title VII of the Charter governing its interpretation and application and with due regard to the explanations referred to in the Charter, that set out the sources of those provisions*"). The amended Charter is published in the *O.J. C* 305, 14 December 2007. Compare Article I-9(1) EU Constitution ("*The Union shall recognise the rights, freedoms and principles set out in the Charter of Fundamental Rights which constitutes Part II*"). For a discussion of the changes in the EU Constitution compared to the Charter, see, e.g. A. Berramdane, 'Les droits fondamentaux dans la Constitution européenne: la constitutionnalisation de la charte des droits fondamentaux', *R.D.U.E.* 2003, pp. 613–645 and H. Brecht, 'Änderungen an der EU-Grundrechtecharta Korrekturen durch Verfassungskonvent und Regierungskonferenz sowie Konsequenzen für die Auslegung der Charta', 8 *Z. Eur. S.* 2005, pp. 355–396. See also R. Barents, 'Een grondwet voor Europa (VI): de grondrechten', 11 *Nederlands tijdschrift voor Europees recht* 2005, pp. 39–45 and T. Schmitz, 'Die Grundrechtecharta als Teil der Verfassung der Europäischen Union', 39 *Europarecht* 2004, pp. 691–713.

1786 See, e.g. Brownlie, pp. 15–19; Malanczuk, pp. 48–50 and Shaw, p. 94. However, the nature of general principles of law is somewhat controversial. E.g. Bossuyt & Wouters, pp. 119–120 consider that these principles *only* include principles derived from domestic legal systems. The view of A. Pellet, *supra* note 1766, is not entirely clear: on the one hand this commentator seems to accept only general principles derived from domestic law (p. 766) but on the other hand he states that general principles of law need not necessarily be recognized under both domestic and international law (p. 768). C. Dominicé, *supra* note 1615, p. 146, distinguishes the two but regards them as both binding on international organizations. L. Caflisch & A.A. Cancado Trindade, 'Les conventions américaine et européenne des droits de l'homme et le droit international général', 108 *R.G.D.I.P.* 2004, pp. 51–59 distinguish both kind of principles, arguing that general principles of international law are not a separate source but rather a number of Member States is much more limited than the number of States in the international community. Despite the fact that the legal systems of the EU Member States include both common law and civil law systems, these systems have much more in common than all the legal systems of the world. This probably is the main reason why the ECJ has been able to recognize so many general principles and uphold them with such force.[1787] Obviously, the ECJ's compulsory jurisdiction and the large number of cases it has decided have also given it much more opportunities to recognize general principles of law. In contrast, such principles play a much less significant role in general international law and in other international organizations.[1788] That being said, there remain some ambiguities in the ECJ's jurisprudence. Most notably, it is not entirely clear to what degree a principle must be common to the Member States (to all Member States, to a majority, to some?).[1789]

Second, and to some extent related to the first aspect, the question arises as to the relationship between general principles in EC and in international law. It results from the preceding point that there will be some overlap in the category of principles derived from domestic law, since such principles of international law will normally also be common to the Member States and are therefore potential candidates for principles of EC law. However, the specific nature of the EC legal order may preclude some of these principles from obtaining this status.[1790] Similarly, general principles of international law proper to international

qualification of rules found in other sources, especially customary international law, but note that the jurisprudence of the European and Inter-American human rights bodies does not always make this distinction.

1787 In this sense A. Leenen, *supra* note 1241, pp. 96–97. Compare A. Toth, *supra* note 1769, pp. 74–75 and A. Pellet, *supra* note 1766, p. 769 (who counters the problem of the diversity of domestic legal systems with the general nature of a general principle).

1788 In this sense A. Toth, *supra* note 1769, pp. 74–75. Compare A. Pellet, *supra* note 1766, pp. 769–772.

1789 E.g. A. Toth, *supra* note 1769, p. 81. For a similar criticism with regard to the International Court of Justice, see A. Pellet, *supra* note 1766, p. 766, noting that the International Court of Justice has only explicitly addressed general principles of law four times and has not accepted the existence of the alleged principle invoked each time. Interestingly, the explanations to the EU's Charter on Fundamental Rights as amended and published in 2007 state that "*The rule of interpretation contained in [Article 52] paragraph 4 has been based on the wording of Article 6(3) of the [EU Treaty] and takes due account of the approach to common constitutional traditions followed by the Court of Justice (...). Under that rule, rather than following a rigid approach of 'a lowest common denominator', the Charter rights concerned should be interpreted in a way offering a high standard of protection which is adequate for the law of the Union and in harmony with the common constitutional traditions*" (*O.J. C* 305, 14 December 2007, p. 34).

1790 See J.-C. Gautron & L. Grard, *supra* note 1667, p. 25, who more generally note that principles derived from other legal orders are only incorporated to the extent that they are adequate and coherent with the overall EC legal framework.

law may also be general principles of EC law but this need not necessarily be the case.[1791]

Third, the ECJ's deriving general principles of EC law from Member State treaties, especially the ECHR in the field of fundamental rights,[1792] is especially interesting. In particular, the Court's statement in *Nold* that "*international treaties for the protection of human rights on which the member States have collaborated or of which they are signatories, can supply guidelines which should be followed within the framework of Community law*" opens up a large potential for binding the EC to a number of provisions in treaties concluded by its Member States.[1793] Nevertheless, it has been pointed out that this judgment was only handed down once all (at the time six) EC Member States had become parties to the ECHR.[1794] It has also been noted that only in 1996 did the ECJ cite case law

---

1791 A principle/rule of international law which has been excluded in the EC legal order is that of reciprocity, as manifested in the *exceptio non adimpleti contractus* (*inter alia* reflected in Articles 60 1969 and 1986 VCLT); see ECJ, Joint Cases 90 and 91/63 (*Commission of the European Economic Community v Grand Duchy of Luxembourg and Kingdom of Belgium*, Judgment of 13 November 1964) and Case 325/82 (*Commission of the European Communities v Federal Republic of Germany*, Judgment of 14 February 1984, §11), also cited by J. Boulois, *supra* note 1616, p. 46, and Cases C-5/94 (*The Queen v Ministry of Agriculture, Fisheries and Food, ex parte: Hedley Lomas (Ireland) Ltd.*, Judgment of 23 May 1996, §§18–21, especially §20) and C-11/95 (*Commission of the European Communities v Kingdom of Belgium*, Judgment of 10 September 1996, §37), also cited by Vanhamme, pp. 90–93. There are differences of opinion as to the concept of general principles of law as a source of international law, but as Meron succinctly points out (T. Meron, *The Humanization of International Law*, Leiden, Nijhoff, 2006, pp. 383–387), the approach limited to principles derived from domestic law has had little success in practice and jurisprudence, wheras more often reference is made to general principles of international law proper, albeit that this raises the question as to the distinction between these principles and customary international law (see on the latter also *infra*, Section F.3 of this chapter, notes 1817–1818 and the accompanying text).

1792 For an overview of the ECJ's case law on the ECHR, see, e.g. E. Guild & G. Lesieur (eds.), *The European Court of Justice on the European Convention on Human Rights. Who Said What, When?*, The Hague, Kluwer Law International, 1998. See also C. Kaddous, *supra* note 1739, pp. 303–318.

1793 Case C-4/73, *supra* note 1776, §13. This was *inter alia* repeated in Case C-540/03 (*supra* note 1784), §35: "*Fundamental rights form an integral part of the general principles of law the observance of which the Court ensures. For that purpose, the Court draws inspiration from ... the guidelines supplied by international instruments for the protection of human rights on which the Member States have collaborated or to which they are signatories*".

1794 France only ratified the ECHR on 3 May 1974 (the other Member States at the time had done so before the conclusion of the EEC Treaty). In *Nold* (*supra* note 1776) the applicant invoked the ECHR but the Court itself did not explicitly mention it. H.G. Schermers, *supra* note 1616, p. 83 submits that the ECJ had not yet taken into account France's ratification in this case. In any event, the ECJ soon explicitly referred to the ECHR, for the first time in its judgment of 28 October 1975 in Case 36/75 (*Roland Rutili v Ministre de l'intérieur*, §32, see F. Sudre, *supra* note 1782, p. 176). The ECJ has also occasionally stressed that all Member States are parties to some of the human rights treaties it has relied on; see, e.g. Case C-540/03, *supra* note 1784, §37.

from the ECHR's supervisory bodies.[1795] Nevertheless, the wording "*on which the member States have collaborated or of which they are signatories*" suggests that it is not necessary for all the Member States to be a party to a given human rights convention.[1796] Indeed, the ECJ discussed the ICCPR at a time when one of the Member States had not even signed this treaty, although it was not decisive in that case.[1797] This confirms the potential for binding the EC to some rules contained in treaties concluded by a significant number of its Member States. However, while the ECJ has thus largely incorporated human rights, especially those found in the ECHR, which is accorded particular significance,[1798] as general principles of EC law, i.e. subject to a transformation,[1799] it has not held

---

1795 See L. Sevon, 'General Principles of Community Law – Concluding Remarks', in U. Bernitz & J. Nergelius (eds.), *supra* note 1769, p. 221, referring to ECJ, Joint Cases C-74/95 and C-129/95 (*Criminal proceedings against X*, Judgment of 12 December 1996, §25). On the relationship between the ECJ and ECtHR, see, e.g. G. Harpaz, 'The European Court of Justice and Its Relations with the European Court of Human Rights: The Quest for Enhanced Reliance, Coherence and Legitimacy', 46 *C.M.L. Rev.* 2009, pp. 105–141.

1796 Compare A. Toth, *supra* note 1769, pp. 82–83, who submits that it is unclear under what conditions other conventions than the ECHR may be taken into account.

1797 See, e.g. Cases 374/87 (*Orkem v Commission of the European Communities*, Judgment of 18 October 1989, §§18 and 31) and 27/88 (*Solvay & Cie v Commission of the European Communities*, same date, ECR 1989-IV, pp. 3355–3358) and Joined cases C-297/88 and C-197/89 (*Massam Dzodzi v Belgian State*, Judgment of 18 October 1990, §68). See also W. Devroe & J. Wouters, *De Europese Unie. Het verdrag van Maastricht en zijn uitvoering: analyse en perspectieven*, Peeters, Leuven, 1996, pp. 95–96 note 542. At the time of this first judgment, Greece had not even signed the ICCPR (it would accede only in 1997) and Ireland had signed but not yet ratified it (it would ratify the ICCPR two months later). It should be noted, however, that the ECJ held that the ICCPR provision that was invoked was not applicable *ratione materiae* in the first case and was not breached in the second case. In Case 249/96 (*Lisa Jacqueline Grant and South-West Trains Ltd*, Judgment of 17 February 1998, §44) the ECJ clearly stated that "*The Covenant is one of the international instruments relating to the protection of human rights of which the Court takes account in applying the fundamental principles of Community law*" (see on the latter case also C. Kaddous, *supra* note 1739, pp. 322–324). Still, it has been pointed out that the ECJ has never annulled any provision on the basis of a (sole) violation of the ICCPR; see F. Sudre, *supra* note 1782, pp. 175–176. Vanhamme, p. 28, points out that some Member States were a party to the ICCPR before they joined the EC/EU and for them Article 307 EC Treaty would entail a priority of the ICCPR over any incompatible EC law.

1798 See, e.g. Joint Cases 46/87 and 227/88 (*Hoechst AG v Commission of the European Communities*, Judgment of 21 September 1989, §13); Opinion 2/94 (*supra* note 1769, §33); Case C-305/05 (*Ordre des barreaux francophones et germanophone and others*, 26 June 2007, §29) and F. Sudre, *supra* note 1782, p. 176.

1799 E.g. F. Sudre, *supra* note 1782, pp. 174–180 and 184–186. This is also the case under Article 6(2) EU Treaty ("*The Union shall respect fundamental rights, as guaranteed by the [ECHR] and as they result from the constitutional traditions common to the Member States,* as general principles of Community law"; F. Sudre, *supra* note 1782, pp. 186–187 describes this as an indirect incorporation) and would remain the case under Article 6(3) (renumbered 6(3)) EU Treaty as it is amended by the Lisbon Treaty (and the identical Article I-9 EU Constitution). This provision reads: "*Fundamental rights, as guaranteed by the [ECHR] and as they result from the constitutional traditions common to the Member States,* shall constitute general principles of the Union's law" (emphasis added). However, since the EU would also strive to that the EC is a party to the ECHR or bound as such.[1800] Nevertheless, it has been argued that in spite of this, the ECJ now *de facto* applies the ECHR as such.[1801] I will further explore the relevance of Article 6 EU Treaty and general principles of EC/EU law for the determination of the law applicable to ESDP operations in Part III below.

The fourth point that merits attention, is that the ECJ has not only bound the EC to human rights as general principles of EC law, but also the Member States when acting within the sphere of EC law.[1802] This has been confirmed, at least to some

---

accede to the ECHR under that provision it would be directly bound too. Some scholars have argued that this transformation does not ensure adequate respect for human rights; see, e.g. H. Rasmussen, 'On Legal Normative Dynamics and Jurisdictional Dialogue in the Field of Community General Principles of Law', in U. Bernitz & J. Nergelius (eds.), *supra* note 1769, pp. 43–45 and A. Toth, *supra* note 1769, pp. 79–87. On the other hand, others have submitted that the ECJ applies the ECHR as a minimum of protection; see, e.g. L. Sevon, *supra* note 1795, p. 221 and *infra* note 1801 and the accompanying text. R. Uerpmann, *supra* note 1616, pp. 41–42 sees the mechanism of general principles as one that permits a certain degree of autonomy from international obligations.

1800 E.g. C. Kaddous, *supra* note 1739, p. 305 and A. Toth, *supra* note 1769, p. 82. R. Uerpmann, *supra* note 1616, p. 39 points out that the Court of First Instance has explicitly held that "*the ECHR is not itself part of Community law*" in Case T-347/94 (*Mayr-Melnhof Kartongesellschaft mbH v. Commission of the European Communities*, Judgment of 14 May 1998, §311) and that "*the [ECHR] as such is not part of Community law*" in Case T-112/98 (*Mannesmannröhren-Werke AG v. Commission of the European Communities*, Judgment of 20 February 2001, §59). That the EC is not (yet) a party to the ECHR is among other things clear from the fact that the ECJ was asked for its opinion on EC accession to the ECHR and held that the EC was not competent to accede to this convention (opinion 2/94, *supra* note 1769). In light of the changed status of human rights in the EC/EU since the Treaty of Amsterdam (*supra* note 1782 and the accompanying text), it is doubtful whether this is still valid; see also in particular the creation of an EU Agency for Fundamental Rights (see Council Regulation (EC) No 168/2007 of 15 February 2007 establishing a European Union Agency for Fundamental Rights, *O.J. L* 53, 22 February 2007, p. 1 and www.fra.europa.eu; its competences are limited to Community law: *id.*, Articles 2–3; see generally G.N. Toggenburg, 'The Role of the New EU Fundamental Rights Agency: Debating the "Sex of Angels" or Improving Europe's Human Rights Performance', 33 *Eur. L. Rev.* 2008, pp. 385–398 and A. von Bogdandy & J. von Bernstorff, 'The EU Fundamental Rights Agency Within the European and International Human Rights Architecture: The Legal Framework and Some Unsettled Issues in a New Field of Administrative Law', 46 *C.M.L. Rev.* 2009, pp. 1035–1068). Compare more generally S. Besson, 'The European Union and Human Rights: Towards A Post-National Human Rights Institution?', 6 *H.R.L.R.* 2006, pp. 323–360.

1801 F. Sudre, *supra* note 1782, pp. 184–186.

1802 See, e.g. ECJ, Cases 222/84 (*Marguerite Johnston v Chief Constable of the Royal Ulster Constabulary*, Judgment of 15 May 1986, §§18–19); 5/88 (*Hubert Wachauf v Bundesamt für Ernährung und Forstwirtschaft*, Judgment of 13 July 1989, §19: "*[the requirement of the protection of fundamental rights in the Community legal order is] also binding on the Member States when they implement Community rules*"); C-260/89 (*Elliniki Radiophonia Tiléorassi AE and Panellinia Omospondia Syllogon Prossopikou v Dimotiki Etairia Pliroforissis and Sotirios Kouvelas and Nicolaos Avdellas and others*, Judgment of 18 June 1991, §§42–45, holding that "*limitations imposed on the power of the Member States to apply the provisions referred to in Articles 66 and 56 [EC] Treaty on grounds of public policy, public security and public health must be appraised in the light of the general principle of freedom of expression embodied in* extent,[1803] in the EU Charter of Fundamental Rights,[1804] in the EU Constitution[1805] and in the Lisbon Treaty.[1806] It is particularly relevant to ESDP operations, assuming it also applies to the EU and not just the EC,[1807] in that it

---

Article 10 [ECHR]"); 159/90 (*The Society for the Protection of Unborn Children Ireland Ltd v Stephen Grogan and others*, Judgment of 4 October 1991, §31, ruling that "*where national legislation falls within the field of application of Community law the Court, when requested to give a preliminary ruling, must provide the national court with all the elements of interpretation which are necessary in order to enable it to assess the compatibility of that legislation with the fundamental rights ... However, the Court has no such jurisdiction with regard to national legislation lying outside the scope of Community law*") and C-2/92 (*The Queen v Ministry of Agriculture, Fisheries and Food, ex parte Dennis Clifford Bostock*, Judgment of 24 March 1994, §16: "*the requirements flowing from the protection of fundamental rights in the Community legal order are also binding on Member States when they implement Community rules*"). See generally K. Lenaerts & P. Van Nuffel, *supra* note 1465, pp. 712 and 723–726; D. Scheuing, 'Zur Grundrechtsbindung der EU-Mitgliedstaaten', 40 *Europarecht* 2005, pp. 162–191 and J. Temple Lang, 'The Sphere in Which Member States are Obliged to Comply with the General Principles of Law and Community Fundamental Rights Principles', 18(2) *Legal Issues of European Integration* 1991, pp. 23–35. See also the references in H.D. Jarass, *EU-Grundrechte: ein Studien- und Handbuch*, Munich, C.H. Beck, 2005, p. 34. Compare T. Kingreen, *supra* note 1773, pp. 70–74, who seems to favour a less extensive binding of the Member States. Compare also with regard to the UN, de Wet, p. 200.

1803 Both texts cited in the next notes are restricted to the implementation of EU law, whereas the ECJ's jurisprudence binds Member States in somewhat broader terms (see *supra*, previous note). However, it would seem that this does not limit the ECJ's existing jurisprudence; see, e.g. R. Barents, *supra* note 1785, pp. 42–43 and D. Scheuing, *supra* previous note, pp. 178 (noting that as long as the Charter has no legal force, it cannot affect the legal situation in this respect) and 182–191 (arguing extensively that the corresponding provision in the EU Constitution does not entail a regression). But see M. Borowski, 'Allgemeine Bestimmungen', in J. Meyer (ed.), *Kommentar zur Charta der Grundrechte der Europäischen Union*, Baden-Baden, Nomos, 2003, pp. 561–564 and 568–570, arguing that the Charter intended to impose a limit compared to the ECJ's jurisprudence. Compare K. Lenaerts & P. Van Nuffel, *supra* note 1465, pp. 731–732; F. Debusseré, *supra* note 1784, section 4.2.1, notes 128–137 and the accompanying text; H.D. Jarass, *supra* note 1802, pp. 37–41 and D. Curtin & R. van Ooik, *supra* note 1773, pp. 108–109. Compare also P. Eeckhout, 'The EU Charter of Fundamental Rights and the Federal Question', 39 *C.M.L. Rev.* 2002, pp. 952–979.

1804 *Supra* note 1783, Article 51(1): "*The provisions of this Charter are addressed to ... the Member States only when they are implementing Union law*". See M. Borowski, *supra* previous note, pp. 561–564 and 568–570 and P. Eeckhout, *supra* previous note, pp. 952–979.

1805 Article II-51(1): "*The provisions of this Charter are addressed to ... the Member States only when they are implementing Union law*".

1806 Article 6(1) (renumbered 6(1)) EU Treaty as it would be amended refers to the "*Charter of Fundamental Rights of 7 December 2000, as adapted at Strasbourg, on 12 December 2007*". The text of the amended Charter is published in the *O.J. C* 305, 14 December 2007 and its Article 51(1) reads "*The provisions of this Charter are addressed to ... the Member States only when they are implementing Union law*". Interestingly, the explanation to this provision is limited to a reference to the ECJ's case law on Member States' human rights obligations under EC law (see *O.J. C* 305, 14 December 2007, p. 32).

1807 K. Lenaerts & P. Van Nuffel, *supra* note 1465, pp. 725–726 seem to take the view that in the implementation of the CFSP, the Member States would not be bound by the human rights obligations of the EU. However, given that the obligations under Article 6 EU Treaty are binding upon the EU, there does not seem to be a good reason why the situation in respect of the EU should differ from that in respect of the EC, even as regards the Member States. The lack of jurisdiction of the ECJ merely concerns the enforcement and cannot have an impact entails that Member States are bound by the EU's human rights obligations when they implement EU Joint Actions, including those concerning ESDP operations (see *infra*, Chapter 9).[1808]

ii. General Principles in the Legal Order of International Organizations Generally

Given the specific features of the EC, it is by no means certain that the ECJ's case law concerning general principles of law can be applied to other international organizations. However, there seems to be no obstacle in principle to such application, subject to appropriate adaptations to the specific nature of every international organization.[1809] Such adaptations would likely include less reliance on general principles derived from the domestic law of Member States,[1810] especially in organizations with a large membership, different principles derived from the proper legal order of each organization and greater reliance on general principles of international law proper, though perhaps less so for 'regional integration organizations'. The ECJ's practice of drawing inspiration from international agreements concluded by all or most Member States in principle lends itself to adoption by other international organizations, but does not seem to be applied very much, an exception being the UN's approach to international humanitarian law[1811] and some traces in the ILO Administrative Tribunal's jurisprudence.[1812]

---

on the substantive obligations. The only convincing argument in favour of a distinction would be if the human rights protection vis-à-vis the Member States in the EC is based on general principles that go beyond Article 6 EU Treaty and cannot be transposed to the EU. While the former may be true, at least to some extent (see *supra* note 1803 and the accompanying text), the latter is questionable.

1808 See also J. Arloth & F. Seidensticker, *The ESDP Crisis Management Operations of the European Union and Human Rights*, Berlin, Deutsches Institut für Menschenrechte, April 2007, p. 15 (available online at http://files.institut-fuer-menschenrechte.de/488/d65_v1_file_4649796b19cd6_Studie%20ESDP%20pdf%20version%2005-2007.pdf).

1809 E.-U. Petersmann, 'Time for a United Nations 'Global Compact' for Integrating Human Rights into the Law of Worldwide Organizations: Lessons from European Integration', 13 *E.J.I.L.* 2002, pp. 621–650, argues in favour of integrating human rights in the law of international organizations.

1810 E.g. Klein, p. 365 writes that general principles derived from domestic law play only a marginal role in the internal legal order of most international organizations. Similarly, A. Reinisch, *supra* note 1615, pp. 539–540.

1811 See *supra*, Section B.2, note 1636 of this chapter.

1812 E.g. *In re Franks (No. 2) and Vollering (No. 2)*, Judgment No. 1333 of 31 January 1994 (considerations, §5: "*The law that the Tribunal applies in entertaining claims that are put to it includes not just the written rules of the defendant organisation but the general principles of law and basic human rights*" – though apparently distinguishing between both); *I. M. B. v. International Atomic Energy Agency*, Judgement No. 2120 of 15 July 2002 (considerations, §§10–11: "*the Tribunal is of the view that paragraph 2(c) of SEC/NOT/1325 is unenforceable because it is contrary to fundamental principles of law. In fact, the provision improperly discriminates ... Discrimination on such grounds is contrary to the Charter of the United*

While it would require a more extensive analysis to compare to what extent other international organizations make use of general principles of law and what status such principles have there, it seems that the use is more limited and the status less.[1813] This may in part be explained by the usual absence or lesser extent of jurisdiction of an international judicial body which may rule that such principles exist[1814] (although their existence does not depend upon a judicial determination, tribunals are most likely to recognize their existence; while legal advisors/services of international organizations may also do so, their advice is often not public and is not necessarily always followed).

3. IUS COGENS

Ius cogens or peremptory norms of international law are not a separate source of international law, but rather a qualification given to a rule laid down in another source.[1815] However, since a rule of *ius cogens* must be (quasi) universally accepted as such,[1816] I would submit that such a rule will usually have the status of customary international law.[1817] Moreover, should such a rule be insufficiently

---

Nations, general principles of law and those which govern the international civil service, as well as international instruments on human rights. The principles of Article 26 of the International Covenant on Civil and Political Rights (1966), although not strictly binding on the Agency are relevant") and *J. M. W. v. European Patent Organisation*, Judgement No. 2292 of 4 February 2004 (consideration 11: "*the EPO as such is not a member of the Council of Europe and is not bound by the [ECHR] in the same way as signatory states. Nevertheless, the general principles enshrined in the Convention, particularly the principles of non-discrimination and the protection of property rights, are part of human rights, which, as declared by both the President of the Office and its Administrative Council in 1994, in compliance with the Tribunal's case law, apply to relations with staff*").

1813 Perhaps with the exception of international administrative law, especially in relation to staff of international organizations; see on this, e.g. AMERASINGHE, pp. 288–290 and the cases cited *supra* previous note. See also R. Kolb, 'General Principles of Procedural Law', in A. Zimmermann *et al.* (eds.), *supra* note 1766, pp. 793–835. However, even in this field their status is often less than within the EC and general principles are generally only used to interpret, supplement and fill gaps (*id.*, p. 290).

1814 This would also explain why precisely in the area of international administrative law, where international tribunals more often have compulsory jurisdiction, general principles of law do play a significant role also in quite a few international organizations (see *supra* previous note).

1815 E.g. BROWNLIE, p. 515 (who regards them as rules of customary law with a special quality); A. Cassese, *International Law*, Oxford, Oxford University Press, 2001, p. 138 (who describes *ius cogens* as an "*an upgrading of certain fundamental rules produced by traditional sources of law*") and A. Pellet, *supra* note 1766, p. 777. SHAW, pp. 65–119 and MALANCZUK, pp. 35–62, treat *ius cogens* under the heading hierarchy of sources after listing the different sources.

1816 See Articles 53 1969 and 1986 VCLT: "*a norm accepted and recognized by the international community of States as a whole as a norm from which no derogation is permitted and which can be modified only by a subsequent norm of general international law having the same character*".

1817 This view seems to be adopted *inter alia* by BROWNLIE, p. 515. See also the references and discussion in G. Cahin, *supra* note 1740, p. 615. Compare MALANCZUK, p. 58 (submitting that reflected in practice despite the presence of *opinio iuris* and a belief that it is a fundamental rule, it would probably constitute a general principle of international law.[1818] In either form, it is binding upon international organizations (see the preceding subsections).

This is confirmed by the inclusion of the *ius cogens* provisions of the 1969 VCLT in the 1986 VCLT (Articles 53 and 64), which also makes it clear that just like States, international organizations cannot derogate from these fundamental rules.[1819] This is also generally accepted in doctrine,[1820] including in respect of the UN Security Council[1821] and was confirmed by the ECJ's Court of First Instance.[1822]

---

ius cogens can be derived from custom and possibly treaties, but probably not from other sources), and Shaw, p. 118 (taking the view that *ius cogens* can be derived from custom and treaties, but not from other sources).

1818 Compare H. Schermers, *supra* note 1615, pp. 401–402, who seems to see a significant overlap between peremptory norms and general principles of law and discusses peremptory norms under a section entitled general principles of law. But see the view of Malanczuk, *supra* previous note (however, at p. 49 Malanczuk does seem to leave open the possibility that *ius cogens* rules may stem from general principles of law) and the explicit opposition to deriving *ius cogens* from general principles of law in Shaw, p. 118. Compare also the reflections by T. Meron, *supra* note 1791, pp. 394–396 (with further references).

1819 See the commentary to Article 53 of the ILC's 1982 draft (that became Article 53 1986 VCLT without any changes) in *Y.I.L.C.* 1982-II, Part 2, p. 56.

1820 According to the ILA in its 2004 *Final Report on the Accountability of International Organisations* (*supra* note 1610), p. 18, "*peremptory norms of international law are applicable to both Member States and [international organisations]*". See also Klein, pp. 362–363; M. Hirsch, *supra* note 1623, pp. 30–31; Lawson, pp. 163–166; H. Schermers, *supra* note 1615, pp. 401–402; S. Skogly, *supra* note 1619, pp. 90–91; Vanhamme, pp. 98–101 and 124–125 and R.A. Wessel, *supra* note 1253, p. 47.

1821 See, e.g. the separate opinion of Judge Lauterpacht to the Order of the International Court of Justice in *Application of the Convention on the Prevention and Punishment of the Crime of Genocide (Bosnia and Herzegovina v. Serbia and Montenegro)* of 13 September 1993, §§99–104; A. Aust, 'The Role of Human Rights in Limiting the Enforcement Powers of the Security Council: A Practitioner's View', in E. de Wet & A. Nollkaemper (eds.), *Review of the Security Council by Member States*, Antwerp, Intersentia, 2003, p. 34; M. Sassoli, *Article 43 of the Hague Regulations and Peace Operations in the Twenty-first Century*, background paper, June 2004 (available online at http://ihl.ihlresearch.org), p. 16; A. Orakhelashvili, 'The Impact of Peremptory Norms on the Interpretation and Application of United Nations Security Council Resolutions', 16 *E.J.I.L.* 2005, pp. 68–69 (arguing that constitutive instruments of international organizations must be interpreted in conformity with *ius cogens* as not permitting a violation of the latter and that such instruments are void under the 1969 VCLT where this is not possible) and A. Orakhelashvili, 'The Post-War Settlement in Iraq: The UN Security Council Resolution 1483 (2003) and General International Law', 8 *J.C.S.L.* 2003, p. 308. But see Zwanenburg, pp. 149–150. Compare E. Lagrange, 'Le Conseil de sécurité des Nations Unies peut-il violer le droit international?', 37 *R.B.D.I./B.T.I.R.* 2004, pp. 568–592, especially pp. 585–591 (who seems to argue that the Security Council might even derogate from *ius cogens*, albeit only in individual decisions, to the extent that the Charter or the relevant rule of *ius cogens* permits it to do so and to the extent that it is strictly necessary).

1822 Cases T-306/01 (*Yusuf and Al Barakaat International Foundation v. Council and Commission*, especially §§231–259 and 277–282) and T-315/01 (*Kadi v. Council and Commission*, especially

G. ONLY EXCEPTIONALLY INTERNATIONAL AGREEMENTS CONCLUDED BY THE MEMBER STATES

1. GENERAL CONSIDERATIONS

Of the topics addressed in this chapter, the question whether international organizations are bound by some of the international agreements concluded by their Member States is one of the few topics on which much has been written, especially in the framework of the EC/EU.[1823] The primary underlying reason why it is often attempted to achieve such a binding seems to be a concern that Member States could otherwise evade their obligations by transferring powers to an international organization without the obligations attached to the exercise of such powers.[1824]

However, a binding as such seems contrary to the relative nature of treaties[1825] – see also the discussion of the reverse question whether Member States are bound by agreements concluded by an international organization[1826] – and is not obvious. Moreover, as I will demonstrate below, there seem to be very few cases in which such a binding has been accepted: to my knowledge only the EC in relation to the GATT and two customs agreements and under strict conditions that are rarely met in other cases,[1827] as well as the case of the European Defence

§§181–208 and 226–231), judgments of 21 September 2005. The Court of First Instance upheld EC anti-terrorism measures that were based on UN Security Council resolutions, ruling that the latter were binding upon the EC and its Member States and that it could not review their legality except under *ius cogens*. The ECJ itself annulled this judgment but did not reject that the UN Security Council is bound by *ius cogens* rules.

1823 Most of the publications cited *supra* note 1616 address this aspect. See also the references in O. Elias, *supra* note 1248, p. 4 note 1 and LAWSON, pp. 138–143.

1824 E.g. M. Hirsch, *supra* note 1623, pp. 53–54 and KLEIN, pp. 338–342. On obligations related to powers transferred to an international organization, see generally M. Hirsch, *supra* note 1623, pp. 38–60.

1825 Although KLEIN, pp. 343–344 is right in stating that the 1986 VCLT does not cover the effect for international organizations of treaties concluded only between States (and that neither does the 1969 VCLT), this convention does cover agreements to which at least one international organization is a party. It is unlikely that a different conclusion than the relativity of treaties would exist according to whether or not an agreement counts an international organization among its parties, all the more so since this rule also exists in the 1969 VCLT and arguably reflects a basic principle of not binding third parties to a treaty without their consent.

1826 *Supra*, Section D.1 of this chapter, notes 1708–1714 and the accompanying text.

1827 KLEIN, pp. 339–340 also mentions Article 3(a)ii of the INTELSAT operating agreement of 20 August 1971 (Washington DC, 1220 *U.N.T.S.* 149 (1981)), which expressly provides for a succession/substitution but relating to a specific transit phase (limited to obligations incurred under a provisional agreement). Moreover, one might wonder whether this provision would have an automatic effect on third parties. T. Ahmed & I. de Jesús Butler, *supra* note 1773,

Community.[1828] Obviously, when Member States conclude an agreement on behalf of an organization, this is a different matter and in such a case the organization will be bound.[1829]

One of the bases for such a binding which has been studied in doctrine is an application by analogy of the rules of State succession in respect of treaties.[1830] However, this is hardly a convincing thesis. First, only in some cases is there a real transfer rather than the creation of new and distinct powers.[1831] Second, even where there is a real transfer of powers to an international organization, this does not, and at least not always or not fully, fit within the definition of State succession, even when applied by analogy. For instance, Article 1(2)b of the 1978 VCSST defines "*succession of States*" as "*the replacement of one State by another in the responsibility for the international relations of territory*", whereas it is clear that international organizations hardly ever, not even in the case of the EC, entirely replace their Member States in the responsibility for their international relations.[1832] It may also be noted that the rules of State succession do not appear

p. 789 also add a fisheries agreement at issue in Cases 3, 4 and 6–76, *Cornelis Kramer and others*, 17 July 1976, but this does not seem to be a case of full substitution.

1828 Article 80 of the EDC Treaty bound the EDC to any Member State treaty concerning the law of armed conflict ("*1. Dans l'exercice de la compétence qui lui est conféré par le présent traité, et sans préjudice des droits et obligations des États membres: ... la Communauté est tenue au respect des règles de droit conventionnel de la guerre qui obligent un ou plusieurs États membres*").

1829 On this mechanism, see Klein, pp. 326–330. This should be distinguished from cases in which Member States are authorized to conclude an agreement in the interest of an organization but not formally on its behalf; see in respect of the EC, *supra*, Chapter 5, note 1255.

1830 See the discussion in Klein, pp. 334–335; Lawson, pp. 85–98; K. Osteneck, *supra* note 1850, pp. 113–115 and H.F. van Panhuys, *supra* note 1616, p. 447 (the latter author submits that a transfer of obligations is not to be assumed too readily).

1831 Similarly Klein, p. 342 and E. Lagrange, *supra* note 1675, pp. 570–571 (who seems to consider that this is always the case). This may have been an implicit underlying factor for the ECtHR in its Kosovo judgment of 31 May 2007 in joined cases *Behrami and Behrami v. France* (No. 71412/01) and *Saramati v. France, Germany and Norway* (No. 78166/01), in which it focused on attribution of conduct in a UN mandated peace operation in Kosovo to the UN, as well as extraterritoriality, to distinguish this case from that in *Bosphorus* (§151). In fact, if the Court absolutely wanted to reach the result which it reached, it could have motivated its judgment far better by stating that in this case there had been no transfer of Member State jurisdiction to the UN as the Member States had no prior jurisdiction to do what the UN authorized them to do in Kosovo (see *infra*, Chapter 9.E). I would not necessarily agree with that view but it is more plausible than the attribution argument on which the Court relied.

1832 Similarly, K. Osteneck, *supra* note 1850, pp. 113–115. Compare Klein, pp. 334–335 and the references there, noting that at best it is only a partial succession. Interestingly, Lawson, p. 87–88, and H.G. Schermers, *supra* note 1616, pp. 87–88, note that a proposal to include specific rules on succession of treaty obligations to international organizations in the work of the ILC and UN was rejected, although Lawson does not seem to see this as decisive. Schermers himself seems to qualify the substitution theory as a kind of succession (*id.*). The 2006 ILA Report on *Aspects of the Law of State Succession* (available online at www.ila-hq.

to be applied to succession between international organizations.[1833] Third, though this is not a conclusive argument, the customary status of the rules on State succession is notoriously unclear[1834] and their application by analogy would be a difficult exercise.[1835]

A few other theories which have been considered relate, in one way or another, to the transfer of powers, either on itself or in combination with the maxim *nemo plus juris transferre potest quam ipse habet.*[1836] However, binding international organizations to agreements concluded by their Member States on this basis poses various difficulties, regardless of whether it is seen as a case of succession or as part of the transfer or grant of powers. For instance, it is doubtful whether it can be applied where there is a creation of new powers rather than the transfer of existing powers, which is often the case with international organizations.[1837] Furthermore, it would depend upon the timing of the transfer of power and would only cover a State's obligations existing before such a transfer and not

org) explicitly states that "*It is clear that the creation of a supranational international organization, e.g. the European Community/European Union, does not amount to a situation of unification of States*" and does not include this under another form of succession either (§9, p. 12, see also §21, p. 15).

1833 See *supra* note 1662 and the accompanying text.

1834 *Id.* See also the 2002 ILA Report on *Aspects of the Law of State Succession* (available online at www.ila-hq.org), p. 2; Lawson, pp. 88–89 (noting that the ICJ left the question open in respect of Article 34 of the 1978 VCSST in its judgment of 25 September 1997 in the *Case concerning the Gabcíkovo-Nagymaros Project* (Hungary/Slovakia), §123) and M. Hartwig, *Die Haftung der Mitgliedstaaten für Internationale Organisationen*, Berlin, Springer, 1993, pp. 83–91 and 337.

1835 Presumably, this kind of succession would be closest to that of a Union of States, see K. Meessen, *supra* note 1616, p. 489 and K. Osteneck, *supra* note 1850, p. 114. But see the ILA's view *supra* note 1832. Compare Lawson, pp. 89–95, who argues in favour of an application of the continuity principle to human rights treaties but seems to consider that in practice what is applied for States is rather a simplified continuity (or succession).

1836 See, e.g. Klein, pp. 341–342 and especially pp. 344–349 (who seems, however, to mix this argument to some extent with the one that international organizations are, as a subject of international law, bound by general international law (at pp. 346–347); the latter argument may well be valid (see *supra*, Section F.1–3 of this Chapter) but cannot simply be extended to treaty obligations) and H. Schermers, *supra* note 1615, pp. 403–404. A variant is the 'Hypothektheorie', according to which any powers transferred to an international organization are transferred with the corresponding obligations; see, e.g. A. von Arnauld, *supra* note 1890, p. 206 and the discussion and references in A. Leenen, *supra* note 1241, p. 214 (deeming this theory inapplicable in respect of external relations); K. Osteneck, *supra* note 1850, p. 115 (who rejects this theory herself); C. Tomuschat, 'Case law – Court of Justice Case T-306/01, Ahmed Ali Yusuf and Al Barakaat International Foundation v. Council and Commission' (annotation), 43 *C.M.L. Rev.* 2006, pp. 542–543 (noting that this theory has now been rejected in German scholarship) and R. Uerpmann, *supra* note 1616, pp. 34–35 (who translates *Hypothek* as a servitude and notes that it is problematic from a time perspective and from the point of view that (some) international organizations exercise a proper jurisdiction and "*not a bunch of Member State jurisdictions*").

1837 See *supra* note 1831.

agreements concluded after such a transfer.[1838] Moreover, it would entail binding an organization to every obligation in force for any of its Member States, at least where it is relevant to the activities of the organization.[1839] That is clearly not accepted in practice[1840] and could lead to incompatible obligations.[1841] Alternatively, it would mean splitting up the organization's exercise of powers according to which Member State would, absent the transfer to the organization, have exercised jurisdiction over a person or entity, which would be impossible to apply in practice. A further alternative is only to take into account agreements to which all (or most) Member States are a party[1842] but this makes it less effective for organizations with a large membership[1843] and, moreover, seems to be at odds with the basis and underlying reason invoked for binding an organization: Member States could perfectly escape their obligations and transfer more rights than they have (by not concurrently transferring obligations) as long as they are not shared by all (or most) Member States. Thus this theory is unworkable if applied in full and a selective application so much departs from its basis that it is hardly convincing.

1838 This problem is recognized by H. Schermers, *supra* note 1615, pp. 403–404, who nevertheless tries to develop some arguments in favour of binding international organizations at least under some circumstances to agreements concluded by Member States after a transfer of powers.

1839 This is recognized by E. Lagrange, *supra* note 1656, p. 428 and H.F. van Panhuys, *supra* note 1616, p. 447, who states that "*the logical implication of this view would be that no institution could perform any act the effects of which would be incompatible with duties binding under international law upon any member State vis-à-vis a third State prior to the coming into force of the relevant treaty and still in force*" and submits that this cannot be assumed. H. Schermers, *supra* note 1615, p. 403 proposes some differentiation according to the nature of the agreements concerned.

1840 For instance, NATO Member States not party to AP I will not accept that NATO is bound by AP I (a number of Member States that have acceded to NATO more recently were parties to AP I before this accession, e.g. Hungary, Latvia and Estonia to name but a few). Likewise, the UN does not feel bound by the ECHR even though this treaty was already in force for Switzerland when this country became a member of the UN. Even within the EC, when the ECJ applies treaty provisions as general principles of law, especially concerning human rights, it requires at least a significant commonality (see *supra*, Section F.2.i of this chapter). H.F. van Panhuys, *supra* note 1616, p. 447 submits, in relation to the EC, that "*[s]uch a far-reaching limitation [i.e. respect for all prior member State treaty obligations] on the jurisdiction of the [EC] is hardly to be assumed*", although he would accept broad participation in a treaty by Member States as presumptive evidence against EC powers that would infringe that treaty.

1841 See also E. Lagrange, *supra* note 1656, p. 428 and E. Lagrange, *supra* note 1675, p. 571.

1842 In this sense Klein, pp. 344–349. H. Schermers, *supra* note 1615, p. 403, takes this into account but argues in favour of a presumption that an organization is bound even where only some of its Member States are bound by a treaty. Compare M. Hirsch, *supra* note 1623, pp. 55–59, who suggests that where a majority of Member States are bound, the international organization will be bound if the Member States that are not bound do not object and there are no other inconsistent obligations. If there is to be a compromise, this may be a workable and acceptable one.

1843 See also Klein, p. 342.

In addition, within the EC Article 307 EC Treaty, which allows a Member State to act contrary to EC law where this is required to comply with obligations it has towards third States under agreements entered into before its entry into the EC,[1844] does not entail that the EC is bound by such agreements but only allows the Member State(s) concerned to invoke them, although it does oblige the EC not to impede that Member State from complying with its obligations.[1845] This provision would be superfluous if the EC were automatically bound by earlier agreements binding its Member States.[1846]

However, the jurisprudence of the ECJ in relation to the ECHR shows that there may be indirect ways of binding an international organization to at least some rules laid down in Member State treaties. Moreover, it must be noted that binding international organizations to agreements concluded by their Member States is not the only way to ensure that Member States do not evade their obligations. Continuing to hold Member States responsible for any violations of their obligations even in respect of powers transferred to an international organization may be an alternative way to achieve this aim. This possibility, which, admittedly, is not without difficulties either, will therefore be discussed in the next section.

1844 This provision has given rise to some discussion and has been clarified to a considerable extent in case law; see generally V. Constantinesco *et al.*, *Traité instituant la CEE: commentaire article par article*, Paris, Economica, 1992, pp. 1497–1508; P. Eeckhout, *supra* note 1431, pp. 333–342; C. Kaddous, *supra* note 1739, pp. 272–300; E.-U. Petersmann & C. Spennemann, 'Artikel 307 EG', in H. von der Groeben & J. Schwarze (eds.), *supra* note 1610, pp. 1643–1665; K. Schmalenbach, 'Article 307', in C. Calliess & M. Ruffert (eds.), *supra* note 1711, pp. 2180–2186 and VANHAMME, pp. 260–265 and the jurisprudence cited there. Compare R. Voss, *supra* note 1616, pp. 166–167, who regards this provision as a manifestation of a constitutional principle of integration in conformity with international law. The applicability of Article 307 to treaties concluded by Member States that acceded after the founding members was consistently included in accession treaties and has now been incorporated in Article 307 EC Treaty (see P. Eeckhout, *supra* note 1431, p. 334). However, Article 307 remains problematic in that the evolution of EC powers may mean that a Member State can lawfully conclude an agreement with a third State in an area that later becomes an (exclusive) Community competence and that Member State can, at least in a strict reading of this provision, not invoke compliance with such an agreement to refuse the application of later EC law: see, e.g. J. Boulois, *supra* note 1616, p. 68 and K. Meessen, *supra* note 1616, pp. 489–491. For recent case law, see the judgments of the ECJ of 3 March 2009 in Cases C-205/06, *Commission v. Austria* and C-249/06, *Commission v. Sweden*. Compare generally H.G. Schermers, 'Constituent Treaties of International Organisations Conflicting with Anterior Treaties', in J. Klabbers & R. Lefeber (eds.), *Essays on the Law of Treaties: A Collection of Essays in Honour of Bert Vierdag*, The Hague, Nijhoff, 1998, pp. 19–30 and See also more generally J. Klabbers, *Treaty Conflict and the European Union*, Cambridge, Cambridge University Press, 2008.

1845 See Case 812/79 (*Attorney General v Juan C. Burgoa*, Judgment of 14 October 1980, §§8–9) and J. Boulois, *supra* note 1616, p. 69; J.-C. Gautron & L. Grard, *supra* note 1667, pp. 88–92 and A. Leenen, *supra* note 1241, pp. 208–211. See also KLEIN, p. 332, writing that this provision makes these treaty rules opposable but not binding upon the EC.

1846 In this sense also K. Meessen, *supra* note 1616, p. 489.

But I will now first turn more extensively to Member State treaties, starting off with the GATT and Customs Agreements as the prominent but isolated examples of the binding of an international organization to such treaties, followed by the ECHR as a marked contrast (and a key human rights treaty that will be crucial in Chapter 9 below), as well as other Member State treaties, in particular the UN Charter (given its primary status in international law and the availability of recent interesting case law), to conclude with the situation in other international organizations.

2. THE EC, GATT AND CUSTOMS AGREEMENTS

To my knowledge, the only cases where an international organization has succeeded or substituted its Member States in respect of treaties concluded by the latter are those of the EC in relation to the GATT and a few customs agreements (compare *infra*, Section G.4.iii of this chapter on the UN Charter in recent terrorism cases). These cases, especially that of the GATT, are well-known[1847] and I will only briefly mention their key features.

As the EC had been granted exclusive competences in the field of external trade relations,[1848] the question soon arose whether the EC itself was bound by the GATT, even though it was not formally the EC but only the Member States that were parties to this treaty. In the celebrated *International Fruit Company* cases, the ECJ held that the EC had taken the place of its Member States in relation to this agreement.[1849] The Court based this conclusion mainly on the following considerations:

> 10. ... at the time when they concluded the [EEC Treaty] the member States were bound by the obligations of the [GATT].
> 11. By concluding a treaty between them they could not withdraw from their obligations to third countries.
> 12. On the contrary, their desire to observe the [GATT undertakings] follows as much from the very provisions of the EEC Treaty as from the declarations made by the member States on the presentation of the Treaty to the [GATT Contracting Parties] ...
> 13. That intention was made clear in particular by Article 110 of the EEC Treaty, ..., as well as by [Article 234 §1].

1847 See, e.g. the references *infra* note 1850; C. Kaddous, *supra* note 1739, pp. 276–281 and Lawson, pp. 80–82.

1848 See especially Article 133 (ex 113) EC Treaty.

1849 Joint Cases 21–24/72, *International Fruit Company NV and others v Produktschap voor Groenten en Fruit*, Judgement of 12 December 1972, especially §§10–18.

> 14. The Community has assumed the functions inherent in the tariff and trade policy, ..., by virtue of Articles 111 and 113 of the Treaty.
> 15 By conferring those powers on the Community, the member States showed their wish to bind it by the obligations entered into under the [GATT].
> 16. Since the entry into force of the EEC Treaty and more particularly, since the setting up of the common external tariff, the transfer of powers which has occurred in the relations between member States and the Community has been put into concrete form in different ways within the framework of the [GATT] and has been recognized by the other Contracting Parties.
> 17. In particular, since that time, the Community, acting through its own institutions, has appeared as a partner in the tariff negotiations and as a party to the agreements ... concluded within the framework [of the GATT], in accordance with ... Article 114 ... EEC Treaty ...
> 18. It therefore appears that, in so far as under the EEC Treaty the Community has assumed the powers previously exercised by member States in the area governed by the [GATT], the provisions of that agreement have the effect of binding the Community.

This has been interpreted as requiring the following elements for such a 'substitution' to take place: all Member States are a party to the agreement, (exclusive and/or exercised) competences in respect of the agreement have been transferred to the EC, the Member States and the EC have intended that the EC substitute them and the third parties to the agreement have accepted this.[1850] Although some authors initially saw room for a broader application of this theory,[1851] most scholars now agree that although it has a potential for extension to other treaties, its conditions will rarely be met.[1852] Indeed, the ECJ has only applied the theory to two other (customs) conventions[1853] and has rejected a broader application thereof put forward in two recent decisions of the Court of First Instance (see *infra*, Section G.4.iii of this chapter).

1850 Similarly KLEIN, pp. 335–336; A. Leenen, *supra* note 1241, pp. 211–215 and 224–230; K. Schmalenbach, *supra* note 1844, p. 2185 and VANHAMME, pp. 107–108. Compare K. Meessen, *supra* note 1616, pp. 489–490, who stresses the consent of all parties concerned and K. Osteneck, 'Die völkerrechtliche Verplichtung der EG zur Umsetzung von UN-Sanktionen', 1 *Z. Eur. S.* 1998, pp. 118–122 (who seems to focus on an external manifestation of the taking over of powers (rather than the will of the Member States) and elaborates on the acceptance of third parties).

1851 See, e.g. P. Pescatore, 'External Relations in the Case-Law of the Court of Justice of the European Communities', 16 *C.M.L. Rev.* 1979, pp. 637–638 and the references in KLEIN, p. 336. See also O. Jacot-Guillarmod, *supra* note 1616, pp. 123–135, arguing that this doctrine could be extended to other substantive law treaty obligations but not to institutional ones.

1852 E.g. M. Bothe, *supra* note 1616, p. 126; G. Cahin, *supra* note 1740, p. 522; J. Boulois, *supra* note 1616, p. 69; KLEIN, pp. 335–340 (though questioning whether this would not be desirable) and K. Meessen, *supra* note 1616, pp. 489–490 (seeing some room for application to other treaties but accepting that for most treaties the criteria will not be met).

1853 Case 38/75 (*Douaneagent der NV Nederlandse Spoorwegen v Inspecteur der invoerrechten en accijnzen*, Judgement of 19 November 1975, §21). See, e.g. A. Leenen, *supra* note 1241, p. 217.

3. THE EC/EU AND THE ECHR[1854]

It has been set out above how the ECJ has in fact incorporated the ECHR in the EC legal order by way of general principles of EC law but that, despite its virtual application of the ECHR as such and the reference to the ECHR in Article 6 EU Treaty, it has not held that the EC/EU is bound by the ECHR as such nor that it is a party thereto (*supra*, Section F.2.i of this chapter). Although some have argued that the substitution theory set out by the ECJ in respect of the GATT could also be applied to the ECHR,[1855] this has clearly not been endorsed.

The European Court of Human Rights too has never ruled that the EC/EU is bound by the ECHR and has always declined jurisdiction to hear applications brought against the EC/EU as such.[1856] However, it has occasionally left open the possibility that the EC/EU Member States might, at least in some circumstances, be responsible for violations of the ECHR by measures adopted in the EC/EU sphere. This will be addressed below in Section H of this chapter.

1854 See also generally D. Frank, *Verantwortlichkeit für die Verletzung der Europäischen Menschenrechtskonvention durch internationale Organisationen: unter besonderer Berücksichtigung der Verantwortlichkeit der EG, EU und von Europol*, Basel, Helbing & Lichtenhahn, 1999; J.-P. Jacqué, 'Communauté européenne et Convention européenne des droits de l'homme', in L.-E. Pettiti, E. Decaux & P.-H. Imbert (eds.), *La Convention européenne des droits de l'homme*, Paris, Economica, 1999 (2nd ed.), pp. 83–100; J-P. Jacqué, 'The Convention and the European Communities', in R. St. J. Macdonald, F. Matscher & H. Petzold (eds.), *The European System for the Protection of Human Rights*, Dordrecht, Nijhoff, 1993, pp. 889–907; G. Ress, 'Die EMRK und das europäische Gemeinschaftsrecht: Überlegungen zu den Beziehungen zwischen den Europäischen Gemeinschaften und der Europäischen Menschenrechtskonvention', 2 *Z. Eur. S.* 1999, pp. 471–485 and J. Vande Lanotte & Y. Haeck (eds.), *Handboek EVRM. Deel 1. Algemene beginselen*, Antwerp, Intersentia, 2005, pp. 753–780. See also J.H. Wiethoff, *Das konzeptionelle Verhältnis von EuGH und EGMR. Unter besonderer Berücksichtigung der aktuellen Verfassungsentwicklung der Europäischen Union*, Baden-Baden, Nomos, 2008.

1855 The European Commission suggested this might already have been the case in its 1979 memorandum on EC accession to the ECHR: see *Bulletin des Communautés européennes*, supplément 2/79, p. 10, also referred to in Klein, p. 336. See also W. Devroe & J. Wouters, *De Europese Unie. Het verdrag van Maastricht en zijn uitvoering: analyse en perspectieven*, Peeters, Leuven, 1996, pp. 96–97 and the references in C. Kaddous, *supra* note 1739, pp. 305–306, especially note 1329. W. Ganshof van der Meersch, *supra* note 1616, p. 194, argued that the EC was bound by the ECHR but it is not clear whether he based this on the substitution theory. *Contra*: J. Boulois, *supra* note 1616, p. 69 and Lawson, pp. 82–85. Compare A. Berramdane, 'La Cour européenne des droits de l'homme juge du droit de l'Union européenne', *R.D.U.E.* 2006, pp. 253–254, who on the one hand seems to argue that the European Court of Human Rights in fact applies the substitution theory to the EC in respect of the ECHR but on the other hand notes that the Court has not accepted complaints against the EC, while the author himself rejects substitution in this case. For a recent argument in favour of succession/substitution in respect of human rights treaties, see T. Ahmed & I. de Jesús Butler, *supra* note 1773, pp. 788–792 (arguing that general international law and the *Kadi* and *Yusuf* cases (see *infra*, Section G.4.iii of this chapter) support this).

1856 See, after an elaborate analysis, Lawson, pp. 39–51 and 518.

The Lisbon Treaty envisages, in addition to the incorporation of a human rights catalogue, that the EU will accede to the ECHR,[1857] which requires an amendment of or protocol to the ECHR,[1858] and will make the EU a party in its own right (thereby arguably also confirming that it is not yet a party).

4. THE EC/EU AND OTHER MEMBER STATE TREATIES, INCLUDING THE UN CHARTER

i. *General*

Where the conditions for substitution are not met and there is no acceptance or incorporation in one way or another, whether imposed on or adopted by the organization, practice and the arguments set out above imply that an international organization is not bound by an international agreement to which (some of) its Member States are a party. Indeed, in practice most international organizations do not consider themselves bound by agreements to which they have not consented in one way or another.[1859]

This is also the case for the EC/EU, as is clear from the ECJ's limited application of the substitution theory, its position towards the ECHR and its interpretation of Article 307 EC Treaty (see the preceding subsections).

ii. *The UN Charter*

For the purpose of this book, it is necessary to consider the position of the UN Charter and of decisions adopted pursuant thereto, especially by the UN Security

---

1857 See Article 6(2) (renumbered 6(2)) EU Treaty as amended by the Lisbon Treaty ("*The Union shall accede to the European Convention for the Protection of Human Rights and Fundamental Freedoms. Such accession shall not affect the Union's competences as defined in the Treaties*") and Protocol No. 5 concerning the modalities of that accession. See also Article I-9(2) EU Constitution. For a wider discussion of one of the modalities that would have to be dealt with, see G. Thallinger, 'The Rule of Exhaustion of Local Remedies in the Context of the Responsibility of International Organisations', 77 *Nordic J.I.L.* 2008, pp. 401–428.

1858 See Article 17 of Protocol No. 14 to the ECHR, Strasbourg, 13 May 2004, *C.E.T.S.* No. 194, which would insert a new paragraph in Article 59 ECHR stipulating that "*The European Union may accede to this Convention*". Because Protocol 14 has not yet entered into force (due to the Russian failure to ratify it so far), the parties to the ECHR have adopted a Protocol 14*bis* (Strasbourg, 27 May 2009, *C.E.T.S.* No. 204, which entered into force on 1 October 2009) to provisionally apply some key provisions of this Protocol. See also the Dutch report in the 2 June 2009 *Kamerbrief inzake het verslag van de 119e ministriële bijeenkomst van de Raad van Europa op 11–12 mei 2009 te Madrid* (www.minbuza.nl/nl/Actueel/Kamerstukken/2009/06/Kamerbrief_inzake_het_verslag_van_de_119e_ministriële_bijeenkomst_van_de_Raad_van_Europa_op_11_12_mei_2009_te_Madrid). Protocol 14*bis* does not include the provision permitting the EU's accession to the ECHR.

1859 See Klein, p. 343. At p. 375 the author admits that his own view to the contrary is not supported by practice neither by the views of most international organizations.

Council.[1860] Two aspects are relevant: on the one hand, does the special position of the UN Charter make it binding on international organizations generally and, on the other hand, does the EC/EU legal order accord a special status to the UN Charter. Also, the EC and EU are bound, pursuant to the thesis defended above, to any rules of UN law that also reflect customary international law.

Concerning the special position of the UN Charter, reflected especially in its Article 103, it must be said first of all that this provision itself does not bind international organizations as such, since they are not a party to the Charter.[1861] Article 2(6) of the Charter offers no solution either, since it only refers to the conduct of third *States*.[1862] Pursuant to Article 25 UN Charter, only members

---

1860 Most of the literature concerns sanctions. See generally N. Angelet, 'La mise en oeuvre des mesures coercitives économiques des Nations Unies dans la Communauté européenne', 26 *R.B.D.I./B.T.I.R.* 1993, pp. 500–533; S. Bohr, 'Sanctions by the United Nations Security Council and the European Community', 4 *E.J.I.L.* 1993, pp. 256–268; I. Canor, '"Can Two Walk Together, Except They Be Agreed?". The Relationship between International Law and European Law: The Incorporation of United Nations Sanctions against Yugoslavia into European Community Law Through the Perspective of the European Court of Justice', 35 *C.M.L. Rev.* 1998, pp. 137–187; W. Devroe & J. Wouters, *supra* note 1797, pp. 625–628; P. Eeckhout, *supra* note 1431, pp. 424–444; C.D. Ehlermann, 'Communautés européennes et sanctions internationales: une réponse à J. Verhoeven', 18 *R.B.D.I./B.T.I.R.* 1984–1985, pp. 96–110; O. Elias, *supra* note 1248, pp. 26–24; R. Fornasier, 'Quelques réflexions sur les sanctions internationales en droit communautaire', No. 402 *R.M.C.U.E.* 1996, pp. 670–677; P. Kapteyn, 'The Role of the ECJ in Implementing Security Council Resolutions', in E. de Wet & A. Nollkaemper (eds.), *Review of the Security Council by Member States*, Antwerp, Intersentia, 2003, pp. 57–62; P.-J. Kuiper, 'Implementation of binding Security Council resolutions by the EU/EC'; in *id.*, pp. 39–55; N. Lavranos, *Legal Interaction between Decisions of International Organizations and European Law*, Groningen, Europa Law Publishing, 2004, pp. 94–100; K. Lenaerts & E. de Smijter, 'The United Nations and the European Union: Living Apart Together', in K. Wellens (ed.), *International Law: Theory and Practice: Essays in Honour of Eric Suy*, The Hague, Nijhoff, 1998, pp. 447–453; K. Osteneck, *supra* note 1850, pp. 103–132; K. Osteneck, *Die Umsetzung von UN-Wirtschaftssanktionen durch die Europäische Gemeinschaft: völker- und europarechtliche Rahmenbedingungen für ein Tätigwerden der Europäischen Gemeinschaft im Bereich von UN-Wirtschaftssanktionsregimen unter besonderer Berücksichtigung der Umsetzungspraxis der EG-Organe*, Berlin, Springer, 2004; R. Pavoni, 'UN Sanctions in EU and National Law: The Centro-Com Case', 48 *I.C.L.Q.* 1999, pp. 582–612; M. Vaucher, 'L'évolution récente de la pratique des sanctions communautaires à l'encontre des Etats tiers', 29 *R.T.D.E.* 1993, pp. 39–59 and J. Verhoeven, 'Communautés européennes et sanctions interntionales', 18 *R.B.D.I./B.T.I.R.* 1984–1985, pp. 79–95. For a general appraisal of the attitude of the EU and its Member States towards the UN Charter, see B. Fassbender, 'The Better Peoples of the United Nations? Europe's Practice and the United Nations', 15 *E.J.I.L* 2004, pp. 857–884, especially pp. 863–872. See also more generally X., 'Symposium: Europe and International Law', 15 *E.J.I.L.* 2004, pp. 857–1040; N.D. White, 'The Ties That Bind: The EU, the UN and International Law', 37 *N.Y.I.L.* 2006, pp. 57–107 and M. Smith, 'The European Union and International Order: European and Global Dimensions', 12 *E.F.A.R.* 2007, pp. 437–456.

1861 See also I. Pernice, *supra* note 1654, pp. 239–241 and R.A. Wessel, *supra* note 1253, pp. 43–44.

1862 It reads: "*The Organization shall ensure that* States *which are not [UN Members] act in accordance with these Principles so far as may be necessary for the maintenance of international* are obliged to accept and carry out UN Security Council decisions. Second, none of the provisions in the Charter contain a clause binding international organizations. In fact, one of the most relevant provisions, namely Article 48(2), provides that decisions of the Security Council for the maintenance of international peace and security "*shall be carried out by the [UN Members]* directly and through their action in *the appropriate international agencies of which they are members*" (emphasis added). Thus no obligation is imposed upon the organizations themselves but rather upon the UN Member States acting within/through these organizations.[1863] Consequently, the Security Council also does not have a legal basis for directly obliging international organizations to implement its decisions,[1864] though it may obviously call upon them to do so.[1865]

Second, the effect of the recognition of the supremacy of the UN Charter in the 1969 and 1986 VCLT needs to be considered.[1866] The safeguarding of the UN Charter supremacy in Article 30(1) of the 1969 VCLT means that at least constituent treaties of international organizations concluded between States only must yield to UN obligations in the case of conflict. However, where such a treaty would nevertheless contain a provision conflicting with a UN obligation (in a manner that cannot be resolved by interpretation in accordance with the latter obligation), it is doubtful whether *the organization* established by that treaty could override this conflicting provision in its constituent treaty. Rather, it would seem that the Member States would incur international responsibility for

---

peace and security" (emphasis added). W. Graf Vitzthum, 'Article 2(6)', in SIMMA, pp. 140–148, does not even address a possible applicability of Article 2(6) with regard to international organizations. Compare K. Osteneck, *supra* note 1850, pp. 129–130, who seems to consider that this provision might apply to international organizations but argues that on the basis of the prohibition to impose obligations on third parties, it can only create a politically binding effect. But see P. Gilsdorf, 'Les reserves de sécurité du Traité CEE à la lumière du Traité sur l'Union Européenne', No. 473 *R.M.C.U.E.* 1994, p. 21 note 24 who does seem to argue that Article 2(6) UN Charter may be a basis for binding the EC.

1863 See O. Corten, 'Article 48', in COT & PELLET, p. 1301; A. Reinisch & B.-O. Bryde, 'Article 48', in SIMMA, pp. 778–779 (noting that to try to achieve a more direct binding effect, the UN has included some provisions in its relationship agreements with a number of international organizations); K. Osteneck, *supra* note 1850, p. 129 and LAWSON, pp. 151–152.

1864 Similarly, U. Villani, 'Les rapports entre l'ONU et les organisations régionales dans le domaine du maintien de la paix', 290 *Rec. Cours* 2001, pp. 345–347.

1865 N. Blokker, 'The Security Council and the Use of Force: on Recent Practice', in N. Blokker & N. Schrijver (eds.), *The Security Council and the Use of Force: Theory and Reality: A Need for Change?*, Leiden, Nijhoff, 2005, pp. 22–23 sees a reluctance by the Security Council to directly address international organizations. Compare N. Lavranos, *supra* note 1860, pp. 94–95, who seems to consider that this has not prevented the Security Council from imposing obligations on international organizations in practice. However, in hardly any of the resolutions which he cites there really is an *obligation*: rather, the organizations are urged, authorized, encouraged or called upon (probably the closest to an obligation) to do something.

1866 See *supra*, Section C.1 of this chapter, notes 1654–1655 and the accompanying text.

breaching their UN obligation when the conditions for Member State responsibility are met.

The EU and EC Treaties contain some references to the UN Charter. In particular, pursuant to Article 11(1) EU Treaty, first and third hyphen, safeguarding the common values, fundamental interests and independence and integrity of the Union and preserving peace and strengthening international security under the CFSP (and thus also the ESDP) shall be in conformity/accordance with "*the principles of the United Nations Charter*". Also, according to Article 19(2) *in fine* EU Treaty, "*Member States which are permanent members of the Security Council will, in the execution of their functions, ensure the defence of the positions and the interests of the Union, without prejudice to their responsibilities under the provisions of the United Nations Charter*". The EC Treaty refers to the UN Charter in the seventh consideration of its preamble, which states that the parties intend "*to confirm the solidarity which binds Europe and the overseas countries and desiring to ensure the development of their prosperity, in accordance with the principles of the Charter of the United Nations*". Moreover, pursuant to Article 177(3) EC Treaty, in the sphere of the EC's development cooperation "*The Community and the Member States shall comply with the commitments and take account of the objectives they have approved in the context of the United Nations and other competent international organisations*".

The provision in Article 19 EU Treaty is addressed to the Member States that are permanent members of the Security Council (the UK and France) and does not impose obligations upon the EU. What remains for the EC is a general reference to a desire to act in accordance with the principles of the UN Charter in the preamble of the EC Treaty. That may be sufficient to interpret EC law as far as possible in accordance with UN obligations,[1867] but hardly seems adequate to bind the EC as such.[1868] Moreover, it is doubtful whether the substitution theory can be extended to UN obligations (see *infra*, Section G.4.iii of this chapter). Only in the area of development cooperation would the more specific provision

---

[1867] See ECJ, Cases C-84/95 (*Bosphorus Hava Yollari Turizm ve Ticaret AS v Minister for Transport, Energy and Communications and others*, Judgment of 30 July 1996, §§11–18) and C-177/95 (*Ebony Maritime SA and Loten Navigation Co. Ltd v Prefetto della Provincia di Brindisi and others*, Judgment of 27 February 1997, §§20–21, 24 and 31); O. Elias, *supra* note 1248, pp. 27–28 and K. Osteneck, *supra* note 1850, p. 126. However, I. Canor, *supra* note 1860, p. 186 considers that the scope of this interpretation in conformity with UN obligations is not yet clear. On interpretation of EC law in conformity with international agreements, including the ECHR, see also A. Peters, *supra* note 1616, pp. 71–73.

[1868] Similarly O. Elias, *supra* note 1248, p. 26; Lawson, p. 159 and A. Leenen, *supra* note 1241, p. 230. Compare K. Osteneck, *supra* note 1850, pp. 103–132, who, in 1998, arrived at the conclusion that the EC had no obligation to implement UN sanctions decisions under *international* law.

of Article 177(3) EC Treaty seem to provide an obligation to comply with commitments undertaken by the EC and its Member States within the UN.[1869] Nevertheless, the ECJ has very recently stated that:

> Observance of the undertakings given in the context of the United Nations is required just as much in the sphere of the maintenance of international peace and security when the Community gives effect, by means of the adoption of Community measures taken on the basis of Articles 60 EC and 301 EC, to resolutions adopted by the Security Council under Chapter VII of the Charter of the United Nations.[1870]

However, it Court went on to say that:

> 295 Next, it is to be noted that the powers provided for in Articles 60 EC and 301 EC may be exercised only in pursuance of the adoption of a common position or joint action by virtue of the provisions of the EC Treaty relating to the CFSP which provides for action by the Community.
>
> 296 Although, because of the adoption of such an act, the Community is bound to take, under the EC Treaty, the measures necessitated by that act, that obligation means, when the object is to implement a resolution of the Security Council adopted under Chapter VII of the Charter of the United Nations, that in drawing up those measures the Community *is to take due account of* the terms and objectives of the resolution concerned and of the relevant obligations under the Charter of the United Nations relating to such implementation.[1871]

By using the expression "*take due account of*", the Court does not seem to say that the EC is bound as such.

In any event, since, for nearly all EC/EU Member States the UN Charter was in force before they entered the EC/EU,[1872] their obligations under the Charter towards third States may be opposed to the EC under Article 307 EC Treaty.[1873] In addition, Article 297 EC Treaty allows Member States to take measures affecting the common market "*in the event of...war, serious international tension*

1869 See also ECJ, Joined Cases C-402/05 P and C-415/05 P, *Yassin Abdullah Kadi and Al Barakaat International Foundation v. Council of the European Union and Commission of the European Communities*, 3 September 2008, §292. However, even here, there may be questions as to the extent to which the EC might have to comply with commitments made by the Member States (does this provision mean that the EC and the Member States each should comply with their own commitments only or also that the EC must comply with the Member States' commitments – and in the latter case, only by those made by all Member States?).

1870 *Id.*, §293.

1871 *Id.*, §§295–296 (emphasis added).

1872 Germany is an exception in this regard.

1873 This provision is also cited by O. Elias, *supra* note 1248, p. 26 and VANHAMME, pp. 27–28. See also T. Ahmed & I. de Jesús Butler, *supra* note 1773, pp. 784–787.

constituting a threat of war, or in order to carry out obligations it has accepted for the purpose of maintaining peace and international security".[1874] Thus, it may be argued that those Member States could, under EC law, violate EC law when this is necessary to comply with their UN obligations.[1875] Obviously, where the EU/EC has taken adequate collective action, as is usually the case,[1876] a Member State may no longer adopt unilateral measures.[1877]

The EC/EU also has a particular system for implementing UN sanctions. When they relate to external economic relations, sanctions normally come within the exclusive competences of the EC and therefore need to be adopted by the EC. However, the present system of implementation of UN (and other) sanctions in the EC/EU is that the Council first adopts a common position under Article 15 *EU* Treaty (i.e. a CFSP instrument) and that the *EC* subsequently implements this on the basis of Articles 301 and 60 (and when necessary also 308) EC Treaty (Article 60 allows a Member State under certain conditions to already adopt provisional measures pending EC action[1878]). Thus, UN sanctions are normally incorporated and transformed into EC law.[1879]

1874 This provision is also cited by O. Elias, *supra* note 1248, p. 26 and is discussed by Vanhamme, pp. 280–286. For an extensive discussion, see M. Trybus, 'At the Borderline between Community and Member States' Competence: The Triple-exceptional Character of Article 297 EC', in T. Tridimas & P. Nebbia (eds.), *European Union Law for the Twenty-first Century: Rethinking the New Legal Order,* Oxford, Hart, 2004, Vol. 2, pp. 137–157.

1875 The ECJ has stressed that there must be an obligation and not a mere permission; see, e.g. Case C-124/95, *The Queen, ex parte Centro-Com Srl v HM Treasury and Bank of England,* Judgment of 14 January 1997, §60 ("*when an international agreement allows, but does not require, a Member State to adopt a measure which appears to be contrary to Community law, the Member State must refrain from adopting such a measure*"). See also C. Kaddous, *supra* note 1739, pp. 297 and 299.

1876 Initially, the EC Member States implemented UN sanctions; see, e.g. P.-J. Kuiper, *supra* note 1860, pp. 39–42. It may also be noted that the EC and its Member States initially did not always implement UN sanctions swiftly, notably in the case of Rhodesia; see, e.g. Lawson, p. 153.

1877 E.g. ECJ, Case C-124/95 (*supra* note 1875), §§46–53 and O. Elias, *supra* note 1248, p. 28.

1878 Article 60 leaves open some questions, including whether it permits Member State action until the Council has adopted measures or only until it has discussed the matter even when it decides not to adopt measures. See J. Bröhmer, 'Article 60', in C. Calliess & M. Ruffert (eds.), *supra* note 1711, pp. 761–762. Likewise, the question arises whether Member State actions are permissible between the adoption of EU measures but pending their EC implementation. J.-M. Hauptmann, 'Article 73G C.E.', in V. Constantinesco, R. Kovar & D. Simon (eds.), *Traité sur l'union européenne (signé à Maastricht le 7 février 1992): commentaire article par article,* Paris, Economica, 1995, p. 196 submits that the scope of this provision (now Article 60 EC Treaty) is limited to that of Article 301 EC Treaty.

1879 This application as EC law is stressed by O. Elias, *supra* note 1248, p. 29. For an extensive discussion of the process of reception and transformation of international law in the EC legal order more generally (and through this medium also in the EC Member States), see N. Lavranos, *supra* note 1860, who names this process 'communitarization' (*inter alia* at pp. 110–111 and 247) – a term also used by A. Peters, *supra* note 1616, pp. 34–35 and 76.

In respect of the EU, there is an obligation to act in accordance with the principles of the UN Charter in the two cases specified by the EU Treaty under the CFSP. While the two cases are those in which respect for the UN Charter is probably the most relevant, one may wonder why this respect has not been stipulated in a more general manner for the entire CFSP (as is the case in the Lisbon Treaty[1880]). Be that as it may, when it comes to action in pursuit of the two objectives specified under the CFSP, including the ESDP, the Union is bound by the principles of the UN Charter. This gives rise to two questions. First, what are these principles? Article 2 of the Charter lists as principles that apply to the Member States the sovereign equality of the UN members, fulfilling in good faith the obligations assumed by members under the Charter, peaceful settlement of disputes, refraining in their international relations from the threat or use of force against the territorial integrity or political independence of any state, or in any other manner inconsistent with the purposes of the UN, giving the UN every assistance in any action it takes in accordance with the Charter and refraining from giving assistance to any State against which the UN is taking preventive or enforcement action.[1881] This does seem to cover the core principles and the main one that could be said to be missing, i.e. respect for human rights,[1882] is already binding for the EU in other ways (see *supra*). Therefore, although one might ask the question whether the obligation goes any further (see the debate on the spirit and principles of international humanitarian law with regard to UN forces[1883]), this seems of little practical value here. Moreover, inasmuch as these principles also reflect rules of customary international law, they bind the EU via that source (see *supra*, Section F.1 of this chapter). However, one of these principles deserves some further study: namely giving the UN every assistance in any action it takes in accordance with the Charter. In particular, through this obligation one can argue that the EU is, at least to some extent, also bound by decisions adopted by the UN Security Council. This may be a plausible argument, but it is uncertain

1880 Articles 3(5) (renumbered 3(5)) ("*In its relations with the wider world, the Union shall ... contribute to ... strict observance and the development of international law, including respect for the principles of the United Nations Charter*") and 10a(1) and (2)c (renumbered 21(1) and (2)c) ("*The Union's action on the international scene shall be guided by the principles which have inspired its own creation, development and enlargement, and which it seeks to advance in the wider world: ... respect for the principles of the United Nations Charter and international law*" and aims to "*preserve peace, prevent conflicts and strengthen international security, in accordance with the purposes and principles of the United Nations Charter*") EU Treaty as they are amended under the Lisbon Treaty. Compare Articles 3(4) and III-292(1) and (2)c EU Constitution.

1881 Compare R.A. Wessel, *supra* note 1253, p. 43, who seems to go further and to equate principles to provisions.

1882 Rather, it is listed as a purpose in Article 1(3) UN Charter.

1883 *Supra* Section B.2 of this chapter.

whether the Member States intended this provision to have this meaning.[1884] The second question is whether this is an obligation only in the internal legal order of the EU or also in the general international legal order. This is open to interpretation: on the one hand, it is part of the EU Treaty with a primarily internal focus, but on the other hand it is included in the provisions on the CFSP and may have been intended in part to affirm the EU's respect for the UN Charter also to the rest of the world.

It may be noted that the EU has confirmed that the ESDP will be developed in accordance with the principles of the UN Charter[1885] and has more generally adopted a positive attitude towards the UN.[1886] Moreover, under the Lisbon Treaty there is a Declaration (No. 13) concerning the common foreign and security policy in which it is stated that "*[The Conference] stresses that the EU and its Member States will remain bound by the provisions of the Charter of the United Nations and, in particular, by the primary responsibility of the Security Council and of its Members for the maintenance of international peace and security*".[1887] As argued above (Chapter 4.A.6[1888]), this is remarkable because of the binding of the *EU* (albeit by the Member States) to the *provisions* of the Charter. While perhaps not intended to be a unilateral act, its precise language and public nature in the context of the Lisbon Treaty may mean it amounts to just that. In addition, it reinforces other provisions of the Lisbon Treaty that require respect for the UN Charter.[1889] Thus under the Lisbon Treaty the EU's binding to the UN Charter is strengthened.

1884 Compare K. Osteneck, *supra* note 1850, p. 131, who, in the context of a discussion of whether UN sanctions can bind the EC via general principles of EC law (through the Member States), submits that the sanctions are too specific to qualify as principles. However, this need not be an obstacle for a binding effect on the basis of a principle that imposes respect for resolutions. Yet the question remains whether the reference to the principles was not intended to be limited to substantive principles and did not exclude this cooperative principle which is closely linked to membership. For a view rejecting further obligations derived from the UN's aims and principles more generally, see E. Sciso, *supra* note 1653, pp. 163–164 and U. Villani, *supra* note 1864, pp. 345–347.

1885 See §2 of the 1999 Cologne Presidency Report: "*The European Union is committed to preserve peace and strengthen international security in accordance with the principles of the UN Charter... as provided for in Article 11 of the [EU Treaty]*" and §26 of the Helsinki European Council Presidency Conclusions, 10–11 December 1999: "*The Union will contribute to international peace and security in accordance with the principles of the United Nations Charter. The Union recognises the primary responsibility of the United Nations Security Council for the maintenance of international peace and security*".

1886 On EU-UN relations, see *supra*, Chapter 2.D.2.

1887 *O.J. C* 306, 17 December 2007, p. 255. Compare B. Fassbender, *supra* note 1860, pp. 878–880 on the EU Constitution and the UN Charter.

1888 Note 1152 and the accompanying text.

1889 See *supra* note 1880.

iii. The Yusuf *and* Kadi *Judgments*

The legal force of the Charter in respect of the EC/EU has been addressed by the ECJ's Court of First Instance in two cases concerning EU/EC anti-terrorism measures: *Yusuf* and *Kadi*.[1890] The essence of these cases concerned the questions

[1890] Cases T-306/01 and T-315/01, *supra* note 1822. For a discussion, see, e.g. R. Brown, 'Kadi v Council of the European Union and Commission of the European Communities: Executive Power and Judicial Supervision at European Level', 11 *E.H.R.L.R.* 2006, pp. 456–469; M. Bulterman, 'Fundamental Rights and the United Nations Financial Sanction Regime: The Kadi and Yusuf Judgments of the Court of First Instance of the European Communities', 19 *Leiden J.I.L.* 2006, pp. 753–772; C. Eckes, 'Judicial Review of European Anti-Terrorism Measures – the Yusuf and Kadi Judgments of the Court of First Instance', 14 *Eur. L. Rev.* 2008, pp. 47–92; G. Harpaz, 'Judicial Review by the European Court of Justice of UN "Smart Sanctions" against Terror in the *Kadi* Dispute', 14 *E.F.A.R.* 2009, pp. 65–88; M.T. Karayigit, 'The Yusuf and Kadi Judgments: The Scope of the EC Competences in Respect of Restrictive Measures', 33 *Legal Issues of Economic Integration* 2006, pp. 379–404; M. Kotzur, 'Eine Bewährungsprobe für die Europäische Grundrechtsgemeinschaft: zur Entscheidung des EuG in der Rs. Yusuf u.a. gegen Rat, EuGRZ 2005, S. 592 ff', 33 *Eur. Gr. R.Z.* 2006, pp. 19–26; J. Klabbers, 'Kadi Justice at the Security Council?', 4 *I.O.L.R.* 2007, pp. 293–304; N. Lavranos, 'UN Sanctions and Judicial Review', 76 *Nordic J.I.L.* 2007, pp. 1–17 (who is very critical); P. Rackow & I. Stegmiller, '"Intelligente Sanktionen" zur Terrorbekämpfung: Yusuf, Kadi, Ayadi und Hassan vor dem EuG', 20 *Humanitäres Völkerrecht* 2007, pp. 68–78; C. Rijken, 'Het Hof als hoeder van de fundamentele rechten in de zaak Kadi en Al Barakaat', 15 *Nederlands Tijdschrift voor Europees Recht* 2009, pp. 140–146; E. Sciso, 'Fundamental Rights and Article 103 of the UN Charter Before the Court of First Instance of the European Communities', 15 *Italian Y.I.L.* 2006, pp. 137–151; S. Steinbarth, 'Individualrechtsschutz gegen Maßnahmen der EG zur Bekämpfung des internationalen Terrorismus. Die Entscheidungen des EuG in den Rs. "Yusuf u.a." sowie "Kadi"', 9 *Z. Eur. S.* 2006, pp. 269–286; C. Tomuschat, *supra* note 1836, pp. 537–551; R. van Ooik & R. Wessel, 'De Yusuf en Kadi-uitspraken in perspectief: nieuwe verhoudingen in de interne en externe bevoegdheden van de Europese Unie', 54 *S.E.W.* 2006, pp. 230–241; A. von Arnauld, 'UN-Sanctionen und gemeinschaftrechtlicher Grundrechtsschutz', 44 *A.V.R.* 2006, pp. 201–216; R.A. Wessel, *The Invasion by International Organizations. De toenemende samenhang tussen de mondiale, Europese en nationale rechtsorde*, Inaugural Lecture, University of Twente, 12 January 2006 (available online at www.bbt.utwente.nl/legs/news/oratie_wessel_web.pdf), pp. 5–13 and R. Wessel, 'Editorial: The UN, the EU and *Jus Cogens*', 3 *I.O.L.R.* 2006, pp. 1–6. See also more generally J. Almqvist, 'A Human Rights Critique of European Judicial Review: Counter-Terrorism Sanctions', 57 *I.C.L.Q.* 2008, pp. 303–331; S. Dewulf & D. Pacquée, 'Protecting Human Rights in the War on Terror: Challenging the Sanctions Regime Originating from Resolution 1267 (1999)', 24 *Netherlands Quarterly of Human Rights* 2006, pp. 607–640; E. Guild, 'The Uses and Abuses of Counter-Terrorism Policies in Europe: The Case of the 'Terrorist Lists'', 46 *J.C.M.S.* 2008, pp. 173–193; D. Halberstam & E. Stein, 'The United Nations, the European Union, and the King of Sweden: Economic Sanctions and Individual Rights in a Plural World Order', 46 *C.M.L. Rev.* 2009, pp. 13–72; B. Kunoy, 'The Jurisdiction of the ECJ to Review the Legality of the Transposition of an International Act in the EC Legal Order', 76 *Nordic J.I.L.* 2007, pp 19–37; N. Lavranos, 'UN Sanctions and Judicial Review', in J. Wouters, A. Nollkaemper & E. De Wet (eds.), *The Europeanisation of International Law: The Status of International Law in the EU and its Member States*, The Hague, T.M.C. Asser Press, 2008, pp. 185–204; D. Pacquée & S. Dewulf, 'Terrorismelijsten: inzichten van het Gerecht van Eerste Aanleg', 5 *Nieuw juridisch weekblad* 2006, pp. 678–683; M. Payandeh, 'Rechtskontrolle des UN-Sicherheitsrates durch staatliche und überstaatliche Gerichte', 66 *Z.a.ö.R.V.* 2006, pp. 41–71; P. Schneider & K. Peiffer, 'Die Terrorlistenpraxis verliert vor Gericht: das EuGH-Urteil und seine Folgen für die gezielten Sanktionen der VN', 22 *Humanitäres Völkerrecht* 2009, pp.

of the EC's competence to adopt sanctions against individuals (in respect of which the Court made an interesting though questionable[1891] link between EC competences under Articles 60, 301 and 308 EC Treaty and EU objectives to promote international peace and security[1892]) and the extent to which the Court could review the legality of certain EC anti-terrorism measures, and, directly or indirectly, UN Security Council measures on which the latter were based, especially in the light of human rights.[1893] However, the points that are relevant for the purpose of this book are to what extent the Court held the EC to be bound by UN obligations as well as its view on *ius cogens* in respect of international organizations, be it the UN or the EC. In respect of these points, the Court ruled that the EC was not directly bound by the UN Charter and Security Council decisions:

> ... unlike its Member States, the Community as such is not directly bound by the Charter of the United Nations and that it is not therefore required, as an obligation of general public international law, to accept and carry out the decisions of the Security Council in accordance with Article 25 of that Charter. The reason is that the Community is *not* a member of the United Nations, or an addressee of the resolutions of the Security Council, *or the successor to the rights and obligations of the Member States for the purposes of public international law* (emphasis added).[1894]

Thus the Court appears to reject a succession theory. However, it goes on to say that the EC is bound to UN obligations by virtue of the EC Treaty. In particular, the Court argued that:

> ... at the time when they concluded the [EC Treaty] the Member States were bound by their obligations under the [UN Charter].

4-14 and T. Tridimas & J.A. Gutierrez-Fons, 'EU Law, International Law, and Economic Sanctions against Terrorism: The Judiciary in Distress', 32 *Fordham I.L.J.* 2009, pp. 660–730.

1891 See E. Sciso, *supra* previous note, pp. 138–141.

1892 *Yusuf*, §§158–170 and Kadi, §122–135. See also M. Kotzur, *supra* note 1890, p. 21. This linkage is interesting from the perspective of consistency between the EC and EU legal order (see *supra*, Chapter 6, notes 1586 and 1592). However, the ECJ rejected this part of the judgments in its appeals judgment, *infra* note 1623, §§195–204 but ruled that "*Articles 60 EC and 301 EC are the expression of an implicit underlying objective, namely, that of making it possible to adopt such measures through the efficient use of a Community instrument. That objective may be regarded as constituting an objective of the Community for the purpose of Article 308 EC*" (*id.*, 226–227). See also Advocate-General Maduro's opinions of 23 and 16 January 2008 in the appeals cases (C-415/05 P and C-402/05 P), both §15.

1893 On UN sanctions and the ECHR generally, see, e.g. I. Cameron, 'UN Targeted Sanctions, Legal Safeguards and the European Convention on Human Rights', 72 *Nordic J.I.L* 2003, pp. 159–214 and I. Cameron, *The European Convention on Human Rights, Due Process and United Nations Security Council Counter-Terrorism Sanctions*, Council of Europe, 6 February 2006 (available online at www.coe.int/t/e/legal_affairs/legal_co-operation/public_international_law/Texts_&_Documents/Docs%202006/I.%20Cameron%20Report%2006.pdf).

1894 *Yusuf*, §242 and Kadi, §192.

By concluding a treaty between them they could not transfer to the Community more powers than they possessed or withdraw from their obligations to third countries under that Charter (…).
On the contrary, their desire to fulfil their obligations under that Charter follows from the very provisions of the [EC Treaty] and is made clear in particular by Article 224 and the first paragraph of Article 234 (…).
Although that latter provision makes mention only of the obligations of the Member States, it implies a duty on the part of the institutions of the Community not to impede the performance of the obligations of Member States which stem from that Charter (…).
It is also to be observed that, in so far as the powers necessary for the performance of the Member States' obligations under the Charter of the United Nations have been transferred to the Community, the Member States have undertaken, pursuant to public international law, to ensure that the Community itself should exercise those powers to that end.
In this context it is to be borne in mind, first, that in accordance with Article 48(2) of the [UN Charter], the decisions of the Security Council 'shall be carried out by the Members of the United Nations directly and through their action in the appropriate international agencies of which they are members' and, second, that according to the case-law (…), the Community must respect international law in the exercise of its powers and, consequently, Community law must be interpreted, and its scope limited, in the light of the relevant rules of international law.
By conferring those powers on the Community, the Member States demonstrated their will to bind it by the obligations entered into by them under the [UN Charter] (…).
Since the entry into force of the Treaty establishing the European Economic Community, the transfer of powers which has occurred in the relations between Member States and the Community has been put into concrete form in different ways within the framework of the performance of their obligations under the [UN Charter] (…).
Thus it is, in particular, that Article 228a of the EC Treaty (now Article 301 EC) was added to the [EU Treaty] in order to provide a specific basis for the economic sanctions that the Community, which has exclusive competence in the sphere of the common commercial policy, may need to impose in respect of third countries for political reasons defined by its Member States in connection with the CFSP, most commonly pursuant to a resolution of the Security Council requiring the adoption of such sanctions.
It therefore appears that, in so far as under the EC Treaty the Community has assumed powers previously exercised by Member States in the area governed by the [UN Charter], the provisions of that Charter have the effect of binding the Community (…).
Following that reasoning, it must be held, first, that the Community may not infringe the obligations imposed on its Member States by the [UN Charter] or impede their performance and, second, that in the exercise of its powers it is bound, by the very

Treaty by which it was established, to adopt all the measures necessary to enable its Member States to fulfil those obligations.[1895]

The Court repeatedly refers to the International Fruit Company cases (five times, the references are omitted in the quote above) and seems to extend the substitution theory to the UN Charter in respect of sanctions, albeit only under EC law: "*in so far as under the EC Treaty the Community has assumed powers previously exercised by Member States in the area governed by the [UN Charter], the provisions of that Charter have the effect of binding the Community*".[1896]

On this point, the judgments seem to depart from the ECJ's established restrictive application of the substitution theory discussed above. A first relaxation is that most but not all EC Member States were UN members before their accession to the EC: Germany was not. However, this may be put in perspective by the fact that Germany was a UN Member State at the time of the unambiguous transfer of sanctions competences to the EC and arguably poses no major problem. As to the other elements, there clearly has been a transfer of some competences to the EC.[1897] The Court's view that "*by conferring those powers on the Community, the Member States demonstrated their will to bind it by the obligations entered into by them under the [UN Charter]*" is, however, less convincing.[1898] First, Article 301 EC Treaty does not even mention the UN and only imposes an obligation on the EC to implement sanctions if required by a CFSP decision, irrespective of

1895 *Yusuf*, §§243–254 and Kadi, §§193–204.

1896 See also T. Ahmed & I. de Jesús Butler, *supra* note 1773, pp. 789–790. Compare KLEIN, pp. 356–357, who notes that Greece invoked this substitution in Case 204/86 (*Hellenic Republic v Council of the European Communities, ECR* 1988--VI, p. 5352, §13). In this case, the ECJ (Judgment of 27 September 1988, §§27–28) dismissed the resolution invoked as being "*completely extraneous to relations between the Community and Turkey in the context of the Association*". KLEIN's argument (on pp. 357–358) that the Council has accepted that the Community is bound via its Member States to UN obligations is not convincing in that the Council only used the argument negatively (i.e. in the absence of an obligation for the Member States, the EC consequently has no obligation) and would not necessarily endorse the inverse position. While the Council seems to come closer to admitting that the EC might be bound by stating that EC organs are not bound by decisions of UN organs where the EC has not assumed powers previously exercised by the EC Member States, thus possibly implying that where this is the case, the EC would be bound (*ECR* 1988--VI, pp. 5334–5335), it is unsure whether it would go this far. Compare K. Osteneck, *supra* note 1850, p. 127, who argues that no conclusions can be drawn from this case.

1897 But see I. Pernice, *supra* note 1654, pp. 240–241, who does not seem to consider that there was (in 1988) a transfer of competences to the EC.

1898 Compare, e.g. K. Osteneck, *supra* note 1850, pp. 122–128, who, in 1998, arrived at the conclusion that the conditions of the substitution theory had not been met in respect of UN sanctions, as did C. Kaddous, *supra* note 1739, pp. 423–424; K. Lenaerts & P. Van Nuffel, *supra* note 1465, p. 756 note 463 and LAWSON, p. 160 (who regards Article 297 as essential in this respect). But see P.-J. Kuiper, *supra* note 1860, pp. 41–42, who, in 2003, argued that "*it may perhaps be possible*" to make the analogy with the ECJ's substitution theory.

whether the latter is taken on the basis of a UN Security Council resolution. One way to read into this provision an obligation to implement UN Security Council resolutions is if one accepts that the EU is under an obligation to implement such decisions. As argued above, this argument is not very strong but can be made if the reference in Article 11(1) EU Treaty to conformity with the "*the principles of the United Nations Charter*" in preserving peace and strengthening international security under the CFSP includes the principle of giving the UN every assistance and would require the implementation of decisions adopted by the UN Security Council. An alternative argument is that the obligation for the EC under Article 307 EC Treaty not to impede the Member States from fulfilling their obligations under the UN Charter includes an obligation to cooperate in implementing UN sanctions.[1899] However, either way one may question whether it was the Member States' intention to so bind the EC/EU also vis-à-vis third parties.[1900] Second, and more importantly, the powers transferred to the EC in relation to the UN are only of a limited nature: not only do they cover only a fraction of the UN's field of activity but they are also limited to the *implementation* of decisions adopted by UN organs in which only the Member States have voting rights.[1901] The former may not pose an obstacle to an application of the substitution theory, as it could arguably be applied partially.[1902] The latter does not sit well with the ECJ's limited acceptance of substitution. Admittedly, it may be argued that there is *some* recognition by the UN of the role of the EU/EC, including in *implementing* UN sanctions and other measures.[1903] Nevertheless, it is doubtful whether the

1899 See A. von Arnauld, *supra* note 1890, pp. 206–207 and compare *supra* note 1845 and the accompanying text. For a similar argument in relation to the ECHR, see R. Uerpmann, *supra* note 1616, pp. 37–38.

1900 K. Lenaerts & E. de Smijter, *supra* note 1860, p. 448 are of the view that the EC is not bound under international law but 'only' under EC/EU law. M. Kotzur, *supra* note 1890, p. 24 also seems to take this view. Compare also R. Uerpmann, *supra* note 1616, pp. 37–38, who, in relation to a similar argument concerning the ECHR, sees this as binding under EC law only. See also P. Stangos & G. Gryllos, 'Le droit communautaire à l'épreuve des réalités du droit international: leçons tirées de la jurisprudence récente relevant de la lutte contre le terrorisme international', 42 *C.D.E.* 2006, pp. 466–467, who argue that the Court *de facto* applies a succession theory in both cases but only as a matter of EC law.

1901 Compare P.J.G. Kapteyn, *supra* note 1860, pp. 42–43, seeing some room for the application of the substitution theory but questioning its use in such a limited case because he perceives it as leading only to a binding of the EC to sanctions decisions to the extent that they have been implemented by the EC.

1902 K. Osteneck, *supra* note 1850, pp. 103–132. But see Lawson, pp. 83–84, who doubts whether a partial substitution is possible.

1903 See P.-J. Kuiper, *supra* note 1860, pp. 42 and 51–52. For instance, in its efforts to combat terrorism, including through the use of sanctions, the Security Council has recognized the important role of international and (sub)regional organizations (see, e.g. UN Security Council Resolution 1631 of 17 October 2005; the Declarations annexed to UN Security Council Resolutions 1377 of 12 November 2001 and 1456 of 20 January 2003 and special meetings with such organizations discussed at www.un.org/sc/ctc/cooperation.html) and the EU has reported to the Security Council's Counter-Terrorism Committee on the measures that it has

UN feels it can bind the EC as such.[1904] Therefore, the argument that all the conditions for substitution set by the ECJ are met is not without merit but is not entirely convincing, even when regarded as a matter of EC law only.

In any event, if substitution, whether merely as a matter of EU law or under international law, can be this 'partial' and relate to non-exclusive competences[1905] and the mere implementation of limited specific international obligations, it would apply to numerous international obligations in force for the Member States which require EC implementing measures, including, arguably, the ECHR. If the ECJ would have followed this line of argument, it would have been a positive development from the perspective of better integrating international law and EU law. In its appeals judgment in these cases, in which the ECJ set aside the Court of First Instance's judgments,[1906] it did not really address this

taken to implement relevant Security Council resolutions (see J. Wouters & F. Naert, 'The European Union and "September 11"', 13 *Indiana International & Comparative Law Review* 2002–2003, p. 755 note 211 and www.un.org/sc/ctc/countryreports/Creports.shtml). Nevertheless, it is clear that this is only a limited recognition.

1904 Compare K. Osteneck, *supra* note 1850, p. 128, who, in 1998, felt that the UN did not perceive its decisions as binding the EC.

1905 T. Ahmed & I. de Jesús Butler, *supra* note 1773, pp. 789–790, see this extension to cases of shared competences as a key difference with the ECJ's case law so far. Lawson, p. 160, regards Article 297 as essential in rejecting the application of the substitution theory to the UN Charter. The EU/EC's sanctions power does not appear to be exclusive: for instance, it does not appear to extend to UN sanctions against Member States (K. Osteneck, *supra* note 1850, pp. 111–113) and, as set out above, leaves some room for Member State measures. P.-J. Kuiper, *supra* note 1860, pp. 45 and 47, submits that for arms embargoes no EC act is required or even possible (in light of Article 296 EC Treaty) but only a CFSP act and that Member State measures are useful and necessary concerning penal sanctions (though noting that the EC is not entirely without competences in the area of penal law, a point recently confirmed by the ECJ in Cases C-176/03, *Commission of the European Communities v Council of the European Union*, Judgment of 13 September 2005, §§38–53 and C-440/05, *Commission of the European Communities v. Council of the European Union*, 23 October 2007, §§63–71). One might add that, unless one accepts that a CFSP act may have direct effect in the Member States' legal orders, national implementing acts would also be necessary. See also R. Pavoni, *supra* note 1860, pp. 601–612 on what competences with regard to UN sanctions are/were still held by the Member States.

1906 Joined Cases C-402/05 P and C-415/05 P, *Yassin Abdullah Kadi and Al Barakaat International Foundation v. Council of the European Union and Commission of the European Communities*, 3 September 2008. For annotations, see, e.g. CEDIN (ed.), 'Actes du colloque sur la rencontre des droits (international, communautaire et interne)', No. 524 *R.M.C.U.E.* 2009, pp. 352–418; P.J. Cardwell, D. French & N. White, 'European Court of Justice, Yassin Abdullah Kadi and Al Barakaat International Foundation v Council and Commission (joined Cases C-402/05 P and C-415/05 P) Judgment of 3 September 2008', 58 *I.C.L.Q.* 2009, pp. 229–240; D. Curtin & C. Eckes, 'The Kadi Case: Mapping the Boundaries Between the Executive and the Judiciary in Europe', 5 *I.O.L.R.* 2008, pp. 365–369; A. Cuyvers, 'Tussen Scyllii en Charybdii: terrorisme, rechtsbescherming en de verhouding tussen rechtsordes in Kadi', 58 *Ars aequi* 2009, pp. 155–164; P. d'Argent, 'Arrêt "*Kadi*": le droit communautaire comme droit interne', *Journal de droit européen* 2008, pp. 265–268; J. d'Aspremont & F. Dopagne, 'Kadi: The ECJ's Reminder of the Elementary Divide between Legal Orders', 5 *I.O.L.R.* 2008, pp. 371–379; G. de Búrca, *The European Court of Justice and the International Legal Order after Kadi*, Jean Monnet Working Paper 01/09, 2009, www.jeanmonnetprogram.org/papers/09/090101.pdf; E. de Wet, 'The Role point.[1907] However, in two other recent judgments, the ECJ has confirmed its restrictive interpretation of the substitution theory.[1908] Hence there is no broader

---

of European Courts in Reviewing Conflicting Obligations under International Law', 5 *I.O.L.R.* 2008, pp. 359–364; A. Gattini, 'Joined Cases C-402/05 P and C-415/05 P, *Yassin Abdullah Kadi and Al Barakaat International Foundation v Council and Commission*, Judgment of the Grand Chamber of 3 September 2008, nyr.', 46 *C.M.L. Rev.* 2009, pp. 213–239; S. Griller, 'International Law, Human Rights and the European Community's Autonomous Legal Order: Notes on the European Court of Justice Decision in Kadi', 4 *European Constitutional Law Review* 2008, pp. 528–553; L.M. Hinojosa Martínez, 'Bad Law for Good Reasons: The Contradictions of the Kadi Judgment', 5 *I.O.L.R.* 2008, pp. 339–357 (addressing the substitution question at pp. 339–341); C. Janssens, 'Het Kadi-arrest van het Hof van Justitie inzake terrorismelijsten: de beslechting van enkele hete hangijzers met betrekking tot interne en externe bevoegdheidsafbakening en rechtsbescherming', 72 *Rechtskundig weekblad* 2009, pp. pp. 1410–1426; J.A. Kämmerer, 'Das Urteil des Europäischen Gerichtshofs im Fall "Kadi": ein Triumph der Rechtsstaatlichkeit?', 44 *Europarecht* 2009, pp. 114–130; M. Kotzur, 'Kooperativer Grundrechtsschutz in der Völkergemeinschaft: zur Rechtmittelentscheidung des EuGH (Große Kammer) vom 3. September 2008 in den verb. Rsn. Kadi u. a.', 35 *Eur. Gr. Z.* 2008, pp. 673–680; N. Lavranos, 'Joined Cases C-402/05 P and C-415/05 *P, Yassin Abdullah Kadi and Al Barakaat International Foundation v. Council of the European Union and Commission of the European Communities* Judgment of the European Court of Justice (Grand Chamber) 3 September 2008, Not Yet Published', 36 *Legal Issues of Economic Integration* 2009, pp. 157–185; S. Menz & T.B. Scholz, 'The Kadi-case or the Legal Protection of Persons Included in the European Union "Anti-terror List"', 17 *European Journal of Crime Criminal Law and Criminal Justice* 2009, pp. 61–68; J.-M. Thouvenin, 'Le choc du droit communautaire et du droit international, encore l'arrêt Kadi', No. 524 *R.M.C.U.E.* 2009, pp. 30–31; T. Tridimas, 'Terrorism and the ECJ: Empowerment and Democracy in the EC Legal Order', 34 *Eur. L. Rev.* 2009, pp. 103–126 (also available at www.carterruck.com/Documents//Terrorism_and_the_ECJ.pdf); L. van den Herik & N. Schrijver, 'Eroding the Primacy of the UN System of Collective Security: The Judgment of the European Court of Justice in the Cases of Kadi and Al Barakaat', 5 *I.O.L.R.* 2008, pp. 329–338; N. Graf Vitzthum, 'Les compétences législatives et juridictionnelles de la Communauté européenne dans la lutte contre le terrorisme – l'affaire "Kadi"', 11 *Z. Eur. S.* 2008, pp. 375–429; R.A. Wessel, 'The Kadi Case: Towards a More Substantive Hierarchy in International Law?', 5 *I.O.L.R.* 2008, pp. 323–327. The Court of First instance had confirmed its findings discussed above in other cases, including Case T-253/02, *Chafiq Ayadi v. Council of the European Union*, judgement of 12 July 2006 (§§115–117; appeal pending – Case C-403/06 P) and Case T-49/04, *Faraj Hassan, v. Council of the European Union and Commission of the European Communities*, judgement of 12 July 2006 (§§91–93; appeal pending – Case C-399/06 P). For an annotation of those two cases, see J. Heliskoski, 'Case T-253/02, *Chafiq Ayadi v. Council*, judgment of the Court of First Instance of 12 July 2006; *Faraj Hassan v. Council and Commission*, judgment of the Court of First Instance of 12 July 2006, nyr', 44 *C.M.L. Rev.* 2007, pp. 1143–1157. However, after the *Kadi* appeals judgment, it followed the ECJ; see, e.g. Case T-318/01, *Omar Mohammed Othman v. Council of the European Union and Commission of the European Communities*, 11 June 2009, especially §§82–99.

1907 E.g. in §307 the Court says "*supposing [Article 300 EC Treaty] to be applicable to the Charter of the United Nations ...*"). Advocate-General Maduro, in his opinions in *Kadi* of 16 January 2008 and in *Al Barakaat* of 23 January 2008 also disagreed with the CFI on various points but did not really address the substitution argument either. See also N. Lavranos, *supra* note 1906, pp. 163, 166 and 177–178.

1908 See Case C-308/06, *International Association of Independent Tanker Owners (Intertanko) and Others*, 3 June 2008, §§48–49 ("*it does not appear that the Community has assumed, under the EC Treaty, the powers previously exercised by the Member States in the field to which Marpol 73/78 applies, nor that, consequently, its provisions have the effect of binding the Community (Case C-379/92 Peralta [1994] ECR I-3453, paragraph 16)*") and Case C-188/07, *Commune de Mesquer*, 24 June 2008, §85 ("*the Community is not bound by the Liability Convention or the* acceptance of this theory, which could have had far-reaching consequences for the EC.

There is another aspect of the *Kadi* appeals judgment which cannot be overlooked: the Court did not feel that it was necessary to determine the extent to which UN Security Council resolutions bind the EC because, essentially, whatever their status is in the EU legal order, they are hierarchically inferior to EU human rights law as enshrined in Article 6 EU Treaty and the autonomy of the EU legal order means that the hierarchy under international law does not matter.[1909] The Court thereby elevated EU human rights to a "*new supra-constitutional law level*" prevailing over other primary EU law.[1910] I will return to the implications of this finding in Chapter 9.C.5 below.

5. OTHER INTERNATIONAL ORGANIZATIONS

I have no knowledge of any international organization that has considered itself to be formally bound by treaties concluded by its Member States absent specific provisions to that effect. Similarly, Cahin submits that only very exceptionally are international organizations bound by Member State treaties.[1911] Morgenstern writes that international organizations are reluctant to accept being bound by treaties to which they are not a party.[1912] For instance, the IMF has rejected the argument that it would be bound by certain human rights treaties despite their broad ratification by its Member States.[1913] Similarly, the ILO Administrative

Fund Convention . it cannot be regarded as having taken the place of its Member States, if only because not all of them are parties to those conventions ..."). On the former case, see F. Dopagne, 'Arrêt "Intertanko": l'appréciation de la validité d'actes communautaires au regard de conventions internationals (Marpol 73/78, Montego Bay)', *Journal de droit européen* 2008, pp. 241–243.

1909 *Supra* note 1906, §§278–330. However, the ECJ does recognize that the rights at stake may be subject to some limitations in the interest of security (see §§338–344 and 355–366).

1910 These words are aptly used by N. Lavranos in his annotation *supra* note 1906, pp. 166 and 176 (see also pp. 163–166 and 174–178 on the autonomy of the EU legal order).

1911 G. Cahin, *supra* note 1740, p. 522.

1912 F. Morgenstern, *supra* note 1229, pp. 33–34, noting that the ILO has felt morally bound to take into account ILO standards but that the applicability of these standards to the UN was rejected by a UN legal opinion.

1913 This view was reportedly taken by the IMF's General Counsel in a legal brief dated 30 May 2001; see A. Clapham, *supra* note 1224, pp. 145–149, especially pp. 146–147. See also F. Gianviti, *Economic, Social and Cultural Rights and the International Monetary Fund*, Paper presented at the IMF Seminar on Current Developments in Monetary and Financial Law, Washington D.C., 7–17 May 2002 (available online at www.imf.org/external/np/leg/sem/2002/cdmfl/eng/gianv3.pdf), pp. 4–5 ("*in the event that some or all members of an international organization adhere to a treaty containing such other objectives or values, this in itself does not result in these objectives or values becoming part of the organization's mandate unless and until agreement is reached to amend the organization's charter*") and 10–31; also cited by E. Denters,

Tribunal (which is also competent for a number of other international organizations) has held that international organizations are not bound by human rights treaties as such,[1914] although it has ruled that some human rights are binding upon them as general principles of law.[1915]

The same can be said in respect of decisions of other international organizations. Even within the UN family, specialized organizations do not generally feel bound by decisions adopted by the UN's principle organs absent specific provisions binding them, e.g. in their relationship agreement.[1916] The World Bank, e.g. only has to "*have due regard for*" Security Council decisions under Articles 41 and 42 UN Charter[1917] and has refused in some cases to apply UN General Assembly resolutions.[1918] Practice to the contrary appears to be limited to a UNIDO legal opinion.[1919] The inclusion of provisions in the relationship agreements, and the fact that some of them do not even impose the binding force of Security Council resolutions, is significant and suggests that absent such provisions an international organization is not bound as such by such decisions.[1920]

H. SOME REFLECTIONS ON THE RESPONSIBILITY OF MEMBER STATES FOR THEIR ACTIONS IN THE FRAMEWORK OF INTERNATIONAL ORGANIZATIONS

As has been noted in the preceding section, most of the arguments put forward in favour of binding international organizations to treaties concluded by its Member States (or Member States' obligations more generally) are based on the

The International Monetary Fund, in J. Wouters (ed.) *International Encyclopaedia of Laws. Intergovernmental Organisations*, The Hague, Kluwer Law International, 2006, p. 62, §156.

1914 E.g. *In re Maugain (No. 6)*, Judgment No. 1144 of 29 January 1992 (considerations, §6: "*... the European Convention on Human Rights ... puts obligations on signatory States, and it is not apparent that it is applicable ...*") and *H.-J. M. v. European Patent Organisation*, Judgement No. 2611 of 7 February 2007 (§8: "*the European Convention on Human Rights, ... appl[ies], according to [its] terms, to Member States not to international organisations*").

1915 See *supra* note 1812 and the accompanying text.

1916 See also A. Reinisch & B.-O. Bryde, 'Article 48', in Simma, pp. 778–780. Compare Klein, pp. 350–359, who, as with treaties (see *supra* this section), argues that in some cases an obligation arises via the obligations of Member States.

1917 See Article VI of the UN-IBRD relationship agreement (15 August 1947, approved by the UN on 15 November 1947 and by the IBRD on 16 September 1947, 16 *U.N.T.S.* 346 (1948)).

1918 See, e.g. A. Reinisch & B.-O. Bryde, *supra* note 1916, pp. 779–780; F. Morgenstern, *supra* note 1229, pp. 28–30 and Klein, pp. 353–354.

1919 Cited in E. Lagrange, *supra* note 1656, pp. 514–515 (seeing it as apparently isolated) and Klein, p. 358.

1920 Similarly, C.W. Jenks, 'Co-ordination: A New Problem of International Organization', 77 *Rec. Cours* 1950-II, pp. 185–186 and Lawson, pp. 151–154, especially note 68.

consideration that a State should not be able to evade its international obligations by transferring powers to an international organization. However, binding the organization to its Member States' (treaty) obligations is not the only way to achieve this desired result. An alternative that has been discussed in doctrine,[1921] seems to be endorsed to some extent by the ILA[1922] and the ILC[1923] and has some support in jurisprudence (see *infra*), is some degree of Member State responsibility for actions in the framework of international organizations. It is not my intention to deal with the responsibility of international organizations themselves (currently under consideration by the ILC) nor with that of Member States for the acts of international organizations generally (also addressed in that context by the ILC) but only to discuss the basic elements of the responsibility of Member States for acts in the framework of international organizations that are contrary to international obligations *of a Member State.*[1924] This did not *appear* to be

1921 See especially the extensive analysis by Lawson, pp. 189–199 and 345–492. See also A. Clapham, *supra* note 1224, p. 135 and R. Wessel in 124 *Mededelingen van de NVIR*, *supra* note 1680, p. 40. Compare the rather critical view of A. Berramdane, *supra* note 1855, pp. 247–251, especially p. 248.

1922 See the ILA's 2004 *Final Report on the Accountability of International Organisations* (*supra* note 1610), *inter alia* pp. 18–19, arguing, among others, that "*Membership of an IO can ... not be considered to imply a corresponding reduction of state responsibility, although an authorisation granted by an IO to one or more Members, could in certain circumstances, prevent the breach of an international obligation by such Members*" and that "*A transfer of powers to an IO cannot ... exclude the responsibility of the States who transferred powers to an IO*". While this seems to be a legal argument this is not necessarily so given the ILA's meta-legal approach in this document (see *supra* note 1610).

1923 The ILC's view on this issue will be addressed in some detail below.

1924 This key distinction is also made by Lawson, especially pp. 280–287. On Member State responsibility more generally, see, e.g. the Institue of International Law's 1995 resolution on 'The Legal Consequences for Member States of the Non-fulfilment by International Organizations of their Obligations toward Third Parties' (available online at www.idi-iil.org/idiE/navig_res_chon.html) and its preparatory report (R. Higgins, 'The Legal Consequences for Member States of the Non-Fulfilment by International Organizations of Their Obligations Towards Third Parties', 66 *A.I.D.I.* 1995-I, pp. 249–469); M. Hartwig, *supra* note 1834; C.F. Amerasinghe, 'Liability to Third Parties of Member States of International Organizations – Practice, Principle and Judicial Precedent', 85 *A.J.I.L.* 1991, pp. 259–280; A. Geslin, 'Réflexions sur la repartition de la responsabilité entre l'organisation internationale et ses Etats membres', 109 *R.G.D.I.P.* 2005, pp. 539–579; R. Higgins, 'The Responsibility of State Members for the Defaults of International Organizations: Continuing the Dialogue', in S. Schlemmer-Schulte & K.-Y. Tung (eds.), *Liber Amicorum Ibrahim F.I. Shihata: International Finance and Development Law*, The Hague, Kluwer Law International, 2001, pp. 441–448; I. Seidl-Hohenveldern, 'Liability of Member States for Acts or Omissions of an International Organization', in *id.*, pp. 727–739; H.G. Schermers, 'The Liability of the Member States for Debts of International Organizations', 1 *Legal Issues of European Integration* 1996, pp. 15–22; I. Seidl-Hohenveldern, 'Der Rückgriff auf die Mitgliedstaaten in Internationalen Organisationen', in R. Bernhardt *et al.* (eds.), *Festschift für Hermann Mosler*, Berlin, Springer, 1983, pp. 881–890 and A. Stumer, 'Liability of Member States for Acts of International Organizations: Reconsidering the Policy Objections', 48 *Harvard I.L.J.* 2007, pp. 553–580. I wil not specifically discuss the *Tin Council* and *Westland Helicopter* cases – for the references to the relevant decisions and arbitral awards and a brief discussion, see, e.g. Amerasinghe, addressed in the ILC's Draft Articles on *State* Responsibility since Article 57 thereof stated that "*These Articles are without prejudice to any question of the responsibility under international law of an international organization, or of any State for the conduct of an international organization*" (but see *infra*, subsection 2 of this Section).[1925]

Member State responsibility in this sense may be argued to arise on a number of different grounds. First, the responsibility of a Member State may result from the very fact of establishing an international organization without binding it to the Member States' obligations and thereby enabling it to commit acts contrary to an international obligation of Member States. Second, the responsibility of a Member State may be based on its own conduct in the framework of an international organization once it has been established. In this case, a further distinction may be made between a Member State's role in decision-making and its role in implementing a decision. Third, further grounds such as complicity and control over an international organization by a State should also be mentioned but will not be discussed here.[1926]

1. RESPONSIBILITY FOR THE ACTIONS OF AN INTERNATIONAL ORGANIZATION RESULTING FROM ITS ESTABLISHMENT

The argument can be made that if States set up an international organization that will exercise certain powers normally exercised by them or exercised to their advantage, without assuring that this organization respects the obligations of these States in the exercise of such powers of which these States cannot derogate among themselves,[1927] the States lay the basis for violations of their obligations and should be responsible themselves when such violations are committed by an international organization.[1928] Although some see this as a piercing of the separate international legal personality of the international organization,[1929] this

pp. 431–436; SANDS & KLEIN, pp. 517–518; SCHERMERS & BLOKKER, pp. 1008–1009, §1588 and C.T. Ebenroth, Shareholders' Liability in International Organizations – the Settlement of the International Tin Council Case, 4 *Leiden J.I.L.* 1991, pp. 171–183.

1925 ILC, Draft Articles on Responsibility of States for Internationally Wrongful Acts, adopted on 31 May and 3 August 2001, *Report of the International Law Commission. Fifty-third session*, UN Doc. A/56/10, pp. 360–363.

1926 See provisional draft Articles 25–27 of the ILC's work on the responsibility of international organizations, UN Doc. A/61/10 (2006), pp. 277–282.

1927 E.g. because they include obligations towards a third State or because derogation was excluded; see *supra* Section C.2 of this chapter, notes 1677–1680 and the accompanying text.

1928 See the discussion in M. Hartwig, *supra* note 1834, pp. 285–287.

1929 E.g. R. Uerpmann, *supra* note 1616, pp. 35–36.

need not necessarily be the case if one argues that the Member States are not simply responsible for the acts of the organization, but rather incur responsibility by virtue of their own initial act of not binding an organization to their own international obligations.

At the domestic level, a State will remain responsible if it transfers governmental powers to an agency even when that agency is independent: Article 5 of the ILC's Draft Articles on State responsibility[1930] stipulates that "*The conduct of a person or entity which is not an organ of the State ... but which is empowered by the law of that State to exercise elements of the governmental authority shall be considered an act of the State under international law, provided the person or entity is acting in that capacity in the particular instance*". The commentary to this provision does not mention international organizations at all and presumably they are not intended to be covered by this provision.[1931] Nevertheless, it has been argued that they can fall within the terms of this provision,[1932] a view which the text itself certainly permits. Indeed, the recent work of the ILC on the responsibility of international organizations seems to endorse this solution, albeit without reference to the State responsibility rules. In particular, draft Article 28(1) as provisionally adopted stipulates that:

> A State member of an international organization incurs international responsibility if it circumvents one of its international obligations by providing the organization with competence in relation to that obligation, and the organization commits an act that, if committed by that State, would have constituted a breach of that obligation.[1933]

The commentary makes it clear that no specific intent is required but seems to leave open an exception where the 'circumvention' is an "*an unwitting result of providing the international organization with competence*".[1934] The latter consideration indicates that, in contrast with a domestic agency, the ILC appears to view the case of international organizations as less absolute. There is some support for this position in the jurisprudence of the European Court of Human Rights, which is also cited by the ILC and which has arguably developed two arguments that soften an absolute rule of Member State responsibility. One is to take into account the importance and needs of international cooperation in

1930 *Supra* note 1925.

1931 See, with respect to a similar provision in an earlier version, LAWSON, p. 272.

1932 See, with respect to a similar provision in an earlier version, V. Lowe, *supra* note 1720, pp. 163–164. The analogy of international organizations with 'indirect state administration' is also mentioned by R. Uerpmann, *supra* note 1616, p. 36, with further references.

1933 UN Doc. A/61/10 (2006), p. 283. See also the Special Rapporteur's proposal that contained the same essence but slightly different wording: UN Doc. A/CN.4/564/Add.1 (2006), pp. 6–11.

1934 Comment 2 to Article 28, UN Doc. A/61/10 (2006), pp. 283–284.

determining whether a particular right has been violated or not, especially through the assessment of proportionality.[1935] The other is to accept that where an international organization is endowed with an equivalent level of human rights protection, the Court will, in principle, accept this as adequate.[1936] The latter approach was recently clearly articulated in *Bosphorus*, where the Court said that:

> State action taken in compliance with [legal obligations flowing from its membership of an international organisation to which it has transferred part of its sovereignty] is justified as long as the relevant organisation is considered to protect fundamental rights, as regards both the substantive guarantees offered and the mechanisms controlling their observance, in a manner which can be considered at least equivalent to that for which the Convention provides (...) However, any such finding of equivalence could not be final and would be susceptible to review in the light of any relevant change in fundamental rights' protection.[1937]

1935 See, e.g. *Beer & Regan v. Germany* and *Waite & Kennedy v. Germany*, both *supra* note 1633, respectively §§54–63 and 64–73. See also, specifically regarding the EC, Lawson, pp. 477–479 and A. Berramdane, *supra* note 1855, pp. 263–266. Compare de Wet, pp. 378–382.

1936 For an extensive and critical discussion, see generally Lawson, pp. 345–492.

1937 *Bosphorus Hava Yolları Turizm ve Ticaret Anonim Şirketi v. Ireland*, 30 June 2005, §155. For a discussion, see, e.g. S. Adam & F. Krenc, 'La responsabilité des états membres de l'Union européenne devant la Cour européenne des droits de l'homme', 125 *J.T.* 2006, pp. 85–87; J. Andriantsimbazovina, 'Harmonie ou disharmonie de la protection des droits de l'homme en Europe? Quelques considérations sur la jurisprudence de la Cour européenne des droits de l'homme depuis 2005', 42 *C.D.E.* 2006, pp. 749–750; F. Benoit-Rohmer, 'À propos de l'arrêt Bosphorus Airlines du 30 juin 2005: l'adhésion contrainte de l'Union à la Convention', 16 *R.T.D.H.* 2005, pp. 827–853 (who is of the view that this permits the ECtHR to exercise a variable measure of control that may depend on the human right concerned); J. Bröhmer, 'Die Bosphorus-Entscheidung des Europäischen Gerichtshofs für Menschenrechte: der Schutz der Grund- und Menschenrechte in der EU und das Verhältnis zur EMRK', 17 *Europäische Zeitschrift für Wirtschaftsrecht* 2006, pp. 71–76; A. Ciampi, 'L'Union européenne et le respect des droits de l'homme dans la mise en œuvre des sanctions devant la Cour européenne des droits de l'homme', 110 *R.G.D.I.P.* 2006, pp. 85–116 (rejecting the Court's view and pleading for a full review); V. Constantinesco, 'C'est comme si ç'était fait?: (observations à propos de l'arrêt de la Cour européenne des droits de l'homme "Grande Chambre", Bosphorus Airlines, du 30 juin 2005)', 42 *C.D.E.* 2006, pp. 363–378; C. Costello, 'The Bosphorus Ruling of the European Court of Human Rights: Fundamental Rights and Blurred Boundaries in Europe', 6 *H.R.L.R.* 2006, pp. 87–130; A. Hinarejos Parga, 'Bosphorus v Ireland and the Protection of Fundamental Rights in Europe', 31 *Eur. L. Rev.* 2006, pp. 251–259; F. Hoffmeister, 'Bosphorus Hava Yollari Turizm ve Ticaret Anonim Sirket v. Ireland: App. No. 45036/98: European Court of Human Rights (Grand Chamber), June 30, 2005', 100 *A.J.I.L* 2006, pp. 442–449 and J. Phelps, 'Reflections on Bosphorus and Human Rights in Europe', 81 *Tulane Law Review* 2006, pp. 251–279. See also *Naletilic v. Croatia* (4 May 2000), in which the Court ruled that the ICTY "*in view of the content of its Statute and Rules of Procedure, offers all the necessary guarantees*" (§1.b). For a recent extentive discussion of Member State responsibility for EC law under the ECHR, see generally P. Schäfer, *Verletzungen der Europäischen Menschenrechtskonvention durch Europäisches Gemeinschaftsrecht und dessen Vollzug: Verantwortlichkeit und Haftung der Mitgliedstaaten*, Baden-Baden, Nomos, 2006.

However, in its later judgment in *Boivin*, the Court appears to have rejected responsibility on the basis of establishment by requiring a direct or indirect intervention of the respondent State:

> … la décision litigieuse a été prise par un tribunal international échappant à la juridiction des Etats défendeurs, dans le cadre d'un conflit du travail qui s'inscrit entièrement dans l'ordre juridique interne d'Eurocontrol, organisation internationale possédant une personnalité juridique distincte de celle de ses Etats membres…. 'à aucun moment la France ou la Belgique ne sont intervenues, directement ou indirectement, dans ce litige, et ne relève en l'espèce aucune action ou omission de ces Etats ou de leurs autorités qui serait de nature à engager leur responsabilité au regard de la Convention. … Contrairement à la situation dans [d'autres] affaires, qui impliquaient toutes une intervention directe ou indirecte de l'Etat ou des Etats mis en cause, on ne saurait dire que le requérant en l'espèce relève de la "juridiction" des Etats défendeurs au sens de l'article 1 de la Convention.[1938]

The principle of Member State responsibility by virtue of establishment seems sound at first sight as Member States should not be able to evade their international obligations. However, an unmitigated theory of Member State responsibility would mean that in order to avoid its responsibility from being engaged, each Member State would have to ensure that an international organization respects all of its international obligations, at least towards those third parties that are entitled to the corresponding rights. This would be very difficult to apply: while it might perhaps be conceivable at the European level (or any regional level more generally), it is difficult to see how it could function at the global level because it would *inter alia* impose regional standards on worldwide international organizations.[1939] Moreover, while in theory it might be possible to require respect only in relation to the beneficiary of the Member State's obligations, this would be very difficult to apply in practice.[1940] It is therefore submitted that a mitigated theory is indeed necessary. It may also be

---

1938 *Boivin v. 34 Members of the Council of Europe*, 9 September 2008 (admissibility decision), pp. 7–8.

1939 This appears to have been one of the considerations taken into account by the ECtHR in relation to its Kosovo decision in the *Behrami & Saramati* cases (*supra* note 1831), see especially §149 ("*the Convention cannot be interpreted in a manner which would subject the acts and omissions of Contracting Parties which are covered by UNSC Resolutions and occur prior to or in the course of such missions, to the scrutiny of the Court. To do so would … be tantamount to imposing conditions on the implementation of a UNSC Resolution which were not provided for in the text of the Resolution itself*").

1940 One can hardly imagine the EU granting more protection to nationals or residents of one Member State than to those of other Member States. Similarly, it is hard to image the UN applying different standards in peacekeeping operations according to where such operations take place, although here a regional differentiation might not be unthinkable (albeit difficult from a sending State perspective where military contingents are concerned). In relation to obligations towards third States rather than individuals, this may be less difficult, although noted that one may draw a parallel with the human rights protection in some EC Member States in which national constitutional Courts have accepted that the human rights protection offered in the framework of international organizations needs to be adequate but not necessarily entirely identical to that on the national level.[1941] Another point of comparison is the European Court of Human Rights' jurisprudence on extradition, in which the Court does not impose full respect of the entire ECHR as a condition for extradition.[1942]

The question then is what mitigation there should be. The European Court of Human Rights seems to have adopted a fairly adequate way of accommodating the different interests involved in cases where there is some Member State intervention. The general equivalent protection test should guarantee a generally adequate protection and encourage Member States to impose such a protection on international organizations. This test is particularly appropriate if one regards the basis for Member State responsibility as relating to Member States' actions when establishing an international organization (or when amending its constituent instruments). However, it should not be limited to cases where there is some Member State intervention.

The question that arises, however, is how to deal with individual violations despite generally equivalent protection. Several options present themselves. A first possibility is to regard the equal protection merely as entailing a presumption of compliance that may be rebutted in any given case for any violation of an obligation. In this case, maximum respect for Member State obligations would be ensured but Member States would be forced to set up a water tight system of respect for their obligations by international organizations. A second option

there respect for conflicting Member State obligations might entail an impossible position for an organization.

1941 E.g. in Germany, see J. Schwarze, *supra* note 1616, p. 2. The comparison between these two levels/situations is also made by R. Uerpmann, *supra* note 1616, p. 33. See also T. Kingreen, *supra* note 1773, pp. 80–84.

1942 Under the ECHR extradition/surrender is clearly prohibited when there is a real risk of torture or inhuman or degrading treatment (ECtHR, *Soering v. UK*, 7 July 1989). The situation for other rights is less clear. E.g. it would appear that a (real threat of a) violation of the right to a fair trial will not normally entail an obligation to refuse extradition/surrender but only exceptionally "*in circumstances where the fugitive has suffered or risks suffering a flagrant denial of justice in the requesting country*" (ECtHR, *Einhorn v. France*, Decision as to the admissibility, 16 October 2001, §32). See also *Drozd and Janousek v. France and Spain* (26 June 1992, §110: "*The Contracting States are, however, obliged to refuse their co-operation if it emerges that the conviction is the result of a flagrant denial of justice*"). Obviously, this is not an ideal solution as it can lead to extradition/surrender in cases where 'lesser' violations are likely. However, any other solution could potentially make extradition/surrender almost impossible between many States. On balance, it may therefore be the only workable solution. Compare Lawson, pp. 244–247.

would be to rely on proportionality as a means of limiting Member State responsibility in the case of violations despite equal protection: in this case only serious violations would outweigh the interests of international cooperation.[1943] This option would combine the two above-mentioned tracks in the European Court of Human Right's jurisprudence and would seem preferable to the first one. It appears to be the option endorsed by the Court in *Bosphorus*.[1944] A third option consists of rejecting Member State responsibility *on the basis of the establishment* in the case of individual violations despite generally equivalent protection. At first sight, this seems difficult to accept in that it leads to a lack of responsibility for certain violations. However, it would least affect the separate legal personality. Moreover, the scope of this gap in protection might be significantly limited if Member States were to incur responsibility for helping adopt and/or implement decisions of international organizations that are contrary to their international obligations (see the following subsection). In that case, the gap in protection would be limited to situations entirely effected by an international organization, which could possibly be covered by the ILC's *unwitting result* exception.

Yet even assuming that one of the above solutions might offer an adequate approach, a number of other difficulties have to be overcome. In particular, while the equal protection may work fairly well in respect of human rights and related areas of law, it is less obvious to assure equal protection in respect of other (very varied and more inter-State) obligations.[1945] More importantly, it is doubtful whether the equivalent protection can be applied to more traditional inter-State obligations: whereas some balancing of interests seems acceptable between two 'common interest regimes' that mostly serve the interests of the international (or European) community and its citizens (e.g. human rights and close European integration), there appears to be little basis for allowing some States to partially

1943 Although it must be admitted that EC/EU integration would thereby justify a lower protection even though the obligations under the ECHR are also owed to non-EC/EU Council of Europe Member States.

1944 *Supra* note 1937, §156: "*If such equivalent protection is considered to be provided by the organisation, the presumption will be that a State has not departed from the requirements of the Convention when it does no more than implement legal obligations flowing from its membership of the organisation. However, any such presumption can be rebutted if, in the circumstances of a particular case, it is considered that the protection of Convention rights was* manifestly *deficient. In such cases, the interest of international co-operation would be outweighed by the Convention's role as a "constitutional instrument of European public order" in the field of human rights*" (emphasis added). A. Berramdane, *supra* note 1855, pp. 261–262 appears to be rather critical of this solution. For a subsequent application, see ECtHR, *Cooperatieve Producentenorganisatie van de Nederlandse Kokkelvisserij U.A. v. the Netherlands*, 20 January 2009 (admissibility decision), pp. 18–21.

1945 A provision such as Article 307 EC Treaty might to some extent solve this problem.

sacrifice their obligations towards a third Party purely for their own interests.[1946] It is therefore submitted that these two situations must be distinguished, although it may be difficult to draw the line between the two.

Finally, from a practical perspective, determining what the ILC qualifies as an act that, if it were committed by that State, would constitute a breach of that obligation, may not always be easy and *inter alia* gives rise to the question in what circumstances Member States would incur individual and/or joint responsibility.[1947] For instance, in the case of treatment by an international organization of its staff that is contrary to human rights obligations of some of its Member States, would all the Member States bound by the obligations concerned be responsible, or only the State in the territory of whom the violation occurs (if it is among those States)?[1948] In the case of responsibility by virtue of the *establishment*, the better view would seem to be that since the staff are employed by an organization set up by all the Member States, all those Member States that are bound by the obligation will incur responsibility.

2. RESPONSIBILITY OF A MEMBER FOR ITS OWN SUBSEQUENT CONDUCT IN THE FRAMEWORK OF AN INTERNATIONAL ORGANIZATION

Apart from the question whether Member States may be held liable for the conduct of an international organization due to their initial role in establishing it, there is also the question to what extent they can be held responsible for their own subsequent conduct in the framework of an international organization, both in adopting decisions and in implementing them.

The ILC, in the present state of its work on the responsibility of international organizations, seems to have proposed to omit this aspect from the latter topic, apparently feeling that it has been adequately addressed in its work on state responsibility.[1949] This would seem to imply that any conduct that is attributable

1946 Compare the argument by L. Caflisch & A.A. Cancado Trindade, *supra* note 1786, pp. 38–39 that the rules of treaty law and State responsibility entail that if a State enters into conflicting treaty obligations that are equal, a State will have to choose which one to obey and will therefore automatically violate the other. The authors see this as the rationale underlying the ECtHR's case law on Member State responsibility in the framework of international organizations.

1947 See on this, e.g. M. Hartwig, *supra* note 1834, pp. 288–289; Lawson, pp. 194–198 and R. Uerpmann, *supra* note 1616, p. 37.

1948 See also Lawson, pp. 195 and 298–300.

1949 The Draft Articles proposed so far, that are relevant, concern the attribution of conduct to international organizations and the circumstances under which a Member State may be to State organs, even when occurring within the framework of an international organization, may lead to the responsibility of that State.[1950] This means that the savings clause in Article 57 of the ILC's Draft Articles on State Responsibility,[1951] which provides that "*These Articles are without prejudice to any question of the responsibility under international law of an international organization, or of any State for the conduct of an international organization*", is to be interpreted restrictively.

While this rule may seem obvious at first sight, State responsibility for conduct within an international organization has been the subject of debate among scholars, especially in relation to decision-making because representatives of States,[1952] especially of governments, in decision-making organs of international organizations act in a dual capacity: they remain State organs but they are also part of an organ of the international organization.[1953] Obviously, this is not the case for truly international (e.g. executive or judicial) offices in respect of which

---

responsible for conduct of an international organization, but hardly the conduct of a Member State in the framework of an international organization. In respect of the latter, it was stated in the Fourth Report of the special rapporteur (UN Doc. A/CN.4/564/Add.1, §54) that "*Not all the questions that may affect the responsibility of a State in connection with the conduct of an international organization should be examined in the present context. For instance, questions relating to attribution of conduct to a State have already been covered in the Articles on State responsibility. It would clearly be preferable not to consider them here again. Thus, if an issue arises as to whether a certain conduct is to be attributed to a State or to an international organization or to both, the current Articles will provide criteria only for settling the question as to whether that conduct is to be attributed to an international organization, while the Articles on State responsibility will say whether that same conduct is to be attributed or not to a State*" (see also UN Doc. A/61/10, pp. 277–278). Also, in the commentaries to draft Articles 25 and 26, which deal with respectively aid or assistance and direction and control by a State to/over the commission of an internationally wrongful act by an international organization, simple "*participation in the decision-making process of the organization according to the pertinent rules of the organization*" seems to be ruled out in principle as a ground for Member State responsibility (for the acts of the organization) under these provisions (UN Doc. A/61/10, pp. 279–281).

1950 Compare A. Geslin, *supra* note 1924, p. 550 ("*le principe selon lequel les membres d'une organisation internationale sont responsables, à l'égard des tiers, de leur propre comportement au sein de cette institution lorsque celui-ci a rendu possible la réalisation de l'acte dommagable semble bien établie et non contesté en pratique*").

1951 *Supra* note 1925.

1952 For instance, I. Pernice, *supra* note 1654, p. 240 note 44, writes that voting engages the Member State's responsibility but questions whether a vote is still an act of a Member State. The ILA's 2004 *Final Report on the Accountability of International Organisations* (*supra* note 1610), p. 25 states that "*the continuing role of Member States qua members of an organ of an IO is neutral as regards Member States' liability if the Organisation has 'une volonté distincte'. … a Member State neither incurs special liability nor avoids existing liability according to whether it is or is not a member of a particular organ*".

1953 For an extensive analysis of the status of State representatives in international organizations, see E. Lagrange, *supra* note 1656, pp. 135–167. See also M. Hartwig, *supra* note 1834, pp. 272–280 and Lawson, pp. 463–471.

the office holder may not take instructions from a State.[1954] Also, the matter becomes more complex in the case of representatives of a State in parliamentary bodies, which represent their State but cannot be said to be subject to its instructions and control in the same way as government representatives (at least in democracies).

It is, however, submitted that the individual conduct (e.g. a vote) of at least government officials that represent States in decision-making bodies of international organizations is attributable to their State and must be distinguished from the collective conduct of an organ (e.g. a decision adopted), which is attributable to the organization.[1955] That the mere vote in itself does not entail any direct consequences, because it only takes effect when it is transformed into a collective decision also reflecting other votes, is not necessarily decisive in my view.[1956] The real question is whether the vote can constitute a breach of an international obligation independently from any breach that might result from the decision adopted. It is submitted that this can be the case but that it will not always be so. In particular, responsibility would arise for a vote that violates a rule which includes an obligation to not tolerate/encourage/incite certain conduct[1957] or an obligation to take all lawful measures to prevent a certain conduct[1958] or to ensure respect for certain rules.[1959] Thus whether a vote may

---

1954 As is, e.g. the case for members of the European Commission or the UN Secretary-General.

1955 Compare Lawson, pp. 463–471, who seems to be in favour of Member State responsibility for votes but notes divergent views in doctrine and the *C.F.D.T.* case to the contrary (see *infra* on the latter). On this distinction between the collective act imputed to the organ and the underlying votes as decisions of individual members of that organ, see also R. Wessel, *supra* note 1253, p. 21 (citing Ruiter) and R. Wessel, *supra* note 1348, pp. 11–14. M. Hartwig, *supra* note 1834, pp. 272–280 seems to be hesitant to admit Member State responsibility for decision-making.

1956 *Contra*: E. Lagrange, *supra* note 1953, pp. 332–343.

1957 E.g. the obligation for States to refrain from "*organising, instigating, assisting or participating in acts of civil strife or terrorist acts in another State or acquiescing in organised activities within its territory directed towards the commission of such acts, when the acts referred to ... involve a threat or use of force*"; see Declaration on Principles of International Law concerning Friendly Relations and Co-operation amongst States in accordance with the Charter of the United Nations (Annex to UN General Assembly Res. 2625(XXV), 24 October 1970), 1.I.9.

1958 E.g. to prevent genocide; see Article 1 Convention on the Prevention and Punishment of the Crime of Genocide (New York, 9 December 1948, 78 *U.N.T.S.* 277): "*The Contracting Parties confirm that genocide, ..., is a crime under international law which they undertake to prevent and to punish*". In its judgment of 26 February 2007 in the *Case concerning the application of the Convention on the Prevention and Punishment of the Crime of Genocide* (Bosnia and Herzegovina *v.* Serbia and Montenegro), the ICJ identified the obligation to prevent genocide as a distinct obligation (§§155–165) and held that Serbia and Montenegro was responsible for violating this obligation (§§425–438) but that it had not committed genocide or complicity thereto because of a lack of attribution (§§379–424).

1959 E.g. the obligation to "*respect and* to ensure respect *for*" the 1949 Geneva Conventions and AP I "*in all circumstances*" (emphasis added), discussed *infra* in Chapter 8.F.

lead to international responsibility depends on the nature of the obligation at stake. Therefore, I argue that a State engages its international responsibility by voting in relation to a decision when the mere vote itself amounts to a violation of an international obligation of that State. This view has some support in the jurisprudence of the European Court of Human Rights, especially the *Matthews* case.[1960] Opponents of this argument in part invoke the older decision of the European Commission of Human Rights in *C.F.D.T.*, in which it was held that the Member States did not exercise their jurisdiction in participating in an EC Council decision.[1961] However, this specific element of this decision does not appear to have been repeated in later jurisprudence and the Court's view in *Matthews*, even though it concerned (quasi) primary EC law, suggests it may no longer be valid. Indeed, in a 2002 decision in the *SEGI* case, the Court clearly regards Member States as responsible for decisions they adopt in the area of the CFSP,[1962] though an exception may have to be made in respect of decisions concerning Chapter VII of the UN Charter.[1963] A similar evolution may be found

1960 *Matthews v. UK*, 18 February 1999, §§32–33, in which the UK was held responsible for an act of EC law to which it had agreed and which required unanimity. The act (Act Concerning the Election of the Representatives of the European Parliament by Direct Universal Suffrage of 20 September 1976, annexed to Council Decision 76/787) was not an ordinary decision of an EC organ, required adoption in accordance with the respective constitutional requirements and was, according to the Court, an international instrument "*freely entered into by the United Kingdom*". The latter element suggests that the same may be true of other decisions of international organizations, at least when adopted by unanimity. Compare M. Breuer, 'Offene Fragen im Verhältnis von EGMR und EuGH. Zur Entscheidung des EGMR im Fall Emesa Sugar', 32 *Eur. Gr. R.Z.* 2005, pp. 229–234 (arguing that the ECtHR may have left open the possibility of reviewing EC secondary law even without Member State implementing Acts in *Emesa Sugar NV v. the Netherlands*, Decision as to admissibility of 13 January 2005) and Uerpmann, *supra* note 1616, pp. 36–37. But see S. Adam & F. Krenc, *supra* note 1937, p. 86, arguing that *Bosphorus* indicates that the *Matthews* ruling is limited to primary EC law.

1961 *C.F.D.T.* v. *the European Communities, alternatively their Member States*, Decision of 10 July 1978, No. 8030/77, §7: "*the Commission considers that an examination of the applicant's complaints is also outside its jurisdiction ratione personae since these States by taking part in the decision of the Council of the European Communities had not in the circumstances of the instant case exercised their "jurisdiction" within the meaning of Article 1 of the Convention*". See E. Lagrange, *supra* note 1656, pp. 337–338. Compare the discussion of this case by Lawson, pp. 363–372.

1962 ECtHR, *SEGI and others & GESTORAS PRO-AMNISTIA and others. v. Germany and others*, 23 May 2002, Decision as to the admissibility ("*CFSP decisions are therefore intergovernmental in nature. By taking part in their preparation and adoption each State engages its responsibility. That responsibility is assumed jointly by the States when they adopt a CFSP decision*"). See on this case J. Andriantsimbazovina, *supra* note 1937, pp. 751–753. An alternative explanation might be that the ECtHR did not consider that the EU, as opposed to the EC, had legal personality and therefore had no option but to attribute the conduct to the Member States. The summary nature of the wording used by the Court does not offer any insight into the reasons supporting its view on this point.

1963 The ECtHR stated in its Kosovo decision in the *Behrami & Saramati* cases (*supra* note 1831) that "*Since operations established by UNSC Resolutions under Chapter VII of the UN Charter are fundamental to the mission of the UN to secure international peace and security ..., the* in the Human Rights Committee's views in this respect: whereas in 1987 it held that "*the recruitment policies of an international organization ... cannot, in any way, be construed as coming within the jurisdiction of the Netherlands or of any other State party to the [ICCPR] and the Optional Protocol thereto*",[1964] it more recently stated that Member States remain bound by their obligations under the ICCPR when they deploy their armed forces in the framework of international organizations,[1965] although the latter concerns the implementation of a decision rather than its adoption.

In addition to responsibility arising from its role in adopting a decision, a Member State may also incur responsibility for implementing a decision of an international organization that is contrary to the Member State's international obligations. Indeed, in most cases where the rights of third parties are affected, Member States will play a role in implementing decisions of international organizations. Although in some respects the question whether the Member State has any discretion or not in this implementation may be relevant,[1966] from the perspective of a Member State's obligation towards third parties this seems irrelevant: if it breaches an obligation from which it could not derogate, the fact

Convention cannot be interpreted in a manner which would subject the acts and omissions of Contracting Parties which are covered by UNSC Resolutions and occur prior to or in the course of such missions, to the scrutiny of the Court.... This reasoning equally applies to voluntary acts of the respondent States such as the vote of a permanent member of the UNSC in favour of the relevant Chapter VII Resolution and the contribution of troops to the security mission: such acts may not have amounted to obligations flowing from membership of the UN but they remained crucial to the effective fulfilment by the UNSC of its Chapter VII mandate and, consequently, by the UN of its imperative peace and security aim" (§149). *A contrario*, in other cases such voluntary acts arguably are attributable to the State concerned.

1964 *H.v.d.P. v. Netherlands*, 8 April 1987, Doc. CCPR/C/29/D/217/1986, §3.2. See on this case D. McGoldrick, 'Extraterritorial Application of the International Covenant on Civil and Political Rights', in F. Coomans & T. Kamminga (eds.), *Extraterritorial Application of Human Rights Treaties*, Antwerp, Intersentia, 2004, pp. 53–54.

1965 General Comment 31 (21 April 2004, CCPR/C/74/CRP.4/Rev.6), §10 ("*a State party must respect and ensure the rights laid down in the Covenant to anyone within the power or effective control of that State Party, even if not situated within the territory of the State Party (...) This principle also applies to those within the power or effective control of the forces of a State Party acting outside its territory, regardless of the circumstances in which such power or effective control was obtained, such as forces constituting a national contingent of a State Party assigned to an international peace-keeping or peace-enforcement operation*").

1966 This may, e.g. be relevant under EC law for determining whether a Member State or a Community institution is responsible for a violation of higher rules of EC law. Compare the ECJ's view that damage suffered as a consequence of EC sanctions adopted pursuant to sanctions imposed by the UN Security Council would not be attributable to the EC but only to the UN; see Case T-184/95 (*Dorsch Consult Ingenieurgesellschaft mbH v Council of the European Union and Commission of the European Communities*, Judgment of 28 April 1998, §§73–74); the appeals judgment (Case C-237/98, *Dorsch Consult Ingenieurgesellschaft mbH v. Council of the European Union and Commission of the European Communities*, Judgment of 15 June 2000) did not address this point.

that it acts in the framework of an international organization is no excuse since it has itself created this organization and enabled it to order the Member State to violate its obligations.[1967] There is case law under the ECHR to this effect,[1968] although it has recently been qualified in *Bosphorus*[1969] and has held to be subject to an exception for Chapter VII of the UN Charter.[1970] The qualification deals with the one circumstance in which it would be harsh to hold a Member State responsible, namely where the Member State had provided for respect of such obligations by the organization but where this has turned out to be ineffective in a specific case. Given the likeness to responsibility resulting from establishment, one could argue for a similar solution (see above). On the other hand, the situation is different because here we have a specific (implementing) action by the Member State, which is in a position to refuse execution and thereby uphold its obligations towards a third party, even if this may entail its responsibility towards the international organization and/or its other Member States. It is submitted that this difference justifies broader Member State responsibility for implementing decisions of international organizations. However, for 'common interest regimes', mitigation via proportionality in those cases where the Member State had provided for equivalent protection and has no discretion to implement the decision in conformity with its obligations, seems acceptable. It is precisely

1967 One may draw a parallel to *force majeure* as a circumstance precluding wrongfulness under the rules of State responsibility as laid down in Article 23 of the ILC's Draft Articles on State Responsibility (*supra* note 1925), which in such a case could not be invoked because there would not be material impossibility and even if there were, it would be due "*either alone or in combination with other factors, to the conduct of the State invoking it*" and that State "*has assumed the risk of that situation occurring*". But see M. Hirsch, *supra* note 1623, pp. 82–88.

1968 See, e.g. ECtHR, *Cantoni v. France*, judgment of 15 November 1996, §30 ("*The fact, pointed to by the Government, that Article L. 511 of the Public Health Code is based almost word for word on Community Directive 65/65 ... does not remove it from the ambit of Article 7 [ECHR]*") and European Commission of Human Rights, Decisions of 9 February 1990 in *M & Co v. Germany* ("*Under Article 1 [ECHR] the Member States are responsible for all acts and omissions of their domestic organs allegedly violating the Convention regardless of whether the act or omission in question is a consequence of domestic law or regulations or of the necessity to comply with international obligations*") and of 16 January 1995 in *Gestra v. Italy* ("*la Commission doit ... controler que les effets de l'application, par les organes internes des Parties contractantes, d'autres conventions internationales conclues par la suite, ne portent pas atteinte aux droits et libertés garantis par la Convention*"); see also Lawson, pp. 473–476; A. Berramdane, *supra* note 1855, pp. 258–261 and M. Breuer, *supra* note 1960, pp. 231–232. S. Adam & F. Krenc, *supra* note 1937, p. 86, consider that the Court was probably so demanding because the Member States had some discretion; however, the language used does not indicate that this matters.

1969 *Supra* note 1937. It was an impoundment by the Irish authorities pursuant to an EC Regulation that was challenged, i.e. Member State implementation. For the view that *Bosphorus* partially overturned *Cantoni*, see A. Haratsch, 'Die Solange-Rechtsprechung des Europäischen Gerichtshofs für Menschenrechte: das Kooperationsverhältnis zwischen EGMR und EuGH', 66 *Z.a.ö.R.V.* 2006, p. 932.

1970 See ECtHR, *Behrami & Saramati* decision (*supra* note 1831) as discussed *supra* note 1963.

such an exception that was recognized by the European Court of Human Rights in *Bosphorus*.[1971]

I would therefore argue that there are three bases for Member State responsibility (leaving aside complicity). First, by virtue of its role in the establishment of an international organization, a Member State incurs international responsibility for an act committed by an international organization that, if committed by that State, would have constituted a breach of an international obligation of that Member State. This is subject to an exception for 'common interest regimes' in respect of which the Member State has provided for equivalent protection, albeit that the Member State will remain responsible where despite such equivalent protection there is a manifest violation that outweighs the interests of international cooperation. Second, a Member State engages its international responsibility by voting in relation to a decision when the mere vote itself amounts to a violation of an international obligation of that State. Third, a Member State is internationally responsible for implementing a decision that violates its international obligations except where it had provided for equivalent protection in relation to a 'common interest regime' and has no discretion to implement the decision in conformity with its obligations and only to the extent that the violation of its obligations is proportionate to the importance of international cooperation.

I. GENERAL CONCLUSIONS

Despite the appearance of general agreement in doctrine and jurisprudence that international organizations are bound by (general) international law, at least in their external relations and inasmuch as the rules are relevant to their competences and are compatible with their proper nature, the reality is more complex and there is no agreement on the basis for this rule. Moreover, international organizations themselves do not always accept this rule when push comes to shove. Furthermore, the distinction between internal and external relations is not always clear in relation to Member States and is not entirely conclusive from the point of view of international law. In particular, Member States are not at liberty to derogate from agreements involving third parties which either affect these parties' rights or which may only be amended by all the parties to such agreements. Also, it may be difficult to establish whether a

1971 *Supra* note 1937. The ECtHR held that compliance with EC law entailed a presumption of conformity with the ECHR to the extent that the EC has an equivalent level of protection but that this may be rebutted if this protection is "manifestly deficient" (§§148–165). See also A. Berramdane, *supra* note 1855, pp. 258–261.

particular act or provision binding an international organization is directed only internally or (also) externally.

A more nuanced analysis is therefore required, looking at different ways in which international organizations may be bound. I have studied this under three headings: obligations undertaken by the organization itself, imposed by its Member States or resulting from general international law.

Obligations undertaken by the organization itself include agreements concluded by the organization, which pose a few specific questions but no fundamental problem for the present purposes in that international organizations are clearly bound by treaties they conclude, and unilateral acts. As to the latter, international organizations may be empowered to adopt decisions, including decisions binding themselves, but in addition, I have argued that they are presumed to have the capacity to perform unilateral acts binding themselves as States may do. Moreover, they may bind themselves to other international instruments through unilateral acts. The particular challenge here is determining whether the organization is bound only in its internal legal order or (also) externally. This question can only be answered on a case-by-case basis.

Obligations imposed by the Member States are essentially those included in the constituent instrument of an organization or in related acts. The main problem in relation to such provisions can be their interpretation.

The most difficult category is obligations resulting from general international law. I submit that in their external relations, international organizations are bound by customary international law inasmuch as the rules are relevant to their competences and are compatible with their proper nature, which means that they may have to be adapted or applied only partially, including with regard to legal capacities. The basis for this binding is that an international organization with international legal personality exists in the international legal order by virtue of this legal order and must accept the rules of that legal order as applicable to it. In addition, as a policy argument, any other view would leave international organizations largely unregulated by international law. The same is true for general principles of law that are part of international law. In addition, general principles of law play a particular role in the internal legal order of international organizations, where they may be based on general principles common to the Member States (the less Member States and the more similar they are, the greater is the potential of this source, which may include similar principles recognized in international law if not contrary to the organization's system), general principles proper to international law (if not contrary to the organization's system), general principles proper to the organization's legal system and general principles derived from treaties to which a significant number of Member States are parties or signatories. This source has mainly been developed in the EC/EU but despite its limited adoption in other international organizations (probably at least partially due to less possibilities for international courts to rule on the matter) offers a significant potential for binding also other international organizations, especially to obligations common to their Member States. Furthermore, it is rarely contested that international organizations are bound by peremptory norms.

In contrast, practice and jurisprudence have only rarely accepted that an international organization is bound by agreements concluded by one or more of its Member States, rejecting theories based on the *nemo plus* … rule or analogies to State succession, despite attempts in the literature in favour of a broader application of this mechanism. The few cases accepting this mechanism that are known concern the EC taking the place of its Member States in relation to the GATT and two customs agreements pursuant to the 'substitution' theory espoused by the ECJ. While the ECJ's Court of First Instance has arguably applied the latter theory to the EC in respect of UN sanctions in *Kadi* and *Yusuf*, albeit only as a matter of EC law, the ECJ itself has rejected this opening to a wider binding of the EC to Member State treaties.

To the extent that international organizations are not bound by treaty obligations of their Member States, there is a risk that Member States evade their international obligations by acting though international organizations. However, this risk can be avoided or minimized if one accepts, at least to some extent, that Member States remain responsible for any violation of their international obligations even if they have transferred competences in respect of such obligations to an international organization. It is submitted that Member State responsibility arises (leaving aside complicity):

- by virtue of establishing an international organization, for acts committed by an international organization that, if committed by that State, would have constituted a breach of an international obligation of that Member State, except for 'common interest regimes' in respect of which the Member State has provided for equivalent protection, with the caveat that where despite such equivalent protection there is a manifest violation that outweighs the interests of international cooperation, the Member State will remain responsible;
- for voting in relation to a decision when the mere vote itself amounts to a violation of an international obligation of that State;

- for implementing a decision of an international organization that violates its international obligations except where it had provided for equivalent protection in relation to a 'common interest regime' and has no discretion to implement the decision in conformity with its obligations and only to the extent that the violation of its obligations is proportionate to the importance of international cooperation.

J. APPLICATION TO THE EU

If these conclusions are applied to the EU, it means that the EU, as an international organization with international legal personality,[1972] is bound by:[1973]

- treaties which it concludes (externally and internally[1974]);
- unilateral acts which it performs to the extent that they create binding obligations (internally and/or externally, depending on the circumstances);
- its constituent instruments and certain related rules (primarily internally);
- agreements between its Member States binding it where this is exceptionally permitted (primarily internally);
- judicial decisions and provisions of other international instruments (whether binding or not and including decisions of other international organizations) made binding by virtue of any of the above sources (internally and/or externally);
- customary international law on matters within its competences subject to any necessary modifications (internally to the extent not set aside by EC/EU law and externally without these limits);[1975]

1972 See *supra*, Chapter 6.

1973 Compare P.J. Kuijper, 'Customary International Law, Decisions of International Organisations and Other Techniques for Ensuring Respect for International Legal Rules in European Community Law', in J. Wouters, A. Nollkaemper & E. de Wet (eds.), *The Europeanisation of International Law: The Status of International Law in the EU and its Member States*, The Hague, T.M.C. Asser Press, 2008, pp. 87–106 and C. Tietje, 'The Status of International Law in the European Legal Order: The Case of International Treaties and Non-binding International Instruments', in *id.*, pp. 55–69.

1974 These expressions as used in this section refer to binding effect under international law or only under EC/EU law.

1975 For a discussion concerning the EC, albeit somewhat dated, see M. Bothe, *supra* note 1616, pp. 128–137. On the EU and customary international law generally, see A. Gianelli, *Unione Europea e diritto internazionale consuetudinario*, Giappichelli, 2004. See also A. Rosas, 'Relations entre les états membres de l'Union européenne: le droit international public y a-t-il encore sa place?', in E. Belliard (ed.), *L'état souverain dans le monde d'aujourd'hui: mélanges en l'honneur de Jean-Pierre Puissochet*, Paris, Pedone, 2008, pp. 255–265.

- general principles of law which are part of international law (internally to the extent not set aside by EC/EU law and externally without these limits);
- general principles of EC/EU law, which may include principles derived from the EC/EU legal order, from general principles of international law or from the Member States' domestic law or their international treaty obligations (primarily internally);
- *ius cogens* (externally and internally);
- (provisions of) treaties concluded by one or more of its Member States where the conditions for 'substitution' are met (internally and/or externally).

In addition, the Member States remain responsible for any violation of their own international obligations, including through or by the EC/EU, within the scope set out above. In respect of EU competences over which the ECJ has no jurisdiction, the equivalent protection test used by the European Court of Human Rights will arguably not be met since it seems to include the procedural guarantees.[1976]

In the next Part, I will analyze the implications of this conclusion for human rights and law of armed conflict obligations in ESDP operations.

1976 See the quote from the *Bosphorus* case, *supra* note 1937. In this sense also L. Wildhaber, 'Europäischer Grundrechtsschutz aus der Sicht des Europäischen Gerichtshofs für Menschenrechte', 32 *Eur. Gr. R.Z.* 2005, p. 692 and M.-G. Garbagnati Ketvel, 'The Jurisdiction of the European Court of Justice in Respect of the Common Foreign and Security Policy', 55 *I.C.L.Q.* 2006, pp. 114–115 and 119.

PART III
APPLICABLE INTERNATIONAL LAW IN ESDP OPERATIONS

GENERAL INTRODUCTION TO THE APPLICABLE LAW

The law applicable to any crisis management operation abroad is a complex combination of domestic and international law.[1977] In this short introduction, I will sketch the main elements of this legal framework, and more particularly of the part governing its conduct (as opposed to its legality and establishment). The general legal framework, including international legal basis and mandate, has already been described above in Chapter 3.A and after this introduction, the applicability of the law of armed conflict and of human rights to ESDP operations will be analyzed *in extenso* in Chapters 8 and 9.

Applicable domestic law will normally include, at least to some extent, the law of the sending State or troop-contributing nation (hereinafter both referred to as 'TCN') as well as the local law of the host State (hereinafter 'local law'). The extent to which the domestic law of the TCN is applicable will be determined by the scope of application of this body of law. Typically, armed forces *inter alia*

1977 See for a discussion of some aspects, R. Arnold & G.-J. Knoops (eds.), *Practice and Policies of Modern Peace Support Operations under International Law*, Ardsley, Transnational, 2006; R. Arnold (ed.), *Law Enforcement within the Framework of PSO*, The Hague, Martinus Nijhoff, 2008 and Häussler, especially pp. 43–78. For a brief summary, see M. Zwanenburg, 'Legal Interoperability in Multinational Forces: A Military Necessity', in College of Europe & ICRC (eds.), *Proceedings of the Bruges Colloquium. Current Challenges to the Law of Occupation. 20th – 21st October 2005 / Actes du colloque de Bruges. Les défis contemporains au droit de l'occupation. 20–21 octobre 2005*, Bruges, College of Europe (*collegium* No. 34, available online at www.coleurop.be/template.asp?pagename=pub_collegium), 2006, pp. 108–110; M. Zwanenburg, 'Pieces of the Puzzle: Peace Operations, Occupation and the Use of Force', 100 *Militair Rechtelijk Tijdschrift* 2007, pp. 65–72, especially pp. 69–72. See also M.J. Kelly, *Restoring and Maintaining Order in Complex Peace Operations*, Kluwer, The Hague, 1999 and D. Fleck (ed.), *The Handbook of the Law of Visiting Forces*, Oxford, Oxford University Press, 2001 (while most of this volume focuses on visiting forces in peacetime, some contributions concern peace operations). For a national perspective, see UK Manual, §§14.1–2; M. Forteau, 'La situation juridique des contingents militaires français chargés d'assurer le maintien de l'ordre public sur un territoire étranger', 107 *R.G.D.I.P.* 2003, pp. 635–676 and G. Scherhaufer, 'Military and Legal Aspects of PSOs: The Example of Austria's Deployment with KFOR', in R. Arnold & G.-J. Knoops (eds.), *supra* this note, pp. 67–87. The law applicable to military operations is sometimes referred to as operational law and some countries have operational law manuals. E.g. the US Judge-Advocate General's *Operational Law Handbook* is available online at https://www.jagcnet.army.mil/JAGCNETPortals/Internet/DocLibs/tjaglcsdoclib.nsf.

take with them their nation's criminal law[1978] as well as all laws and regulations concerning discipline and their military status. This is almost invariably confirmed in the status of forces agreements, especially through the submission of armed forces to the criminal and disciplinary jurisdiction of their sending States.[1979]

The applicability of local law to personnel of international crisis management operations is more complex. On the one hand, the applicability of this body of law will normally be territorial and result from the mere presence in the host State unless the contrary is provided for in agreements or other arrangements.[1980] This is usually reinforced by SOFA provisions stipulating *respect* – although the scope of this notion is not entirely clear[1981] – for local

---

1978 See, e.g. UK MANUAL, §14.1 *in fine*. For instance, in Belgium any person subject to Belgian military law who commits a crime under Belgian law abroad may be prosecuted in Belgium pursuant to Article 10*bis* of the Preliminary Title of the Code of Criminal Procedure, which also stipulates the same rule for any person associated with or authorized to accompany the armed forces abroad.

1979 Depending on the nature of the SOFA the degree of TCN criminal jurisdiction may differ but in operations in a host State it is usually exclusive; see, e.g. section 47(b) UN Model SOFA (UN Doc. A/45/594, 9 October 1990) and §7 SFOR SOFA (Dayton Agreement, Paris, 14 December 1995, 35 *I.L.M.* 1996, p. 75, Appendix B to Annex 1A). Among allies the jurisdiction is often not exclusive; see, e.g. Article VII NATO SOFA (Agreement between the Parties to the North Atlantic Treaty regarding the Status of their Forces, London, 19 June 1951, 199 *U.N.T.S.* 67 (1954), which entered into force on 23 August 1953) and Article 17 EU SOFA.

1980 In Resolution 1502 of 26 August 2006, the UN Security Council reaffirmed "*the obligation of all humanitarian personnel and United Nations and its associated personnel to observe and respect the laws of the country in which they are operating, in accordance with international law and the Charter of the United Nations*". DAVID, p. 209 argues that applicable host State law would include the host State's LOAC obligations. However, this seems questionable in the light of practice.

1981 Within NATO and the EU, it is usually argued that 'respect' does not mean 'comply with' and therefore imposes lesser standards. See also H. Krieger, 'Die Verantwortlichkeit Deutschlands nach der EMRK für seine Streitkräfte im Auslandeinsatz', 62 *Z.a.ö.R.V.* 2002, p. 684 note 81. However, the same term in the Vienna Conventions on Diplomatic Relations (18 April 1961, 500 *U.N.T.S.* 95; Article 41(1)) and on Consular Relations (24 April 1963, 596 *U.N.T.S.* 261; Article 55(1)) are understood as requiring *compliance* with local law; see with regard to the former provision, E. Denza, *Diplomatic Law: A Commentary on the Vienna Convention on Diplomatic Relations*, Oxford, Clarendon Press, 1998 (2nd ed.), pp. 373–374, noting that in older writings the duty to respect was seen as requiring less than a legal duty to obey but that absent specific exceptions, a diplomat is legally bound to comply with local law and that this is also substantiated by the procedural nature of immunities (see *infra*, note 1986), which she considers absurd if there is no underlying duty to comply with the law. Obviously, it may be that the term has retained a distinct meaning in SOFA/SOMAs but this is not obvious and is certainly doubtful when it comes to missions that are in part accorded a diplomatic status (as was the case in some civilian ESDP operations; see *supra* Chapter 3) rather than a distinct one as forces or peacekeepers. Compare more extensively A. Sari, 'The EU Status of Forces Agreement: Continuity and Change in the law of Visiting Forces', 46 *R.D.M.D.G.* 2007, pp. 94–105.

law.[1982] This is also reflected in the 1994 UN Convention on the Protection of United Nations and Associated Personnel.[1983] On the other hand, the applicability of local law is limited by a number of factors. First, SOFAs or other arrangements may contain exceptions where this is deemed necessary to achieve the mandate.[1984] Second, international operations and their staff will often enjoy immunities or exemptions from host State jurisdiction,[1985] even if these are of a mere procedural nature,[1986] and do not affect the applicable substantive law. Third, and most importantly, it seems a distinction must be made between ordinary activities (such as driving, at least in some circumstances, or purchasing everyday goods) on the one hand and activities which amount to an exercise of

---

1982 See, e.g. section 6 UN Model SOFA (*supra* note 1979). See, in respect of peacetime visiting forces, R. Batstone, 'Respect for the Law of the Receiving State', in D. Fleck (ed.), *supra* note 1977, pp. 61–69, especially pp. 64–66 (noting problems with administrative law, including on various permits and licences). The issue is only very briefly discussed in respect of operations in A.P.V. Rogers, 'Visiting Forces in an Operational Context', in D. Fleck (ed.), *supra* note 1977, p. 546. M. Zwanenburg, *supra* note 1977, p. 71, considers that often only lip service is paid to this obligation and identifies the problem of identifying local law in some cases. T. Burkhardt, 'Die Entwicklung der Rechtsverhältnisse auslandischer Streitkräfte in den Aufnahmestaaten, insbesodere außerhalb der NATO', in H. Fischer (ed.), *Krisensicherung und humanitärer Schutz: Festschrift für Dieter Fleck*, Berlin, Berliner Wissenschafts-Verlag, 2004, pp. 47–57, especially pp. 50–53 and 57 suggests that the less military the tasks become, the more local law is decisive.

1983 New York, 9 December 1994, 2051 *U.N.T.S.* 391. Article 6 stipulates that "*1. Without prejudice to such privileges and immunities as they may enjoy or to the requirements of their duties, United Nations and associated personnel shall: (a) Respect the laws and regulations of the host State and the transit State ...*".

1984 E.g. §3 SFOR SOFA (*supra* note 1979) states that "*All personnel enjoying privileges and immunities under this Agreement shall respect the laws of the Republic of Bosnia and Herzegovina insofar as it is compatible with the entrusted tasks/mandate and shall refrain from activities not compatible with the nature of the Operation*". Similarly, section 2(2) of UNMIK Regulation 2000/47 (18 August 2000, available online at www.unmikonline.org/regulations/index_reg_2000.htm) stipulates that "*All KFOR personnel shall respect the laws applicable in the territory of Kosovo and regulations issued by the Special Representative of the Secretary-General insofar as they do not conflict with the fulfilment of the mandate given to KFOR under Security Council resolution 1244 (1999)*". See also section 1.2 of the EU document cited *infra* note 1987. In addition, SOFA/SOMAs include specific exemptions from some local laws and regulations, e.g. concerning entry and registration of international staff, carrying of arms, etc.

1985 See for a recent discussion, A. Dickinson, 'Status of Forces under the UN Convention on State Immunity', 55 *I.C.L.Q.* 2006, pp. 427–436. For UN forces, SOFAs usually partially refer to the Convention on the Privileges and Immunities of the United Nations (13 February 1946, 1 *U.N.T.S.* 15); see, e.g. sections 3–5 and 15 UN Model SOFA (*supra* note 1979). See also D. Fleck, 'Introduction', in D. Fleck (ed.), *supra* note 1977, pp. 3–6.

1986 This is very clear where a waiver of immunity is possible. The procedural nature of international immunities was affirmed in respect of State immunity by the European Court of Human Rights in the cases of *McElhinney v. Ireland*; *Fogarty v. U.K.* and *Al-Adsani v. U.K.*, all three judgments of 21 November 2001, respectively at §25, §26 and §48 ("*The grant of immunity is to be seen not as qualifying a substantive right but as a procedural bar*"). See also R. Batstone, *supra* note 1982, pp. 62–63.

public authority (such as maintaining law and order) on the other hand. As to the former, there appear to be few problems with the duty to respect or observe local law, subject to any specific rules creating exceptions. In contrast, in respect of the latter, i.e. the exercise of public authority, international crisis management operations often have their own rules and certainly do not always apply the local law.[1987] Moreover, in part because the local legal system often does not function anymore and some local legislation may be contrary to human rights, the suggestion has been made to develop a kind of model criminal code that could be applied in post-conflict situations.[1988] Thus in practice, respect for local law is usually limited and one might wonder whether the standard clause should not be replaced by one that more accurately reflects current practice.

Applicable international law may include the law of armed conflict (LOAC). Depending on the nature of the operation this may include the four 1949 Geneva Conventions and/or one of the two 1977 Protocols thereto.[1989] Applicable international law may also include international human rights law, for instance the ICCPR, the UN Convention against Torture and Other Cruel, Inhuman or Degrading Treatment or Punishment[1990] and regional instruments such as the ECHR, the ACHR and the ACHPR. It will also include other rules of public international law of a conventional and customary nature and also decisions of international organizations. For peace operations, the mandate from the UN Security Council and/or other international organizations and SOFA/SOMAs and Participating State agreements will be of great importance.[1991]

1987 In this respect, there are very interesting statements in the Draft Guidelines for criminal procedure in Crisis Management Operations, adopted by the EU's Committee for Civilian Aspects of Crisis Management on 30 May 2002 (EU Council Doc. 9465/02). While the scope of the document is limited to rule of law missions and it has no legally binding value (see §3 of the introduction), its section 1 stipulates that: "*1.1.- International staff deployed to the strengthen the Rule of Law, in the framework of civilian aspects of crisis management under an UN international mandate, will, in principle, have recourse, to local law in their duties*", adding that "*1.2.- Where the local law applicable to the criminal procedure or any of its provisions, recognise to individuals a standard of protection inferior, contrary to or incompatible with the mandate given to the mission, with any other regulation issued by the UN for the mission on international civil administration, with the internationally recognised general principles of law, or with the following guidelines, international staff deployed under the international mandate will apply, on a case-by-case basis, these last regulations, standards or guidelines*".

1988 See *Report of the Panel on United Nations Peace Operations*, UN Doc. A/55/305-S/2000/809, 17 August 2000, §§79–83. For a discussion, see V. O'Connor, 'Traversing the Rocky Road of Law Reform in Conflict and Post Conflict States: Model Codes for Post Conflict Criminal Justice as a Tool for Assistance', 16 *Criminal Law Forum* 2005, pp. 231–255, especially pp. 243–255. The EU Guidelines cited *supra* note 1987 were a contribution to such a concept.

1989 Text, status, reservations and commentaries are available online at www.icrc.org/ihl.

1990 New York, 10 December 1984, 1465 *U.N.T.S.* 85.

1991 For an overview of the instruments usually relevant in a UN operation, see M. Bothe & T. Dörschel, 'The UN Peacekeeping Experience', in D. Fleck (ed.), *supra* note 1977, pp. 491–502.

The applicable law in peace operations is therefore a complex set of rules that originate from different legal orders and that will vary from one operation to another and, in part, from one TCN to another. To get a correct view, it is crucial to understand the interactions between these different rules in any given operation. As an example of the interplay between international and domestic law, detention of pirates in maritime operations may illustrate one of the potential problems.[1992] Pursuant to Article 105 of the UN Convention on the Law of the Sea "*On the high seas, or in any other place outside the jurisdiction of any State, every State may seize a pirate ship or aircraft, or a ship or aircraft taken by piracy and under the control of pirates, and arrest the persons and seize the property on board. The courts of the State which carried out the seizure may decide upon the penalties to be imposed, ...*".[1993] However, a State wishing to exercise this right will need to adopt domestic legislation incorporating piracy as crime, specifying the penalties and establishing the conditions under which its agents and courts may exercise jurisdiction over this crime.[1994] Thus this is a rule which requires implementing measures at the domestic level.[1995]

I will not discuss this overall framework any further but will only further elaborate in Chapters 8 and 9 two particular bodies of law that may provide applicable rules of international law, namely the LOAC and human rights.

1992 This issue has arisen in the context of EUNAVFOR Somalia / Atalanta; see Chapter 3.W.2 above.

1993 UN Convention on the Law of the Sea, Montego Bay, 10 December 1982, 1833 *U.N.T.S.* 3.

1994 While it could be argued that this provision is sufficiently clear to be self-executing in countries that do not require domestic implementing legislation for treaties, a lack of such legislation would be problematic concerning the criminal law aspect of piracy since the principle of legality laid down in human rights instruments requires that the crime *and penalty* be defined by law; see Article 15 ICCPR; Article 7 ECHR; Article 9 ACHR and Article 7.2 ACHPR. See on this issue, in relation to war crimes, crimes against humanity and genocide, F. Naert & L. De Smet, 'Making or Breaking International Law? An International Law Analysis of Belgium's Act concerning the Punishment of Grave Breaches of International Humanitarian Law', 35 *R.B.D.I./B.T.I.R.* 2002, pp. 471–511, especially pp. 483–489.

1995 This requirement also results from human rights law; see, e.g. ECtHR, *Medvedyev and others v. France,* 10 July 2008 (under appeal to the Grand Chamber), especially §§49–63. See also G. Breda & J.P. Pierini, 'Legal Issues Surrounding Maritime Counterdrug Operations and the Related Question of Detention as Highlighted in the *Medvedyev and Others v. France* Decision of the European Court of Human Rights', 47 *Military Law & the Law of War Review* 2008, pp. 167–198.

CHAPTER 8
THE LAW OF ARMED CONFLICT[1996]

A. INTRODUCTION

In this chapter, I will discuss the applicability of the law of armed conflict (LOAC) to ESDP operations, which has not yet received much attention in the literature.[1997] The similar topic of the applicability of the LOAC to UN peace operations has been and still remains the subject of extensive debate and writing.[1998] This is less the case for NATO peace operations,

---

1996 I am grateful to Marten Zwanenburg for his valuable comments on an earlier draft of this chapter.

1997 With the following exceptions: S. Bartelt, *Der rechtliche Rahmen für die neue operative Kapazität der Europäischen Union*, Münster, Lit Verlag, 2003, pp. 161–209 (predating the first ESDP operations); N. Ronzitti, 'L'applicabilità del diritto internazionale umanitario', in N. Ronzitti (ed.), *Le forze di pace dell'Unione Europea*, Roma, Rubbettino, 2005, pp. 165–194 (English summary at pp. 19–20); G.-J. Van Hegelsom, 'Relevance of IHL in the Conduct of Petersberg Tasks', in College of Europe & ICRC (eds.), *Proceedings of the Bruges Colloquium. The Impact of International Humanitarian Law on Current Security Policy Trends. 26th - 27th October 2001 / Actes du colloque de Bruges. L'impact du droit international humanitaire sur l'évolution des politiques de sécurité. 26-27 octobre 2001*, Bruges, College of Europe (*collegium* No. 25, available online at www.coleurop.be/template.asp?pagename=pub_collegium), 2002, pp. 109–120; the very brief discussion in N. Tsagourias, 'EU Peacekeeping Operations: Legal and Theoretical Issues', in Trybus & White, pp. 115–118 and, most recently, M. Zwanenburg, 'Toward a More Mature ESDP: Responsibility for Violations of International Humanitarian Law by EU Crisis Management Operations', in S. Blockmans (ed.), *The European Union and International Crisis Management: Legal and Policy Aspects*, The Hague, TMC Asser Press, 2008, pp. 395–416 and V. Falco, 'Old Continent, New Wars: The European Union and International Humanitarian Law', conference paper available online at www.ies.be/files/repo/conference2008/EUinIA_I_2_Falco.pdf. For a very brief discussion, see also F. Naert, 'The Implementation and the Respect of International Humanitarian Rules in Current International Peace Operations – An EU Perspective', in International Institute of Humanitarian Law (ed.), *International Peace Operations and International Humanitarian Law. …*, Sanremo, IIHL, 2008, pp. 61–63.

1998 See, e.g. M. Bothe, *Le droit de la guerre et les Nations Unies: à propos des incidents armés au Congo*, Geneva, Institut Universitaire de Hautes Études Internationales, 1967; G. Cartledge, 'Legal Constraints on Military Personnel Deployed on Peacekeeping Operations' in H. Durham & T. McCormack (eds.), *The Changing Face of Conflict and the Efficacy of International Humanitarian Law*, The Hague, Nijhoff, 1999, pp. 121–139; L. Condorelli, 'Le statut des forces de l'ONU et le droit international humanitaire', 78 *Rivista di diritto internazionale* 1995, pp. 881–906; L. Condorelli, 'Pertinence du droit international humanitaire pour les organisations internationales et les alliances', in College of Europe & ICRC (eds.), *The Impact of International Humanitarian Law on Current Security Policy Trends: Proceedings of the Bruges Colloquium, 26th-27th October 2001 = L'impact du droit international humanitaire sur l'évolution des politiques de sécurité: actes du Colloque de Bruges, 26-27 octobre 2001*, Bruges, College of Europe, 2002, pp. 25–40; L. Condorelli, A.-M. La Rosa & S. Scherrer (eds.), *Les Nations Unies et le droit international humanitaire: actes du Colloque international à l'occasion du* although they have recently been analyzed extensively by Marten Zwanenburg.[1999] Also, some more recent publications have looked at the LOAC

cinquantième anniversaire de l'ONU (Genève à 19,20 et 21 octobre 1995), Paris, Pedone, 1996; David, pp. 199–212; C. Emanuelli, *Les actions militaires de l'ONU et le droit international humanitaire*, Montreal, Wilson & Lafleur, 1995; H.-P. Gasser, 'Humanitäres Völkerrecht und militärische Operationen der Vereinten Nationen zur Sicherung oder Schaffung des Friedens', 8 *Humanitäres Völkerrecht* 1995, pp. 72–77; H.-P. Gasser, 'Humanitäres Völkerrecht und militärische Operationen der Vereinten Nationen zur Sicherung oder Schaffung des Friedens', in W. Voit (ed.), *Vereinte Nationen und humanitäres Völkerrecht Rechtsentwicklung und Rechtsanwendung – Internationale Rotkreuz-Aktivitäten und Rotkreuz-Operationen in Osteuropa – andere aktuelle Rotkreuz-fragen*, Bochum, Brockmeyer, 1997, pp. 19–32; H.-P. Gasser, 'Die Anwendbarkeit des humanitaren Völkerrechts auf militärische Operationen der Vereinten Nationen', 4 *S.Z.I.E.R.*, 1994, pp. 443–473; R. Glick, 'Lip Service to the Laws of War: Humanitarian Law and United Nations Armed Forces', 17 *Michigan J.I.L.* 1995, pp. 53–107; C. Greenwood, 'International Humanitarian Law and United Nations Military Operations', 1 *Y.I.H.L.* 1998, pp. 3–34; Kolb, Porretto & Vité, especially pp. 117–232; R. Kolb, *Droit humanitaire et opérations de paix internationales: les modalités d'application du droit international humanitaire dans les opérations de maintien ou de rétablissement de la paix auxquelles concourt une organisation internationale (en particulier les Nations Unies)*, Brussels/Geneva, Brulant/Helbing & Lichtenhahn, 2006 (2nd ed.); S. Lüder, *Völkerrechtliche Verantwortlichkeit bei Teilnahme an 'Peace-keeping'-Missionen der Vereinten Nationen*, Berlin, Berliner Wissenschaftsverlag, 2004; S. Oeter, 'Civil War, Humanitarian Law and the United Nations', 1 *M.P.Y.U.N.L.* 1997, pp. 195–229; H. Risse, *Der Einsatz militärischer Kräfte durch die Vereinten Nationen und das Kriegsvölkerrecht*, Frankfurt am Main, Peter Lang, 1988; Y. Sandoz, 'L'Application du Droit Humanitaire par les Forces Armées de l'Organisation des Nations Unies', 60 No. 713 *R.I.C.R.* 1978, pp. 274–284; D. Schindler, 'United Nations Forces and International Humanitarian Law', in C. Swinarski (ed.), *Études et essais sur le droit international humanitaire et sur les principes de la Croix-Rouge en l'honneur de Jean Pictet*, Geneva/The Hague, ICRC/Nijhoff, 1984, pp. 521–530; F. Schwendimann, *Rechtsfragen des humanitären Völkerrechts bei Friedensmissionen der Vereinten Nationen*, Zurich, Schulthess, 2007; F. Seyersted, *United Nations Forces in the Law of Peace and War*, Leiden, Sijthoff, 1966; D. Shraga, 'The United Nations as an Actor Bound by International Humanitarian Law', 5 *International Peacekeeping* 1998, pp. 64–81; D. Shraga, 'UN Peacekeeping Operations: Applicability of International Humanitarian Law and Responsibility for Operations-Related Damage', 94 *A.J.I.L.*, 2000, pp. 406–412; D. Shraga, 'The United Nations as an Actor Bound by International Humanitarian Law', in L. Condorelli, A.-M. La Rosa & S. Scherrer (eds.), *supra* this note, pp. 317–338; B. Tittemore, 'Belligerents in Blue Helmets: Applying International Humanitarian Law to United Nations Peace Operations', 33 *Stanford J.I.L.* 1997, pp. 61–117; G.J. van Hegelsom, 'United Nations Forces and Humanitarian Law. Use of Force and Humanity in Action', 28 *R.D.M.D.G.* 1989, pp. 473–489; M. Zwanenburg, 'Compromise or Commitment: Human Rights and International Humanitarian Law Obligations for UN Peace Forces', 11 *Leiden J.I.L.* 1998, pp. 229–245; M. Zwanenburg, 'VN-troepen en het internationaal humanitair recht', 9 *Zoeklicht* 2000, pp. 12–15; Zwanenburg, also published in an amended version as M . Zwanenburg, *Accountability of Peace Support Operations*, Leiden, Martinus Nijhoff, 2005. See also more generally A. Faite & J. Grenier (eds.), *Report on the Expert Meeting on Multinational Peace Operations. Applicability of International Humanitarian Law and International Human Rights Law to UN Mandated Forces, Organized by the ICRC in cooperation with the University Centre for International Humanitarian Law, Geneva, 11-12 December* 2003 (available online at www.icrc.org/Web/Eng/siteeng0.nsf/htmlall/p0912/$File/ICRC_002_0912.PDF!Open) and A. Faite, 'Multinational Forces Acting Pursuant to a Mandate of the United Nations: Specific Issues on the Applicability of International Humanitarian Law', *11 International Peacekeeping* 2005 *(Yearbook)*, pp. 143–158.

1999 See generally Zwanenburg. Several more specific contributions have been written focusing on the 1999 NATO air campaign in the Kosovo crisis and the ICTY report thereon (ICTY, and international organizations more generally, albeit usually also with a focus on the UN and NATO.[2000] Nevertheless, I submit that the applicability of the LOAC to ESDP operations involves a number of distinct features which justify its examination here. A first such element is the controversial legal status of the EU, which has been examined above in Chapter 6. A second and more important element is the EU's relatively well articulated position vis-à-vis international law in general and human rights in particular, which has already been addressed in general terms in Chapter 7. This specificity has an impact on the mechanisms for applying the LOAC and may reveal mechanisms that might also be relevant for other international organizations. E.g. the question will be examined whether general principles of law recognized in the EU legal order might include some LOAC principles.

In order to provide an overview of all key issues, I will also address some topics where the EU is not in a substantially different position from the UN or NATO, albeit only to a limited extent. These issues include the threshold for an armed conflict and participation therein (section B), the nature of armed conflicts

---

Final Report to the Prosecutor by the Committee Established to Review the NATO Bombing Campaign against the Federal Republic of Yugoslavia, 8 June 2000, available online at www.un.org/icty/pressreal/nato061300.htm and reproduced in 39 *I.L.M.* 2000, pp. 1257–1283 and 21 *H.R.L.J.* 2000, pp. 255–272). See, e.g. P. Benvenuti, 'The ICTY Prosecutor and the Review of the NATO Bombing Campaign against the Federal Republic of Yugoslavia', 12 *E.J.I.L.* 2001, pp. 503–529; M. Bothe, 'The Protection of the Civilian Population and NATO Bombing on Yugoslavia: Comments on a Report to the Prosecutor of the ICTY', 6 *International Peacekeeping* 2000, pp. 158–162 and 12 *E.J.I.L.* 2001, pp. 531–535; J. Burger, 'International Humanitarian Law and the Kosovo Crisis: Lessons Learned or to Be Learned', 82 No. 837 *I.R.R.C./R.I.C.R.* 2000, pp. 129–145; A. Colangelo, 'Manipulating International Criminal Procedure: The Decision of the ICTY Office of the Independent Prosecutor Not to Investigate NATO Bombing in the Former Yugoslavia', 97 *Northwestern University Law Review* 2003, pp. 1393–1436; S.A. Egorov, 'The Kosovo Crisis and the Law of Armed Conflicts', 82 No. 837 *I.R.R.C./R.I.C.R.* 2000, pp. 183–192; P. Kovacs, 'Intervention armée des forces de l'OTAN au Kosovo: fondement de l'obligation de respecter le droit international humanitaire', 82 No. 837 *I.R.R.C./R.I.C.R.* 2000, pp. 103–128; A. Laursen, 'NATO, the War over Kosovo, and the ICTY Investigation', 17 *A.U.I.L.R.* 2002, pp. 765–814; O. Medenica, 'Protocol I and Operation Allied Force: Did NATO Abide by Principles of Proportionality?', 23 *Loyola L.A.I.C.L.R* 2001, pp. 329–426 (though not really elaborating on the applicable law in light of the specificity of a NATO operation); N. Quenivet, 'Report of the Prosecutor of the ICTY Concerning NATO Bombing against the FRY: A Comment', 41 *Indian J.I.L.* 2001, pp. 478–494; A.P.V. Rogers, 'Zero-casualty Warfare', 82 No. 837 *I.R.R.C./R.I.C.R.* 2000, pp. 165–181; N. Ronzitti, 'Is the Non Liquet of the Final Report by the Committee Established to Review the NATO Bombing Campaign against the Federal Republic of Yugoslavia Acceptable?', 82 No. 840 *R.I.C.R./I.R.R.C.* 2000, pp. 1017–1027; P. Rowe, 'Kosovo 1999: The Air Campaign – Have the Provisions of Additional Protocol I Withstood the Test?', 82 No. 837 *I.R.R.C./R.I.C.R.* 2000, pp. 147–164 and T. Voon, 'Pointing the Finger: Civilian Casualties of NATO Bombing in the Kosovo Conflict', 16 *A.U.I.L.R.* 2001, pp. 1083–1113.

2000 See especially Kolb, Porretto & Vité and *Report on the Expert Meeting ...*, *supra* note 1998. For a brief discussion, see, e.g. T.D. Gill, 'Vredesoperaties en humanitair oorlogsrecht', 96 *Militair Rechtelijk Tijdschrift* 2003, pp. 331–347.

involving EU-led forces and the parties thereto (section C), peace operations as occupation (section D) and the impact of UN Security Council intervention (section E). The main parts in which the specificity of the EU comes to the fore are Section F on participating State LOAC obligations in ESDP operations and Section G, which is devoted to the EU's LOAC obligations in ESDP operations. Finally, the main conclusions are summarized in Section H. The relationship between the LOAC and human rights will be analyzed in Chapter 9.D below.

B. THE THRESHOLD FOR AN ARMED CONFLICT AND PARTICIPATION IN AN ARMED CONFLICT

1. THE THRESHOLD FOR ARMED CONFLICT

Any student of the LOAC will know that, with the exception of some rules that also apply in peacetime, the LOAC only applies to situations that amount to an armed conflict or occupation. Indeed, this is clearly stated in Article 2 common to the 1949 Geneva Conventions, which stipulates that:

> In addition to the provisions which shall be implemented in peacetime, the present Convention shall apply to all cases of *declared war or of any other armed conflict* which may arise between two or more of the High Contracting Parties, even if the state of war is not recognized by one of them.
>
> The Convention shall also apply to *all cases of partial or total occupation* of the territory of a High Contracting Party, even if the said occupation meets with no armed resistance. ... (emphasis added).

Even the famous Article 3 common to the 1949 Geneva Conventions only applies to any "armed conflict *not of an international character occurring in the territory of one of the High Contracting Parties*" (emphasis added). This requirement is also repeated in Article 1 of AP I, which states that this Protocol "*shall apply in the* situations referred to in Article 2 common to those Conventions", adding that these situations "include armed conflicts *which peoples are fighting against colonial domination and alien occupation and against racist regimes in the exercise of their right of self-determination*" (emphasis added).

Whether an armed conflict exists is a matter of fact and is hard to define in general terms,[2001] although the ICRC issued an opinion paper on this definition

2001 See, e.g. UK Manual, §3 and C. Greenwood, 'Scope of Application of Humanitarian Law', in D. Fleck (ed.), The *Handbook of Humanitarian Law in Armed Conflict*, Oxford, Oxford University Press, 1995, pp. 42 and 48–49. With regard to peace operations, see Kolb, in 2008[2002] and the ILA is also working on a definition.[2003] That being said, the ICRC Commentary to the Geneva Conventions offers some guidance,[2004] AP II includes a definition but one which is not comprehensive[2005] and the ICTY has given a general definition in the *Tadic* case: "*a resort to armed force between States or protracted armed violence between governmental authorities and organized armed groups or between such groups within a State*".[2006] Some further clarification in treaty law is offered regarding armed conflicts not of an international character (I will return to this notion in the following subsection), in respect of which AP II distinguishes armed conflicts from "*situations of internal disturbances and tensions, such as riots, isolated and sporadic acts of violence and other acts of a similar nature, as not being armed conflicts*".[2007] The

---

Porretto & Vité, pp. 175–183 and Zwanenburg, pp. 197–204. See also generally A.W. Dahl & M. Sandbu, 'The Threshold of Armed Conflict', 45(3–4) *R.D.M.D.G.* 2006, pp. 369–388 and B. Tahzib-Lie & O. Swaak-Goldman, 'Determining the Threshold for the Application of International Humanitarian Law', in L. Lijnzaad, J. van Sambeek & B. Tahzib-Lie (eds.), *Making the Voice of Humanity Heard: Essays on Humanitarian Assistance and International Humanitarian Law in Honour of HRH Princess Margriet of the Netherlands*, Leiden, Nijhoff, 2004, pp. 239–253. For a discussion with regard to non-international armed conflicts, see, e.g. D. Ciobanu, 'The Concept and the Determination of the Existence of Armed Conflicts not of an International Character', 58 *Rivista di diritto internazionale* 1975, pp. 43–79.

2002 ICRC, *How is the Term "Armed Conflict" Defined in International Humanitarian Law?*, Opinion Paper, March 2008, www.icrc.org/web/eng/siteeng0.nsf/htmlall/armed-conflict-Article-170308/$file/Opinion-paper-armed-conflict.pdf, concluding at p. 5 that "*Non-international armed conflicts are* protracted armed confrontations *occurring between governmental armed forces and the forces of one or more armed groups, or between such groups arising on the territory of a State [party to the Geneva Conventions]. The armed confrontation must reach* a minimum level of intensity *and the parties involved in the conflict must show* a minimum of organisation" (the text not in italics was emphasized in the orginal text).

2003 See the *Initial Report on the Meaning of Armed Conflict in International Law*, prepared by the ILA's Committee on the Use of Force for the ILA's 2008 Rio de Janeiro conference (available online at www.ila-hq.org/en/committees/index.cfm/cid/1022), which concludes that "*A state of armed conflict exists if the criteria of organized armed groups and intensity of the hostilities are satisfied*". See also M.E. O'Connel, 'Defining Armed Conflict', 13 *J.C.S.L.* 2008, pp. 393–400.

2004 See especially the ICRC Commentary on Articles 2 and 3 common to the 1949 Geneva Conventions.

2005 Article 1(1) of AP II defines the scope of application of this Protocol as "*all armed conflicts [not covered by Article 1 AP I] and which take place in the territory of a High Contracting Party between its armed forces and dissident armed forces or other organized armed groups which, under responsible command, exercise such control over a part of its territory as to enable them to carry out sustained and concerted military operations and to implement this Protocol*".

2006 *Prosecutor v. Dusko Tadic*, IT-94-1, 2 October 1995, §70.

2007 Article 1(2) AP II. On such excluded situations, see, e.g. A. Eide, 'International Disturbances and Tensions', in Henry Dunant Institute & UNESCO (eds.), *International Dimensions of Humanitarian Law*, Geneva, UNESCO, 1988, pp. 241–256 and several publications by Meron, e.g. T. Meron, 'On the Inadequate Reach of Humanitarian and Human Rights Law and the Need for a New Instrument', 77 *A.J.I.L.* 1983, pp. 589–606; T. Meron, *Human Rights in Internal Strife: Their International Protection*, Cambridge, Grotius, 1987 (describing internal strife at pp. 71–104); T. Meron, 'Internal Strife: Applicable Norms and a Proposed Instrument', latter distinction is restated in the ICC Statute with regard to armed conflicts not of an international character.[2008] Moreover, the latter instrument complicates the picture somewhat by including a definition of armed conflicts not of an international character that seems to differ from the one in AP II.[2009]

The key point I want to make here is that the LOAC is not applicable (with the exception of some peacetime obligations) when this threshold has not been crossed and when there is no occupation either (on occupation, see *infra*, subsection D).[2010] This may seem obvious, but it is sometimes overlooked. In particular, one cannot avoid the impression that sometimes the LOAC is or was looked to as the only body of law that was suitable for peace operations. This was/is reflected to some extent in policy decisions to apply the LOAC even when it was/is not applicable as a matter of law.[2011] It is also reflected in the fact that the UN has (finally) issued some guidance as to respect for the LOAC in UN peace operations, but has not issued similar guidance for respect for human rights, which may be more applicable and more appropriate in most UN

---

in A.J.M. Delissen & G.J. Tanja Abi-Saab (eds.), *Humanitarian Law of Armed Conflict Challenges Ahead: Essays in Honour of Frits Kalshoven*, Dordrecht, Nijhoff, 1991, pp. 249–266; A. Eide, A. Rosas & T. Meron, 'Combating Lawlessness in Gray Zone Conflicts through Minimum Humanitarian Standards', 89 *A.J.I.L.* 1995, pp. 215–223 and T. Meron, 'Towards a Humanitarian Declaration on Internal Strife', 78 *A.J.I.L.* 1984, pp. 859–868. See also *infra*, Chapter 9.C on the applicability of human rights in these situations.

2008 Article 8(2)(d) and (f).

2009 Article 8(2)(f): "*armed conflicts that take place in the territory of a State when there is protracted armed conflict between governmental authorities and organized armed groups or between such groups*".

2010 This corresponds to the view adopted in the UK Manual, §14.3–11. Zwanenburg, pp. 197–204, also clearly makes this argument, as do Kolb, Porretto & Vité, pp. 175–183 and especially pp. 190–199.

2011 E.g. when the son of indicted war criminal Karadzic was detained by NATO-led forces in BiH in July 2005, the NATO Headquarters in Sarajevo declared that he would be treated "*in accordance with international humanitarian law*" (see the press release at www.afsouth.nato.int/NHQSA/PressReleases/2005/PR_10_05.htm), even though the situation in BiH at that time clearly no longer constituted an armed conflict nor an occupation. More generally, I have seen references to the LOAC in a number of operations in which it was clearly not applicable, although this may in part be a precaution for allowing an adequate response in case of escalation. See also the German position as described by H. Krieger, 'Die Verantwortlichkeit Deutschlands nach der EMRK für seine Streitkräfte im Auslandeinsatz', 62 *Z.a.ö.R.V.* 2002, p. 691 and the NATO position cited by Häussler, p. 73 note 230 (not applicable as a matter of law but principles and spirit to be complied with). Compare Häussler, pp. 61–78, especially pp. 64–65 (arguing that even though the LOAC is often not applicable *de iure*, it is more relevant than human rights because the situation in peace operations has more in common with armed conflicts than with peace time) and 72 (submitting that the applicability of the LOAC has not been rejected in any significant way, which is perhaps a little exaggerated).

peacekeeping operations.[2012] It is also worth recalling that not every recourse to armed forces entails the applicability of the LOAC.[2013]

Although such views often seem to be based on laudable motives such as a genuine concern to protect individuals from an unwarranted or unchecked exercise of authority or providing known and relatively clear standards for soldiers on the ground, this approach is in some respects incorrect as a matter of law and may lead to illegal conduct if applied without further limits. In particular, the LOAC, especially the law of international armed conflict, authorizes the killing of combatants and the detention of civilians in a much more liberal manner than human rights law.[2014] Indeed, the recent US qualification of the 'war on terror' as an armed conflict in order to justify broad powers of (targeted) killings and detention illustrates this danger very well, despite the different context.[2015] Obviously a position limited to respecting the LOAC *prohibitions*, as appears to be the policy in the Netherlands,[2016] avoids this problem and is quite acceptable. Fortunately, it appears that there is a growing awareness, including in the framework of the EU, that the deployment of armed forces in peace operations does not necessarily entail the applicability of the LOAC and that human rights may well offer a more adequate legal framework

2012 See in this sense G. Cartledge, *supra* note 1998, pp. 121–139, especially pp. 125–130 and 134–138. On the applicability of human rights in peace operations, see *infra*, Chapter 9.

2013 As also pointed out by K. Watkin, 'Controlling the Use of Force: A Role for Human Rights Norms in Contemporary Armed Conflict', 98 *A.J.I.L.* 2004, p. 26.

2014 I will come back to these examples in Chapter 9.D.2.iv. This point is also made by A. Faite, *supra* note 1998, pp. 155–157 as regards occupation and by A. Zemach, 'Taking War Seriously: Applying the Law of War to Hostilities Within an Occupied Territory', 38 *George Washington I.L.R.* 2006, p. 647. Similarly, H. Borghouts, R. Daverschot & G. Gillissen, *Evaluatie toepassing militair strafprocesrecht bij uitzendingen*, Haarlem, 31 August 2006 (report of a Commission set up by the Dutch Ministries of Justice and of Defence, available online at www.defensie.nl/_system/handlers/generaldownloadHandler.ashx?filename=/media/Rapport_Commissie_Borghouts_tcm46-104611.pdf), p. 22, noting that when the LOAC is not applicable, the competences are limited by the mandate, whereas in an armed conflict or occupation, the LOAC is a basis for the use of force ("*Zolang het internationaal humanitair recht niet van toepassing is op een crisisbeheersingsoperatie, zijn de bevoegdheden van de militairen beperkt tot die welke voortvloeien uit het mandaat of de juridische grondslag voor het optreden. ... In tijd van oorlog of gewapend conflict is het gebruik van geweld gelegitimeerd op grond van het internationaal humanitair recht. Individuele militairen mogen binnen de grenzen van het internationaal humanitair recht geweld toepassen*").

2015 As C. Warbrick, 'The European Response to Terrorism in an Age of Human Rights', 15 *E.J.I.L.* 2004, p. 991 points out, this development post '9/11' is in sharp contrast with the traditional reluctance of States to accept the fact that, especially internal conflicts, had crossed the threshold of an armed conflict.

2016 H. Borghouts, R. Daverschot & G. Gillissen, *supra* note 2014, p. 23 ("*In Nederland geldt als vaststaand beleid dat ook tijdens operaties waarop het internationaal humanitair recht formeel niet van toepassing is, de restricties uit dat recht altijd dienen te worden nageleefd*"). Compare Koninklijke Landmacht (Netherlands Army), *Humanitair oorlogsrecht. Handleiding, s.l., s.n.*, 2005, p. 195, §1210.

for some peace operations. I will extensively analyze the latter aspect in Chapter 9 below.

The essential consideration to keep in mind here is that there has to be an armed conflict or occupation before the LOAC applies and that this is certainly not always the case in peace operations. For instance, operation Althea in BiH clearly does not take place in a situation of armed conflict nor does it constitute an occupation.

This is not to say that the LOAC will be entirely irrelevant. Significant overlaps in substantive rules of the LOAC and human rights mean that parts of the LOAC may well serve as guidance, including in particular for soldiers on the ground. For instance, as regards the *treatment* of detainees, guidance to soldiers to treat detainees as prisoners of war will in most respects be entirely acceptable.[2017]

2. PARTICIPATION IN ARMED CONFLICT

Even assuming that there is an armed conflict in an area of operation, the conclusion is not necessarily that operation personnel are a party to the conflict.[2018] The reason for this is that peace forces may operate in a host State in which an armed conflict is taking place but where they do not themselves take part in the hostilities, notably because they have a limited mandate.[2019] While this again seems obvious, it is not always taken into account.[2020]

It is submitted that this element is correctly reflected in the UN Secretary-General Bulletin on Observance by United Nations Forces of International Humanitarian Law,[2021] which states in its section 1.1 that "*The fundamental*

2017 However, differences should be taken into account as to who may be detained in the first place (i.e. the grounds for and legal basis of detention) and in the case of detention with the purpose of criminal prosecution some additional elements may come into play, such as notification of charges and of the rights related to defence and fair trial in criminal proceedings.

2018 UK Manual, §14.6. See also M. Bothe & T. Dörschel, 'The UN Peacekeeping Experience', in D. Fleck (ed.), *The Handbook of the Law of Visiting Forces*, Oxford, Oxford University Press, 2001, pp. 501–502.

2019 See also R. Murphy, 'United Nations Military Operations and International Humanitarian Law: What Rules Apply to Peacekeepers?', 14 *Criminal Law Forum* 2003, p. 154.

2020 See also Zwanenburg, p. 200, note 267, who also points out that some authors overlook this point.

2021 UN Doc. ST/SGB/1999/13, 6 August 1999, available online at www.icrc.org/Web/Eng/siteeng0.nsf/iwpList367/711A2C1A3BD7FA2EC1256B66005DD94A. For a discussion, see L. Condorelli, 'Les progrès du droit international humanitaire et la circulaire du secrétaire général des Nations Unies du 6 août 1999', in L. Boisson de Chazournes & V. Gowlland-Debbas (eds.), *The International Legal System in Quest of Euity and Uiversality: Liber principles and rules of international humanitarian law set out in the present bulletin are applicable to United Nations forces when in situations of armed conflict they are actively engaged therein as combatants ...*".[2022] In the context of the EU, it was also reflected in the Salamanca Presidency Declaration, which provided that "*Respect for International Humanitarian Law is relevant in EU-led operations when the situation they are operating in constitutes an armed conflict to which the forces are party*".[2023]

However, the remainder of the section cited from the UN Secretary-General's Bulletin is more problematic. It reads "*... to the extent and for the duration of their engagement. They are accordingly applicable in enforcement actions, or in peacekeeping operations when the use of force is permitted in self-defence*". The problem with this wording is twofold. On the one hand, as pointed out by Zwanenburg, it seems to imply that in a given operation one may have occasional and temporary armed conflicts rather than one continuous situation of armed conflict, which seems to be at odds with the prevailing understanding of armed conflicts.[2024] However, there may be some value to this position as far as the use of lethal force is concerned, especially in the context of an armed conflict not of an international character.[2025] The second problem is the final part of the section,

---

Amicorum Georges Abi-Saab, The Hague, Nijhoff, 2001, pp. 495–505; A. Ryniker, 'Respect du droit international humanitaire par les forces des Nations Unies: quelques commentaires à propos de la Circulaire du Secrétaire général des Nations Unies du 6 août 1999', 81 No. 836 *I.R.R.C./R.I.C.R.* 1999, pp. 795–805; Zwanenburg, pp. 181–184; M. Zwanenburg, 'The Secretary-General's Bulletin on Observance by United Nations Forces of International Humanitarian Law: Some Preliminary Oservations', 5 *International Peacekeeping* 1999, pp. 133–139 and M. Zwanenburg, 'The Secretary-General's Bulletin on Observance by United Nations Forces of International Humanitarian Law: A Pyrrhic Victory?', 39 *R.D.M.D.G.* 2000, pp. 13–43.

2022 S. Vité, 'L'applicabilité du droit de l'occupation militaire aux opérations des organisations internationales', in College of Europe & ICRC (eds.), *infra* note 2121, p. 95 points out that this was to some extent confirmed by the UN Security Council in its Resolution 1327 (13 November 2000), Annex, I, 3rd paragraph (bearing in mind "*the need for any provisions for a peacekeeping operation to meet minimum conditions, including ... compliance with the rules and principles of international law, in particular international humanitarian, human rights and refugee law*"). See also Kolb, Poretto & Vité , pp. 140–141. See also the Dutch manual cited *supra* note 2016, p. 195, §1209 (the LOAC *formally* applies when the threshold for participation in an armed conflict has been crossed).

2023 *Infra* note 2239.

2024 Zwanenburg, pp. 200–201. See also, on the similar issue with respect to the 1994 Convention on the Safety of United Nations and Associated Personnel (*infra* note 2045), M. Arsanjani, 'Defending the Blue Helmets: Protection of United Nations Personnel', in L. Condorelli, A.-M. La Rosa & S. Scherrer, *supra* note 1998, p. 145 and M. Frostad, 'Good Guys Wearing Cuffs – The Detention of Peacekeepers', 45 *G.Y.I.L.* 2002, p. 318.

2025 In particular, one could consider to what extent a parallel might be drawn with civilians who take direct part in the hostilities and are legitimate targets only for as long as they so participate. However, it is doubtful whether this analogy can apply: once peacekeepers become a party to the conflict, they would most likely have to be regarded as armed forces i.e. "*in peacekeeping operations when the use of force is permitted in self-defence*". The problem here is not that the LOAC could apply in peacekeeping operations – it clearly can when they escalate – but rather the mentioning of self-defence in this context and its relation to it being "*permitted*". It is submitted that on the basis of the underlying premise in the beginning of the section, this should be read as "*They are accordingly applicable in .... peacekeeping operations when the use of force* reaches such participation even if *it is only* exercised *in self-defence*".[2026] The mere fact that the use of force in self-defence is *permitted* obviously cannot entail the applicability of the LOAC[2027] – as indicated by the beginning of section 1.1. Moreover, even if force is used in self-defence, whether in the strict and ordinary sense of the word[2028] or in the broader UN peacekeeping meaning where it may also include reactions against violent resistance to mission accomplishment,[2029] the LOAC will only apply when the

---

and no longer as civilians (see also *infra*). However, it may be relevant with regard to their opponents/"targets" and the question whether those may be attacked under LOAC rules at all times. Moreover, the direct participation issue, including its temporal aspect, is the subject of divergent opinions and much debate. I will return to this point in Chapter 9.D.2.iv.a below, when addressing the relationship between the LOAC and human rights in such conflicts. The issue is related to the lack of defined combatants in such conflicts and the question whether members of armed (rebel) groups may be targeted everywhere in the State concerned at all times or whether this is only the case for the time that they directly participate in the hostilities. See on this the transcript of the intervention by Jean-Marie Henckaerts in the conference on *The Law of Armed Conflict: Problems and Prospects*, held at Chatham House on 18–19 April 2005 (available online at www.chathamhouse.org.uk/publications/papers/view/-/id/282/), pp. 6–7.

2026 Similarly, O. Engdahl, *Protection of Personnel in Peace Operations: The Role of the 'Safety Convention' against the Background of General International Law*, Leiden, Nijhoff, 2007, p. 101, who also argues that the second sentence of this provision should be interpreted in conformity with its first sentence.

2027 See C. Greenwood, *supra* note 1998 (1 *Y.I.H.L.* 1998), p. 11: "*It is the* fact *of participation in hostilities, not the existence of* authority *to do so which is significant*" (emphasis in original), also quoted in Zwanenburg, pp. 203–204. In the same sense, M. Bothe & T. Dörschel, *supra* note 2018, p. 501 and G.-J. Van Hegelsom, *supra* note 1997, p. 116.

2028 In this sense, self-defence is considered to be inherent and a general principle of criminal law and arguably customary international law; see G.-J. Knoops, *The Prosecution and Defense of Peacekeepers under International Criminal Law*, Ardsley, Transnational Publishers, 2004, pp. 167 and 183, *inter alia* citing ICTY, *Prosecutor v. Dario Kordic and Mario Cerkez*, IT-95-14/2, judgement of 26 February 2001, §§449–451 (also referring to Article 31(1)c ICC Statute).

2029 In EU and NATO practice, (individual – as opposed to inter-State) self-defence broadly speaking means defence against an actual or imminent attack against oneself or one's colleagues and possibly third persons (the precise scope depends on applicable domestic law). Other instances of the use of force, e.g. to detain suspected criminals or to accomplish certain tasks, are covered by rules of engagement (ROE) that are considered to be distinct from self-defence (although there may be some overlap). See also Häussler, pp. 94–96 and for an interesting analysis, see J.F.R. Boddens Hosang, 'Self-Defence in Military Operations: The Interaction between the Legal Bases for Military Self-Defence and Rules of Engagement', 47 *R.D.M.D.G.* 2008, pp. 25–96. In contrast, in UN language, self-defence in an extended sense may include the use of force for mission accomplishment. See on the use of force in UN operations, T. Findlay, *The Use of Force in UN Peace Operations*, Oxford, Oxford University force used crosses the threshold of an armed conflict.[2030] For instance, when a KFOR soldier is attacked by criminals for personal profit and fires his weapon in self-defence, this clearly is not regulated by the LOAC.[2031] The same goes for Althea soldiers who would have to use armed force to arrest a suspected war criminal in BiH. Finally, one might also wonder whether the apparent automatic applicability of the LOAC in peace enforcement operations is correct where, despite being a peace enforcement operation, the operation does not actually become engaged in an armed conflict.[2032]

A further issue that needs to be addressed is the status of peace forces which are not a party to an armed conflict.[2033] Although this primarily concerns their protection against attacks by others rather than standards for their own

---

Press, 2002; S. Chesterman, *The Use of Force in UN Peace Operations*, External Study for the UN Department of Peacekeeping Operations Best Practices Unit, 2004 (available online at http://pbpu.unlb.org/pbps/Library/Chesterman%20External%20Paper%20(31-08-2004).pdf), especially p. 9; S. Chesterman, *You, the People: The United Nations, Transitional Administration, and State-Building*, Oxford, Oxford University Press, 2004, pp. 99–125, especially pp. 103–106; K. Cox, 'Beyond Self-Defence: United Nations Peacekeeping Operations and the Use of Force', 27 *Denver J.I. L. & Policy* 1999, pp. 249–273 (noting at pp. 255–256 that this wide interpretation had, however, rarely been applied by Commanders in practice – it may be noted that this seems to have changed more recently, as evidenced for instance by the robust actions taken by the UN missions in the DRC and Haiti) and R. Zacklin, 'The Use of Force in Peacekeeping Operations', in N. Blokker & N. Schrijver (eds.), *The Security Council and the Use of Force: Theory and Reality: A Need for Change?*, Leiden, Nijhoff, 2005, pp. 91–106 (noting that more recent mandates often specifically include the protection of civilians and that this is reflected in the ROE).

2030 Similarly, O. Engdahl, *supra* note 2026, pp. 98–99 and H. Borghouts, R. Daverschot & G. Gillissen, *supra* note 2014, p. 23 ("*Incidentele of sporadische gevechtshandelingen, bijvoorbeeld in het kader van een crisisbeheersingsoperatie, welke slechts toepassingen betreffen van het recht op zelfverdediging jegens vijandige handelingen, maken de betrokken militairen nog geen partij bij een conflict*"). This is also supported by Article 21 of the 1994 Convention on the Safety of United Nations and Associated Personnel (*infra* note 2045), which provides that "*Nothing in this Convention shall be construed so as to derogate from the right to act in self-defence*"; see on this M. Arsanjani, *supra* note 2024, pp. 140–141 and pp. 201–202 (a discussion further in this book). Compare on the latter provision also S. Lepper, *infra* note 2045, pp. 452–456. *Contra*: M. Frostad, *supra* note 2024, p. 324.

2031 In this respect I would strongly disagree with G.-J. Knoops, *supra* note 2028, pp. 15–16, where he argues that if KFOR forces would have used force to arrest innocent civilians in 2000, this would have been an intentional attack against civilians. First, it is doubtful whether this was a situation of armed conflict or occupation. Second, even assuming it was, it would be a matter of the legality of the arrest rather than 'an attack': to attack a person in the context of the LOAC and war crimes is quite different from using force to arrest him/her (unlike crimes against humanity, in respect of which an 'attack' need not be of a military nature).

2032 This point is made by Zwanenburg, pp. 203–204, citing C. Greenwood, *supra* note 1998, p. 11 (see also *supra* note 2027).

2033 On the protection of peacekeepers, see generally M. Arsanjani, *supra* note 2024, pp. 115–147 and O. Engdahl, *supra* note 2026. See also generally D. Fleck, 'Securing Status and Protection of Peacekeepers', in R. Arnold & G.-J. Knoops (eds.), *Practice and Policies of Modern Peace Support Operations under International Law*, Ardsley, Transnational, 2006, pp. 141–156. For a behaviour, it is worth looking into. In particular, the question arises whether peacekeeping forces (when I use the term forces it refers to armed forces) that are not a party to an armed conflict but who are present in an armed conflict theatre, are to be considered civilians for the purposes of the LOAC despite their military status. A number of elements support the view that they are to be regarded as civilians in this context.[2034] First, military personnel of States not party to an international armed conflict are not covered by the definition of combatants in Article 43 AP I and Article 4(A) GC III because the categories enumerated there only cover armed forces and other groups *belonging to a party to the conflict.*[2035] Consequently, they are civilians pursuant to Article 50(1) AP I[2036] and Article 4 GC IV (though the latter may pose a nationality-based obstacle).[2037] Moreover,

discussion of the protection of peacekeepers from or during detention (including when engaged in armed conflicts), see M. Frostad, *supra* note 2024, pp. 291–330.

2034 This is also the view of A. Faite, *supra* note 1998, p. 156. *Contra*: M. Frostad, *supra* note 2024, p. 325.

2035 Pursuant to Article 43 AP I "*1. The armed forces* of a Party to a conflict *consist of* ..." and "*2. Members of the armed forces* of a Party to a conflict *(other than medical personnel and chaplains covered by Article 33 of the Third Convention) are combatants*" (emphasis added). Pursuant to Article 4(A) GC III, prisoners of war are persons belonging to six listed categories, who have fallen into the power of the enemy. It is via this status that combatants are defined (compare Article 3 Hague Regulations and the ICRC COMMENTARY on Article 4 GC III and Article 43 AP I). The requirement to belong to a party to the conflict is expressly stipulated for members of the armed forces, of militias and volunteer corps ((1) and (2)) and of crews of the merchant marine and of civil aircraft (5). It is implicit for "*Persons who accompany the armed forces without actually being members thereof, ..., provided that they have received authorization*" (4). The only category that might be different is "*Members of regular armed forces who profess allegiance to a government or an authority not recognized by the Detaining Power*" (3). However, here too it is implicit that the non-recognized authority is in fact a party to the conflict (see the *ICRC Commentary* on this provision). The sixth category (spontaneous uprising) is not relevant to peace forces.

2036 This provision reads: "*A civilian is any person who does not belong to one of the categories of persons referred to in Article 4 (A) (1), (2), (3) and (6) of the Third Convention and in Article 43 of this Protocol*".

2037 This provision stipulates that "*Persons protected by the Convention are those who, at a given moment and in any manner whatsoever, find themselves, in case of a conflict or occupation, in the hands of a Party to the conflict or Occupying Power of which they are not nationals*" but excludes nationals of a State which is not bound by the Convention and nationals of a neutral State who find themselves in the territory of a belligerent State as well as nationals of a co-belligerent State as long as the State of which they are nationals has normal diplomatic representation in the State in whose hands they are. The latter may well be an obstacle, as pointed out by C. Greenwood, 'Protection of Peacekeepers: The Legal Regime', 7 *Duke J.C.I.L.* 1996, p. 193, note 40. It also excludes anyone protected under GC I, GC II or GC III. However, the ICTY has somewhat softened this nationality exception in its jurisprudence, as pointed out by H. Duffy, *The "War on Terror" and the Framework of International Law*, Cambridge, Cambridge University Press, 2005, pp. 402–403, *inter alia* citing *The Prosecuter v. Dusko Tadic a/k/a/ 'Dule'* (ICTY- 94–1, 15 July 1999, §§163–168); see also Human Rights Watch, *Genocide, War Crimes and Crimes Against Humanity. A Topical Digest of the Case Law of the International Criminal Tribunal for the Former Yugoslavia*, 2006 (available online at www.unhcr.org/refworld/docid/44c9ed244.html and previously at http://hrw.org/reports/2006/

in non-international armed conflicts, they are even more clearly persons taking no active part in the hostilities.[2038] Second, Article 8(2)(b)iii and (e)iii of the ICC Statute criminalize intentionally directing attacks against personnel, installations, material, units or vehicles involved in a peacekeeping mission in accordance with the Charter of the United Nations "*as long as they are entitled to the protection given to civilians or civilian objects under the international law of armed conflict*". This provision may be read in two ways: either as referring only to civilian personnel of such operations or also to military personnel thereof as long as they are not a party to the conflict. It is submitted that the latter is the better interpretation[2039] and if the former were meant, it would presumably have been explicitly so restricted.[2040] This rule is also reflected in section 1(2) of the above-mentioned UN Secretary-General's Bulletin, which states that the

---

icty0706/ (last consulted in November 2007)), pp. 31–34. Moreover, Part II of GC IV is broader in scope and covers the whole of the populations of the countries in conflict (see Article 13 GC IV).

2038 As rightly pointed out by C. Greenwood, *supra* previous note, p. 191.

2039 Similarly M. Zwanenburg, 'Het Internationaal Strafhof en de bescherming van vredesmachten', 94 *Militairrechtelijk Tijdschrift* 2001, pp. 180–184 and 188 (arguing that this specific offence does not really add anything as attacks against civilians are already prohibited but that it provides an additional emphasis on the protected status of peacekeepers; however, from a discussion with the author it appears that Zwanenburg may no longer maintain this view, at least with regard to international armed conflicts). D. Robinson & H. von Hebel, 'War Crimes in Internal Conflicts: Article 8 of the ICC Statute', 2 *Y.I.H.L.* 1999, p. 201 note 47 see this rule rather as a specific illustration of the prohibition to attack civilians and do not mention a limitation to civilian personnel. Compare C. Greenwood, *supra* note 2037, pp. 189–193, who submits that non-belligerent UN units and their equipment, etc. are not military objectives and may not be attacked in an international armed conflict but takes the view that the UN personnel would normally not be civilian by virtue of the nationality exception in Article 5 GC IV (see *supra* note 2037 on the latter). He also points out that Article 37(1)(d) AP I (prohibiting "*the feigning of protected status by the use of signs, emblems or uniforms of the United Nations or of neutral or other States not Parties to the conflict*") implies a protected status for the UN and its personnel but does not elaborate what this status is.

2040 For a good discussion, see M. Cottier, 'Article 8(2)(b)(iii)', in O. Triffterer (ed.), *Commentary on the Rome Statute of the International Criminal Court*, Nomos, Baden-Baden, 1999, pp. 187–196, who seems to see the issue as unclear but is in favour of regarding all mission personnel as civilians unless there is a level of force exceeding self-defence and entailing the applicability of the LOAC and also points to the question whether some staff could remain civilians in a mission in which other staff have become combatants. The author cites the ICTY's initial indictment of Karadzic & Mladic (IT-95-5-I, 24 July 1995), which states in §14 that "*The UN peacekeepers and civilians referred to in this indictment were, at all relevant times, persons protected by the Geneva Conventions of 1949*". While this is not retained in the latest amended indictment of 11 October 2002 (IT-95-5/18-I), the latter includes a charge of the taking of peacekeepers as hostages contrary to common Article 3 of the Geneva Conventions (count 15) thus also implying they were not combatants. M. Boot, *Nullum Crimen Sine Lege and the Subject Matter Jurisdiction of the International Criminal Court*, Antwerp, Intersentia, 2002, p. 608, argues that this prohibition is arguably superfluous as it covers an attack on civilians not taking a direct part in the hostilities. Compare D. Momtaz, 'War Crimes in Non-International Armed Conflicts under the Statute of the International Criminal Court, 2 *Y.I.H.L.* 1999, pp. 185–186, who submits that the customary basis of this provision is debated.

promulgation of the bulletin "*does not affect the protected status of members of peacekeeping operations under the 1994 Convention on the Safety of United Nations and Associated Personnel or their status as non-combatants, as long as they are entitled to the protection given to civilians under the international law of armed conflict*". Moreover, references by the UN Security Council to the prohibition *under the LOAC* to attack peace forces as long as they are not a party to the conflict also support this view.[2041] It is submitted that on the basis of these arguments, armed peace forces that are not a party to an armed conflict must be considered civilians for the purposes of the LOAC.[2042]

An alternative view is that of Kolb, Porretto and Vité, who argue that the protected status of armed peace forces who are not a party to an armed conflict results from their status as protected personnel of international organizations.[2043] However, this position is not convincing and seems inadequate. First, and in addition to the arguments set out above, while this protected status may be universal for UN forces by virtue of the quasi universal membership of the UN, it is less clear whether and to what extent it is available to personnel of regional organizations deployed in host States that are not members of that organization absent a protected status based on a specific SOFA or other agreement.[2044] Second, while immunity from jurisdiction and especially inviolability certainly imply a prohibition to attack or detain protected persons (though the latter may depend on the exact scope of immunities granted), this obligation rests only upon the host State and its organs and agents. Private individuals or non-State

2041 E.g. when four UNIFIL observers were killed by an Israeli bombardment on their post on 26 July 2006 in south Lebanon, the Security Council issued a Presidential Statement in which it stressed "*that Israel and all concerned parties must comply fully with their obligations under international humanitarian law related to the protection of United Nations and its associated personnel and underlines the importance of ensuring that United Nations personnel are not the object of attack*". Earlier, in Resolution 1502 of 26 August 2006, the UN Security Council reaffirmed "*existing prohibitions under international law against attacks knowingly and intentionally directed against personnel involved in a humanitarian assistance or peacekeeping mission undertaken in accordance with the Charter of the United Nations which in situations of armed conflicts constitute war crimes*".

2042 Compare M. Bothe & T. Dörschel, *supra* note 2018, pp. 501–502, who regard them as non-combatants like any other non-combatant. *Contra*: Kolb, Porretto & Vité, pp. 182–183 and 199–204.

2043 Kolb, Porretto & Vité, pp. 182–183 and 199–204. On the status of UN peacekeepers, see also L. Sanders, 'Het statuut van de militaire peacekeepers', 28 *Transaktie* 1999, pp. 47–67.

2044 In this case only customary international law immunities and other protections would be available but as discussed above (Chapter 5.E.2 and Chapter 7.B.1) it is uncertain to what extent an international organization enjoys immunities under customary international law, especially vis-à-vis non-Member States and the same would be valid for staff of such organizations. Moreover, even if they have a certain protected status in principle, it is doubtful whether this status could also be invoked in the case of a presence of the organization which is not agreed to by the host State, as would be the case in peace enforcement operations.

actors will, at best, be bound only indirectly through a host State's obligation to criminalize attacks on peacekeepers not party to a conflict by virtue of the 1994 UN Convention on the Safety of United Nations and Associated Personnel,[2045] when the host State is a party to this Convention, which is not that widely ratified.[2046] Incidentally, it has been argued that this convention could apply to an ESDP operation when the operation's personnel meets the conditions of "associated personnel" and when the operation supports the mandate of a UN operation.[2047] In this view, a member of a rebel group who would attack a peacekeeper not party to a conflict would not commit any violation of international law (he would not be attacking a civilian) but merely a crime under

2045 New York, 9 December 1994, 2051 *U.N.T.S.* 391 and 34 *I.L.M.* 1995, pp. 482–493. For a discussion of this convention, see E. Bloom, 'Protecting Peacekeepers: The Convention on the Safety of United Nations and Associated Personnel', 89 *A.J.I.L.* 1995, pp. 621–631; M. Bothe & T. Dörschel, *supra* note 2018, pp. 497–499; M.-C. Bourloyannis-Vrailas, 'The Convention on the Safety of United Nations and Associated Personnel', 44 *I.C.L.Q.* 1995, pp. 560–590; A. Bouvier, 'Convention on the Safety of United Nations and Associated Personnel: Presentation and Analysis', 77 No. 309 *I.R.R.C.* 1995, pp. 638–666; O. Engdahl, *supra* note 2026; M. Frostad, *supra* note 2024, pp. 304–320; P. Kirsch, 'The Convention on the Safety of United Nations and Associated Personnel', 2 *International Peacekeeping* 1995, pp. 102–106 and 23 *Proceedings of the Annual Conference of the Canadian Council on International Law* 1994, pp. 182–187; S. Lepper, 'The Legal Status of Military Personnel in United Nations Peace Operations: One Delegate's Analysis', 18 *Houston J.I.L.*1996, pp. 359–464, especially pp. 370–464; R. Murphy, *supra* note 2019, pp. 181–188 and R. Siekmann, 'The Convention on the Safety of United Nations and Associated Personnel: Its Scope of Application', in E. Denters & N. Schrijver (eds.), *Reflections on International Law from the Low Countries: In Honour of Paul de Waart*, The Hague, Nijhoff, 1998, pp. 315-323. On 8 December 2005, the UN General Assembly adopted the Optional Protocol to the Convention on the Safety of United Nations and Associated Personnel (A/RES/60/42); for a discussion, see H. Llewellyn, 'The Optional Protocol to the 1994 Convention on the Safety of United Nations and Associated Personnel', 55 *I.C.L.Q.* 2006, pp. 718–728. The Protocol is not relevant to the LOAC as it essentially extends the scope of application of the 1994 Convention to certain humanitarian operations that are less likely to use force than peace operations.

2046 On 8 November 2009, 88 States were a party to the Convention. Many countries that host peace operations are not a party, including Afghanistan, the DRC, Haiti, Iraq, Sierra Leone and Timor Leste. In contrast, Bosnia and Herzegovina and Côte d'Ivoire are a party. .

2047 See N. Tsagourias, *supra* note 1997, pp. 124–125, referring to Article 2(1) *juncto* Article 1(b)(i). The latter provision covers "*Persons assigned by a Government or an intergovernmental organization with the agreement of the competent organ of the United Nations*" ... "*to carry out activities in support of the fulfilment of the mandate of a United Nations operation*" (obviously subject to the other exclusion rules in the Convention). Article 1(c) defines UN operation as "*an operation established by the competent organ of the United Nations in accordance with the Charter of the United Nations and conducted under United Nations authority and control* ...". See on these provisions also O. Engdahl, *supra* note 2026, pp. 221–22 and 231–233; M. Frostad, *supra* note 2024, pp. 310–314 and M. Arsanjani, *supra* note 2024, pp. 145–146. There were different views during the negotiations as to whether the Convention covers personnel operating under a UN mandate but not under (operational) UN control where no UN forces are co-deployed; see S. Lepper, *supra* note 2045, pp. 383–392. I would argue that the required *establishment* by the UN implies more than a mere authorization and requires at least some UN mission *sensu stricto*.

domestic law except where the 1994 Convention would apply. In fact, the latter convention was adopted precisely because the specific protection of personnel of peace operations was deemed inadequate.[2048] This view is therefore not persuasive.

A further key issue for the purpose of this book is who becomes a party to the armed conflict when peace forces do participate in it: is it their sending State and/or the international organization in the framework of which they operate? I will examine this in Sections F and G below.

C. THE NATURE OF ARMED CONFLICTS AND THE PARTIES THERETO

If peace forces become a party to an armed conflict, a further question needs to be answered: what kind of armed conflict is it? The question arises because the LOAC does not consist of one single set of rules but has rules that differ, at least to some extent, depending on the nature of the armed conflict.

The principle distinction is that between international armed conflicts, defined by Article 2 common to the 1949 Geneva Conventions, as "*all cases of declared war or of any other armed conflict which may arise between two or more of the High Contracting Parties, even if the state of war is not recognized by one of them*" on the one hand, and armed conflicts not of an international character on the other hand.[2049] The latter were initially only governed by Article 3 common to the 1949 Geneva Conventions, which covered any "*armed conflict not of an international character occurring in the territory of one of the High Contracting Parties*".[2050] However, some armed conflicts not of an international character were subsequently made the subject to further regulation by AP II and the ICC

2048 See S. Lepper, *supra* note 2045, pp. 364–365.

2049 See, e.g. D. Schindler, 'The Different Types of Armed Conflicts According to the Geneva Conventions and Protocols', 163 *Rec. Cours* 1979-II, pp. 117–164. See also J. Pejic, 'Status of Armed Conflicts', in E. Wilmshurst & S. Breau (eds.), *Perspectives on the ICRC Study on Customary International Humanitarian Law*, Cambridge, Cambridge University Press, 2007, pp. 77–100.

2050 For developments in such conflicts up to 1949, see L. Moir, 'The Historical Development of the Application of Humanitarian Law in Non-International Armed Conflicts to 1949', 47 *I.C.L.Q.* 1998, pp. 337–361 (discussing common Article 3 at pp. 355–361). Compare for an analysis just before the adoption of AP II, D. Ciobanu, *supra* note 2001, pp. 43–79. On this common Article 3, see also A. Cullen, 'Key Developments Affecting the Scope of Internal Armed Conflict in International Humanitarian Law', 183 *Mil. L. Rev.* 2005, pp. 79–88.

Statute.[2051] Article 1(1) of AP II defines the scope of application of this Protocol as "*all armed conflicts [not covered by Article 1 AP I] and which take place in the territory of a High Contracting Party between its armed forces and dissident armed forces or other organized armed groups which, under responsible command, exercise such control over a part of its territory as to enable them to carry out sustained and concerted military operations and to implement this Protocol*", adding that it "*develops and supplements Article 3 common to the Geneva Conventions* ... without modifying its existing conditions of application" (emphasis added).[2052] Article 8(2)(f) ICC Statute covers "*armed conflicts that take place in the territory of a State when there is protracted armed conflict between governmental authorities and organized armed groups or between such groups*".[2053]

2051 On the law of non-international armed conflicts, see generally R. Abi-Saab, *Droit humanitaire et conflits internes: origines et évolution de la réglementation internationale*, Geneva/Paris, Henry Dunant Institute/Pedone, 1986 (mainly discussing developments up to the adoption of AP II); M. Bothe, 'Conflits armés internes et droit international humanitaire', 82 *R.G.D.I.P.* 1978, pp. 82–102; A. Cassese, 'Le guerre civile et le droit international', 90 *R.G.D.I.P.* 1986, pp. 553–578, especially pp. 558–574; L. Moir, *The Law of Internal Armed Conflict*, Cambridge, Cambridge University Press, 2002; G. Mousourakis, 'Applying Humanitarian Law to Non-International Armed Conflicts', 14 *Anuario de derecho internacional* 1998, pp. 293–319; J. Nguyên Duy-Tân, 'The Law Applicable to Non-International Armed Conflicts', in M. Bedjaoui (ed.), *International Law: Achievements and Prospects*, Paris/Dordrecht, UNESCO/Nijhoff, 1991, pp. 793–809; R. Müllerson, 'International Humanitarian Law in Internal Conflicts', 2 *Journal of Armed Conflict* 1997, pp. 109–133; L. Perna, *The Formation of the Treaty Law of Non-International Armed Conflicts*, Leiden, Martinus Nijhoff, 2006; R. Pinto, 'Les règles du droit international concernant la guerre civile', 114 *Rec. Cours* 1965-I, pp. 524–548; F. Rajower, *Das Recht des bewaffneten nicht-internationalen Konflikts seit 1949*, Zürich, Schulthess, 1990 and the various contributions in 'Coping with Internal Conflicts: Dilemmas in International Law', 13 *Georgia J.I.C.L.* 1983 (Supplement), pp. 179–439, especially pp. 253–301.

2052 The ICRC Commentary to Article 1 AP II makes it clear that the scope of application of AP II is not the same as that of Article 3 common to the Geneva Conventions. This view was also reflected in the statements of various representatives upon the adoption of this provision; see, e.g. the statements by Belgium, Germany, Cameroon and Italy, reproduced in H.S. Levie (ed.), *The Law of Non-International Armed Conflict*, Dordrecht, Martinus Nijhoff, 1987, respectively at pp. 81, 84–85, 88 and 89 (this is an unofficial collection of the preparatory works of AP II; the section on Article 1 counts no less than 67 pages). See also R. Abi-Saab, *supra* note 2051, pp. 145–153, especially p. 152; M. Bothe, *supra* note 2051, pp. 88–91, especially p. 90; A. Cullen, *supra* note 2050, pp. 92–96; David, p. 128 and M. Hess, *infra* note 2089, pp. 96–106. But see F. Rajower, *supra* note 2051, pp. 47–48, who notes that some have argued that the two have the same scope of application but disagrees with this view himself. D.P. Forsythe, 'Legal Management of Internal War: The 1977 Protocol on Non-International Armed Conflicts', 72 *A.J.I.L.* 1978, p. 286, notes that most States were of the view that common Article 3 was wider and that the drafting history supports this, but that some disagreed with this view. B. de Schutter & C. van de Wijngaert, 'Coping with Non-International Armed Conflicts: The Borderline between National and International Law', 13 *Georgia J.I.C.L.* 1983, p. 285, write that despite this wording, many governments seemed to read the conditions for AP II into common Article 3.

2053 See generally M. Boot, *supra* note 2040, pp. 546–556 and 569–578; L. Condorelli, 'War Crimes and Internal Conflict in the Statute of the International Criminal Court', in M. Politi and G. Nesi (eds.), *The Rome Statute of the International Criminal Court. A Challenge to Impunity*,

The latter definition is nearly identical to that given by the ICTY in the *Tadic* case, i.e. "*protracted armed violence between governmental authorities and organized armed groups or between such groups within a State*".[2054] It should also be noted that for States party to AP I "*armed conflicts in which peoples are fighting against colonial domination and alien occupation and against racist regimes in the exercise of their right of self-determination*" are equated to international armed conflicts pursuant to Article 1(4) AP I. I will not take into account the latter aspect below.

Thus treaty law not only recognizes a differences between international armed conflicts and armed conflicts not of an international character, but also seems to contain different kinds of armed conflicts not of an international character that are subject to different LOAC regimes.[2055] However, in respect of the latter it would seem that there is a tendency towards unification of the regime governing armed conflicts not of an international character in respect of which the above-mentioned *Tadic* and ICC Statute definitions arguably reflect the accepted concretization of Article 3 common to the Geneva Conventions,[2056] although it must be admitted that the place of the ICC definition in the overall picture is not very clear.[2057] This appears to be the position adopted in the recent *UK*

Aldershot, Ashgate, 2001, pp. 107–117, especially pp. 111–113; A. Cullen, *supra* note 2050, pp. 102–107; H. Spieker, 'The International Criminal Court and Non-International Armed Conflicts', 13 *Leiden J.I.L.* 2000, pp. 407–408 and A. Zimmermann, 'Article 8 Par 2. Preliminary Remarks on para 2(c) – (f) and para 3: War Crimes Committed in Armed Conflits not of an International Character', in O. Triffterer (ed.), *supra* note 2040, pp. 270–286.

2054 *Prosecutor v. Dusko Tadic*, IT-94-1, 2 October 1995, §70. See also A. Cullen, *supra* note 2050, pp. 98–102 and L. Moir, *supra* note 2051, pp. 134–160.

2055 See generally David, pp. 102–131; F. Rajower, *supra* note 2051, pp. 43–49; D. Schindler, *supra* note 2049, pp. 117–164 and UK Manual, §3.1–3.9.

2056 Similarly, A. Cullen, *supra* note 2050, pp. 79–109, especially pp. 105–109, though this author submits that "*further development is required for its evolution into a more substantive measure for determining the existence of armed conflict*". Compare, with regard to the *Tadic* formula, S. Boelaert-Suominen, 'The Yugoslavia Tribunal and the Common Core of Humanitarian Law Applicable to All Armed Conflicts', 13 *Leiden J.I.L.* 2000, pp. 632–636; R. Murphy, *supra* note 2019, p. 164 and Zwanenburg, p. 194. H. Spieker, *supra* note 2053, pp. 407–408 writes that the ICC definition reflects the modern definition of armed conflict.

2057 The ICC definition can also be read as creating yet another category of non-international armed conflicts (next to common Article 3 and AP II); see, e.g. L. Condorelli, *supra* note 2053, pp. 112–113 (seeing the difference in the protracted element; see also *infra*) and David, pp. 118–119 and 128–129 (focusing on the relationship between the ICC and AP II definitions). I have taken this view myself in the past; see, e.g. F. Naert & J. Wouters, *infra* note 2077, p. 477. However, I am now inclined to see the ICC definition as the modern understanding of common Article 3. The fact that Article 8(2)(c)-(d) ICC Statute covers conflicts in the sense of Article 3 common to the Geneva Conventions and that the more specific *Tadic* definition is adopted separately in Article 8(2)(e)-(f) ICC Statute is not conclusive evidence to the contrary as Article 8(2)b and c similarly distinguish between two sets of rules of international armed conflicts yet clearly do not cover two different kinds of armed conflicts. Rather, the

Manual.[2058] Also, the recent *Sanremo Manual on Non-International Armed Conflicts* offers the following single definition of non-international armed conflicts: "*armed confrontations occurring within the territory of a single State and in which the armed forces of no other State are engaged against the central government*" and excluding internal disturbances and tensions, such as riots, isolated and sporadic acts of violence or other acts of a similar nature.[2059] This

---

qualification that Article 8(2)(e) covers rules "*within the established framework of international law*" and its likeness to the *Tadic* definition imply that this provision did not intend to create a new category. Similarly, T. Meron, *The Humanization of International Law*, Leiden, Nijhoff, 2006, p. 30, submits that it is unlikely that it was the intention to create yet another category of internal armed conflicts. This also seems to be the ICRC's view: its opinion paper *How is the Term "Armed Conflict" Defined in International Humanitarian Law?* (*supra* note 2002, p. 4) states that "*The Statute of the International Criminal Court, in its Article 8, para. 2 (f), confirms the existence of a definition of a non-international armed conflict not fulfilling the criteria of Protocol II. ... the ICTY went on to determine the existence of a NIAC* "whenever there is [...] protracted armed violence between governmental authorities and organised armed groups or between such groups within a State". *The ICTY thus confirmed that the definition of NIAC in the sense of common Article 3 encompasses situations where* "several factions [confront] each other without involvement of the government's armed forces"." (notes omitted; emphasis in the original text). Compare S. Boelaert-Suominen, *supra* note 2056, p. 626 note 22, submitting that the ICC definition did create a new category of non-international armed conflicts (despite its similarity to the *Tadic* definition, which the author does seem to see as an elaboration of common Article 3, see *id.*, pp. 632–636). Compare also M. Bothe, 'War Crimes', in A. Cassese, P. Gaeta & J. Jones (eds.), *The Rome Statute of the International Criminal Court: A Commentary*, Oxford, Oxford University Press, 2002, pp. 419–420 and 423, who is of the view that the definition in Article 8(2)(e)-(f) was deemed to reflect customary law but has a different scope of application than Article 8(2)(c) and thus does not reflect an understanding of common Article 3. L. Moir, *supra* note 2051, pp. 166–167, writes that the ICC threshold is lower than the AP II one, but does not elaborate on the relationship between the ICC and common Article 3 thresholds (although her view of the ICC Statute as a confirmation of customary law (at pp. 160–188) taken together with the lower threshold compared to AP II would seem to imply that she sees the ICC threshold as similar to the common Article 3 one, unless there is a customary law category that differs from both common Article 3 and AP II).

2058 At §15.1, p. 382 note 2 and the accompanying text this manual apparently sees Article 8(2) of the ICC Statute as reflecting customary international law applicable in non-international armed conflicts. Moreover, at Chapter 15.B, pp 384–398, it refers to Article 8(2)(e) ICC Statute and lists a fairly broad range of customary rules applicable in all non-international armed conflicts, i.e. those meant by common Article 3.

2059 M. Schmitt, Y. Dinstein & C. H.B. Garraway, *The Manual on the Law of Non-International Armed Conflict: With Commentary*, San Remo, International Institute of Humanitarian Law, 2006 (available online at www.michaelschmitt.org/images/Manual[1].Final.Brill.pdf), §1.1.1. The commentary discusses the different thresholds under common Article 3 and AP II and mentions the ICC and other treaty provisions as well as customary international law, but does not clarify their mutual impact (except for the former two) nor where the Manual's definition fits in this state of affairs. In fact, an earlier draft contained a broader definition that would have better supported the above argument, namely "*armed confrontations between a state authority and an armed group or among armed groups within the territory of a state*", involving "*significant, intense and sustained use of armed force*" (July 2004 draft, on file with the author).

development is also reflected in the amendment adopted on 21 December 2001 to the Convention on Prohibitions or Restrictions on the Use of Certain Conventional Weapons Which May be Deemed to be Excessively Injurious or to Have Indiscriminate Effects[2060] which extends the scope of application of this convention and the annexed protocols to "*situations referred to in Article 3 common to the Geneva Conventions of 12 August 1949*".[2061] Finally, the recent ICRC study on customary international humanitarian law,[2062] while focusing to a considerable extent on armed conflicts not of an international character,[2063] does not define these conflicts and treats them as one category.[2064] However, a reservation may have to be made to this argument concerning the temporal threshold for armed conflict: while both the *Tadic* and ICC definitions require *protracted* armed violence/conflict, it is a matter of debate whether this requirement is also included in common Article 3 to the Geneva Conventions, especially following the famous *Abella* decision of the Inter-American Commission of Human Rights.[2065] This wide view of common Article 3 could be

2060 Geneva, 10 October 1980.

2061 More generally, L. Perna, *supra* note 2051, pp. 113–134 identifies a dramatic increase since 1980 in the treaty law of non-international armed conflicts.

2062 J.-M. Henckaerts & L. Doswald-Beck (eds.), *Customary International Humanitarian Law*, Cambridge, Cambridge University Press, 2005 (2 Volumes), see also *infra* note 2165.

2063 For an earlier study on this point, see F. Kalshoven, 'Applicability of Customary International Law in Non-International Armed Conflicts', in A. Cassese (ed.), *Current Problems of International Law: Essays on U.N. Law and on the Law of Armed Conflict*, Milan, Giuffre, 1975, pp. 267–285.

2064 J. Pejic, *supra* note 2049, p. 78 also notes that the study doesn't define the notion of armed conflict. Compare the Institute of International Law's Resolution concerning 'The Application of International Humanitarian Law and Fundamental Human Rights, in Armed Conflicts in which Non-State Entities are Parties', adopted at the 1999 Berlin session, which does not distinguish between categories of non-international armed conflicts but seems to leave open the possibility of different legal regimes by listing various sources of applicable law, including treaties – logically each with their own scope of application (although the resolution deals with "*armed conflicts in which non-State entities are parties*" the sources listed clearly imply that these are equated to non-international armed conflicts).

2065 *Juan Carlos Abella v. Argentina*, Report 55/97, Case 11.137, 18 November 1997, §§146–156 (qualifying a 30-hour armed confrontation involving armed forces as an armed conflict). See on this case, e.g. David, pp. 126–127. In the wake of this decision, some commentators have questioned whether common Article 3 requires a protracted armed conflict; see, e.g. R. Cryer, 'The Fine Art of Friendship: Jus in Bello in Afghanistan', 7 *J.C.S.L.* 2002, p. 42 and A. Zimmermann, *supra* note 2053, p. 270. L. Condorelli, *supra* note 2053, pp. 112–113 seems to reject the temporal requirement, as does M. Boot, *supra* note 2040, p. 574, since she regards the ICC definition as a limitation. In contrast, the ICTY has stressed the protracted element; see, e.g. Trial Chamber, *Prosecutor v. Zejnil Delalic, Zdravko Mucic, also known as "Pavo", Hazim Delic and Esad Landzo, also known as "Zenga"* (Celebici), IT-96-21, 16 November 1998, §184 ("*in order to distinguish from cases of civil unrest or terrorist activities, the emphasis is on the protracted extent of the armed violence and the extent of organisation of the parties involved*").

safeguarded if the protracted element in the ICC definition could be regarded as a jurisdictional threshold only.[2066]

This differentiated regime is further complicated by the particular nature of peace operations conducted by international organizations, as these are not explicitly covered as such by any of the existing categories. In this respect, it is submitted that the nature of an armed conflict in which peace forces participate is essentially determined by their opponent.[2067] If the opponent is a High Contracting Party, i.e. armed forces of a government (whether recognized or not), there will be an international armed conflict.[2068] This is clear and does not seem to be contested[2069] when one looks to the peace forces as remaining the armed forces of their sending States. However, it is less clear, though in my view also correct, whether the same is true when looking at them as the armed forces acting on behalf of an international organization (see *infra*, Sections F and G).

2066 In this respect, it may be noted that the ICC Statute, as a criminal law instrument, is primarily a secondary norm, i.e. one criminalizing conduct regulated already by other primary norms of international law, in this case the LOAC. However, these secondary norms may correspond to the primary norms, may lag behind or may be more progressive (i.e they may also determine the primary norm), so that deriving conclusions from it concerning primary norms is tricky. See on this M. Bothe, *supra* note 2057, pp. 417–422. Nevertheless, the reference to "*the established framework of international law*" suggests that the ICC definition was not intended to set new primary norms. The ICC's Pre-Trial Chamber I, in *Prosecutor v Thomas Lubanga Dyilo*, Case No ICC-01/04-01/06, 29 January 2007, www.icc-cpi.int/iccdocs/doc/doc266175.PDF, §234, stated that "*protracted armed conflict...focuses on the need for the armed groups in question to have the ability to plan and carry out military operations for a prolonged period of time*".

2067 Kolb, Porretto & Vité, p. 186. *Contra*: S. Bartelt, *supra* note 1997, pp. 191–192 and 196, arguing that such conflicts are always international.

2068 Kolb, Porretto & Vité, p. 183. See in respect of States also, F. Rajower, *supra* note 2051, p. 31, who, with regard to the UN, however, seems to regard the legal basis of the mandate as determining whether the conflict is international or not (if based on Article 42 UN Charter, he sees it as international, whereas otherwise he is unclear as to what LOAC would apply if the use of force in peacekeeping escalates to participation in an armed conflict).

2069 Except by those who regard UN mandated operations as police operations not subject to the LOAC even when they entail participation in an armed conflict (for a qualification as police actions, albeit with regard to the *ius ad bellum* and not the *ius in bello*, see, e.g. T. Franck & F. Patel, 'Agora: The Gulf Crisis in International and Foreign Relations Law. UN Police Action in Lieu of War: "The Old Order Changeth"', 85 *A.J.I.L.* 1991, pp. 63–74). However, this view ignores the distinction between the *ius ad bellum* and *ius in bello* and is contrary to international instruments (see above) and practice and no longer seems to enjoy much support. See M. Frostad, *supra* note 2024, p. 321 and especially M. Sassoli, 'Collective Security Operations and IHL', in College of Europe & ICRC (eds.), *Proceedings of the Bruges Colloquium. Relevance of International Humanitarian Law to Non-State Actors. 25th – 26th October 2002 / Actes du colloque de Bruges. La pertinence du Droit international humanitaire pour les acteurs non-étatiques. 25–26 octobre 2002*, Bruges, College of Europe (*collegium* No. 27, available online at www.coleurop.be/template.asp?pagename=pub_collegium), 2003, pp. 77–100.

However, when the opponent is an armed group who cannot claim to represent a government or State, not even an unrecognized government,[2070] the nature of the conflict is less certain,[2071] except where the host State government, even though not involved in the armed conflict, opposes it.[2072] In fact, a conflict in which the armed forces of governments are fighting non-governmental armed forces in a third State (since 11 September 2001, the latter are also sometimes referred to as transnational armed groups when they operate in more than one State[2073]) is one which does not really fit within the two traditional categories of armed conflicts. It is neither international *in the sense of the LOAC* because it does not oppose States on both sides nor internal *in the ordinary sense* because it involves armed forces from different States. It usually occurs together with an internal armed conflict and is usually referred to as an 'internationalized' (non-international) armed conflict.[2074]

2070 Where there is a government but it is not recognized, this does not affect the qualification of the armed conflict as international; see Article 4(A)(3) GC III. I will return to the key importance of this factor and its disadvantages *infra* notes 2084–2088 and the accompanying text.

2071 For Kolb, Porretto & Vité, pp. 184–190, the majority view in doctrine is that these conflicts too are international but of a *sui generis* nature but these authors acknowledge that sometimes the law of non-international armed conflicts may be applicable. C. Byron, 'Armed Conflicts: International or Non-International', 6 *J.C.S.L.* 2001, pp. 82–83, argues that a purposive interpretation of the Geneva Conventions entails that such conflicts are international. David, pp 154–158, seems to regard them as international (he seems less clear at p. 160 but that part seems to concern the effect on the internal conflict rather than the conflict in which the UN itself would be engaged). Compare Zwanenburg, pp. 195–196, who does not take a position on this specific issue but adopts a different approach rather than this analogy (see *infra* note 2265). A. Faite, *supra* note 1998, pp. 146–148, rejects the view that the involvement of international forces always entails an international armed conflict.

2072 In this case the conflict may be said to be directed also against the host State and therefore would be international, notwithstanding that the host State would not actually participate in the conflict. Moreover, in any event, where it would lead to the occupation of host State territory without consent, the applicability of the law of occupation and international armed conflict is clear. See also *infra* note 2107 and the accompanying text.

2073 See on this notion, e.g. M. Sassoli, *Transnational Armed Groups and International Humanitarian Law*, HPCR Occasional Paper No. 6, Winter 2006 (available online at www.hpcr.org/pdfs/OccasionalPaper6.pdf); HPCR, *Transnationality, War and the Law. A Report on a Roundtable on the Transformation of Warfare, International Law, and the Role of Transnational Armed Groups*, April 2006 (available online at www.hpcr.org/pdfs/HPCR_-_Transnationality_Roundtable_-_April_2006.pdf) and HPCR, *Non-Linearity of Engagement – Transnational Armed Groups, International Law, and the Conflict between the United States and Al Qaeda*, July 2005 (available online at www.hpcr.org/pdfs/Non-Linearity_of_Engagement.pdf).

2074 See generally on such conflicts R. Bierzanek, 'Quelques remarques sur l'applicabilité du droit international humanitaire des conflits armés aux conflits internes internationalisés', in C. Swinarski (ed.), *supra* note 1998, pp. 281–290; David, pp. 112 and 139–160; H.-P. Gasser, 'Internationalized Non-International Armed Conflicts: Case Studies of Afghanistan, Kampuchea and Lebanon', 33 *American University Law Review* 1983, pp. 145–161 and D. Schindler, 'Le droit international humanitaire et les conflits internes internationales', 64 No. 737 *R.I.C.R.* 1982, pp. 263–272.

It is submitted that such 'internationalized' armed conflicts are at least covered by Article 3 common to the Geneva Conventions because this provision was intended to cover all armed conflicts not covered by Article 2 common to these conventions and its text can be read to cover these conflicts. It suffices to read "*armed conflict not of an international character*" as *not of an international character in the sense of Article 2 common to the Geneva Conventions.*[2075] In fact, this conclusion was recently affirmed by the US Supreme Court in the *Hamdan* case.[2076] Although the case concerned the conflict between the US and Al-Qaeda, i.e. a conflict against a terrorist organization rather than a peace operation, the structure of the conflict is of the same nature: the armed forces of the government of one State against a non-governmental armed group in (one or more) other State(s).[2077] Such a conflict would also be regulated by other treaty provisions that refer to Article 3 common to the Geneva Conventions for their scope of application.[2078] Moreover, it appears that the standards set out in Article 3 common to the Geneva Conventions are not only considered as reflecting

[2075] Similarly, M. Hess, *infra* note 2089, pp. 159–161, regards such conflicts as non-international because of the *a contrario* definition of armed conflicts not of an international character. This also seems to be the view of C. Greenwood, *supra* note 2037, p. 199. G.-J. Knoops, *supra* note 2028, pp. 89–91 also considers that common Article 3 may apply to peace forces.

[2076] US Supreme Court, *Hamdan v. Rumsfeld*, 29 June 2006, available online at www.supremecourtus.gov/opinions/05pdf/05-184.pdf, pp. 66–69 of the online text. On this case, see generally www.hamdanvrumsfeld.com. For annotations, see, e.g. B.C. Baldrate, 'The Supreme Court's Role in Defining the Jurisdiction of Military Tribunals: A Study, Critique, & Proposal for Hamdan v. Rumsfeld', 186 *Mil. L. Rev.* 2005, pp. 1–115 (available online at www.jagcnet.army.mil/JAGCNETInternet/Homepages/AC/MilitaryLawReview.nsf/MLRDisplay?OpenForm); N.K. Katyal, 'Hamdan v. Rumsfeld: The Legal Academy Goes to Practice', 120 *Harvard Law Review* 2006, pp. 66–123; F. Ní Aoláin, '*Hamdan* and Common Article 3: Did the Supreme Court Get It Right?', 91 *Minnesota Law Review* 2007, pp. 1523–1561; P.J. Spiro, 'Hamdan v. Rumsfeld: U.S. Supreme Court Decision on Legality of Military Commissions Established by President Bush', 100 *A.J.I.L* 2006, pp. 888–895 and D. Steiger, *Die CIA, die Menschenrechte und der Fall Khaled el-Masri: Zugleich ein Beitrag zur Frage der Anwendbarkeit des gemeinsamen Article 3 der Genfer Konventionen auf den 'Krieg gegen den Terror'*, Potsdam, MenschenRechtsZentrum der Universität Potsdam, 2007, pp. 73–75.

[2077] For a discussion of these kinds of conflicts in the counter-terrorism context, see F. Naert & J. Wouters, 'Shockwaves through International Law after 11 September: Finding the Right Responses to the Challenges of International Terrorism', in C. Fijnaut, J. Wouters & F. Naert (eds.), *Legal Instruments in the Fight against International Terrorism. A Transatlantic Dialogue*, Martinus Nijhoff, 2004, pp. 476–483. Compare N. Schrijver & L. van den Herik, *Counter-terrorism Strategies, Human Rights and International Law: Meeting the Challenges. Final Report Poelgeest Seminar*, 31 May 2007 (available online at www.minbuza.nl/nl/bestanden/bestanden_hippo/Kamerbrieven_bijlagen/2007/06/236dmvmr_Final_Report_doc).

[2078] Notably the amended Conventional Weapons Convention and its annexed Protocols, see *supra* note 2060 and accompanying text.

customary international law,[2079] but are also deemed applicable in any type of armed conflict.[2080]

However, the question is whether the entire body of customary international humanitarian law applicable in armed conflicts not of an international character[2081] also applies. This will depend upon the question whether the above-mentioned development towards a single definition of armed conflicts not of an international character and corresponding to Article 3 common to the Geneva Conventions rather than AP II (already) reflects existing law. Since this definition is to be understood as clarifying what Article 3 common to the Geneva Conventions covers[2082] and seems to enjoy wide support, this is arguably the case.[2083]

2079 For an extensive discussion, see T. Meron, *Human Rights and Humanitarian Norms as Customary Law*, Oxford, Clarendon Press, 1989, pp. 41–62.

2080 See, e.g. ICJ, *Nicaragua case*, §218 ("*Article 3 ... common to all four Geneva Conventions ... defines certain rules to be applied in the armed conflicts of a non-international character. There is no doubt that, in the event of international armed conflicts, these rules also constitute a minimum yardstick ...; and they are rules which, in the Court's opinion, reflect what the Court in 1949 called 'elementary considerations of humanity' (...)*)" and ICTY, *Prosecutor v. Dusko Tadic*, IT-94-1, 2 October 1995, §102 ("*at least with respect to the minimum rules in common Article 3, the character of the conflict is irrelevant*"). See also A. Cullen, *supra* note 2050, pp. 81–83.

2081 The ICRC's customary international humanitarian law study (*supra* note 2062) and the *Sanremo Manual on Non-International Armed Conflicts* (*supra* note 2059) provide an excellent starting point for determining the content of these rules. See also F. Bugnion, 'Le droit international humanitaire coutumier et les conflits armes non internationaux', in P. Tavernier & J.-M. Henckaerts (eds.), *Droit international humanitaire coutumier: enjeux et défis contemporains*, Brussels, Bruylant, 2008, pp. 179–190; M. Hess, *infra* note 2089, pp. 110–120 and L. Zegveld, *Armed Opposition Groups in International Law: The Quest for Accountability*, Rotterdam, Doctoral thesis, Erasmus University Rotterdam, 2000, pp. 111–119 and 123–131.

2082 This also seems to be the understanding of J. Stewart, 'Towards a Single Definition of Armed Conflict in International Humanitarian Law: A Critique of Internationalized Armed Conflict', 85 No. 850 *I.R.R.C.* 2003, p. 318 and ZWANENBURG, pp. 194–195.

2083 The Institute of International Law's Resolution concerning 'The Application of International Humanitarian Law and Fundamental Human Rights, in Armed Conflicts in which Non-State Entities are Parties', *supra* note 2064, seems to endorse this view by including in its definition of "*armed conflicts in which non-State entities are parties*" "*internal armed conflicts in which peacekeeping forces intervene*" (§I) (while the former category might be distinct from that of non-international armed conflicts, the list of sources of applicable law in §IV clearly implies that they are equated). Also, in the 13th recital of the preamble, the resolution takes the view that the UN Secretary General's Bulletin (*supra* note 2021) can refer to the law of non-international armed conflicts (by stating that it "*provides for the possibility of prosecuting members of the military personnel of such Forces in case of violations of humanitarian law, in particular in situations of internal armed conflicts*"). ZWANENBURG, p. 194, is of the view that "*the customary law of non-international armed conflict has come to be applicable to a broader set of situations than its conventional counterpart*".

The key problem with this view is that, especially in a full civil war, it may no longer be clear who can in fact claim to represent the government/State.[2084] In that case, the link to the legitimate international representative of the State, which has rightly been described as the crucial element in defining international armed conflicts,[2085] becomes its Achilles' heel.[2086] In fact, the problem then becomes very similar to that of the legality of intervention in civil war.[2087] However, absent a central authority to decide on who may legitimately represent a State,[2088] or broad international consensus in specific cases, there is no easy solution to this problem. Nevertheless, it is possible to argue that where there are several contenders to represent a State with roughly equal claims and international support, conflicts with such contenders by third States may be regarded as international (in contrast with the question of the legality of an intervention, accepting multiple parties as belonging to a State for this purpose is less problematic), although it is doubtful whether practice supports this approach.

Moreover, there is the question what happens with an international armed conflict and an armed conflict not of an international character when they occur in the same territory. These situations have been called 'mixed conflicts'.[2089] The prevailing view appears to be that each conflict maintains its own character,[2090] as was held by the International Court of Justice in the *Nicarague* case[2091] and

---

2084 See, e.g. F. Bugnion, 'Jus Ad Bellum, Jus In Bello and Non-International Armed Conflicts', 6 *Y.I.H.L.* 2003, pp. 167–198 (also available at www.icrc.org/Web/eng/siteeng0.nsf/htmlall/francois-bugnion-Article-150306/$File/jus%20ad%20bellum,%20jus%20in%20bello%20and%20non-international%20armed%20conflictsANG.pdf), p. 4 note 12 online version, and J. Stewart, *supra* note 2082, pp. 342–344.

2085 M. Hess, *infra* note 2089, p. 59 and especially pp. 169–182, seeing it as a tension between effectiveness and legitimacy.

2086 *Id.*, pp. 169–182.

2087 Briefly discussed above in Chapter 4.A.6.

2088 The point of this absence is made by M. Hess, *infra* note 2089, pp. 183–192.

2089 See especially M. Hess, *Die Anwendbarkeit des humanitären Völkerrechts, insbesondere in gemischten Konflikten*, Zürich, Schulthess, 1985, who defines these conflicts as involving at least three parties, at least two of which are from within the same State and at least one from a third State (p. 143). See also F. Rajower, *supra* note 2051, pp. 30–33 and J. Stewart, *supra* note 2082, pp. 313–350.

2090 Y. Dinstein, *The Conduct of Hostilities Under the Law of International Armed Conflict*, Cambridge, Cambridge University Press, 2004, pp. 14–15; M. Hess, *supra* note 2089, pp. 150–152 and 159–168 (with further references); Kolb, Porretto & Vité, pp. 185–186 (albeit reluctantly); F. Rajower, *supra* note 2051, p. 31 and H. Risse, *supra* note 1998, pp. 115–120. But see the references to opponents in J. Stewart, *supra* note 2082, pp. 334–335. Also *contra*, David, pp. 146–153 (though less clearly at p. 160).

2091 In §219 of this judgment, the Court stated that "*The conflict between the contras' forces and those of the Government of Nicaragua is an armed conflict which is "not of an international character". The acts of the contras towards the Nicaraguan Government are therefore governed by the law applicable to conflicts of that character; whereas the actions of the United States in and against Nicaragua fall under the legal rules relating to international conflicts*".

seems to have been predominantly accepted by the ICTY.[2092] Nevertheless, even many of the authors who come to this conclusion, often compelled by the strict classification of armed conflicts which States have insisted upon,[2093] regard this solution as regrettable, unfair and not workable in practice.[2094] The latter, however, may be questioned, especially in light of the growing convergence of the law of international and non-international armed conflicts,[2095] in particular as regards methods and means of combat. Thus the practical problems may be limited by instructing soldiers in the field to apply a single set of rules and leave those areas where differences still matter, notably concerning the status of detainees, to higher echelons where the necessary distinctions can be made.[2096] Indeed, while there is clearly an increasing convergence between of the law of

2092 In *Prosecutor v. Dusko Tadic*, IT-94-1, 15 July 1999, §84, the ICTY ruled that "*in case of an internal armed conflict breaking out on the territory of a State, it* may become international (or, depending upon the circumstances, be international in character alongside an internal armed conflict*) if (i) another State intervenes in that conflict through its troops, or alternatively if (ii) some of the participants in the internal armed conflict act on behalf of that other State*" (emphasis added). In its 2 October 1995 decision in the same case, it held that "*the agreements reached ... bear out the proposition that, when the Security Council adopted the Statute of the [ICTY], it did so with reference to* situations that the parties themselves considered at different times and places as either internal or international armed conflicts, or as a mixed internal-international conflict" (§73; emphasis added). The underligned parts clearly imply that the conflicts may keep their separate nature. See also J. Stewart, *supra* note 2082, pp. 333–335, who adds at pp. 323–331 that the ICTY's case law on when the conflict becomes international is unclear and incoherent. On the classification of the Yugoslav conflict(s), see also G. Aldrich, 'Jurisdiction of the International Criminal Tribunal for the Former Yugoslavia', 90 *A.J.I.L.* 1996, pp. 64–69; C. Gray, 'Bosnia and Herzegovina: Civil War or Inter-State Conflict? Characterization and Consequences', 67 *B.Y.I.L.* 1996, pp. 155–197; C. Greenwood, 'International Humanitarian Law and the *Tadic* Case', 7 *E.J.I.L.* 1996, pp. 265–283 and T. Meron, 'Classification of Armed Conflict in the Former Yugoslavia: Nicaragua's Fallout', 92 *A.J.I.L.* 1998, pp. 236–242.

2093 E.g. F. Rajower, *supra* note 2051, p. 31 writes that it is unobjectionable from a strictly legal perspective ("*streng juristisch betrachter, einwandfrei*"). In the same sense M. Hess, *supra* note 2089, pp. 150–152 and J. Stewart, *supra* note 2082, p. 335. C. Greenwood, *supra* note 2092, pp. 269–275, also defends a differentiated analysis per subconflict.

2094 E.g. M. Hess, *supra* note 2089, pp. 159–168 and 280–285 (seeing problems in certain cases, including support for (successful) insurgents and puppet regimes in occupations, a lack of government or competing candidate governments, as well as an unworkable complexity, and pleading for a return to basic principles) and F. Rajower, *supra* note 2051, pp. 30–33 (who pleads for a proper regulation of these conflicts because he sees difficulties in applying all the rules of an international armed conflict too, though he admits that the solution has been rejected and ultimately leaves open the question what law applies to such conflicts despite stressing their international nature in the ordinary sense of the word).

2095 For an analysis of this convergence and its limits, see also L. Moir, 'Towards the Unification of International Humanitarian Law?', in R. Burchill, N.D. White & J. Morris (eds.), *International Conflict and Security Law: Essays in Memory of Hilaire McCoubrey*, Cambridge, Cambridge University Press, 2005, pp. 108–128. On a core of common rules, see S. Boelaert-Suominen, *supra* note 2056, pp. 637–650.

2096 See the example given by Green in a comment in M. Bothe, P. Macalister-Smith & T. Kurzidem (eds.), *National Implementation of International Humanitarian Law: Proceedings of an* international armed conflict and the law of armed conflicts not of an international character,[2097] States still maintain that in some respects there still are differences between both regimes, a reality reflected in the ICC Statute and also acknowledged in the ICRC's recent study on customary international humanitarian law.[2098] Moreover, simply regarding the whole conflict as international does not offer a solution to all problems either, as the law of international armed conflicts cannot fully be applied to armed conflicts not of an international character without some adaptations.[2099] In conclusion, the mixed approach may not be a perfect solution but is the inevitable result of the distinction that States still maintain,[2100] even though it is significantly mitigated by an increased convergence between the law applicable to the different kinds of armed conflicts.[2101]

There are three caveats that must be made in respect of the conclusions reached so far. First, where a non-State party to a conflict is in fact controlled by a third State to such an extent that its actions are attributable to that State, the conflict with that party will become an international one. While this rule is in itself quite simple and does not seem to be contested, the required threshold for such control is controversial, with the International Court of Justice applying a more demanding effective control test in the *Nicaragua*[2102] and *Bosnia-Serbia*

International Colloquium Held at Bad Homburg, June 17-19, 1988, Dordrecht, Kluwer, 1990, pp. 129–130.

2097 See, e.g. J. Stewart, *supra* note 2082, pp. 321–323 and L. Zegveld, *supra* note 2081, pp. 126–131.

2098 *Supra* note 2062. While the great majority of the rules identified in the study apply in both types of armed conflicts, a number apply only to international armed conflicts and a few only to armed conflicts not of an international character. On the limits of this convergence, see also C. Byron, *supra* note 2071, pp. 65–68.

2099 See, e.g. J. Stewart, *supra* note 2082, p. 345 and L. Zegveld, *supra* note 2081, pp. 126–131. For a more extensive analysis, see W.A. Solf, 'Problems with the Application of Norms Governing Interstate Armed Conflict to Non-International Armed Conflicts', 13 *Georgia J.I.C.L.* 1983, pp. 291–301.

2100 Obviously, this could change one day. For a plea to this effect, see J. Stewart, *supra* note 2082, especially pp. 344–349.

2101 R. Bierzanek, *supra* note 2074, pp. 287–288 already wrote in 1984 that the growth of the body of rules applicable in non-international armed conflicts would be one way of solving this problem.

2102 See *Nicaragua* case, §115: "*The Court has taken the view ... that [US] participation, even if preponderant or decisive in the financing, organizing, training, supplying and equipping of the contras, the selection of its ... targets, and the planning of the whole of its operation, is still insufficient in itself, ..., for the purpose of attributing to the [US] the acts committed by the contras ... All the forms of [US] participation mentioned above, and even the general control by the respondent State over a force with a high degree of dependency on it, would not in themselves mean, ..., that the [US] directed or enforced the perpetration of the acts ... alleged by the applicant State .... For this conduct to give rise to legal responsibility of the [US], it would in principle have to be proved that that State had effective control of the military or paramilitary operations in the course of which the alleged violations were committed*".

Genocide[2103] cases than the ICTY's overall control test in *Tadic* (at least in respect of (para)military groups).[2104] It remains to be seen which view will prevail.[2105] Second, when a party is engaged in both an international and a non-international armed conflict, it may have to apply all or some of the rules of the law of international armed conflict in the non-international armed conflict because of the latter's scope of application *ratione loci*.[2106] Third, where the conflict is non-international because one party is a non-State actor but takes place against the will of the host State in which that actor is targeted but without the host State's active military opposition, the conflict is arguably also between two States and thus international, although this may be a matter of debate.[2107]

2103 *Application of the Convention on the Prevention and Punishment of the Crime of Genocide (Bosnia and Herzegovina v. Serbia and Montenegro)*, judgment of 26 February 2007, §§377–415, especially §§396–407, in which the Court expressly disagrees with the ICTY's *Tadic* decision and refers to its own *Nicaragua* judgment. For a critical reading of this 2007 ICJ judgment, see A. Cassese, 'The *Nicaragua* and *Tadic* Tests Revisited in Light of the ICJ Judgment on Genocide in Bosnia', 18 *E.J.I.L.* 2007, pp. 649–668.

2104 Appeals Chamber, *Prosecutor v. Dusko Tadic*, IT-94-1, 15 July 1999, §§97–145 (§145: "*the control ... over these armed forces required by international law for considering the armed conflict to be international was overall control going beyond the mere financing and equipping of such forces and involving also participation in the planning and supervision of military operations. By contrast, international rules do not require that such control should extend to the issuance of specific orders or instructions relating to single military actions*"). See also J. Stewart, *supra* note 2082, pp. 323–331. It has been argued that the ICTY inappropriately applied the *Nicaragua* test: see, e.g. T. Meron, *supra* note 2092, pp. 236–242. However, if the qualification of an armed conflict depends on the parties to the conflict, as it does, the test is one of attribution and therefore it is submitted that the ICTY's approach was correct – see also A. Cassese, *supra* previous note, pp. 649–668.

2105 See also C. Byron, *supra* note 2071, pp. 66–79 and David, pp. 139–146. In its Draft Articles on State Responsibility, the ILC appears to have sided with the International Court of Justice: pursuant to Article 8 of these Draft Articles there is attribution where "*the person or group [...] is in fact acting on the instructions of, or under the direction or control of, that State in carrying out the conduct*" and the commentaries on this provision clarify that "*[s]uch conduct will be attributable to the State only if it directed and controlled the specific operation*" (*Report of the International Law Commission. Fifty-third session*, UN Doc. A/56/10, pp. 105–107). On the other hand, it would appear that developments in the context of combating international terrorism support the ICTY's approach; see on this F. Naert, 'The Impact of the Fight against International Terrorism on the *Ius ad Bellum* after '11 September'', 43(3–4) *R.D.M.D.G.* 2004, pp. 60–61 and 80 (also available as Institute for International Law Working Paper No 68 at www.law.kuleuven.be/iir/nl/onderzoek/wp/WP68e.pdf).

2106 E.g. when a State is occupying part of another State and at the same time is fighting a non-State group in the state it is partially occupying and which is not linked to that State's government, the result of the occupation will be that the law of international armed conflict applies at least in part also to the conflict with the non-State group. This may reduce the fragmentation of applicable law to a significant extent.

2107 This would certainly be the case where such a conflict results in occupation of territory without consent even absent military opposition and it is submitted that the same goes for armed activities short of occupation. See also *supra* note 2072 and the accompanying text.

Furthermore, it is worth looking at some specific instruments on peace forces. The 1994 Convention on the Safety of UN and Associated Personnel[2108] exempts from its scope of application UN operations "*authorized by the Security Council as an enforcement action under Chapter VII of the [UN Charter] in which any of the personnel are engaged as combatants against organized armed forces and to which the law of international armed conflict applies*" (Article 2(2)). This might be read to imply that when UN forces become engaged in an armed conflict, it always becomes an international one.[2109] While it has been argued that this was the view of some of the negotiators,[2110] it does not seem quite correct[2111] and is not entirely conclusive. In fact, the inclusion of the applicability of the law of international armed conflict would be superfluous if it was deemed to be automatically applicable once UN forces became engaged in an armed conflict as combatants.[2112] Moreover, although regarded by most commentators as mutually exclusive with the LOAC,[2113] the Convention is perhaps not necessarily incompatible with the LOAC in non-international armed conflicts, as this body of law does not accord combatant immunity.[2114] Although the situation could be distinguished in that any criminalization of taking up arms in the latter conflicts only occurs under domestic law rather than under international law, unlike with the Convention, it remains to be seen whether this is decisive. Moreover, the savings clause in Article 20(a) makes it clear that the Convention shall not affect the responsibility of UN personnel to respect international humanitarian law. This means that the LOAC might be applicable in other cases than the one which is excluded, e.g. in a non-Chapter VII peacekeeping operation in which the use

2108 *Supra* note 2045.

2109 This seems to be the understanding of Kolb, Porretto & Vité, pp. 186–187.

2110 See P. Kirsch, *supra* note 2045, p. 105, also cited by Zwanenburg, p. 196.

2111 M. Arsanjani, *supra* note 2024, p. 143 note 77 cites an explicit statement by the US representative to the contrary. S. Lepper, *supra* note 2045, pp. 364–365, 374–376 and 378–410, stresses that the US wished to exclude from the Convention only operations covered by the law of *international* armed conflicts, because only in such operations was there an adequate protection by the LOAC. However, it is not very clear whether the inclusion of non-international armed conflicts results from the view that peace forces might be a party to such a conflict or may be affected by it but only while not being a party to it. Also, the author appears to draw a distinction between being a party to and being engaged in an armed conflict, a distinction which is questionable.

2112 M.-C. Bourloyannis-Vrailas, *supra* note 2045, pp. 567–568 states that the conditions listed are cumulative (similarly, M. Arsanjani, *supra* note 2024, pp. 132–133) and also remarks that listing the applicability of the law of international armed conflict as a condition seems to imply that the UN could be engaged in non-international armed conflicts, especially against non-State actors (a view shared by C. Greenwood, *supra* note 2037, p. 199), though she sees no reason why the Convention should apply to such operations. M. Frostad, *supra* note 2024, p. 319 also appears to regard this as a distinct condition.

2113 E.g. M.-C. Bourloyannis-Vrailas, *supra* note 2045, p. 567. But see David, p. 159.

2114 This point is also made by O. Engdahl, *supra* note 2026, pp. 237–240, especially pp. 239–240.

of force nevertheless escalates.[2115] In such cases the conflict need not necessarily be international (see *supra*). Thus the Convention is rather ambiguous on this point.[2116] Moreover, in the later process leading to the adoption of the above-mentioned UN Secretary-General's Bulletin,[2117] it became clear that there were different views on this issue and the Bulletin itself does not fully clarify the matter.[2118]

Finally, it seems that in actual operations, at least in a number of cases contingents have deemed the applicable law to be the law of armed conflicts not of an international character.[2119] For instance, the armed conflict between ISAF forces in Afghanistan on the one hand and Taliban and Al Qaeda fighters on the other hand is no longer regarded as an international armed conflict since the establishment of an internationally recognized Afghan government (by both (some) NATO Member States and the ICRC) but rather as a conflict not of an international character.[2120]

In conclusion, where peace forces are engaged in an armed conflict against the armed forces of a State (i.e. of its government), the conflict is an international one. When the opponent is a non-State actor, the situation is less clear. However, it is submitted that the better view is that this kind of conflict is not of an international character in the sense of the LOAC. Finally, there is also controversy over mixed conflicts, but despite misgivings and shortcomings it seems that in such conflicts each individual conflict retains, in principle, its own character.

2115 This hypothesis is mentioned by C. Greenwood, *supra* note 2037, p. 198 and by M. Zwanenburg, *supra* note 2021 (5 *International Peacekeeping* 1999), p. 136.

2116 See more generally M. Arsanjani, *supra* note 2024, pp. 132–141 and 203, who submits that some assumptions of the negotiators were wrong and that the Convention was drafted and adopted rather quickly without fully considering the relationship with the LOAC. S. Lepper, *supra* note 2045, pp. 373–376 notes that even the US initially overlooked this relationship and (at pp. 393–410) gives an overview of the negotiations on this topic, which shows that it was the subject of considerable debate. D. Shraga, *supra* note 1998 (in L. Condorelli, A.-M. La Rosa & S. Scherrer (eds.)), pp. 334–337 also considers the provisions discussed here unsatisfactory.

2117 *Supra* note 2021.

2118 Zwanenburg, pp. 196–197. But see M. Zwanenburg, *supra* note 2021 (5 *International Peacekeeping* 1999), p. 136, arguing that the use of the term combatants suggests that it deems the law of international armed conflict to be applicable. Given that the term combatants is nowadays also sometimes used in non-international armed conflicts (e.g. in rule 1 of the ICRC's customary international law study (*supra* note 2062)), even if it is not precisely defined in such conflicts, this is not persuasive. Kolb, Porretto & Vité, p. 186 also submit that the Bulletin refers to the law of international armed conflict. In contrast, see the Institute of International Law's view cited *supra* note 2083.

2119 See the discussion in Kolb, Porretto & Vité, pp. 187–188.

2120 This view is reflected in some ISAF and ICRC documents.

D. PEACE OPERATIONS AS OCCUPATION?

The notion of occupation is *defined* in Article 42 of the Hague Regulations, which is still applicable and has achieved a customary law status[2121] and which reads as follows: "*Territory is considered occupied when it is actually placed under the authority of the hostile army. The occupation extends only to the territory where such authority has been established and can be exercised*". This definition is also the one used in practice in military manuals, including by the UK and the US.[2122] At what stage the authority mentioned in Article 42 of the Hague Regulations is established, is a matter of fact[2123] and there is no need for a formal declaration of any kind. In addition to this definition, the *scope of application* of the Geneva Conventions is also crucial. In accordance with Article 2 common to the 1949 Geneva Conventions, GC IV, which deals with occupation, shall apply to any armed conflict between two or more State Parties and "*to all cases of partial or*

2121 This was confirmed by the ICJ in its Advisory Opinion of 9 July 2004 on the *Legal Consequences of the Construction of a Wall in the Occupied Palestinian Territory*, §89 and in its judgment of 19 December 2005 in the *Case concerning armed activities on the territory of the Congo (DRC v. Uganda)*, §172. See also ICTY, Trial Chamber, *Prosecutor v. Dario Kordic and Mario Cerkez*, IT-95-14/2, 26 February 2001, §338. For a recent discussion of occupation, see, e.g. College of Europe & ICRC (eds.), *Proceedings of the Bruges Colloquium. Current Challenges to the Law of Occupation. 20th – 21st October 2005 / Actes du colloque de Bruges. Les défis contemporains au droit de l'occupation. 20–21 octobre 2005*, Bruges, College of Europe (*collegium* No. 34, available online at www.coleurop.be/template.asp?pagename=pub_collegium), 2006; Y. Arai-Takahashi, *The Law of Occupation: Continuity and Change of International Humanitarian Law, and Its Interaction with International Human Rights Law*, Leiden, Martinus Nijhoff, 2009; Y. Dinstein, *The International Law of Belligerent Occupation*, Cambridge, Cambridge University Press, 2009; R. Kolb, *Le droit de l'occupation militaire*, Brussels, Bruylant, 2009 and K. Parameswaran, *Besatzungsrecht im Wandel: Aktuelle Herausforderungen des Rechts der militärischen Besetzung*, Baden-Baden, Nomos, 2008.

2122 See respectively UK MANUAL, p. 275, §11.2 and *US Field Manual 27-10. The Law of Land Warfare*, 1956, as amended later (available online at http://faculty.ed.umuc.edu/~nstanton/FM27-10.htm), §351.

2123 See, e.g. J. Paust, 'The US as Occupying Power Over Portions of Iraq and Relevant Responsibilities Under the Laws of War', *ASIL Insight*, April 2003 (available online at www.asil.org/insigh102.cfm), referring to a standard document of the US Army, and UK, House of Commons Library, *Iraq: Law of Occupation*, Research paper 03/51, 2 June 2003 (www.parliament.uk/commons/lib/research/rp2003/rp03-051.pdf), p. 19. See also ICTY, *Prosecutor v. Dario Kordic and Mario Cerkez, supra* note 2121, §339 ("*The Trial Chamber accepts [the definition from Article 42 of the Regulations attached to Hague Convention IV] and finds that the enquiry as to whether a particular territory is occupied must be conducted on a case-by-case basis*"). The ICTY's jurisprudence offers some guidance, although it is not univocal (see D.A. Mundis, 'Current Developments At The Ad Hoc International Criminal Tribunals', 1 *J.I.C.J.*2003, pp. 704–705). See, in addition to the case cited above in this note (§§338–339), *Prosecutor* v. *Mladen Naletilić and Vinko Martinović*, IT-98-34-T, 31 March 2003, §§215–217 and Trial Chamber, *Prosecutor v. Timohir Blaskic*, IT-95-14, 3 March 2000, §§149–150. See also *Prosecutor v. Ivica Rajic a/k/a/ Viktor Andric*, Decision of 13 September 1996 (Review of the indictment pursuant to Rule 61 of the Rules of Procedure and Evidence), IT-95-12-R61, §§39–42.

total occupation of the territory of a High Contracting Party, even if the said occupation meets with no armed resistance". However, it is generally accepted that consent by the State to the presence of armed forces of another State in its territory precludes occupation.[2124]

On this basis, one might expect peace operations to be occupying powers bound by the law of occupation whenever they exercise actual authority over part or all of the territory of a third State without the consent of that State.[2125] Nevertheless, in practice both States and international organizations involved in peace operations have rarely accepted that they were occupying powers,[2126] despite the fact that in a number of peace operations these conditions were arguably met, in particular in the case of non-consensual Chapter VII operations in which peace forces exercised broad authority.[2127] In addition, there may be cases where the

---

2124 E. Benvenisti, *The International Law of Occupation*, Princeton, Princeton University Press, 2004 (reprint with revised introduction), pp. xvi and 4, defines occupation as "*the effective control of power (be it one or more states or an international organization, such as the United Nations) over a territory to which that power has no sovereign title, without the volition of the sovereign of that territory*". See also Kolb, Porretto & Vité, pp. 207 and 210–211 and UK Manual, §11.1.2, p. 275. For an elaborate discussion of consent and occupation, see A. Roberts, 'What is a Military Occupation?', 55 *B.Y.I.L.* 1984, pp. 276–279, 297–298 and 300.

2125 A. Roberts, *supra* note 2140, p. 604, even seems to argue for the application of the law of occupation as a safety net where there is formal consent but still direct contact between troops and the local population.

2126 The UK Manual, §11.1.2, p. 275, denies that the international administration of a territory is an occupation but states that where troops are sent in to restore law and order in a collapsed State and no agreement has been concluded with the host State authorities, "*there will be* de facto *military rule*" (emphasis in original) to which the law of occupation should be applied by analogy as far as possible.

2127 For a good example of this attitude, see Militair Gerechtshof (Belgian Military Court of Appeal), *Openbaar ministerie / C. en B.*, judgment of 17 December 1997, *J.T.* 1998, pp. 286–289 (also reproduced in J. Wouters, with collaboration of M. Vidal, *Cases van international recht*, Antwerp, Intersentia, 2005, pp. 502–508, especially p. 506; see also Zwanenburg, p. 209), arguing that there was no occupation in Somalia, despite the absence of consent (see M.J. Kelly, *Restoring and Maintaining Order in Complex Peace Operations*, Kluwer, The Hague, 1999, pp. 37–38 and Zwanenburg, p. 207) and the exercise of powers that can hardly be distinguished from those of an occupying power (see the mandate as set out in UNSC Resolutions 794 (3 December 1992), §10; 814 (26 March 1993), §4 and especially 837 (6 June 1993), §5 ("*the Secretary-General is authorized ... to take all necessary measures ... to establish the effective authority of UNOSOM II throughout Somalia*")). In the same sense as the Belgian case, see also the Canadian judgment *R. v. Brocklebank*, Court Martial Appeal Court, 2 April 1996, cited by A. Faite, *supra* note 1998, p. 151 and discussed by K. Boustany, 'Brocklebank: A Questionable Decision of the Court Martial Appeal Court of Canada', 1 *Y.I.H.L.* 1998, pp. 371–374. Compare the discussion by J.M. Simpson, *Law Applicable to Canadian Forces in Somalia*, Ottawa, Canadian Government Publishing, 1997, pp. 26–33 and by R.M. Young & M. Molina, 'IHL and Peace Operations: Sharing Canada's Lessons Learned from Somalia', 1 *Y.I.H.L.* 1998, pp. 362–370.

validity of the consent is questionable.[2128] The exception to this refusal to accept the applicability of the law of occupation which is most commonly cited is Australia's view with regard to its contingent in the Somalia operation.[2129] Another exception, albeit a peculiar one, is the UK and US occupation of Iraq. The latter case is peculiar in that the legal basis for the UK-US-coalition invasion and (initial) occupation of Iraq is controversial[2130] and it may not be entirely

---

2128 E.g. in respect of Kosovo, see the brief discussion by Kolb, Porretto & Vité, pp. 220–221 and Zwanenburg, pp. 207–208. An alternative argument for consent could be that by authorizing the Security Council to take enforcement action, a Member State has given prior treaty-based consent precluding occupation. However, in contrast with prior treaty-based consent as a possible justification from a *ius ad bellum* perspective (see *supra*, Chapter 4.A.6), this argument is not convincing regarding occupation given the different rationale. Compare the discussion in T. Irmscher, 'The Legal Framework for Activities of the United Nations Interim Administration Mission in Kosovo: The Charter, Human Rights, and the Law of Occupation', 44 *G.Y.I.L.* 2001, pp. 377–387, who also seems to conclude against this thesis at p. 385.

2129 See, e.g. the Australian statement at the 1998 Meeting of the Contracting Parties to GC IV cited by Zwanenburg, pp. 208–209 (and previously available online at www.wihl.nl/finals/Australia/AU.G-OC.Discussion%20re.IV%20Conv.%20on%20occupied%20territories.pdf; last consulted in November 2007) ("*The Fourth Convention is a good model to use in peace operations involving deployment without consent ... Australian troops in Somalia found this to be the case when they were deployed into, and given responsibility for, the Bay Province during Operation Restore Hope in 1993.* Following a determination that the Fourth Convention applied to that intervention, *the Australian force relied on the Convention to provide answers to, and a framework for, many initiatives*"; emphasis added). See also M.J. Kelly, *supra* note 2127, pp. 37–63.

2130 See generally 'Agora: Future Implications of the Iraq Conflict', 97 *A.J.I.L.* 2003, pp. 553–642; M. Arcari, 'L'intervention armée contre l'Iraq et la question de l'autorisation du Conseil de Sécurité', 19 *Anuario de derecho internacional* 2003, pp. 5–39; S. Bandopadhyay, 'Kicking up the Sand: The Legality and Consequences of the "Coalition's" Invasion of Iraq', 43 *Indian J.I.L.* 2003, pp. 117–129; A.J. Bellamy, 'International Law and the War with Iraq', 4 *Melbourne J.I.L.* 2003, pp. 497–520; R. Bermejo García, 'El debate sobre la legalidad internacional tras la crisis de Iraq y las Naciones Unidas', 19 *Anuario de derecho internacional* 2003, pp. 41–69; O. Corten, 'Opération Iraqi Freedom: peut-on admettre l'argument de l'"autorisation implicite" du Conseil de Sécurité?', 36 *R.B.D.I./B.T.I.R.* 2003, pp. 205–247; E. de Wet, 'The Illegality of the Use of Force against Iraq Subsequent to the Adoption of Resolution 687 (1991)', 16 *Humanitäres Völkerrecht* 2003, pp. 125–132; I.J. Gassama, 'International Law at a Grotian Moment: The Invasion of Iraq in Context', 18 *Emory I.L.R.* 2004, pp. 1–52; M. Hmoud, 'The Use of Force against Iraq: Occupation and Security Council Resolution 1483', 36 *Cornell I.L.J.* 2004, pp. 435–444; R. Hofmann, 'International Law and the Use of Military Force against Iraq', 45 *G.Y.I.L.* 2002, pp. 9–34; P. MacLain, 'Settling the Score with Saddam: Resolution 1441 and Parallel Justifications for the Use of Force against Iraq', 13 *Duke J.C.I.L.* 2003, pp. 233–291; E. MacWhinney, 'The US/British Invasion of Iraq and the United Nations Charter Prohibition of the Use of Force: The Paradox of Unintended Consequences', 2 *Chinese J.I.L.* 2003, pp. 571–585; S.D. Murphy, 'Contemporary Practice of the United States Relating to International Law: Use of Military Force to Disarm Iraq', 97 *A.J.I.L.* 2003, pp. 419–432; J. Pedigo, 'Rogue States, Weapons of Mass Destruction, and Terrorism: Was Security Council Approval Necessary for the Invasion of Iraq?', 32 *Georgia J.I.C.L* 2004, pp. 199–229; R. Piotrowicz, 'The Use of Force and the Force of Law in Iraq', 77 *Australian Law Journal* 2003, pp. 283–289; J.A. Ramírez, 'Iraq War: Anticipatory Self-Defense or Unlawful Unilateralism?', 34 *California Western I.L.J.* 2003, pp. 1–27; A. Roberts, 'Law and the Use of Force after Iraq', clear whether subsequent resolutions endorsed or merely recognized the fact of the continued occupation until June 2004.[2131] However, since the UK official justification for this war consisted of existing UN Security Council resolutions[2132] and it accepted that it was an occupying power,[2133] this clearly implies that it considers that a UN mandate does not necessarily preclude the applicability of the law of occupation.

Doctrine is divided on the applicability of the law of occupation to peace operations.[2134] Arguments invoked for rejecting the applicability of the law of

---

45 *Survival* 2003, pp. 31–56; G.B. Roberts, 'The UN Charter Paradigm on the Brink: The Legal and Policy Predicates for Use of Force against Iraq', 42 *R.D.M.D.G.* 2003, pp. 441–458; R. Sifris, 'Operation Iraqi Freedom: United States v. Iraq – the Legality of the War', 4 *Melbourne J.I.L.* 2003, pp. 521–560; T. Stein, 'The War against Iraq and the "Ius ad Bellum"', 42 *R.D.M.D.G.* 2003, pp. 459–465; A.E. Wall, 'The Legal Case for Invading Iraq and Toppling Hussein', 32 *Israel Y.H.R.* 2003, pp. 165–192; C. Warbrick, 'The Use of Force against Iraq', 52 *I.C.L.Q.* 2003, pp. 811–814; M.A. Weisburd, 'The War in Iraq and the Dilemma of Controlling the International Use of Force', 39 *Texas I.L.J.* 2004, pp. 522–560; N.D. White & E.P.J. Myjer, 'Editorial: The Use of Force against Iraq', 8 *J.C.S.L.* 2003, pp. 1–8 and R. Wolfrum, 'The Attack of September 11, 2001, the Wars against the Taliban and Iraq: Is There a Need to Reconsider International Law on the Recourse to Force and the Rules in Armed Conflict?', 7 *M.P.Y.U.N.L.* 2004, pp. 30–31.

2131 In particular, resolution 1483 of 22 May 2003 indicates a recognition of the *fact* of occupation and the rights and duties pertaining thereto under the LOAC only: see especially the consideration in the preamble *"Noting the letter of 8 May 2003 from the Permanent Representatives of the [US and UK] to the President of the Security Council (S/2003/538) and recognizing the specific authorities, responsibilities, and obligations under applicable international law of these states as occupying powers under unified command (the 'Authority')"*. It was only in resolution 1511 of 16 October 2003 (§13) that a multinational force with a specific mandate was *authorized.*

2132 See the Attorney General's view of the legal basis for the use of force against Iraq, www.pm.gov.uk/output/Page3287.asp# (later, it was disclosed that a longer and more nuanced advice had been provided by the Attorney-General; see http://news.bbc.co.uk/2/shared/bsp/hi/pdfs/28_04_05_attorney_general.pdf). This was also the Australian view: see Memorandum of advice to the Commonwealth Government on the Use of Force against Iraq by B. Campbell (Office of International Law, Attorney-General's Department) and C. Moraitis (Department of Foreign Affairs and Trade), published in 4 *Melbourne J.I.L.* 2003, pp. 178–182 (available online at www.mjil.law.unimelb.edu.au/issues/archive/2003(1)/06Iraq.pdf). For the US view, see Letter from Ambassador Negroponte to the Security Council President Concerning Commencement of Military Operations in Iraq, 20 March 2003 (UN Doc. S/2003/351, 31 March 2003), also referring to a mandate under existing resolutions, but with additional language that might perhaps indicate an additional claim to self-defence.

2133 This was never contested by the UK.

2134 See the overview in Kolb, Porretto & Vité, pp. 216–219, who themselves seem to accept its applicability to military forces in some cases (the discussion of occupation by Kolb, Porretto & Vité is largely based on and identical to that in S. Vité, 'L'applicabilité du droit international de l'occupation militaire aux activités des organisations internationales', 86 No. 853 *I.R.R.C./R.I.C.R.* 2004, pp. 9–35). Zwanenburg, pp. 204–210 and 222–223, provides a succinct survey of the main arguments and concludes that State practice predominantly rejects the applicability of the law of occupation to peace operations, although he notes it might be a useful regime in such operations. M.J. Kelly, *supra* note 2127, pp. especially pp.

occupation include, in addition to the consensual nature,[2135] which is not always given,[2136] that the aim to change the government and legal system, which may be a part of complex peace operations (e.g. in Kosovo, East-Timor and Iraq), is incompatible with one of the fundamental rules of the law of occupation, namely the prohibition to alter the legal system of occupied territory except for specified and limited reasons[2137]. [2138] The latter issue will be addressed to some extent

167–178, argues in favour of the applicability of the LOAC under certain conditions. C. Emanuelli, *supra* note 1998, p. 40, submits that the UN may be an occupying force if it has no consent. A. Faite, *supra* note 1998, pp. 148–156 seems to lean towards accepting the applicability of the law of occupation but does not take a clear position. L. Green, 'Is there a "New" Law of Intervention and Occupation?', in T. Sparks & G. Sulmasy (eds.), *International Law Challenges: Homeland Security and Combating Terrorism*, Newport, Naval War College (81 International Law Studies), 2006, pp. 167–200 proposes a new and distinct regime, as does C. Stahn, '"Jus ad Bellum", "Jus in Bello" … "Jus Post Bellum"?: Rethinking the Conception of the Law of Armed Force', 17 *E.J.I.L.* 2006, pp. 921–943. S. Wollenberg, *Die Regierung von Konfliktgebieten durch die Vereinten Nationen*, Baden-Baden, Nomos, 2007, pp. 234–239, seems to argue in favour of the applicability to the extent that the rules on occupation are transferable to international administrations. E. Benvenisti, *supra* note 2124, pp. xv-xvii considers that the UN should apply the law of occupation when it exercises effective control without the volition of the Sovereign and sees this body of law as appropriate. J.M. Simpson, *supra* note 2127, pp. 22–33 and 47–49 is uncertain. T. Irmscher, *supra* note 2128, pp. 374–387 argues that the law of occupation may be applicable and was applicable in Kosovo. Compare R. Arnold, 'The Applicability of the Law of Occupation to Peace Support Operations', in R. Arnold & G.-J. Knoops (eds.), *supra* note 2033, pp. 91–115; S. Ratner, 'Foreign Occupation and International Territorial Administration: The Challenges of Convergence', 16 *E.J.I.L* 2005, pp. 695–719 and S. Wills, 'Occupation Law and Multi-National Operations: Problems And Perspectives', 77 *B.Y.I.L.* 2006, pp. 256–332.

2135 E.g. M. Bothe, 'Peacekeeping and International Humanitarian Law: Friends or Foes', 3 *International Peacekeeping*, 1996, p. 92 and J. Cerone, 'Minding the Gap: Outlining KFOR Accountability in Post-Conflict Kosovo', 12 *E.J.I.L.* 2001, pp. 484–485.

2136 E.g. it was debatable in the case of Kosovo given the controversy over the use of force by NATO that led to the Yugoslav consent; see, e.g. T. Irmscher, *supra* note 2128, pp. 385–386. S. Chesterman, *supra* note 2029 (2004), pp. 152–153 submits that the partial inconsistency between means and ends in some international administrations results from a reluctance to accept that its legitimacy ultimately derives from military occupation, not consent.

2137 See especially Articles 43 Hague Regulations and 64 GC IV. For a discussion, see L. Cameron, 'Does the Law of Occupation Preclude Transformational Developments by the Occupying Power?', in College of Europe & ICRC (eds.), *supra* note 2121, pp. 60–66; M. Sassoli, 'Current Developments in the Law of Military Occupation: Maintenance of Public Order and Civil Life in Occupied Territories and Legislative Powers of Occupying Powers', in College of Europe & ICRC (eds.), *Proceedings of the Bruges Colloquium. The Need for Justice and Requirements for Peace and Security. 9th – 10th September 2004 / Actes du colloque de Bruges. Impératifs de Justice et Exigences de Paix et de Sécurité. 9-10 septembre 2004*, Bruges, College of Europe (*collegium* No. 32, available online at www.coleurop.be/template.asp?pagename=pub_collegium), 2005, pp. 105–122; M. Sassoli, *infra* note 2152, and M. Sassoli, 'Legislation and Maintenance of Public Order and Civil Life by Occupying Powers', 16 *E.J.I.L.* 2005, pp. 661–694.

2138 This argument is made by Kolb, Porretto & Vité, pp. 221–225 with regard to interim civilian international administrations mandated by the UN Security Council. In this sense also E. de Wet, 'Beginning and End of Occupation – UN Security Council's Impact on the Law of Occupation', in College of Europe & ICRC (eds.), *supra* note 2121, p. 40 and C. Stahn, below in the course of the discussion of the relationship between human rights and the LOAC in occupation.[2139] At this stage, it is submitted that even in a transformative peace operation,[2140] the law of occupation does not necessarily become entirely inadequate[2141] and that, where it does constitute an obstacle to required changes, the latter may be mandated by an overriding Security Council mandate (see the following section of this chapter).

In conclusion, although the texts of the relevant LOAC conventions imply the applicability of the law of occupation to non-consensual peace operations exercising effective authority, in practice States and international organizations have rarely accepted this.[2142] It is submitted that they have done so wrongly and that the case of Iraq shows that States may exceptionally accept the applicability of the law of occupation. Moreover, this body of law provides a fairly adequate framework that can be supplemented, and if need be, partially set aside, by

---

supra note 2134, pp. 928–929. H.-P. Gasser, 'From Military Intervention to Occupation of Territory: New Relevance of International Law of Occupation', in H. Fischer (ed.), *Krisensicherung und humanitärer Schutz: Festschrift für Dieter Fleck*, Berlin, Berliner Wissenschafts-Verlag, 2004, pp. 139–157, submits that the law of occupation is ill suited for long-term transformative occupations (pp. 146–147) but nevertheless sees it as a (partially) useful regime when combined with human rights (pp. 155–15). For a critique of an overly benevolent view of international administrations, see, e.g. R. Wilde, 'Representing International Territorial Administration: A Critique of Some Approaches', 15 *E.J.I.L.* 2004, pp. 71–96 (*inter alia* stressing that this phenomenon is not as new as is often thought and that the underlying motives are usually more complex than just restoring security and coping with failed States as is often suggested). See also, more extensively, R. Wilde, *International Territorial Administration: How Trusteeship and the Civilizing Mission Never Went Away*, Oxford, Oxford University Press, 2008.

2139 *Infra*, Chapter 9.D.2.iv.d.

2140 I have borrowed this title by analogy from A. Roberts, 'Transformative Military Occupation: Applying the Laws of War and Human Rights', 100 *A.J.I.L.* 2006, pp. 580–622 and from N. Bhuta, 'The Antinomies of Transformative Occupation', 16 *E.J.I.L.* 2005, pp. 721–740. For a critical perspective, see V. Koutroulis, 'Mythes et réalités de l'application du droit international humanitaire aux occupations dites "transformatives"', 40 *B.T.I.R./R.B.D.I.* 2007, pp. 365–400.

2141 Rather to the contrary, it offers a regime tailored to many of the specific security challenges that prevail in such operations, including in respect of detention/internment of individuals for security reasons. See extensively M.J. Kelly, *supra* note 2127, pp. 183–279. See also Zwanenburg, p. 222 and the appraisal by Australia of its application of GC IV in Somalia in the statement cited *supra* note 2129.

2142 In fact, as E. Benvenisti, *supra* note 2124, p. vii, points out, States have more generally been very reluctant to accept that they are occupying powers. This was, e.g. evidenced by the US' initial reluctance to recognize that it was occupying Iraq: e.g. on 7 April 2003, W. Hays Parks, Special Assistant to the (US) Army Judge Advocate General, stated that "*Obviously, we occupy a great deal of Iraq at this time. But we are not, in the technical sense of the law of war, a military occupier or occupation force*" ('Briefing on Geneva Convention, EPW's and War Crimes', available at www.defenselink.mil/transcripts/2003/t04072003_t407genv.html). See also M.J. Kelly, *supra* note 2127, pp. 179–181. On confusion stemming from perceived "liberation" as opposed to occupation, see F. Mini, 'Liberation and Occupation: A Commander's Perspective', in T. Sparks & G. Sulmasy (eds.), *supra* note 2134, pp. 232–234.

overriding powers granted by the UN Security Council.[2143] The latter are addressed in the following section.

E. THE IMPACT OF SECURITY COUNCIL INTERVENTION

The primary importance of a UN Security Council intervention undoubtedly lies in the legality it may confer on a peace operation (see the discussion in Chapter 4.A.6 above). However, the question which we are concerned with in this chapter is to what extent a UN Security Council mandate may affect the law applicable to the conduct of a peace operation. This question may be divided into two aspects: first, does a UN Security Council mandate automatically exclude the applicability of the LOAC – to the extent that it would normally apply – and second, if it does not, may it in specific cases override all or part of the LOAC?

As to the first question, there is little doubt that a UN Security Council mandate does not necessarily entail the exclusion of the LOAC. In addition to the case of Iraq (2003–2004) already discussed in the preceding section, another uncontroversial example is the 1991 coalition war against Iraq.[2144] There are fewer clear cut examples for operations under UN command, but the 1999 Bulletin[2145] and 1994 Convention[2146] as well as UN practice to require troop-contributing nations to respect the LOAC as well as its proper commitment in SOFAs to ensure such respect (all discussed above in Sections B and C of this chapter), clearly imply that the LOAC may indeed apply to these operations too.

2143 Similarly, C. Stahn, 'Lawmaking by International Administrations', 11 *International Peacekeeping* (Yearbook) 2005, p. 104 submits that major changes should be based on a UN Security Council mandate or consent, not the law of occupation. N. Bhuta, *supra* note 2140, p. 740 concludes that the law of occupation is unsuited for transformative occupations but that a refusal to legalize such occupations (presumably with the exception of a UN Security Council mandate) would "*maintain one of the most important legacies of the 19th-century legal order: The formal sovereign equality of states, and a (formal) rejection of any one state's legal entitlement to impose a single model of political order*".

2144 See, e.g. Annex O of the *Final Report to (the US) Congress on the Conduct of the Persian Gulf War*, April 1992 (www.globalsecurity.org/military/library/report/1992/cpgw.pdf), p. 605. Admittedly, there is some discussion over whether the legal basis for this operation was self-defence or Chapter VII UN Charter; see de Wet, p. 281 and more generally K.H. Kaikobad, 'Self-Defence, Enforcement Action and the Gulf Wars, 1980–88 and 1990–91', 63 *B.Y.I.L.* 1992, pp. 299–366. However, this discussion does not seem to have mattered with regard to the applicability of the LOAC. Similarly, in the 2003 war with Iraq, which, according to some Coalition States' official legal argument, was based on a UN Security Council mandate and was not an exercise of the right of self-defence (see F. Naert, *supra* note 2105, pp. 71–73), the applicability of the LOAC was never disputed.

2145 *Supra* note 2021.

2146 *Supra* note 2045.

It is therefore submitted that a UN Security Council mandate clearly does not necessarily entail the exclusion of the applicability of the LOAC.

This brings us to the second question: if the LOAC may apply, can the Security Council decide to set it aside in whole or in part? Except to some extent in the case of Iraq, the Security Council does not appear to have set aside the LOAC or some specific LOAC rules.[2147] In the case of Iraq, firstly, the preamble of Resolution 1483 (22 May 2003), included a paragraph which read "Noting further *that other States that are not occupying powers are working now or in the future may work under the Authority*".[2148] This provision gave rise to some discussion as to whether it was indeed merely "noting" the situation as it was under the LOAC or whether it was in fact a decision altering the situation which would normally have existed under the LOAC.[2149] That being said, the effect was limited anyway by the call in paragraph 5 of the same resolution upon all parties concerned to comply fully with their obligations under international law, and in particular the Geneva Conventions and the Hague Regulations.[2150] Secondly, there was some

---

2147 In 2000, P. Szasz, 'UN Forces and International Humanitarian Law', in M. Schmitt (ed.), *International Law across the Spectrum of Conflict: Essays in Honour of Professor L.C. Green on the Occasion of His Eightieth Birthday*, Newport, Naval War College (75 International Law Studies), 2000, pp. 513–514, wrote that the Security Council had not explicitly or implicitly authorized any violation of the LOAC. On the attitude of the Security Council towards the LOAC, see generally J.D. Fry, 'The UN Security Council and the Law of Armed Conflict: Amity or Enmity?', 38 *George Washington I.L.R.* 2006, pp. 327–347 (noting the Charter's silence on how force should be used as well as the Security Council's lack of guidance in this respect when authorizing force, except for the necessity requirement, but mentioning its calls on others to respect the LOAC). A related issue has arisen with regard to the LOAC and UN sanctions; see, e.g. H.-P. Gasser, 'Collective Economic Sanctions and International Humanitarian Law: An Enforcement Measure under the United Nations Charter and the Right of Civilians to Immunity: An Unavoidable Clash of Policy Goals?', 56 *Z.a.ö.R.V.* 1996, pp. 871–904.

2148 In the previous consideration of the preamble, the US and the UK are considered occupying powers, so the consideration cited presumably concerns all other States.

2149 See F. Naert, with the collaboration of J. Vergauwen, A. Vanheusden & I. Heyndrickx, 'Toepasselijk recht op de conflicten in Irak (1991–2004)', 43(3–4) *R.D.M.D.G.* 2004, pp. 163–165 (with further references). See also M. Zwanenburg, 'Existentialism in Iraq: Security Council Resolution 1483 and the Law of Occupation', 86 No. 856 *I.R.R.C.* 2004, pp. 745–769, especially pp. 755–757 and 763–768. See also generally on this resolution E. Benvenisti, *supra* note 2124, pp. ix-xv (who sees this resolution as revising the law of occupation (pp. x-xi)); L. Lijnzaad, 'How Not to be an Occupying Power: Some Reflections on UN Security Council Resolution 1483 and the Contemporary Law of Occupation', in L. Lijnzaad, J. van Sambeek & B. Tahzib-Lie (eds.), *supra* note 2001, pp. 291–305; A. Orakhelashvili, 'The Post-War Settlement in Iraq: The UN Security Council Resolution 1483(2003) and General International Law', 8 *J.C.S.L.* 2003, pp. 307–314; A. Roberts, 'The End of Occupation: Iraq 2004', 54 *I.C.L.Q.* 2005, pp. 27–48 and M. Starita, 'L'occupation de l'Iraq: le Conseil de sécurité, le droit de la guerre et le droit des peuples à disposer d'eux-mêmes', 108 *R.G.D.I.P.* 2004, pp. 883–916.

2150 Which begged the question whether any provisions of the LOAC had actually been excluded, and if so, which ones; see on this F. Naert, *supra* previous note (with further references) and M. Zwanenburg, *supra* previous note, pp. 764–765.

debate as to whether UN Security Council Resolution 1546 welcoming the end the occupation by 30 June 2004 reflected the legal situation under the LOAC.[2151] Thirdly, some of the Resolutions on Iraq during the period of occupation appear to have granted powers to the occupying powers which they would not have had under the LOAC.[2152] This suggests that the Security Council may indeed set aside some provisions of the LOAC.

This conclusion is also the logical consequence of Article 103 UN Charter and the priority it establishes for obligations under the Charter.[2153] Although the text

---

2151 UNSC Res. 1456 (8 June 2004), §2: "Welcomes *that, also by 30 June 2004, the occupation will end ...and that Iraq will reassert its full sovereignty*". See F. Naert, *supra* note 2149, pp. 170–171. Compare E. de Wet, *supra* note 2138, pp. 40–41 and the discussion at pp. 41–42. Compare also A.E. Wall, 'Civilian Detentions in Iraq', in M. Schmitt & J. Pejic (eds.), *International Law and Armed Conflict: Exploring the Faultlines. Essays in Honour of Yoram Dinstein*, Nijhoff, Leiden, 2007, pp. 428–429, submitting that Coalition forces in Iraq were of the view that there was still an international armed conflict but that the Resolution set aside (at least part of) the LOAC, in particular as regards GC IV with respect to detention of civilians. However, this seems rather questionable and an exclusion would seem to require a clearer wording.

2152 Although the matter is not so clear and has given rise to some debate, see F. Naert, *supra* note 2149, p. 165. In favour of such a setting aside, see, e.g. the UK MANUAL, p. 279, §11.11, note 15; UK, House of Commons Library, *Iraq: Legal Issues at the Handover*, Research paper 04/59, 22 July 2004 (www.parliament.uk/commons/lib/research/rp2004/rp04-059.pdf), p. 16; M. Hmoud, *supra* note 2129, pp. 448–450; T.D. Grant, 'Iraq: How to Reconcile Conflicting Obligations of Occupation and Reform', *ASIL Insight*, June 2003 (www.asil.org/insigh107.cfm) and M.N. Schmitt & C. Garraway, 'Occupation Policy in Iraq and International Law', 9 *International Peacekeeping (Yearbook)* 2005, pp. 53–55 and 61. Furthermore, in a statement to the Security Council, Pakistan referred to "*the delegation of certain powers by the Security Council to the occupying Powers*" and to "*the powers delegated by the Security Council under this resolution*" (UN document S/PV.4761, pp. 11–12) and France in its statement talked about an attribution of authorities (*id.*, p. 4: "*The resolution [...] attributes to the occupying Powers broad authorities in the area of international humanitarian law and the necessary means to exercise those authorities*"). This is only meaningful if it concerns powers that do not already ensue from the law of occupation. The French statement is however somewhat equivocal given that it further states that "*the international community [...] has* recognised the existence *of the rights and obligations of the Authority*" (*id.*, p. 4, emphasis added), which implies a recognition rather than an attribution. D. Scheffer, 'Beyond Occupation Law', 97 *A.J.I.L.* 2003, pp. 845–846 and note 18 and p. 450 seems to doubt it. C. Stahn, *supra* note 2143, pp. 96–98 and *supra* note 2134, p. 929, is also critical. M. Zwanenburg, *supra* note 2149, p. 767 sees it as a problem of interpretation with an unclear result. *Contra*: M. Sassoli, *Article 43 of the Hague Regulations and Peace Operations in the Twenty-first Century*, background paper, June 2004 (available at http://ihl.ihlresearch.org), pp. 16–17, from whom an explicit derogation is necessary.

2153 Similarly, M. Zwanenburg, *supra* note 2149, pp. 759–763. See also HÄUSSLER, pp. 74–76 and T. Irmscher, *supra* note 2128, pp. 376, 387 and 395 (regarding Kosovo). It may be noted that the ICJ considered in its Order of 14 April 1992 in the cases *Questions of Interpretation and Application of the 1971 Montreal Convention arising from the Aerial Incident at Lockerbie (Libya v. UK & Libya v. US)*, Provisional Measures, respectively at §39 and §42, that the obligations under Articles 25 and 103 of the UN Charter extended *prima facie* to the obligations under Resolution 748 (1992) and that this Resolution prevailed *prima facie* over the Montreal Convention. But see J.D. Fry, *supra* note 2147, pp. 344–346 (arguing that Article 103 only refers to the UN Member States and not the Security Council itself but that of Article 103 only covers priority over obligations under any other international agreement, it is submitted that the better view is that the priority of the Charter rules under Article 103 UN Charter also extends to priority over customary international law, although this is not undisputed.[2154] This was arguably

as an organ of an organization with international legal personality, the latter is bound by the customary international law obligation to respect and ensure respect for the LOAC (on the latter, see also *infra*, Section F of this chapter)); T. Christakis & K. Bannelier, 'Acteur vigilant ou spectateur impuissant?: le contrôle exercé par le Conseil de sécurité sur les États autorisés à recourir à la force', 37 *R.B.D.I./B.T.I.R.* 2004, p. 511 (who seem to regard the *ius in bello* as rules of international law which the Security Council must respect but who do not mention Article 103 of the Charter) and A. Orakhelashvili, *infra* note 2158, pp. 66–67 (though it is not clear whether he considers all or only the basic principles of the LOAC as being part of *ius cogens* and binding on the Security Council because of that status). Y. Sandoz, 'Rapport général', in L. Condorelli, A.-M. La Rosa & S. Scherrer (eds.), *supra* note 1998, p. 74, reluctantly seems to accept that the Security Council can override LOAC rules, but argues that such a decision should be explicit and consciously made and should include an obligation to derogate. Compare R. Kolb, 'Jus cogens, intangibilité, intransgressibilité, dérogation "positive" et "negative"', 109 *R.G.D.I.P.* 2005, pp. 312–317 (taking a differentiated stance accepting derogation from some but not all LOAC rules). For a more general discussion on the limits of the powers of the Security Council, see, e.g. de Wet and K. Manusama, *The United Nations Security Council in the Post-Cold War Era: Applying the Principle of Legality*, Leiden, Nijhoff, 2006.

2154 See R. Bernhardt, 'Article 103', in Simma, pp. 1298–1299; A. Cassimatis, 'International Humanitarian Law, International Human Rights Law, and Fragmentation of International Law', 56 *I.C.L.Q.* 2007, p. 636 (on the basis of subsequent practice); de Wet, pp. 182–187; P. Szasz, *supra* note 2147, pp. 513–514 (who sees at least an application to customary international law by analogy) and M. Zwanenburg, *supra* note 2149, p. 761 (with further references). See more generally M. Forteau, 'Le droit international dans la Charte des Nations Unies', in Cot & Pellet, pp. 111–125 and 139–140, arguing that the *ratio legis* of Article 103 is the possibility to override *general* international law (emphasis added) and more generally that the Charter balances between respect for international law and the primacy of UN purposes and principles. *Contra*: the dissenting opinions of Judge Bedjaoui to the ICJ's Orders of 14 April 1992 in the cases *Questions of Interpretation and Application of the 1971 Montreal Convention Arising from the Aerial Incident at Lockerbie* (Libya v. UK and Libya v. USA), both at §29 (""*Article 103 ... does not cover such rights as may have other than conventional sources and be derived from general international law*") and the separate opinion by Judge Rezek to the ICJ's judgment of 27 February 1998 in this case, §2 ("*Article 103 of the Charter is a rule for settling conflicts between treaties ... However, it is not designed to operate to the detriment of customary international law and even less so to the detriment of the general principles of the law of nations*"), also cited by A. Toublanc, 'L'Article 103 et la valeur juridique de la charte des Nations Unies', 108 *R.G.D.I.P.* 2004, pp. 446–450 (who also rejects the applicability of Article 103 to general international law); J. Gardam, 'Legal Restraints on Security Council Military Enforcement Action', 17 *Michigan J.I.L.* 1996, pp. 303–304; J.I. Levitt, 'The Peace and Security Council of the African Union and the United Nations Security Council: The Case of Darfur, Sudan', in N. Blokker & N. Schrijver (eds.), *supra* note 2029, pp. 234–235 and A. Orakhelashvili, *supra* note 2158, p. 69. Italian and French doctrine mainly seems to reject the extension to customary law as such but partly arrives at the same conclusion on the basis of the arguments that the UN Charter is *lex specialis* compared to customary international law (e.g. C. Dominicé, 'L'Article 103 de la Charte de Nations Unies et le droit international humanitaire', in L. Condorelli, A.-M. La Rosa & S. Scherrer, *supra* note 1998, pp. 178–181 and 191; though submitting at pp. 181 and 186–187 that Article 103 does not free the Security illustrated in the context of discussions on Security Council Resolution 1483 since the alleged derogation from the law of occupation does not seem to have been limited to treaty law (which would have been difficult given that much of the law of occupation is part of customary international law). It was also the view put forward by the EU Council and by the European Commission before the ECJ in the *Yusuf* and *Kadi* cases.[2155] I submit that the counter argument that Article 103 UN Charter does not free the Security Council itself but only the Member States[2156] cannot be maintained. First, given the increased convergence between customary international law and treaty law, the effect and rationale of Article 103 would be significantly undermined if it did not cover customary international law[2157] – which undoubtedly explains why practice seems to cover customary international law. Second, the only way the Security Council may authorize Member States to derogate from customary international law is if it is itself free to derogate from this body of law.

Council itself) or that it is *lex posterior* in respect of pre-Charter customary law and for secondary UN law also over post-Charter customary law predating that secondary law (e.g. J.-M. Thouvenin, 'Article 103', in COT & PELLET, pp. 2140–2142). Compare G. Cahin, 'Le droit de la Charte et la coutume internationale', in COT & PELLET, p. 99, who argues that Article 103 is silent on customary law but nevertheless seems to accept that Chapter VII decisions can prevail over customary law. Similarly, E. Lagrange, 'Le Conseil de sécurité des Nations Unies peut-il violer le droit international?', 37 *R.B.D.I./B.T.I.R.* 2004, pp. 575–585, noting that the silence of Article 103 may be interpreted by analogy or *a contrario* but submitting that irrespective of this, Article 24 *juncto* Article 1 UN Charter empower the Security Council to derogate from customary international law in individual decisions but not in general rules. For a recent and fairly extensive discussion of Article 103 UN Charter, see *Fragmentation of International Law: Difficulties arising from the Diversification and Expansion of International Law, Report of the Study Group of the International Law Commission, finalized by M. Koskenniemi*, UN Doc. A/CN.4/L.682, 13 April 2006, pp. 168–181, especially pp. 175–176, concluding that "*the practice of the Security Council has continuously been grounded on an understanding that Security Council resolutions override conflicting customary law. ... it seems sound to join the prevailing opinion that Article 103 should be read extensively – so as to affirm that charter obligations prevail also over United Nations Member States' customary law obligations*". For a very recent discussion of Article 103, see R. Liivoja, 'The Scope of the Supremacy Clause of the United Nations Charter', 57 *I.C.L.Q.* 2008, pp. 583–612.

2155 Cases T-306/01 (*Yusuf and Al Barakaat International Foundation v. Council and Commission*), §207 and T-315/01 (*Kadi v. Council and Commission*) §156, both judgments of 21 September 2005. This is also noted by E. Sciso, 'Fundamental Rights and Article 103 of the UN Charter Before the Court of First Instance of the European Communities', 15 *Italian Y.I.L.* 2006, p. 149, who, however, seems to regard this as the Court's own view, even though the Court simply summarizes the institutions' claims and does not pronounce itself on this point (neither does the ECJ in the appeals judgment, *supra* note 1623). See also J.-M. Thouvenin, *supra* previous note, pp. 2140–2142, writing that the view of the Advocate General in the *Ebony* case before the ECJ (Case C-177/95, *Ebony Maritime SA and Loten Navigation Co. Ltd v Prefetto della Provincia di Brindisi and others*) seems to be based on a priority of Charter law over prior customary international law (*in casu* the freedom of navigation on the high seas).

2156 See the view by Fry and Dominicé *supra* notes 2153 and 2154.

2157 See also M. Forteau, *supra* note 2154, pp. 111–125 and 139–140.

The exception to this power that is usually acknowledged is that the Security Council cannot derogate from *ius cogens*.[2158] In this respect, it has been argued by some that the law of occupation contains less peremptory rules than other parts of the LOAC.[2159]

There is, however, another problem with Article 103: according to its text, this provision only extends priority to *obligations* under the Charter. This would seem to preclude that a mere *right* granted by the Security Council has this same priority.[2160] Yet in the case of peace operations, unlike in the case of sanctions, it

---

2158 See especially the separate opinion of Judge Lauterpacht to the Order of the International Court of Justice in the case *Application of the Convention on the Prevention and Punishment of the Crime of Genocide (Bosnia and Herzegovina v. Serbia and Montenegro)* of 13 September 1993, §§99–104 and ECJ, *Yusuf*, §§277–281, and *Kadi*, §§226–230. See also UN Doc. A/CN.4/L.682, *supra* note 2154, pp. 176–178; C. Dominicé *supra* note 2154, pp. 187–188; De Wet, pp. 187–191 (who also argues at pp. 204–215 that the Security Council is bound by core LOAC principles by virtue of Articles 1(3) and 24(2) UN Charter); A. Orakhelashvili, 'The Impact of Peremptory Norms on the Interpretation and Application of United Nations Security Council Resolutions', 16 *E.J.I.L.* 2005, pp. 59–88; A. Orakhelashvili, *supra* note 2149, p. 308; A.L. Paulus, '*Jus Cogens* in a Time of Hegemony and Fragmentation. An Attempt at a Re-appraisal', 74 *Nordic J.I.L* 2005, pp. 317–319; A. Reinisch, 'Developing Human Rights and Humanitarian Law Accountability of the Security Council for the Imposition of Economic Sanctions', 95 *A.J.I.L* 2001, p. 859; M. Sassoli, *supra* note 2152, p. 16; P. Szasz, *supra* note 2147, pp. 513–514 and M. Zwanenburg, *supra* note 2149, pp. 761–762. But see E. Lagrange, *supra* note 2154, pp. 582–585, questioning whether this is always the case.

2159 Kolb, Porretto & Vité, pp. 225–226. But see David, pp. 94–101 (arguing that most of the LOAC is *ius cogens* and not excepting the law of occupation) and M. Zwanenburg, *supra* note 2149, pp. 762–763. Compare L. Condorelli & L. Boisson de Chazournes, 'Quelques remarques a propos de l'obligation des Etats de 'respecter et faire respecter' le droit international humanitaire en toutes circonstances', in C. Swinarski (ed.), *supra* note 1998, pp. 21–24 and 32–33, who argue that various particular features of the LOAC support its *ius cogens* nature, in particular its unconditional nature and exemption from treaty suspension/termination in reaction to a material breach by another party (Article 60(5) 1969 VCLT states that the provisions governing such suspension/termination "*do not apply to provisions relating to the protection of the human person contained in treaties of a humanitarian character, in particular to provisions prohibiting any form of reprisals against persons protected by such treaties*") or countermeasures more generally (Article 50(1)(c) of the ILC's Draft Articles on Responsibility of States for Internationally Wrongful Acts, adopted on 31 May and 3 August 2001, *Report of the International Law Commission. Fifty-third session*, UN Doc. A/56/10, pp. 57 and 333–340, provides that countermeasures shall not affect "*(c) Obligations of a humanitarian character prohibiting reprisals*"). While certainly significant, it should be noted that these provisions do not cover the entire LOAC. I. Seiderman, *Hierarchy in International Law*, Antwerp, Intersentia/Hart, 2001, pp. 95–98 writes that if a LOAC rule does not entail criminal sanctions when breached, it is unlikely to be *ius cogens*. Compare De Wet, p. 221.

2160 See A. Toublanc, *supra* note 2154, pp. 445–446 and the dissenting opinions of Judge Bedjaoui to the ICJ's Orders of 14 April 1992 in the cases *Questions of Interpretation and Application of the 1971 Montreal Convention Arising from the Aerial Incident at Lockerbie* (Libya v. UK and Libya v. USA), both at §29 (""*Article 103 ... is aimed at "obligations" – whereas we are dealing with alleged "rights" ...*"). Compare more generally R. Kolb, 'Does Article 103 of the Charter of the United Nations Apply only to Decisions or also to Authorizations Adopted by the Security Council?', 64 *Z.a.ö.R.V.* 2004, pp. 21–35.

is on such rights that States rely to justify derogations, e.g. in the case of Iraq or in the case of an "all necessary measures" mandate that is considered to justify a derogation from human rights (see *infra*, Chapter 9.C.5). Here too, governments' practice suggests that Article 103 is interpreted in the sense that when the Security Council authorizes a derogation without imposing it, an ensuing use of that derogation is covered by Article 103. However, judicial decisions have not unequivocally accepted this.[2161] It is submitted that where the Security Council authorizes a derogation, this should be given full effect when relied upon by

[2161] The England and Wales Court of Appeal held in its judgment of 29 March 2006 in *Al-Jedda, R (on the application of) v Secretary of State for Defence* that "*in acting ... pursuant to the authority of UNSCR 1546 ... the [UK] must be taken as performing an obligation within the meaning of Article 25 that was imposed on it by that resolution for the purposes of Article 103*". See [2006] EWCA Civ 327 (available online at www.bailii.org/ew/cases/EWCA/Civ/2006/327.html), §76; see also §§55–87. In §63 of this judgment it is stated that the government's agent argued that "If and in so far as *UNSCR 1546 (2004)* obliged *member states participating ... to intern people in Iraq for imperative reasons of security in order to fulfil the mandate*" (emphasis added). For a critique of this decision, see A. Cassimatis, *supra* note 2154, pp. 635–637. The House of Lords upheld the judgment on 12 December 2007 ([2007] UKHL 58, available online at www.publications.parliament.uk/pa/ld200708/ldjudgmt/jd071212/jedda-1.htm) and addressed the question more explicitly in this judgment, holding that authorizations were covered (see §§30–36, 115–118; 135 and 151–152; but see the questions by Baroness Hale on the scope of the Resolution at §§127–129). For annotations of this case, see A. Breitegger, 'Sacrificing the Effectiveness of the European Convention on Human Rights on the Altar of the Effective Functioning of Peace Support Operations: A Critique of Behrami & Saramati and Al Jedda', 11 *International Community Law Review* 2009, pp. 155–183; J.A.E. Johnston, 'IHL v. Human Rights: The "Al Jedda" Case and Issues arising from an Operational Perspective', in R. Arnold (ed.), *Law Enforcement within the Framework of Peace Support Operations*, Leiden, Nijhoff, 2008, pp. 229–255; F. Messineo, 'The House of Lords in Al-Jedda and Public International Law: Attribution of Conduct to Un-Authorized Forces and the Power of the Security Council to Displace Human Rights', 56 *N.I.L.R.* 2009, pp. 35–62; A. Orakhelashvili, 'R (on the Application of Al-Jedda) (FC) v. Secretary of State for Defence (2007) UKHL 58: House of Lords, Appellate Committee, December 12, 2007', 102 *A.J.I.L.* 2008, pp. 337–345; A. Sari, 'The Al-Jedda Case before the House of Lords', 13 *International Peacekeeping* 2009, pp. 181–196; C. Tomuschat, 'Case Note. R (on the Application of Al-Jedda) v Secretary of State for Defence. Human Rights in a Multi-level System of Governance and the Internment of Suspected Terrorists', 9 *Melbourne J.I.L.* 2008, pp. 391–404 (www.austlii.edu.au/au/journals/MelbJIL/2008/15.html); M. Wood, 'Detention during International Military Operations: Article 103 of the UN Charter and the *Al-Jedda* Case', 47 *R.D.M.D.G.* 2008, pp. 139–165 and M. Zwanenburg, 'De Lords, het EVRM en het Handvest: de zaak Al-Jedda', 101 *Militairrechtelijk tijdschrift* 2008, pp. 133–144. On 31 May 2007, the ECtHR declared inadmissible the applications brought in the cases *Behrami and Behrami v. France* (No. 71412/01) and *Saramati v. France, Germany and Norway* (No. 78166/01). The decision mentions that various State Parties refer to Article 103 UN Charter but phrases it as a priority of UN obligations notwithstanding the authorizing rather than obligating nature of the UN Security Council Resolution at issue (Res. 1244 of 10 June 1999). The Court itself mentions Article 103 but does not really elaborate on the weight it has given to this provision (§147 merely says that "*The Court has therefore had regard to two complementary provisions of the Charter, Articles 25 and 103, as interpreted by the International Court of Justice*"). In contrast, the ECJ has accepted less leeway in its cases concerning the implementation of UN sanctions; see below, Chapter 9.C.5.

States. A different solution might force the Security Council to impose an obligation and lead to greater derogation. What one might expect, however, is that the Security Council is more explicit when it in fact intends to authorize a derogation and also that it better clarifies the scope of any derogation.

F. PARTICIPATING STATE OBLIGATIONS IN ESDP OPERATIONS

1. GENERAL

I have argued in Chapter 7 that there are three bases for Member State responsibility in the framework of international organizations, leaving aside complicity. I will now discuss the implications of each of these bases for Member States in the context of ESDP operations (i-iii), as well as an obligation specific to the LOAC, namely to "*respect and ensure respect*" for LOAC obligations (iv) and the particular implications of ESDP operations conducted by some Member States only (v).

i. Responsibility Resulting from Establishment without Guarantees

First, I concluded that a Member State incurs international responsibility an act committed by an international organization that, if committed by that State, would have constituted a breach of an international obligation of that Member State, except for 'common interest regimes' in respect of which the Member State has provided for equivalent protection, with the caveat that where despite such equivalent protection there is a manifest violation that outweighs the interests of international cooperation, the Member State will remain responsible.

A first point which arises here, is that the universal and fairly detailed nature of the LOAC seems to preclude a balancing with other 'common interests',[2162] with the exception, to some extent, of the interests of international peace and security pursued by the UN Security Council (on the latter, see *supra*, Section E of this chapter). This fairly absolute nature is *inter alia* reflected in the obligation under Article 1 common to the 1949 Geneva Conventions and AP I to "*respect and to ensure respect for the present Convention* in all circumstances" (emphasis added; see *infra*, subsection iv).

[2162] The entire LOAC reflects a balancing between military necessity and humanity and except where specific provisions allow military necessity to override a given rule, no further balancing is possible.

In this context, it should be noted that Member States of international organizations have different treaty obligations in the field of the LOAC,[2163] which complicates the matter for international organizations and gives rise to problems of 'legal interoperability'.[2164] However, the importance of such divergences is limited by the fact that a significant body of treaty rules has become part of customary international humanitarian law on the one hand[2165] and by a marked convergence between EU Member States' treaty obligations in this field on the other hand. As to the latter, all 27 EU Member States at the time of writing are parties to the 1949 Geneva Conventions, AP I, AP II and the ICC Statute,[2166] as well as to the 1980 Convention on Certain Conventional Weapons[2167] and the 1993 Chemical Weapons Convention[2168].[2169] There is significantly greater convergence within the EU than within NATO.[2170] Yet even within the EU, if one looks at the full range of LOAC treaties, there are still some divergences.[2171]

2163 The ICRC's online database at www.icrc.org/ihl provides an extensive overview of all LOAC instruments and their status, including a table with the summary status of the main instruments.

2164 On the latter, see, e.g. David, pp. 209–212; F. Hampson, 'States' Military Operations Authorized by the United Nations and International Humanitarian Law', in L. Condorelli, A.-M. La Rosa & S. Scherrer (eds.), *supra* note 1998, pp. 395–401; M. Zwanenburg, 'Legal Interoperability in Multinational Forces: A Military Necessity', in College of Europe & ICRC (eds.), *supra* note 2121, pp. 108–115, especially pp. 110–115, and the various contributions in A.E. Wall (ed.), *Legal and Ethical Issues of NATO's Kosovo Campaign*, 78 International Law Studies 2002, Newport, US Naval War College, pp. 313–395. For a specific example, see G. Walsh, 'Interoperability of United States and Canadian Armed Forces', 15 *Duke J.I.C.L.* 2005, pp. 315–331, especially pp. 324–331 and K. Watkin, 'Canada/United States Military Interoperability and Humanitarian Law Issues: Land Mines, Terrorism, Military objectives and Targeted Killings', 15 *Duke J.I.C.L.* 2005, pp. 281–314.

2165 See especially the ICRC's study, *supra* note 2062 (see also www.icrc.org/Web/Eng/siteeng0.nsf/html/section_ihl_customary_humanitarian_law#More%20in%20this%20section and the various translations at www.icrc.org/Web/eng/siteeng0.nsf/html/customary-law-translations) and the reactions it has evoked, e.g. by the US (see the 3 November 2006 Letter by John B. Bellinger III, the legal adviser for the State Department, and William J. Haynes II, general counsel of the Department of Defense, to the ICRC, available online at www.defenselink.mil/home/pdf/Customary_International_Humanitiarian_Law.pdf).

2166 The Czech Republic was the last Member State to become a party to the ICC Statute. It deposited its instrument of ratification on 21 July 2009; see UN press release of 22 July 2009 and www.icc-cpi.int/NR/exeres/E3186309-5F6F-462B-8ED5-52A6A8DE9F68.htm.

2167 Convention on Prohibitions or Restrictions on the Use of Certain Conventional Weapons Which May be Deemed to be Excessively Injurious or to Have Indiscriminate Effects, Geneva, 10 October 1980.

2168 Convention on the Prohibition of the Development, Production, Stockpiling and Use of Chemical Weapons and on Their Destruction, Paris, 13 January 1993.

2169 ICRC database, *supra* note 2163, consulted on 11 July 2007.

2170 Where the US and Turkey are not a party to AP I, AP II and the ICC Statute and have not even signed these agreements (the US signed the ICC Statute but later declared that it would not ratify it (the statement is available at http://treaties.un.org), thereby more or less undoing the effects of its signature).

2171 E.g. Finland and Poland are not a party to the Convention on the Prohibition of the Use, Stockpiling, Production and Transfer of Anti-Personnel Mines and on their Destruction

Also, reservations entail differences even where treaties are ratified by all EU Member States.

If a balancing is excluded, what is the extent of the obligations which Member States must assure that an international organization complies with? The key may lie in determining what conduct would otherwise have been committed by that Member State, especially in respect of military operations. In particular, for military contingents it might be argued that in principle, only the conduct of a State's own contingents is conduct that would otherwise have been that Member State's own conduct. This is not problematic in that, as will be explained below (subsection iii of this Section), contingents normally do consider themselves bound by their sending State's law and international obligations. Nevertheless, it might be objected that this may not be decisive in that a Member State might not have participated in an operation if it would not have been led by the international organization concerned; or conversely, that a Member State might have contributed more forces in a coalition framework if it had not been for a collective action. Yet those objections do not offer an alternative objective test that can be used in practice.

However, this still leaves open the question of headquarters, operation and force commanders and civilian missions (though the latter are only likely to be subject to the LOAC in an occupation), as well as that of contingents commanding smaller contingents of other nations. For operation and force commanders, one might argue that they operate at a level which would not otherwise have been that of their sending States and that there is no responsibility by virtue of establishment.[2172] However, there may be issues under the domestic (criminal) law of the State of their nationality.[2173] The same can arguably be said of staff of civilian operations, which retains only a minimal link to their sending State. The most difficult case is probably that of contingents that incorporate units from another Member State. Is the lead contingent required to impose respect for its obligations to elements from other nations under its command?[2174] Subjectively, one might argue that it depends on whether the lead contingent would have

(Oslo, 18 September 1997) and Ireland and Malta are not a party to the Convention for the Protection of Cultural Property in the Event of Armed Conflict (The Hague, 14 May 1954).

2172 The point is raised by H. Risse, *supra* note 1998, pp. 134–146.

2173 For instance, where the domestic law of the State of nationality of a Commander prohibits actions involving the use of anti-personnel landmines but such use is not prohibited for one of the contingents under his command.

2174 L. Condorelli, 'Pertinence du droit international humanitaire pour les organisations internationales et les alliances', in College of Europe & ICRC (eds.), *supra* note 1997, p. 33 cites Daillier as supporting this view but disagrees himself. Compare David, p. 211, who briefly discusses the reverse issue, arguing that the subordinate contingent should comply with its own obligations but mentions the case of forces fully put at the disposal of another replaced the subordinate incorporated contingent if the latter would not have been available, but again this is not a workable test. I would therefore argue that by virtue of establishment, the lead contingent does not have to impose its rules.

The issue is addressed to some extent in the Convention on Cluster Munitions.[2175] Article 21 of this Convention provides that:

> 3. Notwithstanding the provisions of Article 1 of this Convention and in accordance with international law, States Parties, their military personnel or nationals, may engage in military cooperation and operations with States not party to this Convention that might engage in activities prohibited to a State Party.
> 4. Nothing in paragraph 3 of this Article shall authorise a State Party:
> (a) To develop, produce or otherwise acquire cluster munitions;
> (b) To itself stockpile or transfer cluster munitions;
> (c) To itself use cluster munitions; or
> (d) To expressly request the use of cluster munitions in cases where the choice of munitions used is within its exclusive control.[2176]

ii. *Responsibility Resulting from Voting*

Second, I concluded that a Member State engages its international responsibility by voting in relation to a decision if the mere vote itself amounts to a violation of an international obligation of that State. This view has important consequences for the conduct of ESDP operations. It entails that in voting on key decisions such as the mandate, the Operation Plan and the Rules of Engagement, Member States may not violate their LOAC obligations.

This raises the question of how far this obligation goes. In particular, while it is perfectly acceptable that a State has to respect its own obligations, it would be problematic if it were obliged to impose those obligations also on other Member States or on the EU to the extent that the latter are not so bound.[2177] I will come

State (which is very exceptional). I would argue that in that case, they are (also) bound by the latter State's obligations.

2175 Adopted in Dublin on 30 May 2008 and signed on 3 December 2008; text and status available at www.icrc.org/ihl and at www.clusterconvention.org.

2176 For a discussion, see E. Schwager, 'The Question of Interoperability: Interpretation of Articles 1 and 21 of the Convention on Cluster Munitions (CCM)', 21 *Humanitäres Völkerrecht* 2008, pp. 247–250. See also generally T. di Ruzza, 'The Convention on Cluster Munitions: Towards a Balance between Humanitarian and Military Considerations?', 47 *R.D.M.D.G.* 2008, pp. 405–448 and K. Hulme, 'The 2008 Cluster Munitions Convention: Stepping Outside the CCW Framework (Again)', 58 *I.C.L.Q.* 2009, pp. 219–227.

2177 Compare L. Condorelli, *supra* note 2174, pp. 32–33 and the discussion in *id.*, pp. 39–40. Condorelli seems to argue that each contingent has to respect its own obligations but on the other hand states that it is therefore the highest level of obligations that must be respected, which would suggest a binding of all participating nations to any obligation of any back to this in subsection iv below, as there is a specific feature of the LOAC that helps determine the answer to this question.

iii. Responsibility Resulting from Implementing a Decision

Third, I have argued that a Member State is internationally responsible for implementing a decision that violates its international obligations except where it has provided for equivalent protection in relation to a 'common interest regime' and has no discretion to implement the decision in conformity with its obligations and only to the extent that the violation of its obligations is proportionate to the importance of international cooperation.

This poses few problems in respect of the LOAC given the practice of Member States to ensure that their armed forces respect their LOAC obligations even when acting in the framework of an international organization. Indeed, it is the general understanding, confirmed in State practice,[2178] that forces put at the disposal of international organizations by troop-contributing nations are always to comply with the LOAC obligations of their sending State, even if under the effective command and control of an international organization.[2179] This mainly stems from the obligation under Article 1 common to the 1949 Geneva Conventions to "*respect and to ensure respect for the present Convention in all circumstances*" (see *infra*, subsection iv).

Thus the fact that the LOAC seems to leave virtually no room for any balancing with other interests (see subsection i of this Section) is not problematic.

iv. The Obligation to "Respect and to Ensure Respect"

A peculiarity of the LOAC is the obligation under Article 1 common to the 1949 Geneva Conventions to "*respect and to ensure respect for the present Convention in all circumstances*".[2180] This obligation, reaffirmed in Article 1(1) AP I, is also

participating nation. Furthermore, he disagrees with the view of Daillier that the obligations of the State in command are paramount. DAVID, pp. 210–211 accepts, albeit reluctantly, that each State's contingent is bound to its own treaty obligations.

2178 *Inter alia* reflected in UK MANUAL, §14.3, note 2 p. 376. See also the UN Secretary-General Bulletin on Observance by United Nations Forces of International Humanitarian Law, *supra* note 2021, section 2: "*The present provisions ... do not ... replace the national laws by which military personnel remain bound throughout the operation*" – national laws in this sense normally include treaty obligations.

2179 E.g. C. Greenwood, *supra* note 2001, p. 46; N. Ronzitti, *supra* note 1997, p. 166 and ZWANENBURG, p. 192.

2180 On this obligation, see also generally F. Azzam, 'The Duty of Third States to Implement and Enforce International Humanitarian Law', 66 *Nordic J.I.L.* 1997, pp. 55–75; L. Condorelli & L. Boisson de Chazournes, *supra* note 2159, pp. 17–35; L. Boisson de Chazournes & L. Condorelli, widely considered to be part of customary international law[2181] and also seems to be applicable in non-international armed conflicts.[2182]

In the context of Member State responsibility, this obligation reinforces a Member State's other obligations.[2183] In particular, by requiring that a State's armed forces and personnel respect that State's obligations *in all circumstances*, it reinforces the obligation to respect a State's LOAC obligations even when implementing decisions of international organizations. It may also reinforce a State's obligations not to endow international organizations with powers without adequate guarantees.[2184] While this obligation is also understood to require efforts by States to ensure that third parties comply with the LOAC,[2185] this obligation cannot require efforts beyond requiring that such third parties comply

---

'Common Article 1 of the Geneva Conventions Revisited: Protecting Collective Interests', 82 No. 837 *I.R.R.C.* 2000, pp. 67–81 and B. Kessler, 'The Duty to 'Ensure Respect' under Common Article 1 of the Geneva Conventions: Its Implications on International and Non-International Armed Conflicts', 44 *G.Y.I.L.* 2002, pp. 498–516.

2181 In the *Nicaragua* case (*Case Concerning Military and Paramilitary Activities in and Against Nicaragua (Nicar. v. U.S.)*, 27 June 1986 (Merits)), §220, the ICJ considered that the obligation "*in the terms of Article I of the Geneva Conventions, to "respect" the Conventions and even "to ensure respect" for them "in all circumstances" ... does not derive only from the Conventions themselves, but from the general principles of humanitarian law to which the Conventions merely give specific expression*". The Institute of International Law sees this as a basis for affirming that this obligation "*has acquired the status of an obligation of customary international law*", see its Resolution concerning 'The Application of International Humanitarian Law and Fundamental Human Rights, in Armed Conflicts in which Non-State Entities are Parties' (*supra* note 2064), 7th recital of the preamble. See also L. Boisson de Chazournes & L. Condorelli, *supra* note 2181, p. 70.

2182 ICRC study, *supra* note 2062, p. 495. See also B. Kessler, *supra* note 2180, pp. 507–516.

2183 Compare the ILA's 2004 *Final Report on the Accountablity of International Organisations* (available online at www.ila-hq.org), pp. 23–24: "*The obligation for States, under Common Article 1 ... to respect and ensure respect for international humanitarian law applies in all circumstances, whether States are acting individually, collectively or contribute troops to peacekeeping or peace enforcement operations, including those conducted under the auspices of, or under a mandate or authorisation from an [international organization]. The obligation is unconditional. ... primary responsibility by way of effective control is always accompanied by independent, secondary obligations*". See also Kolb, Porretto & Vité, pp. 153–155.

2184 Compare the more extensive discussion by Zwanenburg, pp. 117–128.

2185 E.g. on 20 December 1990, the Security Council, in Resolution 681 (§5), called upon the parties to GC IV "*to ensure respect by Israel, the occupying Power, for its obligations under the Convention in accordance with Article 1 thereof*". Thus the obligation to respect is often regarded as the primary one resting on the actor in control, whereas the obligation to ensure respect is deemed to be a secondary one, resting on other actors. See, e.g. The ILA's 2004 *Final Report on the Accountablity of International Organisations* (available online at www.ila-hq.org), p. 24 ("*primary responsibility by way of effective control is always accompanied by independent, secondary obligations*"). See also L. Condorelli, 'L'obligation de respecter et faire respecter le droit international humanitaire et la responsabilité individuelle', in S. Kolanowski *et al.* (eds.), *Proceedings of the Bruges Colloquium. Current Challenges in International Humanitarian Law. 27–28 October 2000 / Actes du colloque de Bruges. Défis contemporains en droit international humanitaire. 27–28 octobre 2000*, Bruges, College of Europe (*collegium* No. 21, available online at www.coleurop.be/template.asp?pagename=pub_collegium), 2001, pp. 46–50.

with *their own* LOAC obligations. This would mean that the EU Member States are obliged to ensure, within their lawful means, including by voting on decisions and by implementing them, that the EU respects its proper obligations under the LOAC. It would *not* require a State to vote against actions by an international organization and to be carried out by other States which would violate the former State's obligations but not the latter's obligations (e.g. if the former State is a party to AP I and the latter is not).[2186]

In practice, this rule will also be supported by the fact that in most States, personnel of the armed forces will be subject to national criminal law of the sending State even when deployed abroad, at least to the extent that this criminal law includes repression of breaches of LOAC obligations of that State.

Moreover, Article 3 of the 1907 Hague Convention IV stipulates that "*A belligerent party which violates the provisions of the said Regulations shall, if the case demands, be liable to pay compensation. It shall be responsible for all acts committed by persons forming part of its armed forces*" and Article 91 AP I similarly states that "*A Party to the conflict which violates the provisions of the Conventions or of this Protocol shall, if the case demands, be liable to pay compensation. It shall be responsible for all acts committed by persons forming part of its armed forces*". The ICRC commentary to the latter provision explains that this was to ensure that States would not evade their responsibility (as also reflected in Articles 51 GC I, 52 GC II, 131 GC III and 148 GC IV) and places this provision in the context of general State responsibility rules.[2187] It also takes the view that "*Joint or collective responsibility, for example, in cases of coalition, cannot be excluded*".[2188] It is submitted that these provisions reinforce Member States' responsibility, including that to "*respect and to ensure respect for the present Convention in all circumstances*", but do not exclude EU responsibility in addition.[2189]

In fact, State practice within NATO[2190] and within the EU indicates that both these organizations and their Member States primarily perceive LOAC obligations as the responsibility of the Member States. For the EU, this is reflected in the Salamanca Presidency Declaration, which stated that "*The responsibility for complying with International Humanitarian Law, in cases where it applies, in*

2186 See also S. Bartelt, *supra* note 1, pp. 195–201. This corresponds with NATO practice which stresses the differences between Member States' treaty obligations.

2187 ICRC Commentary to AP I, §§3645–3661, pp. 1053–1058.

2188 *Id.*, §3658, p. 1057.

2189 Compare Zwanenburg, pp. 81–86 and 131, who considers that the premises on which these provisions rest are not present in the case of peace support operations.

2190 See Zwanenburg, pp. 189–192, who sees this view as related to the erroneous denial of NATO's international legal personality.

a European Union led-operation, rests primarily with the State to which the troops belong", though adding that "*In exercising the strategic direction and political control, the European Union will ensure that all relevant rules of international law, including humanitarian law as appropriate are duly taken into account*".[2191] Similarly, the Presidency Conclusion of the 19–20 June 2003 Thessaloniki European Council stated that "*The European Council stresses the importance of national armed forces observing applicable humanitarian law*".[2192] For NATO, this also seems to be reflected in the reactions of third parties, including scholars, to the Kosovo air campaign (operation *Allied Force*) and the ICTY's report thereon, as well as in this report itself.[2193] In particular, hardly any attention was paid in this context to whether NATO itself might have been bound by proper obligations under the LOAC and the focus was rather on customary law as AP I was not ratified by a few NATO Member States, including the US.[2194] The main indication to the contrary is that some Member States have on occasion invoked the responsibility of NATO rather than their individual responsibility before international courts, but obviously at a time when it was convenient for them to do so.[2195]

Nevertheless, it is submitted that this focus on the Member States is erroneous where the EU or NATO exercise effective control over an operation.[2196] In this respect, it would seem that NATO and the EU have not come as far as the UN has.[2197]

2191 *Infra* note 2239.

2192 Doc. 11638, 1 October 2003, §74.

2193 See generally the references *supra* note 1999.

2194 The ICTY report itself (*supra* note 1999) hardly addresses the issue (in §42, it is stated that "*Although the Protocol I definition of military objective is not beyond criticism, it provides the contemporary standard which must be used when attempting to determine the lawfulness of particular attacks. That being said, it must be noted once again neither the USA nor France is a party to Additional Protocol I. The definition is, however, generally accepted as part of customary law*"). To some extent this is understandable as the focus is on individual criminal responsibility. For examples of the equally cursory considerations in the literature in this respect, see, e.g. N. Quenivet, *supra* note 1999, pp. 483–484 (*inter alia* arguing at p. 484 that all NATO Member States were responsible for a breach of the LOAC even if they had no control over a specific target selection) and T. Voon, *supra* note 1999, pp. 1091–1093.

2195 See *supra*, Chapter 5.E.3.ii, notes 1434–1435 and the accompanying text. For a discussion of the targeting procedure in NATO after operation *Allied Force*, see, e.g. J.T. Bakker, 'Vredesoperaties en humanitair oorlogsrecht', 96 *Militair Rechtelijk Tijdschrift* 2003, pp. 348–353. On various targeting and LOAC issues during operation Allied Force, see A.E. Wall (ed.), *supra* note 2164.

2196 In this sense also N. Ronzitti, *supra* note 1997, pp. 190–192, seeing primary attribution to the EU under present command arrangements. Compare T. Stein, 'Coalition Warfare and Differing Legal Obligations of Coalition Members under International Humanitarian Law', in A.E. Wall (ed.), *supra* note 2164, pp. 327–335 and the discussion in *id.*, pp. 387–388.

2197 While they except to a greater extent that the forces under their command are bound by all rules of the LOAC when the LOAC is applicable (a point on which the UN is still less

v. *ESDP Operations Conducted by Some Member States Only*

Where does responsibility lie when ESDP operations are conducted by the armed forces of only some Member States? Obviously, only those States participating can incur responsibility for implementing such an operation. In contrast, for the two other grounds of Member State responsibility there does not seem to be any reason to exempt the other Member States as they were/are fully implicated in the establishment of the EU and in the decision-making, including the approval of the mandate, Operation Plan and ROE. However, the matter is somewhat less clear under the Lisbon Treaty, where the Operation Plan and ROE might possibly be adopted by a group of Member States entrusted with the execution of a mission.[2198]

2. THE POSITION OF THIRD STATES PARTICIPATING IN ESDP OPERATIONS

Third States participating in ESDP operations are in a different position from Member States in that they clearly cannot be held liable by virtue of the establishment of the organization. However, their responsibility may arise under the same rules by virtue of the transfer of authority over their forces to the EU as this may also be regarded as a transfer of competences.[2199] In contrast, when they implement an ESDP operation, they can be held liable for that implementation like Member States. As they have no vote on the relevant decisions, except to some extent an influence on certain implementing decisions via a committee of contributors, responsibility for decision-making is rather unlikely.

---

committed, see the limited scope of the Secretary-General's Bulletin; similarly, T.D. Gill, *supra* note 2000, pp. 341–342), they seem to accept much less that both organizations themselves have obligations under the LOAC. For the EU this may perhaps be explained by the controversy over its legal personality and its only recent venture into the realm of military operations. However, for NATO it is less understandable. For a good characterization of the evolution of the UN's position, see R. Zacklin, 'General Report', in L. Condorelli, A.-M. La Rosa & S. Scherrer (eds.), *supra* note 1998, pp. 51–52.

2198 See Articles 27(5) and 29 (renumbered 42(5) and 44) EU Treaty as amended by the Lisbon Treaty. Note also the permanent structured cooperation envisaged in the Protocol (No 4) on permanent structured cooperation established by Article 27 [renumbered 46] EU Treaty as annexed to the Lisbon Treaty. Compare Articles I-41(5), III-310(1) and III-310 and I-41(6) and III-312 EU Constitution and Protocol (No 23) on permanent structured cooperation. Compare N. Ronzitti, *supra* note 1997, pp. 190–192, seeing EU responsibility in this case and possibly joint EU-Member State responsibility in the case of permanent structured cooperation and exclusive Member State responsibility in respect of mutual defence (under the EU Constitution).

2199 I am grateful to Marten Zwanenburg for raising this point.

G. EU OBLIGATIONS IN ESDP OPERATIONS

1. THE EU HAS PROPER OBLIGATIONS UNDER THE LOAC

In the sections above, the focus has been on the applicability of the LOAC with relatively little regard to the specificity of international organizations. In this section, the conclusions of Chapters 6 and 7 on the international legal personality of the EU and the extent to which it is bound by international law will be applied to the LOAC in ESDP operations.

In this subsection, I will first briefly set out why the EU has proper obligations under the LOAC. In the following subsections, I will look into the sources and extent of these obligations.

In Chapter 6.F above, I have argued that ESDP operations have a status independent of the Participating States, most likely as part of the legal personality of the EU, because EU bodies exercise command and control over the EU-led forces put at their disposal. I will now elaborate on this with regard to military operations, as the situation is not so clear in respect of these operations. In particular, it is not settled when or under what circumstances national contingents engage the Union and/or the Sending States.[2200]

Since a significant degree of the authority over the military contingents is transferred to the EU Operation,[2201] these contingents are put at the disposal of

2200 Compare, in respect of the UN and NATO, Zwanenburg, pp. 51–134; Kolb, Porretto & Vité, pp. 327–333 and S. Lüder, *supra* note 1998, pp. 37–138 and 165–180.

2201 Different degrees of command and control are known to military forces. In operations conducted under the command of an international organization, some degree of command and control is normally transferred to the organization. For the command and control (C2) arrangements in military ESDP operations, see Council Doc. 11096/03 EXT 1 (26 July 2006; this is a partially declassified version), especially pp. 6–7 (with definitions of the different kinds of command and control). Compare Zwanenburg, pp. 39–42, especially note 152, citing the NATO definitions which can be found in NATO, *NATO Glossary of Term and Definitions*, presently AAP-6(2006), pp. 2-C-7; 2-F-6 and 2-O-2 (available online at www.nato.int/docu/stanag/aap006/aap6.htm); Kolb, Porretto & Vité, pp. 36–37; D. Fleck, 'Multinational Units', in D. Fleck (ed.), *The Handbook of the Law of Visiting Forces*, Oxford, Oxford University Press, 2001, pp. 39–41 and S. Lüder, *supra* note 1998, pp. 87–90. In the case of the EU there is such a transfer of authority; see Doc. 11096/03 EXT 1 (*supra* this note), pp. 15–16 ("*For the conduct of an EU-led military [crisis management operation], the [Operation Commander] will be vested with the appropriate Command authority, allowing him sufficient flexibility (e.g. [operational control] or possibly [operational command]) over forces by Transfer of Authority (TOA) from the contributing Member States and non-EU [troop contributing nations]*" and "*For the conduct of the operation in theatre, the [Force Commander] will be vested with the appropriate Command authority giving him sufficient flexibility (in principle [operational control]) over the required forces by the [Operation Commander]*"). For instance, Article 10(3) of the EU-Canada framework participation agreement for ESDP operations (*O.J. L* 315, 1 December 2005, p. 21) provides that "*National authorities shall transfer the Operational and Tactical command and/or control of their forces and personnel to the EU* the EU[2202] and the EU, particularly through the Council, PSC and especially the Operation and Force Commanders,[2203] exercises effective control over these forces (including from third States[2204]). Such control is usually regarded as the crucial factor for the purpose of attribution of conduct under international law.[2205] However, it is certainly not uniformly interpreted.[2206]

Operation Commander". The military command and control is transferred to the Operation Commander and subsequently below but not above. In contrast, the political control and strategic direction is exercised by the PSC.

2202 Article 5 of the provisional version of the ILC's Draft Articles on the Responsibility of International Organizations stipulates that "*The conduct of an organ of a State or an organ or agent of an international organization that is placed at the disposal of another international organization shall be considered under international law an act of the latter organization if the organization exercises effective control over that conduct*" (*Report of the 56th Session*, UN Doc. A/59/10, p. 99). In fact, this Article was mainly written with peace operations in mind (see the commentaries, *id*, pp. 110–115). Compare Zwanenburg, pp. 94–95 and 107–115 (writing before the adoption of these Articles but making an analogy with Article 6 of the ILC's Draft Articles on Responsibility of States for Internationally Wrongful Acts (adopted on 31 May and 3 August 2001, *Report of the International Law Commission. Fifty-third session*, UN Doc. A/56/10)) and S. Lüder, *supra* note 1998, pp. 76–105 (also making this analogy and extensively discussing "*Organleihe*" more generally).

2203 Including through the adoption of the mandate, Operation Plan and Rules of Engagement. While most nations may have a number of caveats or reservations to these common rules, such caveats may only be more restrictive than the common rules. On command and control of EU forces, see generally R. Romano, 'Comando e controllo delle orze di Pace dell'Ue', in N. Ronzitti (ed.), *Le forze di pace dell'Unione Europea*, Roma, Rubbettino, 2005, pp. 113–136, especially pp. 129–136, though apparently writing before ESDP operations started (see also the English summary at pp. 18–19). Compare N. Ronzitti, *supra* note 1997, pp. 190–192, seeing attribution to the EU under present command arrangements.

2204 It may be noted that in Pledge P091 made by the EU Member States at the 30th International Conference of the Red Cross and Red Crescent in 2007, there is a commitment by the EU to "*Ensuring implementation of [fundamental procedural guarantees] by third parties involved in EU operations*" (see www.icrc.org/applic/p130e.nsf/pbk/PCOE-79CKFC?openDocument&section =PBP).

2205 See the ILC's view *supra* note 2202 and, e.g. Kolb, Poretto & Vité , pp. 151–173, 285–288 and 423–428 (identifying effective control as decisive at p. 151); Zwanenburg, pp. 51–134, especially pp. 129–134, and S. Lüder, *supra* note 1998, pp. 80–90. See also, specifically regarding the EU, N. Ronzitti, *supra* previous note, pp. 190–192 and N. Tsagourias, *supra* note 1997, pp. 121–122, taking effective control as the decisive criterion but undecided as to whether the EU exercises such control (despite seeming inclined to qualify ESDP operations as EU organs), and citing UN Doc. A/51/389 (20 September 1996), §§17–19 ("*In joint operations, international responsibility for the conduct of the troops lies where operational command and control is vested according to the arrangements ... In the absence of formal arrangements .... responsibility would be determined in each and every case according to the degree of effective control exercised by either party in the conduct of the operation. The principle that in coordinated operations liability ... is vested in the entity in effective command and control of the operation or the specific action reflects a well-established principle of international responsibility*"). See also D. Shraga, *supra* note 2116, pp. 328–333 (seeing operational command and control as decisive in the UN context and regarding it as a manifestation of effective control). See also UN Documents A/CN.4/545, 25 June 2004, pp. 17–18 and A/CN.4/556, 12 May 2005, pp. 4 *juncto* 46.

2206 E.g. S. Bartelt, *supra* note 1, pp. 185–186 and 193, submits that the transfer of operational command is insufficient. However, this author wrongly sees a contrast with the UN, where it is also only such command that is transferred. While section 7 of the Model Agreement

Two recent views on the matter illustrate the complexity. First, the ILA has stated that:

> If ... operational command rests with the IO, the responsibility of the IO will result from non-observance of the same rules, while States have the special responsibility to ensure respect for international humanitarian law by the IO. In cases where strategic control formally rests with the IO but where in practice national commanders choose the targets, both the State and the IO share responsibility for a violation of international humanitarian law. In other words, primary responsibility by way of effective control is always accompanied by independent, secondary obligations.[2207]

Second, the Venice Commission has expressed the opinion that:

> Not all acts by KFOR troops which happen in the course of an operation "under the unified command and control" ... of a NATO Commander must be attributed in international law to NATO but they can also be attributed to their country of origin (...). Thus, acts by troops in the context of a NATO-led operation cannot simply all be attributed either to NATO or to the individual troop-contributing states.[*] There

---

Between the United Nations and Member States Contributing Personnel and Equipment to the United Nations Peace-keeping Operation (UN Doc. A/46/185, 23 May 1991, Annex), provides that ""*During the period of their assignment to [the UN operation], the personnel made available by [the Participating State] shall remain in their national service but shall be under the command of the [UN] .... Accordingly, the [UN Secretary-General] shall have full authority over the deployment, organization, conduct and direction of [UN operation], including the personnel made available by [the Participating State]*", in practice nations certainly do not cede more than operational command to the UN. See also M. Frostad, *supra* note 2024, p. 313. H. Krieger, *supra* note 2011, pp. 677–687, considers that in UN operations the UN is responsible but in NATO operations not NATO but rather the participating States, justifying the difference despite similar transfers of command on the basis on perceived differences in the envisaged consequences as to the mission's external relations. There may be some truth to the latter but it is doubtful whether the difference is significant (see, e.g. the conclusions of SOFAs by the EU and NATO), and even if it is, whether it can be invoked against third parties. In contrast, D. Lorenz, *Der territoriale Anwendungsbereich der Grund- und Menschenrechte – zugleich ein Beitrag zum Individualschutz in bewaffneten Konflikten*, Berlin, Berliner Wissenschafts-Verlag, 2005, pp. 249–293, seems to argue for at least primary Member State responsibility even in UN operations (and seems to be of the view that the UN's acceptance of its responsibility is fine only as long as it ensures that adequate compensation is paid, *id.*, pp. 287–289). There is some support for Member State responsibility in *Bici and Bici v. Ministry of Defence*, 7 April 2004, 2004 EWHC 786 (QB), available online at www.hmcourts-service.gov.uk/judgmentsfiles/j2458/bici-v-mod.htm, §2 ("*The defendant has conceded that it is vicariously liable for any wrongs committed by any of the soldiers. The Crown retained command of the British forces notwithstanding that they were acting under the auspices of the U.N.*"), although this case concerned damages under private (international) law. Compare J. Cerone, 'Human Dignity in the Line of Fire: The Application of International Human Rights Law during Armed Conflict, Occupation, and Peace Operations', 39 *Vanderbilt J.T.L.* 2006, pp. 1456–1457 and 1508–1509. With regard to the EU, see also M. Zwanenburg, *supra* note 1997, pp. 403–406. This is not to say that Participating States may not have their own responsibilities *in addition* to those of the organization, see especially *supra*, Chapter 7.H and Section F of this chapter.

2207 2004 *Final Report on the Accountability of International Organisations* (available online at www.ila-hq.org), p. 24.

> may even be difficult intermediate cases, such as when soldiers are acting on the specific orders of their national commanders which are, however, themselves partly in execution of directives issued by the KFOR commander and partly within the exercise of their remaining scope of discretion.
>
> [*] It is clear, for example, that if the KFOR Commander orders different national contingents to establish a certain number of roadblocks at certain locations this measure, in itself, must be attributed to NATO. This is because the individual troop-contributing states do not have a possibility to influence such a decision by the KFOR Commander, except perhaps by expressly prohibiting their soldiers to follow the order of the KFOR commander. Therefore, should the roadblocks have been ordered for no valid reason and, as such, have caused foreseeable damage, any such damage would have to be borne by NATO and not by the state whose soldiers happened to maintain one particular roadblock. If, on the other hand, a person who happens to be searched at one of the roadblocks is mistreated by one the soldiers, it is, in principle, more plausible to attribute this act to the state of origin of the misbehaving soldiers because in the situation they acted under the supervision and the responsibility of their national commander. In such a situation it is conceivable that jurisdiction of the ECHR is ultimately established after an exhaustion of the judicial remedies provided in the state of the country of origin of the KFOR troops in question.[2208]

This latter opinion seems to fairly correctly apply the effective control test. However, the view expressed on the last example which is quoted here, the mistreatment, is not necessarily convincing in that it would be conduct in direct violation of the NATO commander's instructions (mistreatment is always prohibited by instructions from that level) but not based on national discretionary implementation and hence attributable to NATO rather than the sending State.[2209] In contrast, the failure to exercise disciplinary powers in response may be a distinct violation which would be attributable to the sending State since that is its power and responsibility.

However, according to the 2007 decision of the European Court of Human Rights in joined case *Behrami & Saramati*, if the operation is mandated under Chapter VII UN Charter, the conduct may even be attributable to the UN.[2210]

2208 Opinion No. 280/2004, *Opinion on Human Rights in Kosovo: Possible Establishment on Review Mechanisms*, CDL-AD (2004)033, 11 October 2004, p. 18, §79.

2209 In this sense also Häussler, pp. 153–154, who submits that there is organization responsibility for decisions of their organs and superior commanders as well as lower commanders when they merely apply decisions taken by them but Member State responsibility where lower commanders have discretion that is linked to their sending State's domestic law and policy. This may best reflect where effective control lies but means the test can only be applied on a case-by-case basis, even within a given operation.

2210 ECtHR, decision of 31 May 2007 in joined cases *Behrami and Behrami v. France* (No. 71412/01) and *Saramati v. France, Germany and Norway* (No. 78166/01) concerning the NATO and UN missions in Kosovo. In particular, the Court held that conduct by forces under operational control of NATO (KFOR) was in principle attributable to the UN because it considered that

This is questionable as the Security Council in fact hardly exercises any meaningful control and certainly no effective control.[2211] Indeed, this decision,

the UN (Security Council) "*retained ultimate authority and control*" (§§121–143). In contrast, the Council of Europe's Venice Commission had expressed the view that the attribution of KFOR acts was a complex matter, implicating NATO and the Participating States but not the UN, see *supra* note 2208 and the accompanying text.

2211 In the same sense, K.M. Larsen, 'Attribution of Conduct in Peace Operations: The "Ultimate Authority and Control" Test', 19 *E.J.I.L.* 2008, pp. 509–531. The Court therefore seems to have used a very low threshold of effective control which does not seem to be the one endorsed by the ILC or the ILA. The latter, in its 2004 report, *supra* note 2207, p. 24, states that "*The obligation to abide by international humanitarian law rests wholly on the State when the armed forces remain under its command and control, while the IO that has granted the authorisation, has the special responsibility to ensure respect for international humanitarian law by the State*". Similarly, L. Condorelli, *supra* note 2185, p. 48, also considers that in the case of a mere UN Security Council authorization, the primary responsibility under the LOAC lies with the executing actors while the UN has the obligation to ensure that the executors respect their obligations, as does A. Geslin, 'Réflexions sur la repartition de la responsabilité entre l'organisation internationale et ses Etats membres', 109 *R.G.D.I.P.* 2005, pp. 554–555 ("*il semble désormais assez clairement établi que, lorsque l'opération n'est pas menée sous l'autorité des Nations Unies, le comportement des forces doit être impute aux Etats participants et non à l'organisation, même si celle-ci a autorisé l'opération*"). The Venice Commission (opinion *supra* note 2208, p. 18, §79) was of the view that KFOR actions were attributable to NATO and/or the Participating States but not to the UN. U. Erberich, *Auslandseinsätze der Bundeswehr und Europäische Menschenrechtskonvention*, Cologne, Carl Heymanns, 2004, pp. 64–75, regards the Participating States as responsible when there is only a UN authorization (he sees the UN as exclusively responsible in traditional peacekeeping operations (pp. 75–96) and Participating States exclusively or jointly with the UN or NATO in modern UN or NATO peace operations (pp. 96–156)). See also *Bici and Bici v. Ministry of Defence*, *supra* note 2206, §2 (attribution to the Participating State accepted by the UK though under private law). Kolb, Poretto & Vité , pp. 285–288 even reject NATO responsibility as they believe that NATO has only a coodinating role and consider Participating States to be responsible. T. Christakis & K. Bannelier, *supra* note 2153, pp. 498–527 rightly mention the "*all necessary measures*" (or equivalent) formula as a key factor of discretion as well as a complete freedom as to planning, commanding and conducting operations (pp. 510–512), consider that the only way for the Security Council to be really informed may be by co-deployment (pp. 516–519) and point to the possibility of revoking or changing a mandate and, in order to avoid a "reverse veto" on this point, time limited mandates or defined end states (pp. 519–526). Compare U. Villani, 'Les rapports entre l'ONU et les organisations régionales dans le domaine du maintien de la paix', 290 *Rec. Cours* 2001, pp. 352–353, who sees decisional control for the Security Council rather than operational control in case of authorizations, in particular through modification or termination of a mandate, but admits (at p. 424) that this entails the risk that such control may lead to a lack of control, e.g. if a permanent member of the Security Council is a member of the authorized organization. E. de Wet, 'The Relationship between the Security Council and Regional Organizations during Enforcement Action under Chapter VII of the United Nations Charter', 71 *Nordic J.I.L.* 2002, pp. 10–20 and 36–37, argues that the Security Council must retain overall command and control (because it cannot delegate the discretionary power which States have delegated to it) and sees prior authorization, a limited mandate (and a restrictive interpretation where the mandate is vague or broad) and adequate reporting as means to ensure such control and adds that a time limit may be the most reliable way to ensure control but that a functional expiration may also be possible. She also argues that a mandate unlimited in time becomes illegal once it loses significant support in the Security Council. See also de Wet, pp. 256–310, especially pp. 273–275 and 297–310, also noting the difficulties which the Security Council has occasionally had in keeping this control. N. Blokker, 'The Security Council and the Use of Force: on Recent Practice', in N. Blokker & N. Schrijver (eds.), *The Security Council and the Use of Force: Theory and Reality: A Need for* and especially its reasoning on attribution, has rightly been quite severely criticized.[2212] The case of *Al-Jedda* in the UK House of Lords[2213] illustrates very well how surprising and unconvincing *Behrami & Saramati* is on this point. Based on *Behrami & Saramati*, the UK government invoked the

---

Change?, Leiden, Nijhoff, 2005, p. 24 notes that the most concrete form of Security Council control is the time limit usually attached to an authorization. Notwithstanding this criticism, it should be noted, as mentioned by J.-M. Thouvenin, 'Article 103', in COT & PELLET, pp. 2137–2138, that the ECJ has held that damage suffered as a consequence of EC sanctions adopted pursuant to sanctions imposed by the UN Security Council would not be attributable to the EC but only to the UN; see Case T-184/95 (*Dorsch Consult Ingenieurgesellschaft mbH v Council of the European Union and Commission of the European Communities*, Judgment of 28 April 1998, §§73–74; the appeals judgment, Case C-237/98, *Dorsch Consult Ingenieurgesellschaft mbH v. Council of the European Union and Commission of the European Communities*, Judgment of 15 June 2000, did not address this point). However, this situation is arguably different in that sanctions are more precisely defined and compulsory whereas authorizations for the use of force are usually very general as to the means and not compulsory.

2212 The titles of some of the annotations are quite clear; see, e.g. P. Klein, 'Responsabilité pour les faits commis dans le cadre d'opérations de paix étendue du pouvoir de contrôle de la Cour européenne des droits de l'homme: quelques considérations critiques sur l'arrêt Behrami et Saramati', 53 *A.F.D.I.* 2007, pp. 43–64; B. Knoll, 'Rights without Remedies: The European Court's Failure to Close the Human Rights Gap in Kosovo', 68 *Z.a.ö.R.V.* 2008, pp. 431–451; H. Krieger, 'A Credibility Gap: The Behrami and Saramati Decision of the European Court of Human Rights', 13 *International Peacekeeping* 2009, pp. 159–180 and M. Milanovic & T. Papic, 'As Bad as It Gets: The European Court of Human Rights' Behrami and Saramati and General International Law', 58 *I.C.L.Q.* 2009, pp. 267–296. For further annotations, see P. Bodeau-Livinec, G.P. Buzzini & S. Villalpando, 'Agim Behrami & Bekir Behrami v. France; Ruzhdi Saramati v. France, Germany & Norway. Joined App. Nos. 71412/01 & 78166/01: European Court of Human Rights (Grand Chamber), May 2, 2007', 102 *A.J.I.L.* 2008, pp. 323–331; A. Breitegger, 'Sacrificing the Effectiveness of the European Convention on Human Rights on the Altar of the Effective Functioning of Peace Support Operations: A Critique of Behrami & Saramati and Al Jedda', 11 *International Community Law Review* 2009, pp. 155–183; G. Hafner, 'The ECHR Torn between the United Nations and the States: The Behrami and Saramati Case', in A. Fischer-Lescano *et al.* (eds.), *Frieden in Freiheit / Peace in Liberty / Paix en liberté: Festschrift für Michael Bothe zum 70. Geburtstag*, Baden-Baden, Nomos, 2008, pp. 103–121; P. Lagrange, 'Responsabilité des Etats pour actes accomplis en application du Chapitre VII de la Charte des Nations Unies. Observations à propos de la décision de la Cour européenne des Droits de l'Homme (Grand Chambre) sur le recevabilité des requêtes Behrami et Bahrami c. France et Saramati c. Allemagne, France et Norvège, 31 mai 2007', 112 *R.G.D.I.P.* 2008, pp. 85–110; C. Laly-Chevalier, 'Les opérations militaires et civiles des Nations Unies et la Convention européenne des droits de l'homme (Cour. eur. dr. h., gde ch., décision du 31 mai 2007, Behrami et Saramati)', 40 *B.T.I.R./R.B.D.I.* 2007, pp. 627–661; K.M. Larsen, *supra* note 2211, pp. 509–531; F. Naert, 'ECtHR Dismisses Kosovo Mission Cases', April-May-June 2007 *Newsletter of the International Society for Military Law & the Law of War*, pp. 10–12 (archived at http://home.scarlet.be/~ismllw/publication/bulletin_info.htm); P. Palchetti, 'Azioni di forze istituite o autorizzate delle Nazioni Unite davanti alla Corte europea dei diritti dell'uomo: i casi Behrami e Seramati', 90 *Rivista di diritto internazionale* 2007, pp. 681–704 and S. Valenti, 'La questione dell'applicabilità della Convenzione europea dei diritti dell'uomo alle forze di mantenimento della pace in Kosovo: i casi Behrami e Saramati', 7(1) *Pace diritti umani* 2008, pp. 81–91.

2213 House of Lords, *R (on the application of Al-Jedda) (FC) (Appellant) v Secretary of State for Defence (Respondent)* ([2007] UKHL 58, available online at www.publications.parliament.uk/pa/ld200708/ldjudgmt/jd071212/jedda-1.htm), 12 December 2007. See the annotations *supra* note 2161.

argument that the conduct of UK forces in Iraq (in the post-occupation period in which there was a clear UN mandate) was attributable to the UN and not to the UK even though it had not raised this in the lower courts - presumably because it did not seem plausible. The law Lords rejected this argument by distinguishing the case from *Behrami & Saramati*, but not without difficulty[2214] and with one particularly persuasive dissent.[2215]

The ILC's special rapporteur on the responsibility of international organizations has commented upon the *Behrami & Saramati* decision as follows, in terms that do not require any further comment:

> 26. ... The Court quoted *in extenso* Article 5 of the Commission's draft and summarized various paragraphs of the related commentary. The Court's decision did not contain any criticism of the criterion that was stated by the Commission; however, the Court made use of a different notion of control for reaching its decision. It considered that the decisive point was whether "the United Nations Security Council retained ultimate authority and control so that operational command only was delegated". While acknowledging "the effectiveness or unity of NATO command in *operational* matters", the Court noted that the presence of KFOR in Kosovo was based on a resolution adopted by the Security Council and concluded that "KFOR was exercising lawfully delegated Chapter VII powers of the UNSC so that the impugned action was, in principle, 'attributable' to the UN within the meaning of the word outlined [in Article 3 of the ILC draft]". With regard to UNMIK, the Court stated that it was "a subsidiary organ of the UN created under Chapter VII of the Charter so that the impugned inaction was, in principle, 'attributable' to the UN in the same sense". Several commentators rightly observed that, had the Court applied the criterion of effective control set out by the Commission, it would have reached the different conclusion that the conduct of national contingents allocated to KFOR had to be attributed either to the sending State or to NATO. ...
>
> 30. ... no change should be suggested to Article 5. It is true that the European Court of Human Rights applied a different criterion for attribution and reached, ..., a conclusion that differed from the one that would have been reached on the basis of Article 5, as was specified in the commentary. Without denying the importance of this jurisprudence, it would be difficult to accept, simply on the strength of the judgment in *Behrami and Saramati*, the criterion there applied as a potentially universal rule. Also as a matter of policy, the approach taken by the European Court of Human Rights is unconvincing. It would lead to attributing to the United Nations

[2214] F. Messineo, *supra* note 2161, pp. 43–47, sees an "*uncomfortable distinguishing*" from *Behrami & Saramati.*

[2215] Lord Roger dissented, rejecting the distinction (see §§58–111) and *inter alia* arguing at §100 that the Iraq mandate's time limit arguably entails that the UNSC had greater control over this mission than over KFOR.

conduct which the organization has not specifically authorized and of which it may have little knowledge or no knowledge at all. It is therefore not surprising that in his report of June 2008 on the United Nations Interim Administration Mission in Kosovo, the United Nations Secretary-General distanced himself from that criterion and stated: "It is understood that the international responsibility of the United Nations will be limited to the extent of its effective operational control".[2216]

Obviously a sending State will be responsible if its forces act pursuant to national instructions in violation of EU operational control.[2217]

The EU's command and control over its operations means that the EU exercises powers over armed forces that may be affected by the LOAC, if applicable. For instance, the LOAC, if applicable, will obviously have an impact on the rules of engagement (ROE) that impose limits on the use of force.[2218] Therefore, in

2216 UN Doc. A/CN.4/610 of 27 March 2009, §§26 and 30 (footnotes omitted; see also §27 with references to other ECtHR case law confirming *Behrami & Saramati*).

2217 Similarly, with regard to the UN, Zwanenburg, p. 111.

2218 Within NATO, ROE are defined as "*Directives issued by competent military authority which specify the circumstances and limitations under which forces will initiate and/or continue combat engagement with other forces encountered*" (NATO, NATO Glossary of Term and Definitions, AAP-6(2006), available online at www.nato.int/docu/stanag/aap006/aap6.htm, p. 2-R-8). It may be added that both in NATO and the EU, ROE are approved by a political authority (respectively the North Atlantic Council and the Council or PSC) and are then implemented by military commanders. Both organizations have a (classified) doctrine on ROE (MC 362/1(2003) for NATO) and both include a catalogue of possible ROE. This doctrine and catalogue serve as the basis for selecting the 'ROE profile' (defined by AAP-6(2006) as "*A list of rules of engagement selected for a force assigned to a particular role or operation within defined time and space boundaries*") applicable in a given operation. For the UN's (provisional) ROE catalogue and examples of ROE profiles in UN operations, see T. Findlay, *supra* note 2029, pp. 411–427. On ROE, see generally and for further references J. Boddens Hosang, 'Rules of engagement: het politiek-juridische struikelblok voor de militaire commandant', 96 *Militair Rechtelijk Tijdschrift* 2003, pp. 354–370; G. Coolen, 'Geweldsinstructies vanuit strafrechtelijk oogpunt bezien', 96 *Militair Rechtelijk Tijdschrift* 2003, pp. 376–390; D.-J. Dieben & T. Dieben, *When Does War Become Crime? Aspects of the Criminal Case against Eric O.*', Nijmegen, Wolf Legal Publishers, 2005; C. Gossiaux, 'Les règles d'engagement norme juridique nouvelle?', 40(1/2) *R.D.M.D.G.* 2001, pp. 159–179; A.S. Paphiti, 'Rules of Engagement within Multinational Land Operations', 89 *Militair Rechtelijk Tijdschrift* 1996, pp. 1–12; Studiecentrum voor Militair Recht en Oorlogsrecht (ed.), *De inzetregels. Nieuwe juridische norm? Studiedag van 4 mei 2001/ Règles d'engagement. Norme juridique nouvelle? Journée d'étude du 4 mai 2001*, Brussels, 2001; F. Thomas, 'VN "Rules of Engagement": een strafrechtelijke benadering', in G.J.M. Corstens & M.S. Groenhuijsen (eds.), *Rede en recht: opstellen ter gelegenheid van het afscheid van Prof. mr. N. Keijzer van de Katholieke Universiteit Brabant*, Deventer, Gouda Quint, 2000, pp. 91–101; M. Ubeda-Saillard, 'L'invocabilité en droit interne des règles d'engagements applicables aux opérations militaires multinationales', 108 *R.G.D.I.P.* 2004, pp. 149–176; J.A. van Diepenbrugge, 'Geweldgebruik in het kader van vredesoperaties: leidt de integratie van politieke, juridische en operationele aspecten in de Rules of Engagement in het kader van vredesoperaties tot vage en multi-interpretabele regels?', 96 *Militair Rechtelijk Tijdschrift* 2003, pp. 371–375 and G.A. Wolusky, 'Combat Crime: Rules of Engagement in Military Courts-Martial', 38(1) *R.D.M.D.G.* 1999, pp. 91–118.

addition to any obligations that continue to rest on States providing armed forces to EU-led operations, the EU has its own international LOAC obligations. The extent of these obligations will be explored in the next subsection.

I will not address in detail how the EU gives or could give effect to these obligations.[2219] It may suffice to point out that it largely does so through relevant provisions in the Operation Plan and Rules of Engagement on the basis of existing EU doctrine.[2220] In addition, the Operation and/or Force Commander issue further instructions, including Standard Operating Procedures (SOPs), which may also give effect to LOAC obligations, e.g. concerning detention of non-mission personnel.[2221] Obviously, as discipline and jurisdiction over the forces remains with their sending States, the EU has few competences in these matters, but it could require Member States to investigate alleged crimes or misconduct and to report on this.[2222] Finally, from an EU law perspective, one

---

See also the section on rules of engagement in the questionnaire, general report and country reports in S. Horvat (ed.), *The Rule of Law in Peace Operations. Seventeenth International Congress, The Hague – 16–21 May 2006. Recueil XVII of the International Society for Military Law and the Law of War / La Règle de Droit dans les Opérations de Paix. Dix-septième Congrès International, La Haye (Pays-bas) – 16–21 Mai 2006. Recueil XVII de la Société internationale de Droit militaire et de Droit de la Guerre*, Brussels, Printing House of Defence, 2006. It may be noted that the Institute of International Humanitarian Law (Sanremo, www.iihl.org/) is preparing a public *ROE Manual* for training purposes.

2219 For some aspects, see F. Naert, 'Instruction, Dissemination and Implementation of IHL in Peace Operations. An EU Perspective', in the proceedings of the XXXIst Round Table on Current Issues of International Humanitarian Law on 'International Humanitarian Law and Human Rights in Peace Operations', organized by the ICRC and the International Institute of Humanitarian Law in Sanremo on 4–6 September 2008, pp. 348–350 (available online at www.icrc.org/Web/eng/siteeng0.nsf/htmlall/san-remo-round-table-report-060908/$File/sanremo-2008_Peace%20Ops.pdf).

2220 See also G.-J. Van Hegelsom, *supra* note 1997, p. 115.

2221 Interestingly, see in this respect Pledge P091 made by the EU Member States at the 30th International Conference of the Red Cross and Red Crescent in 2007, which contains a mix of commitments undertaken by the Member States and commitments undertaken by the EU itself concerning 'Fundamental Procedural and other Guarantees' (see www.icrc.org/applic/p130e.nsf/pbk/PCOE-79CKFC?openDocument&section=PBP).

2222 Ensuring adequate investigation and prosecution by sending States has proved to be a problem in the UN context and measures to improve the situation are being discussed at the time of writing. See, e.g. *Report of the Group of Legal Experts on making the standards contained in the Secretary-General's bulletin [on special measures for protection from sexual exploitation and sexual abuse (ST/SGB/2003/13)] binding on contingent members and standardizing the norms of conduct so that they are applicable to all categories of peacekeeping personnel*, UN Doc. A/61/645, and *Report of the Group of Legal Experts on ensuring the accountability of United Nations staff and experts on mission with respect to criminal acts committed in peacekeeping operations*, UN Doc. A/60/980. See also P. Rowe, 'Military Misconduct During International Armed Operations: "Bad Apples" or Systemic Failure?', 13 *J.C.S.L.* 2008, pp. 165–189.

might apply by analogy the requirement of close and loyal cooperation between the EC and its Member States in their external relations.[2223]

A question to be raised here is what consequences there are for EU Member States or third States participating in an EU-led operation when that operation, and hence the EU, becomes a party to the conflict. The position of the EU as a distinct international legal person theoretically means it might be a party to an armed conflict without its Member States being a party to that conflict. Surprisingly, the question does not really seem to have been studied in respect of the UN or NATO.[2224] Presumably, this results from a reluctance to acknowledge that international organizations may be a party to an armed conflict even while admitting that they may be bound by some LOAC obligations.[2225] Moreover, the fact that in most peace operations, the fighting only takes place in the host nation

2223 This argument was made by V. Falco at a colloquium in Nice on 'Le droit international humanitaire et l'Union européenne' on 18–19 June 2009 in her intervention entitled 'L'applicabilité du DIH à l'UE: évolutions normatives' (the proceedings of this colloquium will be published by Pedone). On this duty, see Article 10 EC Treaty and Article 11(2) EU Treaty and ECJ, Opinion 1/91, *Draft agreement between the Community, on the one hand, and the countries of the EFTA, on the other, relating to the creation of the European Economic Area*, 14 December 1991, §§36–38 as well as ECJ (CFI), Case T-228/02, *Organisation des Modjahedines du peuple d'Iran v Council*, judgement of 12 December 2006, §123 (for an application in the Third Pillar).

2224 David, pp. 211–212 briefly discusses part of the problem and mentions that one might argue that in an armed conflict between an international organization and a State, only customary international law would apply, but regards this view as too restrictive and debatable, submitting that the Member States are the real belligerent parties and that their treaty obligations should be applicable. C. Emanuelli, *supra* note 1998, pp. 63–64, seems to consider that the UN could become a party itself as he writes it would substitute the Member States as a party to the armed conflict. C. Greenwood, 'The Applicability of International Humanitarian Law and the Law of Neutrality to the Kosovo Campaign', in A.E. Wall (ed.), *supra* note 2164, pp. 39–40, considers that in operation Allied Force NATO command was irrelevant and that the Member States (implementing the NATO decisions) were the parties to the armed conflict with the Federal Republic of Yugoslavia. However, he does not fully look into whether the requirement that the operation be conducted in conformity with the LOAC might have referred to NATO's proper obligations under the LOAC or may not necessarily have meant that the Member States became a party to the conflict. Also, he seems to leave open whether NATO command may have an impact on State responsibility. J. Gardam, *supra* note 2154, p. 317 surprisingly regards it as "*manifestly incorrect to argue that States supplying the forces are each in a state of armed conflict with the State(s) against whom the action is taken*" including with regard to UN authorized operations.

2225 See, e.g the UN view described in R. Zacklin, *supra* note 2197, p. 51 (stating that the argument that the UN cannot be a party to a conflict remains valid) and D. Shraga, *supra* note 1998 (in L. Condorelli, A.-M. La Rosa & S. Scherrer (eds.)), p. 323. See also S. Lepper, *supra* note 2045, pp. 399–406, citing the ICRC's view that the prevailing view in the international community was that the UN could never be a party to an armed conflict and noting that the US delegation to the conference negotiating the 1994 UN Convention on the Safety of UN and Associated Personnel (*supra* note 2045) took the view that the UN could be a *de facto* party despite not legally being a party (p. 404) – though one may wonder what such a *de facto* party would mean.

and is usually a non-international armed conflict against a party with inferior military capabilities, diminishes the practical importance of the question. Nevertheless, it might be relevant, especially in an international armed conflict with a State that has some capability to strike back in one way or another (e.g. at international shipping in its vicinity). Although it seems unlikely that the EU would be engaged in such a conflict (and if it were, any counter-attack by the opposing State might well lead to NATO involvement in collective self-defence), this cannot be excluded.

In respect of the UN, there seems to be hardly any evidence that the involvement of UN blue helmets in an armed conflict means that all UN Member States – or all UN Security Council Member States – become a party to that conflict (in fact, that would also mean that the targeted State would be engaged in an armed conflict against itself, which would be rather absurd), though there has rarely been an occasion where the issue could arise.[2226] On the other hand, the concurrent and continuing LOAC obligations of Participating States (see the previous section) imply that it is not solely the organization which is a party to the armed conflict. The difficulty is the position of Member States that do not participate in an operation (something which is both feasible and current in the EU; see *supra* Chapter 3, and also in the UN). Perhaps the question may be answered by looking at how the notion of territory and nationality could be applied to international organizations under the LOAC. The way this appears to be applied in other EC/EU contexts[2227] is that these notions cover respectively the territory of the EU's Member States (except those excluded from the scope of application of EU law) and any nationals of a Member State, as in fact formalized through EU citizenship.[2228] This would suggest that all Member States would necessarily become parties to the armed conflict, at least *de facto* through the coverage of their territories and nationals.[2229] Yet the matter seems more complex when it comes to defining the armed forces and combatants of the EU. By

[2226] If only because a government targeted by a UN authorized military enforcement action, which is rare in any event, will most likely direct any resistance it might have at those forces actually attacking it.

[2227] E.g. the law of the sea or competition law. See also P. Torremans, 'Extraterritoriality in Human Rights', in N. Neuwahl & A. Rosas (eds.), *The European Union and Human Rights*, The Hague, Nijhoff, 1995, pp. 281–296, discussing competition law at pp. 285–289 and human rights at pp. 289–296 and pleading for a consistent approach towards extraterritoriality. With regard to extraterritoriality of EC/EU human rights law, see also A. Fischer-Lescano & T. Tohidipur, 'Europäisches Grenzkontrollregime: Rechtsrahmen der europäischen Grenzschutzagentur FRONTEX', 67 *Z.a.ö.R.V.* 2007, pp. 1242–1250.

[2228] See Articles 17–22 EC Treaty. Article 17(1) provides that "*Every person holding the nationality of a Member State shall be a citizen of the Union*".

[2229] Possibly with the exception of Denmark given its opt-out of military cooperation in the ESDP.

analogy with the requirement of belonging to a (State) party to the conflict,[2230] it can be argued that these would only cover the armed forces under EU command, i.e. those which the Member States have put at the EU's disposal at the given time. However, this would seem to lead to a questionable result in that it would shield from attack Member States' armed forces not under EU command but which may well subsequently be transferred to EU command. This would not only pose the practical difficulty that the opponent is unlikely to know exactly which forces are under EU command or scheduled to be under such command, but also would seem extremely unfair. It therefore does not appear to be an acceptable view. Another approach is to look at the decision-making: since EU operations require unanimity, with the exception of Denmark and constructive abstention, all Member States have voted in favour of a military operation. I have argued above (Chapter 7.H) that such a vote is attributable to the Member States. One could argue that the vote for an operation that will entail becoming engaged in an armed conflict makes the State casting that vote a party to that conflict, even if it does not engage in actual hostilities, although this is certainly not evident. If that would be the case, this would only leave open the status of a State availing itself of constructive abstention. I would submit that such a State would not be a party to the conflict.

Finally, by virtue of its obligation to respect and ensure respect for its LOAC obligations,[2231] the EU is probably obliged to ensure that EU forces acting in support of operations by another international organization, even when included in the latter's chain of command,[2232] respect both the EU's and the sending State's LOAC obligations.

2. THE SOURCES AND EXTENT OF THE EU'S LOAC OBLIGATIONS

I will treat, one by one, the sources of EU obligations identified in Chapter 7 as applied to the LOAC: treaties concluded by the EU, binding unilateral acts, the

2230 See *supra* note 2035.

2231 As pointed out by R. Murphy, *supra* note 2019, p. 165, the ICTY held in *Tadic* (*The Prosecuter v. Dusko Tadic a/k/a/ 'Dule'*, ICTY- 94-1, 2 October 1995, §93) that the obligation "*to respect and ensure respect*" for the Geneva Conventions has become a general principle of humanitarian law which "*lays down an obligation that is incumbent, not only on States, but also on other international entities including the United Nations*". Similarly, L. Boisson de Chazournes & L. Condorelli, *supra* note 2181, p. 70, write that "*It is now widely accepted that the obligation contained in common Article 1 is binding on all States and competent international organizations*".

2232 As seems to be the case for the AMIS supporting mission; see *supra*, Chapter 3, note 639 and the accompanying text.

EU's constituent instruments and proper rules; other agreements between the EU Member States binding the EU; provisions of other international instruments and judicial decisions binding by virtue of any of the above sources; customary international law; general principles of international law; general principles of EC/EU law; *ius cogens* and (provisions of) treaties concluded by one or more of its Member States where the conditions for 'substitution' are met. Furthermore, I will briefly look at the position of forces provided by third States.

i. Treaties Concluded by the EU

Obviously, the EU would be bound by any agreement which it concludes and which contains LOAC obligations. However, since the EU is not a party to any LOAC instrument, this entails no obligations.

In contrast, there is more potential for the EU to be bound by LOAC obligations contained in mission-specific agreements which it might conclude, especially in a SOFA. However, the survey of SOFAs concluded so far has revealed that these agreements have rarely included a provision on the LOAC. In fact, this has only been the case for the AMIS Supporting Mission via the AU SOFA and for EUFOR DR Congo via the MONUC SOFA.[2233]

In addition, the EU's possible accession to the ECHR under the Lisbon Treaty[2234] might include a binding to some LOAC obligations (see the link between both regimes discussed below in subsection iii).

The EU therefore seems to partially ignore the ILA's recommendation that "*[International Organizations] should include in the Regulations of the Force and in the Agreements concluded between [International Organizations], troop-contributing States, and troop-receiving States the obligation to observe the applicable principles and rules of international humanitarian law*".[2235] It is submitted that in respect of operations in which the LOAC is or might be applicable, this attitude should be reconsidered.

ii. Binding Unilateral Acts

The EU could unilaterally bind itself to respect certain LOAC obligations.[2236] However, to my knowledge there have been no such acts. The nearest thing to

2233 See *supra*, Chapter 4.B.2. Presumably, the EU's acceptance to apply these agreements would mean it is also bound by the obligations contained therein.

2234 See *supra*, Chapter 7.G.3 *in fine*.

2235 ILA, 2004 *Final Report on the Accountability of International Organisations* (available online at www.ila-hq.org), p. 23.

2236 Compare David, p. 209, with regard to the UN.

such a unilateral act is probably the European Union Guidelines on promoting compliance with international humanitarian law (IHL),[2237] which, while essentially directed at promoting respect for the LOAC by third parties, also state that the "*commitment of the EU and its Member States to IHL ... extends to measures taken by the EU and its Member States to ensure compliance with IHL in their own conduct, including by their own forces*".[2238] However, it is unlikely, given this very general and vague content and the nature of guidelines, that any specific obligations can result from this. In addition, the document seems to primarily have an internal focus.

There was an attempt to specifically address the application of the LOAC to EU-led forces during the Spanish Presidency of the Council in 2002, but it did not lead to a significant result. The outcome was the Salamanca Presidency Declaration,[2239] which stated that the experts present at the seminar leading to the declaration "*invited the Presidency to report to the European Council a number of* considerations" (emphasis added). Moreover, the declaration states that the mentioning of a number of selected topics "*should not be construed as indicating the development of new international obligations*". While the declaration thus clearly cannot serve as a legal instrument or as generating legal obligations, it is interesting to cite some of its content:

> When conducting operations pursuant to Article 17, paragraph 2 of the Treaty on European Union, Forces participating in an EU-led operation will be called upon to respect and apply international law, including international humanitarian law, as appropriate. It follows that the political and military structures of the Union, assisted by experts in international law, should ensure that in exercising the strategic direction and political control, relevant rules of international law, including international humanitarian law are duly taken into account. Participants agreed that although the Union is not a party to, in particular, the Geneva Conventions and their additional Protocols, all measures should be taken in order to assure that EU-led forces are in a position to respect and ensure respect for the relevant international law provisions.
> ...
> 1. Respect for International Humanitarian Law is relevant in EU-led operations when the situation they are operating in constitutes an armed conflict to which the forces

---

2237 *O.J. C* 327, 23 December 2005, p. 4. Compare more generally R. Desgagné, 'European Union Practice in the Field of International Humanitarian Law: An Overview', in V. Kronenberger (ed.), *The European Union and the International Legal Order: Discord or Harmony?*, The Hague, T.M.C. Asser Press, 2001, pp. 455–477.

2238 The note to this sentence states that "*All EU Member States are Parties to the Geneva Conventions and their Additional Protocols and thus under the obligation to abide by their rules*".

2239 The outcome of the international humanitarian law European seminar of 22–24 April 2002 in Salamanca, Doc. DIH/Rev.01.Corrl, on file with the author. See also N. Ronzitti, *supra* note 1997, pp. 178–181 and M. Zwanenburg, *supra* note 1997, p. 402.

> are party. The existence of such situation must be determined on a case by case basis depending on the nature and circumstances of each operation.
> 2. The responsibility for complying with International Humanitarian Law, in cases where it applies, in a European Union led-operation, rests primarily with the State to which the troops belong. In exercising the strategic direction and political control, the European Union will ensure that all relevant rules of international law, including humanitarian law as appropriate are duly taken into account.
> 3. The organs in charge of the European security and defence policy should be adequately supported to ensure awareness and knowledge of the relevant rules of international law.

The only apparent follow up is a short paragraph in the Presidency Conclusion of the 19–20 June 2003 Thessaloniki European Council stating that "*The European Council stresses the importance of national armed forces observing applicable humanitarian law as well as the weight it attaches to dialogue with the ICRC on this matter*".[2240] Clearly, neither instrument amounts to a unilateral act binding the EU.

Similarly, the pledges made by the EU Member States jointly at the International Conferences of the Red Cross and the Red Crescent are probably not intended to be legally binding unilateral acts.[2241] Furthermore, they are not made by the EU as such but by its Member States jointly.[2242]

iii. The EU's Constituent Instruments and Proper Rules

In Chapter 7 (Sections F.2.i and G.3), it has been discussed how the ECJ has bound the EC to human rights via general principles of EC law and that this binding was subsequently explicitly laid down in Article 6 EU Treaty[2243] (and included, subject to some modifications, in the Lisbon Treaty). I have also argued there that in respect of human rights, this reasoning may be extended to the EU.[2244]

2240 Doc. 11638, 1 October 2003, §74. See also N. Ronzitti, *supra* note 1997, pp. 178–181.

2241 For an overview of pledges made at the 30th such Conference in 2007, see www.icrc.org/applic/p130e.nsf/va_navPage/POAI?openDocument&count=-1.

2242 See, e.g. Pledge P091 at the 30th Conference in 2007, which however, contains a mix of commitments undertaken by the Member States and commitments undertaken by the EU itself (see www.icrc.org/applic/p130e.nsf/pbk/PCOE-79CKFC?openDocument&section=PBP).

2243 Article 6(2) EU Treaty reads: "*The Union shall respect fundamental rights, as guaranteed by the European Convention for the Protection of Human Rights and Fundamental Freedoms signed in Rome on 4 November 1950 and as they result from the constitutional traditions common to the Member States, as general principles of Community law*".

2244 See especially Chapter 7.F.2.i, note 1773 and the accompanying text.

The question which arises here is whether Article 6 EU Treaty (and its successor provision in the Lisbon Treaty), although textually only covering human rights, also covers some rules of the LOAC. I submit that this is indeed the case.[2245] A first argument in support of this view is the close connection between human rights and the LOAC that exists in situations of armed conflict. This relationship is explored more extensively below (see Chapter 9.D) and it may suffice here to give the example of the right to life. This right, protected by Article 2 ECHR, is not derogable pursuant to Article 15(2) ECHR except "*in respect of deaths resulting from lawful acts of war*". As will be elaborated below (Chapter 9.C.2.i and 9.D), this is a reference to the LOAC, which includes more specific rules determining when killing is lawful in war. In addition, there are a few cases in which EU instruments[2246] or statements[2247] have regarded the LOAC as part of

2245 Similarly, S. Bartelt, *supra* note 1, pp. 163–164 and 181–182 (though focusing on Article 11 EU Treaty rather than Article 6; moreover, the author regards it as self-binding of the Member States since she rejects the EU's legal personality). See also the argument by Kolb, Poretto & Vité, pp. 130–132 that the LOAC strikes a balance between striving towards peace and security on the one hand and human rights on the other hand and is therefore binding on international organizations that pursue both aims. Compare A. Rosas, 'The Interrelationship between Human Rights and International Humanitarian Law', in S. Kolanowski *et al.* (eds.), *supra* note 2185, pp. 97–98, distinguishing the LOAC from human rights but noting their links.

2246 Council Regulation (EC) No 975/1999 of 29 April 1999 laying down the requirements for the implementation of development cooperation operations which contribute to the general objective of developing and consolidating democracy and the rule of law and to that of respecting human rights and fundamental freedoms and Council Regulation (EC) No 976/1999 of 29 April 1999 laying down the requirements for the implementation of Community operations, other than those of development cooperation, which, within the framework of Community cooperation policy, contribute to the general objective of developing and consolidating democracy and the rule of law and to that of respecting human rights and fundamental freedoms in third countries, *O.J. L* 120, 8 May 1999, respectively pp. 1 and 8, both 8th consideration of the preamble ("*Whereas human rights within the meaning of this Regulation should be considered to encompass respect for international humanitarian law, also taking into account the 1949 Geneva Conventions and the 1977 Additional Protocol thereto, ... and other acts of international treaty or customary law*"). See also the EU Guidelines on promoting compliance with international humanitarian law, *O.J. C* 327, 23 December 2005, p. 4, § 3. See S. Bartelt, *supra* note 1, p. 181 and A. Rosas, *supra* note 2245, pp. 97–98, who also points to the possibility of including the LOAC under the human rights clauses that normally condition EC external cooperation agreements. Compare the discussion of the LOAC as being part of the UN Charter's human rights provisions, *supra* Chapter 7.E, note 1735 and the accompanying text.

2247 Statement by Ms. Anna Sotaniemi, Legal Adviser, Permanent Mission of Finland to the UN on behalf of the EU, UNGA, 61st Session, 6th Committee, Agenda Item 75: Status of the Protocols Additional to the Geneva Conventions of 1949 and relating to the protection of victims of armed conflicts, New York (available online at www.europa-eu-un.org/articles/en/article_6382_en.htm): "*Respect for human rights and fundamental freedoms, as well as the rule of law are key principles that the European Union is founded on. These principles include the goal of promoting compliance with international humanitarian law*". See also M. Zwanenburg, *supra* note 1997, p. 400. See also the Declaration by the Presidency on behalf of the EU on the occasion of the 60th anniversary of the Geneva Conventions, 12 August 2009, www.se2009.eu/en/meetings_news/2009/8/12/declaration_by_the_presidency_on_behalf_ human rights. Moreover, given the widespread ratification of LOAC treaty obligations by the EU Member States, there is no doubt that many of these obligations are shared by the Member States and can be found in their domestic legislation as well as their treaty obligations. Furthermore, the criminalization of a number of war crimes in the ICC Statute, to which all EU Member States are a party[2248] and the constitutional anchoring of this Statute in some Member States,[2249] indicates the constitutional nature of at least some of these rules. Finally, the applicability of human rights, and by extension, part of the LOAC, in external relations, including the ESDP, is reinforced by Article 11(1) EU Treaty,[2250] which states that:

> The Union shall define and implement a common foreign and security policy covering all areas of foreign and security policy, the objectives of which shall be: – to safeguard the common values, fundamental interests, independence and integrity of the Union in conformity with the principles of the United Nations Charter; ... – to develop and consolidate democracy and the rule of law, and respect for human rights and fundamental freedoms.

The equivalent provision under the Lisbon Treaty, Article 10 A (renumbered 21) EU Treaty (see also Article III-292 EU Constitution), contains even stronger language in this respect. It reads:

> 1. The Union' action on the international scene shall be guided by the principles which have inspired its own creation, development and enlargement, and which it

---

of_the_eu_on_the_occasion_of_the_60th_anniversary_of_the_adoption_of_the_four_geneva_conventions_of_1949.

2248 The Czech Republic only ratified the ICC Statute in 2009. The ICC Statute is also mentioned by A. Rosas, *supra* note 2245, pp. 97–98 in this context. In this respect, one may wonder whether the accession of new Member States may affect negatively general principles of EU law which were previously shared by all Member States but no longer are following accession. In this case such an effect was unlikely given that there was only a sole ratification missing and that the State concerned had signed the treaty. However, in other cases the situation may be less clear, unless such principles are to be considered part of the *acquis* which acceding States must accept.

2249 See, e.g. Article 53-3 French Constitution (available online at www.conseil-constitutionnel.fr/conseil-constitutionnel/francais/la-constitution/la-constitution-du-4-octobre-1958/la-constitution-du-4-octobre-1958.5071.html). For an overview of constitutional issues related to the ICC Statute, see generally Council of Europe, Venice Commission, *Report on constitutional issues raised by the ratification of the Rome statute of the International Criminal Court*, 15 January 2001, Doc. CDL-INF(2001)001 (available online at www.venice.coe.int/docs/2001/CDL-INF(2001)001-E.asp).

2250 See S. Bartelt, *supra* note 1, pp. 163–164 and 181–182 (although the author regards it as self-binding of the Member States since she rejected the EU's legal personality) and J. Arloth & F. Seidensticker, *The ESDP Crisis Management Operations of the European Union and Human Rights*, Berlin, Deutsches Institut für Menschenrechte, April 2007 (available online at http://files.institut-fuer-menschenrechte.de/488/d65_v1_file_4649796b19cd6_Studie%20ESDP%20pdf%20version%2005-2007.pdf), p. 15.

> seeks to advance in the wider world: democracy, the rule of law, the universality and indivisibility of human rights and fundamental freedoms, respect for human dignity ... and respect for the principles of the United Nations Charter and international law.
> ...
> 2. The Union shall define and pursue common policies and actions, and shall work for a high degree of cooperation in all fields of international relations, in order to: (a) safeguard its values, ...; (b) consolidate and support democracy, the rule of law, human rights and the principles of international law; ...
> 3. The Union shall respect the principles and pursue the objectives set out in paragraphs 1 and 2 in the development and implementation of the different areas of the Union's external action covered by this Title and Part Five of the Treaty on the Functioning of the European Union, and of the external aspects of its other policies. The Union shall ensure consistency between the different areas of its external action and between these and its other policies.

This goes further than the present EU Treaty in that it not only sets out the aims to protect human rights as one of the fundamental values of the Union and to develop and consolidate respect for human rights, but also imposes human rights as a guideline for the EU's external action and, especially relevant, imposes respect for human rights in the development and implementation of this external action.

I therefore submit that a significant body of LOAC rules forms part of the general principles of EU law binding on the EU and its Member States in the implementation of EU law, including decisions on ESDP and ESDP operations.

From a historical perspective, it may be noted that the EDC Treaty stipulated that the EDC was bound by customary international humanitarian law and by Member State LOAC treaty obligations and that European defence forces were entitled to the same treatment as national armed forces.[2251]

It remains to be elaborated which LOAC rules would be part of these general principles of EU law.[2252] This exercise may perhaps be bypassed since it is argued below that the EU is in any event bound to customary international humanitarian

---

2251 EDC Treaty (French text available online at http://mjp.univ-perp.fr/europe/1952ced.htm), Article 80.

2252 Compare the discussion concerning the UN, *supra*, Chapter 7.B.2. E.g, Part X, section 28 of the Model Agreement between the United Nations and Member States Contributing Personnel and Equipment to the United Nations Peace-keeping Operation (UN Doc. A/46/185, 23 May 1991, Annex) provides that "*[The ... operation] shall observe and respect the principles and spirit of the general international conventions applicable to the conduct of military personnel. The international conventions referred to above include the four Geneva Conventions of 12 August 1949 and their Additional Protocols of 8 June 1977 and the UNESCO Convention of 14 May 1954 on the Protection of Cultural Property in the event of armed conflict.*

law, which is likely to provide a fairly extensive body of rules. However, the source discussed here could cover some rules that do not have a customary status but are widely accepted by EU Member States, e.g. some rules found in the ICC Statue.

Furthermore, inasmuch as the EC and EU Treaties bind the EU to the UN Charter,[2253] including its human rights provisions and through these possibly also part of the LOAC,[2254] this would also constitute a source of obligation for the EU.

iv. Agreements between the EU Member States Binding the EU

To my knowledge, apart from the instruments cited in the preceding subsection (which only indirectly refer to the LOAC), there have been no agreements between the Member States binding the EU to LOAC rules so far.

v. Provisions of Other International Instruments and Judicial Decisions via the Above

The cases where such binding may exist all concern the EU's constituent instruments and proper rules discussed above in subsection iii of this section.

vi. Customary International Law

In light of the extensive body of rules of the LOAC that have achieved the status of customary international law and the conclusion that customary international law is, in principle, binding on the EU in its external relations, this source undoubtedly has great significance.[2255] In this respect, the EU has stated that "*most of the provisions of the [Geneva] Conventions and their 1977 additional protocols are generally recognised as customary law*".[2256] It may also be noted that the applicability of customary LOAC rules to the EDC was explicitly confirmed.[2257] The key question here is whether there are any rules of the LOAC

[The Participating State] shall therefore ensure that the members of its national contingent ... be fully acquainted with the principles and spirit of these Conventions".

2253 See *supra*, Chapter 7.G.4.

2254 See *supra*, Chapter 7.E, especially note 1735 and the accompanying text.

2255 See also N. Tsagourias, *supra* note 1997, p. 117 and M. Zwanenburg, *supra* note 1997, pp. 400–402.

2256 Statement *supra* note 2247, also referred to by M. Zwanenburg, *supra* note 1997, p. 400.

2257 Article 80 EDC Treaty provided that "*1. Dans l'exercice de la compétence qui lui est conféré par le présent traité, et sans préjudice des droits et obligations des États membres: – la Communauté a, en ce qui concerne les Forces européennes de défense et leurs membres, les mêmes droits et* which the EU cannot comply with, or can only comply with subject to certain adaptations, because of its nature as an international organization.

The similar debate in respect of the UN is well-known and it has been recalled above[2258] that the UN initially felt it was unable to comply with (at least part of) the LOAC but has gradually accepted that it is bound by at least part of the LOAC. However, there is still considerable uncertainty over the precise extent to which the UN feels it is so bound, as is obvious from the limited content of the UN Secretary-General's Bulletin[2259] on the matter. In contrast, scholars have for the most part rejected arguments that the UN would be unable to comply with certain LOAC obligations[2260] and some have suggested that there should be a presumption that the UN is bound with the onus of proving the contrary in specific cases resting on the UN.[2261] In the absence of a serious effort by the UN to detail these perceived problems and given its extensive powers, especially those of the Security Council, this approach may well be justified.

In respect of the EU, there have been no efforts to identify (customary) LOAC rules that would be binding on the EU itself. While there certainly are differences in competences between the UN and the EU, it is doubtful whether these are significant in terms of the LOAC. Since the mandate and rules of engagement are adopted at the EU level, the EU clearly has the tools to impose standards of conduct that are compatible with the LOAC. Moreover, any powers it might lack, in particular as regards enforcement, may be accommodated by assuring the troop-contributing States take the necessary measures,[2262] as is the case with the UN.

---

obligations que les États en ce qui concerne leurs forces nationales et les membres de ces Forces, d'après le droit coutumier des gens".

2258 Chapter 7.B.2.

2259 *Supra* note 2021.

2260 See especially the legal opinion in the 1972 *UN Juridical Yearbook*, pp. 153–154, also cited in A. Reinisch, *supra* note 2158, p. 854. Where the UN has no direct competences, it can always, and has indeed, relied on TCNs to make sure that its obligations are complied with, as is the case for prosecution for war crimes. Moreover, in light of the establishment of the International Criminal Tribunals and the UN Administrative Tribunal (see http://untreaty.un.org/UNAT/main_page.htm), it is hard to argue that the UN lacks the competence to itself conduct prosecutions of peacekeepers, although Member States may not permit it to exercise this competence.

2261 See Kolb, Porretto & Vité, pp. 449–450 and R. Kolb, *supra* note 1998, p. vi.

2262 Compare Article 81 EDC Treaty: "*1. La Communauté veille à ce que les Forces européennes de défense et leurs membres conforment leur conduite aux règles du droit des gens. Elle assure la répression de toute violation éventuelle de ces règles qui viendrait à être commise par lesdites Forces ou leurs membres. 2. La Communauté prend, dans le cadre de sa compétence, les mesures de répression pénale et toutes autres mesures appropriées au cas où une telle violation serait commise par les forces d'États tiers ou leurs membres. En outre, les États membres prennent, de leur côté, dans le cadre de leur compétence, les mesures de répression pénale et toutes autres*

A specific point that must be addressed concerns the nature of any armed conflict to which the EU might become a party. As explained above,[2263] for States there are international armed conflicts and armed conflicts not of an international character and the distinction is sometimes controversial, especially in mixed conflicts. The question here is whether an international organization, be it the UN or the EU, can simply be equated to a State for the purposes of the qualification of an armed conflict.[2264] This does not seem to be disputed for conflicts between an international organization and a State.[2265] However, where the opponent is a non-State actor, there is some discussion. For instance, Zwanenburg submits that State sovereignty is the obstacle to the applicability of the full body of the LOAC in non-international armed conflicts and that the lack of such sovereignty for international organizations thus permits the application of the full body of the LOAC to conflicts between international organizations and non-State actors.[2266] However, this is not persuasive in my view. The developments towards increased international regulation of non-international conflicts, including in treaty law, suggest that it is nowadays less the *fact* of international regulation (which, in any event, already occurs under human rights law[2267]) but rather another aspect of State sovereignty, namely the *refusal to legitimize rebellion*, which is the prime consideration of States. The latter aspect is reflected in the fact that prisoner of war status and combatant immunity are still reserved for international armed conflicts. It is submitted that this consideration is also relevant to international organizations given their (inter) governmental nature. Also, they are equally unlikely to wish to legitimize recourse to force by groups opposing them. Indeed, for Kolb, Porretto & Vité, the prisoner of war status seems to be the decisive difference between both types of conflicts and they defend upholding it by either carving out part of the law of international armed conflicts in respect of international organizations (which seems hard to justify) or by applying the law of non-international armed conflicts.[2268] Thus it is submitted that for the purposes of qualification of armed conflicts, international organizations may be equated to States.[2269]

---

mesures appropriées contre toute violation des règles du droit des gens commise envers les Forces européennes de défense ou leurs membres".

2263 Section C of this chapter.

2264 Compare generally David, pp. 199–212.

2265 See on this Zwanenburg, p. 195, who qualifies such conflicts as between two subjects of international law and hence international. Similarly, Kolb, Porretto & Vité, p. 183.

2266 Zwanenburg, pp. 195–196.

2267 On the applicability of human rights and their relationship to the LOAC, see *infra*, Chapter 9.B-D.

2268 Kolb, Porretto & Vité, pp. 189–190.

2269 This would also seem to have been the case for the EDC, as Article 80 of the EDC Treaty (*supra* note 1779) provided that the EDC had the same rights and obligations concerning its forces as States under both customary international law and treaties binding one or more of its Member States and consequently "*les Forces européennes de défense et leurs membres*

vii. General Principles of International Law

Inasmuch as some rules of the LOAC may be considered to be general principles of international law,[2270] they are also binding on the EU.[2271] As with customary rules but even more so given the nature of principles, there seems to be very little room for arguments that the EU could not comply with such principles.

viii. General Principles of EC/EU Law

In Chapter 7.F.2.i, it has been discussed how the ECJ has bound the EU to human rights via general principles of EC law even before this was explicitly laid down in the EC or EU Treaty. I have also argued there that in respect of human rights, this reasoning may be extended to the EU. Given the widespread and largely convergent ratification of LOAC treaty obligations by the EU Member States and the close link between a number of such obligations and human rights (see also *supra*, subsection iii of this Section), I submit that a significant body of LOAC rules forms part of general principles of EU law binding on the EU and its Member States in the implementation of EU law, including decisions on ESDP and ESDP operations. That being said, this obligation may not add much in light of the implications of Article 6 EU Treaty which has now subsumed this source of law.

ix. Ius Cogens

I can be brief about this category of obligations given that it is argued above that they are a quality attached to rules that are either customary international law or general principles of international law, both of which have already been discussed above. It may suffice to add that, as submitted above, some rules of the LOAC are regarded as *ius cogens*, not subject to derogation by the Security Council[2272] and beyond any doubt binding on the EU.

---

jouissent, au point de vue du droit des gens, du même traitement que les forces nationales des États et leurs members".

2270 See for instance the ICJ's *Nuclear Weapons Opinion*, §§78–79, in which the Court held that the distinction between combatants and non-combatants and the corresponding prohibition to make civilians the object of attack, as well as the prohibition to cause unnecessary suffering to combatants, are "*cardinal principles*" of international humanitarian law and constitute "*intransgressible principles of international customary law*". For an earlier discussion, see generally R. Abi-Saab, 'Les "Principes généraux" du droit humanitaire selon la Cour internationale de justice', 69 No. 766 *R.I.C.R.* 1987, pp. 381–389, especially pp. 383–387 and I. Blishchenko, 'Les principes du droit international humanitaire', in C. Swinarski (ed.), *supra* note 1998, pp. 291–300.

2271 Similarly, with respect to NATO, Zwanenburg, pp. 156–161 and 212.

2272 See *supra*, Section E of this chapter.

x. *Member State Treaties through Substitution*

In light of the restrictive scope of the theory of substitution, it does not appear as if this doctrine can be applied to LOAC treaties and there seem to be no indications to the contrary. In contrast, a kind of substitution seems to have been envisaged for the EDC.[2273]

xi. *The Position of Forces Provided by Third States*

The position of third States participating in ESDP operations raises two main questions concerning the LOAC. The first is whether the conduct of these forces may be attributed to the EU. It is submitted that this is the case under the same conditions as for Member States forces, i.e. effective control, usually accomplished through a transfer of operational command.

A second question is to what extent a third Participating State's forces are bound by the EU's LOAC obligations. If these forces come under EU command, the EU should ensure that they respect all the EU's LOAC obligations. If it does not, it may engage its international responsibility. In addition, the EU should also ensure that such forces respect their sending State's LOAC obligations.[2274]

H. CONCLUSIONS

The main findings of this chapter may be summarized as follows.

First, there has to be an armed conflict or occupation before the LOAC applies and this is certainly not always the case in peace operations. Nevertheless, parts of the LOAC, in particular its prohibitions, may well serve as guidance, including in particular for soldiers on the ground, even when they are not applicable *de iure*.

Second, even if the LOAC applies to a given conflict, it will only be binding on EU forces when they are actively engaged in the hostilities (which involves more than isolated cases of limited use of force in self-defence or for mission

---

[2273] Article 80 EDC Treaty provided that "*1. Dans l'exercice de la compétence qui lui est conféré par le présent traité, et sans préjudice des droits et obligations des États membres: … – la Communauté est tenue au respect des règles de droit conventionnel de la guerre qui obligent un ou plusieurs États membres. 2. En conséquence, les Forces européennes de défense et leurs membres jouissent, au point de vue du droit des gens, du même traitement que les forces nationales des États et leurs membres*".

[2274] By virtue of the EU's obligation to "*respect and ensure respect*"; see *supra* note 2274.

accomplishment) – or when they are occupying powers. As long as they are not so engaged and are not occupying powers, they enjoy the protection of civilians under the LOAC and may not be attacked.

Third, when EU forces are actively engaged in hostilities, the conflict will be an international armed conflict if they are fighting the armed forces of another government. In other cases, the conflict will be of a non-international character, unless the EU forces operate on the territory of a third State against the latter's will or their non-State opponent is in fact acting on behalf and under the control of another government. In addition, in the case of concurrent international and non-international armed conflicts, a territorial overlap may lead to part of the law of international armed conflict being applicable to the non-international armed conflict. Furthermore, the development in the law of non-international armed conflict has arguably led to a single definition of such conflicts under customary international humanitarian law covering (protracted) armed violence between organized armed groups and reflecting the current understanding of common Article 3 to the 1949 Geneva Conventions. Moreover, the body of law applicable to such conflicts under customary international humanitarian law is quite expansive, albeit not fully identical to that applicable in international armed conflicts. Thus the relevance of the nature of the armed conflict is rather limited but not irrelevant.

Fourth, while the LOAC implies that peace operations, including EU-led forces, may become occupying powers when they exercise effective authority over an area without the consent of the host State, practice indicates that this conclusion is usually rejected.

Fifth, the UN Security Council may authorize a derogation from both conventional and customary LOAC rules, with the exception of those rules that have achieved the status of *ius cogens*. Not all of the LOAC is *ius cogens* and derogation may be particularly relevant in occupations.

Sixth, even when they put their armed forces under (operational) command or control of the EU and the actions of these armed forces therefore become attributable to the EU, participating Member States remain bound by their own LOAC obligations to a significant extent. The conclusions on Member State responsibility for conduct in the framework of an international organization set out in Chapter 7.H, can be applied to this situation and are reinforced by the specific obligation under the LOAC to "*respect and to ensure respect for*" LOAC obligations "*in all circumstances*". These rules entail that Member State forces continue to be bound by the LOAC obligations binding their sending State even when under EU command or when otherwise implementing an EU mandate. However, this is somewhat difficult to apply in respect of the (Operation and Force) Commanders, civilian staff and, though less so, contingents integrated in lead nation contingents. With regard to voting, this obligation obliges Member States to also ensure that the EU and the other Member States comply with their LOAC obligations. However, it does not require that a Member State impose its own obligations on another Member State's forces or on the EU command when the latter are not bound by these obligations themselves. Fortunately, the problem of international legal interoperability within the EU is limited given the significant convergence of Member States' treaty obligations and the extent to which part of the LOAC has become customary international law. These responsibility rules can also be applied to ESDP operations executed by only some Member States or in which third States participate to the extent that they can be applied, e.g. a Member State not implementing a decision or a third State not voting on it will obviously not be responsible on these respective bases. In fact, as is also the case for NATO, it would seem that in practice the focus in ESDP operations is on Member States' LOAC obligations rather than those of the EU.

Seventh, on the basis of the EU's international legal personality (see *supra*, Chapter 6) and its command and control over the forces and personnel put at its disposal by Member and third States, it has proper obligations under the LOAC. It can implement these through the exercise of its own competences, in particular the adoption of the Operation Plan and ROE, or, for aspects where this is not possible, via the Member States, which have a duty to cooperate loyally. In theory, these premises imply that the EU as such could become a party to an armed conflict, raising the question what the consequences would be for its Member States. This issue has not really been debated so far, not even with respect to NATO or the UN and is of very limited practical importance. While the application of the nationality/citizenship and territoriality factors entail that the Member States are involved anyway, the application by analogy of the link to a party to the conflict for combatants leads to a less obvious outcome.

The application of the conclusions reached in Chapter 7 above as to sources of international obligations for the EU result in a number of ways in which the EU is bound to such obligations. These include mainly:

- EU treaty obligations under SOFAs (so far only limited) or resulting from a possible future accession to the ECHR (via its links with part of the LOAC);

- The EU's obligation under Articles 6 and 11 EU Treaty (and their successor provisions under the Lisbon Treaty) to respect human rights, which can be said to incorporate at least part of the LOAC;
- Customary international humanitarian law, which includes significant parts of the LOAC and is the main source of LOAC obligations of the EU; it is also submitted that for the purpose of qualifying an armed conflict as international or non-international, the EU is to be treated like a State;
- General principles of international humanitarian law;
- General principles of EU law, which can be said to include part of the LOAC via human rights and Member States' ratification and implementation of LOAC treaty obligations;
- A reinforced binding by those LOAC rules that are *ius cogens*.

It is also submitted that if the LOAC applies, there is a presumption that it applies fully and the onus is on the EU to prove that certain rules may only apply subject to changes or may not apply at all.

These obligations are also binding on forces of third States participating in ESDP operations when they are under EU command and control.

It may therefore be concluded that if forces under EU command in an ESDP operation become actively engaged in an armed conflict, the LOAC applies and they are bound to LOAC obligations binding the EU and their sending States.

CHAPTER 9
HUMAN RIGHTS

A. INTRODUCTION

In the preceding chapter, I studied the applicability of the LOAC to ESDP operations and I argued that in many cases, this body of law will not be applicable because the threshold of an armed conflict has not been crossed or because the EU-led forces are not actively engaged as a party to that conflict and there is no occupation either. In this chapter, I will analyze the relevance of the most obvious alternative or complementary (even if the LOAC applies, human rights may also apply) legal regime, namely international[2275] human rights law.[2276] More

[2275] In addition, domestic human rights law may also be relevant but I will limit myself to *international* (including European) human rights law.

[2276] Similarly, F. Mégret & F. Hoffman, 'UN as a Human Rights Violator – Some Reflections on the United Nations Changing Human Rights Responsibilities', 25 *H.R.Q.* 2003, pp. 314–342, especially pp. 331–334. On human rights in peace operations, see generally Kolb, Poretto & Vité , pp. 233–316; S. Parayre, 'Beyond International Humanitarian Law: Aspects of the Applicability of International Human Rights Law' in A. Faite & J. Grenier (eds.), *Report on the Expert Meeting on Multinational Peace Operations. Applicability of International Humanitarian Law and International Human Rights Law to UN Mandated Forces, Organized by the ICRC in cooperation with the University Centre for International Humanitarian Law, Geneva, 11–12 December* 2003, available online at www.icrc.org/Web/Eng/siteeng0.nsf/htmlall/p0912/$File/ICRC_002_0912.PDF!Open, pp. 43–48 and A. Roberts, 'Human Rights Obligations of External Military Forces', in S. Horvat (ed.), *The Rule of Law in Peace Operations. Proceedings of the International Congress of Scheveningen (16–21 May 2006). Recueil XVII of the International Society for Military Law and the Law of War / Le règle de droit dans les operations de la paix, Actes du Congrès international de Scheveningen (16–21 mai 2006). Recueil XVII de la Société internationale de Droit militaire et de Droit de la Guerre*, Brussels, Printing House of Defence, 2006, pp. 429–449. With regard to the UN, see, e.g. also M. Zwanenburg, 'Compromise or Commitment: Human Rights and International Humanitarian Law Obligations for UN Forces', 11 *Leiden J.I.L.* 1998, pp. 229–245 and N. White & D. Klaasen (eds.), *The UN, Human Rights and Post-conflict Situations*, Manchester, Manchester University Press, 2005. Some have labelled the alternative regime police law ("droit de police"); see, e.g R. Kolb, *Droit humanitaire et opérations de paix internationales: les modalités d'application du droit international humanitaire dans les opérations de maintien ou de rétablissement de la paix auxquelles concourt une organisation internationale (en particulier les Nations Unies)*, Brussels/Geneva, Brulant/Helbing & Lichtenhahn, 2006 (2nd ed.), pp. 48–50, arguing that this body of law has hardly been developed so far and that it applies to police type activities but does not exclude the applicability of the LOAC to combat situations. Others have questioned the appropriateness of applying human rights law; see, e.g. C. Emanuelli, *Les actions militaires de l'ONU et le droit international humanitaire*, Montreal, Wilson & Lafleur, 1995, pp. 37–38, who sees it as too general and not adapted and argued that specifically, I will focus on the human rights obligations of EU-led operations and will not address the human rights of mission personnel in such operations.[2277]

The applicability of human rights to ESDP operations raises many difficult questions, some of which have recently been receiving increasing attention in the literature, jurisprudence and practice, albeit usually outside the ESDP context.[2278]

---

peace operations did not have the task to conduct arrests and crowd and riot control. The latter is clearly incorrect, at least for some time now, and the general nature allows flexibility and is limited by jurisprudence (see, e.g. *infra*, Section D.2.iv of this chapter)..

2277 For a recent study of the human rights *of* the armed forces, see P. Rowe, *The Impact of Human Rights Law on Armed Forces*, Cambridge, Cambridge University Press, 2006 and P. Rowe, 'The Obligation of a State under International Law to Protect Members of Its Own Armed Forces during Armed Conflict or Occupation', 9 *Y.I.H.L.* 2006, pp. 3–24. On 18 May 2009, in the case of *Secretary of State for Defence v Smith, R (on the application of)*, [2009] EWCA Civ 441 (www.bailii.org/ew/cases/EWCA/Civ/2009/441.html) the England and Wales Court of Appeals upheld a lower court judgment (*Smith, R (on the application of) v Assistant Deputy Coroner for Oxfordshire & Anor*, [2008] EWHC 694 (Admin), 11 April 2008, www.bailii.org/ew/cases/EWHC/Admin/2008/694.html), which held that the ECHR applies to UK forces also when deployed abroad, even outside military bases abroad, and that the inquest into a death should comply with the requirements of Article 2 ECHR. On accountability for violations of human rights of staff of international organizations generally, see, e.g. R. Borystawska, L. Martinez Lopez & V. Skoric, 'Identifying the Actors Responsible for Human Rights Violations Committed against Staff Members of International Organizations: An Impossible Quest for Justice?', 1 *Human Rights & International Legal Discourse* 2007, pp. 381–423.

2278 For instance, S. Bartelt, *Der rechtliche Rahmen für die neue operative Kapazität der Europäischen Union*, Münster, Lit Verlag, 2003, pp. 163–168 and 176–177 discussed human rights in ESDP operations but hardly mentions the extraterritoriality issue (merely seeming to equate jurisdiction to competence in note 49 at p. 176). I have briefly addressed the issue in F. Naert, 'De binding van NAVO- en EU-strijdkrachten aan mensenrechten bij operaties tegen terrorisme', 30(7) *NJCM-Bulletin* 2005, pp. 909–919 and somewhat more extensively yet still rather concisely in F. Naert, 'Accountability for Violation of Human Rights Law by EU Forces', in S. Blockmans (ed.), *The European Union and International Crisis Management: Legal and Policy Aspects*, The Hague, TMC Asser Press, 2008, pp. 375–393 and it is also touched upon by N. Ronzitti, 'L'applicabilità del diritto internazionale umanitario', in N. Ronzitti (ed.), *Le forze di pace dell'Unione Europea*, Roma, Rubbettino, 2005, pp. 171–172 and 174–178 (English summary at pp. 19–20) and very briefly by N. Tsagourias, 'EU Peacekeeping Operations: Legal and Theoretical Issues', in TRYBUS & WHITE, pp. 118–120. There are a few recent studies specifically on ESDP and human rights: T. Hadden (ed.), *A Responsibility to Assist. Human Rights Policy and Practice in European Union Crisis Management Operations. A COST Report*, Oxford, Hart, 2009 and J. Arloth & F. Seidensticker, *The ESDP Crisis Management Operations of the European Union and Human Rights*, Berlin, Deutsches Institut für Menschenrechte, April 2007 (available online at http://files.institut-fuer-menschenrechte.de/488/d65_v1_file_4649796b19cd6_Studie%20ESDP%20pdf%20version%2005-2007.pdf). However, the latter focuses primarily on how ESDP missions may promote respect for human rights by others and less on how they are bound by human rights themselves (the latter is only briefly dealt with at pp. 15–16). The same is true for the Recommendations of the 8th EU NGO Forum on Human Rights, entitled 'Mainstreaming Human Rights and Democracy in European Union Policies', Helsinki, 7–8 December 2006 (available online at www.europarl.europa.eu/comparl/afet/droi/delegations/07122006_recommendations.pdf). Compare H.

In this chapter, I will look at the key issues involved, namely the extraterritorial scope of application of human rights (section B), the limits on human rights in times of war and in emergencies, including the issue of derogations and the impact of UN Security Council intervention (section C), the relationship between human rights and the LOAC (section D), Participating States' human rights obligations in ESDP operations (section E) and the EU's human rights obligations in ESDP operations (section F). Several of these topics are relevant also for other international organizations but some aspects are specific to the EU. Moreover, despite some recognition of the applicability of human rights in peace operations,[2279] the discussion in this respect has started later than the debate on the applicability of the LOAC in these operations and has yielded less consensus so far.[2280] The EU may therefore be in a good position to advance this issue.

In terms of human rights instruments, I will focus on the ECHR, as the key European human rights treaty which also occupies a prominent place in the EU legal order[2281] and the ICCPR, as its principle worldwide equivalent. In addition, I will also briefly refer to a number of other human rights treaties. The choice for stressing civil and political rights is not meant to downplay the importance of other human rights but is made in light of the primary importance of these 'protection' rights in conflict situations, where the right to life and physical integrity and the prohibition of arbitrary detention are particularly at risk.

Hazelzet, 'Human Rights Aspects of EU Crisis Management Operations: From Nuisance to Necessity', 13 *International Peacekeeping* 2006, pp. 564–581. For an EU document providing an overview of human rights and the ESDP, see General Secretariat of the Council of the EU, *Compilation of Relevant Documents: Mainstreaming Human Rights and Gender into European Security and Defence Policy*, Brussels, 2008, www.consilium.europa.eu/ueDocs/cms_Data/docs/hr/news144.pdf. See also J. Valenius, *Gender Mainstreaming in ESDP Missions*, Paris, EU ISS, Chaillot Paper No. 101, May 2007 and *ESDP Newsletter* No. 4, Summer 2007, p. 15 and *ESDP Newsletter* No. 7, Winter [2008], pp. 27–29 (both www.consilium.europa.eu/showPage.aspx?id=1090&lang=en).

2279 See Article 20 of the UN Convention on the Safety of United Nations and Associated Personnel (New York, 9 December 1994, 2051 *U.N.T.S.* 391 and 34 *I.L.M.* 1995, pp. 482–493): "*Nothing in this Convention shall affect: (a) The applicability of ... universally recognized standards of human rights as contained in international instruments in relation to the protection of United Nations operations and United Nations and associated personnel or the responsibility of such personnel to respect such law and standards*" (see also M. Zwanenburg, *supra* note 2276, pp. 239–240 and A. Clapham, *infra* note 2368, p. 123) and UNSC Res. 1327 (13 November 2000), Annex, I, 3rd paragraph: "*bearing in mind the need for any provisions for a peacekeeping operation to meet minimum conditions, including ... compliance with the rules and principles of international law, in particular international humanitarian, human rights and refugee law*" (see also Kolb, Poretto & Vité , pp. 140–141).

2280 As correctly pointed out by Kolb, Poretto & Vité , pp. 21–22.

2281 The ECtHR has qualified the ECHR as a "*constitutional instrument of European public order*", see *Loizidou v. Turkey,* 23 March 1995 (preliminary objections), §§75 and 93. For its special position within the EU, see the references in Chapter 7, note 1798.

B. EXTRATERRITORIAL SCOPE OF APPLICATION OF HUMAN RIGHTS[2282]

In this section, I will examine to what extent human rights apply extraterritorially to the conduct of State organs, especially the armed forces, outside a State's own territory.[2283] Whether, and if so to what extent, human rights instruments apply extraterritorially, is primarily determined by the scope of application of each of these instruments *ratione loci* and *ratione personae*. In the remainder of this section, I will briefly discuss the scope of application of the ECHR, ICCPR, other selected human rights instruments and customary international human rights.

1. THE EUROPEAN CONVENTION OF HUMAN RIGHTS

Pursuant to Article 1 ECHR "*The High Contracting Parties shall secure to everyone within their jurisdiction the rights and freedoms defined in Section I of this Convention*". There is a considerable body of – mostly relatively recent – jurisprudence on the meaning of "jurisdiction" in this provision and the European Court of Human Rights (ECtHR) has recognized on several occasions

---

2282 This section builds in part on J. Wouters & F. Naert, 'Shockwaves through International Law after 11 September: Finding the Right Responses to the Challenges of International Terrorism', in C. Fijnaut, J. Wouters & F. Naert (eds.), *Legal Instruments in the Fight against International Terrorism. A Transatlantic Dialogue*, Leiden, Martinus Nijhoff, 2004, pp. 514–525. For an extensive comparative study, see J. Cerone, 'Human Dignity in the Line of Fire: The Application of International Human Rights Law during Armed Conflict, Occupation, and Peace Operations', 39 *Vanderbilt J.T.L.* 2006, pp. 1447–1510, especially pp. 1469–1509; F. Coomans & T. Kamminga (eds.), *Extraterritorial Application of Human Rights Treaties*, Antwerp, Intersentia, 2004; M.J. Dennis, 'Application of Human Rights Treaties Extraterritorially in Times of Armed Conflict and Military Occupation', 99 *A.J.I.L.* 2005, pp. 119–141; J. Grenier, 'Extraterritorial Applicability of Human Rights Treaty Obligations to United Nations Mandated Forces', in A. Faite & J. Grenier (eds.), *supra* note 2276, pp. 79–85; D. Lorenz, *Der territoriale Anwendungsbereich der Grund- und Menschenrechte – zugleich ein Beitrag zum Individualschutz in bewaffneten Konflikten*, Berlin, Berliner Wissenschafts-Verlag, 2005; C. Meredith & T. Christou, *Not in My Front Yard: Security and Resistance to Responsibility for Extraterritorial State Conduct*, Nijmegen, Wolf Legal Publishers, 2009; B. Schäfer, *Zum Verhältnis Menschenrechte und humanitäres Völkerrecht. Zugleich ein Beitrag zur extraterritorialen Geltung von Menschenrechtsverträgen*, Potsdam, Menschenrechts-zentrum & Deutsches Institut für Menschenrechte, 2006, pp. 18–34; M. Tondini, 'UN Peace Operations: The Last Frontier of the Extraterritorial Application of Human Rights', 44(1–2) *R.D.M.D.G.* 2005, pp. 175–242 and R. Wilde, 'Triggering State Obligations Extraterritorially: The Spatial Test in Certain Human Rights Treaties', in R. Arnold & N. Quénivet (eds.), *International Humanitarian Law and Human Rights Law: towards a New Merger in International Law*, Leiden, Martinus Nijhoff, 2008, pp. 133–153. For publications dealing with this question regarding specific treaties, see *infra*.

2283 On the question when the conduct of State organs may be attributed to the international organization at the disposal of which they have been placed, see *supra*, Chapter 8.G.1 and *infra*, sections E-F of this chapter.

that the ECHR may apply extraterritorially, but has also limited this extraterritorial reach.[2284] However, the precise scope of this extraterritorial

---

2284 The main cases are discussed below. See generally K. Altiparmak, '*Bankovic*: An Obstacle to the Application of the European Convention on Human Rights in Iraq?', 9 *J.C.S.L.* 2004, pp. 213–240; R. Bakels, *In de vuurlinie: Aansprakelijkheid onder het EVRM voor schendingen van dat verdrag door het Nederlandse contingent in Irak*, Leiden, 2003 (on file with the author); H. Borghouts, R. Daverschot & G. Gillissen, *Evaluatie toepassing militair strafprocesrecht bij uitzendingen*, Haarlem, 31 August 2006 (report of a Commission set up by the Dutch Ministries of Justice and of Defence, available online at www.defensie.nl/_system/handlers/generaldownloadHandler.ashx?filename=/media/Rapport_Commissie_Borghouts_tcm46-104611.pdf), pp. 29–33; M. Bothe, 'Die Anwendung der Europäischen Menschenrechtskonvention in bewaffneten Konflikten: eine Überforderung?', 65 *Z.a.ö.R.V.* 2005, pp. 615–623; J.A. Carrillo-Salcedo, 'Article 1', in L.-E. Pettiti, E. Decaux & P.-H. Imbert (eds.), *La Convention européenne des droits de l'homme*, Paris, Economica, 1999 (2nd ed.), pp. 135–141; J. Cerone, *supra* note 2282, pp. 1481–1494; U. Erberich, *Auslandseinsätze der Bundeswehr und Europäische Menschenrechtskonvention*, Cologne, Carl Heymanns, 2004, especially pp. 5–31; M. Gondek, 'Extraterritorial Application of the European Convention on Human Rights: Territorial Focus in the Age of Globalization?', 52 *N.I.L.R.* 2005, pp. 349–387; E. Guild, *infra* note 2394, pp. 41–54; Y. Haeck & J. Vande Lanotte, 'Artikel 1. Verplichting tot verzekeren verdragsrechten', in J. Vande Lanotte & Y. Haeck (eds.), *Handboek EVRM. Deel 2. Artikelsgewijze commentaar*, Antwerp, Intersentia, 2004, Vol. 1, pp. 3–29 (excluding the applicability of the ECHR to extraterritorial military operations except for occupations at pp. 25–26); H. Krieger, 'Die Verantwortlichkeit Deutschlands nach der EMRK für seine Streitkräfte im Auslandeinsatz', 62 *Z.a.ö.R.V.* 2002, pp. 669–702; E. Lagrange, 'L'application de la Convention de Rome à des actes accomplis par les Etats parties en dehors du territoire national', 112 *R.G.D.I.P.* 2008, pp. 521–565; R. Lawson, 'Life After Bankovic: On the Extraterritorial Application of the European Convention on Human Rights', in F. Coomans & T. Kamminga (eds.), *supra* note 2282, pp. 83–123; R. Lawson, 'The Concept of Jurisdiction in the European Convention on Human Rights', in P.J. Slot & M.K. Bulterman (eds.), *Globalisation and Jurisdiction*, The Hague, Kluwer Law International, 2004, pp. 201–218; R. Lawson, 'Moving Beyond Bankovic: The Gradually Expanding Reach of the European Convention on Human Rights', in S. Horvat (ed.), *supra* note 2276, pp. 473–487; P. Leach, *The British Military in Iraq: The Applicability of the Espace Juridique Doctrine under the European Convention on Human Rights, s.l., s.d.*, www.londonmet.ac.uk/londonmet/library/i86023_24.doc; J. Lett, 'The Age of Interventionism: The Extraterritorial Reach of the European Convention on Human Rights', in R. Arnold & G.-J. Knoops (eds.), *Practice and Policies of Modern Peace Support Operations under International Law*, Ardsley, Transnational, 2006, pp. 117–140; D. Lorenz, *supra* note 2282, pp. 8–35; C. Lush, 'The Territorial Application of the European Convention on Human Rights: Recent Case Law', 42 *I.C.L.Q.* 1993, pp. 898–906; M. O'Boyle, 'The European Convention on Human Rights and Extraterritorial Jurisdiction: A Comment on "Life After Bankovic"', in F. Coomans & T. Kamminga (eds.), *supra* note 2282, pp. 125–139; M.P. Pederson, 'Territorial Jurisdiction in Article 1 of the European Convention on Human Rights', 73 *Nordic J.I.L.* 2004, pp. 279–305 (*inter alia* providing a survey of the (rather short) views expressed on the matter in general commentaries on the ECHR at p. 279 and also discussing other case law not cited below at pp. 284–300); P. Rowe, 'The Application of the European Convention on Human Rights during an International Armed Conflict', in R. Burchill, N.D. White & J. Morris (eds.), *International Conflict and Security Law: Essays in Memory of Hilaire McCoubrey*, Cambridge, Cambridge University Press, 2005, pp. 185–208; A. Uzun, 'Extraterritorial Application of the European Convention on Human Rights – An Overview of the Strasbourg Case-Law', in S. Horvat (ed.), *supra* note 2276, pp. 451–472 and R. Wilde, 'Legal "Black Hole"?: Extraterritorial State Action and International Treaty Law on Civil and Political Rights', 26 *Michigan J.I.L.* 2005, pp. 790–806.

application remains controversial. I will now briefly and critically discuss the main judgments and decisions, as well as a particularly relevant case before the British courts (*Al-Skeini*), and will draw a brief conclusion from them.

First, in *Soering v. the United Kingdom*, the Court held that, while Article 1 ECHR "*sets a limit, notably territorial, on the reach of the Convention*", a decision by a Contracting State to extradite a fugitive "*may ... engage the responsibility of that State under the Convention, where substantial grounds have been shown for believing that the person concerned, if extradited, faces a real risk of being subjected to torture or to inhuman or degrading treatment or punishment in the requesting country*".[2285] Thus the Court read a territorial limit into Article 1 even though this provision only requires "*jurisdiction*". Nevertheless, it recognized a certain extraterritorial effect in respect of persons who are initially on the territory of a State Party. This kind of extraterritorial effect is not the primary concern here, although it is not irrelevant.[2286]

A few years later, in the case of *Drozd and Janousek v. France and Spain*, the Court went further and appeared to equate "*within the jurisdiction*" with being the victim of an act attributable to a State Party, when it stated that:

> The term "jurisdiction" is not limited to the national territory of the High Contracting Parties; their responsibility can be involved because of acts of their authorities producing effects outside their own territory [references omitted]. The question to be decided here is whether the acts complained of by Mr Drozd and Mr Janousek can be attributed to France or Spain or both, even though they were not performed on the territory of those States.[2287]

Indeed, the extraterritorial application of the ECHR was subsequently reaffirmed when the Court held that persons in Northern Cyprus were within the jurisdiction of Turkey, finding that "*although Article 1 ... sets limits on the reach of the Convention, the concept of 'jurisdiction' under this provision is not restricted to the national territory of the ... Parties*" and that "*the responsibility of a ... Party may also arise when as a consequence of military action – whether lawful or unlawful – it exercises effective control [exercised directly or through a subordinate local administration] of an area outside its national territory*".[2288] This was again

2285 7 July 1989, §§86 and 91.

2286 E.g. if the ECHR applies to persons detained in peace operations abroad, this jurisprudence entails limits upon the possibility to transfer these persons to the local authorities (see *infra*, Section D.2.iv.b of this chapter).

2287 26 June 1992, §91.

2288 *Loizidou v. Turkey*, 23 February 1995 (preliminary objections), §62, confirmed in *Loizidou v. Turkey*, 18 December 1996 (merits), §52. See generally A. Husheer, 'Die völkerrechtliche Verantwortlichkeit der Türkei für Menschenrechtsverletzungen in Nordzypern nach den confirmed in the 2001 *Cyprus v. Turkey* judgment.[2289] Moreover, the Court also declared admissible a few cases concerning actions taken by a State's agents outside its territory, *inter alia* by Turkish armed forces in Northern Iraq[2290] and by Russian armed forces in Moldova.[2291]

However, when the Court was faced with complaints brought by victims of the NATO air campaign in the former Yugoslavia during the Kosovo war in 1999 (the *Bankovic* case),[2292] it gave a more restrictive interpretation of the notion "*within the jurisdiction*". The Court stressed that jurisdiction was primarily territorial – other bases of jurisdiction being exceptional. It was also of the opinion that State Parties' lack of derogations under Article 15 ECHR in cases where their forces operated abroad was subsequent practice[2293] indicating "*a lack of any apprehension on the part of the Contracting States of their extra-territorial responsibility in contexts similar to the present case*" (§62). The Court argued that it had only accepted extraterritorial reach in exceptional cases and rejected the notion that ECHR rights could be "*divided and tailored in accordance with the particular circumstances of the extra-territorial act in question*" and also refuted the claim that "*everyone adversely affected by an act imputable to a Contracting State, wherever ... committed or its consequences felt, is thereby brought within the jurisdiction of that State for the purpose of ... the Convention*" (§75). Also, the Court stressed the regional vocation of the ECHR, which operates "*in the legal space (...) of the Contracting Parties*" and which was "*not designed to be applied throughout the world, even in respect of the conduct of Contracting States*" (§80). On the basis of these arguments, the Court found that the applicants were not within the jurisdiction of a State Party (§82).

The judgment has been much debated[2294] and deserves some comment. First, while the Court seems to reason conceptually logical in distinguishing between

Entscheidungen der Europäischen Kommission und des Europäischen Gerichtshofes für Menschenrechte im Fall Loizidou ./. Türkei', 1 *Z. Eur. S.* 1998, pp. 389–422.

2289 10 May 2001, §§75–78. See on this judgment L.G. Loucaides, 'The Judgment of the European Court of Human Rights in the *Case of Cyprus* v. *Turkey*', 15 *Leiden J.I.L.* 2002, pp. 225–236.

2290 *Halima Musa Issa and Others v. Turkey*, 30 May 2000 (decision as to the admissibility; see *infra* note 2309 for the judgment on the merits).

2291 *Ilie Ilaşcu and Others v. Moldova and the Russian Federation*, 4 July 2001 (decision as to the admissibility; see *infra* note 2310 for the judgment on the merits).

2292 In the Grand Chamber decision as to the admissibility of Application No. 52207/99 by *Vlastimir and Borka Bankovic and others v. Belgium, the Czech Republic, Denmark, France, Germany, Greece, Hungary, Iceland, Italy, Luxembourg, the Netherlands, Norway, Poland, Portugal, Spain, Turkey and the United Kingdom*, 12 December 2001, especially §§59–82.

2293 Which may be taken into account for interpreting a treaty provision pursuant to Article 31(3)(b) 1969 VCLT.

2294 For a critical view, see, e.g. R. Lawson, *supra* note 2284 (in Coomans & Kamminga), pp. 83–123; L.G. Loucaides, 'Determining the Extra-territorial Effect of the European Convention:

falling within the jurisdiction of a State and being the victim of an action attributable to that State,[2295] one may wonder whether this view is really correct given that State agents do not normally act merely factually, but, when exercising their functions, almost by definition exercise part of a State's jurisdiction.[2296] The argument that to take a different view than the Court would entail that all the rights in the convention would have to be guaranteed to everyone everywhere, which was clearly not the intention of the drafters,[2297] is not convincing and could easily be accommodated by accepting the view that jurisdiction can be partial or gradual.[2298] In the words of Lorenz: "*effective personal control ...*

Facts, Jurisprudence and the Bankovic Case', 11 *E.H.R.L.R.* 2006, pp. 391–407 and E. Roxstrom, M. Gibney & T. Einarsen, 'The NATO Bombing Case (Bankovic et al. v. Belgium et al.) and the Limits of Western Human Rights Protection', 23 *Boston U.I.L.J.* 2005, pp. 55–136 (extremely critical and qualifying this judgment as "*the most egregious decision in the history of the [Court] ... evinc[ing] a vision of human rights that ... is inimical to the very purpose of human rights*" at p. 56). For a more positive appraisal, see, e.g. D. McGoldrick, *infra* note 2295, pp. 68–72; M. O'Boyle, *supra* note 2284, pp. 125–139 and G. Ress, 'State Responsibility for Extraterritorial Human Rights Violations: The Case of Bankovic', 6 *Z. Eur. S.* 2003, pp. 73–89. For further annotations, see A. Gündüz, 'Creeping Jurisdiction of the European Court of Human Rights: The Bankovic Case vs the Loizidou Case', 24 *Milletlerarasi Hukuk ve Milletlerarasi Özel Hukuk bülteni* 2004, pp. 451–480; M. Happold, 'Bankovic v Belgium and the Territorial Scope of the European Convention on Human Rights' 3 *H.R.L.R.* 2003, pp. 77–90; H.-J. Heintze, 'Las Palmeras v. Bamaca-Velasquez und Bankovic v. Loizidou?: Widersprüchliche Entscheidungen zum Menschenrechtsschutz in bewaffneten Konflikten', 18 *Humanitäres Völkerrecht* 2005, pp. 177–182; P. Pustorino, 'Responsabilità degli Stati parti della Convenzione europea dei diritti dell'uomo per il bombardamento NATO alla radio-televisione Serba: il caso Bankovic', 56 *La Comunità internazionale* 2001, pp. 695–704; G. Ress, 'Problems of Extraterritorial Human Rights Violations: The Jurisdiction of the European Court of Human Rights: The Bankovic Case', 12 *Italian Y.I.L.* 2003, pp. 51–67; A. Rüth & M. Trilsch, 'Bankovic v. Belgium (Admissibility). App. No. 52207/99: European Court of Human Rights, December 12, 2001', 97 *A.J.I.L.* 2003, pp. 168–172 (criticizing some of the arguments while accepting the conclusion) and S. Williams & S. Shah, 'Bankovic and Others v. Belgium and 16 Other Contracting States', 7 *E.H.R.L.R.* 2002, pp. 775–781.

2295 See also D. McGoldrick, 'Extraterritorial Application of the International Covenant on Civil and Political Rights', in F. Coomans & T. Kamminga (eds.), *supra* note 2282, pp. 42–44 and compare the discussion by M.P. Pederson, *supra* note 2284, pp. 303–305, who submits that the purpose of human rights suggests that a link between both notions is more appropriate. The Court repeated the distinction between jurisdiction and attribution in *Mansur Pad and Others v. Turkey*, admissibility decision, 28 June 2007, §52.

2296 In this sense the link between "facticity and normativity" made by M. Scheinin, 'Extraterritorial Effect of the International Covenant on Civil and Political Rights', in in F. Coomans & T. Kamminga (eds.), *supra* note 2282, pp. 75–77. Compare J.A. Carrillo-Salcedo, *supra* note 2284, pp. 135–136 (writing before *Bankovic* that "*il n'est pas nécessaire qu'existe un lien juridique stable comme la nationalité, la residence ou le domicile, car il suffit que l'Etat puisse exercer un certain pouvoir sur l'intéressé*").

2297 Otherwise, e.g. Article 56 ECHR (which requires a notification by State Parties to extend the ECHR to any of the territories for whose international relations it is responsible) would be superfluous.

2298 See R. Lawson, *supra* note 2284 (in Coomans & Kamminga), pp. 120–121 and J. Cerone, 'Minding the Gap: Outlining KFOR Accountability in Post-Conflict Kosovo', 12 *E.J.I.L.* 2001, pp. 479–480.

pertains to single extraterritorial acts which lead to a partial binding to human rights ratione personae".[2299] The latter view would arguably better reflect the multidimensional nature of the concept of jurisdiction in international law[2300] but was, unfortunately, rejected by the Court in *Bankovic*.[2301] However, it has arguably been reversed somewhat in more recent case law.[2302] Second, the

---

2299 D. Lorenz, *supra* note 2282, pp. 105–118, quote from p. 105 (free translation by the author; the original quote reads "*effektiven personalen Kontrolle ... bezieht sich auf extraterritoriale Einzelakte, die eine partielle Menschenrechtsbindung ratione personae auslösen*"). Compare U. Erberich, *supra* note 2284, pp. 29–31, arguing that the ECHR could apply in full even in cases of less than effective control over a territory but that only certain affected rights would come into play in such cases, thus leading to the same result.

2300 The most common distinction is that between legislative (or prescriptive) jurisdiction, judicial (or adjudicative) jurisdiction and enforcement jurisdiction, and it is especially the latter which is more strictly territorial in principle. See, e.g. Malanczuk, pp. 109–110 and Shaw, pp. 572–574 and 576–578. Compare Brownlie, pp. 301–314, who sees few differences between the different forms of jurisdiction. On this multidimensional nature, see also D. Lorenz, *supra* note 2282, pp. 79–83 (arguing that the international law concept of jurisdiction that should be applied here does not lead to territorial limits); M. Gondek, *supra* note 2284, pp. 360–370, especially pp. 364–367 and 385–387 (considering that the Court interpreted jurisdiction wrongly as it is differentiated and not (so) territorial and noting that other human rights bodies have interpreted jurisdiction in a much less territorial sense) and M.P. Pederson, *supra* note 2284, pp. 280–281 and throughout his Article (this author nevertheless concludes at pp. 297–298 that there was no jurisdiction in *Bankovic*, but this seems to be based on his apparent requirement that the jurisdiction be lawful under international law (see especially p. 303), a view which I reject below). Compare H. Krieger, *supra* note 2284, pp. 671–673, who defines jurisdiction in this context as a regular exercise of State authority (over persons or territory) characterized by a certain duration and organization (free translation by the author; the original quote reads "*die regelmäßige Ausübung von Hoheitsgewalt, die von einer gewissen Dauerhaftigkeit und Organisation gekennzeichnet ist*") and regards enforcement jurisdiction as decisive here. Compare also A. Rüth & M. Trilsch, *supra* note 2294, pp. 171–172, who seem to favour a more differentiated approach. B. Schäfer, *supra* note 2282, pp. 31–33 also prefers a more gradual approach and *inter alia* distinguished between negative and positive obligations. N. Tsagourias, *supra* note 2278, p. 120, also advocates a gradual applicability. On the ECHR and international law more generally, see L. Wildhaber, 'The European Convention on Human Rights and International Law', 56 *I.C.L.Q.* 2007, pp. 217–232 (who briefly discusses the jurisdiction debate at pp. 223–224) and L. Caflisch & A.A. Cancado Trindade, 'Les conventions américaine et européenne des droits de l'homme et le droit international général', 108 *R.G.D.I.P.* 2004, pp. 5–62 (discussing the concept of jurisdiction at pp. 34–40 as an example of recourse to general international law – though I would submit it is not a good example as it is questionable whether the Court correctly applied international law).

2301 It was, however, put forward in the concurring opinion of Judge Loucaides in *Assanidze v. Georgia* (8 April 2004): "*To my mind "jurisdiction" means actual authority ... Therefore, a High Contracting Party is accountable under the Convention to everyone directly affected by any exercise of authority by such Party in any part of the world. Such authority may take different forms and may be legal or illegal ... I believe that a reasonable interpretation of the provisions of the Convention in the light of its object must lead to the conclusion that the Convention provides a code of behaviour for every High Contracting Party whenever they act in exercise of their State authority with resulting consequences to individuals*". See also the view of Lord Justice Sedley in the *Al-Skeini* appeals judgement (*infra* note 2323), §§198–202.

2302 See J. Cerone, *supra* note 2282, pp. 1494–1507, especially pp. 1497–1498 and 1502–1504, *inter alia* referring to ECtHR, *Ilie Ilaşcu, Alexandru Leşco, Andrei Ivanţoc and Tudor Petrov-Popa*

Courts' apparent attention for the *legality* under international law of the exercise of extraterritorial jurisdiction[2303] is somewhat puzzling and one can only hope that the Court did not, and will not, consider that only extraterritorial jurisdiction exercised in conformity with international law is to be regarded as jurisdiction in the sense of Article 1 ECHR.[2304] Such a view would create the absurd situation that a State who acts extraterritorially in violation of international law would not be bound by the ECHR only because of that illegality.[2305] Third, the Court's emphasis on the regional application of the

---

v. Moldova and the Russian Federation, 8 July 2004, §333 ("*where a Contracting State is prevented from exercising its authority over the whole of its territory by a constraining de facto situation, ..., it does not thereby cease to have jurisdiction within the meaning of Article 1 of the Convention over that part of its territory temporarily subject to a local authority sustained by rebel forces or by another State. Nevertheless such a factual situation reduces the scope of that jurisdiction in that the undertaking given by the State under Article 1 must be considered by the Court only in the light of the Contracting State's positive obligations towards persons within its territory. The State in question must endeavour, with all the legal and diplomatic means available to it vis-à-vis foreign States and international organisations, to continue to guarantee the enjoyment of the rights and freedoms guaranteed by the Convention*") and also citing jurisprudence from the EComHR that could support a gradual approach. On the situation where a State loses control over part of its territory, compare ECJ, Case C-420/07 (*Meletis Apostolides v. David Charles Orams, Linda Elizabeth Orams*), 28 April 2009.

2303 See, e.g. the Court's consideration in §61 that "*The Court is of the view, therefore, that Article 1 of the Convention must be considered to reflect this ordinary and essentially territorial notion of jurisdiction, other bases of jurisdiction being exceptional and* requiring special justification *in the particular circumstances of each case*" and in §67 that "*In keeping with the essentially territorial notion of jurisdiction, the Court has accepted* only in exceptional cases that acts of the Contracting States performed, or producing effects, outside their territories can constitute an exercise of jurisdiction *by them within the meaning of Article 1 of the Convention*" (emphasis added). See also the British judgment in first instance in *Al-Skeini*, *infra* note 2322, §269: "*jurisdiction ... extend[s] ... only to an extra-territorial jurisdiction which is exceptional and limited and to be found in* specific cases recognised in international law", although that same judgment does not seem to consider the lawful nature as entirely decisive at §272: "*whether* with or without international law approval *or the consent of the home state, the respondent state has in a real sense extended its jurisdiction territorially into another territory, either wholly, ..., or, by reference to a particular location such as a consulate or ship (or perhaps court house or prison), partially*" (emphasis added).

2304 This seems to be the view adopted by M.P. Pederson, *supra* note 2284, p. 303 ("*if a person is kidnapped outside the territory of the contracting States without the involvement or consent of the State where the kidnapping takes place the act will not be within the jurisdiction of the kidnapping State*"). I rather agree with the contrary view, which was eloquently expressed by M. Scheinin, *supra* note 2296, pp. 79–80: "*What the Court is discussing, is the* permissibility *of a State exercising jurisdiction beyond its own territory, not at all the legal* consequences *of the exercise of authority abroad, be it permissible or not*" (emphasis in original). Similarly, J.A. Carrillo-Salcedo, *supra* note 2284, p. 136; U. Erberich, *supra* note 2284, pp. 28–29 and the concurring opinion of Judge Loucaides in *Assanidze v. Georgia*, 8 April 2004 ("*To my mind "jurisdiction" means actual authority ... Such authority may take different forms and may be legal or illegal ...* "). The latter view also seems to be shared by A. Rüth & M. Trilsch, *supra* note 2294, p. 171.

2305 Similarly M. Gondek, *supra* note 2284, p. 364 and U. Erberich, *supra* note 2284, pp. 28–29 ("*Es wäre auch widersinnig, eninen Vertragsstaat gerade bei rechtswidrigem Handeln aus seiner*

ECHR and the "legal space" is also problematic[2306] and seems to be at odds with the *Soering* jurisprudence cited above, in that it would hardly be reasonable to hold that a person suffering torture at the hands of an agent of a State Party in a country outside Europe would not fall under the ECHR but that he would be covered by the ECHR if that same European State transferred him from its own territory to that country with the knowledge that he was likely to be tortured there by local authorities. Nevertheless, there may indeed be some cases where a particular aspect or interpretation of a human right in the ECHR is specifically European and should not be fully applied in some other parts of the world (see *infra*, Section D.2.iv of this chapter).

However, *Bankovic* was not the final word and a few cases decided later by the ECtHR again show a broader acceptance of the extraterritorial application of the ECHR.[2307] Notably, in *Öcalan v. Turkey*, which involved the arrest of PPK-leader Öcalan by Turkish authorities in Kenya, the Court held that it was common ground that "*directly after being handed over to the Turkish officials by the Kenyan officials, the applicant was under effective Turkish authority and therefore within the "jurisdiction" of that State ... even though in this instance Turkey exercised its authority outside its territory*".[2308] Moreover, the alleged regional vocation was set aside in the judgment on the merits in *Issa*, in which the Court did not exclude that "*as a consequence of (...) military action, [a] State could be considered to have exercised, temporarily, effective overall control of a particular portion of*

Verantwortdung zu entlassen"). J. Cerone, *supra* note 2298, p. 478, argues, albeit as a general rule not restricted to the ECHR, that "*the legality of a State's presence abroad [...] is irrelevant*" for the extraterritorial application of human rights and adds (at pp. 480–481) that rejecting the legality requirement would also be in line with the rule that acts done by State agents in their official capacity but *ultra vires* nonetheless are attributable to a State (see Article 7 of the ILC's Draft Articles on State Responsibility, *Report of the International Law Commission on the Work of its fifty-third Session*, UN Doc. A/56/10, 2001, pp. 99–103). See also the ICJ's statement that "*Physical control of a territory, and not sovereignty or legitimacy of title, is the basis of State liability for acts affecting other States*", in §118 of its advisory opinion on *Legal Consequences for States of the Continued Presence of South Africa in Namibia (South West Africa) notwithstanding Security Council Resolution 276 (1970)* of 21 June 1971, also referred to by L. Zegveld, *Armed Opposition Groups in International Law: The Quest for Accountability*, Rotterdam, Doctoral thesis, Erasmus University Rotterdam, 2000, p. 49.

2306 For a discussion, see R. Wilde, 'The "Legal Space" or "Espace Juridique" of the European Convention of Human Rights: Is It Relevant to Extraterritorial State Action?', 10 *E.H.R.L.R.* 2005, pp. 115–124, arguing that this consideration should not be read too broadly. See also J. Cerone, *supra* note 2282, pp. 1492–1494 and D. Lorenz, *supra* note 2282, pp. 119–120 (and pp. 118–126 on regional limitations more generally, pleading in favour of limiting the reach of regional instruments to some extent).

2307 Similarly J. Cerone, *supra* note 2282, pp. 1481–1492, especially p. 1492.

2308 Grand Chamber, 12 May 2005, §91. The wording differs slightly from that in the judgment in first instance (13 March 2003, §93), in which it was unclear to what extent the subsequent transfer to Turkey was conclusive. On this case, see A. Künzli, '*Öcalan v. Turkey*: Some Comments', 17 *Leiden J.I.L.* 2004, pp. 141–154, especially pp. 144–145.

the territory of [another State]" and that "*if (...) at the relevant time, the victims were within that specific area, it would follow logically that they were within the jurisdiction of [that State]*" (the case concerned Iraq).[2309] The extraterritorial application was also confirmed in the *Ilascu* decision on the merits.[2310] While the ECtHR declared inadmissible the application brought by Saddam Hussein against 21 European countries whose troops had joined the US-led military campaign in Iraq for lack of jurisdiction, the decision was based essentially on the lack of evidence that any State Party to the ECHR "*had any ([...]) influence or involvement in [Saddam's] impugned arrest, detention and handover*".[2311] In *Al-Saadoon and Mufdhi v. UK*, the Court accepted that detainees held in custody in a UK-run detention facility in Iraq, both during and after the occupation, were within the UK's jurisdiction "*given the total and exclusive* de facto, *and subsequently also de jure, control exercised by the United Kingdom authorities over the premises in question*".[2312]

Moreover, in its admissibility decision in *Mansur Pad and Others v. Turkey*, the Court restated its jurisprudence as follows:

> Although the words "within their jurisdiction" in Article 1 of the Convention must be understood to mean that a State's jurisdictional competence is primarily territorial (...), in exceptional circumstances the acts of Contracting States which are performed outside their territory or which produce effects there ("extraterritorial act") may amount to the exercise by them of jurisdiction within the meaning of Article 1 (...). Accordingly, a State may be held accountable for violations of the Convention rights and freedoms of persons who are in the territory of another State which does not

---

2309 16 November 2004, §74. See also J. Cerone, *supra* note 2282, pp. 1492–1494 and P. Rowe, *supra* note 2284, pp. 194–195 and 207. See also the Report of a Dutch Parliamentary inquiry into allegations of abuse by Dutch forces in Iraq (*Rapport van de Commissie van onderzoek naar de betrokkenheid van Nederlandse militairen bij mogelijke misstanden bij gesprekken met gedetineerden in Irak*, The Hague, 18 June 2007, available online at http://parlis.nl/pdf/bijlagen/BLG12304.pdf and previously at www.tweedekamer.nl/images/Onderzoek_vermeende_mishandelingen_door_Nederlandse_militairen_in_Irak_in_2003_bijl3_tcm118-129075.pdf; last consulted in November 2007), which states at p. 25 that on the basis of the ECtHR's jurisprudence, the ECHR applied to Dutch forces in Iraq and more generally to these forces when they act abroad ("*Het is de vraag of personen die zich buiten het Koninkrijk in een gebied bevinden waar Nederlandse troepen in een gewapend conflict opereren, (mede) onder de rechtsmacht van Nederland vallen. Of, ruimer gesteld: vallen personen die zich bevinden in een gebied waar vreemde troepen operaties uitvoeren, onder de rechtsmacht van de staat die de troepen heeft gezonden? Deze vraag dient, gelet op de jurisprudentie van het Europese Hof, bevestigend te worden beantwoord*").

2310 8 July 2004, §§386–394, especially §§393–394.

2311 *Saddam Hussein v. Albania, Bulgaria, Croatia, Czech Republic, Denmark, Estonia, Hungary, Iceland, Ireland, Italy, Latvia, Lithuania, the Netherlands, Poland, Portugal, Romania, Slovakia, Slovenia, Turkey, Ukraine and the United Kingdom*, Decision of 14 March 2006 (see www.echr.coe.int/Eng/Press/2006/March/HUSSEIN%20ADMISSIBILITY%20DECISION.htm).

2312 Admissibility decision, 30 June 2009, especially §§84–89.

> necessarily fall within the legal space of the Contracting States, but who are found to be under the former State's authority and control through its agents operating – whether lawfully or unlawfully – in the latter State (...).[2313]

Furthermore, in *Isaak v. Turkey*, the Court, referring also to decisions and opinions of other human rights bodies, stated that:

> a State may also be held accountable for a violation of the Convention rights and freedoms of persons who are in the territory of another State but who are found to be under the former State's authority and control through its agents operating – whether lawfully or unlawfully – in the latter State (...). Accountability in such situations stems from the fact that Article 1 of the Convention cannot be interpreted so as to allow a State party to perpetrate violations of the Convention on the territory of another State, which it could not perpetrate on its own territory (...).[2314]

Applying this to the case at hand, the Court ruled that the victim, who had been killed by a mob including Turkish or Turkish-Cypriot soldiers and/or officials, came under the authority and/or effective control, and therefore within the jurisdiction, of Turkey as a result of the acts of the Turkish and Turkish-Cypriot agents. As the latter had actively taken part in the beating and did nothing to prevent or stop the attack or to help the victim, even if the acts complained of took place in the neutral UN buffer zone, the Court considered that the deceased was under the authority and/or effective control of the respondent State through its agents and accordingly fell within the "jurisdiction" of Turkey.[2315] The Court restated similar considerations in the case of *Solomou v. Turkey*.[2316]

Another decision that must be mentioned here is the ECtHR's Grand Chamber decision of 31 May 2007 declaring inadmissible the applications brought in the

---

2313 Admissibility decision, 28 June 2007, §53. It was disputed whether the alleged killing of seven persons by Turkish security forces took place in Iran or in Turkey and it is not clear whether they were killed by helicopter fire or after having been captured. Turkey claimed the events took place in Turkey. The Court ruled that: "54. *However, in the instant case, it was not disputed by the parties that the victims of the alleged events came within the jurisdiction of Turkey. While the applicants attached great importance to the prior establishment of the exercise by Turkey of extraterritorial jurisdiction with a view to proving their allegations on the merits, the Court considers that it is not required to determine the exact location of the impugned events, given that the Government had already admitted that the fire discharged from the helicopters had caused the killing of the applicants' relatives, who had been suspected of being terrorists (...). 55. Accordingly, the Court finds that the victims of the impugned events were within the jurisdiction of Turkey at the material time*".

2314 Admissibility decision, 28 September 2006, pp. 19–20 of the online version.

2315 *Id.*, pp. 20–21.

2316 24 June 2008 decision on admissibility, §§43–51. For a discussion of both cases, see M. Zwanenburg, 'Isaak v. Turkije en Solomou v. Turkije', 102 *Militairrechtelijk tijdschrift* 2009, pp. 2–14.

cases *Behrami and Behrami v. France*[2317] and *Saramati v. France, Germany and Norway*,[2318] both concerning conduct of personnel of State Parties to the ECHR in the international presence in Kosovo.[2319] The case of *Behrami and Behrami* concerned children who found a number of non-detonated cluster munitions and began playing with them, causing one bomb to detonate, resulting in one of the children's death and seriously injuring another. The victims claimed that France, as lead nation of the multinational Brigade responsible for the area, had breached its obligation under Article 2 ECHR to take positive measures to protect life, namely to mark and/or defuse the non-detonated cluster bombs which KFOR (the NATO-led military Kosovo Force) allegedly had known to be present on the site in question. Claims in Kosovo had not been successful. In the other case, Ruzhdi Saramati, from Kosovo and of Albanian origin, was detained for security purposes pursuant to a detention order by the KFOR Commander (COMKFOR), a Norwegian officer at that time, on 13 July 2001 and was held by KFOR until 26 January 2002 (as of 3 October 2001 under the new French COMKFOR). The applicant complained against Norway and France under Article 5 ECHR (right to liberty and security), Article 13 ECHR (right to an effective remedy) and Article 6(1) ECHR (right to a fair trial, including access to a court). The Chamber dealing with the cases relinquished jurisdiction in favour of the Grand Chamber and the cases were joined.

Remarkably, the Court considered that the question raised by the cases was, less whether the States concerned exercised extraterritorial jurisdiction in Kosovo but, far more centrally, whether the ECtHR was competent to examine under the ECHR those States' contribution to the civil and security presence exercising control of Kosovo (§§69–72). The Court considered that the impugned action of KFOR (detention of Mr. Saramati) and inaction of the United Nations Interim Administration Mission in Kosovo (UNMIK) (the alleged failure to de-mine in the *Behrami* case) could, in principle, be attributed to the UN because both acted under a delegated UN Security Council Chapter VII mandate (§§212–143). The Court then held that is was not competent to review the acts of the States in question carried out on behalf of the UN, interpreting the Convention in the light of other international law applicable in relations between its Contracting Parties, especially the UN Charter (§§144–152). It distinguished these cases from its earlier *Bosphorus* judgment[2320] and considered that the impugned conduct could not be attributed to the respondent States and, moreover, did not take place on the territory of those States or by virtue of a decision of their authorities. Furthermore, it held that there was a fundamental distinction between the

2317 Application No. 71412/01.
2318 Application No. 78166/01.
2319 See the annotations *supra* note 2212.
2320 See *supra*, Chapter 7.H.

international organization/cooperation at issue (§§145 and 150–151). Therefore, the Court did not examine the extraterritoriality issue. While the decision does not provide any guidance on the extraterritoriality as such, its findings on the UN Charter and the question of attribution, although questionable in several respects, have important implications that are discussed above and below.[2321]

In the UK, in the case of *R (Al-Skeini and others) v Secretary of State for Defence* (also referred to in part as the *Mousa* case), British courts up to the House of Lords accepted that the ECHR applied to the British forces in Iraq during the period of occupation but only to a limited extent. While the Courts at all three levels rejected the applicability of the ECHR to combat (like) actions in Iraq and accepted that it applied to a UK-run detention facility there, they differed somewhat on the degree to which the ECHR applied to other actions. The High Court concluded that "*a British military prison, operating in Iraq with the consent of the Iraqi sovereign authorities, and containing arrested suspects, falls within even a narrowly limited exception exemplified by embassies, consulates, vessels and aircraft, and ..., a prison*" and that "*the case of Mr Baha Mousa's death in the custody of British forces in Iraq comes within the scope of the [ECHR] as falling within the jurisdiction of the [UK] ... but that the other claims ... arising out of shootings of Iraqis by British forces in the field fail on the ground that those shootings occurred outside the jurisdiction of the [UK] and thus outside the scope of the [ECHR]*".[2322] The Court of Appeal upheld this decision but recognized a somewhat broader reach of the ECHR and UK Human Rights Act (HRA), accepting that "*the HRA has extra-territorial effect in those cases where a public authority is found to have exercised extra-territorial jurisdiction on the application of [State Agent Authority] principles*").[2323] The relatives of the five applicants killed in the shootings appealed to the House of Lords, as did the Secretary of Defence in respect of the reasoning of the Appeals Court relating to the detention

2321 See *supra*, Chapter 7.H and Chapter 8.F and *infra*, Section E of this chapter. Some aspects of this decision were later confirmed by the ECtHR in *Gajic v. Germany*, 28 August 2007 (admissibility) and *Dusan Beric and Others v. Bosnia and Herzegovina*, 16 October 2007 (admissibility). See also F. Sperotto, 'More on Al Skeini and Extraterritorial Effects of Human Rights Treaties', Issue 11 *NATO Legal Gazette*, 31 January 2008, pp. 2–5.

2322 [2004] EWHC 2911 (Admin), 14 December 2004 (available online at www.bailii.org/ew/cases/EWHC/Admin/2004/2911.html), §§287 en 344. See also T. Abdel-Monem, P. Kennedy, & E. Apostolova, 'R (on the Application of Al Skeini) v. Secretary of Defence: A Look at the United Kingdom's Extraterritorial Obligations in Iraq and Beyond', 17 *Florida J.I.L.* 2005, pp. 345–364 (questioning the judgment's interpretation of the ECtHR's case law at pp. 357–358); S. Horvat, 'The Extension of Jurisdiction of a State to the Territory of Another State in his Effective Control: The Al-Skeini Judgment of the England and Wales High Court of Justice', 43(3–4) *R.D.M.D.G.* 2004, pp. 155–192; R. Wilde, *supra* note 2306, pp. 120–124 and J. Williams, 'Al Skeini: A Flawed Interpretation of Bankovic', 23 *Wisconsin I.L.J.* 2005, pp. 687–729.

2323 [2005] EWCA Civ 1609, 21 December 2005 (available online at www.bailii.org/ew/cases/EWCA/Civ/2005/1609.html), §147.

death case, while accepting the more narrow reasoning of the Divisional Court in respect of the latter. The House of Lords dismissed all the appeals.[2324]

This judgment would seem to mean that anyone held in UK (forces') detention facilities would be within the jurisdiction of the UK, a result that is in line with the ECtHR's case law discussed above, especially *Ocalan*, and which appears to have been questioned no longer by the UK in a further Iraq detention case, namely *Al-Jedda*.[2325] However, the judgment's conclusion that people in an area occupied by UK forces and killed in combat or other shooting incidents there were not within the jurisdiction of the UK[2326] seems questionable given that occupied territory is by definition "*actually placed under the authority of the hostile army [and] extends only to the territory where such authority has been established and can be exercised*"[2327] and given the ECtHR's case law discussed above, especially *Loizidou* and *Issa*.

One may conclude that the ECHR has extraterritorial application where a State Party exercises effective control over another territory or when it detains people abroad.[2328] However, the precise degree of control required may not be so easy to

---

2324 [2007] UKHL 26 (available online at www.publications.parliament.uk/pa/ld200607/ldjudgmt/jd070613/skeini-1.pdf). For annotations, see R. Nigro, 'Il caso Al-Skeini dinanzi alla House of Lords e la nozione di giurisdizione nella Convenzione europea diritti dell'uomo', 90 *Rivista di diritto internazionale* 2007, pp. 1106–1115; T. Thienel, 'The ECHR in Iraq: The Judgment of the House of Lords in R (Al-Skeini) v. Secretary of State for Defence', 6 *J.I.C.J.* 2008, pp. 115–128 and R. Wilde, 'R (on the Application of Al-Skeini) v. Secretary of State for Defence (Redress Trust Intervening): (2007) UKHL 26: UK House of Lords Opinions on Whether the European Convention on Human Rights, as Implemented Through the 1998 Human Rights Act, Has Extraterritorial Effect: United Kingdom House of Lords, June 13, 20007', 102 *A.J.I.L.* 2008, pp. 628–634. The case is pending before the ECtHR.

2325 *Supra* note 2161.

2326 See the appeals judgment (*supra* note 2323), §§124 ("*it is quite impossible to hold that the UK, although an occupying power for the purposes of the Hague Regulations and Geneva IV, was in effective control of Basrah City for the purposes of ECHR jurisprudence at the material time*") and 127 ("*I should make it clear that I reject the arguments by the claimants to the effect that occupation for the purposes of the Hague Regulations must necessarily be equated with effective control of the occupied area for ECHR purposes*").

2327 Article 42 Hague Regulations, which is still in force and has achieved a customary law status; see *supra*, Chapter 8.D.

2328 Compare, with regard to military operations, H. Krieger, *supra* note 2284, pp. 673–688, who makes an analysis based on a distinction between peace enforcement (no human rights in combat but human rights in occupation), "peace consolidating" operations (apparently covering robust peacekeeping; human rights if a direct exercise of powers of government but not in cases of mere support to local authorities), peacekeeping (no human rights in observer missions but possibly for other operations that include law and order tasks) and counter-terrorism operations (human rights in case of detention). However, the mere difficulty of distinguishing between these kinds of operations already illustrates the limited use of this distinction for the purpose of the applicability of human rights. N. Tsagourias, *supra* note 2278, p. 118 is of the view that human rights apply to both non-coercive and coercive peace operations – in the latter case concurrently with the LOAC. See also P. van Dijk, 'The Venice determine, as is clear from the British judgments in *Al-Skeini*. Beyond this, the Court's "all or nothing" approach adopted in *Bankovic* implied that there is little room for application of the ECHR but its more recent case law appears to have overturned this. As argued above, I submit that the latter tendency is the better one and that one should accept that the ECHR may apply partially to the extent of the exercise of jurisdiction, however limited. Thus, in combat situations in areas not under effective control, only the right to life might apply.

2. THE INTERNATIONAL COVENANT ON CIVIL AND POLITICAL RIGHTS

According to Article 2(1) ICCPR "*Each State Party to the present Covenant undertakes to respect and to ensure to all individuals within its territory and subject to its jurisdiction the rights recognized in the present Covenant, without distinction of any kind [...]*".[2329] This provision may be interpreted in two ways: either it covers individuals who are *both* within the territory of a State Party and within its jurisdiction or it covers individuals who are within the territory of a State Party and individuals who are within its jurisdiction.[2330] Although the text rather supports the former interpretation (otherwise it might have read 'within its territory *or* subject to its jurisdiction'), international jurisprudence has overwhelmingly endorsed the latter interpretation.[2331]

This jurisprudence mainly consists of the views of the Human Rights Committee,[2332] which has argued that a literal interpretation would be

---

Commission on the Application of the European Convention on Human Rights Ratione Personae in Case of Peace Keeping and the Fight against Terrorism', in S. Horvat (ed.), *supra* note 2276, pp. 421–428. With regard to detention, see also P. van Dijk *et al.*, *Theory and Practice of the European Convention on Human Rights*, Antwerp, Intersentia, 2006 (4th ed.), pp. 462–463 (pro extraterritoriality).

2329 See generally S. Joseph, J. Schultz & M. Castan, *The International Covenant on Civil and Political Rights. Cases, Materials and Commentary*, Oxford, Oxford University Press, 2000, pp. 59–62 and *id.*, 2004 (2nd ed.), pp. 83–96 and M. Nowak, *U.N. Covenant on Civil and Political Rights. CCPR Commentary*, Kehl, Engel, 1993, pp. 42–43 and *id.*, 2005 (2nd ed.), pp. 43–44. See also D. Lorenz, *supra* note 2282, pp. 35–49.

2330 See D. McGoldrick, *supra* note 2295, pp. 47–49.

2331 For a more extensive discussion, see D. McGoldrick, *supra* note 2295, pp. 41–72; M. Scheinin, *supra* note 2296, pp. 73–81 and R. Wilde, *supra* note 2284, pp. 790–806.

2332 See especially *López Burgos v. Uruguay* (CCPR/C/13/D/52/1979, Communication No. 52/1979, 29 July 1981), §12; *Celiberti de Casariego v. Uruguay* (CCPR/C/13/D/56/1979, Communication No. 56/1979, 29 July 1981), §13 and *Montero v. Uruguay* (CCPR/C/18/D/106/1981, Communication No. 106/1981, 31 March 1983), §5 (it should be noted that in this case the argument rested at least in part on the nature of the right at stake, namely the right to leave any country including one's own country); *Concluding Observations: Netherlands*, 27 August 2001 (CCPR/CO/72/NET), §8 (relating to Dutch peacekeepers in Srebrenica, Bosnia); *Concluding Observations: Israel*, 21 August 2003 (CCPR/CO/78/ISR), §11 (relating to the 'unconscionable'[2333] and 'absurd'[2334] and has very clearly restated its view in its 2004 General Comment 31 as follows: "*States Parties are required by Article 2, paragraph 1, to respect and to ensure the Covenant rights to all persons who may be within their territory and to all persons subject to their jurisdiction. This means that a State party must respect and ensure the rights laid down in the Covenant to anyone within the power or effective control of that State Party, even if not situated within the territory of the State Party*".[2335] Moreover, this view was also adopted by the International Court of Justice, which held in its Advisory Opinion on the *Legal consequences of the construction of a wall in the occupied Palestinian territory* that "*the International Covenant on Civil and Political Rights is applicable in respect of acts done by a State in the exercise of its jurisdiction outside its own territory*".[2336] It is also supported by most authors,

---

occupied territories) and *Concluding Observations on the USA*, 3 October 1995 (CCPR/C/79/Add.50), §384. Various General Comments omit the territorial requirement or read it as an alternative; see, e.g. General Comments Nos. 3 (29 July 1981, §1); 21 (10 April 1992, §2) and 24 (4 November 1994, §12). See also T. Meron, 'Extraterritoriality of Human Rights Treaties', 89 *A.J.I.L.* 1995, p. 79, pointing to General Comment 23 (8 April 1994).

2333 HRC, *López Burgos v. Uruguay* and *Celiberti de Casariego v. Uruguay* (both *supra*, previous note), respectively §12.3 and §10.3 (identical wording): "*it would be unconscionable to so interpret the responsibility under Article 2 of the Covenant as to permit a State party to perpetrate violations of the Covenant on the territory of another State, which violations it could not perpetrate on its own territory*".

2334 *Id.*, concurring opinion of Mr. Tomuschat: "*To construe the words "within its territory" pursuant to their strict literal meaning as excluding any responsibility for conduct occurring beyond the national boundaries would, however, lead to utterly absurd results*". See also D. McGoldrick, *supra* note 2295, p. 48.

2335 21 April 2004, CCPR/C/74/CRP.4/Rev.6, §10.

2336 9 July 2004, §§108–111, especially §111. For a discussion of this advisory opinion, see, e.g. F. Becker, 'IGH-Gutachten über "Rechtliche Konsequenzen des Baus einer Mauer in den besetzten palästinensischen Gebieten"', 43 *A.V.R.* 2005, pp. 218–239; P.H.F. Bekker, 'The World Court's Ruling regarding Israel's West Bank Barrier and the Primacy of International Law: An Insider's Perspective', 38 *Cornell I.L.J.* 2005, pp. 553–568; K. Bradley, 'A Mending Wall: A Critical Look at the International Court of Justice's Analysis in its Advisory Opinion on the Legal Consequences of the Construction of a Wall in the Occupied Palestinian Territory', 19 *Temple International and Comparative Law Journal* 2005, pp. 419–448 (especially pp. 427–429 and 436–437 on this point); S. Breau, 'Legal Consequences of the Construction of a Wall in the Occupied Palestinian Territory: Advisory Opinion, 9 July 2004', 54 *I.C.L.Q.* 2005, pp. 1003–1013 (especially pp. 1010–1011 on this point); K. Calvo-Goller, 'More than a Huge Imbalance: The ICJ's Advisory Opinion on the Legal Consequences of the Construction of the Barrier', 38 *Israel Law Review* 2005, pp. 165–188; R. Kahan, 'Building a Protective Wall around Terrorists: How the International Court of Justice's Ruling in the Legal Consequences of the Construction of a Wall in the Occupied Palestinian Territory Made the World Safer for Terrorists and More Dangerous for Member States of the United Nations', 28 *Fordham I.L.J.* 2005, pp. 827–878 (focusing on self-defence and not treating human rights and the LOAC); M.J. Kelly, 'Critical Analysis of the International Court of Justice Ruling on Israel's Security Barrier', 29 *Fordham I.L.J.* 2005, pp. 181–228; N. Lubell, 'The ICJ Advisory Opinion and the Separation Barrier: A Troublesome Route', 35 *Israel Y.H.R.* 2005, pp. 283–313; M. Mari, 'The ICJ's Advisory Opinion on the Consequences of Israel's Construction of a Separation Barrier in the Occupied Palestinian Territories: A Move in the Right Direction', 7 *Y.I.H.L.* 2004, pp. 373–387; R. O'Keefe, 'Legal Consequences of the Construction of a Wall in the Occupied Palestinian Territory: A Commentary', 37 albeit that they do not always agree on the precise scope of this extraterritorial application.[2337]

R.B.D.I./B.T.I.R. 2004, pp. 92–154; A. Orakhelashvili, 'International Public Order and the International Court's Advisory Opinion on Legal Consequences of the Construction of a Wall in the Occupied Palestinian Territory', 43 *A.V.R.* 2005, pp. 240–256; A. Orakhelashvili, 'Legal Consequences of the Construction of a Wall in the Occupied Palestinian Territory: Opinion and Reaction', 11 *J.C.S.L.* 2006, pp. 119–139; M. Pertile, '"Legal Consequences of the Construction of a Wall in the Occupied Palestinian Territory": A Missed Opportunity for International Humanitarian Law?', 14 *Italian Y.I.L.* 2004, pp. 121–161; N. Strapatsas, 'Case Note on the ICJ Advisory Opinion on the Legal Consequences of the Construction of the Wall in Occupied Palestinian Territority', 35 *Israel Y.H.R.* 2005, pp. 251–282; S. Verhoeven, 'Advisory Opinion on the Legal Consequences of the Construction of a Wall in the Occupied Palestinian Territories', 6 *International Law Forum du droit international* 2004, pp. 106–110; X., 'Agora: ICJ Advisory Opinion on Construction of a Wall in the Occupied Palestinian Territory', 99 *A.J.I.L.* 2005, pp. 1–141; X., 'Special Dossier on the Advisory Opinion of the International Court of Justice on the Legal Consequences of the Construction of a Wall in the occupied Palestinian Territory', 13 *Palestine Yearbook of International Law* 2007, pp. 109–336. See also Oxford Public Interest Lawyers, *Legal Consequences of Israel's Construction of a Separation Barrier in the Occupied Territories*, Oxford, February 2004 (available online at www.law.ox.ac.uk/opbp/OXPIL%20Israel%20Barrier%20Executive%20Summary.pdf) and X., 'Domestic and International Judicial Review of the Construction of the Separation Barrier', 38(1–2) *Israel Law Review* 2005, pp. 6–377 (special double issue). The ICJ later reaffirmed its view on this point in its judgment of 19 December 2005 in the *Case concerning armed activities on the territory of the Congo (DRC v. Uganda)*, §216. On the latter judgment, see J.T. Gathii, 'Armed Activities on the Territory of the Congo: Democratic Republic of the Congo v. Uganda: International Court of Justice, December 19, 2005', 101 *A.J.I.L.* 2007, pp. 142–149; P.N. Okowa, 'Case Concerning Armed Activities on the Territory of the Congo (Democratic Republic of the Congo v Uganda)', 55 *I.C.L.Q.* 2006, pp. 742–753 and G. Zyberi, 'The Development and Interpretation of International Human Rights and Humanitarian Law Rules and Principles Through the Case-Law of the International Court of Justice', 25 *Netherlands Quarterly of Human Rights* 2007, pp. 132–135. The Court's view in the latter case suggests M.J. Dennis, *supra* note 2282, p. 123 was wrong when arguing that the Court's former opinion was best read as only based on the occupied territories being part of Israeli territory for the purpose of the ICCPR. See also A.M. Gross, *infra* note 2512, p. 6 note 25 and compare the reflection by Buergenthal mentioned *infra*, next note.

2337 E.g. F. Becker, *supra* previous note (43 *A.V.R.* 2005), pp. 231–232; T. Buergenthal, 'To Respect and Ensure: State Obligations and Permissible Derogations', in L. Henkin (ed.), *The International Bill of Rights. The Covenant on Civil and Political Rights*, New York, Columbia University Press, 1981, pp. 72–77 (adding, interestingly, that the term "territory" also offers possibilities for a broad interpretation and could cover territory under control of a State that is not formally its own territory); A. Cassese, 'Are International Human Rights Treaties and Customary Rules on Torture Binding upon US Troops in Iraq?', 2 *J.I.C.J.* 2004, pp. 873–874; J. Cerone, *supra* note 2298, pp. 475–476; D. McGoldrick, *supra* note 2295, pp. 47–66; T. Meron, *supra* note 2332, pp. 79–82; M. Scheinin, *supra* note 2296, pp. 73–81 and R. Wilde, *supra* note 2284, pp. 790–806. S. Joseph, J. Schultz & M. Castan, *supra* note 2329 (2000), pp. 59–65, restate the HRC's views and seem to agree as they do not reject these views. *Contra*: M.J. Dennis, *supra* note 2282, pp. 122–127 (also citing other early commentators who adhered to the literal reading and further relying on the preparatory works to reject the applicability to cases of occupation; for a response on the latter point, see Human Rights First, *Memorandum to the Members of the Human Rights Committee*, 18 January 2006 (on file with the author), pp. 6–8). D. Lorenz, *supra* note 2282, pp. 84–88 admits that there is some support for a restrictive interpretation in the preparatory works but does not regard this as conclusive given the limited value of these preparatory works.

This view is also consistent with the Human Rights Committee's view that a State making a decision relating to a person within its jurisdiction of which the "*necessary and foreseeable consequence*" is that "*that person's rights under the Covenant will be violated in another jurisdiction*", may itself be in violation of the Covenant.[2338] It would indeed be absurd that a State were allowed to itself act in violation of the ICCPR outside its territory but would not be allowed to hand over someone to another State which it believes might do the same.

However, one should note that some States have contested this interpretation, or at least its applicability in a specific case.[2339] It has also been argued, similarly to a consideration made in *Bankovic*, that the lack of derogations with regard to military operations indicates that States do not regard the ICCPR as applying to such operations.[2340] On the other hand, some countries have accepted it.[2341] Moreover, as the Human Rights Committee has started to ask States' views on the matter,[2342] these views may well be formally expressed in the replies[2343] and may offer useful insights. Finally, it should also be noted that the extraterritoriality is also a prominent issue in the "war on terror", including with regard to detention centres run abroad and especially the US detention facility at

2338 See, e.g. *Kindler v. Canada* (CCPR/C/48/D/470/1991, Communication No. 470/1991, 18 November 1993), §6.2.

2339 See, e.g. the Netherlands relating to Dutch peacekeepers in Srebrenica, BiH (CCPR/CO/72/NET/Add.1, 29 April 2003) and the US (see, e.g. the HRC's *Concluding Observations on the USA*, CCPR/C/79/Add.50; A/50/40, 3 October 1995, §384; for more details on the US view, see Doc. CCPR/C/USA/3, 28 November 2005, Annex I, pp. 109–112). See also M.J. Dennis, *supra* note 2282, pp. 125–126. See also the short overview in B. Schäfer, *supra* note 2282, pp. 23–24 (who does seem to misrepresent the Belgian view; however, see *infra* note 2341). But see, with regard to the Netherlands, Koninklijke Landmacht (Netherlands Army), *Humanitair oorlogsrecht. Handleiding, s.l., s.n.*, 2005, pp. 158–160 and 196–198, §§1018–1022 and 1211–1212 (recognizing the possible applicability of human rights in operations).

2340 M.J. Dennis, *supra* note 2282, pp. 125–126.

2341 E.g. Belgium has accepted some extraterritorial application of the ICCPR in relation to one of the UN Missions in Somalia; see HRC, *Concluding Observations: Belgium*, CCPR/C/79/Add.99, 19 November 1998, §14: "*The Committee is concerned about the behaviour of Belgian soldiers in Somalia under the aegis of [UNOSOM II], and acknowledges that the State party has recognized the applicability of the Covenant in this respect*".

2342 See, e.g. *Concluding Observations on Germany* (CCPR/CO/80/DEU, 4 May 2004), §11 and *Concluding Observations on Belgium* (CCPR/CO/81/BEL, 12 August 2004), §6.

2343 For the response by Germany, see its statement in CCPR/CO/80/DEU/Add.1, 11 April 2005, p. 3 ("*Pursuant to Article 2, paragraph 1, Germany ensures the rights recognized in the Covenant to all individuals within its territory and subject to its jurisdiction. Wherever its police or armed forces are deployed abroad, in particular when participating in peace missions, Germany ensures to all persons that they will be granted the rights recognized in the Covenant, insofar as they are subject to its jurisdiction. Germany's international duties and obligations, in particular those assumed in fulfilment of obligations stemming from the Charter of the United Nations, remain unaffected. …*").

Guantanamo Bay, which is on Cuban territory but otherwise is under full US jurisdiction.[2344]

Moreover, the Human Rights Committee, contrary to the ECtHR, has endorsed the more nuanced approach permitting a partial extraterritorial application where only limited jurisdiction is exercised extraterritorially. In a case concerning Senegalese nationals who were retired after service in the French armed forces and who lived in Senegal but were affected by a discriminatory French pensions law, the HRC held that "*the authors are not generally subject to French jurisdiction, except that they rely on French legislation in relation to the amount of their pension rights*".[2345]

It may therefore be concluded that, despite a more restrictive text and opposition from some States, the ICCPR has been interpreted by international courts and supervisory organs as having some extraterritorial scope of application, including a partial one in respect of limited extraterritorial jurisdiction.[2346]

3. OTHER HUMAN RIGHTS TREATIES

The International Covenant on Economic, Social and Cultural Rights[2347] does not contain an explicit territorial or jurisdictional limit and its scope of application is not really defined.[2348] However, both the Committee on Economic, Social and Cultural Rights and the International Court of Justice have accepted

---

2344 See generally L. Condorelli & P. De Sena, 'The Relevance of the Obligations Flowing from the UN Covenant on Civil and Political Rights to US Courts Dealing with Guantánamo Detainees', 2 *J.I.C.J.* 2004, pp. 107–120. See also D. Schneider, 'Human Rights Issues in Guantanamo Bay', 68 *Journal of Criminal Law* 2004, pp. 423–439, especially pp. 430–431. However, it seems that arguments based on the ICCPR have played only a minor role, if any, in the key decisions by US courts so far. Nevertheless, the matter has been brought before the IAComHR; see *infra*, next subsection, note 2359 and the accompanying text.

2345 *Ibrahim Gueye et al. v. France*, Communication No. 196/1985, 6 April 1989, CCPR/C/35/D/196/1985, §9.4. See M. Scheinin, *supra* note 2296, pp. 74–75.

2346 Compare T. Meron, *supra* note 2332, p. 80, who argues that only some of the ICCPR rights are, by their nature, intended for extraterritorial application. However, while it does seem correct that certain rights lend themselves more easily to extraterritorial application, e.g. protections such as that against torture, I would argue that it is rather the degree of jurisdiction exercised that matters.

2347 New York, 16 December 1966, 993 *U.N.T.S.* 3.

2348 For a more extensive analysis of extraterritoriality in relation to this treaty, see F. Coomans, 'Some Remarks on the Extraterritorial Application of the International Covenant on Economic, Social and Cultural Rights', in F. Coomans & T. Kamminga (eds.), *supra* note 2282, pp. 183–199 and R. Künneman, 'Extraterritorial Application of the International Covenant on Economic, Social and Cultural Rights', in *id.*, pp. 201–231.

that it may apply extraterritorially.[2349] The International Court of Justice also arrived at the same conclusion with respect to the Convention on the Rights of the Child.,[2350] [2351]

Pursuant to Article 1 ACHR[2352] the State Parties thereto "*undertake to respect the rights and freedoms recognized herein and to ensure to all persons subject to their jurisdiction the free and full exercise of those rights and freedoms*".[2353] The American Declaration on the Rights and Duties of Man,[2354] which is not a treaty but nevertheless a "*source of international obligations*" for the OAS Member States,[2355] contains no jurisdictional limitation in its text, but the IAComHR has held that, with respect to this Declaration, "*each American State is obliged to*

2349 See the ICJ's Advisory Opinion on the *Legal consequences of the construction of a wall in the occupied Palestinian territory* (9 July 2004), §112 and the references therein and the discussion by J. Cerone, *supra* note 2282, pp. 1474 and 1477–1478. But see M.J. Dennis, *supra* note 2282, pp. 127–128, noting that absent specific rules, Article 29 VCLT ("*Unless a different intention appears from the treaty or is otherwise established, a treaty is binding upon each party in respect of its entire territory*") implies a territorial scope of application only. However, the ILC commentary No. 5 to the corresponding earlier draft Article 25 makes it clear that this provision did not concern the possible extraterritorial application ("*The Article was intended by the Commission to deal only with the limited topic of the application of a treaty to the territory of the respective parties; .... In its view, the law regarding the extra-territorial application of treaties could not be stated simply in terms of the intention of the parties or of a presumption as to their intention; and it considered that to attempt to deal with all the delicate problems of extra-territorial competence in the present Article would be inappropriate and inadvisable*"); see *Y.I.L.C.* 1966-II, pp. 213–214.

2350 New York, 20 November 1989, 1577 *U.N.T.S.* 3 and Annex to UNGA Res. 44/25 (20 November 1989). Article 2(1) of this convention stipulates that "*States Parties shall respect and ensure the rights set forth in the present Convention to each child within their jurisdiction without discrimination of any kind* ...".

2351 ICJ, Advisory Opinion on the *Legal consequences of the construction of a wall in the occupied Palestinian territory*, 9 July 2004, §113. Compare M.J. Dennis, *supra* note 2282, p. 129.

2352 American Convention on Human Rights, San José, 22 November 1969, *OAS Treaties Series* No. 36.

2353 For a more extensive analysis of the extraterritoriality of the Inter-American human rights instruments, see D. Cassel, 'Extraterritorial Application of Inter-American Human Rights Instruments', in F. Coomans & T. Kamminga (eds.), *supra* note 2282, pp. 175–181; C.M. Cerna, 'Extraterritorial Application of the Human Rights Instruments of the Inter-American System', in *id.*, pp. 141–174 and D. Lorenz, *supra* note 2282, pp. 49–60. See also J. Cerone, 'The Application of Regional Human Rights Law Beyond Regional Frontiers: The Inter-American Commission on Human Rights and US Activities in Iraq', *ASIL Insight*, 25 October 2005, www.asil.org/insights051025.cfm; J. Cerone, *supra* note 2282, pp. 1478–1481 and J. Cerone, *supra* note 2298, pp. 476–478.

2354 Resolution XXX, Final Act of the Ninth International Conference of American States, Bogota, 30 March – 2 May 1948, available online at www1.umn.edu/humanrts/oasinstr/zoas2dec.htm.

2355 IACtHR, *Interpretation of the American Declaration of the Rights and Duties of Man within the Framework of Article 64 of the American Convention on Human Rights*, Advisory Opinion OC-10/89, 14 July 1989, §§41–47, especially p. 45. This finding was reaffirmed by the IAComHR *inter alia* in *Coard et al. v. United States*, Report No. 109/99, Case 10.951, §36.

uphold the protected rights of any person subject to its jurisdiction".[2356] In 1999, in *Coard et al. v. United States*, the IAComHR held, referring to a number of its previous decisions pertaining to extraterritorial State actions,[2357] that, under the American Declaration on the Rights and Duties of Man, while "*any person subject to its jurisdiction*" most commonly refers to persons within a state's territory, "*it may, under given circumstances, refer to conduct with an extraterritorial locus where the person concerned is present in the territory of one state, but subject to the control of another state – usually through the acts of the latter's agents abroad*" and that "*in principle, the inquiry turns ... on ... whether, under the specific circumstances, the State observed the rights of a person subject to its authority and control*".[2358] This was again reaffirmed in 2002 with regard to persons detained by the US at Guantanamo Bay, Cuba[2359] and in the Commission's report on *Terrorism and Human Rights*.[2360]

The African Charter on Human and Peoples Rights[2361] contains no explicit jurisdictional limit and I have no knowledge of any case law addressing this issue.

While the extraterritorial application of human rights instruments depends on the specific instrument concerned, all conventions discussed above have some degree of extraterritorial application. With the growing awareness of this issue, it is likely that case law will continue to further delimitate the exact scope of this extraterritorial application.

2356 E.g. *Coard et al. v. United States*, *supra* previous note, §37.

2357 For the references, see *id.*, note 7.

2358 *Coard et al. v. United States*, *supra* note 2355, §37.

2359 IAComHR, Decision Authorizing Precautionary Measures in Favor of Detainees Being Held by the United States at Guantanamo Bay, Cuba, 12 March 2002 (previously available online at www.ccr-ny.org/v2/legal/september_11th/docs/3-13-02%20 IACHRAdoptionofPrecautionaryMeasures.pdf): "*These rights ... prescribed under the American Declaration of the Rights and Duties of Man, which constitutes a source of legal obligation for all OAS member states [...] in respect of persons subject to their authority and control*". See also the IAComHR's 2002 annual report, available online at www.cidh.oas.org/annualrep/2002eng/toc.htm, §80. For a discussion of this decision and its follow up, see generally B.D. Tittemore, 'Guantanamo Bay and the Precautionary Measures of the Inter-American Commission on Human Rights: A Case for International Oversight in the Struggle against Terrorism', 6 *H.R.L.R.* 2006, pp. 378–402.

2360 Doc. OEA/Ser.L/V/II.116 Doc. 5 rev. 1 corr., 22 October 2002 (available online at www.cidh.oas.org/Terrorism/Eng/toc.htm), §44: "*a state's human rights obligations are not dependent upon a person's nationality or presence within a particular geographic area, but rather extend to all persons subject to that state's authority and control*".

2361 Nairobi, 27 June 1981.

4. EXTRATERRITORIAL SCOPE OF APPLICATION OF CUSTOMARY INTERNATIONAL HUMAN RIGHTS?

As most States are bound by at least some human rights treaties, the customary status of human rights is not of great importance. However, for international organizations the matter is quite different and, as has become clear in Chapter 7, with the exception of a possible future accession of the EU to the ECHR, no international organization is a party to a human rights treaty. Therefore, in respect of international organizations, customary international human rights law is particularly relevant.

It would exceed the scope of this section to inquire into the extent to which human rights are part of customary international law.[2362] It may suffice to note that in comparison with the LOAC, human rights treaties may be less widely ratified, at least at the universal level and in comparison with the 1949 Geneva Conventions, though less so compared to a number of more specific LOAC treaties.[2363] On the other hand, human rights may be more solidly enshrined in domestic law than the LOAC, a factor which is relevant as evidence of State practice. Moreover, it may well be that the adherence by all or nearly all States in a given region to specific regional human rights instruments[2364] supports the view that these have become regional customary international law.[2365]

2362 For a valiant attempt, see T. Meron, *Human Rights and Humanitarian Norms as Customary Law*, Oxford, Clarendon Press, 1989, pp. 79–135. See also R.B. Lillich, 'The Growing Importance of Customary International Human Rights Law', 25 *Georgia J.I.C.L.* 1996, pp. 1–30 and Kolb, Poretto & Vité , pp. 253–260.

2363 In 1983, B. de Schutter & C. van de Wijngaert, 'Coping with Non-International Armed Conflicts: The Borderline between National and International Law', 13 *Georgia J.I.C.L.* 1983, p. 282, wrote that the ICCPR had only been ratified by a relatively small number of States (70 at the time). See also T. Meron, *supra* note 2374, pp. 4–5 (adding at pp. 4–10 that human rights have achieved customary status to a lesser extent than the LOAC). However, by July 2009 this number had increased to 164 – i.e. about the same number of parties as AP I and AP II, which counted respectively 168 and 164 parties by this date. By this date, the Convention on the Rights of the Child (*supra* note 2350) only trailed the 1949 Geneva Conventions by one party (193 parties v. 194) and does far better than the Convention for the Protection of Cultural Property in the Event of Armed Conflict (The Hague, 14 May 1954) with its 123 parties and the Convention on Prohibitions or Restrictions on the Use of Certain Conventional Weapons Which May be Deemed to be Excessively Injurious or to Have Indiscriminate Effects (Geneva, 10 October 1980) with 109 parties. This information was retrieved from http://treaties.un.org and www.icrc.org/ihl on 25 July 2009.

2364 E.g. the ECHR with its 47 parties (http://conventions.coe.int) covers essentially all of Europe, except Belarus. The African Charter on Human and Peoples' Rights (*supra* note 2361), counts 53 parties (www.africa-union.org/root/au/Documents/Treaties/treaties.htm) – i.e. all AU Member States. The ACHR is less widely ratified in the Americas and counts 'only' 25 parties (www.oas.org/juridico/english/sigs/b-32.html), out of the continent's 35 States.

2365 E. de Wet, 'The Emergence of International and Regional Value Systems as a Manifestation of the Emerging International Constitutional Order', 19 *Leiden J.I.L.* 2006, pp. 617 and 631–632.

In any event, the question that must be addressed here is whether there is any customary international law regarding the scope of application of customary human rights, and if so, what it says. At first sight, one might perhaps argue that customary human rights would not be subject to limitations on their scope of application.[2366] However, that hardly seems convincing. Rather, it would be logical that limitations on the scope of application of human rights in State practice, on which the customary rules are based, also apply to customary human rights.[2367] More specifically, any extraterritorial elements would have to be sufficiently accepted in State practice and accompanied by *opinion iuris* to become customary law.

A detailed analysis would therefore require looking at practice under domestic law and treaty law and the views of States on this matter. Again, this would exceed the scope of this section. However, on the basis of the analysis of the extraterritorial scope of application of the different treaties discussed above, it may be suggested that the customary law scope of application is "*anyone within the jurisdiction*" of a State or an international organization,[2368] including at least situations of effective control over a territory and authority and control over a person.[2369] The reading of this scope of application into the International

Some authors have even argued that the ECHR may have acquired the status of regional *ius cogens*, at least to some extent. See, e.g. *id.*, pp. 617 ("arguably") and 631–632 ("debatable") and F. de Quadros, 'La Convention Européenne des Droits de l'Homme: un cas de ius cogens régional?', in U. Beyerlin *et al.* (eds.), *Recht zwischen Umbruch und Bewahrung – Festschift für Rudolf Bernhardt*, Berlin, Springer, 1995, pp. 555–562.

2366 In this sense J. Cerone, *supra* note 2282, p. 1494, ironically citing the US Judge-Advocate General's *Operational Law Handbook* (2006 edition available online at www.jagcnet.army.mil/TJAGSA), p. 45 (p. 47 of the 2006 edition states: "*If a "human right" is considered to have risen to the status of customary international law, then it is likely considered binding on U.S. State actors wherever such actors deal with human beings. According to the Restatement (Third) of Foreign Relations Law of the United States, international law is violated by any State that "practices, encourages, or condones" a violation of human rights considered customary international law. The Restatement makes no qualification as to where the violation might occur, or against whom it may be directed. Therefore, it is the customary international law status of certain human rights that renders respect for such human rights a legal obligation on the part of U.S. forces conducting operations outside the United States, and not the fact that they may be reflected in treaties ratified by the United States*"). See also N. Lubell, 'Challenges in Applying Human Rights Law to Armed Conflict', 87 No. 860 *I.R.R.C.* 2005, p. 741 and A. Cassimatis, 'International Humanitarian Law, International Human Rights Law, and Fragmentation of International Law', 56 *I.C.L.Q.* 2007, p. 635 (arguing that most customary human rights are not territorially limited).

2367 Similarly to the fact that LOAC rules that become customary international law remain limited to the kind of armed conflict in which they apply (unless they also acquire that status in other kinds of armed conflicts independently from this), see *supra*, Chapter 8.C.

2368 In this sense A. Clapham, *Human Rights Obligations of Non-State Actors*, Oxford, Oxford University Press, 2006, p. 68.

2369 Compare D. Lorenz, *supra* note 2282, p. 61 (who sees a clear acceptance for effective control or personal control but a lack of clarity as to what constitutes effective control (see also *id.*, pp.

Covenant on Economic, Social and Cultural Rights and into the American Declaration on the Rights and Duties of Man absent a defined scope of application in these instruments is particularly instructive in this respect.[2370] The view expressed by the International Court of Justice[2371] and by several scholars[2372] also supports this thesis. However, it must be acknowledged that, as mentioned above, at least some States have resisted these developments.[2373] Should it become clear that the number of States opposing extraterritoriality is significant, *opio iuris* would be lacking and therefore no customary rule of extraterritoriality would exist.

5. CONCLUSION

The question to what extent human rights apply extraterritorially has become the subject of considerable debate, especially the last ten years or so. International jurisprudence supports a significant degree of extraterritorial applicability of human rights based on the notion of persons within the jurisdiction of a State but the precise scope of this applicability has yet to be clarified and may depend to some extent on the specific scope of application of the human rights treaty at

---

88–102) and questions with regard to combat actions and argues that the HRC and IAComHR have rejected *Bankovic*) and B. Schäfer, *supra* note 2282, p. 34.

2370 See *supra*, the preceding subsection of this section.

2371 See especially the judgment of 19 December 2005 in the *Case concerning armed activities on the territory of the Congo (DRC v. Uganda)*, §216: "*The Court further concluded that* international human rights instruments *are applicable "in respect of acts done by a State in the exercise of its jurisdiction outside its own territory"*. This statement seems to have a general scope not limited to any specific instrument and therefore arguably supports a similar conclusion for customary law. Similarly, J. Cerone, *supra* note 2282, pp. 1474–1478, especially pp. 1477–1478.

2372 E.g. A. Cassese, *supra* note 2337, pp. 872–873 and 877 (with respect to the customary law prohibition on torture) and J. Cerone, *supra* note 2298, pp. 478–479 (deducing the rule that a State's human rights obligations extend to individuals outside its territory but under its control). Similarly, T. Meron, *supra* note 2332, pp. 80–82, argues that "*the presumption should be that the state's obligation to respect the pertinent human rights continues [extraterritorially] ... That presumption could be rebutted only when the nature and content of a particular right or treaty language suggest otherwise*". Compare T. Meron, *The Humanization of International Law*, Leiden, Nijhoff, 2006, pp. 462–466.

2373 In some cases, it appears that there are also differences of opinion between government departments. E.g, this appears to be, or has been, the case in the UK; see §208 of the *Al-Skeini* appeals judgment (*supra* note 2323): "*I would also add my appreciation of the disclosure to the court of correspondence manifesting a significant difference of opinion between two departments of state on a matter of importance to these claims. Ordinarily governmental policy positions are simply reflected in the line of argument put forward by Treasury counsel, ... But this is not possible where government itself is divided. It seems to me an honourable thing, as well as a step in the direction of open government, that in such circumstances the court - which means in turn the parties and the public - should be told of the division of view*". I have been told that this was also the case in Germany.

issue. However, there seems to be a growing consensus that effective control over territory and effective control over persons (especially detention) constitute jurisdiction in this sense and lead to the applicability of human rights. Beyond this, including in combat situations and in cases of the exercise of limited authority, the matter is not settled. However, I have argued in this respect that the better interpretation is that even the exercise of limited jurisdiction triggers the applicability of those human rights affected by this exercise of jurisdiction and the case law appears to evolve in that direction.

C. LIMITED SCOPE OF APPLICATION OF HUMAN RIGHTS IN WAR AND EMERGENCIES: DEROGATIONS

1. GENERAL

While human rights treaties are primarily designed for normal peacetime situations, most key human rights treaties contain derogation clauses that permit derogation of most human rights in certain emergency situations,[2374] though

[2374] E.g. Article 4 ICCPR; Article 15 ECHR and Article 27 ACHR (on the latter, see also *Report on Terrorism and Human Rights, supra* note 2360, §§49–52). See generally H. Duffy, *The "War on Terror" and the Framework of International Law*, Cambridge, Cambridge University Press, 2005, pp. 290–301; A. Eide, 'International Disturbances and Tensions', in Henry Dunant Institute & UNESCO (eds.), *International Dimensions of Humanitarian Law*, Geneva, UNESCO, 1988, pp. 241–256; J. Fitzpatrick, *Human Rights in Crisis: The International System for Protecting Rights During States of Emergency*, Philadelphia, University of Pennsylvania Press, 1994; L.C. Green, 'Derogation of Human Rights in Emergency Situations', 16 *C.Y.I.L.* 1978, pp. 92–115; O. Gross & F. Ni Aoláin, *Law in Times of Crisis: Emergency Powers in Theory and Practice*, Cambridge, Cambridge University Press, 2006; J.F. Hartman, 'Derogation from Human Rights Treaties in Public Emergencies – A Critique of Implementation by the European Commission and Court of Human Rights and the Human Rights Committee of the United Nations', 22 *Harvard I.L.J.* 1981, pp. 1–52; R. Higgins, 'Derogations under Human Rights Treaties', 48 *B.Y.I.L.* 1978, pp. 281–320; J.-P. Loof, *Mensenrechten en staatsveiligheid: verenigbare grootheden?: Opschorting en beperking van mensenrechtenbescherming*, Nijmegen, Wolf Legal Publishers, 2005 (available online at https://openaccess.leidenuniv.nl/dspace/handle/1887/4467); T. Meron, *Human Rights in Internal Strife: Their International Protection*, Cambridge, Grotius, 1987; J. Oraa, *Human Rights in States of Emergency in International Law*, Oxford, Clarendon Press, 1992; D. Prémont (ed.). *Droits intangibles et états d'exception. Non-Derogable Rights and States of Emergency.* Brussels, Bruylant, 1996 and S. Schmahl, 'Derogation von Menschenrechtsverpflichtungen in Notstandslagen', in D. Fleck (ed.), *Rechtsfragen der Terrorismusbekämpfung durch Streitkräfte*, Baden-Baden, Nomos, 2004, pp. 125–146. See also the 'Siracusa Principles on the Limitation and Derogation Provisions in the International Covenant on Civil and Political Rights', 7 *H.R.Q.* 1985, pp. 1–14 and the commentary and working paper on the derogation aspect, *id.*, respectively pp. 23–34 and 89–131. See also the references *supra*, Chapter 8.B.1, especially note 2007 and accompanying text.

some do not.[2375] In addition, it may be recalled that most human rights are not absolute but are subject to certain limitations.[2376] Such limitations are typically stipulated in specific provisions[2377] and sometimes more generally.[2378]

In the following subsections, I will look at the derogation clauses under the ECHR and ICCPR and consider the issue of derogation under customary international law, as well as the impact of Security Council intervention. The

2375 The African Charter on Human and Peoples Rights (*supra* note 2361) does not contain a derogation clause; see L. Sermet, 'De la carence dans la Charte africaine des droit de l'homme et des peuples de la clause de dérogation aux droit de l'homme', 109 *R.G.D.I.P.* 2005, pp. 389–406 (analyzing how this may be remedied) and L. Wessels, 'Derogation from Human Rights: A Possible Dispensation for Africa and Southern Africa', 27 *S.A.Y.I.L.* 2002, pp. 120–139, especially pp. 128–137 (arguing that a derogation is nonetheless possible in accordance with customary international law and especially general principles of law). Neither do some of the more specific human rights treaties, e.g. the Convention on the Rights of the Child (*supra* note 2350) and the International Covenant on Economic, Social and Cultural Rights. On the consequences of this lack of derogation mechanism, see F. Ouguergouz, 'L'absence de clause de dérogation dans certains traités relatifs aux droits de l'homme: les réponses du droit international général', 98 *R.G.D.I.P.* 1994, pp. 289–336. See also *infra*, subsection 4 of this Section.

2376 See generally the 'Siracusa Principles ...', *supra* note 2374, pp. 1–14 and the commentary and working paper on the limitation aspect, 7 *H.R.Q.* 1985, respectively pp. 15–22 and pp. 35–88. For a discussion of both limitations and derogations, see also UCL, Centre d'études européennes (ed.), *Les clauses échappatoires en matière d'instruments internationaux relatifs aux droits de l'homme: 4e colloque du Département des Droits de l'homme*, Brussels/Louvain-la-Neuve, Bruylant/Cabay, 1982.

2377 See, e.g. Article 8(2) ECHR ("*There shall be no interference by a public authority with the exercise of [the right to respect for private and family life] except such as is in accordance with the law and is necessary in a democratic society in the interests of national security, public safety or the economic well-being of the country, for the prevention of disorder or crime, for the protection of health or morals, or for the protection of the rights and freedoms of others*"); Article 18 ICCPR ("*3. Freedom to manifest one's religion or beliefs may be subject only to such limitations as are prescribed by law and are necessary to protect public safety, order, health, or morals or the fundamental rights and freedoms of others. 4. The States Parties to the present Covenant undertake to have respect for the liberty of parents and, when applicable, legal guardians to ensure the religious and moral education of their children in conformity with their own convictions*") and Article 15 ACHR ("*No restrictions may be placed on the exercise of [the right of peaceful assembly, without arms] other than those imposed in conformity with the law and necessary in a democratic society in the interest of national security, public safety or public order, or to protect public health or morals or the rights or freedom of others*").

2378 E.g. Article 4 International Covenant on Economic, Social and Cultural Rights ("*The States Parties to the present Covenant recognize that, in the enjoyment of those rights provided by the State in conformity with the present Covenant, the State may subject such rights only to such limitations as are determined by law only in so far as this may be compatible with the nature of these rights and solely for the purpose of promoting the general welfare in a democratic society*"). On the distinction between limitations/restrictions and derogations, see also HRC, General Comment 29 (*State of Emergency (Article 4)*, 31 August 2001), §§4 and 7. For a relativization of this distinction, see I. Seiderman, *Hierarchy in International Law*, Antwerp, Intersentia/Hart, 2001, pp. 70–77.

closely related question of the relationship between human rights and the LOAC will be addressed in the following section.

However, at this stage, some general features of the derogation clauses may be outlined. First, the circumstances that can give rise to derogation are described. Second, a derogation must normally be clearly invoked and officially notified.[2379] Third, a derogation does not give the State *carte blanche*. Some rights are non-derogable, in particular the right to life,[2380] albeit within its limitations, which include lawful acts of war,[2381] and the prohibitions of torture and cruel, inhuman or degrading treatment or punishment,[2382] of slavery[2383] and of punishment not based on criminal offences provided by law at the time the offence was committed.[2384] Under some treaties other rights may also be non-derogable.[2385] Fifth, measures derogating must limited to what is necessary in light of the circumstances.[2386] Sixth, a derogation does not absolve a State from other obligations under international law, including the LOAC, if applicable.[2387] In this respect, it is submitted that even where the LOAC does not apply, there is a presumption that its limits constitute the outer limits for a derogation.[2388] It is

2379 See Article 15(3) ECHR; Article 4(3) ICCPR and Article 27(3) ACHR.

2380 See Article 15(2) *juncto* 2 ECHR; Article 6 *juncto* 4(2) ICCPR and Article 27(2) *juncto* 4 ACHR.

2381 See Article 15(2) ECHR. The ICJ held in its Advisory Opinion on the *Legality of the Threat or Use of Nuclear Weapons* (8 July 1996), §25 that what constitutes an "arbitrary deprivation" under Article 6 ICCPR must, in armed conflicts, be determined according to the LOAC as *lex specialis*. Similarly, with respect to the ACHR, IAComHR, *Juan Carlos Abella v. Argentina* (Report 55/97, Case 11.137, 18 November 1997), §§157–171. Thus, while the right to life is non-derogable under the ICCPR and partially derogable under the ECHR, the effect is the same. See more extensively *infra*, Section D of this chapter.

2382 See Article 15(2) *juncto* 3 ECHR; Article 7 *juncto* 4(2) ICCPR and Article 27(2) *juncto* 5 ACHR.

2383 See Article 15(2) *juncto* 4(1) ECHR; Article 8(1) *juncto* 4(2) ICCPR and Article 27(2) *juncto* 6 ACHR.

2384 See Article 15(2) *juncto* 7 ECHR; Article 15 *juncto* 4(2) ICCPR and Article 27(2) *juncto* 9 ACHR.

2385 E.g. ICCPR Article 4(2) *juncto* Articles 11 (the prohibition of imprisonment for failure to fulfil contractual obligations), 16 (the right to recognition as a person before the law) and 18 (the right to freedom of thought, conscience and religion) and ACHR Article 27(2) *juncto* Articles 3 (the right to juridical personality), 12 (right to freedom of conscience and religion), 18 and 20 (right to a name and to nationality), 17 and 19 (rights of the family and of the child) and 23 (the right to participate in government) and "*the judicial guarantees essential for the protection of such rights*".

2386 J.F. Hartman, *supra* note 2374, p. 3, describes the first and sixth element as the two central standards.

2387 See Article 4(1) ICCPR; Article 27(1) ACHR and Article 15(1) *in fine* ECHR. See also the HRC's General Comment 29, *supra* note 2378, §9.

2388 Similarly, L. Moir, *The Law of Internal Armed Conflict*, Cambridge, Cambridge University Press, 2002, pp. 203–208, argues with respect to judicial guarantees that it would be reasonable to expect these to be no less in internal disturbances than in non-international armed hard to see how limitations on human rights in derogations in situations short of war could be absolutely necessary even though they would exceed the scope of actions permitted in war. Indeed, as the International Court of Justice stated in the *Corfu Channel* case, albeit in a somewhat different context: "*Such obligations are based ... on certain general and well-recognized principles, namely: elementary considerations of humanity,* even more exacting in peace than in war".[2389]

2. THE EUROPEAN CONVENTION ON HUMAN RIGHTS

i. The Derogation Clause

Article 15 ECHR reads as follows:

> 1. In time of war or other public emergency threatening the life of the nation any High Contracting Party may take measures derogating from its obligations under this Convention to the extent strictly required by the exigencies of the situation, provided that such measures are not inconsistent with its other obligations under international law.
>
> 2. No derogation from Article 2, except in respect of deaths resulting from lawful acts of war, or from Articles 3, 4 (paragraph 1) and 7 shall be made under this provision.
>
> 3. Any High Contracting Party availing itself of this right of derogation shall keep the Secretary General of the Council of Europe fully informed of the measures which it has taken and the reasons therefor. It shall also inform the Secretary General of the Council of Europe when such measures have ceased to operate and the provisions of the Convention are again being fully executed.[2390]

---

conflicts. In this sense also the remark by Lord Carswell in *Al-Jedda* (*infra* note 2435), §130 (with regard to the degree of necessity that must exist for security detention).

2389 *Corfu Channel (United Kingdom of Great Britain and Northern Ireland v. Albania)*, judgment of 9 April 1949, *I.C.J. Reports* 1949, p. 22 (emphasis added; the obligations concerned the obligation to notify, for the benefit of shipping in general, the existence of a minefield in a State's territorial waters and the elementary considerations of humanity identified by the Court in this case were the principle of the freedom of maritime communication and every State's obligation not to allow knowingly its territory to be used for acts contrary to the rights of other States). Similarly, A. Eide, *supra* note 2374, pp. 247–248 argues that States should not go beyond the limits of the LOAC in situations that do not reach the threshold of an armed conflict.

2390 See generally E. Chrysler, 'Brannigan and McBride v. U.K.: A New Direction on Article 15 Derogation under the European Convention on Human Rights?', 27 *R.B.D.I./B.T.I.R.* 1994, pp. 603–631; M. El Zeidi, 'The ECHR and States of Emergency: Article 15: A Domestic Power of Derogation from Human Rights Obligations', 11 *Michigan State University - Detroit College of Law Journal of International Law* 2002, pp. 261–306; R. Ergec, *Les droits de l'homme à l'épreuve des circonstances exceptionnelles: étude sur l'article 15 de la Convention européenne des droits de l'homme*, Brussels, Bruylant: Éditions de l'Université de Bruxelles, 1987; O. Gross

There is some case law on this provision, including with regard to Ireland and the UK in respect of Northern Ireland[2391] and with regard to Turkey[2392].[2393] Moreover, since '11 September', it has attracted renewed attention,[2394] especially in light of the UK's derogation concerning the detention of suspected terrorists.[2395]

& F. Ni Aolain, 'From Discretion to Scrutiny: Revisiting the Application of the Margin of Appreciation Doctrine in the Context of Article 15 of the European Convention on Human Rights', 23 *H.R.Q.* 2001, pp. 625–649; O. Gross & F. Ni Aoláin, *supra* note 2374, pp. 268–289; H.-E. Kitz, *Die Notstandsklausel des Article 15 der Europäischen Menschenrechtskonvention*, Berlin, Duncker & Humblot, 1982; R. St. J. Macdonald, 'Derogations under Article 15 of the European Convention on Human Rights', 36 *Colum. J Transn. L.* 1997, pp. 225–267; M. O'Boyle, 'The Margin of Appreciation and Derogation under Article 15: Ritual Incantation or Principle?', 19 *H.R.L.J.* 1998, pp. 23–29; P. Tavernier, 'Article 15', in L.-E. Pettiti, E. Decaux & P.-H. Imbert (eds.), *supra* note 2284, pp. 489–503 and P. van Dijk *et al.*, *supra* note 2328, pp. 1053–1075.

2391 See, e.g. ECtHR, *Lawless v. Ireland*, 1 July 1961; *Ireland v. the United Kingdom*, 13 December 1977 and *Brannigan and McBride v. UK*, 26 May 1993. See generally C. Warbrick, 'Emergency Powers and Human Rights: The UK Experiences', in C. Fijnaut, J. Wouters & F. Naert (eds.), *supra* note 2282, pp. 361–408.

2392 E.g. EComHR, Report of 10 July 1976, *Cyprus v. Turkey*, 4 *E.H.R.R.* 1982, pp. 482–582 and ECtHR, *Aksoy v Turkey*, 18 December 1996.

2393 The list of declarations to the ECHR on the Council of Europe's website (http://conventions.coe.int) reveals that in addition, derogations have, at one time, been notified by Albania and France.

2394 See, e.g. F. Vannneste & N. van Leuven, 'Noodtoestand: een vrijgeleide om terrorisme te bestrijden', in B. Pattyn & J. Wouters (eds.), *Schokgolven. Terrorisme, fundamentalisme en 11 september*, Leuven, Davidsfonds, 2002, pp. 147–158. For a somewhat broader perspective, see H. Duffy, *supra* note 2374, especially pp. 274–378; J. Fitzpatrick 'Speaking Law to Power: The War against Terrorism and Human Rights', 14 *E.J.I.L.* 2003, pp. 241–264; E. Guild, *Security and European Human Rights: Protecting Individual Rights in Times of Exception and Military Action*, Nijmegen, Wolf Legal Publishers, 2007; O. Gross & F. Ni Aoláin, *supra* note 2374, , pp. 365–421; D. Jinks, 'International Human Rights Law and the War on Terrorism', 31 *Denver J.I. L. & Policy* 2002, pp. 101–112; J.-P. Loof, *supra* note 2374; G.L. Neuman, 'Comment, Counter-terrorist Operations and the Rule of Law', 15 *E.J.I.L.* 2004, pp. 1019–1029; C. Warbrick, 'The European Response to Terrorism in an Age of Human Rights', 15 *E.J.I.L.* 2004, pp. 989–1018 and *Assessing Damage, Urging Action: Report of the Eminent Jurists Panel on Terrorism, Counter-terrorism and Human Rights*, 2009, www.icj.org/news.php3?id_Article=4453&lang=en. See also the references *infra*, next note. For an interdisciplinary and more comprehensive approach, see, e.g. B.J Goold & L. Lazarus (eds.), *Security and Human Rights*, Oxford, Hart, 2007.

2395 Declaration contained in a Note Verbale from the Permanent Representation of the United Kingdom, dated 18 December 2001, registered by the (Council of Europe) Secretariat General on 18 December 2001, previously available at the Council of Europe's Treaty Office website (http://conventions.coe.int). See generally E. Bates, 'A "Public Emergency Threatening the Life of the Nation"?: The United Kingdom's Derogation from the European Convention on Human Rights of 18 December 2001 and the "A" Case', 76 *B.Y.I.L.* 2005, pp. 245–335; V.H. Henning, 'Anti-terrorism, Crime and Security Act 2001: Has the United Kingdom Made a Valid Derogation from the European Convention on Human Rights?', 17 *A.U.I.L.R.* 2002, pp. 1263–1297 and C. Warbrick, *supra* note 2391, pp. 392–408. This derogation was withdrawn by a Note Verbale from the Permanent Representation of the United Kingdom dated 16 March 2005 (available http://conventions.coe.int).

I will briefly address those aspects that are most relevant for the purpose of this book. First, what is meant by "*time of war or other public emergency threatening the life of the nation*"? It appears that "war" covers not only war in the (traditional) formal sense, but also, or even rather, armed conflict in the sense of the LOAC, although it is not entirely clear whether this is limited to international armed conflicts or also covers non-international armed conflicts.[2396] It is submitted that, at least with regard to the use of lethal force, reliance on Article 15 ECHR may not be necessary in non-international armed conflicts given that Article 2(2)c ECHR covers death resulting from the use of force strictly necessary "*in action lawfully taken for the purpose of quelling a riot* or insurrection" (emphasis added).[2397] Whether non-international conflicts are excluded has little, if any, relevance as they might fall under other emergencies anyway. However, it might be relevant with regard to the automatic derogation question (see next paragraph).

There is another point here which does not seem quite settled, namely whether the applicability of the LOAC, especially the law of international armed conflict, *automatically* entails a derogation or a right to derogate, or whether even in this case derogations are only permitted if there is a threat to the life of the nation and to the extent strictly required by the situation (see also *infra* this subsection on the consequences of a failure to notify a derogation). The text ("*war or* other *public emergency threatening the life of the nation*"; emphasis added[2398]) and most commentators suggest the latter is the better view.[2399] However, it is doubtful

---

[2396] R. Ergec, *supra* note 2390, pp. 123–134, argues that it covers war in the material sense (which he defines as armed confrontations of a certain duration and scale between organized armies of governments (pp. 125–128), which would only cover international armed conflicts, but accepts that "lawful acts of war" would also cover such acts in non-international armed conflicts (pp. 244–245)). In the *Expert Meeting* ..., proceedings, *infra* note 2579, p. 13, it is stated that "*A number of experts doubted whether this derogation possibility under the [ECHR] was ever meant to encompass the situation of NIAC [non international armed conflicts], especially as NIAC was never referred to as "war" when the Convention was drafted*". P. van Dijk *et al.*, *supra* note 2328, pp. 1059–1060 consider the question as irrelevant since civil war may in any event be covered by other public emergencies threatening the life of the nation.

[2397] There appear to be few discussions of the meaning of insurrection in this provision, a concept which may cover non-international armed conflicts (see the discussion by T.J. Farer, 'The Regulation of Foreign Intervention in Civil Armed Conflict', 142 *Rec. Cours* 1974-II, pp. 318–319 and L. Moir, *supra* note 2388, pp. 4–5). For an exception, see T. Irmscher, 'Menschenrechtsverletzungen und bewaffneter Konflikt: die ersten Tschetschenien-Entscheidungen des Europäischen Gerichtshofs für Menschenrechte', 33 *Eur. Gr. R.Z.* 2006, pp. 12–13 and 17–18, who supports this view. See also G.L. Neuman, *supra* note 2394, p. 1021, who does seem to distinguish between international armed conflicts and 'war' in Article 15 ECHR on the one hand and "riots and insurrections" on the other hand.

[2398] Similarly R. Ergec, *supra* note 2390, p. 126.

[2399] H. Montealegre, *infra* note 2412, pp. 43–44, argues (at least with regard to non-international armed conflicts) that it is required that a war also amounts to a threat to the life of the nation.

whether the LOAC, and at least some of its rules, support this view. For instance, there is clearly a right to take prisoners of war and to detain them to prevent further participation in hostilities even in minor international armed conflicts that may not threaten the life of the nation – to the extent that the latter is possible – and it seems that States have rarely or even never notified derogations in this respect. Moreover, the European Commission and Court of Human Rights also seem to have applied the LOAC *de facto* in right to life cases even absent a derogation (in respect of this right), notably with regard to Cyprus[2400] and Turkey.[2401] This suggests that the applicability of the LOAC is automatic,[2402] even in non-international armed conflicts. However, the European Court of Human Right's recent case law on Chechnya casts some doubt on this.[2403] I would argue that an automatic derogation is the better view for international armed conflicts but that for non-international armed conflicts a derogation should not be automatic because of the lesser clarity of the law applicable to the latter conflicts.[2404] There might be some benefit in a differentiated regime with respect to international armed conflicts where some rules, e.g. on means and

Similarly, H. Krieger, *supra* note 2284, p. 690. This also seems to be the view of T. Irmscher, *supra* note 2396, pp. 16–17.

2400 See the Report of the EComHR of 10 July 1976 in *Cyprus v. Turkey*, 4 *E.H.R.R.* 1982, pp. 482–582, in which the LOAC was held to be applicable in derogation of some provisions of the ECHR (§313) despite the absence of a derogation pertaining to Northern Cyprus (§§525–531).

2401 See, e.g. ECtHR, *Ergi v. Turkey*, 28 July 1998, §§79–81, in which, despite the lack of discussion of any derogation, the Court judged that a security operation had to "*take all feasible precautions in the choice of means and methods of a security operation mounted against an opposing group with a view to avoiding and, in any event, to minimising, incidental loss of civilian life*" – wording closely resembling the wording of Article 57(2)a(ii) AP I (which requires those who plan or decide upon an attack to "*take all feasible precautions in the choice of means and methods of attack with a view to avoiding, and in any event to minimizing, incidental loss or civilian life, injury to civilians and damage to civilian objects*"). Also, the Court does not seem to have aired any concern that an ambush was set up for a PKK group, apparently with the intent to attack rather than capture the PKK members – an approach that can hardly be justified under Article 2 ECHR except by recourse to lawful acts of war as a derogation under Article 15 ECHR or reliance on Article 2(2)c ECHR (see also *infra* note 2403 and *supra* note 2397). I consider that the situation in that region at that time amounted to an armed conflict.

2402 In this sense also one expert in the *Expert Meeting ...*, proceedings, *infra* note 2579, p. 13 ("*One expert asserted that, in the view of States, there is no need for a State to derogate from the Convention in order to engage in an armed conflict and kill enemy combatants or fighters in either IAC or NIAC. The application of IHL is automatic*").

2403 See especially the two *Isayeva* cases (*infra* notes 2550 and 2551), in which the Court applied Article 2 ECHR in full without applying the LOAC and while noting that no derogation had been made despite the fact that there was arguably an armed conflict. However, it appears that Russia did not invoke a derogation, not even in the proceedings before the Court. Even so, however, the Court's view seems to exclude automatic applicability of the LOAC in non-international armed conflicts. See also the discussion *infra*, Section D.2.ii of this chapter.

2404 See also *supra*, Chapter 8.C, including on the different kinds of non-international armed conflicts.

methods of warfare and prisoners of war, might automatically derogate, whereas others, e.g. the treatment of enemy aliens in a State's own territory outside combat areas, would require a (notice of) derogation. However, there does not appear to be any legal basis for such a differentiation.

In addition, case law has clarified to some extent what may be covered by "*other public emergency threatening the life of the nation*".[2405] Points that are particularly relevant in this context, as will become clear below, are that the threat may be geographically limited[2406] and that States have some "margin of discretion/ appreciation".[2407] Also, the threat of terrorism may amount to such an emergency.[2408] Moreover, it no longer appears to be contested that it is possible

2405 See especially ECtHR, *Lawless v. Ireland*, 1 July 1961, section titled 'The Law', §§23–30, especially §28 ("*the natural and customary meaning of the words "other public emergency threatening the life of the nation" is sufficiently clear; whereas they refer to an exceptional situation of crisis or emergency which affects the whole population and constitutes a threat to the organised life of the community of which the State is composed*") and EComHR, "Greek Case" (Report of 5 November 1969), §113 ("*Such a public emergency may then be seen to have, in particular, the following characteristics: (1) It must be actual or imminent. (2) Its effects must involve the whole nation. (3) the continuance of the organised life of the community must be threatened. (4) The crisis or danger must be exceptional, in that the normal measures or restrictions, permitted by the Convention for the maintenance of public safety, health and order, are plainly inadequate*"). See J.F. Hartman, *supra* note 2374, pp. 23–29.

2406 See, e.g. *Aksoy v. Turkey*, 18 December 1996, §70 ("*the particular extent and impact of PKK terrorist activity* in South-East Turkey *has undoubtedly created,* in the region concerned, *a "public emergency threatening the life of the nation""*; emphasis added). Similarly, J.F. Hartman, *supra* note 2374, p. 16, note 87 (not limited to the ECHR) and R. St. J. Macdonald, *supra* note 2390, pp. 239–241.

2407 See, e.g. ECtHR, *Ireland v. the United Kingdom*, 13 December 1977, §207; *Brannigan and McBride v. UK*, 26 May 1993, §§43 and 47 ("*the Court considers there can be no doubt that such a public emergency existed at the relevant time. It does not judge it necessary to compare the situation which obtained in 1984 with that which prevailed in December 1988 since a decision to withdraw a derogation is, in principle, a matter within the discretion of the State* ...") and *Aksoy v. Turkey*, 18 December 1996, §68 ("*it falls to each Contracting State, with its responsibility for "the life of [its] nation", to determine whether that life is threatened by a "public emergency" ... By reason of their direct and continuous contact with the pressing needs of the moment, the national authorities are in principle better placed than the international judge to decide both on the presence of such an emergency ... Accordingly, in this matter a wide margin of appreciation should be left to the national authorities.*"). For a more extensive discussion of this aspect, see O. Gross & F. Ni Aolain, *supra* note 2390, pp. 625–649 and M. O'Boyle, *supra* note 2390, pp. 23–29. But see J.F. Hartman, *supra* note 2374, pp. 27–29, arguing that the EComHR was more demanding in the "Greek case" (Report of 5 November 1969, §§47–125). See also generally R. Ergec, *supra* note 2390, pp. 354–372. See also more generally on this doctrine, R. St. J. Macdonald, 'The Margin of Appreciation', in R. St. J. Macdonald, F. Matscher & H. Petzold (eds.), *The European System for the Protection of Human Rights*, Dordrecht, Nijhoff, 1993, pp. 83–124.

2408 See, e.g. ECtHR, *Lawless v. Ireland*, 1 July 1961, section titled 'The Law', §§28–30 and *Ireland v. the United Kingdom*, 13 December 1977, §§12 and 29–75 *juncto* 205. See also R. St. J. Macdonald, *supra* note 2390, pp. 237–239.

to have a state of emergency justifying derogation but nevertheless not crossing the threshold of an armed conflict.[2409]

Second, any derogation must be "*strictly required by the exigencies of the situation*". While this language suggests that the test is a strict one, it seems the ECtHR has been prepared to grant States a significant "margin of appreciation" in this respect too.[2410] Nevertheless, this requirement clearly does limit States' freedom of manoeuvre.[2411]

Third, derogating measures must not be "*inconsistent with [a State's] other obligations under international law*". This not only refers to human rights obligations that are non-derogable under other human rights treaties, but especially to the LOAC.[2412] I will revisit the relevance of the LOAC below in Section D of this chapter.

2409 See, e.g. T. Meron, *supra* note 2372, pp. 58–59; T. Meron, 'On the Inadequate Reach of Humanitarian and Human Rights Law and the Need for a New Instrument', 77 *A.J.I.L.* 1983, pp. 602–603 and A. Eide, A. Rosas & T. Meron, 'Combating Lawlessness in Gray Zone Conflicts through Minimum Humanitarian Standards', 89 *A.J.I.L.* 1995, p. 217. This alleged gap in protection (there is in fact no complete lack of applicable law as non-derogable and non-derogated rights apply) is sometimes called the "Meron gap". O. Gross & F. Ni Aolain, 'Emergency, War and International Law – Another Perspective', 70 *Nordic J.I.L.* 2001, pp. 55–63, acknowledge this possibility but argue that long time emergencies will normally cross the threshold of an armed conflict. J.F. Hartman, *supra* note 2374, p. 16, notes that natural disasters might also give rise to a state of emergency. On internal strife, see also *supra*, Chapter 8.B.1. In early scholarship, the view was sometimes defended that if there was an emergency leading to a derogation, the threshold of common Article 3 would be crossed; in this sense, e.g. S. MacBride, 'Human Rights in Armed Conflict. The Inter-Relationship between Humanitarian Laws and the Law of Human Rights', 9 *R.D.P.M.D.G.* 1970, p. 383 (arguing that to claim otherwise would be difficult).

2410 See, e.g. *Aksoy v. Turkey*, 18 December 1996, §68 ("*it falls to each Contracting State, with its responsibility for "the life of [its] nation", to determine whether that life is threatened by a "public emergency"* and, if so, how far it is necessary to go in attempting to overcome the emergency. *By reason of their direct and continuous contact with the pressing needs of the moment, the national authorities are in principle better placed than the international judge to decide both on the presence of such an emergency* and on the nature and scope of the derogations necessary to avert it. *Accordingly, in this matter a wide margin of appreciation should be left to the national authorities*"; emphasis added). For a more extensive discussion of this aspect, see O. Gross & F. Ni Aolain, *supra* note 2390, pp. 625–649 (noting at p. 631 that this doctrine initially concerned this aspect); J.F. Hartman, *supra* note 2374, pp. 31–35 and M. O'Boyle, *supra* note 2390, pp. 23–29.

2411 E.g. in *Aksoy v. Turkey*, 18 December 1996, §84, the Court ruled that it was "*not persuaded that the exigencies of the situation necessitated the holding of the applicant on suspicion of involvement in terrorist offences for fourteen days or more in incommunicado detention without access to a judge or other judicial officer*". Similarly, in *Lawless v. Ireland*, 1 July 1961, section titled 'The Law', §36, it opined that "*the sealing of the border would have had extremely serious repercussions on the population as a whole, beyond the extent required by the exigencies of the emergency*".

2412 R. Ergec, *supra* note 2390, p. 223, identifies the LOAC as the key added value of this provision. For a more extensive discussion, see H. Montealegre, 'The Compatibility of a State Party's

Fourth, there must be a notification to the Secretary General of the Council of Europe. The case law seems to require that this notification must be made without delay.[2413] Also, although Article 15 does not explicitly provide for this, such notifications are passed on to the other State Parties to the ECHR.[2414] Furthermore, there must be information on "*the measures ... taken and the reasons therefor[e]*".[2415] A final point, which is particularly relevant for the purposes of this book given the lack of derogations with regard to peace operations despite the possible applicability of the ECHR, is whether the failure to notify a derogation excludes a lawful derogation.[2416] The matter has been discussed but there has not been a definite pronouncement on the issue.[2417] However, the European Commission of human Rights has stated that, in any case, "*some formal and public act of derogation*" is required.[2418] It also seems to have considered that the applicability of the law of international armed conflicts *ipso facto* entailed, at least in some respects, a justification for a derogation.[2419]

Derogation under Human Rights Conventions with Its Obligations under Protocol II and Common Article 3', 33 *A.U.I.L.R.*1983, pp. 41–51. See also S. Bartelt, *supra* note 2278, pp. 178–179; M. El Zeidi, *supra* note 2390, p. 277 and J.F. Hartman, *supra* note 2374, pp. 17–18 (not limited to the ECHR).

2413 J.F. Hartman, *supra* note 2374, p. 19. See *Lawless v. Ireland*, 1 July 1961, §47 (noting that there was no delay but not explicitly stating that this is required).

2414 J.F. Hartman, *supra* note 2374, p. 19 and R. St. J. Macdonald, *supra* note 2390, p. 252, noting that the Committee of Ministers has directed the Secretary-General to do so.

2415 See J.F. Hartman, *supra* note 2374, pp. 18–21 (noting that this is the one remaining difference with the ICCPR, under which what must be reported is the provisions derogated from).

2416 R. Ergec, *supra* note 2390, pp. 316–319, submits that it is a question of opposability rather than validity.

2417 See M. El Zeidi, *supra* note 2390, pp. 285–287, *inter alia* referring to the Irish government's submission in ECtHR, *Lawless v. Ireland*, 1 July 1961 (section titled 'The Law', §46) that "*the Irish Government ... asked the Court to state ... that the letter of 20th July 1957 constituted a sufficient notification ... or, alternatively, to declare that there is nothing in the said paragraph 3 (Article 15-3) which, in the present case, detracts from the Irish Government's right to rely on paragraph 1 of the said Article 15 (Article 15-1)*". R. St. J. Macdonald, *supra* note 2390, pp. 251–252, sees the consequences of a lack of or inadequate notification as unclear but seems to oppose an automatic ineffectiveness in all cases, arguing rather in favour of seeing it as an indication of bad faith. D. Lorenz, *supra* note 2282, pp. 214–215 does not appear to regard a formal derogation as absolutely indispensable. R. Ergec, *supra* note 2390, pp. 315–319, is opposed to automatic ineffectiveness but does not rule out invalidity in cases of bad faith. F. Jacobs & R. White, *The European Convention on Human Rights*, Oxford, Oxford University Press, 2006 (4th ed.), pp. 449–450 submit that a State which fails to notify a derogation may have difficulties proving the case for a derogation. Compare the extensive discussion in J.-P. Loof, *supra* note 2374, pp. 607–681, who seems to argue in favour of a constitutive view of notifications.

2418 *Cyprus v. Turkey*, Report of 10 July 1976, 4 *E.H.R.R.* 1982, p. 556, §§526–528, especially §527. See in this sense also P. van Dijk *et al.*, *supra* note 2328, pp. 1069–1071.

2419 *Cyprus v. Turkey*, Report of 10 July 1976, 4 *E.H.R.R.* 1982, pp. 531–533 (§§309–313) and 555–557 (§§525–531), ruling that the LOAC was applicable to Turkey's actions in Northern Cyprus despite the lack of derogation with regard to this territory. Moreover, in their dissenting

Fifth, "*No derogation from Article 2, except in respect of deaths resulting from lawful acts of war, or from Articles 3, 4 (paragraph 1) and 7 shall be made*". This does not require any elaboration, except with regard to the right to life, which will be addressed below.[2420]

ii. Extraterritorial Applicability?

A question of particular importance for the applicability of the ECHR to peace operations, which take place outside the territory of the Participating States, is whether a derogation can be invoked with regard to the area of operations.

Most of the few commentators who have addressed this issue, reply in the negative, *inter alia* relying on the argument that the life of "the" nation refers to that of the Participating State and that this State will normally not be threatened by the situation in another State in which the operation is conducted.[2421] The ECtHR also seems to have rejected this possibility in *Bankovic*, where it stated that "*the Court does not find any basis upon which to accept the applicants' suggestion that Article 15 covers all "war" and "public emergency" situations generally, whether obtaining inside or outside the territory of the Contracting State*".[2422]

---

opinion in this case, Commission members Sperduti and Trechsel argued that a lack of notification did not affect the validity of a derogation (*id.*, pp. 561–565, especially §3).

2420 *Infra*, Section D.2.iv.a of this chapter.

2421 E.g. U. Erberich, *supra* note 2284, p. 52 (writing that since there is generally no emergency in sending States, a derogation cannot be considered and the ECHR would apply in full) and N. Tsagourias, *supra* note 2278, p. 120. In this sense also M.J. Dennis, *supra* note 2282, p. 136 with regard to the ICCPR. H. Krieger, *supra* note 2284, p. 690 considers that Article 15 ECHR would not normally apply in peace operations, apparently taking the view that the life of the sending State nation must be threatened. Likewise, the two law Lords who specifically addressed derogation in *Al-Jedda* (*infra* note 2435, §§38 and 150), expressed serious doubts as to whether it could apply extraterritorially (although one of them noted that the UK Secretary of State did not accept that the UK could not do so). In contrast, N. Ronzitti, *supra* note 2278, pp. 177–178 seems to consider that a derogation could be invoked regarding ESDP operations. D. Lorenz, *supra* note 2282, p. 111 also appears to consider that it is possible since he argues that the scope of the derogation follows that of the general scope of application (see also *infra*, next paragraph). R. Ergec, *supra* note 2390, pp. 127–129 and 170 seems to take the view that a derogation can apply to an occupation (p. 129) but on the other hand rejects it for wars that are fought far from the State concerned (p. 127, naming the Falklands war as an example) – apparently not considering that the ECHR could apply extraterritorially in the latter case. P. Rowe, *supra* note 2284, submits that a derogation seems difficult in UN operations because there will not normally be a threat (p. 198) but that taking into account derogations would lead to a more realistic framework for applying the ECHR (pp. 207–208). Kolb, Poretto & Vité , pp. 346–347 and 457, seem uncertain as to the possibility of derogations in peace operations but do not seem to rule this out entirely and stress that the limits of derogations have to be respected. Häussler, pp. 69–70 argues that derogation clauses were intended to cover internal crisis, whether or not resulting from an external crisis such as war.

2422 *Supra* note 2292, §62.

However, it is submitted that this reasoning is flawed. If one accepts that the ECHR can apply extraterritorially, especially to entire areas under effective control, it follows that the local "nation" is under the jurisdiction of the "occupying" State.[2423] In that case, it is logical that a threat to the life of *this* nation can justify a derogation.[2424] Indeed, the Court's statement in Bankovic that "*Article 15 itself is to be read subject to the "jurisdiction" limitation enumerated in Article 1*"[2425] can also be turned around: where Article 1 does apply extraterritorially, Article 15 may also do so. Moreover, this view has been endorsed by the European Commission for Human Rights, which stated in respect of Cyprus that "*Turkish armed forces in Cyprus brought any other persons or forces there 'within the jurisdiction' of Turkey, in the sense of Article 1... 'to the extent that they exercise control over such forces or property'... It follows that, to the same extent, Turkey was [...] competent ratione loci for any measures of derogation under Article 15*".[2426] In addition, the obligation to limit measures to what is strictly necessary would support a derogation being limited to the operations area.[2427] Obviously, the situation in the area of operations must be such that there is indeed a threat to the life of the (local) nation.[2428] This may lead to different appreciations by different Participating States,[2429] especially taking into account the margin of appreciation (see preceding subsection), although attempts may be made to overcome this by accepting coordination through or guidance from an international organization in charge.[2430] It may

---

2423 I am using the term in a broad sense here, not restricted to its more narrow meaning under the LOAC.

2424 Compare the *Draft Guidelines for criminal procedure in Crisis Management Operations*, adopted by the EU's Committee for Civilian Aspects of Crisis Management on 30 May 2002 (EU Doc. 9465/02), §1(6): "*In time of public exceptional danger which threatens the life of the nation and the existence of which is officially proclaimed,* or in case of threat to the security of the local population or to the maintenance of law and public order in the mission area, *competent international authorities may take, as provided in their mandate under UN auspices, measures derogating from these guidelines to the extent strictly required by the exigencies of the situation, provided that such measures are not inconsistent with their other obligations under international law*" (emphasis added).

2425 *Supra* note 2292, §62.

2426 *Cyprus v. Turkey*, 4 *E.H.R.R.* 1982, pp. 482–582 §525. In this sense also D. Lorenz, *supra* note 2282, p. 111.

2427 Compare R. Ergec, *supra* note 2390, p. 197 with regard to the duty to geographically limit derogations as much as possible.

2428 I agree with J. Cerone, *supra* note 2298, p. 488 that that the mere presence of a security presence (or, I would add, of a peace operation more generally) does not automatically entail a derogation.

2429 See also N. Ronzitti, *supra* note 2278, p. 171.

2430 See the *Draft Guidelines for criminal procedure in Crisis Management Operations*, *supra* note 2424, §1(6): "*In time of public exceptional danger ... or in case of threat to the security of the local population or to the maintenance of law and public order in the mission area,* competent international authorities *may take, ..., measures derogating from these guidelines ...*". N.

also be noted that the UN Mission in Kosovo has mentioned Article 15 ECHR in an effort to justify broad detention powers.[2431]

As already mentioned, there has (to my knowledge) not been any derogation concerning peace operations. There are various possible explanations for this. First, it seems that States have only relatively recently become aware that the ECHR might apply to such operations. Moreover, when they have been sued on the basis of the ECHR, they have generally denied the ECHR's extraterritorial applicability. Unless States are prepared to explicitly acknowledge the latter, derogations are unlikely as they would imply such recognition.[2432] The ECtHR's *Saramati* and *Behrami* decision[2433] is unlikely to change this. Alternatively, or additionally, States may not deem a notice of derogation absolutely necessary, at least in these cases, possibly because in most cases the derogation is (at least allegedly) based on a UN Security Council mandate, which has a significant public character. Also, it may be recalled that the consequences of a lack of notification are unclear and that notification does not seem to be an absolute requirement in all cases.[2434] In fact, there is a recent British judgment in which a derogation on the basis of a UN Security Council Resolution was deemed to be valid even absent any notification of derogation.[2435]

However, in order to allow for supervision - however marginal - of measures of derogation, some form of publicity does seem necessary.[2436] Given the generally

---

Ronzitti, *supra* note 2278, p. 20, pleads for agreement between the Member States on the applicability of the ECHR more generally.

2431 See Kolb, Poretto & Vité , p. 313. The relevance of this case is not so clear since the UN might perhaps be said to be acting on behalf of the host State or territory in this case.

2432 A. Roberts, *infra* note 2512, p. 609, cites legal advice from the UK Attorney General of 26 May 2003 which mentions as a *"complicating factor"* the *"extent to which the ECHR and other international human rights instruments are likely to apply to any territory of which the UK is the Occupying power"*. This implies the UK was aware that the ECHR was likely to apply. Nevertheless, the UK did not notify any derogation in this respect.

2433 *Supra* notes 2317–2318 and the accompanying text.

2434 See *supra*, preceding subsection, notes 2417–2419 and the accompanying text.

2435 *Al-Jedda, R (on the application of) v Secretary of State for Defence)*, [2006] EWCA Civ 327, 29 March 2006 (available online at www.bailii.org/ew/cases/EWCA/Civ/2006/327.html), §§55–87; upheld by the House of Lords on 12 December 2007 ([2007] UKHL 58, available online at www.publications.parliament.uk/pa/ld200708/ldjudgmt/jd071212/jedda-1.htm). For a criticsm of the 2006 judgment, see A. Cassimatis, *supra* note 2366, pp. 635–637. de Wet, pp. 201–202 and 321–322 argues that the Security Council may derogate from derogable human rights without proclaiming a derogation and has a wider margin of appreciation, at least with regard to sanctions but not in civil administration. Häussler, pp. 75–76, argues that the Security Council does not need to rely on derogation clauses in human rights treaties and argues that the Security Council may have a greater margin of appreciation. However, the latter may be questioned given the broad margin that States already have under the ECHR (see *supra*, preceding subsection).

2436 The possibility of supervision appears to be the main aim of the notification duty; see in this sense, P. Tavernier, *supra* note 2390, p. 493. See also R. Ergec, *supra* note 2390, pp. 297–300, vague nature of UN Security Council mandates,[2437] States should attempt to provide at least in somewhat specific terms what derogations they apply in peace operations.

3. THE INTERNATIONAL COVENANT ON CIVIL AND POLITICAL RIGHTS

i. *The Derogation Clause*

Article 4 ICCPR reads:

> 1. In time of public emergency which threatens the life of the nation and the existence of which is officially proclaimed, the States Parties to the present Covenant may take measures derogating from their obligations under the present Covenant to the extent strictly required by the exigencies of the situation, provided that such measures are not inconsistent with their other obligations under international law and do not involve discrimination solely on the ground of race, colour, sex, language, religion or social origin.
>
> 2. No derogation from Articles 6, 7, 8 (paragraphs 1 and 2), 11, 15, 16 and 18 may be made under this provision.
>
> 3. Any State Party to the present Covenant availing itself of the right of derogation shall immediately inform the other States Parties to the present Covenant, through the intermediary of the Secretary-General of the United Nations, of the provisions from which it has derogated and of the reasons by which it was actuated. A further communication shall be made, through the same intermediary, on the date on which it terminates such derogation.[2438]

---

writing that effective supervision requires publicity and motivation and seeing a balancing exercise between informality and restrictiveness.

2437 See *infra*, subsection 5. Interestingly, the British case dealt with the only case where the measures authorized were in fact fairly specifically set out in an annex to the relevant Security Council Resolution and explicitly included detention: the US letter annexed to Resolution 1546 (8 June 2004) states in part that "*Under the agreed arrangement, the [Multi-National Force] stands ready to continue to undertake a broad range of tasks to contribute to the maintenance of security and to ensure force protection. These include ... internment where this is necessary for imperative reasons of security ...*". Nevertheless, even so it raised questions as to the precise scope and conditions for detention.

2438 See generally T. Buergenthal, *supra* note 2337, pp. 79–89; P.R. Ghandhi, 'The Human Rights Committee and Derogation in Public Emergencies', 32 *G.Y.I.L.* 1989, pp. 323–361; O. Gross & F. Ni Aoláin, *supra* note 2374, pp. 297–304; S. Joseph, J. Schultz & M. Castan, *supra* note 2329 (2004), pp. 823–836; M. Nowak, *supra* note 2329, pp. 72–93 (1993) and 83–110 (2005) and A. Siehr, 'Derogation Measures under Article 4 ICCPR, with Special Consideration of the "War against International Terrrorism"', 47 *G.Y.I.L.* 2004, pp. 545–593.

This provision has been the subject of two General Comments by the Human Rights Committee.[2439] Again, I will briefly address those aspects that are most relevant for the purpose of this book, though much of this is similar to what applies to the ECHR.[2440]

First, what is meant by a "*public emergency which threatens the life of the nation*"? In this respect, it may be noted that the absence of a reference to war obviously does not exclude war and is explained by historic/symbolic reasons.[2441] Furthermore, in light of the similar wording, what has been said about the ECHR in this respect can also be applied to the ICCPR,[2442] including regarding the possibility of a geographically limited threat and derogation[2443] and a threat falling below the threshold of an armed conflict.[2444] However, it appears that the HRC may reject an automatic derogation in case of armed conflict[2445] and does not seem to have recourse to a "margin of appreciation".[2446] In addition, Article 4 ICCPR requires an official proclamation of a public emergency.[2447]

2439 General Comment 29, *supra* note 2378, and the earlier General Comment 5 (*Derogation of Rights*, 31 July 1981).

2440 J.F. Hartman, *supra* note 2374, p. 3, rightly states that both derogation clauses are "*essentially equivalent in criteria, theory, and purpose*". See also L.C. Green, *supra* note 2374, p. 104.

2441 Namely the adoption of the ICCPR under UN auspices, which led to reluctance to acknowledge the possibility of war as the UN Charter was supposed to outlaw war, see T. Buergenthal, *supra* note 2337, p. 79.

2442 T. Buergenthal, *supra* note 2337, pp. 79–80.

2443 *Id.*, p. 80 and J.F. Hartman, *supra* note 2374, p. 16, note 87 (the latter not limited to the ICCPR). Indeed, General Comment 29, *supra* note 2378, §4, correctly points out that a geographically limited derogation may be required by the condition of limitation "*to the extent strictly required by the exigencies of the situation*".

2444 See General Comment 29, *supra* note 2378, §§3 (albeit with some apparent suspicion: "*If States parties consider invoking Article 4 in other situations than an armed conflict, they should carefully consider the justification and why such a measure is necessary and legitimate in the circumstances*") and 5 (referring to a natural catastrophe).

2445 See General Comment 29, *supra* note 2378, §3: "*During armed conflict, whether international or non-international, rules of international humanitarian law become applicable and help, ..., to prevent the abuse of a State's emergency powers. The Covenant requires that even during an armed conflict measures derogating from the Covenant are allowed only if and to the extent that the situation constitutes a threat to the life of the nation*". This statement is, nevertheless, somewhat ambiguous in that its first sentence suggests an automatic application. The entire statement seems to mean the LOAC protections apply automatically but not the rights it grants to States unless there is a derogation. However, it is doubtful whether this splitting up approach is correct.

2446 E.g. this doctrine is not mentioned in General Comment 29 (*supra* note 2378). See also M. Nowak, *supra* note 2329 (2005), p. 101.

2447 See also General Comment 29, *supra* note 2378, §2 ("*The latter requirement is essential for the maintenance of the principles of legality and rule of law at times when they are most needed. When proclaiming a state of emergency with consequences that could entail derogation from any provision of the Covenant, States must act within their constitutional and other provisions of law that govern such proclamation and the exercise of emergency powers; it is the task of the Committee to monitor the laws in question with respect to whether they enable and secure*

Second, any derogation must be "*strictly required by the exigencies of the situation*". Here too, most of what has been mentioned regarding the ECHR is relevant, although again the Human Rights Committee does not seem to have recourse to a margin of appreciation.[2448]

Third, derogating measures must not be "*inconsistent with [a State's] other obligations under international law*". In this respect, there is no difference with the ECHR and these obligations include the LOAC.[2449]

Fourth, there must be a notification via the UN Secretary General. Both the Human Rights Committee[2450] and the International Court of Justice[2451] attach great importance to the notification of derogations. Nevertheless, as under the ECHR,[2452] it may be questioned whether failure to notify a derogation excludes the lawfulness or opposability of a derogation.[2453] In this context, it may be noted that the US has proclaimed a state of emergency after '11 September",[2454] but does not appear to have notified a derogation under the ICCPR[2455] (to which it is a party). In contrast, the UK did notify a derogation from the ICCPR, as well as its subsequent withdrawal.[2456]

---

compliance with Article 4") and M. Nowak, *supra* note 2329 (2005), p. 92 (regarding it as a constitutive element).

2448 Nevertheless, T. Buergenthal, *supra* note 2337, pp. 81–82 sees this doctrine as relevant to the ICCPR too.

2449 General Comment 29, *supra* note 2378, §9; T. Buergenthal, *supra* note 2337, p. 82 and J.F. Hartman, *supra* note 2374, pp. 17–18 (the latter not limited to the ICCPR).

2450 See General Comment 29, *supra* note 2378, §17.

2451 See especially the ICJ's Advisory Opinion on *Legal consequences of the construction of a wall in the occupied Palestinian territory*, 9 July 2004, §136 ("*the communication notified by Israel to the Secretary-General of the United Nations under Article 4 of the International Covenant on Civil and Political Rights concerns only Article 9 of the Covenant, ...; Israel is accordingly bound to respect all the other provisions of that instrument*"). However, this concerns a case where a notification has been made and in that case a strict interpretation may be more warranted than where no notification has been made.

2452 *Supra*, Section C.2.i of this chapter, notes 2417–2419 and the accompanying text.

2453 In General Comment 29, *supra* note 2378, §17 *in fine*, the HRC stated that "*The duty of the Committee to monitor the law and practice of a State party for compliance with Article 4 does not depend on whether that State party has submitted a notification*". This suggests there can be a derogation absent notification. See also M.J. Dennis, *supra* note 2282, pp. 134–135, who argues that a notification should not be decisive, as does T. Meron, *supra* note 2374, pp. 52–53. M. Nowak, *supra* note 2329 (2005), p. 92 is also of the view that the notification is not constitutive. In contrast, D. Schneider, *supra* note 2344, pp. 430–431 considers that a notification is necessary to be able to invoke a derogation. H. Duffy, *supra* note 2374, p. 347 sees a need to clarify the value of the notification.

2454 Declaration of National Emergency by Reason of Certain Terrorist Attacks by the President of the United States of America, 14 September 2001, www.fas.org/irp/news/2001/09/fr091801.html.

2455 See, e.g. H. Duffy, *supra* note 2374, p. 347 and F. Vanneste & N. van Leuven, *supra* note 2394, p. 153 and D. Schneider, *supra* note 2344, pp. 430–431.

2456 See the Notification of the United Kingdom's derogation from Article 9 of the International Covenant on Civil and Political Rights, 18 December 2001, subsequently withdrawn by notification of 15 March 2005 (both available at http://treaties.un.org).

Fifth, here too there is a list of non-derogable rights, which is more extensive than that under the ECHR, and to which the Human Rights Committee has further added elements of other rights.[2457]

ii. Extraterritorial Applicability?

In view of the similar language, the same reasoning may be made for the ICCPR as for the ECHR in this respect. Moreover, the Human Rights Committee has recognized that Article 4 ICCPR may have some extraterritorial scope, albeit in a context where the threat at least partially affected the territory of the State acting extraterritorially.[2458] That being said, no notifications appear to have been made so far regarding extraterritorial measures.[2459]

4. DEROGATION IN CUSTOMARY INTERNATIONAL LAW OR GENERAL PRINCIPLES OF LAW?[2460]

As with the issue of extraterritoriality, it is important in the context of this book to look into whether a derogation mechanism exists under customary international law or general principles of law.

Doctrine often links the derogation mechanism in human rights treaties to the concept of necessity in international law,[2461] although the notions of necessity used vary somewhat.[2462] It is submitted that the most relevant concept of necessity is that of the (state of) necessity as a circumstance precluding

---

2457 General Comment 29, *supra* note 2378, §§13–16 (including a number of procedural safeguards). With regard to implied non-derogable rights, see also generally I. Seiderman, *supra* note 2378, pp. 80–84.

2458 HRC, *Concluding Observations/Comments on Israel*, UN Doc. CCPR/CO/78/ISR, 21 Augustus 2003, §11.

2459 M.J. Dennis, *supra* note 2282, p. 135.

2460 See generally J. Oráa, 'The Protection of Human Rights in Emergency Situations under Customary International Law', in G.S. Goodwin-Gill & S. Talmon (eds.), *The Reality of International Law: Essays in Honour of Ian Brownlie*, Oxford, Clarendon Press, 1999, pp. 413–438. Compare T. Meron, *supra* note 2409, pp. 601–602. Compare, with regard to the UDHR, A. Eide, *supra* note 2374, p. 245.

2461 E.g. R. Ergec, *supra* note 2390, pp. 56–102 (linking it to both derogations in national systems (pp. 61–97) and to necessity in international law (pp. 97–100) and deeming the clause necessary and acceptable given that it limits the possibility of derogation (pp. 100–102)) and J. Oráa, *supra* note 2460, p. 435 (seeing the derogation clauses as a particular application or adaptation of the state of necessity). See also Kolb, Poretto & Vité , pp. 344–347. Compare J.-P. Loof, *supra* note 2374, pp. 113–173.

2462 E.g. J.F. Hartman, *supra* note 2374, pp. 12–13 seems to see necessity as related to military necessity in the LOAC whereas M. El Zeidi, *supra* note 2390, pp. 271–273 sees it rather as linked to a state of necessity.

wrongfulness.[2463] This would imply that under customary international law, derogation would be possible if the conditions for necessity are met.[2464] The key condition that might be difficult to overcome in the case of human rights is that the derogation "*does not seriously impair an essential interest of the State or States towards which the obligation exists, or of the international community as a whole*".[2465] While respect for human rights might be such an essential interest of other States and the international community as a whole, it is unlikely, given derogation mechanisms in human rights treaties, that the same is true for unqualified respect *in all circumstances.*

Further restrictions would be present if it could be ascertained that under customary international law or general principles of law, some rights are non-derogable, so that "*the international obligation in question excludes the possibility of invoking necessity*".[2466] This would once again require a more extensive analysis but is arguably at least the case for those rights that are neither derogable under the ICCPR nor under the ECHR and ACHR.[2467] Similarly, other principles or rules regarding derogations may also have acquired the status of customary international law or of general principles of law and thus impose further restrictions on the possibility to derogate.[2468]

2463 See also H. Duffy, *supra* note 2374, pp. 297–298; M. El Zeidi, *supra* note 2390, pp. 271–273 and J. Oráa, *supra* note 2460, p. 435. See Article 25 of the ILC's Draft Articles on Responsibility of States for Internationally Wrongful Acts (adopted on 31 May and 3 August 2001, *Report of the International Law Commission. Fifty-third session*, UN Doc. A/56/10, pp. 194–206): "*1. Necessity may not be invoked by a State as a ground for precluding the wrongfulness of an act not in conformity with an international obligation of that State unless the act:*
(a) Is the only way for the State to safeguard an essential interest against a grave and imminent peril; and
(b) Does not seriously impair an essential interest of the State or States towards which the obligation exists, or of the international community as a whole.
2. In any case, necessity may not be invoked by a State as a ground for precluding wrongfulness if:
(a) The international obligation in question excludes the possibility of invoking necessity; or
(b) The State has contributed to the situation of necessity".

2464 Compare the situation of human rights treaties that have no explicit derogation mechanism (see *supra* note 2375) and T. Meron, *supra* note 2362, pp. 217–219.

2465 Article 25(1)b ILC Draft Articles on State Responsibility, *supra* note 2463.

2466 *Id.*, Article 25(2)a.

2467 I. Seiderman, *supra* note 2378, p. 81 notes that the four non-derogable rights common to the key human rights treaties are considered to be non-derogable under customary international law by many experts. T. Meron, *supra* note 2374, p. 59, took the view that this was perhaps the case. J. Oráa, *supra* note 2460, p. 437, considers that these core rights are both non-derogable under customary law and *ius cogens*. H. Duffy, *supra* note 2374, p. 296 regards it as unlikely that a customary rule would be broader than the non-derogable rights.

2468 J. Oráa, *supra* note 2460, pp. 413–437 argued (in 1999) that the principles of an exceptional threat, proportionality, non-derogability of fundamental rights and non-discrimination were "*emergent principles of general international law in a very advanced state of crystallisation*" and that the latter three already appeared to be such general principles of international law

5. THE IMPACT OF SECURITY COUNCIL INTERVENTION

In respect of the impact of decisions of the UN Security Council, the position of human rights is largely identical to that of the LOAC: whether conventional or customary, human rights may be set aside by the UN Security Council except for *ius cogens* (see *supra*, Chapter 8.E).[2469] However some specific points need to be addressed.

First, there is the issue of non-derogable rights. To the extent that these rights are not necessarily all *ius cogens*,[2470] it would seem that those rights that do not have this status, may be set aside by the Security Council. However, it is doubtful whether there would ever be a necessity to do so.[2471] Conversely, there may be derogable rights that are *ius cogens*[2472] and may therefore not be set aside.

(and pointed out that the Inter-American Human Rights organs have recognized as general principles of law the principles of an exceptional threat, proportionality, non-derogability of fundamental rights and temporariness). In the same sense, Kolb, Poretto & Vité , p. 457, consider that the criteria for derogations under human rights treaties have become part of customary international law and L. Wessels, *supra* note 2375, pp. 128–129 and 134, argues that they also are general principles of law (citing as principles at p. 134 note 73 an exceptional threat; proportionate measures; core non-derogable rights; non-discrimination and good faith).

2469 But see T. Ahmed & I. de Jesús Butler, 'The European Union and Human Rights: An International Law Perspective', 17 *E.J.I.L.* 2006, p. 787, who argue that the ECJ in *Kadi* and *Yusuf* (*supra*, Chapter 7.G.4.iii) stated that the Security Council is bound by all human rights that are part of the purposes and principles of the UN (Charter). While there is some support for this in these judgments' wordings (see *Kadi*, §§228–229 and *Yusuf*, §§279–280), the Court's conclusion clearly seems to be that *ius cogens* is the only limit (see *Kadi*, §§230, 242 and 288 and *Yusuf*, §§281, 293 and 343). Compare A. Orakhelashvili, 'The Impact of Peremptory Norms on the Interpretation and Application of United Nations Security Council Resolutions', 16 *E.J.I.L.* 2005, pp. 64–66.

2470 See, e.g. General Comment 29, *supra* note 2378, §11 ("*The proclamation of certain provisions of the Covenant as being of a non-derogable nature, ..., is to be seen partly as recognition of the peremptory nature of some fundamental rights ensured in treaty form in the Covenant (e.g., Articles 6 and 7). However, it is apparent that some other provisions of the Covenant were included in the list of non-derogable provisions because it can never become necessary to derogate from these rights during a state of emergency (e.g., Articles 11 and 18)*"). See also I. Seiderman, *supra* note 2378, pp. 77–78 and 84–89. See also J.F. Hartman, *supra* note 2374, pp. 15–16, arguing that the differences in non-derogability between human rights treaties suggest that not all non-derogable rights are fundamental. Compare Kolb, Poretto & Vité , pp. 338–340, and more generally T. Koji, 'Emerging Hierarchy in International Human Rights and Beyond: from the Perspective of Non-derogable Rights', 12 *E.J.I.L.* 2002, pp. 917–941, especially pp. 927–931.

2471 See General Comment 29, *supra* note 2378, §11: "*some ... provisions ... were included in the list of non-derogable provisions because it can never become necessary to derogate from these rights during a state of emergency (e.g., Articles 11 and 18)*". See also I. Seiderman, *supra* note 2378, pp. 77–78.

2472 See General Comment 29, *supra* note 2378, §§11 ("*Furthermore, the category of peremptory norms extends beyond the list of non-derogable provisions as given in Article 4, paragraph 2*") and A. Orakhelashvili, *supra* note 2469, pp. 64–66.

Second, there is the question whether the normal procedures for notifying a derogation must be followed. This has already been discussed to some extent above,[2473] where I have indicated that practice provides some support for the possibility of a derogation without notification but that some form of adequate publicity is required.

Third, the broad and vague nature of many UN Security Council mandates, especially the authorization to use "all necessary measures" to achieve certain objectives, sometimes make it rather difficult to judge if and to what extent[2474] the Security Council has in fact intended to authorize a derogation from certain human rights. It would seem that in practice, Participating States frequently consider that derogations are authorized, e.g. concerning detention.[2475] In contrast, UN sanctions, including in the counter-terrorism sphere, are usually more specific in terms of the measures required.[2476] The treatment by the ECJ of those counter-terrorism measures that do leave considerable discretion suggests

---

2473 *Supra*, Section C.2.ii of this chapter, notes 2435–2437 and the accompanying text.

2474 E.g. while the UK House of Lords accepted in *Al-Jedda* that a UNSC resolution had qualified or displaced Article 5 ECHR, Baroness Hale clearly suggested that the extent to which this was the case remained to be determined. (see *supra* note 2161, especially §§127–129). See also F. Messineo, *supra* note 2161, pp. 51–52.

2475 See on detention *infra*, Section D.2.iv.b of this chapter. For a critical perspective on derogations based on vague mandates, see Kolb, Poretto & Vité , p. 347. Compare J. Cerone, *supra* note 2298, p. 478 note 50, who argues that any derogation should be explicit, as does C. Stahn, 'International Territorial Administration in the Former Yugoslavia: Origins, Developments and Challenges Ahead', 61 *Z.a.ö.R.V.* 2001, p. 153.

2476 On UN sanctions and human rights, see generally I. Cameron, 'UN Targeted Sanctions, Legal Safeguards and the European Convention on Human Rights', 72 *Nordic J.I.L* 2003, pp. 159–214; I. Cameron, *The European Convention on Human Rights, Due Process and United Nations Security Council Counter-Terrorism Sanctions*, Council of Europe, 6 February 2006 (available online at available online at www.coe.int/t/e/legal_affairs/legal_co-operation/public_international_law/Texts_&_Documents/Docs%202006/I.%20Cameron%20Report%2006.pdf); E. de Wet, 'Human Rights Limitations to Economic Enforcement Measures Under Article 41 of the United Nations Charter and the Iraqi Sanctions', 14 *Leiden J.I.L.* 2001, pp. 277–300; B. Fassbender, *Targeted Sanctions and Due Process, The Responsibility of the UN Security Council to Ensure that Fair and Clear Procedures Are Made Available to Individuals and Entities Targeted with Sanctions under Chapter VII of the UN Charter*, 20 March 2006 (available online at www.un.org/law/counsel/Fassbender_study.pdf); I. Couzigou, 'La lutte du Conseil de sécurité contre le terrorisme international et les droits de l'homme', 112 *R.G.D.I.P.* 2008, pp. 49–84; C. Olivier, 'Human Rights Law and the International Fight against Terrorism: How Do Security Council Resolutions Impact on States' Obligations Under International Human Rights Law? (Revisiting Security Council Resolution 1373)', 73 *Nordic J.I.L.* 2004, pp. 399–419 and A. Reinisch, 'Developing Human Rights and Humanitarian Law Accountability of the Security Council for the Imposition of Economic Sanctions', 95 *A.J.I.L* 2001, pp. 851–872. On the Security Council and human rights more generally, see E. Katselli, 'Holding the Security Council Accountable for Human Rights Violations', 1 *Human Rights & International Legal Discourse* 2007, pp. 301–333 and G. Thallinger, 'Sense and Sensibility of the Human Rights Obligations of the United Nations Security Council', 67 *Z.a.ö.R.V.* 2007, pp. 1015–1040.

that there may be a need for greater respect for human rights than States seem to assume and/or a need for more specific Security Council authorizations.

In particular, in cases concerning the lawfulness of EC measures implementing UN Security Council Resolution 1373 (28 September 2001), which leaves it to States and international organizations to determine to whom restrictive measures should be applied, the Court of First Instance ruled that the EC's discretion entails an obligation to fully respect human rights.[2477] In contrast, the ECtHR seems to have ruled that it will not rule on any action in the context of a Chapter VII UN Resolution.[2478] The Strasbourg Court's apparent argument that any State action, even voluntary, in relation to Chapter VII is outside its competence because it would amount to interfering with the UN's mission is hardly convincing and risks entailing a significant gap in human rights protection given the scope of Chapter VII measures adopted so far, including in combating terrorism.[2479] There is much to be said for Lavranos' view that this reflects a "*misguided deferential attitude*" towards the Security Council.[2480] The UK House

---

2477 See especially Case T-228/02 (*Organisation des Modjahedines du peuple d'Iran v. Council of the European Union*, judgment of 12 December 2006, especially §§101–108; stating at §103 that "*unlike the acts at issue in the cases which gave rise to the judgments in Yusuf and Kadi, ..., the acts which specifically apply those restrictive measures to a given person or entity, such as the contested decision, do not come within the exercise of circumscribed powers and accordingly do not benefit from the primacy effect in question*") and the judgments of 11 July 2007 in Cases T-47/03 (*Jose Maria Sison* v *Council of the European Union*, §§137–206) and T-327/03 (*Stichting Al-Aqsa* v *Council of the European Union*, §§53–67). On the former case, see C. Eckes, 'Case T-228/02, *Organisation des Modjahedines du people d'Iran v. Council*, judgment of the Court of First Instance (Second Chamber) of 12 December 2006', annotation in 44 *C.M.L. Rev.* 2007, pp. 1117–1129 and Y. Moiny, 'Le contrôle, par le juge européen, de certaines mesures communautaires visant à lutter contre le financement du terrorisme', 16 *Journal de droit européen* 2008, pp. 137–142. See also C. Lehnardt, 'European Court Rules on UN and EU Terrorist Suspect Blacklists', *ASIL Insight*, 31 January 2007, Volume 11, Issue 1, www.asil.org/insights070131.cfm. For follow-on cases on the scope of the required human rights protection, see Court of First Instance, Case T-229/02, *Osman Ocalan, on behalf of the Kurdistan Workers' Party (PKK) v. Council of the European Union*, 3 April 2008, especially §§62–70; Case T-253/04, *KONGRA-GEL v. Council of the European Union*, 3 April 2008, especially §§95–104; Case T-256/07, *People's Mojahedin Organization of Iran v. Council of the European Union*, 23 October 2008 and Case T-284/08, *People's Mojahedin Organization of Iran v. Council of the European Union*, 4 December 2008, especially §§36–47 and 49–79 (on the latter two cases, see the annotation by E. Spaventa in 46 *C.M.L. Rev.* 2009, pp. 1239–1263). See also, as regards sanctions against Iran, Joined Cases T-246/08 and T-332/08, *Melli Bank plc. v. Council of the European Union*, 9 July 2009, especially §§44–46, 98–114 and 142–153.

2478 See the *Behrami* and *Saramati* decision (*supra* note 1831), especially §§144–152.

2479 See also the mostly critical annotations *supra* note 2212.

2480 N. Lavranos, *supra* note 1906, p. 181, who also considers that the ECJ distantiated itself from this case in *Kadi* (*id.*, pp. 181–182). Compare P. De Sena & M. Chiara Vitucci, 'The European Courts and the Security Council: Between Dedoublement Fonctionnel and Balancing of Values', 20 *E.J.I.L.* 2009, pp. 193–228 and B. Kunoy & A. Dawes, 'Plate Tectonics in Luxembourg: The ménage à trois between EC Law, International Law and the European of Lords' judgment in *Al-Jedda* may be situated in between both positions, in that it accepts a qualification or displacement of a human right on the basis of a UN Security Council resolution, but hasn't expressed a clear view on the precise extent thereof.[2481] Moreover, the ECJ's recent *Kadi* appeals judgment makes it clear that even with regard to specifically mandated measures, EU law imposes quite strict respect for human rights.[2482]

The required respect for human rights could be ensured at the UN level, if applicable, and/or at the EC/EU level and/or at the national level. In fact, in respect of counter-terrorism measures both the EU and the UN have adopted measures towards greater respect for human rights, in an apparent reaction to the ECJ's case law.[2483] In the context of sanctions lists, it would seem that the only solution which can safeguard both the primacy of the UN Charter and (EU) human rights law is to have adequate respect for human rights at the UN level.[2484] This is obviously not solely within the hands of the EU, and more specifically those of its Member States represented in the Security Council, but they are arguably under an obligation to do what they can to achieve this.[2485]

Convention on Human Rights Following the UN Sanctions Cases', 46 *C.M.L. Rev.* 2009, pp. 73–104.

2481 See *supra* note 2161.

2482 See *supra* notes 1906 and 1909–1910 and the accompanying text.

2483 For the EU, see mainly the GAERC Conclusions of 23–24 April 2007, pp. 34–35 (EU Doc. 8425/07 (Presse 80)) and EU Doc. 11309/07 (Presse 158), 29 June 2007 as well as Doc. 7697/07 of 3 April 2007 (entitled 'European Union autonomous/additional restrictive measures (sanctions) – Recommendations for dealing with country-specific EU autonomous sanctions or EU additions to UN sanctions lists'). For an application in a specific case, see EU Council Doc. 5418/3/07 Rev 3, 11 May 2007. For the UN, see, e.g. UNSC Resolutions 1730 (19 December 2006) and 1735 (22 December 2006).

2484 In particular, establishing an adequate review mechanism at the EU or national level for persons on a UNSC terrorist list by definition entails the possibility of arriving at a conclusion different from that reached by the UNSC and thus being faced with the choice of violating either (EU or national) human rights law or UN obligations. See also L. van den Herik & N. Schrijver, 'Eroding the Primacy of the UN System of Collective Security: The Judgment of the European Court of Justice in the Cases of Kadi and Al Barakaat', 5 *I.O.L.R.* 2008, pp. 335–338, who add that the full judicial review required by the ECJ may be difficult to achieve in the UN. See also N. Lavranos, *supra* note 1906, p. 182, submitting that the EC and its Member States are obliged to ensure such respect until it is assured at the UN level.

2485 Compare the considerations of the Court of First Instance in Case T-49/04, *Faraj Hassan v. Council of the European Union and Commission of the European Communities*, 12 July 2006, §§107–124, and especially §§112 ("*Although the Sanctions Committee takes its decisions by consensus, the effectiveness of the procedure for requesting to be removed from the list is guaranteed, on the one hand, by the various formal consultation mechanisms ... provided for in ... the Guidelines and, on the other, by the obligation imposed on all Member States of the United Nations, including the members of that committee, to act in good faith in that procedure in accordance with the general principle of international law*"); 114 ("*particular obligations are imposed on the Member States of the Community when a request for removal from the list is addressed to them*") and 116 ("*both in examining such a request and in the context of the*

D. THE RELATIONSHIP BETWEEN HUMAN RIGHTS AND THE LAW OF ARMED CONFLICT

In the preceding section, it was pointed out that where human rights treaties permit derogations, this is limited by the need to respect other obligations under international law, including especially the LOAC (when applicable). This implies that human rights may, at least to some extent, apply concurrently with the LOAC and raises the question as to what the precise relationship between both regimes is. This has been and still is a much debated topic[2486] that could easily be

---

consultations between States and other actions that may take place under paragraph 8 of the Guidelines, the Member States are bound, in accordance with Article 6 EU, to respect the fundamental rights of the persons involved, as guaranteed by the ECHR and as they result from the constitutional traditions common to the Member States, as general principles of Community law, provided that the respect of those fundamental rights does not seem capable of raising any impediment to the proper performance of their obligations under the Charter of the United Nations").

2486 See, e.g. R. Arnold & N. Quénivet (eds.), *International Humanitarian Law and Human Rights Law: Towards a New Merger in International Law*, The Hague, Martinus Nijhoff, 2008; A. Bos, 'Some Reflections on the Relationship between International Humanitarian Law and Human Rights in the Light of the Adoption of the Rome Statute of the International Criminal Court', in UN Office of Legal Affairs (ed.), *Collection of Essays by Legal Advisers of States, Legal Advisers of International Organizations and Practioners in the Field of International Law*, New York, UN Office of Legal Affairs, 1999, pp. 71–84; M. Bothe, *supra* note 10, pp. 615–623; M. Bothe, 'Humanitäres Völkerrecht und Schutz der Menschenrechte', 21 *Humanitäres Völkerrecht* 2008, pp. 4–8; C. Byron, 'A Blurring of the Boundaries: The Application of International Humanitarian Law by Human Rights Bodies', 47 *Virginia J.I.L.* 2007, pp. 839–896; A. Cassimatis, *supra* note 2366, pp. 623–639; L. Doswald-Beck, 'International Humanitarian Law: A Means of Protecting Human Rights in Times of Armed Conflict', 1 *African Journal of International and Comparative Law* 1989, pp. 595–620; M. El Kouhene, *Les garanties fondamentales de la personne en droit humanitaire et droits de l'homme*, Dordrecht, Nijhoff, 1986; H.-P. Gasser, 'International Humanitarian Law and Human Rights Law in Non-international Armed Conflict: Joint Venture or Mutual Exclusion?', 45 *G.Y.I.L.* 2002, pp. 149–162 and Comment thereto by T. Stein, 45 *G.Y.I.L.* 2002, pp. 163–165; L.C. Green, 'The Relations between Human Rights Law and International Humanitarian Law: A Historical Overview', in S.C. Breau & A. Jachec-Neale (eds.), *Testing the Boundaries of International Humanitarian Law*, London, British Institute of International and Comparative Law, 2006, pp. 49–83; A. Guellali, 'Lex specialis, droit international humanitaire et droits de l'homme: leur interaction dans les nouveaux conflits armés', 111 *R.G.D.I.P.* 2007, pp. 539–574; F. Hampson, 'Other Areas of Customary Law in Relation to the Study', in E. Wilmshurst & S. Breau (eds.), *Perspectives on the ICRC Study on Customary International Humanitarian Law*, Cambridge, Cambridge University Press, 2007, pp. 50–73; F. Hampson & I. Salama, *Working Paper on the Relationship between Human Rights Law and International Humanitarian Law*, UN Doc. E/CN.4/Sub.2/2005/14, 21 June 2005; H.-J. Heintze, 'On the Relationship between Human Rights Law Protection and International Humanitarian Law', 86 No. 856 *I.R.R.C.* 2004, pp. 789–814; H.-J. Heintze, 'Konsequenzen der Konvergenz von Menschenrechtsschutz und humanitärem Völkerrecht', in H. Fischer (ed.), *Krisensicherung und humanitärer Schutz: Festschrift für Dieter Fleck*, Berlin, Berliner Wissenschafts-Verlag, 2004, pp. 243–265; J.-M. Henckaerts & L. Doswald-Beck (eds.), *infra* note 2590, Vol. I, pp. 299–306; J.-M. Henckaerts, 'Concurrent Application of International Human Rights Law and International Humanitarian Law:

the subject of a proper thesis. While its treatment below is more limited and focused on peace operations, I will attempt to cover the key developments, especially the more recent ones. I will first look at the concurrent applicability resulting from the scope of application of both regimes and will then examine how human rights and LOAC rules interact in the case of concurrent applicability.

Victims in Search of a Forum', 1 *Human Rights & International Legal Discourse* 2007, pp. 95–124 (with further extensive references at pp. 95–97 notes 1–2); N.M. Khalil, 'The Treatment of Persons in Armed Conflict and the Universal Declaration of Human Rights', in L. Maybee & B. Chakka (eds.), *Custom as a Source of International Humanitarian Law: Proceedings of the Conference to mark the Publication of the ICRC Study "Customary International Humanitarian Law", held in New Delhi, 8–9 December 2005*, Geneva, ICRC, 2006, pp. 163–196; H. Krieger, 'A Conflict of Norms: The Relationship Between Humanitarian Law and Human Rights Law in the ICRC Customary Law Study', 11 *J.C.S.L.* 2006, pp. 265–291; N. Lubell, *supra* note 2366, pp. 737–754; D. Lorenz, *supra* note 2282, pp. 199–247; S. MacBride, *supra* note 2409, pp. 373–391; G. Melander, 'International Humanitarian Law and Human Rights', 29 *Scandinavian Studies in Law* 1985, pp. 137–148; T. Meron, *supra* note 2372, pp. 45–61; T. Meron, *supra* note 2374, pp. 3–28; A. Migliazza, 'L'évolution de la réglementation de la guerre à la lumière de la sauvegarde des droits de l'homme', 137 *Rec. Cours* 1972-III, pp. 141–241; F. Naert, 'Mensenrechten en internationaal humanitair recht', in Rode Kruis Vlaanderen (ed.), Vol. 4 *Internationaal humanitair recht in de kijker* 2008, pp. 83–95; D. O'Donnell, 'Trends in the Application of International Humanitarian Law by United Nations Human Rights Mechanisms', 38 No. 324 *I.R.R.C.* 1998, pp. 481–503; A. Orakhelashvili, 'The Interaction Between Human Rights and Humanitarian Law: Fragmentation, Conflict, Parallelism, or Convergence?', 19 *E.J.I.L.* 2008, pp. 161–182; S. Perrakis, 'Le droit international humanitaire et ses relations avec les droits de l'homme: quelques considérations', in P. Tavernier & J.-M. Henckaerts (eds.), *Droit international humanitaire coutumier: enjeux et défis contemporains*, Brussels, Bruylant, 2008, pp. 115–137; R. Provost, *International Human Rights and Humanitarian Law*, Cambridge, Cambridge University Press, 2002; N. Prud'homme, 'Lex Specialis: Oversimplifying a More Complex and Multifaceted Relationship?', 40 *Israel Law Review* 2007, pp. 356–395; R. Quentin-Baxter, 'Human Rights and Humanitarian Law: Confluence or Conflict?', 9 *Australian Y.I.L.* 1985, pp. 94–112; G. Ravasi & G.L. Beruto (eds.), *International Humanitarian Law and Other Legal Regimes: Interplay in Situations of Violence: Proceedings of the 27th Round Table in San Remo, 4–6 September 2003 (International Institute of Humanitarian Law and Dragan European Foundation)*, Milan, Nagard, 2005; M.R. Rwelamira, 'Human Rights and International Humanitarian Law: The Link or Common Ground Revisited', 3 *Stellenbosch Law Review* 1992, pp. 329–348; W.A. Schabas, 'Lex specialis? Belt and Suspenders?: The Parallel Operation of Human Rights Law and the Law of Armed Conflict, and the Conundrum of Jus ad Bellum', 40 *Israel Law Review* 2007, pp. 592–613; B. Schäfer, *supra* note 2282; C. Sepúlveda, 'Interrelationships in the Implementation and Enforcement of International Humanitarian Law and Human Rights Law', 33 *American University Law Review* 1983–1984, pp. 117–124; C. Söfker, 'The Inter-American Commission and the Court of Human Rights: Enforcement Mechanisms of International Humanitarian Law?', 20 *Humanitäres Völkerrecht* 2007, pp. 33–36; C. Swinarski, 'On the Relations of International Humanitarian Law and the International Law of Human Rights', 45–46 No. 84–86 *Boletim da Sociedade Brasileira de direto interncaional* 1993, pp. 179–194; R.E. Vinuesa, 'Interface, Correspondence and Convergence of Human Rights and International Humanitarian Law', 1 *Y.I.H.L.* 1998, pp. 69–110 and K. Watkin, 'Controlling the Use of Force: A Role for Human Rights Norms in Contemporary Armed Conflict', 98 *A.J.I.L.* 2004, pp. 1–34.

1. CONCURRENT APPLICABILITY RESULTING FROM THE RESPECTIVE SCOPES OF APPLICATION

The scope of application of both human rights and the LOAC has been analyzed above in this chapter and the preceding one. The main relevant conclusions are the following:

- the LOAC only applies in cases of armed conflict or occupation (with the exception of a few rules that apply also in peace time);
- human rights continue to apply in cases of war or other emergencies but in those cases most human rights may be subject to derogation; this has *inter alia* been confirmed by the International Court of Justice,[2487] the UN Security Council[2488] and General Assembly,[2489] the Human Rights Committee,[2490] the Inter-American Commission on and Court of Human Rights,[2491] the Parliamentary Assembly of the Council of Europe[2492] and implicitly by the European Court of Human Rights;[2493] is the prevailing view in modern

[2487] Advisory Opinions on the *Legality of the Threat or Use of Nuclear Weapons* (8 July 1996), §25 ("*the protection of the [ICCPR] does not cease in times of war, except by operation of Article 4 of the Covenant whereby certain provisions may be derogated from in a time of national emergency*") and on the *Legal consequences of the construction of a wall in the occupied Palestinian territory* (9 July 2004), §§105–106 ("*More generally, ... the protection offered by human rights conventions does not cease in case of armed conflict, save through the effect of provisions for derogation of the kind to be found in Article 4 [ICCPR]*").

[2488] E.g. UNSC Res. 237 of 14 June 1967, preamble ("*Considering that essential and inalienable human rights should be respected even during the vicissitutes of war*").

[2489] E.g. UNGA Res. 2675(XXV) of 9 December 1970, §1 ("*Fundamental human rights, as accepted in international law and laid down in international instruments, continue to apply fully in situations of armed conflict*").

[2490] E.g. General Comment 31, §11 ("*the Covenant applies also in situations of armed conflict to which the rules of international humanitarian law are applicable*").

[2491] IAComHR, *Juan Carlos Abella v. Argentina*, *supra* note 2381, §§157–171, especially §158 ("*The American Convention, as well as other universal and regional human rights instruments, and the 1949 Geneva Conventions share a common nucleus of non-derogable rights and a common purpose of protecting human life and dignity. These human rights treaties apply both in peacetime, and during situations of armed conflict*"); *Report on Terrorism and Human Rights*, *supra* note 2360, §§42 ("*It is also well recognized that the international human rights commitments of states apply at all times, whether in situations of peace or situations of war*") and 61 and IACtHR, *Bámaca Velásquez* Case, 25 November 2000, Series C No. 70 [2000] IACHR 7, §§143 and 207 ("*at the time of the facts of this case, an internal conflict was taking place in Guatemala ... instead of exonerating the State from its obligations to respect and guarantee human rights, this fact obliged it to act in accordance with such obligations*").

[2492] Recommendation 1606(2003), 23 June 2003 (available online at http://assembly.coe.int/Documents/AdoptedText/TA03/EREC1606.htm), §3: "*The ECHR is applicable throughout the territory of member states. It is also applicable in the event of civil war, and even in the event of derogation from the ECHR in application of its Article 15*".

[2493] The ECtHR seems to be very reluctant to openly acknowledge that an armed conflict exists but has continued to apply the ECHR in cases where this was/is arguably the case. See also F. Hampson & I. Salama, *supra* note 2486, p. 18, §72. Compare J.-M. Henckaerts, *supra* note 2486, p. 122. Exceptionally, in *Öcalan v. Turkey*, 12 March 2003, Application No. 46221/99,

doctrine[2494] and has been recognized in some LOAC treaties;[2495] it has also been endorsed by the EU;[2496]
- it is not clear whether the application of the LOAC automatically entails a derogation or only entails a derogation to the extent that one has been notified

§120, the Court acknowledged the existence of an armed conflict with respect to the struggle between Turkey and the PKK ("*a high-profile accused who had been engaged in a lengthy armed conflict with the Turkish military authorities*"); see also ECtHR, *Ahmet Ozkan and others v. Turkey*, 6 April 2004, §305 ("*at the material time there were serious disturbances in south-east Turkey involving armed conflict between the security forces and members of the PKK*"). Chechnya is a similar case: F. Hampson & I. Salama, *supra* note 2486, p. 33, note 58 note that some of the Chechnya cases before the ECtHR concerning military operations there that fall within a conflict which the Russian Constitutional Court has determined, at least at one stage, to have fallen within AP II (citing the judgment of the Constitutional Court of the Russian Federation of 31 July 1995 on the constitutionality of the Presidential Decrees and the Resolutions of the Federal Government concerning the situation in Chechnya, translated in European Commission for Democracy through Law of the Council of Europe, Doc. CDL-INF (96)1, 10 January 1996, available online at www.venice.coe.int/docs/1996/CDL-INF(1996)001-e.asp). However, with regard to Chechnya the ECtHR does not seem to have affirmed the existence of an armed conflict.

2494 See also S. Borelli, *infra* note 2506, pp. 53–55; J.-M. Henckaerts & L. Doswald-Beck (eds.), *infra* note 2590, Vol. I, pp. 299–306; H.-J. Heintze, *supra* note 2486 (*I.R.R.C.* 2004), pp. 789–796; J.-M. Henckaerts, *supra* note 2486, pp. 106–109 (with further references); N. Lubell, *supra* note 2366, pp. 737–738; B. Schäfer, *supra* note 2282, pp. 10–13 and K. Watkin, *supra* note 2486, pp. 1–34, especially pp. 2, 9–10 and 24–34. M.J. Dennis, *supra* note 2282, pp. 136–138 argues that the derogations were intended to cover derogating measures in a State's own territory, especially towards enemy nationals. H. Krieger, *supra* note 2486, pp. 266–268 notes that "*For several decades, it was generally considered that human rights law is not applicable in situations of armed conflict*", adding that the separation between the LOAC and human rights was also "institutionally motivated" as the UN did not want de deal with the LOAC due to its anti-war perspective and the ICRC avoided implication in human rights which it considered largely political, but that perceptions have changed, including with the (legal) refinement of human rights. A. Rosas, 'The Interrelationship between Human Rights and International Humanitarian Law', in S. Kolanowski *et al.* (eds.), *Proceedings of the Bruges Colloquium. Current Challenges in International Humanitarian Law. 27–28 October 2000 / Actes du colloque de Bruges. Défis contemporains en droit international humanitaire. 27–28 octobre 2000*, Bruges, College of Europe (*collegium* No. 21, available online at www.coleurop.be/template.asp?pagename=pub_collegium), 2001, pp. 96–97, submits that in the meantime, human rights have become less political and the LOAC more political. For an analysis of early interaction, also noting the institutional separation, see R. Kolb, 'The Relationship Between International Humanitarian Law and Human Rights Law: A Brief History of the 1948 Universal Declaration of Human Rights and the 1949 Geneva Conventions', 80 No. 324 *I.R.R.C.* 1998, pp. 409–419.

2495 As pointed out by J.-M. Henckaerts, *supra* note 2486, p. 123 and by B. Schäfer, *supra* note 2282, p. 16, Article 72 AP I states that "*The provisions of this Section are additional to … other applicable rules of international law relating to the protection of fundamental human rights during international armed conflict*" and the second consideration of the preamble of AP II recalls that "*international instruments relating to human rights offer a basic protection to the human person*". See also the ICRC COMMENTARY to these provisions.

2496 See the European Union Guidelines on promoting compliance with international humanitarian law (IHL), *O.J. C* 327, 23 December 2005, p. 4, §12 ("*human rights law is applicable to everyone within the jurisdiction of the State concerned in time of peace as well as in time of armed conflict. Thus while distinct, the two sets of rules may both be applicable to a particular situation*").

but I have argued that the better view is that at least in the case of international armed conflicts there is an automatic derogation;[2497]

- measures derogating from human rights may not violate applicable LOAC rules;
- international and some domestic jurisprudence and the majority of doctrine support some extraterritorial application of human rights, though this is opposed by some States to different extents; yet the precise extent of this extraterritorial application is not yet entirely clear.

It should be added that a state may arguably temporarily be exempted, at least in part, from being obliged to respect human rights in parts of its own territory which it no longer controls due to circumstances beyond its control, such as foreign occupation.[2498] I will not further address this below as it only potentially concerns the State in which an operation is being conducted and not directly the sending States or organizations.

From these premises, it results that:[2499]

- a State engaged in a non-international armed conflict on its own territory is bound by both human rights (subject to derogations) and the LOAC;[2500]

2497 Compare R.E. Vinuesa, *supra* note 2486, p. 81, stressing the independence of the scope of application of the LOAC irrespective of any derogation under human rights.

2498 B. Schäfer, *supra* note 2282, pp. 21–22, referring to ECtHR, *Ilie Ilaşcu, Alexandru Leşco, Andrei Ivanţoc and Tudor Petrov-Popa v. Moldova and the Russian Federation*, 8 July 2004, especially §§312–313 ("*the words "within their jurisdiction" ... mean ... that jurisdiction is presumed to be exercised normally throughout the State's territory. This presumption may be limited in exceptional circumstances, particularly where a State is prevented from exercising its authority in part of its territory. That may be as a result of military occupation by the armed forces of another State which effectively controls the territory concerned (...), to acts of war or rebellion, or to the acts of a foreign State supporting the installation of a separatist State within the territory of the State concerned ... The undertakings given by a Contracting State under Article 1 of the Convention include, in addition to the duty to refrain from interfering with enjoyment of the rights and freedoms guaranteed, positive obligations to take appropriate steps to ensure respect for those rights and freedoms within its territory (...). Those obligations remain even where the exercise of the State's authority is limited in part of its territory, so that it has a duty to take all the appropriate measures which it is still within its power to take*"). Compare ECtHR, *Assanidze v. Georgia*, 8 April 2004, §§132–143. See generally K. Mujezinovic Larsen, '"Territorial Non-Application" of the European Convention on Human Rights', 78 *Nordic J.I.L.* 2009, pp. 73–93.

2499 See the similar conclusions by B. Schäfer, *supra* note 2282, pp. 21–23.

2500 B. Schäfer, *supra* note 2282, p. 21, adds liberation wars in the sense of AP I. However, this is not obvious as in such cases the applicability of human rights instruments to colonies or territories otherwise occupied was/is also a question of extraterritoriality (see notably Article 56 ECHR).

- a State engaged in an international armed conflict is bound, in, respect of its own territory, to both human rights (subject to derogations) and the LOAC;[2501]
- a State engaged in an armed conflict, whether of an international or non-international character, is bound, in respect of territory other than its own territory, by the LOAC and by human rights (subject to derogations) to the extent that the latter apply extraterritorially.[2502]

It is therefore submitted that regardless of any doctrinal, philosophical[2503] or other debates about the differences and similarities between human rights and the LOAC and conclusions drawn from this,[2504] present day positive international law, which no longer adheres to a strict distinction between the law of peace and the law of war,[2505] clearly leads to a number of cases of concurrent applicability of human rights and the LOAC.[2506] This is reflected in the European Union

2501 This is primarily relevant for the treatment of 'enemy' civilians in the territory of belligerent States.

2502 Compare H. Krieger, *supra* note 2486, p. 270 note 32, who submits that in the case of an international armed conflict, human rights will often not be applicable, citing *Bankovic*, but that they may apply in occupations.

2503 For a discussion with significant attention for this aspect, see L. Doswald-Beck & S. Vité, 'International Humanitarian Law and Human Rights Law', 75 No. 293 *I.R.R.C.* 1993, pp. 94–119, especially pp. 95–105.

2504 For a succinct overview, see B. Schäfer, *supra* note 2282, pp. 35–42. See also *infra*, subsection 2.iii of this section. The use of the expression "*human rights in armed conflicts*" in the UN in the late 1960s - early 1970s gave rise to debate over whether the LOAC may be qualified as human rights in armed conflict. However, the prevailing view is that this is not the case and that the two are distinct, even though they may overlap. See, e.g. R.E. Vinuesa, *supra* note 2486, p. 75. For an early discussion, see, e.g. K. Suter, 'An Inquiry into the Meaning of the Phrase: "Human Rights in Armed Conflicts"', 15(1–2) *R.D.P.M.D.G.* 1976, pp. 393–439 (noting the political origin of the phrase and its lack of clarity and distinguishing the limited human rights that do apply in armed conflicts from the LOAC).

2505 Similarly H.-J. Heintze, *supra* note 2486 (*I.R.R.C.* 2004), pp. 789–793 and B. Schäfer, *supra* note 2282, pp. 10–17 (citing Ipsen). It may be noted that Article 73 of the 1969 VCLT states that "*The provisions of the present Convention shall not prejudge any question that may arise in regard to a treaty from ...the outbreak of hostilities between States*". The effect of the outbreak of war or other hostilities on treaties is only briefly treated in most treatises, which seem to regard this effect as uncertain but reject a general rule of suspension/termination: see, e.g. Aust, pp. 243–244; Brownlie, p. 621 and Malanczuk, pp. 145–146. In a discussion on the ASIL forum one of the participants cited Article 40 of the Lieber Code (Instructions for the Government of Armies of the United States in the Field, 24 April 1863, available online at www.icrc.org/ihl), which states that "*There exists no law or body of authoritative rules of action between hostile armies, except that branch of the law of nature and nations which is called the law and usages of war on land*" but another participant argued that this "*statement of customary law was not immune to being rendered false by later-in-force human rights instruments*".

2506 Similarly, J. Cerone, *supra* note 2282, pp. 1453–1455 (arguing that "*despite the continuing objections of a handful of States, a consensus is evolving in favor of this ... view*"); U. Erberich, *supra* note 2284, pp. 41–43; H.-J. Heintze, *supra* note 2486 (*I.R.R.C.* 2004), p. 794; J.-M.

Guidelines on promoting compliance with international humanitarian law, which state that "*while distinct, the two sets of rules may both be applicable to a particular situation and it is therefore sometimes necessary to consider the relationship between them*".[2507]

For peace operations generally, and ESDP operations more specifically, it is the last of the above listed conclusions that is particularly relevant: it means that the EU and/or its Member States participating in an ESDP operation in a third State to which the LOAC applies (because it involves engagement in an armed conflict or amounts to an occupation) are also bound by human rights to the extent that these apply extraterritorially.

Until fairly recently, this setting has not been addressed extensively in the literature from this perspective.[2508] Doctrine mostly focused on the relationship between human rights and the LOAC in non-international armed conflicts in the traditional sense (i.e. within a State and not involving outside parties)[2509] and

---

Henckaerts, *supra* note 2486, pp. 119–124 and H. Krieger, *supra* note 2486, p. 268. One of the States rejecting the concurrent applicability is the US; see, e.g. S. Borelli, 'Casting Light on the Legal Black Hole: International Law and Detentions Abroad in the War on Terror', 87 No. 857 *I.R.R.C.* 2005, p. 52.

2507 *O.J. C* 327, 23 December 2005, p. 4, §12.

2508 For exceptions, see, e.g. U. Erberich, *supra* note 2284, pp. 33–60; HÄUSSLER, pp. 61–76 (who argues for a merger of LOAC and human rights principles on the basis of an application by analogy, seen at least in part as a legally binding obligation) and H. Krieger, *supra* note 2284, pp. 690–696. See also T. Irmscher, 'The Legal Framework for Activities of the United Nations Interim Administration Mission in Kosovo: The Charter, Human Rights, and the Law of Occupation', 44 *G.Y.I.L.* 2001, pp 353–395. For a very recent and particularly useful analysis, see J. Cerone, *Jurisdiction and Power: The Intersection of Human Rights Law & the Law of Non-International Armed Conflict in an Extraterritorial Context*, Hebrew University of Jerusalem, Faculty of Law, Research paper No. 12–07, August 2007 (see http://papers.ssrn.com/sol3/papers.cfm?abstract_id=1006833; also published in 40 *Israel Law Review* 2007, pp. 396–452).

2509 See, e.g. R. Abi-Saab, 'Human Rights and Humanitarian Law in Internal Conflicts', in D. Warner (ed.), *Human Rights and Humanitarian Law: The Quest for Universality*, The Hague, Nijhoff, 1997, pp. 107–123; W. Abresch, 'A Human Rights Law of Internal Armed Conflict: The European Court of Human Rights in Chechnya', 16 *E.J.I.L.* 2005, pp. 741–767; M. Freeman, 'International Law and Internal Armed Conflicts: Clarifying the Interplay between Human Rights and Humanitarian Protections', *Journal of Humanitarian Assistance* 2000, available online at www.jha.ac/articles/a059.htm; H.-P. Gasser, *supra* note 2486, pp. 149–162 and Comment thereto by T. Stein, 45 *G.Y.I.L.* 2002, pp. 163–165; F. J. Hampson, 'Human Rights and Humanitarian Law in Internal Conflicts', in M. Meyer & G.F.A. Best (eds.), *Armed Conflict and the New Law*, British Institute of International and Comparative Law, London, 1990, pp. 55–80; W. Heintschel von Heinegg, 'Focus Section: The Non-international Armed Conflict. Fusion or Co-existence of International Human Rights Law and International Humanitarian Law. Introductory Remarks', 45 *G.Y.I.L.* 2002, pp. 55–59; C. Lysaght, 'Scope of Protocol II and Its Relation to Common Article 3 of the Geneva Conventions of 1949 and Other Human Rights Instruments', 33 *American University Law Review* 1983, pp. 9–27; L. Moir, *supra* note 2388, pp. 193–231; L. Perna, *The Formation of the Treaty Law of Non-*

in situations of occupation,[2510] as well as on enforcing the LOAC via human rights bodies.[2511] However, with regard to occupation, the recent Iraq occupation has given rise to renewed attention for the relationship between human rights and the LOAC in occupations and peace operations.[2512]

2. THE INTERACTION IN CASES OF CONCURRENT APPLICATION

In this section, I will inquire how human rights and the LOAC interact when they apply concurrently. I will take as a starting point the general rules on the

International Armed Conflicts, Leiden, Martinus Nijhoff, 2006, pp. 77–91 and R. Müllerson, 'Humanitarian Law, Human Rights and Non-International Armed Conflicts', in K. Koufa (ed.), *International Law at the Turn of the Century*, Thessaloniki, Sakkoulas, 1998, pp. 99–156.

2510 On human rights in occupations, see, e.g. O. Ben-Naftali & Y. Shany, 'Living in Denial: The Application of Human Rights in the Occupied Territories', 37 *Israel Law Review* 2004, pp. 17–118; E.R. Cohen, *Human Rights in the Israeli-Occupied Territories, 1967–1982*, Manchester, Manchester University Press, 1985; J.A. Frowein, 'The Relationship between Human Rights Regimes and Regimes of Belligerent Occupation', 28 *Israel Y.H.R.* 1998, pp. 1–16 and W. Kâlin, Special Rapporteur of the Commission on Human Rights, *Report on the Situation of Human Rights in Kuwait under Iraqi Occupation*, UN Doc. E/CN.4/1992/26, 16 January 1992 (with regard to the latter case, compare G. Alnajjar, 'Human Rights in a Crisis Situation: The Case of Kuwait after Occupation', 23 *H.R.Q.* 2001, pp. 188–209, especially pp. 195–196). H.-P. Gasser, 'From Military Intervention to Occupation of Territory: New Relevance of International Law of Occupation', in H. Fischer (ed.), *Krisensicherung und humanitärer Schutz: Festschrift für Dieter Fleck*, Berlin, Berliner Wissenschafts-Verlag, 2004, pp. 147 and 155–156 submits that in long-term transformative occupations, links develop with human rights and that the law of occupation is the part of the LOAC closest to human rights. For an excellent overview of Israeli jurisprudence on the matter, see A.M. Gross, *infra* note 2512, pp. 9–28.

2511 See, e.g. C. Cerna, 'Human Rights in Armed Conflict: Implementation of International Humanitarian Law Norms by Regional Intergovernmental Human Rights Bodies', in F. Kalshoven & Y, Sandoz (eds.), *Mise en œuvre du droit international humanitaire / Implementation of International Humanitarian Law*, Martinus Nijhoff, Dordrecht, 1989, pp. 31–67 and F. Hampson, 'Using International Human Rights Machinery to Enforce the International Law of Armed Conflicts", 31(1–4) *R.D.P.M.D.G.* 1992, pp. 117–147. See also J.-M. Henckaerts, *supra* note 2486, pp. 95–124, especially pp. 106 and 123–124 (arguing that the relative lack of enforcement mechanisms for victims under the LOAC is likely to lead to greater scrutiny of wartime actions by human rights bodies); M. Bothe, *supra* note 10, pp. 615–623 (who is in favour of human rights bodies applying the LOAC) and N. Lubell, *supra* note 2366, pp. 742–744 (discussing the mandate and expertise of human rights bodies with respect to the LOAC).

2512 See, e.g. A.M. Gross, 'Human Proportions: Are Human Rights the Emperor's New Clothes of the International Law of Occupation?', 18 *E.J.I.L.* 2007, pp. 1–35; N. Lubell, 'Applicability of Human Rights Law in Situations of Occupation', *in* College of Europe & ICRC (eds.), *Proceedings of the Bruges Colloquium. Current Challenges to the Law of Occupation. 20th – 21st October 2005 / Actes du colloque de Bruges. Les défis contemporains au droit de l'occupation. 20–21 octobre 2005*, Bruges, College of Europe (*collegium* No. 34, available online at www.coleurop.be/template.asp?pagename=pub_collegium), 2006, pp. 50–56 and A. Roberts, 'Transformative Military Occupation: Applying the Laws of War and Human Rights', 100 *A.J.I.L.* 2006, pp. 580–622.

relationship and conflicts between different rules of international law (i). I will then look at what international courts and other international organs have said on the matter (ii) and will also study doctrine (iii). I will subsequently analyze the interaction in respect of a few specific rights or situations (iv) and will then draw some conclusions (v).

i. Relationship Rules in International Law

In respect of the two main sources of international law in general (treaties and customary international law), and the LOAC and human rights more specifically, there is no comprehensive set of written rules on how different rules relate to each other. Instead, there are treaty rules on some specific aspects of such relationships, such as Article 30 of the 1969 VCLT concerning successive treaties relating to the same subject matter, Articles 53 and 64 of the 1969 VCLT on *ius cogens* and specific provisions in some treaties that define how they relate to other rules, the most notable being Article 103 UN Charter.

However, given that treaties and custom have, in principle, the same hierarchical status in international law,[2513] these few rules are clearly inadequate. Indeed, they are supplemented by two other relationship principles[2514] that are also known in some other legal systems, namely "*lex specialis (derogat lege generali)*" (i.e. a special law prevails over general law) and "*lex posterior derogat lege priori*"

[2513] See, e.g. *Fragmentation of International Law: Difficulties Arising from the Diversification and Expansion of International Law*, Report of the Study Group of the International Law Commission, finalized by M. Koskenniemi, UN Doc. A/CN.4/L.682, 13 April 2006, p. 166, §324 (but see *id.*, pp. 47–48, §85: "*There is no formal hierarchy between the sources of international law. A number of writers have – correctly, it is submitted – nonetheless suggested that there is a kind of informal hierarchy between them. Inasmuch as "general law" does not have the status of jus cogens, treaties generally enjoy priority over custom and particular treaties over general treaties*"); BROWNLIE, pp. 3–4 ("*it is probably unwise to think in terms of hierarchy dictated by the order (a) to (d) [i.e. the order in which the sources are listed in Article 38 ICJ Statute] in all cases*"); BOSSUYT & WOUTERS, pp. 140–142; A. Cassese, *International Law*, Oxford, Oxford University Press, 2001, pp. 117–118; MALANCZUK, pp. 56–57 (albeit stating in an apparent contradiction that while "*treaties and custom are of equal authority*", nevertheless "*if there is a clear conflict, treaties prevail over custom*") and SHAW, p. 116. Compare A. Pellet, 'Article 38', in A. Zimmermann *et al.* (eds.), *The Statute of the International Court of Justice. A Commentary*, Oxford, Oxford University Press, 2006, pp. 773–783 (noting that treaties are usually given precedence over customary international law but that this is not necessarily always the case and that there is some flexibility).

[2514] I use the term 'relationship' principles/rules rather than 'conflict' principles/rules because the determination of a relationship involves more than just dealing with conflicting rules. Compare UN Doc. A/CN.4/L.682, *supra* note 2513, pp. 10–30, §§5–45 and the heading 'The approach of this Study: seeking relationships' at p. 20. In most general international law treatises, these rules seem to be addressed under the heading of 'hierarchy of sources' yet this also seems too narrow a term.

(i.e. later law prevails over prior law),[2515] to which the principle "*lex posterior generalis non derogate priori speciali*" (i.e. later general law does not prevail over prior special law) is sometimes added.[2516]

However, as is very well illustrated in one of the reports in the framework of the ILC's ongoing work on the fragmentation of international law, the application of these rules is by no means an easy exercise.[2517] In the present context, e.g. it is doubtful whether one can argue that human rights law as a whole is the general law and the LOAC as a whole is the special law. Rather, it might be argued that both are special law/regimes compared to general international law, in which case the *lex specialis* principle can probably only be applied on a case-by-case basis in respect of specific *rules*.[2518] In the following subsections, I will therefore look at how these rules have been applied to the relationship between the LOAC and human rights in case law, doctrine and in respect of a few selected specific rights as well as in occupation.

It may be added first that general principles of law are usually regarded as hierarchically inferior to treaties and custom[2519] and that the hierarchical status of decisions of international organizations will depend on provisions and status of the instrument on which they are based.

2515 See extensively UN Doc. A/CN.4/L.682, *supra* note 2513, pp. 30–166, §§46–323. See also A. Cassese, *supra* note 2513, p. 117; Malanczuk, pp. 56–57 and Shaw, p. 116. See also A. Lindroos, 'Addressing Norm Conflicts in a Fragmented Legal System: The Doctrine of *Lex Specialis*', 74 *Nordic J.I.L.* 2005, pp. 27–66 and E. Vranes, '*Lex Superior, Lex Specialis, Lex Posterior* – Zur Rechtsnatur der "Konfliktlösungsregeln"', 65 *Z.a.ö.R.V.* 2005, pp. 391–405. On the relationship and conflict rules between custom and treaties, see also G. Cahin, *La coutume internationale et les organisations internationales: l'incidence de la dimension institutionnelle sur le processus coutumier*, Paris, Pedone, 2001, pp. 590–613. For treaties, the *lex posterior* rule is reflected in Article 30(3)-(4) 1969 VCLT, which is regarded as customary international law on this point (Aust, p. 181).

2516 Bossuyt & Wouters, p. 141; A. Cassese, *supra* note 2513, p. 117 and Malanczuk, pp. 56–57.

2517 See, e.g. UN Doc. A/CN.4/L.682, *supra* note 2513, pp. 35–36, §58 and pp. 60–65, §§111–122 (noting that general/special is relational and that this can be seen at least in two respects: either the subject matter or the parties).

2518 This point is made more generally by H. Krieger, *supra* note 2486, pp. 268–270. In this sense also A. Orakhelashvili, *supra* note 2486, p. 182. Compare U. Erberich, *supra* note 2284, pp. 44–48, especially p. 46, writing that when different sets of rules apply concurrently, the more general one is (only) replaced by the more specific one when the latter exhaustively regulates a situation and these rules are carved out by the former ("*bei der gleichzeitigen Geltung verschiedener Regelungskomplexe [gilt dass], wenn der eine die Situation erschöpfend und abschließend regelt und diese Regelungen durch die Anwendung des anderen Regelungskomplexes ausgehebelt würden, der allgemeinere dann verdrängt wird*" – emphasis in original; my summary may not fully capture the nuances of this position as expressed in German). For an analysis of the LOAC – human rights relationship in the light of fragmentation, see A. Cassimatis, *supra* note 2366, pp. 623–639.

2519 See, e.g. Bossuyt & Wouters, p. 142; Malanczuk, pp. 56–57 and Shaw, pp. 115–116.

ii. *Jurisprudence*[2520]

The International Court of Justice has explicitly pronounced itself on the relationship between human rights and the LOAC on at least two occasions. First, in its 1996 Advisory Opinion on the *Legality of the Threat or Use of Nuclear Weapons*, it stated that:

> … the protection of the [ICCPR] does not cease in times of war, except by operation of Article 4 of the Covenant whereby certain provisions may be derogated from in a time of national emergency. Respect for the right to life is not, however, such a provision. In principle, the right not arbitrarily to be deprived of one's life applies also in hostilities. The test of what is an arbitrary deprivation of life, however, then falls to be determined by the applicable *lex specialis*, namely, the law applicable in armed conflict which is designed to regulate the conduct of hostilities. Thus whether a particular loss of life, through the use of a certain weapon in warfare, is to be considered an arbitrary deprivation of life contrary to Article 6 of the Covenant, can only be decided by reference to the law applicable in armed conflict and not deduced from the terms of the Covenant itself.[2521]

The Court elaborated on this as follows in its 2004 Advisory Opinion on the *Legal consequences of the construction of a wall in the occupied Palestinian territory*:

> More generally, the Court considers that the protection offered by human rights conventions does not cease in case of armed conflict, save through the effect of provisions for derogation of the kind to be found in Article 4 [ICCPR]. As regards the relationship between international humanitarian law and human rights law, there are thus three possible situations: some rights may be exclusively matters of international humanitarian law; others may be exclusively matters of human rights law; yet others may be matters of both these branches of international law. In order to answer the question put to it, the Court will have to take into consideration both these branches of international law, namely human rights law and, as *lex specialis*, international humanitarian law.[2522]

Whereas the 1996 statement is fairly uncontroversial, albeit perhaps not entirely accurate (see *infra*, subsection iv of this section), the 2004 statement does give rise to a few questions.[2523] For instance, when is a matter exclusively regulated by

---

2520 See also T. Meron, *supra* note 2372, pp. 50–55.
2521 8 July 1996 §25.
2522 9 July 2004, §106.
2523 B. Schäfer, *supra* note 2282, pp. 43–44 even goes so far as to say that this statement doesn't provide much clarification. A. Roberts, *supra* note 2512, p. 597 adds that the Court did not always motivate its views very well in this advisory opinion.

one branch of international law? Also, a matter that is regulated by only one branch may in fact have effects not intended or compatible with the other branch.[2524] E.g. the treatment of prisoners of war is only specifically regulated by the LOAC but may not – at least without derogation – fall within the accepted *legal basis* for deprivation of liberty under Article 5 ECHR.[2525] It is also subject to the prohibition of torture, inhuman and degrading treatment under human rights instruments.[2526] Second, and more importantly, the Court's apparent general qualification of the LOAC as *lex specialis* may be questioned, including from the perspective of *lex posterior*. There may well be instances where a particular human right is more specific, even in armed conflict,[2527] and/or later in time, e.g. the prohibition of the death penalty in all circumstances for parties to Protocol 13 to the ECHR, which clearly intends to supersede any prior conflicting rule on the matter.[2528] Third, it remains to be clarified how the application of the LOAC as *lex specialis* is to be seen: as replacing human rights (in whole or in part) and/or as serving for the interpretation or (partial) modification of human rights.[2529]

2524 B. Schäfer, *supra* note 2282, pp. 44–45.

2525 See also B. Schäfer, *supra* note 2282, pp. 44–45. Compare J.-M. Henckaerts, *supra* note 2486, p. 119, who also points to the incompatibility with human rights in that there is no right for prisoners of war to challenge the legality of their detention but argues that there is no 'complete' incompatibility as the deprivation of liberty is not arbitrary and some procedures for supervision exist. See more extensively *infra*, subsection iv.b of this section.

2526 See U. Erberich, *supra* note 2284, p. 47, who argues that with respect to Article 5 ECHR, the LOAC rules on prisoners of war replace Article 5 ECHR as *lex specialis* but not Articles 2 and 3 ECHR.

2527 Similarly J.-M. Henckaerts, *supra* note 2486, pp. 122–123. See also the arguments in favour of a case-by-case contextual *lex specialis supra* and *infra*, subsections i, iii and iv of this section.

2528 Vilnius, 3 May 2003, *E.T.S.* No. 187. The preamble mentions the "*Wish[...] to strengthen the protection of the right to life guaranteed by the [ECHR]*" and notes "*that Protocol No. 6 to the [ECHR], does not exclude the death penalty in respect of acts committed in time of war or of imminent threat of war*" and Articles 1 to 3 contain an obligation to abolish the death penalty without possibilities of derogation or reservations.

2529 F. Hampson & I. Salama, *supra* note 2486, p. 15, §57 argue that "*It is clear that* lex specialis *is not being used to displace [human rights law]. It is rather an indication that human rights bodies should interpret a human rights norm in the light of LOAC*". Similarly, H.-J. Heintze, *supra* note 2486 (*I.R.R.C.* 2004), pp. 797–798 seems to reject a replacement. It is, however, doubtful whether mere interpretation is always feasible, especially with regard to the ECHR, which contains more specific rules on some key issues such as the right to life and deprivation of liberty; see *infra*, subsection iv of this section. See U. Erberich, *supra* note 2284, pp. 44–48, arguing that in cases of incompatible legal consequences there is a replacement ("*verdrängung*"). See also IAComHR, *Abella* (*supra* note 2381), §157: "*[the Commission] has deemed it necessary at times to* apply directly *rules of international humanitarian law* or to inform its interpretations *of relevant provisions of the American Convention by reference to these rules*" (emphasis added). Compare J.-M. Henckaerts, *supra* note 2486, p. 119, who submits that *most* issues concern the interpretation of an imprecision (emphasis added) and pp. 120–121, arguing that the Court did not mean that the LOAC would replace human rights in its entirety. As to interpretation, N. Lubell, *supra* note 2366, pp. 744–746 points to difficulties resulting from different use of language in both branches (e.g. proportionality

The Human Rights Committee has expressed its view on the matter as follows:

> ... the Covenant applies also in situations of armed conflict to which the rules of international humanitarian law are applicable. While, in respect of certain Covenant rights, more specific rules of international humanitarian law may be specially relevant for the purposes of the interpretation of Covenant rights, both spheres of law are complementary, not mutually exclusive[2530]

This appears to be a more nuanced approach, rejecting *lex specialis* as an exclusion mechanism and leaving open the possibility that in some cases human rights may be more specific.[2531]

The supervisory organs of the Inter-American Human Rights system have also pronounced themselves several times on the relationship between the LOAC and human rights. While the position in respect of their competence to apply the LOAC directly (as opposed to indirectly, e.g. for interpreting human rights) appears to have evolved,[2532] the view on the relationship between the LOAC and human rights seems to have been fairly constant. The key decisions will be cited at some length here as they are probably the most elaborate statements by human rights bodies on the matter. First, in the *Abella* case, the Inter-American Commission on Human Rights held that:

> 157... it useful to clarify the reasons why [the Commission] has deemed it necessary at times to apply directly rules of international humanitarian law or to inform its interpretations of relevant provisions of the American Convention by reference to these rules. A basic understanding of the interrelationship of these two branches of international law - human rights and humanitarian law - is instructive in this regard.
>
> 158. The American Convention, as well as other universal and regional human rights instruments, and the 1949 Geneva Conventions share a common nucleus of non-

means different things in the LOAC and in human rights). M.J. Dennis, *supra* note 2282, pp. 133–134 seems to think rather in exclusion terms.

2530 General Comment 31, §11.

2531 Compare H.-J. Heintze, *supra* note 2486 (*I.R.R.C.* 2004), p. 797.

2532 See, e.g. H.-J. Heintze, *supra* note 2486 (*I.R.R.C.* 2004), pp. 802–805. See also N. Lubell, *supra* note 2366, p. 742. Compare J.-F. Flauss, 'Le droit international humanitaire devant les instances de contrôle des Conventions européenne et interaméricaine des droits de l'homme', in J.-F. Flauss (ed.), *Les nouvelles frontières du droit international humanitaire. Actes du colloque du 12 avril 2002 organisé par l'Institut d'études de droit international de l'Université de Lausanne*, Brussels, Bruylant, 2003, pp. 117–133, especially pp. 126–131. See also generally E.J. Buis, 'The Implementation of International Humanitarian Law by Human Rights Courts: The Example of the Inter-American Human Rights System', in R. Arnold & N. Quénivet (eds.), *International Humanitarian Law and Human Rights Law: towards a New Merger in International Law*, Leiden, Martinus Nijhoff, 2008, pp. 269–293.

derogable rights and a common purpose of protecting human life and dignity. These human rights treaties apply both in peacetime, and during situations of armed conflict .... Although one of their purposes is to prevent warfare, none of these human rights instruments was designed to regulate such situations and, thus, they contain no rules governing the means and methods of warfare.

159. In contrast, international humanitarian law generally ... does not apply in peacetime, and its fundamental purpose is to place restraints on the conduct of warfare in order to diminish the effects of hostilities. It is understandable therefore that the provisions of conventional and customary humanitarian law generally afford victims of armed conflicts greater or more specific protections than do the more generally phrased guarantees in the American Convention and other human rights instruments.

160. It is, moreover, during situations of internal armed conflict that these two branches of international law most converge and reinforce each other. ...

161. For example, both Common Article 3 and Article 4 of the American Convention protect the right to life and, thus, prohibit, *inter alia,* summary executions in all circumstances. Claims alleging arbitrary deprivations of the right to life attributable to State agents are clearly within the Commission's jurisdiction. But the Commission's ability to resolve claimed violations of this non-derogable right arising out of an armed conflict may not be possible in many cases by reference to Article 4 of the American Convention alone. This is because the American Convention contains no rules that either define or distinguish civilians from combatants and other military targets, much less, specify when a civilian can be lawfully attacked or when civilian casualties are a lawful consequence of military operations. Therefore, the Commission must necessarily look to and apply definitional standards and relevant rules of humanitarian law as sources of authoritative guidance in its resolution of this and other kinds of claims alleging violations of the American Convention in combat situations. To do otherwise would mean that the Commission would have to decline to exercise its jurisdiction in many cases involving indiscriminate attacks by State agents resulting in a considerable number of civilian casualties. Such a result would be manifestly absurd in light of the underlying object and purposes of both the American Convention and humanitarian law treaties.

162. Apart from these considerations, the Commission's competence to apply humanitarian law rules is supported by the text of the American Convention, by its own case law, as well as the jurisprudence of the Inter-American Court of Human Rights. ...

164. The Commission believes that in those situations where the American Convention and humanitarian law instruments apply concurrently, Article 29(b) of the American Convention necessarily require the Commission to take due notice of and, where appropriate, give legal effect to applicable humanitarian law rules. Article 29(b) – the so-called "most-favorable-to-the-individual-clause" – provides that no provision of the American Convention shall be interpreted as "restricting the

enforcement or exercise of any right or freedom recognized by virtue of the laws of any State Party of another convention which one of the said states is a party."

165. The purpose of this Article is to prevent States Parties from relying on the American Convention as a ground for limiting more favorable or less restrictive rights to which an individual is otherwise entitled under either national or international law. Thus, where there are differences between legal standards governing the same or comparable rights in the American Convention and a humanitarian law instrument, the Commission is duty bound to give legal effort to the provision(s) of that treaty with the higher standard(s) applicable to the right(s) or freedom(s) in question. If that higher standard is a rule of humanitarian law, the Commission should apply it.

166. Properly viewed, the close interrelationship between human rights law and humanitarian law also supports the Commission's authority under Article 29(b) to apply humanitarian law, where it is relevant. In this regard, the authors of the New Rules make the following pertinent point regarding the reciprocal relationship between Protocol II and the Covenant on Civil and Political Rights: "Protocol II should not be interpreted as remaining behind the basic standard established in the Covenant. On the contrary, when Protocol II in its more detailed provisions establishes a higher standard than the Covenant, this higher standard prevails, on the basis of the fact that the Protocol is "lex specialis" in relation to the Covenant. On the other hand, provisions of the Covenant which have not been reproduced in the Protocol which provide for a higher standard of protection than the protocol should be regarded as applicable irrespective of the relative times at which the two instruments came into force for the respective State. It is a general rule for the application of concurrent instruments of Human Rights – and Part II 'Humane Treatment' [of Protocol II] is such an instrument – that they implement and complete each other instead of forming a basis for limitations".

167. Their point is equally valid concerning the mutual relationship between the American Convention and Protocol II and other relevant sources of humanitarian law, such as Common Article 3.

168. In addition, the Commission believes that a proper understanding of the relationship between applicable humanitarian law treaties and Article 27(1), the derogation clause of the American Convention, is relevant to this discussion. … Article 27(1) requires that any suspension of guarantees not be "inconsistent with that State's other obligations under international law". Thus, while it cannot be interpreted as incorporating by reference into the American Convention all of a State's other international legal obligations, Article 27(1) does prevent a State from adopting derogation measures that would violate its other obligations under conventional or customary international law.

169. … Thomas Buergenthal, has written the following concerning Article 4 [ICCPR]: "Particularly relevant in this connection are humanitarian law treaties because they apply in time of war: a State which purports to derogate from obligation under the

> Covenant which are required also by such other treaty would be violating both Articles. Similarly, a State could not take measures under Article 4 which could violate provisions in other human rights treaties to which it is a party, for example, which such other treaty contains no derogation clause or has a stricter derogation clause forbidding derogation from some rights for which derogation is permitted under Article 4 of the Covenant".
>
> 170. Inasmuch as the content of Article 27(1) of the American Convention is, in most material respects, identical to that of Article 4(1) of the Covenant, ... Professor Buergenthal's analysis applies with equal force to issues involving the interpretation and application of Article 27(1) during situations of armed conflict. Thus, when reviewing the legality of derogation measures taken by a State Party to the American Convention by virtue of the existence of an armed conflict to which both the American Convention and humanitarian law treaties apply, the Commission should not resolve this question solely by reference to the text of Article 27 of the American Convention. Rather, it must also determine whether the rights affected by these measures are similarly guaranteed under applicable humanitarian law treaties. If it finds that the rights in question are not subject to suspension under these humanitarian law instruments, the Commission should conclude that these derogation measures are in violation of the State Parties obligations under both the American Convention and the humanitarian law treaties concerned.[2533]

While the Commission clearly recognizes the need to apply directly some LOAC provisions or to have recourse to the LOAC to interpret some human rights (a distinction which suggests that interpretation alone does not always suffice) (§§157–167), thus affirming the *lex specialis* principle (see especially §§166–167), it seems to contradict itself by also endorsing the "most favourable protection" principle (§§164–167).[2534] This may perhaps be explained by the Commission's apparent belief that "*the provisions of conventional and customary humanitarian law generally afford victims of armed conflicts greater or more specific protections than do the more generally phrased guarantees in the American Convention and other human rights instruments*" (§159), although it also recognizes that the reverse may be true (§§166–167). It is submitted that this view is incorrect, unless limited to non-derogable human rights, and that the *lex specialis* rule clearly implies that in some cases the LOAC will prevail even where it offers less protection.[2535] In other words: more specific does not necessarily equal more

---

2533 *Juan Carlos Abella v. Argentina, supra* note 2381, §§157–171, especially §§158–161. For a fairly critical comment on this case, see L. Zegveld, "The Inter-American Commission on Human Rights and International Humanitarian Law: A Comment on the *Tablada* case"', 80 No. 324 *I.R.R.C.* 1998, pp. 505–511.

2534 D. Lorenz, *supra* note 2282, pp. 211–212 submits that the IAComHR rather follows the integrationist and/or complementary approach.

2535 See T. Meron, *supra* note 2374, p. 30 ("*human rights may be pre-empted by a different, and,* on the whole, less generous lex specialis, *as in the case of prisoners of war*"; emphasis added).

favourable.[2536] It may also be noted that LOAC treaties usually do not contain a general most favourable protection clause covering human rights treaties.[2537]

In the *Las Palmeras* case, the Inter-American Court of Human Rights rejected its competence to *rule on* a violation of the LOAC but did not pronounce itself on the relationship between the LOAC and human rights.[2538] However, soon after this judgment, in the *Bamaca-Velasquez* case, it clarified (or perhaps partially reversed) this, stating that:

> 208. Although the Court lacks competence to *declare* that a State is internationally responsible for the violation of international treaties that do not grant it such competence, it can *observe* that certain acts or omissions that violate human rights, pursuant to the treaties that they do have competence to apply, also violate other international instruments for the protection of the individual, such as the 1949 Geneva Conventions and, in particular, common Article 3.
>
> 209. Indeed, there is a similarity between the content of Article 3, common to the 1949 Geneva Conventions, and the provisions of the American Convention and other international instruments regarding non-derogable human rights (such as the right to life and the right not to be submitted to torture or cruel, inhuman or degrading treatment). This Court has already indicated in the *Las Palmeras Case* (2000), *that the relevant provisions of the Geneva Conventions may be taken into consideration as elements for the interpretation of the American Convention.*[2539]

Compare A.M. Gross, *supra* note 2512, pp. 1–35, who argues that in occupation, applying human rights may lead to lower protection, at least for the occupied population as opposed to that of the occupying State, though he acknowledges that this is not always the case (pp. 26–29 and 31). At p. 35, he also sees the *lex specialis* and most favourable protection rules as incompatible ("*Some may suggest that the courts should apply the most protective norm* rather than *using the* lex specialis *doctrine*"; emphasis added).

2536 B. Schäfer, *supra* note 2282, pp. 47–48 also doubt more generally whether the most favourable protection principle can apply in the LOAC – human rights relationship. But see A. Orakhelashvili, *supra* note 2486, pp. 181–182.

2537 However, some of these treaties contain a number of clauses endorsing this principle with regard to the relationship between certain LOAC rules. See, e.g. Article 75(1) AP I ("*persons ... who do not benefit from more favourable treatment under the Conventions or under this Protocol shall ... enjoy, as a minimum, the protection provided by this Article*").

2538 *Las Palmeras Case*, Preliminary Objections, 4 February 2000, Series C No. 67 [2000] IACHR 4, §§28–34. Interestingly, in §30, it was stated that "*Colombia established the distinction between "interpretation" and "application." The Court may interpret the Geneva Conventions and other international treaties, but it may only apply the American Convention*". For a critical discussion, see F. Martin, "Application du droit internationale humanitaire par la Cour interaméricaine des droits de l'homme", 83 No. 844 *R.I.C.R.* 2001, pp. 1037–1066.

2539 *Bámaca Velásquez Case*, 25 November 2000, *Series C* No. 70 [2000] IACHR 7, §§203–209 (emphasis added). The reference to the *Las Palermas case* is puzzling, as the Court did not say there what it claims to have said (at most, it did not rule out interpretation on the basis of the LOAC, but it did not affirm this).

A further opinion on the matter was issued by the Inter-American Commission on Human Rights with regard to the US detention centre at Guantanamo Bay. It reads in part:

> ... while its specific mandate is to secure the observance of international human rights protections in the Hemisphere, this Commission has in the past looked to and applied definitional standards and relevant rules of international humanitarian law in interpreting the American Declaration and other Inter-American human rights instruments in situations of armed conflict.
>
> ... It is well-recognized that international human rights law applies at all times, in peacetime and in situations of armed conflict. ... in situations of armed conflict, the protections under international human rights and humanitarian law may complement and reinforce one another, sharing as they do a common nucleus of non-derogable rights and a common purpose of promoting human life and dignity. In certain circumstances, however, the test for evaluating the observance of a particular right, such as the right to liberty, in a situation of armed conflict may be distinct from that applicable in time of peace. In such situations, international law, including the jurisprudence of this Commission, dictates that it may be necessary to deduce the applicable standard by reference to international humanitarian law as the applicable *lex specialis*.
>
> Accordingly, where persons find themselves within the authority and control of a state and where a circumstance of armed conflict may be involved, their fundamental rights may be determined in part by reference to international humanitarian law as well as international human rights law.[2540]

Here the Commission only cited the *lex specialis* principle and does not mention the most favourable treatment principle. Finally, the relationship human rights – LOAC is discussed at some length in the Commission's *Report on Terrorism and Human Rights*:

> 45. When interpreting and applying the provisions of inter-American human rights instruments, it is both appropriate and necessary to take into account member states' obligations under other human rights and humanitarian law treaties, which together create an interrelated and mutually reinforcing regime of human rights protections. These treaties include, but are not limited to, ... the 1949 Geneva Conventions, ... and the 1977 Additional Protocols thereto ... Under this interconnected regime of treaty obligations, one instrument may not be used as a basis for denying or limiting other favorable or more extensive human rights that individuals might otherwise be entitled to under international or domestic law or practice. ...

2540 Decision Authorizing Precautionary Measures in Favor of Detainees Being Held by the United States at Guantanamo Bay, Cuba, 12 March 2002, *supra* note 2359 (notes omitted).

> 61. In situations of armed conflict, both international human rights law and international humanitarian law apply ... Nevertheless, the American Convention and other universal and regional human rights instruments were not designed specifically to regulate armed conflict situations and do not contain specific rules governing the use of force and the means and methods of warfare in that context. Accordingly, in situations of armed conflict, international humanitarian law may serve as *lex specialis* in interpreting and applying international human rights instruments ... Consequently, in such circumstances, one must necessarily look to and apply definitional standards and relevant rules of international humanitarian law as sources of authoritative guidance in the assessment of the respect of the inter-American Instruments in combat situations ...
>
> 62. It is therefore appropriate, and indeed imperative, for the Commission to consider all relevant international norms, including those of international humanitarian law, while interpreting the international human rights law instruments for which it is responsible ... International humanitarian law is also pertinent to the Commission's interpretation of and application of human rights protection to the extent that, as described previously, states' treaty obligations in these regimes of international law prescribe interrelated and mutually reinforcing standards of protection ...[2541]

Here we again find the combination of the *lex specialis* principle (§61) and the most favourable treatment principle (§45), which, as argued above, may conflict.

The European Commission of Human Rights dealt with the LOAC – human rights relationship in one of the early Cyprus cases. In particular, it did not deem it necessary to inquire whether the internment of prisoners of war by Turkey was compatible with Article 5 ECHR (on deprivation of liberty) because this was regulated by GC III (§313), despite no derogation being found to be applicable in this respect (§§312 and 529–531) and despite its conclusion that this internment was not in conformity with Article 5 ECHR (§309). In contrast, with regard to interned civilians, it held that Article 5 ECHR was violated (§310) and ruled that no derogation was in force in this respect either (§§312 and 525–531) but did not refer to the LOAC on this point. It concluded that there was a violation of Article 5 ECHR with regard to the detention of civilians and that it was not necessary to examine whether Article 5 had been violated by the internment of prisoners of war.[2542] This apparent and striking inconsistency of ignoring LOAC rules on the internment of civilians while accepting LOAC rules on prisoners of war was rightly criticized by Commission members Sperduti and Trechsel in their dissenting opinion, in which they argued that the LOAC rules on internment of

---

2541 *Supra* note 2360.

2542 *Cyprus v. Turkey*, Report of 10 July 1976, 4 *E.H.R.R.* 1982, pp. 482–582, especially pp. 529–533 and 555–559, including points II.2–3 of the conclusions in Part IV.

civilians should have been taken into account for determining whether an acceptable derogation had been made (they rejected the view that there was no derogation).[2543] In addition, the majority's conclusion not to consider whether GC III was correctly applied with regard to prisoners of war implies a separatist or at least exclusionary *lex specialis* view.

Since this case, the supervisory organs of the ECHR have not explicitly applied or referred to the LOAC until very recently, neither have they stated any views on the relationship between human rights and the LOAC.[2544] Nevertheless, as mentioned above, they have ruled that human rights apply in some situations of armed conflict. Consequently, how they have decided these cases is relevant.[2545]

First, in at least one of the Turkish PKK cases, namely *Ergi*, the Court used language very closely resembling that of the LOAC, which it seemed to apply implicitly (in the absence of a derogation). In particular, the Court judged that a security operation had to "*take all feasible precautions in the choice of means and methods of a security operation mounted against an opposing group with a view to avoiding and, in any event, to minimising, incidental loss of civilian life*".[2546] This is obviously inspired by Article 57(2)a(ii) AP I, which provides that those who plan or decide upon an attack shall "*take all feasible precautions in the choice of means and methods of attack with a view to avoiding, and in any event to minimizing, incidental loss or civilian life, injury to civilians and damage to civilian objects*". This was therefore seen by most commentators as a *de facto* application of the LOAC.[2547] In addition to the ruling regarding the incidental

2543 *Id.*, pp. 561–565, especially §§6–7. See on this also F. Martin, *supra* note 2538, pp. 1061–1062.

2544 H.-J. Heintze, *supra* note 2486 (*I.R.R.C.* 2004), pp. 806–812 rightly mentions that the Court did not have recourse to the LOAC in the more recent Cyprus cases but that it applied the LOAC *de facto* in *Ergi* (see *infra*, next paragraph and note 2546). N. Lubell, *supra* note 2366, p. 743 writes that after the early Cyprus case, there has been reluctance to have recourse to the LOAC but that it has been applied *de facto* in some cases. See also J.-F. Flauss, *supra* note 2532, pp. 120–126 (noting the organs' reluctance to apply the LOAC but perceiving some implicit taking into account of the LOAC) and H.-J. Heinze, 'The European Court of Human Rights and the Implementation of Human Rights Standards During Armed Conflicts', 45 *G.Y.I.L.* 2002, pp. 60–77 (also noting this reluctance at pp. 75–76) and Comment thereto by R. Haßenpflug, 45 *G.Y.I.L.* 2002, pp. 78–81.

2545 For an overview, albeit predating the important Chechnya cases, see A. Reidy, 'The Approach of the European Commission and Court of Human Rights to International Humanitarian Law', 80 No. 324 *I.R.R.C.* 1998, pp. 513–529.

2546 ECtHR, *Ergi v. Turkey*, 28 July 1998, §§79–81.

2547 E.g. A.M. Gross, *supra* note 2512, p. 32; H.-J. Heintze, *supra* note 2486 (*I.R.R.C.* 2004), p. 810; H. Krieger, *supra* note 2284, p. 692; A. Reidy, *supra* note 2545, pp. 4–5 of the online version printout, and K. Watkin, *supra* note 2486, p. 24. But see, albeit with hindsight in light of the ECtHR's recent Chechnya cases, W. Abresch, *supra* note 2509, pp. 742 and 746 (doubting whether the Court applied the LOAC and writing that if it did so, it did so "*in a highly imprecise manner*").

civilian loss of life, the Court does not seem to have aired any concern that an ambush was set up for a PKK group, apparently with the intent to attack rather than to capture the PKK members, an approach that can hardly be justified under Article 2 ECHR except by recourse to lawful acts of war as a derogation under Article 15 ECHR,[2548] unless one considers that Article 2(2)c ECHR covers such acts.[2549] I should clarify that I consider that the situation in that region at that time amounted to an armed conflict.

Second, the more recent Chechnya cases regarding the conduct of hostilities are also of great significance, notably the 24 February 2005 judgments in *Isayeva, Yusupova and Bazayeva v. Russia*[2550] and in *Isayeva v. Russia*[2551].[2552]

In the former case, Russian military airplanes bombed several vehicles in a convoy in Chechnya on 29 October 1999. The applicants claimed that it had been announced that there would be a humanitarian corridor that day for civilians wanting to leave the area (including Red Cross staff, see §183) but that a large convoy of civilians who wanted to make use of this corridor (a substantial number of cars and thousands of people spread over several kilometres, see §184) were turned back at a roadblock (see also §185) and were subsequently attacked by airplanes, leading to many deaths and injuries as well as the destruction of a number of vehicles (§§13–24). Russia claimed that in the course of counter-terrorist operations in the area that *inter alia* aimed to prevent transportation of rebel personnel and supplies, the airplanes were attacked from a truck with large-calibre infantry firearms, which they then attacked upon having obtained permission and that this was followed by a second attack on another similar truck and it conceded that 14 civilian vehicles were destroyed or damaged and 16 civilians killed as well as 11 wounded but argued that the civilian vehicles only appeared after the rockets had been fired (§§25–30). The ICRC stated that five Chechen Red Cross vehicles, all marked, including one on the roof, were in the

2548 On this point, see also *infra*, subsection iv.a of this section on the right to life.

2549 This provision refers to "*action lawfully taken for the purpose of quelling a riot or insurrection*"; see *supra* note 2397 for a brief discussion of its usually overlooked relevance.

2550 Applications Nos. 57947/00, 57948/00 and 57949/00.

2551 Application No. 57950/00.

2552 There was also a judgment in *Khashiyev and Akayeva v. Russia* (Applications Nos. 57942/00 and 57945/00) but this concerned torture and extra-judicial executions by the Russian military. For a brief summary, see the 19 March 2005 issue of *International Law in Brief* (available at www.asil.org/ilibmenu.cfm) and the 27 February 2005 issue of *Sentinelle* (available at www.sfdi.org/actualites/Sentinelle8.html#russie). There have been further cases since then, including *Musayev and Others v. Russia*, 26 July 2007 (applications Nos. 57941/00, 58699/00 and 60403/00), which concerned the unlawful killing of civilians in what does not appear to have been an immediate combat situation. See also generally P. Rowe, 'Non-International Armed Conflict and the European Court of Human Rights: Chechnya from 1999', 4 *New Zealand Yearbook of International Law* 2007, pp. 205–226.

convoy that was attacked and that two Red Cross staff were killed and one was wounded (§31). Two journalists also died from the injuries they sustained while filming a bus with refugees being hit (§33).

The Court restated that the right to life is one of the most fundamental ECHR provisions from which in peacetime no derogation is permitted under Article 15 and that the circumstances in which deprivation of life may be justified must therefore be strictly construed (§168), recalling that any use of force must be no more than "absolutely necessary" for the achievement of one or more of the purposes set out in sub-paragraphs (a) to (c) (§169). It noted that "*No state of emergency or martial law has been declared in Chechnya. No federal law has been enacted to restrict the rights of the population of the area. No derogation under Article 15 of the Convention has been made*" (§125) and added that Russia's failure to "*invoke the provisions of domestic legislation at any level which would govern the use of force by the army or security forces in situations such as the present one, while not in itself sufficient to decide on a violation of the positive obligation of the State to protect the right to life, in the circumstances of the present case is also directly relevant to the proportionality of the response to the alleged attack*" (§198). The LOAC was invoked by the applicants, who submitted that the aerial bombardment was "*an indiscriminate attack on civilians, which could not be justified under international humanitarian law*", referring to common Article 3 of the Geneva Conventions (§157), and by some intervening third parties, who argued for construing the LOAC in the light of human rights (§§161–167). Russia did not rely on the LOAC and argued that the pilots "*had not intended to cause harm to the civilians, because they did not and could not have seen the convoy*", that "*the attack and its consequences were legitimate under Article 2 §2 (a) [ECHR]*" and that "*the use of air power was justified by the heavy fire opened by members of illegal armed formations, which constituted a threat not only to the pilots, but also to the civilians who were in the vicinity*" (§160). While the judgment contains further guidance on the right to life under the ECHR, this aspect will be addressed below. Here the focus is on the relationship LOAC – human rights generally. In this respect, the following excerpts are relevant:

> 171. In particular, it is necessary to examine whether the operation was planned and controlled by the authorities so as to *minimise, to the greatest extent possible, recourse to lethal force*. The authorities must take appropriate care to ensure that *any risk to life is minimised*. The Court must also examine whether the authorities were not negligent in their choice of action (...)....
>
> 174. It is undisputed that the applicants were subjected to an aerial missile attack, during which the first applicant's two children were killed and the first and the second applicant were wounded. This brings the complaint, in respect of all three applicants, within the ambit of Article 2 (see §171 above). The Government suggested

> that the use of force was justified in the present case under paragraph 2 (a) of Article 2 and that the harm done was not intentional. …
>
> 177. … the documents submitted by the parties and the investigation file nevertheless allow the Court to draw certain conclusions as to *whether the operation was planned and conducted in such a way as to avoid or minimise, to the greatest extent possible, damage to civilians.*
>
> 178. The Court accepts that *the situation that existed in Chechnya at the relevant time called for exceptional measures on behalf of the State in order to regain control over the Republic and to suppress the illegal armed insurgency. These measures could presumably include employment of military aviation equipped with heavy combat weapons.* The Court is also prepared to accept that *if the planes were attacked by illegal armed groups, that could have justified use of lethal force*, thus falling within paragraph 2 of Article 2. … (emphasis added).

On the facts, the Court doubted that the airplanes had been attacked but assumed that "*the military reasonably considered that there was an attack or a risk of attack from illegal insurgents, and that the air strike was a legitimate response to that attack*" (§181). It found that the authorities must have known that there were many civilians and civilian vehicles in the vicinity, did not believe that the air controller (who was not at the scene – there was no forward air controller) only learned of this one year after the facts and held that the pilots must have seen, at least in the attacks following the initial one (the entire attack lasted several hours), the civilians present, despite allegedly not being aware of the humanitarian corridor (§§186–194). It stated that "*All this had placed the civilians on the road, including the applicants, at a very high risk of being perceived as suitable targets by the military pilots*" (§189). Moreover, the fact that several civilian vehicles suffered direct hits "*excludes accidental damage by shrapnel due to a large impact radius*" (§193) and the use of twelve S-24 non-guided air-to-ground missiles, which on explosion, each create several thousand pieces of shrapnel with an impact radius exceeding 300 metres and possibly even 600–800 metres, meant that due to several explosions on a relatively short stretch of the road filled with vehicles, "*Anyone who had been on the road at that time would have been in mortal danger*" (§195). It concluded that even assuming that the military were pursuing a legitimate aim, "*the Court does not accept that the operation near the village of Shaami-Yurt was planned and executed with the requisite care for the lives of the civilian population*" (§199; emphasis added) and found that Article 2 ECHR had been violated (§200).

The Court seems to completely ignore the LOAC, despite it being invoked, and bases its judgment on Article 2 without regard to derogation – there being none.[2553] This is reflected in the Court's emphasis on minimizing any lethal use of force and any risk to life. Nevertheless, the Court's willingness to assume that "*the military reasonably considered that there was an attack or a risk of attack from illegal insurgents, and that the air strike was a legitimate response to that attack*" (§181; emphasis added) suggests that it does see some room for attacking rebels, which might leave some room for looking towards the LOAC.[2554] Moreover, the actual findings would most likely have been identical under the LOAC.

The other *Isayeva* case concerned an operation by Russian armed forces in early 2000 in Chechnya. On 4 February 2000, a group of Chechen fighters entered the village of Katyr-Yurt, which was perceived to be a safe zone (§186), early in the morning (§§10–28). The Russian military appears to have had advance knowledge that this was likely to happen and to have planned an attack in advance (§§185–188), but it did not warn the some 18,000 to 25,000 civilians (§189) in advance. Only after an initial bombing, it seems that a corridor was opened for civilians to leave (§193). However, the applicant claimed that as she and other family members left by minibus, planes reappeared and bombed cars on the road, killing the applicant's son and wounding others (§§17–18). The government claimed that any civilians killed was the result of their being forced to stay and their being used as human shields by the Chechen fighters (§§23–26).

The Court restated the same principles as in the former case (§§172–173), including the lack of derogation (§133, see also §191) and the failure to invoke the provisions of domestic legislation which would govern the use of force in these situations (§199). Again, while the judgment contains further guidance on the right to life under the ECHR, this aspect will be addressed below and what is crucial here, is how the absence of a derogation, despite a situation of (non-international) armed conflict, was stressed by the Court which therefore felt it had to apply Article 2 ECHR with its limited exceptions to the right to life and hence for the use of lethal force. This does not seem to have been contested by Russia,[2555] which may have strengthened the Court's inclination to approach the issue from a law enforcement perspective. The key excerpts from the judgment in this respect state:

2553 Compare more generally L. Moir, *supra* note 2388, pp. 195–197, arguing that absent a derogation, human rights apply in full in non-international armed conflicts.

2554 See also *supra* note 2397 on the potential significance of Article 2(2)c ECHR, which might perhaps have allowed for application of the law of non-international armed conflict on lethal use of force without the need for a derogation.

2555 According to §179 of the judgment "*The Government suggested that the use of force was justified in the present case under paragraph 2 (a) of Article 2 of the Convention*". This suggests that Russia did not invoke a derogation nor the LOAC (indeed, the judgment does not mention any such claims). Nor does Russia appear to have invoked Article 2(2)c ECHR.

180. The Court accepts that *the situation that existed in Chechnya at the relevant time called for exceptional measures by the State in order to regain control over the Republic and to suppress the illegal armed insurgency.* Given the context of the conflict in Chechnya at the relevant time, *those measures could presumably include the deployment of army units equipped with combat weapons, including military aviation and artillery.* The presence of a very large group of armed fighters in Katyr-Yurt, and their active resistance to the law-enforcement bodies, which are not disputed by the parties, *may have justified use of lethal force* by the agents of the State, thus bringing the situation within paragraph 2 of Article 2.

181. Accepting that the use of force may have been justified in the present case, it goes without saying that a balance must be achieved between the aim pursued and the means employed to achieve it. The Court will now consider whether the actions in the present case were no more than absolutely necessary for achieving the declared purpose. In order to do so the Court will examine ...whether the planning and conduct of the operation were consistent with Article 2 of the Convention. ...

189. The Court regards it as evident that when the military considered the deployment of aviation equipped with heavy combat weapons within the boundaries of a populated area, they also should have considered the dangers that such methods invariably entail. There is however no evidence to conclude that such considerations played a significant place in the planning. ...

189. ... The planes ... carried heavy free-falling high-explosion aviation bombs ... with a damage radius exceeding 1,000 metres. ... bombs and other non-guided heavy combat weapons were used against targets both in the centre and on the edges of the village ...

191. The Court considers that using this kind of weapon in a populated area, *outside wartime* and without prior evacuation of the civilians, is impossible to reconcile with *the degree of caution expected from a law-enforcement body in a democratic society. No martial law and no state of emergency has been declared in Chechnya, and no derogation has been made under Article 15 of the Convention (see § 133). The operation in question therefore has to be judged against a normal legal background. Even when faced with a situation where, as the Government submit, the population of the village had been held hostage by a large group of well-equipped and well-trained fighters, the primary aim of the operation should be to protect lives from unlawful violence. The massive use of indiscriminate weapons stands in flagrant contrast with this aim and cannot be considered compatible with the standard of care prerequisite to an operation of this kind involving the use of lethal force by State agents. ...*

200. To sum up, accepting that the operation in Katyr-Yurt on 4–7 February 2000 was pursuing a legitimate aim, the Court does *not accept that it was planned and executed with the requisite care for the lives of the civilian population.* (Emphasis added.)

While the law enforcement paradigm is thus pre-eminent, there are some hints that the Court might perhaps accept that groups of armed rebels may be subject to attack rather than capture, at least in some cases (especially §180). In fact, the bases on which the Court found that there had been violations all pertained to the lack of discrimination and precautions (§§191 and 200).

Thus, while in both cases the Court applied human rights and not the LOAC, this may have been influenced by the apparent Russian failure to invoke the LOAC and the lack of derogation. Moreover, with regard to the points on which the Court had to rule, i.e. the deaths of innocent civilians, an application of the LOAC would probably have led to the same conclusions. It is therefore submitted that these judgments should not necessarily be seen as a total rejection of the LOAC as *lex specialis* with regard to (the right to life in) non-international armed conflicts.[2556] However, they may well mean that a State that does not invoke a derogation, not even when sued before the Court, is likely to be held to stricter human rights standards and may lose the benefit of LOAC provisions that might have given it more latitude.[2557]

In two cases decided in 2008, the Court did have explicit recourse to the LOAC in the context of Article 7 ECHR (concerning the requirement that criminal offences be laid down by law in force at the time of the offence) but these cases did not really raise the relationship between the ECHR and the LOAC.[2558] However, on 18 September 2009, the Court stated in *Varnava and Others v. Turkey* that:

2556 Similarly, D. de Bijl, *infra* note 2585, pp. 104–106. But see H. Krieger, *supra* note 2486, pp. 274–275 and 290–291 and W. Abresch, *supra* note 2509, especially pp. 742–743 and 767 (who argues that these judgments constitute a break with the predominant approach and a rejection of the application of the LOAC). A.M. Gross, *supra* note 2512, pp. 31–32, describes the ECtHR's decisions as a "more mixed" view that is different from the ICJ's view on *lex specialis* with regard to the right to life. Compare Krieger's earlier analysis that the Court/Commission's jurisprudence rather supported the *lex specialis* view (*supra* note 2284, pp. 693–695).

2557 Compare W. Abresch, *supra* note 2509, pp. 750, 752–757 and 767, who sees the ECtHR's approach of rejecting the application of the LOAC as a promising strategy notably given States' reluctance to accept that a non-international armed conflict exists on their territory. Although this approach may be criticized in that the Court could also rather have chosen to challenge this reluctance where it is not reasonable (and could arguably have relied on Article 2(2)c ECHR to apply the LOAC even absent a derogation, see *supra* note 2397 and accompanying text), it does make States pay a price for not recognizing the applicability of the LOAC.

2558 *Kononov v. Latvia*, 24 July 2008 (appeal to the Grand Chamber pending), §§55–70 and 117–148 and *Korbely v. Hungary*, 19 September 2008, §§49–53 and 74–95.

> … Article 2 must be interpreted in so far as possible in light of the general principles of international law, including the rules of international humanitarian law which play an indispensable and universally-accepted role in mitigating the savagery and inhumanity of armed conflict […] (…). The Court therefore concurs with the reasoning of the Chamber in holding that in a zone of international conflict Contracting States are under obligation to protect the lives of those not, or no longer, engaged in hostilities. This would also extend to the provision of medical assistance to the wounded; where combatants have died, or succumbed to wounds, the need for accountability would necessitate proper disposal of remains and require the authorities to collect and provide information about the identity and fate of those concerned, or permit bodies such as the ICRC to do so.[2559]

This explicit interpretation in light of the LOAC is a welcome development but the wording "*in so far as possible*" raises the question of how far the Court will be willing to go. Perhaps the Court will express itself in more detail on the matter in the cases that have been brought in relation to the 2008 Russian-Georgian war.[2560]

International jurisprudence thus endorses the LOAC as *lex specialis* when it deals with matters also regulated by human rights but it appears that the European Court of Human Rights and Inter-American Commission on Human Rights interpret this as leading, at least in some cases and notably in non-international armed conflicts, to the application of the highest level of protection. It is submitted that the latter does not necessarily correspond to a proper application of the *lex specialis*.

iii. Doctrine

In a recent monograph on the subject, Schäfer has succinctly summed up the main doctrinal schools as 'separatist' (i.e. excluding concurrent applicability), 'integrationist' (i.e. seeing both as part of one broader 'humanitarian law' or seeing one branch as part of the other) and 'complementarist' (i.e. regarding both regimes as complementing each other) and regards the latter as the majority view at present.[2561] Henckaerts is part of that majority and endorses a complementary

---

2559 Grand Chamber (on appeal), §185.

2560 The Court has decided to treat seven such cases (out of over 3,300 similar cases) as a matter of priority, see ECtHR press release of 14 January 2009 (http://cmiskp.echr.coe.int/tkp197/view.asp?action=html&documentId=845593&portal=hbkm&source=externalbydocnumber&table=F69A27FD8FB86142BF01C1166DEA398649).

2561 B. Schäfer, *supra* note 2282, pp. 35–42 (who supports this majority view, though not without some sympathy for the 'integrationist' theory). See also D. Lorenz, *supra* note 2282, pp. 200–207.

view.[2562] Both authors also stress that this complementarity works both ways, thus requiring a case-by-case analysis.[2563] In addition, mention should be made of the convergence theory, although it appears to have different meanings and may overlap with the integrationist and complementarity doctrines.[2564] Erberich also opts for a case-by-case decision but adds some criteria for deciding when the *lex specialis* replaces the *lex generalis*: namely when the legal consequences of the two rules are incompatible.[2565]

Roberts has argued for a somewhat more nuanced approach, seeing a stronger case for the concurrent applicability of human rights in occupations or with respect to detention than regarding armed conflict and has described the relationship as complex, rejecting a one-way *lex specialis* and offering some guidance as to the interaction in occupation in the form of a balanced mix.[2566] Krieger also endorses the *lex specialis* approach, but stresses that this principle is contextual and is usually applied to a conflict between two rules rather than between two (specialized) regimes[2567] and focuses on interpreting the LOAC, especially in non-international armed conflicts and international administrations and peace operations, in the light of human rights rather than the other way around, *inter alia* noting that the contextual element and regional specificities in many human rights provisions may render human rights less valuable in this respect as might be thought.[2568] She adds the very pertinent observation that the LOAC cannot be applied as *lex specialis* in peace operations in which the LOAC is only applied by analogy.[2569] Watkin too supports the *lex specialis* approach and also sees this as a case-by-case matter, noting for instance that in occupation the use of force for policing would rather be subject to human rights whereas

2562 J.-M. Henckaerts, *supra* note 2486. This view is also shared by N. Tsagourias, *supra* note 2278, p. 118.

2563 J.-M. Henckaerts, *supra* note 2486, pp. 122–123 (citing the deprivation of liberty and penal prosecutions in non-international armed conflicts as examples of cases in which human rights law is more specific) and B. Schäfer, *supra* note 2282, pp. 48–52 (though concluding nevertheless that the LOAC will generally be *lex specialis* in case of conflict). See also D. Lorenz, *supra* note 2282, pp. 209–210 and 214–227.

2564 See, e.g. A.M. Gross, *supra* note 2512, pp. 2–4, especially p. 4 note 14 (who uses it for a concurrent application of both regimes regardless of how this concurrent application is further detailed).

2565 U. Erberich, *supra* note 2284, pp. 44–48, especially p. 46 ("*Eine verdrängung der allgemeinen Norm finded dann statt, wenn die von den Normen vorgesehenen Rechtsfolden miteinander unvereinbahr sind, da ansonsten der Spezialnorm kein eigenere Anwendungsbereich zukäme*").

2566 A. Roberts, *supra* note 2512, pp. 580–622, especially pp. 594–595, 599–601 and 619.

2567 H. Krieger, *supra* note 2486, pp. 268–270 generally and 270–276 specifically as regards the LOAC and human rights. See also *supra*, subsection (i) of this Section.

2568 H. Krieger, *supra* note 2486, pp. 265–291.

2569 H. Krieger, *supra* note 2284, pp. 695–696.

combat actions in occupation would be governed by the LOAC.[2570] Abresch takes this further and argues in favour of the approach the European Court of Human Rights seems to have taken in the *Isayeva* cases, i.e. ignoring the LOAC in non-international armed conflicts and only applying human rights, at least in some respects.[2571]

In contrast, Dennis submits that the "*precise relationship between the two bodies of law remains unclear*" and argues for a clear separation between human rights and the LOAC.[2572] Stein also seems to plead for keeping the two regimes apart.[2573] Lattanzi seeks to demarcate human rights from the LOAC through the criterion of jurisdiction and thus seems to defend, at least to some extent, a separatist view.[2574] Gasser also stresses the distinct nature of both regimes, though he rejects mutual exclusion.[2575]

Generally, the focus is clearly on the *lex specialis* principle and little attention is paid to the *lex posterior* principle, although it is given a limited role by some authors.[2576] The most favourable treatment clause common in human rights treaties is sometimes mentioned but less often endorsed – though it is reflected to some extent in the views of those who support the convergence or integrationist theory. However, as argued above, it does not seem appropriate for the relationship between human rights and the LOAC unless when it is explicitly stipulated in this respect.[2577]

2570 K. Watkin, *supra* note 2486, pp. 24–34, especially pp. 26–28. Watkin more generally sees stronger pressure to apply human rights to governance issues than to combat situations (*id.*, p. 2) and sees the main areas of direct interface as being non-international armed conflicts, occupations and counter-terrorism actions (*id.*, pp. 9–10 and 24–30).

2571 W. Abresch, *supra* note 2509, especially pp. 742–743 and 767.

2572 M.J. Dennis, *supra* note 2282, pp. 120 and 133–141 (arguing at p. 138 that this is what States wanted when they concluded AP II).

2573 T. Stein, *supra* note 2486, pp. 163–165, especially p. 165.

2574 F. Lattanzi, 'La frontière entre le droit international humanitaire et droits de l'homme', in E. Decaux, A. Dieng & M. Sow (eds.), *From Human Rights to International Criminal Law. Studies in Honour of an African Jurist, the Late Judge Laïty Kama / Des droits de l'homme au droit international pénal: études en l'honneur d'un juriste africain, feu le juge Laïty Kama*, Leiden, Nijhoff, 2007, pp. 519–770, who opposes the application of the LOAC by human rights organs in international armed conflicts (*id.*, pp. 569–570).

2575 H.-P. Gasser, *supra* note 2486, pp. 149–162, especially p. 162.

2576 B. Schäfer, *supra* note 2282, p. 46 only sees a role for the *lex posterior* principle where there is a clear intention to change an older rule.

2577 In this sense B. Schäfer, *supra* note 2282, pp. 47–48. But see the view of the IAComHR (and my criticism thereon), *supra* subsection (ii) of this Section, and H.-J. Heintze, *supra* note 2486 (*I.R.R.C.* 2004), pp. 794 and 812–813 ("*Research shows that there is a convergence between the protection offered by human rights law and that of international humanitarian law. Both bodies of law can be applied in armed conflicts in order to achieve the greatest possible protection in the sense of the Martens Clause*"). Compare A.M. Gross, *supra* note 2512, p. 35, noting that

iv. Specific Rights or Situations

I will now examine in more detail the precise relationship between the LOAC and human rights in respect of three specific rights, namely the right to life (and the use of force more generally), the prohibition of arbitrary deprivation of liberty and the prohibition of torture, inhuman and degrading treatment or punishment, as well as the relationship between the LOAC and human rights in the specific situation of occupation.[2578]

a. The Right to Life and the Use of Force

As to the right to life,[2579] it is usually argued that the LOAC is the *lex specialis* when applicable, as implied by the ECHR[2580] and *inter alia* affirmed by the International Court of Justice with regard to the ICCPR[2581].[2582]

---

even if one prefers the most favourable protection rule, in occupations the question arises most favourable to whom? Compare also H. Krieger, *supra* note 2486, p. 274.

2578 For an overview of the kind of operations which peace operations often conduct and the rights that may be affected by these operations, see Häussler, pp. 91–124 (mentioning *inter alia* the use of force in self-defence and for mission accomplishment, arrest of persons suspected of war crimes, vetting of public officials and crowd and riot control and intelligence gathering and surveillance (raising privacy and data protection issues)).

2579 For a good overview of various issues and perspectives, see University Centre for International Humanitarian Law (Geneva) (ed.), *Expert Meeting on the Right to Life in Armed Conflicts and Situations of Occupation, Convened in Geneva on 1-2 September 2005*, proceedings available online at www.adh-geneve.ch/pdfs/3rapport_droit_vie.pdf and N. Quénivet, 'The Rights to Life in International Humanitarian Law and Human Rights Law', in R. Arnold & N. Quénivet (eds.), *International Humanitarian Law and Human Rights Law: towards a New Merger in International Law*, Leiden, Martinus Nijhoff, 2008, pp. 331–353. For an early analysis, see F. Hampson, *supra* note 2511, pp. 127–135. See also more generally M. Bertrand, *The Right to Life in European Constitutional and International Case-Law*, Strasbourg, Council of Europe Publishing, 2006 and B.G. Ramcharan (ed.), *The Right to Life in International Law*, The Hague, Nijhoff, 1985.

2580 See the reference to "*lawful acts of war*" in Article 15(2) ECHR.

2581 Advisory Opinion on the *Legality of the Threat or Use of Nuclear Weapons*, 8 July 1996, §25 ("*In principle, the right not arbitrarily to be deprived of one's life applies also in hostilities. The test of what is an arbitrary deprivation of life, however, then falls to be determined by the applicable* lex specialis, *namely, the law applicable in armed conflict which is designed to regulate the conduct of hostilities. Thus whether a particular loss of life, through the use of a certain weapon in warfare, is to be considered an arbitrary deprivation of life contrary to Article 6 of the Covenant, can only be decided by reference to the law applicable in armed conflict and not deduced from the terms of the Covenant itself*"). On the right to life under the ICCPR generally, see M. Nowak, *supra* note 2329 (2005), pp. 120–156.

2582 See also IAComHR, *Abella*, *supra* note 2381, §§161 and 176–178 and 189 and T. Meron, *supra* note 2372, p. 46. In contrast, F.F. Martin, 'Using International Human Rights Law for Establishing a Unified Use of Force Rule in the Law of Armed Conflict', 64 *Saskatchewan Law Review* 2001, pp. 347–396, pleads for a single standard, but this does not seem to reflect the law as it stands nor does it seem feasible or desirable, for the reasons set out below, although his view has gained some support in the ECtHR's Chechnya cases (see *infra*).

However, while correct in the context of the conduct of hostilities in an international armed conflict, this is not necessarily always the case in other circumstances.[2583] In particular, in restoring and ensuring public order in cases of occupation[2584] and more generally in respect of tasks of a law and order nature rather than combat-related tasks, e.g. in peace operations, human rights law is arguably more tailor-made.[2585] However, with the exception

---

[2583] See also L. Doswald-Beck, 'The Right to Life in Armed Conflict: Does International Humanitarian Law Provide All the Answers?', 88 No. 864 *I.R.R.C.* 2006, pp. 881–904.

[2584] This is a duty under Article 43 Hague Regulations. But see A. Zemach, 'Taking War Seriously: Applying the Law of War to Hostilities Within an Occupied Territory', 38 *George Washington I.L.R.* 2006, pp. 645–695, pleading for applying the LOAC when the occupant faces guerrilla forces.

[2585] See also H. Krieger, *supra* note 2486, pp. 273–274 and K. Watkin, *supra* note 2486, pp. 9 and 26–28 (noting that distinguishing between both types of actions may not always be easy), adding at pp. 9 and 32 the issue of non-lethal or less than lethal weapons as well as the restrictions on the use of riot control agents (e.g. tear gas) resulting from the Chemical Weapons Convention. This convention (Convention on the Prohibition of the Development, Production, Stockpiling and Use of Chemical Weapons and on their Destruction, Paris, 13 January 1993) prohibits the use of riot control agents "*as a method of warfare*" in its Article I(5). Many States consider that this does not prohibit their use in peace operations for non-combat tasks such as crowd and riot control, where they may offer the possibility of a proportionate response. However, some States have a more restrictive view and/or are faced with restrictions resulting from domestic law. See Häussler, p. 115. It may be noted that the ECtHR seemed to require consideration of non-lethal means in some cases; see *Erdogan and others v. Turkey*, 25 April 2006, §79. On the use of proportionate means, see also ECtHR, *Gülec v. Turkey*, 27 July 1998, §§69–73, especially §71 ("*The gendarmes used a very powerful weapon because they apparently did not have truncheons, riot shields, water cannon, rubber bullets or tear gas. The lack of such equipment is all the more incomprehensible and unacceptable because the province of Şırnak, as the Government pointed out, is in a region in which a state of emergency has been declared, where at the material time disorder could have been expected*"). For a discussion of the right to life under Article 2 ECHR in peace operations, see D. de Bijl, 'Recht op leven voor opposing forces? Rechtvaardiging van geweldstoepassing in vredesmissies onder artikel 2 EVRM', 100 *Militair Rechtelijk Tijdschrift* 2007, pp. 97–110, especially pp. 106–110, who concludes that while this provision was not made to be applied in peace operations it is sufficiently flexible to allow its application in such operations and that the Court's jurisprudence should dispel fears of unrealistic judgments. For a domestic case on the use of force in peace operations, see *Bici and Bici v. Ministry of Defence*, 7 April 2004, 2004 EWHC 786 (QB), available online at www.hmcourts-service.gov.uk/judgmentsfiles/j2458/bici-v-mod.htm (see also D. Lorenz, *supra* note 2282, p. 268 and H. Krieger, *supra* note 2486, pp. 273–274). At §102 of this judgment, the court qualifies (some) KFOR actions as "*carrying out essentially a policing and peacekeeping function*". Compare Häussler, pp. 92–97, arguing that in peace operations a more robust use of force may be required. With regard to the right to life in occupations, see *Expert Meeting …*, proceedings, *supra* note 2579, pp. 20–29.

of the ECHR, which has some more specific provisions in this respect,[2586] detailed guidance can only come from jurisprudence[2587] and

---

[2586] Article 2 (right to life) reads as follows: "*1 Everyone's right to life shall be protected by law. No one shall be deprived of his life intentionally save in the execution of a sentence of a court following his conviction of a crime for which this penalty is provided by law.*
2 Deprivation of life shall not be regarded as inflicted in contravention of this Article when it results from the use of force which is no more than absolutely necessary:
a) in defence of any person from unlawful violence;
b) in order to effect a lawful arrest or to prevent the escape of a person lawfully detained;
c) in action lawfully taken for the purpose of quelling a riot or insurrection". The exhaustive nature of this list (see, e.g. EComHR, *Stewart v. UK*, decision of 10 July 1984, §13 of the section 'The Law'), except for lawful acts of war pursuant to Article 15(2) ECHR, poses some problems in peace operations, e.g. in respect of the use of lethal force to protect property in cases not also covered by one of the other grounds. It seems that State Parties have different views on the permissibility of such use of force, which is regularly authorized in peace operations for specific categories of properties, e.g. (some of) the property of the force itself or "property with special designated status". See also very briefly D. de Bijl, *supra* note 2585, p. 108; HÄUSSLER, pp. 120–122 and M. Kelly, T. McCormack, P. Muggleton & B. Oswald, *infra* note 2634, pp. 128–130. Compare on national territory for the Netherlands, Rijkswet van 24 februari 2003, houdende regels met betrekking tot het geweldgebruik bij de bewaking van militaire objecten, *Staatsblad* 2003, 134 of 3 April 2003 (available online at www.st-ab.nl/wetten/1008_Rijkswet_geweldgebruik_bewakers_militaire_objecten.htm). For a discussion of the Dutch legislation on this matter and its evolution, see G.L. Coolen, *Militair straf- en strafprocesrecht*, Kluwer, 2004 (4th ed.), pp. 52–64. Compare also T. Opsahl, 'The Right to Life', in R. St. J. Macdonald, F. Matscher & H. Petzold (eds.), *supra* note 2407, pp. 207–223 (pointing to a rejection of a proposal to specifically include the use of lethal force to prevent entry in secure areas in Article 2 at p. 213 note 27 and arguing for the exclusion of the use of lethal force to protect property at p. 216). Compare with regard to the ICCPR, T. Meron, *supra* note 2374, pp. 65–66. On Article 2 ECHR, see also generally G. Guillaume, 'Article 2', in L.-E. Pettiti, E. Decaux & P.-H. Imbert (eds.), *supra* note 2284, pp. 143–154; Y. Haeck, 'Artikel 2. Recht op leven', in J. Vande Lanotte & Y. Haeck (eds.), *supra* note 2284, Vol. 1, pp. 31–121 (with further references) and S. Trechsel, 'Spotlights on Article 2 ECHR, The Right to Life', in W. Benedek, H. Isak & R. Kicker (eds.), *Development and Developing International and European Law: Essays in Honour of Konrad Ginther on the Occasion of His 65th Birthday*, Frankfurt am Main, Lang, 1999, pp. 671–686 (with interesting reflections on the question how immediate/direct a threat to life must be for the purpose of its defence with lethal force under Article 2(2)a ECHR at pp. 682–683).

[2587] See, e.g. EComHR, *Stewart v. UK*, decision of 10 July 1984 (use of plastic baton rounds in crowd and riot control) and ECtHR, *McCann and Others v. UK*, 27 September 1995 (planning and conduct of an anti-terrorist operation); *Andronicou and Constantinou v. Cyprus*, 9 October 1997 (forcible intervention in a hostage situation); *Gülec v. Turkey*, 27 July 1998 (use of force in crowd and riot control); *Ergi v. Turkey*, 28 July 1998 (planning and conduct of an anti-terrorist/insurgency operation); *Osman v. UK*, 28 October 1998 (regarding positive obligations to protect life); *Ogur v. Turkey*, 20 May 1999 (planning and conduct of an anti-terrorist/insurgency operation); *Makaratzis v. Greece*, 20 December 2004 (use of force to arrest driver for traffic violation and adequacy of legal and regulatory framework on the use of force); *Bubbins v. UK*, 17 March 2005, §§134–151 (shooting of a suspected burglar who appeared to be armed and ready to fire at policemen); *Nachova and Others v. Bulgaria*, 6 July 2005 (limits on lethal force in arrests); the *Isayeva* cases (*supra* notes 2550–2551; discussed above and below; on conduct and planning of anti-terrorist/insurgency operations); *Erdogan and others v. Turkey*, 25 April 2006, §§70–87 (use of force in arrest and allegations of a shoot to kill operation); *Isaak v. Turkey*, judgment of 24 June 2008, §§103–120 (manifestly disproportionate use of force to detain a person posing no threat who entered a buffer zone in the course of a demonstration) and *Solomou v. Turkey*, 24 June 2008 (decision on admissibility), §§63–79 guidelines[2588] rather than treaty texts.[2589]

Moreover, even with regard to combat, the right to life poses a challenge in non-international armed conflicts: in these conflicts, there are no legitimate combatants who are entitled to participate in the hostilities and may also be legitimately attacked and killed.[2590] On the one hand, the significant extension of LOAC rules concerning the conduct of hostilities to non-international armed conflicts, including those protecting civilians, suggest that there is a combatant-like status that entails being a legitimate subject of attacks (including attacks to kill rather than to capture).[2591] On the other hand, the lack of combatant status combined with normal human rights rules suggest that attacks to kill are only exceptionally justified and capture should be the standard aim.[2592] This has led to different views

---

(directed fire at an individual in a restricted zone posing no threat not justified; as regards a related riot, "*a potential illegal or violent action from a group of persons cannot, as such, justify the immediate shooting and killing of one or more other individuals who are not themselves posing a threat*"). See also W. Abresch, *supra* note 2509, pp. 760–764; D. de Bijl, *supra* note 2585, pp. 97–110 and P. van Dijk *et al.*, *supra* note 2328, pp. 395–403.

2588 See especially the Basic Principles on the Use of Force and Firearms by Law Enforcement Officials (adopted by the 8th UN Congress on Prevention of Crime and Treatment of Offenders in 1990, available online at www.smallarmsnet.org/docs/saun17.pdf). See also more generally the Body of Principles for the Protection of All Persons under Any Form of Detention or Imprisonment (Annex to UNGA Res. 43/173 of 9 December 1988); the Code of Conduct for Law Enforcement Officials (Annex to UNGA Res. 34/169 of 17 December 1979) and the European Code of Police Ethics (Annex to Recommendation (2001)10 of the Committee of Ministers to Member States on the European Code of Police Ethics, 19 September 2001, available online at www.coe.int/t/e/legal_affairs/legal_co-operation/police_and_internal_security/documents/Rec(2001)10_ENG4831-7.pdf). See also K. Watkin, *supra* note 2486, pp. 18–20.

2589 Compare T. Meron, *supra* note 2374, pp. 68–69, who submits more generally that human rights are vague on the level of force permitted and that IHL is more developed and appropriate in this respect. For further guidance, see generally R. Crawshaw, 'International Standards on the Right to Life and the Use of Force by Police', 3 *International Journal of Human Rights* 1999, pp. 67–91. See also the 2003 Israeli Or Commission (Official Commission of Inquiry into the October 2000 Events) report, available online at www.adalah.org/eng/commission.php.

2590 See, e.g. W. Abresch, *supra* note 2509, pp. 746–748; N. Lubell, *supra* note 2366, pp. 746–750; J.-M. Henckaerts & L. Doswald-Beck (eds.), *Customary International Humanitarian Law*, Cambridge, Cambridge University Press, 2005, Vol. I, pp. 17–24 and *Expert Meeting ...*, proceedings, *supra* note 2579, pp. 35–42. See generally M. Bothe, 'Töten und getötet werden: Kombattanten, Kämpfer und Zivilisten im bewaffneten Konflikt', in K. Dicke *et al.* (ed.), *Weltinnenrecht: liber amicorum Jost Delbrück*, Berlin, Duncker & Humblot, 2005, pp. 67–84; J. Mallein, *La situation juridique des combattants dans les conflits armés non internationaux*, Grenobles, Service de reproduction des thèses de l'Université des sciences sociales de Grenoble, 1978 and W.A. Solf, 'The Status of Combatants in Non-International Armed Conflicts under Domestic Law and Transnational Practice', 33 *American University Law Review* 1983, pp. 53–65. Recently, F. Bugnion, 'Jus Ad Bellum, Jus In Bello and Non-International Armed Conflicts', 6 *Y.I.H.L.* 2003, pp. 167–198, has argued that the law of non-international armed conflicts remains incomplete because of the lack of combatant status and that this may need to change for this body of law to become more successful.

2591 See also L. Perna, *supra* note 2509, p. 106.

2592 See W. Abresch, *supra* note 2509, especially pp. 742–743 and 757–760.

on when attacks to kill are justified, the options including *inter alia* an application of or analogy to direct participation in hostilities by civilians (a matter of much debate in itself[2593]),[2594] the permissibility of attacks based on group status and differentiated solutions requiring arrest when reasonably possible.[2595] Thus there is a combined problem of imprecision in the LOAC on this point[2596] and of LOAC – human rights interaction. The issue is not unrelated to "targeted killings" and some of the issues arising in that context are also relevant here.[2597] The law is

2593 See also K. Watkin, *supra* note 2486, pp. 16–17 and J.-M. Henckaerts & L. Doswald-Beck (eds.), *supra* note 2590, Vol. I, pp. 22–23. See generally the debate conducted on this topic in the framework of the ICRC (which issued 'interpretive guidance' on this notion in May 2009; see www.icrc.org/web/eng/siteeng0.nsf/htmlall/direct-participation-ihl-feature-020609?opendocument and especially www.icrc.org/Web/eng/siteeng0.nsf/htmlall/direct-participation-report_res/$File/direct-participation-guidance-2009-icrc.pdf) and M.N. Schmitt, '"Direct Participation in Hostilities" and 21st Century Armed Conflict', in H. Fischer *et al.* (eds.), *Krisensicherung und humanitärer Schutz. Festschrift für Dieter Fleck*, Berlin, Berliner Wissenschafts-Verlag, 2004, pp. 505–529 (available online at www.michaelschmitt.org/images/Directparticipationpageproofs.pdf). The issue was addressed by the Israeli Supreme Court on 13 December 2006 (HJC 769/02, *Public Committee against Torture in Israel and others v. the Government of Israel and others*, available online at http://elyon1.court.gov.il/Files_ENG/02/690/007/a34/02007690.a34.pdf); see W.J. Fenrick, 'The Targeted Killings Judgment and the Scope of Direct Participation in Hostilities', 5 *J.I.C.J.* 2007, pp. 332–338; H. Moodrick Even-Khen, 'Can We Now Tell What "Direct Participation in Hostilities" Is?: HCJ 769/02 the Public Committee against Torture in Israel v. the Government of Israel', 40 *Israel Law Review* 2007, pp. 213–244. On targeted killings, see the further references *infra* note 2597.

2594 This was the approach adopted by the IAComHR in *Abella*, supra note 2381, §§176–178 ("*when civilians, such as those who attacked the Tablada base, assume the role of combatants by directly taking part in fighting, whether singly or as a member of a group, they thereby become legitimate military targets. As such, they are subject to direct individualized attack* to the same extent as combatants. *Thus, by virtue of their hostile acts, the Tablada attackers* lost *the benefits of the above mentioned precautions in attack and against the effects of indiscriminate or disproportionate attacks pertaining to* peaceable *civilians*" (emphasis in original) and 189 ("*the persons who participated in the attack on the military base were legitimate military targets only* for such time as they actively participated in the fighting. *Those who surrendered, were captured or wounded and ceased their hostile acts, fell effectively within the power of Argentine state agents, who could no longer lawfully attack or subject them to other acts of violence*").

2595 See generally K. De Groof, 'Targeted killing en het onderscheid burger-strijder', 2 *IHR in de kijker* 2006, pp. 37–50.

2596 N. Lubell, *supra* note 2366, p. 750. See also W. Abresch, *supra* note 2509, especially pp. 746–748.

2597 See generally (not limited to a human rights perspective), O. Ben-Naftali & K.R. Michaeli, '"We Must Not Make a Scarecrow of the Law": A Legal Analysis of the Israeli Policy of Targeted Killings', 36 *Cornell I.L.J.* 2003, pp. 233–292; C. Downes, '"Targeted Killings" in an Age of Terror: The Legality of the Yemen Strike', 9 *J.C.S.L.* 2004, pp. 277–294; W.J. Fisher, 'Targeted Killing, Norms, and International Law', 45 *Colum. J. Transn. L.* 2007, pp. 711–758; A. Guiora, 'Targeted Killing as Active Self-Defense', 36 *Case Western Reserve Journal of International Law* 2004, pp. 319–334; D. Kretzmer, 'Targeted Killing of Suspected Terrorists: Extra-Judicial Executions or Legitimate Means of Defence?', 16 *E.J.I.L.* 2005, pp. 171–212; N. Melzer, *Targeted Killing in International Law*, Oxford, Oxford University Press, 2008; N. Melzer, 'Targeted Killing or Less Harmful Means? – Israel's High Court Judgment on Targeted Killing and the Restrictive Function of Military Necessity', 9 *Y.I.H.L.* 2006, pp. 87–113; A. Plaw, *Targeting Terrorists. A License to Kill?*, Aldershot, Ashgate, 2008; V.-J. Proulx, certainly not settled,[2598] but it appears that practice in peace operations that are considered to amount to participation in non-international armed conflicts offers some support for the permissibility of attacks to kill based on group status, at least in combat areas.[2599] That appears to be the approach accepted by the Inter-American Commission on Human Rights in *Abella*.[2600] There also seems to be some room for this view under the case law of the European Court of Human Rights, though this is less certain after the *Isayeva* cases.[2601]

'If the Hat Fits, Wear It, if the Turban Fits, Run for Your Life: Reflections on the Indefinite Detention and Targeted Killing of Suspected Terrorists', 56 *Hastings Law Journal* 2005, pp. 801–900; T. Ruys, 'Licence to Kill?: State-sponsored Assassination under International Law', 44(1–2) *R.D.M.D.G.* 2005, pp. 13–49; M.N. Schmitt, 'Targeted Killings and International Law: Law Enforcement, Self-defense and Armed Conflict', in R. Arnold & N. Quénivet (eds.), *International Humanitarian Law and Human Rights Law: towards a New Merger in International Law*, Leiden, Martinus Nijhoff, 2008, pp. 525–553; G. Solis, 'Targeted Killing and the Law of Armed Conflict', 60 *Naval War College Review* 2007, pp. 127–146 and *Expert Meeting* ..., proceedings, *supra* note 2579, pp. 29–35. See also the Israeli court decision *supra* note 2593 and the annotations cited in that note.

2598 See F. Hampson & I. Salama, *supra* note 2486, pp. 33–34, note 61: "*It is not clear whether in non-international conflicts a party can target the fighters of the other side without the need for them to be posing a threat*". Compare N. Lubell, *supra* note 2366, pp. 746–750, for a thoughtful overview of the main options. Lubell notes the risk of authorizing too much force if the LOAC is applied too readily but the impossibility of applying strict human rights norms in high intensity conflicts and has difficulty finding a legal basis for requiring arrest if possible when the LOAC applies. See also the different views in *Expert Meeting* ..., proceedings, *supra* note 2579, pp. 35–42.

2599 See for instance offensive actions by ISAF in Afghanistan (see, e.g. a July 2009 tactical directive on the use of force in ISAF partially released to the public and available at www.nato.int/isaf/docu/official_texts/Tactical_Directive_090706.pdf) and by MONUC in the DRC (see *supra* note 458). Compare the definition of 'ex- and would-be-belligerents' and the notion of 'forces' in Häussler, pp. 91–92.

2600 See *supra* note 266.

2601 See the discussion of the ECtHR's main decisions pertaining to armed conflicts, *supra* subsection ii of this Section. D. de Bijl, *supra* note 2585, pp. 104–106 argues that the Court's case law, including the *Isayeva* cases (*supra* notes 2550–2551 and the accompanying text), suggests that opposing forces may be attacked under LOAC standards. He also cites ECtHR, *Ahmet Ozkan and others v. Turkey*, 6 April 2004, especially §305. In that case the Court accepted that fairly heavy fire ("*intensive firing, including the use of RPG-7 missiles and various grenades*") aimed at points from which the security forces had been fired upon after they had fired warning shots was not disproportionate in the circumstances of the case (which included "*serious disturbances in south-east Turkey involving armed conflict between the security forces and members of the PKK*"). The Court does, however, not really address the targeting of the opposing forces in this case (in fact, the recourse to warning shots suggests the aim was not an attack to kill) but its acceptance of the level of force does suggest an application of the LOAC in this respect. In contrast, W. Abresch, *supra* note 2509, pp. 742–743 and 752–760, argues that this case law endorses unified use of force rules requiring capture if possible, albeit that that possibility is to be evaluated taking into account different circumstances. However, at p. 759 he acknowledges that the Court's focus on 'civilians' could be interpreted as leaving room for applying the LOAC, though he argues against such an interpretation. Compare N. Quénivet, 'Isayeva v. the Russian Federation and Isayeva, Yusupova and Bazayeva v. the Russian Federation: Targeting Rules According to Article 2 of the European Convention on Human Rights', 18 *Humanitäres Völkerrecht* 2005, pp. 219–226.

In any event, when persons may legitimately be attacked, it is submitted that the LOAC as *lex specialis* determines the legality of the modalities of an attack.[2602] While some have argued that in non-international armed conflict, human rights can adequately deal with this,[2603] this is doubtful, especially in high intensity conflicts.[2604] Moreover, the increased regulation of non-international armed conflicts by the LOAC (see *supra*, Chapter 8.C) means that the (perceived) imprecision of the LOAC in such conflicts is diminishing.

A final point that is sometimes raised as a challenge to applying the right to life under human rights in armed conflicts is the obligation for States to effectively investigate cases of killings.[2605] I would argue that if interpreted flexibly, taking into account the circumstances of each case, this should not be a major obstacle. Moreover, if a gradual approach to jurisdiction is accepted, this obligation may not apply or apply to a much more limited extent in combat situations in areas outside overall control.[2606]

b. The Prohibition of Arbitrary Deprivation of Liberty

Second, there is the prohibition of arbitrary deprivation of liberty. In this respect, various issues arise. First, detention (I use this term in a broad sense covering all cases of deprivation of liberty) is one of the two cases (the other one is effective control over a territory), in which there is a fairly large consensus that it

---

Compare also G.C. Bruno, '"Collateral Damages" of Military Operations: is Implementation of International Humanitarian Law Possible using International Human Rights Law Tools?', in R. Arnold & N. Quénivet (eds.), *International Humanitarian Law and Human Rights Law: towards a New Merger in International Law*, Leiden, Martinus Nijhoff, 2008, pp. 295–307.

2602 K. Watkin, *supra* note 2486, p. 24 also clearly argues for respecting the more appropriate nature of the LOAC rules in this respect. See also the discussion *supra* note 2601 of *Ahmet Ozkan and others v. Turkey*. Compare F. Hampson & I. Salama, *supra* note 2486, p. 18, §72: "*There is a reason particular to the European Convention why LOAC/IHL needs to be taken into account. The provisions dealing with unlawful killings and unlawful detention are drafted differently in Articles 6 and 9 of ICCPR. The ECHR lists exhaustively the only grounds upon which resort may be made to potentially lethal force and the only grounds upon which a person may be detained. In these circumstances, ridiculous results flow from a failure to recognize the applicability of LOAC/IHL, at least where the State has not derogated*". But see H. Krieger, *supra* note 2486, pp. 274–275 and 290–291, arguing that in non-international armed conflicts, human rights are the better standard and that the use of force rules should take into account the specific context but be based on "*regular legal standards of human rights law*", despite acknowledging the differences in meaning of proportionality in the LOAC and in human rights (pp. 280–281).

2603 W. Abresch, *supra* note 2509, especially pp. 750–757, arguing that there are unified use of force rules but that they may be varied in their application.

2604 In this sense N. Lubell, *supra* note 2366, p. 749.

2605 See, e.g. H. Krieger, *supra* note 2486, pp. 282–283 and K. Watkin, *supra* note 2486, pp. 19–20 and 33–34.

2606 H. Krieger, *supra* note 2486, pp. 282–284 considers that *Bankovic* excludes this.

constitutes an exercise of jurisdiction triggering the applicability of human rights.[2607]

Second, as with regard to the right to life, the ICCPR contains a rather general rule in respect of the grounds for detention ("*Everyone has the right to liberty and security of person. No one shall be subjected to arbitrary arrest or detention. No one shall be deprived of his liberty except on such grounds and in accordance with such procedure as are established by law*"[2608]), which more easily allows for an interpretation in the light of the LOAC. In contrast, the ECHR contains a more specific and exhaustive list of accepted grounds for detention: it states:

> 1. Everyone has the right to liberty and security of person. No one shall be deprived of his liberty save in the following cases and in accordance with a procedure prescribed by law:
> a) the lawful detention of a person after conviction by a competent court;
> b) the lawful arrest or detention of a person for non-compliance with the lawful order of a court or in order to secure the fulfilment of any obligation prescribed by law;
> c) the lawful arrest or detention of a person effected for the purpose of bringing him before the competent legal authority on reasonable suspicion of having committed an offence or when it is reasonably considered necessary to prevent his committing an offence or fleeing after having done so;
> d) the detention of a minor by lawful order for the purpose of educational supervision or his lawful detention for the purpose of bringing him before the competent legal authority;
> e) the lawful detention of persons for the prevention of the spreading of infectious diseases, of persons of unsound mind, alcoholics or drug addicts or vagrants;
> f) the lawful arrest or detention of a person to prevent his effecting an unauthorised entry into the country or of a person against whom action is being taken with a view to deportation or extradition.[2609]

This means that recourse to a derogation seems necessary under the ECHR for certain armed conflict-related detentions (see *infra*).[2610] While Article 5 ECHR is

2607 See *supra*, Section B of this chapter. See also D. Lorenz, *supra* note 2282, pp. 105–118; H. Krieger, *supra* note 2284, pp. 673, 688 and 695; A. Roberts, *supra* note 2512, p. 594 and P. Rowe, *supra* note 2284, pp. 191 and 196.

2608 See generally S. Joseph, J. Schultz & M. Castan, *supra* note 2329 (2004), pp. 303–347 and M. Nowak, *supra* note 2329 (2005), pp. 210–240.

2609 See generally S. Trechsel, 'Liberty and Security of Person', in R. St. J. Macdonald, F. Matscher & H. Petzold (eds.), *supra* note 2407, pp. 277–344 and the comments (per paragraph) by J. De Meyer, R. de Gouttes, P. Pirard & P. Titian and R. Koering-Joulin in L.-E. Pettiti, E. Decaux & P.-H. Imbert (eds.), *supra* note 2284, pp. 189–238.

2610 This also seems to be the view of A. Reidy, *supra* note 2545, pp. 3–4 of the online version printout. In this sense more generally A. Roberts, *supra* note 2512, p. 593, arguing that not listed as non-derogable, it may be argued that its core content, i.e. the prohibition of arbitrary detention coupled with some procedural safeguards to ensure this right, is non-derogable and may even have acquired a *ius cogens* status.[2611] Indeed, this core content is non-derogable under the ICCPR according to the Human Rights Committee.[2612] However, this does not (yet) seem to have been explicitly recognized by the European Court of Human Rights with regard to the ECHR.[2613]

---

internment in occupation is contrary to human rights but that the latter could be limited by a derogation.

2611 On the non-derogable nature, see, e.g. H. Duffy, *supra* note 2374, p. 296. Compare the remark by T. Meron, *supra* note 2374, pp. 62–63 that it would be "*incongruous that due process under human rights could be derogated from (to the extent ...) whereas for armed conflicts non derogable rights exist*". As regards due process, in *Kadi*, §288 and *Yusuf*, §343 (both *supra*, Chapter 7, note 1822), the EU's Court of First Instance ruled that the right of access to a court is, at least in part, *ius cogens*. See also C. Olivier, 'Revisiting General Comment No. 29 of the United Nations Human Rights Committee: About Fair Trial Rights and Derogations in Times of Public Emergency', 17 *Leiden J.I.L.* 2004, pp. 405–419. The ICJ has stated, in its judgment in the case concerning the *United States Diplomatic and Consular Staff in Tehran (United States of America v. Iran)* of 24 May 1980 that "*Wrongfully to deprive human beings of their freedom and to subject them to physical constraint in conditions of hardship is in itself manifestly incompatible with the principles of the Charter of the United Nations, as well as with the fundamental principles enunciated in the Universal Declaration of Human Rights*" (§91).

2612 See notably General Comment 29, *supra* note 2378, §11: "*States parties may in no circumstances invoke Article 4 of the Covenant as justification for acting in violation of humanitarian law or peremptory norms of international law, for instance ... through arbitrary deprivations of liberty or by deviating from fundamental principles of fair trial, including the presumption of innocence*". On the right to judicial remedies in the context of detentions and derogations, see also L. Condorelli & P. De Sena, *supra* note 2344, pp. 114–116. On judicial guarantees concerning detention, see also R.E. Vinuesa, *supra* note 2486, pp. 81–87. For a discussion in the context of terrorism, see, e.g. A. de Zayas, 'Human Rights and Indefinite Detention', 87 No. 857 *I.R.R.C.* 2005, pp. 15–38 and C. Maierhöfer, '"... dem man nichts beweisen kann": Terrorismus, präventiver Freiheitsentzug und die Rolle des Völkerrechts', 32 *Eur. Gr. R.Z.* 2005, pp. 460–463. See also IACtHR, advisory opinions OC-8/87 (*Habeas Corpus in Emergency Situations*, 30 January 1987) and OC-9/87 (*Judicial Guarantees in States of Emergency*, 6 October 1987).

2613 In *Ireland v. UK*, 13 December 1977, §204, the Court stated that "*Article 5 (Article 5) does not appear amongst the entrenched provisions listed in paragraph 2 of Article 15 (Article 15-2) and is therefore one of the Articles subject to the 'right of derogation' reserved by the Contracting States, the exercise of which is regulated by paragraphs 1 and 3 (Article 15-1, Article 15-3)*". Nevertheless, it might be argued that Article 5(4) ECHR is part of this core (this provision reads "*Everyone who is deprived of his liberty by arrest or detention shall be entitled to take proceedings by which the lawfulness of his detention shall be decided speedily by a court and his release ordered if the detention is not lawful*"). Compare IAComHR, Decision Authorizing Precautionary Measures in Favor of Detainees Being Held by the United States at Guantanamo Bay, Cuba, 12 March 2002 (*supra* note 2359): "*according to international norms applicable in peacetime and wartime, ..., a competent court or tribunal, as opposed to a political authority, must be charged with ensuring respect for the legal status and rights of persons falling under the authority and control of a state*" (notes omitted). R. Ergec, *supra* note 2390, pp. 191–196 writes that the safeguards that are required under the ECHR will normally include *judicial* guarantees. He cites *Klass and others v. Germany*, 6 September 1978, §55. This judgment,

Third, in respect of international armed conflicts and occupation, it seems to be generally considered that the LOAC is *lex specialis* as regards the detention/internment of prisoners of war and civilians.[2614] Yet, as already suggested above, this needs to be nuanced in that it is correct with regard to the legal basis for deprivation of liberty and the minimum safeguards,[2615] but does not necessarily extend to all issues relating to the detention of these categories of persons.[2616] For instance, prohibitions on torture, cruel or degrading treatment under human rights remain fully applicable (see also *infra*, next paragraph)[2617] and States that have accepted the prohibition of the death penalty under all circumstances cannot apply it to such detained/interned persons even where the LOAC permits it.[2618] Moreover, one may wonder whether in cases of prolonged occupations, at least when the situation is somewhat normalized, the safeguards under the LOAC for the internment of civilians are still adequate or whether the strictly required test for derogating from human rights does not demand stronger procedural safeguards than those provided for under the LOAC.[2619]

---

which concerned surveillance rather than detention but is nonetheless relevant, states that "*The rule of law implies, inter alia, that an interference by the executive authorities with an individual's rights should be subject to an effective control which should normally be assured by the judiciary, at least in the last resort, judicial control offering the best guarantees of independence, impartiality and a proper procedure*" but accepted in that case that another form of independent supervision was adequate. HÄUSSLER, pp. 130–131 and 134–136 argues that the supervision need not necessarily be of a judicial nature, relying in part on LOAC provisions that permit administrative review and noting that the Venice Commission (see Opinion No. 280/2004, *Opinion on Human Rights in Kosovo: Possible Establishment on Review Mechanisms*, CDL-AD (2004)033, 11 October 2004, pp. 27–28) did also not require a judicial review (this opinion emphasized above all the requirements for independence). Compare G.L. Neuman, *supra* note 2394, pp. 1026–1029.

2614 See, e.g. U. Erberich, *supra* note 2284, pp. 44–48 and H. Krieger, *supra* note 2486, p. 272.

2615 For an extensive discussion of detention in armed conflicts, including both LOAC and human rights aspects, see University Centre for International Humanitarian Law (Geneva) (ed.), *Expert Meeting on the Supervision of the Lawfulness of Detention During Armed Conflict, Convened in Geneva on 14–15 July 2004*, proceedings available online at www.adh-geneve.ch/pdfs/4rapport_detention.pdf. See also A. Jachec-Neale, 'Status and Treatment of Prisoners of War and other Persons Deprived of their Liberty', in E. Wilmshurst & S. Breau (eds.), *Perspectives on the ICRC Study on Customary International Humanitarian Law*, Cambridge, Cambridge University Press, 2007, pp. 302–336 and F. Hampson, 'Fundamental Guarantees', in *id.*, pp. 282–301.

2616 See also U. Erberich, *supra* note 2284, pp. 44–48 and A. Reidy, *supra* note 2545, pp. 3–4 of the online version printout.

2617 Similarly, U. Erberich, *supra* note 2284, pp. 44–48.

2618 See, e.g. Articles 100–101 GC III and Article 68 GC IV.

2619 Compare A.M. Gross, *supra* note 2512, pp. 26–29, who argues that due process and procedural safeguards for detention are areas in which human rights may offer more protection than the LOAC in occupations. Compare also F. Messineo, *supra* note 2161, pp. 57–58. On detention of civilians in armed conflicts, see, e.g. R. Goodman, 'Editorial Comment. The Detention of Civilians in Armed Conflict', 103 *A.J.I.L.* 2009, pp. 48–74.

Fourth, with regard to detention in non-international armed conflicts the relationship between the LOAC and human rights is less clear and there seems to be a tendency towards regarding human rights as the *lex specialis* in this case because the LOAC says very little on this.[2620]

Fifth, it would seem that with regard to the limitations imposed on transferring detainees to a third party, LOAC[2621] and human rights[2622] rules should be

2620 See, e.g. J.-M. Henckaerts & L. Doswald-Beck (eds.), *supra* note 2590, Vol. I, pp. 347–352 and H. Krieger, *supra* note 2486, pp. 275–276. See also IACtHR, *Bámaca Velásquez* Case, 25 November 2000, Series C No. 70 [2000] IACHR 7, §143 ("*Efraín Bámaca Velásquez was detained by the Guatemalan army in clandestine detention centers for at least four months, thus violating Article 7 of the Convention (...). Although this is a case of the detention of a guerrilla during an internal conflict (...), the detainee should have been ensured the guarantees that exist under the rule of law, and been submitted to a legal proceeding. This Court has already stated that, although the State has the right and obligation to guarantee its security and maintain public order, it must execute its actions 'within limits and according to procedures that preserve both public safety and the fundamental rights of the human person.'*").

2621 See Article 12 GC III ("*Prisoners of war may only be transferred by the Detaining Power to a Power which is a party to the Convention and after the Detaining Power has satisfied itself of the willingness and ability of such transferee Power to apply the Convention. ... Nevertheless, if that Power fails to carry out the provisions of the Convention in any important respect, the Power by whom the prisoners of war were transferred shall, upon being notified by the Protecting Power, take effective measures to correct the situation or shall request the return of the prisoners of war. Such requests must be complied with*") and Article 45 GC IV (which contains the same rule for interned civilians).

2622 See especially ECtHR, *Soering v. UK*, 7 July 1989, §§91 and 113 and HRC, *Kindler v. Canada* (CCPR/C/48/D/470/1991, Communication No. 470/1991, 18 November 1993), §6.2. See also ECtHR, *Einhorn v. France*, Admissibility, 16 October 2001, §32 and *Drozd and Janousek v. France and Spain*, 26 June 1992, §110. Specifically as regards "diplomatic assurances" in case of transfer, see ECtHR, *Saadi v. Italy*, judgment, 28 February 2008. See also A. Deeks, *Promises Not to Torture: Diplomatic Assurances in US Courts*, ASIL Discussion Paper Series, December 2008, www.asil.org/files/ASIL-08-DiscussionPaper.pdf; G. Noll, 'Diplomatic Assurances and the Silence of Human Rights Law', 7 *Melbourne J.I.L.* 2006, pp. 104–126; V. Pergantis, 'Soft Law, Diplomatic Assurances and the Instrumentalisation of Normativity: Wither a Liberal Promise?', 56 *N.I.L.R.* 2009, pp. 137–166 and L. Skoglund, 'Diplomatic Assurances Against Torture: An Effective Strategy?: A Review of Jurisprudence and Examination of the Arguments', 77 *Nordic J.I.L.* 2008, pp. 319–364. For a case on transfer of detainees in a peace operation, see ECtHR, *Al-Saadoon and Mufdhi v. UK*, admissibility decision, 30 June 2009. In this case, on 30 December 2008, the Court of Appeal upheld the High Court's decision of 19 December 2008 (*R (Saadoon & Mufdhi) v. Secretary of State for Defence*, [2008] EWHC 3098 (Admin), www.judiciary.gov.uk/docs/judgments_guidance/r-al-saadoon-mufdhi-v-ssdefence.pdf), allowing British forces in Iraq to hand over two Iraqi criminal justice detainees to the Iraqi authorities for trial before the Iraqi High Tribunal, even though there was a real risk of the death penalty being imposed (full appeals judgment delivered on 21 January 2009; see *R (on the application of (1) Faisal Attiyah Nassar Al-Saadoon (2) Khalaf Hussain Mufdhi) v. Secretary of State for Defence*, [2009] EWCA Civ 7, www.bailii.org/ew/cases/EWCA/Civ/2009/7.html). Also on 30 December 2009, the ECtHR issued a Rule 39 order to prevent the handover of the two men to the Iraqi authorities. UK forces nevertheless handed them over on 31 December 2008, saying that they had no legal powers to hold them. See M. Wood, *supra* note 2161, p. 142 note 8 and http://news.bbc.co.uk/2/hi/uk_news/7806445.stm. See also M.E. Cross & S. Williams, 'Between the Devil and the Deep Blue Sea: Conflicting Thinking in the applied concurrently.[2623] This may have significant implications in peace operations,[2624] where the transfer of detainees to the local authorities is often envisaged but where the local authorities may not be in a position to assure adequate respect for minimum safeguards, at least in the short term. This can pose a difficult dilemma for peace operations,[2625] which in such cases and where release is not an option may need to either obtain sufficient assurances of respect for fundamental rights by local authorities[2626] or to detain persons themselves. With regard to the latter, the question arises what legal basis is available and what safeguards have to be put in place. This is particularly problematic under the ECHR because its Article 5 is rather detailed[2627] and includes exhaustively[2628] the grounds for which detention is permissible. As detention for security reasons

Al-Saadoon Affair', 58 *I.C.L.Q.* 2009, pp. 689–702. Transfer of detainees has been addressed in the context of operation Atalanta: see above, Chapter 3.W.2.

2623 H. Krieger, *supra* note 2284, p. 695. Compare on the similar issue of transfers/renditions of detainees in the "war on terror", J. Fitzpatrick 'Rendition and Transfer in the War against Terrorism: Guantánamo and Beyond', 25 *Loyola L.A.I.C.L.R.* 2003, pp. 457–492. On detentions abroad in the "war on terror", see more generally H. Duffy, *supra* note 2374, pp. 379–442 and S. Borelli, *supra* note 2506, pp. 39–68. For an outspoken criticism on US detentions in Guantanamo Bay, see Lord J. Steyn, 'Guantanamo Bay: The Legal Black Hole', 53 *I.C.L.Q.* 2004, pp. 1–15 (for a summary, see Lord J. Steyn, 'Guantánamo: A Monstrous Failure of Justice', *The International Herald Tribune*, 28 November 2003, available online at www.nytimes.com/2003/11/27/opinion/27iht-edsteyn_ed3_.html). See also F. de Londras, 'The Right to Challenge the Lawfulness of Detention: An International Perspective on US Detention of Suspected Terrorists', 12 *J.C.S.L.* 2007, pp. 223–260.

2624 On detention in peace operations more generally, see, e.g. P.M. Dupont, 'Detention of Individuals during Peacekeeping Operations: Lessons learned from Kosovo', in R. Arnold & G.-J. Knoops (eds.), *supra* note 2284, pp. 249–252; U. Erberich, *supra* note 2284, pp. 166–171; Häussler, pp. 125–163; F. Naert, 'Detention in Peace Operations: The Legal Framework and Main Categories of Detainees', 45(1–2) *R.D.M.D.G.* 2006, pp. 51–78 (also available online at www.law.kuleuven.be/iir/eng/research/wp.html as KU Leuven, Institute for International Law, Working Paper No. 94) and B. Oswald, 'Detention in Military Operations: Some Military, Political and Legal Aspects', 46 *R.D.M.D.G.* 2007, pp. 341–361. See also the Copenhagen process, *infra* note 2639 and accompanying text.

2625 See also P. Rowe, *supra* note 2284, pp. 202–204.

2626 This has been the focus of particular attention in Afghanistan. See on this F. Naert, *supra* note 2624, pp. 62 and 64–65 (including the text of an Afghan-Dutch MOU) and A. Roberts, *supra* note 2276, pp. 440–445. See also Arrangement for the Transfer of Detainees between the Canadian Forces and the Ministry of Defence of the Islamic Republic of Afghanistan, Kabul, 18 December 2005 (previously available online at www.forces.gc.ca/site/operations/archer/agreement_e.asp; last consulted in November 2007), later supplemented by an additional informal agreement (following a controversy over allegations of abuse); see 'Canada to get access to Afghan detainees: O'Connor', 26 April 2007, www.ctv.ca/servlet/ArticleNews/story/CTVNews/20070424/afghanistan_abuse_070425?s_name=&no_ads=.

2627 See above in this section. See also Article 5(3) ECHR: "*Everyone arrested or detained in accordance with the provisions of paragraph 1.c of this Article shall be brought promptly before a judge or other officer authorised by law to exercise judicial power and shall be entitled to trial within a reasonable time or to release pending trial. Release may be conditioned by guarantees to appear for trial*".

2628 ECtHR, *Labita v. Italy*, 6 April 2000, §170 ("*the list of exceptions to the right to liberty secured in Article 5 §1 is an exhaustive one and only a narrow interpretation of those exceptions is* does not seem to be covered by these grounds,[2629] a derogation seems indispensable.[2630] In addition, the UN Security Council mandates on the basis of

consistent with the aim of that provision, namely to ensure that no one is arbitrarily deprived of his or her liberty").

2629 ECtHR, *Jecius v. Lithouania*, 31 July 2000, §§47–51 ("*The Government stated that the applicant's preventive detention was compatible with Article 5 §1 (c) of the Convention as ... the Code of Criminal Procedure had permitted detention with a view to preventing the commission of banditry, criminal association and terrorising a person. ... The Court observes that a person may be deprived of his liberty only for the purposes specified in Article 5 §1. A person may be detained under Article 5 §1 (c) only in the context of criminal proceedings, for the purpose of bringing him before the competent legal authority on suspicion of his having committed an offence (...). The Court considers therefore that preventive detention of the kind found in the present case is not permitted by Article 5 §1 (c)*"). See also Kolb, Poretto & Vité, p. 310. U. Erberich, *supra* note 2284, pp. 170–171 regards the grounds for detention as the main challenge to applying Article 5 ECHR in peace operations.

2630 Compare C. Warbrick, *supra* note 2394, p. 1014, noting the UK's acknowledgement that its post '11 September' detention regime for suspected terrorists required a derogation. Compare P. Rowe, *supra* note 2284, pp. 202–204, arguing that in the absence of a derogation, perhaps recourse may be had to detention "*to secure the fulfilment of any obligation prescribed by law*" (Article 5(1)b ECHR). This basis is also invoked by Häussler, p. 134. However, while leading commentators have pointed out the potential of this provision as a basis for preventive detention, they also stress that it must concern a specific obligation which is not respected. See notably ECtHR, *Engel and others v. The Netherlands*, 8 June 1976, §69: "*the words "secure the fulfilment of any obligation prescribed by law" concern only cases where the law permits the detention of a person to compel him to fulfil a specific and concrete obligation which he has until then failed to satisfy. A wide interpretation would entail consequences incompatible with the notion of the rule of law from which the whole Convention draws its inspiration ... It would justify, for example, administrative internment meant to compel a citizen to discharge, in relation to any point whatever, his general duty of obedience to the law*". These commentators also point out that any detention must be limited in duration to what is necessary for ensuring respect for the obligation. See, e.g. ECtHR, *Vasileva v. Denmark*, 25 September 2006, §§36–43 (detention to establish identity following refusal to prove identity as legally required was justified but not for 13.5 hours). See F. Jacobs & R. White, *supra* note 2417, pp. 141–142 and P. van Dijk *et al.*, *supra* note 2328, pp. 469–471. See also C. Maierhöfer, *supra* note 2612, p. 462. Indeed, all of the law Lords in *Al-Jedda* (*supra* note 2435) seem to have shared the view that security detention would be in violation of Article 5(1) ECHR unless there is a derogation and/or UNSC authorization (e.g. §§37–39 and 138–139) and the UK does not seem to have invoked this provision to argue otherwise. For case law on detention under derogation, see generally, e.g. ECtHR, *Aksoy v. Turkey*, 18 December 1996, §§65–87, especially §84 ("*The Court has taken account of the unquestionably serious problem of terrorism in South-East Turkey and the difficulties faced by the State in taking effective measures against it. However, it is not persuaded that the exigencies of the situation necessitated the holding of the applicant on suspicion of involvement in terrorist offences for fourteen days or more in incommunicado detention without access to a judge or other judicial officer*"). See also C. Warbrick, *supra* note 2394, pp. 1005–1006. The ECJ's focus on the autonomy of the EU legal order in the *Kadi* appeals judgment (see above, Section C.5 of this chapter and *supra* notes 1906 and 1909–1910 and accompanying text) may imply that Member States should formally invoke derogations when they wish to derogate from Article 5 ECHR in an ESDP operation in which the ECHR applies. While the ECJ has no jurisdiction in this area, this does not affect the substantive law. On the duration of detention absent a derogation, see, e.g. ECtHR, *Brogan and Others v. UK*, 29 November 1988, merits, §§57–62. See also *infra* note 2637. On prisoners of war and interned civilians, see also EComHR, *Cyprus v. Turkey*, Report of 10 July 1976, 4 *E.H.R.R.*

which detention powers are usually claimed are often rather broad in nature (very few have explicitly mentioned detention so far[2631]) and may lack the required precision expected of the legal basis in this context.[2632] While peace operations do make efforts to provide safeguards against arbitrary detention,[2633]

1982, pp. 482–582, especially pp. 529–533 and 555–559, including points II.2–3 of the conclusions in Part IV (treating prisoner of war rules as *lex specialis* yet ignoring internment rules for civilians altogether) and the dissenting opinions at *id.*, pp. 561–565 (arguing that the LOAC should have been applied consistently as *lex specialis*), discussed *supra* Section D.2.ii of this chapter. See on the latter also F. Hampson & I. Salama, *supra* note 2486, p. 32, note 62. Useful lessons may be drawn from post '11 September' measures to detain suspected terrorists and the legal controversies to which they have given rise, notably in the UK (see, e.g. the developments summarized in the 2005/1, 2005/4, 2006/2, 2006/3 and 2007/1 issues of the *Newsletter* of the International Society for Military Law and the Law of War, available online at http://home.scarlet.be/~ismllw/publication/bulletin_info.htm) and the US (although these seem to be much more concerned with US domestic law; they also continue to evolve at a high pace; see the sections on US developements in virtually all *Newsletters* of the International Society for Military Law and the Law of War (*id.*) from 2005 onwards).

2631 In the letter of the US Secretary of State annexed to UNSC Res. 1546 of 8 June 2004 on Iraq and endorsed in the resolution (see §10), it is stated that "*the [Multinational Force] stands ready to continue to undertake a broad range of tasks to contribute to the maintenance of security and to ensure force protection. These include … internment where this is necessary for imperative reasons of security …*". On detention in Iraq, see generally A.E. Wall, 'Civilian Detentions in Iraq', in M. Schmitt & J. Pejic (eds.), *International Law and Armed Conflict: Exploring the Faultlines. Essays in Honour of Yoram Dinstein*, Nijhoff, Leiden, 2007, pp. 413–438, especially pp. 428–429. Bruce Oswald has identified (at a presentation at the 31st Sanremo Roundtable on 4–6 September 2008) 3 other UNSC resolutions explicitly mentioning detention: Resolutions 169 (24 November 1961, §4; on the Congo); 837 (6 June 1993, §5; on the perpetrators of attacks against UNOSOM II in Somalia) and 1638 (11 November 2005, §1; concerning former President Charles Taylor of Liberia).

2632 See the critical view by Kolb, Poretto & Vité, p. 347. See also the critical questions by Baroness Hale in *Al-Jedda* (*supra* note 2435), §§125–129. See on this requirement ECtHR, *Jecius v. Lithouania*, 31 July 2000, §56 ("*the standard of "lawfulness" set by the Convention … requires that all law be sufficiently precise to allow the person – if need be, with appropriate advice – to foresee, to a degree that is reasonable in the circumstances, the consequences which a given action may entail*"). Compare U. Erberich, *supra* note 2284, p. 170. I would agree with Erberich (*id.*, p. 170) and Häussler, pp. 133–134 that "by law" can include international law. However, while Häußler's view on detention power being widely accepted in practice as implied in UN Security Council mandates (Häussler, pp. 137–138) undoubtedly reflects practice, this does not necessarily mean that it is adequate in terms of human rights. Compare also above, Chapter 9.C.5 and note 2161 on the required respect for human rights, especially where UN Security Council resolutions leave some discretion. In a maritime context, see ECtHR, *Medvedyev and others v. France,* 10 July 2008 (under appeal to the Grand Chamber), §§49–63. See G. Breda & J.P. Pierini, 'Legal Issues Surrounding Maritime Counterdrug Operations and the Related Question of Detention as Highlighted in the *Medvedyev and Others v. France* Decision of the European Court of Human Rights', 47 *Military Law & the Law of War Review* 2008, pp. 167–198.

2633 On such safeguards, see generally J. Pejic, 'Procedural Principles and Safeguards for Internment/Administrative Detention in Armed Conflict and other Situations of Violence', 87 No. 858 *I.R.R.C.* 2005, pp. 375–391. Compare the views expressed by some of the law Lords in *Al-Jedda* (*supra* note 2435), especially at §§39 and 125–129. With regard to the EU, see also Pledge P091 made by the EU Member States at the 30th International Conference of the Red these have varied[2634] and it is questionable whether they have always been adequate. In particular, the review mechanisms that are put in place may well lack sufficient independence from the operation.[2635] While the feasibility of an

Cross and Red Crescent in 2007, which contains a mix of commitments undertaken by the Member States and commitments undertaken by the EU itself concerning Fundamental Procedural and other Guarantees and in which "*The EU Member States reaffirm their determination to respect fundamental procedural guarantees for al persons detained in relation with armed an armed conflict or other situation of violence as enshrined in relevant IHL and/or international human rights law, as applicable*" and "*The EU therefore pledges to promote respect of fundamental procedural guarantees through a wide range of measures including: - Training for staff participating in EU military and civilian crisis management operations in fundamental procedural guarantees*" (see www.icrc.org/applic/p130e.nsf/pbk/PCOE-79CKFC?openDocument&section=PBP).

2634 E.g. detention in Kosovo by both UNMIK and KFOR has been criticized, notably by the OSCE (see, e.g. *A Review of the Criminal Justice System (February – July 2000)*, www.osce.org/documents/mik/2000/08/970_en.pdf, pp. 19–20 and 25–26 and *A Review of the Criminal Justice System (September 2001 – February 2002)*, www.osce.org/documents/mik/2002/04/965_en.pdf, pp. 9 and 45–50); by the Ombudsperson institution in Kosovo (see *Special Report No. 3 on the Conformity of Deprivations of Liberty under 'Executive Orders' with Recognised International Standards addressed to Mr. Hans Haekkerup Special Representative of the Secretary General of the United Nations*, 29 June 2001 (available online at www.ombudspersonkosovo.org/repository/docs/E4010629a.pdf), concluding at §29 that "*The Ombudsperson, therefore, concludes that deprivations of liberty imposed under 'Executive Orders' do not conform with recognised international standards*") and by the Venice Commission (see Opinion No. 280/2004, *Opinion on Human Rights in Kosovo: Possible Establishment on Review Mechanisms*, CDL-AD (2004)033, 11 October 2004, pp. 11–12 and 27–28). See also E. Abraham, 'The Sins of the Savior: Holding the United Nations Accountable to International Human Rights Standards for Executive Order Detentions in its Mission in Kosovo', 52 *American University Law Review* 2003, pp. 1291–1337; Kolb, Poretto & Vité, pp. 308–316; H. Krieger, *supra* note 2486, pp. 289–290 and C. Stahn, *supra* note 2475, pp. 152–154. On detention in KFOR, see also M. Johnson, 'Headquarters KFOR', in D. Fleck (ed.), *The Handbook of the Law of Visiting Forces*, Oxford, Oxford University Press, 2001, pp. 342–343. In contrast, the detention by the International Force for East Timor (INTERFET) has been praised. It was regulated by the INTERFET Detainee Ordinance issued by the INTERFET Commander, dated 21 October 1999 (on file with the author, obtained via the ASIL's email list). See M. Kelly, T. McCormack, P. Muggleton & B. Oswald, 'Legal Aspects of Australia's Involvement in the International Force for East Timor', 83 No. 841 *I.R.R.C.* 2001, pp. 130–136. This regime has been described in some detail in a few publications. See, e.g. M. Kelly, *INTERFET Detainee Management Unit in East Timor*, paper presented at the Swiss Seminar on the Law of Armed Conflict in 2000 on 27 October 2000 (on file with the author and obtained via the ASIL's email list); B. Oswald, 'The INTERFET Detainee Managment Unit in East Timor', 3 *Y.I.H.L.* 2000, pp. 347–361; M.Kelly, T. McCormack, P. Muggleton & B. Oswald, *supra* this note, pp. 130–136 and S. Linton, 'Rising From The Ashes: The Creation Of A Viable Criminal Justice System In East Timor', 5 *Melbourne University Law Review* 2001, pp. 122–180 (available online at www.austlii.edu.au/au/journals/MULR/2001/5.html).

2635 See Venice Commission Opinion, *supra* note 2634, p. 27, §129 ("*the KFOR Commander has already provided for an embryonic form of review procedure by requiring that any decision on extending detention beyond an initial period of 72 hours must be made upon a request by the Legal Adviser. The disadvantage of this review procedure is not so much that it is purely advisory, but that the review is conducted only by a soldier who remains within the chain of command and within the administrative hierarchy. It is therefore currently not institutionally* independent review sometimes appears to be questioned, this does not seem convincing,[2636] especially in complex peace operations that include rule of law elements. That being said, it is clear that the review mechanism need not be the same as in a normal peacetime situation.[2637]

In any event, it is clear that with regard to detention, one cannot generally designate either the LOAC or human rights as *lex specialis*.[2638] Rather, the relationship will vary from case to case. It may also be noted that the Legal Service of the Danish Ministry of Foreign Affairs has launched the 'Copenhagen Process on the Handling of Detainees in International Military Operations' in October 2007 in order to attempt to identify a horizontal and multilateral solution to the challenge of how troop-contributing States can ensure that they act in accordance with their international obligations when handling detainees – including when transferring detainees to local authorities or to other troop-contributing countries.[2639]

---

ensured that the Commander receives an independent legal advice, although experience shows that most Legal Advisers perform admirably in their position").

2636 Similarly, U. Erberich, *supra* note 2284, p. 171. See, e.g. the proposals put forward in the Venice Commission Opinion, *supra* note 2634, pp. 27–28, §§130–133.

2637 See H. Krieger, *supra* note 2486, pp. 285–286 for this argument more generally but also specifically regarding detention. For a similar view with regard to detention in the context of the fight against international terrorism, see F. de Londras, *supra* note 2623, pp. 223–260, especially p. 260. There is also a parallel with the question of judicial review of terrorist lists. On the latter, see, e.g. Section C.5 of this chapter above. For the permissibility of a longer than normal period before a detainee appears before a judge in light of the specific circumstances in martime operations, see ECtHR, *Medvedyev and others v. France*, 10 July 2008 (under appeal to the Grand Chamber), §§64–69 ("*Il reste certes que la détention imposée aux requérants à bord du Winner n'était pas sous la supervision d'une "autorité judiciaire" au sens de l'article 5 ... ils n'ont pas bénéficié de la protection contre l'arbitraire qu'offre un encadrement de cette nature. Cet élément, que la Cour a dûment examiné à l'aune du premier paragraphe de l'article 5, ne met toutefois pas en cause le fait que la durée de la privation de liberté subie par les requérants se trouve justifiée par les "circonstances tout à fait exceptionnelles" susexposées, notamment par l'inévitable délai d'acheminement du Winner vers la France*") and *Rigopoulos v. Spain*, 12 January 1999, admissibility decision ("*the applicant had been detained on the orders and under the strict supervision of the Central Investigating Court, and in compliance with the relevant legislation ...having regard to the wholly exceptional circumstances of the instant case, the time which elapsed between placing the applicant in detention and bringing him before the investigating judge [16 days] cannot be said to have breached the requirement of promptness in paragraph 3 of Article 5*"). This would be relevant in the context of EUNAVFOR Somalia / Atalanta (see Chapter 3.W.2 below).

2638 But see D. Lorenz, *supra* note 2282, pp. 219–222, who appears to generally see the LOAC as prevailing in the case of conflict.

2639 See Danish Ministry of Foreign Affairs, Legal Service, Copenhagen Conference on 'The Handling of Detainees in International Military Operations', 11–12 October 2007, *Non-Paper on Legal Framework and Aspects of Detention*, 4 October 2007 with accompanying note on the 'Copenhagen Process on The Handling of Detainees in International Military Operations, 46 *R.D.M.D.G.* 2007, pp. 363–392. See also B. Oswald, *supra* note 2624.

c. The Prohibition of Torture, Inhuman and Degrading Treatment or Punishment

The third right which is addressed here is the prohibition of torture, inhuman and degrading treatment or punishment.[2640] This rule suffers no exceptions, as is clear from its non-derogable nature[2641] and is reaffirmed in treaties specifically dealing with this right.[2642]

Moreover, it is, albeit often in slightly different forms, contained in various LOAC treaties and rules. For instance, pursuant to common Article 3 of the 1949 Geneva Conventions, persons taking no active part in the hostilities "*shall in all circumstances treated humanely*" and shall not be subjected to "*violence to life and person, in particular ..., mutilation, cruel treatment and torture*" nor to "*outrages upon personal dignity, in particular humiliating and degrading treatment*" and the grave breaches provisions of these Conventions cover "*torture or inhuman treatment, including biological experiments, wilfully causing great suffering or serious injury to body or health*" committed against persons or property protected by the Conventions.[2643] Similar protections, sometimes including more specific rules, are included with regard to other protected persons in Articles 12 GC I; 12 GC II; 13 and 14 GC III; 27 and 32 GC IV; 10, 11 and 75 AP I and 4 and 7 AP II. The ICRC's customary international humanitarian law

---

2640 See Article 7 ICCPR; Article 3 ECHR; Article 5 ACHR and Article 5 African Charter on Human and Peoples' Rights (*supra* note 2361). See also the UN Convention against Torture and Other Cruel, Inhuman or Degrading Treatment or Punishment (New York, 10 December 1984, 1465 *U.N.T.S.* 85 and Annexed to UNGA Res. 39/46, 10 December 1984); European Convention for the Prevention of Torture and Inhuman or Degrading Treatment or Punishment (Strasbourg, 27 November 1987, *E.T.S.* 126) and Inter-American Convention to Prevent and Punish Torture (Cartagena, 12 September 1985, *O.A.S. Treaty Series* No. 67).

2641 See, e.g. Articles 7 *juncto* 4(2) ICCPR; Articles 3 *juncto* 15(2) ECHR and Articles 5 *juncto* 27(2) ACHR.

2642 See, e.g. Article 2 Convention against Torture and Other Cruel, Inhuman or Degrading Treatment or Punishment (*supra* note 2640) ("*2. No exceptional circumstances whatsoever, whether a state of war or a threat of war, internal political instability or any other public emergency, may be invoked as a justification of torture. 3. An order from a superior officer or a public authority may not be invoked as a justification of torture*") and Article 5 Inter-American Convention to Prevent and Punish Torture (*supra* note 2640) ("*The existence of circumstances such as a state of war, threat of war, state of siege or of emergency, domestic disturbance or strife, suspension of constitutional guarantees, domestic political instability, or other public emergencies or disasters shall not be invoked or admitted as justification for the crime of torture. Neither the dangerous character of the detainee or prisoner, nor the lack of security of the prison establishment or penitentiary shall justify torture*"). While Article 17(3) European Convention for the Prevention of Torture and Inhuman or Degrading Treatment or Punishment (*supra* note 2640) does stipulate that the European Committee for the Prevention of Torture and Inhuman or Degrading Treatment or Punishment "*shall not visit places which representatives or delegates of Protecting Powers or the [ICRC] effectively visit on a regular basis by virtue of the Geneva Conventions ... and the Additional Protocols ... thereto*", this only affects the supervision and not the applicability of the substantive right.

2643 Articles 50 GC I; 51 GC II; 130 GC III and 147 GC IV. See also Article 85 AP I.

study contains rules stipulating that "*Civilians and persons* hors de combat *must be treated humanely*" (Rule 87) and that "*Torture, cruel or inhuman treatment and outrages upon personal dignity, in particular humiliating and degrading treatment, are prohibited*" (Rule 90).[2644]

This is one of the cases where the most favourable protection rule seems appropriate and where a cumulative application of human rights and the LOAC is generally accepted.[2645] This was *inter alia* reflected in the ICTY's judgment in the *Furundzija* case, in which the court stated that:

> 134. Torture in times of armed conflict is specifically prohibited by international treaty law, in particular by the Geneva Conventions of 1949 [common Article 3; Articles 12 and 50 GC I; Articles 12 and 51 GC II; Articles 13, 14 and 130 GC III; Articles 27, 32 and 147 GC IV] and the two Additional Protocols of 1977 [Article 75 AP I and Article 4 AP II] …
>
> 137. … the proposition is warranted that a general prohibition against torture has evolved in customary international law…
>
> 143. The prohibition of torture laid down in international humanitarian law with regard to situations of armed conflict is reinforced by the body of international treaty rules on human rights: these rules ban torture both in armed conflict and in time of peace…
>
> 144. It should be noted that the prohibition of torture laid down in human rights treaties enshrines an absolute right, which can never be derogated from, not even in time of emergency (on this ground the prohibition also applies to situations of armed conflicts). This is linked to the fact, …, that the prohibition on torture is a peremptory norm or jus cogens.
>
> 159. International humanitarian law, while outlawing torture in armed conflict, does not provide a definition of the prohibition. Such a definition can instead be found in Article 1(1) of the 1984 Torture Convention whereby:
>
> For the purposes of this Convention, the term 'torture' means any act by which severe pain or suffering, whether physical or mental, is intentionally inflicted on a person for such purposes as obtaining from him or a third person information or a confession, punishing him for an act he or a third person has committed or is suspected of having committed, or intimidating or coercing him or a third person, or for any reason based on discrimination of any kind, when such pain or suffering is inflicted by or at the instigation of or with the consent or acquiescence of a public official or other person acting in an official capacity. It does not include pain or suffering arising only from, inherent in or incidental to lawful sanctions.

2644 J.-M. Henckaerts & L. Doswald-Beck (eds.), *supra* note 2590, Vol. I, respectively pp. 306–308 and 315–319.

2645 See, e.g. U. Erberich, *supra* note 2284, pp. 50–51. Compare H. Krieger, *supra* note 2486, pp. 275–276 on the meaning of degrading treatment in relation to the merger of both regimes.

160. This definition was regarded by Trial Chamber I of ICTR, in Prosecutor v. Jean-Paul Akayesu, hereafter "Akayesu", as sic et simpliciter applying to any rule of international law on torture, including the relevant provisions of the ICTR Statute. [...] ... Trial Chamber II of the International Tribunal has rightly noted in Delalic that indeed the definition of torture contained in the 1984 Torture Convention ... "thus reflects a consensus which the Trial Chamber considers to be representative of customary international law".[...] This Trial Chamber shares such conclusion, ...

161. The broad convergence of the aforementioned international instruments and international jurisprudence demonstrates that there is now general acceptance of the main elements contained in the definition set out in Article 1 of the Torture Convention.

162. The Trial Chamber considers however that while the definition referred to above applies to any instance of torture, whether in time of peace or of armed conflict, it is appropriate to identify or spell out some specific elements that pertain to torture as considered from the specific viewpoint of international criminal law relating to armed conflicts. ... As is apparent from this enumeration of criteria, the Trial Chamber considers that among the possible purposes of torture one must also include that of humiliating the victim. This proposition is warranted by the general spirit of international humanitarian law: the primary purpose of this body of law is to safeguard human dignity. The proposition is also supported by some general provisions of such important international treaties as the Geneva Conventions and Additional Protocols, which consistently aim at protecting persons not taking part, or no longer taking part, in the hostilities from "outrages upon personal dignity". The notion of humiliation is, in any event close to the notion of intimidation, which is explicitly referred to in the Torture Convention's definition of torture.[2646]

However, the ICTY later overruled this judgment in part, notably in the *Kunarac* case, in which it ruled that:

482. ... the Trial Chamber is of the view that the definition of torture contained in the Torture Convention cannot be regarded as the definition of torture under customary international law which is binding regardless of the context in which it is applied. ... The definition was also meant to apply only in the context of that Convention, and only to the extent that other international instruments or national laws did not give the individual a broader or better protection. The Trial Chamber, therefore, holds that the definition of torture contained in Article 1 of the Torture Convention can only serve, for present purposes, as an interpretational aid. ...

496. The Trial Chamber concludes that the definition of torture under international humanitarian law does not comprise the same elements as the definition of torture generally applied under human rights law. In particular, the Trial Chamber is of the view that the presence of a state official or of any other authority-wielding person in

[2646] *Prosecutor v. Furundzija*, ICTY-95–17/1, 10 December 1998 (notes omitted). See also L. Moir, *supra* note 2388, pp. 200–201.

the torture process is not necessary for the offence to be regarded as torture under international humanitarian law.[2647]

This latter judgment thus explicitly confirms the most favourable protection rule with regard to torture.

d. Occupation

Fourth, occupation also merits a brief specific analysis.[2648] As with detention, it must be noted first that occupation arguably by definition entails effective control over territory,[2649] since it is defined as "*territory actually placed under the authority of the hostile army*" and extends only to "*the territory where such authority has been established and can be exercised*",[2650] thus leading to the applicability of human rights.[2651] The rejection of this link in *Al-Skeini* is not convincing.[2652]

2647 *Prosecutor v. Dragoljub Kunarac, Radomir Kovac and Zoran Vukovic*, IT-96-23 & 23/1, 22 February 2001. See also J.-M. Henckaerts & L. Doswald-Beck (eds.), *supra* note 2590, Vol. I, pp. 317–318.

2648 See also the references *supra* notes 2510 and 2512; Y. Arai-Takahashi, *The Law of Occupation: Continuity and Change of International Humanitarian Law, and Its Interaction with International Human Rights Law*, Leiden, Martinus Nijhoff, 2009; E. Benvenisti, *The International Law of Occupation*, Princeton, Princeton University Press, 2004 (reprint with revised introduction), pp. viii-xi, xvi, 16 and 187–189; C. MacCarthy, 'Legal Reasoning and the Applicability of International Human Rights Standards during Military Occupation', in R. Arnold & N. Quénivet (eds.), *International Humanitarian Law and Human Rights Law: towards a New Merger in International Law*, Leiden, Martinus Nijhoff, 2008, pp. 121–132 and T. Ruys & S. Verhoeven, 'DRC v. Uganda: The Applicability of International Human Law and Human Rights Law in Occupied Territories', in R. Arnold & N. Quénivet (eds.), *International Humanitarian Law and Human Rights Law: towards a New Merger in International Law*, Leiden, Martinus Nijhoff, 2008, pp. 155–195. For a discussion with respect to the right to property, see L. Loucaides, 'The Protection of the Right to Property in Occupied Territories', 53 *I.C.L.Q.* 2004, pp. 677–690. On the right to education, see J.T. Horowitz, 'The Right to Education in Occupied Territories: Making More Room for Human Rights in Occupation Law', 7 *Y.I.H.L.* 2004, pp. 233–277.

2649 In this sense, R. Ergec, *supra* note 2390, p. 129 and P. Rowe, *supra* note 2284, pp. 195–196. This also seems to be the view of D. Lorenz, *supra* note 2282, p. 92.

2650 Article 42 Hague Regulations. See also *supra*, Chapter 8.D.

2651 In this sense, R. Ergec, *supra* note 2390, p. 129 and P. Rowe, *supra* note 2284, pp. 195–196. See also E. Benvenisti, *supra* note 2648, pp. viii-xi and xvi (seeing UNSC Res. 1483 on Iraq as a revision of the law of occupation taking into due account the relevancy of human rights and noting the affirmation of the applicability of human rights in occupation by the ICJ in its 9 July 2004 advisory opinion on the *Legal consequences of the construction of a wall in the occupied Palestinian territory*) and 16 and 187–189 (seeing a probability that political and civil rights will be curtailed but that this should decrease if and when the security situation improves). On the extraterritorial applicability of human rights resulting from effective control over a territory, see *supra*, Section B of this chapter.

2652 In this British case, the Appeals Court ruled that "*it is quite impossible to hold that the UK, although an occupying power for the purposes of the Hague Regulations and Geneva IV, was in effective control of Basrah City for the purposes of ECHR jurisprudence at the material time*"

However, the applicability of the sending State's human rights obligations may conflict with another fundamental rule of the law of occupation, namely that the existing local law must be respected by the occupying power, subject to only limited exceptions.[2653] Thus Article 43 Hague Regulations provides that the occupant "*shall take all the measures in his power to restore, and ensure, as far as possible, public order and safety, while respecting, unless absolutely prevented, the laws in force in the country*".[2654] Similarly, Article 64 GC IV stipulates that:

> The penal laws of the occupied territory shall remain in force, with the exception that they may be repealed or suspended by the Occupying Power in cases where they constitute a threat to its security or an obstacle to the application of the present Convention. Subject to the latter consideration and to the necessity for ensuring the effective administration of justice, the tribunals of the occupied territory shall continue to function in respect of all offences covered by the said laws.
>
> The Occupying Power may, however, subject the population of the occupied territory to provisions which are essential to enable the Occupying Power to fulfil its obligations under the present Convention, to maintain the orderly government of the territory, and to ensure the security of the Occupying Power, of the members and property of the occupying forces or administration, and likewise of the establishments and lines of communication used by them.

The reasons listed for altering local law do not appear to include ensuring respect for human rights that are in force for the occupying power, although an evolutionary interpretation may not exclude an interpretation to this effect.[2655]

(*supra* note 2323, §§112–128, quote from §124). This was affirmed as to the result in the House of Lord's judgment in the case (*supra* note 2324, §§129–132), although it seems rather based on the relationship with the LOAC (see *infra* in this paragraph).

2653 See also D. Lorenz, *supra* note 2282, pp. 93–94 and compare T. Irmscher, *supra* note 2508, pp. 390–394.

2654 On this provision, see generally E. Benvenisti, *supra* note 2648, pp. 7–31; M. Sassoli, *Article 43 of the Hague Regulations and Peace Operations in the Twenty-first Century*, background paper, June 2004 (available online at at http://ihl.ihlresearch.org/); M. Sassoli, 'Legislation and Maintenance of Public Order and Civil Life by Occupying Powers', 16 *E.J.I.L.* 2005, pp. 661–694; M. Sassoli, 'Current Developments in the Law of Military Occupation: Maintenance of Public Order and Civil Life in Occupied Territories and Legislative Powers of Occupying Powers', in College of Europe & ICRC (eds.), *Proceedings of the Bruges Colloquium. The Need for Justice and Requirements for Peace and Security. 9th – 10th September 2004 / Actes du colloque de Bruges. Impératifs de Justice et Exigences de Paix et de Sécurité. 9–10 septembre 2004*, Bruges, College of Europe (*collegium* No. 32, available online at www.coleurop.be/template.asp?pagename=pub_collegium), 2005, pp. 105–122 and Y. Dinstein, 'The Israel Supreme Court and the Law of Belligerent Occupation: Article 43 of the Hague Regulations', 25 *Israel Y.H.R.* 1995, pp. 1–20.

2655 Compare E. Benvenisti, *supra* note 2648, pp. viii-ix and 16 and A. Roberts, *supra* note 2512, pp. 586–589, who *inter alia* notes a suggestion allowing change in case of violations of the Universal Declaration of Human Rights that was, however, not acted upon.

Indeed, the ICJ seems to have espoused the latter approach.[2656] In any event, the extent to which this may pose an obstacle to the application of the sending State's human rights obligations will depend on the extent to which these obligations correspond to those of the occupied State.[2657] Where they coincide, there will be no obstacle. Where they do not, the sending State's human rights obligations may apply only to a limited extent. This will particularly be the case with regard to regional human rights treaties outside their region.[2658] In fact, the matter was addressed in the *Al-Skeini* case. In this case, the Appeals Court said:

> 124. In my judgment it is quite impossible to hold that the UK … was in effective control of Basrah City for the purposes of ECHR jurisprudence at the material time. If it had been, it would have been obliged … to secure to everyone in Basrah City the rights and freedoms guaranteed by the ECHR. One only has to state that proposition to see how utterly unreal it is … as an occupying power it was bound to respect the laws in force in Iraq unless absolutely prevented (see Article 43 of the Hague Regulations cited in para 113 above)….
>
> 126. And it is in any event very much open to question whether an effort by an occupying power in a predominantly Muslim country to inculcate what the ECtHR has described (…) as "the common spiritual heritage of the member states of the country of Europe" during its temporary sojourn in that country would have been consistent with the Coalition's goal, which was to transfer responsibility to representative Iraqi authorities as early as possible….[2659]

This view was later also expressed by the House of Lords in this case:

> During the period in question here it is common ground that the UK was an occupying power in Southern Iraq and bound as such by Geneva IV and by the Hague Regulations. Article 43 of the Hague Regulations provides that the occupant "shall take all the measures in his power to restore and ensure, as far as possible, public

2656 *Case concerning armed activities on the territory of the Congo (DRC v. Uganda)*, judgment of 19 December 2005, §178 ("*[the] obligation, according to Article 43 of the Hague Regulations of 1907, to take all the measures in its power to restore, and ensure, as far as possible, public order and safety in the occupied area, while respecting, unless absolutely prevented, the laws in force in the DRC. This obligation comprised the duty to secure respect for the applicable rules of international human rights law and international humanitarian law …*").

2657 Compare M.J. Dennis, *supra* note 2282, pp. 131–132, who argues that on the basis of Article 43 Hague Regulations, in occupation human rights treaties of the sending State may not be applicable unless they are also binding on the host State.

2658 See also H. Krieger, *supra* note 2486, pp. 284–286. See more generally D. Lorenz, *supra* note 2282, pp. 118–126, arguing for some limitations on the extraterritorial application of regional human rights instruments beyond 'their' region. But see E. Roxstrom, M. Gibney & T. Einarsen, *supra* note 2294, pp. 56–66 and 131–136. Compare also U. Häußler, 'Regional Human Rights vs. International Peace Missions: Lessons Learned from Kosovo', 20 *Humanitäres Völkerrecht* 2007, pp. 238–244.

2659 *Supra* note 2652.

> order and safety, while respecting, unless absolutely prevented, the laws in force in the country." The appellants argue that occupation within the meaning of the Hague Regulations necessarily involves the occupant having effective control of the area and so being responsible for securing there all Convention rights and freedoms. So far as this being the case, however, the occupants' obligation is to respect "the laws in force", not to introduce laws and the means to enforce them (for example, courts and a justice system) such as to satisfy the requirements of the Convention. Often (for example where Sharia law is in force) Convention rights would clearly be incompatible with the laws of the territory occupied.[2660]

Roberts has noted that human rights are not tailored to occupations but acknowledged the case for their applicability and has offered some guidance as to the interaction between human rights and the LOAC in occupation in the form of a balanced mix of both.[2661] Moreover, Gross has argued that human rights may in some cases lead to less protection than would be available under the law of occupation, especially when the human rights of the occupying State and its nationals are taken into account (although his findings may be of limited value outside the situation of the Palestinian occupied territories which are the focus of his Article),[2662] and sees a fundamental problem in trying to apply human rights to a situation of occupation which is considered as structurally at odds with the values underlying human rights.[2663]

It may be concluded that despite a strong case for the applicability of human rights to occupations, the obligation to respect existing local law in principle limits the applicability of the sending State's human rights obligations, albeit to varying degrees depending on the extent to which these obligations are in line with those of the occupied State.

v. Conclusions

It has been argued above that the general relationship rules do not offer a generic answer on how human rights and the LOAC interact. While doctrine and

---

2660 *Supra* note 2652, §129.

2661 A. Roberts, *supra* note 2512, pp. 580–622, especially pp. 589–590, 599–601 and 619 (see also his overview of doctrine at pp. 590–593 and of specific cases of occupation at pp. 595–599 and 605–618).

2662 A.M. Gross, *supra* note 2512, pp. 1–35. He does acknowledge that sometimes human rights may offer more protection (pp. 26–29 and 31), notably as regards detention and due process and procedural safeguards. On the latter, see also Y. Arai-Takahashi, 'Fair Trial Guarantees in Occupied Territory: The Interplay between International Humanitarian Law and Human Rights Law', in R. Arnold & N. Quénivet (eds.), *International Humanitarian Law and Human Rights Law: towards a New Merger in International Law*, Leiden, Martinus Nijhoff, 2008, pp. 449–474.

2663 *Id.*, p. 32.

international case law largely support the *lex specialis* principle, they are not always on the same line as to how this should be applied. Moreover, there is also some support in doctrine and especially jurisprudence for the most favourable protection principle, especially in non-international armed conflicts, either in the alternative or in addition to the *lex specialis* rule – despite the fact that the latter may be contradictory. In contrast, the separatist view has very few supporters. An analysis of a number of specific rights and of the interaction in occupations has demonstrated that the exact relationship depends on the specific right at stake and the circumstances of each case. It is therefore submitted that the relationship between both regimes cannot be determined by way of a general rule,[2664] not even in respect of different rights or situations/qualifications and that a case-by-case analysis is required.

E. PARTICIPATING STATE OBLIGATIONS IN ESDP OPERATIONS: MEMBER STATE RESPONSIBILITY

There is not much that can be added to what has been said about Member State responsibility in Chapters 7.H and 8.F above, especially since the general considerations in Chapter 7.H in this respect are based to a considerable extent on the jurisprudence of the European Court of Human Rights. For the sake of convenience, it is recalled that I argue in Chapter 7.H that there are three bases for Member State responsibility (leaving aside complicity). First, a Member State incurs international responsibility for an act committed by an international organization that, if committed by that State, would have constituted a breach of an international obligation of that Member State, except for 'common interest regimes' in respect of which the Member State has provided for equivalent protection, with the caveat that where despite such equivalent protection there is a manifest violation that outweighs the interests of international cooperation, the Member State will remain responsible. Second, a Member State engages its international responsibility by voting in relation to a decision when the mere vote itself amounts to a violation of an international obligation of that State. Third, a Member State is internationally responsible for implementing a decision that violates its international obligations except where it had provided for equivalent protection in relation to a 'common interest regime' and has no

2664 See also the thoughtful analysis of C. MacCarthy, 'Legal Conclusion or Interpretative Process?: Lex Specialis and the Applicability of International Human Rights Standards', in R. Arnold & N. Quénivet (eds.), *International Humanitarian Law and Human Rights Law: towards a New Merger in International Law*, Leiden, Martinus Nijhoff, 2008, pp. 101–118, who makes a persuasive case that *lex specialis* operates as an interpretative process rather than as a conclusive rule.

discretion to implement the decision in conformity with its obligations and only to the extent that the violation of its obligations is proportionate to the importance of international cooperation.

Nevertheless, three particular points deserve some attention here. The first is that of the equivalent protection. In particular, while the European Court of Human Rights has accepted that the EC offers such equivalent protection, at least in principle, it demands that this protection be equivalent in terms of both substance *and procedural protection*. As the Court said in *Bosphorus*:

> State action taken in compliance with [legal obligations flowing from its membership of an international organisation to which it has transferred part of its sovereignty] is justified as long as the relevant organisation is considered to protect fundamental rights, as regards both the substantive guarantees offered *and the mechanisms controlling their observance*, in a manner which can be considered at least equivalent to that for which the Convention provides (...) However, any such finding of equivalence could not be final and would be susceptible to review in the light of any relevant change in fundamental rights' protection.[2665]

Given the lack of jurisdiction of the ECJ in the area of the CFSP and the ESDP, it is submitted that this implies that the EU does not offer equivalent protection in these areas.[2666] Thus Member States cannot be absolved on this ground.

2665 *Bosphorus Hava Yolları Turizm ve Ticaret Anonim Şirketi v. Ireland*, 30 June 2005, §155 (emphasis added).

2666 Similarly, with regard to the Third Pillar, E. Spaventa, 'Remembrance of Principles Lost: on Fundamental Rights, the Third Pillar and the Scope of Union Law', 25 *Y.E.L.* 2006, pp. 153–176 and J. Andriantsimbazovina, 'Harmonie ou disharmonie de la protection des droits de l'homme en Europe? Quelques considérations sur la jurisprudence de la Cour européenne des droits de l'homme depuis 2005', 42 *C.D.E.* 2006, p. 753, who cites the Opinion of Advocate-General Mengozzi of 26 October 2006 in Cases C-354/04 (*Gestoras Pro Amnistía and Others v Council*) and C-355/04 (*Segi Araitz Zubimendi Izaga Aritza Galarraga v Council*), both §86 (who writes that "*it is entirely improbable that the European Court of Human Rights would extend to the third pillar of the Union the presumption of equivalence in the protection of the fundamental rights that it has established between the ECHR and Community law, or the 'first pillar' of the Union, and which leads that Court to carry out only a 'marginal' review of the compatibility of acts adopted by the Community institutions with the ECHR*"). This view is also shared with regard to the Third Pillar by S. Peers, 'Salvation Outside the Church: Judicial Protection in the Third Pillar After the Pupino and Segi Judgments', *C.M.L. Rev.* 2007, pp. 883–929 (who also discusses these two cases). Compare ECJ, Cases C-354/04 and C-355/04 (both *supra* this note, both 27 Februari 2007), §§50–51 (on the *Segi* case, see also B. Davies, '*Segi* and the Future of Judicial Rights Protection in the Third Pillar of the EU', 14 *European Public Law* 2008, pp. 311–321). This is the case even if the standard of comparison is remedies that exist in the Member States concerning military operations abroad, since in at least some Member States legal proceedings are not altogether precluded (see, e.g. the UK cases *Al-Skeini*, *supra* notes 2322–2324, *Al-Jedda*, *supra* note 2435, and *Bici*, *supra* note 2585), and where they are available, may open recourse to the ECtHR. Similarly, with regard to KFOR, H. Krieger, *supra* note 2284, pp. 684–686. Compare F. Benoit-Rohmer, 'À propos de l'arrêt Bosphorus

The second point concerns the European Court of Human Right's consideration in *Behrami* and *Saramati* that:

> ... the circumstances of the present cases are essentially different from those with which the Court was concerned in the *Bosphorus* case. In its judgment in that case, the Court noted that the impugned act (...) had been carried out by the respondent State authorities, on its territory and following a decision by one of its Ministers (...). The Court did not therefore consider that any question arose as to its competence, notably *ratione personae*, vis-à-vis the respondent State despite the fact that the source of the impugned seizure was an EC Council Regulation which, in turn, applied a UNSC Resolution. In the present cases, the impugned acts and omissions of KFOR and UNMIK cannot be attributed to the respondent States and, moreover, did not take place on the territory of those States or by virtue of a decision of their authorities. The present cases are therefore clearly distinguishable from the *Bosphorus* case in terms both of the responsibility of the respondent States under Article 1 and of the Court's competence *ratione personae*.
>
> There exists, in any event, a fundamental distinction between the nature of the international organisation and of the international cooperation with which the Court was there concerned and those in the present cases. As the Court has found above, UNMIK was a subsidiary organ of the UN created under Chapter VII and KFOR was exercising powers lawfully delegated under Chapter VII of the Charter by the UNSC. As such, their actions were directly attributable to the UN, an organisation of universal jurisdiction fulfilling its imperative collective security objective.[2667]

Clearly, the attribution to the UN, or more generally an international organization, cannot have been decisive since the equivalent protection test precisely concerns the conditions for a transfer of competences to an international organization. Rather, it is the Court's deference to the UN (Charter) that seems to have been crucial, although I have argued above that it is not convincing (*supra*, Section C.5 of this chapter). There remains the question of the effect of the combination of extraterritoriality and the transfer of powers. While the Court does not address this, as it ignores the extraterritoriality issue altogether, this is an issue worth exploring a little further. It can be argued in this respect that where a State transfers competences to an international organization which that organization subsequently exercises over persons and/or territory that were not previously within the jurisdiction of the State having transferred these powers, the State concerned is not obliged to ensure equivalent protection by the

Airlines du 30 juin 2005: l'adhésion contrainte de l'Union à la Convention', 16 *R.T.D.H.* 2005, p. 852, who is of the view that the standard is not limited to EC law and covers all EU law but does not discuss the specificity of the CFSP with regard to judicial review.

2667 *Supra* notes 2317–2318 and the accompanying text, §151.

organization concerned.[2668] Obviously, the organization itself would be bound by its own human rights obligations (see *infra*, next Section of this chapter). Also, this is without prejudice to Member State responsibility for a Member State's own acts that are not attributed to the international organization, notably in respect of decision-making and implementing measures.[2669] It is submitted that this argument would have offered a more plausible basis for the Court's conclusions – which it seemed intent on drawing – in *Behrami* and *Saramati* than the ones on which it has in fact relied in this case.

Third, in the framework of the ESDP, the obligation for Member States to respect human rights recognized as part of EU law in the implementation of EU law means that Member States participating in an ESDP operation are bound to respect these human rights in any event.[2670]

F. EU OBLIGATIONS IN ESDP OPERATIONS

1. THE EU HAS PROPER OBLIGATIONS UNDER HUMAN RIGHTS LAW

In the sections above, the focus has been on the applicability of human rights with little regard to the specificity of international organizations. In this section, the conclusions of Chapters 6 and 7 on the international legal personality of the EU and the extent to which it is bound by international law will be applied to human rights in ESDP operations.

In this subsection, I will first briefly set out why the EU has proper obligations under human rights. In the following subsections, I will look into the sources and extent of these obligations.

2668 In this sense, H. Krieger, *supra* note 2284, pp. 683–684, on the basis of a combination of *Bankovic* and *Matthews* and *Waite and Kennedy*. However, she does seem to accept that where the ECHR would already apply in the territory concerned, e.g. on the basis of a peace agreement, this exemption would not apply.

2669 Compare Häussler, pp. 73–74 (seeing Member State responsibility for policy decisions and discretion in implementation), 144 (seeing Member State responsibility for decision-making, transfer of command and implementation based on national policy considerations when there is a discretion) and 153–154 (seeing organization responsibility for decisions of their organs and superior commanders as well as lower commanders when they merely apply decisions taken by them but Member State responsibility where lower commanders have discretion that is linked to their sending State's domestic law and policy).

2670 See *supra*, Chapter 7.F.2.i *in fine*. On judicial review in this context, see also *infra* note 2713 and the accompanying text.

That the EC has proper human rights obligations is no longer disputed. I have argued above that this is also the case for the EU, including in the conduct of its ESDP operations.[2671] Moreover, in Chapters 6.F and 8.G.1 above, I argued that ESDP operations have a status independent of the Participating States, most likely as part of the legal personality of the EU, and that EU bodies exercise command and control over the EU-led forces put at their disposal. This means that the EU exercises powers over armed forces that may be affected by human rights, if applicable. For instance, human rights, if applicable, will obviously have an impact on the rules of engagement and other directives that impose limits on detention.[2672] Therefore, in addition to any obligations that continue to rest on States providing armed forces to EU-led operations, the EU has its own international human rights obligations. The way in which these can be implemented is the same as for the LOAC.[2673]

As with regard to the LOAC, there is, however, a question proper to the applicability of human rights to international organizations, namely that of its territoriality, to the extent that this may limit the scope of application of human rights (see *supra*, Section B of this chapter). Three views seem possible: first, the territory of an international organization is equated with that of its Member States, as I have argued is the case under the LOAC;[2674] second, it is limited to the territory of its host State; and third, the notion is inapplicable and must be replaced by that of functional jurisdiction. The second view, while it may perhaps not be unsuited to the human rights of staff of international organizations in general, seems too limited. Indeed, with regard to the EC, there is no such limit. The rationale underlying the territoriality for States, namely that they are presumed to have complete jurisdiction over their territory, is clearly inapplicable for international organizations, which normally only have limited functional jurisdiction. Admittedly, they may exercise more or less all the powers of a State as interim administrators, e.g. in east Timor or Kosovo[2675] (although even then these powers may be split between different organizations, as in Kosovo), but this

---

2671 Chapter 7.F.2.i, note 1773 and the accompanying text.

2672 See on rules of engagement *supra*, Chapter 8.G.1, note 2218.

2673 See *supra*, Chapter 8.G.1. For some of these mechanisms, see J. Arloth & F. Seidensticker, *supra* note 2278, pp. 19–24 (standards of behaviour for mission personnel and pre-deployment training).

2674 See *supra*, Chapter 8.G.1.

2675 On the UN mission in Kosovo and human rights, see, e.g. M. Brand, 'Institution-Building and Human Rights Protection in Kosovo in the Light of UNMIK Legislation', 70 *Nordic J.I.L.* 2001, pp. 461–488; M. Brand, 'Effective Human Rights Protection when the UN "Becomes the State": Lessons from UNMIK', in N. White & D. Klaasen (eds.), *The UN, Human Rights and Post-conflict Situations*, Manchester, Manchester University Press, 2005, pp. 347–375 and J. Nilsson, 'UNMIK and the Ombudsperson Institution in Kosovo: Human Rights Protection in a United Nations "Surrogate State"', 22 *N.Q.H.R.* 2004, pp. 389–411.

is the exception. It is therefore suggested that for international organizations, from a human rights perspective territoriality is irrelevant and jurisdiction is the determining factor. In this case, this coincides with the applicability condition I have defended above for States.

2. THE SOURCES AND EXTENT OF THE EU'S HUMAN RIGHTS OBLIGATIONS

As in Chapter 8.G.2 above, I will treat, one by one, the sources of EU obligations identified in Chapter 7 as applied to human rights: treaties concluded by the EU, binding unilateral acts, the EU's constituent instruments and proper rules; other agreements between the EU Member States binding the EU; provisions of other international instruments and judicial decisions binding by virtue of any of the above sources; customary international law; general principles of international law; general principles of EC/EU law; *ius cogens* and (provisions of) treaties concluded by one or more of its Member States where the conditions for 'substitution' are met.[2676] Furthermore, I will briefly look at the position of forces provided by third States.

i. Treaties Concluded by the EU

So far, the EU is not a party to any human rights treaty.[2677] However, this may well change with the EU's envisaged accession to the ECHR under the Lisbon Treaty.[2678] If this accession were to come about, it raises the question whether the EU could notify a derogation with respect to an ESDP operation, which could

---

2676 Compare with regard to the EC/EU generally T. Ahmed & I. de Jesús Butler, *supra* note 2469, pp. 771–802 (the authors do not seem to distinguish between the EC and the EU). Compare also with regard to international organizations and human rights more generally the ILA's 2004 *Final Report on the Accountablity of International Organisations* (available online at www.ila-hq.org), p. 22: "*Human rights obligations, which are increasingly becoming an expression of the common constitutional traditions of States, can become binding upon IO-s in different ways: through the terms of their constituent instruments; as customary international law; or as general principles of law or if an IO is authorised to become a party to a human rights treaty. The consistent practice of IO-s points to a recognition of this. Moreover, certain human rights obligations may have attained the status of peremptory norms*".

2677 However, the European Commission has submitted a proposal that the *EC* should become a party to the Convention on the Rights of Persons with Disabilities (New York, 13 December 2006 (Annex to UNGA Res. 61/106; entered into force on 3 May 2008)), which permits the accession of regional integration organizations in its Article 44 (within the limits of their competence). See Proposal for a Council Decision concerning the conclusion, by the European Community, of the Optional Protocol to the United Nations Convention on the Rights of Persons with Disabilities, COM/2008/530 final, 28 August 2008.

2678 See *supra*, Chapter 7.G.3 *in fine*.

ensure a uniform position in this respect. This would depend on the terms of the accession and should not *a priori* be excluded.[2679]

In addition, there is the potential for the EU to be bound by human rights obligations contained in mission-specific agreements which it might conclude, especially in a SOFA or SOMA. However, the survey of agreements concluded so far has revealed that these agreements have not included a provision referring to respect for human rights except the Atalanta transfer agreements.[2680] It is submitted that this is regrettable. Whereas a lack of reference to the LOAC (see Chapter 8 above) may in most cases be explained by the nature of ESDP operations and these not being a party to an armed conflict nor occupying forces, there is no equally valid rationale for not mentioning human rights. Presumably, it has either simply been overlooked or the EU and/or the Member States are not yet ready to openly acknowledge the applicability of human rights in these operations. In light of the developments outlined above, that will be increasingly difficult to maintain. However, the lack of jurisdiction of the European Court of Justice in the area of the ESDP and the European Court of Human Rights' large exemption in respect of UN-mandated operations may mean that there may be no judicial forum in which this can be settled, except in domestic courts if the latter were to assert jurisdiction.

ii. Binding Unilateral Acts

There are no unilateral statements specifically on respect for human rights in ESDP operations that might bind the EU, except the EULEX Kosovo and Atalanta Joint Actions.[2681]

2679 Protocol 14 to the ECHR (Strasbourg, 13 May 2004, *E.T.S.* 194) merely adds a clause stipulating that "*The European Union may accede to this Convention*" (Article 17(1)). There is no reason why this should not include a derogation power. The Protocol No. 5 adopted under the Lisbon Treaty includes a clause stating that "*The agreement relating to the accession of the Union to the European Convention on the Protection of Human Rights and Fundamental Freedoms (hereinafter referred to as the 'European Convention') provided for in Article 6(2) of the Treaty on European Union shall make provision for preserving the specific characteristics of the Union and Union law, in particular with regard to: (a) the specific arrangements for the Union's possible participation in the control bodies of the European Convention* ...". Interestingly, the explanations to the EU's Charter of Fundamental Rights as amended in 2007 state that "*The Charter does not affect the possibilities* of Member States *to avail themselves of Article 15 ECHR, ..., when they take action in the areas of national defence in the event of war and of the maintenance of law and order, in accordance with their responsibilities recognised in Article 4(1) of the Treaty on European Union and in Articles 72 and 347 of the Treaty on the Functioning of the European Union*" (*O.J.* C 305, 14 December 2007, p. 33; emphasis added).

2680 See *supra*, Chapter 4.B.2 and especially Chapter 3.W.2.

2681 See *supra* Chapter 3.T.2 and 3.W.2. It may be recalled that there was the Joint Declaration by the European Parliament, the Council and the Commission of 5 April 1977 on respect for

There are a number of guidelines in relation to human rights and the CFSP or even ESDP, but they mostly concern how the EU should deal with respect for human rights by third parties and not with respect by the EU itself.[2682] Moreover, even where they do relate to the EU's and/or the Member States' own obligations,[2683] it is doubtful that they are intended to be legally and externally binding – the term guidelines is indicative in this respect.

There is also more generally the EU's Charter of Fundamental Rights, which was solemnly proclaimed by the European Parliament, the Council and the Commission in Nice on 7 December 2000.[2684] However, its legal nature was deliberately left open[2685] and has not yet been determined.[2686] It is therefore unlikely that it would qualify as a unilateral act legally binding the EU as a distinct source. It is made binding under the Lisbon Treaty by incorporation.[2687]

iii. *The EU's Constituent Instruments and Proper Rules*[2688]

In Chapter 7.F.2.i), it has been discussed how the ECJ has bound the EC to human rights via general principles of EC law and that this binding was

human rights by the EC (*O.J. C* 103, 27 April 1977, p. 1) but this is no longer relevant since the explicit language in Article 6 EU Treaty.

2682 See, e.g. the more general guidelines on the death penalty (1998), torture and other cruel, inhuman or degrading treatment (Doc. 7369/01, 3 April 2001), human rights dialogues with third countries (14469/01, 3 December 2001), children and armed conflict (Doc. 15634/03, 4 December 2003; which contains specific sections on ESDP operations) and human rights defenders (Doc. 10056/1/04 REV 1, 9 June 2004), all available at http://consilium.europa.eu/cms3_fo/showPage.asp?id=822&lang=EN&mode=g.

2683 See, e.g. the Draft guidelines on protection of civilians in EU-led crisis management operations (Doc. 14805/03, 14 November 2003) and various documents on the implementation of UNSC Res. 1325 in the context of the ESDP (listed in the Council's register). See also J. Arloth & F. Seidensticker, *supra* note 2278, pp. 16–19 and N. Ronzitti, *supra* note 2278, p. 179.

2684 Charter of Fundamental Rights of the European Union, *O.J. C* 364, 18 December 2000, p. 1.

2685 In §2 of the Presidency Conclusions of the 7–9 December Nice European Council, it is stated that "*the question of the Charter's force will be considered later*".

2686 See *supra*, Chapter 7.F.2.i, note 1784.

2687 Article 6(1) (renumbered 6(1)) EU Treaty Charter as it is amended by the Lisbon Treaty ("*The Union recognises the rights, freedoms and principles set out in the Charter of Fundamental Rights of 7 December 2000, as adapted at Strasbourg, on 12 December 2007, which shall have the same legal value as the Treaties*") *juncto* the adapted Charter (published in the *O.J. C* 305, 14 December 2007). But see the Protocol on the application of the Charter of Fundamental Rights of the [EU] to Poland and the [UK]. See generally A. Moriceau, 'Le Traité de Lisbonne et la Charte des droits fondamentaux', No. 519 *R.M.C.U.E.* 2007, pp. 361–364. Compare Article I-9 and Part II EU Constitution. On the latter, see generally L. Burgorgue-Larsen, A. Levade & F. Picod (eds.), *Traité établissant une Constitution pour l'Europe, Tome 2: Partie II: La Charte des droits fondamentaux de l'Union. Commentaire article par article*, Brussels, Bruylant, 2005.

2688 See also briefly N. Ronzitti, *supra* note 2278, pp. 171 and 180.

subsequently explicitly laid down in Article 6 EU Treaty[2689] (and included, subject to some modifications, in the Lisbon Treaty). I have also argued there that in respect of human rights, this reasoning may be extended to the EU.[2690]

Moreover, and as already mentioned in Chapter 8 (Section G.2.iii), the applicability of human rights in external relations, including the ESDP, is reinforced by Article 11(1) EU Treaty,[2691] which states that:

> The Union shall define and implement a common foreign and security policy covering all areas of foreign and security policy, the objectives of which shall be: – to safeguard the common values, fundamental interests, independence and integrity of the Union in conformity with the principles of the United Nations Charter; ... – to develop and consolidate democracy and the rule of law, and respect for human rights and fundamental freedoms.

There is, however, one key question that needs to be addressed, namely that of the extraterritorial scope of application. Essentially, the question is whether the rights derived from other sources, including the ECHR, keep the scope of application of those sources or are given a proper scope of application due to their transformation into general principles of EC/EU law. In addition to the submission above (subsection 1 of this section) that for international organizations territoriality is irrelevant when it comes to human rights, it is submitted that given that these rights only apply as general principles of EC/EU law, their scope of application follows that of EC/EU law. Consequently, in the case of the CFSP and ESDP, they apply extraterritorially to the extent of the EU's extraterritorial exercise of jurisdiction.[2692] To the extent that the ECHR or other human rights treaties also apply extraterritorially to any exercise of jurisdiction (see *supra*, Section B of this chapter), there is no difference. However, to the extent that such treaties are interpreted more narrowly, there may be differences.

2689 Article 6(2) EU Treaty reads: "*The Union shall respect fundamental rights, as guaranteed by the European Convention for the Protection of Human Rights and Fundamental Freedoms signed in Rome on 4 November 1950 and as they result from the constitutional traditions common to the Member States, as general principles of Community law*".

2690 See especially Chapter 7.F.2.i, note 1773 and the accompanying text.

2691 See also S. Bartelt, *supra* note 2278, pp. 163–164 and 181–182 (although the author regards it as a self-binding of the Member States since she rejects the EU's legal personality) and J. Arloth & F. Seidensticker, *supra* note 2278, p. 15.

2692 Compare A. Fischer-Lescano & T. Tohidipur, *supra* note 2227, pp. 1242–1250 (concluding in favour of extraterritorial application) and P. Torremans, 'Extraterritoriality in Human Rights', in N. Neuwahl & A. Rosas (eds.), *The European Union and Human Rights*, The Hague, Nijhoff, 1995, pp. 281–296 (who argues for some extraterritorial effect of human rights in the EU consistent with the extraterritoriality in other areas of EC/EU law).

The equivalent provision under the Lisbon Treaty, Article 10 A (renumbered 21) EU Treaty (compare Article III-292 EU Constitution), contains even stronger language in this respect. It reads:

> 1. The Union' action on the international scene shall be guided by the principles which have inspired its own creation, development and enlargement, and which it seeks to advance in the wider world: democracy, the rule of law, the universality and indivisibility of human rights and fundamental freedoms, respect for human dignity … and respect for the principles of the United Nations Charter and international law. …
>
> 2. The Union shall define and pursue common policies and actions, and shall work for a high degree of cooperation in all fields of international relations, in order to: (a) safeguard its values, …; (b) consolidate and support democracy, the rule of law, human rights and the principles of international law; …
>
> 3. The Union shall respect the principles and pursue the objectives set out in paragraphs 1 and 2 in the development and implementation of the different areas of the Union's external action covered by this Title and Part Five of the Treaty on the Functioning of the European Union, and of the external aspects of its other policies. The Union shall ensure consistency between the different areas of its external action and between these and its other policies.

As already noted in Chapter 8.G.2.iii, this goes further than Article 11 EU Treaty in that it not only sets out the aims to protect human rights as one of the fundamental values of the Union and the aim to develop and consolidate respect for human rights, but also imposes human rights as a guideline for the EU's external action and, especially relevant, imposes respect for human rights in the development and implementation of this external action.

I therefore submit that a significant body of human rights is part of EU law binding on the EU in the adoption and implementation of EU law, including decisions on the ESDP and the conduct of ESDP operations, to the extent that the EU exercises jurisdiction, both under the pre- and post-Lisbon EU Treaty.

In addition, on the political level – at least as long as it is not incorporated in the EU Treaty – one may add the Charter of Fundamental Rights (see *supra*, preceding subsection).[2693] As to its scope of application, the Charter's Article 52(3) states that "*In so far as this Charter contains rights which correspond to rights guaranteed by the [ECHR], the meaning and scope of those rights shall be the same as those laid down by the said Convention. This provision shall not*

[2693] See also F. Naert, *supra* note 2278, pp. 914–915.

prevent Union law providing more extensive protection". Depending on whether 'scope' is also intended to cover scope of application *ratione personae/loci*, these rights keep their original scope of application or get the scope of application of EC/EU law. Given the submission above (subsection 1 of this section) that for international organizations territoriality is irrelevant when it comes to human rights, it is submitted that the latter view is the better one.

Inasmuch as the EC and/or EU Treaties bind the EU to the UN Charter,[2694] including its human rights provisions,[2695] this would also constitute a source of obligation for the EU.[2696]

iv. Agreements between the EU Member States Binding the EU

To my knowledge, apart from the instruments cited in the preceding subsection, there have been no agreements between the Member States binding the EU to human rights so far.

v. Provisions of Other International Instruments and Judicial Decisions via the Above

The cases where such binding may exist all concern the EU's constituent instruments and proper rules discussed above in subsection iii of this section.

vi. Customary International Law

In light of the conclusion that customary international law is, in principle, binding on the EU in its external relations, this source undoubtedly has significant potential.[2697] However, given the greater uncertainty over the extent to which human rights are part of customary international law, this source is less important than it is with regard to the LOAC. Moreover, in light of the explicit and strong foundations that bind the EU to human rights law via general principles of EC/EU law, including the ECHR, it is unlikely to add much, except perhaps in that it undoubtedly binds the EU also externally vis-à-vis any third State or international organization (with legal personality).[2698]

2694 See *supra*, Chapter 7.G.4.

2695 See *supra*, Chapter 7.E.

2696 See T. Ahmed & I. de Jesús Butler, *supra* note 2469, p. 787.

2697 See also N. Tsagourias, *supra* note 2278, p. 119. Similarly, with regard to the UN, T. Irmscher, *supra* note 2508, pp 369–370 and M. Zwanenburg, *supra* note 2276, pp. 234–235. See also more generally Kolb, Poretto & Vité, pp. 253–260 and A. Clapham, *supra* note 2368, pp. 118–124.

2698 Compare T. Ahmed & I. de Jesús Butler, *supra* note 2469, pp. 778–781 (also arguing that the EU is bound by customary international human rights law) and 792–800 (seeing possible

As with the LOAC, the question arises whether there are any rules of customary international human rights law which the EU cannot comply with, or can only comply with subject to certain adaptations, because of its nature as an international organization. The main obstacle here would seem to be that the EU has only limited competences. Therefore it can only ensure respect for human rights to the extent that it exercises jurisdiction. As this is precisely the criterion for the applicability of human rights to international organizations put forward above (subsection 1 of this section), and, to a significant extent, also for States,[2699] this should not pose real problems.

Since the mandate and rules of engagement are adopted at the EU level, the EU clearly has the tools to impose standards of conduct that are compatible with human rights. Moreover, any powers it might lack, in particular as regards enforcement, may be accommodated by assuring the troop-contributing States take the necessary measures, as is the case under the LOAC.

vii. *General Principles of International Law*

Inasmuch as some human rights may be considered to be general principles of international law,[2700] they are also binding on the EU and would apply in ESDP operations.[2701] As with customary rules but even more so given the nature of principles, there seems very little room for arguments that the EU could not comply with such principles.

viii. *General Principles of EC/EU Law*

In Chapter 7.F.2.i, it has been discussed how the ECJ has bound the EU to human rights via general principles of EC law even before this was explicitly laid down in the EC or EU Treaty. I have also argued there that in respect of human rights, this reasoning may be extended to the EU. Thus a significant body of human rights forms part of general principles of EU law binding on the EU and its Member States in the implementation of EU law, including decisions on ESDP and ESDP operations.[2702] However, this obligation may not add much in light of the implications of Article 6 EU Treaty which has now subsumed this source of law. Moreover, it might be argued that the very nature of principles supports a

---

additional obligations compared to Article 6 EU Treaty, though mostly derived from the argument that the EU would also be bound by some Member State human rights treaties).

2699 See *supra*, Section B of this chapter.

2700 See, e.g. HÄUSSLER, p. 65 and the reference in note 203.

2701 Similarly, with regard to the UN, M. Zwanenburg, *supra* note 2276, pp. 235–236 and more generally HÄUSSLER, p. 65.

2702 In this sense also N. Tsagourias, *supra* note 2278, p. 119. See more generally HÄUSSLER, pp. 65 and 72.

broad interpretation of their scope of application to the detriment of the importance of territoriality.

ix. Ius Cogens

I can be brief about this category of obligations given that it is argued above that they are a quality attached to rules that are either customary international law or general principles of international law, both of which have already been discussed above. It may suffice to add that some core human rights are regarded as *ius cogens*,[2703] not subject to derogation by the Security Council[2704] and beyond any doubt binding on the EU. Furthermore, the nature of these rights arguably implies that they are not subject to a restrictive scope of application.

x. Member State Treaties through Substitution

In Chapter 7.G.3, it has been discussed how the ECJ has not accepted substitution in respect of the ECHR. Nor is this the case for any other human rights treaty, and it does not appear that this will change despite the ECJ's Court of First Instance's reasoning in *Kadi* and *Yusuf*.[2705]

xi. The Position of Forces Provided by Third States

In this respect there is no difference with the LOAC (see *supra*, Chapter 8,G.2.xi), except that the obligation to "*respect and ensure respect*" under the LOAC does not apply in the field of human rights.

G. CONCLUSIONS

In this Chapter, I have analyzed the applicability of human rights in ESDP operations. This is of key importance as I have concluded in Chapter 8 above that in many cases, the LOAC will not be applicable because the threshold of an

2703 For some case law holding specific human rights to be *ius cogens*, see, e.g. ICTY, *Prosecutor v. Furundzija*, ICTY-95-17/1, 10 December 1998, §§153–157 (the prohibition of torture) and ECJ (Court of First Instance), *Kadi*, §288 and *Yusuf*, §343, both *supra*, Chapter 7, note 1822 (regarding at least the core of the right of access to a court, as part of the right to a fair trial, as *ius cogens*). Which human rights are *ius cogens* is a matter of debate, but one other human right most often mentioned in this context is the prohibition of slavery; see, e.g. Brownlie, p. 515; Shaw, p. 117 and Malanczuk, p. 58. See also Kolb, Poretto & Vité , pp. 338–340 and A. Orakhelashvili, *supra* note 2469, pp. 64–66.

2704 See *supra*, Section C.5 of this chapter.

2705 Compare T. Ahmed & I. de Jesús Butler, *supra* note 2469, pp. 788–792, who argue in favour of a broader succession/substitution under international law, including for human rights treaties.

armed conflict has not been crossed or the EU-led forces are not actively engaged as a party to that conflict and are not occupying forces either. In such cases, human rights law is the most obvious alternative regime. Moreover, even if the LOAC does apply, this does not preclude that human rights may also apply.

A first relevant aspect, which remains much debated, is the question to what extent human rights apply extraterritorially. International jurisprudence supports a significant extent of extraterritorial applicability of human rights based on the notion of persons within the jurisdiction of a State but the precise scope of this applicability has yet to be clarified and may depend to some extent on the specific scope of application of the human rights treaty at issue. However, there seems to be a growing consensus that effective control over territory and effective control over persons (i.e. especially detention) constitute jurisdiction in this sense. Beyond this, including in combat situations and in other cases of the exercise of limited authority, the matter is not settled. However, I have argued that a gradual notion of jurisdiction triggering corresponding human rights obligations would be most in line with the multidimensional notion of jurisdiction in general international law and the case law seems to evolve in that sense.

Second, as the situation in most peace operations, especially in military ESDP operations, is far from normal peace time conditions, emergency clauses and derogations have been looked at. It is submitted that applying human rights in these circumstances is possible only when due account is taken of the possibility of derogating from certain human rights (and that derogations may apply extraterritorially in parallel with the scope of application of human rights), of the impact of overriding UN Security Council Resolutions (except in relation to *ius cogens*) and of the possible concurrent applicability of the LOAC, which may be more suitable as *lex specialis*, although this has to be determined on a case-by-case basis in respect of each individual right and situation.[2706]

Under these conditions, the EU and its Member States should have nothing to fear from the application of human rights in ESDP operations.[2707] I therefore subscribe to the view expressed by Watkin that: "*The long-term solution to this*

2706 Similarly, with regard to the fight against international terrorism, C. Warbrick, *supra* note 2394, pp. 989–993 and especially the abstract at p. 989 (insisting on the applicability of human rights but accepting that they may have to be modified *in extremis*).

2707 Similarly H. Krieger, *supra* note 2284, pp. 697–698. Compare C. Warbrick, *supra* note 2394, p. 999, praising the ECtHR's achievement to extensively review compliance with human rights (though with regard to peace operations it would seem that the Court has rather tried very hard to avoid having to exercise any review at all) but at the same time be sufficiently flexible to keep States within the ECHR and limit their recourse to derogations.

issue may not be to "bar the door" to human rights principles and their advocates but, rather, to ensure that human rights accountability mechanisms take into consideration both the nature of warfare and the unique aspects of international humanitarian law".[2708] This is also supported by the recognition of the applicability of human rights in peace operations in the 1994 UN Convention on the Safety of United Nations and Associated Personnel and in UN Security Council Resolution 1327.[2709]

Moreover, in respect of human rights, the EU is in a unique position by virtue of its strong commitment to human rights and its legally binding obligations to respect human rights in the exercise of its jurisdiction, especially under Article 6 EU Treaty and as general principles of EU law and in the future possibly its accession to the ECHR. In addition, like other international organizations, it is bound by human rights that are part of customary international law, general principles of international law and *ius cogens*. In contrast, the EU is not bound by its Member States' human rights treaty obligations. Neither has the EU entered into binding treaty obligations (including in SOFA/SOMAs) nor has it issued unilateral statements or acts binding it to human rights in ESDP operations, except in two cases. Also, the extraterritoriality debate is less relevant to international organizations given the functional nature of their jurisdiction.

As regards Member State responsibility, little needs to be added to the conclusions reached in Chapter 7, especially since these were based to a significant extent on human rights jurisprudence. Nevertheless, three points may be made. First, given the lack of jurisdiction of the ECJ in the area of the CFSP and the ESDP, it is submitted that the EU does not offer equivalent protection in these areas. Second, it can be argued that where a State transfers competences to an international organization which that organization subsequently exercises over persons and/or territory that were not previously within the jurisdiction of the State having transferred these powers, the State concerned is not obliged to ensure equivalent protection by the organization concerned. However, this is without prejudice to the organization's own human rights obligations and to Member State responsibility for a Member State's own acts that are not attributed to the international organization, notably in respect of decision-making and implementing measures. Third, in the framework of the ESDP, the obligation for Member States to respect human rights recognized as part of EU law in the implementation of EU law means that Member States participating in an ESDP operation are bound to respect these human rights in any event.

2708 K. Watkin, *supra* note 2486, p. 24.

2709 See *supra* notes 2279–2280 and the accompanying text.

In addition to these legal considerations, as a matter of policy, it is difficult to see how the EU could not accept that it is bound by human rights in peace operations, which usually at least in part aim at promoting the rule of law and human rights[2710] as part of the EU's foreign policy objectives, without losing its credibility.[2711] Accountability for individual violations that occur despite efforts to ensure respect for human rights should not be rejected. As a British court stated with regard to a shooting by some UK KFOR forces:

> The British Army can justifiably be proud of the operation it carried out in Kosovo.... It displayed professionalism and discipline of the highest quality. The soldiers on the ground had to carry out difficult and highly responsible tasks which required a combination of courage and sensitivity. In general, they discharged their duties with considerable credit. But soldiers are human; from time to time mistakes are inevitable, and even the most rigorous discipline will crack. In this case the fall from the Army's usual high standards led to tragic consequences for the victims and their families. The Queen's uniform is not a licence to commit wrongdoing, and it has never been suggested that it should be. The Army should be held accountable for such shortcomings, even where the victims are from the very community which has benefited so much from the Army's assistance. A proper system of justice requires no less.[2712]

It is submitted that a clear recognition of the applicability of human rights and their scope of application in peace operations is highly desirable. However, absent coordinated attempts to this effect, the law is likely to be clarified only gradually and essentially on the basis of jurisprudence. It is therefore all the more regrettable that the European Court of Human Rights' stance in *Saramati* and *Behrami* has probably closed the door to Strasbourg for large categories of cases.

2710 See more generally Kwa Hong Ip, 'PSOs: Establishing the Rule of Law through Security and Law Enforcement Operations', in R. Arnold & G.-J. Knoops (eds.), *supra* note 2284, pp. 3–34 and N. Quénivet, 'Promoting and Abiding by the Rule of Law: UN Involvement in Post-conflict Justice', in *id.*, pp. 35–66.

2711 In this sense (though not limited to the EU), H. Krieger, *supra* note 2284, p. 698. See also D. de Bijl, *supra* note 2585, pp. 109–110. Compare S. Chesterman, *You, the People: The United Nations, Transitional Administration, and State-Building*, Oxford, Oxford University Press, 2004, pp. 145–153, who argues with regard to transitional administration that international administrations do not accept the very rules they impose, points to the balancing act between security and human rights and concludes that the inconsistency between means and ends in part stems from a reluctance to accept that their legitimacy derives ultimately from military occupation and not consent. I would rather ague that such considerations may justify derogations from normal peacetime rules but not derogations that fall short of basic human rights altogether. With regard to international administrations, see also L. Cameron, 'Human Rights Accountability of International Civil Administrations to the People Subject to Administration', 1 *Human Rights & International Legal Discourse* 2007, pp. 267–300 and de Wet, pp. 311–337, especially pp. 319–322.

2712 *Bici and Bici v. Ministry of Defence*, *supra* note 2585, §113.

It remains to be seen whether the Court will not limit the scope of this decision (as it did with *Bankovic*) or even overturn it in light of the harsh criticism of this decision. In contrast, the Human Rights Committee seems more willing to supervise respect for human rights in peace operations but it has less authority. Given this situation, national courts are bound to play an important role. Moreover, it may be noted that the Lisbon Treaty inserts an Article 9 F (renumbered 19(1)) into the EU Treaty stipulating that "*Member States shall provide remedies sufficient to ensure effective legal protection in the fields covered by Union law*".[2713] Several British cases illustrate that this approach may be a viable option to some extent, although it risks leading to divergent case law. However, when responsibility lies with international organizations, as I have argued is the case to a significant extent for the EU in ESDP operations, this option may not be available due to these organizations' immunities before domestic courts. Thus, there is a need for adequate internal or international supervision, which could partially be achieved through the EU's envisaged accession to the ECHR, at least to the extent that the ECtHR would not attribute conduct in ESDP operations to the UN when there is a UN mandate, in order to avoid a serious gap in protection.[2714]

That being said, my experience with ESDP operations is that human rights are taken into account to a significant extent in both generic and mission specific documents, including the Operation Plan and the Rules of Engagement,[2715] even though the precise extent of the applicability of human rights as a matter of law

---

2713 Compare T. Corthaut, 'An Effective Remedy for All?: Paradoxes and Controversies in Respect of Judicial Protection in the Field of the CFSP under the European Constitution', 12 *Tilburg Foreign Law Review* 2004, pp. 116–117 with regard to the corresponding provision under the EU Constitution (Article I-29(1), subparagraph 2). See also under current EU law, ECJ, Case C-354/04, *Gestoras Pro Amnistía and Others v Council of the European Union*, 27 February 2007, §§49–57, especially §51 ("*the institutions are subject to review of the conformity of their acts with the treaties and the general principles of law, just like the Member States when they implement the law of the Union*") and 56 ("*it is for the Member States and, in particular, their courts and tribunals, to interpret and apply national procedural rules governing the exercise of rights of action in a way that enables natural and legal persons to challenge before the courts the lawfulness of any decision or other national measure relating to the drawing up of an act of the European Union or to its application to them and to seek compensation for any loss suffered*"). For a recent and more extensive appraisal of the role of Member States in ensuring judicial review in the EU, see K. Lenaerts, 'The Rule of Law and the Coherence of the Judicial System of the European Union', 44 *C.M.L. Rev.* 2007, pp. 1625–1659, who also specifically addresses this provision in the Lisbon Treaty at pp. 1629–1630.

2714 Compare A. Breitegger, 'Sacrificing the Effectiveness of the European Convention on Human Rights on the Altar of the Effective Functioning of Peace Support Operations: A Critique of Behrami & Saramati and Al Jedda', 11 *International Community Law Review* 2009, pp. 181–183.

2715 For an overview of relevant documents in the public domain, see General Secretariat of the Council of the EU, *Compilation of Relevant Documents: Mainstreaming Human Rights and Gender into European Security and Defence Policy, supra* note 2278.

is often left open. It is, however, unfortunate that the documents that could illustrate this are classified. I can therefore only state that this is my sincere appraisal of the EU's practice.

Finally, it cannot be stressed enough that human rights training for the armed forces is crucial.[2716] My experience in this regard confirms that while the LOAC is still generally known better by the armed forces than human rights, these forces are increasingly being trained in human rights too.

2716 L. Moir, *supra* note 2388, p. 195, submits that armed forces are quite familiar with the LOAC but much less with human rights.

SUMMARY, GENERAL CONCLUSIONS, FINAL REFLECTIONS AND RECOMMENDATIONS

In *Chapter 1*, I briefly traced the development of the ESDP, in which the WEU has played an important role, including as a link between the EU and NATO in the period between the establishment of the EU with its nascent CFSP and the formal launching of the ESDP at the 1999 Cologne and Helsinki European Councils. However, since the EU has taken over the WEU's crisis management functions, the WEU's remaining role has been marginal and is essentially limited to that of a secretariat overseeing a collective self-defence clause that is not implemented within the WEU anyway (see also Chapter 4). As for the EU, following this launch of the ESDP, which was made possible by the Amsterdam Treaty, it very quickly developed the institutional setup, financing mechanism and the necessary doctrine and strategy (including the European Security Strategy) and the Member States have committed the required headquarters and forces, as well as civilian capabilities, to declare the ESDP operational. This culminated in the launch of the first ESDP operations in 2003.

In *Chapter 2*, I gave an overview of the main features and present status of the ESDP. This included the following basic principles:

- the ESDP includes the progressive framing of a common defence policy, which *includes* humanitarian and rescue tasks, peacekeeping tasks and tasks of combat forces in crisis management, including peacemaking and which might lead to a common defence if the European Council so decides; it essentially includes military and civilian crisis management and has an outward focus;
- the EU may conduct ESDP operations either autonomously or with recourse to NATO assets, the obligations in the framework of, and the role of, NATO are not affected, there will be no unnecessary duplication and the EU will only act when NATO as a whole is not engaged, although the latter must be nuanced and increasingly parallel and complementary EU and NATO operations take place in the same theatres of operations (see Chapters 3–4);
- the ESDP shall respect the principles of the United Nations Charter and the primary role of the UN Security Council (see also Chapter 7);
- the ESDP is part of the CFSP but is subject to some specific rules.

The key EU institutions in the ESDP are the Council, the Political and Security Committee, the EU Military Committee, the EU Military Staff, the Committee for Civilian Aspects of Crisis Management, the Civilian Planning and Conduct Capability and the chain of command in operations. The ESDP is also supported by the EU Satellite Centre, EU Institute for Security Studies, the European Defence Agency and the European Security and Defence College.

Furthermore, this chapter addressed the crucial cooperation with NATO, currently held hostage to the Turkish-Cypriot dispute which has started to also affect operational cooperation, as well as cooperation with other actors, including third States which participate in many ESDP operations (and include States from outside Europe), the UN (with which an important partnership is being further developed), the OSCE and the AU (which receives significant support from the EU, including for AU operations).

It also briefly covered capabilities (both civilian and military), the European Defence Agency and defence industry and procurement, financing and the status of forces.

In *Chapter 3*, I first offered a short introduction to and overview of the legal framework for ESDP operations and then discussed in some detail the EU's ESDP operations launched up to 31 August 2009 more or less in chronological order, namely EUPM (BiH), CONCORDIA (FYROM), ARTEMIS (DRC), PROXIMA (FYROM), EUJUST THEMIS (Georgia), ALTHEA (BiH), EUPOL KINSHASA (DRC), EUSEC DRC (DRC), EUJUST LEX (Iraq), EU Support AMIS II (Sudan); EU AMM (Indonesia), COPPS (Palestinian Territories), EUPAT (FYROM), EU BAM Rafah (Palestinian Territories); EUFOR DR Congo (DRC); EUPOL Afghanistan; EUPOL RD Congo; EUFOR Tchad/RCA, EULEX Kosovo; EU SSR Guinea-Bissau; EUMM Georgia and EU NAVCO – EUNAVFOR Somalia/Atlanta. In principle, each time, in addition to a general description, the focus is on the mandate, legal status and applicable law and the participation of third States, if applicable, and an attempt was made to point to both particular and recurrent features. I have submitted that this overview shows that the ESDP works in practice and is developing rapidly.

Chapter 4 is the first chapter which is predominantly analytical rather than descriptive and draws some conclusions, including from the two preceding chapters. It is divided into two sections: the first examining the scope of the ESDP and the second dealing with the legal status of and applicable law in ESDP operations.

With regard to the scope of the ESDP, I successively discussed the scope of the ESDP under the text of the present EU Treaty, its scope in practice (i.e. the ESDP operations), the scope of the CSDP under the Lisbon Treaty, the integration of the WEU, the issue of solidarity, neutrality and the way towards a common defence and the international legal basis for ESDP operations.

I have concluded that the ESDP as it stands is operational, as manifested through its rapidly increasing number and variety of operations, which constitute part of the progressive framing of a common defence policy within the CFSP. However, the ESDP would probably better be described as a common security policy with a civilian and military component as it presently excludes a common defence, thereby remaining compatible with the neutral status of some of its Member States. The ESDP does include at least peacekeeping with peace enforcement elements and in my view also pure peace enforcement, as well as a broad range of other consensual tasks. I have argued that when the Lisbon Treaty enters into force, its mutual assistance clause will also take over the WEU's sole remaining function and the WEU should be abolished (the role of its Parliamentary Assembly can just as well be performed by the European Parliament and by Conferences involving national Parliaments' relevant Committees or their chairpersons).

Under the Lisbon Treaty, the key innovations are the solidarity clause – providing for a common reaction to terrorist attacks – and a mutual defence clause, albeit one that would exempt the neutral Member States and that would not yet constitute a common defence, as well as the possibility for some Member States to accept more far-reaching commitments via permanent structured cooperation. There are also various less fundamental changes (that in part codify existing practice), e.g. the possibility of entrusting the execution of an operation to a group of Member States, the commitment to improve capabilities, the role of the EDA and the possibility of enhanced cooperation on military and defence matters.

The international legal basis for ESDP operations is to some extent an independent topic, which has not raised problems so far given that there has always been host State consent or a UN Security Council mandate (although there was some controversy with regard to the Kosovo mission). Nevertheless, and especially since I concluded that the scope of the ESDP includes peace enforcement, the question may one day arise whether there are other legal bases. In this respect I have argued that the following elements are relevant. First, the scope of international customary law on the use of force, as this is binding on the EU (see Chapter 7). Second, the question to what extent the EU is bound to the

UN Charter rules on the use of force (in respect of which a Declaration annexed to the Lisbon Treaty and stating that the *EU* is bound by the *provisions* of the UN Charter may have binding effect). Third, the question whether the EU is a regional agency under Chapter VIII of the UN Charter and the implications thereof, including in relation to treaty-based intervention rights – however, for the EU with an outward looking ESDP, this is of little relevance and the Chapter VIII status does not seem to entail any significant consequences. Fourth, the issue of consent to intervention in cases of civil war or serious unrest in the State in which the intervention takes place (in respect of this, I have argued that the EU can arguably rely on host government consent as long as there is an established government that is internationally recognized, even in cases of civil war, unless there is a conflict with the right to self-determination).

As to the legal status of and applicable law in ESDP operations, the SOFA/SOMAs address the usual issues such as privileges and immunities, albeit with some peculiarities, especially in early cases, claims, and respect for local law (after initial omissions in this respect). However, except for a few references to the LOAC in SOFAs concluded by other organizations and extended to EU missions (and the recent provisions on respect for human rights in the EULEX Kosovo and Atalanta Joint Actions[2717]), there are no references to the LOAC or to human rights. I have therefore analyzed the applicability of these two bodies of international law in Part III.

In *Chapter 5* the legal status of international organizations was examined. I first defined the following key concepts as follows:

- international organizations: "*forms of international cooperation founded on an international instrument creating a new entity, usually a legal person, having at least one organ with a will of its own and not established under the domestic law of a State*";
- a subject of international law: "*an entity possessing rights and/or duties directly under international law*";
- international legal personality: "*the ability to possess rights and duties directly under international law and to exercise proper powers on the international plane and/or enter into international legal relation*".

I then argued briefly that virtually all international organizations have at least some rights and duties under international law with essentially two kinds of exceptions: those established on the basis of non-legal international commitments and those who only act on behalf of the Member States and do not possess any

[2717] See above, Chapter 3, respectively Sections T.2 and W.2.

proper rights and duties. I have looked at the former in respect of the OSCE and have concluded that despite claims to the contrary, the OSCE has international legal personality, especially because of its treaty-making power as exercised in practice.

Next, I illustrated that it is no longer contested that international organizations may possess international legal personality and that this personality may be granted implicitly. In contrast, there is still debate over the elements and consequences of international legal personality. I have argued in this respect that presumptive personality may be the most accurate view subject to the possibility of rebuttal except where Member States enable an organization to perform certain acts that necessarily imply international legal personality. Nevertheless, in that case the expressed denial should be taken into account when considering the legal capacities of an international organization.

As to the *indicia* of international legal personality of international organizations, it is submitted that two capacities stand out and are each sufficient: the power to take legally binding decisions and treaty-making capacity. Both are examined in relation to the EU in Chapter 6. In this chapter, the treaty-making capacity was analyzed with respect to NATO (which has international legal personality and concludes international treaties) and the Eurocorps (which does not seem to conclude international agreements in its own name).

As to the consequences of the international legal personality of international organizations, I submit that a number of legal capacities are inherent, in particular the right to bring an international claim, international responsibility and the right to conduct international relations. The treaty-making capacity is probably better described as presumptive and the better view is that privileges and immunities are customary and proper to the international legal personality of international organizations. Inherent capacities may be limited by the Member States but only to some extent vis-à-vis third parties.

Furthermore, I argued that the international legal personality of international organizations is objective in the sense that the *existence* of an organization with such personality is opposable to all and the rights and obligations resulting from it must be respected by other international legal persons. In contrast, rights and obligations resulting from the specific constituent instrument are not so opposable without recognition.

In *Chapter 6*, I examined the legal status of the EU. I argued that from its establishment, the EU has been an international organization and that it has rights and duties itself under international law, has the power to adopt binding decisions and has treaty-making capacity. A clear recognition of its privileges and immunities has not yet occurred but this has only been possible because of the single institutional framework granting the EU's organs privileges and immunities as *EC* organs, even if this is inaccurate in some cases. I also submitted that the establishment of EU agencies with a distinct legal personality by the EU confirms that the EU itself has legal personality. As to the relationship between the EU and the EC and between the EU and the agencies, I argued that it is the EU as an overarching entity which has international legal personality and not a 'CFSP EU'. This construction does not affect the EC's distinct legal personality and resembles in some respects the situation of the UN family. I also concluded that ESDP operations have a legal status, probably as a kind of *de facto* organs of the EU or alternatively an independent legal status. On the basis of these findings, I concluded that the EU is a subject of international law with international legal personality, despite any doubts that may still be uttered by some. In any event, with the entry into force of the Lisbon Treaty, the debate will be settled and the EU's legal personality will be explicitly recognized and will clearly include *international* legal personality.

Pursuant to the conclusions reached in Chapter 5, this means that the EU's legal personality is opposable to all States and international organizations and that the EU possesses a right to bring international claims (e.g. in ESDP operations), may be held internationally responsible (e.g. for breaching its treaty obligations) and may maintain international relations. Its treaty-making capacity is now beyond doubt. In respect of its privileges and immunities it arguably would be entitled to customary privileges and immunities if the present solution via the EC organs were to pose a problem.

The main conclusion of *Chapter 7* is that international organizations are bound by international law to the extent that it is relevant to their functioning and activities if they have international legal personality. The EU is a subject of international law and has international legal personality and is therefore also bound by international law in this manner. However, some rules of international law may apply only partially or in a modified manner. The sources of the legal obligations of international organizations are many and are varied and include *inter alia*:

- their constitutive instruments and related acts;
- other elements of their internal law, including general principles of law that are part thereof and relevant decisions and other unilateral acts of their competent organs that (intend to) create legal commitments;

- treaties which they conclude;
- customary international law;
- general principles of law recognized in international law;
- only exceptionally Member State treaties.

In addition, I have argued that there are three bases for the responsibility of Member States for their conduct in the framework of international organizations (leaving aside complicity). First, by virtue of establishing an international organization, a Member State incurs international responsibility for an act committed by an international organization that, if committed by that State, would have constituted a breach of an international obligation of that Member State, except for 'common interest regimes' in respect of which the Member State has provided for equivalent protection, with the caveat that where despite such equivalent protection there is a manifest violation that outweighs the interests of international cooperation, the Member State will remain responsible. Second, a Member State engages its international responsibility by voting in relation to a decision when the mere vote itself amounts to a violation of an international obligation of that State. Third, a Member State is internationally responsible for implementing a decision that violates its international obligations except where it had provided for equivalent protection in relation to a 'common interest regime' and has no discretion to implement the decision in conformity with its obligations and only to the extent that the violation of its obligations is proportionate to the importance of international cooperation.

In the introduction to *Part III*, I illustrated that the law applicable to ESDP operations is a complex mixture of domestic law (of the sending States and of the host State), EU law and international law.

In *Chapter 8*, I reached the following conclusions with regard to the LOAC.

First, specific questions proper to this body of law, including its cope of application and the nature/qualification of armed conflicts (especially the international v. non-international distinction), are equally relevant to ESDP operations and entail that the LOAC will only apply if EU-led forces become actively engaged in an armed conflict or occupy a third State's territory without its consent, which will usually not be the case.

Second, if this occurs and the LOAC applies, customary international law is of particular significance and general principles of EU law and the EU Treaty arguably also encompass some LOAC obligations that bind the EU.

Third, it is submitted that the nature of command and control transferred to the EU means that the EU itself will be primarily responsible (though this is an area of law that is far from settled) but participating Member States also continue to have obligations, including by virtue of the specific LOAC obligation to respect and ensure respect for certain LOAC rules in all circumstances.

In *Chapter 9*, I analyzed the applicability of human rights in ESDP operations. This is of key importance as I concluded in Chapter 8 that in many cases, the LOAC will not be applicable because the threshold of an armed conflict has not been crossed or the EU-led forces are not actively engaged as a party to a conflict. In such case, human rights law is the most obvious alternative regime. Moreover, even if the LOAC does apply, this does not necessarily mean that human rights do not apply as well. In this respect, I came to the following conclusions with regard to human rights.

First, human rights apply to some extent extraterritorially and may apply to peace operations. It is submitted that this is the case to the extent that these operations exercise jurisdiction over persons or territory, however partial, and that for international organizations territoriality if less relevant in any event given their functional nature.

Second, with the exception of some rights, human rights may be derogated from in time of war or certain emergencies. This possibility arguably also applies extraterritorially in peace operations if the conditions are met. Furthermore, the UN Security Council may derogate from a number of human rights.

Third, the relationship between human rights and the LOAC is primarily regulated by the *lex specialis* principle. However, it is submitted that this principle can only be applied on a case-by-case basis so that no general rules can be formulated, neither on the basis of the rights at stake nor on that of the situation or its legal qualification.

Fourth, it is well established that the EC is bound by a significant body of human rights law via Article 6 EU Treaty and general principles of EC law and it is submitted that this can be extended to the EU, including with regard to the ESDP.

Fifth, customary international human rights law also binds the EU but its scope is not settled.

Sixth, accession by the EU to the ECHR would also entail relevant human rights obligations for the EU, although the ECtHR's case law may limit the applicability in ESDP operations, especially in operations under a mandate based on Chapter VII of the UN Charter.

Seventh, with regard to the responsibilities of the EU and the Member States, the same applies as for the LOAC, except that the participating Member States' obligations are less extensive than under the LOAC and appear to be different under the ECHR and ICCPR, at least as interpreted by their supervisory bodies. However, this is mitigated by the duty to respect human rights that are part of EU law when Member States implement EU law, including when they conduct ESDP operations. Furthermore, I argued that due to the lack of judicial supervision over the CFSP and ESDP at EU level, the ECtHR's equivalent protection rule does not apply with regard to the ESDP. However under the Lisbon Treaty m*ember States shall have to "provide remedies sufficient to ensure effective legal protection in the fields covered by Union law*" (renumbered Article 19(1)) and this would seem to cover the ESDP.

By way of *general conclusions*, it is worth stressing six points.

First, the response to the first main research question, namely to what extent and how are international organizations in general and the EU in particular bound by international law, is that international organizations with international legal personality are indeed subject to international law to a considerable extent by virtue of this legal personality and through a variety of sources, some of which are applicable to all international organizations and some of which are specific to each organization (see the conclusions of Chapter 7 for more details).

Second, on the basis of the EU's international legal personality, it has distinct rights and obligations under international law, including in the field of the LOAC and human rights. These obligations result from various sources, which include primarily Article 6 EU Treaty, general principles of EU law and customary international law and in the future perhaps accession to the ECHR. Of these sources, customary international law is particularly relevant with respect to the LOAC and the other sources with regard to human rights, although there are overlaps between them and they mutually reinforce each other. While international law may require adaptation in order to be applied to/by international organizations, with respect to the LOAC and human rights, few adaptations seem necessary and it is submitted that there is a presumption that both regimes apply fully and that the onus is on the EU to prove that certain rules may only apply subject to changes or may not apply at all. Moreover, with regard to human rights it is submitted that the territoriality debate is less relevant to international organizations to the benefit of the (functional) jurisdictional element.

Third, the response to the second main research question, namely what international law is applicable to the conduct of ESDP operations, in particular what rules, if any, of the law of armed conflict and of international human rights law, is a complex mix of EU and international law, including in some cases human rights and the LOAC. Both of the latter apply to an ESDP operation if this operation falls within the scope of application that is proper to these two regimes, i.e. respectively participation in an armed conflict or occupying territory without consent on the one hand and exercising jurisdiction over persons or territory, even when only to a limited extent, on the other hand (see the conclusions of Chapters 8 and 9 for more details).

Fourth, as to human rights, the specific circumstances in which ESDP operations are conducted must be taken into account. This may result in limitations or derogations by virtue of an emergency situation, the impact of a UN Security Council resolution and the applicability of the LOAC, which may be the *lex specialis* in some respects (though not necessarily in all respects), as well as, to some extent, the regional nature of (the specific scope of) some human rights rules. If these elements are duly taken into account, human rights can be applied in ESDP operations without affecting the ability to carry out the mandate and mission.

Fifth, by virtue of its command and control over ESDP operations, the EU is in principle the main entity responsible for any conduct of ESDP operations. However, the respective responsibilities are not yet well settled in international law and Participating/Member States are also responsible to some extent for their own conduct in the framework of these operations. In addition, the responsibility of Member States is reinforced by the LOAC obligation *to respect and ensure respect* for their LOAC obligations on the one hand and by the obligation under EU law to respect human rights that are part of the general principles of EU law in the implementation of ESDP operations on the other hand. Since both the EU and the Participating/Member States thus have LOAC and human rights obligations in ESDP operations, and since these obligations are largely similar, there should be no significant gaps in applicable LOAC and human rights.

Sixth, while the extent to which the EU and the Member States have recognized these obligations is difficult to establish given the classified nature of key documents relevant to these issues, it appears that there has been limited recognition of the EU's own obligations, as opposed to those of the Member States. However, it is difficult to assess to what extent this is the result of the lingering resistance to the EU's legal personality or of Member States' and the EU's views on the question of attribution and responsibility. Moreover, it seems that there is some reluctance to recognize the *de iure* applicability of human rights. In contrast, the applicability of the LOAC, within its scope of application, does not seem to be seriously contested.

On this basis, I make the following four *recommendations*:

First, following the entry into force of the Lisbon Treaty, Member States and the EU should fully recognize the EU's international legal personality and accept that this entails distinct rights and obligations of the EU, including in the area of the ESDP and under the LOAC and human rights.

Second, Member States and the EU should recognize that human rights apply to the extent that they exercise jurisdiction – however limited – over territory and/or persons in ESDP operations, albeit subject to the limits set out above. This applicability is based on legal considerations and is reinforced by a crucial policy argument: how could the EU not accept that it is bound by human rights in peace operations, which usually in part aim at promoting the rule of law and human rights as part of the EU's foreign policy objectives, without losing its credibility? This recognition should be reflected in SOFA/SOMAs and other legal instruments for ESDP operations to publicly confirm the EU's commitment to human rights. Moreover, this is the key point on which the EU can and should set an example and can help shape international law in this area.[2718] The references to human rights in the Joint Actions on EULEX Kosovo and Atalanta are therefore welcome precedents.[2719] Similarly, the EU's accession to the ECHR, as envisaged by the Lisbon Treaty, would constitute a milestone precedent[2720] and would set an example that could open the way for other international organizations to also accede to treaties on human rights – and why not also LOAC treaties.

Third, SOFAs and other legal instruments for EU-led military operations that might become engaged in an armed conflict should include a clause requiring compliance with the LOAC inasmuch as it is applicable.

Fourth, States and international organizations should undertake efforts to clarify how they divide or share responsibility in peace operations, including in the

2718 On the EC/EU contribution to international law generally, see F. Hoffmeister, 'The Contribution of EU Practice to International Law', in M. Cremona (ed.), *Developments in EU External Relations Law. Vol. XVII/1 Collected Courses of the Academy of European Law*, Oxford, Oxford University Press, 2008, pp. 37–127.

2719 See above, Chapter 3, respectively Sections T.2 and W.2.

2720 It may in fact be preceded by the *EC*'s accession to the Convention on the Rights of Persons with Disabilities, see *supra* note 2677.

framework of the ILC's ongoing work on the responsibility of international organizations.

On a final note, I wish to stress again that my experience with ESDP operations is that human rights and the LOAC are very much taken into account. However, a clear and public position on this subject would enhance the EU's credibility and contribute to the reaffirmation and development of the LOAC and human rights and is therefore desirable, especially at a time when both bodies of law are being challenged.

REFERENCES, CITATIONS AND TABLE OF CASES

1. SOME REMARKS ON REFERENCES AND CITATIONS

In respect of references and citations, I have omitted the place of publication in a number of instances where materials are readily available on the internet. While the internet publications are not normally authentic, I have no knowledge of problems in this respect and trust that for most readers, the online publication will be more readily accessible than a publication in the official records. In order not to have to include the internet address every time, I will here indicate where certain categories of decisions and instruments may be accessed. Some of them, especially in the UN and EU, are also available in other languages than English.

UN Security Council Resolutions (by year and number):
www.un.org/documents/scres.htm
UN General Assembly Resolutions (by session, year and number):
www.un.org/documents/resga.htm
UN Documents by organ, category and date:
www.un.org/en/documents
UN Documents by document number (searchable):
http://documents.un.org
U.N.T.S.:
http://treaties.un.org/
ICJ judgements and advisory opinions:
www.icj-cij.org (go to 'cases')
ICC situations and cases:
www.icc-cpi.int/Menus/ICC/Situations+and+Cases/
ICTY cases:
www.icty.org/action/cases/4
ILC (most ILC documents, including all annual reports and the Y.I.L.C.):
www.un.org/law/ilc/
http://untreaty.un.org/ilc/research.htm
ILO Administrative Tribunal (including decisions):
www.ilo.org/public/english/tribunal/
ECtHR case-law (searchable, click on 'case-law' or 'jurisprudence' and then on 'HUDOC'):
www.echr.coe.int/echr
(C.)E.T.S.:
http://conventions.coe.int

Most EU legislation (including EC/EU Treaties, case-law, treaties concluded by the EC and legislation in force):
http://eur-lex.europa.eu
EC/EU Official Journal (by date and issue as of 1998):
http://eur-lex.europa.eu/JOIndex.do?ihmlang=en
ECJ case-law (including by case number and searchable):
http://curia.europa.eu
EU Council documents (unless indicated otherwise, all documents cited are public):
http://register.consilium.europa.eu
International agreements concluded by the EC/EU (Council website):[2721]
www.consilium.europa.eu/showPage.aspx?id=252&lang=EN
North Atlantic Council Communiqués (Summit & Ministerial Meetings by year):
www.nato.int/docu/comm.htm
Inter-American Commission for Human Rights (including reports and cases):
www.cidh.oas.org/DefaultE.htm
Inter-American Court of Human Rights: jurisprudence:
www.corteidh.or.cr/buscadores.cfm
CSCE and OSCE Documents (incl. Summit & Ministerial Council documents):
www.osce.org/mc/documents.html

Moreover, a number of key instruments, cases and publications are cited in abbreviated form; all sources so cited are listed in the Table of Abbreviations and Abbreviated Citations. All internet addresses cited in this book were active in June or July 2009, unless indicated otherwise.

2. TABLE OF CASES AND OPINIONS OF (QUASI-)JUDICIAL BODIES

International Court of Justice[2722]

Advisory Opinions

- *Legal consequences of the construction of a wall in the occupied Palestinian territory*, 9 July 2004;
- *Legality of the Threat or Use of Nuclear Weapons*, 8 July 1996;

[2721] Usually, the Council decision concerning the conclusion of an agreement immediately precedes the agreement or is at least published earlier in the same issue of the *O.J.* In such cases, I have cited a double *O.J.* page number with a / in between, the first number referring to the page of the Council decision and the second to that of the (first page of the) agreement. For data on the entry into force of agreements, I have relied on the data provided in this database (i.e. where the date is still left open I have assumed the agreement has not yet entered into force).

[2722] Separate or dissenting opinions are listed separately.

- *Legality of the Use by a State of Nuclear Weapons in Armed Conflict*, 8 July 1996 (preliminary objections);
- *Interpretation of the Agreement of 25 March 1951 between the WHO and Egypt*, 20 December 1980;
- *Legal Consequences for States of the Continued Presence of South Africa in Namibia (South West Africa) notwithstanding Security Council Resolution 276 (1970)*, 21 June 1971;
- *Certain Expenses of the United Nations*, 20 July 1962;
- *Reparation for Injuries Suffered in the Service of the United Nations*, 11 April 1949;

Contentious Cases

- *Corfu Channel Case*, 9 April 1949;
- *Barcelona Traction, Light and Power Company Ltd. (Belgium v. Spain)*, 5 February 1970;
- *Fisheries Jurisdiction Case (United Kingdom v Iceland)*, 2 February 1973;
- *Nuclear Test (Australia v. France)*, 20 December 1974;
- *United States Diplomatic and Consular Staff in Tehran*, 24 May 1980;
- *Military and Paramilitary Activities in and against Nicaragua*, 27 June 1986 (Merits);
- *Questions of Interpretation and Application of the 1971 Montreal Convention Arising from the Aerial Incident at Lockerbie (Libya v. UK & Libya v. US)*:
  - Orders of 14 April 1992;
  - Judgments of 27 February 1998;
- *Case concerning the Maritime Delimitation and Territorial Questions between Qatar and Bahrain (Qatar v. Bahrain)*, 1 July 1994;
- *Case concerning the Gabcíkovo-Nagymaros Project (Hungary/Slovakia)*, 25 September 1997;
- *Case concerning armed activities on the territory of the Congo (DRC v. Uganda)*, 19 December 2005;
- *Application of the Convention on the Prevention and Punishment of the Crime of Genocide (Bosnia and Herzegovina v. Serbia and Montenegro)*:
  - Order of 13 September 1993;
  - Judgment of 26 February 2007;

ILO Administrative Tribunal

- *In re Franks (No. 2) and Vollering (No. 2)*, Judgment No. 1333 of 31 January 1994;
- *In re Maugain (No. 6)*, Judgment No. 1144 of 29 January 1992;
- *I. M. B. v. International Atomic Energy Agency*, Judgement No. 2120 of 15 July 2002;
- *J. M. W. v. European Patent Organisation*, Judgement No. 2292 of 4 February 2004;
- *H.-J. M. v. European Patent Organisation*, Judgement No. 2611 of 7 February 2007;

Arbitral Awards

- Award of 29 June 1990, *European Molecular Biology Laboratory v. Germany* (105 *I.L.R.* 1997);

Human Rights Committee

General Comments

- General Comment 3, Implementation at the National Level (1981);
- General Comment 5, Derogation of Rights (1981);
- General Comment 21, Humane Treatment of Persons Deprived of Liberty (1992);
- General Comment 23, Rights of Minorities (1994);
- General Comment 24, Reservations (1994);
- General Comment 29, State of Emergency (2001);
- General Comment 31, The Nature of the General Legal Obligation Imposed on States Parties to the Covenant (2004);

Reports and Observations

- *López Burgos v. Uruguay*, 29 July 1981, No. 52/1979;
- *Celiberti de Casariego v. Uruguay*, 29 July 1981, No. 56/1979;
- *Montero v. Uruguay*, 31 March 1983, No. 106/1981;
- *H.v.d.P. v. Netherlands*, 8 April 1987, No. 217/1986;
- *Ibrahim Gueye et al. v. France*, 6 April 1989, No. 196/1985;
- *Kindler v. Canada*, 18 November 1993, No. 470/1991;
- *Concluding Observations on the USA*, 3 October 1995, CCPR/C/79/Add.50;
- *Concluding Observations: Belgium*, 19 November 1998, CCPR/C/79/Add.99;
- *Concluding Observations: Netherlands*, 27 August 2001, CCPR/CO/72/NET;
- *Concluding Observations: Israel*, 21 August 2003, CCPR/CO/78/ISR;
- *Concluding Observations on Germany*, 4 May 2004, CCPR/CO/80/DEU;
- *Concluding Observations on Belgium*, 12 August 2004, CCPR/CO/81/BEL;

European Commission/Court of Human Rights

Commission

- *Greek Case*, 5 November 1969;
- *Cyprus v. Turkey*, 10 July 1976;
- *C.F.D.T.* v. *the European Communities, alternatively their Member States*, 10 July 1978;
- *Stewart v. UK*, 10 July 1984;
- *M & Co v. Germany*, 9 February 1990;
- *Gestra v. Italy*, 16 January 1995;

Court

- *Lawless v Ireland* (Merits), 1 July 1961;
- *Engel and Others v. The Netherlands*, 30 April 1976;
- *Ireland v UK*, 13 December 1977;
- *Klass and others v. Germany*, 6 September 1978;
- *Brogan and Others v. UK*, 29 November 1988;
- *Soering v. the UK*, 7 July 1989;
- *Drozd and Janousek v. France and Spain*, 26 June 1992;
- *Brannigan and McBride v UK*, 26 May 1993;
- *Loizidou v. Turkey*, preliminary objections, 23 February 1995 (merits *infra*);
- *McCann v UK*, 27 September 1995;
- *Cantoni v. France*, 15 November 1996;
- *Loizidou v. Turkey*, 18 December 1996 (merits; preliminary objections *supra*);
- *Aksoy v Turkey*, 18 December 1996;
- *Andronicou and Constantinou v. Cyprus*, 9 October 1997;
- *Gülec v. Turkey*, 27 July 1998;
- *Ergi v. Turkey*, 28 July 1998;
- *Osman v. UK*, 28 October 1998;
- *Rigopoulos v. Spain*, 12 January 1999 (admissibility);
- *Matthews v. UK*, 18 February 1999;
- *Beer and Regan v. Germany*, 18 February 1999;
- *Waite en Kennedy v. Germany*, 18 February 1999;
- *Ogur v. Turkey*, 20 May 1999;
- *Labita v. Italy*, 6 April 2000;
- *Naletilić v. Croatia*, 4 May 2000 (admissibility);
- *Halima Musa Issa and Others v. Turkey*, 30 May 2000 (admissibility; merits *infra*);
- *Jecius v. Lithouania*, 31 July 2000;
- *Cyprus v. Turkey*, 10 May 2001;
- *Ilie Ilaşcu, Alexandru Leşco, Andrei Ivanţoc and Tudor Petrov-Popa v. Moldova and the Russian Federation*, 4 July 2001 (admissibility; merits *infra*);
- *Einhorn v. France*, 16 October 2001 (admissibility);
- *McElhinney v. Ireland*, 21 November 2001;
- *Fogarty v. UK*, 21 November 2001;
- *Al-Adsani v. UK*, 21 November 2001;
- *Vlastimir and Borka Bankovic´ and Others v. Belgium, the Czech Republic, Denmark, France, Germany, Greece, Hungary, Iceland, Italy, Luxembourg, the Netherlands, Norway, Poland, Portugal, Spain, Turkey and the United Kingdom*, 12 December 2001 (admissibility);
- *SEGI e.a. & GESTORAS PRO-AMNISTIA and others. v. Germany and others*, 23 May 2002 (admissibility);
- *Ocalan v. Turkey*, 12 March 2003 (appeal: Grand Chamber, 12 May 2005);
- *Ahmet Ozkan and others v. Turkey*, 6 April 2004;
- *Assanidze v. Georgia*, 8 April 2004;

- *Ilie Ilaşcu, Alexandru Leşco, Andrei Ivanţoc and Tudor Petrov-Popa v. Moldova and the Russian Federation*, 8 July 2004 (merits; admissibility *supra*);
- *Halima Musa Issa and Others v. Turkey*, 16 November 2004 (merits; admissibility *supra*);
- *Makaratzis v. Greece*, 20 December 2004;
- *Emesa Sugar NV v. the Netherlands*, 13 January 2005 (admissibility);
- *Isayeva, Yusupova and Bazayeva v. Russia*, 24 February 2005;
- *Isayeva v. Russia*, 24 February 2005;
- *Khashiyev and Akayeva v. Russia*, 24 February 2005;
- *Bubbins v. UK*, 17 March 2005;
- *Bosphorus Hava Yolları Turizm ve Ticaret Anonim Şirketi v. Ireland*, 30 June 2005;
- *Nachova and Others v. Bulgaria*, 6 July 2005;
- *Saddam Hussein v. Albania and Others*, Decision of 14 March 2006 (admissibility);
- *Erdogan and others v. Turkey*, 25 April 2006;
- *Vasileva v. Denmark*, Judgment of 25 September 2006;
- *Isaak v. Turkey*, 28 September 2006 (admissibility);
- Joined cases *Behrami and Behrami v. France* and *Saramati v. France, Germany and Norway*, 31 May 2007 (admissibility);
- *Mansur Pad and Others v. Turkey*, 28 June 2007 (admissibility);
- *Musayev and Others v. Russia*, 26 July 2007;
- *Gajic v. Germany*, 28 August 2007 (admissibility);
- *Dusan Beric and Others v. Bosnia and Herzegovina*, 16 October 2007 (admissibility);
- *Saadi v. Italy*, 28 February 2008;
- *Solomou v. Turkey*, 24 June 2008 (admissibility);
- *Medvedyev and others v. France*, 10 July 2008 (under appeal to the Grand Chamber);
- *Kononov v. Latvia*, 24 July 2008 (under appeal to the Grand Chamber);
- *Boivin v. 34 Members of the Council of Europe*, 9 September 2008 (admissibility);
- *Korbely v. Hungary*, 19 September 2008;
- *Al-Saadoon and Mufdhi v. UK*:
  - 30 December 2008 (Rule 39 order);
  - 30 June 2009 (admissibility);
- *Cooperatieve Producentenorganisatie van de Nederlandse Kokkelvisserij U.A. v. the Netherlands*, 20 January 2009 (admissibility);
- *Varnava and Others v. Turkey*, 18 September 2009 (Grand Chamber on appeal);

European Court of Justice (incl. Court of First Instance)

- Case 1/58, *Friedrich Stork & Cie v High Authority of the European Coal and Steel Community*, 4 February 1959;
- Case 26/62, *Van Gend en Loos / Administratie der Belastingen*, 5 February 1963;
- Case, 6/64, *Costa / E.N.E.L.*, 15 July 1964;
- Joint Cases 90 and 91/63, *Commission v Grand Duchy of Luxembourg and Kingdom of Belgium*, 13 November 1964;
- Case 29/69, *Erich Stauder v City of Ulm – Sozialamt*, 12 November 1969;
- Case 38/69, *Commission v Italian Republic*, 18 February 1970;

- Case 11/70, *Internationale Handelsgesellschaft mbH v Einfuhr- und Vorratsstelle für Getreide und Futtermittel*, 17 December 1970;
- Case C-22/70, *Commission v Council, European Agreement on Road Transport (AETR)*, 31 March 1971;
- Joint Cases 21–24/72, *International Fruit Company NV and others v Produktschap voor Groenten en Fruit*, 12 December 1972;
- Case C-4/73, *J. Nold, Kohlen- und Baustoffgroßhandlung v Commission*, 14 May 1974;
- Case 36/75, *Roland Rutili v Ministre de l'intérieur*, 28 October 1975;
- Case 38/75, *Douaneagent der NV Nederlandse Spoorwegen v Inspecteur der invoerrechten en accijnzen*, 19 November 1975;
- Opinion 1/76, *Draft Agreement establishing a European laying-up fund for inland waterway vessels*, 26 April 1977;
- Cases 3–4/76 and 6/76, *Cornelis Kramer and others*, 14 July 1976;
- Case 41/74, *Yvonne van Duyn v Home Office*, 4 December 1974;
- Case 44/79, *Liselotte Hauer v Land Rheinland-Pfalz*, 13 December 1979;
- Case 812/79, *Attorney General v Juan C. Burgoa*, 14 October 1980;
- Case 104/81, *Hauptzollamt Mainz v C.A. Kupferberg & Cie KG a.A.*, 26 October 1982;
- Case 325/82, *Commission v Federal Republic of Germany*, 14 February 1984;
- Case 222/84, *Marguerite Johnston v Chief Constable of the Royal Ulster Constabulary*, 15 May 1986;
- Case 68/86, *United Kingdom of Great Britain and Northern Ireland v Council*, 23 February 1988;
- Case 85/86, *Commission of the European Communities v Board of Governors of the European Investment Bank*, 3 March 1988;
- Case T-184/95, *Dorsch Consult Ingenieurgesellschaft mbH v Council and Commission*, 28 April 1998 (appeal: Case C-237/98, *Dorsch Consult Ingenieurgesellschaft mbH v. Council and Commission*, 15 June 2000);
- Case 204/86, *Hellenic Republic v Council*, 27 September 1988;
- Case 5/88, *Hubert Wachauf v Bundesamt für Ernährung und Forstwirtschaft*, 13 July 1989;
- Case 374/87, *Orkem v Commission of the European Communities*, 18 October 1989;
- Joint Cases 46/87 and 227/88, *Hoechst AG v Commission*, 21 September 1989;
- Case 27/88, *Solvay & Cie v Commission of the European Communities*, 18 October 1989;
- Joined Cases C-297/88 and C-197/89, *Massam Dzodzi v Belgian State*, 18 October 1990;
- Case C-260/89, *Elliniki Radiophonia Tiléorassi AE and Panellinia Omospondia Syllogon Prossopikou v Dimotiki Etairia Pliroforissis and Sotirios Kouvelas and Nicolaos Avdellas and others*, 18 June 1991;
- Case 159/90, *The Society for the Protection of Unborn Children Ireland Ltd v Stephen Grogan and others*, 4 October 1991;
- Opinion 1/91, *Draft agreement between the Community, on the one hand, and the countries of the EFTA, on the other, relating to the creation of the European Economic Area*, 14 December 1991;

- Case C-286/90, *Anklagemyndigheden v Peter Michael Poulsen and Diva Navigation Corp.*, 24 November 1992;
- Opinion 2/91 (*ILO Convention 170*), 19 March 1993;
- Case C-158/91, *Criminal proceedings against Jean-Claude Levy*, 2 August 1993;
- Case C-364/92, *SAT Fluggesellschaft mbH v Eurocontrol*, 19 January 1994;
- Case C-2/92, *The Queen v Ministry of Agriculture, Fisheries and Food, ex parte Dennis Clifford Bostock*, 24 March 1994;
- Case 327/91, *French Republic v Commission*, 9 August 1994;
- Joint Cases C-46/93 and C-48/93, *Brasserie du Pêcheur SA v Bundesrepublik Deutschland* and *The Queen v Secretary of State for Transport, ex parte: Factortame Ltd and others*, 5 March 1996;
- Case C-5/94, *The Queen v Ministry of Agriculture, Fisheries and Food, ex parte: Hedley Lomas (Ireland) Ltd.*, 23 May 1996;
- Cases C-84/95, *Bosphorus Hava Yollari Turizm ve Ticaret AS v Minister for Transport, Energy and Communications and others*, 30 July 1996;
- Case C-11/95, *Commission v Kingdom of Belgium*, 10 September 1996;
- Case C-124/95, *The Queen, ex parte Centro-Com Srl v HM Treasury and Bank of England*, 14 January 1997;
- Case C-177/95, *Ebony Maritime SA and Loten Navigation Co. Ltd v Prefetto della Provincia di Brindisi and others*, 27 February 1997;
- Case 249/96, *Lisa Jacqueline Grant and South-West Trains Ltd*, 17 February 1998;
- Case T-347/94, *Mayr-Melnhof Kartongesellschaft mbH v. Commission*, 14 May 1998;
- Case C-162/96, *Racke / Hauptzollamt Mainz*, 16 June 1998;
- Case C-414/97, *Commission v. Spain*, 16 September 1999;
- Case T-112/98, *Mannesmannröhren-Werke AG v. Commission*, 20 February 2001;
- Case T-54/99, *Max.mobil Telekommunikation Service GmbH v. Commission*, 30 January 2002;
- Case C-186/01, *Dory*, 11 March 2003;
- Case T-26/01, *Fiocchi Munizioni SpA v Commission*, 30 September 2003;
- Case T-177/01, *Jégo-Quéré et Cie SA v. Commission*, 3 May 2002, set aside by Case C-263/02, *Commission v. Jégo-Quéré et Cie SA*, 1 April 2004;
- Case C-233/02, *French Republic v. Commission*, 23 March 2004;
- Case C-160/06, *Kingdom of Spain v. Eurojust*, Opinion of Advocate General Maduro, 16 December 2004;
- Case C-105/03, *Maria Pupino*, 16 June 2005;
- Case C-176/03, *Commission v Council*, 13 September 2005;
- Case T-306/01, *Yusuf and Al Barakaat International Foundation v. Council and Commission*, 21 September 2005 (appeal: see case C-415/05 P *infra*);
- Case T-315/01, *Kadi v. Council and Commission*, 21 September 2005 (appeal: see case C-402/05 P *infra*);
- Opinion 1/03 (*Competence of the Community to conclude the new Lugano Convention on jurisdiction and the recognition and enforcement of judgments in civil and commercial matters*), 7 February 2006;
- Case C-540/03, *European Parliament v. the Council*, 27 June 2006;
- Case T-253/02, *Chafiq Ayadi v. Council*, 12 July 2006;

- Case T-49/04, *Faraj Hassan, v. Council and Commission*, 12 July 2006;
- Case T-228/02, *Organisation des Modjahedines du peuple d'Iran v. Council*, 12 December 2006;
- Case C-354/04, *Gestoras Pro Amnistía and Others v Council*:
  - judgment, 27 February 2007;
  - Opinion of Advocate-General Mengozzi, 26 October 2006;
- Case C-355/04, *Segi Araitz Zubimendi Izaga Aritza Galarraga v Council*:
  - judgment, 27 February 2007;
  - Opinion of Advocate-General Mengozzi, 26 October 2006;
- Case T-47/03, *Jose Maria Sison* v *Council*, 11 July 2007;
- Case T-327/03, *Stichting Al-Aqsa* v *Council*, 11 July 2007;
- Case C-440/05, *Commission v. Council*, 23 October 2007;
- Case C-305/05, *Ordre des barreaux francophones et germanophone and others*, 26 June 2007;
- Case T-229/02, *Osman Ocalan, on behalf of the Kurdistan Workers' Party (PKK) v. Council*, 3 April 2008;
- Case T-253/04, *KONGRA-GEL v. Council*, 3 April 2008;
- Case C-337/05, *Commission v. Italian Republic*, 8 April 2008;
- Case C-91/05, *Commission v. Council*:
  - judgment, 20 May 2008;
  - Opinion of Advocate-General Mengozzi, 19 September 2007;
- Case C-402/05 P, *Kadi v. Council and Commission* (see appealed decision in case T-315/01*supra*);
  - judgment, 3 September 2008;
  - Opinion of Advocate-General Maduro, 16 January 2008;
- Case C-415/05 P, *Al Barakaat International Foundation v. Council and Commission* (see appealed decision in case T-306/01 *supra*):
  - judgment, 3 September 2008;
  - Opinion of Advocate-General Maduro, 23 January 2008;
- Case C-157/06, *Commission v. Italy*, 2 October 2008;
- Case T-256/07, *People's Mojahedin Organization of Iran v. Council*, 23 October 2008;
- Case T-284/08, *People's Mojahedin Organization of Iran v. Council*, 4 December 2008;
- Case C-205/06, *Commission v. Austria*, 3 March 2009;
- Case C-249/06, *Commission v. Sweden*, 3 March 2009;
- Case C-420/07 (*Meletis Apostolides v. David Charles Orams, Linda Elizabeth Orams*), 28 April 2009;
- Case T-318/01, *Omar Mohammed Othman v. Council and Commission*, 11 June 2009;
- Joined Cases T-246/08 and T-332/08, *Melli Bank plc. v. Council*, 9 July 2009;

Inter-American Court of / Commission on Human Rights

Court

- Advisory Opinion OC-8/87, *Habeas Corpus in Emergency Situations*, 30 January 1987;

- Advisory Opinion OC-9/87, *Judicial Guarantees in States of Emergency*, 6 October 1987;
- *Las Palmeras Case*, Preliminary Objections, 4 February 2000;
- *Bámaca Velásquez*, 25 November 2000;
- Advisory Opinion OC-10/89, *Interpretation of the American Declaration of the Rights and Duties of Man [...]*, 14 July 1989;

Commission

- *Juan Carlos Abella v. Argentina*, 18 November 1997;
- *Coard et al. v. United States*, 29 September 1999;
- *Decision on Precautionary Measures (Detainees at Guantanamo Bay, Cuba)*, 12 March 2002;
- *Report on Terrorism and Human Rights*, Doc. OEA/Ser.L/V/II.116 Doc. 5 rev. 1 corr., 22 October 2002;

ICC

Pre-Trial Chamber I, *Prosecutor v Thomas Lubanga Dyilo*, Case No ICC-01/04-01/06, 29 January 2007;

ICTY

- *Karadzic & Mladic*:
  - IT-95-5-I, 24 July 1995 (initial indictment);
  - IT-95-5/18-I, 11 October 2002 (amended indictment);
- *The Prosecuter v. Dusko Tadic a/k/a/ 'Dule'*, ICTY- 94-1:
  - 2 October 1995;
  - 15 July 1999;
- *Prosecutor v. Ivica Rajic a/k/a/ Viktor Andric*, Review of the indictment pursuant to Rule 61 of the Rules of Procedure and Evidence, IT-95-12-R61, 13 September 1996;
- *Prosecutor v. Zejnil Delalic, Zdravko Mucic, also known as "Pavo", Hazim Delic and Esad Landzo, also known as "Zenga"* (Celebici), IT-96-21, 16 November 1998;
- *Prosecutor v. Furundzija*, ICTY-95-17/1, 10 December 1998;
- *Prosecutor v. Timohir Blaskic*, IT-95-14, 3 March 2000;
- *Prosecutor v. Blagoje Simic, Milan Simic, Mirosllav Tadic, Stevan Todorovic and Simo Zaric*, Decision on Motion for judicial Assistance to be provided by SFOR and others, IT-95-9, 18 October 2000;
- *Prosecutor v. Dario Kordic and Mario Cerkez*:
  - IT-95-14/2-T, Order for the Production of Documents by the European Community Monitoring Mission and its Member States, 4 August 2000;
  - IT-95-14/2, 26 February 2001;
- *Prosecutor v. Dragoljub Kunarac, Radomir Kovac and Zoran Vukovic*, IT-96-23&23/1, 22 February 2001;

- *Prosecutor v. Dragan Nikolic*, Decision on Defence Motion Challenging the Exercise of Jurisdiction by the Tribunal, IT-94-2-PT, 9 October 2002;
- *Prosecutor* v. *Mladen Naletilić and Vinko Martinović*, IT-98-34-T, 31 March 2003;
- *Final Report to the Prosecutor by the Committee Established to Review the NATO Bombing Campaign against the Federal Republic of Yugoslavia*, 8 June 2000 (39 *I.L.M.* 2000, pp. 1257–1283);

Domestic Case Law

Belgium

- Brussels labour appeals court (*Arbeidshof*), 27 November 1996;
- Military Court of Appeal (Militair Gerechtshof), *Openbaar ministerie / C. en B.*, 17 December 1997;
- Cour de cassation, 12 March 2001, *Arab League*;

Canada

- Court Martial Appeal Court, *R. v. Brocklebank*, 2 April 1996;

Germany

- BVerfG, 12 October 1993, *BVerfGE* 89, 155 (Maastricht Treaty);
- BVerfG, 22 November 2001, 2 BvE 6/99 (NATO);
- BVerfG, 30 June 2009, 2 BvE 2/08 (Lisbon Treaty);

Israel

- Supreme Court, *Public Committee against Torture in Israel and others v. the Government of Israel and others*, HJC 769/02, 13 December 2006;

Italy

- Corte Suprema di Cassazione, *FAO v. Colagrossi*, 19 May 1992, No. 5942 (101 *I.L.R.* 1995, pp. 385–394);

Russia

- Constitutional Court, *Constitutionality of the Presidential Decrees and the Resolutions of the Federal Government concerning the situation in Chechnya*, 31 July 1995 (translated in Council of Europe Doc. CDL-INF (96)1, 10 January 1996);

UK

- *Bici and Bici v. Ministry of Defence*, 7 April 2004, 2004 EWHC 786 (QB);

- *R (Al-Skeini and others) v Secretary of State for Defence* ([2004] EWHC 2911 (Admin)), 14 December 2004, upheld on appeal on 21 December 2005 in [2005] EWCA Civ 1609, upheld by the House of Lords on 13 June 2007 ([2007] UKHL 26);
- *Al-Jedda, R (on the application of) v Secretary of State for Defence* (([2006] EWCA Civ 327), 29 March 2006; upheld by the House of Lords on 12 December 2007 ([2007] UKHL 58);
- *Smith, R (on the application of) v Assistant Deputy Coroner for Oxfordshire & Anor* ([2008] EWHC 694 (Admin)), 11 April 2008, upheld by the England and Wales Court of Appeal on 18 May 2009 in *Secretary of State for Defence v Smith, R (on the application of)* ([2009] EWCA Civ 441);
- *R (Saadoon & Mufdhi) v. Secretary of State for Defence*, [2008] EWHC 3098 (Admin), 19 December 2008; appeal dismissed by the Court of Appeal on 30 December 2008 with the full judgment delivered on 21 January 2009 (*R (on the application of (1) Faisal Attiyah Nassar Al-Saadoon (2) Khalaf Hussain Mufdhi) v. Secretary of State for Defence*, [2009] EWCA Civ 7);

US

- US Supreme Court, *Hamdan v. Rumsfeld*, 29 June 2006.

www.ingramcontent.com/pod-product-compliance
Ingram Content Group UK Ltd.
Pitfield, Milton Keynes, MK11 3LW, UK
UKHW051846100926
8556IPUK00005B/470